Pearson New International Edition

Exceptional Children
An Introduction to Special Education
William L. Heward
Tenth Edition

Pearson Education Limited
Edinburgh Gate
Harlow
Essex CM20 2JE
England and Associated Companies throughout the world

Visit us on the World Wide Web at: www.pearsoned.co.uk

© Pearson Education Limited 2014

ISBN 10: 1-292-02202-7
ISBN 13: 978-1-292-02202-4

British Library Cataloguing-in-Publication Data
A catalogue record for this book is available from the British Library

ARP impression 98

Printed in Great Britain by Ashford Colour Press Ltd.

Table of Contents

A Personal View of Special Education

MY PRIMARY GOAL IN WRITING THIS TEXT
is to describe the history, practices, advances,
challenges, and opportunities that make up the
complex and dynamic field of special education in
as complete, clear, current, and accurate a manner
as possible. This, of course, is much easier said
than done: an author's descriptions of anything
he holds dear are influenced by personal views.
Because my personal beliefs and assumptions
about special education—which are by no means
unique, but neither are they held by everyone
in the field—affect both the substance and the
tone of this text, I believe I owe you, the reader,
an explicit summary of those views. So, here are
10 assumptions that underlie and guide my efforts
to understand, contribute to, and convey the field
of special education.

*People with disabilities have a fundamental
right to live and participate in the same
settings and programs—in school, at home, in
the workplace, and in the community—as do
people without disabilities.* That is, the settings
and programs in which children and adults with
disabilities learn, live, work, and play should,
to the greatest extent possible, be the same
settings and programs in which people without
disabilities participate. People with disabilities
and those without have a great deal to contribute
to one another and to society. We cannot do that
without regular, meaningful interactions in shared
environments.

*People with disabilities have the right to
as much self-determination as they can achieve.*

Special educators have no more important
teaching task than that of helping students with
disabilities learn how to increase their level of
autonomy over their own lives. Self-determination
and self-advocacy skills should be featured
curriculum components for all students with
disabilities.

*Special education must expand and
improve the effectiveness of its early
identification and prevention efforts.* When
a disability or a condition that places a child
at risk for a disability is detected early, the
chance of lessening its impact (or preventing
it altogether) is greater. Great strides
have been made in the early detection of
physical disabilities, sensory impairments,
and developmental delays in infants and
preschoolers. Although systematic programs
of early identification and prevention of less
visible disabilities, such as learning disabilities
and emotional and behavioral disorders, are
less well developed, the field has made a
commitment to doing just that with an approach
called *responsiveness to intervention.*

*Special education must do a better job of
helping students with disabilities transition from
school to adult life.* Although increasing numbers
of special education students are leaving high
school for college or a job, a place to live on their
own, and friends with whom to share recreation
and leisure activities in the community, such
positive outcomes still elude far too many young
adults with disabilities. Special education cannot

From Chapter 1 of *Exceptional Children* and *An Introduction to Special Education*, Tenth Edition. William L. Heward.

be satisfied with improving students' achievement on classroom-based measures only. We must work equally hard to ensure that the education students receive during their school years prepares them to cope with and enjoy the multifaceted demands and opportunities of adulthood.

Special education must continue to improve its cultural competence. When a student with disabilities has the additional challenge of learning in a new or different culture or language, it is critically important that her teachers provide culturally responsive curriculum and instruction. Teachers who are most effective in helping these children combine fundamentally sound instructional methods with sensitivity to and respect for their students' heritage and values.

School and family partnerships enhance both the meaningfulness and the effectiveness of special education. Professionals have too long ignored the needs of parents and families of exceptional children, often treating them as patients, clients, or even adversaries instead of realizing that they are partners with the same goals. Some special educators have given the impression (and, worse, believed it to be true) that parents are there to serve professionals, when in fact the opposite is more correct. We must recognize that parents are a child's first—and, in many ways, best—teachers. Learning to work effectively with parents is one of the most important skills the special educator can acquire.

The work of special educators is most effective when supplemented by the knowledge and services of all of the disciplines in the helping professions. It is foolish for special educators to argue over territorial rights when more can be accomplished for our students when we work together within an interdisciplinary team that includes our colleagues in psychology, medical and health services, counseling, social services, and vocational rehabilitation.

All students have the right to an effective education. An educator's primary responsibility is designing and implementing instruction that helps students with special needs learn useful academic, social, vocational, and personal skills. These skills are the same ones that influence the quality of our own lives: working effectively and efficiently at our jobs, being productive members of our communities, maintaining a comfortable lifestyle in our homes, communicating with our friends and family, and using our leisure time meaningfully and enjoyably. Instruction is ultimately effective when it helps students acquire and maintain positive lifestyle changes. To put it another way, the proof of the process is in the product. Therefore, . . .

Teachers must demand effectiveness from the curriculum materials and instructional tools they use. For many years, conventional wisdom has fostered the belief, still held by some, that teaching children with disabilities requires unending patience. I believe this notion does a great disservice to students with special needs and to the educators—both special and general education teachers—who teach them. A teacher should not wait patiently for an exceptional student to learn, attributing lack of progress to some inherent attribute or faulty process within the child, such as intellectual disabilities, learning disability, attention-deficit disorder, or emotional disturbance. Instead, the teacher should select evidence-based practices and then use direct and frequent measures of the student's performance as the primary guide for modifying those methods as needed to improve their effectiveness. This, I believe, is the real work of the special educator. Numerous examples of instructional strategies and tactics demonstrated to be effective through rigorous scientific research are described and illustrated throughout this text. Although you will not know how to teach exceptional children after reading this or any other introductory text, you will gain an appreciation for the importance of explicit, systematic instruction and an understanding of the kinds of teaching skills a competent special educator must have. And finally, I believe that . . .

The future for people with disabilities holds great promise. We have only begun to discover the myriad ways to improve teaching, increase learning, prevent and minimize the conditions that cause and exacerbate the effects of disabilities, encourage acceptance, and use technology to compensate for disabilities. While I make no specific predictions for the future, I am certain that we have not come as far as we can in learning how to help exceptional children and adults build and enjoy fuller, more independent lives in the school, home, workplace, and community.

The Purpose and Promise
of Special Education

Katelyn Metzger/Merrill

- When is special education needed? How do we know?
- If disability labels do not tell us what and how to teach, why are they used in special education?
- Why have court cases and federal legislation been required to ensure that children with disabilities receive a free appropriate education?

- How can a special educator provide all three kinds of intervention—preventive, remedial, and compensatory—on behalf of an individual child?
- In what ways do general and special education differ? Are those differences important? If so, why and how?

▼ FEATURED TEACHER

MEGAN MENCINSKY

North Elementary School • District 84, Franklin Park, Illinois

EDUCATION—TEACHING CREDENTIALS—EXPERIENCE

- B.A., special education, Elmhurst College, 2007
- Currently pursuing M.S., special education (Curriculum Adaptation and Behavior Intervention), Northeastern Illinois University
- Illinois, Learning Behavior Specialist (LBS) I/Type 10, all disabilities except Deaf and Blind, preschool to age 21; LBS II (Certificate in Curriculum Adaptation); Standard Sign Language interpreter
- 5 years of experience as a special education teacher

WHY I CHOSE TO BE A SPECIAL EDUCATOR

When I was in college, a friend's concerned mother told me I would be "wasting my talents" as a special educator. Why, she wondered, would an intelligent and ambitious young person want to spend her time with students who struggled to learn? I said that I wanted a profession where I was challenged daily and had both the opportunity and responsibility to make a difference in people's lives. Special education is that profession and then some. To be a great special educator requires a myriad of talents and skills to teach the most difficult-to-teach students in schools. As my principal likes to say, "Other students will succeed despite us. Our special education students will succeed *because* of us."

When people find out I am a special education teacher, they'll often remark that I must be extremely patient and kind. If anything, I am impatient—not with my students, but with poorly designed lessons and weak instructional procedures. Being a special education

teacher requires a vast skill set, one that I continue to try to develop and enhance every day. Every time I think I have mastered a strategy or content area, something new comes along: a new strategy, a new book to supplement the curriculum, a new website to use. The responsibilities of the job require knowledge of general education curriculum and state learning standards at various grade levels, how to modify and adapt curriculum, how to identify and write goals, and how to keep data that accurately track students' progress toward those goals. I must collaborate with outside service providers, administer district and state assessments, plan lessons, direct my paraprofessionals, manage my classroom effectively, provide positive behavior support—and oh, yes, I have to teach as well! A special educator's job is never boring, that's for sure. Every day is different, and every day is the chance to teach my students something new (and I learn something new every day!).

MY CURRENT CLASSROOM AND STUDENTS

I currently teach seven early primary students in a cooperative-run self-contained classroom in a typical elementary school. My students are eligible for special education under the disabilitiy categories of emotional and behavior disorders, autism, learning disabilities, and other health impairments. Among my biggest accomplishments this year were helping a student progress from "significantly below average" on his initial reading benchmark to "average," and teaching another student the coping skills that prevented him from being hospitalized for his mental health issues the entire time he was with me. I know I am not solely responsible for these accomplishments; my students are the ones putting in the effort. I'm the facilitator who constructs the environment that supports their learning. Detecting and helping my students see their small successes are a key part of my job.

My classroom is a portal for new experiences for my students, which I create using a balance of technology and hands-on materials, and traditional texts. The Internet enables my students to see pictures of people from the past to supplement our history lessons, view videos of a butterfly's metamorphosis, and take virtual field trips to national parks.

TUNEFUL ROUTINES, REINFORCEMENT, AND PROGRESS DATA I teach routines from day 1 of the school year. For example, I give students a tour to show them where everything is in class. I use music as cues for classroom routines. When I play "Yellow Submarine" by the Beatles, students know they have until the end of the song to complete whatever activity they are working on, clean up, and come sit at the carpet. The "Inspector Gadget" theme song means it is time to switch centers. A song gives the students a minute or two to process what they need to do and then time to clean up and get where they need to be without my saying a word. For my students who have anxiety, the music allows them a chance to complete their activity without panicking that they don't have enough time. I also use visual timers so students can see how long they have to complete a task.

I have incorporated a classroom token economy for positive behavior. I find that overcorrecting students does not get the behavior to stop, but that encouraging those who are doing the right thing usually leads the others to follow suit. I also use visuals on a lanyard that I show to students while I teach to give directions. For example, if a student is out of his seat, I will show him the card that says "Please sit down" with a picture of a student sitting. This way, I don't have to stop my instruction, and the student can process what I am asking him to do. This works exceptionally well with my students who are second-language learners or have a hard time processing information auditorally. It is also more subtle than verbally correcting students.

I also use self-monitoring techniques in my class. Students graph their daily point totals, spelling test scores, and how long they can read independently. Their graphs are hung where they can easily access them. Students always want to better their scores when they can see how they are actually doing. I also share their monthly curriculum-based measurement scores and graphs with them, so they can see what they need to do to "get their lines going up" on their graphs. This motivates them to improve, rather than always working for a tangible reward.

Using a combination of best practices—following teaching routines, using visual prompts, reinforcing on-task behavior, and having students self-monitor their progress—makes the classroom run smoothly, which enables me to effectively use the curriculum assigned by our district. When time is spent on-task rather than on behaviors, we often end up finishing early, which allows me to plan supplemental lessons to the general education curriculum to take my students even deeper into the material.

Ms. Mencinsky shared her experiences during the 2010–2011 school year on Reality 101, the Council for Exceptional Children's blog for new special education teachers. To read Megan's entries and those of other beginning special educators, go to http://www.cecreality101.org.

CONSIDERING SPECIAL EDUCATION AS A CAREER? If you are considering becoming a special education teacher, get as much hands-on experience with children with special needs as you can. Special education is a vast field. Involvement in local special recreation associations, volunteering, and other related activities will help you realize if this is an area of education you want to pursue, and even what age group and areas of special education might be your niche. Ask lots of questions and do research ahead of time, particularly when looking at different teacher preparation programs. I would always suggest attending a program whose graduates are enthusiastic about teaching and the training they received—merely satisfied is not enough.

MyEducationLab™

Visit the **MyEducationLab** for *Exceptional Children* to enhance your understanding of chapter concepts with a personalized Study Plan. You'll also have the opportunity to hone your teaching skills through video- and case-based Assignments and Activities, IRIS Center Resources, and Building Teaching Skills and Dispositions lessons.

EDUCATING EXCEPTIONAL CHILDREN IS A DIFFICULT CHALLENGE. Teachers like Megan Mencinsky who have accepted that challenge—special educators—work in a dynamic and exciting field. To begin to appreciate some of the action and excitement, as well as the persistent and emerging challenges and controversies that characterize special education, it is necessary to examine some concepts and perspectives that are basic to understanding exceptional children.

WHO ARE EXCEPTIONAL CHILDREN?

All children exhibit differences from one another in terms of their physical attributes (e.g., some are shorter, some are stronger) and learning abilities (e.g., some learn quickly and use what they have learned in new situations; others need intensive instruction and have difficulty maintaining and generalizing new knowledge and skills). The differences among most children are relatively small, enabling them to benefit from the general education program. The physical attributes and/or learning characteristics of **exceptional children** differ from the norm (either below or above) to such an extent that they require an individualized program of special education and related services to fully benefit from education. The term *exceptional children* includes children who experience difficulties in learning as well as those whose performance is so advanced that modifications in curriculum and instruction are necessary to help them fulfill their potential. Thus, *exceptional children* is an inclusive term that refers to children with learning and/or behavior problems, children with physical disabilities or sensory impairments, and children with superior intellectual abilities and/or special talents. The term *students with disabilities* is more restrictive than *exceptional children* because it does not include gifted and talented children. Learning the definitions of several related terms will help you better understand the concept of exceptionality.

Although the terms *impairment*, *disability*, and *handicap* are sometimes used interchangeably, they are not synonymous. **Impairment** refers to the loss or reduced function of a particular body part or organ (e.g., a missing limb). A **disability** exists when an impairment limits a person's ability to perform certain tasks (e.g., walk, see, add a row of numbers). A person with a disability is not *handicapped*, however, unless the disability leads to educational, personal, social, vocational, or other problems. For example, if a child who has lost a leg learns to use a prosthetic limb and functions in and out of school without problems, she is not handicapped, at least in terms of her functioning in the physical environment.

Handicap refers to a problem or a disadvantage that a person with a disability or an impairment encounters when interacting with the environment. A disability may pose a handicap in one environment but not in another. The child with a prosthetic limb may be handicapped (i.e., disadvantaged) when competing against nondisabled peers on the basketball court but experience no disadvantage in the classroom. Many people with disabilities experience handicaps that are the result of negative attitudes and inappropriate behavior of others who needlessly restrict their access and ability to participate fully in school, work, or community activities.

The term **at risk** refers to children who, although not currently identified as having a disability, are considered to have a greater than usual chance of developing one. Educators often apply the term to infants and preschoolers who, because of biological conditions, events surrounding their births, or environmental deprivation, may be expected to experience developmental problems at a later time. The term is also used to refer to students who are experiencing significant learning or behavioral problems in the general education classroom and are therefore at risk of being diagnosed with a disability.

Definition of *exceptional children*

Content Standards for Beginning Teachers—Initial Common Core: Similarities and differences of individuals with and without exceptional learning needs (ICC2K5).

Definition of *impairment, disability, handicap, and at-risk*

Content Standards for Beginning Teachers—Initial Common Core: Similarities and differences of individuals with and without exceptional learning needs (ICC2K5).

Certain physical characteristics and/or patterns of learning and behavior are shared by subgroups of exceptional children. These characteristics fall into the following categories of exceptionality:

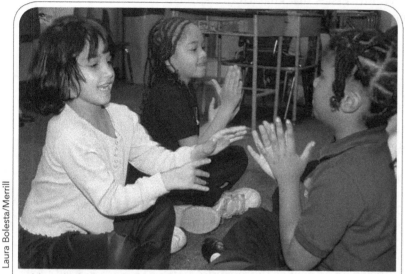

Although children with disabilities have special instructional needs, they are more like other children than they are different.

Laura Bolesta/Merrill

- Intellectual disabilities
- Learning disabilities
- Emotional or behavioral disorders
- Autism
- Speech or language impairments
- Hearing impairments
- Visual impairments
- Physical or health impairments
- Traumatic brain injury
- Multiple disabilities
- Giftedness and special talents

As stated previously, all children differ from one another in individual characteristics along a continuum; exceptional children differ markedly from the norm so that an individually designed program of instruction—special education—is required if they are to benefit fully from education. Although exceptional children are more like other children than they are different, an exceptional child differs in important ways from his same-age peers without disabilities. And whether and how those differences are recognized and responded to will have a major impact on the child's success in school and beyond.

HOW MANY EXCEPTIONAL CHILDREN ARE THERE?

Nearly 6 million children and youth with disabilities, from birth through age 21, received special education services during the 2009–2010 school year (U.S. Department of Education, 2011). Here are some demographic facts about special education in the United States:

- Children with disabilities in special education represent approximately 12% of the school-age population ages 6 to 17. Table 1 shows the number of school-age students in each of the 13 disability categories used by the federal government.
- About twice as many males as females receive special education.
- Early intervention programs have been major contributors to the increases since 1986. During the 2009–2010 school year, 731,250 preschoolers (ages 3 to 5) and 348,143 infants and toddlers (birth through age 2) were among those receiving special education.
- The number of children who receive special education increases from age 3 through age 9. The number served decreases gradually with each successive age year after age 9 until age 17. Thereafter, the number of students receiving special education decreases sharply.
- Since the federal government began reporting child count data in 1976–1977, the percentage of students receiving special education under the learning disabilities category has almost doubled (from 23.8% to 42.3%), whereas the percentage of students with intellectual disabilities has decreased to just one-third (from 24.9% to 7.8%).

TABLE 1 • **Number of students ages 6–21 who received special education services under the federal government's disability categories (2009–2010 school year)**

DISABILITY CATEGORY	NUMBER	PERCENT OF TOTAL
Learning Disabilities	2,483,391	42.3
Speech or Language Impairment	1,107,029	18.8
Other Health Impairment	678,970	11.6
Intellectual Disability	460,964	7.8
Emotional Disturbance	405,293	6.9
Autism	333,022	5.7
Multiple Disabilities	124,380	2.1
Developmental Delay	104,432	1.8
Hearing Impairment	70,548	1.2
Orthopedic Impairment	57,930	1.0
Visual Impairment	25,813	0.4
Traumatic Brain Injury	24,395	0.4
Deaf-Blindness	1,359	<0.1
All Disabilities	5,877,196	100.0

Source: From U.S. Department of Education. (2011). *Individuals with Disabilities Education Act (IDEA) data* (Table 3). Washington, DC: Author.

- The number of school-age students with autism in 2009–2010 was 10 times the number of students classified with autism just 10 years earlier.
- Although each child receiving special education is classified under a primary disability category, many children are affected by more than one disability condition. In a nationwide study of more than 11,000 elementary school students in special education, school staff reported that 40% of the students were affected by an additional or secondary disability (Marder, 2009).
- About 1 in 6 students with disabilities ages 6 to 13 are "declassified" and no longer receiving special education services 2 years later (SRI International, 2005).
- Although federal law does not mandate special education for children who are gifted and talented, approximately 3 million academically gifted and talented students were in pre-K to grade 12 gifted programs during the 2008–2009 school year (National Association for the Gifted, 2010).

WHY DO WE LABEL AND CLASSIFY EXCEPTIONAL CHILDREN?

Centuries ago, labeling and classifying people were of little consequence; survival was the main concern. Those whose disabilities prevented full participation in the activities necessary for survival were left on their own to perish and, in some instances, were even killed (Berkson, 2004). In later years, derogatory words such as *dunce, imbecile,* and *fool* were applied to people with intellectual disabilities or behavior problems, and other demeaning words were used for people with health impairments or physical disabilities. These terms shared a common function: to exclude people with disabilities from the activities and privileges of everyday life.

Labeling and Eligibility for Special Education

Under the federal Individuals with Disabilities Education Act (IDEA), to receive special education and related services, a child must be identified as having a disability (i.e., labeled) and, in most cases, further classified into one of that state's categories, such as learning disabilities or orthopedic impairments. (IDEA allows children ages 3 to 9 to be identified as *developmentally delayed* and receive special education services without the use of a specific disability label.) In practice, therefore, a student becomes eligible for special education and related services because of membership in a given disability category.

Some educators believe that the labels used to identify and classify exceptional children stigmatize them and serve to deny them opportunities in the mainstream (e.g., Harry & Klingner, 2007; Kliewer, Biklen, & Kasa-Hendrickson, 2006). Others argue that a workable system of classifying exceptional children (or their exceptional learning needs) is a prerequisite to providing needed special educational services and that using more "pleasant" terms minimizes and devalues the individual's situation and need for supports (e.g., Anastasiou & Kauffman, 2011; Keogh, 2005a, 2005b). As Kauffman (2003) noted, the stigma of cancer was not eliminated by referring to those affected as people with prolific cells or challenging tissue.

Labeling and classification are complex issues involving emotional, political, and ethical considerations in addition to scientific, fiscal, and educational interests (Florian et al., 2006; McLaughlin et al., 2006). As with most complex issues, valid perspectives and arguments exist on both sides of the labeling question. The reasons most often cited for and against the labeling and classification of exceptional children follow.

Possible Benefits of Labeling and Classification

- Labeling recognizes meaningful differences in learning or behavior and is a first and necessary step in responding responsibly to those differences. As Kauffman (1999) points out, "Although universal interventions that apply equally to all . . . can be implemented without labels and risk of stigma, no other interventions are possible without labels. Either all students are treated the same or some are treated differently. Any student who is treated differently is inevitably labeled. . . . Labeling a problem clearly is the first step in dealing with it productively" (p. 452).
- A disability label can provide access to accommodations and services not available to people without the label. For example, some parents of secondary students seek a learning disability label so their child will be eligible for accommodations such as additional time on college entrance exams.
- Labeling may lead to a protective response in which peers are more accepting of the atypical behavior of a child with disabilities than they would be of a child without disabilities who emitted that same behavior.
- Classification helps practitioners and researchers communicate with one another and classify and evaluate research findings (e.g., National Autism Center, 2009).
- Funding and resources for research and other programs are often based on specific categories of exceptionality (e.g., Interagency Autism Coordinating Committee, 2011).
- Labels enable disability-specific advocacy groups to promote specific programs and spur legislative action (e.g., Autism Speaks, http://www.autismspeaks.org).
- Labeling helps make exceptional children's special needs more visible to policy makers and the public.

Pros and cons of labeling

 Council for Exceptional Children Content Standards for Beginning Teachers—Initial Common Core: Issues in definition and identification of individuals with exceptional learning needs (ICC1K5).

Possible Disadvantages of Labeling and Classification

- Because the labels used in special education usually focus on disability, impairment, or performance deficits, they may lead some people to think only in terms of what the individual cannot do instead of what she can do or might be capable of doing (Terzi, 2005).
- Labels may stigmatize the child and lead peers to reject or ridicule the labeled child.
- Teachers may hold low expectations for a labeled student (Beilke & Yssel, 1999; Bianco, 2005) and treat her differentially as a result, which may lead to a self-fulfilling prophecy. For example, in one study, student teachers gave a child labeled "autistic" more praise and rewards and fewer verbal corrections for incorrect responses than they gave a child labeled "normal" (Eikeseth & Lovaas, 1992). Such differential treatment could impede the rate at which a child learns new skills and contribute to a level of performance consistent with the label's prediction.
- Labels may negatively affect the child's self-esteem.
- Disability labels are often misused as explanatory constructs (e.g., "Sherry acts that way *because* she is emotionally disturbed").
- Even though membership in a given category is based on a particular characteristic (e.g., deafness), there is a tendency to assume that all children in a category share other traits as well, thereby diminishing the detection and appreciation of each child's uniqueness (J. D. Smith & Mitchell, 2001).
- Labels suggest that learning problems are primarily the result of something inherently wrong with the child, thereby reducing the systematic examination of and accountability for instructional variables as causes of performance deficits. This is an especially damaging outcome when a label provides a built-in excuse for ineffective instruction (e.g., "Jalen's learning disability prevents him from comprehending printed text.").
- A disproportionate number of children from some minority and diverse cultural groups are included in special education programs and thus have been assigned disability labels (Sullivan, 2011).
- Classifying exceptional children requires the expenditure of a great amount of money and professional and student time that might be better spent in delivering and evaluating the effects of early intervention for struggling students (L. S. Fuchs & Fuchs, 2007a).

Although the pros and cons of using disability category labels have been widely debated for several decades (Hobbs, 1976a, 1976b), neither conceptual arguments nor research has produced a conclusive case for the total acceptance or absolute rejection of labeling practices. Most of the studies conducted to assess the effects of labeling have produced inconclusive, often contradictory evidence and have generally been marked by methodological weakness.

Alternatives to Labeling and Classification

Educators have proposed a number of alternative approaches to classifying exceptional children that focus on educationally relevant variables (e.g., Hardman, McDonnell, & Welch, 1997; Iscoe & Payne, 1972; Sontag, Sailor, & Smith, 1977; Terzi, 2005). For example, Reynolds, Zetlin, and Heistad (1996) proposed that the lowest-achieving 20% and the highest-achieving 20% of students be eligible for broad (noncategorical) approaches to improvement of learning opportunities.

Some noted special educators have suggested that exceptional children be classified according to the curriculum and skill areas they need to learn. For example:

> But if we shouldn't refer to these special children by using those old labels, then how should we refer to them? For openers, call them Rob, Amy, and

Effects of labels on behavior of others

 Council for Exceptional Children

Content Standards for Beginning Teachers—Initial Common Core: Teacher attitudes and behaviors that influence behavior of individuals with exceptional learning needs (ICC5K4).

Quotes by Thomas C. Lovitt (personal communication). Reprinted with permission.

11

FUTURE TRENDS

CURRENT ISSUES **AND**

▶ What's in a Name? The Labels and Language of Special Education

SOME YEARS AGO AT THE ANNUAL CONVENTION OF THE COUNCIL FOR EXCEPTIONAL CHILDREN, hundreds of attendees were wearing big yellow and black buttons that proclaimed "Label jars, not children!" Wearers of the buttons were presumably making a statement about one or more of the criticisms leveled at labeling and categorizing exceptional children: labeling is bad because it focuses on the child's deficits, labeling makes it more likely that others will expect poor performance or bad behavior from the child, and labels may damage the child's self-esteem.

Labels, in and of themselves, are not the problem. Most special educators agree that a common language for referring to children who share instructional and related service needs is necessary. The words that we use as labels do, however, influence the degree to which those words effectively and appropriately communicate variables relevant to the design and delivery of educational and other human services. For example, blanket labels such as *the handicapped* or *the retarded* imply that all people in the group being labeled are alike; individuality has been lost. At the personal level, describing a child as a "physically handicapped boy" suggests that the disability is the most important thing to know about him.

How, then, should we refer to exceptional children? At the personal level, we should follow Tom Lovitt's advice and call them by their names: Linda, Shawon, and Jackie. Referring to "Mitch, a fifth-grade student with learning disabilities" helps us focus on the individual

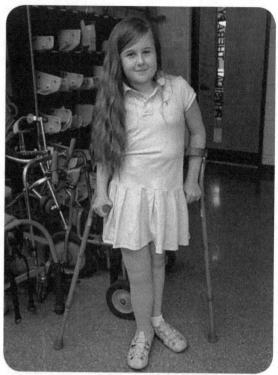

Katelyn Metzger/Merrill

Changing the label used to identify Charlotte for her special education eligibility won't lessen the impact of her disability. But referring to her as "Charlotte, a fifth grader who likes to read mysteries," helps us recognize her strengths and abilities—what she can do—instead of focusing on a disability label as if it were the most important thing to know about her.

Jose. Beyond that, refer to them on the basis of what you're trying to teach them. For example, if a teacher wants to teach Brandon to compute, read, and comprehend, he might call him a student of computation, reading, and comprehension. We do this all the time with older students. Sam, who attends Juilliard, is referred to as "the trumpet student"; Jane, who attends Harvard, is called "the law student." (T. C. Lovitt, personal communication, August 7, 2011)

For continued discussion of labeling, including the perspectives of several people with disabilities, see *Current Issues and Future Trends*, "What's in a Name? The Labels and Language of Special Education."

child and his primary role as a student. Such a description does not ignore or gloss over Mitch's learning problems but acknowledges that there are other things we should know about him.

It is important for everyone, not just special educators, to speak, write, and think about exceptional children and adults in ways that respect each person's individuality and recognize strengths and abilities instead of focusing only on disabilities. Simply changing the way we talk about a person with a disability, however, will not make the problems posed by her disability go away. Some people with disabilities have spoken out against the efforts of those without disabilities to assuage their feelings with language that may be politically correct but that ignores the reality of a disability. Judy Heumann (1994), a former director of the U.S. Office of Special Education and Rehabilitation Services and a person who has used a wheelchair since she was 18 months old, explains her position:

> As our movement has evolved, we have been plagued by people, almost always not themselves disabled, attempting to change what we call ourselves. If we are "victims" of anything, it is of such terms as "physically challenged, able-disabled, differently-abled, handi-capables, and people with differing abilities," to name just a few. Nondisabled people's discomfort with reality-based terms such as disabled led them to these euphemisms. I believe these euphemisms have the effect of depoliticizing our own terminology and devaluing our own view of ourselves as disabled people. . . . Let the disabled people who are politically involved and personally affected determine our own language. . . . A suggestion to those of you who do not know what to call me: ask! (p. 1)

Professional and advocacy organizations have taken differing views on disability labels. On the one hand, the National Federation of the Blind adopted a resolution against the use of terms such as *visually challenged* and *people with blindness*, stating that such politically correct euphemisms are "totally unacceptable and deserving only ridicule because of their strained and ludicrous attempt to avoid such straightforward, respectable words as *blindness, blind, the blind, blind person*, or *blind persons*" (Jernigan, 1993, p. 867). The American Association on Mental Retardation (AAMR) changed its name to the American Association on Intellectual and Developmental Disabilities (AAIDD) because it considered *intellectual disabilities* to be less stigmatizing than *mental retardation* (Prabhala, 2007). In 2010, President Barack Obama signed into law Rosa's Law, which changed all references to *mental retardation* in federal statutes to *intellectual disabilities*.

Changing the label for a disability or need for special education will not lessen prejudice or stigma (real or imagined). In a discussion of the pros and cons of replacing *mental retardation* with *intellectual disabilities*, Eidelman called for a public education campaign to foster more positive attitudes towards people with disabilities: "Changing the term will make many people happy. That happiness will quickly fade when the new term is used as a pejorative. Without a long-term effort to include everyone and to educate those with negative or neutral attitudes toward our constituents, a change in terminology will become the new pejorative very quickly" (in Turnbull, Turnbull, Warren, Eidelman, & Marchand, 2002, p. 68). And a change in terminology will not reduce the effects of the condition on the person's life.

WHAT DO YOU THINK?

1. From the perspective of a school-age child (or the parent or sibling of a child) who needs special education, what labels would you find most appropriate for each category of exceptionality listed earlier in this chapter?

2. What should prospective teachers learn about the types and function of disability labels used in special education?

3. How can teachers minimize the potential of disability labels to stigmatize and prejudice?

WHY ARE LAWS GOVERNING THE EDUCATION OF EXCEPTIONAL CHILDREN NECESSARY?

An Exclusionary Past

It is said that a society can be judged by the way it treats those who are different. By this criterion, the U.S. educational system has a less than distinguished history. Children who are different because of race, culture, language, gender, socioeconomic status, or exceptionality have often been denied full and fair access to educational opportunities (Banks & Banks, 2013). It's important, however, to note that past practices were not entirely negative. Long before there was any legal requirement to do so, many children with special needs were educated by devoted teachers and parents (Brownell, Sindelar, Kiely, & Danielson, 2010).

In the not so distant past, many children with disabilities were entirely excluded from any publicly supported program of education. Before the 1970s, laws in many states permitted public schools to deny enrollment to children with disabilities (Murdick, Gartin, & Crabtree, 2006). One state law, for example, allowed schools to refuse to serve "children physically or mentally incapacitated for school work"; another state had a law stipulating that children with "bodily or mental conditions rendering attendance inadvisable" could be turned away. When these laws were contested, the nation's courts generally supported exclusion. In a 1919 case, for example, a 13-year-old student with physical disabilities (but normal intellectual ability) was excluded from his local school because he "produces a depressing and nauseating effect upon the teachers and school children" (J. D. Smith, 2004, p. 4).

When local public schools began to accept a measure of responsibility for educating certain exceptional students, a philosophy and practice of segregation prevailed. Children with disabilities were confined to segregated classrooms, isolated from the students and teachers in the general education program. One special education teacher describes the crude facilities in which her special class operated and the sense of isolation she felt in the 1960s:

> I accepted my first teaching position, a special education class in a basement room next door to the furnace. Of the 15 "educable mentally retarded" children assigned to work with me, most were simply nonreaders from poor families. One child had been banished to my room because she posed a behavior problem to her fourth-grade teacher.
>
> My class and I were assigned a recess spot on the opposite side of the play yard, far away from the "normal" children. I was the only teacher who did not have a lunch break. I was required to eat with my "retarded" children while other teachers were permitted to leave their students. . . . Isolated from my colleagues, I closed my door and did my thing, oblivious to the larger educational circles in which I was immersed. Although it was the basement room, with all the negative perceptions that arrangement implies, I was secure in the knowledge that despite the ignominy of it all I did good things for children who were previously unloved and untaught. (Aiello, 1976, p. 14)

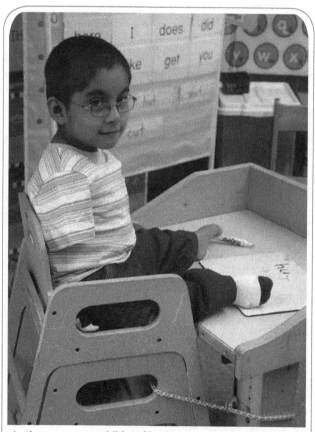

In the past, many children like Jose were denied access to education in public schools.

Children with mild learning and behavioral problems usually remained in general education classrooms but received no special help. Those who did not make satisfactory academic progress were termed "slow learners" or simply "failures." If their deportment in class exceeded the teacher's tolerance for misbehavior, they were labeled "disciplinary problems" and suspended from school. Children with more severe disabilities—including many with visual, hearing, and physical or health impairments—were placed in segregated schools or institutions or kept at home. Gifted and talented children seldom received special attention in schools. It was assumed they could make it on their own without help.

Society's response to exceptional children has come a long way. As our concepts of equality, freedom, and justice have expanded, children with disabilities and their families have moved from exclusion and isolation to inclusion and participation. Society no longer regards children with disabilities as beyond the responsibility of the local public schools. No longer may a child with disabilities be turned away from school because someone believes he is unable to benefit from education. Federal legislation and court rulings have made it clear that all children with disabilities have the right to a free appropriate program of public education in the least restrictive environment (Yell, 2012).

Separate Is Not Equal

The history of special education is closely related to the civil rights movement. Special education was strongly influenced by social developments and court decisions in the 1950s and 1960s, especially the landmark case *Brown v. Board of Education of Topeka* (1954), which challenged the practice of segregating students according to race. In its ruling in the *Brown* case, the U.S. Supreme Court declared that education must be made available to all children on equal terms:

> Today, education is perhaps the most important function of state and local governments. Compulsory school attendance laws and the great expenditure for education both demonstrate our recognition of the importance of education to our democratic society. It is required in the performance of our most basic responsibilities. . . . In these days, it is doubtful that any child may reasonably be expected to succeed in life if he is denied the opportunity of an education. (*Brown v. Board of Education*, 1954)

The *Brown* decision began a period of intense questioning among parents of children with disabilities, who asked why the same principles of equal access to education should not apply to their children. Parents and other advocates dissatisfied with an educational system that denied equal access to children with disabilities initiated numerous court cases in the 1960s and early 1970s. Generally, the parents based their arguments on the 14th Amendment to the Constitution, which provides that no state shall deny any person within its jurisdiction the equal protection of the law and that no state shall deprive any person of life, liberty, or property without due process of law.

Equal Protection

In the past, children with disabilities were denied access to certain educational programs or received special education only in segregated settings. Basically, when the courts have been asked to rule on the practice of denial or segregation, judges have examined whether such differential treatment is rational and necessary. One of the most historically significant cases to examine these questions was the class action suit *Pennsylvania Association for Retarded Children (PARC) v. Commonwealth of Pennsylvania* (1972). *PARC* challenged a state law that denied public school education to children considered "unable to profit from public school attendance."

The lawyers and parents supporting *PARC* argued that even though the children had intellectual disabilities, it was neither rational nor necessary to assume they were ineducable. Because the state was unable to prove that the children were, in fact, ineducable or to demonstrate a rational need for excluding them from public school programs, the court decided that the children were entitled to receive a free, public education. In addition, the court ruled that parents had the right to be notified before any change was made in their children's educational program.

The wording of the *PARC* decision proved particularly important because of its influence on subsequent federal legislation. Not only did the court rule that all children with intellectual disabilities were entitled to a free appropriate public education, but it also stipulated that placements in general education classrooms and regular public schools were preferable to segregated settings.

> It is the Commonwealth's obligation to place each mentally retarded child in a free, public program of education and training appropriate to the child's

capacity. . . . Placement in a regular public school class is preferable to placement in a special public school class and placement in a special public school is preferable to placement in any other type of program of education and training. (*PARC v. Commonwealth of Pennsylvania*, 1972)

The *Brown* and *PARC* cases had far-reaching effects on special education (Yell, 2012). The rulings from these landmark cases were incorporated into subsequent federal legislation, most notably IDEA.

THE INDIVIDUALS WITH DISABILITIES EDUCATION ACT

In 1975, Congress passed Public Law 94-142, the Education for All Handicapped Children Act. This piece of legislation completely changed the face of education in this country. Congress has reauthorized and amended PL 94-142 five times. The 1990 amendments renamed the law the Individuals with Disabilities Education Act—most often referred to by its acronym, IDEA. The most recent reauthorization of IDEA, PL 108-466, is titled *The Individuals with Disabilities Education Improvement Act of 2004.*

IDEA exerts a profound influence on what takes place in every school building in the country and has changed the roles and responsibilities of general and special educators, school administrators, parents, and students with disabilities in the educational process. The law reflects society's concern about treating people with disabilities as full citizens with the same rights and privileges all other citizens enjoy.

The purposes of IDEA are

1. (A) to ensure that all children with disabilities have available to them a free appropriate public education that emphasizes special education and related services designed to meet their unique needs and prepare them for further education, employment, and independent living; (B) to ensure that the rights of children with disabilities and parents of such children are protected; and (C) to assist States, localities, educational service agencies, and Federal agencies to provide for the education of all children with disabilities;

2. to assist States in the implementation of a statewide, comprehensive, coordinated, multidisciplinary, interagency system of early intervention services for infants and toddlers with disabilities and their families;

3. to ensure that educators and parents have the necessary tools to improve educational results for children with disabilities by supporting system improvement activities; coordinated research and personnel preparation; coordinated technical assistance, dissemination, and support; and technology development and media services; and

4. to assess, and ensure the effectiveness of, efforts to educate children with disabilities. (PL 108-466, Sec. 601 [d])

Major Principles of IDEA

The majority of the many rules and regulations defining how IDEA operates fall within six major principles, most of which have remained basically unchanged since 1975 (Turnbull, Huerta, & Stowe, 2009; Yell, 2012):

ZERO REJECT Schools must educate *all* children with disabilities. No child with disabilities may be excluded from a free public education, regardless of the nature or severity of the disability. The requirement to provide special education to all students with disabilities is absolute between the ages 6 and 17. If a state provides educational services to children without disabilities who are the ages of 3 to 5 and 18 to 21, it must also educate all children with disabilities in those age groups. Each state's education agency is responsible for locating, identifying, and evaluating all children, from birth to

Major principles of IDEA

Content Standards for Beginning Teachers—Initial Common Core: Rights and responsibilities of students, parents, teachers and other professionals, and schools related to exceptional learning needs (ICC1K4).

age 21, residing in the state with disabilities or who are suspected of having disabilities. This requirement of IDEA is called the *child find system*.

NONDISCRIMINATORY EVALUATION Schools must use nonbiased, multifactored methods of evaluation to determine whether a child has a disability and, if so, whether the child needs specially designed instruction to benefit from education. Testing and evaluation procedures must not discriminate on the basis of race, culture, or native language. All tests must be administered in the child's native language, and identification and placement decisions cannot be made on the basis of a single test score. These provisions of IDEA are known as *protection in evaluation procedures*.

FREE APPROPRIATE PUBLIC EDUCATION All children with disabilities, regardless of the type or severity of their disability, shall receive a **free appropriate public education (FAPE)**. This education must be provided at public expense—that is, without cost to the child's parents. An **individualized education program (IEP)** must be developed and implemented to meet the unique needs of each student with a disability. The IEP specifies the child's present levels of performance, identifies measurable annual goals, and describes the specific special education and related services that will be provided to help the child attain those goals and benefit from education.

Children with disabilities have sometimes been prevented from attending their neighborhood schools or benefiting from educational activities by circumstances that impede their access or participation. A child who uses a wheelchair, for example, may require a specially equipped school bus. A child with special health needs may require medication several times a day. A child with an orthopedic impairment may need physical therapy to maintain sufficient strength and flexibility in her arms and legs. IDEA requires that schools provide any related services and assistive technology that a child with a disability may need to access and benefit from special education. Types of related services included in the IDEA regulations are shown in Table 2.

LEAST RESTRICTIVE ENVIRONMENT IDEA requires schools to educate students with disabilities with children without disabilities to the maximum extent appropriate and

School districts must provide related services and assistive technology to students with disabilities—such as this device that enlarges printed material—so they may have access to and benefit from a public education.

Katelyn Metzger/Merrill

TABLE 2 • **Types and definitions of related services that students with disabilities may need to benefit from special education**

RELATED SERVICE	IDEA DEFINITION
Audiology	(1) Identification of children with hearing loss; (2) Determination of the range, nature, and degree of hearing loss, including referral for medical or other professional attention for the habilitation of hearing; (3) Provision of habilitative activities, such as auditory training, speech reading (lipreading), hearing evaluation, and speech conservation; (4) Creation and administration of programs for prevention of hearing loss; (5) Counseling and guidance of children, parents, and teachers, regarding hearing loss; and (6) Determining the child's need for group and individual amplification, selecting and fitting an appropriate hearing aid, and evaluating the effectiveness of amplification.
Counseling Services	Services provided by qualified social workers, psychologists, guidance counselors, or other qualified personnel.
Early Identification and Assessment	Implementation of a formal plan for identifying a disability as early as possible in a child's life.
Interpreting Services	(1) The following, when used with respect to children who are deaf or hard of hearing: Oral transliteration services, cued language transliteration services, sign language transliteration and interpreting services, and transcription services, such as communication access real-time translation (CART), C-Print, and TypeWell; and (2) Special interpreting services for children who are deaf-blind.
Medical Services	Services provided by a licensed physician for diagnostic or evaluation purposes to determine a child's medically related disability that results in the child's need for special education and related services.
Occupational Therapy	(1) Services provided by a qualified occupational therapist; and (2) includes (A) Improving, developing, or restoring functions impaired or lost through illness, injury, or deprivation; (B) Improving ability to perform tasks for independent functioning if functions are impaired or lost; and (C) Preventing, through early intervention, initial or further impairment or loss of function.
Orientation and Mobility Services	Services provided to blind or visually impaired children by qualified personnel to enable those students to obtain systematic orientation to and safe movement within their environments in school, home, and community.
Parent Counseling and Training	(1) Assisting parents in understanding the special needs of their child; (2) Providing parents with information about child development; and (3) Helping parents to acquire the necessary skills that will allow them to support the implementation of their child's IEP or IFSP.
Physical Therapy	Services provided by a qualified physical therapist.
Psychological Services	(1) Administering psychological and educational tests, and other assessment procedures; (2) Interpreting assessment results; (3) Obtaining, integrating, and interpreting information about child behavior and conditions relating to learning; (4) Consulting with other staff members in planning school programs to meet the special needs of children as indicated by psychological tests, interviews, and behavioral evaluations; (5) Planning and managing a program of psychological services, including psychological counseling for children and parents; and (6) Assisting in developing positive behavioral intervention strategies.
Recreation	(1) Assessment of leisure function; (2) Therapeutic recreation services; (3) Recreation programs in schools and community agencies; and (4) Leisure education.
Rehabilitative Counseling Services	Services provided by qualified personnel in individual or group sessions that focus specifically on career development, employment preparation, achieving independence, and integration in the workplace and community.
School Health Services and School Nurse Services	Health services designed to enable a child with a disability to receive FAPE as described by the child's IEP. School nurse services are provided by a qualified school nurse or other qualified person. School health services are services provided by either a qualified school nurse or other qualified person.

TABLE 2 • (Continued)

RELATED SERVICE	IDEA DEFINITION
Social work services in the schools	(1) Preparing a social or developmental history on a child with a disability; (2) Group and individual counseling with the child and family; (3) Working in partnership with parents and others on those problems in a child's living situation (home, school, and community) that affect the child's adjustment in school; (4) Mobilizing school and community resources to enable the child to learn as effectively as possible; and (5) Assisting in developing positive behavioral intervention strategies.
Speech-language pathology services	(1) Identification of children with speech or language impairments; (2) Diagnosis and appraisal of specific speech or language impairments; (3) Referral for medical or other professional attention necessary for the habilitation of speech or language impairments; (4) Provision of speech and language services for the habilitation and prevention of communicative problems; and (5) Counseling and guidance of parents, children, and teachers regarding speech and language impairments.
Transportation	(1) Travel to and from school and between schools. (2) Travel in and around school buildings. (3) Specialized equipment (such as special or adapted buses, lifts, and ramps), if required to provide special transportation for a child with a disability.
Exception—services that apply to children with surgically implanted devices, including cochlear implants	(1) Related services do not include a medical device that is surgically implanted, the optimization of that device's functioning (e.g., mapping), maintenance of that device, or the replacement of that device. (2) Nothing in paragraph (b)(1) of this section—(i) Limits the right of a child with a surgically implanted device (e.g., cochlear implant) to receive related services that are determined by the IEP Team to be necessary for the child to receive FAPE; (ii) Limits the responsibility of a public agency to appropriately monitor and maintain medical devices that are needed to maintain the health and safety of the child, including breathing, nutrition, or operation of other bodily functions, while the child is transported to and from school or is at school; or (iii) Prevents the routine checking of an external component of a surgically implanted device to make sure it is functioning properly.

Source: IDEA Regulations, 34 Code of Federal Regulations (CFR) §300.34; Authority: 20 USC §1401 (26).

that students with disabilities be removed to separate classes or schools only when the nature or severity of their disabilities is such that they cannot receive an appropriate education in a general education classroom with supplementary aids and services. IDEA creates a presumption in favor of inclusion in the general education classroom by requiring that a student's IEP contain a justification and explanation of the extent, if any, to which the student will not participate with nondisabled peers in the general academic curriculum, extracurricular activities, and other nonacademic activities (e.g., lunch, recess, transportation, dances). To ensure that each student with disabilities is educated in the least restrictive environment (LRE) appropriate for her needs, school districts must provide a continuum of alternative placements and service alternatives (e.g., consultation with general education classroom, resource room, special class, special schools).

PROCEDURAL SAFEGUARDS Schools must follow an extensive set of procedures to safeguard and protect the rights and interests of children with disabilities and their parents. Parental consent must be obtained for initial and all subsequent evaluations and placement decisions regarding special education. Schools must maintain the confidentiality of all records pertaining to a child with disabilities and make those records available to the parents. When parents of a child with disabilities disagree with the results of an evaluation performed by the school, they can obtain an independent evaluation at public expense. When the school and parents disagree on the identification, evaluation, placement, or provision of a FAPE and related services for the child, the parents may request a **due process hearing.** States also must offer parents an opportunity to resolve the matter through mediation by a third party before holding a due process

Due process safeguards

 Council for Exceptional Children

Content Standards for Beginning Teachers—Initial Common Core: Issues, assurances, and due process rights related to assessment, eligibility, and placement within a continuum of services (ICC1K6).

hearing. If parents prevail in due process or judicial proceedings under IDEA, the state must reimburse their attorneys' fees. The law also allows the court to award reasonable attorneys' fees to the prevailing school district against the attorney of a parent, or the parent who files a complaint that the court determines to be frivolous, unreasonable, without foundation, or filed for any improper purpose, such as to harass.

Although most conflicts between school districts and parents are resolved without resorting to a due process hearing, hearings occur with increasing frequency (Bateman, 2010). Zirkel and D'Angelo (2002) reviewed all reported hearing decisions in the United States from 1998 to 2000 and found that schools received a favorable decision in 55% of hearings, parents prevailed in 23%, and 22% of the decisions were mixed results.

PARENT PARTICIPATION AND SHARED DECISION MAKING Schools must collaborate with parents and students with disabilities in the planning and implementation of special education and related services. The parents' (and, whenever appropriate, the student's) input and wishes must be considered in determining IEP goals, related-service needs, and placement decisions.

Other Provisions of IDEA

SPECIAL EDUCATION SERVICES FOR PRESCHOOLERS Noting that states were serving at most about 70% of preschool children with disabilities and that early intervention services for infants and toddlers with disabilities from birth through age 2 were scarce or nonexistent in many states, Congress included provisions in the Education of the Handicapped Act Amendments in 1986 (PL 99-457) to expand services for these segments of the population. Beginning with the 1990–1991 school year, PL 99-457 required each state to fully serve all preschool children with disabilities ages 3 to 5—that is, to provide the same services and protections available to school-age children.

EARLY INTERVENTION FOR INFANTS AND TODDLERS PL 99-457 included an incentive grant program to encourage states to provide early intervention services to infants and toddlers with disabilities and their families. The children served are those from birth through age 2 who need early intervention services because they are experiencing developmental delays or have a diagnosed biological condition likely to result in developmental delays. Rather than mandate special services for this age group, IDEA encourages each state to develop and implement a statewide, comprehensive, coordinated, multidisciplinary, interagency program of early intervention services for infants and toddlers with disabilities and their families. The encouragement is in the form of a gradually increasing amount of federal money awarded to states that identify and serve all infants and toddlers with disabilities. Various education and human services agencies within each state work together to provide services such as medical and educational assessment, physical therapy, speech and language intervention, and parent counseling and training. These early intervention services are prescribed and implemented according to an **individualized family services plan (IFSP)** written by a multidisciplinary team that includes the child's parents.

ASSISTIVE TECHNOLOGY IDEA requires IEP teams to consider whether assistive technology is necessary in order for a child to receive a FAPE. The law defines **assistive technology** as "any item, piece of equipment, or product system, whether acquired commercially off the shelf, modified, or customized, that is used to increase, maintain, or improve functional capabilities of a child with a disability" (20 USC 1401, Sec. 602[1]). Assistive technology includes devices and services such as alternative and augmentative communication devices, low-vision aids, positioning and mobility devices, and adaptive toys and games (Bryant & Bryant, 2012).

SCIENTIFICALLY BASED INSTRUCTION An important addition to IDEA 2004 was the stipulation that the special education and related services prescribed in a child's IEP be "based on peer-reviewed research to the extent practicable." For example, a large body of peer-reviewed research supports the use of instructional activities that build students' fluency with tool skills such as reading and math computation (Kubina & Hughes, 2005). See *Teaching & Learning*, "It's Good to Go Fast!"

UNIVERSAL DESIGN FOR LEARNING The concept of universal design originated in architecture, with the design and construction of barrier-free physical environments (e.g., installing ramps and curb cuts for wheelchair users). IDEA 2004 defines *universal design* consistent with the Assistive Technology Act as "a concept or philosophy for designing and delivering products and services that are usable by people with the widest possible range of functional capabilities, which include products and services that are directly accessible (without requiring assistive technologies) and products and services that are interoperable with assistive technologies" (Sec. 3[19]).

The basic idea of **universal design for learning (UDL)** is that new curricular materials and learning technologies should be designed from the beginning to be flexible enough to accommodate the learning styles of a wide range of individuals, including children with disabilities. UDL applied to curriculum and instruction encompasses three principles: (a) multiple means of representation to to give diverse learners options for acquiring information and knowlege (e.g., presenting material in different formats such as print, print with audio pictures, accessible web pages); (b) multiple means of action and expression to provide learners options for demonstrating what they know (e.g., students can respond, such as speaking, writing, and using voice-operated switches); and (c) multiple means of engagement to tap into students' interests, offer appropriate challenges, and increase motivation (National Center on Universal Design for Learning, 2011).

Legal Challenges to IDEA

Although IDEA has resulted in dramatic increases in the number of students receiving special education services and greater recognition of the legal rights of children with disabilities and their families, it has also resulted in numerous disputes concerning the education of students with disabilities. Parents and other advocates have brought about thousands of due process hearings and hundreds of court cases. Due process hearings and court cases place parents and schools in confrontation and are expensive and time-consuming (Getty & Summey, 2004; Yell, Katsiyannis, & Bradley, 2009).

It is difficult to generalize how courts have resolved the various legal challenges based on IDEA. Many different judicial interpretations exist for *free appropriate public education* and *least restrictive environment*. The federal statute and regulations use these terms repeatedly; but in the view of many parents, educators, judges, and attorneys, they are not defined with sufficient clarity. Thus, the questions of what is appropriate and least restrictive for a particular child and whether a public school district should be compelled to provide a certain type of instructional program or service must often be decided by judges and courts based on the evidence presented. Some of the key issues that courts have ruled on are the extended school year, FAPE and related services, disciplinary procedures, and the fundamental right to an education for students with the most severe disabilities.

EXTENDED SCHOOL YEAR Most public schools operate for approximately 180 days per year. Parents and advocates have argued that, for some children with disabilities, particularly those with severe and multiple disabilities, a 180-day school year is not sufficient to meet their needs. In *Armstrong v. Kline* (1979), the parents of five students with severe disabilities claimed that their children tended to regress during the usual breaks in the school year and called on the schools to provide a period of instruction longer than 180 days. The court agreed and ordered the schools to extend the school year for these students. As a result of this and other related judicial rulings, the IDEA regulations require school districts to provide extended school years services if an IEP team determines they are necessary for a student to receive a FAPE (34 *CFR* § 300.309).

It's Good to Go Fast!
Fluency-Building Activities
Promote Student Achievement

Ask 100 teachers, "Is practice important?" and every one will answer, "Yes" (and more than a few will give you a funny look for asking a question with such an obvious answer). Then ask the same 100 teachers, "What is the purpose of practice?" Their answers to this question will vary considerably, but responses such as the following will be common: practice should help students "internalize the knowledge," "attain a deep or rich understanding," and "gain confidence" with the skill. These are worthy outcomes, but what does the performance of a student who has "internalized" a concept look like, and what types of practice will help students "gain confidence"?

Here's another purpose of practice: practice should help students achieve fluency.

WHAT IS FLUENCY, AND WHY DOES IT MATTER?

Fluency is the combination of accuracy and speed that characterizes competent performance. A person who is fluent performs a skill automatically, without hesitations, as if by second nature. Accuracy, typically in the form of percent correct, is commonly used to assess student performance; fluency gives a more complete picture of learning than accuracy alone. Whereas two students might each complete a page of math problems with

100% accuracy, the one who finishes in 2 minutes is much more accomplished than the one who needs 7 minutes to answer the same problems. Fluency also has important functional implications. Many of the skills we use every day in school, home, community, or the workplace must be performed at a certain rate or speed to be useful. The student who needs 5 minutes to read the directions on a worksheet that his classmates read in 1 minute may not be able to finish the task in the time allotted.

A student who is fluent with a particular skill or knowledge is likely to exhibit the following outcomes (Binder, 1996; Kubina, 2005; Kubina & Morrison, 2000; Lin & Kubina, 2005; Smyth & Keenan, 2002):

- **Better retention.** The ability to use the skill or knowledge at a later point in time, even when no opportunities to emit the behavior have occurred since prior practice.
- **Greater endurance.** The ability to stay at the task for longer periods of time and stay engaged. Fluent performers are also less likely to be distracted by minor events in the environment.
- **Improved application and generalization.** For example, a student who has achieved fluency in

How many directional arrows can you correctly identify in 1 minute? "See-say" time trials are helping Robert attain fluency with this map-reading skill.

component skills (e.g., multiplication facts and subtraction) may learn composite skills (e.g., long division) more quickly.

THREE FLUENCY-BUILDING TECHNIQUES

The three fluency-building techniques described next—repeated reading, time trials, and SAFMEDS—can be conducted as teacher-directed practice activities one-on-one in small groups or with the whole class. Each technique can also be used as peer-managed or independent practice activities.

Repeated Reading. Oral reading fluency is a key component of reading success (National Reading Panel, 2000a). Students who can read fast can cover more material, and their comprehension is better than slower readers (Daane, Campbell, Grigg, Goodman, & Oranje, 2005). One of the most often-used interventions to improve reading fluency is repeated reading. With **repeated reading**, the student orally reads the same passage, usually three to five times during each session. With each successive reading, the student tries to increase the number of words read correctly per minute. The student first listens to the teacher, who models reading the passage; the student may read the passage silently, before beginning; and the teacher provides feedback and practice on missed words and phrases (Alber-Morgan, 2007). When the student achieves the fluency criterion on a given passage, the teacher introduces a new passage. The difficulty level of successive passages gradually increases over time. The set goal is slightly higher than the current reading rate (Bursuck & Damer, 2011). Numerous studies report that repeated reading is an effective means for improving oral reading fluency for students with and without disabilities in elementary, middle, and high school (Alber-Morgan, Ramp, Anderson, & Martin, 2007; Tam, Heward, & Heng, 2006; Yurick, Robinson, Cartledge, Lo, & Evans, 2006).

Time Trials. Giving students the opportunity to perform a skill as many times as they can in a brief period—**time trials**—can be an excellent way to build fluency. Practice in the form of 1-minute time trials helps students with and without disabilities achieve fluency with a wide range of academic, vocational, and other skills (e.g., Beck, Conrad, & Anderson, 2010; Codding, Burns, & Lukito, 2011; Johnson & Layng, 1994; Miller, Hall, & Heward, 1995; Smith, Marchand-Martella, & Martella, 2011).

SAFMEDS. *Say All Fast a Minute Each Day Shuffled* (**SAFMEDS**) consist of a deck of cards with a question, vocabulary term, or problem on one side of each card and the answer on the other side. A student answers as many items in the deck as he can during 1 minute. The student looks at the question or problem, states the answer, flips the card over to reveal the correct answer, and puts the card on either a "correct" or "incorrect" pile. Eshleman (2000) provides examples and guidelines for using SAFMEDS.

HOW TO GET STARTED

When planning and conducting fluency-building activities, teachers should consider these guidelines:

- **Use fluency building during the practice stage of learning.** During the initial acquisition stage of learning, the student should focus on learning to perform the skill correctly. A student who tries to "go fast" before she can perform the skill correctly more often than incorrectly might end up "practicing errors" instead of building fluency. (Because they reveal the correct answer to each question, SAFMEDS can help build fluency during the acquisition stage of learning.)
- **The time for each fluency-building trial should be brief.** One minute is sufficient for most academic skills. Brief interval sprints of 10 seconds, then 15 seconds, 20 seconds, and so on, can help students gradually build their fluency (Kostewicz & Kubina, 2010).
- **Do fluency-building activities daily.** For example, a series of two or three 1-minute oral reading time trials could be conducted at the end of each day's lesson.
- **Make fluency building fun.** Time trials should not be presented as a test; they are a learning activity that can be approached like a game.
- **Follow fluency-building activities more relaxed activities.**
- **Feedback should emphasize proficiency** (total number correct), not simply accuracy (percentage correct).
- **Encourage each student to set goals and try to beat his or her own best performance.**
- **Have students keep track of their progress** by self-graphing their best performance each day.
- **Consider using a performance feedback chart** to provide both individual students and the class with feedback during a fluency-building program.

MyEducationLab™

To watch students and teachers engaged in fluency-building activities in math, reading, writing, and social studies, go to MyEducationLab, Chapter 1, and click on Fluency Building videos.

FAPE AND RELATED SERVICES The related-services provision of IDEA has been highly controversial, creating much disagreement about what kinds of related services are necessary and reasonable for the schools to provide a FAPE and what services should be the responsibility of the child's parents. The first case based on IDEA to reach the U.S. Supreme Court was *Board of Education of the Hendrick Hudson Central School District v. Rowley* (1982). Amy Rowley was a fourth grader who, because of her hearing loss, needed special education and related services. The school district had originally provided Amy with a hearing aid, speech therapy, a tutor, and a sign language interpreter to accompany her in the general education classroom. The school withdrew the sign language services after the interpreter reported that Amy did not make use of her services: Amy reportedly looked at the teacher to read her lips and asked the teacher to repeat instructions rather than get the information from the interpreter. Amy's parents contended that she was missing up to 50% of the ongoing instruction (her hearing loss was estimated to have left her with 50% residual hearing) and was therefore being denied an appropriate public school education. The school district's position was that Amy, with the help of the other special services she was still receiving, was passing from grade to grade without an interpreter. School personnel thought, in fact, that an interpreter might hinder Amy's interactions with her teacher and peers. It was also noted that this service would cost the school district as much as $25,000 per year. The Supreme Court ruled that Amy, who was making satisfactory progress in school without an interpreter, was receiving an adequate education and that the school district could not be compelled to hire a full-time interpreter.

DISCIPLINING STUDENTS WITH DISABILITIES Some cases have resulted from parents' protesting the suspension or expulsion of children with disabilities. The case of *Stuart v. Nappi* (1978), for example, concerned a high school student who spent much of her time wandering in the halls even though she was assigned to special classes. The school sought to have the student expelled on disciplinary grounds because her conduct was considered detrimental to order in the school. The court agreed with the student's mother that expulsion would deny the student an FAPE as called for in IDEA. In other cases, expulsion or suspension of students with disabilities has been upheld if the school could show that the grounds for expulsion did not relate to the student's disability. In 1988, however, the Supreme Court ruled in *Honig v. Doe* that schools could not recommend expulsion or suspend a student with disabilities for more than 10 days.

The IDEA amendments of 1997 (PL 105-17) contained provisions that enable school districts to discipline students with disabilities in the same manner as students without disabilities, with a few notable exceptions. If the school seeks a change of placement, suspension, or expulsion in excess of 10 days, the IEP team and other qualified personnel must review the relationship between the student's misconduct and her disability. This review is called a **manifestation determination** (Katsiyannis & Maag, 2001). If the team determines that the student's behavior is not related to the disability, the same disciplinary procedures used with other students may be imposed. However, the school must continue to provide educational services in the alternative placement.

IDEA 2004 revised the discipline provisions of the law such that under special circumstances (e.g., student brings to or possesses a weapon at school; possesses, uses, or sells illegal drugs at school; inflicts serious injury upon someone at school or a school function), school personnel have the authority to remove a student with disabilities to an interim alternative educational setting for up to 45 school days, whether or not the misconduct was related to the child's disability.

RIGHT TO EDUCATION The case of *Timothy W. v. Rochester School District* (1989) threatened the zero-reject philosophy of IDEA. In July 1988, Judge Loughlin of the district court in New Hampshire ruled that a 13-year-old boy with severe disabilities and quadriplegia was ineligible for education services because he could not benefit from special education. The judge ruled in favor of the Rochester School Board, which claimed that IDEA was not intended to provide educational services to "all

Manifestation determination

Council for Exceptional Children

Content Standards for Beginning Teachers—Initial Common Core: Laws, policies, and ethical principles regarding behavior management planning and implementation (ICC1K2).

handicapped students." In his decision, the judge determined that the federal law was not explicit regarding a "rare child" with severe disabilities and declared that special evaluations and examinations should be used to determine "qualifications for education under PL 94-142."

In May 1989, a court of appeals overturned the lower court's decision, ruling that public schools must educate all children with disabilities regardless of how little they might benefit or the nature or severity of their disabilities. The three-judge panel concluded that "schools cannot avoid the provisions of EHA [Education of the Handicapped Amendments] by returning to the practices that were widespread prior to the Act's passage . . . of unilaterally excluding certain handicapped children from a public education on the ground that they are uneducable" (U.S. Court of Appeals, 875 F.2d 954 [1st Cir.]).

Related Legislation

JAVITS GIFTED AND TALENTED STUDENT EDUCATION ACT IDEA does not apply to children who are gifted and talented. The Jacob K. Javits Gifted and Talented Student Education Act (PL 100-297), enacted in 1988, is the only federal program that addresses the needs of the nation's 3 million gifted and talented students. This act provides federal support for demonstration programs at a national research center on the gifted and talented, competitive grants to institutions of higher education and state and local school districts to develop and expand models serving students who are underrepresented in gifted and talented programs, and competitive grants for state agencies and school districts to enhance gifted education curricula and programs. While the purpose of the Javits Act is laudable, it has been "chronically underfunded" (Council for Exceptional Children, 2011). The $7.5 million Congress appropriated for the act in fiscal year 2010 represents less than 2 cents of every $100 of the federal K–12 education budget.

SECTION 504 OF THE REHABILITATION ACT OF 1973 Another important law that extends civil rights to people with disabilities is Section 504 of the Rehabilitation Act of 1973, which states that "no otherwise qualified handicapped individual shall . . . solely by reason of his handicap, be excluded from the participation in, be denied the benefits of, or be subject to discrimination under any program or activity receiving federal financial assistance" (Sec. 504, 29 USC § 794[a]). This law, worded almost identically to the Civil Rights Act of 1964 (which prohibited discrimination based on race, color, or national origin), expanded opportunities to children and adults with disabilities in education, employment, and various other settings. It requires provision of "auxiliary aids for students with impaired sensory, manual, or speaking skills"—for example, readers for students who are blind and people to assist students with physical disabilities in moving from place to place. This requirement does not mean that schools, colleges, and employers must have all such aids available at all times; it simply means that no person with disabilities may be excluded from a program because of the lack of an appropriate aid.

Section 504 is not a federal grant program; unlike IDEA, it does not provide any federal money to assist people with disabilities. Rather, it "imposes a duty on every recipient of federal funds not to discriminate against handicapped persons" (T. P. Johnson, 1986, p. 8). "Recipient," of course, includes public school districts, virtually all of which receive federal support. Most colleges and universities have also been affected; many students in private institutions receive federal financial aid. The Office of Civil Rights conducts periodic compliance reviews and acts on complaints when parents, individuals with disabilities, or others contend that a school district is violating Section 504.

Architectural accessibility for students, teachers, and others with physical and sensory impairments is an important feature of Section 504; however, the law does not call for a completely barrier-free environment. Emphasis is on accessibility to programs, not on physical modification of all existing structures. If a chemistry class is required for a pre-med program of study, for example, a college might make this program accessible to a student with physical disabilities by reassigning the class to an accessible location or providing assistance to the student in traveling to an otherwise inaccessible location. Not all sections of all courses need to be made accessible, but a college should not segregate students with disabilities by assigning them all to a particular section. Like IDEA, Section 504 calls for nondiscriminatory placement in the "most integrated setting appropriate" and has served as the basis for many court cases over alleged discrimination against individuals with disabilities, particularly in their right to employment. For a discussion of what teachers need to know about Section 504, see T. E. C. Smith (2002).

AMERICANS WITH DISABILITIES ACT The Americans with Disabilities Act (ADA) was signed into law in 1990 and amended in 2008. Patterned after Section 504 of the Rehabilitation Act of 1973, ADA extends civil rights protection of people with disabilities to private sector employment, public services and accommodation, transportation, and telecommunications. A persons with a disability is defined in ADA as a person (a) having a physical or mental impairment that substantially limits one or more major life activities (e.g., caring for oneself, walking, communicating, working); (b) having a record of such an impairment (e.g., a person who no longer has heart disease but who is discriminated against because of that history); or (c) who is regarded as having such an impairment (e.g., a person with significant facial disfiguration due to a burn who is not limited in any major life activity but is discriminated against). The major provisions of ADA fall under four areas:

- *Employment.* Employers with 15 or more workers may not discriminate against a qualified individual with a disability in the application and hiring process or in opportunities for advancement. Employers must make reasonable accommodations that will allow a person with a disability to perform essential job functions. The employer must make reasonable accommodations in job requirements or situation if they will not impose "undue hardship" or expense on the employer.
- *Public entities (including public transportation).* ADA regulations detail accommodations requirements for making public transportation accessible to people with disabilities. New vehicles purchased by public transit authorities must be accessible to people with disabilities. All intercity and commuter rail services must be accessible and usable.
- *Public accommodations and commercial facilities.* Businesses open to the public, such as hotels, restaurants, grocery stores, and parks and recreation facilities, must not discriminate against people with disabilities. New buildings must be made accessible, and existing facilities must remove barriers if doing so is "readily achievable." The law recognizes that what might be readily achievable by a large company might not be so for a small, local business.
- *Telecommunications.* Companies offering telecommunications services to the general public must offer telecommunications relay services (TRS) to consumers with disabilities, notably those who are deaf or hard of hearing, 24 hours per day, 7 days per week. In TRS, communication assistants translate between the signed/typed words of a consumer and the spoken words of others.

The Americans with Disabilities Act requires employers to make reasonable accommodations to allow a person with disabilities to perform essential job functions.

ELEMENTARY AND SECONDARY EDUCATION ACT (A.K.A. NO CHILD LEFT BEHIND ACT) The Elementary and Secondary Education Act (ESEA) was first enacted in 1965 as part of President Lyndon Johnson's war on poverty. The law's first part, Title I, includes criteria and formulas for determining schools' eligibility for funding for programs serving children from low-income families. Congress appropriates funds for ESEA annually, and the law is to be reauthorized every 5 to 6 years. When Congress reauthorized ESEA in 2001, it renamed it the No Child Left Behind Act (NCLB). The intent of NCLB is to improve the achievement of all students, with a particular emphasis on children from low-income families. The ultimate goal of NCLB was that all children would be proficient in reading and math by 2014 and be taught by qualified teachers highly trained in their subjects. Two major provisions of NCLB stress accountability for student learning and scientifically based programs of instruction.

Accountability for Student Learning. States are expected to make annual progress toward the 100% goal by 2014. NCLB requires annual assessments of at least 95% of all students in each school district in reading/language arts and math in grades 3 through 8 and at least once in grades 10 through 12. States must report disaggregated test results for students by poverty levels, race, ethnicities, disabilities, and limited English proficiency. Each school and children from each category must achieve state-determined pass rates that gradually rise each year toward the 100% goal. Annual school "report cards" provide comparative information on the performance of each school. These report cards are intended to show not only how well students are doing on meeting standards but also the progress that disaggregated groups are making in closing achievement gaps. Districts and schools that repeatedly fail to make **adequate yearly progress (AYP)** toward state proficiency goals for 2 consecutive years are subject to increasingly intrusive corrective actions and ultimately restructuring. Schools whose test results meet or exceed a state's pass rates are eligible for academic achievement awards such as public commendations.

Scientifically Based Instruction. NCLB puts a special emphasis on using educational programs and practices that rigorous scientific research has demonstrated to be effective. The NCLB-funded Reading First program is a prime example of the emphasis on research-based practices. Reading First is designed to help states, school districts, and schools ensure that every child can read at grade level or above by the end of grade 3 through the implementation of instructional programs and materials, assessments, and professional development grounded in scientifically based reading research. Lyon and Riccards (2007) used data from Washington state as an example of "just one of many success stories across the nation" for the Reading First program. They reported that even though the poverty rate in Reading First schools is 84% compared to the statewide average of 36%, reading achievement scores in Reading First schools increased by 22% compared to an 11% increase across the state.

Implications for Students with Disabilities. The provisions of NCLB apply to all students, including those with disabilities. When Congress reauthorized IDEA in 2004, it aligned many provisions of the law with NCLB. Although IDEA already required students with disabilities to participate in state- and districtwide assessments, the inclusion of all students' scores in a school district's report card has resulted in higher expectations for achievement by students receiving special education and increased the accountability of schools to help them attain it. Some students with mild to moderate disabilities are provided with **accommodations** (e.g., additional time, large print) when taking district- and statewide tests (Carter, Prater, & Dyches, 2009). Students with severe disabilities for whom standard academic achievement tests would be inappropriate can take **alternative assessments** (e.g., a video portfolio demonstrating improvements in language or adaptive behavior) if their IEP team recommends them (Thompson, Quenemoen, Thurlow, & Ysseldyke, 2001).

While recognizing that NCLB is a complex, powerful law, Yell (2012) describes it as a "a logical step" in a progression of federal laws intended to improve the academic achievement of our nation's students. Strongly divided opinions over the merits of NCLB, particularly with respect to how test scores of students with disabilities and those with limited English proficiency are used to determine schools' effectiveness, will likely lead Congress to make significant revisions in the next reauthorization of ESEA. This author hopes that Yell is correct in his prediction that two provisions of the law will remain unchanged: the emphasis on evidence-based instruction and holding schools accountable for student learning. Table 3 summarizes federal legislation regarding the education of exceptional children and rights of individuals with disabilities.

WHAT IS SPECIAL EDUCATION?

Special education is a complex enterprise that can be defined and evaluated from many perspectives. One may, for example, view special education as a legislatively governed enterprise whose practitioners are concerned with issues such as due process procedures for informing parents of their right to participate in decisions about their children's education and the extent to which the school district's IEPs include each component required by IDEA. From a sociopolitical perspective, special education can be seen as an outgrowth of the civil rights movement and society's changing attitudes about people with disabilities. Each of these perspectives has some validity, and each has had and continues to play an important role in defining special education and its practice. Neither view, however, reveals the fundamental purpose of special education as *instructionally based intervention*.

Special Education as Intervention

Special education is, first of all, purposeful intervention designed to prevent, eliminate, and/or overcome the obstacles that might keep a child with disabilities from learning and from full and active participation in school and society. Special education provides three basic types of intervention: preventive, remedial, and compensatory.

PREVENTIVE INTERVENTION Special educators design preventive intervention to keep a potential or minor problem from becoming a disability. Preventive interventions include actions that stop an event from happening and those that reduce the negative outcomes of a disability or condition that has already been identified. Prevention can occur at three levels:

- *Primary prevention* is designed to reduce the number of new cases (**incidence**) of a disability; it consists of efforts to eliminate or counteract risk factors so that a child never acquires a disability. Educators use primary prevention efforts for all people who could be affected by the targeted problem. For example, in a school-wide program to prevent behavior disorders, primary prevention would include building- and classroomwide systems of positive behavior support for all students (Sugai et al., 2010).
- *Secondary prevention* is aimed at individuals who have already been exposed to or are displaying specific risk factors and is intended to eliminate or counteract the effects of those risk factors. Secondary prevention in a schoolwide program to prevent behavior disorders would entail specialized interventions for those students exhibiting early signs of troubled behavior.
- *Tertiary prevention* is aimed at individuals with a disability and intended to prevent the effects of the disability from worsening. For example, intensive interventions would be provided for students identified with emotional or behavioral disorders.

Preventive efforts are most promising when they begin as early as possible—even before birth, in many cases. Later we describe some of the promising methods for preventing and minimizing the effects of disabilities. Unfortunately, widespread primary and secondary prevention programs are rare in this country, and it is likely that it will be decades before a significant reduction in the incidence and prevalence of most disabilities is achieved. In the meantime, we must rely on remedial and

Preventive, remedial, and compensatory interventions

 Council for Exceptional Children

Content Standards for Beginning Teachers—Initial Common Core: Models, theories, and philosophies that form the basis for special education practice (ICC1K1).

TABLE 3 • **Federal legislation concerning the education of exceptional children and rights of individuals with disabilities**

DATE	LEGISLATION	EDUCATIONAL IMPLICATIONS
1958	National Defense Education Act (PL 85-926)	Provided funds for training professionals to train teachers of children with mental retardation
1961	Special Education Act (PL 87-276)	Provided funds for training professionals to train teachers of deaf children
1963	Mental Retardation Facility and Community Center Construction Act (PL 88-164)	Extended support given in PL 85-926 to training teachers of children with other disabilities
1965	Elementary and Secondary Education Act (PL 89-10)	Provided money to states and local districts for developing programs for economically disadvantaged and disabled children
1966	Amendment to Title I of the Elementary and Secondary Education Act (PL 89-313)	Provided funding for state-supported programs in institutions and other settings for children with disabilities
1966	Amendments to the Elementary and Secondary Education Act (PL 89-750)	Created the federal Bureau of Education for the Handicapped (today's Office of Special Education)
1968	Handicapped Children's Early Assistance Act (PL 90-538)	Established the "first chance network" of experimental programs for preschool children with disabilities
1969	Elementary, Secondary, and Other Educational Amendments (PL 91-230)	Defined learning disabilities and provided funds for state-level programs for children with learning disabilities
1970	Education Amendments of 1970 (PL 92-318)	Mandated a study of the gifted that resulted in the *Marland Report* (1972), which many states used as a basis for building programs for gifted and talented students
1973	Section 504 of the Rehabilitation Act (PL 93-112)	Declared that a person cannot be excluded on the basis of disability alone from any program or activity receiving federal funds
1974	Education Amendments (PL 93-380)	Extended previous legislation; provided money to state and local districts for programs for gifted and talented students for the first time; protected the rights of children with disabilities and their parents in placement decisions
1975	Developmental Disabilities Assistance and Bill of Rights Act (PL 94-103)	Affirmed the rights of citizens with mental retardation (MR) and cited areas in which services must be provided for people with MR and other developmental disabilities
1975	Education for All Handicapped Children Act (EAHCA) (PL 94-142)	Mandated free appropriate public education for all children with disabilities ages 6 to 21; protected the rights of children with disabilities and their parents in educational decision making; required the development of an IEP for each child with a disability; stated that students with disabilities must receive educational services in the least restrictive environment
1978	Gifted and Talented Children's Education Act of 1978 (PL 95-561)	Provided funds for in-service training programs, research, and other projects aimed at meeting the needs of gifted and talented students
1983	Amendments to the Education of the Handicapped Act (PL 98-199)	Required states to collect data on the number of youth with disabilities exiting their systems and to address the needs of secondary students making the transition to adulthood; gave incentives to states to provide services to infants and preschool children with disabilities
1984	Developmental Disabilities Assistance and Bill of Rights Acts (PL 98-527)	Mandated the development of employment-related training activities for adults with disabilities

(Continues)

TABLE 3 • (Continued)

DATE	LEGISLATION	EDUCATIONAL IMPLICATIONS
1986	Handicapped Children's Protection Act (PL 99-372)	Provided authority for the reimbursement of attorney's fees to parents who prevail in a hearing or court case to secure an appropriate education for their child
1986	Education for the Handicapped Act Amendments of 1986 (PL 99-457)	Required states to provide free appropriate education to all 3- to 5-year-olds with disabilities who were eligible to apply for federal preschool funding; included incentive grants to encourage states to develop comprehensive interdisciplinary services for infants and toddlers (birth through age 2) and their families
1986	Rehabilitation Act Amendments (PL 99-506)	Set forth regulations for the development of supported employment programs for adults with disabilities
1988	Jacob K. Javits Gifted and Talented Students Education Act (PL 100-297)	Provided federal funds in support of research, teacher training, and program development for the education of gifted and talented students
1988	Technology-Related Assistance for Individuals with Disabilities Act of 1988 (PL 100-407)	Created statewide programs of technology assistance for people of all ages with disabilities
1990	Americans with Disabilities Act (PL 101-336)	Provided civil rights protection against discrimination to citizens with disabilities in private sector employment; provided access to all public services, public accommodations, transportation, and telecommunications
1990	Individuals with Disabilities Education Act (IDEA) Amendments of 1990 (PL 101-476)	Renamed the EAHCA; added autism and traumatic brain injury as new categories of disability; required all IEPs to include a statement of needed transition services no later than age 16; expanded the definition of related services to include rehabilitation counseling and social work services
1994	Goals 2000: Educate America Act (PL 103-227)	Provided federal funds for the development and implementation of educational reforms to help achieve eight national education goals by the year 2000
1997	Individuals with Disabilities Education Act (IDEA) of 1997 (PL 105-17)	Added several major provisions including: a regular education teacher must be a member of the IEP team; students with disabilities must have access to the general education curriculum; the IEP must address positive behavior support plans where appropriate; students with disabilities must be included in state- or districtwide testing programs; if a school seeks to discipline a student with disabilities resulting in change of placement, suspension, or expulsion for more than 10 days, a "manifestation determination" by the IEP team must find that the student's misconduct was not related to the disability
2001	No Child Left Behind Act of 2001 (Reauthorization of the Elementary and Secondary Education Act (PL 107-110)	NCLB's ultimate goal is that all children will be proficient in all subject matter by the year 2014. School districts are expected to make adequate yearly progress (AYP) toward the 100% goal, ensure that all children are taught by "highly qualified" teachers, and use curriculum and instructional methods validated by rigorous scientific research. Schools that do not make AYP are initially targeted for assistance and then subject to corrective action and ultimately restructuring
2004	Individuals with Disabilities Education Improvement Act of 2004 (PL 108-446)	Retained major components and principles of IDEA; key changes include benchmarks and short-term objectives required only in IEPs for students who take alternative assessments related to alternative achievement standards; pilot program for multiyear IEPs; "response-to-instruction" may be used to identify learning disabilities; "highly qualified" special education teacher defined; under special circumstances (e.g., brings a weapon to school) a student with disabilities may be removed from school to an interim setting for up to 45 school days whether or not the misconduct was related to the child's disability

compensatory efforts to help individuals with disabilities achieve fuller and more independent lives.

REMEDIAL INTERVENTION Remediation attempts to eliminate specific effects of a disability. The word *remediation* is primarily an educational term; social service agencies more often use the word *rehabilitation*. Both terms have a common purpose: to teach the person with disabilities skills for independent and successful functioning. In school, those skills may be academic (reading, writing, computing), social (initiating and maintaining a conversation), self-care (eating, dressing, using the toilet without assistance), or vocational (career and job skills to prepare secondary students for the world of work). The underlying assumption of remedial intervention is that a person with disabilities needs special instruction to succeed in typical settings.

COMPENSATORY INTERVENTION Compensatory intervention involves teaching a substitute (i.e., compensatory) skill that enables a person to engage in an activity or perform a task in spite of a disability. For example, although remedial instruction might help a child with cerebral palsy learn to use her hands in the same way that others do for some tasks, a headstick and a template placed over a computer keyboard may compensate for her limited fine-motor control and enable her to type instead of write lessons by hand. Compensatory interventions give the person with a disability an asset that nondisabled individuals do not need, including, for example, assistive devices or special training such as orientation and mobility instruction for a child who is blind.

Special Education as Instruction

Ultimately, *teaching* is what special education is most about. But the same can be said of all of education. What, then, is *special* about special education? One way to answer that question is to examine special education in terms of the who, what, how, and where of its teaching.

WHO We have already identified the most important *who* in special education: exceptional children whose educational needs necessitate an individually planned program of instruction. Teachers provide the instruction that is the heart of each child's individualized education program. These teachers include both general education classroom teachers and special education teachers—teachers "with a special certification who [are] specially trained to do special things with special students" (Zigmond, 2007, p. 151). Working with special educators and general education teachers are many other professionals (e.g., school psychologists, speech-language pathologists, physical therapists, counselors) and paraprofessionals (e.g., classroom aides) who help provide the educational and related services that exceptional children need. This interdisciplinary team of professionals, working together with parents and families, bears the primary responsibility for helping exceptional children learn despite their special needs.

WHAT Special education can sometimes be differentiated from general education by its curriculum—that is, by *what* is taught. Although every student with disabilities needs access to and support in learning as much of the general education curriculum as appropriate, the IEP goals and objectives for some special education students will not be found in state standards or the school district's curriculum guide. Some children need intensive, systematic instruction to learn skills that typically developing children acquire without instruction. Educators often use the term **functional curriculum** to describe the knowledge and skills that some students with disabilities need in order to achieve as much success and independence as they can in school, home, community, and work settings. Skills such as dressing, toileting, making a purchase, preparing a snack are a critically important component of the special education received by many students with severe disabilities. Also, as discussed previously, some children are taught certain skills, such as reading braille or using a voice-output device, to compensate for or reduce the effects of a disability.

HOW Special education also differs from general education by its use of specialized, or adapted, materials and methods. This difference is obvious when you observe a special educator use sign language with students who are deaf. When watching a special educator gradually and systematically withdraw verbal and physical prompts while helping a student learn to perform the steps of a task, you may find the differentiated nature of special education instruction less obvious, but it is no less specialized.

Other features that often distinguish special education teaching from instruction in general education are its precision, focus, intensity, and frequency of student progress measures. For example, Mellard, McKnight, and Jordan (2011) identified 10 different dimensions by which the intensity of instruction can be varied, including dosage (number of minutes, frequency, and duration of instruction), group size, number of response opportunities, and immediacy of feedback.

WHERE Special education can sometimes be identified (but not defined) by where it takes place. Although the majority of children with disabilities spend most of the school day in general education classrooms, others are in separate classrooms or separate residential and day schools. And many of the students in general education classrooms spend a portion of each day in a resource room, where they receive individualized instruction. Table 4 lists the definitions of six educational placements used by the U.S. Department of Education.

Special educators also teach in many settings not usually thought of as school. An early childhood special educator may spend much of his time teaching parents how to work with their infant or toddler at home. Special education teachers of students with severe disabilities often conduct community-based instruction, helping their students learn and practice functional daily living and job skills in the actual environments where those skills must be used.

Approximately four out of five school-age children with disabilities received at least part of their education in general education classrooms during the 2009–2010

TABLE 4 • **Federal government's definitions of educational environments for students with disabilities**

EDUCATIONAL SETTING	DEFINITION
Regular Classroom*	Student spends at least 80% of the school day inside regular class.
Resource Room (Pull-Out)	Student spends at least between 40% and 79% of the school day inside regular class.
Separate Classroom	Student spends less than 40% of the school day inside regular class.
Separate School	Student receives special education and related services in a public or private separate day school for students with disabilities, at public expense, for more than 50% of the school day.
Residential Facility	Student receives special education and related services in a public or privately operated residential facility in which children receive care or services 24 hours a day.
Homebound/Hospital	Student receives special education and related services in a hospital or homebound program.

Source: Adapted from U.S. Department of Education. (2011). *Twenty-second annual report to Congress on the implementation of the Individuals with Disabilities Education Act* (p. II-14). Washington, DC: Author.

*Most educators use the term *general education classroom* instead of *regular classroom*. Note that the federal government's definition of "regular classroom" placement enables a student to leave the classroom for supplemental instruction and related services for up to one full day per week.

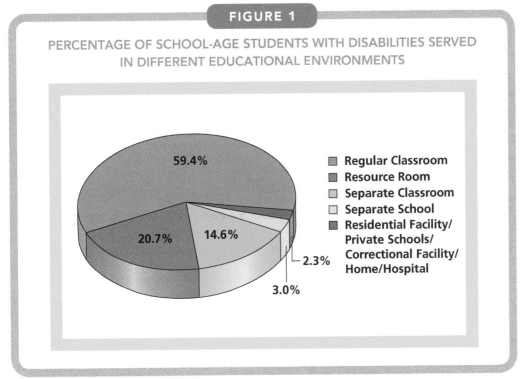

FIGURE 1

PERCENTAGE OF SCHOOL-AGE STUDENTS WITH DISABILITIES SERVED IN DIFFERENT EDUCATIONAL ENVIRONMENTS

- ■ Regular Classroom
- ■ Resource Room
- ■ Separate Classroom
- □ Separate School
- ■ Residential Facility/ Private Schools/ Correctional Facility/ Home/Hospital

Source: From U.S. Department of Education. (2011). *Individuals with Disabilities Education Act (IDEA) data* (Table 2-2). Washington, DC: Author.

school year (see Figure 1). This includes 59% who were served in a general education classroom and 21% who were served for part of each school day in a resource room, a special setting in which a special educator provides individualized instruction. About one in seven children with disabilities are educated in separate classrooms within a regular public school. About 3% of school-age students with disabilities—usually those with severe disabilities—are educated in special schools. Residential schools serve less than 1% of all children with disabilities, as do nonschool environments such as homebound or hospital programs.

A Definition of Special Education

At one level, special education is an important part of society's response to the needs of exceptional children and the rights of individuals with disabilities—a response brought about by parent advocacy, litigation, legislation, and, increasingly, self-advocacy by people with disabilities. At another level, special education is a profession with its own history, cultural practices, tools, and research base focused on the learning needs of exceptional children and adults. But at the level where exceptional children most meaningfully and frequently contact it, *special education is individually planned, specialized, intensive, goal-directed instruction.* When practiced most effectively and ethically, special education is also characterized by the use of evidence-based teaching methods, the application of which is guided by direct and frequent measures of student performance. Table 5 shows the fundamental dimensions and defining features of special education.

Special education is not general education, and efforts to "blur" the identity of special education are not in the best interest of children with disabilities who need specially designed instruction (Fuchs, Fuchs, & Stecker, 2010; Zigmond, Kloo, & Volonino, 2009). See *Current Issues and Future Trends,* "General Education and Special Education Are (and Should Be) Different."

Defining features of special education

 Council for Exceptional Children — Content Standards for Beginning Teachers—Initial Common Core: Models, theories, and philosophies that form the basis for special education practice (ICC1K1).

TABLE 5 • **Dimensions and defining features of special education instruction**

DIMENSION	DEFINING FEATURES
Individually Planned	• Learning goals and objectives selected for each student based on assessment results and input from parents and student • Teaching methods and instructional materials selected and/or adapted for each student • Setting(s) where instruction will occur determined relative to opportunities for student to learn and use targeted skills
Specialized	• Sometimes involves unique or adapted teaching procedures seldom used in general education (e.g., constant time delay, token reinforcement, self-monitoring) • Incorporates a variety of instructional materials and supports—both natural and contrived—to help student acquire and use targeted learning objectives • Related services (e.g., audiology, physical therapy) provided as needed • Assistive technology (e.g., adapted cup holder, head-operated switch to select communication symbols) provided as needed
Intensive	• Instruction presented with attention to detail, precision, structure, clarity, and repeated practice • "Relentless, urgent" instruction (Zigmond & Baker, 1995) • Efforts made to provide incidental, naturalistic opportunities for student to use targeted knowledge and skills
Goal-Directed	• Purposeful instruction intended to help student achieve the greatest possible personal self-sufficiency and success in present and future environments • Value/goodness of instruction determined by student's attainment of learning outcomes
Research-Based Methods	• Recognition that not all teaching approaches are equally effective • Instructional programs and teaching procedures selected on basis of research support
Guided by Student Performance	• Systematic, ongoing monitoring of student progress • Results of frequent and direct measures of student learning used to inform modifications in instruction

Special education is individually planned, specially designed, intensive instruction.

Katelyn Metzger/Merrill

CURRENT AND FUTURE CHALLENGES

Special educators have legitimate reason to feel good about progress their field has made. Much has been accomplished in terms of making a free appropriate education available to children with disabilities. Educators have learned much about how to effectively teach children with severe disabilities, whom many previously had assumed were incapable of learning. Special educators and families are learning to work as partners on behalf of exceptional children. Technological advances have helped many students overcome physical impairments and communication disabilities.

Of the many challenges faced by the field of special education, none is more critical than getting effective teaching practices more widely implemented.

Close the Research-to-Practice Gap

Special education can be nothing more, or less, than the quality of instruction (Heward & Dardig, 2001). Contrary to the contentions of some observers, special education research has produced a significant and reliable knowledge base about effective teaching practices (e.g., Cook, Tankersley, & Landrum, 2009; Coyne, Kame'enui, & Carnine, 2011). No knowledgeable person will argue that research has discovered everything important to know about teaching exceptional students. Far from it: a great many questions remain to be answered, the pursuit of which will no doubt lead to other questions yet to be asked.

While a significant gap remains between what is relatively well understood and what is poorly understood or not understood at all, the more distressing gap may be between research findings about teaching and learning and practices in many classrooms (Heward, 2005). Researchers have discovered and continue to refine reliable, scientifically based knowledge about effective teaching practices for students with disabilities. For example, we know what features of early reading instruction will reduce the number of children who later develop reading problems (Simmons, Kame'enui, Coyne, Chard, & Hairrell, 2011); how to use a teaching tactic called **time delay** to help students with severe intellectual disabilities learn new skills (Browder, Ahlgrim-Delzell, Spooner, Mims, & Baker, 2009); and the components of secondary special education programs that increase the success of youth with disabilities in transitioning from school to adult life (Sitlington, Neubert, & Clark, 2010). Sadly, the instruction received by many students with disabilities not only fails to take advantage of that knowledge (e.g., McLesky & Waldron, 2011; Zigmond, 2007) but often embraces approaches and methods scientific studies have shown to be ineffective (see Botts, Hershfeldt, & Christensen-Sandort, 2008; Cox, Gast, Luscre, & Ayers, 2009; Heward, 2003).

It is critically important for special education to close the gap between the field's knowledge of evidence-based practices and the curriculum and instruction that students receive (Carnine, 1997; Cook et al., 2009; Deshler, 2005; Heward & Silvestri, 2005; Odom et al., 2005). Instructional practices supported by scientific research are described throughout this text and featured in the *Teaching & Learning* boxes.

Getting available knowledge to work in the classroom is by no means the only problem and challenge facing special education today. The field faces numerous other challenges. For example:

- Improve the quality of pre- and in-service training programs to ensure that all special educators meet professional standards (CEC, 2009).
- Increase the availability and quality of special education programs for gifted and talented students.
- Help secondary students with disabilities transition to adult life. When special education is judged by its ultimate product—the youth who leave secondary school programs—it becomes clear how much further the field must progress. Too many young adults with disabilities are unsuccessful and unhappy in their postschool adjustment. Special education must improve the transition of youth with disabilities from school to life in their communities.

CURRENT ISSUES AND FUTURE TRENDS

▶ General Education and Special Education
Are (and Should Be) Different

BY NAOMI ZIGMOND

THE LAST TWO DECADES have witnessed increasing calls for combining general and special education into a single system of education (e.g., Arnold & Dodge, 1994; National Association of State Boards of Education, 1992; National Education Association, 1992). Many advocates for a single system assume that, if we are not there already, there should soon come a time when there will no longer be a need for certain students to be singled out for a special education. I believe they are wrong and offer 10 major differences between general and special education that are historic and worth preserving:

1. *The reach of general and special education are distinctly different.* General education is an entitlement for all students; it is the universal, basic, compulsory, and free education developed in the United State to offer opportunity to all, regardless of race, class, or social standing. Special education, on the other hand, is reserved for students with disabilities who need a unique, different, and special education.

2. *The governance of general and special education is distinctly different.* In the U.S. Constitution, individual states, not the federal government, have primary authority over public education. Every state has a department of education and laws that regulate school finance, hiring of school personnel, student attendance, and curriculum. In contrast, federal laws (IDEA, primarily) require each state to ensure that all of its students with disabilities receive nondiscriminatory testing, evaluation and placement, the right to due process, education in the least restrictive environment, and a free and appropriate public education (FAPE). Federal laws also require strict monitoring of every state's compliance with these requirements. No such federal oversight exists for general education.

3. *Decisions about what children need to learn are made very differently in general and special education.* Local school boards or the state legislature dictates the curriculum for general education

and sets curriculum standards for schools and school graduates of general education; their concern is with knowledge and skills that everyone should possess. By contrast, special education pays attention to the unique needs of the individual student and confirms, in an individualized education program plan (IEP), the school's commitment to meeting those unique needs.

4. *The focus of general and special education is different.* General education is oriented to the group. Students are placed in classes and grades and, while there continue to be lively debates about optimal class size, these debates do not question the basic premise that general education is delivered to groups. In contrast, special education is directed to the individual. The right to a special education is based on individualized decision making and involves individualized educational programming.

5. *General and special education respond differently to differences in students' background knowledge, readiness to learn, language proficiency, and interests.* General education teachers begin with a group goal in mind and then utilize "differentiated instruction" to accommodate the diversity among students. General education teachers provide multiple options for taking in information and making sense of ideas so that everyone in the class can access the same lesson. Special educators begin by planning for the unique needs of the individual. Special education is not just about access and accommodations; it is about delivering specially designed instruction that is explicit, intensive, and supportive and meets each individual student's specific learning needs.

6. *In general education, we know what to expect in yearly academic growth.* Yearly learning outcomes for general education students have been established through large-scale testing programs and other normative data. We use these expectations to gauge the quality and success of

schools, teachers, and students. However, expectations for achievement for students with disabilities are not nearly as clear-cut. Students with disabilities become eligible for special education services because they score poorly on academic achievement tests; if their disability did not adversely affect school achievement, these students would not qualify for special education. Some special education reformers suggest that we should have the same high standards and expectations for academic growth for all students, including students with disabilities in need of a special education; others believe that is an unrealistic expectation. No definitive studies have established expected academic growth rates for students in special education, thus, standard methods of measuring program effectiveness for these students are inappropriate.

7. *General education and special education teachers are differently prepared and differently skilled.* General education teachers are well prepared to teach standard curriculum content to large groups of diverse students. Teacher training programs in general education prepare teachers to teach specific content subject matter. In contrast, pedagogy—instructional skills—is the focus of special education teacher preparation, not subject matter. Special education teachers need a very specialized set of skills because the structure, intensity, precision, and relentlessness with which these teachers must plan, deliver, monitor, and adapt instruction is well beyond that which would be possible in a regular classroom.

8. *Highly qualified general education teachers are generalists.* That is as it should be. But a highly qualified generalist does not have the same expertise as a specialist, and special education teachers are (and should be) specialists. Special educators must possess in-depth understanding of the specialized methodologies and instructional techniques needed to support the learning of students with exceptional learning difficulties and differences. They must have the know-how to make their teaching intensive, urgent, and goal directed.

9. *General education is strongly influenced by a culture of ideology, faddishness, and opinion, but not research.* In contrast, special education practice has a long history of being research based. General education has only recently embraced the need to ground teaching and learning in scientific research findings; "evidence-based practice" is little more than a recent buzzword to many in general education.

10. *General education is a place.* It is the "normal" educational setting. It is where everyone goes to school. Special education is not a place; it is a service. The service can be delivered in any number of places from mainstream classroom to residential school. And no matter the place, students with disabilities in need of a special education should be receiving instruction that is specialized, individualized, and intensive.

From the start, general and special education evolved from different premises (public education of the masses vs. education of individuals with special needs), and with different emphases in teacher preparation (learning to teach subject matter vs. learning to teach individual students). Some have argued that special education be merged with general education, with no separate mission, budget, or personnel (McLaughlin, 1995). Some believe that special education is so not-special that it can be delivered by a generalist, busy teaching 25 to 30 other students a standardized curriculum determined at the school district, or state, or federal level.

We cannot let this happen. Advocates for students with disabilities did not press for just equal educational opportunity; they fought to have some students with disabilities treated differently, receiving more opportunity, more intensive instruction, more individually tailored curriculum, more carefully designed instruction. That's what special education is. It's time to renew our commitment to students with disabilities and ensure the programs and resources necessary to fulfill that commitment.

WHAT DO YOU THINK?

1. If you are preparing to be a general (or special) education teacher, do you think maintaining the differences between general and special education as outlined here would be good for your future profession?

2. Which of the 10 differences between general and special education do you think are most and least important? Why?

3. As a student with disabilities, or a parent/family member of a student with disabilities, how do these 10 differences affect you?

About the Author

Naomi Zigmond, Distinguished Professor of Special Education at the University of Pittsburgh, has been a special education researcher and teacher educator for more than 40 years. Her focus has been on the organization of special education service delivery for students with disabilities in elementary and secondary schools and the impact of program organization on student achievement.

- Apply advances in technologies that reduce or eliminate the disabling effects of physical and sensory impairments.
- Increase access to assistive technology that enhances the educational performance and personal independence of individuals with disabilities.
- Increase funding for special education. Teaching children with disabilities is very expensive. Laws and regulations calling for special education and related services have limited value if the schools lack the financial resources to provide them. When Congress passed IDEA in 1975, it promised to provide federal funds for 40% of the "excess costs" of educating children with disabilities. Congress has never appropriated more than about 18% of the national average (Sack-Min, 2007).
- Improve the behavior and attitudes of people without disabilities toward those with disabilities.
- Open more opportunities for individuals with disabilities to participate in the full range of residential, employment, and recreational options available to people without disabilities.

Only time will tell how successful special education will be in meeting these challenges. And, of course, special education does not face these challenges alone. General education, adult service agencies (e.g., vocational rehabilitation and social work), the science and practice of medicine, government agencies, and society as a whole must all help find solutions.

▼ TIPS FOR BEGINNING TEACHERS

Hit the Ground Running

BY MEGAN MENCINSKY

BE YOUR OWN PROFESSIONAL DEVELOPMENT COACH

Your education doesn't end when you step into your own classroom. It is only just beginning.

- **Attend as many professional development opportunities as possible, and always walk away with at least one usable idea.** Don't limit your opportunities; if you teach students with learning disabilities, don't turn down a chance to go to a seminar on students with autism or vice versa. You may find an idea that you can modify to use in your current situation.
- **Join professional organizations.** Membership in the Council for Exceptional Children at both the national and state chapter levels, as well as other organizations for special education professionals, affords numerous opportunities to continue learning about your field though conferences, journals, newsletters, and members-only websites.
- **Observe master teachers at work.** Visit other classrooms, particularly those at current grade levels of your students and where they will most likely be the next school year. Watching skilled teachers and what their students are working on will give you many good ideas.
- **Keep an idea notebook.** Whenever you read, see, hear, or think of something that might be useful later on, jot it down. At least once a month, review the ideas in your notebook.

BUILD A PERSONAL SUPPORT NETWORK

No one has all the answers. It is essential to have people you can turn to when you need support.

- **Be involved in the life of your school.** Make yourself known in the school. Tutor general education students, volunteer for committees, and attend school functions. The professional relationships you develop with colleagues will be invaluable.
- **Maintain contact with your classmates and professors from your teacher preparation program.** It is great to have a network of colleagues outside school you can go to for ideas and suggestions.
- **Introduce yourself to the custodians, secretaries, and other support personnel.** You never know when you may need shelves hung, an extra desk for a new student, or the thermostat set to a more desirable temperature. Make sure to be friendly, and remember all the support personnel in your building!

STRIVE FOR BALANCE

Juggling demanding professional responsibilities with a personal life can be especially difficult for beginning teachers. Find ways to make your work environment a positive place where you and your students feel welcomed.

- **Incorporate your personality into your classroom.** Make your room a place where your students and you like to be.

If you like music, play songs by an artist of the week when students are working independently. If quotations inspire you, post some outside your door and on the walls.

- **Work hard, work efficiently, and then leave the building.** My first year teaching I found myself staying later and later each day after school trying to get everything done. Working hard wasn't a problem, but I had to learn to work more efficiently, realize that everything will never be done, and walk away at a certain time. You need to be replenish yourself; you can't give all of yourself if you are exhausted.
- **Reserve and guard time for non-school activities.** Spend time with your friends; go to a movie; keep up your favorite hobbies. You don't have a hobby? Get one!

BE PREPARED, BE PREPARED, BE PREPARED!

Any and all types of unannounced situations occur. You will have peace of mind (and gain respect from others) if you are calm, flexible, and prepared as situations arise.

- **Keep a collection of backup lessons in a binder**—In case you go through plan A, plan B, all the way down to plan Z. Have a lesson that is interactive and handy for days when there is a surprise meeting and you have a sub, students are restless, or the superintendent drops by for a surprise visit.
- **Keep a freshen-up kit in your desk.** Toothpaste/mouthwash, cologne/perfume, and deodorant will come in handy. This kit is particularly beneficial on nights where you are required to stay late at school for parent–teacher conferences, choir concerts, and the like.
- **Develop a personal system of organization.** It is daunting at first, but make sure you label and sort things so that they are easily stored and easily accessible. Sort lessons by subject, or create a different binder for each day of the week, with lessons and materials included. Label bins or binders by subject, and then label subtopics; create a cache of materials you can easily get to.

▼ KEY TERMS AND CONCEPTS

accommodations
adequate yearly progress (AYP)
alternative assessments
assistive technology
at risk
disability
due process hearing
exceptional children
free appropriate public education
functional curriculum

handicap
impairment
incidence
individualized education program (IEP)
individualized family services plan (IFSP)
manifestation determination
repeated reading
SAFMEDS
time trials
universal design for learning (UDL)

▼ SUMMARY

Who Are Exceptional Children?

- Exceptional children are those whose physical attributes and/or learning abilities differ from the norm, either above or below, to such an extent that an individualized program of special education is necessary.
- *Impairment* refers to the reduced function or loss of a particular body part or organ.
- A *disability* exists when an impairment limits a person's ability to perform certain tasks in the same way that most people do.
- *Handicap* refers to the problems a person with a disability encounters when interacting with the environment.
- A child who is *at risk* is not currently identified as having a disability but is considered to have a greater than usual chance of developing one if intervention is not provided.

How Many Exceptional Children Are There?

- About 6 million children with disabilities, birth through age 21, received special education services in 2009–2010.
- Children in special education represent approximately 12% of the school-age population.
- Children receiving special education under the two largest disability categories, learning disabilities and speech or language impairments, make up 60% of all school-age special education students.

Why Do We Label and Classify Exceptional Children?

- Some educators believe that disability labels have negative effects on the child and on others' perceptions of her and can lead to exclusion; others believe that labeling is a necessary first step to providing needed intervention and is important for comparing and communicating about research findings.

- Alternative approaches to classifying exceptional children that do not rely on disability labels have been proposed (e.g., classifying students by the curriculum and skill areas they are learning).

Why Are Laws Governing the Education of Exceptional Children Necessary?

- Before the 1970s, many states had laws permitting public schools to deny enrollment to children with disabilities. When local public schools began to accept a measure of responsibility for educating certain exceptional students, a philosophy of segregation prevailed.
- Special education was strongly influenced by the case of *Brown v. Board of Education* in 1954, in which the U.S. Supreme Court declared that education must be made available to all children on equal terms.
- In the class action lawsuit *PARC* (1972), the court ruled that all children with intellectual disabilities were entitled to a free appropriate public education and that placements in regular classrooms and regular public schools were preferable to segregated settings.
- All children with disabilities have the right to equal protection under the law, which has been interpreted to mean the right to a free appropriate public education in the least restrictive environment.
- All children with disabilities and their parents have the right to due process under the law, which includes the rights to be notified of any decision affecting the child's educational placement, to have a hearing and present a defense, to see a written decision, and to appeal any decision.

Individuals with Disabilities Education Act

- IDEA, first enacted by Congress in 1975 and amended and reauthorized most recently in 2004, encompasses six major principles:
  - **Zero reject**. Schools must educate all children with disabilities. This principle applies regardless of the nature or severity of the disability.
  - **Nondiscriminatory identification and evaluation.** Schools must use nonbiased, multifactored methods of evaluation to determine whether a child has a disability and, if so, whether special education is needed.
  - **Free appropriate public education.** All children with disabilities shall receive a free appropriate public education at public expense. An IEP must be developed and implemented for each student with a disability that addresses the student's unique needs by providing specially designed instruction and related services based on peer-reviewed research to the extent practicable.
  - **Least restrictive environment.** Students with disabilities must be educated with children without disabilities to the maximum extent appropriate, and they should be removed to separate classes or schools only when the nature or severity of their disabilities is such that they cannot receive an appropriate education in a general education classroom.
  - **Procedural safeguards.** Schools must follow certain procedures to safeguard and protect the rights and interests of children with disabilities and their parents.
  - **Parent participation and shared decision making.** Schools must collaborate with parents and with students with disabilities in the design and implementation of special education services.
- IDEA requires states to provide special education services to all preschoolers with disabilities ages 3 to 5. This law also makes federal money available to states that develop early intervention programs for disabled and at-risk infants and toddlers from birth through age 2. Early intervention services must be coordinated by an IFSP.
- IDEA requires that schools provide related services and assistive technology that a child with a disability needs to access and benefit from special education.
- IDEA encourages the use of universal design for learning (UDL) to ensure that new curricular materials and learning technologies accommodate the learning needs of the widest possible range of individuals, including children with disabilities.
- Court cases have challenged the way in which particular school districts implement specific provisions of IDEA. Rulings from the various cases have established the principle that each student with disabilities is entitled to a personalized program of instruction and related services that will enable him to benefit from an education in as integrated a setting as possible.
- The Javits Gifted and Talented Children's Education Act provides financial incentives to states for developing programs for gifted and talented students.
- Section 504 of the Rehabilitation Act forbids discrimination in all federally funded programs, including educational and vocational programs, on the basis of disability.
- The Americans with Disabilities Act extends the civil rights protections for people with disabilities to private sector employment, all public services, public accommodations, transportation, and telecommunications.
- NCLB requires that all children must be taught by "highly qualified" teachers, emphasizes use of evidence-based teaching methods, and requires schools to make annual progress toward the ultimate goal of all children being proficient in all subject matter by 2014.

What Is Special Education?

- Special education consists of purposeful intervention efforts at three levels: preventive, remedial, and compensatory.
- Special education is individually planned, specialized, intensive, goal-directed instruction. When practiced most effectively and ethically, special education uses research-based teaching methods and is guided by direct and frequent measures of student performance.

Current and Future Challenges

- The field of special education faces many challenges, but none is more important than reducing the gap between what scientific research tells us about effective teaching practices and what exceptional children experience in the classroom.

MyEducationLab™

Go to Topic 1, Special Education Law, in the MyEducationLab (www.myeducationlab.com) for *Exceptional Children*, where you can

- Find learning outcomes for special education law along with the national standards that connect to these outcomes.
- Complete Assignments and Activities that can help you more deeply understand the chapter content.
- Apply and practice your understanding of the core teaching skills identified in the chapter with the Building Teaching Skills and Dispositions learning units.
- Examine challenging situations and cases presented in the IRIS Center Resources.
- Access video clips of CCSSO National Teachers of the Year award winners responding to the question "Why do I teach?" in the Teacher Talk section.
- Check your comprehension of the content covered in the chapter with the Study Plan. Here you will be able to take a chapter quiz, receive feedback on your answers, and then access Review, Practice, and Enrichment activities to enhance your understanding of chapter content.
- Use the Online Lesson Plan Builder to practice lesson planning and integrating national and state standards into your planning.

▼ GLOSSARY

accommodation: The adjustment of the eye for seeing at different distances; accomplished by muscles that change the shape of the lens to bring an image into clear focus on the retina.

adequate yearly progress (AYP): The measure by which schools, districts, and states are held accountable for meeting student performance standards in reading/language arts and math under Title I of the No Child Left Behind Act of 2001 (NCLB); states must measure and report student progress on those standards yearly in grades 3 to 8 and in one grade in high school; graduation rates are included in calculation of AYP for high schools.

alternative assessment: instrument used to obtain standards-based performance and progress measures of students with severe disabilities for whom taking standard district and statewide achievement tests would be inappropriate; often a portfolio of student work samples or other evidence demonstrating mastery or improvements in key skills over time.

assistive technology: "Any item, piece of equipment, or product system, whether acquired commercially off the shelf, modified, or customized, that is used to increase, maintain, or improve the functional capabilities of children with disabilities" (the Individuals with Disabilities Education Act [IDEA] regulations, 34 *CFR* § 300.5).

at risk: A term used to refer to children who are not currently identified as disabled but are considered to have a greater than usual chance of developing a disability. Physicians use the term *at risk* or *high risk* to refer to pregnancies with a greater than normal probability of producing a baby with disabilities.

disability: A condition characterized by functional limitations that impede typical development as the result of a physical or sensory impairment or difficulty in learning or social adjustment.

due process: A set of legal steps and proceedings carried out according to established rules and principles; designed to protect an individual's constitutional and legal rights.

exceptional children: Children whose performance deviates from the norm, either below or above, to the extent that special education is needed.

free appropriate public education (FAPE): As guaranteed by the Individuals with Disabilities Education Act (IDEA), schools must provide each qualifying child with disabilities a program of education and related services individually designed to meet that child's unique needs and from which the child receives educational benefit including being prepared for further education, employment, and independent living; this provision of education and related services is without cost to the child's parents or guardians, except for fees equally imposed on the parents or guardians of children without disabilities.

handicap: Refers to the problems a person with a disability or impairment encounters in interacting with the environment. A disability may pose a handicap in one environment but not in another.

impairment: Refers to the loss or reduced function of a particular body part or organ (e.g., a missing limb); compare to *disability* and *handicap*.

incidence: The percentage of people who, at some time in their lives, will be identified as having a specific condition. Often reported as the number of cases of a given condition per 1,000 births or people of a given age.

individualized education program (IEP) team: The group of people who create the IEP for a student with a disability. The team must include (a) the parents of the child with a disability; (b) at least one regular education teacher of the child; (c) at least one special education teacher; (d) a representative of the local education agency who is qualified to provide, or supervise the provision of, specially designed instruction to meet the unique needs of children with disabilities; (e) an individual who is knowledgeable about the general curriculum and the availability of resources of the local education agency; (f) an individual who can interpret the instructional implications of evaluation results, who may be a member of the team described in clauses (b) through (f); (g) at the discretion of the parent or the agency, other individuals who have knowledge or special expertise regarding the child, including related service personnel as appropriate; and (h) whenever appropriate, the child with a disability.

individualized family services plan (IFSP): A requirement of the Individuals with Disabilities Education Act for the coordination of early intervention services for infants and toddlers with disabilities from birth to age 3. Similar to the individualized education program (IEP), which is required for all school-age children with disabilities.

manifestation determination: A review of the relationship between a student's misconduct and his disability conducted by the individualized education program (IEP) team and other qualified personnel. Required by the Individuals with Disabilities Education Act (IDEA) amendments of 1997 when school officials seek to discipline a student with disabilities in a manner that would result in a change of placement, suspension, or expulsion in excess of 10 days.

repeated reading: A technique for increasing reading fluency in which a student orally reads the same a passage, usually three to five times, during each session. With each successive reading, the student tries to increase the number of words read correctly per minute. When the student achieves a predetermined fluency criterion on a given passage, a new passage is introduced. The difficulty level of successive passages gradually increases over time.

SAFMEDS (Say All Fast a Minute Each Day Shuffled): A deck of cards with a question, vocabulary term, or problem printed on one side of each card and the answer on the other side. A student answers as many

items in the deck as he can during 1-minute practice trials by looking at the question or problem, stating an answer, flipping the card over to reveal the correct answer, and putting each card on a "correct" or "incorrect" pile.

time trials: A fluency-building activity in which students correctly perform a particular skill (e.g., segmenting sounds, identifying animal species, writing answers to addition and subtraction problems) as many times as

they can in a brief period, usually no longer than 1 minute.

universal design for learning (UDL): An approach to developing curriculum materials and lessons that incorporates concepts from architecture and product design to make access and interaction with the materials accessible, motivating, and engaging for all learners

Planning and Providing Special Education Services

From Chapter 2 of *Exceptional Children* and *An Introduction to Special Education*, Tenth Edition. William L. Heward.

Planning and Providing Special Education Services

Lori Whitley/Merrill

- Why must the planning and provision of special education be so carefully sequenced and evaluated?

- What are the intended functions of prereferral intervention?

- What does the disproportionate representation of students from diverse cultural and linguistic groups in special education say about the field?

- How do collaboration and teaming impact the effectiveness of special education?

- How should the quality of a student's individualized education program (IEP) be judged?

- Is the least restrictive environment always the general education classroom? Why or why not?

- What elements must be in place for a student with disabilities to receive an appropriate education in inclusive classrooms?

- In what ways has special education been most successful? What are the field's greatest shortcomings and challenges?

▼ FEATURED TEACHER

SHEENA WASHINGTON

Annapolis Middle School • Annapolis, Maryland

EDUCATION—TEACHING CREDENTIALS—EXPERIENCE

- B.A. in Political Science with concentration in African and African Diaspora Studies, St. Mary's College of Maryland, 2004

- M.Ed. in Special Education, Notre Dame of Maryland University, 2012

- Maryland State Certification in Special Education and Humanities, grades 7–12

- 3 years of teaching experience; 2 years Peace Corps volunteer in Niger, West Africa

MY STUDENTS AND SCHOOL I work with about 60 seventh-grade students, who are eligible for special education and related services under the disability categories of specific learning disabilities, intellectual disabilities, emotional disturbances, autism, and other health impairments. All of my students are fully included in general education classes and I am a co-teacher in those classrooms.

Many of my students have ADHD, which impacts their ability to stay on task and perform academically, but we have been working toward effective self-monitoring of behavior. Several of my students are English language learners, which, combined with their disabilities, makes vocabulary development and reading comprehension extremely difficult. Some of my

students receive counseling services for social skills training or anger management.

Of the nearly 600 students at our school, 43% are African American, 36% Caucasian, 18% Hispanic, and 4% Asian/Pacific Islander. We have a growing population of students coming to us directly from Spanish-speaking countries without any English skills. Our students come from a range of socioeconomic and cultural backgrounds. Many of our students have behavioral and disciplinary challenges that result from issues such as poverty, parents struggling with addictions, and homelessness. Over half of the our school's students are eligible to receive free and reduced meals.

DIFFERENTIATED INSTRUCTION Differentiating instruction to make learning engaging and meaningful for all students has been a focus at our school this year. The thoughtful use of fluid student learning groups enables us to provide each student with instructional materials according to his or her skill levels, while teaching and assessing the same skills. Our students have become so habituated to fluid groupings that they cannot tell whether the groups were formed by heterogeneous or homogeneous academic reading levels. I have found that letting students choose among several options for how their work will be assessed increases their commitment to and engagement in the lesson.

Differentiating instruction ultimately benefits students; and for co-teaching partners, it is a process of effective teacher collaboration in planning sessions and in the classroom. In the beginning of the year, many of the general education content teachers were hesitant about, and some even resistant to, the idea of fluid student groups according to readiness levels. By midyear, with a significant amount of professional development, teachers are more familiar with the approach and willing to try new strategies in the classrooms; the result is increased student engagement, collaboration, and learning.

COLLABORATION IS KEY A successful inclusive classroom is built upon a foundation of collaboration between the general education and special education teachers. As a beginning special education teacher, I find that co-teaching presents both the biggest opportunity and the most difficult challenge. In my first year, I worked with four very different content teachers in algebra, social studies, language arts, and science. The match with one of these teachers was perfect. Although our personalities were very different, we complemented each other and truly collaborated to create lessons that all of our students could master. One of those teachers was an extremely controlling person who viewed any idea that deviated from what he had always done as a threat. The most difficult aspect of co-teaching is asserting myself as an equal partner with general education teachers not yet ready for this equality of roles; some teachers tend to view the special educator's role as "helper" or "teacher's assistant." The ongoing process of building and nurturing a productive relationship with each teacher entails respect, open communication, and compromise from both partners as they learn and adapt to each other's teaching style, personality, and expectations for classroom norms.

I work very closely with our school psychologist and social worker to help make our school a positive environment for students with special needs. Together, we conduct functional behavioral assessments and develop behavior intervention plans to support the needs of my students. One student diagnosed with an anxiety disorder eventually felt safe enough in our school to disclose past traumatic abuse. Through almost daily communication with the psychologist, school social worker, and other members of the students' IEP team, the student understood that she had a team of adults who cared and supported her well-being. This made all the difference in that initial period of building relationships and trust before academic learning could even be addressed. Seeing this child begin to regain self-confidence and trust in adults was one of my most meaningful accomplishments as a special educator.

Last year, our school began an initiative where teachers and school staff walk through the communities of our students to introduce ourselves to family members and welcome students back before the school year begins. We make it a priority to visit our students' families who live in government-supported housing and hand out pencils, Popsicles, and fliers with important school information. I think this community walk says a lot about the dedication and commitment that our school staff has for our students.

WHAT I LIKE MOST ABOUT BEING A SPECIAL EDUCATOR I love building relationships with students and breaking down the walls of previous negative experiences that have allowed apathy and poor attitudes to survive. I cherish the moments when a student begins to believe that he or she is capable and shows a willingness to try. My parents have always said that they thought I should be a lawyer who advocates for the disadvantaged. I feel strongly that the most important aspect of my job is advocating for my students and empowering them with self-efficacy and confidence.

We special educators need to be dependable, resilient, and dedicated to our work and to our students. We need to be idealists and believe that regardless of the realities of our students' lives at home and regardless of their disabilities, they can learn and we can inspire them to achieve and experience worlds beyond their immediate realities.

Ms. Washington shared her experiences during the 2010-2011 school year on Reality 101, the Council for Exceptional Children's blog for new special education teachers. To read Sheena's entries and those of other beginning special educators, go to http://www.cecreality101.org.

MyEducationLab™

Special education is defined as individually planned, specialized, intensive, goal-directed instruction. But how do teachers know what kinds of modifications to curriculum and instruction an individual child needs? And toward what goals should that specialized instruction be directed? In this chapter, we examine the process by which special education is planned, devoting particular attention to four critical aspects of educating students with disabilities: (a) the importance of teaming and collaboration among professionals, (b) the individualized education program (IEP), (c) least restrictive environment (LRE), and (d) inclusive education.

THE PROCESS OF SPECIAL EDUCATION

The Individuals with Disabilities Education Act (IDEA) mandates a sequence of events schools must follow to identify and educate children with disabilities. Although the federal rules and regulations that state and local education agencies must follow are lengthy, detailed, and sometimes redundant for legal purposes, the process they specify is designed to answer a sequence of questions that makes both educational and common sense:

- Which students might need special education?
- Does this particular child have a disability that adversely affects his educational performance? In other words, is this student eligible for special education? If the answer is yes, then. . . .
- What specific educational needs result from the child's disability?
- What specialized methods of instruction, accommodations, curricular modifications, related services, and/or supplementary supports are necessary to meet those needs so the student can achieve increased levels of academic achievement and functional performance and participate in the life of the school?
- What educational setting is the least restrictive environment in which the student can receive an appropriate education?
- Is special education helping? If not, what changes should be made in the student's program?

Figure 1 identifies the major steps in the sequence of planning, implementing, and evaluating special education and highlights some of the key procedures, elements, and requirements of each step.

Prereferral Process

A child who may need special education usually comes to the school's attention because (a) a teacher or parent reports concern about differences in learning, behavior, or development or (b) the results of a screening test suggest a possible disability. Screening tests are relatively quick, inexpensive, and easy-to-administer assessments given to large groups of children to find out who might have a disability and need further testing (Elliott, Huai, & Roach, 2007). For example, most schools administer vision screening tests to all elementary children.

    Before referring the child for formal testing and evaluation for special education, most schools initiate a **prereferral intervention** process. Although IDEA does not

Prereferral intervention

Initial Level Content Standards for Special Education Teachers: Screening, prereferral, referral, and classification procedures (ICC8K3).

FIGURE 1 THE BASIC STEPS IN PLANNING, PROVIDING, AND EVALUATING
SPECIAL EDUCATION

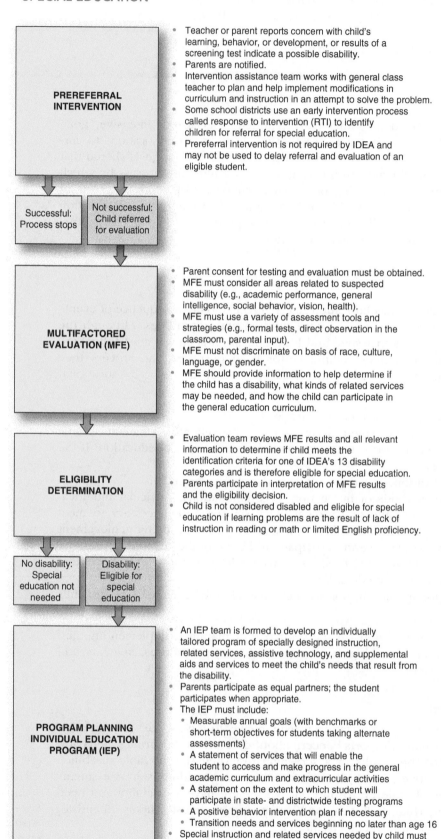

PREREFERRAL INTERVENTION

- Teacher or parent reports concern with child's learning, behavior, or development, or results of a screening test indicate a possible disability.
- Parents are notified.
- Intervention assistance team works with general class teacher to plan and help implement modifications in curriculum and instruction in an attempt to solve the problem.
- Some school districts use an early intervention process called response to intervention (RTI) to identify children for referral for special education.
- Prereferral intervention is not required by IDEA and may not be used to delay referral and evaluation of an eligible student.

Successful: Process stops

Not successful: Child referred for evaluation

MULTIFACTORED EVALUATION (MFE)

- Parent consent for testing and evaluation must be obtained.
- MFE must consider all areas related to suspected disability (e.g., academic performance, general intelligence, social behavior, vision, health).
- MFE must use a variety of assessment tools and strategies (e.g., formal tests, direct observation in the classroom, parental input).
- MFE must not discriminate on basis of race, culture, language, or gender.
- MFE should provide information to help determine if the child has a disability, what kinds of related services may be needed, and how the child can participate in the general education curriculum.

ELIGIBILITY DETERMINATION

- Evaluation team reviews MFE results and all relevant information to determine if child meets the identification criteria for one of IDEA's 13 disability categories and is therefore eligible for special education.
- Parents participate in interpretation of MFE results and the eligibility decision.
- Child is not considered disabled and eligible for special education if learning problems are the result of lack of instruction in reading or math or limited English proficiency.

No disability: Special education not needed

Disability: Eligible for special education

PROGRAM PLANNING INDIVIDUAL EDUCATION PROGRAM (IEP)

- An IEP team is formed to develop an individually tailored program of specially designed instruction, related services, assistive technology, and supplemental aids and services to meet the child's needs that result from the disability.
- Parents participate as equal partners; the student participates when appropriate.
- The IEP must include:
  - Measurable annual goals (with benchmarks or short-term objectives for students taking alternate assessments)
  - A statement of services that will enable the student to access and make progress in the general academic curriculum and extracurricular activities
  - A statement on the extent to which student will participate in state- and districtwide testing programs
  - A positive behavior intervention plan if necessary
  - Transition needs and services beginning no later than age 16
- Special instruction and related services needed by child must be identified without regard to cost or availability in district.

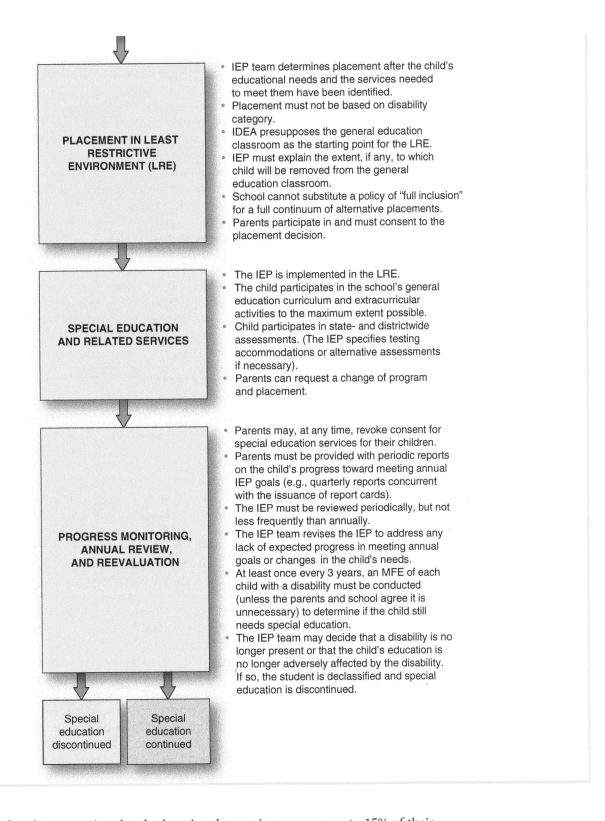

require prereferral intervention, local educational agencies may use up to 15% of their IDEA funds "to develop and implement coordinated, early intervening services . . . for students in kindergarten through grade 12 (with a particular emphasis on students in kindergarten through grade 3) who have not been identified as needing special education or related services but who need additional academic and behavioral support to succeed in a general education environment" (PL 108-466, Sec. 613[f][1]).

Prereferral intervention is often conducted by a building-based *early intervening assistance team* (also called *student support team, teacher assistance team,* or *problem-solving team*), which helps teachers devise and implement interventions for students who are experiencing academic or behavioral difficulties in the general education classroom. Early intervening teams typically consist of the school principal or designated administrator; school nurse; guidance counselor; several classroom teachers with experience across different grade levels; and one or more special education teachers, at least one of whom is skilled in designing behavior intervention plans. The classroom teacher describes the academic and/or behavior problems the student has been experiencing to the team, and together the group "brainstorms not only on the possible etiology of the problem, but more importantly, on possible solutions to it" (Spinelli, 2012, p. 6). The team develops an intervention strategy and assists the classroom teacher in implementing and evaluating it with student progress data (Bahr & Kovalesk, 2006).

Increasingly, school districts have begun using a more formal and systematic pre-referral process called **response to intervention (RTI)**. How a student responds to increasingly intensive, scientifically validated instruction can help determine whether the child's struggles to learn are the result of poor or insufficient instruction or of a disability for which special education is needed. "If the child responds poorly to validated instruction, the assessment eliminates instructional quality as a viable explanation for poor academic growth and instead provides evidence of a disability. For children who do respond nicely, RTI serves a critical prevention function" (L. S. Fuchs, Fuchs, & Hollenbeck, 2007, p. 13).

The idea of RTI is to provide early intervention in the form of scientifically validated instruction to all children whose performance suggests they are at risk for school failure. RTI involves universal screening, continuous monitoring of student progress on key performance indicators, and several levels or tiers of increasingly intensive instructional interventions before referral for assessment for special education eligibility (National Center on Response to Intervention, 2010; Shapiro, Zigmond, Wallace, & Marsten, 2011). Numerous models for implementing RTI have been developed. The most common RTI framework embodies three tiers of intervention corresponding to the three levels of prevention. Tier 1 (primary prevention) consists of high-quality curriculum and instruction intended to meet the needs of most students. Tier 2 (secondary prevention) consists of moderately intensive evidence-based interventions designed to address the learning or behavioral difficulties of students whose lack of progress in Tier 1 identifies them as at risk for a disability. Tier 2 interventions are typically provided to small groups of students. Tier 3 (tertiary prevention) is highly intensive, individualized intervention for students who show minimal response to Tier 2 interventions. In some RTI models, Tier 3 is special education. To learn about two research-based practices that can make Tier 1 instruction more effective for all students, see *Teaching & Learning,* Choral Responding and Response Cards: Two Research-Based Practices for Increasing Student Participation and Achievement.

RTI was conceived and is most often used as an early intervening system for reading difficulties and for identifying students with learning disabilities. Most states permit local school districts to use RTI to identify students with learning disabilities, and 12 states require districts to implement RTI to identify students with learning disabilities (Zirkel & Thomas, 2010). The logic of RTI has been extended to other literacy skills (Alber Morgan, 2010), mathematics (Gersten, 2011), and social behavior support for students who exhibit problem behaviors in the classroom (Cheney, Flower, & Templeton, 2009).

Regardless of its form, prereferral intervention is designed to achieve the following purposes and benefits (Brown & Doolittle, 2008; L. S. Fuchs & Fuchs, 2005; Macy & Hoyt-Gonzales, 2007; Salvia, Ysseldyke, & Bolt, 2013):

- Provide immediate instructional and/or behavior management assistance to the child and teacher.
- Reduce the frequency of identifying children for special education whose learning or behavioral problems are the result of not receiving appropriate instruction rather than a disability.

Information, implementation guidelines, and case study examples for RTI from pre-K through secondary school can be found at the National Center on Response to Intervention (http://www.rti4success.org/), the National Research Center on Learning Disabilities (http://www.nrcld.org/), the RTI Action Network (http://www.rtinetwork.org/), and the IRIS Center (http://iris.peabody.vanderbilt.edu/tutorials.html).

- Prevent relatively minor problems from worsening to a degree that would eventually require special education.
- Strengthen teachers' capacity to effectively intervene with a greater diversity of problems, thereby reducing the number of future referrals for special education.
- Prevent the costly and time-consuming process of assessment for special education eligibility by solving the problems that originally caused teachers or parents to be concerned about the child.
- Provide IEP teams

Response to intervention entails several tiers of increasingly intensive instruction.

Laura Bolesta/Merrill

with valuable baseline data for planning and evaluating special education and related services for students who are referred and found eligible for special education.

A school district may not use RTI or any other form of prereferral intervention to delay formal evaluation and assessment of a student who is eligible for special education (Yell, 2012). At any time during the prereferral process, parents have the right to request that their child receive a comprehensive evaluation for identification/eligibility for special education services.

Evaluation and Eligibility Determination

To be eligible for special education and related services, a child must have a disability and need specially designed instruction. IDEA requires that all children suspected of having a disability receive a nondiscriminatory **multifactored evaluation (MFE)**. Either the school or the parents can request that a child be evaluated for special education. Regardless of the source of the referral, the parents must be notified of the school's intent to test their child, and they must give their consent to the evaluation. Within 60 days of receiving parental consent for evaluation, the school district must complete the evaluation to determine whether the child has a disability and identify the educational needs of the child (IDEA, Sec. 614[a][1][C]).

IDEA is explicit in describing some do's and don'ts that school districts must follow when evaluating a child for special education:

In conducting the evaluation, the local educational agency shall—

(A) use a variety of assessment tools and strategies to gather relevant functional, developmental, and academic information, including information provided by the parent, that may assist in determining—
   (i) whether the child is a child with a disability; and
   (ii) the content of the child's individualized education program, including information related to enabling the child to be involved in and

Multifactored evaluation

 Council for Exceptional Children

Initial Level Content Standards for Special Education Teachers: Legal provisions and ethical principles regarding assessment of individuals (ICC8K2).

Choral Responding and Response Cards:
Two Research-Based Practices for Increasing Student Participation and Achievement

Rashawn raised his hand for the last time. He wanted to answer several of his teacher's questions, especially when she asked whether anyone could name the clouds that look like wispy cotton. But it wasn't his day to get called on. He tried to follow along but soon lost interest and laid his head on his desk.

Dean did get called on once, but he didn't raise his hand too often. It was easier just to sit there. If he were quiet and still like Rashawn, then he wouldn't have to think about learning all this weather stuff. But it got too hard for Dean to just sit, so he started acting out. This got his teacher's attention.

"Dean, please pay attention!"

"Stop that, Dean!"

"Dean, how do you expect to learn this material for tomorrow's test if you're not part of the group?"

The next day, Rashawn and Dean did poorly on the test of meteorology concepts. Each boy had a history of poor school achievement; and teachers sometimes wondered if their lack of success was due to a *learning disability* or *attention deficit disorder*. But perhaps their chronic underachievement was directly influenced by the quality of instruction they received. Neither boy had actively participated during the previous day's lesson. Instead of being active learners who responded frequently to the lesson's content, both students were at best passive observers. Decades of educational research has shown that students who respond actively and often learn more than do students who passively attend to instruction (Ellis, Worthington, & Larkin, 2002; L. Fuchs et al., 2010; Greenwood, Delquadri, & Hall, 1984; Swanson & Hoskyn, 2001).

Although most teachers recognize the importance of actively engaging students, it is difficult during group instruction. Posing a question or problem to the entire class and then calling on one student to answer is the most commonly used method for student participation during group instruction. This provides an active learning opportunity only for the student who is called on and often results in more frequent responses by high-achieving students and few or no responses by low-achieving students. Two research-based alternatives to handraising (HR) and one-student-at-a-time participation are choral responding and response cards.

CHORAL RESPONDING

Choral responding (CR)—all students in the group responding orally in unison to a question or item presented by the teacher—has been around since the days of the one-room schoolhouse. It is the simplest, fastest way to increase student participation in group instruction (Heward, Courson, & Narayan, 1989). In his book *Teach Like a Champion: 49 Techniques That Put Students on the Path to College,* Lemov (2010) refers to CR as the "call and response" technique. Choral responding can be used to review or to check students' maintenance of previously learned concepts. For example, a high school history teacher could use CR to review the day's Civil War lesson. "Okay, class. I'm going to ask a series of questions about what we've covered in today's lesson. Your response will be 'Confederate' or 'Union.'" Teachers can also use CR to teach new knowledge and skills. Whether a lesson primarily reviews or teaches new content or skills is determined by the type and sequence of CR questions.

CR has been the response mode in numerous studies demonstrating a strong relationship between frequent student response during instruction and improved learning outcomes (e.g., Cihak, Alberto, Taber-Doughty, & Gama, 2006; Maheady, Michielli-Pendl, Mallette, & Harper, 2002; Sterling, Barbetta, Heward, & Heron, 1997), and it is a primary means for student participation in the evidence-based Direct Instruction programs to teach language, reading, math, and spelling (Carnine, Silbert, Kame'enui, & Tarver, 2010; Flores & Ganz, 2009).

RESPONSE CARDS

Response cards (RCs) are cards, signs, or items that all students simultaneously hold up to display their responses to a question or problem. There are two basic types of RCs: preprinted and write-on. When using *preprinted RCs,* each student selects from a personal set of cards the one with the answer she wishes to display. Examples include yes/true and no/false cards, numbers, colors, traffic signs, molecular structures, and parts of speech. Instead of using a set of different cards, teachers can distribute a single preprinted RC with multiple answers to each student (e.g., a card with clearly marked sections identified as proteins, fat, carbohydrates, vitamins, and minerals for use in a lesson on healthful eating habits). In its humblest version, the preprinted RC with multiple responses is a "pinch card": the student responds by holding up the card with her fingers pinching the part displaying her answer. Colored clothespins also make good pinching tools. Preprinted RCs may also have built-in devices for displaying answers, such as a cardboard clock with movable hour and minute hands.

When using write-on RCs, students mark their answers on blank cards that they erase between learning

Carl Harris/Merrill

Preprinted response cards

trials. Teachers can make a set of 40 durable write-on RCs from a 4-by-8-foot sheet of white laminated bathroom board (available from builders' supply stores). The cost is about $25, including the charge for cutting the sheet into 9-by-12-inch RCs. Dry-erase markers are available at most office supply stores, and paper towels or tissues will easily wipe the RCs clean.

Students can also use small chalkboards as write-on RCs, but responses may be difficult for the teacher to see in a full-size classroom. Write-on RCs can be custom-made to provide background or organizing structure for responses. For example, music students might mark notes on an RC that has permanent treble and bass clef scales; students in a driver's education class could draw where their car should go on RCs with permanent street intersections.

Research. A study comparing write-on RCs with HR during whole-class science lessons in an inner-city fifth-grade classroom produced three major findings (Gardner, Heward, & Grossi, 1994). First, with RCs, each student responded to teacher-posed questions an average of 21.8 times per 30-minute lesson, compared to a mean of 1.5 academic responses when the teacher called on individual students. The higher participation rate takes on major significance when its cumulative effect is calculated over the course of a 180-day school year. If the teacher used RCs instead of HR for just 30 minutes per day, each student in the class would make more than 5,000 additional academic responses during the

William Heward

Students using write-on response cards in a math lesson

school year. Second, all 22 students scored higher on next-day quizzes and 2-week review tests that followed lessons with RCs than they did on quizzes and tests that followed lessons with HR. Third, all but one student preferred RCs over hand raising. Numerous studies that have evaluated the effects of RCs with general and special education students at the elementary, middle, and secondary levels have produced a similar pattern of findings (e.g., Cavanaugh, Heward, & Donelson, 1996; George 2010; Horn, 2010; Randolph, 2007; Skibo, Mims, & Spooner, 2011).

In addition to increased participation and learning outcomes for students, several studies have found improved on-task behavior and/or decreases in the frequency of disruptions and inappropriate behavior when students used RCs (e.g., Armendariz & Umbreit, 1999; Christle & Schuster, 2003; Davis & O'Neill, 2004; Lambert, Cartledge, Lo, & Heward, 2006).

HOW TO GET STARTED WITH RESPONSE CARDS
Suggestions for All Types of RCs
- Model several question-and-answer trials and give students practice on how to use RCs.
- Maintain a lively pace throughout the lesson; keep intervals between trials short.
- Give clear cues when students are to hold up and put down their cards.
- Students can learn from watching others; do not let them think it is cheating to look at classmates' RCs.

Suggestions for Using Preprinted RCs
- Design the cards to be as easy to see as possible (e.g., consider size, print type, color codes).
- Make the cards easy for students to manipulate and display (e.g., put answers on both sides of the cards; attach a group of related cards to a ring; see photo).
- Begin instruction on new content with a small set of fact/concept cards (perhaps only two), gradually adding cards as students' skills improve.

Suggestions for Using Write-On RCs
- Limit language-based responses to one to three words.
- Keep a few extra markers on hand.
- Be sure students do not hesitate to respond because they are concerned about making spelling mistakes: (a) provide several practice trials with new terms before the lesson begins; (b) write new terms on the chalkboard, and tell students to refer to them during the lesson; and/or (c) use the "don't worry" technique, telling students to try their best but that misspellings will not count against them.
- Students enjoy doodling on their response cards. After a good lesson, let students draw on the cards for a few minutes.

MyEducationLab™

To observe teachers conducting various lessons with choral responding and response cards, go to the book resources for this text on MyEducationLab.

progress in the general education curriculum, or, for preschool children, to participate in appropriate activities;

(B) not use any single measure or assessment as the sole criterion for determining whether a child is a child with a disability or determining an appropriate educational program for the child; and

(C) use technically sound instruments that may assess the relative contribution of cognitive and behavioral factors, in addition to physical or developmental factors.

Additional Requirements—Each local educational agency shall ensure that

(A) assessments and other evaluation materials used to assess a child—
  (i) are selected and administered so as not to be discriminatory on a racial or cultural basis;
  (ii) are provided and administered in the language and form most likely to yield accurate information on what the child knows and can do academically, developmentally, and functionally, unless it is not feasible to so provide or administer;
  (iii) are used for purposes for which the assessments or measures are valid and reliable;
  (iv) are administered by trained and knowledgeable personnel; and
  (v) are administered in accordance with any instructions provided by the producer of such assessments;

(B) the child is assessed in all areas of suspected disability;

(C) assessment tools and strategies that provide relevant information that directly assists persons in determining the educational needs of the child are provided; and

(D) assessments of children with disabilities who transfer from one school district to another school district in the same academic year are coordinated with such children's prior and subsequent schools, as necessary and as expeditiously as possible, to ensure prompt completion of full evaluations. (PL 108-446, Sec. 614[b][2])

The MFE is conducted by a school-based *multidisciplinary evaluation team*, sometimes called a *student study team*, which includes the child's parents. The team examines the test results and all other relevant information to determine if the child has a disability that adversely affects his or her educational performance and is therefore entitled to special education. IDEA stipulates that a child shall not be identified as a child with a disability if the child's learning difficulties are the result of a "lack of appropriate instruction in reading . . .; lack of instruction in math; or limited English proficiency" (PL 108-446, Sec. 614[b][4]). An MFE must do more than provide information on the existence of a disability for determining eligibility for special education. IDEA requires that evaluation reports also provide information about the child's educational needs and how to meet them.

One study found that 40% of elementary and middle school students receiving special education services had at least one additional (nonprimary) disability (Marder, 2009). To read an example of a case in which a child was determined to have a disability but not eligible for special education because he was doing well in school, see D. F. Bateman (2008).

DISPROPORTIONATE REPRESENTATION OF STUDENTS FROM CULTURALLY AND LINGUISTICALLY DIVERSE GROUPS IN SPECIAL EDUCATION Disproportionate representation exists when a particular group receives special education at a rate significantly higher or lower than would be expected based on the proportion of the general student population that group represents. Culturally and linguistically diverse students are both overrepresented and underrepresented in special education, depending on the group and disability category (De Valenzuela, Copeland, Huaqing Qi, & Park, 2006; Kalyanpur, 2008; Waitoller, Artiles, & Cheney, 2010). Table 1 shows the risk ratios for students from five race/ethnicity groups for receiving special education by each of the federal government's disability categories. A *risk ratio* is the relative likelihood of a member of a given group to be, in this case, receiving special education, compared

to members of the general population. A risk ratio of 1.0 means that the number of students identified with a given disability matches the proportion of the overall student population represented. A risk ratio greater than 1.0 indicates overrepresentation; a risk ratio less than 1.0 indicates underrepresentation.

When all disability categories are combined, African American and Native American students are overrepresented (risk ratios of 1.5) and Asian American students are underrepresented (risk ratio, 0.5) in the special education population. Hispanic and white students are generally represented among the special education population at an overall rate close to their proportion of the resident school-age population. Some disparities are especially evident when the data are examined by disability category. An African American student is more than twice as likely to be identified with emotional

TABLE 1 ● Risk ratios for students ages 6 through 21 served under IDEA by disability category and race/ethnicity

DISABILITY	AMERICAN INDIAN/ ALASKA NATIVE	ASIAN/PACIFIC ISLANDER	BLACK/AFRICAN AMERICAN	HISPANIC	WHITE
Specific learning disabilities	1.8	0.4	1.4	1.2	0.8
Speech or language impairments	1.4	0.7	1.0	0.9	1.1
Intellectual disabilities	1.3	0.5	2.9	0.7	0.6
Emotional disturbance	1.6	0.3	2.3	0.6	0.8
Multiple disabilities	1.7	0.6	1.5	0.7	1.0
Hearing impairments	1.3	1.2	1.1	1.3	0.8
Orthopedic impairments	1.0	0.8	1.0	1.2	0.9
Other health impairments	1.2	0.4	1.7	0.5	1.5
Visual impairments	1.4	1.0	1.2	0.9	0.9
Autism	0.7	1.3	1.0	0.6	1.3
Deaf-blindness	1.7	1.1	0.8	1.1	1.0
Traumatic brain injury	1.5	0.6	1.2	0.7	1.2
All disabilities	**1.5**	**0.5**	**1.5**	**0.9**	**0.9**

Notes: Ratios rounded to nearest one-tenth. States now report IDEA child count data by seven race/ethnicity categories: American Indian or Alaskan Native, Asian, Black or African American, Hispanic/Latino, Native Hawaiian or other Pacific Islander, White, and Two or more races.

Source: U.S. Department of Education. (2010). *Twenty-ninth annual report to Congress on the implementation of the Individuals with Disabilities Education Act* (Table 1-13). Washington, DC: Author.

and behavioral disorders than is a student in the general population and nearly three times as likely to be identified with intellectual disabilities. Even larger differences in proportional representation by race are sometimes apparent when special education enrollment data are examined at the state and local levels. (Hetzner, 2007).

For decades, reports and census studies have shown that three groups of culturally different students—African American, Hispanic American, and Native American— have consistently been underrepresented in gifted education programs (Donovan & Cross, 2002; Ford, 1998, 2010b; Ford, Grantham, & Whiting, 2008).

Is this disproportionate representation appropriate? Identification and classification for special education should be based entirely on the presence of a disabling condition that adversely affects the child's educational performance. The fact that culturally and linguistically diverse students are identified as having a disability is not, in itself, a problem. All students with disabilities that adversely affect their educational performance have the right to special education services, whatever their racial, cultural, or linguistic backgrounds. Disproportionate representation is problematic if it means that children have been wrongly placed in special education programs that deny them appropriate educational interventions that match their full learning capacities, stigmatize them, or segregate them (Artiles & Bal, 2008). For example, Skiba, Poloni-Staudinger, Galine, Simmons, and Feggins-Azziz (2006) found that African American students with disabilities were more likely to be placed in more restrictive educational settings than were white students with disabilities. Figure 2 shows the percentage by race/ethnicity of school-age students served in four different educational environments.

Disproportionate representation is also a problem if it means students with disabilities are overlooked because of their membership in a racial or ethnic minority group, resulting in their being denied access to needed special education (De Valenzuela et al., 2006).

The causes of disproportionate representation have been difficult to pinpoint and often controversial (Cullinan & Kauffman, 2005; Harry & Klingner, 2006, 2007; Osher et al., 2004). Are students from some culturally and linguistically diverse groups more likely to have a disability than are white children? For example, a much greater proportion of students from diverse groups are born to mothers without access to maternal health care and live in poverty—factors that are associated with an increased incidence of disability. Half of the nation's Latino fourth graders and almost half of African American fourth graders attend public schools in which more than three-fourths of the students come from low-income families (based on federal eligibility criteria for free or reduced-price school lunch). By comparison, only 5% of white fourth graders attend schools with poverty rates this high (Kober, 2006). Or, as some researchers have suggested, do inherent problems in the referral and placement process bias the identification of minority children (Harry & Klingner, 2006; Osher et al., 2004)? The answer to these controversial and complex questions is that probably both explanations are partly true (Serna, Forness, & Nielson, 1998).

Recognizing and Combating Cultural and Racial Bias in Referral and Identification Procedures. Understanding the reasons for the disproportionality phenomenon in special education is not simple. Numerous factors must be considered, and educators have identified three areas as integral to this problem: (a) incongruity between teachers and culturally and linguistically diverse students and families, which may lead to biased referrals; (b) inaccurate assessment of culturally diverse students; and (c) ineffective curriculum and instructional practices for culturally diverse students.

Today's teachers are mostly white (87%) and female (70%) (National Education Association, 2010), and these predominately middle-class educators are teaching an increasingly diverse student population. For example, with respect to the overrepresentation of African American students in the emotional and behavior disorders category, some researchers contend that an African American behavioral style conflicts

FIGURE 2

PERCENTAGE OF SCHOOL-AGE STUDENTS SERVED UNDER IDEA BY RACE/ETHNICITY AND EDUCATIONAL ENVIRONMENT.

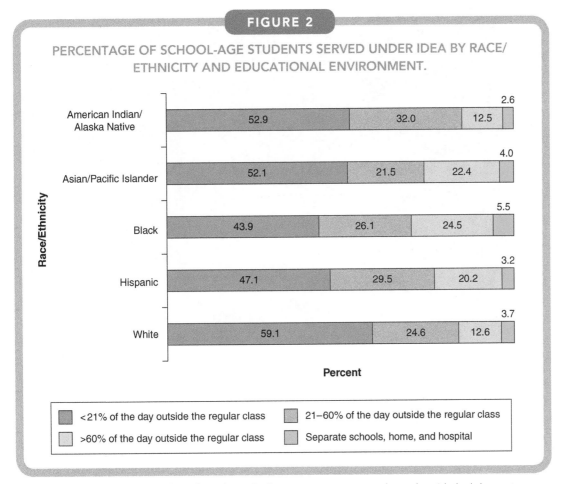

Note: The colored bars represent, from left to right, regular class, resource room, separate class, and special school placements.

Source: U.S. Department of Education. (2010). Twenty-ninth annual report to Congress on the implementation of the Individuals with Disabilities Education Act (Figure 1-28). Washington, DC: Author.

with white teachers' expectations for classroom behavior (Hale, 2001; Townsend, 2000). "When African American students 'behave' in modes affirmed and sanctioned by dimensions of African American culture (Boykin, 1983) and those modes are unfamiliar to or misinterpreted by teachers, most of whom are white, their behavior is often perceived as inappropriate" (Webb-Johnson, 2003, p. 5).

Bias in the assessment process may contribute to the disproportionate numbers of culturally diverse students in special education. The methods used to identify students for services are an inexact science; and many authors have argued that the likelihood of obtaining valid, accurate, and unbiased assessment results is lower when the student in question is from a culturally or linguistically different background (Ford, 2004a, 2010a Langdon, Novak, & Quintanar, 2000; Ortiz, 1997; Utley & Obiakor, 2001).

Inappropriate referral to special education can occur if educators and school psychologists cannot separate the presence of unrecognized diversity or deficits from disability. Barrera (1995) noted three potential sources of learning problems in children from culturally and linguistically diverse backgrounds: (a) unrecognized cultural/linguistic diversity, (b) deficits stemming from chronic poverty or trauma, and (c) disabilities. She contended that special education services are neither appropriate nor most efficient for learning difficulties that are not the result of inherent disabilities.

If, for example, a child has experienced trauma that remains unaddressed, simply reducing task complexity will not be a sufficient response. . . . It is

Teachers are most effective when curriculum content and instructional methods are responsive to the cultural, ethnic, and linguistic diversity among their students.

important, therefore, to understand the specific difficulties that may stem from unrecognized diversity or deficits. Once understood, pre-referral intervention can be directed toward eliminating their impact and assessing whether any difficulties remain. It is these difficulties, that remain after diversity and deficit have been addressed, that are the appropriate target for special education. (p. 64)

Understanding the complex issues related to culturally diverse students in special education requires that educators understand the problems with incongruity of a teacher's interactions with students and families from diverse cultures, the assessment and referral process in special education, and ineffective instructional and discipline practices (Salend & Garrick Duhaney, 2005; Townsend, 2000; West, Leon-Guerrero, & Stevens, 2007). To better meet the needs of students with disabilities from diverse backgrounds, schools should address three issues. First, staff must become culturally responsive to students and families (Cartledge & Kourea, 2008; Harry, 2008; Tam & Heng, 2005). Second, staff must implement appropriate assessment strategies for determining the educational needs of culturally diverse students. Third, educators should implement culturally responsive practices that support a multicultural approach to curriculum and instruction (Banks & Banks, 2013; Cartledge, Gardner, & Ford, 2009; Hoover, Klingner, Baca, & Patton, 2008; Obiakor, 2007). Fiedler and colleagues (2008) have developed a checklist to help school personnel identify and consider factors at the referral, assessment, and eligibility determination stages that lead to disproportionate representation.

Program Planning

If the evaluation team determines that a child has a disability that is adversely affecting his or her educational performance, an individualized education program (IEP) is formed. The IEP team determines the what (learning goals and objectives), how (specialized instruction and related services), who (teachers and related-service providers), and when (frequency of specialized instruction and related services) of a child's special education program. The IEP is the centerpiece of the special education process. A detailed description of the IEP appears later in this chapter.

Placement

After the IEP team determines the child's educational needs and the special education and related services necessary to meet those needs, the team then determines an educational setting in which the child can receive an appropriate education in the least restrictive environment (LRE). Where children with disabilities are taught is one of the most debated and often misunderstood aspects of special education and IDEA, and it is discussed in depth later in this chapter and throughout the text.

Progress Monitoring, Annual Review, and Reevaluation

In addition to being specialized, intensive, and goal-directed instruction, special education is also continuously evaluated education.

ONGOING PROGRESS MONITORING No matter how appropriate the goals on a student's IEP and well-conceived the specially designed instruction and related services identified to meet those goals, the document's usefulness is limited without ongoing monitoring of student progress. Schools are accountable for providing a free appropriate education to all children with disabilities, and accountability requires measurement (Heward, 2003; Kauffman & Konold, 2007). Direct and frequent measurement of student performance provides the most meaningful information about student progress and the effectiveness of instruction (Greenwood & Maheady, 1997; McDonough et al., 2005).

ANNUAL REVIEW A child's IEP is <u>not</u> intended to be a permanent document. All aspects of an IEP—the annual goals and outcomes, delivery of specially designed instruction and related services, appropriateness of placement—must be thoroughly reviewed periodically, at least annually. The IEP team revises the IEP to address any lack of expected progress in meeting annual goals or changes in the child's needs.

REEVALUATION For some students, the specially designed instruction and related services they receive may ameliorate a problem (e.g., speech therapy for an articulation disorder) or accommodate an impairment (e.g., a prosthesis or mobility device) such that they no longer need, or are eligible for, special education. At least once every 3 years, the school must conduct an MFE of each child with a disability (unless the parents and school agree it is unnecessary) to determine if the child still needs special education. If the IEP team decides that a disability is no longer present or that the child's education is no longer adversely affected by the disability, the student is declassified, and special education discontinues.

Although special education is sometimes characterized as a "one-way street" down which "it's relatively easy to send children . . . but they rarely return" (Finn, Rotherham, & Hokanson, 2001, p. 339), a nationwide study of more than 11,000 students in special education ages 6 to 12 found 17% of the students had been declassified after 2 years and were no longer receiving special education services (SRI International, 2005). Another study based on a nationally representative sample of children found that 16% of preschoolers who had received special education services were declassified after 2 years. (Daley & Carlson, 2009).

In 2008, IDEA regulations were amended to give parents the right to revoke their consent for special education for their child at any time. After receipt of parents' written request for revocation, the school must cease the provision of all special education and related services to the child.

Monitoring student progress

Council for Exceptional Children

Initial Level Content Standards for Special Education Teachers: Evaluate instruction and monitor progress of individuals with exceptional learning needs (ICC8S8).

Online tutorials and a variety of practical and efficient procedures for obtaining and using student performance data are available from the National Center on Student Progress Monitoring (http://www.studentprogress.org/).

Direct and frequent measures of student performance provide the most meaningful information about student progress and the effectiveness of instruction.

Katelyn Metzger/Merrill

COLLABORATION AND TEAMING

Special education is a team game. The team that plans, delivers, and evaluates the program of specially designed instruction and related services to meet the unique needs that arise from 10-year-old Jessica's disability might include the following: the third-grade teacher who works with Jessica in the general education classroom; the speech-language pathologist who meets with Jessica's teacher each week to co-plan language activities; the special education teacher who provides Jessica with intensive reading instruction each day in the resource room and collaborates with her general education teacher on instructional modifications for Jessica in math and science; the adapted physical education teacher who works with Jessica in the gymnasium; and Jessica's parents, who help with homework and keep everyone informed of their daughter's progress at home. Without open, honest, and frequent communication and collaboration between and among the members of Jessica's team, the quality of her education is likely to suffer.

Paraeducators—also known as *paraprofessionals, teacher aides*, and *instructional assistants*—play important roles in delivering special education services to students with disabilities (Carnahan, Williamson, Clarke, & Sorensen, 2009). IEP teams must be careful, however, that a paraprofessional's proximity does not have inadvertent adverse effects, such as limiting a student's independence (Causton-Theoharis, 2009).

Collaboration

Types of collaboration

 Initial Level Content Standards for Special Education Teachers: Models and strategies of consultation and collaboration (ICC10K1).

Collaboration has become a common and necessary practice in special education (Lingo, Barton-Arwood, & Jolivette, 2011; Sayeski, 2009). Teachers are better able to diagnose and solve learning and behavior problems in the classroom when they work together. Three ways in which team members can work collaboratively are through coordination, consultation, and teaming (Bigge, Stump, Spagna, & Silberman, 1999).

*Coordinati*on is the simplest form of collaboration, requiring only ongoing communication and cooperation to ensure that services are provided in a timely and systematic fashion. Although an important and necessary element of special education, coordination does not require service providers to share information or specifics of their efforts with one another. Fortunately for Jessica, the four educators on her IEP team do much more than simply coordinate who is going to work with her when.

In *consultation*, team members provide information and expertise to one another. Consultation is traditionally considered unidirectional, with the expert providing assistance and advice to the novice. However, team members can, and often do, switch roles from consultant to consultee and back again. Jessica's third-grade teacher, for example, receives expert advice from the speech-language pathologist on strategies for evoking extended language from Jessica during cooperative learning groups but takes the consultant's role when explaining details of the science curriculum to Jessica's resource room teacher.

Teaming

Intervention assistance *team*, child study *team*, IEP *team*: each step of the special education process involves a group of people who must work together for the benefit of a child with special needs. For special education to be most effective, these groups must become functioning and effective teams (Correa, Jones, Thomas, & Morsink, 2005; Hunt, Soto, Maier, & Doering, 2003). Teaming is the most difficult level of collaboration to achieve; it also pays the most dividends. Teaming "bridges the two previous modes of working together and builds on their strengths while adding the component of reciprocity and sharing of information among all team members through a more equal exchange" (Bigge et al., 1999, p. 13).

Although the team approach has many variations, each member of a team generally assumes certain clearly assigned responsibilities and recognizes the importance of learning from, contributing to, and interacting with the other members of the team. Many believe that the consensus and group decisions arising from a team's involvement provide a form of insurance against erroneous or arbitrary conclusions in the complex issues that face educators of students with disabilities. In practice, three team models have emerged (McGonigel, Woodruff, & Roszmann-Millican, 1994)—multidisciplinary, interdisciplinary, and transdisciplinary—and these are discussed next.

MULTIDISCIPLINARY TEAMS *Multidisciplinary teams* are composed of professionals from different disciplines who work independently of one another. Each team member conducts assessments, plans interventions, and delivers services. Teams that operate according to a multidisciplinary structure risk the

By teaming, these teachers are better able to diagnose and solve learning problems.

Laura Bolesta/Merrill

danger of not providing services that recognize the child as an integrated whole; they must be careful not to "splinter" the child into segments along disciplinary lines. (An old saying described the child with disabilities as giving "his hands to the occupational therapist, his legs to the physical therapist, and his brain to the teacher" [Williamson, 1978].) Another concern is the lack of communication among team members.

INTERDISCIPLINARY TEAMS *Interdisciplinary teams* are characterized by formal channels of communication between members. Although each professional usually conducts discipline-specific assessments, the interdisciplinary team meets to share information and develop intervention plans. Each team member is generally responsible for implementing a portion of the service plan related to his or her discipline.

TRANSDISCIPLINARY TEAMS The highest level of team involvement, but also the most difficult to accomplish, is the *transdisciplinary team*. Members of transdisciplinary teams seek to provide services in a uniform and integrated fashion by conducting joint assessments, sharing information and expertise across discipline boundaries, and selecting goals and interventions that are discipline-free (Friend & Cook, 2010; Giangreco, Edelman, & Dennis, 1991). Members of transdisciplinary teams also share roles (often referred to as *role release*); in contrast, members of multidisciplinary and interdisciplinary teams generally operate in isolation and may not coordinate their services to achieve the integrated delivery of related services. Regardless of the team model, team members must learn to put aside professional rivalries and work collaboratively for the benefit of the student (Zigmond,, Kloo, & Lemons, 2011).

Co-Teaching

Co-teaching—a general education teacher and special education teacher planning and delivering instruction together in an inclusive classroom—has become increasingly common. Co-teaching takes many different forms depending on the purpose of the lesson, the individualized objectives and needed supports for students with disabilities, and the teachers' relative levels of expertise with the content (Ploessl Rock, Schoenfeld, & Blanks, 2010; Potts & Howard, 2011). Five co-teaching formats are commonly used:

- *One teaching/one helping.* One teacher instructs the whole class while the other circulates to collect information on student performance and to offer help. This arrangement takes advantage of the expertise of one teacher in a specific subject area.

Teaming models

Council for Exceptional Children Initial Level Content Standards for Special Education Teachers: Models and strategies of consultation and collaboration (ICC10K1).

- *Parallel teaching.* When it is necessary to lower the student–teacher ratio, both teachers teach the same materials to two equal-sized groups of students.
- *Station teaching.* When teaching material that is difficult but not sequential, both teachers present different content at the same time to two equal groups of students and then switch groups and repeat the lesson.
- *Alternative teaching.* When teachers need to individualize instruction, remediate skills, promote mastery, or offer enrichment, one teacher works with a smaller group or individual students while the other teacher works with the rest of the class.
- *Team teaching.* When it is desirable to blend the talents and expertise of teachers, both teachers plan and teach a lesson together. (adapted from Salend, 2011)

As Sheena Washington emphasized in her Featured Teacher essay, meticulous planning, open communication, and flexibility are keys to successful co-teaching. It is a mistake, however, to assume that two teachers in the classroom instead of one will automatically improve the effectiveness of a lesson. While the rationale and suggested techniques for co-teaching are logical, much more outcome research on the effects of co-teaching is needed (Friend & Hurley-Chamberlain, 2011; Zigmond, 2007; Zigmond & Magiera, 2001).

Suggestions for effective co-teaching can be found in Howard and Potts (2009); Murawaski and Dieker (2008); Potts and Howard (2011); Sileo (2010); and Sileo and van Garderen (2010).

INDIVIDUALIZED EDUCATION PROGRAM

The IEP is "the heart of IDEA" and "the make or break component of FAPE for every child with a disability" (Bateman & Herr, 2006, p. 10). IDEA requires that educators develop and implement an IEP for each student with disabilities between the ages of 3 and 21. (Educators develop an *individualized family service plan* [IFSP] for each infant and toddler [from birth through age 2] with disabilities.) IDEA is specific about who is to develop the IEP and what it must include.

IEP Team

Each IEP must be the product of the collaborative efforts of the members of an **IEP team**, the membership of which is specified in IDEA as the following:

The term "individualized education program team" or "IEP Team" means a group of individuals composed of—

1. The parents of a child with a disability;
2. not less than 1 regular education teacher of the child (if the child is, or may be, participating in the regular education environment);
3. not less than 1 special education teacher, or where appropriate, at least 1 special education provider of the child;
4. a representative of the local education agency who—
    (i) is qualified to provide, or supervise the provision of, specially designed instruction to meet the unique needs of children with disabilities;
    (ii) is knowledgeable about the general curriculum; and
    (iii) is knowledgeable about the availability of resources of the local education agency;
5. an individual who can interpret the instructional implications of evaluation results, who may be a member of the team described in clauses (2) through (6);
6. at the discretion of the parent or the agency, other individuals who have knowledge or special expertise regarding the child, including related service personnel as appropriate; and
7. Whenever appropriate, the child with a disability. (PL 108-446, Sec. 614 [d][1][B])

IEP Components

Each IEP must include the following seven components:

1. A statement of the child's present levels of academic achievement and functional performance, including—
   (a) how the child's disability affects the child's involvement and progress in the general education curriculum;
   (b) for preschool children, as appropriate, how the disability affects the child's participation in appropriate activities; and
   (c) for children with disabilities who take alternate assessments aligned to alternate achievement standards, a description of benchmarks or short-term objectives;

2. A statement of measurable annual goals, including academic and functional goals, designed to—
   (a) meet the child's needs that result from the child's disability to enable the child to be involved in and make progress in the general education curriculum; and
   (b) meet each of the child's other educational needs that result from the child's disability;

3. A description of how the child's progress toward meeting the annual goals described in subclause (2) will be measured and when periodic reports on the progress the child is making toward meeting the annual goals (such as through the use of quarterly or other periodic reports, concurrent with the issuance of report cards) will be provided;

4. A statement of the special education and related services and supplementary aids and services, based on peer-reviewed research to the extent practicable, to be provided to the child, or on behalf of the child, and a statement of the program modifications or supports for school personnel that will be provided for the child—
   (a) to advance appropriately toward attaining the annual goals;
   (b) to be involved in and make progress in the general education curriculum in accordance with subclause (1) and to participate in extracurricular and other nonacademic activities; and
   (c) to be educated and participate with other children with disabilities and nondisabled children in the activities described in this subparagraph;

5. An explanation of the extent, if any, to which the child will not participate with nondisabled children in the regular class and in the activities described in subclause (4)(c);

6. (a) a statement of any individual appropriate accommodations that are necessary to measure the academic achievement and functional performance of the child on State and districtwide assessments consistent with section 612(a)(16)(A); and (b) if the IEP Team determines that the child shall take an alternate assessment on a particular State or districtwide assessment of student achievement, a statement of why—
   (aa) the child cannot participate in the regular assessment; and
   (bb) the particular alternate assessment selected is appropriate for the child;

7. The projected date for the beginning of the services and modifications described in subclause (4), and the anticipated frequency, location, and duration of those services and modifications. (PL 108-446, Sec. 614 [d][1][B])

IEPs for students age 16 and older must include information on how the child's transition from school to adult life will be supported:

8. Beginning not later than the first IEP to be in effect when the child is 16, and updated annually thereafter—
   (a) appropriate measurable postsecondary goals based upon age appropriate transition assessments related to training, education, employment, and, where appropriate, independent living skills;

Participation and progress in the general curriculum

Initial Level Content Standards for Special Education Teachers: Identify and prioritize areas of the general curriculum and needed accommodations (ICC7S1).

> (b) the transition services (including courses of study) needed to assist the child in reaching those goals; and
>
> (c) beginning not later than 1 year before the child reaches the age of majority under State law, a statement that the child has been informed of the child's rights under this title, if any, that will transfer to the child on reaching the age of majority under section 615(m). (PL 108-446, Sec. 614 [d][1][A][i])

When developing a child's IEP, the IEP team must consider the following factors:

1. *General.* The IEP Team must consider (i) the strengths of the child; (ii) the concerns of the parents for enhancing the education of their child; (iii) the results of the initial or most recent evaluation of the child; and (iv) the academic, developmental, and functional needs of the child.

2. *Consideration of special factors.* The IEP Team must—

   i. In the case of a child whose behavior impedes the child's learning or that of others, consider the use of positive behavioral interventions and supports, and other strategies, to address that behavior;

   ii. In the case of a child with limited English proficiency, consider the language needs of the child as those needs relate to the child's IEP;

   iii. In the case of a child who is blind or visually impaired, provide for instruction in Braille and the use of Braille unless the IEP Team determines, after an evaluation of the child's reading and writing skills, that instruction in Braille or the use of Braille is not appropriate for the child;

   iv. Consider the communication needs of the child, and in the case of a child who is deaf or hard of hearing, consider the child's language and communication needs; and

   v. Consider whether the child needs assistive technology devices and services. (PL 108-446, Sec. 614 [d][3][A & B])

IEP Functions and Formats

An IEP spells out where the child is, where she should be going, how she will get there, how long it will take, and how to tell if and when she has arrived. An IEP provides teachers and families with the opportunity—and the responsibility—to first be realistic about the child's needs and goals and then to be creative about how to meet them. Being realistic does not mean taking a pessimistic or limited view of the child's current capabilities or potential to reach improved levels of academic achievement or functional performance; it means analyzing how specially designed instruction and related services can help the child get from her present levels of performance to future goals.

The IEP is also a measure of accountability for teachers and schools. Whether a particular school or educational program is effective will be judged, to some extent, by how well it is able to help children meet the goals and objectives set forth in their IEPs. Like other professionals, teachers are being called on to demonstrate effectiveness, and the IEP provides one way for them to do so. Although a child's teacher and school cannot be prosecuted in the courts if the child does not achieve his IEP goals, the school

Each area of functioning that is adversely affected by the student's disability must be represented by an annual goal on the IEP.

Katelyn Metzger/Merrill

district is legally bound to provide the special education and related services identified in the IEP, and the school must be able to document that it made a conscientious and systematic effort to achieve those goals (Bartlett, Etscheidt, & Weisentstein, 2007; Wright, Wright, & O'Connor, 2010).

IEP formats vary widely across school districts, and schools may exceed the requirements of the law and include additional information. Bateman and Linden (2006) cautioned against overreliance on standardized forms and computers for creating IEPs. "Forms by their very nature tend to interfere with true individualization. . . . [A] proper form will contain all the required elements in the simplest way possible, allowing for the most flexibility and creativity" (pp. 82–83). Figure 3 shows portions of the IEP for Curt, a ninth grader and low achiever seen by the school district as a poorly motivated student with a disciplinary problem and a bad attitude. Curt's parents see their son as a discouraged and frustrated student with learning disabilities, especially in written language.

FIGURE 3 PORTIONS OF AN IEP FOR CURT, A NINTH GRADER WITH LEARNING DISABILITIES AND A HISTORY OF DISCIPLINARY PROBLEMS

Unique educational needs, characteristics, and measured present levels of academic achievement and functional performance (PLOPs)	Special education, related services and supplemental aids and services (based on peer-reviewed research to the extent practicable); assistive technology and modifications or personnel support	Measurable annual goals and short-term objectives (progress markers),[1] including academic and functional goals to enable the student to be involved in and make progress in the general curriculum and to meet other needs resulting from the disability
(Including how the disability affects student's ability to participate and progress in the general curriculum)	(Including anticipated starting date, frequency, duration and location for each)	(Including progress measurement method for each goal)

Study skills/organizational needs:
- How to read text
- Note taking
- How to study notes
- Memory work
- Be prepared for class, with materials
- Lengthen and improve attention span and on-task behavior

Present level: Curt currently lacks skills in all these areas.

1. Speech/lang. therapist, resource room teacher, and content area teachers will provide Curt with direct and specific teaching of study skills, i.e.
   - Note taking from lectures
   - Note taking while reading text
   - How to study notes for a test
   - Memorization hints
   - Strategies for reading text to retain information

2. Assign a "study buddy" for Curt in each content area class.

3. Prepare a motivation system for Curt to be prepared for class with all necessary materials.

4. Develop a motivational plan to encourage Curt to lengthen his attention span and time on task.

5. Provide aide to monitor on-task behaviors in first month or so of plan and teach Curt self-monitoring techniques.

6. Provide motivational system and self-recording form for completion of academic tasks in each class.

Goal: At the end of academic year, Curt will have better grades and, by his own report, will have learned new study skills.

Obj. 1: Given a 20–30 min lecture/oral lesson, Curt will take appropriate notes as judged by that teacher.

Obj. 2: Given 10–15 pgs. of text to read, Curt will employ an appropriate strategy for retaining info., i.e. mapping, webbing, outlining, notes, etc. as judged by the teacher.

Obj. 3: Given notes to study for a test, Curt will do so successfully as evidenced by his test score.

(continued)

FIGURE 3 *Continued*

Academic needs/written language: Curt needs strong remedial help in spelling, punctuation, capitalization, and usage.

Present level: Curt is approximately 2 grade levels behind his peers in these skills.

1. Provide direct instruction in written language skills (punctuation, capitalization, usage, spelling) by using a highly structured, well-sequenced program. Services provided in small group of no more than four students in the resource room, 50 minutes/day.

2. Build in continuous and cumulative review to help with short-term rote memory difficulty.

3. Develop a list of commonly used words in student writing (or use one of many published lists) for Curt's spelling program.

Adaptations to regular program:
- In all classes, Curt should sit near the front of the class.
- Curt should be called on often to keep him involved and on task.
- All teachers should help Curt with study skills as trained by spelling/language specialist and resource room teacher.
- Teachers should monitor Curt's work closely in the beginning weeks/months of his program.

Goal: Within one academic year, Curt will improve his written language skills by 1.5 or 2 full grade levels to a 6.0 grade level as measured by a standardized test.

Obj. 1: Given 10 sentences of dictation at his current level of instruction, Curt will punctuate and capitalize with 90% accuracy (checked at the end of each unit taught).

Obj. 2: Given 30 sentences with choices of usage, at his current instructional level, Curt will make the correct choice in 28 or more sentences.

Obj. 3: Given a list of 150 commonly used words in 6th grade writing, Curt will spell 95% of the words correctly.

[1]For students who take an alternative assessment and are assessed against other than grade level standards, the IEP **must** include short-term objectives (progress markers). For other students, the IEP **may** include short-term objectives. The IEP **must** for all students clearly articulate how the student's progress will be measured, and that progress must be reported to parents at designated intervals.

Source: Reprinted from Bateman, B. D., & Linden, M. L. (2006). *Better IEPs: How to develop legally correct and educationally useful programs* (4th ed., pp. 153–155). Verona, WI: Attainment Company, Inc. Used by permission.

One of the most difficult tasks for the IEP team is determining how inclusive the IEP document should be. It is important for educators and parents to recognize that an IEP is not the same as a curriculum. "IEP objectives are not comprehensive enough to cover the entire scope and sequence of what a student is to learn. The content taught by most special educators goes far beyond what is written in the IEP. Sometimes special educators try to incorporate an entire curriculum into the IEP, resulting in an overly long, detailed IEP" (Browder, 2001, p. 35).

Remembering that special education is "specially designed instruction" will help IEP teams determine the content of a student's IEP (Strickland & Turnbull, 1993). Adaptations to curriculum and instruction that differ significantly from the range of adaptations normally made for general education students or that the IEP team deems necessary to remediate or compensate for the adverse affects on the child's educational performance should be considered "specially designed instruction" and be included as part of the student's IEP.

Each area of functioning that is adversely affected by the student's disability must be represented by an annual goal on the IEP. Annual goals are statements of what the IEP team believes the student can accomplish in 1 year if the special services provided are effective. Too often, IEP teams' hard work and best intentions for a child's progress are muddled at best, or lost altogether, by IEP goals that are impossible to measure.

Figure 4 presents some examples of nonmeasurable IEP goals and how IEP teams might change them into measurable goals.

IEP Problems and Potential Solutions

Since its inception, the IEP process has been problematic. J. J. Gallagher (1984) wrote that the IEP is "probably the single most unpopular aspect of the law, not only because

---

FIGURE 4   TURNING NONMEASURABLE IEP GOALS INTO MEASURABLE GOALS

"Measurable" is the essential characteristic of an IEP goal or objective. When a goal isn't measurable, it cannot be measured. If it cannot be measured, it violates IDEA and may result in denial of FAPE to the child. A measurable goal contains a given or condition, the learner's performance, and the desired level of performance or criteria. The learner's performance must be an observable, visible, or countable behavior.

Not Observable or Countable	Observable and Countable
enjoying literature	reading orally
understanding history	constructing a time line
becoming independent	dressing oneself
respecting authority	speaking to adults without vulgarities
improving, feeling, knowing	pointing, drawing, identifying, writing, etc.

Not-Measurable Goals Made Measurable

Rebecca will increase her active listening skills. This goal has no criterion to indicate the level at which Rebecca must perform to reach the goal, nor does it specify the behavior of "active listening." We could not tell if Rebecca has "improved" without knowing the previous level of her skills. Thousands and thousands of goals have used this "student will improve X" format. It is not measurable, not acceptable, and not useful. To improve this goal, we must ask what the writer meant by "active listening." Perhaps "following oral directions" would be an acceptable visible learner performance. If so, this measurable version is probably closer to what was intended: "Given 5 simple, two-step oral directions such as 'Fold your paper and hand it in,' Rebecca will correctly complete 4 directions."

Sara will make wise choices in her use of leisure time. Sara may, indeed, "make wise choices," but we really can't see her doing this. This goal does not describe a visible learner performance and does not include a criterion. Perhaps the writer meant something like "Sara will attend a supervised, school-sponsored extracurricular activity at least once a week."

Beth will show an appropriate level of upper body strength. This goal is easily fixed. The goal writer may well have meant, "Beth will pass the XYZ test of upper body strength at her age level."

The following two objectives appeared under the totally nonmeasurable goal of "develop functional academics" on the IEP for Alex, a highly intelligent, 16-year-old nonreader who has severe dyslexia and a high level of anger and confusion about why he can't read, write, or spell.

Given 10 words, Alex shall group letters and pronounce letter sounds in words with 80% accuracy. How do we determine whether Alex has met this progress marker? Clearly, we give 10 words to Alex (perhaps a list) and ask him to do something, but what? Is it possibly as simple as "Alex, would you read these aloud"? That's a good guess, but does the list look like "sit, bun, log, cat," or does it look like "exegesis, ophthalmology, entrepreneur"? What is 80% accuracy in reading the list? If the word "palace" were read as "place" or "tentative" as "tantative" or "when" as "where," what percentage of accuracy do we assign to each effort? Or did the writer really mean that Alex should read 80% of the words accurately? How long a time frame is Alex to be allowed to read the words? Perhaps the objective writer meant something like this: "Given 10 unfamiliar, regular CVC words, Alex will decode 9 of 10 correctly in 20 seconds."

Alex will research the history and culture of the given country with 80% accuracy. Remembering that Alex reads at a mid-first-grade level and is presently working on letter sounds and decoding, what are we to make of this objective? If Alex comes to school tomorrow morning and says, "I researched the history and culture of China without any mistakes last night," are we to check off the objective as complete? Is that what the writer intended? What about something like this: "Given a 1-hour PBS video on the history and culture of China and a tape recorder, after viewing the tape, Alex will dictate and record 10 things he learned about China, with no more than one factual error."

Source: Adapted from Bateman, B. D., & Herr, C. M. (2006). *Writing measurable IEP goals and objectives* (pp. 153–155). Verona, WI: Attainment Company, Inc. Used by permission.

it requires a great deal of work, but also because the essence of the plan itself seems to have been lost in the mountains of paperwork" (p. 228). More than 20 years later, Bateman and Linden (2006) expressed a similar opinion:

> Sadly, many IEPs are horrendously burdensome to teachers and nearly useless to parents and children. Far from being a creative, flexible, data-based, and individualized application of the best of educational interventions to a child with unique needs, the typical IEP is "empty," devoid of specific services to be provided, and its goals are often not measurable. (p. 87)

Studies of actual IEPs seem to support such harsh descriptions. For example, Grigal and colleagues (1997) examined IEPs for high school students and found that transition-related goals included vague outcomes (e.g., "will think about best place to live," "will explore jobs"), no evaluation procedures, and very few adaptations in activities or materials. Properly including all of the mandated components in an IEP is no guarantee that the document will guide the student's learning and teachers' teaching in the classroom, as intended by IDEA. Although most educators support the idealized concept of the IEP, inspection of IEPs often reveals inconsistencies between what is written on the document and the instruction that students experience in the classroom (S. W. Smith & Brownell, 1995).

Although IDEA requires parents to participate in IEP meetings and encourages student participation, research on parent and student involvement in the IEP process has produced mixed results (Test et al., 2004). In a study of 109 middle school and high school IEP meetings, Martin and colleagues (2006) concluded that students' "presence can at best be viewed as tokenism because of the very low levels of student engagement and low student [expression of] opinions of their IEP meetings" (p. 197).

On the bright side, numerous studies have shown that students with widely varying disabilities can learn to be actively involved in the IEP process, even to the point of leading the meeting (e.g., Arndt, Konrad, & Test, 2006; Kelley, Bartholomew, & Test, 2011; Martin, Van Dycke, et al., 2006). Some research suggests a positive correlation between students' participation in the IEP process and academic achievement (Barnard-Brak & Lechtenberger, 2010).

General education teachers also benefit from instruction in the IEP process. In a study of 393 middle school and high school IEP meetings, general education teachers rated themselves lower than all other IEP meeting participants, including students, on the extent to which they helped make decisions and knew what to do next (Martin, Huber Marshall, & Sale, 2004). General education teachers ranked second lowest (only to students) in knowing the reason for the meetings, talking at the meetings, feeling comfortable saying what they thought, understanding what was said, and feeling good about the meeting.

Regardless of the level of parent and student participation, the appropriateness and measurability of the goals, and the IEP team's satisfaction with the document, without instruction of the highest quality, many children with disabilities will make little progress. This reality led to the requirement in IDEA 2004 that teachers must use evidence-based practices (EBPs) to ensure their students receive the highest quality instruction. See *Current Issues and Future Trends*, "Evidence-Based Practice: Easier Said Than Done."

LEAST RESTRICTIVE ENVIRONMENT

IDEA requires that every student with disabilities be educated in the **least restrictive environment (LRE)**. Specifically, the law stipulates that

> to the maximum extent appropriate, children with disabilities, including children in public or private institutions or other care facilities, are educated with children who are not disabled, and special classes, separate schooling, or other removal of children with disabilities from the regular educational environment occurs only when the nature or severity of the disability of a child is such that

Excellent resources, curricula, and strategies for involving students and their families in their IEPs are available from Giangreco, Cloninger, and Iverson (2011); Konrad (2008); Thoma and Wehman (2010); A. Turnbull and colleagues (2010); and Van Dycke, Martin, and Lovett (2006).

Resources and tools to help IEP teams develop IEPs that comply with the law and serve as meaningful guides for the specially designed instruction are Bateman and Herr (2006); Capizzi (2008); Jung (2007); Lytle and Bordin (2001); and Wright et al., (2010).

The least restrictive environment is a relative concept; the LRE for one child may be inappropriate for another.

education in regular classes with the use of supplementary aids and services cannot be achieved satisfactorily. (PL 108-446, Sec. 612 [a][5][A])

The LRE is the setting that is most similar to a general education classroom and also meets the child's special educational needs. *Least restrictive environment* is a relative and wholly individualized concept; it is not to be determined by disability category. The LRE for one 10-year-old student who is blind might be inappropriate for another 10-year-old with the same type and degree of visual impairment. And the LRE for both students may change over time. Since the passage of IDEA, there have been many differences of opinion over which type of setting is least restrictive and most appropriate for students with disabilities. Some educators and parents consider any decision to place a student with disabilities outside the general education classroom to be overly restrictive; most, however, recognize that full-time placement in a general education classroom is restrictive and inappropriate if the child's educational needs cannot be adequately met in that environment.

Least restrictive environment

Initial Level Content Standards for Special Education Teachers: Principles of normalization and concept of least restrictive environment (IGC1K8).

Continuum of Alternative Placements

IDEA requires schools to provide a **continuum of alternative placements**—that is, a range of placement and service options—to meet the individual needs of all students with disabilities.

Continuum of alternative placements.
(a) Each public agency must ensure that a continuum of alternative placements is available to meet the needs of children with disabilities for special education and related services. (b) The continuum required in paragraph (a) of this section must—(1) Include the alternative placements listed in the definition of special education under §300.38 (instruction in regular classes, special classes, special schools, home instruction, and instruction in hospitals and institutions); and (2) Make provision for supplementary services (such as resource room or itinerant instruction) to be provided in conjunction with regular class placement. (Authority: 20 USC 1412 §300.115 [a] [5])

The continuum can be depicted symbolically as a pyramid, with placements ranging from the general education classroom at the bottom to special schools, residential

Continuum of placement alternatives and services

Initial Level Content Standards for Special Education Teachers: Continuum of placement and services available for individuals with disabilities (IGC1K5).

FUTURE TRENDS

▶ Evidence-Based Practice: Easier Said Than Done

Should science guide practice in special education? Most individuals would say "Yes." However, the "devil is in the details." (Odom et al., 2005, p. 137)

WHEN CONGRESS REAUTHORIZED IDEA IN 2004, one of the most significant changes was the stipulation that the special education and related services prescribed in a child's IEP be "based on peer-reviewed research to the extent practical." Thus, Congress made a legal requirement of something many special educators had always strived to do: use the results of scientific research to ensure their students receive the highest-quality instruction. It is unfortunate that a federal law is required to motivate educators to use scientifically sound teaching practices with children whose learning is most dependent upon effective instruction. The reality, however, is that far too few teachers use evidence-based practices in their classrooms (Burns & Ysseldyke, 2009), many students with disabilities have been the recipients of teaching methods that are misguided at best, and some students have been subjected to practices that research has shown repeatedly to be not only benignly ineffective but also harmful (Heward, 2003; Jacobson, Foxx, & Mulick, 2005).

While the mandate to use evidence-based practices (EBPs) may appear straightforward, it is not. Just some of the questions that the field must address are the following: What criteria should educators use to define EBPs? Who will apply those criteria to determine which practices teachers should use and which ones they should avoid? What are the most effective and efficient ways to disseminate information about EBPs to IEP teams and teachers? How can a teacher determine the validity and trustworthiness of an EBP for her students?

DEFINING EVIDENCE-BASED PRACTICES

No universal standards exist for defining an EBP. The field of special education, and education in general, is working to develop criteria for determining whether a practice should be considered evidence based. Two fundamental issues are determining criteria for the type and amount of research evidence required for a practice to be considered an EBP (Kretlow & Blatz, 2011). The Department of Education's Institute for Education Sciences and What Works Clearinghouse have identified the **randomized control trial (RCT)** (also called a *randomized experimental group design)* as the gold standard for research methodology to show evidence of an instructional technique's effectiveness. While there is no doubt that well-conducted RCTs provide strong experimental tests of an intervention's effects, much of special education's research base has been produced with other research methodologies, most notably nonrandomized group designs, single-subject research, and correlational studies (Odom et al., 2005). More recently, information obtained from qualitative studies has provided conceptual frameworks and support for emerging practices that can be analyzed and evaluated further with experimental studies. Examples of quality indicators for special education research using each of these four methodologies can be found in Gersten et al. (2005); Horner et al. (2005); Thompson et al. (2005); and Brantlinger, Jimenez, Klingner, Pugach, and Richardson (2005), respectively. Five teams of authors applied these quality indicators to published research in the Spring 2009 issue of the journal *Exceptional Children.*

Another issue to be resolved is who will determine what practices are designated as evidence based. Traditionally, peer-reviewed literature reviews and meta-analyses (a sophisticated statistical comparison and assessment of the results produced by a group of studies that evaluated the same practice) by scholars who have examined a given topic provide one source of expert opinion (e.g., Bellini & Akullian, 2007; Lewis, Hudson, Richter, & Johnson, 2004). It is not uncommon, however, that after reviewing the existing research for a given practice, one author concludes the evidence base to be very strong while another's assessment of the same set of studies yields a much lower rating (e.g., Kavale & Forness, 1996; McIntosh, Vaughn, & Zaragoza, 1991).

Professional organizations and nonprofit groups are also contributing to the discussion of EBPs. For example, the Council for Exceptional Children (CEC) (2006a) proposed a process and criteria by which practices would be classified at three levels:

- *Research-based practice:* recommended for special educators' repertoire
- *Promising practice:* may be included in special educators' repertoire with clear caveats for following the developing literature
- *Emerging practice:* informative, but research base does not yet lead to recommended use

More recently CEC (2008) classified practice evidence bases as: *positive evidence base*, *insufficient evidence base* (three levels: potentially positive, mixed effects, and no discernable effects), and *negative evidence base*.

CEC's Division for Research and Division for Learning Disabilities co-produces a periodic series of Practice Alerts (available at www.TeachingLD.org) to inform teachers about practices at two levels of research support: "Go For It" for practices with significant amounts of consistent evidence and "Use Caution" for practices with limited or mixed research evidence (e.g., Reading Recovery [Denton & Mathes, 2002]). Examples of practices that have received the "Go For It" designation are using graphic organizers (Ellis & Howard, 2007), fluency instruction (Kubina & Hughes, 2007), classwide peer tutoring (Maheady, Mallette, & Harper, 2003), and phonics instruction (Pullen & Lloyd, 2007).

Descriptions of instructional programs and practices that have met the criteria considered by various government and nonprofit professional organizations sufficient to be identified as evidence based can be found at these websites:

- What Works Clearinghouse, www.whatworks.ed.gov/
- Doing What Works, http://dww.ed.gov/site/
- National Center for the Dissemination of Disability Research, http://www.ncddr.org/
- The Wing Institute, http://winginstitute.org/
- The IRIS Center, http://iris.peabody.vanderbilt.edu/index.html
- The Campbell Collaboration, http://www.campbellcollaboration.org/
- Center on Positive Behavioral Interventions and Supports, http://www.pbis.org/
- NICHCY Research to Practice Database, http://research.nichcy.org/search.asp
- National Secondary Transition Technical Assistance Center, http://www.nsttac.org/
- The National Professional Development Center on Autism Spectrum Disorders, http://autismpdc.fpg.unc.edu/
- National Autism Center's National Standards Project, www.nationalautismcenter.org/nsp/

EVIDENCE-BASED USE OF EVIDENCE-BASED PRACTICES

No matter how much scientific evidence supports a given a curriculum program or instructional technique, a teacher should never assume effectiveness (Dietrich, Keyworth, & States, 2008). A list of EBPs will never replace the need for professional judgment and wisdom (Cook, Tankersley, & Landrum,

2009). To maximize outcomes for students, teachers should do the following when implementing any EBP:

- *Be consistent.* Treatment fidelity is paramount. The full and intended effects of any practice will not be realized unless it is implemented as designed. Researchers use the term "with complete fidelity" when evaluating a practice.
- *Beware of eclecticism.* It is tempting to think that a combination of practices will be more effective than any single practice. Eclecticism, however, is often a recipe for failure because (a) the most important and effective parts of each model might be rejected in favor of weaker, ineffective components; (b) some components of a given practice may not be effective when implemented without other elements of the practice; (c) elements from different practices may be incompatible with one another; (d) an eclectic mix might prevent any of the included models from being implemented with sufficient duration and intensity to obtain significant effects; and (e) teachers who use elements of multiple practices may not learn to implement any of the methods with the precision necessary for optimal results (Heward, 2003).
- *Test it yourself.* The most important and generally useful EBP of all may be direct and frequent measurement of student progress. Teachers can go a step further and conduct a mini-experimental analysis (Maheady & Jabot, 2011).
- *If you must modify the program, change only one variable at a time.* Modification or variation may be necessary to obtain desired levels of learning for a given student. Begin by implementing the published procedure as consistently and rigorously as possible. Then, if data show insufficient progress, change one, but only one, aspect of the program while continuing to measure student performance.

WHAT DO YOU THINK?

1. Why is use of EBPs a current issue in special education?
2. Identify and rank-order five criteria you believe most important in determining whether an instructional program or teaching method should be designated an EBP.
3. Like television viewers who are barraged with a steady stream of commercials touting amazing results from one wonder drug after another, teachers are told by every publisher and in-service workshop presenter that the programs and methods they are pitching are "scientifically proven" to be effective. How can educators protect themselves from being taken in by false claims?

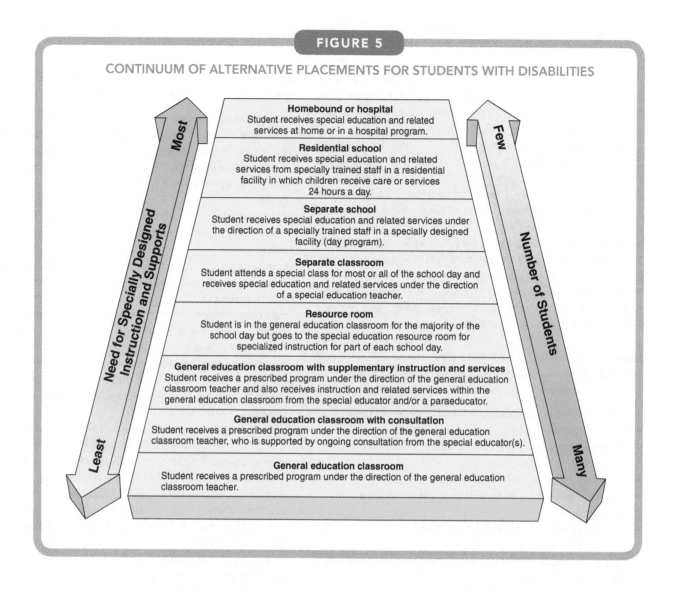

FIGURE 5

CONTINUUM OF ALTERNATIVE PLACEMENTS FOR STUDENTS WITH DISABILITIES

Homebound or hospital
Student receives special education and related services at home or in a hospital program.

Residential school
Student receives special education and related services from specially trained staff in a residential facility in which children receive care or services 24 hours a day.

Separate school
Student receives special education and related services under the direction of a specially trained staff in a specially designed facility (day program).

Separate classroom
Student attends a special class for most or all of the school day and receives special education and related services under the direction of a special education teacher.

Resource room
Student is in the general education classroom for the majority of the school day but goes to the special education resource room for specialized instruction for part of each school day.

General education classroom with supplementary instruction and services
Student receives a prescribed program under the direction of the general education classroom teacher and also receives instruction and related services within the general education classroom from the special educator and/or a paraeducator.

General education classroom with consultation
Student receives a prescribed program under the direction of the general education classroom teacher, who is supported by ongoing consultation from the special educator(s).

General education classroom
Student receives a prescribed program under the direction of the general education classroom teacher.

Most — Least — Need for Specially Designed Instruction and Supports

Few — Many — Number of Students

facilities, and homebound or hospital placements at the top (see Figure 5). The fact that the pyramid is widest at the bottom indicates that most children with disabilities are served in *general education classrooms* and that the number of children who require more intensive instruction and highly specialized services decreases as we move up the continuum.

Five of the eight placement options depicted in Figure 5 are available in regular public school buildings. Children at the first three levels on the continuum have full-time placements in general education classrooms and receive various degrees and types of support by special teachers who consult or co-teach with the general education teachers. In a *resource room*, a special educator provides instruction to students with disabilities for part of the school day. Children who require full-time placement in a *separate classroom* (also called a *self-contained classroom*) are with other children with disabilities for most of the school day and participate with children without disabilities only at certain times, such as during lunch, recess, or perhaps art and music. Although the separate classroom provides significantly fewer opportunities for interaction with children without disabilities than does the general education classroom, it provides more integration than does placement in *separate schools* or *residential schools,* which are attended only by children with disabilities. A child in a *homebound* or *hospital* setting receives special education and related services on an individual basis and may have few opportunities to interact with other children.

Determining LRE

The IEP team determines the proper placement for a child after determining the child's needs that result from the disability and the special education and related services necessary to meet those needs. The legally mandated and educationally sound sequence is as follows: (a) the school determines whether the child has a disability and is therefore eligible for special education, (b) the IEP team determines the child's individual needs and develops an IEP that specifies the special education and related services needed to meet those needs, and (c) the child is placed in the LRE in which educators can provide an appropriate program and the child can make satisfactory educational progress.

The general education classroom is the starting point for the IEP team's discussion of placement. Removal of a child with disabilities from the general education classroom is to occur only if the IEP team determines that the specially designed instruction and related services necessary for the student to achieve her IEP goals cannot be provided in that setting. Mercer, Mercer, and Pullen (2011) suggest that IEP teams think of LRE as the *most enabling environment* for the child with disabilities.

Placement of a student with disabilities should not be viewed as all-or-nothing at any one level on the continuum. The IEP team should consider the extent to which the student can effectively be included into each of three dimensions of school life: the general academic curriculum, extracurricular activities (e.g., clubs), and other school activities (e.g., recess, mealtimes). IDEA allows IEP teams to determine that total integration is appropriate in one dimension and partial integration best meets the student's needs in another dimension (H. R. Turnbull, Huerta, & Stowe, 2009).

A student's placement must not be regarded as permanent. The continuum concept is intended to be flexible, with students moving from one placement to another as dictated by their individual educational needs. The IEP team should periodically review the specific goals and objectives for each child—they are required to do so at least annually—and make new placement decisions if warranted. The child's parents must be informed whenever the school considers any change in placement so that the parents can either consent or object to the change and present additional information if they wish.

INCLUSIVE EDUCATION

Although often confused, the terms *inclusion* and *least restrictive environment* are not synonymous. **Inclusion** means educating students with disabilities in general education classrooms; the LRE principle requires that students with disabilities be educated in settings as close to the regular class as possible in which an appropriate program can be provided and the child can make satisfactory educational progress. For many students with disabilities, an inclusive classroom and the LRE are one and the same; but that is not always so.

Much discussion and controversy and many misconceptions have arisen regarding the inclusion of students with disabilities in general education classrooms. Although many parents of children with disabilities strongly support inclusion, others have resisted it just as strongly, thinking that the general education classroom does not offer the intense, individualized education their children need (Garrick Duhaney & Salend, 2000). For example, studies of parents of children with severe disabilities have found some parents in favor of and some against inclusion (Gallagher et al., 2000; Palmer, Fuller, Arora, & Nelson, 2001). Havey (1999) reported that in 67% of the cases in which parents contested the schools' placement decision, the parents sought a more restrictive educational setting (e.g., parents wanted the child to attend a resource room for part of each day instead of full-time placement in a general education class).

As we have seen, IDEA calls for the education of each child with a disability in the LRE, removed no farther than necessary from the general education public school program. The law does not require placement of all children with disabilities in general education classes or suggest that general education teachers should educate students with disabilities without the necessary support services, including help from special educators and other specialists. Although not all children with disabilities attend general education classes, general education classroom teachers are expected to teach a much wider range of learning, behavioral, sensory, and physical differences among their students than ever before. Thus, provision of in-service training for general

Determining LRE

 Council for Exceptional Children

Initial Level Content Standards for Special Education Teachers: Issues, assurances, and due process rights related to assessment, eligibility, and placement within a continuum of services (ICC1K6) (also ICC5S3, ICC5S4, ICC5S5, IGC5S3).

educators is an important (and sometimes overlooked) requirement of IDEA. General education teachers are understandably wary of having students with disabilities placed in their classes if the school provides little or no training or support (DeSimone & Parmar, 2006). The role of general education classroom teachers is already a highly demanding one; they do not want their classes to become any larger, especially if they perceive children with special needs as unmanageable (Cook, Cameron, & Tankersly, 2007). General education teachers are entitled to be involved in decisions about children who are placed in their classes and to be offered continuous consultation and other support services from administrators and their special education colleagues (Kennedy & Fisher, 2001; Kochhar-Bryant, 2008).

Although some educators have expressed concern that the presence of students with disabilities impairs the academic achievement of students without disabilities, no evidence supports this. In fact, Cole, Waldron, and Majd (2004) reported that 334 students without disabilities in inclusive classrooms actually made greater gains in reading and math than did a comparison group of 272 students without disabilities who were educated in "traditional" classrooms. When considering the results of studies such as these, it is important to consider that the most critical factor affecting student achievement is most likely to be quality of instruction and not the presence or absence of students with disabilities.

Placing a child with disabilities in a resource room or separate class is no guarantee that child will receive the specialized instruction he needs (e.g., Maggin, Wehby, Moore Partin, Robertson, & Oliver, 2011; McLeskey & Waldron, 2011). We also know that simply including a child with disabilities in a general education classroom does not mean that she will learn and behave appropriately or be socially accepted by the teacher or by children without disabilities (Cook, 2004; Siperstein, Parker, Norins Bardon, & Widaman, 2007). It is important for special educators to teach appropriate social skills and behavior to the child with disabilities and to educate children without disabilities about their classmates with special needs. Examples of effective inclusion programs can be found at age levels ranging from preschool (Sandall, Schwartz, & Joseph, 2000) to high school (Cobb Morocco, Clay, Parker, & Zigmond, 2006), and they include children with high-incidence disabilities (Hock, Schumaker, & Deshler, 1999) and severe disabilities (Ryndak & Fisher, 2007).

Promoting Inclusion with Cooperative Learning

As Sheena Washington indicated at the beginning of this chapter, cooperative learning activities provide a strategic approach for differentiating instruction and integrating students with disabilities into both the academic curriculum and the social fabric of the classroom. Cooperative learning can take many forms, but in most models all students in the class are assigned to small heterogeneous groups and help one another achieve a shared academic goal (Johnson & Johnson, 2009). According to Slavin (1995), cooperative learning arrangements should include the following:

1. *Group goals*. All members of the group work together to earn grades, rewards, or other recognition of success for the group.
2. *Individual accountability*. Each student within the group must demonstrate his or her learning and contribute in a specific way for the group to obtain success. However, the manner in which group members contribute may differ to meet individualized needs and learning objectives.

Well-designed cooperative learning activities keep students actively engaged and motivated to succeed. In addition to improved academic outcomes, cooperative learning can also promote positive social relationships, friendships, and mutual supports among students with and without disabilities in the classroom, which are vital to successful inclusion (Dion, Fuchs, & Fuchs, 2007; Maheady et al., 2006; Plumer & Stoner, 2005).

Classwide peer tutoring is a form of cooperative learning with more than three decades of research demonstrating its effectiveness as an instructional approach for

Facilitating Inclusion

Council for Exceptional Children

Initial Level Content Standards for Special Education Teachers: Use strategies to facilitate integration into various settings (ICC4S1) (also ICC5K1, ICC5S1, ICC5S2, ICC5S3, ICC5S4, ICC5S5, ICC5S9, and IGC5S3).

Numerous strategies for including students with disabilities in the general education program can be found in Friend and Bursuck (2012); Giangreco and Doyle (2007); Lewis and Doorlag (2011); Mastropieri and Scruggs (2011); McLeskey, Rosenberg, and Westling, (2010); and Salend (2011).

teaching reading, math, social studies, and a wide range of specialized subject areas to (and by) students with and without disabilities in inclusive classrooms (Gardner, Nobel, Hessler, Yawn, & Heron, 2007; Mackiewicz, Wood, Cooke, & Mazzotti, 2011; Maheady & Gard, 2010). See *Teaching & Learning*, "Classwide Peer Tutoring."

Arguments For and Against Full Inclusion

Some special educators believe that the continuum of alternative placements should be dismantled and all students with disabilities placed in general education classes. For example, in a paper widely cited by advocates of full inclusion, S. J. Taylor (2005) contends that the LRE model

- *Confuses segregation and integration with intensity of services.* The LRE principle assumes that the intensive services needed by people with severe disabilities cannot be provided in the most integrated settings. Segregation and integration and intensity of services are separate dimensions.
- *Requires a readiness model.* LRE implies that people with disabilities must earn the right to move to the least restrictive environment.
- *Sanctions infringements on students' rights.* LRE asks not whether people with disabilities should be restricted but to what extent.
- *Requires people to move as they develop and change.* LRE expects people with disabilities to move through a series of progressively less restrictive environments. Even if people move smoothly through a continuum, their lives would be a series of stops between transitional placements.
- *Directs attention to physical settings rather than to the services and supports people need.* LRE emphasizes facilities and environments designed specifically for people with disabilities. The field created "facilities," first large ones and now smaller ones, and "programs," rather than providing the services and supports to enable people with disabilities to participate in the same settings as other people. (adapted from Taylor, 2005)

Some authors view full inclusion as a matter of social justice (e.g., Artiles, Harris-Murri, & Rostenberg, 2006; Sapon-Shevin, 2007; Stainback, Stainback, & Ayres, 1996). No clear consensus exists in the field about the meaning of inclusion. To some, *inclusion* means full-time placement of all students with disabilities in general education classrooms; to others, the term refers to any degree of integration into the mainstream. Stainback and Stainback (1996), strong advocates and leaders of the inclusion movement, define an inclusive school as "a place where everyone belongs, is accepted, supports, and is supported by his or her peers and other members of the school community in the course of having his or her educational needs met" (p. 3). Giangreco (2011) states that inclusive education exists only when each of the six characteristics shown in Figure 6 "occurs on an ongoing, daily basis" (p. 4).

Virtually all special educators support the responsible inclusion of students with disabilities in general education classrooms and the development and evaluation of new models for working more cooperatively with general educators to serve all students (e.g., D. Fuchs, Fuchs, & Stecker, 2010; Kochhar-Bryant, 2008; McLeskey & Waldron, 2011; Smith & Hilton, 1997). Throughout this text, you will find descriptions of many research-based model programs and strategies for successfully and meaningfully including students with disabilities as full members of the academic and social life of general education classrooms.

Shared activities with individualized outcomes and a sense of belonging and group membership for all students are two defining features of inclusive education.

Scott Cunningham/Merrill

Classwide Peer Tutoring
Collaborative Learning for All Students in Inclusive Classrooms

The idea of students teaching one another is not new (Lancaster, 1806). In traditional approaches to peer tutoring, the teacher identifies a high-achieving student to help a classmate who has not mastered a particular skill. In contrast, contemporary classwide peer tutoring (CWPT) models include low achievers and students with disabilities as full participants in an ongoing, whole-class activity in which all students help one another learn new curriculum content.

FOUR EVIDENCE-BASED MODELS

Four classwide peer tutoring models have emerged from more than three decades years of solid empirical research (Alber Morgan, 2006).

Juniper Gardens Children's Project CWPT. The Juniper Gardens Children's Project CWPT model was the brainchild of Greenwood, Delquadri, and Carta (1997). The whole class is divided into two weekly competing teams that are further broken into tutoring dyads and triads. Tutors present individual items, evaluate tutees' performance, and provide feedback and points. Daily and weekly public posting of team points serves as motivation.

A 12-year longitudinal study that compared groups of at-risk and nonrisk students who had or had not received CWPT instruction found that CWPT increased students' active engagement during instruction in grades 1 to 3; improved pupil achievement in grades 2, 3, 4, and 6; reduced the need for special education services by 7th grade; and decreased the number of students who dropped out of school by the end of 11th grade (Greenwood, Maheady, & Delquadri, 2002).

Peer-Assisted Learning Strategies. The Peer-Assisted Learning Strategies (PALS) program was developed by researchers at Vanderbilt University working collaboratively with local school districts (Morgan, Young, & Fuchs, 2006). The original PALS program was designed for use in reading and math by students in grades 2–6 (D. Fuchs, Fuchs, Mathes, & Simmons, 1996). K-PALS for kindergarten, First Grade PALS for beginning reading instruction, and High School PALS for content-area instruction have been added (D. Fuchs et al., 2001). PALS tutors and tutees interact in a set of structured activities for three 35-minute sessions per week. Examples of reading activities include Partner Reading with Retell, Paragraph Shrinking, and Prediction Relay. Teachers use brief scripted lessons to train all students to implement the activities independently. Over 15 years of research has demonstrated the effectiveness of this CWPT program in improving the reading performance of students at all performance levels, including students with disabilities and English language learners, from kindergarten through high school (McMaster, Fuchs, & Fuchs, 2006; McMaster, Kung, Han, & Cao, 2008).

SUNY Fredonia Classwide Student Tutoring Teams. The SUNY Fredonia Classwide Student Tutoring Teams (CSTT) model combines elements of Slavin's (1986) Student Team Learning approach with components from the Juniper Gardens CWPT model. Pupils work in four-member, heterogeneous learning teams and take turns reading and responding to items on teacher-developed study guides and/or concept cards. Tutor roles rotate clockwise on each item, and the process continues until a predetermined time limit (e.g., 20 to 30 minutes) has elapsed (Maheady, Mallette, & Harper, 2006). One study compared CSTT instruction to conventional teacher-led instruction on the math performance of 91 low-achieving ninth- and tenth-grade pupils enrolled in a program for potential high school dropouts (Maheady, Sacca, & Harper, 1987). During CSTT instruction, students' weekly math quiz scores increased by an average of 20 percentage points.

The Ohio State University Model. The Ohio State University CWPT model evolved from research in the late 1970s and early 1980s aimed at finding a low-cost approach for individualizing instruction of beginning reading and math skills for diverse groups of learners in the primary grades (Heron, Heward, Cooke, & Hill, 1983; Heward, Heron, & Cooke, 1982; Parson & Heward, 1979). The OSU model has been replicated and extended by hundreds of teachers in elementary, middle, and secondary classrooms across a wide range of curriculum areas such as spelling, science facts and vocabulary, algebra, geometry, reading fluency, foreign language vocabulary, and social studies (e.g., Gardner et al., 2001; Miller, Barbetta, & Heron, 1994; Wright, Cavanaugh, Sainato, & Heward, 1995). Daily sessions last about 20 minutes, with each student serving as both tutor and tutee during the session. When in the role of tutee, the child responds to questions presented by his or her partner (tutor) using a set of individualized task cards of unknown facts, problems, or items determined by a teacher-given pretest. The basic elements of the OSU model follow.

Tutoring Folders and Task Cards. Each student in the class has a tutoring folder (see Figure A) containing a set of task cards on specific curriculum content. Each card identifies one word, problem, concept, or fact to be taught

PEER TUTORING FOLDER

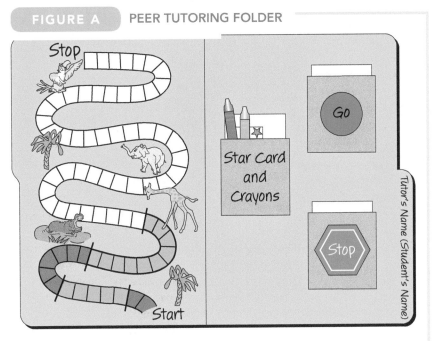

Source: Adapted from "Total Tutoring for Special and General Educators [Instructor's Manual]" by T. E. Heron & W. L. Heward, 2000. Columbus, OH: The Ohio State University Special Education Program. Used by permission.

to the child's tutoring partner. The task cards are in a GO pocket on one side of the folder. Also in the folder are a STOP pocket to collect learned cards, a track chart to record the tutee's progress, and markers to use for recording.

Practice. One child begins in the role of tutor, presenting the task cards as many times as possible during a 5-minute practice period and shuffling the set of cards after each round. The teacher trains tutors to praise their partners' correct responses and to say, "Try again," when the tutee makes an error. If the tutee still does not respond correctly, the tutor says, for example, "This word is *tree;* say *tree.*" A timer signals the end of the first practice period, and the partners switch roles. While students are tutoring, the teacher walks around the room, prompting and rewarding good tutoring behaviors, answering questions, and generally supervising the activity.

Testing. After the second practice period, the students reverse roles again; and the first tutor tests her partner by presenting each task card once with no prompts or cues. The teacher gives tutors about 5 minutes each to test and record their tutees' progress.

- The tutor places cards that a tutee reads or answers correctly in one pile and missed cards in another.
- The students then switch roles again, and the first tutor is now tested on the words she practiced.
- The tutors then mark the back of each card to identify if it was "correct" or "incorrect" during the test. Each tutor records his tutee's daily progress on the chart.
- When a child correctly responds to a task card on the test for three consecutive sessions, that item is

considered learned, and the tutor moves it to the folder's STOP pocket.
- When the students have learned all 10 cards, the teacher places a new set of words in the GO pocket.
- Each session ends with the partners praising and complimenting each other for their good work.

CHARACTERISTICS COMMON TO ALL FOUR MODELS

- **Clearly defined learning tasks/responses.** CWPT programs are based on clearly defined learning tasks and explicitly defined peer tutoring roles and teaching responsibilities. Tutoring procedures are often scripted, and each tutor is expected to use standard procedures with little variation.
- **Individualized instruction.** Frequent pre- and post-tests are used to determine individualized learning tasks for each student. Additionally, because CWPT uses one-to-one instruction, each learner's performance can be observed, checked, and redirected in ways more frequent and continuous than in teacher-led group instruction.
- **High rates of active student responding (ASR).** Well-designed CWPT programs provide each student with many opportunities to respond. Depending on the curriculum content, a student may make 50 or more responses during a 10-minute peer tutoring session. Total ASR increases further in reciprocal CWPT programs because each student responds to each item in the role of tutee (initial responses to tutor's prompts, repeating missed items) and tutor

(prompting responses, discriminating between correct and incorrect responses, and providing feedback).

- **Immediate feedback and praise for correct responses.** Peer tutors provide feedback and praise to their tutees, and the teacher provides feedback to the tutors as a means of promoting high-quality peer teaching and learning during CWPT sessions.
- **Systematic error correction.** Tutors immediately and systematically correct mistakes by their tutees. Materials that reveal the correct response to the tutor enable students who are themselves learning the material to detect and correct errors.
- **Continuous monitoring of student progress.** All evidence-based CWPT models incorporate direct and frequent measurement of students' progress. These data are obtained in a variety of ways, such as end-of-session assessments by tutors, regularly scheduled, teacher-administered "check-outs" of students' performances, weekly pre- and posttests, and curriculum-based measures. In some models, items missed on follow-up assessments are returned to the student's folder for additional practice and relearning.
- **Motivation.** Students have fun doing CWPT. Participation and learning are motivated by game-like formats, individual and team goals, charting their progress, and point/reward systems.

HOW TO GET STARTED

1. **Identify curriculum area and measurable learning outcome.** What should students know or be able to do as a result of CWPT?

2. **Design a practice activity that will provide tutors and tutees with direct and repeated practice with this knowledge and/or skill.**

3. **Determine the sequence of steps that will make up each CWPT session.** For example, students obtaining materials and setting up, tutoring practice trials, testing, recording performance, and clean-up/putting materials away. For each component, specify (a) materials needed, (b) what the tutors and tutees will do, (c) what the teacher (you) will do, and (d) how many minutes it should take.

4. **Create tutoring folders, task cards, and other necessary materials.** Consider having students make their CWPT materials from models you provide.

5. **Build in a motivation component.** Specify how you will reinforce desired behavior by tutors (e.g., providing tutees with frequent response opportunities) and tutees (e.g., acquiring targeted knowledge and skills). Consider incentive systems such as "Mystery Motivators."

6. **Train students to carry out the CWPT procedures.** Teach peer tutoring skills as you would any other skill: be explicit, provide models, have students discriminate correct and incorrect procedures, provide guided practice, give feedback, reinforce accurate responses, and correct errors.

7. **Implement and evaluate.** Collect data to answer three questions: Are students implementing the tutoring procedures correctly? Are students acquiring and maintaining targeted knowledge and skills? Do students enjoy the CWPT program? CWPT should be fun for students and their teacher.

MyEducationLab™

To observe teachers who have adapted the OSU CWPT model to fit the needs of their students, go to the book resources for this text on MyEducationLab.

For thoughtful discussions of the full range of assumptions, perspectives, practices, potential benefits, and realities of inclusion, see D. Fuchs, et al., (2010); Giangreco (2011); Kauffman and Hallahan (2005); Kavale and Forness (2000); McLeskey and Waldron (2011); Mitchell (2004a, 2004b); Simpson (2004b); Zigmond (2003); and Zigmond et al. (2009).

Very few special educators support eliminating the continuum of alternative placements in favor of a universal policy of full inclusion. The Council for Exceptional Children (CEC), the major professional organization in special education, supports inclusion as a "meaningful goal" to be pursued by schools but believes that the continuum of services and program options must be maintained and that IEP planning teams must make placement decisions based on the student's individual educational needs (see Figure 7). The discussion of inclusion continues throughout the text.

Zigmond (2003) reminds us that asking what is the "best place" to educate students with disabilities misses the point of what special education is all about.

The bedrock of special education is instruction focused on individual needs. The very concept of "one best place" contradicts this commitment to individualization.

I can say with some certainty that place is not what makes special education "special" or effective. Effective teaching strategies and an individualized approach are the more critical ingredients in special education, and neither of these is associated solely with one particular environment. (pp. 196, 198)

Excerpt from Zigmond: From "Where should students with disabilities receive special education services? Is one place better than another?" By N. Zigmond, 2003. *Journal of Special Education*, 37, 193-199. Copyright 2003 by the Hammill Institute on Disability. Reprinted by permission.

FIGURE 6 ELEMENTS OF INCLUSIVE EDUCATION

1. All students are welcomed in general education. The first placement options considered are the general education classes in the school that the students would attend if they did not have a disability.

2. Disability is recognized as a form of human diversity. Hence, students with disabilities are accepted as individuals and are not denied access because of their disabilities.

3. Appropriate supports, regardless of disability type or severity, are available. Supports are provided in typical environments instead of sending students to specialized settings to receive supports.

4. The composition of classrooms reflects the naturally occurring proportion of students with and without disabilities. The percentage of students without disabilities is substantially higher than the percentage of students with disabilities.

5. Students, irrespective of their developmental or performance levels, are educated with peers in the same age groupings available to those without disability labels instead of with younger students.

6. Students with and without disabilities participate in shared educational experiences while pursuing individually appropriate learning outcomes with necessary supports. Educational experiences are designed to enhance valued life outcomes that seek an individualized balance between both the academic-functional and the social-personal aspects of schooling.

Source: From Giangreco, M. F. (2011). Educating students with severe disabilities: Foundational concepts and practices. In M. E. Snell & F. Brown (Eds.), *Instruction of students with severe disabilities* (7th ed., p. 4). Upper Saddle River, NJ: Pearson. Used by permission.

FIGURE 7 CEC'S POLICY ON INCLUSION

The Council for Exceptional Children believes all children, youth, and young adults with disabilities are entitled to a free and appropriate education and/or services that lead to an adult life characterized by satisfying relations with others, independent living, productive engagement in the community, and participation in society at large. To achieve such outcomes, there must exist for all children, youth, and young adults a rich variety of early intervention, educational, and vocational program options and experiences. Access to these programs and experiences should be based on individual educational need and desired outcomes. Furthermore, students and their families or guardians, as members of the planning team, may recommend the placement, curriculum option, and the exit document to be pursued.

CEC believes that a continuum of services must be available for all children, youth, and young adults. CEC also believes that the concept of inclusion is a meaningful goal to be pursued in our schools and communities. In addition, CEC believes children, youth, and young adults with disabilities should be served whenever possible in general education classrooms in inclusive neighborhood schools and community settings. Such settings should be strengthened and supported by an infusion of specially trained personnel and other appropriate supportive practices according to the individual needs of the child.

Source: Reprinted from *What every special educator must know: Ethics, standards, and guidelines* (6th ed., p. 255). Copyright 2009 by the Council for Exceptional Children. Arlington, VA. Used by permission.

WHERE DOES SPECIAL EDUCATION GO FROM HERE?

The promise of a free appropriate public education for all children with disabilities is an ambitious one. The process of bringing about this goal has been described in such lofty terms as a "new Bill of Rights" and a "Magna Carta" for children with disabilities (Goodman, 1976). Weintraub and Abeson (1974) wrote in support of IDEA before the bill's passage: "At the minimum, it will make educational opportunities a reality for all handicapped children. At the maximum, it will make our schools healthier learning environments for all our children" (p. 529). Today, most observers acknowledge that substantial progress has been made toward fulfillment of that promise.

IDEA has had far-reaching effects. In place of the once-prevalent practice of excluding children with disabilities, schools now seek the most appropriate ways of including them. As A. P. Turnbull and colleagues (2011) observe, the student is no longer required to meet the requirements of the school, but the school is required to fit the needs of the student. Today's schools provide far more than academic instruction. Schools are expected to provide wide-ranging services to children from diverse backgrounds and with different learning needs. In effect, they have become diversified agencies offering services such as medical support, physical therapy, vocational training, parent counseling, recreation, special transportation, and in-service education for staff members.

Most people—both within and outside the field of education—have welcomed the inclusion and participation of children with disabilities in their schools and communities. Despite ample evidence of progress toward providing equal educational opportunity, it is equally true that many people—again, inside and outside the field of education—have detected significant problems and concerns with the very nature of special education (e.g., D. Fuchs et al., 2010; D. Gallagher, Heshusius, Iano, & Skrtic, 2004) or the implementation of IDEA (e.g., Finn et al., 2001; McLaughlin, 2010). States and local school administrators maintain that the federal government has never allocated sufficient funds to cover its promised share of the high costs of educating students with disabilities (Council for Exceptional Children, 2011). Special education teachers express dissatisfaction about excessive paperwork, unclear guidelines, and inappropriate grouping of students with disabilities. Many are concerned that too many students from culturally diverse groups are identified for special education. General education teachers contend that they receive little or no training or support when students with disabilities are placed in their classes. There are many other problems, real and perceived, and no quick fix or easy solution can be offered.

Special education is at a crossroads. Once, access to educational opportunity was the primary issue for children with disabilities. Would they receive an education at all? Could they be served in their local community and neighborhood schools? While some access problems persist (e.g., particularly for children who live in poverty or in extremely isolated areas and for children of migrant and homeless families), the primary concern today is about the appropriateness and effectiveness of special education.

Today, all children with disabilities receive special education and related services. Some children benefit from a special education that includes curricular elements and instructional technologies that were unavailable just a few years ago. . . . While special education can rightfully be proud of its accomplishments, the educational outcomes for many students with disabilities are disappointing. As a group, students with disabilities fare poorly on virtually every measure of academic achievement and social adaptation. . . .

Regardless of where services are delivered, the most crucial variable is the quality of instruction that each student receives.

Anthony Magnacca/Merrill

We believe that these poor outcomes for students with disabilities reflect not so much the field's lack of knowledge about how to teach these students, as they are testament to education's collective failure to systematically implement available knowledge.... As a result, many children with disabilities are receiving a special education that is not nearly as effective as it could be. In essence, the potential effectiveness of the special education received by many of the more than 6 million children who participate in special education today is neutralized by the presence of weak approaches that are selected on the basis of ideology instead of research results. (Heward & Silvestri, 2005, p. 193)

Can special education fulfill the promise of a free appropriate public education for all students with disabilities? The answer depends in part on the ability of professionals to work together; assume new roles; communicate with each other; and involve parents, families, and students with disabilities themselves. But above all, special educators must realize that the most crucial variable in the effectiveness of special education is the quality of instruction that children receive. They must rediscover "special education's necessary and noble mission" of teaching the most difficult-to-teach children (D. Fuchs et al., 2010).

Special education is serious business. The learning and adjustment problems faced by students with disabilities are real; and their prevention, remediation, and compensation require intensive, systematic intervention. Regardless of who does it or where it takes place, good teaching must occur. Exceptional children deserve no less.

▼ TIPS FOR BEGINNING TEACHERS

Relationships Are Key

BY SHEENA WASHINGTON

My biggest lesson during my first year of teaching was that I could not reach students who needed help the most unless the students knew that I genuinely cared about them as people. One of the most important aspects of being a teacher is being a positive adult in a child's life, and building relationships is the key to any open, accepting, and cooperative classroom.

BUILD RELATIONSHIPS WITH YOUR STUDENTS

Create an environment of trust, and let students know who you are as a person.

- **Something about me.** A dynamic art teacher taught me this strategy for creating an environment of interpersonal trust and caring among students and teachers. Each student and the two co-teachers write the ending to a series of personal statements (e.g., "Something you would never know about me is...," "One of my biggest challenges this year will be...," "One of my happiest moments was when...", "The thing that I am so proud of is ..."), and then share their responses with the whole class.
- **Put some of yourself in lessons.** During a poetry unit, I had students reflect on a poem by my favorite singer, Jill Scott. In a language arts activity, I told students about my love for traditional Indian music and had them write an essay about the mood created by the melody of instruments and Hindu words. During a science unit on population growth, I shared pictures of my community in Niger, West Africa, during my Peace Corps service. This helps students connect the lesson to something real and see their teacher as an authentic person.

BUILD RELATIONSHIPS WITH YOUR CO-TEACHERS

Successful co-teaching means both teachers share enforcement of classroom rules, procedures, and discipline; both teachers plan differentiated lessons; both teachers instruct the class and take turns working with small groups and the whole class.

- **Communicate before the school year begins.** This is when you share your goals and expectations, strengths and weaknesses. If you are new partners, request copies of curriculum materials and lesson plans, and ask the general education teacher to point out the most challenging concepts for students to master. Make sure you understand the state standards for each content area. Suggest ways that lessons could be modified to increase student engagement and success.
- **Create and keep sacred a schedule of planning times with each co-teacher.** I meet with all four of my co-teachers and mapped out team teaching planning times with each teacher during the week.
- **Be flexible but firm.** Flexibility and compromise are key components to collaborative partnerships. Present your ideas and the rationale for them, listen to your co-teacher's ideas, and look for areas of agreement. If repeated efforts to be flexible and compromise do not result in necessary modifications to curriculum and instruction and students continue to struggle, use student progress data as a support.

FIND A MENTOR

Nothing is more gratifying in my day than having a student recognize a problem and ask for my guidance. Just as students benefit from the guidance and support of a trusted adult, beginning teachers can benefit from a mentor.

- **Look for a professional whose work and work ethic you respect and admire.** The primary prerequisite for a mentor is genuine interest in your growth and development.
- **Don't be afraid to ask.** Most people love to give advice. I know I do! But we especially like to offer advice when

we know our help is appreciated. Tell your prospective mentor that you are new to the field and are looking for some guidance as you develop.

- **Specify some personal goals and a communication plan.** Discuss your goals, the type of support that the mentor can provide, and when and how you will communicate.

▼ KEY TERMS AND CONCEPTS

choral responding (CR)
continuum of alternative placements
disproportionate representation
IEP team
inclusion
least restrictive environment (LRE)

multifactored evaluation (MFE)
prereferral intervention
randomized control trial
response cards
response to intervention (RTI)

▼ SUMMARY

The Process of Special Education

- IDEA mandates a particular sequence of events that schools must follow to identify and educate children with disabilities.
- Prereferral intervention is a problem-solving process used to (1) provide immediate instructional and/or behavior management assistance to the child and teacher, (2) reduce the chances of identifying a child for special education who may not be disabled, and (3) identify students for evaluation.
- Response to intervention (RTI) is a form of prereferral intervention that measures a student's response to increasingly intensive, scientifically validated instruction to determine whether the child's struggles to learn are the result of poor or insufficient instruction or of a disability for which special education is needed.
- Any child suspected of having a disability must receive a nondiscriminatory multifactored evaluation (MFE) to determine eligibility for special education and to provide information about the child's educational needs and how to meet them.
- Culturally and linguistically diverse students are both underrepresented and overrepresented in special education, depending on the cultural/ethnic group and disability category.
- Inappropriate referral to special education and false identification of a disability can occur if educators and school psychologists cannot separate the presence of unrecognized diversity or deficits from disability.
- Schools must plan and provide an individualized education program (IEP) for each child with a disability.
- After identifying the child's educational needs and the services required to meet them, the IEP team determines the least restrictive environment (LRE) in which the child can receive an appropriate education.

- The IEP team must review the IEP periodically, but not less frequently than annually.
- At least once every 3 years, the IEP team conducts an evaluation to determine if the child still needs special education.
- Parents may at any time revoke their consent for special education services for their child.

Collaboration and Teaming

- Coordination, consultation, and teaming are three modes of collaboration that team members can use.
- Three models for teaming are multidisciplinary, interdisciplinary, and transdisciplinary.
- Co-teaching is two or more teachers planning and delivering instruction together. Co-teaching arrangements include one teaching/one helping, parallel teaching, station teaching, alternative teaching, and team teaching.

Individualized Education Program

- An IEP planning team must include (1) the parents of the child with a disability; (2) at least one general education teacher of the child; (3) at least one special education teacher; (4) a representative of the local education agency; (5) an individual who can interpret the instructional implications of evaluation results; (6) at the discretion of the parent or school, other individuals who have knowledge or special expertise regarding the child; and (7) whenever appropriate, the child.
- Each IEP must include these seven components:
  1. A description of the child's present levels of educational performance
  2. Measurable annual goals, including benchmarks or short-term objectives for students who take alternative assessments aligned to alternative standards

3. How the child's progress toward the annual goals will be measured and when reports on the child's progress toward meeting the annual goals will be provided

4. The special education and related services and supplementary aids and services, based on peer-reviewed research to the extent practical, to be provided to the child

5. An explanation of the extent, if any, to which the child will not participate with nondisabled children in the regular class

6. Any individual accommodations that are necessary to measure the academic achievement and functional performance of the child on state- and districtwide assessments (or alternative assessment selected if appropriate)

7. The projected date for the beginning of the services and modifications described in number 4 and the anticipated frequency, location, and duration of those services and modifications

- Beginning when the student reaches age 16, IEPs must also include information on how the educational program will support the child's transition from school to adult life.

- Without direct and ongoing monitoring of student progress toward IEP goals and objectives, the document's usefulness is limited.

- The IEP provides teachers and parents with the opportunity—and the responsibility—to first be realistic about the child's needs and goals and then to be creative about how to meet them.

- IEP formats vary widely across school districts, and schools may exceed the requirement of the law and include additional information.

- Each area of functioning that is adversely affected by the student's disability must be represented by an annual goal on the IEP.

Least Restrictive Environment

- The LRE is the setting closest to the general education classroom that also meets the child's special educational needs.

- The LRE is a relative concept; the LRE for one child might be inappropriate for another child with the same disability.

- The continuum of alternative placements is a range of placement and service options to meet the individual needs of students with disabilities.

- The IEP team must determine the LRE after it has designed a program of special education and related services to meet the child's unique needs.

- Removal of a child with disabilities from the general education classroom is to occur only if the IEP team determines that the specially designed instruction and related services necessary for the student to achieve her IEP goals cannot be provided in that setting.

Inclusive Education

- Inclusion is the process of integrating children with disabilities into the academic and social activities of regular schools and general education classes.

- Well-planned, carefully conducted inclusion can generally be effective with students of all ages, types, and degrees of disability.

- Some special educators believe that the LRE principle and continuum of alternative placements should be replaced with a policy of full inclusion, in which all students with disabilities are placed full-time in general education classrooms.

- Cooperative learning activities in which students work in small heterogeneous groups to help one another achieve a common academic goal or product can be an effective strategy for integrating students with disabilities into the academic and social fabric of the classroom.

Where Does Special Education Go From Here?

- Special education has made substantial progress toward fulfilling the promise of a free appropriate public education for all children with disabilities.

- Implementation of IDEA has brought problems of funding, inadequate training and support for teachers, and opposition by some to including children with disabilities in general education classes.

- Regardless of where special education services are delivered, the most crucial variable is the quality of instruction that each child receives.

MyEducationLab™

Go to Topic 2, Individualized Education Programs, in the MyEducationLab (www.myeducationlab.com) for *Exceptional Children*, where you can:

- Find learning outcomes for individualized education programs along with the national standards that connect to these outcomes.
- Complete Assignments and Activities that can help you more deeply understand the chapter content.
- Apply and practice your understanding of the core teaching skills identified in the chapter with the Building Teaching Skills and Dispositions learning units.
- Examine challenging situations and cases presented in the IRIS Center Resources.
- Access video clips of CCSSO National Teachers of the Year award winners responding to the question, "Why Do I Teach?" in the Teacher Talk section.
- Check your comprehension of the content covered in the chapter with the Study Plan. Here you will be able to take a chapter quiz, receive feedback on your answers, and then access Review, Practice, and Enrichment activities to enhance your understanding of chapter content.
- Use the Online Lesson Plan Builder to practice lesson planning and integrating national and state standards into your planning.

▼ GLOSSARY

choral responding: Each student in the class or group responds orally in unison to a question, problem, or item presented by the teacher.

continuum of alternative placements: A range of placement and instructional options for children with disabilities. Often depicted as a pyramid, with placements ranging from the general education classroom at the bottom to special schools, residential facilities, and homebound or hospital placements at the top. The Individuals with Disabilities Education Act (IDEA) requires schools to provide a continuum of alternative placements to meet the individual needs of students with disabilities.

disproportionate representation: When a particular group receives special education at a rate significantly higher or lower than would be expected based on the proportion of the general student population that group represents students.

inclusion: Educating students with disabilities in general education classrooms.

individualized education program (IEP): The written document required by the Individuals with Disabilities Education Act (PL 94-142) for every child with a disability; includes statements of present performance, annual goals, short-term instructional objectives, specific educational services needed, extent of participation in the general education program, evaluation procedures, and relevant dates; and must be signed by parents as well as educational personnel.

least restrictive environment (LRE): The educational setting that most closely resembles a regular school program and also meets the child's special educational needs. For many students with disabilities, the general education classroom is the LRE; however, the LRE is a relative concept and must be determined for each individual student with disabilities.

multifactored evaluation (MFE): Assessment and evaluation of a child with a variety of test instruments and observation procedures. Required by the Individuals with Disabilities Education Act (IDEA) when assessment is for educational placement of a child who is to receive special education services. Prevents the misdiagnosis and misplacement of a student as the result of considering only one test score.

prereferral intervention: Individualized intervention for a student experiencing academic or behavioral difficulties in the general education classroom before referring the student for formal testing and evaluation for special education eligibility. Usually coordinated by a building-based team that helps teachers devise and implement the additional academic or behavioral supports. See *response to intervention (RTI)*.

randomized controlled trial: A research study in which participants are randomly assigned to the experimental group (which receives the intervention or treatment being evaluated) or to the control group (which does not receive the treatment). Also called *randomized experimental group design*.

response cards: Cards, signs, or other items that are simultaneously held up by all students to display their response to a question or problem presented by the teacher; response cards enable every student in the class to respond to each question or item.

response to intervention (RTI): A systematic prereferral and early intervention process that consists of universal screening and several tiers of increasingly intensive trials of research-based interventions before referral for assessment for special education eligibility. The Individuals with Disabilities Education Act (IDEA) of 2004 stipulates that schools can use RTI to determine a child's eligibility for special education under the specific learning disabilities category.

Collaborating with Parents and Families in a Culturally and Linguistically Diverse Society

From Chapter 3 of *Exceptional Children* and *An Introduction to Special Education*, Tenth Edition. William L. Heward.

Collaborating with Parents and Families in a Culturally and Linguistically Diverse Society

- What can a teacher learn from the family of a child with disabilities?
- In what ways might a child's disability affect the family system and parents' roles?
- How can teachers who are not parents of children with disabilities communicate effectively and meaningfully with parents of exceptional children?

- How can a teacher communicate effectively and meaningfully with families from diverse cultures?
- What forms of home–school communication are likely to be most effective?
- How much parent involvement is enough?

▼ FEATURED TEACHER

JOSHUA HOPPE

Ma'ili Elementary School • Leeward District (Campbell, Kapolei, Wai'anae), Hawaii

EDUCATION—TEACHING CREDENTIALS— EXPERIENCE

- B.A. in Psychology 2005, University of Hawaii
- M.A. in Special Education 2007, University of Phoenix; M.Ed. in Curriculum Studies 2009, University of Hawaii
- Hawaii— Elementary, Special Education K–12 Mild, Moderate, and Severe
- 7 years of experience as a special education teacher

CURRENT TEACHING POSITION AND STUDENTS This year I teach 11 students from ages 6 to 12, in grades 1 to 6. Most of my students are eligible for special education under the disabilitiy categories of autism or intellectual disability, though I have two students with orthopedic or health impairments. My students function significantly below their same-aged peers in all areas: academic, communication, social, and self-care skills. Most speak in one- or two-word pharases, while some can hold conversations, and others are functionally nonverbal. Some like to play with their peers and participate with minimal assistance in nonacademic activities in the general education environment; others have significant social skills deficits and behavioral problems.

While we spend most of the school day in a self-contained classroom, for some of my students the class is like a resource room. They come to me during scheduled core academic periods and return to their homeroom for general education classes with or without an instructional assistant during lunch, recess, Hawaiian studies, PE, library, computers, science, and homeroom activities such as art and music. Some of my higher-functioning students do parallel or modified lessons during the general education writing block in their homeroom classes. Our bell schedule is staggered, and students are out and about at different times. I will often go with a group of students to recess or the cafeteria, as well as rotate between the inclusion classes and homeroom activities while an educational assistant or two work with the students that remain in the room.

About 75% of the general population of students at Ma'ili Elementary, including those in my classroom, meet the requirements for the federal free or reduced lunch program. While most of my students live in two-parent households, several live with single parents due to a parent passing away, a parent having fled from an abusive spouse, or divorce.

A RAINBOW OF DIFFERENT CULTURES Hawaii is often described as a melting pot of cultures. The majority of families whose children attend our school are multiracial. In addition to a large population of "Islanders," which includes Native Hawaiians and other Pacific Islanders, the dominant immigrant populations at Ma'ili are Filipino, Samoan, and

Micronesian. We also have students from Japanese, Chinese, Korean, Caucasian, African American, and Hispanic families.

People born and raised in Hawaii belong to a distinct general culture often referred to as "local." Some common threads of being "local" are knowledge of local foods, familiarity with various places and activities, a generally laid-back attitude, and the ability to speak and understand Pidgin English (properly Hawaiian Creole English, or HCE). Most people in Wai'anae, the portion of Honolulu County where Ma'ili Elementary is located, consider themselves American, but more specifically they see themselves as Hawaiians. However, some Native Hawaiians do not consider themselves American due to the technically illegal way in which Hawaii was brought into the union. As a teacher, my place is not to judge the validity of families' cultural views. To facilitate open communication with my students' families and to appreciate the influences that have shaped them, I need to understand as many nuances of these varied perspectives as possible.

RESPECTING CULTURAL DIFFERENCES

Hawaii's incredibly diverse student population presents wonderful opportunities for cross-cultural learning and challenges teachers. Growing up here gives me a considerable advantage in communicating with parents and families. A lot of teachers who come to Hawaii from the mainland leave after a year or two because they are unable to adapt to the local culture. I have some colleagues from the mainland who are wonderful at their jobs but lack an understanding of local culture. A coworker from the mainland once did a mocking impression of a parent's "pidgin accent" and said it sounded "dumb and ignorant." I told her that her impression was dumb and ignorant and that HCE speakers were neither, based solely on their language. I told her that as great a teacher as she was, she needed to learn to listen to what people were saying, not how they were saying it. I also told her that HCE is considered its own language by the University of Hawaii, and that while I agreed with her that students need to hear standard English modeled in the classroom, her attempt to speak HCE (though her impression was terrible enough to be comical) was denigrating the language that most of her students' families spoke at home.

I have had many students whose parents are learning English but who are not yet comfortable or fluent enough to use it with school personnel. In these situations, I always use translated notices of procedural safeguards and make sure a skilled interpreter attends IEP meetings. Aside from being required by IDEA, these steps show families that I am on their side. I have found that as soon as you develop rapport with a parent of a special needs child, regardless of his or her cultural background, life gets easier for everyone. For example, a parent may tell me about something their child does at home that explains puzzling behaviors in school. It gives me a better understanding of the student as a whole, which improves my ability to teach the student and helps prioritize IEP objectives.

COMMUNICATING WITH PARENTS AND FAMILIES

Embracing a parent's preferred means of communication is crucial. I have some parents who respond only to face-to-face contact, others who prefer exchanging written notes in home–school tablets, some who prefer phone conversations, and even some who prefer e-mail and text messaging. I like text messaging because it is quick, it is accessible in multiple settings, and it leaves a record. I had a family with a young boy with autism who were having problems with him at home. They were able to send detailed e-mails to me about what was happening that I reviewed and responded to while having a cup of coffee at home on a Saturday morning. These e-mails also provided a record of what we had tried and what the results were, and they helped us decide if we were getting to the issue or not. This information was reviewed at team meetings and used as a basis for further collaboration.

I also make myself available after school hours via e-mail or my cell phone. A lot of teachers are shocked that I give parents my cell number. "You have to have boundaries!" they say. I agree, but don't think parents having my phone number is a big deal. Parents understand I don't have to answer, they can leave a message, and I will get back to them when I set some time aside to do so. Parents have not abused this. I have been able to extend my help to parents who were having difficulty with their children on the weekend as well. One of my students was really distressed about something related to a toy in school. His mother could not understand what he was saying and called me for help. She put her son on the phone, and I was able to understand what he was saying, and calm him down. It does not take a lot of effort to do little things like this, and it pays dividends in building trustful partnerships with parents and families.

COLLABORATIVE COLLABORATION One of my most challenging parents was a mother from the Philippines whose son was a student with autism I had been teaching for the past 5 years. We had some communication breakdowns over the years but have also experienced numerous success stories. She did not trust the school district's transportation department and insisted on driving her son to school every day. She sometimes arrived to school late, which disrupted her son's routine and triggered an emotional outburst. When this occurred and I was not in the room, she would yell at staff, "What kind of school is this!" Other times she would linger when she dropped off her son and say things like, "I can't be perfect, sometimes he doesn't want to get up." It took some time for her to understand what autism is and how it was affecting her son. When she saw progress, she would say, "He's getting better. How long you think until he is normal?" For quite some time, whenever I would start explaining, in plain language, what his disability was and how it affected him, she would change the subject to how she didn't get a good education growing up in the Philippines, how her teacher used to hit her with a stick and call her stupid.

Her husband, a retired navy lieutenant, had passed away 2 years ago. He was skilled in communicating calmly and clearly with the school and with his son. The loss of this man is a very significant one for this family. So I understand that a lot of what this mother was doing was a product of the stress of losing this breadwinner/communicator/partner that she had relied on so much and being thrust into many new roles while still taking care of an autistic child. There were some tearful hugs some mornings before she left and then again in the afternoons. I made it clear that we were here to support her through this process. I also tried to assess what kind of outside help she could access.

Luckily, there is a wonderful Filipina teacher at our school who speaks perfect Visayan, Tagalog, and English. I enlisted her help at IEP meetings and conferences with this parent. My colleague encouraged this mother to enroll in classes at the community school for adults, since one of the mother's chief complaints was not being educated. I had also been trying to get her some respite care through the department of health. She kept refusing, because she somehow thought if they were involved, the department would take her son away. With the help of my colleague, she finally called the case manager I had referred her to and got the ball rolling.

As this mother's trust in me grew, we targeted two problems she was having with her son in the community: stealing items and running away from her in the grocery store. To avoid the stress caused by these behaviors, she had stopped taking him anywhere other than to and from school. I told her to make a shopping list with check marks for each item they needed at the store with the last on the list being the thing he wanted and would often steal (usually tape or candy). Mom and I created a simple social story for the expected behaviors in the store. By having her son push the shopping cart and keep track of the list, he no longer ran off and didn't need to steal because he knew they were going to get the items on the list.

She still brings him to school late sometimes. I made a schedule for him to follow at home and told her to set the alarm 15 minutes earlier in the morning. I also suggested making him mini-schedules when she was going to do something different, like visiting a friend or going to an evening church service. I told her to make it simple, just place names or activities, and to put something he really wanted last, right before going home or something that would occur at home. She reports that she sometimes tries this approach, and it seems to work.

I feel that we are now in a place where we communicate well and work effectively with each other despite our cultural differences. I know there are times when she does not completely understand what I'm trying to get across, but I always do my best to make sure I understand what she is trying to get across to me. I want her to continue to feel that I am someone who will always listen to her and help her to the best of my ability.

MyEducationLab™

Visit the **MyEducationLab** for *Exceptional Children* to enhance your understanding of chapter concepts with a personalized Study Plan. You'll also have the opportunity to hone your teaching skills through video and case based Assignments and Activities, IRIS Center Resources (optional), and Building Teaching Skills and Disposition lessons.

FAMILY IS THE MOST POWERFUL AND PERVASIVE INFLUENCE in a young child's life. Long before a professional with the job title "teacher" arrives, a child has learned countless skills from parents and family members. With rare exceptions, no one ever knows or cares about a child as much as a parent does.

Too often in the past, educators viewed parents as either troublesome (if they asked too many questions or, worse, offered suggestions about their child's education) or uncaring (if they did not jump to attention whenever the professional determined the parent needed something—usually advice from the professional). Today, parent involvement and family support are understood as essential elements of special education.

SUPPORT FOR FAMILY INVOLVEMENT

Although many factors have contributed to the increased emphasis on collaboration between parents and teachers in the education of exceptional children, three issues are clear: (a) parents want to be involved, (b) educational outcomes are enhanced when parents are involved, and (c) federal law requires collaboration between schools and families.

Parents: Advocating for Change

Parents of exceptional children have long advocated for equal access to educational opportunities for their children, and they have done so with impressive effectiveness. As you know, parents are primarily responsible for the litigation and legislation that established the right to a free and appropriate public education for all children with disabilities.

The first parent group on behalf of children with disabilities was the National Society for Crippled Children, organized in 1921. The United Cerebral Palsy Association, founded in 1948, and the National Association for Retarded Citizens (now called The Arc), organized in 1950, are two national parent organizations largely responsible for making the public aware of the special needs of children with disabilities. The Learning Disabilities Association of America, formed in 1963, also organized by and consisting mostly of parents, has been instrumental in bringing about educational reform. Parent members of the Association for Persons with Severe Handicaps (TASH), founded in 1975, have been effective advocates for family-focused educational services and the inclusion of students with severe disabilities in neighborhood schools and general education classrooms. The mission of the Association for Science in Autism Treatment, founded in 1998 by parents and professionals, is to disseminate accurate, scientifically sound information about autism and its treatment. Many other parent-led organizations continue today to advocate for effective education, community acceptance, needed services, and the rights of individuals with disabilities.

Educators: Seeking Greater Effectiveness

Research shows a strong correlation between parent involvement and improvements in a variety of measures of academic achievement and school performance such as better attendance, higher grades, better scores on standardized tests, higher graduation rates, and improved social skills (Fan & Chen, 2001; Hoover-Dempsey et al., 2005; Pomerantz, Moorman, & Litwack, 2007; Speth, Saifer, & Forehand, 2008; Westat and Policy Studies Associates, 2001). The effectiveness of educational programs for children with disabilities is

A parent is a child's first teacher.

increased when parents and families are actively involved (e.g., Newman, 2004; Resetar, Noell, & Pellegrin, 2006).

To meet the needs of children with disabilities, educators must expand the traditional role of the classroom teacher beyond that of instructing academic skills in the classroom. Effective special educators design and implement instructional programs that enable students with disabilities to use and maintain academic, language, social, self-help, recreation, and vocational skills in school, home, and community settings. In their home and community lives, children may participate in some 150 different kinds of social and physical settings (Dunst, 2001). The large number of nonschool settings in which children live, play, and learn illustrates two important points. First, the many different settings and situations exemplify the extent of the challenge teachers face in helping children use newly learned skills throughout their daily lives. Second, the many different settings and social situations children experience in home and community provide extended opportunities for learning and practicing important skills. To be maximally effective, teachers must look beyond the classroom for assistance and support, and parents and families are natural and necessary allies.

At the very least, teachers and students benefit when parents provide information about their children's use of specific skills outside the classroom. Families know certain aspects of their children better than anyone else does (Meadan, Sheldon, Appel, & DeGrazia, 2010). It is helpful for teachers to remind themselves that they spend roughly half the days of the year with their students, seeing them for less than a third of each of those days (Giangreco, Cloninger, & Iverson, 2011). Parental reports on what their children do (and do not do) during nonschool time, and information such as their children's interests, motivations, habits, fears, routines, pressures, needs, and health status, have tremendous educational implications.

But parents can do much more than just report on their children's activities and interests. They can provide extra skill practice and teach their children new skills in the home and community (Harte, 2009; Park, Alber Morgan, & Fleming, 2011). When parents are involved in identifying what skills their children need to learn (and, just as important, what they do not need to learn), the hard work expended by teachers is more likely to produce outcomes with real significance in the lives of children and their families. Another powerful argument for making active family involvement the cornerstone of educational planning is that families must live with the outcomes of decisions made by IEP teams (Giangreco et al., 2011). Over the course of a child's years in school, a great many educators and other professionals will come and go, but family is the constant in the child's life.

Family involvement as cornerstone for planning

 Content Standards for Beginning Teachers—Common Core: Collaborate with families and others in the assessment of individuals with exceptional learning needs (ICC10S2) (also ICC10K3, ICC2K4).

Legislators: Mandating Parent and Family Involvement

Congress made parent involvement a key component of the Education of the Handicapped Children Act (PL 94–142), the original federal special education law. Each reauthorization of the law has strengthened and extended parent and family participation in the education of children with disabilities. In the introduction to the Individuals with Disabilities Education Act (IDEA) of 2004, Congress reaffirmed and made clear its belief in the importance of parent and family involvement: "Over 30 years of research and experience has demonstrated that the education of children with disabilities can be made more effective by . . . strengthening the role and responsibility of parents and ensuring that families of such children have meaningful opportunities to participate in the education of their children at school and at home" (20 USC 601[c][5][B]).

Parent participation in the form of shared decision making is one of the basic principles of IDEA that provide the general framework for carrying out national policies for the education of children with disabilities. IDEA stipulates procedures schools must follow to ensure parents of children with disabilities have input with regard to referral, testing, program planning, placement, and evaluation. In addition, the law mandates due process procedures if parents believe that their child's needs are not being met.

The No Child Left Behind Act of 2001 also views parent involvement as a key to academic success of students and spells out three parent involvement components: schools

IDEA and parent participation

 **Content Standards for Beginning Teachers—Common Core:** Rights and responsibilities of students, parents, teachers, other professionals, and schools related to exceptional learning needs (ICC1K4).

The following organizations provide educators and families with parent involvement resources: the National Coalition for Parent Involvement in Education (http://ncpie.org/), the National Parental Teacher Association (http://www.pta.org/), and the National Parental Information and Resource Coordination Center (http://www.nationalpirc.org).

must (a) notify parents of their improvement status; (b) collaborate with parents in developing and implementing a school improvement plan in which parents, school staff, and students share responsibility for improving academic achievement; and (c) include strategies that promote "effective" parent involvement in the plan (though "effective" strategies are not defined).

So, parents want to be involved, teachers know that family involvement is a good thing, and the law requires it. But the most important reasons that families and educators should develop and maintain collaborative partnerships are that children with disabilities will benefit from

- increased likelihood of targeting meaningful IEP goals;
- greater consistency and support in their two most important environments—home and school;
- increased opportunities for learning and development; and
- access to expanded resources and services.

UNDERSTANDING FAMILIES OF CHILDREN WITH DISABILITIES

Teachers and parents working together for the benefit of a child with disabilities make a powerful team. To work together, they must communicate with one another. Effective communication is more likely when each party understands and respects the responsibilities and challenges faced by the other. For educators, an important initial step in partnering with families is to strive for an understanding of how a child's disability might influence the family system and the many interrelated roles of parenthood.

Family Responses to a Child with Disabilities

Parental responses to disability

Council for Exceptional Children

Content Standards for Beginning Teachers—Common Core: Concerns of families of individuals with exceptional learning needs and strategies to help address these concerns (ICC10K3).

The birth of a baby is an emotionally powerful, joyous event that simultaneously brings new challenges and responsibilities. The birth of a child with disabilities, or the onset or diagnosis of a child's disability, is a traumatic "change in plans" that ushers in an additional set of challenges and stresses (Van Riper, 2007). Early research on parents' responses to having children with disabilities identified mostly negative outcomes as parents went through three stages of adjustment some call a grief cycle: confronting, adjusting, and accepting or adapting (e.g., Anderegg, Vergason, & Smith, 1992; Blacher, 1984; Ferguson, 2003). First, parents experience a period of emotional crisis characterized by shock, denial, and disbelief. This initial reaction is followed by a period of alternating feelings of anger, guilt, depression, shame, lowered self-esteem, rejection of the child, and overprotectiveness. Eventually, parents reach a third stage in which they accept and adapt to their child's disability. Firsthand reports by parents describe a similar sequence of experiences (e.g., Boushey, 2001; Holland, 2006).

Poyadue (1993) suggested a stage beyond acceptance or adaptation that involves appreciation of the positive aspects of family life with a child with a disability. Many parents report not only coping successfully with the challenges posed by a child with disabilities but also experiencing benefits to the family (Blacher & Baker, 2007; Hastings, Beck, & Hill, 2005; Lalvani, 2008). For example, Patterson and Leonard (1994) interviewed couples whose children required intensive home care routines because of chronic and complex health care needs and found roughly equal numbers of positive and negative responses. Positive responses included increased closeness among couples and stronger family bonds. In another study, the majority of 1,262 parents of children with disabilities agreed with the following statements: "The presence of my child is very uplifting. Because of my child, I have many unexpected pleasures. My child is the reason I am a more responsible person" (Behr, Murphy, & Summers, 1992, p. 26). As the mother of a child with Down syndrome in another study noted: "[People] think you're overwhelmed, . . . They think if you're a family with a disabled kid that you, your family, doesn't have fun. . . . I disagree totally. We have a lot of fun" (Lalvani, 2008, p. 441).

After a period of uncertainty, most families of children with disabilities reestablish healthy family functioning. With strength and resilience they become determined to do whatever they can to meet their children's needs as well as possible and to move forward with an enlightened sense of optimism (King, Baxter, Rosenbaum, Zwaigenbaum, & Bates, 2009; Van Riper, 2007). Figure 1 shows a five-stage "resilience model" that identifies experiences and tasks for parents as they move from learning of their child's disability through acceptance and appreciation. Kochhar-Bryant (2008) developed this model based on the following:

- Parents and family members are the best sources of knowledge about their child, their own strengths and needs.
- Parents' resilience may not be immediately appreciable but should be identified and supported.
- Parents are engaged in a continuous adjustment process that can be facilitated by sensitive, caring professionals.

FIGURE 1

A RESILIENCE MODEL TOWARD FAMILY STRENGTH

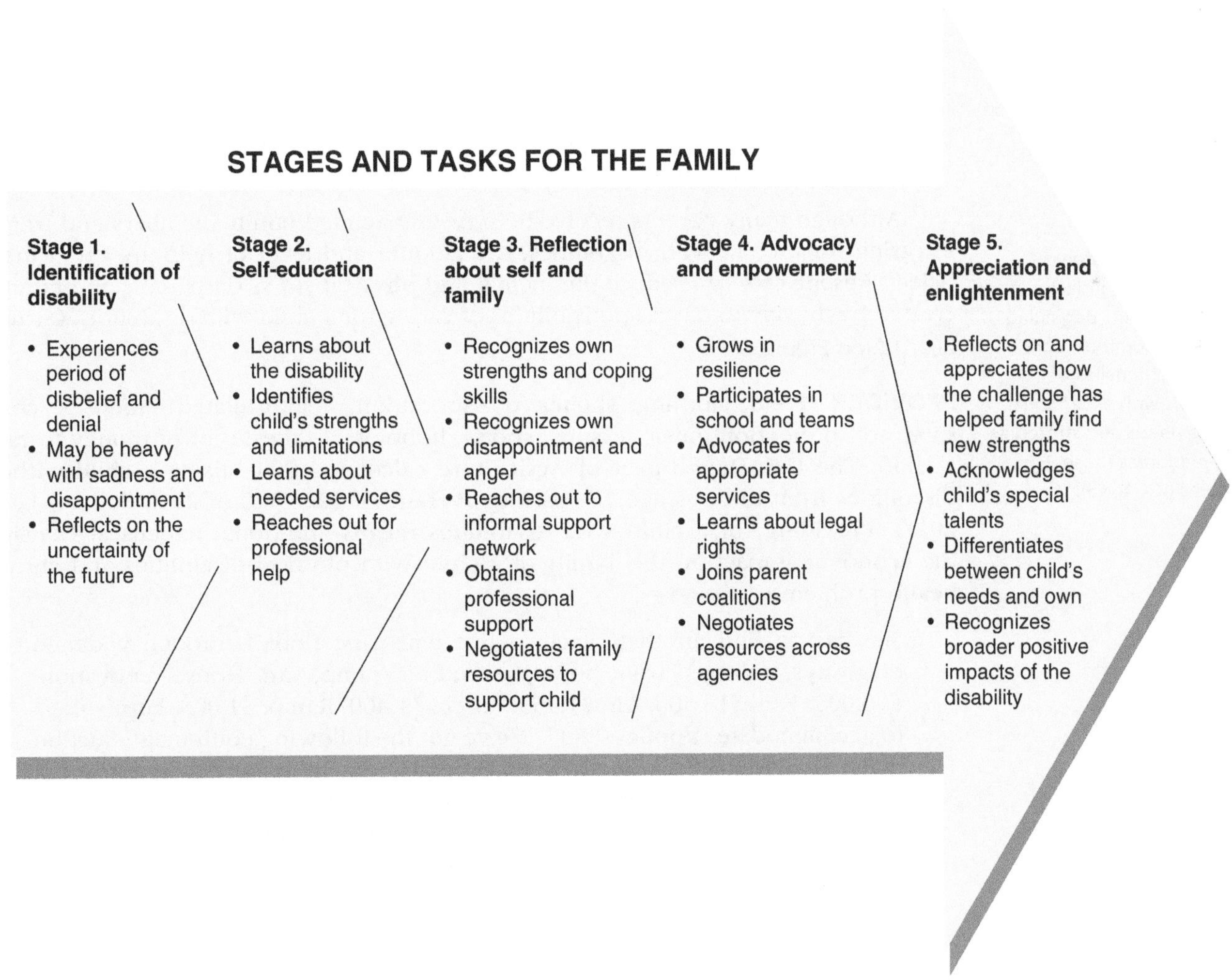

STAGES AND TASKS FOR THE FAMILY

Stage 1. Identification of disability

- Experiences period of disbelief and denial
- May be heavy with sadness and disappointment
- Reflects on the uncertainty of the future

Stage 2. Self-education

- Learns about the disability
- Identifies child's strengths and limitations
- Learns about needed services
- Reaches out for professional help

Stage 3. Reflection about self and family

- Recognizes own strengths and coping skills
- Recognizes own disappointment and anger
- Reaches out to informal support network
- Obtains professional support
- Negotiates family resources to support child

Stage 4. Advocacy and empowerment

- Grows in resilience
- Participates in school and teams
- Advocates for appropriate services
- Learns about legal rights
- Joins parent coalitions
- Negotiates resources across agencies

Stage 5. Appreciation and enlightenment

- Reflects on and appreciates how the challenge has helped family find new strengths
- Acknowledges child's special talents
- Differentiates between child's needs and own
- Recognizes broader positive impacts of the disability

Source: From Kochhar-Bryant, C. A. (2008). *Collaboration and system coordination for students with special needs: From early childhood to the postsecondary years* (p. 213). Upper Saddle River, NJ: Merrill/Prentice Hall. Used by permission of Pearson Education, Inc.

The Many Roles of the Exceptional Parent

Roles of exceptional parents

 Content Standards for Beginning Teachers—Common Core: Concerns of families of individuals with exceptional learning needs and strategies to help address these concerns (ICC10K3) (also ICC2K4).

Parenting any child demands tremendous physical and emotional energy. All parents have a great deal in common. Hart and Risley (1995), who conducted a longitudinal study of 42 families with young typically developing children, noted, "All the babies had to be fed, changed, and amused. As we went from one home to another we saw the same activities and lives centered on caregiving. . . . Most impressive of all that the parents had in common was the continual and incredible challenge a growing child presents" (pp. 53, 55).

Parents of children with disabilities, however, experience added physical, emotional, and financial stress (Chiasson & Reilly, 2008). Educators who are not parents of children with disabilities, chronic illness, or severe problem behavior cannot possibly know the 24-hour, 7-day reality of being the parent of such a child (Hutton & Caron, 2005). Nonetheless, educators should strive to understand as much as possible how a child with special needs affects (and is affected by) the family system. In addition to providing love and affection, parents of children with disabilities fulfill at least nine other varied and demanding roles.

CAREGIVER   Caring for any young child is a demanding task. But the additional caregiving requirements of children with disabilities can be tremendous and cause added stress (Osborne & Reed, 2009; Quintero & McIntyre, 2010). And the level of care needed by some children with severe disabilities or chronic health conditions can be nonstop:

> Mike sleeps when he wants to, mostly during the day. He sleeps with a heart monitor on which alarms several times per night, because he stops breathing frequently. Usually I'm up by 8:00 and often cannot go to bed until 12:00 or 1:00 because of Mike's feedings, medication. It's hard to fit all of this into a day and still have time for sleep. (Bradley, Knoll, & Agosta, 1992)

Respite care

 Content Standards for Beginning Teachers—Common Core: Concerns of families of individuals with exceptional learning needs and strategies to help address these concerns (ICC10K3).

Although many parents receive help from extended family members and friends in caring for a child with disabilities, the amount and level of help are often insufficient. **Respite care** can reduce the mental and physical stress on parents and families created by the day-to-day responsibilities of caring for a child with disabilities (Strunk, 2010) (see Figure 2).

PROVIDER   Food, clothing, shelter, transportation, health-related expenses, childcare, not to mention music lessons, sports, hobbies: it takes a lot of money to raise a child. The U.S. Department of Agriculture calculated that raising a child without disabilities from birth to age 17 costs an average of $226,920 in 2010 dollars (Leno, 2011). Providing for a child with disabilities means additional expenses. Consider the economic impact on this family of a child with physical disabilities and chronic health problems:

> We had to find another place to live with first floor bedroom, widened doorways, enlarged front porch, central air, ramp, van. House renovation: $10,000. Van: $18,500. Air: $1,450. Porch: $1,400. Ramp: $1,000. Furnishings to accommodate supplies: $800. We've got the following equipment: Suction machine, portable suction machine, generator for emergency power, hospital bed, air pressure mattress, wheelchair, room monitor, humidifier, bath chair, oxygen, air cleaner, gastronomy tube pump, breathing treatment machine. And all the following expenses have gone up: formula, diapers, appliances, utility bills, medications. (Bradley et al., 1992)

It is not just families of children with physical disabilities or health conditions who face financial burdens. Many parents of children with learning and behavioral problems pay thousands of dollars for specific treatments, behavioral intervention programs, and in-home therapy. While some families receive financial assistance from

---

FIGURE 2   RESPITE: SUPPORT FOR FAMILIES

Parents of nondisabled children frequently hire others to care temporarily for their children. For parents of children with disabilities, however, the range of child care options is limited. Many parents of children with severe disabilities identify the availability of reliable, high-quality child care as their single most pressing need (Warfield & Hauser-Cram, 1996). In response to this need, many communities have developed respite care programs. **Respite care** is the short-term care of a family member with disabilities to provide relief for parents from caretaking duties.

Quality respite care can reduce the mental and physical stress on parents and families created by the day-to-day (in some cases, moment-to-moment) responsibilities of caring for a child with disabilities. The most frequently requested support service by families, "respite can make difference between a struggling or thriving family" (Solomon, 2007, p. 39). The mother of a son born with a neurological condition that produces frequent seizures and extreme hyperactivity describes her family's experience with respite care:

> During the first 4 years of Ben's life, we averaged 4 hours of sleep a night. We were wearing ourselves out; I have no doubt we would have completely fallen apart. My husband, Roger, used his vacations for sleeping in. The respite program came along just in time for us. It was hard at first. There's an overwhelming guilt that you shouldn't leave your child. We didn't feel like anyone else could understand Ben's problems. But we had to get away. Our church gave us some money, with orders to take a vacation. It was the first time Roger and I and our 12-year-old daughter, Stacy, had really been together since Ben was born.

Families and their advocates can locate respite service providers in their communities through the National Respite Locator Service at www.respitelocator.org/.

---

federal, state, and/or local agencies, those sources seldom cover the costs (Worcester, Nesman, Mendez, & Keller, 2008). On top of the additional expenses, families of children with disabilities often have reduced income because one parent works part-time instead of full-time or must withdraw from the workforce altogether to care for the child (Davenport & Eidelman, 2008; Solomon, 2007).

TEACHER   Most children learn many skills without anyone teaching them. Children with disabilities, however, often do not acquire new skills as naturally or independently as their typically developing peers do. In addition to learning systematic teaching techniques (Ozcan & Cavkaytar, 2009), some parents must learn to use and/or teach their children to use special equipment and assistive devices such as hearing aids, braces, wheelchairs, and adapted eating utensils (Parette, Brotherson, & Huer, 2000).

COUNSELOR   All parents are counselors in the sense that they deal with their children's changing emotions, feelings, and attitudes. But parents of a child with disabilities must also deal with their child's feelings that result from his particular disability: "Will I still be deaf when I grow up?" "I'm not playing outside anymore; they always tease me." "Why can't I go swimming like the other kids?" Parents play a critical role in how a child with disabilities comes to feel about himself. Their interactions can help develop an active, outgoing child who confidently tries new experiences or a withdrawn child with negative attitudes toward himself and others.

BEHAVIOR SUPPORT SPECIALIST   All parents are challenged and frustrated from time to time by their children's noncompliance and misbehavior. But the frequency and severity of challenging behaviors exhibited by some children with disabilities can make it nearly impossible for their families to experience and enjoy normal routines of daily life (Fox, Vaughn, Wyatte, & Dunlap, 2002). Turnbull and Ruef (1996) interviewed 14 families with children with intellectual disabilities who frequently exhibited problem behavior. The children's problem behavior fell into one of two domains, according to the behavior's impact on the child and the family: dangerous behavior (e.g., "He punches his face a lot on the jaw line—his cheek bone, his mouth, occasionally his forehead. . . . He will eventually bleed from his mouth") and difficult behavior (e.g., "When I am around him it is constant noise. He talks or squawks. By afternoon I am frazzled") (p. 283). Such behavior demands specialized and consistent treatment, and some parents must become skilled in behavior-support techniques to achieve a semblance of normal family life (e.g., Becker-Cottrill, McFarland, & Anderson, 2003; Park, Alber-Morgan, & Fleming, 2011).

PARENT OF SIBLINGS WITHOUT DISABILITIES Children are deeply influenced by having a brother or a sister with special needs (McHugh, 2003); the nature of that influence, however, is varied. Some studies have found negative effects, such as a higher incidence of emotional or behavioral problems (Orsillo, McCaffrey, & Fisher, 1993), lower self-esteem (McHale & Gamble, 1989), or resentment or jealousy (Hutton & Caron, 2005) in siblings of children with disabilities. But researchers have also reported many instances of siblings displaying nurturing and affection toward their brother or sister with disabilities (Hannah & Midlarsky, 2005; Moyson & Roeyers, 2011). Research on peer-mediated interventions shows that a brother or sister without disabilities can help their sibling with disabilities learn new social behaviors/skills in the home (Zhang & Wheeler, 2011). The positive relationships between a sibling and his or her brother or sister with disabilities often last well into adulthood (Orsmond & Seltzer, 2000).

Brothers and sisters of a child with disabilities often have concerns about their sibling's disability: uncertainty regarding the cause of the disability and its effect on them, uneasiness about the reactions of friends, and a feeling of being left out or being required to do too much for the child with disabilities (Moyson & Roeyers, 2011). Parents play key roles in determining the nature of the relationship between their children and the extent to which their children without disabilities are happy and well adjusted (Quintero & McIntyre, 2010).

MARRIAGE PARTNER Having a child with disabilities can put stress on a marriage. Specific stressors can be as diverse as arguing over who is to blame for the child's disability; disagreeing about expectations for the child's behavior; and spending so much time, money, and energy on the child with disabilities that little is left for each other (Brobst, Clopton, & Hendrick, 2009; Florian & Findler, 2001; Meadan et al., 2010). It is a mistake, however, to assume that the presence of a child with disabilities has a negative effect on marital relationships. Most families of children with disabilities experience average to above-average levels of marriage adjustment (e.g., Flaherty & Glidden, 2000; Stoneman & Gavidia-Payne, 2006), and studies have found that a child with disabilities can strengthen a marriage in part because of a couple's shared commitment to the child (Bauer, 2008; Scorgie & Sobsey, 2000).

INFORMATION SPECIALIST Grandparents, aunts and uncles, neighbors, the school bus driver: all of these people can be important influences on a child's development. While parents of children without disabilities can reasonably expect them to receive certain kinds of treatment from significant others, parents of children with disabilities know they cannot depend on appropriate actions and reactions from others. These parents must try to ensure that other people interact with their child in ways that support their child's dignity, acceptance, opportunities for learning, and maintenance of adaptive

Brothers and sisters without disabilities often have special needs and concerns because of their sibling's disability.

behaviors. One mother of a child with Down syndrome describes her response to anyone who stares at her son: she looks the person squarely in the eye and says, "You seem interested in my son. Would you like to meet him?" (Schulz, 1985, p. 6). This usually ends the staring and often creates an opportunity to provide information or begin a friendship.

ADVOCATE   IDEA not only defines the rights of parents of children with disabilities, it also requires specific efforts and responsibilities. Although involvement in their child's education is desirable for all parents, participation is a must for parents of children with disabilities. They must acquire special knowledge (e.g., about different kinds of related services) and learn special skills (e.g., how to participate effectively in IEP meetings). They must be consistent and firm in presenting their concerns and wishes regarding learning goals, placement options, and career development opportunities for their children (Lindstrom, Doren, Metheny, Johnson, & Zane, 2007; Neely-Barnes, Graff, Marcenko, & Weber, 2008; Wright & Wright, 2006a). They must often advocate for effective educational services and opportunities for their children in a society that devalues people with disabilities. As one mother put it: "If I don't do it, he's going to get lost out there. And so I've got to button up my boot straps and make sure that I know everything that I need to know about this, and take the bull by the horns" (King et al., 2009, p. 58).

Changing Needs as Children Grow

Another way to increase our understanding of how a child with disabilities might affect his or her family and vice versa is to examine the likely impact of the child's and family's changing needs at various ages (Ankeny, Wilkins, & Spain, 2009; Turnbull, Turnbull, Erwin, Soodak, & Shogren, 2011). Table 1 identifies some of the major issues and concerns that parents and siblings face during four life-cycle stages and suggests strategies for supporting families at each stage. And the demands of parenting a child with disabilities often do not end when the child reaches adulthood. Many parents in their 70s and 80s continue to care for their adult children with disabilities (Llewellyn, Gething, Kendig, & Cant, 2004).

Family life-cycle stages

 Content Standards for Beginning Teachers—Common Core: Concerns of families of individuals with exceptional learning needs and strategies to help address these concerns (ICC10K3).

Developing and Maintaining Family–Professional Partnerships

Turnbull and colleagues (2011) define a family–professional *partnership* as

> A relationship in which families (not just parents) and professionals agree to build on each other's expertise and resources, as appropriate, for the purpose of making and implementing decisions that will directly benefit students and indirectly benefit other family members and professionals. (p. 137).

To better understand the characteristics of effective family–professional partnerships, Blue-Banning, Summers, Frankland, Nelson, and Beegle (2004) conducted in-depth focus groups and interviews with 137 adult family members of children with and without disabilities and 53 professionals. The participants represented a wide range of ethnic groups and socioeconomic levels and resided in Kansas, North Carolina, and Louisiana. The results suggested that partnerships are facilitated by professional behaviors clustered around these six dimensions: communication, commitment, equality, skills, trust, and respect.

The study by Blue-Banning and colleagues (2004) gives empirical support to something that educators have long known but too seldom practiced: Effective home–school partnerships are characterized by family members and professionals jointly pursuing shared goals in a climate of mutual respect and trust. Families receive supports in the form of the knowledge and resources that empower them to participate as full partners, and professionals receive input from families that helps them be more effective teachers.

TABLE 1 • **Issues faced by family members during four life-cycle stages of a person with disabilities and ways that professionals can help**

LIFE-CYCLE STAGES		
	BIRTH AND EARLY CHILDHOOD	**CHILDHOOD**
Issues for Parents	• Discovering and coming to terms with exceptionality • Obtaining an accurate diagnosis • Informing siblings and relatives • Locating early intervention services • Participating in IFSP meetings • Seeking to find meaning in the exceptionality • Clarifying a personal ideology to guide decisions • Addressing issues of stigma • Identifying positive contributions of exceptionality • Setting great expectations	• Establishing routines to carry out family functions • Adjusting emotionally to educational implications • Clarifying issues of mainstreaming versus special class placement • Advocating for inclusive experiences • Participating in IEP conferences • Locating community resources • Arranging for extracurricular activities • Developing a vision for the future
Issues for Siblings	• Less parental time and energy for sibling needs • Feelings of jealousy because of less attention • Fears associated with misunderstandings about exceptionality	• Division of responsibility for any physical care needs • Oldest female sibling may be at risk • Limited family resources for recreation and leisure • Informing friends and teachers • Possible concern about younger sibling surpassing older • Issues of mainstreaming into same school • Need for basic information on exceptionality
Enhancing Successful Transitions	• Advise parents to prepare for the separation of preschool children by periodically leaving the child with others. • Gather information and visit preschools in the community. • Encourage participation in Parent-to-Parent programs. (Veteran parents are matched in one-to-one relationships with parents who are just beginning the transition process.) • Familiarize parents with possible school (elementary and secondary) programs, career options, or adult programs so they have an idea of future opportunities.	• Provide parents with an overview of curricular options. • Ensure that IEP meetings provide an empowering context for family collaboration. • Encourage participation in Parent-to-Parent matches, workshops, or family support groups to discuss transitions with others.

Principles of Effective Communication

Principles of effective communication

 Council for Exceptional Children

Content Standards for Beginning Teachers—Common Core: Foster respectful and beneficial relationships between families and professionals (ICC10S3).

Ongoing two-way communication is the key operational element of the family–professional partnership. The family members in the study by Blue-Banning and colleagues (2004) said they needed frequent communication, but they also highlighted the importance of the quality of communication. "Family members stressed that communication should be honest and open, with no hidden information and no 'candy-coating' of bad news" (p. 173). Family members and professionals emphasized the need for two-way communication, stating that both professionals and parents should listen carefully and nonjudgmentally to what each has to say. One father stated it like this: "The first thing is to listen to us . . . because we know our kids better than anybody. . . . I think some of these people have preconceived notions about

LIFE-CYCLE STAGES		
	ADOLESCENCE	**ADULTHOOD**
Issues for Parents	• Adjusting emotionally to possible chronicity of exceptionality • Identifying issues of emerging sexuality • Dealing with physical and emotional changes of puberty • Addressing possible peer isolation and rejection • Planning for career/vocational development • Arranging for leisure activities • Expanding child's self-determination skills • Planning for postsecondary education	• Addressing supported employment and living options • Adjusting emotionally to any adult implications of dependency • Addressing the need for socialization opportunities outside the family • Initiating career choice or vocational program • Planning for possible need for guardianship
Issues for Siblings	• Overidentification with sibling • Greater understanding of differences in people • Influence of exceptionality on career choice • Dealing with possible stigma and embarrassment • Participation in sibling training programs • Opportunity for sibling support groups	• Possible issues of responsibility for financial support • Addressing concerns regarding genetic implications • Introducing new in-laws to exceptionality • Need for information on career/living options • Clarify role of sibling advocacy • Possible issues of guardianship
Enhancing Successful Transitions	• Assist families and adolescents to identify community leisure activities. • Incorporate into the IEP skills that will be needed in future career and vocational programs. • Visit or become familiar with a variety of career and living options. • Develop a mentor relationship with an adult with a similar exceptionality and an individual who has a career that matches the student's strengths and preferences.	• Provide preferred information to families about guardianship, estate planning, wills, and trusts. • Assist family members in transferring responsibilities to the individual with an exceptionality, other family members, or service providers as appropriate. • Assist the young adult or family members with career or vocational choices. • Address the issues and responsibilities of marriage and family for the young adult.

Source: Adapted from Turnbull, A., & Turnbull, H., Erwin, E. J., Soodak, L. C., & Shogren, K. A. (2011). *Families, professionals, and exceptionality: Positive outcomes through partnership and trust* (5th ed., p. 93), and Turnbull, A. P., & Turnbull, H. R. (1990, 1997, 2001). *Families, professionals, and exceptionality: Collaborating for empowerment* (2nd ed., pp. 134–135; 3rd ed., p. 149; 4th ed., p. 173). Upper Saddle River, NJ: Pearson. Used by permission.

everything. . . . So if I tried to say to them [professionals] something, it'd be LISTEN TO ME" (p. 175).

When asked to voice their perceptions of and preferences for interactions with education professionals, a group of parents of children with autism said they wanted frequent, honest, and open communication between home and school (Stoner et al., 2005). "Parents wanted to be informed of achievements, but they also wanted to know of any problems that the teachers had encountered" (p. 46).

C. L. Wilson (1995) recommends five principles for effective communication between educators and parents.

ACCEPT PARENTS' STATEMENTS Accepting parents' statements means conveying through verbal and nonverbal means that parents' input is valued. Parents are more likely to speak freely and openly when they believe that what they say is respected. Acceptance means conveying "I understand and appreciate your point of view." It does not mean the teacher must agree with everything that a parent says.

Active listening

 Content Standards for Beginning Teachers—Common Core: Foster respectful and beneficial relationships between families and professionals (ICC10S3).

LISTEN ACTIVELY Good listeners attend and respond to a conversation partner in a sincere and genuine manner. A good listener pays attention to content, noting who said it and how. For example, in an IFSP/IEP conference attended by extended family members, an educator should notice if a grandparent seems to be speaking for the child's parents or if the mother and father express different opinions about an issue through tones of voice or body language. An active listener not only comprehends, interprets, sorts, and analyzes what the speaker says but also responds to the speaker's message with animation and interest (Howard, Williams, & Lepper, 2010; McNaughten & Vostal, 2010). Figure 3 illustrates the kind of communication problems that occur when only one party is actively listening.

QUESTION EFFECTIVELY Educators should ask mostly open-ended questions when communicating with parents. An open-ended question such as "What did Shareena do with her homework project last week?" is more likely to evoke a descriptive and informative reply from parents than is the closed-ended question "Is Shareena having trouble with her homework?" which might result in a yes or no response. Questions to parents should not focus solely on problems or deficits, and teachers must respect families' desire to keep some things private and "in the family" (Turnbull et al., 2011).

FIGURE 3 EXAMPLE OF COMMUNICATION PROBLEMS BETWEEN AN ACTIVE AND A PASSIVE LISTENER

Actively Listening Parent	Passively Listening Preschool Teacher
"I would very much like to have my child use his communication board on a more regular basis. Currently, he becomes very frustrated because he can't tell us what he needs." The parent frowns and looks sad.	"All the students in my class are able to speak. We will have the speech language pathologist work with Andy so that he can speak as well." The teacher is fiddling with papers she needs for her next parent conference.
"Perhaps you didn't read Andy's file carefully. His cerebral palsy is so involved that he is not able to make any understandable speech sounds. We have already had him evaluated by a speech therapist at St. Luke's and they created the communication board for him so he could develop his language skills." The parent shakes her head and pushes a catalogue of language devices toward the childcare provider.	(Still looking at her other papers.) "We have an excellent speech language pathologist. She will have Andy talking in no time. Andy can work with her during circle time since that is oral and Andy wouldn't be able to participate."
"We don't want Andy to miss out on circle time. He loves to be a part of the group. We can choose appropriate pictures to put on his communication board so he can respond with the rest of the children. He gets very frustrated when he is not allowed to be with the rest of the students." The parent's shoulders tighten and she leans forward, thumping the catalogue of language devices to emphasize the use of the communication board.	"Oh, we don't let the children bring toys to the circle. He has to be able to speak up like everyone else. Also, I've been meaning to talk to you about his behavior. He has been refusing to cooperate with our group activities. I'd like to send him to time out when this happens."
(She gives a big sigh.) "As I said, he gets very frustrated when he isn't able to communicate and when he isn't a part of the group. I don't think time out would be the right answer for this problem."	"Well, if you don't allow us to control his behavior, I don't know how Andy is ever going to be able to be a part of our class." She looks at her watch, ready to end the meeting.
"We seem to have a different understanding of Andy's problems. Perhaps we need to meet as a team again, so the speech-language pathologist can also be involved. I'm concerned that you are not addressing Andy's communication needs." The parent's face is red, her hands are shaking as she pulls the catalogue back to her bag. The parent takes a deep breath, pulls her bag over her shoulder, and leaves, shaking her head as she goes.	"That would be fine, because I have another parent coming now and can't talk any longer. It has been a pleasure meeting with you today." The childcare provider smiles and shakes the parent's hand as she shuffles her papers together and heads toward the door to greet the next parent.

Source: Adapted from Howard, V. F., Williams, B. F., & Lepper, C. (2010). *Very young children with special needs: A foundation for educators, families, and service providers* (4th ed., p. 71). Upper Saddle River, NJ: Pearson. Used by permission.

ENCOURAGE It is important for parents to hear good news about their son or daughter. Describing or showing parents specific instances of their child's good behavior or improved performance encourages parental involvement.

STAY FOCUSED Although greetings and some small talk are desirable before getting down to business, conversations between parents and teachers should focus on the child's educational program and progress. Educators must be sensitive to cultural differences and the idiosyncratic conversational styles of individual families (Gonzalez-Mena, 2006; Lynch & Hanson, 2011). But teachers must also learn to notice when extended small talk is drifting too far from the purpose at hand so that they can refocus the conversation.

Parent–teacher communication is enhanced when teachers actively listen to what parents say.

Michael Newman/PhotoEdit

Identifying and Breaking Down Barriers to Parent–Teacher Partnerships

Let's face it: parents and teachers do not always communicate effectively and cooperate with one another. They may sometimes even seem to be on opposite sides, battling over what each thinks is best for the child. The child, unfortunately, never wins that battle. She needs to have the people responsible for the two places where she spends most of her life—home and school—work together to make those environments consistent with and supportive of her job of learning. Teachers should work to increase the likelihood that their interactions with parents and families are characterized by cooperation. They must be responsive to the practices and beliefs of families from diverse cultural backgrounds and identify and eliminate attitudes and behaviors that block family involvement.

PROFESSIONAL ROADBLOCKS TO COMMUNICATION Parents' and teachers' assumptions about and attitudes toward one another are sometimes counterproductive. Teachers sometimes complain that parents are uninterested, uncooperative, or hostile. Parents may complain that educators are negative, unavailable, or patronizing. We should examine factors that cause friction between parents and teachers, not to assign fault but to identify what we can change and improve. Professionals who recognize that some of their own behaviors may diminish the potential for productive partnerships with parents are in a better position to change their actions and obtain the benefits that such relationships can provide (Hanhan, 2008; Matuszny, Banda, & Coleman, 2007).

Although educators cannot directly change the attitudes of parents, they can—and, as professionals, must—identify and eliminate personal behaviors that may serve as barriers to communication with families. Some professionals hold stereotypes and false assumptions about what parents of children with disabilities must

Roadblocks to communication

Council for Exceptional Children Content Standards for Beginning Teachers—Common Core: Foster respectful and beneficial relationships between families and professionals (ICC10S3).

be feeling and what they must need (Dyson, 1996; Voltz, 1994). Such attitudes often lead to poor relationships between families and professionals. We should not be surprised if parents feel intimidated, confused, angry, hostile—or just terminate their involvement altogether—when professionals interact with them in any of the following ways:

- *Treating parents as vulnerable clients instead of equal partners.* Professionals who see parents only as people who need their help make a grave mistake. Teachers need parents and what they have to offer as much as parents need teachers.
- *Keeping professional distance.* Most professionals in human services develop some degree of distance to avoid getting too involved with a client—supposedly to maintain objectivity and credibility. But aloofness or coldness in the name of professionalism has hindered or terminated many parent–teacher relationships. Parents must believe that the educators working with their children really care about them (Nelson, Summers, & Turnbull, 2004).
- *Treating parents as if they need counseling.* Some professionals make the faulty assumption that having a child with disabilities causes a parent to need therapy or parent education. A mother of a child who attended a preschool for students with developmental delays described her frustration: "Everybody who came here was aimed at me. Everybody is telling me 'You need parent counseling.' I mean, I have lived for 30 years. I never needed help and all of a sudden I need help on how to do this and help on how to do that. I feel like they are saying John is not the problem, I am the problem" (Rao, 2000, p. 481).
- *Blaming parents for their child's disability.* Some parents do feel responsible for their child's disability and, with a little encouragement from a professional, can be made to feel completely guilty. A productive parent–professional relationship focuses on collaborative problem solving, not blame.
- *Disrespecting parents as less intelligent.* Teachers sometimes give too little recognition to parents' information and suggestions. They consider parents too biased, too involved, or too unskilled to make useful observations (Lake & Billingsley, 2000). Some professionals concede that parents have needed information but contend that parents cannot, or should not, make any decisions based on what they know. "They treat me like I'm uneducated. They break down things into real small pieces and then ask me to repeat things. I have gone to nursing school. I can read. Maybe they met other people who cannot read but they can ask me 'Rose, can you read?' They treat you like you are a child" (Rao, 2000, p. 481).
- *Treating parents as adversaries.* Some teachers expect the worst whenever they interact with parents. Even when that attitude can be partially explained by previous unpleasant encounters with unreasonable parents, it usually becomes a self-fulfilling prophecy and is at best a negative influence on new relationships.
- *Labeling parents.* Some educators seem eager to label parents (Sonnenschein, 1981). If parents disagree with a diagnosis or seek another opinion, they are denying; if parents refuse a suggested treatment, they are resistant; and if parents insist that something is wrong with their child despite test evidence to the contrary, they are anxious.

CONFLICT RESOLUTION   Not all ineffective parent–teacher relationships are caused by professional mishandling. Some parents are genuinely difficult to work with or unreasonable. Parents sometimes fight long and hard for services for their child. But after securing services and seeing that their child is receiving an appropriate education, the parents continue their intense advocacy until minor issues with professionals become major confrontations. One mother stated, "For years I have scrapped and fought for services. Now I come on like gangbusters over issues that are really not that important. I don't like what has happened to me. I've ended up to be an aggressive, angry person" (Bronicki & Turnbull, 1987, p. 10).

Although some teachers voice concern that parents of children with disabilities are unrealistic and make too many demands of schools (e.g., Chesley & Calaluce, 1997), most recognize that these parents, like all parents, are simply advocating for the best possible educational services and outcomes for their children. When someone sees things differently from us and we both have vested interests in the outcome, we often resort to argument in an attempt to resolve our differences. Although a teacher may "win" an argument with parents—if one defines winning as forcing the parents to agree verbally or simply give up their perspective—arguing is rarely a useful tool in a partnership.

Dialoguing. Dialoguing is an approach to conflict resolution in which both parties try to see each other's point of view. Gonzalez-Mena (2006) points out differences between a dialogue and an argument:

- The object of an argument is to win; the object of a dialogue is to gather information.
- The arguer tells; the dialoguer asks.
- The arguer tries to persuade; the dialoguer seeks to learn.
- The arguer tries to convince; the dialoguer wants to discover.
- The arguer sees two opposing views and considers hers the valid or best one; the dialoguer is willing to understand multiple viewpoints. (p. 117)

Most of us are better at arguing than we are at dialoguing. That's probably because we have had much more practice with the former. We tend to argue first and think rationally later. But later might be too late if in "winning" the argument, we have damaged the parent–teacher relationship. Gonzalez-Mena (2006) recommends using the RERUN approach—reflect, explain, reason, understand, and negotiate:

- *Reflect.* Acknowledge what you perceive the other person is thinking or feeling. If you understand what the person is feeling, you might say, "I think you're looking at it this way." If you perceive that the other person is very emotional, acknowledge your perception: "You sound really upset." These two openers are invitations for the person to talk more. People who know that their feelings and thoughts are received and accepted are more likely to be open to listening—if not right away, eventually.
- *Explain.* Explain your perspective concisely. But do not lecture. Remember, we have two ears and only one mouth—a reminder that we should listen twice as much as we talk.
- *Reason.* The explanation of your perspective should include the reason you believe or feel the way that you do.
- *Understand.* Next comes the hardest part. Tune in to both your own and the parent's thoughts and feelings, and try to understand the situation from both points of view. You don't have to say anything out loud at this point; just be sure you have clarity. You may have to talk inwardly to yourself to get it. Self-reflection is an important part of the process. When you think you understand, you're ready for the next step.
- *Negotiate.* Try brainstorming together until you can find a mutually satisfying solution. Don't give up. Refuse to take an either–or attitude. If you don't get stuck in a dualistic frame of mind, you can probably find a third or fourth solution that differs from or combines both of your stances on the matter. Creative negotiators can open up new avenues of action that no one has ever thought of before. (adapted from Gonzalez-Mena, 2006, p. 119)

Dialoguing to resolve conflicts

 Council for Exceptional Children

Content Standards for Beginning Teachers—Common Core: Foster respectful and beneficial relationships between families and professionals (ICC10S3).

Additional suggestions for effective communication and conflict resolution with parents can be found at the National Center on Dispute Resolution in Special Education (http://www.directionservice.org/cadre/), from the Pennsylvania Department of Education (2011), and in Dyches, Carter, and Prater (2012); McLamed and Reiman (2011); Montgomery (2005); Sileo and Prater (2012).

WORKING WITH CULTURALLY AND LINGUISTICALLY DIVERSE FAMILIES

Differences in the cultural beliefs and linguistic practices of professionals and families can serve as barriers to family involvement (Harry, 2008). Teachers who fail to recognize and respect differences between their own cultural perspectives and the values and beliefs of families are prone to biased and faulty judgments about parents that weaken the parent–teacher partnership.

Understanding and Respecting Cultural Differences

Cultural and linguistic differences

 Council for Exceptional Children

Content Standards for Beginning Teachers—Common Core: Potential impact of differences in values, languages, and customs that can exist between the home and school (ICC1K10) (also ICC3K3, ICC6K3, ICC10K4).

The demands and challenges faced by families who may be less educated, poor, or isolated from the dominant American culture may prevent them from becoming actively involved in school partnerships. The literature on culturally diverse families supports the following notions about these families (Araujo, 2009; Banks & Banks, 2013; Brandon & Brown, 2009; Cartledge, Kea, & Ida, 2000; Correa, Jones, Thomas, & Morsink, 2005; Gollnick & Chinn, 2009; Lynch & Hanson, 2011; Olivos, 2009):

Many families are English-language learners (ELL). In 2000, one in five people in the United States 5 years old and older spoke a language other than English at home. From the 1997–98 school year to the 2008–09 school year, the number of English-language learners enrolled in public schools increased from 3.5 million to 5.3 million, or by 51% (National Clearinghouse for English Language Acquisition, 2011). During the same period, the general population of students grew by 7.2%, to 49.5 million. Inability to understand the language of the school is a major deterrent to parents who have not achieved full English proficiency. In these cases, interactions with the schools are difficult at best and often practically nonexistent. Schools should provide materials in both the native language and in English and preferably communicate with the family directly through home visits or by telephone. Many parents of English language learner (ELL) students believe that their participation does not help schools perform their jobs as educational institutions; as a result, they separate themselves from the process.

In some cultures, such as many Hispanic ones, teaming with the school is not a tradition. Education has been historically perceived as the responsibility of the schools, and parent intervention is viewed as interference with what trained professionals are supposed to do.

Many families live in low-income and poverty. In 2010, 22% of all children in the United States were living in poverty (Annie E. Casey Foundation, 2011). But the situation is worse for children with disabilities and those from families who are English language learners. In 2000, Fujira and Yamaki reported that 28% of children with disabilities lived below the federal poverty line, and material hardships for families raising children with disabilities have worsened since then (Parish, Rose, Grinstein-Weiss, Richman, & Andrews, 2008). Two-thirds of children of ELL parents come from low-income families (Comacho, 2007).

Practitioners should understand that although the parents may not have finished school or cannot read, they are "life educated" and know their child better than anyone else does. In Spanish, the term *educado* (educated) does not mean "formal schooling" but means that a child is skilled in human relations, well mannered, respectful of adults, and well behaved.

If families are undocumented immigrants, they are naturally fearful of interaction with anyone representing authority. Building families' trust and cooperation, even if they are undocumented immigrants, is important. The special educator's role is not to engage in the activities of the Office of Immigration and Naturalization Services. The school's focus is on educating children, who by law are not a suspect class (Correa, Gollery, & Fradd, 1988).

Families from culturally diverse backgrounds tend to be family oriented. Extended family members—*compadre*s or *padrinos* (godparents) in the Hispanic culture—may play important roles in child rearing and family decisions. A child's disability or even a mild language problem may be an extremely personal subject for discussion with outsiders, and families may seek solutions for problems within the family structure. It is important for educators to respect this informal kinship system of support and to understand that schooling may represent a much more formal and impersonal support service for some families. The close, insular aspect of a family is a strength that helps the family function and cope with the stresses sometimes associated with raising a child with a disability (Bailey, Skinner, Correa, Arcia, et al., 1999; Rueda, Monzo, Shapiro, Gomez, & Blacher, 2005).

Culturally diverse families may have different experiences with and views about disability, and some may hold idiosyncratic ideologies and practices about the cause and treatment of disability. For example, in some Hispanic cultures, parents may believe that God sent the child with disabilities to them as a gift or blessing, while others may believe the child was sent as a test or a punishment for previous sins. In studies on Latino families, parents acknowledged transforming their lives since the birth of their child by becoming better parents (Bailey, Skinner, Correa, Arcia, et al., 1999; Bailey, Skinner, Correa, Blanes, et al., 1999). Many Native American cultural/tribal groups do not consider the birth of a child with a disability to be a negative or tragic event. Health and physical characteristics that might be defined as disabilities in mainstream culture may be framed as special strengths rather than deficiencies. "Native American societies have an uncanny gift for tolerance" (Boyd-Ball, 2007, n.p.).

A culturally responsive educator strives to develop awareness of and respect for the beliefs and values held by parents and family members from diverse cultural groups.

© Blend Images/Alamy

Although previous studies have reported the existence of folk beliefs and alternative treatments for disabilities in some cultural groups, more recent research finds that for Puerto Rican and Mexican families such beliefs are not prevalent (Bailey, Skinner, Correa, Blanes, et al., 1999; Skinner, Correa, Skinner, & Bailey, 2001). Families did report knowing about *el mal ojo* (the evil eye) or *el susto* (a scare or fright experienced by the pregnant mother) as explanations given for disabilities but did not believe them to be true of their own children. They reported that some family members (usually the elders) might believe that to cure the child, the family must make *mandas* (offerings to God or a Catholic saint) or seek the help of a *curandero* (a local healer). However, almost all families interviewed used traditional Western medicine to treat their children with disabilities.

Many low-income parents view schooling as an incomprehensible and purposely exclusionary system. Lack of trust is often the result of misunderstanding the perceived intentions of each party. Sending home communications in English only and scheduling meetings at times when parents cannot attend serve to reinforce parent apprehension. Professionals often misperceive parents' lack of involvement that results from mistrust and apprehension as a lack of concern for the children's education.

Many parents from culturally and linguistically different families have had negative education experiences of their own, and these memories linger through adulthood. In some cases, these parents have fallen victim to racial and linguistic discrimination by the schools. Negative feelings toward home–school interaction are often reinforced when schools communicate with parents only to share bad news about their children. Parents who feel uncomfortable in the school setting are less likely to be involved than those who have developed a sense of equal partnership are.

The educational system—in particular, the special education system—may be intimidating to the family. Although this may be true for any family, regardless of cultural or linguistic background, for a non-English-speaking family or one that is less well educated and poor, a professional's use of educational jargon may be especially intimidating. Some families may even put the professional on a pedestal and, believing the professional is the expert, not question or comment on their own wishes for their child's education.

Although it is important that professionals understand the cultural and linguistic practices of the community and families they serve, an important caveat must be stated: Just as professionals should refrain from making assumptions about how the parents of a child with a disability feel based on some model or theory of adjustment, educators must also avoid the error of assuming that all members of a cultural or ethnic group share the same experience, values, or beliefs.

Culturally Responsive Services for Families

Educators can increase the involvement of families from culturally and linguistically diverse backgrounds by using strategies such as the following (Al-Hassan & Gardner, 2002; Araujo, 2009; Brandon & Brown, 2009; Harry, 2008; Matuszny et al., 2007; Olivos, 2009; Tam & Heng, 2005):

- Have native-speaking staff members make initial contacts.
- Provide trained, culturally sensitive interpreters during parent–teacher conferences and IEP/IFSP meetings.
- When a language interpreter is not available, use a **cultural interpreter** whenever possible for conferences and family interviews. A cultural interpreter does not have to speak the family's native language, but must "have enough of a basic understanding of the home culture to help the school understand that home culture and to help the family understand school culture, policies, and practices" (Gabel, 2004, p. 23).
- Conduct meetings in family-friendly settings.
- Identify and defer to key decision makers in the family.
- Recognize that families from diverse cultures may view time differently from the way professionals do, and schedule meetings accordingly.
- Provide transportation and child care to make it easier for families to attend school-based activities.

CULTURAL RECIPROCITY Educators should also work toward **cultural reciprocity,** understanding how differing values and belief systems may influence families' perspectives, wishes, and decisions. For example, a special educator who views disability as a physical phenomenon that can be assessed and treated objectively may have difficulty developing an effective partnership with parents who view disability as a blessing or a punishment that is to be treated with a spiritual perspective (Bailey, Skinner, Correa, Arcia et al., 1999; Harry, Rueda, & Kalyanpur, 1999).

Recognizing differences between our own perspectives and those of people from other cultures and ethnic groups requires careful examination of our own cultural background and belief system. "Understanding that our own beliefs and practices are but one cultural variation should make it easier to respect, and therefore to serve, the wide diversity of families whose children are served by special education programs" (Harry, 2003, p. 138). See Figure 4, "Building Cultural Reciprocity."

FIGURE 4   BUILDING CULTURAL RECIPROCITY

Professionals who seek to make a difference for children must be willing to take the initiative in building a bridge between the cultures of diverse families and the culture of schools. To build this bridge, Beth Harry recommends that professionals initiate a two-way process of information sharing and understanding called *cultural reciprocity*. The process is recursive, meaning that each step informs the others.

- **Step 1.** Identify the cultural values embedded in your interpretation of a student's difficulties or in a recommendation for service. Ask yourself which values underlie your recommendation. Next, analyze experiences that have contributed to your holding of these values. Consider the roles of nationality, culture, socioeconomic status, and professional education in shaping your values.
- **Step 2.** Find out whether the family being served recognizes and values your assumptions and, if not, how family members' views differ from yours.
- **Step 3.** Acknowledge and give explicit respect to any cultural differences identified, and fully explain the cultural basis of your assumptions.
- **Step 4.** Through discussion and collaboration, determine the most effective way of adapting your professional interpretations or recommendations to the value system of this family.

Harry points out that "by developing your own cultural self-awareness, you are able to recognize the cultural underpinnings of your professional practice. This, in turn, enables you to facilitate conversations with the families." Through the process, families also acquire knowledge about the special education system, which supports them in making informed decisions about services. "With cultural reciprocity, we find not only better relationships, but more reasonable goals that are implemented."

Source: Adapted from ERIC/OSEP Special Project. (2001). *Family involvement in special education* (Research Connections in Special Education, no. 9, pp. 4–5). Arlington, VA: ERIC Clearinghouse on Disabilities and Gifted Education.

Cultural reciprocity

 Content Standards for Beginning Teachers—Common Core: Culturally responsive factors that promote effective communication and collaboration with individuals with exceptional learning needs, families, school personnel, and community members (ICC10K4) (also ICC3K4, ICC6K3).

HOME–SCHOOL COMMUNICATION METHODS

No single method of communication will be effective or even appropriate with every parent and family. By making a variety of communication avenues available to families, teachers can increase the number of families they reach and the frequency and quality of communications. Some families prefer face-to-face meetings; others appreciate receiving written messages or phone calls; still others feel more comfortable communicating with teachers through e-mail messages (Stuart, Flis, & Rinaldi, 2006). Teachers should ask parents which methods of communication they prefer.

Parent–Teacher Conferences

Parent–teacher conferences are a universal method of home–school communication. In a face-to-face meeting, teachers and parents can exchange information and coordinate their efforts to assist the child with disabilities in school and at home. Unfortunately, parent–teacher conferences are often stiff, formal affairs with anxious teachers and worried parents wondering what bad news they will hear this time. With some thoughtful planning and a systematic approach to conducting parent–teacher conferences, however, teachers can improve the productivity and comfort for all participants.

PREPARING FOR THE CONFERENCE   Preparation is the key to an effective parent–teacher conference. It entails establishing specific objectives for the conference, reviewing a record of the student's recent grades, selecting examples of the student's work, perhaps creating a graph or chart showing his cumulative progress, and preparing an agenda for the meeting (Dardig, 2008; Kroth & Edge, 2007). Figure 5 shows an outline that teachers can use to prepare an agenda and record notes of a parent–teacher conference.

CONDUCTING THE CONFERENCE   The child's classroom is an appropriate setting for most parent–teacher conferences because it provides ready access to student records and curriculum materials and reminds the teacher and parents that the purpose of the

Planning and conducting parent–teacher conferences

 Content Standards for Beginning Teachers—Common Core: Plan and conduct collaborative conferences with individuals with exceptional learning needs and their families (ICC10S5) (also ICC7S3).

FIGURE 5   OUTLINE FOR A PARENT–TEACHER CONFERENCE

Conference Outline

Date _____ 2-11-13 _____   Time _____ 4:30 - 5:30 _____

Student's Name _____ Jeremy Wright _____
Parents' Name(s) _____ Barbara and Tom Wright _____
Teacher's Name _____ Tim G. _____
Other Staff Present _____ None _____

Objectives for Conference: (1) Show graph of J's reading progress, (2) find out about spelling program,
    (3) get parents' ideas: intervention for difficulties on playground/in gym, (4) share list of books for leisure reading

Student's Strengths   • good worker academically, wants to learn
    • excited about progress in reading fluency

Area(s) Where Improvement Is Needed: • continue w/spelling @ home
    • arguments & fighting w/other kids

Questions to Ask Parents: • Interactions w/friends while playing in neighborhood?
    • How would they feel about f'dback from classmate re: playground/gym behavior?
    • Consequences?

Parents' Responses/Comments: • very pleased w/reading - want to build on it.
    • wondering how long w/in-home spelling?
    • willing to give rewards @ home: playground/gym

Examples of Student's Work/Interactions: • graph of corrects/errors per min.: reading
    • weekly pre- & post-test scores: spelling.

Current Programs and Strategies Used by Teacher: • reading: silent read, two 1-min. time trials, self-charting
        comprehension practice
    • spelling: practice w/tape recorder, self-checking

Suggestions for Parents: • continue spelling games (invite friends)
    • Show interest in/play fantasy games (Dung. & Dragons) w/J

Suggestions from Parents: • Try using some high-interest spelling words (e.g., joust, castle)
    • Matt & Amin could help with playground/gym program

Follow-up Activities: (Agreed to in conf)
    Parents: • Continue to play spelling game 2 nights per week
        • Take J to library for adventure books
    Teacher: • Ask J for high-interest words & use 3-4 in his weekly list.
        • Develop peer intervention strategy w/Matt, Amin & J (group contingency?)

Date to Call for Follow-up:
        Feb. 21 (Tuesday) _____ (check when called)

conference is to work together to improve the child's education. Wherever parent conferences are held, the area should be arranged so that it is conducive to partnership interactions. Teachers should not sit behind their desks, creating a barrier between themselves and the parents, or have parents sit in undersized children's chairs.

A four-step sequence for conducting parent–teacher conferences recommended by Stephens and Wolf (1989) more than 20 years ago remains sound advice today:

1. *Build rapport.* Establishing mutual trust and the belief that the teacher really cares about the student is important to a good parent–teacher conference. A minute or two devoted to relevant small talk helps build rapport. Instead of beginning with a superficial statement about the weather or traffic, the teacher might begin by commenting on some recent news or community or national event that is likely to be of interest to the family or their child.

2. *Obtain information.* Parents can provide teachers with important information for improving instruction. As suggested earlier, teachers should use open-ended questions that cannot be answered with a simple yes or no. For example, "Which school activities has Felix mentioned lately?" is better than "Has Felix told you what we've been doing in school?" The first question encourages parents to provide more information; the teacher is trying to build a conversation, not preside over a question-and-answer session. Throughout the conference, the teacher should show

genuine interest in listening to parents' concerns, avoid dominating the conversation, and stay focused on the purpose of the meeting. Teachers should refrain from making gestures, facial expressions, and other forms of "body language" that suggest frustration, suspicion, confrontation, or defensiveness. Above all, professionals should not make comments that lecture ("Do you realize . . ."), criticize or judge ("That was a mistake . . ."), or threaten ("Unless you take my advice . . .") (Fiedler, Simpson, & Clark, 2007; Hanhan, 2008).

Showing parents examples of their children's progress sets the occasion for parental praise and approval of student effort.

© Michael Newman/PhotoEdit

3. *Provide information.* The teacher should give parents concrete information about their child in jargon-free language. The teacher should share examples of schoolwork and data on student performance—what the student has already learned and what he needs to learn next. If the student has made insufficient progress, the teacher and parents should discuss ways to improve it.

4. *Summarize and follow up.* The conference should end with a concise summary of the discussion and any decisions that were made. The teacher should review strategies agreed on during the conference and indicate the activities that either party has agreed to do to help carry out those strategies. Some teachers record notes on a laptop computer during the conference and at the conclusion of the meeting print a copy so that parents will also have a record of what was said or agreed to.

These strategies are relevant for all types of parent–teacher meetings. However, IEP, IFSP, and transition planning meetings entail additional procedural requirements. You can find detailed suggestions for planning and conducting parent–teacher conferences in Dardig (2008), Hanhan (2008), and Kroth and Edge (2007).

Written Communication

Although much can be accomplished in a face-to-face meeting, parent–teacher conferences should not be the sole means of home–school communication. Written messages, especially when part of a systematic program of ongoing information exchange, can be an effective way to maintain home–school communication.

Teachers should never rely on written messages, regardless of their form, as the sole method of communicating with parents. Educators must also be sensitive to the cultural and linguistic backgrounds and educational levels of parents (Al-Hassan & Gardner, 2002). A study of parents' rights documents published by state departments of education found that only 4% to 8% of the materials were written at the recommended reading level for parents (Fitzgerald & Watkins, 2006). Up to 50% of the documents were written at the college reading level or higher, and "nearly all lacked additional organizational and textual features that would make them more readable" (p. 507). If parents must spend a great deal of time trying to understand the written

Home–school written communications

Council for Exceptional Children

Content Standards for Beginning Teachers—Common Core: Involve the individual and family in setting instructional goals and monitoring progress (ICC7S3).

109

messages from their child's school, they may view those messages as a nuisance and be discouraged from active involvement in their child's education.

HAPPY GRAMS AND SPECIAL ACCOMPLISHMENT LETTERS   The simplest type of home–school written message is a brief note informing parents of something positive their child has accomplished at school. Many teachers regularly send students home with such "happy grams," giving parents an opportunity to praise the child at home and stay abreast of activities in the classroom.

A letter to parents detailing the accomplishment of an important milestone or special achievement by their child is an excellent way to build a partnership. For an example of such a letter and suggestions for developing a system for writing them, see *Teaching & Learning*, "A Parent Appreciation Letter."

TWO-WAY HOME–SCHOOL REPORTING FORMS   Teachers can build a two-way, parent–teacher communication system around a reporting form or a notebook that the child carries between home and school. Teachers can develop and use a standard form or checklist such as the one shown in Figure 6 to inform parents about their child's

> A book by M. L. Kelly (1990) includes tear-out masters of school–home notes that teachers can duplicate and use for a variety of communication purposes.

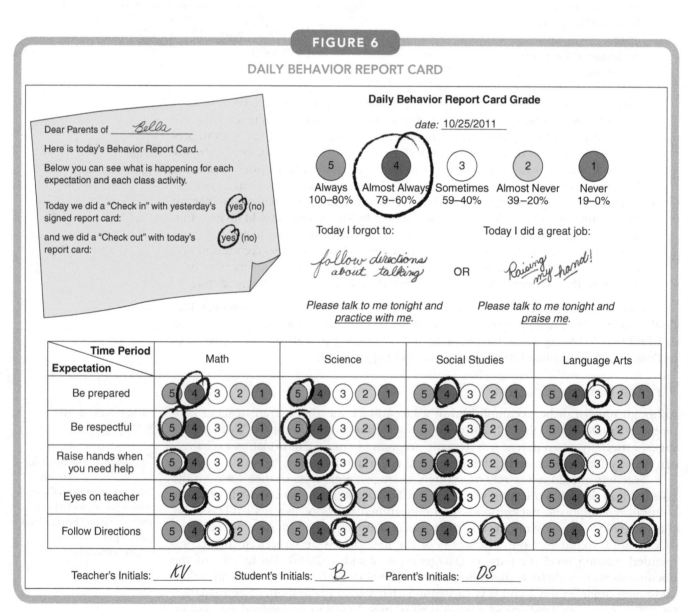

FIGURE 6

DAILY BEHAVIOR REPORT CARD

Source: Figure from ELECTRONIC DAILY BEHAVIOR REPORT CARD (E DBRC): A WEB BASED SYSTEM FOR PROGRESS MONITORING by Tufan Adiguzel, Denise Soares and Kimberly Vannest. Copyright © 2011 by Adiguzel, Soares and Vannest. Reprinted with permission.

homework assignments, behavior in the classroom, progress on IEP goals (Olympia, Andrews, Valum, & Jensen, 1993; Vannest, Burke, Payne, Davis, & Soares, 2011; Vannest, Davis, Davis, Mason, & Burke, 2010). Parents sign the form to indicate they have received it and can use the form themselves to provide information or request assistance from the teacher(s). To be most effective, home–school communication forms should be simple to use, with spaces for teachers and parents to circle or check responses and to write short notes to one another.

DIALOGUE NOTEBOOKS Home–school dialogue notebooks offer another form of written communication between parents and teachers (Davern, 2004; Hall, Wolfe, & Bollig, 2003). Teachers and parents write observations about the child's behavior or progress each day and write comments or questions to each other. Dialogue notebooks are the most time-consuming but are very effective with some families. In describing a notebook system that a teacher used to communicate regularly with the parents of children with emotional and behavioral disorders. Williams and Cartledge (1997) emphasize the importance of being organized, persistent, and flexible in expectations for parent participation.

HOME–SCHOOL CONTRACTS A home–school contract specifies parent-delivered rewards for the child contingent on her behavior or academic performance in the classroom. For example, Kerr and Nelson (2010) describe a home–school contract developed by the teacher and parents of a child who disrupted a daily academic "warm-up" activity with singing and other attention-getting behavior. The parents agreed to help their son with textbook reading each night so he was prepared for the warm-up activity and to buy him a ticket for the high school football game each week he completed all of the warmups correctly. Home–school contracts use parent-controlled rewards, build in parent recognition and praise of the child's accomplishments, and involve the teacher and parents together in a positive program to support the child's learning.

CLASS NEWSLETTERS AND WEBSITES Class newsletters and websites are additional methods of fostering home–school communication. Although producing a newsletter or designing a website requires a lot of work, it can be worth the effort. Most teachers today have access to a computer and word-processing software. A one- or two-page monthly newsletter can provide parents information that is too long or detailed to give over the telephone. A newsletter is also an excellent way to recognize parents who participate in various activities. Featuring student-produced stories, photos, and news items in a class newsletter or website transforms a teacher task into an enjoyable and meaningful learning activity for the entire class.

Telephone Communication

PHONE CALLS Regular telephone calls can be an effective and efficient way to maintain home–school communication and parent involvement. A brief conversation that focuses on a child's positive accomplishments lets parents and teachers share the child's success and recognize each other's contributions. Short, positive calls from the teacher also reduce parents' fear that calls from school always indicate a problem. Teachers should set aside time on a regular basis so that each child's parent receives a call at least once every 2 or 3 weeks. Teachers should ask parents what times they prefer to receive calls. Keeping a log helps to maintain the schedule and reminds teachers of any necessary follow-up.

VOICE MAIL Telephone answering machines are a convenient, low-cost technology for home–school communication. By recording daily messages on an answering machine, teachers can give parents a great deal of information for relatively little cost. Parents can call and listen at their convenience, literally 24 hours a day. Recorded telephone messages can provide schoolwide and classroom-by-classroom information, good news (e.g., citizen of the month), serve as a homework hotline (Dardig, 2008), and provide parents with suggestions for working with their children at home

Additional examples of Daily Behavior Report Cards such as the one shown in Figure 6, and guidelines for using them are available at http://edbrc.tamu.edu/.

Englund (2009) details procedures for designing a website where parents can access an e-portfolio of their child's progress.

A Parent Appreciation Letter

JILL C. DARDIG

Once in a while I receive a thank-you note from a student. Sometimes these notes are handwritten; nowadays most are e-mailed. No matter what the mode of transmission, getting one of these letters really makes my day—a little positive recognition goes a long way!

A student's note might thank me for doing a small thing such as writing a reference letter, for taking the time to listen about a problem or challenge with which they are dealing, for teaching a class they really enjoyed, or for helping with something more substantial such as helping them obtain a summer job, teaching position, or another significant matter over the course of their college experience.

Like teaching, parenting can be a challenging and exhausting enterprise, especially when parenting a child whose special needs require extended energy and intensive support. In addition, many parents of children with disabilities have a history of receiving negative or problem-oriented letters and phone calls from school concerning their child. And when they do,

these parents may feel that their children's difficulties reflect poorly on them, making their jobs as parents even more stressful.

What can a teacher do to recognize and show appreciation for the efforts, endurance, and successes of parents of children with special needs? A Parent Appreciation Letter, which celebrates their child's achievement, whether big or small, is a wonderful way to tell parents that you share in their joy when their child takes a step forward, and to congratulate them on their contribution to this happy event.

How to Get Started

Make a "Special Accomplishments Chart." Set up a "Special Accomplishments Chart" to record special achievements of all of the students in your class on an ongoing basis. Keep the chart on a clipboard or in a notebook in a handy place in your classroom. The chart shown here includes examples of entries by teachers across a range of grade levels.

Student	Accomplishment and Significance	Date	Letter Sent to Parents?
Laura—preschool	Put her coat on without help and quickly while in her wheelchair before recess; this may seem like a small thing, but it's a big step towards her achieving independence and fitting in with her peers.	10/6	Yes, 10/6
Martha—2nd grade	Inserted and kept her hearing aid in and turned on to proper volume every day without reminders; this enables her to comprehend instructions and lesson content; she's on top of everything this week!	10/6	Yes, 10/6
Akeelah—4th grade	Spelling test improvement—earned 100% on advanced grade-level tests 3 weeks in a row in a subject she had been struggling with; she showed motivation and commitment to study every day at school and at home— her regular class teacher noted this progress.	10/6	Not yet
Carlo—7th grade	Orientation & mobility—using his cane, Carlo successfully traveled from resource room to inclusion class on a different floor of the school building by himself; I know he's working on independent travel at home and out in the community; he expressed pride in his accomplishment and has mentioned that he may not need a buddy to accompany him to the restroom and lunchroom anymore!	10/9	Not yet
Lee—8th grade	Social behavior—on several occasions, chose appropriate option (calmly moved on to the next section, came back later to work on difficult problem) when frustrated with written	10/15	Yes, 10/15

	work, then tried again and was successful; politely asked teacher for help on another occasion; also helped a classmate make an appropriate choice; these behaviors will serve him well next year in high school.		
Branden— sophomore in high school	Vocational—at nursing home work-study placement, increased speed and accuracy of serving lunches to residents; served entire floor in a half hour and still had time for some very nice conversations with the residents (they love and appreciate Branden and his nice sense of humor); got a rave review from his supervisor, possible future career?	10/16	Yes, 10/19
Jordan—senior in high school	Excelled in our math unit on handling checking and savings accounts; these skills will be so useful for her in the near future; she expressed an interest in having an actual bank account and learning more about budgeting.	10/16	Not yet

Transform Notes on Chart to Letters. Each week or two, select one or more students whose parents will receive a Parent Appreciation Letter. Each letter should state its purpose, identify and provide some interesting detail about the student's achievement, explain the importance of the achievement, thank the parents for helping their child succeed in school, and provide a link between the current accomplishment and future successes. (See the letter, below.)

If you send a Parent Appreciation Letter by surface mail or with the student (rather than by e-mail), don't be surprised if your student tells you that the letter is on the refrigerator door at home for the entire family to enjoy.

Mrs. Stacy Walker
School
Address
Phone and E-mail

Dear Mr. and Mrs. Gonzales,

I want to let you know that Martha has responded so well to our program that teaches her to insert her hearing aid and keep it in place and turned to the correct volume all day.

After several weeks of practice both at school and at home, Martha is now completely independent on this task and does not have to be reminded to do so. The checklist Martha uses every morning and after lunch has allowed her to successfully monitor her own behavior, and I think the reminder should not even be necessary after she is successful for a few more weeks.

For the past few weeks, I have noticed that Martha responds to my instructions immediately, is following oral directions about her schoolwork correctly the first time they are given, and is interacting more with her classmates during small group work and during specials. To a great extent, her progress seems to have eliminated most of her confusion and frustration about what she needs to do while in class and what her classmates are saying to her that she previously misunderstood or missed entirely.

Please keep me informed after Martha's next visit to the audiologist so that I can make any necessary modifications to the use and care of her hearing aid.

Martha is a lovely girl and a delight to have in my class. Thanks for all you have done to work with Martha and me on her "Aid-In" program.

Sincerely,
Mrs. Stacy Walker

Source: Excerpts from INVOLVING PARENTS OF STUDENTS WITH SPECIAL NEEDS: 25 READY TO USE STRATEGIES by Jill C. Dardig, 2008, 1st Edition. Copyright © 2008 by Jill C. Dardig. Reprinted with permission by SAGE Publications.

(Heward, Heron, Gardner, & Prayzer, 1991). Parent callers can also leave messages on the machine, pose a question, offer an idea or suggestion for the teacher, and so on. Contrast these 10 guidelines with the professional roadblocks to communication described earlier.

E-MAIL AND TEXT MESSAGING   Educators and families are increasingly communicating with one another via e-mail, text messaging and "Internet-based" options (Bouffard, 2008).

Teachers have developed other strategies for home–school communication in addition to the methods described here (e.g., classroom bulletin board that informs parents and families of upcoming events and curriculum foci [Dardig, 2005, 2008]). Whatever system of home–school communication a school or teacher uses, it should not be "one size fits all families" but tailored to meet each family's needs and preferences (Stuart et al., 2006, p. 48).

Regardless of the mode of parent–teacher communication or differences in cultural experiences and language backgrounds of the participants, educators should follow the suggestions shown in Figure 7 in their interactions with parents and families.

Companies now offer Internet-based communication options for schools are now offered by several companies such as HomeworkNow (http://www.homeworknow.com/).

Guidelines for communicating with parents

 Content Standards for Beginning Teachers—Common Core: Foster respectful and beneficial relationships between families and professionals (ICC10S3) (also ICC1K7, ICC9S7).

FIGURE 7   TEN GUIDELINES FOR COMMUNICATING WITH PARENTS AND FAMILIES

1. *Don't assume that you know more about the child, his needs, and how those needs should be met than his parents do.* If you make this assumption, you will usually be wrong and, worse, miss opportunities to obtain and provide meaningful information.

2. *Junk the jargon.* Educators whose speech is laced with technical terminology will have difficulty communicating effectively with parents (or with anyone else, for that matter). Speak in clear, everyday language and avoid the "alphabet soup" of special education (e.g., FAPE, IFSP, MFE).

3. *Don't let assumptions and generalizations about parents and families guide your efforts.* Do not assume a parent is in the *x, y,* or *z* stage of adjustment and therefore needs *a, b,* or *c* type of support or program. If you are genuinely interested in what a father or mother feels and wants, and you should be, ask.

4. *Be sensitive and responsive to the cultural and linguistic backgrounds of parents and families.* The information and support services desired by families from diverse cultural and ethnic groups vary, and majority educators must work to be sensitive to those differences.

5. *Don't be defensive or intimidated.* Unless you are one, you cannot ever really know what parenting a child with disabilities is like. But as a trained teacher, you do know something about helping children with disabilities learn. That's your job; it's what you do every day. Offer families the knowledge and skills you have without apology, and welcome their input.

6. *Refer families to other professionals when needed.* As a teacher, you interact with parents and families in an effort to improve the child's educational progress. You are not a marriage counselor, therapist, or financial advisor. If a parent or a family member indicates the need for non–special education services, offer to refer him or her to professionals and agencies qualified to provide them.

7. *Help parents strive for a realistic optimism.* Children with disabilities and their families benefit little from professionals who are doom-and-gloom types or who minimize the significance of a disability. Help parents analyze, plan, and prepare for their child's future.

8. *Start with something parents can be successful with.* When parents show an interest in helping their child at home, don't set them up to fail by giving them complicated materials, complex instructions, and a heavy schedule of nightly tutoring. Begin with something simple that is likely to be rewarding to the parent and the child.

9. *Respect a parent's right to say no.* Most educators are eager to share what they know and to help families plan and carry out shared teaching goals. But professionals sometimes "fail to recognize the more basic needs of families, one of which is to not need a professional support person! . . . there comes a time when parents and other members of the family wish to be left alone" (J. S. Howard et al., 2005, p. 124).

10. *Don't be afraid to say, "I don't know."* Sometimes parents will ask questions that you cannot answer or request services you cannot provide. A mark of a true professional is knowing the limits of your expertise and when you need help. It is okay to say, "I don't know." Parents will think more highly of you.

OTHER FORMS OF PARENT INVOLVEMENT

Lim's (2008) definition of parent involvement as "any activities that are provided and encouraged by the school and that encourage parents in working on behalf of their children's learning and development" (p. 128) is a good one because it recognizes the wide variety of forms and levels at which parent involvement can occur and focuses on benefits for the child. Parents as tutors, parent education and support groups, and parents as research partners represent three very different types of parent involvement with a common purpose of educational benefits for children.

Parents as Tutors

Typically developing children acquire many skills that children with disabilities do not learn without systematic instruction. For children with disabilities, the casual routines of everyday life at home and in the community may not provide enough practice and feedback to teach them important skills. Many parents of exceptional children have responded to this challenge by systematically teaching their children self-help and daily living skills (e.g., Cavkaytar, 2007), assisting their children with homework (Patton, Jayanthi, & Polloway, 2001), providing home-based academic tutoring to supplement classroom instruction (Resetar et al., 2006), and teaching language and communication skills (Cooke, Mackiewicz, Wood, & Helf, 2009; Park, Alber Morgan, & Cannella-Malone, 2011)

The majority of parents who participate in systematic home tutoring programs organized by their child's teacher or school describe it as a positive experience for them and their children. A mother and father wrote: "We really enjoyed teaching M. to tell time, and he enjoyed working with us. He learned so quickly and we were so happy and proud to see the progress he was making. We have two other children. Doing this program allowed us to spend time alone with M" (Donley & Williams, 1997, p. 50).

Properly conducted home-based parent tutoring can enhance a child's educational progress and give enjoyment to both child and parent. Guidelines for home-based parent tutoring include the following:

- *Keep sessions short.* Aim for 15- to 20-minute sessions 3 or 4 days per week.
- *Make the experience positive.* Parents should praise the child's attempts.
- *Provide frequent opportunities for the child to respond.* Tutoring materials and activities should evoke numerous responses from the child rather than require the child to passively attend to a great deal of explanation and demonstration by the parent.

Parents as tutors

 Content Standards for Beginning Teachers—Common Core: Assist individuals with exceptional learning needs and their families in becoming active participants in the educational team (ICC10S4) (also ICC1K7).

When properly conducted, home-based parent tutoring sessions strengthen the child's educational programs and are enjoyable for the child and the parent.

© Blend Images/Alamy

- *Keep parent responses to the child consistent.* By praising the child's correct responses (materials and activities at the child's appropriate instructional level are a must) and providing a consistent, unemotional response to errors (e.g., "Let's read that word again, together"), parents can prevent the frustration and negative results that can occur when home tutoring is mishandled.

- *Use tutoring to practice and extend skills already learned in school.* For example, parents can use spelling or vocabulary words from school as the questions or items for adapted board games (Wesson, Wilson, & Higbee Mandelbaum, 1988), and parents can read storybooks to promote literacy skills (e.g., Tardáguila-Harth & Correa, 2007).

- *Keep a record.* Parents, like classroom teachers, can never know the exact effects of their teaching unless they keep records. A daily record enables both parents and child to see gradual progress that might be overlooked if subjective opinion is the only basis for evaluation. Most children do make progress under guided instruction, and a record documents that progress, perhaps providing the parent with an opportunity to see the child in a new and positive light. To read about a home-based parent-tutoring program that illustrates these recommendations, see *Teaching & Learning*, "A Talking Photo Album Helps Parents with Limited English Proficiency Teach Their Children English."

If parents wish to tutor their children at home, they should be helped to do so. Teachers should recognize, however, that not all parents want to teach their children at home. Some parents may feel that home tutoring will compete with other activities in the home and negatively affect their family's overall quality of life (Parette & Petch-Hogan, 2000). Others may not have the time to learn and use the necessary teaching skills. Professionals must not interpret such situations as indications that parents do not care enough about their children.

Parent Education and Support Groups

Parent education and parent support groups

Content Standards for Beginning Teachers—Common Core: Concerns of families of individuals with exceptional learning needs and strategies to help address these concerns (ICC10K3).

Education for parenting is not new; such programs date back to the early 1800s. Parent education programs can serve a variety of purposes and occur in different formats: from one-time-only events that inform parents of a new school policy, to make-it-and-take-it workshops in which parents make instructional materials to use at home (e.g., a math facts practice game), to multiple-session programs on IEP/IFSP planning or behavior support strategies. Research shows benefits of systematic parent education, particularly in programs that teach parents ways to interact with their children (McIntyre, 2008; Schultz, Schmidt, & Stichter, 2011).

Parents should be involved in planning and conducting parent groups as much as possible (Kroth & Edge, 2007; Turnbull et al., 2011). Educators can use both open and closed needs assessment procedures to determine what parents want from a parent program. An *open needs assessment* consists of questions such as these:

The best family time for my child is when we _____.
I will never forget the time that my child and I _____.
When I take my child to the store, I am concerned that she will _____.
The hardest thing about having a special child is _____.
I wish I knew more about _____.

A *closed needs assessment* asks parents to select from a list of topics they would like to learn more about. For example, educators can give parents a list of topics (e.g., bedtime behavior, interactions with siblings, homework, making friends, planning for the future) and ask them to check any item that is something of a problem and circle any topic that is a major concern or interest. Parents' and families' needs and preferences can also be assessed with an instrument that combines open and closed format items (Matuszny et al., 2007).

Parent-to-Parent Groups

Parent-to-parent (P2P) programs help parents of children with special needs become reliable allies for one another (Santelli, Poyadue, & Young, 2001). The programs give parents of children with disabilities the opportunity to receive support from a parent who has experienced similar circumstances and challenges. It carefully matches trained and experienced parents in a one-to-one relationship with parents who have been newly referred to the program. "Because the two parents share so many common disability and family experiences, an immediacy of understanding is typically present in the match. This makes the informational and emotional support from the veteran parents all the more meaningful" (Santelli, Turnbull, Marquis, & Lernet, 1997, p. 74). The first parent-to-parent program, called Pilot Parents, was formed in 1971 by the parent of a young child with Down syndrome in Omaha, Nebraska.

Parents as Research Partners

Researchers in special education are concerned about the social validity of their studies (Horner, Carr, et al., 2005). Are they investigating socially significant variables? Are the methods used to change student performance acceptable? Did the changes observed make any real difference in the child's life? Who better than parents to identify meaningful outcomes, observe and measure performance in the home and community, and let researchers know if their ideas and findings have any real validity?

When helping families assess their strengths and needs, professionals should not overlook the importance of leisure time.

© Jeff Greenberg/PhotoEdit

A model research-partnership program conducted at the Fred S. Keller School in New York embraces parents as full partners in conducting action research with their children. "The parents are the scientists, and they conduct empirical studies under the supervision of the schools' parent educators" (Donley & Williams, 1997, p. 46). Parents are assisted in the development of their research projects by their child's teachers, other parents, and a paid parent educator. The experience culminates with a poster session presentation at the end of the school year during which the parent-scientists display the academic, social, and affective gains that their children achieved. Donley and Williams recognize that some school programs do not have the resources to hire a parent educator. They provide several suggestions for schools with more limited resources to approximate their model.

Parent to Parent USA is a national nonprofit organization that supports the activities of hundreds of local parent-to-parent groups and 36 statewide programs (www.p2pusa .org).

How Much Parent Involvement?

It is easy to get carried away with a good concept, especially one like parent and family involvement, which has so much promise for positive outcomes. But teachers and other professionals who provide special education services to children with disabilities must not take a one-sided, unidirectional view of parent involvement. Sometimes the time and energy required for parents to participate in home-based tutoring programs or parent education groups cause stress among family members or guilt if the parents cannot fulfill teachers' expectations (Callahan, Rademacher, & Hildreth, 1998;. Turnbull et al., 2011). The time required to provide additional help to a child with disabilities may take too much time and attention away from other family members (Parette & Petch-Hogan, 2000).

A Talking Photo Album Helps Parents with Limited English Proficiency Teach Their Children English

BY ALLISON G. KRETLOW, SARA M. MACKIEWICZ, CHARLES L. WOOD, JACKLYN V. MIRABAL, AND NANCY L. COOKE

Ms. Reed, a school psychologist in an elementary school with a growing population of students who were learning English as a second language, faced a great challenge. Several new teachers asked her for guidance in teaching students who are learning English. Some of their students had recently moved to the United States and were still learning common English vocabulary words. Ms. Reed knew that increasing students' common English vocabulary would immediately impact their success in the classroom. Teachers often ask parents to practice at home the concepts taught at school; however, this approach was not an option because these students' parents were also English language learners.

A CHALLENGE FOR TEACHERS AND PARENTS

Ms. Reed felt frustrated because she knew the parents were interested in helping their children learn and succeed in school. These parents regularly attended parent–teacher conferences and participated in after school workshops. Ms. Reed needed to find a way for parents to help their children learn without requiring them to be proficient English speakers.

The challenges the parents at Ms. Reed's school faced are not unique, unfortunately. Many parents of students who are not proficient English speakers face similar challenges to providing home support to their children. In particular, studies have demonstrated that Hispanic parents, just like the parents in Ms. Reed's school, face many barriers to helping their children learn English and academics in the home (Klimes-Dougan, Lopez, Nelson, & Adelman, 1992).

Researchers have documented several reasons why these parents have difficulty helping their children learn (Johnson & Viramontez Anguiano, 2004; Ramirez, 2003). First, many parents of students who are learning English are not proficient English speakers themselves, which makes it very difficult for them to interact with their children's teachers, to get involved in school activities, and to help their children develop English vocabulary at home. For example, parents may not be able to read the directions on their children's homework, read or write notes about academic progress, or speak with their children's teachers about ways to help them at home.

Second, many parents who are learning English have limited formal education, which, when combined with limited English, increases the parents' difficulty in providing academic support in the home. Though research has shown that parent tutoring can be highly effective (e.g., Resetar et al., 2006), many parents with limited formal education may not read well in Spanish or English, which limits their adeptness to tutor their children using the typical tutoring materials a teacher might send home (e.g., workbooks, teacher-created materials in English).

Third, parents who are learning English may not have access to appropriate materials to help their children learn English (e.g., tutoring programs in Spanish and English, technology). Though some commercial materials for tutoring exist, many parents do not know they exist, do not know where to get them, or cannot afford to purchase them.

One afternoon while observing a classroom including students with and without special needs, Ms. Reed noticed a student using an assistive technology device called a Talking Photo Album™ (TPA) (Attainment Company, 2007) to communicate with his teacher and

---

Mirror model for parent involvement

Council for Exceptional Children

Content Standards for Beginning Teachers—Common Core: Models and strategies of consultation and collaboration (ICC10K1).

Kroth and Edge (2007) describe the mirror model for parent involvement (see Figure 8), which recognizes that parents have a great deal to offer as well as a need to receive services from special educators. The model attempts to give parents an equal part in deciding what services they need and what services they might provide to professionals or other parents. The top half of the model assumes that professionals have certain information, knowledge, and skills that they should share with parents to help them with their children. The bottom half of the model assumes that parents have information, knowledge, and skills that can help professionals be more effective

Charles L. Wood

Mother and daughter use a Talking Photo Album™ to learn English vocabulary together.

peers. Suddenly the idea came to her. "I bet parents could use these at home to tutor their children in English vocabulary."

PARENT TUTORING WITH A TALKING PHOTO ALBUM

A TPA is a battery-operated recording and playback device that looks like a small picture album. The book has 24 pages, and each page contains a recording device that can record up to 10 seconds of audio material. Pushing a button embedded on the edge of each page plays the recorded information. Teachers place pictures into each page by sliding a card into a clear pocket. The parent shows the child a picture, the child says the name of the picture (e.g., "umbrella"), the parent presses the button to hear the recording in English, and the parent provides appropriate feedback (e.g., "yes, umbrella" or "try again").

SUCCESS WITH PARENT TUTORING

Ms. Reed and the teachers were thrilled. Some students learned almost 100 new English vocabulary words in just a few months of parent tutoring with a TPA (Cooke et al., 2009). But that's not all: the parents acquired many new English words, too. Ms. Reed also learned

that her students' siblings, eager to participate, sometimes "chimed in" during home tutoring sessions or played "tutor and tutee" with the materials. This was a great success.

HOW TO GET STARTED

Educators interested in offering a TPA for home-based parent tutoring in English vocabulary will need to prepare the materials, teach parents how to use the materials, and evaluate the success of the program.

1. **Prepare the TPA.** Make a list of vocabulary words commonly found in the classroom, home, and/or community. Target 10 to 12 words at a time to use in the album. Place pictures of targeted vocabulary on each page and match the same pictures on the opposite sides. Make a clear audio recording of the corresponding English and Spanish words on each page. For more details, see Wood, Mackiewicz, Van Norman, and Cooke (2007).

2. **Teach parents how to tutor with a TPA.** Teach parents to use effective tutoring behaviors such as brisk pacing and corrective feedback. Send the prepared TPA home with students. Ask parents to tutor their children at least five times a week. Ask parents to send the TPA back to school at the end of each week.

3. **Evaluate the tutoring program.** Assess each student's mastery of new vocabulary frequently. This can be done using accuracy (i.e., the number of pictures named correctly) or fluency (i.e., the number of pictures named correctly in a preset number of minutes). Measure students' generalization of learned words by testing students to see if they can name the "real thing" (e.g., a refrigerator, a window) represented in the pictures they have learned. Replace cards with new pictures when students demonstrate that they have learned the words. For example, after checking students' progress weekly, replace learned cards with new cards and send any "not yet mastered" cards back home for more practice.

in assisting children. The model assumes that not all parents need everything that professionals have to offer and that no parent should be expected to provide everything. All parents should be expected to provide and obtain information, most will be active participants in IEP planning, and fewer will participate in or contribute to workshops and extended parent education groups.

Parents and family are the most important people in a child's life. Skilled and caring teachers should be next in importance. Working together, teachers, parents, and families can and do make a difference in the lives of exceptional children.

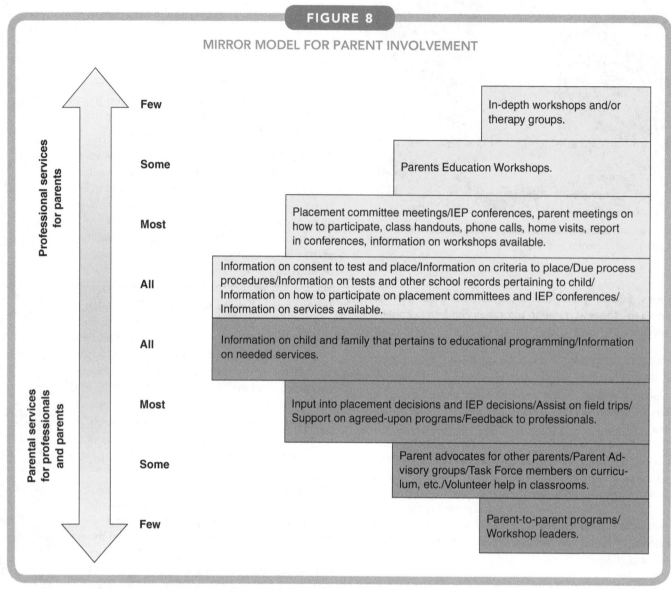

FIGURE 8

MIRROR MODEL FOR PARENT INVOLVEMENT

Source: Figure from COMMUNICATING WITH PARENTS AND FAMILIES, 4th Edition, by R.L. Kroth and D. Edge. Copyright © 2007 by Kroth and Edge. Reprinted with permission.

▼ TIPS FOR BEGINNING TEACHERS

Collaborating with Parents and Families

BY JOSHUA HOPPE

The most effective special educators create and nourish strong and comfortable partnerships with the families of their students. They do so by building rapport, communicating and listening effectively, and respecting where families are coming from in their wishes for their children.

BUILD RAPPORT

The importance of establishing and maintaining good rapport with the parents and families cannot be overstated. When rapport is established, parents will be more receptive to your suggestions and more willing to share more information about their child.

- **Take initiative.** Make contact with parents as soon as possible. Consider it your job to keep the lines of communication open. Call just to check in and see how everything is going at home and update parents on what is happening in school. If parents feel that you care about them and their child, you are well on your way to establishing rapport.

SPEAK PLAINLY, LISTEN FULLY, AND GET HELP WHEN NEEDED

Maximum effectiveness as a special educator requires meaningful two-way communication with parents and families. At minimum, a special educator should always do the following:

- **Speak in straightforward language.** When I first started teaching, I was nervous about my role and overcompensated. Wanting to sound knowledgeable and authoritative, I used far too much jargon and acronyms when speaking with parents. This was a misguided practice that I learned to avoid. You are required in IEP meetings to speak in plain, everyday language for a reason. Take the core concepts and frameworks you have learned in school to inform what you are saying, but say them as you would in a real world conversation.

- **Listen fully to what parents are saying.** Parents know their children better than anyone. By listening to them, you will gain a wealth of information. When parents feel that you really listen to them, they feel comfortable telling you their dreams and concerns for their child's future.

- **Get a translator when needed.** If you cannot communicate with a parent in his or her native tongue, find a resource who can. I was lucky enough to have a teacher who taught only one classroom away from me who was from the Philippines. When I started having difficulty communicating with a parent from the Philippines, I enlisted this teacher's help and was very grateful I did. If you are not so fortunate in having a resource this easily accessible, you will have to branch out. Talk to your administration or district resources and find an interpreter.

BE AWARE OF AND RESPECT DIFFERENT CULTURAL BELIEFS AND PRACTICES

Families' cultural beliefs and practices often affect their relationship with the school and the dominant culture. Educators who learn about and respect those differences will be more effective.

- **Learn how families' cultural differences affect students' participation in school activities and make adaptations.** The religious beliefs of one of my student's family did not include celebrating birthdays or holidays. Rather than eliminate holiday themed activities all together or exclude the child while the rest of my students enjoyed them, I spoke with the child's mother and found her reasonable and easy to work with. We decided that whenever a planned activity compromised the family's religious beliefs, we would come up with an adaptation to remove any connections that the family objected to. For example, if the other kids were making an Easter basket, she would just make a basket.

- **Understand how cultural differences influence parents' perceptions of Western service delivery models and search for comfortable mediums.** I had a student whose impulsivity and inattention to task severely hampered learning. Doctors recommended medication but the mother refused because her cultural belief was that taking medication might cause her son to become possessed by the devil or demons. Though I did not agree with her belief, I respected it, and we worked on other means of providing environmental support and shaping appropriate behavior. It is now a few years later, and her son has made tremendous progress without medication. This parent also had beliefs in a lot of other areas that affected service delivery. She did not want to accept outside help from the department of health for respite services because she thought they were going to take her son away. When a new individual support staff was assigned to her son, she became anxious and wanted the previous staff member reassigned, even though the new staff was full-time and trained in working with students with autism. Over time, she gained trust and was very happy with the new staff member and more open to receiving additional help at home.

- **Understand where to draw the line with respect to cultural practices and seek compromise.** One Pacific Island boy's family had a cultural belief about discipline that involved spanking the child with objects. This boy's extremely challenging behaviors frustrated and caused great stress for the family, and they employed a method to control his behavior at home they believed was effective and appropriate. When the student came to school with bruises, I had to intercede. I initiated a call to Child Protective Services and the school intervened. We were able to express that her cultural view of discipline was her right, but that a student showing up to school with bruises crossed a line.

I created a self-monitoring sheet on which the student would rate himself after each scheduled activity on how well he followed the behavioral and task expectations. I would guide him through and also write comments if he did exceptionally well or was exceptionally challenging. He took the self-monitoring sheet home and his mother signed it. If he did well for the entire day he received a reward at home. If he exhibited certain challenging behaviors, he was unable to engage in a preferred activity at home that evening. He would lose access to preferred activities for misbehavior and receive differential reinforcement with attention and access to preferred items for good behavior at home too. By adding these interventions to her parenting style, this mother was able to rely less on punishment to achieve behavioral change.

EXPECTATIONS

If you become a special educator, do not expect your job to be easy. You might find it helpful to create an identity for yourself that embodies all of the professional characteristics needed to do your job effectively. My mentor teacher went by a sort of *nom de guerre* to separate his work identity from his home identity. While at work he played a character that exemplified the tirelessly positive, attentive, and dedicated person a special education teacher needs to be. When he finished work, he could take that hat off and relax.

- Do expect to be amazed by what your students can achieve when you and their parents work together.

▼ KEY TERMS AND CONCEPTS

cultural interpreter
cultural reciprocity

respite care

▼ SUMMARY

Support for Family Involvement

- Three factors are responsible for the increased emphasis on parent and family involvement in the education of children with disabilities: parent advocacy, educators' desire to increase their effectiveness, and legislative mandates.
- A successful parent–teacher partnership provides benefits for the professional, the parents, and, most important, the child.

Understanding Families of Children with Disabilities

- Many parents experience similar sequences of emotions and challenges as they react and adjust to the birth or diagnosis of a child with a disability (e.g., shock, denial, grief, reflection, advocacy, appreciation).
- After a period of uncertainty, most families of children with disabilities exhibit strength and resilience, reestablish healthy family functioning, and become determined to do whatever they can to meet their children's needs and to move forward with an enlightened sense of optimism.
- Parents of children with disabilities fulfill at least nine roles and responsibilities: caregiver, provider, teacher, counselor, behavior support specialist, parent of siblings without disabilities, marriage partner, information specialist/trainer for significant others, and advocate for school and community services.
- A child's disability affects parents and siblings without disabilities in different ways during the different life-cycle stages of the family.
- Respite care—the temporary care of an individual with disabilities by nonfamily members—is a critical support for many families of children with severe disabilities.

Developing and Maintaining Family–Professional Partnerships

- Five principles of effective communication between educators and parents are accepting what is being said, active listening, questioning appropriately, encouraging, and staying focused.
- Attitudes of and behaviors by professionals that serve as barriers to communication with parents and families include making assumptions about the services and information that parents need, treating parents as clients or adversaries instead of partners, keeping professional distance, acting as if parents need counseling, blaming parents for their child's disability or performance, disrespecting parents' suggestions, and labeling parents who don't act the way the professionals believe they should.

- Dialoguing is an approach to conflict resolution in which both parties try to see each other's point of view.

Working with Culturally and Linguistically Diverse Families

- Differences in the cultural beliefs and linguistic practices of professionals and families often serve as barriers to parent involvement.
- Cultural interpreters help school personnel understand the home culture and help the family understand school culture, policies, and practices.
- Understanding differences between our own perspectives and those of people from other cultures and ethnic groups requires careful examination of our own cultural background and belief system.

Home–School Communication Methods

- The most common modes of home–school communication are parent–teacher conferences, written messages, and telephone calls. Teachers are using class newsletters, websites, and e-mail to communicate with families with increasing frequency and effectiveness.
- Ten guidelines for communicating with parents of children with disabilities:
  - Don't assume you know more about a child than the parents do.
  - Junk the jargon, and speak in plain, everyday language.
  - Don't let assumptions or generalizations guide your efforts.
  - Be sensitive and responsive to cultural and linguistic differences.
  - Don't be defensive toward or intimidated by parents.
  - Refer families to other professionals when needed.
  - Help parents strive for a realistic optimism.
  - Start with something that parents can be successful with.
  - Allow and respect parents' right to say no.
  - Don't be afraid to say, "I don't know."

Other Forms of Parent Involvement

- Many parents can help teach their child with disabilities.
- Parents and professionals should work together in planning and conducting parent education groups.
- Parent-to-parent groups provide new parents of children with disabilities support from parents who have experienced similar circumstances and challenges.

- Parents who serve as research partners help brainstorm research questions, collect performance data on their children, and share those data with other parents and teachers.

- The mirror model of parent involvement assumes that not all parents need everything that professionals have to offer and that no parent should be expected to participate in every form of school involvement.

MyEducationLab™

Go to Topic 4, Parents and Families, in the MyEducationLab (www.myeducationlab.com) for *Exceptional Children*, where you can

- Find learning outcomes for parents and families along with the national standards that connect to these outcomes.
- Complete Assignments and Activities that can help you more deeply understand the chapter content.
- Apply and practice your understanding of the core teaching skills identified in the chapter with the Building Teaching Skills and Dispositions learning units.
- Examine challenging situations and cases presented in the IRIS Center Resources.
- Access video clips of CCSSO National Teachers of the Year award winners responding to the question, "Why Do I Teach?" in the Teacher Talk section.
- Check your comprehension of the content covered in the chapter with the Study Plan. Here you will be able to take a chapter quiz, receive feedback on your answers, and then access Review, Practice, and Enrichment activities to enhance your understanding of chapter content.
- Use the Online Lesson Plan Builder to practice lesson planning and integrating national and state standards into your planning.

▼ GLOSSARY

cultural interpreter: An individual who helps school personnel and family members from a diverse culture communicate effectively; may or may not speak the family's home language, but has sufficient understanding of both the home culture and school culture, policies, and practices to help the family and school understand one another.

cultural reciprocity: A two-way process between professionals and families of information sharing, understanding, and respecting how their differing values and belief systems may influence perspectives, wishes, and decisions. Requires careful examination of each party's own cultural background and belief system.

respite care: The temporary care of an individual with disabilities by nonfamily members; provides much-needed support for many families of children with severe disabilities.

Intellectual Disabilities

From Chapter 4 of *Exceptional Children* and *An Introduction to Special Education*, Tenth Edition. William L. Heward.

Intellectual Disabilities

© Paula Solloway/Alamy

- What are the implications for special education in viewing intellectual disabilities as an inherent trait within the individual or as a state of functioning that reflects the fit between a person's capacities and the contexts in which the person is to function?
- What should teachers know about IQ tests and the assessment of intellectual functioning?
- Which is more important in determining a person's level of adaptive functioning: intellectual capability or a supportive environment? Why?
- How are the characteristics of students with intellectual disabilities relevant to planning and delivering instruction?

- What factors might account for the wide differences in the prevalence of intellectual disabilities within the school-age population across states and school districts?
- Why has the prevention of intellectual disabilities proven so difficult?
- What should curriculum goals for students with intellectual disabilities emphasize?
- What are the most important features of effective instruction for students with intellectual disabilities?
- What is needed to make education for a student with intellectual disabilities appropriate in a general education classroom?

▼ FEATURED TEACHER

SANDIE TRASK-TYLER

Blendon Middle School • Westerville, Ohio

EDUCATION—TEACHING CREDENTIALS—EXPERIENCE

- B.S., special education, Ohio Dominican University, 1983
- M.A., special education and applied behavior analysis, The Ohio State University, 1989
- Ohio developmental handicaps, K–12; multiple handicaps, K–12
- 27 years of teaching: first 6 years teaching secondary students with visual impairments and intellectual disabilities at the Ohio State School for the Blind

CURRENT TEACHING POSITION AND STUDENTS
The eight sixth and seventh graders in my self-contained classroom have a wide range of abilities and educational needs associated with mild to severe intellectual disabilities. Most have additional disabilities, such as communication disorders or physical and motor problems, and remain in my classroom throughout their middle school years. Each student receives individualized instruction and supports in self-help and daily living skills, social and communication skills, and functional academics.

CLASSROOM SUPPORT
The students spend most of the school day in my classroom working on both individual lessons and group activities. Three classroom assistants help me with instructional activities and accompany students to lunch and general education classes such as art, physical education, and music. The assistants implement behavior interventions, provide student instruction, and collect data. A speech-language therapist, an occupational therapist, and a physical therapist team with me on classroom activities and contribute their expertise to promote student success and independence. My students have opportunities throughout the school day to interact with other middle school peers. In addition to eating lunch in the cafeteria and attending assemblies, my students complete reading and math activities as well as play video or board games with other students who come to our classroom. This is a wonderful social and learning opportunity for all participants.

FUNCTIONAL CURRICULUM My job is to prepare students for life in their community and eventual transition into the real world. All of my students have individualized daily schedule checklists or picture schedules with icons on their desks that list/identify their various activities to be completed. The students' individualized education program (IEP) goals provide the foundation for all of the instruction that occurs in the classroom. I keep a notebook for each student indexed by subject area that includes a color-coded data collection sheet for each IEP goal and objective. To track lesson implementation, I check off the dates we work on each student objective in the class attendance book. This helps me quickly identify which IEP goals we have or have not worked on each day.

Within each curricular area, I target functional activities and skills that will promote each student's independence. We practice skills over and over and work on generalizing across settings, staff, materials, and situations. I plan classroom activities that integrate many curricular areas so students can practice their skills in natural contexts. One of the students' favorite activities is food preparation. I create recipes that use various sight words, kitchen vocabulary, equipment, and measurements. Students must use their safety skills to use cooking equipment and their social skills to communicate with one another when sharing ingredients. Food preparation is a wonderful activity to work on fine-motor skills and the use of both hands. Before the cooking activity, students write out their shopping lists, look through a grocery circular to find needed items, and shop for the items. At the store, students read their shopping lists, write down prices, unload carts, and pay for their groceries. The best part is when students get to eat their completed recipes!

Our class auction provides another fun and meaningful opportunity to practice a variety of skills. I videotaped an actual auction and then had the auctioneer visit our classroom to talk about his job. We then practiced bidding as we would at an auction. I developed a classroom reinforcement program using the auction concept. Students earn classroom money for completing homework, completing jobs, and getting "caught being good." At the end of each week, we hold an auction and students bid on items of interest. One of the skills that students practice with this activity is withdrawing and depositing money into their savings accounts. Students who have difficulty writing use deposit, withdrawal, date, and number stamps. Students also work on calculator skills, writing skills, money management skills (e.g., "Do I have enough money to bid?"), and group interaction skills. It is very exciting to watch the students learn about handling money.

One of our past service learning projects included working with other seventh-grade students to grow plants and share them with residents of a local nursing home. We learned about different types of flowers and vegetables and conducted a science experiment growing seeds in different types of soil. Each student picked a seed to follow as it sprouted and grew, and each and was responsible for planting, watering, and measuring and recording data on their plants' growth. Students entered their data into the computer and graphed the growth of their flowers, vegetables, and herbs. As the plants were growing, students created and decorated clay pots. They also designed gift tags using their writing and word-processing skills. When the plants were mature, we walked to a nearby nursing home and gave the residents plants in our handmade pots. We also planted vegetable and herb plants in a separate garden area so the residents could enjoy fresh tomatoes and cucumbers. This was an awesome activity that integrated community service, student cooperation and teamwork, science activities, language arts skills, creativity, and math skills.

WHAT I LIKE BEST ABOUT BEING A SPECIAL EDUCATION TEACHER The best part of my job is creating fun activities that provide meaningful practice of learned skills and develop new ones. A class necklace business has been a wonderful activity to incorporate many students' IEP goals and objectives into a functional outcome. We live in "Buckeye Country," where a lot of people are avid fans of The Ohio State University Buckeyes. As a class activity several years ago, my students made Buckeye necklaces to wear during the football season. When other teachers started asking us to make necklaces for them and their friends, a class business was born! This project allows students at all ability levels to participate. It is exciting to watch the students build skills and self-esteem through making and selling their product. The students take turns performing different jobs such as production manager, marketing manager, and quality-control manager. As a result, they learn about the process of buying the materials needed, producing the product, and selling the product. The students manage the money for expenses and decide how to use the profits.

A consultant colleague says he never knows what he'll see when visiting my classroom. He mentions the

To meet Ms. Sandie Trask-Tyler and see her classroom, go to the book resources for this text on MyEducationLab.

"campsite," a tent one student uses as a quiet retreat from the busy classroom; the "vending machine," where students can buy a treat with classroom money they've earned; the claw-foot bathtub where students can relax and read or complete independent work; and the "Barnes and Noble area," a student-created nook where they can sit in soft chairs with a drink and read and/or listen to books on tape, CDs, or vintage Elvis records. His praise challenges me to think of other ways to enhance my classroom environment to better support the needs and interests of my students.

MyEducationLab™

Visit the **MyEducationLab** for *Exceptional Children* to enhance your understanding of chapter concepts with a personalized Study Plan. You'll also have the opportunity to hone your teaching skills through video- and case-based Assignments and Activities, IRIS Center Resources, and Building Teaching Skills and Dispositions lessons.

THE HISTORY OF SPECIAL EDUCATION IS DEEPLY ROOTED in the education and treatment of people with intellectual disabilities. In the United States, the first public school special education classes were for children with intellectual disabilities. The first federal legislation in support of special education provided funds for training professionals to prepare teachers for children with mental retardation.

When they hear the words "special education," many people think of a child with Down syndrome. Most people have a notion of what people with intellectual disabilities are like. Unfortunately, much of that awareness consists of misconceptions, oversimplifications, and fear. When an undergraduate special education major told a fellow waitress about her career plans to teach children labeled as having mental retardation—a disability now referred to by the term *intellectual disabilities*—her coworker's response was "Why would you want to teach children who cannot learn?" (Danforth & Navarro, 1998, p. 36).

In spite of misguided and negative perceptions still held by some, people with intellectual disabilities are increasingly enjoying the benefits and responsibilities of participating in the educational and societal mainstream. This chapter presents some key factors in understanding the complex concept of intellectual disability and looks at some contemporary instructional practices that have greatly improved educational outcomes for students with intellectual disabilities.

DEFINITIONS

Various terms for and definitions of intellectual disability have been proposed, adopted, and debated over the years (Goodey, 2005; Trent, 1994). In early times, people with severe deficits in cognitive functioning were identified with the term *idiocy* (derived from a Greek word meaning "people who did not hold public office"). In the 19th century, the label *imbecile* (derived from the Latin word for "weak and feeble") indicated a less severe degree of intellectual disability. The terms *feebleminded* and *simpleton* were eventually added to refer to people with mild intellectual disability (Clausen, 1967). Although grossly inappropriate and stigmatizing today, each of those terms was used by professionals in medicine, psychology, and education to label and refer to people with intellectual disabilities. Over the years, *mental deficiency* (Doll, 1941) and, later, *mental retardation* (Heber, 1961) were introduced and considered appropriate terminology.

In 2007, the American Association on Mental Retardation, the leading professional organization concerned with the study, treatment, and prevention of mental retardation, changed its name to the American Association on Intellectual and Developmental Disabilities (AAIDD). Consistent with the practice of most special educators today, this text uses the term *intellectual disabilities*, except for instances where the terminology itself is being discussed.

First, we will look at the traditional and still most commonly used approach to defining and classifying intellectual disability as an inherent trait within the individual. Then we will examine the most recent conception of intellectual disability as a state of functioning that reflects the fit between a person's capabilities and his environment.

IDEA Definition

Definitions of ID

 Content Standards for Beginning Teachers of Individuals with DD and/or Autism—Definitions and issues related to the identification of individuals with developmental disabilities (DD1K1).

In 1973, the American Association on Mental Retardation (AAMR) published a definition of mental retardation that, with minor rewording, was incorporated into the Individuals with Disabilities Education Act (IDEA) and continues to serve today as the basis by which most states identify children for special education services under the disability category of intellectual disabilities. In IDEA, **intellectual disability** is defined as "significantly subaverage general intellectual functioning, existing concurrently with deficits in adaptive behavior and manifested during the developmental period, that adversely affects a child's educational performance" (34 CFR, §300.8[c][6]).

The definition specifies three criteria for a diagnosis of intellectual disability. First, "significant subaverage intellectual functioning" must be demonstrated. The word *significant* refers to a score of ≥2 standard deviations below the mean on a standardized intelligence test (a score of approximately 70 or less; IQ testing is discussed later in the chapter). Second, an individual must also have significant difficulty with tasks of everyday living (adaptive behavior). Third, the deficits in intellectual functioning and adaptive behavior must occur during the developmental period to help distinguish intellectual disability from other disabilities (e.g., impaired intellectual performance due to traumatic brain injury). A child who exhibits substantial limitations in intellectual functioning and adaptive behavior will automatically meet the IDEA requirement that the disability "adversely affects a child's educational performance."

AAIDD's Definition

In 1992, the AAMR published a system for diagnosing and classifying mental retardation that represented a conceptual shift from viewing mental retardation as an inherent trait or permanent condition to a description of an individual's functioning in the context of his present environment and the supports needed to improve it. That definition was revised slightly in 2002 and, with replacement of the term *mental retardation* with *intellectual disability,* reads in the AAIDD's most recent manual on definition and classification as follows:

> Intellectual disability is characterized by significant limitations in both intellectual functioning and in adaptive behavior as expressed in conceptual, social, and practical adaptive skills. This disability originates before age 18.

© moodboard/Alamy

Which student has intellectual disabilities? The terms *mental retardation* and *intellectual disabilities* identify substantial limitations in functioning, not something inherent within the individual.

The following five assumptions are essential to the application of this definition:

1. Limitations in present functioning must be considered within the context of community environments typical of the individual's age peers and culture.
2. Valid assessment considers cultural and linguistic diversity as well as differences in communication, sensory, motor, and behavioral factors.
3. Within the individual, limitations often coexist with strengths.
4. The purpose of describing limitations is to develop a profile of needed supports.
5. With appropriate personalized supports over a sustained period, the life functioning of the person with intellectual disability generally will improve. (AAIDD Ad Hoc Committee on Terminology and Classification, 2010, p. 1)

The AAIDD definition is based on the conceptual framework shown in Figure 1. Five factors that influence human functioning are listed in the left column. The center of the figure depicts the mediational role that supports play between the multidimensional aspects of intellectual disability and individual functioning. Supports are defined as "resources and strategies that aim to promote the development, education, interests, and personal well-being of a person and that enhance individual functioning" (AAIDD Ad Hoc Committee, 2010, p. 18).

Supports needed by a student with intellectual disabilities are identified as part of the IEP process. For adults, an interdisciplinary team can use the AAIDD's Supports Intensity Scale to develop a profile of the types and intensity of needed supports within each of five factors that influence human functioning shown in Figure 1 (Thompson et al., 2004).

Classification of Intellectual Disability

Intellectual disability and people so diagnosed have traditionally been classified by the degree or level of intellectual impairment as measured by an IQ test. The most widely used classification system consists of four levels of severity according to the range of IQ scores shown in Table 1. The range of scores at the low and high ends of each

Classification of ID

 Content Standards for Beginning Teachers of Individuals with DD and/or Autism—Screening, prereferral, and classification procedures (ICC8K3)

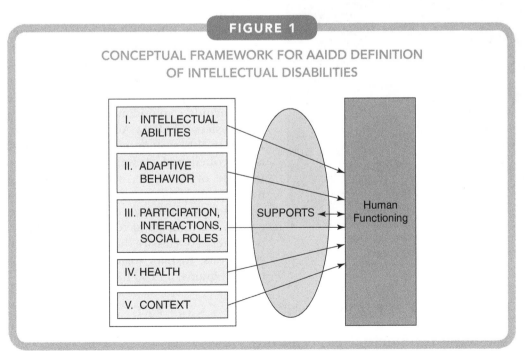

FIGURE 1

CONCEPTUAL FRAMEWORK FOR AAIDD DEFINITION OF INTELLECTUAL DISABILITIES

I. INTELLECTUAL ABILITIES

II. ADAPTIVE BEHAVIOR

III. PARTICIPATION, INTERACTIONS, SOCIAL ROLES

IV. HEALTH

V. CONTEXT

SUPPORTS

Human Functioning

Source: Intellectual Disability: Definition, Classification, and Systems of Supports (11th ed.) by AAIDD Ad Hoc Committee on Terminology and Classification (p. 14). Copyright 2010 by American Association on Intellectual and Developmental Disabilities. Reproduced with permission of AAIDD.

TABLE 1 • Classification of Intellectual Disabilities by IQ Score

LEVEL	IQ SCORE
Mild	50–55 to approximately 70
Moderate	35–40 to 50–55
Severe	20–25 to 35–40
Profound	Below 20–25

Source: Diagnostic and Statistical Manual of Mental Disorders (DSM-IV-TR) (American Psychological Association, 2000).

level represents the inexactness of intelligence testing and highlights the importance of clinical judgment in diagnosis and classification.

For many years, students with intellectual disabilities were classified as *educable mentally retarded (EMR)* or *trainable mentally retarded (TMR)*. These terms referred to mild and moderate levels of intellectual disability, respectively. This two-level classification system did not include children with severe and profound intellectual disabilities, because they were often denied a public education and were likely to reside in a state-operated institution. The terms *EMR* and *TMR* are considered archaic and inappropriate because they suggest predetermined achievement limits (Beirne-Smith, Patton, & Kim, 2006).

Two previous AAIDD manuals on definition and classification provided rationale and procedural recommendations for classifying intellectual disabilities according to an individual's profile of needed supports (Luckasson et al., 1992, 2002). This approach represented a change from classifying intellectual disabilities on the basis of estimates of an individual's intellectual deficiencies to estimating the intensities of supports needed to improve functioning in her school, home, community, and work environments. The four levels of intensity of supports—intermittent, limited, extensive, and pervasive—essentially paralleled the four-level classification system based on IQ scores.

Concerned about pejorative connotations of previously acceptable clinical terms and possibly stigmatizing labels that often emerge from classification categories, and recognizing that classification serves multiple purposes, the AAIDD currently recommends a multidimensional classification system (AAIDD Ad Hoc Committee, 2010). In this system, intellectual disability is described and classified specific to the purpose of doing so, such as identifying needed supports to enable the provision and funding of services, to describe and categorize learning characteristics for research purposes, to classify health and medical conditions, to plan treatment and prevention programs, and so forth.

Laura Bolesta/Merrill

Although Kaitlyn needs extensive supports in some areas of life functioning, she needs only limited supports in other areas.

IDENTIFICATION AND ASSESSMENT

Assessing Intellectual Functioning

Assessment of a child's intellectual functioning requires the administration of an intelligence (IQ) test by a school psychologist or other trained professional. An IQ test consists of a series of questions (e.g., vocabulary, similarities), problem solving (e.g., mazes, block designs), memory, and other tasks assumed to require certain degrees of intelligence to answer or solve correctly. The child's performance on those items is entered into a formula that yields a score representing her intelligence.

IQ tests are *standardized tests*; that is, the same questions and tasks are always presented in a prescribed way, and the same scoring procedures are used each time the test is administered. IQ tests are also norm-referenced tests. During its development, a **norm-referenced test** is administered to a large sample of people selected at random from the population for whom the test is intended. Developers then use the scores of people in the norming sample to represent how scores on the test are generally distributed throughout that population.

IQ scores seem to be distributed throughout the population according to a phenomenon called the *bell-shaped curve,* or **normal curve,** shown in Figure 2. A mathematical concept called the **standard deviation** describes how a particular score varies from the mean, or average, of all the scores in the norm sample. Test developers apply an algebraic formula to the scores achieved by the norm sample on a test to determine what value equals 1 standard deviation for that test. A child's IQ test score can then be described in terms of how many standard deviations above or below the mean it is. Theoretically, an equal number of people score above and below the mean, and about 2.3% of the population falls ≥2 standard deviations below the mean.

The AAIDD's criterion for "significant limitations of intellectual functioning," a requirement for a diagnosis of intellectual disability, is an IQ score approximately 2 standard deviations below the mean, which is a score of 70 or below on the two most widely used intelligence tests, the Wechsler Intelligence Scale for Children (WISC-IV) (Wechsler, 2003) and the Stanford-Binet Intelligence Scales (Roid, 2003a). According to the AAIDD, the IQ cutoff score of 70 is intended as a guideline and should not be interpreted as a hard-and-fast requirement. A higher IQ score of 75 or more may also be associated with intellectual disabilities if, according to a clinician's judgment, the child exhibits deficits in adaptive behavior thought to be caused by impaired intellectual functioning.

Although IQ tests have been widely criticized, they can provide useful information. IQ tests are particularly useful for objectively identifying an overall deficit in cognitive functioning, and IQ score has proven to be a strong predictor of school achievement. Because IQ tests are composed largely of verbal and academic tasks—the same things a child must master to succeed in school—they correlate highly with school achievement.

Standardized tests, norm-referenced tests, the normal curve, and standard deviation

 Council for Exceptional Children — Content Standards for Beginning Teachers of Individuals with DD and/or Autism—Basic terminology used in assessment (ICC8K1)

IQ scores and diagnosis of ID

 Council for Exceptional Children — Content Standards for Beginning Teachers of Individuals with DD and/or Autism—Specialized terminology used in the assessment of individuals with DD (DD8K1) (also ICC8K4).

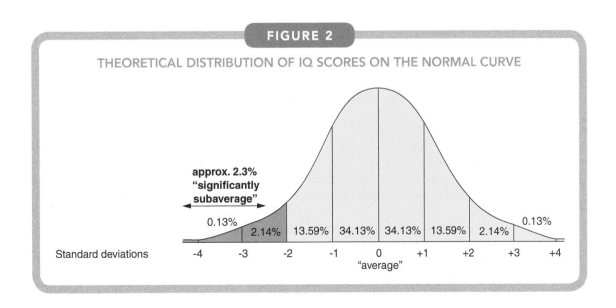

FIGURE 2

THEORETICAL DISTRIBUTION OF IQ SCORES ON THE NORMAL CURVE

approx. 2.3% "significantly subaverage"

0.13% 2.14% 13.59% 34.13% 34.13% 13.59% 2.14% 0.13%

Standard deviations   -4   -3   -2   -1   0   +1   +2   +3   +4
"average"

Even though the major intelligence tests are among the most carefully constructed and researched psychological assessment instruments available, they are still far from perfect and have both advantages and disadvantages. Following are several additional important considerations (Overton, 2012; Salvia, Ysseldyke, & Bolt, 2011; Venn, 2007):

- *Intelligence is a hypothetical construct.* No one has ever seen a thing called intelligence; we infer it from observed performance. We assume it takes more intelligence to perform some tasks at a given age than it does to perform others.
- *An IQ test measures only how a child performs at one point in time on the items included on the test.* An IQ test samples only a small portion of an individual's skills and abilities; we infer from that performance how a child might perform in other situations.
- *IQ scores can change significantly.* IQ scores often increase over time, particularly in the 70–80 range where diagnostic decisions are not so clear-cut (Whitaker, 2008). Examiners are hesitant to give a diagnosis of intellectual disabilities on the basis of an IQ score that might increase after a period of intensive, systematic intervention.
- *Intelligence testing is not an exact science.* The standard error of IQ tests is 3 to 5 points in either direction. Among the many variables that can affect a person's IQ score are motivation, the time and location of the test, inconsistency or bias by the test administrator in scoring responses that are not precisely covered by the test manual, which IQ test was selected, and which edition of that test was used. Because each of the widely used IQ tests measures a child's performance on a different set of tasks, when "an IQ score appears in isolation we must ask the question, 'IQ as measured by which test?'" (Venn, 2007, p. 145). IQ scores on the Wechsler series of intelligence tests increased steadily during the 20th century at a rate of about .3 IQ points per year (Flynn, 1987, 2006, 2007; Kanaya, Scullin, & Ceci, 2003). This rise, known at the "Flynn effect," has been masked by the periodic renorming of IQ tests to reset the mean at 100 (Scullin, 2006).
- *Intelligence tests can be culturally biased.* The Binet and Wechsler IQ tests tend to favor children from the population on which they were normed—primarily white, middle-class children. Some of the questions may tap learning that a middle-class child is more likely to have experienced. Both the Binet and Wechsler, which are highly verbal, are especially inappropriate for children for whom English is a second language (Venn, 2007).
- *An IQ score should never be used as the sole basis for making a diagnosis of intellectual disability or a decision to provide or deny special education services.* An IQ score is just one component of a multifactored, nondiscriminatory assessment.
- *An IQ score should not be used to determine IEP objectives.* The results of a student's performance on criterion-referenced tests of curriculum-based knowledge and skills are a more appropriate and useful source of information for IEP objectives.

Assessing Adaptive Behavior

Adaptive behavior is "the collection of conceptual, social, and practical skills that have been learned by people in order to function in their everyday lives" (AAIDD Ad Hoc Committee on Terminology and Classification, 2010, p. 43). The systematic assessment of adaptive behavior is important for reasons beyond the diagnosis of intellectual disabilities. The adaptive skills exhibited by a person with intellectual disabilities—as well as the nature and severity of maladaptive behaviors—are critical factors in determining the supports a student requires for success in school, work, community, and home environments (Schalock, 1999; Thompson et al., 2004). Numerous instruments for assessing adaptive behavior have been developed. Most consist of a series of questions that a person familiar with the individual (e.g., a teacher, parent, or caregiver) answers.

AAMR ADAPTIVE BEHAVIOR SCALE A frequently used instrument for assessing adaptive behavior by school-age children is the AAMR Adaptive Behavior Scale—School

(ABS-S:2) (Lambert, Nihira, & Leland, 1993). The ABS-S:2 consists of two parts. Part 1 contains 10 domains related to independent functioning and daily living skills (e.g., eating, toilet use, money handling, numbers, time); Part 2 assesses the individual's level of maladaptive (inappropriate) behavior in seven areas (e.g., trustworthiness, self-abusive behavior, social engagement). Another form, the ABS-RC:2, assesses adaptive behavior in residential and community settings (Nihira, Leland, & Lambert, 1993).

AAIDD DIAGNOSTIC ADAPTIVE BEHAVIOR SCALE   The Diagnostic Adaptive Behavior Scale (DABS), designed for use with individuals from 4 to 21 years old, includes a cutoff point at which an individual is considered to have significant limitations in adaptive behavior. Thus, the DABS provides critical information on determining a diagnosis of intellectual disability.

VINELAND ADAPTIVE BEHAVIOR SCALES   The Vineland Adaptive Behavior Scales are available in three versions. The Interview Editions in Survey Form or Expanded Form are administered by an individual who is very familiar with the person being assessed, such as a parent, teacher, or a direct caregiver (Sparrow, Balla, & Cicchetti, 2005).

ADAPTIVE BEHAVIOR ASSESSMENT SYSTEM-II   The ABAS-II provides a comprehensive assessment of 10 specific adaptive skills in three domains (conceptual, social and practical) (Harrison & Oakland, 2003). Five different forms are available for use with individuals from birth to age 89.

Measurement of adaptive behavior has proven difficult in large part because of the relative nature of social adjustment and competence: Actions that may be considered appropriate in one situation or by one group may not be in another situation or by another group. No universal agreement exists concerning exactly which adaptive behaviors everyone should exhibit. As with IQ tests, cultural bias can be a problem in adaptive behavior scales; for instance, one item on some scales requires a child to tie a laced shoe, but some children have never had shoes with laces.

CHARACTERISTICS

Intellectual disability is seldom a time-limited condition. Although some children with intellectual disabilities make tremendous advancements in adaptive skills (some to the point of functioning independently and no longer being considered under any disability category), most are affected throughout their life span (Beadle-Brown, Murphy, & Wing, 2005; Bernheimer, Keogh, & Guthrie, 2006).

Many children with mild intellectual disabilities are not identified until they enter school, and some not until they reach the second or third grade, when more difficult academic work is required. Most students with mild intellectual disabilities master academic skills up to about the sixth-grade level and can learn vocational and daily living skills well enough to support themselves independently or semi-independently in the community.

Children with moderate intellectual disabilities show significant delays in development during their preschool years. As they grow older, discrepancies in overall intellectual development and adaptive functioning generally grow wider between these children and age-matched peers without disabilities. People with moderate intellectual disabilities are more likely to have health and behavior problems than are individuals with mild intellectual disabilities.

Individuals with severe and profound intellectual disabilities are almost always identified at birth or shortly afterward. Most of these infants have significant central nervous system damage, and many have

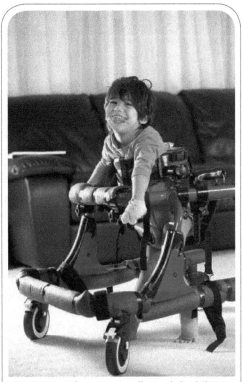

Students with severe intellectual disabilities often have additional disabilities or health conditions.

© Jaren Wicklund/Fotolia

additional disabilities and/or health conditions (Heikua et al., 2005).

Cognitive Functioning

Cognitive functioning of students with ID

 Content Standards for Beginning Teachers of Individuals with DD and/or Autism—Psychological, social/emotional, and motor characteristics of individuals with DD (DD2K5) (also ICC2K2).

Deficits in cognitive functioning and learning characteristics of individuals with intellectual disabilities include poor memory, slow learning rates, attention problems, difficulty generalizing what they have learned, and lack of motivation.

MEMORY Students with intellectual disabilities have difficulty remembering information (Carlin et al., 2003). As would be expected, the more severe the cognitive impairment, the greater the memory problems. *Short-term memory,* or *working memory*, is the ability to remember one thing while performing another task (Lanfranchi, Baddeley, Gathercole, & Vianello, 2011). It is also the ability to recall and use information that was encountered just a few seconds to a couple of hours earlier—for example, remembering a specific sequence of job tasks an employer stated a few minutes before. Students with intellectual disabilities have trouble retaining information in short-term memory (Henry, 2008).

Children with intellectual disabilities take longer than do chronological age-matched peers without disabilities to automatically recall information and therefore have more difficulty handling larger amounts of cognitive information at one time (Bergeron & Floyd, 2006). Early researchers suggested that once people with intellectual disabilities learned a specific item of information sufficiently to commit it to *long-term memory*—information recalled after a period of days or weeks—they retained that information about as well as people without cognitive disability (Belmont, 1966; Ellis, 1963).

Some recent research has focused on teaching children with intellectual disabilities metacognitive or executive control strategies, such as rehearsing and organizing information into related sets, which many children without disabilities learn to do naturally (Carlin, Soraci, & Strawbridge, 2005). Students with intellectual disabilities do not tend to use such strategies spontaneously but can be taught to do so, with improved performance on memory-related and problem-solving tasks as an outcome of such strategy instruction (Merrill, 2005).

LEARNING RATE The rate at which children with intellectual disabilities acquire new knowledge and skills is well below that of typically developing children. A frequently used measure of learning rate is *trials to criterion*—the number of practice or instructional trials needed before a student can respond correctly without prompts or assistance. For example, while 2 or 3 trials with feedback may be required for a typically developing child to learn to discriminate between two geometric forms, a child with intellectual disabilities may need 20 to 30 or more trials to learn the same discrimination.

Because students with intellectual disabilities learn more slowly, some educators have assumed that instruction should be slowed down to match their lower rate of learning. Research has shown, however, that students with intellectual disabilities, like all learners, benefit from opportunities to learn to "go fast" (Jolivette, Lingo, Houchins, Barton-Arwood, & Shippen, 2006; Miller, Hall, & Heward, 1995).

ATTENTION Efficient learners attend to critical features of a task (e.g., to the outline of geometric shapes instead of dimensions such as their color or position on the page). Students with intellectual disabilities are typically slower to attend to relevant features of a learning task than are students without disabilities (Merrill, 2005) and instead may focus on distracting irrelevant stimuli (Carlin, Chrysler, & Sullivan, 2007; Dickson, Deutsch, Wang, & Dube, 2006). In addition, individuals with intellectual disabilities often have difficulty sustaining attention to learning tasks (Tomporowski & Hagler, 1992). These attention problems compound and contribute to a student's difficulties in acquiring, remembering, and generalizing new knowledge and skills.

Effective instructional design for students with intellectual disabilities must systematically control for the presence and saliency of critical stimulus dimensions as well as the presence and effects of distracting stimuli. After initially directing a student's attention to the most relevant feature of a simplified task and reinforcing correct responses, the teacher can gradually increase the complexity and difficulty of the task. A student's selective and sustained attention to relevant stimuli will improve as she succeeds (Huguenin, 2000).

GENERALIZATION AND MAINTENANCE Many students with disabilities, especially those with intellectual disabilities, have trouble using their new knowledge and skills in settings or situations that differ from the context in which they first learned those skills. Such transfer, or generalization, of learning occurs without explicit programming for many children without disabilities but may not be evident in students with intellectual disabilities without specific programming to facilitate it. One of the most important and challenging areas of contemporary research in special education is the search for strategies and tactics for promoting the generalization and maintenance of learning by individuals with intellectual disabilities (Cooper, Heron, & Heward, 2007).

MOTIVATION Some students with intellectual disabilities exhibit an apparent lack of interest in learning or in problem-solving tasks (Glidden & Switzky, 2006). Some individuals with intellectual disabilities develop *learned helplessness,* which describes an individual's expectation of failure, regardless of his efforts, based on experiences of repeated failure. In an attempt to minimize or offset failure, the person may set extremely low expectations for himself and not appear to try very hard. When faced with a difficult task or problem, some individuals with intellectual disabilities may quickly give up and turn to or wait for others to help them (Fidler, Hepburn, Mankin, & Rogers, 2005). Some acquire a problem-solving approach called *outer-directedness,* which describes an individual's distrust of her own responses to situations and reliance on others for assistance and solutions (Fidler, Philofsky, Hepburn, & Rogers, 2005; Zigler, 1999).

Rather than an inherent characteristic of intellectual disabilities, the apparent lack of motivation may be the product of frequent failure and prompt dependency acquired as the result of others' caretaking. After experiencing success, individuals with intellectual disabilities do not differ from people without intellectual disabilities on measures of outer-directedness (Bybee & Zigler, 1998). The current emphasis on teaching self-determination skills to students with intellectual disabilities is helping more and more of these students become self-reliant problem solvers who act upon their world rather than passively wait to be acted upon (Fowler, Konrad, Walker, Test, & Wood, 2007; Wehmeyer et al., 2007). (See *Current Issues and Future Trends,* "Self-Determination: The *Most* Natural Support.")

Adaptive Behavior

By definition, children with intellectual disabilities have substantial deficits in adaptive behavior. These limitations can take many forms and tend to occur across domains of functioning. Limitations in self-care skills and social relationships as well as behavioral excesses are common characteristics of individuals with intellectual disabilities.

SELF-CARE AND DAILY LIVING SKILLS Individuals with intellectual disabilities who require extensive supports must often be taught basic self-care skills such as dressing, eating, and hygiene. Direct instruction and environmental supports such as added prompts and simplified routines are necessary to ensure that deficits in these adaptive areas do not seriously limit one's quality of life. Most people with mild intellectual disabilities learn to take care of their basic needs, but they often benefit from training in self-management skills to achieve the levels of performance necessary for independent living and successful employment (e.g., Grossi & Heward, 1998).

Learned helplessness and outer-directedness

 Content Standards for Beginning Teachers of Individuals with DD and/or Autism—Psychological, social/emotional, and motor characteristics of individuals with DD (DD2K5) (also ICC2K2).

Adaptive behavior of individuals with ID

 Content Standards for Beginning Teachers of Individuals with DD and/or Autism—Psychological, social/emotional, and motor characteristics of individuals with DD (DD2K5) (also ICC2K2).

AND FUTURE TRENDS

▶ *Self-Determination: The Most Natural Support*

BY MICHAEL L. WEHMEYER

CURRENT ISSUES

IF YOU LISTED WHAT YOU think students with intellectual disability need most to transition successfully from high school to their adult life, what would be on that list? It would, most likely, look something like this:

- Job skills and workplace supports
- Independent living and community inclusion skills
- Postsecondary education and training
- Transportation
- Health care
- Friends, family, and supports

Those (and other items) are all, obviously, important to enable students with intellectual disability to become independent, self-sufficient young adults. Another item that should be on the list may not be as obvious. Research has shown that students with disabilities, including students with intellectual disability, who are more self-determined when they leave high school, achieve more positive employment, independent living, and quality-of-life outcomes than do their peers with disabilities who are less self-determined.

What does "being self-determined" mean? Have you met people who you just knew would make it in life? These people had goals and plans to achieve them. They could identify barriers to success and solve problems to remove them. They knew what they were good at and capitalized on their strengths. They take charge of their own learning, work toward self-set goals, and are ready when opportunities become available. Perhaps these qualities even describe you. These people are self-determined.

As you will learn from this text, people who are self-determined *act* in ways that enable them to solve problems in their lives, set and attain goals, make decisions, advocate on their own behalf, and generally improve the quality of their lives. In our own work, we have defined self-determination as "volitional actions that enable one to act as the primary causal agent in one's life and to maintain or improve one's quality of life" (Wehmeyer, 2006, p. 117). The ideas of "volitional action" and "causal agent" are central to understanding what is meant by being self-determined. By acting volitionally, we mean that people who are self-determined act based on their preferences and interests and not based on coercion or someone else's preferences and interests. There's more

to being self-determined, though, than simply doing what you want rather than what someone else wants. The word *volition* is defined as the exercise of the capability of a person to make a *conscious* choice or decision with *intention*. Acting volitionally implies that one does so consciously and with intention. Self-determined behavior is not just acting to gratify instant needs or acting recklessly for short-term pleasure; it is acting consciously and with intention based on one's preferences and interests to choose, make decisions, advocate, and, generally, self-govern and self-regulate one's behavior in pursuit of one's goals.

The second part of this definition implies that self-determined people are causal agents in their lives. The noun *determination* in the term *self-determination* originates from the philosophical doctrine of *determinism*, which proposes that all events—including human behavior—are in some way *caused* (i.e., determined). Obviously, causes of human behavior are varied, from genes to environment; the meaning of *self*-determination (or self-determinism) is that one's actions are *caused* by oneself as opposed to something or someone else (i.e., other-determination). Self-determination refers to self-caused action.

People who are self-determined are causal agents in their lives. The adjective *causal* means expressive of or indicative of cause—showing the interaction of cause and effect. The term *agent* is a noun that refers to one who acts or has the authority to act. Self-determined people act "with authority" to make or cause something to happen in their lives. Causal agency implies more, however, than just causing action; it implies that people who make or cause things to happen in their lives do so with an eye toward *causing* an effect to accomplish a specific end or to cause or create change; in other words, they act volitionally and intentionally.

Does all this fussing about terms and definitions matter? Well, it does to people with intellectual disability. People too often equate self-determination with physically acting independently, without help, and with "controlling" one's own life. People with intellectual disability have limitations to their capacity to solve difficult problems or make complex decisions and in many meaningful ways, to "control" their lives. The important point to understand, though, is that being self-determined

© Paula Solloway/Alamy

Self-determination may be the most important factor in ensuring a good quality of life for students with intellectual disablities as they transition to adulthood.

is *not* about doing things independently; it is about making things happen in one's life by acting volitionally and being a causal agent. Even if a student cannot independently make a decision, for example, she can be actively supported to engage in the decision-making process; and if the student needs others' support to make that decision, he can still be "self-determined" as long as the ultimate decision takes into account, to the maximum degree practicable, the student's preferences, interest, beliefs, values, skills, abilities, and long-term goals.

In too many cases, the way others understand self-determination limits the degree to which educators work to promote the self-determination of students with intellectual disability. This is in spite of the fact that research has shown that students with intellectual and other disabilities can acquire the knowledge and skills to make more effective decisions, solve problems, set and attain goals, and self-advocate (Chambers et al., 2007) and become more self-determined (Wehmeyer, Palmer, Shogren, Williams-Diehm, & Soukup, in press). In fact, a host of evidence-based practices have been shown to enhance the knowledge and skills that enable students to become more self-determined (Cobb, Lehmann, Newman-Gonchar, & Alwell, 2009). My research with my colleagues has focused on developing and establishing an evidence base for a model of teaching to enable teachers to, in essence, teach students to teach themselves! This model, the Self-Determined Learning Model of Instruction, teaches students to self-direct the learning process and engage in a self-regulated problem-solving process to enable them to set goals, create plans to address those goals, and to self-monitor and self-evaluate their progress toward those goals. Research has shown that students with intellectual and other disabilities who are provided instruction using the model can

learn to self-regulate the learning process, achieve academic and transition-related goals and greater access to the general education curriculum (Shogren, Palmer, Wehmeyer, Williams-Diehm, & Little, in press), and attain higher self-determination (Wehmeyer et al., in press). Relatedly, a substantial literature base shows that students with intellectual disability can learn to self-regulate behavior or self-direct learning when taught skills such as self-instruction, self-monitoring, antecedent cue regulation, self-evaluation, and self-reinforcement (e.g., Fowler et al., 2007). For tips on promoting student-directed learning in inclusive settings, see Agran, King-Sears, Wehmeyer, and Copeland (2003).

Also, a visible component of many school districts' emerging efforts to promote student self-determination involves promoting student involvement in educational planning and decision making. These activities range from teaching students to use presentation software, such as Microsoft's Power-Point, to present information about themselves during an IEP meeting to the implementation of more systematic, curricular efforts that promote self-determination by teaching students skills to run their IEP meeting (see Wehmeyer et al., 2007, for a discussion of such programmatic efforts).

Promoting self-determination has become a critical issue in the education of students with intellectual disability, and there is every reason to believe that this will be the case in the future. So, I suggest that if you haven't done so already, add one more item to your list of items you "must teach" to students with intellectual disability:

- Self-determination

WHAT DO YOU THINK?

1. What is the relationship between self-determined learning goals and the motivation to achieve them? Think of your own life.
2. Should the components and purposes of self-determination for students with intellectual disability differ from those for students with other types of disabilities? For students without disabilities? If so, how and why?
3. What should a teacher do if she believes that a self-determined learning goal expressed by a student with intellectual disability is inappropriate or maladaptive?

About the Author

Michael Wehmeyer is a professor of special education and the director of the Kansas University Center on Developmental Disabilities, both at the University of Kansas, and immediate past-president of the American Association on Intellectual and Developmental Disabilities. His research interests include access to the general education curriculum by students with intellectual disability, self-determination, and technology use by people with disabilities.

SOCIAL DEVELOPMENT Making and sustaining friendships and personal relationships present significant challenges for many children with intellectual disabilities (Guralnick, Connor, Neville, & Hammond, 2006). Poor communication skills, inability to recognize the emotional state of others, and unusual or inappropriate behaviors when interacting with others can lead to social isolation (Matheson, Olsen, & Weisner, 2007; Williams, Wishart, Pitcarin, & Willis, 2005). It is difficult at best for someone who is not a professional educator or paid caretaker to want to spend the time necessary to get to know a person who stands too close, interrupts frequently, does not maintain eye contact, and strays from the conversational topic. Teaching appropriate social and interpersonal skills to students with intellectual disabilities is one of the most important functions of special education (Carter, 2011).

BEHAVIORAL EXCESSES AND CHALLENGING BEHAVIOR Students with intellectual disabilities are more likely to exhibit behavior problems than are children without disabilities (Dekker, Koot, van der Ende, & Verhulst, 2002). While youth with mild or borderline intellectual disabilities exhibit more antisocial behavior than do adolescents without disabilities (Douma, Dekker, de Ruiter, Tick, & Koot, 2007), in general, the more severe the intellectual impairment, the higher the incidence and severity of problem behavior. Difficulty accepting criticism, limited self-control, and bizarre and inappropriate behaviors such as aggression or self-injury are observed more often in children with intellectual disabilities than in children without disabilities. Some genetic syndromes associated with intellectual disabilities tend to include atypical and maladaptive behavior. For example, children with Prader-Willi syndrome (described in Table 2, later in the chapter) often engage in self-injurious, obsessive-compulsive behavior and **pica** (eating nonnutritive substances such as string, hair, dirt) (Ali, 2001; Dimitropoulos, Feurer, Butler, & Thompson, 2001; Symons, Butler, Sanders, Feurer, & Thompson, 1999).

Individuals with intellectual disabilities and psychiatric conditions requiring mental health supports are considered as dual-diagnosis cases. Data from one report showed that approximately 10% of all people with intellectual disabilities had mental health problems. The incidence of mental illness and behavior disorders in children and adults with intellectual disabilities is about two to three times higher than that of the general population (Dosen & Day, 2001). Although comprehensive guidelines are available for treating psychiatric and behavioral problems of people with intellectual disabilities (Rush & Francis, 2000), much more research is needed on how best to support this population (Didden, Korzilius, van Oorsouw, & Sturmey, 2006).

Positive Attributes

Descriptions of the learning characteristics and adaptive behavior of individuals with intellectual disabilities focus on limitations and deficits and paint a picture of a monolithic group of people whose most important characteristics revolve around the absence of desirable traits. But individuals with intellectual disabilities are a huge and disparate group composed of people with highly individual personalities (Haywood, 2006; J. D. Smith & Mitchell, 2001a, 2001b). Many children and adults with intellectual disabilities display tenacity and curiosity in learning, get along well with others, and are positive influences on those around them (Bauer, 2008; Reiss & Reiss, 2004; J. D. Smith, 2000).

Although challenged by significant limitations in learning and adaptive behavior, people with intellectual disabilities also possess many positive attributes.

PREVALENCE

Many factors contribute to the difficulty of estimating the number of people with intellectual disabilities. Some of these factors include changing definitions of intellectual disabilities, the schools' reluctance to label children with mild intellectual impairment, and the changing status of schoolchildren with mild intellectual disabilities (some are declassified during their school careers; others are no longer identified after leaving school) (Drew & Hardman, 2007). Historically, the federal government estimated the prevalence at 3% of the general population, although recent analyses find little objective support for this figure. If prevalence figures were based solely on IQ scores, 2.3% of the population theoretically would have intellectual disabilities (see Figure 2).

Basing prevalence estimates on IQ scores only, however, ignores the other necessary criterion for intellectual disabilities—deficits in adaptive functioning and the need for supports. Some professionals believe that if adaptive behavior is included with intellectual ability when estimating prevalence, the figure drops to about 1%. In fact, two national studies estimated the prevalence of intellectual disabilities at 0.78% (Larson et al., 2001) and 1.27% of the U.S. population (Fujiura, 2003).

During the 2009–10 school year, 460,964 students ages 6 through 21 received special education under the disability category of intellectual disabilities (U.S. Department of Education, 2011). These students represented about 7.8% of all school-age children in special education. Intellectual disability is the fourth-largest disability category after learning disabilities, speech or language impairments, and other health impairments.

Prevalence rates vary greatly from state to state. For example, the prevalence of intellectual disabilities as a percentage of the school-age population in 2008–09 ranged from a low of 0.29% (Maine) to a high of 2.18% (West Virginia) (U.S. Department Education, 2010e). Such differences in prevalence are in large part a function of the widely differing criteria for identifying students with intellectual disabilities (Denning, Chamberlain, & Polloway, 2000; Scullin, 2006). Prevalence figures also vary considerably among districts within a given state (Hetzner, 2007).

CAUSES AND PREVENTION

Causes

More than 350 risk factors associated with intellectual disabilities have been identified (Dykens, Hodapp, & Finucane, 2000). Approximately 35% of cases have a genetic cause, another third involve external trauma or toxins, and etiology remains unknown for another third of cases (Heikua et al., 2005; Szymanski & King, 1999). Nevertheless, knowledge of etiology is critical to efforts designed to lower the incidence of intellectual disabilities and may have implications for some educational interventions (Hodapp & Dykens, 2007; Powell, Houghton, & Douglas, 1997).

Figure 3 lists etiologic factors associated with intellectual disabilities that the AAIDD categorizes as **prenatal** (occurring before birth), **perinatal** (occurring during or shortly after birth), or **postnatal** (occurring after birth). Each of these etiologic factors can be classified further as biomedical or environmental (social, behavioral, educational). However, a combination of biological and environmental factors is often involved in individual cases of intellectual disabilities, making specific determination of etiology extremely difficult (Heikua et al., 2005; van Karnebeek et al., 2005).

BIOMEDICAL CAUSES Researchers have identified specific biomedical causes for about two-thirds of individuals with more severe levels of intellectual disabilities (Batshaw, Pellegrino, & Roizen, 2007). Table 2 describes some of the more common prenatal conditions that often result in intellectual disabilities. The term *syndrome* refers to a number of symptoms or characteristics that occur together and provide the defining features of a given disease or condition. **Down syndrome** and **fragile X syndrome** are the two most common genetic causes of intellectual disabilities (Roberts et al., 2005).

Causes of ID

 Content Standards for Beginning Teachers of Individuals with DD and/or Autism— Medical aspects of developmental disabilities and their implications for learning (DD2K1).

FIGURE 3 ETIOLOGIC RISK FACTORS FOR INTELLECTUAL DISABILITIES

Timing	Biomedical	Social	Behavioral	Educational
Prenatal	1. Chromosomal disorders 2. Single-gene disorders 3. Syndromes 4. Metabolic disorders 5. Cerebral dysgenesis 6. Maternal illnesses 7. Parental age	1. Poverty 2. Maternal malnutrition 3. Domestic violence 4. Lack of access to prenatal care	1. Parental drug use 2. Parental alcohol use 3. Parental smoking 4. Parental immaturity	1. Parental cognitive disability without supports 2. Lack of preparation for parenthood
Perinatal	1. Prematurity 2. Birth injury 3. Neonatal disorders	1. Lack of access to birth care	1. Parental rejection of caretaking 2. Parental abandonment of child	1. Lack of medical referral for intervention services at discharge
Postnatal	1. Traumatic brain injury 2. Malnutrition 3. Meningoencephalitis 4. Seizure disorders 5. Degenerative disorders	1. Impaired child caregiver 2. Lack of adequate stimulation 3. Family poverty 4. Chronic illness in the family 5. Institutionalization	1. Child abuse and neglect 2. Domestic violence 3. Inadequate safety measures 4. Social deprivation 5. Difficult child behaviors	1. Impaired parenting 2. Delayed diagnosis 3. Inadequate early intervention services 4. Inadequate special-educational services 5. Inadequate family support

Source: Intellectual Disability: Definition, Classification, and Systems of Supports (11th ed.) by AAIDD Ad Hoc Committee on Terminology and Classification (p. 60). Copyright 2010 by American Association on Intellectual and Developmental Disabilities. Reproduced with permission of AAIDD.

It is important to understand that none of the etiologic factors shown in Figure 3 and Table 2 *is* intellectual disability. These conditions, diseases, and syndromes are commonly associated with intellectual disabilities, but they may or may not result in the deficits of intellectual and adaptive functioning that define intellectual disabilities. "Because intellectual disability is characterized by impaired functioning, its etiology is whatever causes this impairment in functioning" (AAIDD Ad Hoc Committee, 2010, p. 61). Any risk factor, such as low birth weight or Trisomy 21 (Down syndrome), causes intellectual disability only when it results in impaired functioning sufficient to meet the criteria for diagnosis.

Some of the health conditions and disorders shown in Table 2 require special education and related services as disabilities in their own right and/or are causes of other disabilities whether or not intellectual disability is also involved.

Psychosocial disadvantage

 Council for Exceptional Children

Content Standards for Beginning Teachers of Individuals with DD and/or Autism—Characteristics and effects of the cultural and environmental milieu of the individual with exceptional learning needs and the family (ICC2K3).

ENVIRONMENTAL CAUSES Individuals with mild intellectual disabilities, those who require less intensive supports, make up about 90% of all people with intellectual and developmental disabilities (Drew & Hardman, 2007). The vast majority of those individuals show no evidence of organic pathology—no brain damage or other biological problem. When no biological risk factor is evident, the cause is presumed to be *psychosocial disadvantage*, environmental influences such as poverty, minimal opportunities to develop early language, child abuse and neglect, and/or chronic social or sensory deprivation. Professionals sometimes use the term to *intellectual disability of cultural-familial origin* when referring to the result of a poor social environment early in the child's life (AAIDD Ad Hoc Committee, 2010).

Although no direct evidence proves that social and environmental deprivation causes intellectual disability, researchers generally believe that these influences cause many cases of mild intellectual disabilities. Empirical support for the causal influence of poverty is found in research showing that children who live in poverty have a higher than normal chance of being identified as having intellectual disabilities (Fujiura & Yamaki, 2000).

Prevention

Medical advances have noticeably reduced the incidence of intellectual disabilities caused by some of the known biological factors. Probably the biggest single preventive strike against intellectual disabilities (and many other disabling conditions, including blindness and deafness) was the development of an effective rubella vaccine in 1962. When **rubella** (German measles) is contracted by mothers during the first 3 months of pregnancy, it causes severe damage in 10% to 40% of unborn children. Fortunately, this cause of intellectual disabilities can be eliminated if women are vaccinated for rubella before becoming pregnant.

Advances in medical science have enabled doctors to identify certain genetic influences associated with intellectual disabilities. Genetic disorders are detected during pregnancy by two types of tests: screening procedures and diagnostic tests. Obstetricians routinely provide noninvasive screening procedures, such as ultrasound and maternal serum alpha-fetoprotein (AFP), to women whose pregnancy is considered at risk for a congenital disability. Maternal serum screening measures the amount of AFP

TABLE 2 • **Some Prenatal Conditions Associated with Intellectual Disabilities**

SYNDROME	DEFINITION/CAUSE	REMARKS/CHARACTERISTICS
Down syndrome	Caused by chromosomal abnormality; most common of three major types is trisomy 21, in which the 21st set of chromosomes is a triplet rather than a pair. Most often results in moderate level of intellectual disability, although some individuals function in mild or severe range. Affects about 1 in 691 live births; incidence of Down syndrome increases with age of mother to approximately 1 in 30 for women at age 45.	Best-known and well-researched biological condition associated with intellectual disability; estimated to account for 5%–6% of all cases. Characteristic physical features: short stature; flat, broad face with small ears and nose; upward slanting eyes; small mouth with short roof, protruding tongue may cause articulation problems; hypotonia (floppy muscles); heart defects common; susceptibility to ear and respiratory infections. Older people at high risk for Alzheimer's disease.
Fetal alcohol spectrum disorder (FASD)	FASD incorporates fetal alcohol syndrome (FAS), fetal alcohol effect (FAE), and alcohol-related neurodevelopmental disorder (ARND). Mother's excessive alcohol use during pregnancy has toxic effects on fetus, including physical defects and developmental delays. FAS is diagnosed when the child has two or more craniofacial malformations and growth is below the 10th percentile for height and weight. Children who have some but not all of the diagnostic criteria for FAS and a history of prenatal alcohol exposure are diagnosed with FAE, a condition associated with hyperactivity and learning problems.	A leading cause of intellectual disability, FAS has an incidence higher than Down syndrome and cerebral palsy. In addition to cognitive impairments, some children experience sleep disturbances, motor dysfunctions, hyperirritability, aggression, and conduct problems. Although risk of FASD is highest during the first trimester of pregnancy, pregnant women should avoid drinking alcohol at any time.
Fragile X syndrome	A triplet, repeat mutation on the X chromosome interferes with production of the FMR-1 protein, which is essential for normal brain functioning; majority of males experience mild to moderate intellectual disability in childhood and moderate to severe deficits in adulthood; females may carry and transmit the mutation to their children but tend to have fewer disabilities than affected males.	Affects approximately 1 in 4,000 males; the most common inherited cause of intellectual disability and the most common clinical type of intellectual disability after Down syndrome. Characterized by social anxiety and avoidance (avoiding eye contact, tactile defensiveness, turning the body away during face-to-face interactions, and stylized, ritualistic forms of greeting); preservative speech often includes repetition of words and phrases.

(Continues)

TABLE 2 • (Continued)

SYNDROME	DEFINITION/CAUSE	REMARKS/CHARACTERISTICS
Phenylketonuria (PKU)	Genetically inherited condition in which a child is born without an important enzyme needed to break down an amino acid, phenylalanine, found in many common foods; failure to break down this amino acid causes brain damage that often results in aggressiveness, hyperactivity, and severe intellectual disability.	Widespread screening has virtually eliminated intellectual disability resulting from PKU in the United States. By analyzing the concentration of phenylalanine in a newborn's blood plasma, doctors can diagnose PKU and treat it with a special diet. Most children with PKU who receive a phenylalanine-restricted diet have normal intellectual development.
Prader-Willi syndrome	Caused by deletion of a portion of chromosome 15. Infants have hypotonia (floppy muscles) and may have to be tube fed. Initial phase is followed by development of insatiable appetite; constant preoccupation with food can lead to life-threatening obesity if food seeking is not monitored. Affects 1 in 10,000 to 25,000 live births.	Associated with intellectual and learning disabilities; behavior problems common: impulsivity, aggressiveness, temper tantrums, obsessive-compulsive behavior; some forms of self-injurious behavior, such as skin picking; delayed motor skills, short stature, small hands and feet, underdeveloped genitalia.
Williams syndrome	Caused by deletion of material on the seventh chromosome; cognitive functioning ranges from normal to mild and moderate levels of intellectual disability.	Characteristic elfin-like facial features; physical features and manner of expression exudes cheerfulness and happiness; described as "overly friendly," lack of reserve toward strangers; often have uneven profiles of skills, with strengths in vocabulary and storytelling skills and weaknesses in visual-spatial skills; often hyperactive, may have difficulty staying on task and low tolerance for frustration or teasing.

Sources: AAIDD Ad Hoc Committee on Terminology and Classification (2010); Astley & Clarren (2000); Beirne-Smith et al. (2006); Dimitropoulos et al. (2001); Fidler, Hepburn, Most, Philofsky, & Rogers (2007); Hall, Lightbody, & Reiss (2008); Levine & Wharton (2000); Mervis, Klein-Tasman, & Mastin (2001); National Down Syndrome Society (2011); J. E. Roberts et al. (2005).

and other biochemical markers in the mother's bloodstream and can identify pregnancies at risk for disabilities such as Down syndrome and spina bifida.

Diagnostic tests, such as amniocentesis and chorionic villi sampling, can confirm the presence of various disorders associated with intellectual disabilities. **Amniocentesis** requires withdrawing a sample of fluid from the amniotic sac surrounding the fetus during the second trimester of pregnancy (usually the 14th to 17th week). Fetal cells are removed from the amniotic fluid and grown in a cell culture for about 2 weeks. At that time, a chromosome and enzyme analysis is performed to identify the presence of about 80 specific genetic disorders before birth. Many of these disorders, such as Down syndrome, are associated with intellectual disabilities.

In **chorionic villi sampling (CVS),** a small amount of chorionic tissue (a fetal component of the developing placenta) is removed and tested. CVS can be performed earlier than amniocentesis (during the 8th to 10th week of pregnancy). Because fetal cells exist in relatively large numbers in the chorion, they can be analyzed immediately without waiting 2 to 3 weeks for them to grow. Although CVS is being used more often, it has been associated with a miscarriage rate of about 10 in 1,000 (compared with 2.5 in 1,000 for amniocentesis).

Amniocentesis and CVS are invasive procedures that entail some risk of miscarriage. A recently developed simple blood test that detects fetal DNA and RNA in the mother's bloodstream in the first trimester (Papageorgiou et al., 2011; Wright & Burton, 2009) can determine a baby's gender and the presence of numerous genetic and chromosomal abnormalities. The test can be done as early as 5 weeks into the pregnancy and is reported to be 100% accurate.

Women who are at risk for giving birth to a baby with a disability on the basis of the parents' genetic backgrounds are commonly referred for **genetic counseling** (Roberts, Stough, & Parrish, 2002). Genetic counseling consists of a discussion between a specially trained medical counselor and the prospective parents about the possibility that they may give birth to a child with disabilities.

Newborn screening tests for inherited conditions and biomedical risk factors are now mandatory in every state. A procedure called *tandem mass spectrometry*, developed in the late 1980s, measures various components of blood, urine, or plasma in about 2 minutes for 20 to 30 different metabolic disorders (U.S. Department of Health and Human Services, 2011). A simple blood test administered to virtually every baby born in the United States has drastically reduced the incidence of intellectual disabilities caused by **phenylketonuria (PKU).** By analyzing the concentration of phenylalanine in a newborn's blood plasma, doctors can diagnose PKU and treat it with a phenylalanine-restricted diet. Most children with PKU who receive treatment have normal intellectual development.

Toxic exposure through maternal substance abuse such as alcohol (Ryan & Ferguson, 2006) and environmental pollutants (e.g., lead poisoning) are two major causes of preventable intellectual disabilities that can be combated with education and training.

For discussions of ethical considerations of genetic testing for disabilities, see Bauer (2008), Beirne-Smith and colleagues (2006), Drew and Hardman (2007), Kuna (2001), Smith and Mitchell (2001a), and Zucker (2004).

EDUCATIONAL APPROACHES

The search for effective methods for educating students with intellectual disabilities began in France more than 200 years ago, when Jean Marc Gaspard Itard kept a detailed diary of his efforts to teach a young boy who was found in the woods and thought to be a feral child. Itard showed that systematic intervention could produce significant gains with a child thought to be incapable of learning (Itard, 1806/1962).

Since Itard's time, researchers and practitioners working with students with intellectual disabilities have developed numerous methods of specialized instruction, some of which have contributed to improved practice in all other areas of education. Similarly, efforts by early advocates on behalf of children and adults with intellectual disabilities blazed trails for advocacy groups representing individuals with other disabilities. Some key historical events and their implications for the education and treatment of children and adults with intellectual disabilities are highlighted in Figure 4.

History of ID

 Content Standards for Beginning Teachers of Individuals with DD and/or Autism—Historical foundations and classic studies of DD (DD1K3).

Curriculum Goals

What do students with intellectual disabilities need to learn? Too often in the past, children with mild intellectual disabilities were presented with a slowed- and/or watered-down version of the general education curriculum that focused largely on traditional academic subjects. For example, a group of children with mild intellectual disabilities might spend several weeks learning the 50 states and their capitals. Students with more severe intellectual impairments often spent hours putting pegs into pegboards and sorting plastic sticks by color because educators believed these isolated skills were developmental prerequisites for more meaningful activities. Unfortunately, knowing that Boise is the capital of Idaho or being able to sort by color did not help these students function more capably.

Wiser curricular decisions combined with increasingly effective instructional techniques and supports are enabling many students with intellectual disabilities to participate meaningfully in the general education curriculum (Soukup, Wehmeyer, Bashinski, & Bovaird, 2007; Wehmeyer, 2006).

ACADEMIC CURRICULUM All students with intellectual disabilities should receive instruction in the basic skills of reading, writing, and math (Allor, Mathes, Jones, Champlin, & Cheatham, 2010; Browder, Spooner, Ahlgrim-Delzell, Harris, & Wakeman, 2008; Cooper-Duffy, Szedia, & Hyer, 2010). Functional academics are "the most useful parts" of reading, writing, arithmetic, and science for the student (Browder & Spooner,

FIGURE 4   KEY HISTORICAL EVENTS IN THE EDUCATION OF CHILDREN
WITH INTELLECTUAL DISABILITIES

Date	Historical Event	Educational Implication
1806	Jean Marc Gaspard Itard published an account of his work with Victor, the Wild Boy of Aveyron.	Itard showed that intensive treatment could produce significant learning. Many consider Itard the father of special education.
1848	Edouard Seguin, who had studied and worked under Itard, helped establish the Pennsylvania Training School.	This was the first educational facility for people with intellectual disabilities in the United States.
1850	Samuel Gridley Howe began the School for Idiotic and Feeble Minded Youth.	This was the first publicly funded residential school in the United States.
1896	The first public school class for children with intellectual disabilities began in Providence, RI.	This began the special class movement, which grew to 1.3 million children in 1974, the year before IDEA.
1905	Alfred Binet and Theodore Simon developed a test in France to screen those students not benefiting from the general education classroom.	The test enabled empirical identification of students with intellectual disabilities and contributed to the growth of the special class movement.
1916	Lewis Terman, of Stanford University, published the Stanford-Binet Intelligence Scale in the United States.	Most schools adopted IQ testing as a means of identifying children with below-average general intelligence.
1935	Edgar Doll published the Vineland Social Maturity Scale.	It provided a standardized method for assessing a person's adaptive behavior, which later became part of the definition of intellectual disabilities.
1950	Parents formed the National Association for Retarded Children (known today as The Arc).	The Arc remains a powerful and important advocacy organization for people of all ages with intellectual disabilities.
1958	National Defense Education Act (PL 85–926) enacted.	Provided funds for training professionals to train teachers of children with intellectual disabilities.
1959	AAMR published its first manual on the definition and classification of mental retardation, with diagnosis based on an IQ score of 1 standard deviation below the mean (approximately 85).	Many students were identified in the borderline category of mental retardation and served in special classes for "slow learners" or EMR students.
1961	John F. Kennedy established the first President's Panel on Mental Retardation. (Today, the President's Committee for People with Intellectual Disabilities).	The panel's first report (Mayo, 1962) made recommendations that helped guide national policy with respect to intellectual disabilities (e.g., citizenship, education, prevention).
1969	Bengt Nirje published a key paper defining normalization. Wolf Wolfensberger championed normalization in the United States.	Normalization became a leading philosophy guiding the development and delivery of educational, community, vocational, and residential services for people with intellectual disabilities.
1973	AAMR published a revised definition that required a score on IQ tests of 2 standard deviations below the mean (approximately 70 or less) and concurrent deficits in adaptive behavior.	This eliminated the category of borderline intellectual disabilities.
1992	AAMR published "System '92," a radically different definition of mental retardation with a classification system based on intensities of supports.	New definition and classification system generated cautious support by some and concern by others.
2007	AAMR changed its name to the American Association on Intellectual and Developmental Disabilities (AAIDD) and replaced the term *mental retardation* with *intellectual disabilities*.	According to the AAIDD, the term *intellectual disability* (a) reflects current practices that focus on functional behaviors and contextual factors; (b) provides a logical basis for providing individualized supports due to its social-ecological framework; (c) is less offensive to people with disabilities; and (d) is more consistent with international terminology.
2010	"Rosa's Law" (PL 111-256) signed by President Barack Obama in October 2010.	Amends language in federal statutes by replacing all references to "mental retardation" and "mentally retarded individual" to "intellectual disability" and "individual with an intellectual disability." Law named after 9-year-old girl with Down syndrome, who fought with her parents to have a similar law passed in her home state of Maryland.

2006). Choosing functional academic targets is not as simple as it might seem. The most useful part of writing for one student (e.g., making a grocery list) may not be a functional writing skill for another student (e.g., writing the number of items packaged on the job). Teachers must carefully assess each student's current routines to find those skills that the student requires and/or could use often. Educators should also consider skills that future environments are likely to require.

Teachers must be on guard against the faulty assumption that a traditional academic skill cannot be functional because it is not a typical activity or learning outcome for students with intellectual disabilities. For example, while *crystal* and *limestone* would not appear on any lists of functional sight words, such words might be extremely functional for a student with a rock collection (Browder, 2000).

Complete immersion in the academic curriculum, however, can be a restrictive and ineffective education for a student with intellectual disabilities. Care must be taken that a student's involvement in the academic portions of the general education curriculum does not limit opportunities to learn the skills that will help him function independently and successfully in current and future environments.

Laura Bolesta/Merrill

Serving as salesclerk for the Buckeye Necklaces business that she and her classmates created helps Kaitlyn learn functional skills.

FUNCTIONAL CURRICULUM Learning functional curriculum content increases a student's independence, self-direction, health and fitness, and enjoyment in everyday school, home, community, and work environments. Special educators have taught students with intellectual disabilities a wide range of practical skills, such as using public transportation (Mechling & O'Brien, 2010), shopping (Bramlett, Ayres, Douglas, & Cihak, 2011), ordering in a restaurant (Mechling, Pridgen, & Cronin, 2005), cooking and food safety (Madaus et al., 2010; Mechling, 2008), telling time (Horn, Shuster, & Collins, 2006), and nutrition and fitness (Simpson, Swicegood, & Gaus, 2006).

Teachers determine whether a particular knowledge or skill is functional by seeking answers to questions such as:

- Will learning this knowledge/skill help the student be more independent and successful in his home, school, or community?
- Will failure to learn this knowledge/skill have any negative consequences to the student?

The ultimate approach to determining if a given skill qualifies as functional curriculum is to contemplate this question from the student's perspective: "Will I need it when I'm 21?" (Beck, Broers, Hogue, Shipstead, & Knowlton, 1994). The answer to this question is critical, because when educators fail to relate curriculum for a student with intellectual disabilities to outcomes with direct relevance to that student's eventual independence and quality of life, "years of valuable opportunities for meaningful learning can be wasted" (Knowlton, 1998, p. 96).

Neither teachers nor students should view decisions about what to teach as academic or functional, one or the other. General and special educators who teach students with intellectual disabilities should seek to align the academic and functional curricula in ways that allow each student to benefit as much as possible from access to the general education curriculum while learning from a personalized curriculum of functional skills across life domains (Browder, Ahlgrim-Delzell, Courtade-Little, & Snell, 2006; Browder et al., 2004).

Functional curriculum goals

Council for Exceptional Children Content Standards for Beginning Teachers of Individuals with DD and/or Autism—Plan instruction for independent functional life skills relevant to the community, personal living, sexuality, and employment (DD7S1).

Bouck (2011) shares a content analysis of 10 commercially available functional curriculum models for secondary students with mild to moderate intellectual disabilities.

Examples of lessons that blend effective instruction of both functional skills and academic goals can be found in Collins, Karl, Riggs, Galloway, and Hager (2010).

Integrating life skills into curriculum

Content Standards for Beginning Teachers of Individuals with DD and/or Autism—Integrate affective, social, and life skills with academic curricula (ICC7S7).

Self-determination

Content Standards for Beginning Teachers of Individuals with DD and/or Autism—Use procedures to increase the individual's self-awareness, self-management, self-control, self-reliance, and self-esteem (ICC5S8) (also ICC4S5, ICC7S14).

Information on research-validated curriculum models, instructional materials, and lesson plans for teaching self-determination and self-advocacy to students with disabilities are available from the National Self-Determination Synthesis Project (www.uncc.edu/sdsp/sd_lesson_plans.asp; see also Konrad, Walker, Fowler, Test, & Wood (2008); and the Kentucky Youth Advocacy Project at http://www.kyap.org/).

As students with intellectual disabilities reach middle and secondary school, the emphasis on learning functional skills that will help them transition to adult life in the community becomes especially critical (Wehman, 2011). Several models and taxonomies of adult functioning provide frameworks from which to build functional curriculum activities. For example, Life Skills Instruction includes 147 major life demands that are associated with a variety of specific life skills and organized around six domains of adult functioning (Cronin, Patton, & Wood, 2005).

SELF-DETERMINATION Self-determined learners set personal goals, plan steps for achieving those goals, choose and implement a course of action, evaluate their performance, and make adjustments in what they are doing to reach their goals. Self-determination learners are self-advocates (Kleinert, Harrison, Fisher, & Kleinert, 2010). Learning self-determination skills can serve as a curriculum goal in its own right as well as a means to help students achieve other learning outcomes (Wehmeyer et al., 2007). For example, Agran, Blanchard, Wehmeyer, and Hughes (2002) taught four middle school students with intellectual disabilities a four-step problem-solving sequence to achieve self-set goals related to their participation and success in the general education classroom. The students were taught to (a) verbalize, "What is the problem?" and to say out loud what it was (e.g., "I need to say at least one sentence during class."); (b) ask, "What can I do about it?" and verbalize the proposed solution; (c) implement the proposed solution; and (d) ask, "Did that fix the problem?"

Teaching students to take responsibility for their learning is an important component of self-determination. Students should be taught to take an active role in their learning at an early age. Teaching students with disabilities to recruit assistance from the classroom teacher is one strategy for helping them succeed in general education classrooms and take an active role in their education. For example, Craft, Alber, and Heward (1998) taught four fourth graders with intellectual disabilities to recruit teacher attention while they worked on spelling assignments in a general education classroom. The students learned to show their work to the teacher two to three times per session and to make statements such as "How am I doing?" or "Look, I'm all finished!" Recruitment training, which was conducted in the special education classroom, increased the frequency of each student's recruiting, the frequency of teacher praise, the percentage of worksheet items completed, and the accuracy with which the students completed the assignments. After the study, the general education teacher stated, "They fit in better, they were more a part of the group, and they weren't being disruptive because they were working." To learn more about this strategy for teaching students to take an active role in their learning, see *Teaching & Learning*, "Look, I'm All Finished!' Recruiting Teacher Attention."

Self-determination requires a complex set of skills and is a lofty goal for any student. However, students with intellectual disabilities can learn self-determination skills, and those who do are more likely to achieve IEP goals and make a successful transition from school to adult life (Agran et al., 2005; Fowler, Konrad, Walker, Test, & Wood, 2007; Test, Fowler, Brewer, & Wood, 2005; Shogren, Palmer, Wehmeyer, Williams-Diehm, & Little, 2011).

Instructional Methods

Students with intellectual disabilities learn best when their teachers use instructional methods derived from empirical research, such as the following practices (Heward, 2003):

- Assess each student's present levels of performance to identify and prioritize the most important instructional targets.
- Define and task-analyze the new knowledge or skills to be learned.
- Design instructional materials and activities so the student has frequent opportunities to respond in the form of guided and independent practice.
- Provide and then fade prompts and cues so the student can respond to naturally occurring stimuli.

- Provide systematic consequences for student performance in the form of contingent reinforcement, instructional feedback, and error correction.
- Incorporate fluency-building activities into lessons.
- Use strategies to promote the generalization and maintenance of newly learned skills.
- Conduct direct and frequent measurements of student performance, and use those data to inform instructional decisions.

Some of these components of effective instruction are described here.

TASK ANALYSIS   Task analysis means breaking down complex or multistep skills into smaller, easier-to-learn subtasks. The subskills or subtasks are then sequenced, either in the natural order in which they are typically performed or from easiest to most difficult. Assessing a student's performance on a sequence of task-analyzed subskills helps pinpoint where instruction should begin. Figure 5 shows a task analysis and

Task analysis

 Content Standards for Beginning Teachers of Individuals with DD and/or Autism—Use task analysis (ICC7S5).

FIGURE 5   TASK ANALYSIS DATA COLLECTION FORM FOR A STUDENT'S MORNING ARRIVAL ROUTINE

Teachers: Wharton, Kwan   **Instructional cue:** Arrival at school by school bus; Bus stops, kids stand up
Student: Marc   **Settings:** Bus arrival area, sidewalk, lobby, hallway, classroom   **Target:** Morning arrival routine
Day(s): Daily at arrival   **Stage of learning:** Acquisition   **Teaching method:** Constant time delay (0, 4 seconds)
Probe Schedule: First Tuesday each month   **Baseline/Probe method:** Multiple opportunity task analytic assessment (4-sec. latency)

Dates →	9/21	9/22	9/23	9/24	9/27	9/28	9/30	10/1	10/4	10/5								
Delayed prompt →			0	0	4	4	4	4	4									
Task Steps ↓																		
1. Get off bus	−	−	√	√	√	√	√	√	+	+								
2. Open and walk through door (help OK)	−	−	√	√	√	√	√	√	√	−								
3. Walk down the hallway (thru lobby to left)	+	−	√	√	√	√	√	√	√	−								
4. Open Ms. Kwan's door, go in	−	−	√	√	√	√	√	√	√	−								
5. Wave to Ms Kwan*	−	−	√	√	√	√	√	+	+	+								
6. Find empty cubby, take off backpack	−	−	√	√	+	+	+	+	+	+								
7. Put backpack inside cubby (on floor)	+	−	√	√	√	+	+	+	+	+								
8. Take off jacket	−	−	√	√	√	√	√	√	+	−								
9. Hang it up (empty hook)	−	−	√	√	√	√	+	√	+	−								
10. Go to your schedule get card (first card)	+	+	√	√	√	+	+	+	+	+								
11. Go to _____ and get started (first card)	−	−	√	√	√	√	√	√	√	−								
12. Go to your schedule, get rainbow rug card (when teacher rings bell)	−	−	√	√	√	√	√	√	√	−								
13. Go sit on rainbow rug (criss-cross)	−	+	√	√	√	√	+	+	+	+								
14. Listen and do _____ (use circle schedule)	−	−	√	√	√	√	√	√	√	√								
15. Go to schedule, get Ms. Wharton's room card (when circle done)	−	−	√	√	√	√	+	+	+	+								
16. Find Ms. Kwan, say good-bye*	−	−	√	√	√	√	√	+	+	+								
17. Go to Ms. Wharton's room	−	−	√	√	√	+	√	+	√	−								
Total independent	3	2	0	0	1	4	6	7	10	8								
Baseline/Teach/Probe	B	B	T	T	T	T	T	T	T	P								

Date	Teacher	Anecdotal Comments
9/23	JW	Waited for help on most steps
9/25	JW	Sleepy, ear infection meds
10/4	LK	He's more sure
10/5	LK	Great probe!

[Located on back of task analysis]

Materials: Arrival schedule, backpack, jacket
Latency Period: 0 seconds, 4 seconds
Criterion: 10 of 15 steps correct (67%) for 3 of 5 teaching days

Recording Key: Test: + correct, − incorrect; Teach: + unprompted correct, √ prompted correct (gestural/partial physical prompt), − unprompted/prompted error; NR no response
* Social enrichment steps

Source: From M. E. Snell & F. Brown (Eds.) (2011), *Instruction of students with severe disabilities* (7th ed., p. 154). Reproduced by permission of Pearson Education, Inc., Upper Saddle River, NJ.

"Look, I'm All Finished!"
Recruiting Teacher Attention

BY SHEILA R. ALBER-MORGAN AND WILLIAM L. HEWARD

Preparing any student with disabilities for inclusion in a general education classroom should include explicit instruction in classroom survival skills such as staying on task during a lesson, following teachers' directions, and completing assigned seat work. These skills are likely to enhance any student's acceptance and success in the classroom. Because teachers value such "good student" behaviors, students are also likely to receive teacher praise and attention for exhibiting them (Lane, Givner, & Pierson, 2004; Lane, Wehby, & Cooley, 2006).

Many students with disabilities are very good at getting their teachers' attention. Unfortunately, that attention is often for the wrong behaviors. A penchant for disruptive behavior and academic skill deficits make many students with disabilities prone to negative interactions with teachers and poor achievement in general education classrooms. Teaching students to politely recruit positive teacher attention for academic efforts can reverse this pattern of negativity. Teachers may be willing to spend more time with students who politely seek assistance and are receptive to feedback, and they will have more time to devote to instruction.

Students who are still, quiet, and docile are easy to overlook and may receive little attention and support. Classrooms are busy places, and teachers can easily overlook students' important academic and social behaviors. It is hard for teachers to be aware of students who need help, especially low-achieving ones who are less likely to ask; a disruptive student is more likely to get his teacher's attention than is the student who is working quietly and productively.

Although teachers in general education classrooms are expected to adapt instruction to serve students with disabilities, this is not always the case. For example, the secondary teachers interviewed in one study believed that students with disabilities should take responsibility for obtaining the help they need (Schumm et al., 1995). Thus, politely recruiting teacher attention and assistance can help students with disabilities function more independently and actively influence the quality of instruction they receive.

Students with intellectual disabilities (Craft et al., 1998; Mank & Horner, 1987), learning disabilities (Alber, Heward, & Hippler, 1999; Wolford, Alber, & Heward, 2001), and emotional or behavior disorders (Alber, Anderson, Martin, & Moore, 2004; Lo & Cartledge, 2006; Smith & Sugai, 2000) have learned to recruit teacher and peer attention for performing academic tasks in general education classrooms.

Politely recruiting teacher attention and assistance is one way that students can influence the quality of the instruction they receive.

WHO SHOULD BE TAUGHT TO RECRUIT?

While politely obtaining teacher assistance is a valuable skill for any student, it is particularly important for students such as the following:

Withdrawn Willamena. Willamena seldom asks a teacher anything. Because she is so quiet and well behaved, her teachers sometimes forget she's in the room. Withdrawn Willamenas are prime candidates for recruitment training.

In-a-Hurry Harry. Harry is usually half-done with a task before his teacher finishes explaining it. Racing through his work allows him to be the first to turn it in. But his work is often incomplete and error filled, so he doesn't hear much praise from his teacher. Harry would benefit from recruitment training that includes self-checking and self-correction.

Shouting Shelly. Shelly has just finished her work, and she wants her teacher to look at it—right now! But Shelly doesn't raise her hand. She gets her teacher's attention—and disrupts most of her classmates—by shouting across the room. Students like Shelly should be taught appropriate ways to solicit teacher attention.

Pestering Pete. Pete always raises his hand, waits quietly for his teacher to come to his desk, and then politely asks, "Have I done this right?" But sometimes he repeats this routine a dozen times in a 20-minute period, and his teachers find it annoying. Positive teacher attention often turns into reprimands. Recruitment training for Pete, and for all students, will

TEACHING & LEARNING

teach him to limit the number of times he cues his teachers for attention.

HOW TO GET STARTED

1. **Identify target skills.** Students should recruit attention for behaviors that are valued by teachers and therefore likely to be reinforced—for example, writing neatly and legibly, working accurately, completing assigned work, cleaning up at transitions, and making contributions when working in a cooperative group.

2. **Teach self-assessment.** Students should self-assess their work before recruiting teacher attention (e.g., Harry asks himself, "Is my work complete?"). After the student can reliably distinguish between complete and incomplete work samples, she can learn how to check the accuracy of her work with answer keys or checklists of the steps or components of the academic skill. Or she can spot-check two or three items before asking the teacher to look at it.

3. **Teach appropriate recruiting.** Teach students when, how, and how often to recruit and how to respond to the teacher after receiving attention.

   - **When?** Students should signal for teacher attention after they have completed and self-checked a substantial part of their work. Students should also be taught when not to try to get their teacher's attention (e.g., when the teacher is working with another student, talking to another adult, taking the lunch count).

   - **How?** The traditional hand raise should be part of every student's recruiting repertoire. Depending on teacher preferences and the routines in the general education classroom, students should be taught other methods of gaining attention (e.g., signaling the need for help or feedback by standing up a small flag on their desks or bringing their work to the teacher's desk).

   - **How often?** While helping Withdrawn Willamena learn to seek teacher attention, don't turn her into a Pestering Pete. How often a student should recruit varies across teachers and activities (e.g., independent seat work, cooperative learning groups, whole-class instruction). Direct observation in the classroom can establish a desired rate of recruiting. It is also a good idea to ask the general education classroom teacher when, how, and with what frequency she prefers students to ask for help.

   - **What to say?** Students should be taught several statements that are likely to evoke positive feedback from the teacher (e.g., "Please look at my work." "Did I do a good job?" "How am I doing?"). Keep it simple, but teach the student to vary her verbal cues so she will not sound like a parrot.

   - **How to respond?** Students should respond to their teacher's feedback by establishing eye contact, smiling, and saying, "Thank you." Polite appreciation is very reinforcing to teachers and will increase the likelihood of more positive attention the next time.

4. **Model and role play the complete recruiting sequence.** Begin by providing students with a rationale for recruiting (e.g., the teacher will be happy you did a good job, you will get more work done, your grades might improve). Thinking aloud while modeling is good way to show the recruiting sequence. While performing each step, say, "Okay, I've finished my work. Now I'm going to check it. Did I put my name on my paper? Yes. Did I do all the problems? Yes. Did I follow all the steps? Yes. Okay, my teacher doesn't look busy right now. I'll raise my hand and wait quietly until she comes to my desk." Have another student pretend to be the general education classroom teacher and come over to you when you have your hand up. Say, "Mr. Patterson, please look at my work." The helper says, "Oh, you did a very nice job." Then smile and say, "Thank you, teacher." Role play with praise and offer corrective feedback until the student correctly performs the entire sequence on several consecutive trials.

5. **Prepare students for alternative responses.** Not every recruiting response by a student will result in teacher praise; some efforts may even be followed by criticism (e.g., "This is all wrong. You need to pay better attention."). Use role playing to prepare students for these possibilities, and have them practice polite responses (e.g., "Thank you for helping me with this.").

Politely recruiting teacher attention and assistance is one way students can actively influence the quality of instruction they receive. For more information on teaching students to recruit teacher attention, see Alber and Heward (2000).

Sheila Alber-Morgan is a faculty member in the special education program at The Ohio State University.

data collection form developed for teaching a preschooler with disabilities a routine for arriving at his classroom each morning.

During the task-analysis stage of instructional planning, it is important to consider the extent to which the natural environment requires performance of the target skill for a certain duration or at a minimum rate. For example, Test, Spooner, Keul, and Grossi (1990) included specific time limits for each of the 17 steps in a task analysis used to teach two secondary students with severe intellectual disabilities to use the public telephone to call home. The authors determined the specific sequence of steps and the time limit for each step by observing two adults without disabilities use the telephone.

ACTIVE STUDENT RESPONSE Research in general and special education has been unequivocal in its support of the positive relationship between students' active engagement with academic tasks and their achievement (Ellis, Worthington, & Larkin, 2002; Greenwood, Delquadri, & Hall, 1984; Heward, 1994; Swanson & Hoskyn, 2001). Providing instruction with high levels of active student participation is important for all learners, but it is particularly important for students with disabilities: "The pedagogical clock continues to tick mercilessly, and the opportunities for these students to advance or catch up diminish over time" (Kame'enui, 1993, p. 379).

Researchers have used terms such as *academic learning time, opportunity to respond,* and *active student response* to refer to this important variable. Heward (1994) defined **active student response (ASR)** as

> an observable response made to an instructional antecedent. . . . ASR occurs when a student emits a detectable response to ongoing instruction. The kinds of responses that qualify as ASR are as varied as the kinds of lessons that are taught. Depending upon the instructional objective, examples of ASR include words read, problems answered, boards cut, test tubes measured, praise and supportive comments spoken, notes or scales played, stitches sewn, sentences written, workbook questions answered, and fastballs pitched. The basic measure of how much ASR a student receives is a frequency count of the number of responses emitted within a given period of instruction. (p. 286)

When all variables are held constant (e.g., quality of curriculum materials, students' prerequisite skills, motivational variables), an ASR-rich lesson will result in more learning than will a lesson in which students make few or no responses. Choral responding (Flores & Ganz, 2009), response cards (Horn, 2010), and classwide peer tutoring (Maheady, Mallette, & Harper, 2006) are research-based methods for increasing ASR for all students, including those with intellectual and other disabilities, during group instruction (Horn, 2010).

SYSTEMATIC FEEDBACK Instructional feedback—information provided to students about their performance—falls into two broad categories: (a) praise and/or other forms of confirmation or **positive reinforcement** for correct responses, and (b) error correction for incorrect responses. Feedback is most effective when it is specific, immediate, positive, frequent, and differential (comparing the student's present performance with past performance; e.g., "You read 110 words today, Jermon. That's five more than yesterday.").

Effective instruction for all students, with or without disabilities, is characterized by frequent opportunities for active student response and systematic feedback.

A special type of feedback that Werts and colleagues call *instructive feedback* can increase the efficiency of instruction for students with intellectual and other disabilities (Werts, Wolery, Gast, & Holcomb, 1996). When giving feedback on students' responses to targeted items, the teacher intentionally presents "extra information." For example, after a student correctly reads the word *corn,* the teacher might say, "Right, this word is *corn;* it is a vegetable." The instructive feedback is the statement "it is a vegetable." Several studies have found that instructive feedback did not impede students' acquisition of the target information and that students also learned much of the additional information (e.g., Gursel, Tekin-Iftar, & Boxkurt, 2006; Werts, Hoffman, & Darcy, 2011).

Using feedback effectively is one of the most important skills for teachers (Konold, Miller, & Konold, 2004). Effective teachers change both the focus and the timing of their feedback as students progress from initial attempts at learning a new skill through practicing a newly acquired skill. When a student is first learning a new skill or content knowledge, feedback should follow each response (see Figure 6). Feedback during this **acquisition stage of learning** should focus on the accuracy and form of the student's response (e.g., "Very good, Kathy. Two quarters equal 50 cents."). Providing feedback after each response in the acquisition stage reduces the likelihood that students will practice errors by responding in the absence of feedback.

When a student begins to perform a new skill with some consistent accuracy (at minimum correct responses outnumber errors), she should begin making a series of responses before the teacher provides feedback. Feedback during this **practice stage of learning** should emphasize the correct rate at which the student performs the target skill (e.g., "Dominique, you correctly answered 28 problems in 1 minute. Way to go!"). Feedback after each response during the practice stage may have a detrimental effect on learning because it blocks the student's opportunity to develop fluency.

TRANSFER OF STIMULUS CONTROL   Trial-and-error learning is inefficient and frustrating for students without disabilities. For students with intellectual disabilities and other learning problems, it is likely to be a complete waste of time. Instead of waiting to see whether the student will make a correct response, the effective teacher provides

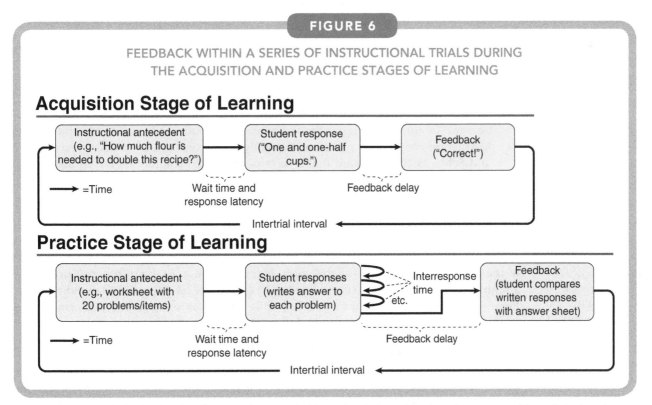

FIGURE 6

FEEDBACK WITHIN A SERIES OF INSTRUCTIONAL TRIALS DURING THE ACQUISITION AND PRACTICE STAGES OF LEARNING

Notes: Wait time is the time between the presentation of a question/problem and teacher's signal that the student may respond; *latency* is the elapsed time between the signal to respond and student's initiation of the response; *interresponse time* is the time between two consecutive responses.

a prompt (e.g., physical guidance, verbal directions, pictures, prerecorded auditory prompts) that makes a correct response very probable (Dogoe & Banda, 2009). The correct response is reinforced, the prompt is repeated, and another correct student response is reinforced. The response prompts are then gradually and systematically withdrawn so that the student's responding comes under the stimulus control of natural cues that occur in the learner's everyday environment.

GENERALIZATION AND MAINTENANCE   Generalization and maintenance refer to the extent to which students use what they have learned across settings and over time. Although much remains to be learned about helping students with intellectual other disabilities get the most out of what they learn, researchers have developed the promising beginnings of a reliable "technology of generalization" (Cooper et al., 2007). Three of many strategies for promoting generalization and maintenance are described here:

Promoting generalization and maintenance

Content Standards for Beginning Teachers of Individuals with DD and/or Autism—Use strategies to facilitate maintenance and generalization of skills across learning environments (ICC4S4).

- *Maximize contact with naturally occurring reinforcement contingencies.* The most basic strategy for promoting generalization and maintenance is to increase the probability that a student's performance of a newly learned skill will be reinforced in the natural environment (e.g., the general education classroom, the playground, the community, recreational and work settings) (Baer, 1999). Teachers can accomplish this by (a) teaching functional skills that students need and that the people in the student's natural environment are likely to value and (b) teaching students to perform new skills with the accuracy and fluency necessary to produce reinforcement in the natural environment.
- *Program common stimuli.* If the generalization setting differs greatly from the setting where teaching takes place, the student may not perform the new behavior. Teachers can program common stimuli in two basic ways: (a) incorporate into the teaching situation as many typical features of the generalization setting as possible and (b) create a new common stimulus that the student learns to use in the teaching setting and can transport to the generalization setting, where it prompts or assists performance of the target skill. (To learn how iPods can function as common stimuli that help secondary students with intellectual disabilities generalize skills across settings, see *Teaching & Learning*, "'So That's What I Do Next': Video Modeling and Prompting with iPods and iPads."
- *Community-based instruction.* Teaching in the actual setting where students are ultimately to use their new skills increases the probability of generalization and maintenance. A review of 23 research studies, however, showed that simply conducting instruction in the community is no guarantee of generalization and maintenance (Walker, Richter, Uphold, & Test, 2010). Poorly designed instruction will be ineffective regardless of where it is conducted. And community-based instruction can be expensive and typically is not available on a daily basis. Morse and Schuster (2000) found that 2 days per week of community-based instruction supplemented by simulation training in the classroom were effective in teaching students with intellectual disabilities to shop for groceries.

Direct and frequent measurement

Content Standards for Beginning Teachers of Individuals with DD and/or Autism—Evaluate instruction and monitor progress of individuals with exceptional educational needs (ICC8S8) (also ICC7S13).

DIRECT AND FREQUENT MEASUREMENT   Teachers should verify the effects of their instruction by measuring student performance directly and frequently. Measurement is *direct* when it objectively records the learner's performance of the behavior of interest in the natural environment for that skill. Measurement is *frequent* when it occurs on a regular basis; ideally, measurement should take place as often as instruction occurs. Figure 5 shows how teachers recorded daily measures of student's performance of each step of the morning routine, including the degree of independence and whether an adult provided a prompt or assistance.

Teachers who do not collect direct and frequent measures of their students' performance are prone to two mistakes: (a) continuing ineffective instruction even though no real learning has occurred (e.g., perhaps a teacher believes a certain type of instruction is effective) and (b) discontinuing or changing an effective program of instruction because the teacher's subjective judgment detects no improvement (Heward, 2005).

Without counting, would you know if a student's reading has improved from 70 words read correctly per minute to 80 words per minute?

EDUCATIONAL PLACEMENT ALTERNATIVES

Children with mild intellectual disabilities were traditionally educated in self-contained classrooms in the public schools, and students with moderate and severe intellectual disabilities were routinely placed in special schools. Today many children with intellectual disabilities are educated in general education classrooms.

During the 2008–09 school year, 17% of students with intellectual disabilities were educated in the general education classroom, with 27% being served in resource room programs and 48% in separate classes (U.S. Department of Education, 2010b). About 7% of students with intellectual disabilities are educated in separate schools, residential facilities, or home/hospital environments. Sometimes a number of small neighboring school districts pool their resources to offer a special school program for students with moderate, severe, and profound intellectual disabilities. However, some special educators believe that separate schools prohibit students from obtaining an education in the least restrictive environment and that all children should attend their local neighborhood schools regardless of the type or severity of their disability (e.g., Stainback & Stainback, 1996; Taylor, 2005).

Simply putting a child with disabilities into a general education classroom does not mean that he will be accepted socially or receive the most appropriate and needed instructional programming (Siperstein, Parker, Norins Bardon, & Widamon, 2007). Many special and general educators, however, are developing programs and methods for teaching students with intellectual disabilities alongside their classmates without disabilities. Systematically planning for the student's inclusion in the classroom through team games and collaborative learning and group investigation projects and directly training all students in specific skills for interacting with one another are just some of the methods for increasing the chances of a successful general education class placement (Giangreco & Doyle, 2007; Grenot-Scheyer, Fisher, & Staub, 2001; Ryndak & Fisher, 2007; Salend, 2011; Snell & Janney, 2005). Peer tutoring and peer buddy programs can also promote the instructional and social inclusion of students with intellectual disabilities into general education classrooms (Campbell Miller, Cooke, Test, & White, 2003; Copeland et al., 2004; Hughes & Carter, 2006).

Students with intellectual disabilities often benefit from similar programs for students who are not disabled. During the early elementary grades, students with intellectual disabilities as well as their chronological-age peers need instruction in basic academic skills. During this period, most students with intellectual disabilities benefit from full or partial inclusion in general education classroom settings.

The relative appropriateness of spending the entire school day in a general education classroom changes for some students as they move from the elementary grades to high school, when opportunities for community-based instruction in vocational and life skills are critical (Bouck, 2011; Hartman, 2009). The extent to which a general education classroom is an appropriate placement for a student with intellectual disabilities, as with any student with disabilities, should be determined by the student's individual needs. "School inclusion can then be seen as a means (as opposed

Placement alternatives for students with ID

Council for Exceptional Children — Content Standards for Beginning Teachers of Individuals with DD and/or Autism—Continuum of placement services available for individuals with DD (DD1K2).

Facilitating inclusion for students with ID

Council for Exceptional Children — Content Standards for Beginning Teachers of Individuals with DD and/or Autism—Approaches to creating positive learning environments for individuals with DD (ICC5K1) (also ICC5S3, ICC5S4).

Community-based instruction lets students with intellectual disabilities learn vocational skills in real-world work settings.

© Fotosearch/SuperStock

"So That's What I Do Next":
Video Modeling and Prompting with iPods and iPads

BY RYAN O. KELLEMS AND TOBIAS H. RICKARD

Thomas, a secondary student with intellectual disabilities, was experiencing difficulty doing important tasks while working as a clerk, where his responsibilities included restocking the shelves at his community job placement site in a grocery store. For example, Thomas would begin to restock the laundry detergent but falter along the way, requiring numerous prompts to complete the task.

The problem was not motivation. Thomas enjoyed working at the store and the transition goals on his self-directed IEP included competitive employment and independent living. Nor was he resistant to instruction and feedback from teachers or supervisor and coworkers on the job site. Thomas always responded positively to assistance and corrections. The problem was that Thomas required a great deal of supervision and frequent prompts to complete the task. Like many students with cognitive disabilities, when faced with multiple-step tasks, Thomas has difficulty remembering what to do next.

Another common characteristic Thomas shares with today's students, with or without disabilities, is being tech-savvy. He needs no instruction or any reminders on how to use the iPod that plays his favorite music.

We sought an instructional strategy that would take advantage of Thomas's familiarity with mobile technology devices to help him, and other students like him, learn to perform functional tasks. We found it in video modeling.

WHAT IS VIDEO MODELING?
With video modeling the learner watches a brief video of a person performing the target skill or task and then imitates the model's behavior. In video self-modeling, the learner watches a video of himself (Buggey, 2007). Video prompting is a form of video modeling where the learner watches a series of videos with each one depicting a single step. The learner then performs that step before the next step is shown (Sigafoos, O'Reilly, Cannella et al., 2007). Numerous peer-reviewed studies have demonstrated the effectiveness of video modeling and video prompting for teaching a wide range of social skills, domestic routines, and vocational tasks to children and adults with developmental disabilities and autism (Mechling, Gast, & Gustafson, 2009; Mechling & Stephens, 2009; Van Laarhoven, Johnson, Van Laarhoven-Myers, Grider, & Grider, 2009; Sigafoos, O'Reilly, Cannella, et al., 2007). Bellini and Akullian

(2007) conducted a meta-analysis of video modeling research and concluded that video modeling meets the criteria for an evidence-based instructional practice.

ADVANTAGES OF iPOD VIDEO MODELING
Early video modeling research and practice usually had the learner view and imitate the videotaped model in a controlled, instructional setting, prior to performing the targeted task or skill in the natural setting without the video model (Ayres & Langone, 2008). Recently several researchers have reported successful use of video modeling using iPods, iPads, and other portable electronic devices (Kellems, 2011; Mechling, in press). Those studies and our experience suggest the following advantages of iPod video modeling:

- Learners can take video models with them to use as reminders and prompts in community, home, and work environments.
- Students think using mobile devices is cool, and it is socially acceptable in most settings.
- Students can view the entire video or replay any part as needed.
- Auditory prompts can be included and, if appropriate to the setting, listened to with ear buds so as to not distract others.
- It lessens the amount of teacher and staff time required to supervise and prompt students to complete tasks.
- It is cost-effective as videos for commonly required tasks can be used by multiple students.
- Videos can be individualized based on a learner's needs and preferences.
- It allows students maximum control and independence, leading to higher levels of self-determination.

THOMAS MAKES TEA
Thomas and other secondary students with disabilities enrolled in the Community Living Program (CLP) practice daily living skills such as meal preparation, cleaning, and budgeting in community-based apartments rented by the school district. Like many of their peers with intellectual disabilities, CLP students need a great deal of practice and guided support to learn functional skills. With the introduction of the iPad, routines that instructional staff previously had to model and prompt repeatedly are now being demonstrated using video via iPods and iPads.

Thomas loves to make iced tea for himself and others, but he required a number of prompts to complete the task. By using his iPad to watch video prompts of the steps needed to correctly make iced tea, he can do it. iPod and iPad video modeling is enabling other CLP students to complete vocational tasks at various community-based work sites.

HOW TO GET STARTED

An excellent source of practical information on preparing and using video modeling and prompting can be found in Sigafoos, O'Reilly, and de la Cruz (2007). The following steps will help you get started using video modeling/prompting with portable electronic devices:

1. **Obtain necessary equipment to accomplish three functions:** (a) capturing video (using a camcorder or digital camera), (b) video editing (using computer software such as iMovie for Mac or Windows Movie Maker for PC), and (c) video playback by the student (using portable electronic devices such as iPod or iPad, smartphone, or other mobile electronic device). The iPad2 can accomplish all three functions.

2. **Identify target tasks or skills to be learned.** Individual student needs based on transition plans, IEP goals, and students', parents', and employer's input. Targeted task can be functional, vocational, and social.

3. **Task-analyze the skill.** Conduct a task analysis (see Figure 5). If the task is to be performed in a community-based employment setting, ask the employer or a coworker to verify the accuracy and completeness of the task analysis.

4. **Observe the student performing the task without any assistance or prompts.** Note which steps the student struggles with or does not complete correctly. This information will help determine which steps to emphasize with video.

5. **Make a video of someone performing each step of the task.** The model might be the teacher, a coworker, or the student himself. The model should be as close to the age and appearance of the student as possible. Have the model emphasize or explain any steps or techniques that the student has difficulty with. For steps the student can already complete correctly, a still image of the student doing that step may be used instead of video.

6. **Edit the video into a sequence of brief clips, one clip for each step.** Add text and/or voiceover instructions at the beginning of each step and

provided by Ryan Kellems

Thomas viewing video model on iPad.

provided by Ryan Kellems

"Rinse out tea pitcher." iPad provides text or audio prompt and video clip of each step in a task.

a "stop" cue at the end. For steps that must be repeated a certain number of times or until a certain outcome is obtained, provide explicit instructions that state when the step is completed and when to move on to the next step.

7. **Load video into iPod, iPad, or similar mobile device, and observe the student performing the task with the device.** Edit/refine the video as needed (the video will need to be formatted for the specific mobile device to be used).

8. **Reduce the video.** As the student's performance of targeted tasks improves, edit out steps and fade use of video models and prompts to promote maximum independence.

About the Authors

Ryan O. Kellems is a research associate in the Secondary Special Education and Transition Research Unit at the University of Oregon; Tobias H. Rickard is an autism specialist working with the Community Living Program in the 4J School District, Eugene, Oregon.

to just a goal unto itself) toward the ultimate objective of community inclusion and empowerment" (Polloway, Smith, Patton, & Smith, 1996, p. 11).

Acceptance and Membership

Since the early 1970s, the principle of **normalization** has provided a conceptual foundation and touchstone for improving the life experiences of people with intellectual disabilities. The concept, which originated in Scandinavia, was first described in an American publication by Nirje (1969) in a book published by the President's Committee on Mental Retardation. Nirje's idea of nomalization contained "eight planks": a normal rhythm of the day, a normal routine of life (e.g., living in one place and working in another); a normal rhythm of the year (e.g., observing holidays, personal religious days, and relaxation days); a normal developmental experience of the life cycle (e.g., experiencing the settings and atmospheres enjoyed by typical peers); valuing individual choices (e.g., allowing the dignity and freedom to fail); living in a sexual world; normal economic standards; and living, learning, and recreating in the same community facilities others enjoy (Perske, 2004)

Wolfensberger (1972), one of the first and best-known champions of normalization in the United States, wrote that the principle refers to the use of progressively more normal settings and procedures "to establish and/or maintain personal behaviors which are as culturally normal as possible" (p. 28). Normalization is not a technique or a set of procedures but an overriding philosophy. It says that people with intellectual disabilities should, to the greatest extent possible, be both physically and socially integrated into everyday society regardless of their degree or type of disability.

While the principle of normalization has helped individuals with intellectual disabilities who are physically present in many school, community, and work settings today, it has not gained them acceptance and true membership (Lemay, 2006). Wolfensberger (1983) proposed the concept of *social role valorization (SRV)* as a necessary and natural extension of the normalization principle.

> The key premise of SRV is that people's welfare depends extensively on the social roles they occupy: People who fill roles that are positively valued by others will generally be afforded by the latter the good things of life, but people who fill roles that are devalued by others will typically be badly treated by them. This implies that in the case of people whose life situations are very bad, and whose bad situations are bound up with occupancy of devalued roles, then if the social roles they are seen as occupying can somehow be upgraded in the eyes of perceivers, their life conditions will usually improve, and often dramatically so. (Wolfensberger, 2000, p. 105)

Perhaps the greatest current expression and extension of the normalization/SRV concept in special education can be found in the growing movement toward teaching self-determination skills to individuals with intellectual disabilities. In his presidential address to the AAMR, Wagner (2000) offered this example of the relationship between self-determination and social role valorization:

> How do we . . . implement this dream of highly valued roles in society? One thing we need to do is . . . celebrate the people who, in fact, currently have highly valued roles. . . . [For example] . . . there is Christina. She has big dreams. . . . About 6 years ago, she was mainstreamed into a large high school. In central Louisiana. . . . [S]he went out for the cheerleading squad and became a cheerleader. Then, a few years later when she was a senior, Christina decided that she wanted to be Homecoming Queen. She saw no problem at all with the fact that she has Down syndrome. . . . [S]he ran for Homecoming Queen and won. Christina is my heroine of big dreams. She did not let her handicaps stand in the way of realizing her dreams. I think it is also a testament to that high school that they did not let her handicaps stand in the way either. (p. 442)

One of the most important things that special educators can do is to help students like Christina identify their goals and provide the instruction and supports that will enable them to pursue those goals. As support for self-determination and social role valorization grows among both educators and the public, the time draws nearer when all people with intellectual disabilities will experience the benefits of valued membership in integrated school, community, and employment settings.

▼ TIPS FOR BEGINNING TEACHERS

Organization Is Key

BY SANDIE TRASK-TYLER

GET TO KNOW YOUR STUDENTS BEFORE THE SCHOOL YEAR BEGINS

- Send a welcome note to all of your students in the middle of the summer and include a picture of yourself. Highlight something they can look forward to when school starts.
- Organize a class get-together for your students and their families before the start of school. This is a great opportunity for everyone to meet each other and a wonderful way for parents to network.

BE PREPARED TO BUY EXTRA CLASSROOM SUPPLIES

- Stock up on classroom supplies during the back-to-school sales in the summer.
- Save your personal spending receipts for classroom purchases. You may be able to use these expenditures on your taxes.
- Shop at yard sales and auctions for all types of items you can use in your classroom at a great price.

CREATE AN ORGANIZATIONAL SYSTEM THAT WORKS FOR YOU

- Label boxes, shelves, and cabinets with words and/or pictures of what belongs there to assist staff and students in locating and replacing items.

- Create a spreadsheet of student and staff information such as phone numbers, addresses, parents' names, and so forth and keep a copy at home and school for easy access.
- Create a spreadsheet with students' school information, including date of birth, multifactored evaluation due date, IEP due date, related services, and so on.
- Set up a notebook or clipboard for each student with his corresponding IEP data sheets. You can group them into the different curricular areas and even insert student work samples so all of their learning information is in one location.
- Color-code student data sheets and other student information. This helps all of the classroom staff easily identify student forms and makes paperwork colorful.
- Set up a teacher binder that includes general substitute teacher information, overall class schedule, student transportation information, copies of emergency information, drill procedures, each student's IEP, and other classroom information (such as the previously mentioned spreadsheets).

▼ KEY TERMS AND CONCEPTS

acquisition stage of learning
active student response (ASR)
adaptive behavior
amniocentesis
chronic villi sampling (CVS)
Down syndrome
fragile X syndrome
generalization
genetic counseling
intellectual disability
maintenance
normal curve

normalization
norm-referenced test
perinatal
phenylketonuria (PKU)
pica
positive reinforcement
postnatal
practice stage of learning
prenatal
rubella
standard deviation
task analysis

▼ SUMMARY

Definition

- IDEA defines *intellectual disability* as significantly sub-average general intellectual functioning existing concurrently with deficits in adaptive behavior and manifested during the developmental period that adversely affects a child's educational performance.
- According to the AAIDD, intellectual disability is characterized by significant limitations in both intellectual functioning and adaptive behavior as expressed in conceptual, social, and practical adaptive skills. This disability originates before age 18.
- A traditional and still widely used method of classifying intellectual disabilities consists of four categories of the degree or level of intellectual impairment as determined by IQ score: mild, moderate, severe, and profound.
- The AAIDD previously recommended classifying intellectual disabilities according to the intensity of supports needed by an individual: intermittent, limited, extensive, and pervasive—an approach that essentially paralleled the four-level classification system based on IQ scores. AAIDD's current approach is a multidimensional classification system that recognizes varied purposes of classification.

Identification and Assessment

- An IQ test consists of a series of questions (e.g., vocabulary, similarities), problem solving (e.g., mazes, block designs), memory, and other tasks assumed to require certain amounts of intelligence to answer or solve correctly.
- IQ scores seem to be distributed throughout the population according to a phenomenon called the *normal curve.* Theoretically, about 2.3% of the population falls ≥2 standard deviations below the mean, which the AAIDD calls "significantly subaverage."
- The IQ cutoff score of 70 is intended only as a guideline and should not be interpreted as a hard-and-fast requirement. An IQ score of 75 or higher may be associated with intellectual disability if, according to a clinician's judgment, the child exhibits deficits in adaptive behavior thought to be caused by impaired intellectual functioning.
- Because IQ tests are composed largely of verbal and academic tasks—the same things a child must master to succeed in school—they correlate highly with school achievement.
- Adaptive behavior consists of the conceptual, social, and practical skills that people need to function in their everyday lives.
- Systematic assessment of adaptive behavior is important because the exhibited adaptive skills—as well as the nature and severity of maladaptive behaviors—of a person with intellectual disabilities are critical factors in determining the nature and degree of supports she requires for success in school, work, community, and home environments.
- Most instruments for assessing adaptive behavior consist of a series of questions answered by someone familiar with the individual.

- Measurement of adaptive behavior has proven difficult, in large part because of the relative nature of social adjustment and competence: behavior that is considered appropriate in one situation or by one group may not be appropriate in or by another.

Characteristics

- Children with mild intellectual disabilities may experience substantial performance deficits only in school. Their social and communication skills may be normal or nearly so. They are likely to become independent or semi-independent adults.
- Most children with moderate intellectual disabilities show significant developmental delays during their preschool years.
- Most children with severe and profound intellectual disabilities are identified at birth or shortly thereafter and may have additional disabilities and/or health conditions.
- The cognitive functioning of students with intellectual disabilities is characterized by
  - memory deficits, especially working memory and short-term memory;
  - rarely used metacognitive or executive control strategies such as rehearsing and organizing information;
  - a slow learning rate compared to typically developing age-mates;
  - trouble attending to relevant features of a learning task, perhaps focusing instead on distracting irrelevant stimuli, and often difficulty sustaining attention;
  - difficulty generalizing and maintaining newly learned knowledge and skills;
  - expecting failure regardless of their efforts (learned helplessness);
  - distrusting their own responses to situations and relying on others for assistance and solutions (outer-directedness).
- Children with intellectual disabilities have substantial deficits in adaptive behavior that take many forms and tend to occur across domains of functioning. Limitations in self-care skills and social relationships as well as behavioral excesses are common characteristics of individuals with intellectual disabilities.
- Many children and adults with intellectual disabilities display positive attributes such as tenacity and curiosity in learning, getting along well with others, and being a positive influence on those around them.

Prevalence

- Theoretically, 2.3% of the population would score 2 standard deviations or more below the norm on IQ tests; but this does not account for adaptive behavior, the other criterion for diagnosis of intellectual disability. Many experts now cite an incidence figure of approximately 1% of the total population.
- During the 2009-2010 school year, approximately 7.8% of all students receiving special education did so under the category of intellectual disabilities.

Causes and Prevention

- More than 350 causes and risk factors associated with intellectual disabilities have been identified.
- Each risk factor for intellectual disabilities is classified by when it occurs (i.e., prenatal, perinatal, or postnatal) and whether its influence is biomedical or environmental (social, behavioral, educational).
- Biomedical causes are identified for about two-thirds of individuals with severe and profound levels of intellectual disabilities.
- Although etiology is unknown for most individuals with mild intellectual disabilities, psychosocial disadvantage in early childhood is suspected as a causal factor in many cases.
- Virus vaccines, amniocentesis, CVS, genetic counseling, and early screening tests have reduced the incidence of intellectual disabilities caused by some genetic disorders.

Educational Approaches

- Students with intellectual disabilities need instruction in basic academic skills that are required and/or could be used often in their current and future environments.
- Curriculum should focus on functional skills that will help the student succeed in self-care, vocational, domestic, community, and leisure domains.
- Major components of explicit systematic instruction are task analysis, active student response, systematic feedback, transfer of stimulus control from teacher-provided cues and prompts to natural stimuli, programming for generalization and maintenance, and direct and frequent measurement of student performance.

Educational Placement Alternatives

- During the 2008–09 school year, approximately 17% of students with intellectual disabilities were educated in general education classrooms; 27% in resource rooms; 48% in separate classrooms; and about 7% in separate schools, residential facilities, or home/hospital environments.
- During the early elementary grades, many students with intellectual disabilities benefit from full or partial inclusion in general education classroom settings.
- Strategies for facilitating successful placement in a general education class include planning for the student's inclusion through team games, collaborative learning, group investigation projects, and by directly training all students in specific skills for interacting with one another.
- The relative appropriateness of inclusion in the general education classroom may change for some students with intellectual disabilities as they move from the elementary grades to the secondary level, when opportunities for community-based instruction in vocational and life skills are critical.
- Teachers should determine the extent to which a general education classroom is an appropriate placement for a student with intellectual disabilities based on the student's individual needs.
- The principles of normalization, social role valorization, and self-determination are important in helping people with intellectual disabilities achieve acceptance and membership in society.

MyEducationLab™

Go to Topic 10, Intellectual Disabilities, in the MyEducationLab (www.myeducationlab.com) for *Exceptional Children*, where you can

- Find learning outcomes for intellectual disabilities along with the national standards that connect to these outcomes.
- Complete Assignments and Activities that can help you more deeply understand the chapter content.
- Apply and practice your understanding of the core teaching skills identified in the chapter with the Building Teaching Skills and Dispositions learning units.
- Examine challenging situations and cases presented in the IRIS Center Resources.
- Access video clips of CCSSO National Teachers of the Year award winners responding to the question "Why Do I Teach?" in the Teacher Talk section.
- Check your comprehension of the content covered in the chapter with the Study Plan. Here you will be able to take a chapter quiz, receive feedback on your answers, and then access Review, Practice, and Enrichment activities to enhance your understanding of chapter content.
- Use the Online Lesson Plan Builder to practice lesson planning and integrating national and state standards into your planning.

▼ GLOSSARY

acquisition stage of learning: The initial phase of learning when the student is learning how to perform a new skill or use new knowledge; feedback should focus on the accuracy and topography of the student's response. Compare with *practice stage of learning*.

active student response (ASR): A frequency-based measure of a student's active participation during instruction; measured by counting the number of observable responses made to an ongoing lesson or to curriculum materials.

adaptive behavior: Conceptual, social, and practical skills that people have learned in order to function in their everyday lives; refers to typical performance of people without disabilities in meeting the expectations of everyday environments.

amniocentesis: The insertion of a hollow needle through the abdomen into the uterus of a pregnant woman. Used to obtain amniotic fluid in order to determine the presence of genetic and chromosomal abnormalities. It also confirms the gender of the fetus.

chorionic villi sampling (CVS): A procedure for prenatal diagnosis of chromosomal abnormalities that can be conducted during the first 8 to 10 weeks of pregnancy; fetal cells are removed from the chorionic tissue, which surrounds the fetus, and directly analyzed.

Down syndrome: A chromosomal anomaly that often causes moderate to severe mental retardation, along with certain physical characteristics such as a large tongue, heart problems, poor muscle tone, and a broad, flat bridge of the nose.

fragile X syndrome: A chromosomal abnormality associated with mild-to-severe mental retardation. Thought to be the most common known cause of inherited intellectual disabilities. Affects males more often and more severely than females; behavioral characteristics are sometimes similar to individuals with autism. Diagnosis can be confirmed by studies of the X chromosome.

generalization: The extent to which previously learned knowledge or skill either occurs under conditions different from those under which it was originally learned or is performed in a different but functionally equivalent manner. Situation or setting generalization occurs when a student performs a behavior in the presence of stimuli other than those that were present originally. Response generalization occurs when a person performs behaviors that were never directly trained but have the same effect on the environment as the original trained behavior.

genetic counseling: A discussion between a specially trained medical counselor and people who are considering having a baby about the chances of having a baby with a disability, based on the prospective parents' genetic backgrounds.

intellectual disabilities: A disability characterized by significant limitations in both intellectual functioning and adaptive behavior as expressed in conceptual, social, and practical adaptive skills; the disability originates before age 18 (AAIDD, 2007). Refers to the same population of individuals who were diagnosed previously with mental retardation. (See *mental retardation*.)

maintenance: The extent to which a learner continues to exhibit a previously learned behavior after a portion or all of the instructional intervention originally used to teach the skill has been terminated.

normal curve: A mathematically derived curve depicting the theoretical probability or distribution of a given variable (e.g., as a physical trait or test score) in the general population. Indicates that approximately 68% of the population will fall within 1 standard deviation above or below the mean; approximately 27% will fall between 1 and 2 standard deviations either above or below the mean; and less than 3% will achieve more extreme scores of more than 2 standard deviations in either direction.

normalization: As a philosophy and principle, the belief that individuals with disabilities should, to the maximum extent possible, be physically and socially integrated into the mainstream of society regardless of the degree or type of disability. As an approach to intervention, the use of progressively more normal settings and procedures "to establish and/ or maintain personal behaviors which are as culturally normal as possible" (Wolfensberger, 1972, p. 28).

norm-referenced test: A test constructed so that a person's score can be compared to others of same age or grade level; contrast with *criterion-referenced test*.

perinatal: Occurring at or immediately after birth.

phenylketonuria (PKU): An inherited metabolic disease that can cause severe mental retardation; can now be detected at birth, and the detrimental effects can be prevented with a special diet.

pica: A form of self-injurious behavior in which the person ingests nonnutritive substances (e.g., dirt, rocks, sticks, plastic, string, feces); exhibited by some people with moderate and severe mental retardation.

positive reinforcement: Presentation of a stimulus or event immediately after a response has been emitted, which has the primary effect of increasing the occurrence of similar responses in the future.

postnatal: Occurring after birth.

practice stage of learning: After a student has learned how to perform a new skill, she should work to develop fluency with the target skill. Feedback during the practice stage of learning should emphasize the rate or speed with which the student correctly performs the skill. Compare with *acquisition stage of learning*.

prenatal: Occurring before birth.

rubella: German measles; when contracted by a woman during the first trimester of pregnancy, may cause visual impairments, hearing impairments, intellectual disabilities, and/or other congenital impairments in the child.

standard deviation: A descriptive statistic that shows the average amount of variability among a set of scores. A small standard deviation indicates that the scores in the sample are distributed close to the mean; a larger standard deviation indicates that more scores in the sample fall farther from the mean.

task analysis: Breaking a complex skill or chain of behaviors into smaller, teachable units.

Learning Disabilities

Learning Disabilities

- Why has the concept of learning disabilities proven so difficult to define?
- What characteristic encompasses all students with learning disabilities?
- What factors might account for the huge increase in the prevalence of students identified with learning disabilities since the category was officially recognized in the mid-1970s?
- Are the achievement deficits of most students diagnosed with learning disabilities the result of neurological impairment or poor instruction?

- What can a student's responsiveness to evidence-based instruction reveal about the need and focus of special education?
- How can academic tool skills and learning strategies relate to each other?
- What skills are most important to the success of an elementary-age student with learning disabilities in the general education classroom? for a secondary student?

▼ FEATURED TEACHER

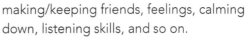

ANGELA PRESTON

Carl A. Furr Elementary School • Cabarrus County Schools, Concord, North Carolina

EDUCATION—TEACHING CREDENTIALS—EXPERIENCE

- B.A., Special Education, Appalachian State University, 2004
- M.Ed., Special Education, University of North Carolina at Charlotte, 2011
- North Carolina Teaching Licenses in Specific Learning Disabilities, General Curriculum, and Adapted Curriculum
- 8 years of experience as a special education teacher

CURRENT TEACHING POSITION AND STUDENTS I am an exceptional child (EC) resource teacher and the EC department chair for my school. I teach students who are pulled out of the general education classroom for specialized instruction in reading, writing, math, and/or social skills in my resource room. I teach 32 different students. If you count the number of students in and out of my room each day, I teach 53 students (e.g., James comes three different times for reading, writing, and math).

Academically, most of my students are 1 to 3 years below grade level. If that does not sound so bad, think about being a fourth or fifth grader with the reading or math skills of a first or second grader.

Most of my students get along well with their peers, but several receive social skills instruction to address making/keeping friends, feelings, calming down, listening skills, and so on.

Most of my students take the end-of-grade (EOG) state assessments. A student can receive accommodations such as extra time, a separate room, read aloud, and multiple test sessions to assist with showing what they know. A few of my students take the Extend 2 alternative assessment, a grade-level assessment that uses simpler language, shorter passages, and provides three answer choices instead of four.

I use a model-lead-test ("I do, we do, you do") approach for teaching all subjects (reading, writing, and math). I also use it when I want students to remember more than one direction. The model-lead-test format is a research-based instructional strategy that has been proven to be effective.

WHAT I LIKE MOST ABOUT BEING A SPECIAL EDUCATOR Being a teacher means you have chosen to make a difference in the lives of students. Being a special education teacher means not only making a difference, but also providing a foundation for unique students who continually struggle. The best part of being a special educator is building relationships with students and guiding them to success. Even the smallest achievements bring joy to students, their families, and teachers. Teaching students in a small-group, resource setting allows you to get to know each student personally. It also provides a chance to teach some of the same students from first through fifth grades.

I love building relationships with kids and watching them grow. The growth in my field can seem much slower than in other classes, which makes even the smallest steps feel like huge accomplishments. The groups I teach are never larger than nine students, so I can really get to know each student individually and find out his or her interests. I love helping students make good life decisions. My students will often talk with me about what is going on outside my room, and together we can make a plan on how they can address those issues.

It is an incredible moment when you can build a relationship that unlocks how a student thinks, teach something, and see that student apply it. I had a student who was learning that everyone makes mistakes. We had been working all year on saying, "No big deal," if he made a mistake. One spring day he walked in my room and said, "I made a mistake today. No big deal." I could barely contain my excitement. We started dancing around the room singing, "No big deal. No big deal." He was beginning to understand the important life lesson that no one is perfect.

PERSONAL QUALITIES OF AN EFFECTIVE SPECIAL EDUCATOR

Special educators need to be compassionate, organized, staunch advocates for their students and able to make decisions under pressure. Compassionate teachers build relationships with their students. They understand the child has a disability and is willing to work with the child. Yet, they still set high goals. Organization is key! There are so many IEP dates, evaluation dates, meeting dates, and so on, to keep up with. Staying organized will keep the stress to a minimum. Advocating for a child can be difficult if you are not an assertive person. Sometimes you are the child's only advocate, and your decisions must always have the child's best interest at heart. The last quality is just as important as the others. Special education can be unpredictable. Great teachers are able to think on their feet and make quick decisions under pressure.

But all of these nice personal qualities will mean little if the teacher does not provide systematic, intensive instruction thoughtfully aimed at each child's unique needs. I recall a few years ago when a student was placed in our program and I was told, "Good luck—he just does not understand how to read." He began the year reading 20 words per minute (wpm) on a grade-level text. We worked daily on reading using a Direct Instruction program. He worked hard in my room and with his general education teacher. On his final reading assessment he gave it his all and finished the year reading 72 wpm! He then impressed his teachers (including me) by passing both his Extend 2 reading and his math EOG tests. His teacher and I could not wait to tell him. He just beamed as we explained how he passed both tests and how much growth he had made. Later at his IEP meeting, I teared up when I told his mom how well he did this year. His growth in just 1 year was incredible!

ADVICE TO SOMEONE CONSIDERING A CAREER IN SPECIAL EDUCATION

Being a special education teacher is a rewarding but difficult occupation. Spend time with kids with disabilities by volunteering or mentoring. Volunteer at Special Olympics or in a special education class at a local school. This will help you decide if being a special education teacher is right for you. In high school, I was a student mentor to a student with Down syndrome. Working with him helped me realize I wanted a career in special education. Teaching is more effective and rewarding for people who have a true passion for children with disabilities. Once you have decided, you can't imagine your life spent as anything except a special education teacher. Be ready for truly one of the most rewarding jobs of all.

After the newness of teaching wears off, it can be easy to fall into a routine of monotony and lower expectations. Keep your spirits high by making your career enjoyable and full of laughter. At our school the EC teachers offer an incentive for all the EC third through fifth graders who take the EOG test. If they give 100% effort on the EOGs by reading every question and answer choices, trying each math problem by writing something down, looking back over their answers, and taking their time, they earn a pie ticket. At the end of the year, we pass out the tickets and the kids can throw whip cream pies at their EC teachers. Some kids will only earn one or two, but all kids can earn up to three for the three tests. Tickets are earned by the effort each student makes, not the score received. We also let the second graders watch so they can see what they can earn next year.

The EC teachers also keep things light by pranking each other on our birthdays. The kids love the excitement, and sometimes it's all we need to recharge the teachers and the kids. Over the years we have been known to remove all items from a classroom (chairs, tables, even posters), fill a room with metal folding chairs, and much more. Once, I even found a goldfish swimming in one of my plastic drawers!

It is important to stay serious about teaching by using explicit instruction and maintaining focus on building students' skills. But it is also important to enjoy the uniqueness of the students and your fellow colleagues. I had a group of students who were learning short vowel sounds. At the end of our reading lesson, we would play "Karaoke Vowels!" I would give a student a fake microphone, flash them a vowel, and they would sing the vowel sound. One of my students was so excited he ran across the room, fell to his knees, arched his back, and sang, "Aaaaa!" at the top of his lungs. From that point forward, we sang "Rock Star Vowels!"

To observe a teacher using Direct Instruction techniques such as those used by Angela Preston, go to the book resources for this text on MyEducationLab.

MyEducationLab™

Visit the **MyEducationLab** for *Exceptional Children* to enhance your understanding of chapter concepts with a personalized Study Plan. You'll also have the opportunity to hone your teaching skills through video- and case-based Assignments and Activities, IRIS Center Resources, and Building Teaching Skills and Dispositions lessons.

BY THE LATE 1950S, most public schools had established special education programs (or at least offered some type of special service) for children with intellectual disabilities, children with physical disabilities, children with sensory impairments, and those with emotional or behavioral disorders. But there remained a group of children with serious learning problems who did not fit into the existing categories of exceptionality. The children seemed physically intact, yet they seemed unable to learn certain basic skills and subjects at school. Because the schools at that time had no programs for these children, parents searching for help for their children turned to physicians and psychologists. Understandably, these professionals viewed the children from the vantage points of their respective disciplines and used terms such as *brain damage, minimal brain dysfunction, neurological impairment, perceptual handicap, dyslexia*, and *aphasia* to describe or account for the children's learning problems. Some of these terms are still used today because a variety of disciplines continue to influence the field of learning disabilities.

The term *learning disabilities* was coined by Samuel Kirk in a 1963 address to a group of parents whose children were experiencing serious difficulties in learning to read, write, spell, or solve math problems. The parents liked the term and that very evening voted to form the Association for Children with Learning Disabilities. Today, the organization's name is Learning Disabilities Association of America (LDA), and it is a powerful advocacy group for people with learning disabilities. In 1975, learning disabilities was included as a special education category in IDEA.

Considerable confusion and disagreement exist among professionals and parents on even the most basic question: What is a learning disability? In some ways, learning disabilities has brought out both the worst and the best that special education has to offer. Learning disabilities has served as a breeding ground for fads and miracle treatments ("New Diet Regimen Cures Learning Disabilities!"). At the same time, some of the most innovative and productive researchers in special education have devoted their careers to the study and treatment of learning disabilities. Many instructional strategies that were developed for students with learning disabilities have influenced and benefited the entire field of education.

DEFINITIONS

Many definitions of learning disabilities have been proposed and debated over the years. Although none has been universally accepted, the two definitions that have had the most influence are the federal definition in IDEA and a definition proposed by the National Joint Committee on Learning Disabilities (NJCLD).

Federal Definition

IDEA defines **specific learning disability** as follows:

> *In General*—The term "specific learning disability" means a disorder in 1 or more of the basic psychological processes involved in understanding or in using language, spoken or written, which disorder may manifest itself in an imperfect ability to listen, think, speak, read, write, spell, or to do mathematical calculations.
>
> *Disorders Included*—Such term includes such conditions as perceptual disabilities, brain injury, minimal brain dysfunction, dyslexia, and developmental aphasia.
>
> *Disorders Not Included*—Such term does not include a learning problem that is primarily the result of visual, hearing, or motor disabilities, of mental retardation, of emotional disturbance, or of environmental, cultural, or economic disadvantage. (PL 108-466, Sec. 602[30])

OPERATIONALIZING THE FEDERAL DEFINITION When using the federal definition to identify students with learning disabilities, most states require three criteria:

1. A severe discrepancy between the student's intellectual ability and academic achievement
2. An exclusion criterion: the student's difficulties are not the result of another known condition that can cause learning problems
3. A need for special education services

Ability–Achievement Discrepancy. Children with learning disabilities exhibit an unexpected difference between general ability and achievement—a discrepancy that would not be predicted by the student's general intellectual ability. Children who are having minor or temporary difficulties in learning should not be identified as learning disabled. According to federal guidelines that accompanied the original IDEA, only children with a "severe discrepancy between achievement and intellectual ability" were to be identified as learning disabled (U.S. Office of Education, 1977).

The most common practice for identifying children with learning disabilities is to determine if a severe discrepancy exists between their expected and actual achievement. This involves comparing a student's score on an IQ test with her score on a standardized achievement test. While such a comparison seems simple on the surface, in practice it is fraught with problems (Fletcher et al., 2002; Kavale, 2002). The federal government proposed several mathematical formulas for determining a severe discrepancy. All of the proposed formulas were eventually rejected, and the final rules and regulations for IDEA did not contain a specific definition of and formula for determining a severe discrepancy. This confusion and disagreement about exactly how a severe discrepancy should be determined led to widely differing procedures for identifying and classifying students as learning disabled (Fuchs & Young, 2006).

Recognizing the problems inherent in the discrepancy approach to determining eligibility for special education and with concern for the large and growing number of children being identified under the learning disabilities category, when Congress reauthorized IDEA in 2004, it significantly changed the way that states could determine a child's eligibility for special education under the specific learning disabilities category:

> When determining whether a child has a specific learning disability . . . a local educational agency shall not be required to take into consideration whether a child has a severe discrepancy between achievement and intellectual ability. . . . [And] a local educational agency may use a process that determines if the child responds to scientific, research-based intervention as a part of the evaluation procedures." (PL 108-466, Sec. 614[b][6][A–B])

This approach to identifying students with learning disabilities, called *response to intervention (RTI)*, shifts identification from a "wait-to-fail" model to one of early identification and prevention (Vaughn & Fuchs, 2003b). RTI is discussed in detail later in this chapter.

Exclusion. The IDEA definition of learning disabilities identifies students with significant learning problems that are not "primarily the result" of other conditions that can impede learning, such as another recognized disability or lack of opportunity to learn due to cultural factors, environmental or economic disadvantage, or limited English proficiency. The word *primarily* in the definition recognizes that learning disabilities can coexist with other disabilities; in that case, the student typically receives services under the other disability category.

Need for Special Education. Students with learning disabilities show specific and severe learning problems despite standard educational efforts and therefore need specially designed instruction to meet their unique needs. This criterion is meant to avoid the overidentification of children who have not had the opportunity to learn. Such children should progress satisfactorily as soon as they receive effective instruction at a curricular level appropriate to their current skills.

National Joint Committee on Learning Disabilities Definition

The NJCLD is a group composed of representatives from 12 professional organizations concerned with the education, treatment, and rights of children and adults with learning disabilities. The NJCLD (1990/2001) believes that the federal definition of learning disabilities contains several inherent weaknesses:

NJCLD definition of LD

 Content Standards for Beginning Teachers of Students with LD: Current definitions and issues related to the identification of individuals with LD (LD1K5).

- *Exclusion of adults.* Learning disabilities can occur across the life span.
- *Reference to "basic psychological processes."* This phrase invites debate on how to teach students with learning disabilities, a curricular issue, not a definitional one.
- *Inclusion of spelling as a learning disability.* Spelling can be subsumed under "written expression."
- *Inclusion of obsolete terms.* Terms such as *minimal brain dysfunction, perceptual impairments,* and *developmental aphasia* have proven difficult to define and only add confusion to the definition.
- *Wording of the exclusion clause.* The IDEA definition suggests that learning disabilities cannot occur along with other disabilities. However, a person may have a learning disability along with another disability but not *because of* another disability.

In response to these problems with the federal definition, the NJCLD (1991) developed the following definition:

> *Learning disabilities* is a general term that refers to a heterogeneous group of disorders manifested by significant difficulties in the acquisition and use of listening, speaking, reading, writing, reasoning, or mathematical abilities.
>
> These disorders are intrinsic to the individual and presumed to be due to central nervous system dysfunction, and may appear across the life span. Problems in self-regulatory behaviors, social perception, and social

© Blend Images/Shutterstock

Students with learning disabilities have significant learning problems that cannot be explained as primarily the result of another recognized disability or lack of opportunity to learn due to environmental, cultural, or economic conditions.

interaction may exist with learning disabilities but do not themselves constitute a learning disability.

Although learning disabilities may occur concomitantly with other handicapping conditions (for example, sensory impairment, mental retardation, serious emotional disturbance) or with extrinsic influences (such as cultural differences, insufficient or inappropriate instruction), they are not the result of those conditions or influences. (p. 1)

The NJCLD (2011) recently reaffirmed its position that "learning disabilities (LD) represents a valid, unique, and heterogeneous group of disorders [that] are neurobiologically based, involve cognitive processes, and affect learning" (p. 1). Some authorities, however, contend that the concept of learning disabilities is poorly defined and functions as a catchall category for any student who is experiencing learning problems and does not meet eligibility requirements for other disability categories (Kavale, Holdnack, & Mostert., 2006).

CHARACTERISTICS

Early in the field's history, a task force commissioned to identify the characteristics of children with learning disabilities found that 99 separate characteristics were reported in the literature (Clements, 1966). An inherent danger in such lists is to assume, or to look for, each of those characteristics in every child with learning disabilities. This danger is especially troublesome with learning disabilities because the category includes children who exhibit a wide range of learning, social, and emotional problems. In fact, Mercer and Pullen (2009) suggest that it is theoretically possible for an individual with learning disabilities to exhibit one of more than 500,000 combinations of cognitive or socioemotional problems.

Learning disabilities are associated with problems in listening, reasoning, memory, attention, selecting and focusing on relevant stimuli, and the perception and processing of visual and/or auditory information. These perceptual and cognitive processing difficulties are assumed to be the underlying causes of the following characteristics that students with learning disabilities experience, either individually or in combination: reading problems, deficits in written language, underachievement in math, poor social skills, attention deficits and hyperactivity, behavior problems, and low self-esteem/self-efficacy.

Reading Problems

Dyslexia/reading disabilities

 Council for Exceptional Children Content Standards for Beginning Teachers of Students with LD: Educational implications of characteristics of various exceptionalities (ICC2K2).

Difficulty with reading is by far the most common characteristic of students with learning disabilities. About 80% of all children identified as learning disabled are referred for special education because of reading problems. Children who fail to learn to read by the first grade tend to fall farther and farther behind their peers, not only in reading but in general academic achievement as well (Kame'enui, Good, & Harn, 2005).

Evidence suggests that specific reading disability, sometimes called dyslexia, is a persistent deficit, not simply a developmental lag in linguistic or basic reading skills (Lyon, Shaywitz, & Shaywitz, 2003). The International Dyslexia Association defines **dyslexia** as

a specific learning disability that is neurobiological in origin. It is characterized by difficulties with accurate and/or fluent word recognition and by poor spelling and decoding abilities. These difficulties typically result from a deficit in the phonological component of language that is often unexpected in relation to other cognitive abilities and the provision of effective classroom instruction. (2008, p. 1)

The most severe reading problems of children with learning disabilities lie at the word level of processing (i.e., inability to accurately and fluently decode single words), and the most common cognitive limitation of these children is dysfunction in the awareness of the phonological structure of spoken words (Torgesen & Wagner, 1998). **Phonological awareness** refers to the "conscious understanding and knowledge that language is made up of sounds" (Simmons, Kame'enui, Coyne, Chard, & Hairrell, 2011, p. 54). The most important aspect of phonological awareness for learning to read is **phonemic awareness,** the knowledge that words consist of separate sounds, or phonemes, and the ability to manipulate these individual sound units. A child with phonemic awareness can do these things:

Phonological awareness

Council for Exceptional Children

Content Standards for Beginning Teachers of Students with LD: Effects of phonological awareness on the reading abilities of individuals with LD (LD3K2).

- *Orally blend sounds to make words* (e.g., "What word do you have if you put these sounds together: /c/, /aaaa/, /t/?"—*cat*)
- *Isolate sounds at the beginning, middle, and ending of words* (e.g., "What is the first sound in *rose*?"—/*rrrrr*/)
- *Segment a word into sounds* (e.g., "Say the sounds in the word *sat*"—/ssss/—/aaaa/—/t/)
- *Manipulate sounds within a word* (e.g., "What word do you have if you change the /ssss/ in *sat* to /mmmm/?—*mat*) (adapted from Simmons et al., 2011, p. 54)

Recent research suggests that children with severe reading disabilities, particularly those who are resistant to interventions effective for the majority of struggling readers, may share a second processing problem in addition to deficits in phonological awareness. Many children and adults with dyslexia show a significant deficit in *visual naming speed* (the ability to rapidly name visually presented stimuli) compared to a typical reader (Lovett, Steinbach, & Frijters, 2000). When asked to state the names of visually presented material such as letters, many individuals with reading disabilities have difficulty rapidly retrieving and stating the names of the letters, even though they know the letter names. The term *double-deficit hypothesis* is used to describe children who exhibit underlying deficits in phonological awareness and rapid naming speed (Wolf & Bowers, 2000).

Of course, comprehension is the goal of reading. And comprehension lies at the phrase, sentence, paragraph, and story level, not in identifying single words. But the inability to rapidly identify words impairs comprehension in at least two ways. First, faster readers encounter more words and idea units, thereby having the opportunity to comprehend more. Second, assuming that both word recognition and comprehension consume finite cognitive processing resources, a struggling reader who devotes more processing resources to identifying words has "fewer cognitive processing resources . . . available for comprehension" (Jenkins & O'Conner, 2001, pp. 1–2).

Comprehension and beginning reading instruction

Council for Exceptional Children

Content Standards for Beginning Teachers of Students with LD: Relationships among reading instruction methods and LD (LD7K1) (also LD3K3).

Extensive research over the past 35 years has produced more than 2,000 peer-reviewed journal articles about early reading acquisition and reading difficulties. This research has revealed a great deal about the nature of children's reading disabilities and the kind of interventions most effective in preventing and remediating reading problems (Bursuck & Damer, 2011; Foorman, 2007; King-Sears & Bowman-Kruhm, 2010; Ming & Dukes, 2010). Figure 1 describes key principles of effective beginning reading instruction consistent with recommendations based on a review of that research by the National Institute of Child Health and Human Development (2000). To learn more about effective beginning reading instruction, see *Teaching & Learning*, "Explicit Instruction."

FIGURE 1   RESEARCH-BASED PRINCIPLES OF EARLY READING INSTRUCTION

1. **Begin teaching phonemic awareness directly in kindergarten.** Many children and adults who cannot read are not aware of phonemes. If phonemic awareness does not develop by age 5 or 6, it is unlikely to develop later without instruction. Activities such as the following help develop children's phonemic awareness:

   - *Phoneme deletion.* What word would be left if the /k/ sound were taken away from *cat*?
   - *Word-to-word matching.* Do *pen* and *pipe* begin with the same sound?
   - *Phoneme counting.* How many sounds do you hear in the word *cake*?
   - *Odd word out.* What word starts with a different sound: *bag, nine, beach, bike*?

   Teachers should start teaching phonemic awareness before beginning instruction in letter–phoneme relationships and continue phonemic awareness activities while teaching the letter–phoneme relationships.

2. **Teach each letter–phoneme relationship explicitly.** Only about 40 to 50 letter–sound relationships are necessary to read. Telling children explicitly what single sound a given letter or letter combination makes will prevent reading problems better than encouraging children to figure out the sounds for the letters by giving clues. Many children have difficulty figuring out the individual letter–phoneme correspondences if they hear them only in the context of words and word parts. Therefore, teachers should separate phonemes from words for instruction. For example, the teacher shows the children the letter *m* and says, "This letter says /mmm/."

   A new phoneme and other phonemes the children have learned should be practiced for about 5 minutes each day in isolation. The rest of the lesson should use these phonemes in words and stories composed of only the letter–phoneme relationships the children have learned in isolation up to that point.

3. **Teach frequent, highly regular letter–sound relationships systematically.** To teach systematically means coordinating the introduction of the letter–phoneme relationships with the material the children are asked to read. The words and stories should be composed of only the letter–phoneme relationships the children have learned. The order of the introduction of letter–phoneme relationships should be planned to allow reading material composed of meaningful words and stories as soon as possible. For example, if the first three letter–phoneme relationships the children learn are /a/, /b/, /c/, the only real word the children can read is *cab*. But if the first three letter–phoneme relationships are /m/, /a/, /s/, the children can read *am, Sam, mass, ma'am*.

4. **Show children exactly how to sound out words.** After children have learned two or three letter–phoneme relationships, teach them how to blend the sounds into words. Show them how to move sequentially from left to right through spellings as they sound out each word. Every day practice blending words composed of only the letter–phoneme relationships the children have learned.

5. **Give children connected, decodable text to practice the letter–phoneme relationships.** Children need extensive practice in applying their knowledge of letter–sound relationships to reading. The most effective integration of phonics and reading occurs with *decodable text*—text composed of words that use the letter–phoneme relationships the children have learned to that point and a limited number of sight words that have been systematically taught. As the children learn more letter–phoneme relationships, the texts become more sophisticated.

   Texts that are less decodable do not integrate phonological knowledge with actual reading. For example, "*The dog is up*" is the first sentence children read in one meaning-based program with an unintegrated phonics component. The sound-letter relationships the children had learned up to this point were /d/, /m/, /s/, /r/, /t/. By applying their phonics knowledge, the children could read only "_____ d_____ _____ _____." But if children have learned /a/, /s/, /m/, /b/, /t/, /h/, /f/, /g/, /i/, they can read "*Sam has a big fist.*" The sentence is 100% decodable because the phonics component has been integrated properly into the child's real reading.

   Text that is less decodable requires children to use prediction or context to figure out words. Although prediction is valuable in comprehension for predicting the next event or predicting an outcome, it is not useful in word recognition. The use of predictable text rather than decodable text might allow children to use prediction to figure out a passage. However, the strategy does not transfer to real reading. Predictable text gives children false success. While such success may motivate many children, ultimately they will not be successful readers if they rely on text predictability to read.

6. **Use interesting stories to develop language comprehension.** Research does not rule out the use of interesting, authentic stories to develop language comprehension. But it does recommend not using these stories as reading material for nonreaders. Teacher-read stories play an important role in building children's oral language comprehension, which ultimately affects their reading comprehension. Story-based activities should be structured to build comprehension skills, not decoding skills.

   During the early stages of reading acquisition, children's oral language comprehension level is much higher than their reading comprehension level. The stories teachers read to children to build their comprehension should be geared to their oral language comprehension level. The material used to build children's decoding should be geared to their decoding skills, with attention to meaning. Teachers should teach comprehension strategies and new vocabulary using orally presented stories and texts that are more sophisticated than the early decodable text the children read. The teacher should read these stories to the children and discuss the meaning with them. After the children become fluent decoders, they can apply these comprehension strategies to their own reading.

Source: Adapted from Grossen, B. (2006). Six principles for early reading instruction. In W. L. Heward, *Exceptional children: An introduction to special education* (8th ed., pp. 186–188). Upper Saddle River, NJ: Pearson.

Written Language Deficits

Many students with learning disabilities have problems writing and spelling. Students with learning disabilities perform significantly lower than their age-matched peers without disabilities on all written expression tasks, including the transcription of handwriting, spelling, punctuation, vocabulary, grammar, and expository writing (Graham & Harris, 2003; Troia, 2007). Some students with learning disabilities are competent readers but struggle mightily with written language. For example, Figure 2 shows the story written by a 10-year-old student when shown an illustration of prehistoric cavemen. Sean's oral reading of his story reveals a huge disparity between his written and oral language abilities.

Explicit instruction of letter–phoneme relationships prevents reading problems better than encouraging children to figure out the sounds for the letters by giving clues.

Compounding the weak language base that many students with learning disabilities bring to the writing task is an approach to the writing process that involves minimal planning, effort, and metacognitive control (Englert, Wu, & Zhao, 2005). Many students with learning disabilities use a "retrieve-and-write" approach in which they retrieve from immediate memory "whatever seems appropriate and write it down" (De La Paz & Graham, 1997, p. 295). They seldom use the self-regulation and self-assessment strategies of competent writers: setting a goal or plan to guide their writing, organizing their ideas, drafting, self-assessing, and rewriting. As a result, they produce poorly organized compositions containing a few poorly developed ideas.

Fortunately, teachers can help most students with learning disabilities to improve their writing and spelling skills by explicit instruction on specific writing skills and strategic approaches to writing and giving frequent opportunities to practice with systematic feedback and motivation (e.g., Alber-Morgan, Hessler, & Konrad, 2007; Lienemann, Graham, Leader-Janssen, & Reid, 2006; Schumaker & Deshler, 2009).

Written language deficits

 Council for Exceptional Children Content Standards for Beginning Teachers of Students with LD: Educational implications of characteristics of various exceptionalities (ICC2K2) (also LD3K3).

Math Underachievement

Numerical reasoning and calculation pose major problems for many students with learning disabilities. Students with learning disabilities perform lower than typically achieving children on every type of arithmetic problem at every grade level (Cawley,

---

FIGURE 2 WRITTEN LANGUAGE SAMPLE FROM A 10-YEAR-OLD STUDENT WITH LEARNING DISABILITIES

Sean's Written Story	Sean's Oral Reading of His Story
A loge tine ago they atene a cosnen they head to geatthere on fesee o One day tere were sane evesedbeats all gaseraned tesene in cladesn they hard a fest for 2 meanes.	A long time ago there were ancient cave men. They had to get their own food. One day there were some wildebeests. They all gathered them and killed them. They had a feast for two months.

Source: Courtesy of Timothy E. Heron, The Ohio State University.

Explicit Instruction

BY NANCY E. MARCHAND-MARTELLA AND RONALD C. MARTELLA

Although most teachers have read or heard about the importance of explicit instruction, many are unsure about how to include the fundamental principles and practices of explicit instruction into their daily lessons.

EXPLICIT INSTRUCTION DEFINED

Explicit, or direct, instruction is "a systematic method of teaching with emphasis on proceeding in small steps, checking for student understanding, and achieving active and successful participation by all students" (Rosenshine, 1987, p. 34). This type of instruction is also referred to as "demonstration-prompt-practice" (Stevens & Rosenshine, 1981) or "I do, we do, you do" (Martella, Nelson, Marchand-Martella, & O'Reilly, 2012). Rosenshine (1986) provides highlights of research on explicit instruction of well-defined knowledge and skills such as math procedures, grammatical rules, and vocabulary. These highlights include the following:

- Start every lesson by correcting the previous day's homework and reviewing what students have recently been taught.
- Describe the goals of today's lesson.
- Present new material in small steps, giving clear and detailed explanations of the skill(s) to be learned (modeling), checking often for student understanding through strategic questioning.
- Provide repeated opportunities for students to practice in an active manner and to obtain feedback on their performance (guided practice).
- Monitor student learning through varied exercises (e.g., seat work).
- Continue providing practice opportunities until students are performing skills independently and with ease (independent practice).
- Review the previous week's lesson at the beginning of each week; review what students have learned over the past 4 weeks at the end of each month.

Explicit instruction is a "deceptively simple strategy" that includes the following: teachers show students what to do, give them opportunities to practice with teacher feedback, and then provide opportunities for students to apply these skills on their own over time (Hempenstall, 2004). It is not trial-and-error learning, discovery, exploration, facilitated learning, or some other approach where teachers assist or facilitate performance; rather, the teacher's "direct actions have a direct and instructional influence on students' learning" (Carnine, Silbert, Kame'enui, & Tarver, 2010, p. 5).

WHY EXPLICIT INSTRUCTION IS IMPORTANT

Students qualify for special education because they are significantly behind their peers in one or more academic areas. These students must be accelerated in their learning to catch up, so teachers must do more in less time. The most effective way of shortening the learning time for these students is through the direct teaching of skills.

"Instructional approaches that have yielded significant outcomes for students with LD are characterized as being well specified, explicit, carefully designed, and closely related to the area of instructional need (reading, spelling, math)" (Vaughn & Fuchs, 2003, p. 140). For example, instruction found to be most effective in teaching students to read involves systematic and explicit techniques (i.e., instruction includes a carefully selected set of skills organized into a logical sequence) (Armbruster, Lehr, & Osborn, 2006; National Institute of Child Health and Human Development, 2000; National Institute for Literacy, 2007). Additionally, explicit instructional techniques are fundamental for students who are acquiring math skills. "The teacher reveals or makes transparent the connections between knowledge acquisition and knowledge application, rather than leaving the student to discover those connections more incidentally" (L. S. Fuchs & Fuchs, 2001, p. 93). Therefore, in explicit instruction, teachers initially take full responsibility for student learning but gradually relinquish responsibility to students as they become successful. "This progression can be seen as a continuum that moves from teacher modeling, through guided practice using prompts and cues, to independent and fluent performance by the learner" (Rosenshine, 1986, p. 69).

EXAMPLES OF EXPLICIT INSTRUCTION IN PUBLISHED CURRICULA

Several curricular programs feature explicit instruction. The most well known are the Direct Instruction programs in reading, math, and language published by Science Research Associates. Figure A shows Exercise 5 from Lesson 4 of *Reading Mastery Signature Edition, Grade K* (Engelmann & Bruner, 2008). In this lesson, the sound for the letter *m* (/m/) is introduced by the teacher (modeling) and practiced by the students (guided practice). The /m/ is reviewed in the same lesson and over subsequent lessons during independent practice activities.

Figure B shows a phonemic awareness activity from Voyager Passport, Level A, Lesson 7 (Voyager Expanded Learning, 2008). As you can see, final sound discrimination is introduced by the teacher (modeling); it is practiced by the students with the teacher assisting (guided practice), and then done independently during the lesson and in subsequent lessons for review.

TEACHING & LEARNING

SCRIPT FROM A DIRECT INSTRUCTION LESSON USING EXPLICIT INSTRUCTION
TO INTRODUCE A NEW LETTER–SOUND CORRESPONDENCE

SOUNDS
EXERCISE 5

Introducing the new sound **mmm** as in **mat**

a. (Touch the first ball of the arrow.) Here's a new sound. My turn to say it. When I move under the sound, I'll say it. I'll keep on saying it as long as I touch under it. Get ready. (Move quickly to the second ball of the arrow. Hold for two seconds.) mmm.

b. (Touch the first ball of the arrow.) My turn again. Get ready. (Move quickly to the second ball of the arrow. Hold for two seconds.) mmm.

c. (Touch the first ball of the arrow.) My turn again. Get ready. (Move quickly to the second ball of the arrow. Hold for two seconds.) mmm.

d. (Touch the first ball of the arrow.) Your turn. When I move under the sound, you say it. Keep on saying it as long as I touch under it. Get ready. (Move quickly to the second ball of the arrow. Hold for two seconds.) *mmm.* Yes, mmm.

To Correct
(If the children do not say *mmm:*)
1. mmm.
2. (Touch the first ball of the arrow.) Say it with me. Get ready. Move quickly to the second ball of the arrow. Hold for two seconds. Say mmm with the children.) mmm.
3. (Touch the first ball of the arrow.) Your turn. Get ready. (Move quickly to the second ball of the arrow. Hold for two seconds.) mmm.

e. (Touch the first ball of the arrow.) Again. Get ready. (Move quickly to the second ball of the arrow. Hold for two seconds.) *mmm.* Yes, mmm.

f. (Repeat *e* until firm.)

g. (Call on individual children to do *d.*)

h. Good saying mmm.

Source: From Reading Mastery—Reading Presentation Book A—Grade K, 6e © 2008 (Exercise 5 from Lesson 4). Used by permission from The McGraw-Hill Companies, Inc.

HOW TO GET STARTED

Following are guidelines and suggestions for teachers who want to incorporate principles of explicit instruction into nonexplicit lessons:

1. **Determine whether or not a lesson is explicit.**
   Teachers can recognize if a lesson is explicit or not by considering the directedness of the information provided to the students. For example, if students are expected to find answers on their own without previous instruction, the lesson is not likely to be explicit. Phrases such as "encourage children to identify," "challenge children to say," "help children focus," "work with children to build," "help them discover," and "facilitate learning by" are used in nonexplicit programs.

   Explicit programs are more likely to use phrases such as "My turn to say it," "I'm going to show you," "Watch me," "This is," and "Let's say it together." In explicit programs and instruction, teachers model or show students how to do something, provide students with practice and

teacher feedback, and include independent activities for students to practice on their own.

2. **Once you identify nonexplicit instructional formats, make them more explicit.** For example, the following sample illustrates nonexplicit instruction from Rigby Literacy, Grade 1, Level 4, Day 1, "The animal walk" (Rigby, 2004):

   > **Initial and final consonant sounds.** Find the words like and little in the book. What is the same about these words? Let's say the words aloud. What sound do you hear at the beginning of each word? Find the words slug and bug. What is the same about these words? Let's say the words aloud. What sound do you hear at the end of each word? (p. 94)

   Teachers can make this lesson more explicit by

   a. *Modeling* what is the same about these words (e.g., "Find the words like and little in the book. Both of these words begin with the sound /l/.)

FIGURE B

EXAMPLE OF LESSON USING EXPLICIT INSTRUCTION FOR PHONEMIC AWARENESS SKILLS

Looking for the Last Sound

cat/can **cup**/cut

mat/**mad** **man**/map

pen/**pet** sit/**sip**

sad/sun **pin**/pig

58 • Adventure 3 Lesson 7

Phonemic Awareness (10 min.)
Final Sound Discrimination
Materials: letter squares *d, n, p, t*; Individual Reading Mat A (1 per student and teacher)

Source: From Adventure 3 Phonemic Awareness *Voyager Passport*, Level A (Lesson 7, p. 118). Copyright 2008 by Voyager Expanded Learning. Used by permission from Voyager Expanded Learning.

b. *Providing guided practice* (e.g., "What sound is the same in both of these words?" "Yes, /l/.")

c. *Including independent practice activities* (e.g., students complete independent assignments focused on /l/)

To observe teachers implementing Direct Instruction lessons in reading and spelling, go to the book resources for this text on MyEducationLab.

About the Authors

Nancy E. Marchand-Martella and Ronald C. Martella are professors of special education at Eastern Washington University.

Parmar, Foley, Salmon, & Roy, 2001). Deficits in retrieving number facts and solving story problems are particularly evident (L. S. Fuchs et al., 2010; Geary, 2004). The math competence of students with learning disabilities progresses about 1 year for every 2 years in school, and the skills of many children plateau by age 10 or 12 (Cawley, Parmar, Yan, & Miller, 1998).

Given these difficulties, it is not surprising that more than 50% of students with learning disabilities have IEP goals in math (Kavale & Reese, 1992). As with reading and writing, research shows that explicit, systematic instruction of thoughtfully sequenced skills sequences that incorporates guided practice, fluency training, and feedback can improve the math performance of students with learning disabilities (e.g., Codding, Burns, & Lukito, 2011; L. S. Fuchs et al., 2010; Gersten et al., 2009; Misquitta, 2011).

Social Skills Deficits

Students with learning disabilities are prone to social problems. After reviewing 152 studies, Kavale and Forness (1996) concluded that about 75% of students with learning disabilities exhibit deficits in social skills. Poor social skills often lead to rejection, low social status, fewer positive interactions with teachers, difficulty making friends, and loneliness—all of which are experienced by many students with learning disabilities regardless of classroom placement (Estell, Jones, Pearl & Van Acker, 2009; Wiener, 2004). The poor social skills of students with learning disabilities may be due to the ways they interpret social situations relative to their own experiences and inability to perceive the nonverbal affective expressions of others (Meadan & Halle, 2004; Most & Greenbank, 2000).

Although researchers who studied messages by children on a website for people with learning disabilities found "rare instances" when children described positive social relationships (e.g., "I have lots of friends."), the children overwhelmingly expressed social difficulties (Raskind, Margalit, & Higgins, 2006).

Some students with learning disabilities, however, experience no problems getting along with their peers and teachers. For example, Sabornie and Kauffman (1986) reported no significant difference in the sociometric standing of 46 high school students with learning disabilities and 46 peers without disabilities. Moreover, they discovered that some of the students with learning disabilities enjoyed socially rewarding experiences in inclusive classrooms.

One interpretation of these contradictory findings is that social competence and peer acceptance are not characteristics of learning disabilities but are outcomes of the different social climates created by teachers, peers, parents, and others with whom students with learning disabilities interact (Vaughn, McIntosh, Schumm, Haager, & Callwood, 1993). Researchers have begun to identify the types of problems experienced by children with learning disabilities who are ranked low in social acceptance and to discover instructional arrangements that promote the social status of students with learning disabilities in the general education classroom (Bryan, 2005; Court & Givon, 2003).

Attention Problems and Hyperactivity

Some students with learning disabilities have difficulty attending to a task and/or display high rates of hyperactivity. Children who consistently exhibit these problems may be diagnosed with attention-deficit/hyperactivity disorder (ADHD). A high degree of **comorbidity** (two conditions occurring in the same individual) between learning disabilities and ADHD has frequently been reported (Smith & Adams, 2006). A national study examining the demographics of elementary and middle school students with disabilities found that of 28% of parents whose children were receiving special education under the category of learning disabilities reported their children as also having ADHD (Wagner & Blackorby, 2002).

Behavioral Problems

Researchers have consistently found a higher-than-usual incidence of behavioral problems among students with learning disabilities (Cullinan, 2007). A comparative study of more than 600 adolescents with and without learning disabilities found a higher frequency of risk-taking behaviors such as smoking, marijuana use, delinquency, acts of aggression, and gambling among the youth with learning disabilities (McNamara & Willoughby, 2010). Although research clearly shows increased behavioral problems among children with learning disabilities, the relationships between the students' behavior problems and academic difficulties are not known. In other words, we do not know whether the academic deficits or the behavioral problems cause the other

Social, attention, and behavioral problems

 Content Standards for Beginning Teachers of Students with LD: Psychological, social, and emotional characteristics of individuals with LD (LD2K3) (also ICC2K2).

difficulty, or whether both are products of other causal factors. And it is important to note that many children with learning disabilities exhibit no behavioral problems.

Regardless of the interrelationships of these characteristics, teachers and other caregivers responsible for planning educational programs for students with learning disabilities need skills for dealing with social and behavioral difficulties as well as academic deficits.

Low Ratings of Self-Efficacy

Students with learning disabilities are more likely to report lower levels of self-efficacy, mood, effort, and hope than are their peers without learning disabilities. It is not known whether a tendency for negative self-perceptions is an inherent characteristic of learning disabilities or the result of a painful history of frustration and disappointment with academic and social situations (Cosden, Brown, & Elliott, 2002), "day-to-day struggles, and/or future worries" (Lackaye, Margalit, Ziv, & Ziman, 2007, p. 111).

The Defining Characteristic

Although students with learning disabilities are an extremely heterogeneous group, it is important to remember that the fundamental, defining characteristic of students with learning disabilities is the presence of specific and significant achievement deficits seemingly in spite of adequate overall intelligence. The difference between what students with learning disabilities "are expected to do and what they can do . . . grows larger and larger" over time (Deshler et al., 2001, p. 97). The performance gap becomes especially noticeable and handicapping in the middle and secondary grades, when the academic growth of many students with disabilities plateaus. By the time they reach high school, students with learning disabilities are the lowest of the low achievers, performing below the 10th percentile in reading, written language, and math (Hock, Schumaker, & Deshler, 1999).

The difficulties experienced by children with learning disabilities—especially for those who cannot read at grade level—are substantial and pervasive and usually last across the life span (Price, Field, & Patton, 2003). The tendency to think of learning disabilities as a "mild" disability erroneously supports "the notion that a learning disability is little more than a minor inconvenience rather than the serious, life-long condition it often is [and] detracts from the real needs of these students" (Hallahan, 1998, p. 4).

Although an objective awareness of the learning and behavioral problems faced by children with learning disabilities is necessary for effective intervention, teachers should not focus solely on students' deficits. It is equally important to recognize and value the useful skills and interests possessed by each child with learning disabilities and help that child maintain a positive outlook (see Figure 3).

PREVALENCE

Learning disabilities is by far the largest of all special education categories. During the 2009–10 school year, nearly 2.5 million students ages 6 to 21 received special education under the specific learning disabilities category (U.S. Department of Education, 2011). This figure represents 42.3% of all school-age children with disabilities and about 4% of the school-age population. As a result of different methods employed by the states for

Academic achievement of students with LD

 Content Standards for Beginning Teachers of Students with LD: Educational implications of characteristics of various exceptionalities (ICC2K2) (also LD3K3).

Creatas Images/Thinkstock

Teachers of students with learning disabilities should not be so focused on remediating their students' skill deficits that they fail to recognize and nurture the negotiable skills and positive qualities of each student.

FIGURE 3 **THE IMPORTANCE OF MAINTAINING A POSITIVE FOCUS**

Tom Lovitt is a pioneer in the education of children's learning disabilities and one of the field's more productive teachers and scholars. His carefully conducted research and thoughtful writing have spanned five decades and dealt with virtually every aspect of special education. In one of his classic books on teaching children with learning problems, *In Spite of My Resistance . . . I've Learned from Children,* Lovitt (1977) wrote that, all things being equal, a teacher who imparts many skills to many children is good, and one who does not is not. After all, teaching is helping children learn new things.

Although Lovitt consistently declares that the development of children's academic and social skills is the primary purpose for teachers and students to come together, he also warns us not to become so concerned with fixing everything we believe is wrong with the student that we forget about recognizing and building upon all that is positive.

> We teachers, in all good faith, set out to remediate as many of the "shortfalls" as possible so that youth with learning disabilities will be as normal and wonderful as we are. We should reconsider this total remedial approach to learning disabilities. One reason for considering an alternative should be obvious if we thought of a day in the life of a student with learning disabilities. First, the teacher sets out to remediate his reading, then his math, and then his language, social skills, and soccer playing. Toward the end of the day, she attempts to remediate his metacognitive deficits. That lad is in a remediation mode throughout the day. Is it any wonder that some of these youngsters have self-concepts, self-images, self-esteems, and attributions that are out of whack?
>
> We should spend some time concentrating on these youngsters' positive qualities. If a girl is inclined toward mechanics, or a boy to being a chef, we should nurture those skills. And if a child doesn't have a negotiable behavior, we should locate one and promote it. I can't help but think that if every youngster, LD or otherwise, had at least one trade, skill, or technique at which he or she was fairly competent, that would do more for that youngster's adjustment than would the many hours of remediation to which the child is subjected. Perhaps that accent on the positive would go a long way toward actually helping the remediation process. If children knew they could excel in something, that might help them become competent in other areas as well.

(T. C. Lovitt, August 7, 2011, personal communication)

diagnosing learning disabilities, the percentage of children served in this special education category ranges widely, from a low of 1.5% of the school-age population in Kentucky to a high of 5.6% in Iowa (U.S. Department of Education, 2009). Across grade levels, males with learning disabilities outnumber females by a 3:1 ratio.

The number of students identified with learning disabilities grew tremendously from 1976–1977, the first school year the federal government reported such data, through the 2002–03 school year, until students with learning disabilities represented approximately one-half of all school-age children receiving special education. The rising incidence of children with learning disabilities fueled the ongoing debate over the nature and validity of the learning disability category, and led some scholars to suggest it be considered an epidemic (Swanson, 2000). Recent years have seen a slight decrease in the identification rates for learning disabilities (McLeskey, Landers, Hoppey, & Williamson, 2011).

Although some believe the increase in the number of children identified as learning disabled indicates the true extent of the disability, others contend that too many low achievers—children without a disability who are doing poorly in school because they have not received effective instruction—have been improperly diagnosed as learning disabled, placing a severe strain on the limited resources available to serve those students challenged by a true disability. Lyon (1999), of the National Institute of Child and Human Development, suggested that learning disabilities has become "a sociological sponge to wipe up the spills of general education" (p. A1).

CAUSES

In most cases, the cause (etiology) of a child's learning disability is unknown. Many causes have been proposed, which probably reflects the diverse characteristics of students with learning disabilities. Just as there are different types of learning disabilities (e.g., language disabilities, math disabilities, reading disabilities), there are likely to

Causes of LD

 Content Standards for Beginning Teachers of Students with LD: Etiologies of learning disabilities (LD2K1).

be different causes. Four classes of suspected causes are brain damage, heredity, biochemical imbalance, and environmental agents.

Brain Damage or Dysfunction

Some professionals believe that all children with learning disabilities suffer from some type of neurological injury or dysfunction. This belief is inherent in the definition of learning disabilities by the National Joint Committee on Learning Disabilities (1991), which states that learning disorders are "presumed to be due to central nervous system dysfunction" (p. 19). When evidence of brain damage is not found (which is the case for the majority of children with learning disabilities), the term *brain dysfunction* is sometimes used, especially by physicians. This wording implies brain damage by asserting that the child's brain does not function properly.

Advances in neuroimaging technologies such as magnetic resonance imaging (MRI) and functional magnetic resonance imaging (fMRI) have enabled researchers to discover that specific regions of the brains of some individuals with reading and language disabilities show activation patterns (i.e., function) during phonological processing tasks that differ from the patterns found in the brains of people without disabilities (e.g., Miller, Sanchez, & Hynd, 2003; Richards, 2001; Simos, Breier, Fletcher, Bergman, & Papanicolaou, 2000). Other studies have found that the brain structure of some children with reading disabilities differs slightly from that of children without disabilities (Collins & Rourke, 2003; Leonard, 2001). Collectively, neuroimaging research has been reasonably consistent in revealing functional and/or structural differences in the left temporal lobe of individuals with dyslexia (Gabrieli, 2009).

This research holds promise for understanding the neurobiological bases of dyslexia and other specific learning disabilities. As Leonard (2001) points out, however, we do not yet know how and to what extent the brain's neural networks are affected by the child's experiences (i.e., learning) and vice versa. Thus, we do not know whether neurobiological factors associated with learning disabilities contribute to the learning problems of children, are the product of an unstimulating environment, or are a combination of the two. However, growing evidence indicates that intensive remedial reading instruction reduces differences in the ways that the brains of children with reading disabilities and those of children without reading problems are activated (Rourke, 2005). For example, Shaywitz and colleagues (2004) reported that an average of 105 hours of individual tutoring that focused on teaching the **alphabetic principle** (how letters and combinations of letters represent the small segments of speech called *phonemes*) and oral reading fluency practice not only improved children's reading fluency but "facilitated the development of the neural systems that underlie skilled reading" (p. 933).

Special educators should refrain from placing too much emphasis on theories linking learning disabilities to brain damage or brain dysfunction. There are three major reasons for such caution. First, not all children with learning disabilities display clinical (medical) evidence of brain damage, and not all children with brain damage have learning disabilities. Second, assuming a child's learning problems are caused by a dysfunctioning brain may serve as a built-in excuse for continuing to provide ineffective instruction. When a student with suspected brain damage fails to learn, his teachers may be quick to presume that the brain injury prevents him from learning and slow to analyze and change instructional variables. Third, whether a child's learning disability results from brain injury or other central nervous system dysfunction will not, given our present state of knowledge, essentially alter the form or intensity of instructional interventions.

Heredity

Siblings and children of people with reading disabilities have a slightly greater than normal likelihood of having reading problems. Growing evidence indicates that genetics may account for at least some family links with dyslexia (Fisher & Francks, 2006; Galaburda, 2005; Grigorenko, 2003). Research has located possible chromosomal loci for the genetic transmission of phonological deficits that may predispose a child for reading problems later (Kaplan et al., 2002).

Biochemical Imbalance

Several popular theories advanced in the 1970s, and that continue to find traction from time to time in the popular media, hold that biochemical disturbances within a child's body cause learning disabilities. For example, Feingold (1975, 1976) claimed that artificial colorings and flavorings in many of the foods children eat can cause learning disabilities and hyperactivity. He recommended a treatment for learning disabilities consisting of a diet with no foods containing synthetic colors or flavors. In a comprehensive review of research studies that tested the special diet, Spring and Sandoval (1976) concluded that very little scientific evidence supported Feingold's theory.

Research also has suggested that learning disabilities can be caused by the inability of a child's bloodstream to synthesize a normal amount of vitamins (Cott, 1972). As a result, some children with learning disabilities received *megavitamin therapy,* which consists of massive daily doses of vitamins in an effort to overcome the child's suspected vitamin deficiencies. A study designed to test the effects of megavitamin treatment on children with learning disabilities and hyperactivity found that huge doses of vitamins did not improve the children's performance (Arnold, Christopher, Huestis, & Smeltzer, 1978). Most professionals today give little credence to biochemical imbalance as a significant cause of learning disabilities or to regimented diets and heavy doses of vitamins as treatment.

Some professionals advocate specialized diets and vitamin therapies as treatments for autism. See Schreibman (2005) for a discussion.

Environmental Factors

Although virtually impossible to document as primary causes of learning disabilities, environmental factors—particularly impoverished living conditions early in a child's life and limited exposure to highly effective instruction in school—probably contribute to the learning problems experienced by many children who receive special education. The tendency for learning disabilities to run in families also suggests a correlation between environmental influences on children's early development and subsequent achievement in school. Evidence for this relationship can be found in longitudinal research such as that conducted by Hart and Risley (1995), who found that infants and toddlers who received infrequent communication exchanges with their parents were more likely to show deficits in vocabulary, language use, and intellectual development before entering school.

Another environmental variable that is likely to contribute to children's learning problems is the quality of instruction they receive. Many special educators today believe that Engelmann (1977) was correct when he claimed more than 35 years ago that the vast majority of "children who are labeled 'learning disabled' exhibit a disability not because of anything wrong with their perception, synapses, or memory, but because they have been seriously mistaught" (pp. 46–47).

Although the relationship between the absence of effective instruction and learning disabilities is not clear, a great deal of evidence shows that many students' learning problems can be remediated by heavy doses of intensive, systematic instruction. It would be naive, however, to think that the achievement problems of all children with learning disabilities are caused entirely by inadequate instruction. Nevertheless, from an educational perspective, intensive, systematic instruction should be the intervention of first choice for all students with learning disabilities.

IDENTIFICATION AND ASSESSMENT

Assessments commonly used with students with learning disabilities include standardized intelligence and achievement tests, criterion-referenced tests, curriculum-based measurement, and direct and daily measurement. Because curriculum-based measurement (CBM) plays a central role in distinguishing between children who are struggling academically and those who may have a learning disability, and in the ongoing assessment of the progress of identified children, CBM is described first and in some detail.

Curriculum-Based Measurement

CBM

 Council for Exceptional Children

Content Standards for Beginning Teachers of Students with LD: Terminology and procedures used in the assessment of individuals with LD (LD8K1) (also ICC8K4, ICC8S4, ICC8S5).

Any measurement system must be valid and reliable. Repeatedly putting a ruler in a pot of water might yield a reliable measure of 3 inches, but it would not produce a valid measure of the water's temperature. As silly as that example might seem, too often, measures used in education assess something other than the skills students need to progress in the curriculum. **Curriculum-based measurement (CBM)** (also called *progress monitoring*) entails measuring the growth of students' proficiency in the core skills that contribute to success in school (Deno, Lembke, & Anderson, n.d.). CBM is characterized by multiple, ongoing measures of child performance over time and instructional decision making based on visual inspection of graphs of those data.

CBM is a **formative evaluation** method in that it provides information on student learning as instruction takes place over time. By contrast, the results of a **summative evaluation** cannot be used to inform instruction, because it is conducted after instruction has been completed (e.g., at the end of a grading period or school year). One study found that teachers who used CBM made an average of 2.5 changes in students' instructional plans over the course of 20 weeks, compared to an average of just 0.27 changes by teachers who were not using CBM (L. S. Fuchs, Fuchs, Hamlett, & Stecker, 1991). Other studies have reported that students whose teachers tailor instruction plans on CBM data perform and achieve better academically than do students whose teachers do not use CBM (Stecker & Fuchs, 2000; Wesson, 1991).

Detailed guidelines for tools for conducting CBMs are available at the National Center on Student Progress Monitoring (http://www.studentprogress.org/) and the Research Institute on Progress Monitoring (http://www.progressmonitoring.net).

In addition to being valid and reliable, CBMs should be easy to administer; cost- and time-efficient; and, perhaps most important, sensitive to small, incremental changes in student performance over time (Hessler & Konrad, 2008). One set of CBMs with these attributes is the Dynamic Indicators of Basic Early Literacy Skills (DIBELS) (Good, Kaminski, et al., 2011). DIBELS was developed to be an efficient indicator of key reading skills for early identification of children at risk for reading difficulties and to assess the effects of interventions designed to prevent such failure. DIBELS consists of a set of 1-minute fluency measures used to regularly monitor the development of prereading and early reading skills. Research has demonstrated that children who meet or exceed the benchmark goal for each measure are likely (odds greater than 80%–90%) to become proficient readers (Good, Kaminski, et al., 2011).

The most recent version, DIBELS Next, consists of six individual measures and a composite score:

- *First Sound Fluency.* The assessor says words, and the student says the first sound for each word. Benchmark: 30 or more first sounds per minute by the middle of kindergarten.
- *Letter Naming Fluency.* The student is presented with a sheet of letters and asked to name the letters. There is no benchmark for this measure.
- *Phoneme Segmentation Fluency.* The assessor says words, and the student says the individual sounds in each word. Benchmark: 40 or more phonemes per minute by the end of kindergarten.
- *Nonsense Word Fluency.* The student is presented with a list of VC and CVC nonsense words (e.g., *ov, sig, rav*) and asked to read the words. This test of the alphabetic principle assesses a child's letter–sound correspondence and ability to blend letters together to form unfamiliar "words." For example, if the stimulus word is *vaj*, the student could say, "/v/–/a/–/j/" or say the word /vaj/ to obtain a total of three letter sounds correct. Benchmark: 58 or more letter sounds per minute by the end of first grade.
- *DIBELS Oral Reading Fluency.* The student is presented with a reading passage and asked to read aloud. The student is then asked to retell what she just read.

The DIBELS measures are free and can be downloaded in English and Spanish at http://dibels.uoregon.edu. Also available on this website are video clips showing an examiner administering each of the DIBELS measures to a student.

The number of words read correctly in 1 minute is the oral reading fluency rate. The student receives 1 point for each word in her retell that is related to the passage. Benchmarks by the end of first, second, and third grade, respectively: 47, 87, and 100 words read correctly per minute and 15, 27, and 30 retell points.

- *Daze.* The student is presented with a reading passage in which some words are replaced by a multiple-choice box that includes the original word and two distractors. The student reads the passage silently and selects the word in each box that best fits the meaning of the sentence. The student receives 1 point for each correct word, minus half a point for each incorrect word. Benchmarks by the end of third and fourth grade are 19 and 24 points, respectively. (adapted from Good, Kaminski, et al., 2011)
- *Composite Score.* Composite Score is a combination of multiple DIBELS scores and provides the best overall estimate of a student's reading proficiency. The scores used to calculate the composite vary by grade and time of year. (adapted from Good, Kaminski, et al., 2011)

Numerous peer-reviewed studies have demonstrated the predictive validity of DIBELS for screening children who are likely to develop reading problems and for tracking the reading progress of children with disabilities, those who are at risk for reading failure, and struggling readers from low-performing high-poverty schools (e.g., Baker et al., 2008; Burke, Hagan-Burke, Kwok, & Parker, 2009; Goffreda, Diperna, & Pedersen, 2009).

DIRECT DAILY MEASUREMENT Direct daily measurement, the cornerstone of the behavioral approach to education, is, in a sense, CBM on steroids. It entails recording a measure of the student's performance each time a specific skill is taught. In a program teaching multiplication facts, for example, the student's performance of multiplication facts would be assessed each day that multiplication was taught. Measures such as correct rate (e.g., number of multiplication facts stated or written correctly per minute), error rate, and percent correct would be recorded. Direct daily measurement provides information about student learning on a continuous basis, enabling the teacher to modify instruction in accordance with changing (or unchanging) performance, not because of intuition, guesswork, or the results of a test that measures something else (Heward, 2003).

Some teachers of students with learning disabilities use a special system of direct daily measurement called **precision teaching**. Precision teachers make instructional decisions based on changes in the frequency of a student's performance (e.g., number of words read correctly per minute) as plotted on a standard celeration chart. Information about precision teaching and the standard celeration chart can be found at the Standard Celeration Society's website: http://celeration.org/.

Identifying Learning Disabilities by Assessing Response to Intervention

The basic premise of **response to intervention (RTI)** is that measuring a low-achieving student's response to increasingly intensive, scientifically validated instruction can determine whether the child's struggles to learn are the result of poor or insufficient instruction or of a disability for which special education is needed. Researchers who have implemented intensive programs of remedial instruction for struggling readers in the early grades report that a small percentage of those students (5% to 7%) fail to make adequate progress (e.g., O'Conner, 2000; Torgesen, 2001). "It is reasonable to think that these students, whose response to treatment is significantly lower than expected, could be identified with reading/learning disabilities" (Vaughn, Linan-Thompson, & Hickman, 2003, p. 393).

Self-recording direct and daily measures of academic performance is an excellent way to involve students in their own learning.

Response to intervention

 Council for Exceptional Children

Content Standards for Beginning Teachers of Students with LD: Screening, prereferral, referral, and classification procedures (ICC8K3) (also ICC8K4, ICC8S4, ICC8S5).

When done well, RTI has two functions: screening/identification and prevention. A child's positive response to scientifically validated instruction eliminates instructional quality as a viable explanation for poor academic growth and suggests evidence of a disability (L. S. Fuchs, Fuchs, & Hollenbeck, 2007). Children who respond favorably to RTI's increasingly intensive instruction benefit from the preventive aspect of the approach.

The trustworthiness of RTI depends on two equally important elements: (a) the consistent, rigorous implementation of research-based interventions and (b) an accurate, reliable, easy-to-use measure for monitoring student progress. CBM is the primary approach of progress monitoring in RTI. Although there are numerous approaches to RTI, a three-tiered model is most common (L. S. Fuchs & Fuchs, 2007a, 2007b; Johnson, Mallard, Fuchs, & McKnight, 2006). A student who moves through each tier of the model experiences all three levels of preventive intervention. The following examples describe how RTI can be used to prevent reading problems and identify children who need special education for reading disabilities.

TIER 1: PRIMARY INTERVENTION IN THE GENERAL EDUCATION CLASSROOM

Primary prevention is provided to all students in the form of evidence-based curriculum and instruction in the general education classroom (Foorman, 2007). Frequent progress monitoring assesses the performance of students whose scores on a screening test fall below benchmarks for critical reading skills. Students are considered at risk if both their level of performance and rate of growth on the CBM are well below those of their classmates. At-risk students who continue to struggle during Tier 1 instruction are moved to Tier 2 (see Figure 4).

TIER 2: SECONDARY INTERVENTION

Students who are struggling in the general education program receive an intensive fixed-duration trial (e.g., 10 to 12 weeks) of small-group supplemental tutoring using a research-validated program (Vaughn & Roberts, 2007). A student who makes satisfactory progress during this intensive prevention trial, such as Jordan in Figure 4, "is deemed disability-free (and remediated); he or she then is returned to the original classroom environment" (Vaughn & Fuchs, 2003, p. 139).

L. S. Fuchs and Fuchs (2007a, 2007b) recommend using a **dual discrepancy criterion** and designating a student as nonresponsive only when the student (a) fails to make adequate growth in the presence of instruction and (b) completes Tier 2 intervention(s) below the benchmark criteria. A student who is not responsive to Tier 2 intervention may receive a second trial of Tier 2 intervention (with some modifications to the intervention based on observations of the student during the first trial) or move directly to a multifactored evaluation to determine the presence of disability and special education eligibility (as with the case example of Taylor in Figure 5).

TIER 3: TERTIARY INTERVENTION

In most RTI models, Tier 3 is special education (Stecker, 2007). Some special educators recommend that students who do not make progress with small-group intervention in Tier 2 receive intensive individualized interventions prior to a determination of special education eligibility (e.g., Reschly, 2005).

Potential benefits and goals of RTI include the following (Alber-Morgan, 2010; Bradley, Danielson, & Doolittle, 2007; Johnson et al., 2006; L. S. Fuchs & Fuchs, 2007a, 2007b):

- Earlier identification of students using a problem-solving approach, instead of a "wait-to-fail" approach
- Reduction in the number of students referred for special education

Response to intervention begins with primary prevention for all students in the form of evidence-based curriculum and instruction in the general education classroom.

FIGURE 4

EXAMPLE PROFILE OF A STUDENT WHO IS NONRESPONSIVE TO TIER 1 INTERVENTION AND RESPONSIVE TO TIER 2 INTERVENTION

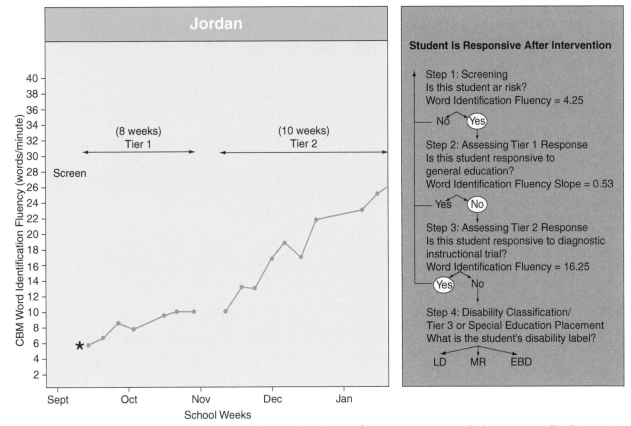

Jordan's case represents an assessment made during Tier 1 with indication of nonresponsiveness and advancement to Tier 2 instruction with assessment made and no indication of continued nonresponsiveness. Jordan began with an oral reading fluency of five words per minute, which flagged Jordan as being at risk. As he progressed through Tier 1 instruction, he failed to make adequate progress, which suggests that Jordan requires more intensive intervention than can be offered through the school's Tier 1 instructional program. Continued progress monitoring during Tier 2 intervention shows that Jordan is responding to the diagnostic instructional trial and that no further level of intervention is warranted. Jordan's progress will continue to be monitored with the following possible outcomes:

1. Student will reach the targeted goal for oral reading fluency (ORF) and return to Tier 1 instruction.
2. Student will continue with Tier 2 instruction as long as he/she makes adequate progress.

Source: National Research Center on Learning Disabilities. (2007). *Responsiveness to intervention in the SLD determination process.* [Brochure]. Lawrence, KS: Author. Website: http://www.nrcld.org.

- Reduction in the overidentification of minority students
- Provision of more instructionally useful data than those provided by traditional methods of assessment and identification
- Increased likelihood that students are exposed to high-quality instruction in the general education classroom by stipulating that schools use evidence-based instructional practices and routinely monitor the progress of all students
- Service to all students with achievement problems, so that only those students who fail to respond to multiple levels of intervention efforts receive the label learning disabled

Many leading special educators, including some who have helped develop the RTI concept and methodology, have expressed concerns with RTI (e.g., Division for Learning Disabilities, 2011; D. Fuchs & Deshler, 2007; L. S. Fuchs, 2011; Kavale & Spaulding, 2008). Practitioners are also cautious. One survey found that although 75% of school psychologists endorsed using RTI and phonemic awareness as components

FIGURE 5

EXAMPLE PROFILE OF A STUDENT WHO IS NONRESPONSIVE TO TIER 1 INTERVENTION
AND NONRESPONSIVE TO TIER 2 INTERVENTION

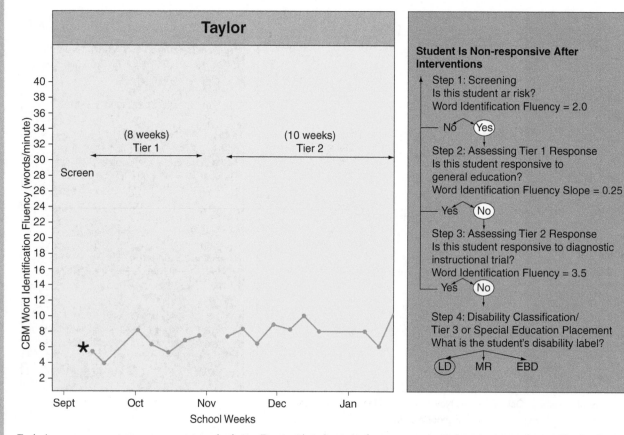

Taylor's case represents an assessment made during Tier 1 with indication of non-responsiveness and advancement to Tier 2 instruction with assessment made and indication of continued non-responsiveness resulting in a learning disability classification. Taylor began with an ORF of five words per minute, which identified Taylor as at risk for reading failure. As Taylor continued in the general class (Tier 1), Taylor failed to make adequate progress and was referred for Tier 2 intervention. The initial assessment in Tier 2 showed Taylor had an ORF of seven words per minute. As Taylor continued with Tier 2 instruction, Taylor failed to make adequate progress. This suggests the need for a student-centered, comprehensive evaluation and problem-solving approach that ensures individualized instruction to address Taylor's specific learning disability (i.e., Tier 3 or special education).

Source: National Research Center on Learning Disabilities. (2007). *Responsiveness to intervention in the SLD determination process.* [Brochure]. Lawrence, KS: Author. Retrieved October 17, 2007, from http://www.nrcld.org

Implementation guidelines, and case study examples for RTI from pre-K through secondary school can be found at the National Center on Response to Intervention (http://www.rti4success.org/), the National Research Center on Learning Disabilities (http://www.nrcld.org/), and the RTI Action Network (http://www.rtinetwork.org/).

of diagnosis of learning disabilities, 62% also endorsed the IQ–achievement discrepancy criterion (Machek & Nelson, 2007). Although legitimate concerns have been raised about RTI—notably the fact that high-fidelity applications of evidence-based instruction do not occur in many classrooms (McLesky & Waldron, 2011)—Kame'enui (2007) stated, "Arguably, RTI, at least the essence of it as a concept, is thoroughly consistent with the statutory intent and practice of special education" (p. 7).

Intelligence and Achievement Tests

Standardized intelligence and achievement tests are widely used as diagnostic tools with children with learning disabilities because a discrepancy between general intellectual ability and achievement remains a primary factor in determining eligibility for special education services (Zirkel & Thomas, 2010). These norm-referenced tests are constructed so that one student's score can be compared with the scores of other students of the same age who have taken the test. Widely used standardized tests for assessing a student's overall academic achievement include the Iowa

Tests of Basic Skills (Hoover, Dunbar, & Frisbie, 2007), the Peabody Individual Achievement Test (Markwardt, 1998), the Woodcock-Johnson III Tests of Achievement (Woodcock, Shrank, McGrew, & Mather, 2007), and the Wide Range Achievement Test—4 (WRAT-4) (Wilkinson & Robertson, 2006). Scores on these and similar tests are commonly reported by grade level; a score of 3.5, for example, means that the student's score equals the average score of the students in the norm group who were halfway through the third grade.

Some norm-referenced tests are designed to measure achievement in certain academic areas. Frequently administered reading achievement tests include the Gates-MacGinitie Reading Tests (MacGinitie, MacGinitie, Maria, & Dreyer, 2006), the Gray Oral Reading Tests (Wiederholt & Bryant, 2001), the Test of Reading Comprehension (Brown, Wiederholt, & Hammill, 2008), and the Woodcock Reading Mastery Test (Woodcock, 1998). Norm-referenced tests used to assess mathematics achievement include KeyMath—3: A Diagnostic Inventory of Essential Skills (Connolly, 2007), the Stanford Diagnostic Mathematics Test (Beatty, Madden, Gardner, & Karlsen, 2003), and the Test of Mathematical Abilities (Brown, Cronin, & McEntire, 1994).

Criterion-Referenced Tests

Criterion-referenced tests differ from norm-referenced tests in that a child's score on a criterion-referenced test is compared with a predetermined criterion, or mastery level, rather than with normed scores of other students. The value of criterion-referenced tests is that they identify the specific skills the child has already learned and the skills that require instruction. One criterion-referenced test widely used by special educators is the Brigance Comprehensive Inventory of Basic Skills (Brigance, 2010), which includes nearly 400 criterion-referenced assessments in reading, language arts, and math. Some commercially distributed curricula now include criterion-referenced test items for use as both a pretest and a posttest. The pretest assesses the student's entry level to determine which aspects of the program she is ready to learn; the posttest evaluates the effectiveness of the program. Criterion-referenced tests can be, and often are, informally developed by classroom teachers.

EDUCATIONAL APPROACHES

Not long ago, instruction of students with learning disabilities emphasized the remediation of basic skill deficits, often at the expense of providing opportunities for students to express themselves, learn problem-solving skills, or access the general education curriculum in meaningful ways. "The overemphasis on the 'basics' with the exclusion of any creative or cognitively complex activities provides many students with LD an unappealing intellectual diet" (Gersten, 1998, p. 163). In recent years, however, the field has shifted its instructional focus from a remediation-only mode to an approach designed to give students with learning disabilities meaningful access to and success with the core curriculum. By incorporating the six principles of effective instructional design shown in Figure 6, general class teachers and special educators can make curriculum and instruction more effective for students with and without disabilities (Coyne, Kame'enui, & Carnine, 2011).

Many students with learning disabilities (a) bring weak academic tool skills and limited background knowledge to academic activities, (b) have difficulty organizing information on their own, and (c) do not approach learning tasks in effective and efficient ways. Thus, contemporary best practice in educating students with learning disabilities is characterized by explicit instruction, the use of content enhancements, and teaching students to be strategic learners.

Content Enhancements

Educating students with learning disabilities at the middle and secondary levels is particularly difficult. Most are "ill-prepared for high school" and have reading and language skills at the fourth- to fifth-grade level (Deshler et al., 2001). Lectures and assigned readings in textbooks are widely used in middle and high school classrooms to present academic content to students. The teacher talks and assigns a portion of

Standardized achievement tests

 Content Standards for Beginning Teachers of Students with LD: Use and limitations of assessment instruments (ICC8K4) (also LD8K3, ICC8S2, ICC8S5, LD8S1).

Criterion-referenced tests

 Content Standards for Beginning Teachers of Students with LD: Use and limitations of assessment instruments (ICC8K4) (also LD8K3, ICC8S2, ICC8S5, LD8S1).

History of LD

 Content Standards for Beginning Teachers of Students with LD: Historical foundations, classical studies, and major contributors in the field of LD (LD1K1).

Some key historical events and their implications for the education of students with learning disabilities are shown in Figure 7. More detailed accounts of the history of the learning disabilities field can be found in Bateman (2005); Chamberlain (2010a, 2010b); Keogh (2005b); Lerner and Johns (2008); and Mercer and Pullen (2009).

SIX MAJOR PRINCIPLES OF EFFECTIVE INSTRUCTIONAL DESIGN

Big Ideas
Highly selected concepts, principles, rules, strategies, or heuristics that facilitate the most efficient and broadest acquisition of knowledge.

Conspicuous Strategies
Sequence of teaching events and teacher actions that make explicit the steps in learning. They are made conspicuous by the use of visual maps or. models, verbal directions, full and clear explanations, and so forth.

Mediated Scaffolding
Temporary support for students to learn new material. Scaffolding is faded over time.

Strategic Integration
Planful consideration and sequencing of instruction in ways that show the commonalities and differences between old and new knowledge.

Primed Background Knowledge
Related knowledge, placed effectively in sequence, that students must already possess in order to learn new knowledge.

Judicious Review
Sequence and schedule of opportunities learners have to apply and develop facility with new knowledge. The review must be adequate, distributed, cumulative, and varied

Source: From Kame'enui, E. J., Carnine, D. W., & Dixon, R. C. (2011). Introduction. In M. D. Coyne, E. J. Kame'enui, & D. W. Carnine (Eds.), *Effective teaching strategies that accommodate diverse learners* (4th ed., p. 13). © 2011. Reproduced by permission of Pearson Education, Inc., Upper Saddle River, NJ.

Content enhancements: Graphic organizers, note-taking strategies, and mnemonics

 Council for Exceptional Children

Content Standards for Beginning Teachers of Students with LD: Methods for guiding individuals in identifying and organizing critical content (LD4K5).

a high-vocabulary, content-dense text; and students are held responsible for obtaining, remembering, and using the information later (usually on a quiz or a test). A combination of poor reading, listening, note-taking, and study skills, compounded by a limited store of background knowledge, makes obtaining needed information from reading, lectures, and homework assignments a daunting task for students with learning disabilities.

Content enhancement is the general term for a wide range of techniques teachers use to enhance the organization and delivery of curriculum content so that students can better access, interact with, comprehend, and retain that information (Deshler et al., 2001; Bulgren, 2006). To effectively use a content-enhancement approach, teachers need to be thoughtful about the curriculum content to be covered and what learning approaches students need to be successful with that content. The teacher, in effect, must plan a lesson that effectively teaches "what the students should learn as well as how" (Baker, Gersten, & Scanlon, 2002, p. 67). Content enhancements often helpful to students with learning disabilities include graphic organizers and visual displays, note-taking strategies, and mnemonics.

GRAPHIC ORGANIZERS AND VISUAL DISPLAYS *Graphic organizers* are visual-spatial arrangements of information containing words or concepts connected graphically that help students see meaningful hierarchical, comparative, and sequential relationships (Dye, 2000; Ellis & Howard, 2007; Ives, 2007). Story mapping, visually representing the elements of a narrative story with graphic organizers, can help students with learning disabilities improve their comprehension (Stetter & Hughes, 2010).

Visual displays can be effective for teaching abstract concepts to students with disabilities. For example, the visual maps in Figure 8 help students see how the "big idea" of convection operates in similar fashion across a number of applications.

NOTE-TAKING STRATEGIES Traditional lecture is widely used in middle and high school classes to present curriculum content to students. The teacher talks, and students are held responsible for obtaining, remembering, and using the information at a later time (usually on a quiz or test). Students who take good notes and study them later consistently receive higher test scores than do students who only listen to the lecture and read the text (Kiewra, 2002).

FIGURE 7 **KEY HISTORICAL EVENTS IN THE EDUCATION OF CHILDREN WITH LEARNING DISABILITIES**

DATE	HISTORICAL EVENT	EDUCATIONAL IMPLICATIONS
1920s–1940s	Research by Alfred Strauss and others (Cruickshank, Doll , Kephart, Kirk, Lehtinen, Werner) with children with intellectual disabilities and brain injury at the Wayne County Training School in Michigan found relationships between brain injury and disorders that interfered with learning: perceptual disorders, perseveration, disorders of conceptual thinking, and behavioral problems such as hyperactivity and impulsivity.	In the book *Psychopathology and Education of the Brain-Injured Child*, Strauss and Lara Lehtinen (1947) recommended strategies for relieving perceptual and conceptual disturbances of children with brain injury and thus reducing their symptomatic learning problems,
1950s–1960s	By the early 1950s, most public schools had established special education programs for children with intellectual disabilities, sensory impairments, physical disabilities, and behavioral disorders. But there remained a group of children who were having serious learning problems at school, yet did not fit into any of the existing categories of exceptionality. They did not "look" disabled; the children seemed physically intact, yet they were unable to learn certain basic skills and subjects at school.	In searching for help with their children's problems, parents turned to other professionals—notably doctors, psychologists, and speech and language specialists. Understandably, these professionals viewed the children from the perspectives of their respective disciplines. As a result, terms such as *brain damage, minimal brain dysfunction, neurological impairment, perceptual handicap, dyslexia,* and *aphasia* were often used to describe and to account for the children's learning and behavior problems.
1963	Samuel Kirk used the term *learning disabilities* in an address to a group of parents whose children were experiencing serious difficulties in learning to read, were hyperactive, or could not solve math problems.	The parents liked the term and, that very evening, voted to form the Association for Children with Learning Disabilities. Today this organization's name is the Learning Disabilities Association of America (LDA).
1966	A national task force identified 99 different characteristics of children with *minimal brain dysfunction* (the term used at the time) (Clements, 1966).	An inherent danger of such lists is a tendency to assume that each of those characteristics is exhibited by *all* of the children considered to be in the category. This danger is especially troublesome with learning disabilities, because the children who make up the category are an extremely heterogeneous group.
mid-1960s–1970s	The concept of process, or ability, testing grew out of the belief that learning disabilities are caused by a basic underlying difficulty of the child to process, or use, environmental stimuli in the same way that children without disabilities do. Two of the most widely used process tests for diagnosing and assessing learning disabilities were developed during this time: the Illinois Test of Psycholinguistic Abilities (ITPA) (Kirk, McCarthy, & Kirk, 1968) and the Marianne Frostig Developmental Test of Visual Perception (Frostig, Lefever, & Whittlesey, 1964).	The ability training approach dominated special education for children with learning disabilities, from the field's inception through the 1970s. The three most widely known ability training approaches were psycholinguistic training, based on the ITPA; the visual-perceptual approach (Frostig & Horne, 1973); and the perceptual-motor approach (Kephart, 1971).
1968	The National Advisory Committee on Handicapped Children drafted and presented to Congress a definition of learning disabilities.	This definition was later incorporated into IDEA and used to govern the disbursement of federal funds for support of services to children with learning disabilities.
1968	The Division for Children with Learning Disabilities (DCLD) was established within the Council for Exceptional Children (CEC).	DCLD is the largest division of CEC.
1969	Congress passed the Children with Learning Disabilities Act (part of PL 91-230).	This legislation authorized a 5-year program of federal funds for teacher training and the establishment of model demonstration programs for students with learning disabilities.
late 1970s–early 1980s	Reviews of research showing the ineffectiveness of psycholinguistic training (Hammill & Larsen, 1978), the visual-perceptual approach (Myers & Hammill, 1976), and perceptual-motor approaches (Kavale & Mattson, 1983) were published.	Process testing and ability training gradually gave way to increased use of a skill training approach. If a student has not learned a complex skill and has had sufficient opportunity and wants to succeed, a skill trainer would conclude that the student has not learned the necessary prerequisite skills and provide direct instruction and practice on those prerequisite skills.

(Continued)

FIGURE 7   *(Continued)*

DATE	HISTORICAL EVENT	EDUCATIONAL IMPLICATIONS
1975	Congress passed the Individuals with Disabilities Education Act (PL 94–142).	*Learning disabilities* was included as one of the disability categories in IDEA.
1980s–1990s	Research on instructional design, content enhancements, and learning strategies provided additional knowledge on effective teaching methods for students with learning disabilities.	Skill training approach is supplemented with increased emphasis on helping students with learning disabilities have meaningful contact with the general curriculum.
2001	In response to concerns about the large number of children identified as learning disabled, the U.S. Office of Special Education sponsored a Learning Disabilities Summit in Washington, DC.	Nine white papers were developed on topics such as diagnostic decision making, classification models, early identification, and the nature and legitimacy of learning disabilities as a disability. Recommendations included in these papers played an influential role in how learning disabilities were treated in the reauthorization of IDEA in 2004.
2004	IDEA Improvement Act of 2004 changed the rules for determining whether a child has a specific learning disability. Schools are no longer required to document that a severe discrepancy between achievement and intellectual ability exists and may instead use an identification process based on a child's responsiveness to research-based instruction.	Schools using a response to intervention (RTI) model provide systematic help for all students struggling with basic skills (usually reading) in the early grades. Referral for special education evaluation and possible diagnosis of a learning disability is reserved for students who fail to make satisfactory progress after one or two 10- to 12-week trials of intensive small-group intervention using research-based instructional programs.

Many secondary teachers consider the ability to take notes a key ingredient for success in high school and beyond. Because content classes at the middle and secondary levels tend to be delivered in traditional lecture format, an emphasis on note taking qualifies as a "signature practice" for engaging and supporting all students in challenging content learning (Morocco, Brigham, & Aguilar, 2006). Students learn to organize information, focus on important content, and create a database from which to study as they prepare for tests (Brigham, Parker, Morocco, & Zigmond, 2006).

The listening, language, and, in some cases, motor skill deficits of many students with learning disabilities make it difficult for them to identify what is important during a lecture and write it down correctly and quickly enough to keep up. While trying to choose and write one concept in a notebook, the student with learning disabilities might miss the next two points. One study found that middle school students with learning disabilities accurately recorded only 13% of science lecture content (Boyle, 2010).

Strategic note taking and guided notes are two methods by which teachers can organize and enhance lecture content so that students with disabilities and their general education peers can take good notes. *Strategic note taking* involves specially designed note paper containing cues such as "What do you already know about this topic?" or "List new vocabulary and terms" that help students organize information and combine new knowledge with prior knowledge (Boyle, 2001). In one study, middle school students who were trained to use strategic note taking performed better than students who used conventional note taking on measures of note-taking completeness and accuracy, immediate recall, and comprehension of the lecture content (Boyle, 2011).

Guided notes are teacher-prepared handouts that provide an outline of the lecture content, which students complete during class by writing in key facts, concepts, and/or relations (Heward, 2001). A variation of guided lecture notes, *structured reading worksheets* are teacher-prepared supplements that help students study and comprehend assigned reading from content-rich textbooks by prompting them to find and write key points (Alber, Nelson, & Brennan, 2002). See *Teaching & Learning*, "Guided Notes: Helping All Students Succeed in the General Education Curriculum."

FIGURE 8

SIMPLE VISUAL MAPS SHOWING HOW THE "BIG IDEA" OF CONVECTION APPLIES ACROSS APPLICATIONS

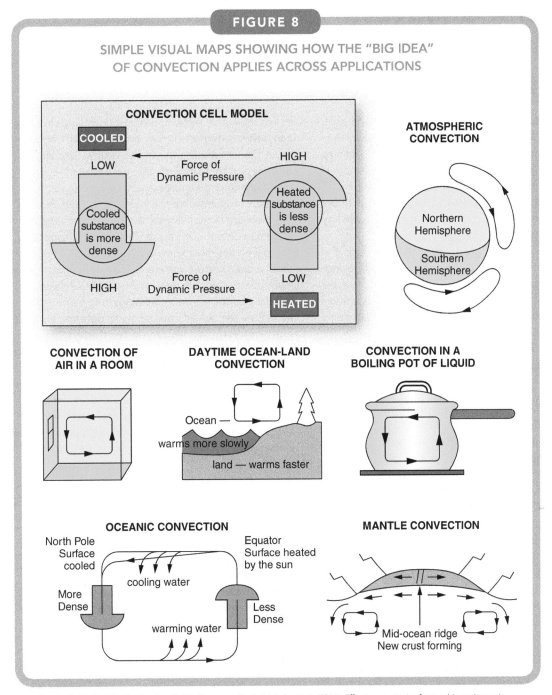

Source: From Grossen, B., Carnine, D. W., Romance, N. R., & Vitale, M. R. (2011). Effective strategies for teaching science. In M. D. Coyne, E. J. Kame'enui, & D. W. Carnine (Eds.), *Effective teaching strategies that accommodate diverse learners* (4th ed., p. 189). © 2011. Reproduced by permission of Pearson Education, Inc., Upper Saddle River, NJ.

MNEMONICS Research has demonstrated that memory-enhancing strategies called *mnemonics* can help students with learning disabilities recall specific academic content (Wolgemuth, Cobb, & Alwell, 2008). Mnemonic strategies combine special presentation of information with explicit strategies for recall and are most often used to help students remember large amounts of unfamiliar information or make connections between two or more facts or concepts. Three of the most commonly used mnemonic strategies by special education teachers are letter strategies, keyword method, and pegword method.

Letter strategies are acronyms and acrostics. Common examples of acronym mnemonics are HOMES to remember the names of the Great Lakes (Huron, Ontario, Michigan, Erie, and Superior) and FACE to remember the four notes in the spaces between the lines on a music staff. Acrostics are sentences in which the first letter of each word stands for

Guided Notes: Helping All Students Succeed in the General Education Curriculum

TEACHING & LEARNING

Traditional lecture is widely used in middle and high school classes. Most successful students take notes during lectures and study them later. Note taking serves two functions: a *process function* (the note taker interacts with the curriculum content during the lecture by listening, looking, thinking, and writing) and a *product function* (the note taker produces a summary/list of key points for later study) (Boyle, 2001).

Many students with learning disabilities lack the complex set of skills necessary for effective note taking. Effective note taking requires the ability to discriminate between relevant and irrelevant content and facts, attend to teachers' "verbal signposts," organize information, and record information accurately and fluently (Boyle, 2010; Kiewra, 2002). These skills are noticeably lacking in the repertoires of many students without disabilities as well.

WHAT ARE GUIDED NOTES?

Guided notes (GNs) are teacher-prepared handouts that "guide" a student through a lecture with standard cues and specific space in which to write key facts, concepts, and/or relationships. Guided notes help students succeed with both functions of note taking. With regard to the process function, GNs take advantage of one of the most consistent and important findings in recent educational research: students who make frequent, relevant responses during a lesson learn more than students who are passive observers. To complete their GNs, students must respond throughout the lecture by listening, looking, thinking, and writing about the lesson's content. Guided notes assist students with the product function of note taking because they are designed so that all students can produce a standard and accurate set of lecture notes for study and review (see Figure A).

Numerous studies have found that students at all achievement levels in elementary through postsecondary classrooms perform better on tests of retention of lecture content when they used GNs than on tests based on lectures when they took their own notes (e.g., Hamilton, Seibert, Gardner, & Talbert-Johnson, 2000; Konrad, Joseph, & Eveleigh, 2009; Musti-Rao, Stephen, Kroeger, & Schumacher-Dyke, 2008; Patterson, 2005; Sweeney et al., 1999).

Other Advantages of Guided Notes In addition to requiring students to actively respond to curriculum, helping them produce an accurate set of notes, and improving retention of course content, other advantages of GNs include the following (Heward, 2001):

- Students can easily identify the most important information. Because GNs cue the location and number

of key concepts, facts, and/or relationships, students can better determine if they are "getting it" and are more likely to ask the teacher to clarify. Teachers often report that students ask more content-specific questions during lectures when GNs are used.

- Teachers must prepare the lesson or lecture carefully.
- Teachers are more likely to stay on task with the lecture's content and sequence. Teachers, especially those who are most knowledgeable and interested in their subject matter, sometimes get sidetracked from main points students need to know. While these tangential points may be interesting, they make it difficult for even skilled note takers to determine what's most important in a lecture/demonstration.
- GNs can improve students' independent note-taking skills. Gradually fading the use of GNs can help students learn to take notes in classes in which GNs are not used. For example, after several weeks of providing students with GNs for the entire lecture, the teacher might give GNs for only three quarters of the lecture, then one half of the lecture, and so on.

HOW TO GET STARTED

Here are steps and suggestions for creating and using GNs:

1. **Examine existing lecture outlines to identify the most important course content that students must learn and retain via lectures.** Remember: less can be more. Student learning is enhanced by lectures with fewer points supported by additional examples and opportunities for students to respond to questions or scenarios.

2. **Include all facts, concepts, and relationships students are expected to learn on guided notes.**

3. **Include background information so that students' note taking focuses on the important facts, concepts, and relationships they need to learn.**

4. **Delete the key facts, concepts, and relationships from the lecture outline, leaving the remaining information to provide structure and context for students' note taking.**

5. **Insert cues such as asterisks, bullets, and blank lines to show students where, when, and how many facts or concepts to write and provide students with a legend that explains each symbol.** (See Figure B for an example.)

6. **Leave ample space for students to write.** Providing three to four times the space needed to

GUIDED NOTES FOR A LESSON ON CLOUDS COMPLETED
BY AN ELEMENTARY STUDENT WITH LEARNING DISABILITIES

Clouds

Directions: Follow along with your teacher and till in your guided notes.

What Are Clouds?

★ Clouds are tiny drops of condensing _Water vapor_ or
Ice crystals that settle on particles of dust in the atmosphere.

What Are the Different Kinds of Clouds?

★ Although there are many different types of clouds, there are _three_ main types:

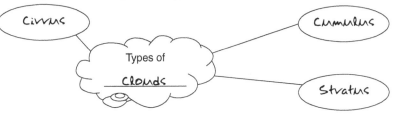

How Do I Know What Type of Clouds Are in the Sky?

- Cirrus clouds
  - Most common
  - Usually made of _Ice crystals_
  - Look like feathers
  - Thin and _Wispy_

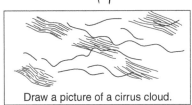

Draw a picture of a cirrus cloud.

- Cumulus clouds
  - White and _Puffy_
  - Look like cotton balls
  - Usually predict _Fair weather_ but can develop into
    cumulonimbus clouds which may produce rain,
    lightning strong winds, and bail

Draw a picture of a cumulus cloud.

Source: Courtesy of Moira Konrad, The Ohio State University.

type the content will generally leave enough room for students' handwriting.

7. **Don't require students to write too much.** Using GNs should not unduly slow down the pace of the lesson.

8. **Enhance GNs with supporting information, resources, and additional opportunities to respond.** Insert diagrams, illustrations, photos, high-lighted statements, or concepts that are particularly

For more details on these and additional suggestions for developing and using guided notes, see Heward (2001); Konrad, Joseph, and Itoi (2011); and Lazarus (1996).

important, and resources such as websites into GNs. Interspersing sets of questions or practice problems within the GN gives students additional opportunities to respond and receive teacher feedback during the lesson. Guided notes can be designed so that students create a set of study cards for subsequent review and practice. (To observe a middle school teacher using guided note study cards, go to the book resources for this text on MyEducationLab.)

9. **Use PowerPoint slides or other visuals to project key content.** Visually projecting the key facts, definitions, concepts, and relationships enhances student access to the most critical content and improves the pace of the lecture.

10. **Intersperse opportunities for other forms of active student response during lesson.** Stop lecturing from time to time, and ask a series of questions, to which the students respond chorally or with response cards, referring to their GNs for answers as needed.

11. **Consider gradually fading the use of guided notes to help students learn to take notes in classes in which they are not used.**

12. **Provide follow-up activities to ensure that students study and review their notes,** such as daily quizzes, collaborative review activity, and random study checks.

a different word. For example, "Kids playing croquet on freeways get smashed" can help students remember the life sciences classification system: kingdom, phylum, class, order, family, genus, and species (Kleinheksel & Summy, 2003); and "Every good boy deserves fudge" reminds them of the notes on the five lines of the music staff.

The *keyword method* is used to link a new, unfamiliar word with familiar information. Mastropieri and Scruggs (2010) give the following example of how a teacher could use a keyword mnemonic to help a student remember that the Italian word *strada* means "road." First, identify a keyword for *strada* that sounds like the new word but is familiar and easy to picture. In this case, "straw" would be a good keyword because it sounds like strada and is easy to picture. Next, draw (or ask students to imagine) a picture of the keyword and its referent doing something together. In this case, the interactive picture could show straw lying on a road (see Figure 9). Finally, the teacher instructs the student to look at the picture and begins the following dialogue to help the student acquire the keyword strategy:

> The Italian word *strada* means road. The keyword for strada is *straw* [show picture]. Remember this picture of straw lying on a road? Remember this picture of what? Good, straw lying on a road. Now, when I ask you for the meaning of *strada*, think first of the keyword, *straw*. Then think back to the picture with the straw in it, remember that the straw was on a road, and then retrieve the answer, *strada* means road. Now what does *strada* mean? Good, *strada* means road. And how did you remember that? Good, you thought of the key word, *straw*, and remembered the picture of *straw* on the road. (Mastropieri & Scruggs, 2010, p. 237)

FIGURE 9

MNEMONIC PICTURE FOR REMEMBERING THAT THE ITALIAN WORD
STRADA MEANS "ROAD"

Strada (Straw)   Road

Straw →

Source: Mastropieri, M. A., & Scruggs, T. E. (2010). *The inclusive classroom: Strategies for effective instruction* (4th ed., p. 237). © 2010. Reproduced by permission of Pearson Education, Inc., Upper Saddle River, NJ.

The *pegword method* employs rhyming words for numbers (1 is "bun," 2 is "shoe," 3 is "tree," etc.) when information to be remembered is numbered or ordered. For example, to remember that Newton's first (or number 1) law of motion is that objects at rest tend to stay at rest, show a picture of a bun (1) resting. To remember that insects have six legs, create a picture of insects on sticks (6).

Learning Strategies

Proficient learners approach tasks and problems systematically. They identify what needs to be done, make a plan, and evaluate their progress. An accomplished writer knows how to identify and organize the content of a paper to enhance its persuasiveness. When adding a series of unlike fractions, a skilled math student immediately looks to see if all of the denominators are even numbers. Unless they are explicitly taught, however, many students with learning disabilities are unaware of the strategies, or "tricks of the trade," used by proficient learners (Schumaker & Deshler, 2006).

A **learning strategy** can be defined as "an individual's approach to a learning task. A strategy includes how a person thinks and acts when planning, executing, and evaluating performance on a task and its outcomes" (Deshler & Lenz, 1989, p. 205). Donald Deshler and Jean Schumaker and their colleagues at the University of Kansas (Schumaker & Deshler, 1992) have conducted extensive research on how to help students with learning disabilities acquire and use effective learning strategies. They have developed, field-tested, and validated a learning strategies curriculum for adolescents with learning disabilities (Bui, Schumaker, & Deshler, 2006; Deshler & Schumaker, 2006; Ellis, Deshler, Lenz, Schumaker, & Clark, 1991).

Students use task-specific strategies to guide themselves successfully through a learning task or problem. A mnemonic is often used to help students remember the steps of the strategy. For example, Test and Ellis (2005) taught students the *LAP*

Learning strategies

 Council for Exceptional Children   Content Standards for Beginning Teachers of Students with LD: Methods for teaching individuals to independently use cognitive processing to solve problems (LD4K4).

strategy for adding and subtracting fractions: *L*ook at the denominator and sign; *A*sk yourself if the denominators will divide evenly; and *P*ick a fraction type. A well-researched strategy for writing is POW-TREE (*P*ick my idea, *O*rganize my thoughts/notes, *W*rite and say more–*T*opic sentence (tell what you believe), *R*easons (3 or more), *E*nding (wrap it up), *E*xamine (have I included all the parts?) (Sandmel et al., 2009).

EDUCATIONAL PLACEMENT ALTERNATIVES

General Education Classroom

Placement alternatives

Content Standards for Beginning Teachers of Students with LD: Demands of learning environments (ICC5K1).

IDEA requires that students with disabilities be educated with students without disabilities, have access to the core curriculum to the maximum extent possible, and that they be removed from the general education classroom only to the extent that their disability necessitates. During the 2008–09 school year, 62% of students with learning disabilities were educated in general education classrooms (U.S. Department of Education, 2009).

Research on the academic achievement of students with learning disabilities in inclusive classrooms is mixed. Some studies have reported better learning outcomes for students with learning disabilities in general education classrooms than in pull-out programs (e.g., Baker, Wang, & Walberg, 1995; Rea, McLaughlin, & Walther-Thomas, 2002). Other studies of students with learning disabilities in the general education classroom have reported disappointing achievement results (e.g., Schumm, Moody, & Vaughn, 2000), concerns about inadequate instruction (e.g., Chard & Kame'enui, 2000), teachers' limited understanding of learning needs of students with LD (DeSimone & Parmar, 2006), and poor acceptance by teachers and/or peers (e.g., Cook, 2001; Cook, Tankersley, Cook, & Landrum, 2000).

Many studies have compared the social functioning and self-concepts of students with learning disabilities in different educational placements. The contention of advocates of full inclusion for students with learning disabilities is that pull-out services such as resource room and special class placement stigmatize students, thus damaging self-concept and limiting opportunities to develop relationships with typical peers. For example, Wiener and Tardif (2004) studied 117 children with learning disabilities in different educational placements and found a "slight superiority of the more inclusive programs" (p. 30) with respect to peer acceptance, number of friends, self-perceptions of mathematics competence, and behavior problems. The authors noted, however, that the differences between groups were not large and were "especially small" when compared to the differences between children with and without learning disabilities." Wiener and Tardif warned, "It would be inappropriate to conclude that the major variable influencing the social and emotional adjustment of children with LD is the special education placement" (p. 30).

Elbaum (2002) conducted a meta-analysis of 36 studies examining the self-concept of students with learning disabilities in different placements and concluded that, "contrary to the stigmatization perspective, students with LD placed in general education classrooms did not, overall, have higher self-concepts than students placed in either part-time or full-time special education classrooms" (p. 222). But Elbaum properly noted that, while no one placement is preferable in terms of self-concept for all students with learning disabilities, individual students may be "profoundly affected by a placement that jeopardized their self-esteem" and that, when making placement decisions for a child, individualized education program (IEP) teams "should guard against a priori assumptions about the benefit or detriment of specific placements to students' self-concept. Each student's social and emotional needs, as well as the student's own preference with regard to placement options, ought to be taken into account" (pp. 222–223).

All of the methods described in the previous section for enhancing the general education curriculum help promote the success of students with learning disabilities in general education classrooms. Special educators can facilitate the success of these students in inclusive classrooms by teaching them behaviors that are valued by general education teachers. For example, when asked to rate which of 30 different social skills were critical for success in the classroom, the majority of 366 teachers in grades K–12 rated self-control (controlling temper in conflict situations) and cooperation (complying with teacher's directions) as the most essential (Lane, Givner, & Pierson, 2004). In another study, 89 general education high school teachers identified following directions in class, coming to class prepared with materials, and treating teachers and peers with courtesy among the most important skills for success in the general education classroom (Ellet, 1993).

Consultant Teacher

A consultant teacher provides support to general education classroom teachers and other staff members who work directly with students with learning disabilities. The consultant teacher helps the general education teacher select assessment devices, curriculum materials, and instructional activities. The consultant may even demonstrate teaching methods or behavior management strategies. A major advantage of this model is that the consultant teacher can work with several teachers and thus indirectly serve many children. A major drawback is that most consultant teachers have little direct contact with students.

Resource Room

A resource room is a specially staffed and equipped classroom where students with learning disabilities come for one or several periods during the school day to receive individualized instruction. A resource room teacher serves an average of 20 students with disabilities. During the 2008–09 school year, 28% of students with learning disabilities were served in resource rooms (U.S. Department of Education, 2009).

The resource teacher is a certified special educator whose primary role is to teach needed academic skills, social skills, and learning strategies to the students who are referred to the resource room. Students typically attend their general education classrooms for most of the school day and come to the resource room for one or more periods of specialized instruction in the academic and/or social skill areas in which they need the most help. In addition to teaching students with learning disabilities, the resource teacher also works closely with each student's general education teacher(s) to suggest and help plan each student's program in the general education classroom.

Some advantages of the resource room model are that (a) students do not lose their identity with their general education class peer group; (b) students can receive the intensive, individualized instruction they need every day, which may not be possible in the general education classroom; and (c) flexible scheduling allows the resource room to serve a fairly large number of students. Some disadvantages of resource rooms are that they (a) require students to spend time traveling between classrooms, (b) may result in inconsistent instructional approaches between settings, and (c) can make it difficult to determine whether and how students should be held accountable for what they missed while out of the general education classroom.

Separate Classroom

During the 2008–09 school year, 8% of students with learning disabilities were served in separate classrooms (U.S. Department of Education, 2009). In a separate classroom, a special education teacher is responsible for all educational programming for 8 to 12 students with learning disabilities. The academic achievement deficiencies of some children with learning disabilities are so severe that they need full-time placement in a setting with a specially trained teacher. In addition, poor

Heron and Harris (2001) describe how consultant teachers can increase their effectiveness in supporting children in general education classrooms, and Learned, Dowd, and Jenkins (2009) offer tips for instructional conferences with included students.

In a resource room, students with learning disabilities can receive intensive, specialized instruction on the academic and social skills in which they need the most help.

197

work habits and inappropriate social behaviors make some students with learning disabilities candidates for the separate classroom, where distractions can be minimized and individual attention stressed. Generally, IEP teams are not to view a student's placement in a separate classroom (or any other educational setting) as permanent. A student should be placed in a separate classroom only after legitimate and supported attempts to serve her effectively in less restrictive environments have proven unsuccessful.

Should All Students with Learning Disabilities Be Educated in the General Education Classroom?

Perspectives on full inclusion

Content Standards for Beginning Teachers of Students with LD: Philosophies, theories, models, and issues related to individuals with LD (LD1K2) (also ICC5K1).

For many students with learning disabilities, the least restrictive environment for all or most of the school day is the general education classroom attended by their same-age peers. The movement toward full inclusion of all students with disabilities in general education classrooms, however, has many leading researchers and advocates for students with learning disabilities worried. They think that although the full-inclusion movement is based on strong beliefs and has the best intentions at heart, little research supports it (D. Fuchs & Fuchs, 1994, 2009; Kauffman & Hallahan, 2005; McLeskey & Waldron, 2011; Mock & Kauffman, 2005; Zigmond, Kloo, & Volonino, 2009). They fear that the special education services for students with learning disabilities guaranteed by IDEA—particularly the meaningful development and implementation of IEPs and the identification of the least restrictive environment for each student along a continuum of placement options—will be lost if full inclusion becomes reality. They wonder, for example, how a high school student with disabilities who reads at the fourth-grade level and spends the entire school day in general education subject-matter classes will receive the individualized, intensive reading instruction that she needs. They note, for example, that 40% of students with learning disabilities have general education teachers who have received no information about their instructional needs and that only 11% of general education teachers make substantial modification to curriculum and instruction to meet the needs of students with disabilities (Wagner, Newman, Cameto, Levine, & Marder, 2003).

All of the major professional and advocacy associations concerned with the education of children with learning disabilities have published position papers against full inclusion. Each group supports the placement of students with learning disabilities in general education classrooms to the maximum extent possible, given that the instructional and related services required to meet each student's individualized educational needs are provided; but they strongly oppose any policy that mandates the same placement and instruction for all students with learning disabilities. Each group believes that special education for students with learning disabilities requires a continuum of placement options that includes the possibility of some or even all instruction taking place outside the general education classroom.

For some students with learning disabilities, the general education classroom may actually be more restrictive than a resource room or special class placement when the instructional needs of the student are considered—and remember that academic deficit is the primary characteristic and remedial need of students with learning disabilities. However, placing a student with learning disabilities in a resource room or special class does not guarantee that he will receive the intensive, specialized instruction he needs. For example, Moody, Vaughn, Hughes, and Fischer (2000) found that only three of the six resource room teachers they observed provided differentiated reading materials and instruction to match the individual needs of their students. Similarly, Swanson (2008) found that students spent most of their time in resource rooms in nonreading activities and undifferentiated seat work.

The collective message of research on outcomes for students with learning disabilities in inclusive classrooms and other settings is consistent with the findings for students with other disabilities: where a student is taught is not as important as the quality of instruction that student receives.

▼ TIPS FOR BEGINNING TEACHERS

Becoming an Exceptional Teacher

BY ANGELA PRESTON

ORGANIZATION: THE PAPERWORK SIDE

My mentor once told me, "Special education is like having two full-time jobs. The first is teaching; the second is paperwork." When you begin teaching, there are times you may feel overwhelmed. Following these tips will help keep you feeling organized and confident.

- **Write due dates for all IEPs and reevaluations in your planner/calendar.** Once you know which students are on your caseload, write all of their IEP and reevaluation due dates in your calendar or planner. Back up 10 more days and write "send IEP invitation for student" in your calendar. This reminder will keep you from missing any IEP due dates.
- **Make lists and use a notebook.** Keep a notebook for yourself. Bring the notebook to staff meetings, staff development, special education team meetings, or other meetings. Use the notebook to keep all your information in one place. Make lists of what you need to do, and continually cross them off and update the lists. Don't worry if your list never seems to end. There will always be more things to do; the lists just help you stay organized. I sometimes write down a few things I have already completed that day and cross them off. This way I feel as if I've already accomplished a few things on my ever-growing list.
- **Document everything.** Someone once told me, "If you didn't write it down, it didn't happen." Document all parent phone calls; attempts at calling doctors, parents, teachers, other schools, etc; observations; important e-mails; and dates students transfer to or from your school. Keep samples of student work that addresses IEP goals. It is better to have too much information than not enough.

ORGANIZATION: THE TEACHING SIDE

As a resource teacher, I have many groups of students flowing in and out of my door each day. The best way to keep from feeling like a train wreck is to keep your room organized. Follow the same schedule each day, and make sure your students understand the procedures and expectations. Once you've established your routine, your day will run like a well-oiled machine.

- **Organize your classroom setup.** I prefer using plastic bins/drawers for each of my classes. I have the drawers labeled by time and subject. All the materials for that class are in the drawer (workbooks, textbooks, notebooks, teacher books, etc.). I also have baskets with pencils so we don't waste time trying to find pencils at the beginning of class. Other types of setups include giving a specific space for each student to keep their books on shelves. This also helps older elementary students by getting them ready for lockers in middle school.
- **Manage your time.** Time management is essential. If students show up early for class, let them finish work they missed or read a book. Use warmups to review previously learned information. Have extra review work for students to complete if they finish the lesson before the rest of the class. Don't waste a moment of their time because they are already behind and need the most instruction during the day.
- **Reserve time for yourself.** It is easy to become over-ambitious when you start teaching, wanting to re-create everything new, spending hours working before, during, and after school. Set limits for what you can accomplish in a day. Prioritize things and keep a list of what you want to create over the summer (see the tip on making lists and keeping a notebook). Pick one day a week that you will put manipulatives together for the following week. Pick another day a week that you will leave "on time" or at least within an hour. Keep a hobby, work out, and spend time with friends each week so as not to become another new-teacher burnout statistic.

PARENT COMMUNICATION

With parent support, your job as a teacher becomes reassuring and brings much satisfaction. Teaching as a collaborative effort between parents and school provides the most success for students.

- **Meet face-to-face.** The first time you meet a parents, plan to meet in person. This allows you to establish an immediate connection and express your care and support for their child. Remember, parents know their child better than anyone. Be ready to listen to their concerns and address them at meetings. Most parents ask what they can do to help at home. Have lists of simple activities they can do in the car, in the kitchen, or around the house to help their child. Also, don't forget to have a translator present at all meetings with parents who are not fluent in English.
- **Start on a positive note.** Begin each phone call, e-mail, meeting, or conversation with a positive comment. Parents understand their child has a disability, and it can be easy to always talk about his difficulties at school. Before you know it, the parent begins to dread receiving phone calls from school. Starting off each conversation with a positive comment—"Your son helped another student find a pencil today," or "She has many friends and is very social in class"—before addressing the concern you have. If you can't think of anything positive, don't call the parents yet.
- **Address the acronym abyss.** It seems as if education has a tendency to make words as small as possible. We hear these acronyms on a daily basis and use them without hesitation. Explain what the acronyms mean to parents, and use language they understand. Write down the acronyms they need to know, and give the list to the parents at meetings to help them understand sentences like: "At this IEP meeting your son's EC and GE teachers, LEA rep, along with yourself, will discuss his DD re-eval results and determine if he is eligible for EC services under LD, OHI, or ED with OT as a related service."

STUDENT RELATIONSHIPS

Building student relationships can be rewarding for both the teacher and the student. Students work harder for teachers they respect, and teachers work harder for students who respect them.

- **Make each student believe he or she is your favorite.** I firmly believe the more a student feels cared for, the harder they will work, the more they will behave appropriately, and the quicker they will respond to their teacher. Finding similarities to talk about, making up secret handshakes, greeting students as they come in/leave class, or making positive comments all help foster strong relationships. Once a positive relationship has been established, students will work hard and begin believing in themselves because their teacher believes in them, too.

- **Talk about why they come to your class.** This works best for older students, and I would not mention anything about a disability or special education without parent permission. Talk to the students about why they are in your class. I usually start with strengths we all have and weaknesses I have. Then I'll ask who has a hard time reading. After a few seconds everyone will raise their hand. Then I'll discuss why it is important to know how to read and that we are all here to work on being better readers. I usually end by making them a promise that I will give 100% effort into teaching reading, but that they must devote 100% effort in learning how to read. Giving students a chance to understand why they are pulled out and setting personal goals result in higher achievement for students.

- **Balance procedures, instruction, and relationships.** When you first start off, make sure the students understand your procedures, and have procedures for everything. Practice your procedures daily. Keep your expectations consistent to help students understand what to expect. It is possible to find a balance between maintaining strong systematic instruction with building strong student relationships. Use procedures to help students define your role as a teacher, but use small moments for encouragement during instruction. Once the balance has been made, you are on your way to being an exceptional teacher with a rewarding career.

▼ KEY TERMS AND CONCEPTS

alphabetic principle
comorbidity
criterion-referenced tests
curriculum-based measurement (CBM)
dual discrepancy criterion
dyslexia
formative evaluation
guided notes

learning strategy
phonemic awareness
phonological awareness
precision teaching
response to intervention (RTI)
specific learning disability
summative evaluation

▼ SUMMARY

Definition

- The federal definition of *specific learning disability* is a disorder in one or more of the basic psychological processes involved in understanding or in using language, spoken or written, which may manifest in an imperfect ability to listen, think, speak, read, write, spell, or perform mathematical calculations and is not due to a sensory, motor, or intellectual disability, to emotional disturbance, or to environmental or economic disadvantage.

- There is no universally agreed-on definition of learning disabilities. Most states require that three criteria be met: (a) a severe discrepancy between potential or ability and actual achievement, (b) learning problems that cannot be attributed to other disabilities, and (c) special educational services needed to succeed in school.

Characteristics

- Difficulty reading is the most common characteristic of students with learning disabilities. It is estimated that 80% of all children identified as learning disabled are referred for special education services because of reading problems.

- Many students with learning disabilities show one or more of the following characteristics: deficits in written language, underachievement in math, poor social skills, attention deficits and hyperactivity, behavior problems, and low self-esteem/self-efficacy.

- The fundamental, defining characteristic of students with learning disabilities is specific and significant achievement deficits in the presence of adequate overall intelligence.

- In addition to their academic and social-skills deficits, students with learning disabilities possess positive attributes and interests that teachers should identify and try to strengthen.

Prevalence

- Learning disabilities make up the largest category in special education. Students with learning disabilities represent almost one half of all students receiving special education.

- About three times as many boys as girls are identified as learning disabled.
- Some educators believe that the high prevalence of learning disabilities is the result of overidentification and misdiagnosis of low-achieving students.

Causes

- Although the actual cause of a specific learning disability is seldom known, four suspected causal factors are brain damage, heredity, biochemical imbalance, and environmental factors.
- Specific regions of the brains of some individuals with reading and language disabilities show abnormal activation patterns during phonological processing tasks.
- Genetics may account for at least some family links with dyslexia. Research has located possible chromosomal loci for the genetic transmission of phonological deficits that may predispose a child for reading problems later.
- Biochemical imbalance due to artificial colorings and flavorings in a child's diet or vitamin deficiencies have been suggested as causes of learning disabilities. Most professionals today give little credence to these causes.
- Environmental factors—particularly impoverished living conditions early in a child's life and poor instruction—are likely contributors to the achievement deficits of many children with learning disabilities.

Identification and Assessment

- Five forms of assessment are frequently used with students with learning disabilities:
  - Norm-referenced tests compare a child's score with the scores of age mates who have taken the same test.
  - Criterion-referenced tests, which compare a child's score with a predetermined mastery level, are useful in identifying specific skills the child has learned as well as skills that require instruction.
  - Curriculum-based measurement (CBM) is a formative evaluation method that measures a student's progress in the actual curriculum in which she is participating. CBM is the primary means of assessment in RTI models.

- Direct and daily measurement involves assessing a student's performance on a specific skill each time it is taught.
- Response to intervention (RTI), a promising approach to the prevention and early identification of learning disabilities, uses curriculum-based measurement of at-risk children's progress during one or two 10- to 12-week trials of intensive individual or small-group instruction with scientifically validated instruction. Failure to respond to this treatment suggests a learning disability.

Educational Approaches

- Contemporary best practice in educating students with learning disabilities is characterized by explicit instruction, the use of content enhancements, and teaching students to be strategic learners.
- Explicit instruction is unambiguous, clear, direct teaching of targeted knowledge or skills: Students are shown what to do and given frequent opportunities to practice with teacher feedback and later to apply what they have learned.
- Content enhancements such as graphic organizers, note-taking strategies, and mnemonics help make curriculum content more accessible to students with learning disabilities.
- Learning strategies help students guide themselves successfully through specific tasks or general problems.

Educational Placement Alternatives

- About 65% of students with learning disabilities are educated in general education classrooms.
- In some schools, a consultant teacher helps regular classroom teachers work with children with learning disabilities.
- In the resource room, a special educator provides specialized instruction to students for one or more periods in the academic and/or social skill areas in which they need the most help.
- Approximately 1 in 10 students with learning disabilities is educated in separate classrooms.
- Many researchers and advocates for students with learning disabilities do not support full inclusion, which would eliminate the continuum of service delivery options.
- Where a student is taught is not as important as the quality of instruction that student receives.

MyEducationLab

Go to Topic 9, Learning Disabilities, in the MyEducationLab (www.myeducationlab.com) for *Exceptional Children*, where you can

- Find learning outcomes for learning disabilities along with the national standards that connect to these outcomes.
- Complete Assignments and Activities that can help you more deeply understand the chapter content.
- Apply and practice your understanding of the core teaching skills identified in the chapter with the Building Teaching Skills and Dispositions learning units (optional).
- Examine challenging situations and cases presented in the IRIS Center Resources.
- Access video clips of CCSSO National Teachers of the Year award winners responding to the question "Why do I teach?" in the Teacher Talk section.
- Check your comprehension of the content covered in the chapter with the Study Plan. Here you will be able to take a chapter quiz, receive feedback on your answers, and then access Review, Practice, and Enrichment activities to enhance your understanding of chapter content.
- Use the Online Lesson Plan Builder to practice lesson planning and integrating national and state standards into your planning.

▼ GLOSSARY

alphabetic principle: The understanding that words are composed of letters that represent sounds and the ability to pronounce and blend the sounds of letters into words (decoding) and to recode sounds into letters (spelling). See *phonics*.

comorbidity: Two or more conditions occurring in the same person (e.g., learning disabilities and ADHD).

criterion-referenced test: A test constructed so that a child's score can be compared with a predetermined criterion, or mastery level; contrast with *norm-referenced test*.

curriculum-based measurement: A type of formative evaluation consisting of frequent measures of a student's progress in learning the objectives that comprise the curriculum in which the student is participating.

dual discrepancy: A criterion for identifying a student as unresponsive in a response to intervention (RTI) approach when the student (a) fails to make adequate growth in the presence of instruction and (b) completes Tier 2 intervention(s) below the benchmark criteria (Fuchs & Fuchs, 2007).

dyslexia: A specific language-based disorder of constitutional origin characterized by difficulties in single-word decoding, usually reflecting insufficient phonological processing. These difficulties, which are not the result of generalized developmental disability or sensory impairment, are often unexpected in relation to age and other

cognitive and academic abilities and severely impair the individual's ability to read (Orton Dyslexia Society Research Committee, 1994).

formative evaluation: Any type of ongoing evaluation of student performance or learning that occurs as instruction takes place over time; results can be used to modify instruction to make it more effective. See *curriculum-based measurement*.

guided notes: Teacher-prepared handouts that provide background information and standard cues with specific spaces where students can write key facts, concepts, and/ or relationships during a lecture.

learning strategy: A systematic approach to a learning task or problem solving; specifically, what a person does when planning, executing, and evaluating his or her performance on a task.

phonemic awareness: The ability to hear and manipulate the sounds of spoken language; critical prerequisite for learning to read. A child with phonemic awareness can orally blend sounds to make a word; isolate beginning, middle, and ending sounds in words; segment words into component sounds; and manipulate sounds within words.

phonological awareness: The "conscious understanding and knowledge that language is made up of sounds" (Simmons, Kame'enui, Coyne, & Chard, 2007, p. 49). See *phonemic awareness*.

precision teaching: An instructional approach that involves (a) pinpointing the skills to be learned; (b) measuring the initial frequency or rate per minute at which the student can perform those skills; (c) setting an aim, or goal, for the child's improvement; (d) using direct, daily measurement to monitor progress made under an instructional program; (e) charting the results of those measurements on a *standard celeration chart*; and (f) changing the program if progress is not adequate.

response to intervention (RTI): A systematic prereferral and early intervention process that consists of universal screening and several tiers of increasingly intensive trials of research-based interventions before referral for assessment for special education eligibility. The Individuals with Disabilities Education Act (IDEA) of 2004 stipulates that schools can use RTI to determine a child's eligibility for special education under the specific learning disabilities category.

specific learning disability: See *learning disabilities*.

summative evaluation: Any type of evaluation of student performance or learning that occurs after instruction has been completed (e.g., a test given at the end of a grading period or school year).

Emotional or Behavioral Disorders

From Chapter 6 of *Exceptional Children* and *An Introduction to Special Education*, Tenth Edition. William L. Heward.
Copyright © 2013 by Pearson Education, Inc. All rights reserved.

Emotional or Behavioral Disorders

© Gabe Palmer/Alamy

► **FOCUS QUESTIONS**

- What are the points of agreement and disagreement between the definition of emotional disturbance in the Individuals with Disabilities Education Act (IDEA) and the definition of emotional or behavioral disorders by the Council for Children with Behavior Disorders?

- Whose disability is more severe: the acting-out, antisocial child or the withdrawn child?

- What factors might account for the disparity between the number of children receiving special education under the emotional disturbance category and researchers' estimates of the prevalence of emotional or behavioral disorders?

- How can research findings about the cumulative interplay of risk factors for behavioral problems in

adolescence and adulthood guide the development and implementation of prevention programs?

- Although screening and assessment tools for emotional or behavioral disorders are becoming increasingly sophisticated and efficient, schools seldom use them. Why?

- What are the most important skills for teachers of students with emotional or behavioral disorders?

- Why might the inclusion of children with emotional or behavioral disorders in general education classrooms be more (or less) intensely debated than the inclusion of children with other disabilities?

- What are the largest current impediments to children with emotional or behavioral disorders receiving the most effective education possible?

▼ FEATURED TEACHER

KIMBERLY RICH

Snow Horse Elementary School • Davis School District, Kaysville, Utah

EDUCATION—TEACHING CREDENTIALS—EXPERIENCE

- Para-Education Certificate, Salt Lake Community College, 1999

- B.S. in Elementary and Special Education, Weber State University, 2003

- Utah Level 2 Professional Educator License in Elementary Education grades 1–8 and Special Education Mild/Moderate Disabilities grades K–12

- 9 years teaching students with emotional or behavior disorders; 5 years staff at a group home for youth in state custody

- 2010 Utah Council for Exceptional Children Teacher of the Year

CURRENT POSITION AND STUDENTS My room is one of four self-contained special education classrooms at Snow Horse Elementary, an urban school with an enrollment of approximately 750 students. This year I have a classroom of 12 African American and Caucasian third and fourth graders from middle-income families. My students

receive special education services under the disability categories of emotional disturbance, autism, learning disabilities, and other health impairment. Their academic skills span a tremendous range: in reading, from beginning reader to seventh-grade level; in math, from simple addition and subtraction to long division skills. In addition to their academic needs, many of my students also receive speech and language services, psychological services, occupational therapy, and adaptive physical education services. Each morning I teach reading, writing, and math in the special education classroom. In the afternoon our students receive science and social studies instruction in general education classrooms. They also attend physical education, computer, art, and library with their general education classes. A paraeducator or I accompany and support the students as needed in the general education classes.

All of my students participate in district- and statewide assessments with accommodations as determined appropriate by their IEP teams, such as flexible scheduling, small-group settings, having math and science tests read to them, and a reduction in distractions.

CURRICULUM AND INSTRUCTION The curriculum in our classroom consists of grade-level core academic skills, social skills, and the goals on each student's individualized education program (IEP). To ensure that our students' needs are being met and addressed, we continually monitor each student's progress toward meeting his or her IEP goals. Each student's IEP includes both academic and behavioral goals. Here's one of the IEP goals for Katie, an 8-year-old girl who has difficulty following directions: "In all school settings, Katie will follow directions in 5 seconds with no more than 2 incidents of noncompliance per week for 4 consecutive school weeks."

The teaching approach I have found most effective is direct instruction, which allows for students to have a high rate of response, immediate correction, and an increased engagement in the lesson. Direct instruction is often delivered based on student need and ability. Small-group or one-to-one instruction is a typical delivery pattern.

CLASSROOM MANAGEMENT The classroom management system implemented in my classroom is a level system. Green is the highest level, followed by blue, yellow, orange, with red as the lowest level. The higher levels entail greater privileges, and students gain or lose the privileges as they move up or drop down the system based on their daily behavior at school. Each student has a daily level sheet that lists our classroom responsibilities (rules) on the positive side and the misbehavior opposite of our classroom responsibilities on the negative side. Throughout the school day, students earn positive points each time they demonstrate a classroom responsibility. When students exhibit misbehaviors, they receive negative points. My paraprofessionals and I use tally marks to record these points on the students' daily level sheets.

A student who receives 10 negative marks drops one level. Students can receive an automatic level drop for a single occurrence of certain behaviors such as excessive verbal aggression, physical aggression, stealing, not returning their daily home note, or not completing daily reading or homework. When a student receives a level drop, I note the time on their daily level sheet. The student will then stay on that level for 1 day, after which he can buy his way back up to level blue at a cost of 20 points per level. A bulletin board shows students' current levels, providing a visual reminder of their privileges.

At the end of each week, students can purchase a dice roll with points they have earned during the week. We have a menu with six rewards, numbered from 1 to 6. Students roll a single die and then receive the reward on the menu that matches the number rolled. When students on level green arrive at school each morning, one student is selected to spin the spinner to earn bonus points for the group and a chance at a Mystery Motivator. (For a complete description of Mystery Motivators, see *Teaching & Learning*, "Mystery Motivators Can Improve Students' Social and Academic Behavior" later in this chapter.) If on any level students have a day with zero misbehaviors, they choose a simple reinforcement from what we call the "Fab-Bag."

To ensure that the items on the reward menu are of high interest to the students, the class chooses the rewards at the beginning of the year. Their favorite things are mechanical pencils, popcorn, no-homework coupons, extra recess coupons, computer game time, rolling chair coupon (allowing them to switch chairs with a teacher for a day), and a free book. We change the items on the reward menu at the beginning of every month.

To meet Kimberly Rich and observe some of these classroom management and motivation techniques, go to the book resources for this text on MyEducationLab.

Daily, my students take home a note that goes to parents informing them of exactly the number of times their student demonstrated both positive and negative behaviors at school that day. The note has a place for the parent/guardian's signature and space for parents to write a comment or question for me. When students return their note the next day signed by a parent, they receive points. The daily home notes build a trusting relationship with parents and reduce miscommunication among student, family, and school staff.

SCHOOL- AND DISTRICTWIDE COLLABORATION I serve as a member of the district Least Restrictive Environment Committee, which helps school teams review whether a change of placement is best for students. Another district assignment is to serve as a coach to new teachers in the same classroom as mine on an elementary level. I help them get their classrooms set up, answer any questions, and help them learn the curriculum. In addition, as a member of the school Multidisciplinary Special Education Team, we meet weekly to discuss special education students' assessments and progress.

Other professionals I work with are the school psychologist, speech/language pathologist, occupational therapists, and occasionally an adapted physical education specialist. The school psychologist services may include weekly sessions for social skills or anger management. The speech/language pathologist services may include weekly sessions for articulation or understanding of language skills. The adapted physical education specialist works with students on basic physical education skills such as throwing a ball, skipping, jumping rope, bouncing a ball, and so on, as decided on by assessments and included as a goal on the IEP.

My classroom serves as a training site for teachers and administrators in our district to learn strategies for effective social skills instruction. Teachers observe social skills instruction in my classroom. I then observe these teachers conducting social skills instruction in their classrooms and offer suggestions and support.

WHY I ENJOY BEING A SPECIAL EDUCATION TEACHER I have the privilege of seeing my students make noticeably great progress, usually in a short time frame. My students usually come into my classroom having experienced little to no success in school. As we address their diverse academic and behavior needs, they feel success and begin to enjoy attending school. A parent of one of my students shared the following conversation with me. The parent had asked Jake what it was like to have me as a teacher. Jake responded with "She has that something special, not sure actually what it is, but you know she has it. In times of doubt she gets me motivated, when I doubt myself that I can do something. You just trust her thoughts, ideas, and what she tells you to do. I used to be nervous and scared at school, but not with her." Students like Jake give me the motivation to continue to strive to help other students feel successful and recognize their potential.

MyEducationLab™

Visit the **MyEducationLab** for *Exceptional Children* to enhance your understanding of chapter concepts with a personalized Study Plan. You'll also have the opportunity to hone your teaching skills through video- and case-based Assignments and Activities, IRIS Center Resources, and Building Teaching Skills and Dispositions lessons.

CHILDHOOD SHOULD BE A HAPPY TIME: a time to play, make friends, and learn—and for most children it is. But some children's lives are in constant turmoil. Some children strike out at others, sometimes with disastrous consequences. Others are so shy and withdrawn that they seem to be in their own worlds. In either case, playing with others, making friends, and learning all the things a child must learn are extremely difficult for these children. These are children with emotional or behavioral disorders.

Many children with emotional or behavioral disorders are disliked by their classmates and teachers; even their siblings and parents may reject them. Sadder still, they often do not even like themselves. The child with behavioral disorders is difficult to be around, and attempts to befriend him (most are boys) may lead to rejection, verbal abuse, or even physical attack. Although most children with emotional or behavioral disorders are of sound mind and body, their noxious or withdrawn behavior is as serious an impediment to their functioning as are the intellectual, learning, sensory, and physical disabilities that challenge other children.

DEFINITIONS

A clear and widely accepted definition of emotional or behavioral disorders is lacking for numerous reasons. First, disordered behavior is a social construct; no clear agreement exists about what constitutes good mental health. All children behave inappropriately at times. How often, with how much intensity, and for how long must a student exhibit problem behavior before he is considered disabled because of the behavior? Second, different theories of emotional disturbance use concepts and terminology that do little to promote meaning from one definition to another. Third, expectations and norms for appropriate behavior are often quite different across ethnic and cultural groups. Finally, emotional or behavioral disorders sometimes occur in conjunction with other disabilities (most notably learning disabilities), making it difficult to determine whether one condition is an outcome or the cause of the other.

Of the many definitions of emotional or behavioral disorders that have been proposed, the two that have had the most influence are the definition in the Individuals with Disabilities Education Act (IDEA) and one proposed by a coalition of professional associations concerned with children with behavior problems.

Federal Definition of Emotional Disturbance

IDEA definition of E/BD

 Council for Exceptional Children

Content Standards for Beginning Teachers of Students with E/BD: Issues in definition and identification of individuals with exceptional learning needs, including those from culturally and linguistically diverse backgrounds (ICC1K5) (also BD1K1).

Emotional disturbance is one of the disability categories in IDEA under which a child is eligible to receive special education services. IDEA defines **emotional disturbance** as:

(i) [a] condition exhibiting one or more of the following characteristics over a long period of time and to a marked degree that adversely affects educational performance:

(A) An inability to learn which cannot be explained by intellectual, sensory, and health factors;

(B) An inability to build or maintain satisfactory interpersonal relationships with peers and teachers;

(C) Inappropriate types of behavior or feelings under normal circumstances;

(D) A general pervasive mood of unhappiness or depression; or

(E) A tendency to develop physical symptoms or fears associated with personal or school problems.

(ii) Emotional disturbance includes schizophrenia. The term does not apply to children who are socially maladjusted, unless it is determined that they have an emotional disturbance under paragraph (i) of this section. (PL 108-446, 20 *CFR* §300.8[c][4])

At first glance, this definition may seem straightforward enough. It identifies three conditions that must be met: *chronicity* ("over a long period of time"), *severity* ("to a marked degree"), and *difficulty in school* ("adversely affects educational performance"); and it lists five types of problems that qualify. But in fact, this definition is extremely vague. What do terms such as *satisfactory* and *inappropriate* really mean? Differing degrees of teacher tolerance for student behavior (Walker, Ramsey, & Gresham, 2005), differences between teachers' and parents' expectations for student behavior (Konold, Walthall, & Pianta, 2004), and the fact that expectations for behavior vary across ethnic and cultural groups (Cullinan & Kauffman, 2005) make the referral and identification of students with emotional or behavioral disorders a highly subjective process.

And how does one determine that some behavior problems represent "social maladjustment," whereas others indicate true "emotional disturbance"? Many children experiencing significant difficulties in school because of their behavior are ineligible for special education under IDEA because their problems are considered to be "merely" conduct disorders or discipline problems (Forness & Kavale, 2000). The federal definition was derived from a single study conducted by Eli Bower (1960) in the Los Angeles County schools more than 50 years ago. Bower himself never intended to make a distinction between emotional disturbance and social maladjustment. Indeed, he stated that the five components of the definition were, in fact, meant to be indicators of social maladjustment (Bower, 1982).

It is difficult to conceive of a child who is sufficiently socially maladjusted to have received that label but who does not display one or more of the five characteristics (especially "B") included in the federal definition. As written, the definition seemingly excludes children on the very basis for which they are included. The federal definition's illogical criterion for ineligibility, the dated and arbitrary list of the five characteristics, and the subjective wording that enables school districts to not serve many children with behavioral problems have produced strongly voiced criticism (e.g., Forness & Kavale, 2000; Kauffman & Landrum, 2009).

CCBD Definition of Emotional or Behavioral Disorder

In response to the problems with the federal definition, the Council for Children with Behavioral Disorders (CCBD, 2000) drafted a new definition using the term *emotional or behavioral disorder*. The CCBD definition was later adopted by the National Mental Health and Special Education Coalition (a group of 30 education, mental health, and child advocacy organizations) and subsequently submitted to the U.S. Congress as a proposed replacement for the IDEA definition. The CCBD definition of **emotional or behavioral disorder** reads as follows:

1. The term "emotional or behavioral disorder" means a disability that is characterized by emotional or behavioral responses in school programs so different from appropriate age, cultural, or ethnic norms that the responses adversely affect educational performance, including academic, social, vocational or personal skills; more than a temporary, expected response to stressful events in the environment; consistently exhibited in two different settings, at least one of which is school-related; and unresponsive to direct intervention in general education, or the condition of the child is such that general education interventions would be insufficient.
2. The term includes such a disability that co-exists with other disabilities.
3. The term includes a schizophrenic disorder, affective disorder, anxiety disorder, or other sustained disorder of conduct or adjustment, affecting a child if the disorder affects educational performance as described in paragraph (1). (*Federal Register*, February 10, 1993, p. 7938)

Advantages of this definition, according to the CCBD (2000), are that it clarifies the educational dimensions of the disability; focuses directly on the child's behavior in school settings; places behavior in the context of appropriate age, ethnic, and cultural norms; and increases the possibility of early identification and intervention. Perhaps most important, the revised terminology and definition do not require "meaningless distinctions between social and emotional maladjustment, distinctions that often waste diagnostic resources when it is already clear that serious problems exist" (p. 7).

CHARACTERISTICS

Children with emotional or behavioral disorders are characterized primarily by behavior that falls significantly beyond the norms of their cultural and age group on two dimensions: externalizing (aggression, acting out) and internalizing (anxiety, social withdrawal). Either pattern of abnormal behavior has adverse effects on a child's academic achievement and social relationships.

Externalizing Behaviors

The most common behavior pattern of children with emotional or behavioral disorders consists of antisocial, or externalizing, behaviors. In the classroom, children with **externalizing behaviors** frequently do the following (adapted from Walker, 1997):

- Get out of their seats
- Yell, talk out, and curse
- Disturb peers

Externalizing behaviors and noncompliance

 Content Standards for Beginning Teachers of Students with E/BD: Range of characteristics within and among individuals with emotional and/or behavioral disorders (BD2K2) (also BD1K1).

209

- Hit or fight
- Ignore the teacher
- Complain
- Argue excessively
- Steal
- Lie
- Destroy property
- Do not comply with directions
- Have temper tantrums

Rhode, Jenson, and Reavis (1998) describe noncompliance as the "king-pin behavior" around which other behavioral excesses revolve. "Noncompliance is simply defined as not following a direction within a reasonable amount of time. Most of the arguing, tantrums, fighting, or rule breaking is secondary to avoiding requests or required tasks" (p. 4). Antisocial, noncompliant children "can make our teaching lives miserable and single-handedly disrupt a classroom" (Rhode et al., 1998, p. 3).

All children sometimes cry, disrupt others, and refuse to comply with requests of parents and teachers; but children with emotional or behavioral disorders do so with disturbing frequency. Also, their antisocial behavior often occurs with little or no apparent provocation. Aggression takes many forms—verbal abuse toward adults and other children, destructiveness and vandalism, and physical attacks on others. These children seem to be in continuous conflict with those around them. It is no wonder that children with emotional or behavioral disorders find it difficult to establish and maintain friendships.

Many believe that most children who exhibit deviant behavioral patterns will grow out of them with time and become normally functioning adults. Although this optimistic outcome holds true for some children who exhibit problems such as withdrawal, fears, and speech impairments (Rutter, 1976), research indicates that it is not so for children who display consistent patterns of aggressive, coercive, antisocial, and/or delinquent behavior (Dunlap et al., 2006; Montague, Enders, Cavendish, & Castro, 2011; Nelson, Stage, Duppong-Hurley, Synhorst, & Epstein, 2007). A pattern of antisocial behavior early in a child's development is the best single predictor of delinquency in adolescence. Children who enter adolescence with a history of aggressive behavior stand a very good chance of dropping out of school, being arrested, abusing drugs and alcohol, having marginalized adult lives, and dying young (Lipsey & Derzon, 1998; Walker et al., 2005).

Internalizing Behaviors

Some children with emotional or behavioral disorders are anything but aggressive. Their problem is the opposite—too little social interaction with others. They are said to exhibit **internalizing behaviors**. Although children who consistently act immaturely and withdrawn do not present the threat to others that antisocial children do, their behavior creates a serious impediment to their development. These children seldom play with others their own age. They lack the social skills needed to make friends and have fun, and they often retreat into daydreams and fantasies. Some are extremely fearful of certain things without reason (i.e., phobia), frequently complain of being sick or hurt, and go into deep bouts of depression (King, Heyne, & Ollendick, 2005; Maag & Swearer, 2005). Obviously, such behavior limits a child's chances to take part in and learn from the typical school and leisure activities that children participate in and enjoy. Table 1 describes the most common types of anxiety disorders and mood disorders seen in school-age children.

Because children who exhibit the internalizing behaviors characteristic of some types of anxiety and mood disorders may be less disturbing to classroom teachers than are antisocial children, they are in danger of not being identified (Lane & Menzies, 2005). Happily, the outlook is fairly good for the child with mild or moderate degrees of withdrawn and immature behavior who is fortunate enough to have competent teachers and other school professionals responsible for his development. Carefully targeting the social and self-determination skills the child should learn and systematically arranging opportunities for and reinforcing those behaviors often prove successful (Morris & March, 2004).

It is a grave mistake, however, to believe that children with emotional disorders characterized primarily by internalizing behaviors have only mild and temporary problems. The severe anxiety and mood disorders that some children experience not only cause pervasive impairments in their educational performance but also threaten their very existence. Indeed, without identification and effective treatment, the extreme emotional disorders of some children can lead to self-inflicted injury or even death from substance abuse, starvation, or suicidal behavior (Spirito & Overholser, 2003).

Internalizing behaviors limit a child's chances to take part in the school and leisure activities in which most children participate.

Academic Achievement

Most students with emotional or behavioral disorders perform one or more years below grade level academically (Cullinan, 2007). Studies of the academic achievement of students with emotional or behavioral disorders have reported dismal outcomes such as the following (Benner, Nelson, Ralston, & Mooney, 2010; Cullinan & Sabornie, 2004; Landrum, Katsiyannis, & Archwamety, 2004; Lane, Carter, Pierson, & Glaeser, 2006; Nelson, Benner, Lane, & Smith, 2004; Reid, Gonzalez, Nordness, Trout, & Epstein, 2004; Wagner, Kutash, Duchnowski, Epstein, & Sumi, 2005):

- Two-thirds cannot pass competency exams for their grade level.
- They are more likely to receive grades of D and F than are students with other disabilities.
- Achievement deficits tend to worsen as students grow older.
- They have the highest absenteeism rate of any group of students.
- Only one in three leaves high school with a diploma or certificate of completion, compared to 50% of all students with disabilities and 76% of all youth in the general population.
- An alarming 60% drop out of high school.

The strong correlation between behavior problems and low academic achievement is a reciprocal relationship (Landrum, Tankersley, & Kauffman, 2003). Disruptive and defiant behavior interrupts instruction and limits participation in classroom activities and assignment completion. As a result of this lack of engagement with the curriculum, students with emotional or behavioral disorders may fail to learn. The problem is further exacerbated when a student with emotional or behavioral disorders receives ineffective instruction from teachers who are unaware of the student's academic skills deficits or who cannot address the deficits. The student becomes frustrated, which leads to misbehavior in the form of avoidance and escape that in turn causes the student to fall yet further behind academically (Payne, Marks, & Bogan, 2007).

In addition to the challenges to learning caused by their behavioral excesses and deficits, many students with emotional or behavioral disorders also have learning disabilities and/or language delays, which compound their difficulties in mastering academic skills and content (Glassberg, Hooper, & Mattison, 1999; Nelson, Benner, & Cheney, 2005).

Academic achievement of students with E/BD

 Council for Exceptional Children Content Standards for Beginning Teachers—Common Core: Educational implications of characteristics of various exceptionalities (ICC2K2) (also BD2K1, BD3K2).

TABLE 1 • **Types of anxiety, mood, and other emotional disorders in children**

CONDITION	CHARACTERISTICS/SYMPTOMS	REMARKS
Anxiety Disorders	Maladaptive emotional state or behaviors caused by excessive and often irrational fears and worries.	
Generalized anxiety disorder	Excessive, unrealistic worries, fears, and tension that lasts 6 months or more; in addition to chronic anxiety, symptoms include restlessness, fatigue, difficulty concentrating, muscular aches, insomnia, nausea, excessive heart rate, dizziness, and irritability.	Excessive worrying interferes with normal activities. Children tend to be very hard on themselves, striving for perfection, sometimes redoing tasks repeatedly; they may also seek constant approval or reassurance from others. Usually affects children between the ages of 6 and 11.
Phobias	Intense fear reaction to a specific object or situation (e.g., snakes, dogs, or heights); level of fear is inappropriate to the situation and is recognized by the person as being irrational; can lead to the avoidance of common, everyday situations.	Most phobias can be treated successfully with behavior therapy techniques such as systematic desensitization (gradual and repeated exposure to feared object or situation while relaxing) and self-monitoring.
Obsessive/ compulsive disorder (OCD)	Persistent, recurring thoughts (obsessions) that reflect exaggerated anxiety or fears; typical obsessions include worry about being contaminated, behaving improperly, or acting violently. The obsessions may lead an individual to perform a ritual or routine (compulsions)—such as washing hands, repeating phrases, or hoarding—to relieve the anxiety caused by the obsession.	OCD most often begins in adolescence or early adulthood. Most individuals recognize their obsessions are irrational and that the compulsions are excessive or unreasonable. Behavioral therapy is effective in treating most cases of OCD; medications are often effective.
Anorexia nervosa	Refusal to maintain body weight at or above a minimally normal weight for age and height. Obsessive concern with body weight or shape. Intense anxiety about gaining weight or becoming fat, even though severely underweight. Two subtypes: restricting food intake by starving oneself down to an abnormal weight and binge eating/ purging.	Anorexia and bulimia (see below) are primarily disorders of females, particularly adolescent girls. Early in the course of anorexia, the person often denies the disorder. Depression, anxiety, compulsive exercise, social withdrawal, obsessive/compulsive symptoms, and substance abuse are often associated with eating disorders.
Bulimia nervosa	Recurrent episodes of (a) binge eating (eating in a discrete period of time an amount of food much larger than most people would eat under similar circumstances while feeling that one cannot stop eating) and (b) inappropriate compensatory behavior in order to prevent weight gain (e.g., self-induced vomiting, misuse of laxatives or other medications, fasting, excessive exercise).	Preoccupation with weight and shape and excessive self-evaluation are primary symptoms of both anorexia and bulimia. Many patients demonstrate a mixture of both anorexic and bulimic behaviors.
Posttraumatic stress disorder (PTSD)	Prolonged and recurrent emotional reactions after exposure to a traumatic event (e.g., sexual or physical assault, unexpected death of a loved one, natural disaster, witnessing or being a victim of acts of war or terrorism). Symptoms: flashbacks and nightmares of the traumatic event; avoiding places or things related to the trauma; emotional detachment from others; and difficulty sleeping, irritability, or poor concentration.	Increased recognition of PTSD in children has occurred in the U.S. since the terrorist attacks of September 11, 2001. Individual and group counseling and support activities can be helpful. Teachers can help by providing an environment in which the child with PTSD feels safe and positive social attention for the child's involvement with normal activities.
Selective mutism (also called *elective mutism, speech phobia*)	Child speaks normally to specific person or group (e.g., family members) but refuses to talk to others. May be a response to trauma, more often caused by anxiety or fear of speaking in certain settings or to certain individuals or groups.	Treatment uses positive approach, no attention or punishment for not speaking, reinforcement for approximations of speaking (e.g., participation in class activities, nonspeech vocalizations).

TABLE 1 • (Continued)

CONDITION	CHARACTERISTICS/SYMPTOMS	REMARKS
Mood Disorders	Characterized by impaired functioning due to episodes of abnormally depressed or elevated emotional state.	
Depression	Marked by pervasive sad mood and sense of hopelessness. Symptoms include social withdrawal; irritability; feelings of guilt or worthlessness; inability to concentrate; loss of interest in normal activities; drastic change in weight, appetite, or sleeping pattern; prolonged crying bouts; recurring thoughts of suicide. Several symptoms must be exhibited over a period of time and not be temporary, reasonable responses to life circumstances (e.g., grief over death of a family member).	Researchers estimate that 15% to 20% of adolescents experience depression at one time or another; adolescent girls are twice as likely as boys to be depressed. Depression is often overlooked in children, especially when symptoms are overshadowed by externalizing behavioral disorders. Teachers should be attentive for signs of possible depression and refer students for evaluation.
Bipolar disorder (formerly called *manic-depressive disorder*)	Alternating episodes of depressive and manic states. During manic episodes, person is in an elevated mood of euphoria—a feeling of extraordinary elation, excitement—and exhibits three or more of the following symptoms: excessive egotism; very little sleep needed; incessant talkativeness; rapidly changing thoughts and ideas in uncontrolled order; easily distracted; agitated, "driven" activities; and participation in personally risky activities. The peak age at onset of first symptoms falls between the ages of 15 and 19. Five years or more may elapse between the first and second episodes, but the time periods between subsequent episodes usually narrow.	Some patients are reluctant to participate in treatment because they find the experience of mania very enjoyable. Patients often recall this experience and minimize or deny entirely the devastating features of full-blown mania or the demoralization of a depressive episode. Regular patterns of daily activities, including sleeping, eating, physical activity, and social and/or emotional stimulation may help. Medications are often effective in treating acute episodes, preventing future episodes, and providing stabilizing moods between episodes.
Other Disorders		
Schizophrenia	A severe psychotic disorder characterized by delusions, hallucinations (hearing voices), unfounded fears of persecution, disorganized speech, catatonic behavior (stupor and muscular rigidity), restricted range and intensity of emotional expression (affective flattening), reduced thought and speech productivity, and decreased initiation of goal-directed behavior. Affects males and females with equal frequency. Onset typically occurs during adolescence or early adulthood. Most people with schizophrenia alternate between acute psychotic episodes and stable phases with few or no symptoms.	Although no cure exists, most children with schizophrenia benefit from a variety of treatments, including antipsychotic medication, behavioral therapy, and educational interventions such as social skills training. The general goals of treatment are to decrease the frequency, severity, and psychosocial consequences of psychotic episodes and to maximize functioning between episodes.
Tourette syndrome	An inherited neurological disorder characterized by motor and vocal tics (repeated and involuntary movements) such as eye blinking, facial grimacing, throat clearing or sniffing, arm thrusting, kicking, or jumping. About 15% of cases include coprolalia (repeated cursing, obscene language, and ethnic slurs). Symptoms typically appear before age 18; males affected 3 to 4 times more often than females. Many students also have attentional problems, impulsiveness, compulsions, ritualistic behaviors, and learning disabilities.	Tics are experienced as irresistible; student may seek a secluded spot to release symptoms after delaying them. Tics are more likely during periods of tension or stress, and decrease with relaxation or when focusing on an absorbing task. Tolerance and understanding of symptoms are of paramount importance to students; untimed exams (in a private room if vocal tics are a problem) and permission to leave the classroom when tics become overwhelming are often helpful.

Sources: American Psychiatric Association (2006); American Psychological Association (2011); Anxiety Disorders Association of America (2011); Cullinan (2007); Kauffman and Landrum (2009); Morris and March (2004); Rutherford, Quinn, and Sathur (2004); Schum (2002); Tourette Syndrome Association (2011).

Intelligence

Many more children with emotional or behavioral disorders score in the slow learner or mild intellectual disabilities range on IQ tests than do children without disabilities. Two research groups who reviewed a total of 25 studies on performance of students with emotional and behavioral disorders on IQ tests published between 1991 and 2000 reported a mean score of 96 across the studies (Reid et al., 2004; Trout et al., 2003). No studies have found an average IQ of 100 or higher.

Whether children with emotional or behavioral disorders actually have any less real intelligence than do children without disabilities is difficult to say. An IQ test measures how well a child performs certain tasks at the time and place the test is administered. It is almost certain that the disruptive behavior exhibited by a child with emotional or behavior disorders has interfered with past opportunities to learn many of the tasks included on the test. Rhode and colleagues (1998) estimate that the average student actively attends to the teacher and to assigned work approximately 85% of the time, but that students with behavior disorders are on task only about 60% or less of the time. This difference in on-task behavior can have a dramatic impact on learning. Off-task and disruptive behavior frequently produces teacher attention, which can have the unintended effect of reinforcing the undesired behavior. Teaching students to obtain teacher attention when they have completed some work is one strategy for breaking this pattern.

Social Skills and Interpersonal Relationships

The ability to develop and maintain interpersonal relationships during childhood and adolescence is an important predictor of future adjustment. As might be expected, students with emotional or behavioral disorders are often rejected by peers and experience great difficulty in making and keeping friends (Bierman, 2005; Gresham, Lane, MacMillan, & Bocian, 1999). The findings of a study (Schonert-Reichl, 1993) comparing the social relationships of secondary students with behavioral disorders with those of same-age peers without disabilities is typical of much of the published literature on social skills of students with emotional or behavioral disorders: the students with behavioral disorders reported lower levels of empathy toward others, participation in fewer curricular activities, less frequent contacts with friends, and lower-quality relationships than were reported by their peers without disabilities.

Juvenile Delinquency

Students with emotional or behavioral disorders are 13.3 times more likely to be arrested during their school careers than are students without disabilities (Doren, Bullis, & Benz, 1996a). More than one-third of students with emotional or behavioral disorders are arrested during their school years (Henderson & Bradley, 2004). In 2008, U.S. law enforcement agencies made about 2.1 million arrests of people under the age of 18 (Office of Juvenile Justice and Delinquency Prevention [OJJDP], 2009). As staggering as this number may seem, it represents 19% fewer juvenile arrests than in 1999. Although males are generally arrested for crimes involving aggression (e.g., assault, burglary) and females have been associated with sex-related offenses (e.g., prostitution), females accounted for 30% of all juvenile arrests and 17% of juvenile violent crime arrests in 2008.

Arrest rates for juveniles increase sharply during the junior high years. This pattern probably reflects both the greater harm adolescents can cause to society by their inappropriate behavior and the fact that younger children are often not arrested (and therefore do not show up on the records) for committing the same acts that lead to the arrest of an older child. Younger children, however, are being arrested, and they are committing serious crimes. Youth under the age 15, for example, accounted for 27% of all violent and property crime arrests in 2008 (OJJDP, 2009).

About half of all juvenile delinquents are *recidivists* (repeat offenders). A report of chronic offenders in Lane County, Oregon, found that 15% of juvenile offenders committed 64% of all new crimes by juveniles (Wagner, 2009). An encouraging finding from a longitudinal study of 1,354 serious adolescent offenders found that most youth who commit felonies greatly reduce their rate of offending over time (Mulvey, 2011). This study also found that longer stays in juvenile detention facilities do not reduce recidivism but that community-based supervision after release from detention is effective in reducing repeat offenses.

PREVALENCE

Estimates of how many children have emotional or behavioral disorders vary tremendously. A review of 50 epidemiological studies of mental health problems in children found an average prevalence of 8.3% (Roberts, Attkisson, & Rosenblatt, 1998). Another review of 30 studies of behavior problems of preschoolers from low-income families found a mean prevalence of 30% (Qi & Kaiser, 2003). Such wide-ranging estimates suggest that different criteria are being used to decide what constitutes emotional or behavioral disorders (Feil et al., 2005). Differences in prevalence figures, however, stem as much from how the data are collected as they do from the use of different definitions and instruments (Cullinan, 2007). Most surveys ask teachers to identify students in their classes who display behavior problems at that point in time. Many children exhibit inappropriate behavior for short periods, and such one-shot screening procedures will identify them.

Credible studies indicate that from 3% to 6% of school-age children have emotional or behavioral problems that are sufficiently serious and persistent to warrant intervention (Kauffman & Landrum, 2009). Annual reports from the federal government, however, show that far fewer children are being served than the most conservative prevalence estimates. The 405,293 children ages 6 to 21 who received special education under the IDEA category of emotional disturbance during the 2009–2010 school year represented less than 1% of the school-age population (U.S. Department of Education, 2011).

The number of children being served represents less than half of the 2% estimate the federal government used previously in its estimates of funding and personnel needs for students with emotional and behavioral disorders. Kauffman (2005) believed that social policy and economic factors caused the government to first reduce its estimate of the prevalence of behavioral disorders (from 2% to 1.2%) and then to stop publishing an estimate altogether. "The government obviously prefers not to allow wide discrepancies between prevalence estimates and the actual number of children served. It is easier to cut prevalence estimates than to serve more students" (p. 50).

Gender

More than three-fourths of children identified for special education because of emotional or behavioral disorders are boys (Wagner et al., 2005). Boys identified as emotionally or behaviorally disordered are likely to have externalizing disorders in the form of antisocial, aggressive behaviors (Furlong, Morrison, & Jimerson, 2004). Although girls with emotional or behavioral disorders are more likely to show internalizing disorders such as anxiety and social withdrawal, research shows that girls have problems with aggression and antisocial behavior as well (Talbott & Thiede, 1999).

Students in Juvenile Detention Facilities

In 2008, about 81,000 juveniles, or 263 for every 100,000 juveniles in the general population, were in residential detention facilities (Sickmund, 2010). A national survey of principals of juvenile corrections facilities found that 40% of all of committed youth were classified with a disability (Gagnon, Barber, Van Loan, & Leone, 2009). Another national study reported that nearly one half (47%) of incarcerated youth were classified with emotional disturbance (Quinn, Rutherford, Leone, Osher, & Poirier, 2005).

CAUSES

Causes of E/BD

Content Standards for Beginning Teachers of Students with E/BD: Typical and atypical human growth and development (ICC2K1) (also IGC2K4, ICC1K7).

The behavior of some children with emotional or behavioral disorders is so self-destructive and apparently illogical that it is difficult to imagine how they got that way. We shake our heads in bewilderment and ask, "Where did that behavior come from?" Numerous theories and conceptual models have been proposed to explain abnormal behavior (see Bigby, 2007; Cullinan, 2007; Kauffman & Landrum, 2009; Webber & Plotts, 2008). Regardless of the conceptual model used to view emotional or behavioral disorders, the suspected causes can be grouped into two major categories: biological and environmental.

Biological Factors

BRAIN DISORDERS Many individuals who have brain disorders experience problems with emotion and behavior. Brain disorders are the result of either *brain dysgenesis* (abnormal brain development) or *brain injury* (caused by influences such as disease or trauma that alter the structure or function of a brain that had been developing normally up to that point). For the vast majority of children with emotional or behavioral disorders, however, there is no evidence of brain disorder or injury.

GENETICS Evidence indicates the presence of genetic links to some forms of emotional or behavioral disorders (Rhee & Waldman, 2002; Rutter, 2006). The disorder with the strongest research support for a genetic risk factor is schizophrenia, a severe and debilitating form of mental illness characterized by auditory hallucinations (hearing voices), delusions, unfounded fears of persecution, and disordered speech. Relatives of schizophrenics have an increased risk of acquiring schizophrenia that cannot be explained by environmental factors alone; and the closer the relation, the higher the probability of acquiring the condition (Pennington, 2002). However, genetics alone has not been found to cause schizophrenia. A person in either of the two highest-risk groups (a child of two parents with schizophrenia or an identical twin of a sibling with the condition) still has a less than 50% chance of developing schizophrenia (Plomin, 1995).

TEMPERAMENT No agreed-on definition of **temperament** exists, but it is generally conceived to be a person's behavioral style or typical way of responding to situations. Because physiological differences or markers are associated with differences in infants' temperament, it is considered an inborn biological influence (Kagan & Snidman, 2004). An infant who seldom cries but smiles and coos when passed from one person to another might be said to have an easygoing temperament. In contrast, an infant who is distractible, frequently fusses, and withdraws from new situations might show signs of a difficult temperament.

Some research shows that an easy or positive temperament is correlated with resilience to stress (Smith & Prior, 1995) and that a difficult temperament at an early age increases the likelihood of behavior problems in adolescence (Caspi, Henry, McGee, Moffitt, & Silva, 1995). In one study, children with an inhibited temperament style characterized by withdrawing from novel situations, playing alone, and spending time on the periphery of social action in the second year of life were more likely to develop social phobias and symptoms of anxiety by age 13 (Schwartz, Snidman, & Kagan, 1999).

Although a child's temperament is unlikely in itself to cause emotional or behavior problems, it may predispose the child to problems by interacting with environmental factors, such as making parenting interactions more difficult (Nelson et al., 2007). Thus, certain events that might not produce problem behavior in a child with an easygoing temperament might result in disordered behavior by the child with a difficult temperament (Rimm-Kaufman & Kagan, 2005; Teglasi, 2006).

Environmental Factors

Three primary environmental factors contribute to the development of conduct disorder and antisocial behavior: (a) an adverse early rearing environment, (b) an aggressive pattern of behavior displayed when entering school, and (c) social rejection by peers. Considerable evidence shows that these causal factors occur in sequence (Dodge, 1993; Pennington, 2002; Walker et al., 2005). The settings in which these events occur are home, school, and the community.

HOME The relationship children have with their parents, particularly during the early years, is critical to the way they learn to behave. Observation and analysis of parent–child interaction patterns show that parents who treat their children with love, are sensitive to their children's needs, and provide praise and attention for desired behaviors tend to have children with positive behavioral characteristics. Decades of research show clearly that children with emotional or behavior problems are more likely to come from homes in which parents are inconsistent disciplinarians, use harsh and excessive punishment, spend little time engaged in prosocial activities with their children, do not monitor the whereabouts and activities of their children, and show little love and affection for good behavior (McEvoy & Welker, 2000; Patterson, Reid, & Dishion, 1992; Watson & Gross, 2000). When such conditions are present in the home, a young child may be "literally trained to be aggressive during episodes of conflict with family members" (Forgatch & Paterson, 1998, p. 86).

Because of the research on the correlation between parental child-rearing practices and behavior problems, some mental health professionals have been quick to pin the blame for children's behavior problems on parents. But the relationship between parent and child is dynamic and reciprocal; in other words, the behavior of the child affects the behavior of the parents just as much as the parents' actions affect the child's actions. Therefore, at best it is not practical and at worst it is wrong to blame parents for the emotional or behavior problems of their children. Instead, professionals must work with parents to help them systematically change certain aspects of the parent–child relationship in an effort to prevent and modify those problems (Park, Alber-Morgan, & Fleming, 2011; Lien-Thorne & Kamps, 2005; Ryan, Boxmeyer, & Lochman, 2009).

SCHOOL School is where children spend the largest portion of their time outside the home. Therefore, it makes sense to observe carefully what occurs in schools in an effort to identify factors that may contribute to problem behavior. Also, because most children with emotional or behavioral disorders are not identified until they are in school, it seems reasonable to question whether school contributes to the incidence of behavioral disorders. Educational practices that contribute to the development of emotional or behavioral problems in children include ineffective instruction that results in academic failure, unclear rules and expectations for appropriate behavior, inconsistent and punitive discipline practices, infrequent teacher praise and approval for academic and social behavior, and failure to individualize instruction to accommodate diverse learners (Furlong et al., 2004; Lago-Delello, 1998; Sprague & Walker, 2000).

A teacher's actions can maintain and actually strengthen deviant behavioral patterns even though the teacher is trying to help the child. Consider the all-too-common interaction between teacher and student illustrated in Figure 1 (Rhode et al., 1998). It begins with a teacher request that the student ignores and follows a predictable and escalating sequence of teacher pleas and threats that the student counters with excuses, arguments, and eventually a

Influence of home and community

 Council for Exceptional Children

Content Standards for Beginning Teachers—Common Core: Family systems and the roles of families in supporting development (ICC2K4).

Even though the teacher is trying to help, a child's problem behavior can be maintained and actually strengthened by what takes place in the classroom.

© Radius Images/Alamy

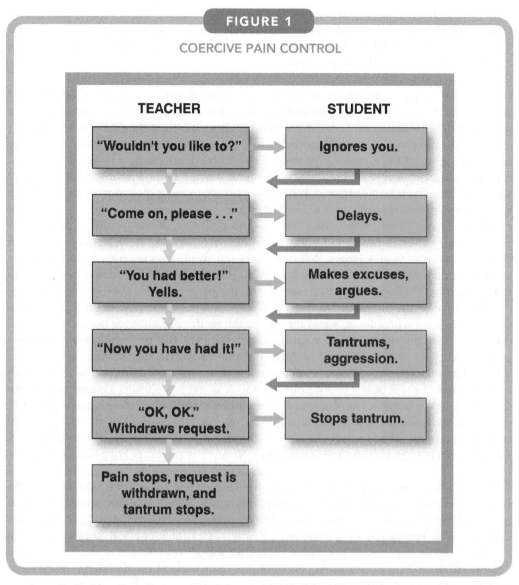

Source: Reprinted from Rhode, G., Jensen, W. R., & Reavis, H. K. (1998). *The tough kid book: Practical classroom management strategies* (p. 5). Longmont, CO: Sopris West. Used with permission.

Teacher's reaction to noncompliance

 Council for Exceptional Children

Content Standards for Beginning Teachers—Common Core: Teacher attitudes and behaviors that influence behavior of individuals with exceptional learning needs (ICC5K2).

full-blown tantrum. The escalating aggression and tantruming become so aversive to the teacher that she withdraws the task demand (thereby reinforcing and strengthening the student's disruptive behavior) so the student will stop tantruming (thereby reinforcing the teacher's withdrawing the request) (Gunter, Denny, Jack, Shores, & Nelson, 1993; Maag, 2001). This process teaches the child to argue, make excuses, tantrum, destroy property, and even use physical aggression to get what he wants.

COMMUNITY Students who associate with peers who exhibit antisocial behavior are likely to experience trouble in the community and at school. Gang membership, drug and alcohol abuse, and deviant sexual behavior are community factors that contribute to the development and maintenance of an antisocial lifestyle (Karnick, 2004; Walker et al., 2005).

A Complex Pathway of Risks

It is impossible to identify a single factor or isolated event as the cause of a child's emotional or behavioral disorder. Most chronic behavior problems are the accumulated effect of exposure to a variety of family, neighborhood, school, and societal risk factors. The greater the number of risk factors and the longer a child's exposure to them, the greater the probability that the child will experience negative outcomes (Sprague & Walker, 2000). Figure 2 illustrates this pattern of antisocial behavior development as originally conceived by Patterson and his colleagues (Patterson, 1982; Patterson et al., 1992). Although the interplay of these risk factors is complex and the specific contribution of any given risk factor cannot be determined, the outcome is, sadly, highly predictable.

Although knowledge of these risk factors provides information necessary for planning and implementing prevention programs (Conroy & Brown, 2006), precise knowledge of etiology is not required to effectively treat children's existing behavior problems. Attempting to determine the extent to which various factors in a child's past

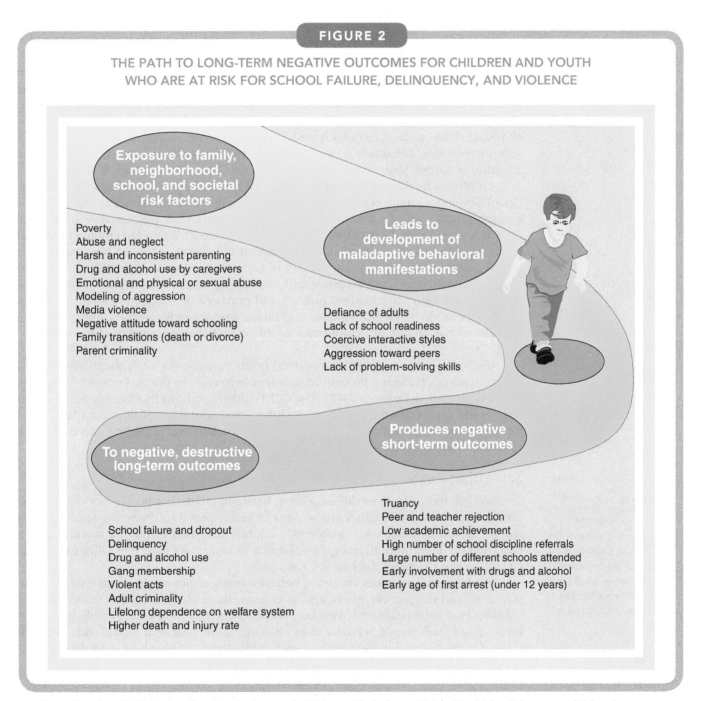

FIGURE 2

THE PATH TO LONG-TERM NEGATIVE OUTCOMES FOR CHILDREN AND YOUTH WHO ARE AT RISK FOR SCHOOL FAILURE, DELINQUENCY, AND VIOLENCE

Exposure to family, neighborhood, school, and societal risk factors

Poverty
Abuse and neglect
Harsh and inconsistent parenting
Drug and alcohol use by caregivers
Emotional and physical or sexual abuse
Modeling of aggression
Media violence
Negative attitude toward schooling
Family transitions (death or divorce)
Parent criminality

Leads to development of maladaptive behavioral manifestations

Defiance of adults
Lack of school readiness
Coercive interactive styles
Aggression toward peers
Lack of problem-solving skills

Produces negative short-term outcomes

To negative, destructive long-term outcomes

School failure and dropout
Delinquency
Drug and alcohol use
Gang membership
Violent acts
Adult criminality
Lifelong dependence on welfare system
Higher death and injury rate

Truancy
Peer and teacher rejection
Low academic achievement
High number of school discipline referrals
Large number of different schools attended
Early involvement with drugs and alcohol
Early age of first arrest (under 12 years)

Source: Figure from "The Path to Long Term Negative Outcomes for Children and Youth who are at Risk for School Failure, Delinquency, and Violence" by Jeffrey R. Sprague and Hill M. Walker, from INTERVENTION IN SCHOOL AND CLINIC, November 1999, Volume 35(2). Copyright © 1999 by Sprague and Walker. Reprinted with permission by SAGE publications.

are responsible for his current behavior problems is "an impossible and quite unnecessary task. Disruptive child behavior can be changed very effectively without knowing the specific, original causes for its acquisition and development" (Walker, 1997, p. 20).

IDENTIFICATION AND ASSESSMENT

Assessment of emotional or behavioral disorders, as with all disabilities, should answer four basic questions concerning special education services:

1. Who might need help?
2. Who really does need help (who is eligible)?
3. What kind of help is needed?
4. Is the help benefiting the student?

In practice, however, many school districts do not use any systematic method for identifying children with emotional or behavioral disorders. This is because most children with emotional or behavioral disorders identify themselves. Antisocial children seldom go unnoticed: "To have one in your classroom is to recognize one" (Rhode et al., 1998, p. 3). This does not mean, however, that identification is a sure thing. Identification is always more difficult with younger children because the behavior of all young children changes quickly and often. Also, there is danger that some children with internalizing behaviors go undetected because their problems do not draw the attention of parents and teachers (Lane & Menzies, 2005; Morris, Shah, & Morris, 2002).

Children who display patterns of antisocial behavior when entering school run the risk of developing more serious and long-standing behavior problems as they progress through school and life. Unfortunately, many students with emotional or behavioral disorders experience delay between the onset of the disability and beginning of special education services (Wagner et al., 2005), which only serves to make it more difficult to reverse this all-too-common trajectory of behavior problems early in life, leading to tragic outcomes during adolescence and adulthood. Conroy and Brown (2006) stated that it is "imperative that current policies and practices be changed from a *reactive* to a *proactive* mode by identifying young children who are either chronically exposed to established risk factors or demonstrate problematic behavior patterns at an early age" (p. 225).

Responsiveness to intervention (RTI) holds promise for early identification and intervention of children who exhibit problem behaviors in the classroom (Fairbanks, Sugai, Guardino, & Lathrop, 2007). The CCBD (2008) cautions that interventions under RTI should not be used as a substitute for special education evaluation and referral for a student suspected of having an emotional/behavioral disability and that using suspension and expulsion "in the name of RTI" is not appropriate.

Screening Tests

Screening tools for E/BD

Content Standards for Beginning Teachers of Students with E/BD: Screening, prereferral, referral, and classification procedures (ICC8K3) (also ICC8K4).

Screening is the process of differentiating between children who are not likely to be disabled and those who either show signs of behavioral disturbance or seem to be at risk for developing behavior problems. Children identified through a screening process then undergo more thorough assessment to determine their eligibility for special education and their specific educational needs.

Most screening devices consist of behavior rating scales or checklists that are completed by teachers, parents, peers, and/or children themselves. Teachers' ratings of child behavior tend to be consistent over time, and teachers' ratings of young children's behavior are good predictors of behavior at an older age (Montague et al., 2011). Brief descriptions of three widely used screening tests for emotional or behavioral disorders follow.

CHILD BEHAVIOR CHECKLIST (CBCL) The CBCL is one of several assessment tools included in the Achenbach System of Empirically Based Assessment (ASEBA) (Achenbach & McConaughy, 2003), a widely used and researched collection of checklists and assessment devices (Konold et al., 2004). This school-age version comes in teacher report, parent report, and self-report forms and can be used with children ages 6 through 18. The teacher's report form includes 112 behaviors (e.g., "sudden changes in mood or feelings," "not liked by other pupils") that are rated on a 3-point scale: "not true," "somewhat or sometimes true," or "very true or often true." The CBCL also includes items representing social competencies and adaptive functioning such as getting along with others and acting happy.

BEHAVIORAL AND EMOTIONAL RATING SCALE (BERS) The BERS assesses a student's strengths in 52 items across five areas of functioning: interpersonal strengths (e.g., reacts to disappointment in a calm manner); family involvement (e.g., participates in family activities); intrapersonal strengths (e.g., demonstrates a sense of humor); school functioning (e.g., pays attention in class); and affective strengths (e.g., acknowledges painful feelings of others) (Epstein, 2004). Data from a strength-based assessment such as the BERS may be used to present positive attributes of students in IEP meetings, as an aid in writing IEP goals and objectives, and as an outcome measure to document a student's progress on strength-related IEP goals and objectives (Epstein, Hertzog, & Reid, 2001).

SYSTEMATIC SCREENING FOR BEHAVIORAL DISORDERS (SSBD) The SSBD employs a three-step **multiple gating screening** process for progressively narrowing down the number of children suspected of having serious behavior problems (Walker & Severson, 1992). In Gate I, classroom teachers rank order every student in their classrooms according to behavioral profiles on two dimensions: externalizing problems and internalizing problems. The top three students on each teacher's list progress to Gate II, the Critical Events Index.

Critical events are behaviors of high salience and concern even if their frequency is low. Any occurrence of these target behaviors is an indicator of major disruption of social-behavioral adjustment processes in school. The 33 items that make up the Critical Events Index include externalizing behaviors such as "is physically aggressive with other students" and "makes lewd or obscene gestures" and internalizing behaviors such as "vomits after eating" and "has auditory or visual hallucinations." Students who exceed normative criteria on the Critical Events Index advance to Gate III of the SSBD, which consists of direct and repeated observations during independent seat-work periods in the classroom and on the playground during recess. Children who meet or exceed cutoff criteria for either or both observational measures are referred to child study teams for further evaluation to determine their eligibility for special education.

Direct Observation and Measurement of Behavior

In assessment by direct observation and measurement, the actual behaviors that cause concern about a child are clearly specified and observed in the settings in which they normally occur (e.g., in the classroom, on the playground). Behavior's measurable dimensions include frequency, duration, latency, topography, and magnitude (see Figure 3).

The advantage of assessing and describing emotional or behavioral disorders in terms of these dimensions is that identification, design of intervention strategies, and evaluation of treatment effects can all revolve around direct and objective measurement. This approach leads to a direct focus on the child's problem—the behavior that is adversely affecting his life—and ways of dealing with it such as strengthening a desired alternative behavior as opposed to concentrating on some presumed (and unreachable) problem within the child (Cullinan, 2007). Detailed procedures for various techniques for observing and measuring behavior can be found in Cooper, Heron, and Heward (2007).

Functional Behavioral Assessment

Functional behavioral assessment (FBA) is a systematic process for gathering information to understand why a student may be engaging in challenging behavior. School

Measurable dimensions of behavior

 Content Standards for Beginning Teachers of Students with E/BD: Assess social behaviors of individuals with emotional and/or behavioral disorders (BD8S2) (also ICC8K1).

FIGURE 3 FIVE MEASURABLE DIMENSIONS OF BEHAVIOR

FREQUENCY OR RATE: how often a particular behavior occurs, usually expressed as a count per standard unit of time (e.g., 6 talkouts per minute). All children cry, get into fights with other children, and sulk from time to time; yet we are not apt to think of them as emotionally disturbed. The primary difference between children with behavioral disorders and other children is the frequency with which these behaviors occur. Although disturbed children may not do anything their nondisabled peers do not do, they do certain undesirable things too often (e.g., crying, hitting others) and/or engage in adaptive behaviors too infrequently (e.g., playing with others).

DURATION: how long a child engages in a given activity (e.g., worked on math problems for 12 minutes). The amount of time children with behavioral disorders engage in certain activities is often markedly different—either longer or shorter—from that of other children. For example, most young children have temper tantrums, but the tantrums generally last no more than a few minutes. A child with emotional or behavioral disorders may tantrum for more than an hour at a time. The problem may also be one of too short a duration—for example, a child who cannot stick to an academic task for more than a few seconds at a time.

LATENCY: the time that elapses between the opportunity to respond and the beginning of the behavior. The latency of a child's behavior may be too long (e.g., several minutes elapse before he begins to comply with the teacher's request) or too short (e.g., the child immediately begins screaming and tantruming at the slightest provocation or frustration, thus having no time to consider more appropriate alternative behaviors).

TOPOGRAPHY: the physical shape or form of behavior. Printing your name in block letters and signing your name in cursive have different topographies. Some children with emotional or behavioral disorders emit behaviors that are seldom, if ever, seen in typical children (e.g., setting fires, cruelty to animals). These behaviors may be maladaptive, bizarre, or dangerous to the child or others.

MAGNITUDE: the force or intensity with which behavior is emitted. The magnitude of a child's responses may be too little (e.g., talking in a volume so low that she cannot be heard) or too much (e.g., slamming the door).

Functional behavioral assessment

 Council for Exceptional Children

Content Standards for Beginning Teachers of Students with E/BD: Conduct functional behavior assessments (BD8S1) (also BD8S3, ICC7S4).

psychologists, special educators, and behavior analysts use this information to generate hypotheses about what the behavior's function, or purpose, is for the student. Two common functions of problem behavior are (a) to get something the student wants (positive reinforcement) (e.g., hitting other students produces attention from the teacher) and (b) to avoid or escape something the student doesn't want (negative reinforcement) (e.g., disruptive behavior when the teacher presents academic tasks results in task removal).

Knowledge of a behavior's function can point to the design of an appropriate and effective **behavioral intervention plan (BIP)**, a required IEP component for all students with disabilities whose school performance is adversely affected by behavioral issues (Etscheidt, 2006). For example, knowing that a student's tantruming is maintained by teacher attention suggests a different intervention than one indicated for challenging behavior maintained by escape from academic tasks. Recent research literature contains numerous examples of using FBA to guide the successful intervention for extremely challenging and disruptive behavior (e.g., Heckaman, Conroy, Fox, & Chait, 2000; Lo & Cartledge, 2006; Turton, Umbreit, & Mathur, 2011; Umbreit, Ferro, Liaupsin, & Lane, 2007; Wright-Gallo, Higbee, Reagon, & Davey, 2006). FBA entails one or more of three assessment methods: indirect assessment, direct assessment, and functional analysis (Neef & Peterson, 2007).

INDIRECT FUNCTIONAL BEHAVIOR ASSESSMENT The easiest and quickest form of FBA involves asking teachers, parents, and others who know the child well about the circumstances that typically surround the occurrence and nonoccurrence of the problem behavior and the reactions the behavior usually evokes from others. A number of instruments for conducting indirect FBA via structured interview, questionnaire, or checklist have been published (e.g., the Motivation Assessment Scale [Durand & Crimmins, 1992]; Questions About Behavioral Function [Paclawsky, Matson, Rush, Smalls, & Vollmer, 2000]). One widely used empirically validated tool for indirect FBA, the Functional Assessment Interview, includes a student-assisted form so students can serve as their own informants (O'Neill et al., 1997). The interview questions the informant to identify behavior(s) that cause trouble for the student at school, describe the student's class schedule and its relation to problem behavior, rate the intensity of behaviors across class periods and times of day, describe the situation in which the problem behavior typically occurs (e.g., difficult, boring, or unclear material; peer teasing; teacher reprimands), and describe the events that often follow the behavior and may function to maintain it.

DESCRIPTIVE FUNCTIONAL BEHAVIOR ASSESSMENT Descriptive FBA entails direct observation of the problem behavior under naturally occurring conditions. Using a technique called **ABC recording,** an observer records a temporally sequenced account of each occurrence of the problem behavior(s) in context of the antecedent conditions and events and consequences for those behaviors as those events unfold in the student's natural environment (Cooper et al., 2007). This assessment technique is so named because it obtains information on (**A**) the antecedent events that occasion or trigger problem behavior (e.g., transitions from one classroom or activity to another, task difficulty), (**B**) the nature of the behavior itself (e.g., duration, topography, intensity), and (**C**) the consequences that may function to maintain the behavior (e.g., teacher attention, withdrawal of task demands).

IEP teams often combine the results of indirect and direct FBAs to obtain a picture of function. Figure 4 shows the hypothesized functions of aggression, property destruction, and tantrums by Brian, a 13-year-old student diagnosed with oppositional defiant disorder and attention-deficit/hyperactivity disorder as determined by the results of a Functional Assessment Interview and ABC recording. In some cases, the results of an indirect and/or descriptive FBA lead to an effective treatment plan. Revealing the controlling variables for many chronic problem behaviors, however, requires a functional analysis.

FUNCTIONAL ANALYSIS Functional behavioral assessment might also include a **functional analysis,** the experimental manipulation of several antecedent or consequent events surrounding the target behavior in an attempt to verify the hypothesized functions of the behavior (e.g., systematically varying the difficulty of academic tasks to test if the child's oppositional behavior is triggered by difficult tasks) (Iwata, Dorsey, Slifer, Bauman, & Richman, 1994). The same or similar antecedent conditions and consequences identified through indirect and descriptive FBA are used in a functional analysis, but those variables are manipulated in a controlled or analog setting rather than the natural environment. This allows better control of the variables, and the safety of child and others can be ensured. Functional analysis purposely results in occurrences of the problem behavior; therefore, only highly trained personnel who have attained appropriate consents from parents/guardians and have ensured that adequate safeguards are in place to protect the student and others from any harm should conduct it.

FIGURE 4 HYPOTHESIZED FUNCTIONS OF AGGRESSION, PROPERTY DESTRUCTION, AND TANTRUMS BY A 13-YEAR-OLD STUDENT DIAGNOSED WITH OPPOSITIONAL DEFIANT DISORDER AND ATTENTION-DEFICIT/HYPERACTIVITY DISORDER

Antecedent	Behavior	Consequence	Function
When adult or peer attention is diverted from Brian . . .	he engages in a variety of problem behaviors, which result in . . .	attention from adults and peers.	Gain attention from adults and peers
When Brian's access to preferred toys and activities is restricted . . .	he engages in a variety of problem behaviors, which result in . . .	gaining access to preferred toys and activities.	Gain access to preferred toys and activities
When Brian is required to perform difficult or undesirable tasks . . .	he engages in a variety of problem behaviors, which result in . . .	the tasks being removed.	Escape from difficult and/or nonpreferred tasks

Source: From Neef, N. A., & Peterson, S. M. (2007). Functional behavior assessment. In J. O. Cooper, T. E. Heron, & W. L. Heward, *Applied behavior analysis* (2nd ed., pp. 515). Upper Saddle River, NJ: Pearson Education, Inc. Used by permission.

FIGURE 5	INTERVENTIONS FOR ATTENTION AND ESCAPE FUNCTIONS OF AGGRESSION, PROPERTY DESTRUCTION, AND TANTRUMS BY A 13-YEAR-OLD STUDENT DIAGNOSED WITH OPPOSITIONAL DEFIANT DISORDER AND ATTENTION-DEFICIT/HYPERACTIVITY DISORDER

ATTENTION FUNCTION

Intervention	Antecedent	Behavior	Consequence
Teach a new behavior	When adult or peer attention is diverted from Brian . . .	he will raise his hand and say, "Excuse me . . ."	and adults and peers will provide attention to Brian.
Teach a new behavior	When adult or peer attention is diverted from Brian . . .	he will self-monitor his appropriate independent work and match teacher recordings . . .	and the teachers will provide him with one-on-one time if he meets a specific criterion.
Change the antecedent	During independent work times, adults will provide attention to Brian every 5 minutes . . .	to increase the probability that Brian will appropriately work independently . . .	which will increase adult opportunities to praise and attend to appropriate behavior.
Change the antecedent	Allow Brian to play with peers during leisure times . . .	to increase the probability that Brian will play appropriately . . .	which will increase adult opportunities to praise appropriate behavior and for peers to respond positively.

ESCAPE FUNCTION

Intervention	Antecedent	Behavior	Consequence
Teach a new behavior	When Brian is required to perform a difficult or undesirable task . . .	he will say, "May I take a break now?" . . .	And the teacher will allow Brian to take a break from the task.
Change the reinforcement contingency	When Brian is required to perform difficult or undesirable tasks . . .	and he engages in a variety of problem behaviors . . .	he will be required to continue working on the task and the time out intervention will be discontinued.

Source: From Neef, N. A. & Peterson, S. M. (2007). Functional behavior assessment. In J. O. Cooper, T. E. Heron, & W. L. Heward, *Applied behavior analysis* (2nd ed., p. 517). Upper Saddle River, NJ: Pearson Education, Inc. Used by permission.

A functional analysis with Brian confirmed and clarified the hypothesized functions of his problem behaviors and led to the design of a successful multicomponent intervention shown in Figure 5. Detailed descriptions of how to conduct FBAs can be found in Neef and Peterson (2007) and Umbreit, Ferro, Liaupsin, and Lane (2007).

EDUCATIONAL APPROACHES

Curriculum Goals

What should students with emotional or behavioral disorders be taught? An obvious but only partially correct answer is that students with externalizing problems should learn to control their antisocial behavior and that those with internalizing problems should learn to have fun and make friends. However, if programs serving children with emotional or behavioral disorders treat maladaptive behavior at the expense of academic instruction, students who already possess deficient academic skills fall even further behind their peers. Special education for students with emotional or behavioral disorders must include effective instruction in the personal, social, and academic skills required for success in school, community, and vocational settings.

ACADEMIC SKILLS Systematic instruction in reading, writing, and arithmetic is as important to students with emotional or behavioral disorders as it is to any student who hopes to function successfully in school and society (Hodge, Riccomini, Buford, & Herbst, 2006;

Wehby, Lane, & Falk, 2003). With No Child Left Behind's emphasis on the academic achievement of all students, the academic course schedules of nearly all secondary students with emotional or behavior disorders closely resemble those of students in the general population. Nearly all secondary school youth with emotional or behavior disorders take language arts, math, and social studies in a given semester, and 84% take science (Wagner & Cameto, 2004). Only foreign language is taken at a markedly lower rate by youth with emotional or behavior disorders than by youth in the general population.

Until recently, relatively few studies on academic interventions with students with emotional or behavioral disorders appeared in the peer-reviewed research literature (see Hodge et al., 2006; Pierce, Reid, & Epstein, 2004). The authors of one review found only 55 teacher-mediated academic interventions published over 30 years (Mooney, Epstein, Reid, & Nelson, 2003). However, increasing awareness of the crucial role effective instruction plays in the treatment of children with emotional and behavioral disorders is leading to more research on curriculum and instruction (Lane & Menzies, 2010). Fortunately, this research shows that most students with emotional or behavioral disorders make excellent progress when provided with explicit, systematic instruction (e.g., Benner et al., 2010; Billingsley, Scheuermann, & Webber, 2009; Lingo, Bott Slaton, & Jolivette, 2006; Mooney et al., 2003).

Good instruction is the foundation for effective behavior management in the classroom. Teachers must guard against the tendency to avoid noncompliance and disruptive outbursts by providing students with behavior problems with limited academic instruction in the form of easier tasks, fewer opportunities to respond, and lowered expectations (Sutherland, Alder, & Gunter, 2003; Wehby et al., 1998).

SOCIAL SKILLS Social skills instruction is an important curriculum component for students with emotional or behavioral disorders. Many of these students have difficulty holding a conversation, expressing their feelings, participating in group activities, and responding to failure or criticism in positive and constructive ways. They often get into fights and altercations because they lack the social skills needed to handle or defuse provocative incidents. The slightest snub, bump, or misunderstood request—which would be laughed off or ignored by most children—can precipitate an aggressive attack by some students.

Learning the social and nonacademic skills that match teacher expectations for student behavior is especially important for children with emotional or behavioral disorders (Meier, DiPerna, & Oster, 2006). A survey of 717 teachers across grade levels identified the following five skills as critical to success in general education classrooms (Lane, Wehby, & Cooley, 2006):

- Controls temper in conflict situations with peers
- Controls temper in conflict situations with adults
- Follows/complies with directions
- Attends to teacher's instructions
- Easily makes transitions from one classroom activity to another

Many studies on teaching social skills to students with emotional or behavioral disorders have been published. A review by Gresham, Cook, Crews, and Kern (2004) concluded that social skills training is generally effective and is an essential component of a comprehensive program for students with emotional and behavior disorders. Based on his review of published research on teaching social skills, Maag (2006) recommended that schools make social skills training an integral and ongoing curriculum component for the benefit of all students.

Numerous social skills curricula and training programs have been published, such as the following:

- *Taking Part: Introducing Social Skills to Children* (Cartledge & Kleefeld, 2009) helps students in preschool classrooms through third grade learn social skills in six units: making conversation, communicating feelings, expressing oneself, cooperating with peers, playing with peers, and responding to aggression and conflict.

Social skills instruction and curricula

 Content Standards for Beginning Teachers—Common Core: Social skills needed for educational and other environments (ICC5K5).

- *The Prepare Curriculum: Teaching Prosocial Competencies* (Goldstein, 2000) is designed for students who are aggressive, withdrawn, or otherwise deficient in social competencies. Activities and materials for middle and high school students are provided in 10 areas, such as problem solving, anger control, stress management, and cooperation.
- *The Walker Social Skills Curriculum* includes ACCEPTS: A Curriculum for Children's Effective Peer and Teacher Skills (Walker, McConnell, et al., 1988), for children in grades K–6, and ACCESS: Adolescent Curriculum for Communication and Effective Social Skills (Walker, Todis, Holmes, & Horton, 1988), for students at the middle and high school levels.

Television programs (Bryan & Ryan, 2001) and children's books are sometimes used to provide examples and content for social skills instruction for students with emotional and behavioral disorders (Brame, 2000; Marchant & Womack, 2010). Regardless of the social skills targeted, instruction should include examples and nonexamples modeled, opportunities for role playing, guided practice with feedback, and strategies to promote generalization to the natural environment (Elksnin & Elksnin, 2006; Lane, Menzies, Barton-Arwood, Doukas, & Munton, 2005; McIntosh & MacKay, 2008).

Research-Based Instructional Practices

Contingent teacher praise and positive reinforcement

 Content Standards for Beginning Teachers of Students with E/BD: Principles of reinforcement theory in serving individuals with E/BD (BD1K4) (also BD4S1).

A four-phase review process to identify scientifically supported teaching methods for students with emotional or behavioral disorders revealed these four strategic approaches (Lewis, Hudson, Richter, & Johnson, 2004):

- teacher praise (reinforcement);
- high rates of active response by students;
- clear instructional strategies, including direct instruction; and
- positive behavior support, including schoolwide, functional assessment-based individual plans and self-management.

Functional behavior assessment was explained earlier in this chapter. Schoolwide positive behavioral support and self-management are described in the remainder of this section. Proactive, positive classroom management and the use of peer mediation and support are also described. To read about the importance of contingent teacher praise as an instructional tool, see *Teaching & Learning*, "The Power of Teacher Praise."

SCHOOLWIDE POSITIVE BEHAVIORAL SUPPORT Traditionally, discipline in the schools has focused on the use of punishment in an effort to control the misbehavior of specific students. Not only are such strategies generally ineffective in achieving long-term reductions in problem behavior or increases in overall school safety (Morrison & D'Incau, 2000; Skiba, 2002), but they also do not teach students desired, prosocial behaviors. The development of schoolwide positive behavior support (SWPBS) represents a tremendous advance in achieving student discipline and establishing positive school climate procedures. SWPBS is not a particular method or model but a strategic framework made up of of organizational systems and research-based, scientifically validated intervention

Katelyn Metzger/Merrill

Research has repeatedly shown that the systematic use of praise and attention and other forms of positive reinforcement for desired behaviors is a powerful classroom management and instructional tool.

practices for establishing a positive school culture, and teaching and supporting appropriate behaviors that enable the academic and social behavior success of all students (Sugai et al., 2010). Over 11,000 schools in the United States have implemented SWPBS. A wide range of resources and training materials to help schools implement SWPBS are available at no cost at the OSEP Center on Positive Behavioral Interventions & Supports (http://www.pbis.org/).

SWPBS is conceptualized and implemented from a prevention perspective, with a continuum of instructional interventions and behavioral supports that become more targeted and intensive as indicated by students' needs (Sugai & Horner, 2005). Most implementations entail three tiers of supports, as illustrated in Figure 6.

Tier 1—Primary Prevention: Universal Supports for All Students. All teachers and school staff participate in a team effort to teach appropriate behavior to all students across all school settings within school.

- *Behavioral expectations are stated and defined.* A small number of behavioral expectations are clearly defined. These often are simple, positively framed rules such as "Be respectful of self, others, and surroundings"; "Be responsible"; and "Be safe." Specific examples are provided for behavioral expectations (e.g., "Being respectful in class means raising your hand when you want to speak or get help. During lunch or in the hall, being respectful means using a person's name when you talk to him or her.").
- *Behavioral expectations are explicitly taught.* The behavioral expectations are taught to all students in the building. Behavioral expectations are taught directly with a systematic format: the general rule is presented, the rationale for the rule is discussed, positive examples ("right way") are described and rehearsed, negative examples ("wrong way") are described and modeled, and students practice the "right way" until they demonstrate fluent performance.
- *Appropriate behaviors are acknowledged and rewarded.* Appropriate behaviors are acknowledged and rewarded on a regular basis. Some schools do this through

Schoolwide positive behavior support

Council for Exceptional Children Content Standards for Beginning Teachers of Students with E/BD: Use prevention and intervention strategies for individuals at risk for emotional and/or behavioral disorders (BD4S3) (also ICC5S2, ICC5S3, ICC5S10, ICC5S11).

FIGURE 6

CONTINUUM OF SCHOOLWIDE POSITIVE BEHAVIORAL SUPPORT

Tertiary prevention:
Specialized individualized systems for students with high-risk behavior

~5%

Secondary prevention:
Specialized group systems for students with at-risk behavior

~15%

Primary prevention:
School- /classroom-wide systems for all students, staff, & settings

~80% of Students

Source: Figure adapted from SCHOOL WIDE POSITIVE BEHAVIOR SUPPORT: IMPLEMENTERS' BLUEPRINT AND SELF ASSESSMENT, 2010, by Rob Horner and George Sugai for the OSEP Center on Positive Behavioral Interventions and Support, www.pbis.org. Copyright © 2010 by Horner and Sugai. Reprinted with permission.

The Power of Teacher Praise

Social approval, often conveyed through verbal praise, is a powerful reinforcer for most people. The original experimental demonstrations of the power of adults' social attention as reinforcement for children's behavior took place in a series of four studies designed by Montrose Wolf and carried out by the preschool teachers at the University of Washington's Institute of Child Development in the early 1960s (Allen, Hart, Buell, Harris, & Wolf, 1964; Harris, Johnston, Kelly, & Wolf, 1964; Hart, Allen, Buell, Harris, & Wolf, 1964; Johnston, Kelly, Harris, & Wolf, 1966). Describing those early studies, Risley (2005) wrote:

> We had never seen such power! The speed and magnitude of the effects on children's behavior in the real world of simple adjustments of something so ubiquitous as adult attention was astounding. Forty years later, social reinforcement (positive attention, praise, "catching them being good") has become the core of most American advice and training for parents and teachers—making this arguably the most influential discovery of modern psychology. (p. 280)

Numerous studies since have shown repeatedly the positive effects of contingent praise on the behavior of infants (e.g., Poulson & Kymissis, 1988), preschoolers (e.g., Wolery, 2000), and school-age students with and without disabilities (e.g., Kratochwill & Stoiber, 2000; Sutherland, Wehby, & Copeland, 2000). Yet many educators do not appreciate that the systematic use of contingent praise and attention may be the most powerful motivational and classroom management tool they have (Flora, 2004). Teacher praise and attention are especially important for students with learning and behavior problems.

MISGUIDED ADVICE

Some argue against the use of praise and rewards for student performance (Deci, Koestner, & Ryan, 1999). Alfie Kohn (1993), in particular, has gained considerable attention for claiming that extrinsic motivators such as incentive plans, grades, and verbal praise damage the intrinsic motivation of students to perform and learn. Using faulty interpretations of research of questionable validity, Kohn argues that praise is not only ineffective but actually harmful to children. In an article titled "Five Reasons to Stop Saying 'Good Job!'" Kohn (2001) warned early

childhood teachers that praising and rewarding students for their accomplishments manipulates children, creates praise junkies, steals their pleasure, causes children to lose interest, and reduces achievement. Not only does this stand in stark contrast to the extensive, decades-long research literature showing the positive benefits of such practices (Chance, 1992, 1993), but the "planned use of positive reinforcement is antithetical to [Kohn's pejorative description of the practice as] blurted-out judgments, slathered-on praise, knee-jerk tendencies, and evaluative eruptions" (Strain & Joseph, 2004, p. 58).

Research conducted in classrooms and laboratories does not support Kohn's contention that students are "punished by rewards" (Cameron, 2005). Cameron, Banko, and Pierce (2001) conducted a meta-analysis of 145 experimental studies and concluded that no scientific evidence indicated any detrimental effects of reward on intrinsic motivation.

VERY LOW RATES OF TEACHER PRAISE

Kohn and others concerned that teachers are praising their students too frequently need not worry. In spite of its documented effectiveness in increasing academic performance and desired student behaviors, studies over the past three decades have consistently found very low rates of teacher praise. In a study of 104 teachers in grades 1 through 12, White (1975) found that rates of teacher praise dropped with each grade level; and in every grade after second, the rate at which teachers delivered statements of disapproval to students exceeded the rate of teacher approval. Numerous studies have reported similar low rates of teacher praise in general and special education classrooms (e.g., Deno, Maruyama, Espin, & Cohen, 1990; Harrop & Swinson, 2000; Maggin, Wehby, Moore Partin, Robertson, & Oliver, 2011). Especially discouraging are studies in classrooms for students with emotional or behavioral disorders that found teachers' rates of praise as low as one per hour or less (Van Acker, Grant, & Henry, 1996; Wehby, Symons, & Shores, 1995).

FOUR POSSIBLE REASONS FOR INFREQUENT TEACHER PRAISE

Some teachers worry that students will expect to be praised or rewarded. They believe students should want

formal systems (tickets, rewards); others do it through social events. Schools strive to establish a ratio of four positive adult interactions with students for every one that is negative.

- *Behavioral errors are corrected.* When students violate behavioral expectations, clear procedures are needed for showing them that their behavior was unacceptable and preventing unacceptable behavior from resulting in inadvertent rewards.

to learn for intrinsic reasons. It would be wonderful if all students came to school prepared to work hard and to learn for "intrinsic" reasons. The ultimate intrinsic motivator is success itself (Skinner, 1989)—using new knowledge and skills effectively enough to enjoy control over one's environment, be it solving a new algebra problem or reading a mystery with sufficient fluency and endurance to find out who did it. But it is naive and irresponsible for educators to expect children with few skills and a history of failure to work hard without positive consequences. Contingent teacher praise and other extrinsic motivators such as points toward a grade or slips of paper as entries in a classroom lottery are proven ways of helping students attain the performance levels necessary to meet the naturally existing reinforcement contingencies of success.

Some teachers believe that praising takes too much time away from teaching. Detecting and praising performance improvements, particularly by low-achieving students who have experienced little academic success, are among the most effective and important forms of teaching. It is unfortunate that some educators believe they are not teaching when they are praising student accomplishments.

Some teachers feel it is unnatural to praise. Teachers who think it is unnatural to praise students' good behavior are, in some respects, correct. The natural contingencies of the classroom undermine the use of praise and strengthen reprimanding. Teacher reprimands typically produce an immediate change in student behavior (e.g., the child stops disrupting class), which negatively reinforces reprimanding (Alber & Heward, 2000). By contrast, when a teacher praises a student for behavior, such as working quietly in class, usually no immediate consequence reinforces the teacher's praising behavior (e.g., the student just continues working as before). The pervasiveness of these naturally occurring contingencies is supported by the fact that while few teachers must be taught to identify misbehavior and issue reprimands, many teachers need help learning to catch students being good.

Classrooms are busy places, and many student behaviors worthy of praise and attention go unnoticed. Teachers may not notice many desirable behaviors if students do not call attention to themselves. Teachers are more likely to notice and pay attention to a disruptive student than to a student who is working quietly and productively.

HOW TO GET STARTED

1. **Always be on the lookout for student behavior worthy of praise.** Even the most unskilled and unruly student is correct or obedient sometimes. Don't miss these critical teaching moments.

2. **Arrange opportunities for students to do something well just so you can give approval.** For example, an easy way to provide a low-achieving student with an opportunity to succeed in front of his classmates is to ask a question he is likely to know and then call on him to answer.

3. **Don't worry about sounding wooden and unnatural at first.** Teachers are often concerned their students will think they are not being genuine. Practice four or five praise statements you can say when you observe specific behaviors or performance improvements by your students. Providing specific praise and approval is like any other skill; you'll get better with practice.

4. **Provide prompts for praise.** Prompt yourself to praise desired student behavior by marking reminders in your lesson plan or by playing an audio recording of randomly spaced beeps. Each time you see or hear a prompt, look for a student or group behaving well and praise that behavior. Several smart phone apps that help educators remember to praise good behavior have come on the market, such as R+Remind and iPraiseU (http://www.pecsusa.com/apps.php).

5. **Use self-monitoring to increase your praise rate.** Set a goal to give a certain number of praise statements in a class period. Self-record your praising behavior by marking a card or moving pennies from one pocket to another. Reward yourself with a treat after school for meeting your goal. Start small, and gradually increase your daily goal as your praising skills improve.

6. **Don't worry about overpraising.** Of all the mistakes a teacher might make, providing too much praise and approval for students' good academic and social behaviors is not likely to be one of them.

Additional ideas for increasing the frequency and effectiveness of teacher praise can be found in Fullerton, Conroy, and Correa (2009); Keller and Duffy (2005); Musti-Rao and Haydon (2011); and Stormount and Reinke (2009).

All teachers and school staff participate in teaching and rewarding desired student behavior, consequences for rule violations are clearly defined and consistently applied, and objective data are used to evaluate and continually improve the system. Well-implemented universal supports are usually effective for about 80% of students.

Tier 2—Secondary Prevention: Targeted Interventions for Students with At-Risk Behavior. In a typical school, about 15% of students will require more focused behavioral support due to chronic misbehavior and minor rule violations. Tier 2 supports are often delivered in a small-group format. Check in/check out (CICO) is an example of a tier 2 intervention. The basic components of CICO are (a) a brief meeting at the beginning of the day to set behavioral goals, (b) a point card on which teachers record points based on the student's meeting defined criteria and give the student feedback at different times during the day, (c) a brief meeting at the end of the day to review how the day went, and (d) rewards for earning a predetermined number of points (Crone, Horner, & Hawken, 2004). A number of studies have found that CICO effectively reduced problem behavior in the classroom and the number of office discipline referrals (e.g., Filter et al., 2007; Hawken & Horner, 2003).

Tier 3—Tertiary Prevention: Intensive, Individualized Interventions for Students with High-Risk Behavior. Students who exhibit serious problem behaviors such as major rule violations that put the student or others in danger or who are unresponsive to secondary-level interventions, or about 5% of students in most schools, require intensive, individualized interventions and ongoing behavioral supports, which may also include wraparound supports outside school to address quality-of-life issues. A team conducts a functional behavior assessment (described earlier) and creates an individualized behavior intervention plan (BIP). Dunlap and colleagues (2010) provide numerous tips and research-based strategies for creating and implementing BIPs within a SWPBS system.

SELF-MANAGEMENT Many children with emotional or behavioral disorders believe they have little control over their lives. Things just seem to happen to them, and being disruptive is their means of reacting to an inconsistent and frustrating world. These students can learn responsibility and achieve self-determination through **self-management**—making responses to increase or decrease the future frequency of a target behavior one wishes to change. Self-management is also an important tool for promoting the generalization and maintenance of treatment gains from one setting to another.

Of the many forms of self-management, self-monitoring and self-evaluation are the most widely used and most researched. **Self-monitoring** is a relatively simple procedure in which a person observes his own behavior and records the occurrence or nonoccurrence of a specific target behavior. A person using **self-evaluation** compares his performance against a predetermined standard or goal. With both strategies, a self- or teacher-delivered reward may be contingent upon meeting performance criteria.

Numerous studies have demonstrated that students with various disabilities can use self-monitoring and self-evaluation to regulate social and academic behavior (e.g., Anderson, Fisher, Marchant, Young, & Smith, 2006; Levendoski & Cartledge, 2000; Mooney, Ryan, Uhing, Reid, & Epstein, 2005; Sheffield & Waller, 2010).

"Countoons" are self-management tools that remind young children not only what behavior to record but also what consequences will follow if they meet predetermined performance criteria. Daly and Ranalli (2003) created six-frame countoons that enable students to self-record an inappropriate behavior and an incompatible appropriate behavior. In the countoon shown in Figure 7, Frames 1 and 4 show the student doing her math work, appropriate behavior that is counted in Frame 5. The criterion number of math problems to meet the contingency, in this case 10, is also indicated in Frame 5. Frame 2 shows the student talking with a friend, the inappropriate behavior to be counted in Frame 3. The student must not chat more than six times to meet the contingency. The "What Happens" frame (F6) depicts the reward the student will earn by meeting both parts of the contingency. For a review of principles and strategies for self-management, see Cooper and colleagues (2007). Detailed procedures and materials for teaching self-monitoring and other self-management skills to students

Self-monitoring
and self-evaluation

Content
Standards for
Beginning
Teachers—Common Core:
Use procedures to promote
individual's self-awareness,
self-management, self-
control, self-reliance, and
self-esteem (ICC4S5) (also
ICC4S2, ICC4S4).

FIGURE 7

EXAMPLE OF A COUNTOON THAT CAN BE TAPED TO A STUDENT'S DESK AS A REMINDER OF TARGET BEHAVIORS, THE NEED TO SELF-RECORD, AND THE CONSEQUENCE FOR MEETING THE CONTINGENCY

My Count

1	2	3	4
5	6	7	8
9	10	11	12

F3

Do my math work	Chat with my friend	What I Do	What Happens
		Do my math work	5 minutes of my favorite game on Friday
F1	F2	F4	F6

What I Do

F5

My Count

1	2	3	4	5
6	7	8	9	10
11	12	13	14	15

My Count

Source: From "Using Countoons to Teach Self-Monitoring Skills" by P. M. Daly and P. Ranalli, 2003, *Teaching Exceptional Children, 35*(5), p. 32. Copyright 2003 by the Council for Exceptional Children. Reprinted by permission.

can be found in Joseph and Konrad (2009); Patton, Jolivette, and Ramsey (2006); and Rafferty (2010). "KidTools" and "KidSkills," free software programs that children can use to create self-management tools, can be downloaded at http://kidtools.missouri .edu. Training modules for teachers with video demonstrations and practice materials are also available at this site.

PROACTIVE, POSITIVE CLASSROOM MANAGEMENT Teachers of students with emotional or behavior disorders must design and manage classroom environments that decrease antisocial behavior and increase the frequency of positive teacher–student interactions as a basis for building positive behavior and academic success. This is a very tall order. Fortunately, teachers can turn to a strong base of clearly defined, evidence-based practices for guidance on effective classroom management (e.g., Cipani, 2008; Kerr & Nelson, 2010; Lane, Falk, & Wehby, 2006; Rhode, Jensen, & Morgan, 2003).

Most classroom behavior problems can be prevented by the use of proactive behavior management. *Proactive strategies* are preplanned interventions that anticipate behavior problems and stop them before they occur. "It is much more difficult to

Proactive classroom management

 Council for Exceptional Children

Content Standards for Beginning Teachers—Common Core: Basic classroom management theories and strategies for individuals with exceptional learning needs (ICC5K2) (also BD4S1, BD4S2).

remediate the problems caused by a Tough Kid than to prevent them. Once a teacher has lost the management tempo in a classroom and things are out of control, it is far more difficult to reestablish control" (Rhode et al., 1998, p. 19).

Proactive strategies include the following: structuring the physical environment of the classroom (e.g., have the most difficult students sit nearest the teacher); establishing clear rules and expectations for appropriate behavior (Kostewicz, Kubina, & Ruhl, 2008); planning lessons and managing transitions to minimize downtime; providing students with opportunities make choices (Green, Mays, & Jolivette, 2011); presenting instruction to students in ways that increase the probability of compliance (Lee, Belifore, & Budin, 2008); keeping students actively engaged during instruction (Lambert, Cartledge, Lo, & Heward, 2006); using praise and positive reinforcement to motivate desired behavior (Kennedy & Jolivette, 2008; Witzer & Mercer, 2003); and anticipating and addressing problem behaviors before they occur (Stormont & Reinke, 2009).

In addition to the strategies already mentioned, teachers must know when and how to use a large set of behavior change tactics and tools such as *shaping, contingency contracting, extinction* (ignoring disruptive behavior), *differential reinforcement of alternative or incompatible behavior, response cost* (a loss of reinforcers as a consequence for misbehavior, like a fine), *time-out* (restricting a student's access to reinforcement for a brief time following an inappropriate behavior [Ryan, Saunders, Katsiyannis, & Yell, 2007]), and *overcorrection* (requiring restitution beyond the damaging effects of the antisocial behavior,—e.g., when a child who takes another child's cookie must return it plus one of her own [Cooper et al., 2007]). These techniques should not be implemented as isolated events but incorporated into an overall instructional and classroom management plan that includes the previously mentioned proactive strategies and perhaps a **token economy** or **level system** in which students access greater independence and more privileges as they demonstrate increased behavioral control (Cruz & Cullinan, 2001).

When designing and implementing classroom management strategies, teachers of students with emotional or behavioral disorders must be careful not to create an environment in which coercion is the primary means by which students are motivated to participate and follow rules. In addition to promoting escape and avoidance behavior by those being coerced, coercive environments do not teach what to do as much as they focus on what not to do (Sidman, 1989).

Peer-mediated support and interventions

Content Standards for Beginning Teachers—Common Core: Basic classroom management theories and strategies for individuals with exceptional learning needs (ICC5K2) (also ICC4S2, BD4S3).

PEER MEDIATION AND SUPPORT The power of the peer group can be an effective means of producing positive changes in students with behavioral disorders. Strategies for teaching peers to help one another replace inappropriate behavior with positive alternative behavior include the following:

- *Peer monitoring.* A student is taught to observe and record a peer's behavior and provide the peer with feedback (Anderson et al., 2006; Christensen, Young, & Marchant, 2004).
- *Positive peer reporting.* Students are taught, encouraged, and reinforced for reporting each other's positive behaviors (Nelson, Caldarella, Young, & Webb, 2008).
- *Peer tutoring.* In serving as academic or social skills tutors for one another, students with emotional or behavioral disorders may also learn better social skills (Blake, Wang, Cartledge, & Gardner, 2000; Spencer, 2006).
- *Peer support and confrontation.* Peers are trained to acknowledge one another's positive behaviors, and when inappropriate behavior occurs or is about to occur, peers are trained to explain why the behavior is a problem and to suggest or model an appropriate alternative response (Bullock & Foegen, 2002; Nelson, Martella, & Marchand-Martella, 2002).

Implementing a peer support, or group process, model is much more complicated than bringing together a group of children and hoping they will benefit from positive peer influence. Most children with serious emotional or behavioral disorders have not been members of successfully functioning peer groups in which appropriate behavior is modeled and valued, nor have many such children learned to accept responsibility for their actions (Rockwell & Guetzloe, 1996). The teacher's first and most formidable challenge is helping promote group cohesiveness.

Although group process treatment programs take many forms, most incorporate group meetings and group-oriented contingencies. Two types of group meetings are usually held daily. A planning meeting is held each morning in which the group reviews the daily schedule, each group member states a behavioral goal for the day, peers provide support and suggestions to one another for reaching their goals, and a group goal for the day is agreed on. An evaluation meeting is held at the end of each day to discuss how well the individual and group goals were met, and each group member must give and receive positive peer comments. Problem-solving meetings are held whenever any group member, including the teacher, feels the need to discuss a problem.

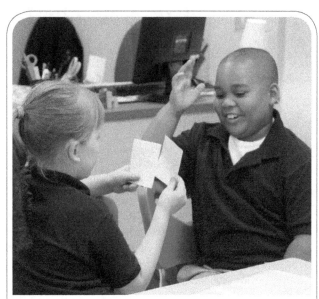

Peer tutoring can be an excellent way for children to learn valuable social skills.

Katelyn Metzger/Merrill

Group contingencies specify certain rewards and privileges that are enjoyed by the group if their behavior meets certain criteria (Heering & Wilder, 2006; Lannie & McCurdy, 2007). Popkin and Skinner (2003) conducted an interesting application of a group contingency with students with emotional or behavioral disorders. The researchers wrote *spelling* and a performance criterion on each of a set of 30 index cards (e.g., five cards with 75%, eight cards with 80%, and five cards with 95%). At the end of the school day, the teacher randomly selected one of the cards. If the students' average performance as a class exceeded the criterion shown on the card, the entire group received a reward. The students who had been doing well in spelling improved (e.g., B students became A students), and the students who had done poorly showed large increases in their performance (e.g., failing students earned As and Bs). After several weeks, similar sets of cards with *mathematics* and *grammar* were added to the deck. Students contributed ideas for the rewards. The students helped determine the rewards and the criteria for earning them. See *Teaching & Learning*, "Mystery Motivators Can Improve Students' Social and Academic Behavior."

Fostering Strong Teacher–Student Relationships

In addition to academic and behavior management skills, the teacher of children with emotional or behavioral disorders must establish healthy and positive child–teacher relationships. William Morse (1985), one of the pioneers in the education of children with emotional or behavioral disorders, identified two important affective characteristics necessary for teachers to relate effectively and positively to students with behavior problems. Morse called these traits differential acceptance and empathetic relationship.

Differential acceptance means the teacher can receive and witness frequent and often extreme acts of anger, hate, and aggression from children without responding similarly. This is much easier said than done. But the teacher of students with emotional or behavioral disorders must view disruptive behavior for what it is—behavior that reflects the student's past frustrations and conflicts with himself and those around him—and try to help the child learn better ways of behaving. Acceptance should not be confused with approving or condoning antisocial behavior; the child must learn that he is responding inappropriately. Instead, this concept calls for understanding without condemning.

Having an *empathetic relationship* with a child refers to a teacher's ability to recognize and understand the many nonverbal cues that often are the keys to

Differential acceptance and empathetic relationship

 Council for Exceptional Children

Content Standards for Beginning Teachers—Common Core: Establish and maintain rapport with individuals with and without exceptional learning needs (ICC5S7) (also ICC5K4).

Mystery Motivators Can Improve Students' Social and Academic Behavior

BY NATALIE ALLEN WILLIAMS

There are three important things to remember about education. The first one is motivation, the second is motivation, and the third is motivation. (Terrell Bell, former U.S. secretary of education)

The ability to motivate students is important for all teachers; for teachers who work with children with emotional or behavioral disorders it is essential. Mystery Motivators are a fun and effective way to motivate students to learn difficult curriculum content and achieve new levels of performance.

WHAT ARE MYSTERY MOTIVATORS?

Mystery Motivators are special rewards for appropriate student behavior presented in a gamelike format. Students know that when they meet the performance criteria for specific academic or social behaviors they will have an opportunity to receive a Mystery Motivator, but they do not know what the Mystery Motivator is or when the game will make it available. The suspense surrounding the identity and availability of the Mystery Motivator builds students' anticipation and incentive to perform well (Rhode et al., 1998). Mystery Motivator incentive systems take a wide variety of forms and can be used with individual students, small groups or teams within a class, or the whole class to improve academic and social behaviors.

DO THEY WORK?

Teachers have conducted Mystery Motivator incentive systems with students from preschool to secondary classrooms. Teachers have used Mystery Motivators to decrease a wide range of disruptive behaviors (e.g., De Martini-Scully, Bray, & Kehle, 2000; Kehle, Bray, Theodore, Jenson, & Clark, 2000; Murphy, Theodore, Aloiso, Alric-Edwards, & Hughes, 2006), to improve in-school academic performance (Skinner, Williams, & Neddenriep, 2004), and to increase the completion and accuracy of homework (Madaus, Kehle, Madaus, & Bray, 2003). Parents also have used Mystery Motivators to reduce disruptive behavior and noncompliance at bedtime (Mottram & Berger-Gross, 2004; Robinson & Sheridan, 2000). Mystery Motivators are sometimes so effective that "remarkable reductions of disruptive behavior" occur (Murphy et al., 2006, p. 53).

HOW TO GET STARTED

1. **Define target behaviors and performance criteria.** Identify the academic and/or social behaviors you want to motivate students to change (e.g., arriving on time to class, completing homework, participating in class discussions, following class rules, exhibiting positive behaviors on the playground or in the cafeteria), and define them in observable and measurable terms. Specify the performance levels students must achieve to be eligible for the Mystery Motivator (e.g., all students in class complete assigned academic work during the school day and have no rule infractions). Do not make the initial performance criteria too high.

2. **Create a pool of rewards.** Observe what students do in their free time, listen to the things they talk about, and ask the students to suggest rewards that they would like to work for. Have the students check or rank their preferences from a list of activities, privileges, and tangible items (e.g., no homework pass, pencils, trading cards, computer time, 10 minutes' free time, bubble gum party). Rhode and colleagues (1998) provide many ideas and examples of possible rewards that can serve as Mystery Motivators.

3. **Select the Mystery Motivator rewards.** Unknown to the students, write the names of the most preferred rewards on index cards. Create a few additional Mystery Motivators that will be complete surprises to the students—include some fun and silly things, such as the teacher will sing a song chosen by the students, do 25 sit-ups, or wear a wig and funny glasses while teaching a lesson!

4. **Print a big "?" on the outside of an envelope, and seal one of the Mystery Motivator cards inside.** Display the envelope in a conspicuous place in your classroom, for example, taped to the middle of the chalkboard or hung from the ceiling by a string. When students see the envelope, their interest and anticipation for what's inside will build.

5. **Create a device and procedure by which students will reveal the availability of Mystery Motivator.** Spinners and charts with "invisible ink" markers are two effective and motivating ways for students to find out if they will receive a Mystery Motivator.

   • **Spinners.** Students who meet the criteria for the target behavior gain access to a spinner and a corresponding reward menu (see photo). Each item on the reward menu has a corresponding numbered section on the spinner based on its relative value to the students. Landing on the larger-sized sections of the spinner gains access

TEACHING & LEARNING

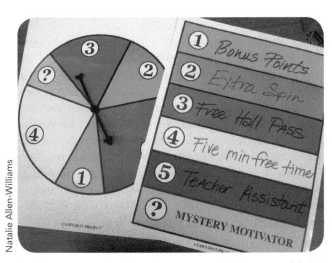

Natalie Allen-Williams

Students enjoy using the spinner to reveal what reward they or the class will receive.

to the less valuable rewards on the menu. When the spinner lands on the smallest slice, which is marked with the "?", the student immediately receives the Mystery Motivator. (Instead of using a spinner, students can roll dice to determine which reward on the menu they will receive.)

- **Chart and invisible markers.** The method uses a special set of colorful markers that contains a pen that writes in invisible ink and several colorful "developer pens" in different colors that "magically" reveal the invisible writing when rubbed over it. (Crayola® Changeables is a widely available brand of these markers.) Create a simple chart of squares labeled with the days of the week and a bonus square. Using the "ghost writer" pen, mark a "?" in several randomly selected squares. Each day the student meets the performance criteria, he is allowed to select one of the developer

Get Wild for a Mystery Motivator

If coloring in a square with the "magic" pen reveals a "?" the student or group receives the Mystery Motivator.

pens and color in that day's square on the chart. If a "?" appears, the student receives the Mystery Motivators. Students who meet the performance criteria each day of the week could be allowed to color in a "bonus square" for a chance at another Mystery Motivator as shown here or they could gain access to a spinner and reward menu.

6. **Introduce the program to students.** Point to the envelope and say, "You're probably wondering what this envelope with the big question mark is all about." Then explain that the students can earn rewards for good behavior including the possibility of the Mystery Motivator. Demonstrate how the spinner or chart works. Describe and model examples and nonexamples of the target behavior and performance criteria. It may be helpful to have students role-play the target behaviors.

   Teacher hype is a key to the success of the program (Rhode et al., 1998). Refer to the Mystery Motivator often ("It's squiggly and really cool!") but keep its identity a secret. Tell students the Mystery Motivator is something they really want, something you have heard them talking about, something they have told you they would be willing to work for, and so on.

7. **Evaluate the program, and use the data to revise and improve it.** While Mystery Motivator incentive systems are fun for students and teachers alike, they have a serious purpose and should be evaluated in terms of their effects on student behavior and learning. As you would when implementing any new curriculum or instructional method, take data on the students' performance of the target behaviors during the Mystery Motivator program, and compare it to their performance levels before the program. Ask students for their opinions and perceptions of the program. Do they like it? Would they like to see changes in the program? Use all of this information to continually evaluate and make improvements in the program's effectiveness.

About the Author

Natalie Allen Williams is a faculty member in the teacher education department at Weber State University and a former teacher of students with emotional and behavioral disorders. Her research interests include proactive classroom management, functional behavior assessment, and reading strategies for students with EBD. Dr. Allen Williams appears on the video "Including Students with EBD in General Education" in the Book Resources for this text on MyEducationLab.

MyEducationLab™

To see how the Mystery Motivators technique is applied in the classroom, go to the Book Resources for this text on **MyEducationLab**.

TEACHING & LEARNING

understanding the individual needs of children with emotional or behavioral disorders. Teachers should communicate directly and honestly with behaviorally troubled children. Many of these children have already had experience with supposedly helpful adults who have not been honest with them. Children with emotional or behavioral disorders can quickly detect someone who is not genuinely interested in their welfare.

The teacher of children with emotional or behavioral disorders must also realize that his actions serve as a powerful model. Therefore, it is critical that the teacher's actions and attitudes be mature and demonstrate self-control. At the same time, teachers who take themselves too seriously risk overreacting to emotionally charged situations with students and risk burnout (Abrams, 2005). Richardson and Shupe (2003) suggest that teachers use an appropriate sense of humor to build relationships with students, defuse conflict, engage learners, and help manage their own stress levels.

Focus on Alterable Variables

Alterable variables

Content Standards for Beginning Teachers—Common Core: Effective management of teaching and learning (ICC5K3).

The twofold task of the teacher of children with emotional or behavioral disorders is helping students (a) replace antisocial and maladaptive behaviors with more socially appropriate behaviors and (b) acquire academic knowledge and skills. The frequent displays of antisocial behavior, the absence of appropriate social skills, and the academic deficits exhibited by many students with emotional or behavioral disorders make this a staggering challenge. The challenge is all the more difficult because the teacher can never control (or even know) all of the factors affecting a student's behavior. Typically, a host of contributing factors exists over which the teacher can exert little or no influence (e.g., the delinquent friends with whom the student associates before and after school). But it does little good to bemoan the student's past (which no one can alter) or to use all of the negative factors in the student's current life that cannot be changed as an excuse for failing to help the student in the classroom.

Special educators should focus their attention and efforts on those aspects of a student's life that they can effectively control. Bloom (1980) used the term *alterable variables* to refer to things that both make a difference in student learning and can be affected by teaching practices. Alterable variables include key dimensions of curriculum and instruction such as the amount of time allocated for instruction; the sequence of activities within the overall lesson; the pacing of instruction; the frequency with which students actively respond during instruction; how and when students receive praise or other forms of reinforcement for their efforts; and the manner in which errors are corrected. The teachers who focus on the identification and systematic management of alterable variables are those most likely to make a difference in the lives of children with emotional or behavioral disorders.

EDUCATIONAL PLACEMENT ALTERNATIVES

Placement alternatives

Content Standards for Beginning Teachers of Students with E/BD: Advantages and disadvantages of placement options for individuals with E/BD (BD5K1).

Students with emotional or behavioral disorders are served across the continuum of educational placements. During the 2008–2009 school year, approximately 39% of school-age children with emotional or behavioral disorders were educated in general education classrooms, 19% in resource rooms, 23% in separate classrooms, 13% in special schools, 2% in correctional facilities, 2% in residential schools, and 1% in home or hospital placements (U.S. Department of Education, 2010). Although the trend in recent years has been for increased placement of students with emotional and behavior disorders in general education classrooms, about 40% of all students in this disability category receive their education in separate classrooms, special schools, and residential facilities.

The relatively high proportion of students with emotional or behavioral disorders who are served in more restrictive settings compared to students in most other disability categories probably reflects the fact that only students with the most severe behavioral problems are identified and served. As a result, most students receiving special education because of emotional or behavioral disorders have serious, long-standing problems that require intensive interventions in highly structured environments (Landrum et al., 2004). Consistent implementation of the specialized supports and programming needed by these students can be very difficult in the regular classroom (Kauffman, Bantz, & McCullough, 2002; Maggin et al., 2011).

A major challenge of educating students with emotional or behavioral disorders is arranging an environment in which academic and social skills can be learned at acceptable rates and the safety of all students is protected. Supporters of full inclusion believe that the general education classroom can be made into such an environment for all students with disabilities. Some positive outcomes have been reported for students with emotional or behavioral disorders in general education classrooms. For example, a study comparing middle

A major challenge of educating students with emotional or behavioral disorders is arranging an environment in which academic and social skills can be learned at acceptable rates.

© Benis Arapovic/Shutterstock

school students who spent the entire school day in separate classrooms with students who participated in various classes in general education classrooms for at least 1 hour per day found that the students who spent part of the day in regular classrooms had better academic records and better work habits than did the students who spent the entire day in special classes (Meadows, Neel, Scott, & Parker, 1994). Although these results seem to support the contention that students with emotional or behavioral disorders should be educated in general education classrooms, the authors point out that the students included in the general education classrooms did not exhibit the extreme aggression, lack of self-control, or degree of withdrawal that the students who stayed in the separate classrooms did. They also noted that placement in general education classrooms typically represents "a major reduction, . . . if not a complete cessation, of differential programming" (p. 178). That is, the general education teachers did not make instructional or management accommodations to meet the needs of the students with behavior problems. Without specialized instruction or accommodations, it is hard to imagine how students with severe emotional or behavioral disorders would receive an appropriate education in the general education classroom.

While supporting the education of students with emotional or behavioral disorders in the general education classroom when their individual needs can be met, the CCBD does not believe that the general education classroom is the most appropriate placement for all students with emotional and behavioral disorders.

> CCBD supports a full continuum of mental health and special education services for children and youth with emotional or behavioral disorders. We believe that educational decisions depend on individual student needs. Consequently, . . . CCBD does not support the notion that all . . . students with emotional or behavioral disorders are always best served in general education classrooms. (CCBD, 1993, p. 1)

Meticulous planning, coordination, and support needed are often unavailable to make inclusion effective. When an IEP team makes the decision to place a student with emotional or behavioral disorders in a general education classroom or to transition a student from a more restrictive setting to the general education classroom, it is imperative that the student and the general education teacher be prepared before and supported after the placement. Preparation includes identifying the social and academic expectations in the general education classroom, assessing the student's current social and academic skills against those expectations, teaching the student additional skills needed to meet those expectations, and in-service training for the teacher on special techniques of behavior management (Meier, DiPerna, & Oster, 2006; Nelson, 2000). Support following the general class placement should include a crisis intervention support plan and ongoing consultation and in-class modeling and intervention by a special educator trained to work with students with behavioral disorders (Shapiro, Miller, Swaka, Gardill, & Handler, 1999; Simpson, 2004; Walker et al., 2005).

CHALLENGES, ACHIEVEMENTS, AND ADVOCACY

Special education for students with emotional or behavioral disorders faces a number of critical and ongoing issues. A continuing concern of many advocates for children with emotional or behavioral disorders is revising the federal definition of this disability so that all children with emotional and behavioral problems that adversely affect their educational performance are eligible to receive the special education and related services they need. Although IDEA mandates that all children with disabilities receive an individualized program of special education and related services, in practice, determination of whether a child is disabled under the category of emotional disturbance is often more a function of a school district's available resources to provide needed services than a function of the child's actual needs for such services.

Despite public concern over school safety and youth violence and widespread recognition that antisocial behavior is a chronic disabling condition that exacts tremendous social and financial costs for society, we do little to prevent it. Instead of intervening early when problems are small and more likely to respond to intervention, we wait until children are older and their antisocial behavior is well established and much more difficult to change (Kauffman, 2010). The knowledge and tools for early detection and prevention are available (e.g., Strain & Timm, 2001; Walker et al., 2009). What is needed is the national resolve and commitment of resources sufficient for a large-scale program of early detection and prevention.

The issues presented here are not new. Most have been recognized, discussed, and debated for decades. And each will likely remain problems well into the future. Many other issues and problems could be added to the list (Gage et al., 2010; Katsiyannis & Yell, 2004). Although the challenges faced by those who work with and advocate for students with emotional or behavioral disorders appear daunting and unrelenting, the field has experienced significant advances and successes to help guide the future.

The field has identified specific program components and instructional practices that, when used in combination, are likely to result in successful outcomes for students with emotional or behavioral disorders (Dunlap et al., 2006; Lewis et al., 2004). Many of those achievements and best practices have been described in this chapter. We must now work diligently to close the gap between what is known about effective special education for students with emotional or behavioral disorders and what those students experience each day in the classroom.

▼ TIPS FOR BEGINNING TEACHERS

Working with Students with Emotional and Behavioral Disorders

BY KIMBERLY RICH

BE CONSISTENT

Students learn to trust you as you are consistent with them.

- **Set up class procedures and expectations clearly right from the beginning.** Have students repeat these at the beginning of each day, reminding them what you expect from them.

- If students earn a privilege, make sure they get it.
- If students lose a privilege, make sure they lose it.

We are never as consistent as we think we are. Use some sort of device to prompt you to positively reinforce students, such as: A MotivAider®, a get device you wear like a pager that vibrates to prompt you; get 'Em On Task, a computer program you can use to prompt you; beep tapes, still a means of prompting you to reinforce students.

PURCHASE A DIGITAL TIMER

Using a digital timer throughout the day requires you to be honest about "time," especially as it relates to monitoring task completion and transitions. A timer frees you from having to guess how much time has passed since you directed students to begin or change tasks.

- **Use it to measure academic progress such as repeated readings or math timings.**
- **Use it to implement behavior expectations.** Give students a specific time frame to complete a task or assignment.
- **Use it to decrease transition time.** For example, give students 1 minute to clean off their desks.

KEEP AND USE YOUR SENSE OF HUMOR

It is very difficult to work with students who have many academic and behavior needs.

- **Laugh at yourself from time to time.** Your students need to see you enjoying yourself.
- **Create a Sunshine folder.** Collect great thoughts or things students have given to you that put a smile on your face. When you've had a rough day, pull the folder out.

STAY IN CONTROL

When in control in stressful situations, you are providing a positive role model for your students.

- **Never take personally anything students do or say when they are escalated.** Know they are lashing out at you because you are there.
- **When you make a mistake with a student, and you will, apologize.** For example, yesterday, another staff member gave James permission to go to the bathroom. I stopped James as he was walking out of the door and told him he was not allowed to leave the classroom without permission. Then my staff member told me James had asked for and received permission from her. I immediately apologized to James for stopping him and then praised him for asking permission the correct way.

EACH DAY SPEND TIME WITH YOUR STUDENTS IN A NONACADEMIC SITUATION

Spending time with your students in nonacademic settings and situations will strengthen your relationship with them.

- **Join your students on the playground.** You will learn many things about your students from the way they interact with others and their conversations. You will also be much more approachable to your students.
- **Eat lunch with your students.** The conversations that you will have will teach you about their likes and dislikes, how their night before went, what their morning was like, and what things they hope for themselves.

▼ KEY TERMS AND CONCEPTS

ABC recording
behavior intervention plan (BIP)
duration (of behavior)
emotional disturbance
emotional or behavioral disorder
externalizing behaviors
frequency (or rate) (of behavior)
functional analysis
functional behavior assessment
group contingencies
internalizing behaviors

latency (of behavior)
level system
magnitude (of behavior)
multiple gating screening
self-evaluation
self-management
self-monitoring
temperament
token economy
topography (of behavior)

▼ SUMMARY

Definitions

- No single, widely used definition of emotional and behavioral disorders exists. Most definitions require a child's behavior to differ markedly (extremely) and chronically (over time) from current social or cultural norms.

- Many leaders in the field do not like the definition of "emotional disturbance" in IDEA because students who are "socially maladjusted" are not eligible for special education services.
- The CCBD proposed a definition of emotional or behavioral disorders as a disability characterized by "behavioral

or emotional responses in school programs so different from appropriate age, cultural, or ethnic norms that they adversely affect educational performance."

Characteristics

- Children with externalizing problems exhibit antisocial and aggressive behavior.
- Children with internalizing problems are withdrawn and lack social skills needed to interact effectively with others.
- As a group, students with emotional or behavioral disorders perform academically 1 or more years below grade level.
- A large number of students with emotional or behavioral disorders also have learning disabilities and/or language delays.
- Students with emotional or behavioral disorders generally score slightly below average on IQ tests.
- Many students with emotional or behavioral disorders have difficulty developing and maintaining interpersonal relationships.
- About one-third of students with emotional or behavioral disorders are arrested during their school years.

Prevalence

- Estimates of the prevalence of behavioral disorders vary tremendously. Credible studies indicate that 3% to 6% have emotional and behavioral problems that warrant special education.
- Far fewer children with emotional or behavioral disorders are receiving special education than the most conservative prevalence estimates.

Causes

- Biological factors related to development of behavioral disorders include brain disorders, genetics, and temperament.
- Environmental etiologic factors occur in the home, school, and community.
- Although knowledge of causes is necessary for planning and implementing prevention programs, effective intervention and treatment of children's existing behavior problems do not require precise knowledge of etiology.

Identification and Assessment

- Systematic screening should be conducted as early as possible to identify children who are at risk for developing serious patterns of antisocial behavior.
- Most screening instruments consist of behavior rating scales or checklists that are completed by teachers, parents, peers, and/or children themselves.
- Direct observation and measurement of specific problem behaviors within the classroom can indicate whether and for which behaviors intervention is needed. Five measurable dimensions of behavior are rate, duration, latency, topography, and magnitude.

- Functional behavioral assessment (FBA) is a systematic process for gathering information to discover a problem behavior's function, or purpose, for the student. Two major types of behavioral functions of problem behaviors are (a) to get something the student wants (positive reinforcement) and (b) to avoid or escape something the student doesn't want (negative reinforcement).
- Results of FBA can point to the design of an appropriate and effective behavior intervention plan (BIP).

Educational Approaches

- Students with emotional or behavioral disorders require systematic instruction in social skills and academics.
- Schoolwide positive behavior support is a preventive based framework for establishing a positive school culture and promoting the academic and social behavior success of all students. SWPBS entails universal supports for all students, targeted interventions for students with at-risk behavior, and intensive, individualized interventions for students with high-risk behavior.
- A good classroom management system uses proactive strategies to create a positive, supportive, and noncoercive environment that promotes prosocial behavior and academic achievement.
- Self-management skills can help students develop control over their environment, responsibility for their actions, and self-direction.
- Group process approaches use the influence of the peer group to help students with emotional or behavioral disorders learn to behave appropriately.
- Two important affective traits for teachers of students with emotional or behavioral disorders are differential acceptance and empathetic relationship.
- Teachers should concentrate their resources and energies on alterable variables—those things in a student's environment that the teacher can influence that make a difference in student learning and behavior.

Educational Placement Alternatives

- Although the trend in recent years has been for increased placement of students with emotional and behavior disorders in general education classrooms, 40% of all students in this disability category receive their education in separate classrooms, special schools, and residential facilities.
- Comparing the behavioral and academic progress of students with emotional or behavioral disorders in different educational placements is difficult because students with milder disabilities are included first and more often, whereas those students who exhibit more severe behavioral disturbances tend to remain in more restrictive placements.
- When a student with emotional or behavioral disorders is placed in a general education classroom, it is imperative that the student and the general education teacher be prepared before and supported after the placement.

Challenges, Achievements, and Advocacy

- Two of the most pressing challenges for the field of emotional or behavioral disorders are (a) ensuring that all students with emotional or behavioral problems that adversely affect their educational performance receive special education services, and (b) developing large-scale programs of early detection and prevention.

MyEducationLab™

Go to Topic 11, Emotional/Behavioral Disorders, in the **MyEducationLab** (www.myeducationlab.com) for *Exceptional Children*, where you can:

- Find learning outcomes for emotional/ behavioral disorders along with the national standards that connect to these outcomes.
- Complete Assignments and Activities that can help you more deeply understand the chapter content.
- Apply and practice your understanding of the core teaching skills identified in the chapter with the Building Teaching Skills and Dispositions learning units.
- Examine challenging situations and cases presented in the IRIS Center Resources.
- Access video clips of CCSSO National Teachers of the Year award winners responding to the question "Why do I teach?" in the Teacher Talk section.
- Check your comprehension of the content covered in the chapter with the Study Plan. Here you will be able to take a chapter quiz, receive feedback on your answers, and then access Review, Practice, and Enrichment activities to enhance your understanding of chapter content.
- Use the Online Lesson Plan Builder to practice lesson planning and integrating national and state standards into your planning.

▼ GLOSSARY

ABC recording: A form of direct observation often used as a part of functional behavior assessment. The observer records a descriptive, temporally sequenced account of all behaviors of interest and the antecedent conditions and consequences for those behaviors as those events occur in the client's natural environment.

behavioral intervention plan (BIP): A statement of specific strategies and procedures to prevent the occurrence of a child's problem behavior and intervene when necessary; based upon results of a *functional behavior assessment*. Required in the individualized education program (IEP) for all students with disabilities whose school performance is adversely affected by behavioral issues.

duration (of behavior): The measure of how long a person engages in a given activity.

emotional disturbance: A disability defined in the Individuals with Disabilities Education Act (IDEA) as a condition exhibiting one or more of the following characteristics over a long period of time and to a marked degree that adversely affects educational performance: inability to build or maintain satisfactory interpersonal relationships; inappropriate types of behavior or feelings under normal circumstances; a general pervasive mood of unhappiness or depression; or a tendency to develop physical symptoms or fears associated with personal or school problems. Many professionals prefer the term *emotional or behavioral disorders*.

emotional or behavioral disorders: Defined by the Council for Children with Behavioral Disorders as a disability characterized by emotional or behavioral responses in school programs so different from appropriate age, cultural, or ethnic norms that the responses adversely affect educational performance; more than a temporary, expected response to stressful events in the environment; consistently exhibited in two different settings, at least one of which is school related; and unresponsive to direct intervention in general education, or the condition of the child is such that general education interventions would be insufficient. Contrast with the Individuals with Disabilities Education Act (IDEA) definition of *emotional disturbance*.

externalizing behaviors: Antisocial, disruptive behaviors (e.g., aggression, noncompliance, property destruction) characteristic of many children with emotional or behavioral disorders.

frequency (or rate of behavior): A measure of how often a particular response is emitted; usually reported as the number of responses per standard unit of time (e.g., 5 per minute).

functional analysis: Experimental manipulation of antecedent or consequent events representing those observed in the child's natural environment to verify their function in either triggering or maintaining problem behavior.

functional behavior assessment (FBA): A systematic process of gathering information about the purposes (functions) a problem behavior serves for an individual; that information then guides the design of interventions. Three basic types of FBA are indirect assessment (structured interviews with significant others), direct descriptive assessment (systematic observations), and functional analysis (see *functional analysis*).

group contingencies: A type of behavior management and motivation procedure in which consequences (rewards and/or penalties) are applied to the entire group or class of students contingent upon the behavior of selected students or the entire group.

internalizing behaviors: Immature and withdrawn behaviors (e.g., social withdrawal, irrational fears, depression) characteristic of some children with emotional or behavioral disorders.

latency: The time that elapses between the opportunity to respond and the beginning of the response.

level system: A behavior management system in which students access greater independence and more privileges as they demonstrate increased behavioral control; see also *token economy*.

magnitude (of behavior): The force with which a response is emitted.

multiple-gating screening: A multistep process for screening children who may have disabilities. The initial step casts the broadest net (e.g., a multiple-gated screening for children who may have emotional or behavior problems might begin with teacher nominations); children identified in the first step are assessed more closely in a second step (e.g., a behavior checklist); children who have passed through the first two "gates" are screened further (e.g., direct observations in the classroom).

self-evaluation: A procedure in which a person compares his performance of a target behavior with a predetermined goal or standard; often a component of self-management. Sometimes called *self-assessment*.

self-management: The personal application of behavior change tactics that produces a desired change in behavior. This is an intentionally broad, functional definition in that the desired change in the target behavior must occur for self-management to be demonstrated (see Cooper, Heron, & Heward, 2007, p. 578).

self-monitoring: A procedure whereby a person systematically observes his behavior and records the occurrence or nonoccurrence of a target behavior. (Also called *self-recording* or *self-observation*.)

temperament: A person's behavioral style or typical way of responding to situations.

token economy (token reinforcement system): An instructional and behavior-management system in which students earn tokens (e.g., stars, points, poker chips) for performing specified behaviors. Students accumulate their tokens and exchange them at prearranged times for their choice of activities or items from a menu of backup rewards (e.g., stickers, hall monitor for a day).

topography (of behavior): The physical shape or form of a response.

Autism Spectrum Disorders

Autism Spectrum Disorders

Lori Whitley/Merrill

▶ FOCUS QUESTIONS

- What are the defining features—the clinical symptoms—for a diagnosis of autism spectrum disorder?

- How might some of the characteristic behaviors of autism spectrum disorders become assets for the child as a learner?

- What factors might account for the enormous increase in the prevalence of autism spectrum disorders in recent years?

- How have etiologic theories and the search for causes of autism changed from the first reports of the disability to today?

- Why are research and development of tools for early screening and diagnosis of autism spectrum disorder so critical?

- What skills are most important for teachers of children with autism spectrum disorders?

- What features of an educational environment (a general education classroom, resource room, or special class) will enable a child with autism spectrum disorder to benefit optimally from placement in that setting?

- Why are fads and unproven interventions so prevalent in the education and treatment of children with autism?

▼FEATURED TEACHERS

KAZUKO YAMAMOTO AND BETH MUENINGHOFF

Winterset Elementary School • Columbus, Ohio

EDUCATION—TEACHING CREDENTIALS— EXPERIENCE

Kazuko Yamamoto:

- B.S. and M.A., special education, The Ohio State University, 1995 and 1998

- Ohio certificates in Education of Developmentally Handicapped (K–12), Multiply Handicapped (K–12), and Early Education of the Handicapped

- 9 years as a primary-grade resource room teacher for students with high-incidence disabilities and 8 years teaching in a special needs preschool

Beth Mueninghoff:

- B.A., psychology, Western Kentucky University, 1988

- Special education certification program in multiple/severe disabilities, Ohio Dominican University, 2000

- Ohio certificates in Education of Developmentally Handicapped (K–12) and Multiply Handicapped (K–12)

- 11 years as special education teacher; 13 years teaching self-help skills to adults with disabilities in residential settings

Kazuko Yamamoto

OUR SCHOOL, CLASSROOMS, AND STUDENTS Winterset Elementary is an urban public school with an enrollment of about 280 culturally and socioeconomically diverse children in grades K–5.

Kazuko: My special needs preschool classroom is a full-day unit for 5-year-

Beth Mueninghoff

olds with multiple disabilities. This year, each of my five students has a diagnosis of autism spectrum disorder. Two of the students are from families whose primary language is not English. All of my students this year show delays in cognition, communication, social emotional, adaptive behavior and motor development, and qualify for speech, occupational and physical therapy. The students' communication skills vary tremendously, ranging from having no functional oral language to speaking in three-word phrases. Their skill levels in other areas also cover a wide spectrum. Two of my students are just beginning to imitate the simple actions and verbalizations of others, while others are learning to identify letters and count to 20 or higher with one-to-one correspondence. However, there is one objective common to all the students: learning to relate to and interact with the world around them in more appropriate, meaningful, and "happy" ways, which, I believe, is the foundation of all learning.

Beth: I teach one of our school's two primary special education classes. My students are 6 to 9 years old in grades K–2. One student comes from a home in which Somali is spoken. The socioeconomic levels of my students range from poverty to middle class. Six of my eight students this year have a diagnosis of autism. All of my students have communication/speech needs and receive support services from a speech pathologist. There are many different skill levels in the room. Four students go to general education classrooms for some or all academic instruction, and four receive all academic instruction in my classroom. Seven of the eight students in my class spend time in a general education class for music and physical education instruction. They are accompanied to the general education classrooms by a teaching assistant who helps them as needed to function socially or academically with typically developing peers. One student is fully included and receives instruction in a general education class for the entire day. He is supported as needed for behavioral/social issues.

TEACHING STRATEGIES We have found that several teaching strategies or methods are consistently effective with our the students:

Visual Supports. Many children with autism have difficulties comprehending spoken language but respond well to visual stimuli. Picture cards are one way to make words and abstract concepts more concrete. We place picture cards all around our classrooms to help the children learn vocabulary (e.g.,

"shelf"), directions (e.g., "first-then"), and classroom expectations (e.g., "quiet").

Picture cards provide an alternative method of communication for a nonverbal child or reluctant speaker. In some instances, systematic pairing of picture cards with spoken language eventually evokes speech from a nonverbal or reluctant child.

Picture cards can also be incorporated into interventions for problem behavior. Sometimes the more you speak to a child who is having a tantrum, the more the child's behavior escalates into a real meltdown. Using the picture cards seems to help the child deescalate, reminding him of the appropriate behaviors. Kazuko calmly holds up the "quiet" and "stop" picture cards in front of a tantruming child and models those behaviors. From the first day of school in the fall, she reinforces the children's exhibition of self-control.

Picture activity schedules are another effective instructional tool. Many children with autism function more independently and successfully when visual supports provide some predictability in their environment. Having a visual schedule seems to give them a sense of security and control. It also lets them know what comes next so that transitions from one activity to another are not so difficult.

Modeling, Frequent Opportunities to Respond, and Reinforcement. Our children have difficulty acquiring and generalizing new skills to the extent with which those skills become meaningful and useful to them. The children need to be provided with multiple and repeated opportunities to practice whatever they are learning.

Telling a student with autism what to do is often ineffective. Instead of saying, "Zach, stop bothering Cordy and wait for your turn" and expecting him to understand and comply, we demonstrate exactly what the desired behavior looks like, by sitting up straight, putting our hands together, being quiet, watching the child whose turn it is, and so forth. Immediately after modeling the skill, we have the student imitate it. Then we follow up with numerous opportunities to practice the skill in meaningful contexts across sessions. We "catch them being good," stop, and reinforce, reinforce, reinforce. It may seem like common sense, but we continually remind ourselves of these basic but important strategies.

Functional Analysis and Problem Solving. Some children with autism sometimes present challenging behaviors such as self-stimulating behaviors, extreme and long-lasting temper tantrums, aggression toward others, and even self-injury. One of our most important roles as special education teachers is to be problem solvers. We work as a team, and with the help of our instructional assistants, we assess the environment and identify what antecedent conditions or events may be triggering the problem behavior and what consequence may be sustaining it. We are fortunate to have three other special education teachers in our school. We often brainstorm as a group to create effective interventions for a child's problem behavior. It is also important to teach the child an alternative appropriate behavior and reinforce it while trying to decrease the inappropriate behavior.

TEACHING PHILOSOPHIES Kazuko: "It is better to light candles than to curse the darkness." I am not sure whose quote this is, but it has been my guiding philosophy since the day I first heard it. Teaching a child with autism is no easy task, and one can be easily overwhelmed by the enormity of a child's skill deficits and behavioral excesses. Every child has a set of skills, or strengths, and it is our job to find those strengths and build on them. I constantly ask myself three questions: "What can this child do now?" "What is the next step?" and "Where do I want to see this child at the end of the school year?" Continually asking and answering these questions help me develop purposeful, goal-oriented lesson plans and activities that meet each child's current skills. Children with autism seem to be often "stuck" in activities or routines they perceive as "happiness" and "security." I believe that one of my important roles as their teacher is to expand their horizon and help them realize that "the outside world" is not such a bad place to be.

Beth: I begin with having high expectations for my students. I believe all students can learn and that we just need to tap into what motivates each student to achieve his highest level of performance. We need to teach the students the power of choice, no matter how simple the choice. I give my students many opportunities to make choices throughout the day. I observe their choices, and then I use those choices to motivate them to learn.

Although we both have much more to learn about teaching children with special needs, we each feel good about where we are in our careers as special education teachers. There are some difficult days when I feel like quitting, and yet, I honestly think this is one of the most rewarding jobs anyone could have. When Kazuko and I step back and see how far our students have come, we know that what we are doing is making a real difference in their lives.

To see Ms. Yamamoto's and Ms. Mueninghoff's classrooms and watch them use some of the teaching strategies they've described here, go to the book resources for this text on MyEducationLab.

MyEducationLab™

Visit the **MyEducationLab** for *Exceptional Children* to enhance your understanding of chapter concepts with a personalized Study Plan. You'll also have the opportunity to hone your teaching skills through video- and case-based Assignments and Activities, IRIS Center Resources, and Building Teaching Skills and Dispositions lessons.

AUTISM, AN INTRIGUING AND PUZZLING DEVELOPMENTAL DISORDER of childhood, can be a frightening, exhausting, and heartbreaking experience for the parents and families of children affected with the condition. Until recently, the prognosis for children with autism was extremely poor, with problems of daily living persisting into adulthood and requiring intensive supervision and supports for more than 90% of individuals (Bristol et al., 1996). The good news is that research has improved our understanding of autism, and effective education and treatment are producing much better futures for many children with autism and their families.

In a fairly short time autism has moved from being a relatively unrecognized disability, even within the field of special education, to one of widespread interest in education and society in general. Still, much remains unknown about the disability. Richard Simpson (2004a), who, like most people, was "both fascinated and spellbound" (p. 137) by children with autism when he first began working with them more than 30 years ago, has written:

In spite of the extraordinary recent media coverage and other attention that autism has received, it continues to have the same mystique that it had when I first entered the field. That is, in spite of significant advancements in treating and understanding individuals with autism spectrum disorders, the disability remains a mystery. Even when viewed through a disability lens, individuals with ASD are a particularly challenging and enigmatic group. (p. 138)

DEFINITIONS

While people with autism have no doubt always been part of the human community, the condition was not described or named until 1943, when Leo Kanner, a psychiatrist at Johns Hopkins Hospital in Baltimore, published case reports on a group of 11 children. He wrote that the children displayed behaviors that differed "so markedly and uniquely from anything reported so far, that each case merits . . . a detailed consideration of its fascinating peculiarities" (Kanner, 1943, p. 217). The children Kanner described, eight boys and three girls, shared the following characteristics:

- Difficulty relating to others in a typical manner
- Extreme aloneness that seemed to isolate the child from the outside world
- Resistance to being picked up or held by parents
- Significant speech deficits, including mutism and echolalia
- In some cases, exceptional memorization skills
- Early specific food preferences
- Monotonous, obsessive desire for repetition and sameness
- Bizarre, repetitive behavior such as rocking back and forth and spinning objects
- Explosive temper tantrums
- Lack of imagination and few spontaneous behaviors such as typical play
- Normal physical appearance

Kanner concluded that this unusual group of characteristics, especially the "inability to relate themselves in the ordinary way to people and situations" (1943, p. 242), constituted a pathogenic syndrome. He called this condition *early infantile autism*.

Unaware of Kanner's work, Hans Asperger, a pediatrician in Vienna, used the term *autistic psychopathology* in 1944 to describe a behavioral syndrome he found among a group of older children and adolescents (Wing, 1998). Asperger's "little professors" (as he called them) had good language skills and often above-average to superior intelligence, but they were socially naive and inappropriate and used odd intonation and body language while giving monologues about specialized interests.

Many of the behavioral deficits and excesses first reported by Kanner and Asperger are key diagnostic criteria in contemporary definitions of **autism spectrum disorder,** a group of neurodevelopmental disorders marked by persistent deficits in social communication and interaction, and by restricted, repetitive patterns of behavior and interests.

IDEA Definition of Autism

IDEA definition of autism

Content Standards for Beginning Teachers of Individuals with DD and/or Autism— Definitions and issues related to the identification of individuals with developmental disabilities (DD1K1) (also, DD2K3).

When Congress reauthorized IDEA in 1990 (PL 101-476), autism was added as a disability category under which children were entitled to special education. IDEA defines the disability as follows:

(i) *Autism* means a developmental disability affecting verbal and nonverbal communication and social interaction, generally evident before age three, that adversely affects a child's educational performance. Other characteristics often associated with autism are engagement in repetitive activities and stereotyped movements, resistance to environmental change or change in daily routines, and unusual responses to sensory experiences.

(ii) Autism does not apply if a child's educational performance is adversely affected primarily because the child has a serious emotional disturbance as defined in paragraph (c) (4) of this section.

(iii) A child who manifests the characteristics of autism after age three could be identified as having autism if the criteria in paragraph (c) (1) (i) of this section are satisfied. (34 CFR, Part 300 §300.8[c][1][i–iii] [August 14, 2006])

American Psychiatric Association Definition of Autism Spectrum Disorder

Most children receiving special education under the IDEA disability category of autism have received a diagnosis of one of four related pervasive developmental disorders that constitute the *autism spectrum*—autistic disorder, Asperger's disorder, childhood disintegrative disorder, or pervasive developmental disorder not otherwise specified (PDD-NOS)—per criteria published in the American Psychiatric Association's *Diagnostic and Statistical Manual of Mental Disorders (DSM-IV)* (2000). These related disorders, which constitute the *autism spectrum,* are differentiated from one another primarily by the age of onset and the severity of various symptoms.

AUTISTIC DISORDER (AUTISM) Autistic disorder is marked by three defining features with onset before age 3: (a) qualitative impairment of social interaction (e.g., lack of social or emotional reciprocity and affect); (b) qualitative impairment of communication (e.g., delay or total absence of spoken language); and (c) restricted, repetitive, and stereotyped patterns of behavior, interests, and activities (e.g., stereotypic or repetitive speech or motor behavior, excessive adherence to routines, preoccupation with unusual objects). The combination of behavioral deficits (e.g., inability to relate to others, lack of functional language), behavioral excesses (e.g., self-stimulation, bizarre and challenging behaviors), and unusual responses to or interest in sensory aspects of their environment makes children with autism stand out as strikingly different from most children.

ASPERGER'S DISORDER At the mild end of the autism spectrum is Asperger's disorder or, more commonly, **Asperger syndrome**. The most distinctive feature of Asperger syndrome is impairment in social areas, particularly an inability to understand how to interact socially. Deficits in the use of nonverbal behaviors related to social interaction such as eye gaze, facial expression, gestures, body posture, and judging personal space are common. Children with Asperger syndrome do not have general language delay, and most have average or above-average intelligence.

CHILDHOOD DISINTEGRATIVE DISORDER
Childhood disintegrative disorder shares behavioral characteristics with autistic disorder, but the condition does not begin until after age 2 and sometimes not until the child has reached age 10. Medical complications are common, and the prognosis for significant improvement is usually very poor.

PERVASIVE DEVELOPMENTAL DISORDER NOT OTHERWISE SPECIFIED (PDD-NOS)
Children who meet some, but not all, of the qualitative or quantitative criteria for autistic disorder are often diagnosed as having **pervasive developmental disorder not**

DSM definition of autistic spectrum disorder

 Content Standards for Beginning Teachers of Individuals with DD and/or Autism—Definitions and issues related to the identification of individuals with developmental disabilities (DD1K1) (also, DD2K3).

A child with autism might focus his attention on one object or activity for hours.

© Losevsky Pavel/Shutterstock

249

otherwise specified (PDD-NOS). Children with PDD-NOS have significant impairments in socialization with difficulties in either communication or restricted interests.

PROPOSED DSM-5 DEFINITION OF AUTISM SPECTRUM DISORDER The American Psychiatric Association (2011a) had earlier made available for public comment a proposed definition of autism spectrum disorder to be included in the fifth edition of the *Diagnostic and Statistical Manual of Mental Disorders (DSM-5)*, scheduled for publication in May 2013. The work group that developed the proposed definition noted that distinctions among the related disorders had been inconsistent over time, variable across sites, and often influenced by issues such as language competence or intelligence rather than core features of the disorder (American Psychiatric Association, 2011b). The group determined that autism is best represented as a single diagnostic category defined by a common set of behaviors manifested in early childhood within two domains: (a) persistent deficits in social communication and social interaction, and (b) restricted, repetitive patterns of behavior, interests, or activities.

The proposed *DSM-5* definition combines two core deficit areas—impairments in social interaction and impairments in communication—into a single domain of social/communication deficits and subsumes Asperger's disorder into a single diagnostic category of autism spectrum disorder. In *DSM-IV*, Asperger syndrome is a separate category with its own diagnostic criteria. Several studies have found that the majority of children diagnosed with Asperger syndrome also meet the diagnostic criteria for autism (Howlin, 2003; Tryon, Mayes, Rhodes, & Waldo, 2006)—a finding that supports Wing's (1998) contention that "Asperger syndrome and high-functioning autism are not distinct conditions" (p. 23.)

Adoption of the term *autism spectrum disorder* reflects the growing consensus in the field that the social and communication impairments fall on a spectrum, or continuum, of severity, with autistic disorder representing the most severe form and Asperger syndrome representing the mildest form. The work group that developed the *DSM-5* definition proposed that a child diagnosed with autism spectrum disorder be ascribed one of three levels of severity based on the amount of support required to counteract the limitations and impairments to everyday functioning as a result of the disorder.

> While changes, if any, to the diagnostic criteria for autism spectrum disorder recommended by the DSM-5 work group are likely to be minor, readers should consult the DSM-5 for the final version officially adopted by the American Psychiatric Association.

CHARACTERISTICS

As you read about the characteristics of children with autism spectrum disorder (ASD), remember these important points: Some children on the spectrum are very severely affected in most or all domains of everyday functioning, while others are only mildly affected. Although many children with ASD behave in similar ways, any two children on the spectrum may be more distinguished by their differences than by their similarities. "There is no single behavior that is always typical of autism and no behavior that would automatically exclude an individual child from a diagnosis of autism" (National Research Council, 2001, p. 11).

> Characteristics of autism
>
> Content Standards for Beginning Teachers of Individuals with DD and/or Autism—Psychological, social/emotional, and motor characteristics of individuals with developmental disabilities (DD2K2) (also, ICC2K2, ICC2K5, ICC2K6).

Impaired Social Interactions

Many children with autism exhibit extreme aloofness. Parents often report that their attempts to cuddle and show affection to the child are met with a profound lack of interest by the child. The child seems not to know or care whether he is alone or in the company of others. Many children with ASD have difficulty perceiving the emotional state of others, expressing emotions, and forming attachments and relationships. They seldom use social gestures such as showing and pointing things out to others or waving and nodding their head at others. Although some children with ASD will pull, push, or lead others by the hand to get things they want, the use of these gestures typically lacks any social component; the child seems to be using the other person just as a means to an end (Professional Development in Autism Center, 2004).

Young children with ASD often show deficits in **joint attention,** a social communication skill typically developing children begin to display in infancy (Dawson et al., 2004). Joint attention is evident when two people use gestures and gaze to share, follow, or direct each other's attention to interesting objects or events (Jones & Carr, 2004). A typically developing child looks where someone else is looking, as when a child notices that his mother has turned her head to look at something and does the same, or when a child turns his head or eyes in the direction someone is pointing. Joint attention allows the young child and another person to interact with their shared environment in the same frame of reference, an important factor in the development of language and social skills.

Deficits in joint attention is one of the reasons children with autism have difficulty learning by observing others. To find out how to help students with autism learn by observation, see *Teaching & Learning*, "'Do This, but Don't Do That.'"

Communication and Language Deficits

About half of children with autistic disorder are mute; they do not speak, but they may hum or occasionally utter simple sounds. The speech of many who do talk consists largely of **echolalia**—verbatim repetitions of what people around them have said—and noncontextual speech phrases without any apparent communicative purpose. Echolalia may be immediate or delayed. For example, Murphy (2003) reported that throughout the day a 7-year-old boy with autism repeated phrases he had heard from movies, cartoons, television shows, announcers of sporting events, and teachers during math instruction, such as the following:

"Hermione, we need to go find Harry!"
"Hi, Squidward!"
"Angelica, help me!"
"Today's Noggin show was brought to you by your good friends at McDonald's."
"Jeff Gordon rounds the far outside turn!"
"Add five carry the one." (p. 22)

Some children with ASD have an impressive vocabulary but do not use it in appropriate or useful ways. A common characteristic of children with autism is the concrete or literal processing of verbal information. They understand straightforward cause-and-effect relationships and questions that have a definite answer more easily than they do abstract concepts, idiomatic expressions, or humor. For example, a child with autism may understand the idea that an umbrella is used to stay dry in the rain but find an idiomatic figure of speech such as "It's raining cats and dogs" incomprehensible (Professional Development in Autism Center, 2004).

Many children with ASD can learn to request and label items, but understanding the subtleties of humor is often something that remains confusing into adulthood. That's why we were so excited one day when Sammy came up with a new response to an old question. Sammy had been taught to answer the question "What is your mommy's name?" Then one day in December he surprised us when instead of answering, "Chris Hall," he looked right at us with a serious face and responded, "Chris—mis." Three seconds later he started cracking up and saying, "Mommy is Christmas!" "Mommy is Christmas!" We all laughed along; and since then, Sammy has come up with many more jokes to delight everyone around him. (Michelle Hickman, personal communication, August 16, 2011)

Mustafa's token board reminds him to use his developing speech and social skills when interacting with others.

Laura Bolesta/Merrill

"Do This, but Don't Do That":
Teaching Children with Autism to Learn by Observation

BY BRIDGET A. TAYLOR

First-grade teacher Miss Jane is giving a lesson on how seeds grow into plants. Most of the children are actively engaged in the lesson, but Lucas, a 7-year-old with autism, stares at the wall clock, seemingly mesmerized by the second hand circling around the numbers. Lucas's support aide directs him to look at Miss Jane, who has asked a student to come to the front of the class to demonstrate how to sow seeds in a pot. The student places the seeds in the pot and gently covers them with soil. Miss Jane praises the student for doing such a good job and then asks Lucas to take a turn. Lucas picks up the seeds but doesn't seem to know what to do with them. Miss Jane guides Lucas's hand to place the seeds in the pot and then asks him to return to his seat. Miss Jane then asks who can tell her what the seeds need in order to grow. A student says, "French fries." The children laugh, but Miss Jane isn't amused. She informs the wisecracking student that his answer is incorrect and asks Lucas the same question. Lucas replies, "French fries."

Like many children with autism, Lucas has difficulty acquiring new skills by observing his peers. To learn by observing others Lucas must first learn some important foundational skills. He will need to learn to visually attend to the actions and vocalizations of others for extended periods of time, to imitate complex responses demonstrated by his peers, and to learn which responses he should and should not imitate based on his teacher's feedback to others.

WHAT IS OBSERVATIONAL LEARNING?

Observational learning was first defined by Albert Bandura (1962) as the acquisition of new responses by observing the behavior of a model. In a famous experiment, Bandura demonstrated that children who had observed adults being aggressive toward a BoBo doll were more likely to behave aggressively later. Many subsequent experiments have shown that children and adults readily acquire adaptive and positive skills by observational learning (Browder, Schoen & Lentz, 2001).

Researchers in applied behavior analysis have demonstrated that effective observational learning requires not only imitating a model, but also discriminating between positive and negative consequences received by the model (Catania, 2007). To know which responses he should and should not imitate, Lucas needs to learn the difference between his teacher's praise statements and her corrective statements toward other students.

WHY DO CHILDREN WITH AUTISM HAVE TROUBLE LEARNING BY OBSERVATION?

Core diagnostic features of autism—poor eye contact and joint attention, weak or absent imitation, and difficulty understanding language—impede observational learning (Taylor & Hoch, 2008). Whereas typically developing children can imitate facial expressions as early as 32 hours old, hand movements as early as 6 months, and can imitate actions after a 6-month delay as young as 12 months (Barr, Dowden, & Hayne, 1996), children with autism overall showed significant deficits in imitative behavior (Williams, Whiten, & Singh, 2004).

Children with autism often show more interest in objects than people and do not attend to the actions of others for extended periods of time. In the opening vignette example, Lucas is unable to sustain his attention to Miss Jane and then to his peers' responses. As a result, when it is his turn, Lucas is unable to imitate the response demonstrated by his peer of putting the seeds in the pot. In addition, if Lucas does pay attention when Miss Jane shows her displeasure at a student's response, he does not comprehend Miss Jane's displeasure and, as a result, may imitate the student's response without attending to the consequences provided by Miss Jane.

WHAT SKILLS ARE NEEDED FOR OBSERVATIONAL LEARNING?

To learn by observation, a child with autism, like anyone, must be able to do the following:

- **Attend.** The child will need to be able to look at people performing complex actions for extended periods of time. For example, to learn how to plant seeds properly, Lucas would need to watch his classmate pick up the seeds, place them in the pot, and cover the seeds with soil.
- **Imitate.** The child will need to be able to duplicate behavior demonstrated by a model. For example, Lucas would need to imitate what the peer demonstrated in order to plant the seeds correctly.
- **Discriminate.** The child will need to know the difference between positive feedback (praise) and negative feedback (corrective feedback). To know which responses to imitate, Lucas will need to attend to the consequences that the model (in this case the peer) receives from the teacher. He will need to know if the teacher praises a response that response should be imitated, whereas if the modeled behavior leads to correction from the teacher, he should not imitate that response.

TEACHING & LEARNING

HOW TO GET STARTED

Some emerging research provides some guidance on teaching the components of observational learning.

1. **Teach attending skills.** Start with teaching the child to make eye contact when you call his name, or when you provide a directive such as "Look at me" or "Look here." For example, say the child's name and provide a gesture of guiding your finger from his eyes to yours and when the child establishes eye contact with you, provide praise and something the child likes as a reward. Once the child can make eye contact with you for extended periods of time, teach the child to visually monitor the behavior of others. For example, seat the child in front of another child performing an action and provide the direction "Look at [peer's name]." When the child looks in the direction of the peer, provide praise and something the child likes as a reward. You can ensure the child is looking at the peer by asking relevant questions about the peer behavior, such as "What is [peer's name] doing?" Over time, make sure the child can look at the peer for longer periods of time. In the case of Lucas, during the school day, Miss Jane should ensure that Lucas is observing the behavior of his peers. For example, when calling on another student to perform an action, Miss Jane can provide a directive to Lucas such as "Lucas, look at what [peer's name] is doing," and provide praise and a reward for doing so. In addition, his support aide could monitor Lucas's attending behavior and provide subtle prompts (e.g., written reminders on his desk) to look in the direction of his peers.

2. **Teach imitation of peers' responses.** Start with simple motor actions that the target child already can perform. Seat the child across from a peer. Ask the peer to model an action (e.g., rolling a toy car back and forth on the table), and then guide the child's hands to imitate the peer's response. Provide praise and a preferred item after he imitates the action. Gradually fade your guidance over several trials until the child imitates the peer's actions on his own. Over time, make the actions to be imitated more complex (e.g., placing a doll in the car and moving the car to a specific location), include vocal responses (e.g., have the child say "zoom-zoom" when he moves the car), and have different children be the peer model. For Lucas, Miss Jane could enhance Lucas's imitation skills by having Lucas come to the front of the class to more closely observe the behavior of his peers to enhance the likelihood that he would imitate the behavior. She could also provide a directive to Lucas such as "Do what [peer's name] just did," before having him perform the response.

"Do what she is doing." Start by having the child imitate simple motor actions modeled by a peer.

3. **Teach imitation of new responses.** Teach the child to learn a new response by imitating the response modeled by the peer. Begin with simple responses such as labels for novel objects. Collect items that the child is unable to label but the peer can. Seat the child next to a peer. Guide the child to look in the direction of the peer (e.g., point in the direction of the peer). Present the peer with the item and ask him to label the item (e.g., hold up a stapler and ask, "What is this?"); when the peer responds correctly, provide praise and a preferred item to the peer. Then ask the child with autism to label the item. If he does, provide praise and a preferred item. If he doesn't, provide another opportunity for the peer to model the correct label of the item, and then provide the child with autism another opportunity to label the item correctly. The goal is that the child will imitate the response demonstrated by the peer rather than you telling the child the answer. In the case of Lucas, Miss Jane could, when Lucas is unable to answer a question accurately, ask one of his peers to provide the correct answer. Miss Jane could then ask Lucas to answer the question again. In this case, Miss Jane is ensuring that Lucas learns the correct information by observing his peer's response, rather than her having to tell him the correct answer.

4. **Teach the child to identify positive and negative or corrective consequences provided by the teacher.** Have the child observe a teacher instructing a peer in learning a new response (e.g., learning labels for several past presidents). Initially, the teacher should provide very obvious praise when the response is accurate (e.g., "That's right—that's Bill Clinton!") and inaccurate (e.g., "No, that's Abraham Lincoln"). After each response, ask the child to identify if the peer is correct or incorrect. When the child correctly

Bridget A. Taylor

The goal is for the child to imitate correct responses by observing his peers.

child observe the teacher instructing a peer in a task (e.g., how to color a picture using particular colors). While the peer is completing the response, have the teacher provide praise for a particular response (e.g., have the teacher say, "I like how you are using yellow to color the sun!"). Then have the teacher provide corrective feedback about a particular response (e.g., have the teacher say, "Don't use green to color the flower"). Then provide the child with autism an opportunity to complete the response and see if the child completes the responses the teacher praised, and assess if the child inhibits doing the response the teacher discouraged. When the child imitates the responses based on the differential feedback from the teacher, provide praise to the child. In the case of Lucas, Miss Jane should provide feedback to Lucas when he imitates behavior that he shouldn't. For example, when Lucas imitated the peer's inaccurate response of "French fries," Miss Jane could point out her response to the peer by saying, "Lucas, did I say he was correct or incorrect?" Miss Jane and the support aide will need to ensure that Lucas is able to accurately discriminate Miss Jane's consequences to the other students, and respond accordingly.

labels the accurate consequence, provide praise and a preferred item. For Lucas, Miss Jane could provide very obvious cues as to when a student is correct and incorrect by providing explicit praise statements to other students when they respond, such as "You are correct—the answer is [correct answer]!" and very obvious corrective statements such as "That's not correct—the answer is [correct answer]." In addition, to enhance Lucas's attention toward her consequences, Miss Jane could ask Lucas if a peer's response was correct or incorrect after she provides a consequence to the peer. For example, after she praises a peer, she could ask Lucas, "Was he correct?" and when Lucas answers accurately, Miss Jane can praise Lucas.

5. **Teach the child to identify which behavior he should and should not imitate.** Have the

About the Author

Bridget A. Taylor is the cofounder and executive director of Alpine Learning Group, a program providing comprehensive evidence-based education and treatment of children with autism (www.alpinelearninggroup.org). Her research interests include increasing language, social skills, and observational learning in children with autism.

Repetitive, Ritualistic, and Unusual Behavior Patterns

The repetitive behaviors and ritualistic routines of some children with autism are strikingly conspicuous. They may exhibit **stereotypy,** a pattern of persistent and repetitive behaviors such as rocking their bodies when in a sitting position, twirling around, flapping their hands at the wrists, flicking their fingers, sniffing at the air, or humming a set of three or four notes over and over again. A child may spend hours at a time gazing at his cupped hands, staring at lights, spinning objects, clicking a ballpoint pen, and so on. These odd, distracting behaviors not only dominate much of the child's time, making it difficult at best to participate and learn from lessons, they are social stigma that inhibit others from interacting with the child in a normal way (Loftin, Odom, & Lantz, 2007).

Insistence on Sameness and Perseveration

Children with autism often have issues about routines. They may insist on having everything in the same place all the time and get very upset if anything is moved. Even slight changes in their routines at home or in the classroom can trigger explosive "meltdowns" in some children. Sometimes a verbal child with autism may show this desire for sameness in a preoccupation with a certain subject or area of interest to the exclusion of all others. This child may talk incessantly about one topic, regardless of how bored his listeners are with it, and show no interest in anything else. He may ask the same question over and over, regardless of the reply.

Unusual Responsiveness to Sensory Stimuli

About 70% to 80% of individuals with autism exhibit abnormal reactions to sensory stimulation (Harrison & Hare, 2004). This takes the form of over- and underresponsiveness to sensory stimulation (Leekam et al., 2007). An *overresponsive* (hypersensitive) individual may not be able to stand certain sounds, dislike being touched or the feel of certain textures, and refuse to eat foods with certain smells or tastes. For example, Temple Grandin, an adult with autism who has a Ph.D. in animal science and designs environments and equipment to improve the humane and healthful handling of livestock, describes in her autobiography (*Thinking in Pictures and Other Reports of My Life with Autism*) how overly sensitive skin and certain sounds bothered her as a child:

> Washing my hair and dressing to go to church were two things I hated as a child. Scratchy petticoats were like sandpaper scraping away at raw nerve endings. . . . [L]oud noises were also a problem, often feeling like a dentist's drill hitting a nerve. They actually caused pain. I was scared to death of balloons popping because the sound was like an explosion in my ear. Minor noises that most people can tune out drove me to distraction. . . . My ears are like microphones picking up all sounds with equal intensity. (1995, pp. 66–68)

An *underresponsive* (hyposensitive) child appears oblivious to sensory stimulation to which most people react. Some children with autism do not seem to feel pain in a normal way. Some underresponsive children will spin round and round, rock back and forth, or rub and push things hard into their skin, perhaps to create additional forms or higher intensities of stimulation (Gabriels et al., 2008). It is not uncommon for an individual with autism to display a combination of both over- and underresponsiveness—for example, being hypersensitive to tactile stimulation but unresponsive to many sounds. The child's responses (or lack thereof) to sensory stimulation may be highly variable across settings or situations and from day to day, or even moment to moment. Fortunately, some fairly simple interventions (e.g., gradually increasing the intensity of stimulation so the person can habituate, or get used to the sensation [Koegel, Openden, & Koegel, 2004]) have been shown to help reduce fearful and avoidance responses to sensory stimulation by individuals with autism (Stiegler & Davis, 2010).

Intellectual Functioning

Although autism spectrum disorders occur across the full range of intellectual abilities, epidemiological surveys show that about 70% to 80% of individuals with autistic disorder also meet the diagnostic criteria for intellectual disabilities (Chakrabarti & Fombonne, 2001; Coolican, Bryson, & Zwaigenbaum, 2008). About one-half of those individuals function in the severe or profound range of intellectual disabilities. Some professionals use the terms *low-functioning autism* and *high-functioning autism* to differentiate individuals with and without intellectual disabilities.

Uneven skill development is a common characteristic of ASD, and about 10% to 15% of children exhibit "splinter skills"—areas of relatively superior performance that are unexpected compared to other domains of functioning. For example, a child may draw very well or remember things that were said a week before but have no functional language and refrain from eye contact.

Some experts estimate that 10% of people with autism have **savant syndrome,** an extraordinary ability or knowledge in a particular area such as memorization, mathematical calculations, drawing, sculpture, or music ability while functioning at the intellectually disabled level in all other areas (Heaton & Wallace, 2004; Kelly, Macaruso, & Sokol, 1997; Rimland & Fein, 1988). Although the term *autistic savant* is commonly used to

To learn more about the remarkable abilities of people with savant syndrome, go to "Savant Profiles" at http://www .wisconsinmedicalsociety .org/savant_syndrome/ savant_profiles.

refer to this phenomenon, only about half of people with savant syndrome have autism; and half have other forms of intellectual or developmental disabilities, central nervous system injury, or disease (Treffert, 2011a). The amazing betting calculations by Raymond in the movie *Rain Man* are illustrative of savant syndrome (although Kim Peek, the man on whom the movie character was based, did not have autism; Treffert, 2011b).

Many children with ASD exhibit *overselectivity,* the tendency to focus on a minute feature of an object or a person rather than the whole. For example, if shown a guitar for the first time, a child might focus on the sound hole and not consider anything else about the instrument, such as its size, shape, other parts, or even the sound that it makes. This overselectivity interferes with the child's understanding of what a guitar is—the totality of its parts and function. The tendency to overselect hinders learning new concepts and interferes with the child's ability to interpret relevant meaning from the environment. The tendency to attend to individual details rather than integrate them into a gestalt or "big picture" is a key element of a neuropsychological theory in autism called *weak central coherence* (Noens & van Berckelaer-Onnes, 2005).

Obsessive attention on a specific object or activity is another characteristic often seen in individuals with autism spectrum disorder. This focused attention may last for a long time and can be very difficult to break. For instance, if a child with autism has focused her attention on trains, she may continually choose to play with trains and resist playing with other toys. Focused attention may impede the child's ability to shift attention to other people or activities, such as a parent who is entering the room or another child who is attempting to join her play.

Some children with autism possess a strong aptitude for rote memory for certain things. For example, a child with autism may be able to name all of the Cy Young Award winners in the major leagues and repeat the script of an entire movie verbatim. Yet the same child may not recall what he did during recess or remember the sound that the letter *k* makes.

Problem Behavior

Some students with autism exhibit behavior problems in the form of property destruction, aggression toward others, and even self-injury.

> Often the parents report that the child sometimes bites himself so severely that he bleeds, or that he beats his head against walls or sharp pieces of furniture so forcefully that large lumps rise and his skin turns black and blue. He may beat his face with his fists. . . . Sometimes the child's aggression will be directed outward against his parents or teachers in the most primitive form of biting, scratching, and kicking. Some of these children absolutely tyrannize their parents by staying awake and making noises all night, tearing curtains off the window, spilling flour in the kitchen, etc. (Lovaas & Newsom, 1976, p. 309)

Many individuals with autism experience a variety of sleep problems, such as delayed onset of sleep, brief sleep duration, and night walking (Hoffman, Sweeney, Gilliam, & Lopez-Wagner, 2006). Food and eating problems are also common in children with autism spectrum disorders. Some children have extremely narrow food preferences, often sensory based (e.g., refusing foods with greater texture), some refuse to eat altogether, or choke, gag, and spit out food (Williams & Foxx, 2007). Some children with autistic disorder engage in **pica,** the compulsive, recurrent consumption of nonfood items (e.g., paper, dirt, pebbles, feces, hair). Stiegler (2005) cited the following account of one parent's experience with his child's pica:

> Over the last couple years we have pulled out of [our son's] throat: a set of keys, large bulldog clips, sticks, rocks, wads of paper, opened safety pins, wire (from the screen). Plus add the stuff that he gets down before we can get it out: magnets from the fridge, Barbie parts, paper, money, paper clips, etc. (Menard, 1999, n.p.)

The frequent, high-intensity, and sometimes dangerous behavior problems of some children with autism create tremendous stress on parents and can lead to family dysfunction if not brought under control (Long, Gurka, & Blackman, 2008; Osborne & Reed, 2011). Frequent behavior problems are also a major difficulty in effectively including students in general education classrooms.

Asperger Syndrome

While children with Asperger syndrome do not have the deficits in language and overall intellectual functioning typical of children with autistic disorder, they share many characteristics. Following are other characteristics exhibited by many individuals with Asperger syndrome (Attwood, 2007; Ritvo, 2006; Smith Myles & Simpson, 2001):

- Intense interest in a particular subject, often atypical things or parts of things (e.g., deep-fat fryers, ZIP codes, washing-machine motors), to the exclusion of everything else
- Clumsiness, difficulty with fine- and/or gross-motor activities
- Inflexible adherence to routines
- Fascination with maps, globes, and routes
- Superior rote memory, tendency to amass many related facts
- Speech and language impairments in the areas of semantics, pragmatics, and prosody (volume, intonation, inflection, and rhythm); pedantic, odd speech patterns; formal style of speaking
- Difficulty understanding others' feelings
- Extensive vocabulary, reading commences at an early age (*hyperlexia*)
- Perfectionist, frustrated when asked to submit work they believe is below standard

Their peculiarities and social skills deficits make it difficult for children with Asperger syndrome to develop and maintain friendships. Because they are highly verbal and often have superior intelligence, students with Asperger syndrome are considered slackers by teachers and peers and often misdiagnosed as having obsessive-compulsive disorder or attention-deficit/hyperactivity disorder (ADHD).

Positive Attributes and Strengths of Students with ASD

After reading graphic descriptions of the social and communication impairments, skill deficits, and behavioral excesses exhibited by individuals with ASD, it is easy to overlook their strengths and positive attributes. Not all individuals with ASD are always unattached to those around them or consistently behave in a stilted or inappropriate manner. As Greenspan and Weider (1997) remind us, many children with autism are "quite loving and caring, thoughtful and creative" (p. 88).

As we might expect, a noticeable difference exists between descriptions of autism and Asperger syndrome by people with and without the conditions (Grandin, 1995; Kluth, 2004; Willey, 2003). While people without disabilities tend to focus on the social, communication, and cognitive differences compared to typical functioning, many people with autism and Asperger syndrome have described positive features associated with their disability. For example, Temple Grandin (2006) describes some of the positive features associated with her disability:

> I think in pictures and sounds. I don't have the ability to process abstract thought the way that you do. Here's how my brain works: It's like the search engine Google for images. If you say the word "love" to me, I'll surf the Internet inside my brain. Then, a series of images pops into my head. What I'll see, for example, is a picture of a mother horse with a foal, or I think of "Herbie the Lovebug," scenes from the movie *Love Story* or the Beatles song, "Love, love, all you need is love...."
>
> [O]ne of the features of being autistic is that I'm good at synthesizing lots of information and creating systems out of it.

Thompson (2009) details practical, research-based interventions to prevent meltdowns and other behavior problems by children with autism in home, school, and community settings.

Difficulty reading other people's feelings makes developing romantic relationships especially hard for teens and young adults with Asperger syndrome.

257

TEACHING & LEARNING

Caught in a Behavior Trap:
From Unwanted Obsession to Motivational Key

Many students with Asperger syndrome are enthralled with particular subjects or things. Such special interest areas (SIAs) are a dominant characteristic of over 90% of individuals with Asperger syndrome (Attwood, 2003). Because the child spends so much time talking about or fiddling with the object of his interest, these SIAs are often viewed as a deficit. However, teachers can take advantage of students' obsessions, be it tarantulas or toilet brushes, and can turn a perceived deficit into a strength (Winter-Messiers, 2007).

BEHAVIOR TRAPS

Behavior traps are especially powerful contingencies of reinforcement that produce substantial, long-lasting behavior changes (Baer & Wolf, 1970). Behavior traps are particularly evident in the activities we just cannot get (or do) enough of. Alber and Heward (1996) described how a teacher created a behavior trap that took advantage of a fifth grader's obsession with baseball cards:

> Carlos experiences school as tedious and unrewarding. But he does find solace in his baseball cards, often studying, sorting and playing with them in class. His teacher, Ms. Greene, long ago lost count of the number of times she had to stop an instructional activity to separate Carlos and his beloved baseball cards. Then one day, when she approached Carlos' desk to confiscate his cards in the middle of a lesson on alphabetization, Ms. Greene discovered that Carlos had already alphabetized all the left-handed pitchers in the National League!

Ms. Greene realized she'd found the secret to sparking Carlos' academic development.

> Carlos was both astonished and thrilled to learn that Ms. Greene not only let him keep his baseball cards at his desk, but also encouraged him to "play with them" during class. Before long, Ms. Greene had incorporated baseball cards into learning activities across the curriculum. In math, Carlos calculated batting averages; in geography, he located the hometown of every major leaguer born in his state; and in language arts, he wrote letters to his favorite players requesting an autographed photo. Carlos began to make significant gains academically and an improvement in his attitude about school was also apparent. (p. 285)

The most effective behavior traps share four essential features: (a) they are "baited" with virtually irresistible reinforcers that "lure" the student to the trap; (b) only a low-effort response already in the student's repertoire is necessary to enter the trap; (c) interrelated contingencies of reinforcement inside the trap motivate the student to acquire, extend, and maintain targeted academic and/or social skills; and (d) they can remain effective for a long time because the student shows few, if any, satiation effects.

HOW TO GET STARTED

1. **Identify the child's SIA.** This is the easiest assessment a teacher will ever conduct. The objects, events, people, or things that qualify

Teachers must not overlook the many positive attributes and strengths of children with autism spectrum disorders.

Some people might think if I could snap my fingers I'd choose to be "normal." But I wouldn't want to give up my ability to see in beautiful, precise pictures. I believe in them. (n.p.)

Lianne Willey (2001), a woman with Asperger syndrome, writes:

> We can describe a situation like no one else. We can tell you what intangibles feel like and secret flavors taste like. We can describe for you, in unbelievable depth, the intricate details of our favorite obsessions. (p. 29)

Many educators view the intense preoccupation by students with ASD toward their favorite obsessions as an eccentric

as SIAs are known to anyone who has spent any time with the child. Tyler, for example, loves maps and will endlessly talk about, look at, and draw maps.

2. **Incorporate the SIA across the curriculum.** Tyler's fascination with maps could be integrated easily into math, reading, writing, science, and social studies lessons.

3. **Make entering the trap easy.** A student does not have to earn his way into a behavior trap. In a behavior trap, the student has free access to the SIA. Provide materials that may be required to engage in the SIA, and prompt the student to use them in ways that will incorporate the targeted skills (e.g., "Tyler, would you show me how many different types of structures are identified on this map?").

4. **Start small, and use the trap judiciously.** Use the SIA to help the student improve skills with which he has experienced some success, then gradually add new skills. Even though Tyler is crazy about maps, requiring him to write a 10-page research report on the topic (especially if his writing skills are poor) could destroy the effectiveness of maps as behavior trap bait. Better to begin by asking Tyler to label and classify his favorite map components, then write brief descriptions about them, then compare and contrast the functions of the components, and so on. In time, Tyler may write reports with all the detail of an experienced cartographer.

5. **Don't be in a hurry to eliminate the SIA.** Remember that you're not trying to eliminate the student's interest in his SIA, but use it to motivate the student to learn new academic and social skills, which may eventually lead to the student developing other interests.

6. **Involve the target student's peers.** Encourage peers to participate in SIA-related curriculum activities. Peer involvement gives the target student opportunities to practice social and language skills. A bonus may be that peers acquire interest in and useful knowledge about their classmate's SIA.

7. **Periodically change the curriculum areas and activities associated with the SIA.** Although a student may not tire of his SIA outside the trap (that is possible, however, and something to watch for), an SIA may lose its effectiveness as bait if a trap focuses solely on a single curriculum area or activity.

8. **Evaluate the effects.** Look for improvements in the student's skills and knowledge the behavior trap was designed to "catch." Collect data on the amount of time the student actively engages with the SIA-related curriculum, the completion and accuracy of academic products, and the student's comments. The student's behavior will suggest ways that an ineffective trap can be revised. Over time, the student's interest in the curriculum area(s) baited with the SIA may grow to the point where the trap is no longer necessary.

MyEducationLab™

Go to the book resources for this text on **MyEducationLab**. As you watch the video, consider how Tyler's teachers could use his special interests as motivation to further extend his academic and social skills.

---

foible at best and as an impediment to the development of social relationships and to engagement with the academic curriculum at worst. However, encouraging students' involvement with their special interest areas can lead to positive outcomes and strengths in other areas of functioning (Winter-Messiers et al., 2007). To learn about one strategy for using a student's eccentricity or obsession as the basis for building strengths in academic, social, and other areas, see *Teaching & Learning*, "Caught in a Behavior Trap: From Unwanted Obsession to Motivational Key."

PREVALENCE

Not long ago, autism was considered an extremely rare disorder, with an estimated incidence of just 3 in 10,000 children in the 1970s. More recent population studies have reported much higher incidence rates, ranging from 30 to 121 cases per 10,000 people (Kadesjo, Gillberg, & Hagberg, 1999; Yeargin Allsopp et al., 2003; Kogan et al., 2009). The incidence of autism has increased so much and so fast that some states have reported it to be an epidemic (Feinberg & Vacca, 2000). The number of students in California schools tripled from 2002 to 2010 (Lin, 2001). The most recent estimate by the Centers for Disease Control and Prevention (CDC, 2011a) is that 1 in 110 children have autism. The rise in autism prevalence is an international phenomenon,

Prevalence of autism

 Council for Exceptional Children

Content Standards for Beginning Teachers of Individuals with DD and/or Autism— Definitions and issues related to the identification of individuals with developmental disabilities (DD1K1)

with recent studies from Asia, Europe, and North America reporting approximate prevalence rates of 0.6% to more than 1%, including a recent study in South Korea of 2.6% (CDC, 2011b). This makes autism far more common than childhood cancer, Down syndrome, or diabetes. Boys are affected about four to five times more often than girls are (Autism and Developmental Disabilities Monitoring Network, 2007).

In the 2009–10 school year, 333,022 students ages 6 to 21 received special education services under the IDEA category of autism (U.S. Department of Education, 2011). This figure represents nearly 4.2 times the number of students with autism (78,717) served during 2000–2001. Autism has overtaken learning disabilities as the fastest-growing disability category in special education. As was the case with the increase in the number of children diagnosed with learning disabilities from the early 1980s through the turn of the century, the factors responsible for the dramatic increase in the number of children receiving special education under the category of autism in the last decade are unclear. The increase is likely due to a confluence of factors, including greater awareness of ASD, changes in federal and state policy and law favoring better identification and reporting of autism, improved screening and assessment procedures, greater availability of services for the diagnostic category, and changes in the definition and diagnostic criteria to a spectrum of related disorders that includes children with milder forms of autism who would not have been identified in earlier years (Fombonne, 2003; Gurney et al., 2003). Another contributing factor may be diagnosis shift; while the number of students with autism has increased, the number in the disability categories of learning disabilities, emotional and behavioral disorders, and intellectual disabilities have all decreased in recent years.

Most experts believe, however, that all of these factors together do not account for the total increase in the prevalence of autism and that an increase in the true incidence of ASD has occurred (Blaxhill, 2004; Hertz-Picciotto & Delwihe, 2009). Regardless of causes, the increased number of children being identified with ASD presents a public health and educational challenge for society and schools that must develop the infrastructure and expertise to serve them. It also heightens the need for research into causes of autism and for development of ever more effective treatments.

CAUSES

Causes of autism

Council for Exceptional Children

Content Standards for Beginning Teachers of Individuals with Exceptional Learning Needs in Individualized Independence Curricula—Etiologies and medical aspects of conditions affecting individuals with disabilities (ICC2K3).

Autism is a neurodevelopmental disorder with no medical or physiological marker. Ninety to 95% of cases are *idiopathic autism*, meaning that the etiology, or cause, is unknown (Grice & Buxbaum, 2006). As Schreibman (2005) noted, "When a definite etiology for a disorder is unknown, theories of etiology proliferate. Nowhere is that more apparent than in the field of autism" (p. 75). So many causes of autism have been proposed over the years that "it's a dull month without a new cause for autism" (Rutter, 2002).

From the 1950s to the mid-1970s, many professionals believed that parents who were indifferent to the emotional needs of their children caused autism. This notion may have had its beginnings in Kanner's (1943) observations that many of the parents of his original "autistic" group were preoccupied and that "there were very few really warmhearted fathers and mothers" (p. 50).

During the 1950s and 1960s, Bruno Bettelheim perpetuated the notion that autism could be attributed to inadequate parenting. Bettelheim's (1967) theory of *psychogenesis* claimed that autism was an outcome of uninterested, cold parents who were unable to develop an emotional bond with their children. Mothers of children with autism were called "refrigerator mothers" and led to believe they had caused their children's disability. For parents, the idea that they are to blame creates a great deal of guilt on top of the grief already experienced when they find their toddler exhibiting the disturbing behavioral markers of autism.

Although no causal link between parenting style and autism has ever been discovered, the misconception still receives media attention from time to time (Yavorcik, 2008), and many parents must battle the unnecessary guilt associated with that initial blame (Scheuermann & Weber, 2002).

Current biomedical research on the causes of autism pursues one of three theories: neuropathology, genetic inheritance, and environmental toxins that invade the central nervous system (Williams & Williams, 2011).

Recent research shows a clear biological origin for autism in the form of abnormal brain development, structure, and/or neurochemistry (Akshoomoff, 2000; Hyman & Towbin, 2007). Although the precise neurobiological mechanisms that cause autism have not been discovered, "it is clear that autism reflects the operation of factors in the developing brain" (National Research Council, 2001, p. 11). Studies of brain function point out differences in processing in different regions of the brain but also possible differences in connectivity. Overall, however, credible neurobiological hypotheses of the origins or risks for autism still remain few (Lord, 2007).

Genetic Inheritance

Autism clearly has a genetic component; having one child with autism greatly increases the chances of having another child with autism. A recent study found that parents who have a child with autism have a 19% chance overall (26% for males and 9% for females) of having a second child who will also be affected (Ozonoff et al., 2011). These findings are considerably higher than the level of risk of 3% to 8% reported in previous sibling recurrence studies (Boyle, Van Naarden Braun, & Yeargin-Allsopp, 2005).

Numerous genetic links to autism have been identified, but we still do not completely understand their causal relationships (Autism Research Institute, 1998; Mueller & Courchesne, 2000; NIH, 2007). However, a genetic factor is not the single cause, because if one identical twin has autism, the other twin may not. Because identical twins share the same genes, some other factor must be contributing to the presence of autism. The current theory among autism genetics researchers supports the idea of complex inheritance. This means that multiple genetic factors are likely to be involved, which in combination may predispose an individual to developing autism. In addition to the presence of a necessary, but currently still-unknown, combination of autism-related genes, exposure to certain environmental factors might lead to the development of autism in some individuals (Interactive Autism Network, 2011a). What these environmental factors are is still unknown.

In 1998, an English physician, Andrew Wakefield, suggested the measles-mumps-rubella (MMR) vaccine insulted children's gastrointestinal system, which led to regressed development and autism. Wakefield's hypothesis received tremendous media coverage worldwide. Worried parents elected not to have their children vaccinated, which in turn caused a spike in MMR diseases in children, including several deaths. No research has found a connection between the MMR vaccine (or vaccines containing thimerosal used for protection against diphtheria, tetanus, pertussis, and hepatitis B) and autism (Institute of Medicine, 2004). Numerous questions about the legitimacy of the study on which Wakefield derived his "gut theory" of autism (Wakefield et al., 2008) led to an investigation by Britain's General Medical Council, which discovered that Wakefield had a financial conflict of interest with a lawyer planning to bring suit against vaccine manufacturers for causing autism (Deer, 2010). *The Lancet,* the British medical journal that had published the article, retracted the paper (Editors of *The Lancet,* 2010).

Although the cause of autism is unknown at this time, research continues to bring us closer to answering that question. Autism might best be viewed as a behavioral syndrome that may be produced by multiple biological causes (Berney, 2000; Mueller & Courchesne, 2000).

Accounts of the Wakefield MMR vaccine scare by Ahearn (2010) and Deer (2010) are vivid examples of the importance of reliable science. Two excellent sources of reliable, science-based information about causes and proposed biological treatments for autism are Autism Speaks (http://www.autismspeaks. org) and the Interactive Autism Network (http// www.iancommunity.org).

IDENTIFICATION AND ASSESSMENT

Because the specific neurobiological causes of autism are not known, no medical test is available for ASD. Determining whether a child has an ASD is based on professional assessment of behavioral characteristics per the DSM.

Autism-specific screening tools detect early warning signs of autism, such as lack of joint attention, the failure to look at what a parent looks or points at.

© AISPIX/Shutterstock

The parents of 21 children diagnosed with autism reported that the average age of their child when the parents first recognized something was wrong was 15 months (Hutton & Caron, 2005). The changes in behavior associated with autism may be gradual or quite sudden, as shown in the following parent's account reported by Fleischmann (2004):

> It wasn't a gradual change that happened. It was an Invasion of the Body Snatchers experience. One day he looked the same and that's the only way I recognized him. He no longer made eye contact, spoke, sang, interacted. . . . He screamed and cried and stayed awake and stomped and hid under mattresses and pillows and ate dirt. (p. 39)

Autism can be reliably diagnosed at 18 months, and researchers are actively pursuing reliable methods for detecting warning signs in children as young as 14 months (Goin & Myers, 2004; Landa, Holman, & Garrett-Mayer, 2007). For no other disability is early identification more critical. Early diagnosis enables early intervention, which is highly correlated with dramatically better outcomes than are typically obtained when intervention begins later in the child's life.

Unfortunately, many children are not formally diagnosed with autistic disorder until the age of 5 or older (Wiggins, Baio, & Rice, 2006). Children with Asperger syndrome are on average 5.5 years older when diagnosed than are children with autism (Goin-Kochel, Mackintosh, & Myers, 2006).

Screening

Many parents of children with autism report that their baby developed in typical fashion for the first year or more, acquiring some meaningful communication skills and enjoying cuddling and hugging. But then between 12 and 15 months of age, the child began showing an oversensitivity to certain sounds or touch; no longer seemed to understand even simple words or gestures; and became increasingly withdrawn, aimless, and perseverative (Wetherby et al., 2004). Sometimes the early warning signs appear well before the baby's first birthday. When they do appear during the first year of life, they usually are not in the form of delays in major motor milestones (Landa et al., 2007). Many babies who are later diagnosed with autism often sit, crawl, and start to walk on time but show delayed or unusual development in social and communication domains.

Signs that warrant concern during the first year and a half of life include lack of pointing or gestures, infrequent or poor-quality imitation of the caregiver's facial expression, no single words by 16 months, lack of smiling, not responding to name being called, lack of joint attention (e.g., not looking at what parent looks at or points to), and loss of previously acquired language or social skills at any age (Landa, 2007; Plauché Johnson, Myers, & the Council on Children with Disabilities, 2007). In addition to these early markers, very young children with ASD may engage in repetitive and stereotyped patterns of specific behaviors by, for example, repeating certain behaviors over and over; saying scripted verses from familiar videos or TV shows again and again; or showing obsessive interest in certain objects, activities, or parts of objects.

The American Academy of Pediatrics recommends that all children be screened with a standardized autism-specific screening tool at the 18-month preventive care visit and again at 24 months of age to identify children whose development may have

For more information about the early warning signs of autism and other developmental disorders, go to First Signs at http://www.firstsigns.org and the CDC's "Learn the Signs/Act Early" at http://www.cdc.gov/ncbddd/actearly/milestones/index.html.

regressed (Plauché Johnson et al., 2007). Brief descriptions of four widely used screening instruments for ASD follow.

CHECKLIST FOR AUTISM IN TODDLERS (CHAT)   The CHAT identifies children at age 18 months who are at risk for social-communication disorders (Baron-Cohen, Allen, & Gillberg, 1992). It is a short questionnaire with nine items filled out by the parents and five items by a primary health care worker. The CHAT looks at (a) joint attention, including pointing to show and gaze monitoring (e.g., looking to where a parent is pointing), and (b) pretend play (e.g., pretending to pour tea from a toy teapot). Any child who fails the CHAT should be rescreened approximately 1 month later. If he fails the CHAT for a second time, the child should be referred to a specialist for a diagnostic evaluation.

If a child passes the CHAT on the first administration, no further action needs to be taken. However, passing the CHAT does not guarantee that a child will not go on to develop a social-communication problem of some form. If parents are worried, they should seek referral.

MODIFIED CHECKLIST FOR AUTISM IN TODDLERS (M-CHAT)   The M-CHAT (Robins, Fein, Barton, & Green, 2001) is an expanded American version of the original CHAT, which was developed in the U.K. Its goal is to improve the sensitivity of the CHAT for an American audience. Of the M-CHAT's 23 questions, those found to best discriminate between children diagnosed with and without ASD are 9 items pertaining to social relatedness and communication, such as the following:

- "Does your child ever use his/her index finger to point, to indicate interest in something?"
- "Does your child ever bring objects over to you (parent) to show you something?"
- "Does your child imitate you? (e.g., if you make a face, will your child imitate it?)"
- "If you point at a toy across the room, does your child look at it?" (Robins et al., 2001)

A child fails the M-CHAT when she fails two or more of the critical items or any three items. A child who fails the M-CHAT should be evaluated in more depth by the physician or referred for a developmental evaluation with a specialist. Not all children who fail the M-CHAT will meet criteria for a diagnosis on the autism spectrum.

SOCIAL COMMUNICATION QUESTIONNAIRE (SCQ)   The SCQ is a 40-item screening tool completed by a parent or other primary caregiver in less than 10 minutes (Rutter, Bailey, & Lord, 2003). Although the SCQ was developed for screening children age 4 years and up, a study found that it correctly identified 89% of children ranging in age from 17 to 45 months and made no false-positives (an incorrect diagnosis of a person who does not have the disability) if a cutoff score of 11 was used (Wiggins, Bakeman, Adamson, & Robins, 2007).

AUTISM SPECTRUM SCREENING QUESTIONNAIRE (ASSQ)   The ASSQ is a 27-item checklist that is completed by parents and teachers when screening symptoms characteristic of Asperger syndrome and other high-functioning ASDs in children (Ehlers, Gillberg, & Wing, 1999).

Diagnosis

Children who fail screening tests or whose parents or professionals have reason for concern undergo a complete diagnostic evaluation. A diagnosis of autism should be given by a professional with expertise in autism. That professional could be a developmental pediatrician, a psychologist, a psychiatrist, or a neurologist. In addition to administering an autism diagnostic tool with proven validity and reliability, it is vital that the clinician directly observe the child.

Following are brief descriptions of several of the growing number of rating scales, observation checklists, and diagnostic interviews that have been developed to aid the examiner's evaluation of a child suspected of having ASD. Professionals and parents should remember, however, that no single test or assessment device is failproof, especially when diagnosing a disability with such a wide range of expression.

CHILDHOOD AUTISM RATING SCALE (CARS)   The CARS is one of the most widely used instruments for diagnosing autism. It consists of 15 items rated on a 1 to 4 scale based on information from a parent report, records, and direct observation of the child (Schopler, Van Bourgondien, Wellman, & Love, 2009).

AUTISM DIAGNOSTIC INTERVIEW—REVISED (ADI-R) AND AUTISM DIAGNOSTIC OBSERVATION SCHEDULE (ADOS)   The ADI-R is a semistructured interview of the primary caregivers of a child or adult suspected of having autism (Lord, Rutter, & Le Couteur, 1994). A trained examiner conducts a detailed interview with the child's primary caregiver, typically requiring at least 2 hours to complete. Questions cover communication, social development and play, repetitive and restrictive behaviors, behavior problems, and family characteristics. The ADI-R has been called the "gold standard" for diagnosis of autism for research purposes (Filipek et al., 2000). Results from the ADI-R ideally are supplemented by the ADOS, which consists of a trained examiner working with the child in a prescribed set of interactions designed to evoke behaviors characteristic of autism (Lord et al., 2000).

ASPERGER SYNDROME DIAGNOSTIC SCALE (ASDS)   The ASDS is designed to identify Asperger syndrome in children ages 5 through 18 (Smith Myles, Jones-Bock, & Simpson, 2000). It consists of 50 yes/no items that can be answered by parents, family members, teachers, speech-language pathologists, psychologists, and other professionals familiar with the child. The ASDS yields a quotient that predicts the likelihood that the individual assessed has Asperger syndrome.

EDUCATIONAL APPROACHES

Children with autism are among the most difficult students to teach. They may focus on irrelevant stimuli while seeming oblivious to instructional stimuli, show little or no apparent interest in their teachers and peers, and with little or no warning have a "meltdown" that includes aggression, property destruction, self-injury, or all three. Seldom does a child with autism progress without an education that is truly special. Such children require instruction that is meticulously planned, skillfully delivered, and continually evaluated and analyzed for its effectiveness.

The good news is that a great deal of exciting research is providing professionals with tools to significantly improve educational outcomes for children with autism (e.g., Odom, Collet-Klingenberg, Rogers, & Hatton, 2010; Simpson, 2005; Williams & Williams, 2011). This section examines the importance of early intervention, introduces applied behavior analysis as a fundamental source of science-based intervention, and describes several instructional strategies for teaching children with autism.

Critical Importance of Early Intensive Behavioral Intervention

Early intensive behavioral intervention (EIBI) has helped some children with autism learn communication, language, and social skills so that they have been able to succeed in general education classrooms. One of the earliest and most powerful examples of the potential of systematic early intervention on the lives of children with autism is the work of Ivar Lovaas and his colleagues at the University of California, Los Angeles (Lovaas, 1987; Smith, Eikeseth, Klevstrand, & Lovaas, 1997; Smith & Lovaas, 1998). In 1987, Lovaas reported the results of a study that provided a group of 19 children with autism with an intensive early intervention program of one-to-one behavioral treatment for 40 hours per week for 2 years or more prior to age 4. Intervention also included parent training and inclusion in a preschool setting with typically developing children. When compared with a group of 19 similar children at age 7, the children in

---

History of education
and treatment in autism

Council for Exceptional Children

Content Standards for Beginning Teachers of Individuals with DD and/or Autism—Historical foundations and classic studies of developmental disabilities (DD1K3) (also DD1K4, DD9K1).

Figure 1 identifies some key events in the history of understanding and treating autism spectrum disorders. More detailed treatments of the history of autism can be found in Firth, 2003; Rimland, 1994; and Wing, 1998.

the early intervention group had gained an average of 20 IQ points and made major advances in educational achievement. Nine of the children had moved from first to second grade in general education classrooms and were considered by their teachers to be well adjusted.

Follow-up evaluations of the same group of 19 children several years later, at the average age of 11.5 years, showed that the children had maintained their gains (McEachin, Smith, & Lovaas, 1993). In particular, 8 of the 9 "best-outcome" children were considered "indistinguishable from average children on tests of intelligence and adaptive behavior" (p. 359). Although some have raised important questions about the validity and generality of this research (e.g., Gresham & MacMillan, 1997a, 1997b), replications of the "UCLA model," including a study in which children were randomly assigned to early intensive behavioral intervention or an alternate intervention, have produced similar results (Cohen, Amerine-Dickens, & Smith, 2006; Smith, Groen, & Wynn, 2000).

The work of Lovaas and colleagues was a landmark accomplishment in the education of children with autism (Baer, 2005). First, they discovered and validated at least some of the factors that can be controlled to help children with autism achieve normal functioning in a general education classroom. Second, the dramatic improvements that were previously considered unattainable in the children's social, communication, and cognitive functioning helped spur wide-ranging interest and research funding for a disorder for which custodial care was thought to be the only option (National Institute of Mental Health, 2004). Third, the successful outcomes provided a legitimate basis for hope and encouragement for parents and teachers desperate to learn how to help children with autism.

Applied Behavior Analysis

The teaching methods used in the Lovaas early intervention project were derived from **applied behavior analysis (ABA)**. ABA provides a scientific approach to designing, conducting, and evaluating instruction based on empirically verified principles describing functional relationships between events in the environment and behavior change (i.e., learning) (Cooper, Heron, & Heward, 2007). ABA uses behavioral principles such as positive reinforcement to teach children skills in a planned, systematic manner. Children receive repeated opportunities to practice and use their new skills across the day, settings, people, and situations.

Treatments based on other models can yield beneficial outcomes for children with autism. For example, an intervention derived from developmental psychology and designed to improve joint attention and symbolic play enhanced mother–child interactions and raised children's scores on standardized tests of IQ and language (Kasari, Freeman, & Paparella, 2006). However, no other form of treatment for children with autism has the amount or quality of scientific evidence attesting to its effectiveness that treatment informed by ABA has (Eikeseth, 2009; Eldevik et al., 2010; Myers, Plauché Johnson, & the Council on Children with Disabilities, 2007). Intervention programs consisting of an eclectic mix of components from different treatment models are not as effective as programs based on ABA (e.g., Eikeseth, Smith, Jahr, & Eldevik, 2002; Howard, Sparkman, Cohen, Green, & Stanislaw, 2005). After an extensive review of the research on autism treatments, the National Autism Center (2009a) concluded that 11 treatments have been thoroughly researched and have sufficient evidence to be confidently considered "established treatments" (e.g., joint attention intervention, modeling, naturalistic teaching strategies, peer training package, pivotal response treatment, self-management).

Approximately two-thirds of the Established Treatments were developed exclusively from the behavioral literature (e.g., applied behavior analysis, behavioral psychology, and positive behavioral supports). Of the remaining one-third, 75% represent treatments for which research support comes predominantly from the behavioral literature. (p. 16)

ABA

Council for Exceptional Children

Content Standards for Beginning Teachers of Individuals with DD and/or Autism—Evidence-based practices for teaching individuals with pervasive developmental disabilities, autism, and autism spectrum disorders (DD4K4) (also, ICC4S4, ICC4S5, DD4S1, ICC5K2, ICC5K3).

FIGURE 1   KEY HISTORICAL EVENTS IN THE EDUCATION OF CHILDREN WITH AUTISM SPECTRUM DISORDERS

Date	Historical Event	Educational Implication
1911	Eugen Bleuler, a Swiss psychiatrist, coins the term *autism*—from the Greek word *autos* (self)—to describe patients with schizophrenia who actively withdraw from social contact.	When used later to name a condition in children who displayed behaviors similar to Bleuler's patients, the term *autism* implied that children purposively withdrew from those around them.
1943	Leo Kanner, a child psychiatrist at Johns Hopkins University, describes the characteristics of a childhood disorder he calls *early infantile autism.*	Kanner's observation that "there were very few really warmhearted fathers and mothers" may have caused some to speculate that indifferent, nonresponsive parents were responsible for the disorder.
1944	Hans Asperger, an Austrian pediatrician with a special interest in "psychically abnormal" children, publishes a paper describing a pattern of behavior based on his work with more than 400 children with "autistic psychopathy."	The combination of behaviors and abilities he described later came to be known as *Asperger syndrome*.
1965	Autism Society of America (ASA) is founded (originally National Society for Autistic Children).	ASA's mission is to promote lifelong access and opportunity for all individuals within the autism spectrum and their families to be fully participating, included members of their communities.
1967	Bruno Bettleheim's book, *An Empty Fortress*, advances the notion that children with autism actively or purposively withdraw into their own worlds because of cold and uncaring parents.	Bettleheim's theory that autism was caused by "refrigerator mothers" led to much professional blaming and mistreatment of parents and devastating guilt.
1981	Lorna Wing publishes an article in Great Britain in which the term *Asperger syndrome* is used for the first time.	Wing's seminal paper generated renewed interest in Asperger syndrome, especially in Europe.
1987	Ivar Lovaas publishes results of the Young Autism Project, in which children with autism participated in an intensive early intervention program of one-to-one behavioral treatment for more than 40 hours per week for 2 years or more before age 4.	This was the first study to show that early, intensive, behavioral intervention could enable some children with autism to achieve normal functioning. It gave hope to parents and provided other researchers and practitioners with principles on which to build.
1990	Congress passes the Individuals with Disabilities Education Act (IDEA) Amendments of 1990 (PL 101-476).	Autism is added as a new disability category under which children are entitled to special education.
1993	Catherine Maurice's *Let Me Hear Your Voice: A Family's Triumph over Autism* is published.	This powerful account of a mother's efforts to find help for her two children brought attention to the importance of science-based treatment for autism, especially treatment based on applied behavior analysis (ABA).
1994	Asperger syndrome is officially recognized in the *Diagnostic and Statistical Manual of Mental Disorders (DSM-IV)* as a pervasive developmental disability within the autism spectrum.	This created increased awareness of Asperger syndrome among clinicians, researchers, and educators.
1994	The National Alliance for Autism Research (NAAR) is founded, the first organization in the United States dedicated to promoting research seeking to identify causes and potential biomedical cures for autism.	NAAR-funded research has been leveraged into more than $48 million in autism research awards by the National Institutes of Health and other funding sources and has led to advances in the neurosciences and other scientific fields.
1998	The Association for Science in Autism Treatment (ASAT) is founded (www.asatonline.org).	ASAT's mission is to educate parents, professionals, and policymakers by disseminating accurate, scientifically sound information about autism and its treatment and by combating inaccurate or unsubstantiated information.
2000	Behavior Analyst Certification Board begins credentialing Board Certified Behavior Analyst (BCBA) (www. bacb.com).	The BACB gives parents, schools, and agencies assurance that a BCBA has achieved a certain level of knowledge/skills regarding effective and ethical practice based on ABA.
2005	Autism Speaks is founded through a $25 million gift by the grandparents of a child with autism.	Autism Speaks is the nation's largest autism science and advocacy organization, dedicated to funding research into the causes, prevention, treatment, and a cure for autism; increasing awareness of ASD; and advocating for the needs of individuals with ASD and their families.

FIGURE 1 *(Continued)*

2002	CEC's Division on Developmental Disabilities (DDD) includes ASD within its purview and changes it's name to the Division on Autism and Developmental Disabilities (DADD).	Special educators with interests in ASD have a centralized source of information and a voice within CEC.
2006	Interactive Autism Network (IAN) is established at the Kennedy Krieger Institute (http://www.iancommunity.org).	IAN Community is an online library and meeting place where everyone concerned with autism spectrum disorders can learn more about autism research. IAN Research matches willing individuals with ASD and their families with appropriate local and national research projects.
2006	Combating Autism Act of 2006 (PL 109-416) is enacted.	This act authorized nearly $1 billion over 5 years to combat autism through research, screening, early detection, and early intervention, increasing federal spending on autism by at least 50%. It includes provisions relating to the diagnosis and treatment of people with ASD and expands biomedical research on autism, including a focus on possible environmental causes.
2009	National Autism Center (NAC) publishes results of its National Standards Project: a review of existing research literature by an expert to identify evidence-based treatment approaches for autism.	NAC also published a handbook for educators and parents outlining specific evidence-based program components, procedures, and implementation strategies. See www.nationalautismcenter.org.
2013	The American Psychiatric Association publishes a revised definition of autism spectrum disorder (ASD) in the *DSM-5*.	Autistic disorder and Asperger's disorder were subsumed within ASD; three levels of severity were added depending on the extent of supports needed for everyday functioning.

Because of the documented accomplishments of some children with autism after receiving intensive ABA therapy, many parents and practitioners have advocated for ABA programs and services for children with autism. However, misunderstandings about ABA are widespread, and many educators and parents have a narrow or incorrect view of what ABA is and is not. (See Figure 2, "What Is ABA?")

One of the most common misconceptions is that ABA consists only of **discrete trial training (DTT),** one-on-one sessions during which a routinized sequence of contrived learning trials is presented as teacher and child sit at a table. For example, an item or instruction is presented (e.g., "Touch the spoon"), the child responds, and reinforcement is provided for a correct response. Each sequence of antecedent stimulus, child response, and consequence (or feedback) is a trial.

As Baer (2005) points out,

The discrete trial method of teaching, or DTT, is as old as teaching and much older than education. It can be described as follows:

1. The teacher prepares a set of problems to present to a student one at a time.
2. This sequence is usually in an optimum order for teaching and learning, to the best of the teacher's ability.
3. The student responds or fails to respond to each problem.
4. The teacher responds to each of the student's responses or nonresponses, rewarding or acknowledging correct responses; ignoring, correcting, or reproving incorrect responses; and either ignoring or prompting responses after nonresponses.
5. The cumulative effect of this teaching is to impart a new set of integrated facts, a concept, or a skill.

The discrete trial method is the method whereby children learn games and parents teach children language. It is commonly used in school classrooms for teaching any subject matter. DTT is the method of Socratic

Discrete trial training

 Content Standards for Beginning Teachers of Individuals with DD and/or Autism—Evidence-based practices for teaching individuals with pervasive developmental disabilities, autism, and autism spectrum disorders (DD4K4) (also, ICC4S4, DD4S1, ICC5K3).

Teaching methods derived from ABA are effective not only with learners with autism and other disabilities but also with students in general education. See Alberto and Troutman [2009] and Heward et al. [2005].

dialogue, it is often how law students are taught their most useful skills, and it is often how medical interns are taught clinical and diagnostic skills. (p. 10)

[DTT] is used in countless variations. Whether DTT is drudgery or sublimely informative depends not on its format, but on how skillfully the teacher has prepared what the student will encounter and how skillfully the teacher can answer whatever response to the encounters the student may make. (p. 24)

DTT is not ABA, and ABA can be done without DTT. However, DTT plays an important role in ABA-based programming for children with autism, and it is a teaching method that special educators should know how to use with a high degree of skill (Fazzio, Martin, Arnal, & Yu, 2009). It is also important to know that

---

FIGURE 2   WHAT IS ABA?

ABA stands for *applied behavior analysis*, a science devoted to improving and understanding human behavior. ABA focuses on objectively defined, observable behaviors that are important in the daily lives of the participants, and it seeks to improve those behaviors while demonstrating reliable relationships between the procedures employed and the improvements in behavior.

WHAT ABA IS

ABA is individualized. (This is the *applied* of ABA.) Teaching goals are determined by a careful assessment of the current skills and behavioral deficits of the individual in the context of his environment. Skills to be taught are not selected from a predetermined list, but are selected on an individual basis. Behaviors that are most likely to produce beneficial outcomes for the child and his family are the primary focus of ABA-based teaching.

ABA is data-based evaluation and decision making. (This is the *behavior* of ABA.) Direct and frequent measurement is the foundation of ABA. Measurement is direct when a learner's performance of the target behavior is observed and recorded as it occurs in the natural environment for that skill. Frequent measurement is better than infrequent measurement. Ideally, measurement occurs as often as instruction occurs.

ABA is designed to be effective. (This is the *analysis* of ABA.) Because data are collected directly and frequently during instruction, assessment of learning is continuous. By examining the data, teachers, therapists, and parents can determine whether or not the instruction is working. If the child is not making reasonable progress, instruction is modified.

ABA is doable. Although ABA requires far more than learning to administer a few simple procedures, it is not so complicated as to be prohibitive. Parents can learn the basic principles of ABA and can incorporate teaching strategies based on those principles into daily interactions with their children. For example, a parent can work on her child's greeting behavior throughout the day. Whenever the child encounters a new person or a parent or sibling greets the child, she can prompt the child to wave and make eye contact and then praise and reinforce that behavior.

ABA is, in the words of one mother of a young child with autism, "Good old-fashioned hard work." ABA is not a magic bullet or a miracle cure. It requires diligent, continuous analysis of the relationship between behavior and the environment in which behavior occurs. Because behavior is always happening, teaching is always happening. ABA is certainly intensive; but when used correctly as the basis for designing and evaluating treatment for young children with autism, ABA can produce meaningful, life-changing results.

WHAT ABA IS NOT

ABA does not prescribe instructional settings, teaching formats, or materials. ABA can be used to guide discrete trial instruction for reading skills delivered by a teacher while sitting at a table with a child. ABA can also guide a parent's provision of incidental learning trials for language acquisition while giving her child a bath. ABA does not require that certain items be used as rewards or consequences for behavior. The items and activities to be used as rewards (technically called *reinforcers*) are determined by the child's preferences and by the effects those items and activities have when provided as consequences for the child's behavior.

Because ABA does not dictate any specific type of instructional method or format, the phrase "ABA method" is a misnomer. ABA is broader than any "brand name" method of behaviorally based instruction or therapy (e.g., Lovaas method, PECS, verbal behavior method). Many service providers and parents mistakenly believe that ABA is one of these ABA-based brand names. However, training in a brand name is no substitute for in-depth training in the science of applied behavior analysis.

ABA is not bribery. Every effort is made to increase children's motivation and make learning fun. Naturally occurring consequences are used as reinforcers whenever possible. For example, instead of using just teacher praise or edible items when teaching play and social skills to children, naturally occurring consequences, such as access to favorite toys and interacting with other children, are provided as reinforcers for appropriate play and socialization behaviors.

ABA is not punitive. Positive strategies are used until they are exhausted, and reinforcers are delivered systematically to increase appropriate behavior. The goal of ABA is not to decrease maladaptive behavior but to increase the occurrence and strength of appropriate behavior. An important element of ABA is to determine the function of behavior. For example, does a child tantrum and hit himself or others because he wants attention? Does he throw things because he needs help? Knowing why a child exhibits challenging behaviors allows parents and teachers to teach appropriate replacement behaviors, such as tapping a person on the shoulder to get attention or using spoken words or a communication device to say, "I need help."

Source: Adapted from Silvestri, S. M., Wood, C. L., Allen, N. J., Anderson, M. A., Murphy, C. M., & Heward, W. L. (2009). What is ABA? In E. A. Boutot & M. Tincani (Eds.), *Autism encyclopedia: The complete guide to autism spectrum disorders* (pp. 83-87). Waco, TX: Prufrock Press.

using DTT is just one type of teaching arrangement, and ABA programming uses a variety of procedures to help individuals with autism acquire and generalize new skills (Sulzer-Azaroff & Associates 2008; Thompson, 2011). Following is a partial list of strategies for teaching students with autism derived from ABA:

- Strategies for shifting control over a student's responses from contrived stimuli used in training to naturally occurring stimuli in the student's environment. (Reeve, Reeve, Townsend, & Poulson, 2007)
- Alternative forms of communication such as the Picture Exchange Communication System (PECS)
- Teaching practices for spoken and written language based on a functional analysis of verbal behavior (Barbera, 2007).
- Peer tutoring interventions for building academic and social relationships (Kamps, Barbetta, Leonard, & Delquadri, 1994; Petursdottir, McComas, McMaster, & Horner, 2007)
- Strategies to increase active student responding during group instruction (Cihak, Alberto, Taber-Doughty, & Gama, 2006)
- Self-management tactics (Southall & Gast, 2011)
- Methods of errorless discrimination learning (Jerome, Frantino, & Sturmey, 2007)
- Functional assessment of challenging behavior (Neef & Peterson, 2007)
- Functional communication training (Mancil, 2006)
- Naturalistic strategies for teaching language and social skills (Koegel & Koegel, 2006)

Lessons featuring discrete trial training are an important part of Ayah's school day.

Laura Bolesta/Merrill

Visual Supports: Helping Students with Autism Cope with Social Situations and Increase Their Independence in the Classroom

Visual supports encompass a wide variety of interventions that involve visual cues and prompts that help students perform skills with greater independence and accuracy (Meadan, Ostrosky, Triplett, Michna, & Fettig, 2011). Picture activity schedules and social stories are two strategies for students with ASD that entail visual supports.

PICTURE ACTIVITY SCHEDULES Some level of independent performance is needed for success in inclusive classrooms. For preschoolers with autism, a lack of play skills "might prevent opportunities for learning and successful participation in inclusive classrooms. The impending isolation might serve to perpetuate the children's deficits in socialization and communication" (Morrison, Sainato, BenChaaban, & Endo, 2002, p. 58). Numerous studies have shown that children with autism can be taught to use picture activity schedules to increase their independence in selecting and carrying out a sequence of activities in the classroom (e.g., Bevill, Gast, MaGuire, & Vail, 2001; Goodman & Williams, 2007; McClannahan & Krantz, 1999; Morrison et al., 2002; Spriggs, Gast, & Ayres, 2007). Activity schedules have also helped older students learn social and transition related skills (Banda & Grimmett, 2008). Video modeling can be incorporated into activity schedules (Stromer, Kimball, Kinney, & Taylor, 2006); see *Teaching & Learning*, "Multimedia Activity Schedules Promoting Independence among Children with Autism."

The Ohio Center for Autism and Low Incidence, in partnership with other autism service centers, and research centers has developed a series of training modules on how to use discrete trial training and many other behavioral teaching techniques. The modules are free and can be accessed at http://www.autisminternetmodules.org.

Excellent descriptions of a variety of teaching methods based on ABA for children with autism can be found in Scheuermann and Webber (2002); Sulzer-Azaroff and Associates (2008); and Williams and Williams (2011).

Visual supports and picture activity schedules

 Council for Exceptional Children

Content Standards for Beginning Teachers of Individuals with DD and/or Autism—Specialized materials for individuals with developmental disabilities (DD4K2) (also, DD4K1, DD4S1, ICC4S3, ICC4S4, ICC4S5).

Multimedia Activity Schedules:
Promoting Independence Among Children with Autism

BY JONATHAN W. KIMBALL AND ROBERT STROMER

Devon and two friends are playing with the train set in their preschool classroom. A timer suddenly beeps from across the room, and Devon scurries from the play center toward the sound. The beeping comes from a computer, and the monitor displays a photograph of Devon playing with a locomotive. Devon uses the mouse to click a large button in the corner of the screen and watches as a new photo appears, depicting the classroom's sand table. This photo also has a button. When he clicks it, Devon sees a 10-second video clip of one child inviting another to play at the sand table. A new photo appears showing Devon at the sand table with other children. Devon leaves the computer, approaches a peer, and says, "Come play." Together, the two children head toward the sand table.

In this vignette, Devon, a 4-year-old with autism, is using an activity schedule presented on a computer. Before learning to follow such a schedule, Devon had received intensive teacher instruction in a number of play skills: playing with trains and sand, building with blocks, playing a picture-matching memory game, and "cooking" on the toy stove.

Before learning to use an activity schedule, Devon, like many children with autism, would not spontaneously demonstrate even the skills he had mastered during guided practice. Instead, during free time he remained alone and engaged in repetitive, nonfunctional rituals known as stereotypy—for instance, rapidly flapping his hands or stacking Legos in a particular pattern—until an adult asked him to participate in one of the centers. In the vignette, however, adults are conspicuously absent.

ACTIVITY SCHEDULES AND ACTIVE KIDS

Part of a larger class of assistive technology known as visual supports, an activity schedule traditionally is a series of separate images—photos, icons, or words depicting activities a child can perform—presented in sequence in a notebook or on cards. Once a child like Devon can complete three or four activities in isolation, he may be ready to learn how to follow an activity schedule to perform these activities in a sequence. Activity schedules (not unlike day planners and smart phones used by adults) have an excellent track record in helping children

1. Click on Activity Photo

2. Look at Video

3. Look at Cue to Play

4. Initiate Activity

5. Do Activity

6. Put Materials Away

Robert Stromer

Devon's independence and social interactions with classmates have increased dramatically since he learned to use multimedia activity schedules.

with autism remain engaged in a sequence of activities, for extended periods of time, without adult prompting. Students with disabilities have successfully employed activity schedules

- for work tasks and leisure,
- at school or at home,
- for finite (a worksheet or a puzzle) or open-ended (reading or ball play) tasks, and
- in a group or alone.

Once children become competent with a schedule, they often can follow it when the images are rearranged or when new ones are substituted or added.

SOCIAL STORIES Learning to tolerate change and how and when to use communication and social interaction skills within the typical rules that govern social situations is a major challenge for many students with autism (Charlop-Christy, 2007). **Social stories** explain social situations and concepts, and the expected behaviors of the people involved, in a format understandable to an individual with ASD. Social stories can answer

TEACHING & LEARNING

An activity schedule essentially exchanges one form of prompting for another. But this is a distinction with a real difference: The child who has learned to employ a portable visual schedule no longer requires a teacher or a parent to tell her when to initiate one activity and when to move on to the next. Thus, a child who previously relied on adults for direction may become more self-directed. Beyond simply being a prompting mechanism, an activity schedule can be a significant means of building independence and self-determination.

Multimedia Activity Schedules. Children with autism have difficulty understanding or responding appropriately to complex stimuli such as spoken words or the human face. Research has shown, however, that these children attend very well to two-dimensional images such as what appears on television or computer monitors; in fact, Devon, like many children with autism, often watches videos and plays on computers to the exclusion of most other activities. If visual prompts such as those in activity schedules must be attended to in order to be effective, and if children with autism are naturally motivated to attend to computers, then it is reasonable to conclude that children with autism may readily learn to follow activity schedules presented via computer. Having brought activity schedules to the computer, it is a short step to bringing the audiovisual capabilities of computers to activity schedules.

The combination of these two technologies is greater than the sum of their parts. More than an expensive toy, the computer becomes a means of delivering instruction; more than a prompting system, the activity schedule becomes a context for embedding auditory and visual instructional material. In other words, once a child has acquired the skill of schedule following, she may then learn additional skills while following a multimedia schedule. The computer integrates two forms of instructional and assistive technology that have usually been researched and developed separately: activity schedules and video modeling (Bellini & Akullian, 2007; Nikopoulos & Keenan, 2004). Children with autism not only have learned to independently follow computer schedules but in doing so also have learned skills such as the following (Kimball, Kinney, Taylor, & Stromer, 2004):

- Sight-word reading
- Spelling
- Daily living skills
- Functional play routines

- Social-communication skills such as asking for help or, like Devon, seeking a playmate

Because lack of social skills is a defining feature of autism, Devon's accomplishment is truly significant. Importantly, once children have learned new skills while following computer activity schedules, they have retained those skills when the same pictures are presented in portable notebooks.

HOW TO GET STARTED

1. **Notebook schedules.** Lynn McClannahan and Patricia Krantz (2010) provide an excellent guide for developing and using notebook activity schedules. The closest thing to a manual for this type of technology, their book discusses prerequisite skills, preparing a first schedule, proceeding from teaching a child to follow a schedule to using schedules to foster social skills, and troubleshooting.

2. **Multimedia schedules.** Teaching with multimedia schedules requires a few more steps for teachers. Teachers should be comfortable with using Microsoft PowerPoint and Apple Keynote and with handling digital cameras and images. Step-by-step procedures for developing schedules in PowerPoint that include sounds, videos, and even built-in beeping timers like Devon's are detailed in Rehfeldt, Kinney, Root, and Stromer (2004). While multimedia schedules have the potential to capitalize on the naturally motivating properties of computers and video, children with autism also should be able to imitate actions from videos and use a computer mouse or touchscreen. Devon's teacher, using the steps outlined by McClannahan and Krantz, taught him his first activity schedule on a computer before he learned to complete the same activities following a notebook schedule. Now when Devon moves from one activity to the next in his schedule, a stranger might have difficulty distinguishing him from his typically developing classmates.

About the Author

Jonathan W. Kimball is a senior behavior analyst at Woodfords Family Services in Portland, Maine. Robert Stromer is a professor at the School of Social and Community Services, George Brown College, Toronto, Canada. They gratefully acknowledge the contributions of Elizabeth M. Kinney and Bridget A. Taylor to the development of multimedia activity schedules.

a child's questions about concepts and provide information about social behavior that she is not likely to ask for or obtain in other ways (Gray & Garand, 1993). Teachers and parents can use social stories to describe a situation and expected behaviors, explain simple steps for achieving certain goals or outcomes, and teach new routines and anticipated actions (Gray & Attwood, 2010). Providing social stories before an event or

TEACHING & LEARNING

activity can decrease a child's anxiety, improve his behavior, and help him understand the event from others' perspectives.

Social stories are written at the student's level of comprehension and usually contain four basic types of sentences written from the perspective of the student (Sansosti Powell-Smith, & Kincaid, 2004):

- *Descriptive sentences* identify the contextual variables of the target situation. Example: *I can't interrupt when others are having a conversation or are busy with something.*
- *Perspective sentences* describe the reactions and feelings of others about the situation. Example: *Interrupting makes people angry because you stop them from talking and they might forget what they were talking about.*
- *Directive sentences* describe the desired behavior with respect to a specific social cue or situation. Example: *If it's extremely important, I can tap the person on the shoulder and say excuse me, otherwise I must be patient and wait until they're finished.*
- *Affirmative sentences* express shared beliefs or reference a rule or law about the situation to reassure the individual. Example: *Everyone deserves to talk without being interrupted.*

(Examples adapted from Barry Morris [2011], "Social Stories," at http://www.autism-help.org/communication-social-stories-autism.htm.)

Social stories are usually constructed with one sentence per page. Photographs or line drawings depicting key information and important aspects of the events are sometimes added to illustrate the sentence on each page (see Figure 3). Comic book conversation is a modification of a social story that uses pictures, simple figures, and comic strip components such as speech bubbles instead of text (Glaeser, Pierson, & Fritschman, 2003; Rogers & Myles, 2001). Social stories containing self and peer video models can be presented via computers and smart boards (Sansosti & Powell-Smith, 2008; Xin & Sutman, 2011).

Several studies have reported improvements in children's behavior after systematic exposure to social stories. For example, Ivey, Heflin, and Alberto (2004) found that three 5- to 7-year-old boys with autism increased their independent and appropriate participation in novel activities when parents read social stories to the children once a day for 5 days before the events. However, the research base for social stories is limited, and the mechanisms for how social stories affect behavior are not fully understood. After reviewing 28 published studies on social stories, Test, Richter, Knight, and Spooner (2011) concluded that social stories could not currently be considered an evidence-based practice. Special education teachers are encouraged to provide accountability through the use of formative data collection to determine whether the practice is effective for individual students.

Sufficient positive outcomes have been attained with social story interventions to date, however, and the method should be considered a promising practice (Reynhout & Carter, 2006; Sansosti et al., 2004). Social stories may be most effective when part of a multicomponent intervention that includes other elements such as response prompts, feedback, reinforcement, and self-recording of desired behaviors (Sansosti & Powell-Smith, 2008; Scattone, Wilczynski, Edwards, & Rabian, 2002). For example, Crozier and Tincani (2005) found that a social story supplemented by occasional verbal prompts (e.g., "Remember to raise your hand when you want to talk to a teacher," p. 153) was more effective than the social story alone.

EDUCATIONAL PLACEMENT ALTERNATIVES

During the 2008–09 school year, approximately 36% of students with autism were educated in general education classrooms, with 18% served in resource room programs and 36% in separate classes (U.S. Department of Education, 2010d). About 10% of students with autism attended special schools or residential facilities.

FIGURE 3

SAMPLE SOCIAL STORY ABOUT WAITING IN THE LUNCH LINE AT THE
SCHOOL CAFETERIA WITH PICTURES ILLUSTRATING THE TEXT

At my school, students eat lunch in the cafeteria. p. 1

The cafeteria can be very crowded at lunch. p. 2

When I go to the cafeteria, I get my tray and stand at the end of the line. I stay in line and wait with everyone else to get my lunch. p. 3

When I have to wait I can think of other things. I can think of a song or my favorite book. p. 4

Soon it will be my turn and I can choose my lunch. p. 5

Waiting in line is hard but I try my best to wait calmly. Everyone feels good when people wait their turn. p. 6

Source: From Crozier, S., & Sileo, N. M. (2005). Encouraging positive behavior with social stories: An intervention for children with autism spectrum disorders. *Teaching Exceptional Children, 37*(6), p. 30. Used by permission.

General Education Classroom

Students with autism are increasingly placed in general education classrooms for the purpose of improved social integration. Under the right conditions, students with autism become "accepted, visible members" of peer groups (Boutot & Bryant, 2005). A strong argument for educating children with autism in inclusive settings is that socially competent children are an essential ingredient for peer-mediated interventions, an evidence-based practice for children with autism (Odom et al., 2010). Schwartz, Billingsley, and McBride (1998) described five strategies essential to providing effective education for young children with autism in inclusive classrooms (see Figure 4).

Javan's improving ability to participate in group activities is helping him benefit from the increasing amount of time he spends in the general education classroom.

Lori Whitley/Merrill

While some children who have received early intensive behavioral intervention (EIBI) make a smooth transition to public school classrooms, many others struggle mightily with the demands of a new and highly complex environment. Perhaps the biggest shock for a child with autism who has transitioned from an EIBI program to a public school classroom is going from being the star of the show with multiple adults focusing on meeting the child's individual needs from moment to moment to being part of a group of 25 or 30 students. As children move from kindergarten into the primary grades, meaningful progress in academics are added to social interaction. Lovaas (1994) found that children with autism doing well in first grade have a much greater chance of continued success in school than do those who struggle in the first grade.

I recently asked 41 autism experts—educators, clinicians, and researchers who together had more than 500 years of experience teaching children with ASD—to name the three or four most important skills needed by a student with ASD for success in the regular classroom (Heward, 2011). Their answers to this informal survey encompassed a wide range of challenges and issues, and included skills such as transitioning from one activity to another without fuss, being able to retain large amounts of auditory information, dealing with thin schedules of adult attention and reinforcement, and self-care skills such as toileting and eating. The collective wisdom of these experts, determined by tallying how many of them mentioned a given skill, is that success in the regular classroom for a student with ASD depends on the child's ability to reliably do the following:

Display near-zero levels of problem behavior	16
Participate and learn in group lessons	16
Complete assigned tasks independently (or with minimal teacher assistance)	15
Interact with peers appropriately	13
Comply with classroom rules/follow the teacher's directions	12
Get the teacher's attention/assistance appropriately	11

The classroom skills needed by a student with ASD are not fundamentally different from those expected of any student. Doing all of the above is a tall order for any child with autism, but an especially difficult challenge for children on the severe end of the autism spectrum. But there are good reasons for optimism. Early intervention programs are increasingly aware of teaching children how to participate effectively in

FIGURE 4 FIVE STRATEGIES FOR EFFECTIVE EDUCATION OF YOUNG CHILDREN WITH AUTISM IN INCLUSIVE CLASSROOMS

Teach Communication and Social Competence Without communication and social interactions among children, an inclusive program may provide little more than parallel instruction

- *Provide systematic instruction in imitation skills.* Imitation is critical to learning from and relating to others. Embed imitation training throughout the day—in small groups, opening circle, gym, and outdoor play.

- *Plan opportunities for students with disabilities to interact directly with typically developing peers.* For example, at opening circle, begin with a desirable toy such as a jar of bubbles and then help all children share the toy directly with other children instead of passing the toy from child to teacher to child.

Use Instructional Strategies That Maintain the Class's Natural Flow Instead of isolating children with disabilities to provide individualized instruction, teach within the context of developmentally appropriate activities and routines.

- *Use naturalistic teaching procedures.* Instruction should involve activities that are interesting to students, take advantage of child-initiated interactions, and use naturally occurring consequences.

- *Use different cues and prompts to ensure that each child receives adequate support.* Provide only what help is required so the children do not become dependent on teacher assistance.

Teach and Provide Opportunities for Independence While interdependence is appropriate and normal in human relationships, we expect children to become increasingly independent as they grow.

- *Give children choices whenever possible, and teach choice making when necessary.*

- *Picture schedules can help some children learn to follow the sequence and duration of daily activities.*

- *Because it is easy to overlook nonverbal children, give them frequent chances to respond to teacher initiations.*

- *Maintain high expectations for all children.* Celebrate small victories, and immediately "up the ante," all the while believing that the child has the ability to reach the next objective.

Build a Classroom Community That Includes All Children Classrooms should be learning communities where everyone makes a valuable contribution and has something to learn.

- *Use activities that will engage children with a large range of abilities.* Plan open-ended activities that use preferred materials, support many responses, and address strengths of children with disabilities.

- *Allow every child to have a turn and play a role.* For example, every child, including children with autism, can take a turn being in charge of handing out materials. This puts the children with disabilities on an equal footing with others in the group and requires them to be communicative partners with peers.

Promote Generalization and Maintenance of Skills Unless children demonstrate skills across a variety of situations and maintain them over time, they will have limited ability to participate meaningfully in inclusive environments.

- *Target skills that will be useful in each child's life.* Skills a child needs in many situations and those typically enjoyed by same-age children are likely to be generalized and maintained because they are frequently practiced and produce naturally reinforcing outcomes.

- *Use instructional prompts judiciously, and fade them rapidly.* To keep children from depending on adult assistance and direction, use the least directive and intrusive prompt that ensures successful skill performance. Fade the prompt as quickly as possible without disrupting performance.

- *Distribute learning trials naturally.* Capitalize on teaching opportunities that occur within natural school routines and activities.

- *Use common materials for instruction.* Teach with materials frequently found in preschools, child-care settings, and the homes of young children. Arrange for children to practice with these materials across many settings in the classroom.

Source: Adapted from Ilene S. Schwartz, Felix F. Billingsley, & Bonnie M. McBride, "Including Children With Autism in Inclusive Preschools: Strategies That Work." *Young Exceptional Children,* January 1998, 1, pages 19–26,

group lessons before they transition to classrooms (e.g., Charania, LeBlanc, Carr, & Gunby, 2010). Teachers' implementation of evidence-based practices for preventing challenging behavior and replacing it with adaptive responses (e.g., Dunlap et al., 2010; Thompson, 2009) are enabling many children with autism to spend increasing portions of the school day in inclusive classrooms.

Researchers have developed and continue to refine evidence-based practices that special and general education teachers can use to help children with ASD learn each of these skill areas (Odom et al., 2010). An advantage of many of these practices is that they can be applied with typically developing students in the class in addition to their use with the student with ASD. It is easier for a teacher to implement the same technique with the entire class than it is do "something special" for a student with disabilities while doing something different with the rest of the class. Improved student behavior and academic performance, especially if the teacher sees all or most students in the classroom benefiting, increases the likelihood of the teacher continuing to use the intervention.

Techniques that can be implemented with the entire class and that have been shown to help students with ASD learn the skills they need to be successful in general education classrooms include choral responding (Cihak et al., 2006) and response cards (Horn, 2010) for participating in group instruction; self-management (Southall & Gast, 2011) for completing assigned tasks and following rules and directions; collaborative learning activities such as classwide peer tutoring (Kamps et al., 1994) for interacting with appropriately with classmates; and teaching children how to recruit teacher attention/assistance (Alber & Heward, 2000). While more research is needed to refine and improve the effectiveness of all of these strategies, teachers can use these tools to help students with ASD.

Teaching & Learning features elsewhere in this text explain how to start using choral responding, response cards, and classwide peer tutoring, and how to teach children to self-monitor and recruit teacher attention.

Resource and Special Classrooms

The general education classroom is not the least restrictive environment for all students with ASD. Many children at the severe end of the autism spectrum are best served in a setting where they can receive a highly individualized program of intensive, specialized instruction focused on the social/communication, self-control, and independence skills necessary for maximal benefit from placement in a general education classroom. "To assign children with autism who do not possess those skills to the usual public school classroom is to assign them to regression" (Baer, 2005, p. 9).

Because instructional time is such a precious commodity for students with disabilities, it must be used wisely. For no group of children is this more true than it is for students with autism. Because the potential is high for significant improvements in functioning by children with autism who receive early intensive behaviorally based education and treatment, the phrase "make every minute count" is more than just a slogan. In addition to using words such as *intensive, specialized,* and *focused,* invoking the word *urgent* is not an exaggeration when describing the special education needed by children with autism. Many students with autism spend a portion of each school day in the general education classroom with same-age peers and part of the day in a resource room where they receive intensive, specialized instruction focused on their individualized education program (IEP) goals and objectives.

Instruction in a special class or resource room typically features a high frequency of instructional trials per minute; careful specification of and planning for transferring the control of students' responses from teacher-contrived antecedent and consequent stimuli to naturally occurring events; specific strategies for promoting the generalization of newly learned skills to the regular classroom, the community, and the home; continuous recording of data on each child's performance of targeted skills; and the daily review of those data as the basis for making curricular and instructional decisions.

Providing supplemental or booster lessons in the resource room using the same curriculum materials the students encounter in the general education classroom can enhance students' success with those materials in the regular classroom. A resource room can provide an effective setting in which to conduct small-group learning activities with typically developing peers from the regular classroom. The presence of general classroom peers while practicing and learning new skills, especially social and language skills, can make generalization to the regular classroom more natural and likely.

DISTINGUISHING UNPROVEN TREATMENTS FROM EVIDENCE-BASED PRACTICES

Evidence-based practices

Content Standards for Beginning Teachers of Individuals with DD and/or Autism—Professional and ethical practice (ICC9S13) (also, ICC9K4, ICC9S5).

While the popularity of unproven interventions has always been a problem in special education (Jacobson, Foxx, & Mulick, 2005a), the tremendous range of behavioral deficits, excesses, and peculiarities by which autism spectrum disorder is manifested has made autism especially fertile ground for the proliferation of treatments promising remediation or cure. The Interactive Autism Network (2011) reported that families were using 381 different autism treatments, and that children were receiving an average of 5 simultaneous treatments (one child received 56 concurrent treatments!). In another study, parents reported that their children with autism were receiving 7 simultaneous treatments (Green et al., 2006).

Many treatments claimed to help children with autism are backed by little or no scientific evidence (see Metz, Mulick, & Butter, 2005; Schreibman, 2005). Taking megadoses of vitamins and diet supplements, wearing weighted vests, receiving hormone injections, having one's skin brushed, and spending time in a room with colorful, flashing lights and soothing sounds are just some of the widely used autism treatments for which little or no credible research exists. Because educators need to understand this issue, we look at two examples of unproven treatments, facilitated communication and secretin therapy, that promised great outcomes and were used widely; identify several factors that contribute to the continued appearance and popularity of dubious interventions; and then suggest several resources that special educators and parents can consult for objective information.

To read one parent's perspectives on the anguish of trying to separate unsubstantiated claims from scientifically validated treatments for her two children, see *Current Issues and Future Trends,* "The Autism Wars."

Facilitated Communication

Facilitated communication (FC) is a process by which a communication partner, called a facilitator (most often a teacher; sometimes a friend or parent), provides physical support to assist an individual who cannot speak or whose speech is limited to typing on a keyboard or pointing at pictures, words, or other symbols on a communication board. Facilitated communication was developed in Australia for use with people with cerebral palsy (Crossley, 1988; Crossley & Remington-Guerney, 1992). It was brought to the United States and used primarily with people with autism and intellectual disabilities by Douglas Biklen, who claimed that individuals with autism and other severe disabilities can carry on typed conversations on complex topics such as current events and economics after training with FC.

Advocates reported that FC has produced dramatically more sophisticated language than the user can produce by speech, signing, or gestures (Biklen, 1990, Crossley, 1988), which led to speculations of an "undisclosed literacy" consistent with "normal intellectual functioning" by individuals previously thought to have severe or profound intellectual disabilities.

Facilitated communication produced tremendous interest and controversy, both in the professional literature and in the popular media. Claims of meaningful

CURRENT ISSUES AND

FUTURE TRENDS

▶ The Autism Wars

BY CATHERINE MAURICE

Many parents I know, as well as many researchers and clinicians, routinely use the phrase "the autism wars." We know what we're talking about, but people unfamiliar with the politics of autism diagnosis and treatment might not. Briefly, "the autism wars" refers to the fierce infighting and conflicting claims of individuals or groups, each of whom claims to know how best to treat children with autism and derides the theories and methods of the other camps. In an environment where funding is scarce, fear and passion run high, and children's futures are at stake, the autism wars can generate much rancor, to say nothing of confusion.

On Monday, for example, a parent may consult one doctor and be told to place her child in a therapeutic nursery. The doctor will tell the parent to avoid at all costs any program based on behavior analysis because such programs are manipulative, damaging, and tantamount to dog training. On Tuesday, the parent might be told that therapeutic nurseries have little impact on autistic behaviors and often reinforce such behaviors in spite of their warm and fuzzy talk about "nurturing the whole child" and "finding the hidden child within the autistic shell." On Wednesday, the parent is informed by another parent writing on the Internet that massive doses of vitamin B6 can produce meaningful language in the child or that an injection of secretin can have a positive effect on the symptoms of autism.

In the course of hearing or reading these recommendations, the parent learns that professionals are "not to be trusted" and that parents should always "trust their own instincts" and "follow their hearts" when it comes to selecting autism treatments. On Thursday, the same parent is advised to try "an eclectic approach: a little of this and a little of that." Finally, on Friday, the parent is told that there is not a whole lot that anyone can do for autism anyway, so why not come to a weekly support group to discuss "coping" and "feelings" with a coping facilitator?

For a parent of a newly diagnosed child or for a young person intending to teach students with autism, the barrage of conflicting messages can produce frustration, fear, and even despair. It is nothing short of outrageous that the organizations and individuals to whom parents and caregivers have turned for help have by and large failed to produce a set of clear, strong, discriminatory guidelines based on sound scientific principles as well as humanitarian concerns to lead people through the morass of so-called options for autism treatments.

Instead, many experts have tolerated, even encouraged, this time-consuming and expensive experimentation on our children—perhaps to remain popular with parents, who love anyone who gives them hope. But if my child is diagnosed with cancer, I could presumably go to a reputable cancer center and find out which treatments have solid empirical research behind them, which are still experimental, which are "alternative" (an unfortunate euphemism for "there are no scientific data supporting this treatment"), and which are known to cause harm. A reputable cancer treatment center would give me the objective information I needed to make a truly informed choice about my child's well-being. But with autism, bogus therapies have been allowed free rein. The situation is perhaps now beginning to change; but for far too long, too much money, time, and energy have been wasted on fads and "breakthroughs." Colleagues have estimated that more than 100 such miracle cures and "exciting new interventions" currently are being marketed to an extremely vulnerable population (Lockshin, Gillis, & Romanczyk, 2005).

I have had two children diagnosed with autism. The sudden loss of language, the increasingly odd and stereotypic behaviors, the avoidance of eye contact, the tantrums, the toe walking, the crying, the withdrawal into absence and staring—only a parent who has been through this can understand what it means to watch your child slip away into some foreign world, where she herself seems increasingly frustrated and frightened by her inability to communicate her most basic needs. When my daughter and then later my son received this terrifying diagnosis, many people, both professionals and parents, told me how "expert" they were in autism. I was told about their degrees, their far-flung reputations, and their personal experience. But few people had ever bothered to read, much less refer me to, published data in peer-reviewed, science-based journals. All was opinion; all was anecdote; all was theory.

Through the grace of God, I managed to stumble my way through many deviations, mistakes, and wrong turns until I found the program and the people who could truly help my children. Although I was told that applied behavior analysis was cold and harmful, that autism was lifelong, severe, and incurable, I managed somehow to hold onto a little flame of reason in the face of opinion and ideology. The research was there. The data were there. None of the other saviors and experts had anywhere close to the 30-year history of empirical evidence that the field of behavior analysis has accrued.

In 1995, both my daughter and my son were reevaluated (by the same people who first diagnosed them) and were found to have "no significant residua of autism." Throughout their school years, they have been enrolled in general education, without the need for any special services. My daughter, 18 years old, has just graduated from high school and will be attending a 4-year, selective liberal arts college. My son, age 16, has completed his sophomore year in high school, earning high honors for the year. And yes, they have friends; they have their own personalities and opinions about everything; and they know what it means to empathize with another, to feel another's joy or pain or fear.

No, recovery does not happen to all families who choose intensive behavioral intervention, and that truth cannot be stated often enough. There is still so much work to do in order to understand clearly what causes autism and how to prevent it, cure it, or help children recover from it. So far, only a minority of children who receive intensive early intervention are reaching a level of functioning where they are no longer considered autistic. I am glad that the National Alliance for Autism Research (NAAR) was founded to advance the search for a biological understanding of autism. I am glad that other groups, organizations, and research centers around the country are focusing more money and time on the biomedical side of autism. We need serious scholarship and research if we are ever to alleviate the symptoms of autism in every child who receives this diagnosis. One day, I know, such efforts will lead to treatments that may be more effective, less costly, and less labor-intensive than treatment based on applied behavior analysis (ABA).

However, as such research is going forward, let us not abandon the children who are alive today or leave them floundering in a sea of controversial alternative therapies. At the moment, it appears that ABA offers the best hope for progress. No, not all children will recover under intensive ABA, but virtually all children seem to make appreciable progress. Most develop some level of meaningful language, even if problems remain. Today, I know many families who delight in their children's ever-growing capacity to communicate verbally, to learn, and to love; and even as their children grow older, the learning never ceases.

Does that mean that I believe that ABA is the only current worthwhile treatment for autism? It is not a question of what I or anyone else believes. It is a question of what objective data exist to back up any treatment claim. The education and treatment of children with autism should be based on scientific research, on logic, on common sense, on ethics—not on belief. "Belief" is what has produced those scores of "exciting new breakthrough treatments" that you can find on the Internet. Today, more than ever, it is incumbent on all of us to turn to science—the hard science, not the pseudo-science that abounds in popular books, newsletters, and Internet chat rooms—for guidance on how to help children with autism. And for the sake of all our children, we should never just accept at face value what anyone tells us about research. We need to ask for that research, read it, and find out where it was published. Find out about relevant peer review, control groups, intake evaluations, outcome data, and independent confirmation of findings. Beware of self-published research or research that relies heavily on parent surveys.

One of the hallmarks of good research is finding every possible way to eliminate observer bias. A survey that parents fill out and submit over the Internet about what they think works or not, when so many families are combining three or more treatments at once, is not considered an objective piece of data; and it is irresponsible for anyone to publish the results of such surveys as research. In the history of autism, many bogus treatments have been rushed to market before demonstrating anywhere near enough evidence of their safety and effectiveness. The profiteers are not going to voluntarily curb their behavior. As long as parents are willing to pay thousands of dollars for snake oil, people will sell them snake oil. Only consumers can decide whether or not to keep the purveyors of such marginal treatments in business. It is up to all of us to bring the same kind of critical thinking to autism treatments as we would, at the very least, to the purchase of a used car.

Reason and tenderness can walk hand in hand. Judgment, intelligence, compassion, and mercy all have their place in autism treatment. We parents love our children. That's a given. We owe it to them to separate profiteering from progress, sense from nonsense, hope from hype.

WHAT DO YOU THINK?

1. If a child or family member of yours was diagnosed with autism, how would you find the most effective treatment and support?
2. What reasons might account for strong opinions held by some educators against the use of intensive behavioral intervention for educating children with autism?
3. Do you think parents of children with autism may be more vulnerable or inclined to use unproven treatments than parents of children with other disabilities? Why or why not?

About the Author

Catherine Maurice holds a Ph.D. in French literature and literary criticism from New York University. She is the author of *Let Me Hear Your Voice; A Family's Triumph over Autism* (Knopf, 1993), published in multiple languages throughout the world, and the principal editor of two books on research-based interventions for autism: *Behavioral Intervention for Young Children with Autism: A Manual for Parents and Professionals* (Maurice, Green, & Luce, 1996) and *Making a Difference: Behavioral Intervention for Autism* (Maurice, Green, & Foxx, 2001). She is a founding member of the Association for Science in Autism Treatment and continues to serve on its advisory board. In 2001, *Psychology Today* named her the recipient of its Mental Health Award.

and extensive communication and vocabulary use by individuals with autism or intellectual disabilities whose use of language had previously been nonexistent or extremely limited generated understandable excitement that a powerful and widely effective new treatment might have been discovered. Even though little or no scientific evidence supported these claims, FC was soon being widely implemented in special education and adult human services programs serving individuals with disabilities. During the 1990s, many state education and developmental disability agencies and school districts hired FC experts and sent their teachers to be trained in the new technique. Many children and adults with disabilities were "facilitated" on a daily basis. All of this was done in the absence of any rigorous, scientific evaluation of FC.

Although some educators and many parents raised questions from the beginning about the efficacy and appropriateness of FC, asking for data supporting its use, many more were too excited about the promises of this new wonder therapy to ask many questions. But as the uniformly negative results of carefully controlled empirical studies on FC accumulated (e.g., Oswald, 1994; Simpson & Myles, 1995; Wheeler, Jacobson, Paglieri, & Schwartz, 1993), more began to question its use. Research designed to validate FC has repeatedly demonstrated either facilitator influence (correct or meaningful language is produced only when the facilitator "knows" what should be communicated) or no unexpected language competence compared with the participants' measured IQ or a standard language assessment (for a review, see Jacobson, Foxx, & Mulick, 2005b).

In the light of the overwhelming scientific evidence showing that the communication attributed to individuals with severe disabilities during FC was influenced by the facilitator (Rimland, 1993), several prominent professional organizations passed resolutions or position statements cautioning that FC is unproven and that no important decisions should be made regarding a student's or client's life that are based on the process unless authorship can be confirmed (e.g., American Association on Mental Retardation, 1994; American Psychological Association, 1994). Additional studies since the mid-1990s have failed to produce any credible scientific support for FC, and have produced a great deal of evidence against it (Mostert, 2001, 2010). Nevertheless, advocates still promote the use of FC (often now calling it *supported typing*), and it is used in various schools and programs serving children with autism and other developmental disabilities (e.g., Biklen, 2005; Institute on Communication and Inclusion at Syracuse University, 2011).

Secretin Therapy

Secretin therapy is a good example of how a systematic line of carefully controlled experiments can help separate fact from fiction and hype from legitimate hope. Secretin is an amino acid hormone released within the proximal duodenum in response to gastric acid secretion. Horvath and colleagues (1998) reported improvements in function in three children with autism who were experiencing gastrointestinal problems and had received intravenous infusions of purified porcine secretin to assess their pancreatic functioning. This report was followed by an explosion of interest in secretin as a treatment for autism, with multiple Internet sites devoted to its use and availability. However, numerous highly controlled studies employing **double-blind, placebo-controlled** studies have found no significant differences on any measure of language, behavior, or autism symptom severity after treatment with secretin compared to treatment with a placebo (e.g., Coniglio et al., 2001; Coplan et al., 2003; Dunn-Geier et al., 2000; Molloy et al., 2002).

Another study reported that children with autism with chronic, active diarrhea exhibited a reduction in aberrant behavior when treated with secretin but that problem behaviors of children with autism/PDD who did not have gastrointestinal problems were unaffected by the treatment (Kern, Miller, Evans, & Trivedi, 2002). If discomfort from gastrointestinal problems is a causal factor for some of a child's problem behaviors and secretin relieves that discomfort, it is possible that secretin therapy is correlated with a reduction in problem behavior in such children—but not because it is related to autism. Williams, Wray, and Wheeler (2009) reviewed 13 randomized control trial studies comparing secretin with a placebo treatment and found "no evidence that single or multiple dose intravenous secretin is effective" and concluded that it "should not currently be recommended or administered as a treatment for autism" (p. 2).

Children with autism need and deserve an education derived from scientific research, not unproven treatments and fads.

Lori Whitley/Merrill

Why Are Unproven Autism Treatments So Widely Used?

Unproven treatment fads for children with autism thrive

- when the available treatments are not producing cures for the majority of those treated;
- when the underlying cause of a disorder is unknown or mysterious;
- because hope and need are far stronger motivators than reason or skepticism;
- when we lean too much on the authority, fame, or niceness of those promoting the fads;
- because often, neither parents nor the professionals they consult understand what constitutes credible evidence. (adapted from Maurice, 2004)

Parents and teachers of children with autism are easy targets for interventions that promise cures. As many authors and families have noted, who among us, parent or teacher, wouldn't look for anything that might help (Maurice & Taylor, 2005; Zane, 2011)?

> On the Internet, and in huge conferences, parents are encouraged to mix up chemical cocktails for their children, to put them on radical diets, to subject them to hours of brushing and stroking, even to inject them with unproven substances. Often, the promoters of these fads encourage parents to submit testimonials, and these testimonials are then published as "research." (Maurice, 2004, n.p.)

Educators are equally susceptible, often gullibly so, to testimonials, advertised promises, and pseudoscientific "evidence" (Kauffman, 2011; Stephenson & Carter, 2011). And instead of using legitimate measures of learning to evaluate a curriculum or instructional method, some programs consider staff and students reports of "having fun" a measure of success (Downs & Downs, 2010). Schools and programs that adopt unproven autism treatments not only risk wasting financial resources and encouraging parents to cling to unrealistic expectations based on claims made for those treatments, but also risk slowing, or even harming, students' progress (Zane, Davis, & Rosswurm, 2008).

How can professionals discriminate innovative interventions for autism that hold promise for effectiveness from those based on exaggerated claims, fads, ideology, and pseudoscience? By staying abreast of developments in autism treatment research from credible sources that base their conclusions and recommendations on peer-reviewed science and that have no ideological bent or financial interest favoring a particular treatment or approach. Organizations such as the American Academy of Pediatrics (Myers et al., 2007), the National Professional Development Center on Autism Spectrum Disorders (http://autismpdc.fpg.unc.edu/), the Association for Science in Autism Treatment (http://www.asatonline.org), and the Interactive Autism Network (http://www.iancommunity.org) are sources of reliable information.

The knowledgeable selection of an evidence-based treatment from those that are fashionable and false is a necessary but insufficient step in providing the most effective education for children with autism. A poorly implemented treatment, no matter how much research supports it, is unlikely be very effective. Teachers should learn as much as they can about a new instructional practice and then implement it with as much professional care and fidelity as possible. Finally, and perhaps most important, regardless of the source and amount of research supporting a particular practice, teachers should collect direct and frequent measures of student learning to evaluate its effects on their students.

Children with autism spectrum disorders deserve nothing less.

▼ TIPS FOR BEGINNING TEACHERS

Working with Students with Autism Spectrum Disorders

BY KAZUKO YAMAMOTO AND BETH MUENINGHOFF

INDIVIDUALIZE TO THE MAX

For students with autism, the need to individualize cannot be overstated.

- **Each student will have many more learning needs than you can meet.** You will not be able to teach everything at once, or even everything—ever. Observe each child during academic, social, and other routines during the school day, and ask yourself which skills will be immediately useful and have the greatest positive impact on her daily life.
- **Careful observation often reveals effective reinforcers.** Many children with autism have their own unique special interests, and often they seem content in their own world as long as they have what they want. Some autistic children appear to lack a desire to reach out to the world outside. We often use their autism to work for us in teaching important skills to our children. For example, if John has a fixation for wheels, we can use cars and other toys with wheels to teach him to make a request using a sign or a picture card.

FOCUS ON TEACHING SKILLS, NOT DECREASING BEHAVIORS

Some students with autism have frequent tantrums, are aggressive toward others, make stereotypic movements, or engage in self-injurious behaviors. Children with autism, like all children, may engage in challenging and harmful behaviors because they have not learned appropriate ways in which to meet their needs.

- **Instead of telling a student what not to do, teach him what to do.** Interventions that focus solely on reducing the frequency of negative behaviors are often ineffective and shortsighted because they do not teach the children alternative, appropriate ways to control their world. If a student grabs a book from another student, explain that the student should ask for the book, model the appropriate behavior and then have the student imitate it.
- **Try to determine what function a negative behavior has for a student.** For example, when James throws a tantrum, is he usually involved in a difficult task or an undesirable activity? After you have discovered this function, then teach an appropriate replacement behavior (e.g., teach James how to signal or ask for a break from a task).

TAKE ADVANTAGE OF TEACHABLE MOMENTS

Naturally occurring situations or events provide the opportunity to teach a lesson on the spot.

- **Always be on the lookout for teachable moments.** A child spilling his milk during snack time, for example, provides his teacher with a wonderful chance to prompt and instruct a variety of language, emotional, communication, and social skills—in addition to the real-world practice of motor, self-help, and vocational skills involved in cleaning up the mess!
- **Don't just wait for teachable moments to occur; contrive them.** During a snack or play activity, hide the juice or part of a toy so that the child has to communicate to obtain the desired item.

COMMUNICATE AND CELEBRATE WITH PARENTS

We both use home–school communication journals to inform parents of how their children did at school. Kazuko also sends home a daily activity sheet to encourage socialization as well as communication between parent and child.

- **Home–school dialogue journal.** This notebook goes back and forth between home and school. At the beginning of a school year, make a daily entry to inform parents about their child's school day. As the school year progresses, make entries on an as-needed basis. The parents also write in the journal to bring whatever they feel is important to the teacher's attention. It is also a good way to celebrate together even the tiniest progress a child makes at home or school. The notebook can also be sent via e-mail.

- **Daily home–school report with picture symbols.** Kazuko's daily activity sheet consists of numerous picture symbols representing activities at school. Circle the activities the students enjoyed at school such as speech, cooking, and art. Also write a word or two to give parents more details for each activity, for example, circle "cooking" and write "We made red Jell-O" next to it. Ask the parents to go over the sheet and talk about what happened at school with their child. The pictures help the children "talk about" what they did at school with their parent. It is also informative for the parents, because the report includes information such as their child's behavior, activities, and supplies that need to be sent to school.

- **Celebrate accomplishments.** Each time a student moves another step toward reaching your high expectations for success, celebrate that achievement with the student and his family.

▼ KEY TERMS AND CONCEPTS

applied behavior analysis (ABA)
Asperger syndrome
autism spectrum disorder
autistic disorder
behavior traps
childhood disintegrative disorder
discrete trial training (DTT)
double-blind, placebo-controlled
echolalia
facilitated communication (FC)

joint attention
pervasive developmental
    disorder not otherwise
    specified (PDD-NOS)
pica
savant syndrome
social stories
stereotypy

▼ SUMMARY

Definitions

- Autism spectrum disorder (ASD) is a group of related neurodevelopmental disorders of childhood marked by persistent deficits in social communication and interaction, and by restricted, repetitive patterns of behavior and interests.
- Autistic disorder is marked by three defining features, with onset before age 3 years: (a) qualitative impairment of social interaction; (b) qualitative impairment of communication; and (c) restricted, repetitive, and stereotyped patterns of behavior, interests, and activities.
- Asperger syndrome is marked by impairments in all social areas, particularly an inability to understand how to interact socially. Children with Asperger syndrome do not have general language delay, and most have average or above-average intelligence.
- Childhood disintegrative disorder shares characteristics with autistic disorder, but the condition does not begin until after age 2 and sometimes not until age 10.
- Pervasive developmental disorder not otherwise specified (PDD-NOS) is the diagnosis given to children who meet some, but not all, of the criteria for autistic disorder. PDD-NOS is marked by significant impairments in socialization with difficulties in either communication or restricted interests.

Characteristics

- Some children with ASD are severely affected in most or all domains of functioning, while others are only mildly affected.
- Impaired social interactions include difficulty in perceiving the emotional state of others, expressing emotions, and forming attachments and relationships, as well as deficits in joint attention (e.g., not looking at what a parent points to).
- Many children with ASD do not speak. Echolalia is common among those who do talk.
- Children with ASD tend to exhibit concrete or literal processing of verbal information and have difficulty understanding the social meanings of language.
- A diagnosis of ASD can be made for a child with severe or profound intellectual disabilities as well as for one who is intellectually gifted.

- Many children with ASD exhibit the following cognitive and learning characteristics:
  - Overselectivity—the tendency to focus on a minute feature of an object or a person rather than the whole
  - Obsessive attention on a specific object or activity for long periods of time
  - Strong aptitude for rote memory for certain things but difficulty recalling recent events
  - Uneven skill development—areas of relatively superior performance that are unexpected compared to other domains of functioning
  - Very rarely, autism savant syndrome—an extraordinary ability in a specific area or skill while functioning at the intellectual disabilities level in all other areas
  - Unusual responsiveness to sensory stimuli: overresponsiveness (hypersensitivity)—for example, intense dislike of certain sounds, being touched, or the feel of certain textures—and/or underresponsiveness (hyposensitivity)—for example, no reaction to stimuli that are painful to most people.
  - Obsess about having everything in their environment stay the same and become very upset when items are moved or when routines change.
  - Stereotypic and self-stimulatory behaviors, such as rocking their bodies when in a sitting position, twirling around, flapping hands, flicking fingers, or spinning things.
  - Aggressive and self-injurious behavior.
- Some people with autism spectrum disorders have described positive aspects of their disability, such as sensitivity to detail and intense interest in topics, which can be assets to functioning in some environments.

Prevalence

- Although once considered a rare disorder, recent studies show that autism occurs in about 1% of all children.
- Boys are affected about four to five times more often than are girls.
- Reasons for the dramatic increase in the incidence of ASD are not clear but may include greater awareness of the disability, more widespread screening and better assessment procedures, greater availability of services via the disability category, and an actual increase in the true incidence of the disability.

Causes

- For many years, it was widely thought that parents who were indifferent to the emotional needs of their children caused autism. However, no causal link between parental personality and autism has been ever discovered.
- Recent research shows a clear biological origin for autism in the form of abnormal brain development, structure, and/or neurochemistry.
- Some experts believe that certain genes may make a child more susceptible to autism but that exposure to certain environmental factors may lead to the development of the disorder in some individuals.

Identification and Assessment

- No medical test for autism spectrum disorders is available; a diagnosis is most often made according to criteria in the DSM.
- Autism can be reliably diagnosed at 18 months of age, with research currently developing methods for diagnosis by the child's first birthday.
- Screening babies for early warning signs of autism is critical because early diagnosis is correlated with dramatically better outcomes.
- Signs that warrant concern during the first 18 months of life include lack of pointing or gestures, infrequent or poor imitation, no single words by 16 months, lack of smiling, not responding to name, lack of joint attention, and loss of previously acquired language or social skills.

Educational Approaches

- Children with autism are among the most difficult to teach of all students; they require carefully planned, meticulously delivered, and continually evaluated and analyzed instruction.
- Although the prognosis for children with autistic disorder was traditionally extremely poor, early intensive behaviorally based education and treatment has helped some children achieve communication, language, and social skills so they can succeed in general education classrooms.
- Among the many treatments and therapies available for helping children with autism, interventions based on applied behavior analysis (ABA) have the clearest and most consistent research evidence supporting their effectiveness.
- Discrete trial training (DTT) is an important part of ABA-based programming for children with autism. However, DTT alone does not constitute ABA, and ABA can be done without DTT.
- ABA programming uses a variety of procedures to help individuals with autism acquire and generalize new skills, such as strategies for shifting stimulus control, the Picture Exchange Communication System (PECS), peer-mediated interventions, functional assessment, and naturalistic teaching strategies, to name a few.
- Picture activity schedules—a series of images, photos, icons, or video clips depicting activities a child can perform, presented in sequence—can help children with autism independently select and carry out a sequence of activities in the classroom.
- Social stories, which explain social situations and the expected behaviors of the people involved in a format understandable to a student with ASD, can decrease a child's anxiety about an event, improve his behavior, and help him understand events from the perspective of others.

Educational Placement Alternatives

- Approximately 36% of students with ASD are educated in general education classrooms, 18% in resource rooms, 36% in separate classrooms, and 10% in special schools or residential facilities.
- Strategies for providing effective education for young children with ASD in inclusive classrooms include
  - teaching communication and social competence;
  - using instructional strategies that maintain the class's natural flow;
  - teaching and providing opportunities for independence;
  - building a classroom community that includes all children; and
  - promoting the generalization and maintenance of skills.
- According to one group of autism experts, success in the regular classroom for a student with ASD depends on the child's ability to
  - display near-zero levels of problem behavior,
  - participate and learn in group lessons,
  - complete assigned tasks independently (or with minimal teacher assistance),
  - interact with peers appropriately,
  - comply with classroom rules/follow the teacher's directions, and
  - get the teacher's attention/assistance appropriately.

- Instruction in a resource room or other specialized setting should feature a high frequency of instructional trials, procedures for transferring control of student responses from teacher-contrived events to naturally occurring events, strategies for promoting the generalization and maintenance of newly learned skills, and daily review of data on each child's performance for making curricular and instructional decisions.
- Regardless of the setting in which a child with ASD is served, the presence of socially competent children is helpful because peer-mediated interventions are among the most effective types of interventions for teaching communication and social skills to children with ASD.
- Whatever the child's educational placement, parent involvement and consistency between home and school are critical components for optimal learning.

Distinguishing Unproven Interventions from Evidence-Based Practices

- Most of the many treatments that promise to cure or relieve the symptoms of autism are based on little or no scientific evidence.
- Many children with autism receive unproven treatments at home and at school.
- Autism treatments should be chosen based on a review of the scientific evidence for their effectiveness, implemented with fidelity, and evaluated by direct and frequent measures of student learning.

MyEducationLab™

Go to Topic 14, Autism, in the MyEducationLab (www.myeducationlab.com) for *Exceptional Children*, where you can

- Find learning outcomes for autism along with the national standards that connect to these outcomes.
- Complete Assignments and Activities that can help you more deeply understand the chapter content.
- Apply and practice your understanding of the core teaching skills identified in the chapter with the Building Teaching Skills and Dispositions learning units.
- Examine challenging situations and cases presented in the IRIS Center Resources.
- Access video clips of CCSSO National Teachers of the Year award winners responding to the question "Why Do I Teach?" in the Teacher Talk section.
- Check your comprehension of the content covered in the chapter with the Study Plan. Here you will be able to take a chapter quiz, receive feedback on your answers, and then access Review, Practice, and Enrichment activities to enhance your understanding of chapter content.
- Use the Online Lesson Plan Builder to practice lesson planning and integrating national and state standards into your planning.

▼ GLOSSARY

applied behavior analysis (ABA): "The science in which tactics derived from the principles of behavior are applied systematically to improve socially significant behavior and experimentation is used to identify the variables responsible for behavior change" (Cooper, Heron, & Heward, 2007, p. 20).

Asperger syndrome: A developmental disorder characterized by normal

cognitive and language development with impairments in all social areas, repetitive and stereotypic behaviors, preoccupation with atypical activities or items, pedantic speech patterns, and motor clumsiness; included in *autism spectrum disorders*.

autism spectrum disorders: Group of five related developmental disorders that share common core deficits or difficulties in social relationships, communication, and

ritualistic behaviors; differentiated from one another primarily by the age of onset and severity of various symptoms; includes autistic disorder, Asperger syndrome, Rett syndrome, childhood disintegrative disorder, and pervasive developmental disorder not otherwise specified (PDD-NOS).

autistic disorder: A pervasive developmental disorder marked by three defining features with onset before age 3: (a) impairment of social interaction; (b) impairment of communication; and (c) restricted, repetitive, and stereotypic patterns of behavior, interests, and activities.

behavior trap: An interrelated set of contingencies of reinforcement that can be especially powerful, producing substantial and long-lasting behavior changes. Effective behavior traps include four essential features: (a) They are "baited" with virtually irresistible reinforcers that "lure" the student to the trap; (b) only a low-effort response already in the student's repertoire is necessary to enter the trap; (c) once inside the trap, the student is motivated by interrelated contingencies of reinforcement to acquire, extend, and maintain targeted academic and/or social skills; and (d) they can remain effective for a long time because students show few, if any, satiation effects (see Cooper, Heron, & Heward, 2007, p. 691).

childhood disintegrative disorder: Shares behavioral characteristics with autistic disorder, but does not begin until after age 2 and sometimes not until age 10; medical complications are common; one type of autism spectrum disorder.

discrete trial training: An instructional format involving a series of three-part trials: (a) an antecedent stimulus (e.g., flashcard with "2 + 2 = ?"), (b) student response (e.g., "four"), and (c) feedback (reinforcement for a correct response; ignoring or correcting an incorrect response; and providing a response prompt or ignoring nonresponses).

double-blind, placebo-controlled study: A procedure used to control for expectancy effects by subjects and bias by researchers in studies evaluating the effects of a treatment or intervention. Some subjects receive the actual treatment being tested; others receive a placebo (fake) designed to appear like the actual treatment; subjects do not know whether they are receiving the real treatment or a placebo (they are "blind"); the researchers do not know which subjects received the treatment (making it a "double-blind" experiment).

echolalia: The repetition of what other people have said as if echoing them; characteristic of some children with delayed development, autism, and communication disorders.

facilitated communication (FC): A type of augmentative communication in which a "facilitator" provides assistance to someone in typing or pointing to vocabulary symbols; typically involves an alphanumeric keyboard on which the user types out a message one letter at a time. To date, research designed to validate FC has repeatedly demonstrated either facilitator influence (correct or meaningful language is produced only when the facilitator "knows" what should be communicated) or no unexpected language competence compared to the participants' measured IQ on a standard language assessment.

joint attention: A social communication skill in which two people interact with their shared environment in the same frame of reference. Joint attention is evident when a child looks where someone else is looking or turns head or eyes in the direction someone is pointing.

pervasive developmental disorders—not otherwise specified (PDD-NOS): Children who meet some but not all of the criteria for autistic disorder are often diagnosed as having PDD-NOS; included in the autism spectrum disorders.

pica: A form of self-injurious behavior in which the person ingests nonnutritive substances (e.g., dirt, rocks, sticks, plastic, string, feces); exhibited by some people with moderate and severe mental retardation.

savant syndrome: Extraordinary ability or knowledge in a particular area (e.g., memorization, mathematical calculations, drawing, music) while functioning at the intellectually disabled level in all other areas.

social stories: An intervention for teaching social skills that uses individualized stories usually constructed with one sentence per page accompanied by photographs or simple line drawings depicting a social situation from the viewpoint of the student. Often used with children with autism spectrum disorders to decrease anxiety about the situation, help the child learn relevant social cues and the expected behaviors, explain how to behave to achieve desired outcomes from the situation, and help understand the event from the perspective of others.

stereotypy: Repetitive, nonfunctional movements (e.g., hand flapping, rocking).

Communication Disorders

From Chapter 8 of *Exceptional Children* and *An Introduction to Special Education*, Tenth Edition. William L. Heward.

Communication Disorders

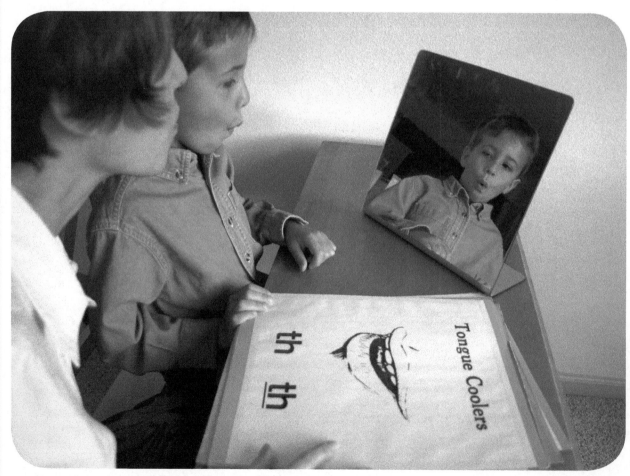

© Christina Kennedy/PhotoEdit

▶ FOCUS QUESTIONS

- How are speech and language impairments related to one another and to typical language development?
- What types of communication disorders might statements such as "The dogs runned home" and "That foop is dood" signal?
- How are causes of speech and language impairments classified?
- What are the major components of a comprehensive evaluation to detect the presence and extent of a communication disorder?

- What are the basic goals and common elements of effective interventions for speech-sound errors? For language disorders?
- What is augmentative and alternative communication (AAC), and who can it help?
- How does the role of the speech-language pathologist change as a function of the setting in which a child with communication disorders is served?

▼ FEATURED TEACHER

STEVEN EVERLING

Northwest Elementary School • Pinellas County School District, Largo, Florida

EDUCATION—TEACHING CREDENTIALS— EXPERIENCE

- B.A., communication sciences and disorders, University of South Florida, 1995
- M.S., speech-language pathology, University of South Florida, 2000
- Florida, speech and language impaired, K–12; Florida, exceptional student education, K–12; Florida, prekindergarten/primary education, age 3– grade 3; Florida, licensure as a speech-language pathologist; certificate of clinical competence in speech-language pathology from the American Speech-Language-Hearing Association
- 16 years of experience as a speech-language pathologist

CURRENT TEACHING POSITION AND STUDENTS

I've been a speech-language pathologist in the Pinellas County Schools for 16 years. My first 4 years were in a middle school. For 3 years I taught the entire academic curriculum—language arts, reading, math, science, and social studies—in a self-contained classroom for students with severe language impairments. The emphasis was on promoting language development across the curriculum. The next

year, I taught language arts to students who were in the language-impaired resource program and provided pull-out speech therapy services to students with impairments of articulation, voice, and fluency. For the past 11 years, I have delivered speech and language services in both a resource room and an inclusion setting at Northwest Elementary, a K–5 building with about 700 students.

The 50 students I'm serving this year are 3 to 12 years old in grades preK–5, and classified as speech and/or language impaired. Some of my students also receive special education services because of developmental delay, learning disability, or emotional disturbance.

Intervention for children with language needs must be specific to the individual child. In general, I have found that many children with language disabilities have significant problems making inferences in both the oral and print domains. For example, Brian, an 11-year-old with specific learning disabilities and language impairments, could not organize the structure of a storybook. Brian's special education teacher and I collaborated on teaching him several ways to organize text-based information. These strategies included story search procedures to find important information and story maps and other graphic organizers to arrange key information so that he could make reasonable inferences. I help students with articulation, voice, or fluency problems develop techniques and strategies that enable them to communicate more effectively in their everyday school and home environments.

COLLABORATION AND TEAMING I work and interact with several different professionals daily. I collaborate with general education and special education teachers to help them become aware of the unique communication needs of students with speech and/or language impairments. I also explain and demonstrate techniques they can use to facilitate language learning and assist in the generalization of skills and strategies the students have learned in speech and language therapy. The school psychologist and I talk frequently because the speech and language assessments I administer are often a component of the multifactored assessment conducted whenever a student is referred for an evaluation. On occasion, I interact with the occupational and physical therapists on ways we can assist each other with skill carryover for students.

WHAT I LIKE MOST ABOUT BEING A SPECIAL EDUCATOR There are two things I like most about being a special educator. First, I enjoy working with a variety of students, each of whom presents a unique set of speech and/or language needs. From the student who stutters, to the student who exhibits speech-sound errors, to the student who has difficulties with language-based concepts, finding effective strategies for communicative success is always rewarding. Second, I appreciate collaborating with other educators and school personnel who share a similar desire to help students achieve their potential.

ADVICE TO SOMEONE CONSIDERING A CAREER IN SPECIAL EDUCATION My main advice for anyone considering a career in special education is first and foremost to set high, yet realistic, expectations for students in both academics and behavior. In my experience, students generally strive to reach the standards expected of them. Second, it is important to be flexible, because each day you'll be confronted with new situations and challenges. Third, open communication with parents can make

all the difference. Involving parents in their child's education encourages appropriate student behavior and increases the likelihood that the skills you are teaching in the classroom will be practiced and reinforced at home.

THE MOST DIFFICULT THING ABOUT BEING A SPECIAL EDUCATOR The hardest thing about this job is finding time to get everything accomplished: student instruction, lesson planning, individualized education programs (IEPs) and related paperwork, parent contacts, schoolwide faculty duties and responsibilities, to name just a few. However, I have found that the longer I work in the school system, the more efficiently and effectively I can manage the multiple responsibilities of a special educator's typical school day.

MOST MEANINGFUL ACCOMPLISHMENTS AS A SPECIAL EDUCATOR My most meaningful accomplishments occur when my students improve in their ability to be effective communicators. For example, John, a first grader who was receiving services for both specific learning disabilities and speech impairments, had such a severe phonological impairment that his speech was nearly impossible to understand. John produced most speech sounds in the front of his mouth while omitting sounds at the end of words, which made his speech unintelligible to most listeners. For example, toward the end of our first therapy session, when John said, "Ti to toe," I had to ask him to repeat himself several times before I realized he was trying to say, "Time to go." All of John's utterances exhibited similar speech patterns. Over the course of his first- and second-grade years, I saw John 2 hours per week for speech therapy. At the beginning of his first-grade year, his reluctance to speak was a clear effect of his not being understood by his parents, teachers, and friends. One can imagine John's frustration: always being asked to repeat himself and then still not being understood. By the end of John's second-grade year, his speech, while still noticeably in error, was for the vast majority of utterances intelligible to those with whom he most commonly interacted. By that time, John had become a much more verbal and assertive child as a result, at least partially, of his now being able to more effectively communicate with others. Students like John make my responsibilities as a speech-language pathologist real and meaningful.

COMMUNICATION—THE SENDING AND RECEIVING OF INFORMATION—is such a fundamental part of the human experience that we cannot stop communicating even when we want to. You may decide to say nothing, but sometimes saying nothing communicates a great deal. Still, imagine trying to go through an entire day without speaking. How would you make contact with other people? You would be frustrated when others did not understand your needs and feelings. By the end of the day, besides feeling exhausted from trying to make yourself understood, you might even start to question your ability to function adequately in the world.

Although relatively few people with communication disorders are completely unable to express themselves, an exercise like the one just described would increase your awareness of some of the problems and frustrations faced every day by children and adults who cannot communicate effectively. Children who cannot express their desires, thoughts, and feelings are virtually certain to encounter difficulties in their schools and communities. When communication disorders persist, it may be hard for children to learn and develop and to form satisfying relationships with other people.

MyEducationLab

Visit the **MyEducationLab** for *Exceptional Children* to enhance your understanding of chapter concepts with a personalized Study Plan. You'll also have the opportunity to hone your teaching skills through video- and case-based Assignments and Activities, IRIS Center Resources, and Building Teaching Skills and Dispositions lessons.

DEFINITIONS

Before we define communication disorders, a discussion of some basic terms is necessary.

Communication

Communication is the interactive exchange of information, ideas, feelings, needs, and desires. Each communication interaction includes three elements: (a) a message, (b) a sender who expresses the message, and (c) a receiver who responds to the message. Although communication most often involves at least two participants, each playing the dual roles of speaker and listener, intraindividual communication occurs when the same person is both sender and receiver of the same message (e.g., when we talk to ourselves or write a note to remind ourselves to do something when we read it later). In addition to enabling some degree of control in a social environment, communication serves several important functions, particularly between teachers and children.

NARRATING   Children need to be able to tell (and follow the telling of) a story—a sequence of related events connected in an orderly, clear, and interesting manner. Five-year-old Cindy tells her teacher, "I had a birthday party. I wore a funny hat. Daddy made a cake, and Mommy took pictures." Fourteen-year-old Ian tells the class about the events leading up to Christopher Columbus's first voyage to America.

EXPLAINING/INFORMING   Teachers expect children to interpret the explanations of others in speech and writing and to put what they understand into words so that their listeners or readers will be able to understand it, too. In a typical classroom, children must frequently respond to teachers' questions: "Which number is larger?" "How do you suppose the story will end?" "Why do you think George Washington was a great president?"

REQUESTING   Children are expected to communicate their wishes and desires to others in socially appropriate ways. A child who has learned to state requests clearly and politely is more likely to get what she wants and less likely to engage in inappropriate behavior to communicate her needs.

EXPRESSING   It is important for children to express their personal feelings and opinions and to respond to the feelings of others. Speech and language can convey joy, fear, frustration, humor, sympathy, anger. A child writes, "I have just moved. And it is hard to find a friend because I am shy." Another tells her classmates, "Guess what?

Scott Cunningham/Merrill

Good communicators use nonlinguistic cues such as body posture and gestures and pragmatic conversational skills such as turn taking.

I have a new baby brother!" Through such communicative interactions, children gradually develop a sense of self and an awareness of other people.

Although speech and language form the message system most often used in human communication, spoken or written words are not necessary for communication to occur. Both paralinguistic behaviors and nonlinguistic cues play major roles in human communication. *Paralinguistic behaviors* include speech modifications (e.g., variations in stress, pitch, intonation, rate of delivery, pauses) and non-language sounds (e.g., "oohh," laughter) that change the form and meaning of the message. *Nonlinguistic cues* include body posture, facial expressions, gestures, eye contact, head and body movement, and physical proximity. Some researchers estimate that two-thirds or more of the information in some face-to-face interactions may be communicated by non-speech means (Zeuschner, 2003).

Language

A **language** is a formalized code used by a group of people to communicate with one another. All languages consist of a set of abstract symbols—sounds, letters, numbers, elements of sign language—and a system of rules for combining those symbols into larger units. Languages are not static; they grow and develop as tools for communication as the cultures and communities of which they are part change. Nearly 7,000 living languages are spoken in the world (Lewis, 2009).

No matter what language is spoken, the symbols and rules governing language are essentially arbitrary. The arbitrariness of language means there is no logical, natural, or required relationship between a set of sounds and the object, concept, or action it represents. The word *whale,* for example, brings to mind a large mammal that lives in the sea; but the sound of the word has no apparent connection with the creature. *Whale* is merely a symbol we use for this particular animal. A small number of *onomatopoeic words*—such as *tinkle, buzz,* and *hiss*—sound like what they represent, but most words have no such relationship. Likewise, some hand positions or movements in American Sign Language are *iconic:* they look like the object or event they represent (e.g., tipping an imaginary cup to one's lips is the sign for *drink*).

FIVE DIMENSIONS OF LANGUAGE Language can be described by five dimensions that define its *form* (phonology, morphology, syntax), *content* (semantics), and *use* (pragmatics). **Phonology** refers to the linguistic rules governing a language's sound system. Phonological rules describe how sounds are sequenced and combined. A **phoneme** is a speech sound capable of differentiating meaning. Only the initial phoneme prevents the words *pear* and *bear* from being identical, for example; yet in one case we think of a fruit, in the other a large animal. The English language uses approximately 42 to 45 phonemes (Small, 2012).

The **morphology** of a language is concerned with the basic units of meaning and how those units are combined into words. **Morphemes,** the smallest elements of language that carry meaning, can be sounds, syllables, or whole words. *Free morphemes* can stand alone (e.g., *fit, slow*). *Bound morphemes* do not carry meaning by themselves; they are grammatical markers that change the meaning of words when attached to free morphemes (e.g., *unfit, slowly*). The word *baseballs* consists of two free morphemes (*base* and *ball*) and one bound morpheme (*s*).

Syntax is the system of rules governing the meaningful arrangement of words. If morphemes could be strung together in any order, language would be an unintelligible tangle of words. Syntactical rules are language-specific (e.g., Japanese and English have different rules); and they specify the acceptable (i.e., grammatical) relationships among subject, verb, object, and other sentence elements. The meaning of a sentence cannot be derived from the congregate meanings of the individual words; it is found in the interactive meanings of those words as the result of their grammatical and sequential relationships with one another. For example, "Help my chicken eat" conveys a meaning much different from "Help eat my chicken."

Semantics concerns the meaning of words and combinations of words. The semantic knowledge of competent language users includes vocabulary and concept development, connotative meanings by context (*hot* refers to temperature when discussing the weather but something else when talking about an athlete's recent performance), categories (*collies* and *beagles* are *dogs*), and relationships among words (such as antonyms and synonyms).

Pragmatics govern the social use of language. There are three kinds of pragmatic skills: (a) using language for different purposes (e.g., greeting, informing, demanding, promising, requesting); (b) changing language according to the needs of a listener or situation (e.g., talking differently to a baby than to an adult, giving background information to an unfamiliar listener, speaking differently in a classroom than on a playground); and (c) following rules for conversations and storytelling (e.g., taking turns, staying on topic, rephrasing when misunderstood, how close to stand when someone is talking, how to use facial expressions and eye contact) (American Speech-Language-Hearing Association, 2011). Pragmatics vary across and within cultures, and a good communicator understands and respect the rules of his communication partner.

Speech

Speech is the oral production of language. Although speech is not the only vehicle for expressing language (e.g., gestures, manual signing, pictures, and written symbols are also used), it is the fastest, most efficient method of communication by language. Speech sounds are the product of four separate but related processes (Hulit, Howard, & Fahey, 2011): *respiration* (breathing provides the power supply for speech); *phonation* (the production of sound when the vocal folds of the larynx are drawn together by the contraction of specific muscles, causing the air to vibrate); *resonation* (the sound quality of the vibrating air, shaped as it passes through the throat, mouth, and sometimes nasal cavities); and *articulation* (the formation of specific, recognizable speech sounds by the tongue, lips, teeth, and mouth). Figure 1 shows the organs used to produce speech sounds.

Speech is one of the most complex human behaviors. Hulit and colleagues (2011) describe just some of what happens in speaking a single word, *statistics*.

The tip of the tongue is lifted from a resting position to an area on the roof of the mouth just behind the upper teeth called the alveolar ridge to produce the *s* sound. The tongue is pressed against the alveolar ridge hard enough to produce constriction but not so hard as to stop the airflow altogether. As the speaker slowly contracts the muscles of exhalation under precise control, air is forced between the tip of the tongue and the alveolar ridge. Leaving the tongue in the same area, the speaker now presses a little harder to stop the airflow and then quickly releases the contact for the production of the *t* sound. The tongue drops to a neutral position and the vocal folds in the larynx vibrate to produce the vowel *a*. The speaker turns off the voice and lifts the tongue to the alveolar ridge for the next *t*, then vibrates the vocal folds for the vowel *i* while the tongue stays in a forward but slightly lowered position. The speaker turns voicing off again and moves the tongue to the alveolar ridge yet again to produce the controlled constriction for the next *s*, followed by increased pressure to stop the air flow and release it for the *t*.

FIGURE 1

SPEECH ORGANS

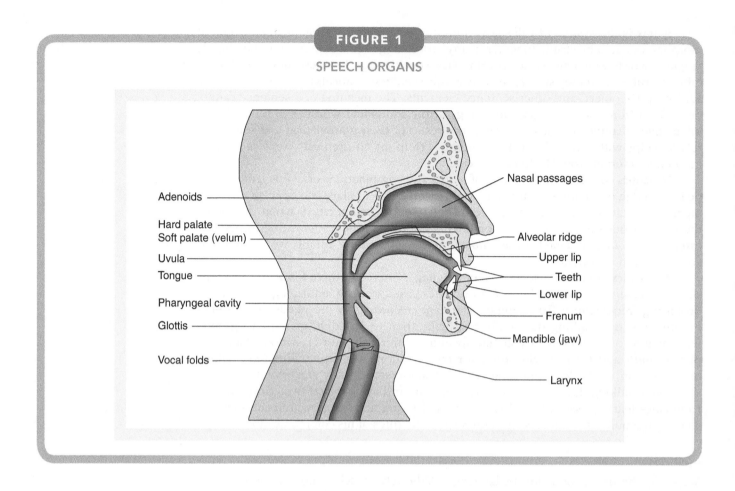

The voice is turned on one more time and the tongue lowered to a neutral position for the *i*, and then turned off as the tongue arches to the back of the mouth where it contacts the velum, or fleshy part of the roof of the mouth, for the *k*. Finally, the tongue tip darts to the alveolar ridge for the production of the final *s* sound.

All of this occurs in the production of *one* word! (p. 5)

Most languages begin in spoken form, the product of people talking with each other. Writing is a secondary language form that uses graphic symbols to represent the spoken form. There is no one-to-one correspondence, however, between **graphemes** (print symbols or letters) and phonemes.

Typical Speech and Language Development

Typical language development

Council for Exceptional Children

Content Standards for Beginning Teachers—Common Core: Educational implications of characteristics of exceptionalities (ICC2K2).

Despite the enormous complexity of speech and language, most children, without any formal instruction, learn to talk during the first few years of life. Language learning is a remarkable process, and one not fully understood.

Most children follow a predictable sequence in the acquisition of speech and language skills. Knowledge of the speech and language milestones acquired by typically developing children helps professionals determine whether a particular child is simply developing language at a slower than usual rate or whether the child shows an atypical pattern of language development. Figure 2 identifies some of the key indices of typical speech and language development. The ages at which children acquire certain speech and language skills are not rigid and inflexible. Children's early environments and opportunities vary widely, and all these factors exert tremendous influence on language development.

As the descriptions in Figure 2 indicate, words and sentences by children differ from adult forms. Children who use structures such as "All gone sticky" and "Where

FIGURE 2   OVERVIEW OF TYPICAL LANGUAGE DEVELOPMENT

Birth to 6 months
- Infant first communicates by crying, which produces a reliable consequence in the form of parental attention.
- Different types of crying develop—a parent can often tell from the baby's cry whether she is wet, tired, or hungry.
- Comfort sounds—coos, gurgles, and sighs—contain some vowels and consonants.
- Comfort sounds develop into babbling, sounds that in the beginning are apparently made for the enjoyment of feeling and hearing them.
- Vowel sounds, such as /i/ (pronounced "ee") and /e/ (pronounced "uh"), are produced earlier than consonants, such as /m/, /b/, and /p/.
- Infant does not attach meaning to words she hears from others but may react differently to loud and soft voices.
- Infant turns eyes and head in the direction of a sound.

7 to 12 months
- Babbling becomes differentiated before the end of the first year and contains some of the same phonetic elements as the meaningful speech of 2-year-olds.
- Baby develops inflection—her voice rises and falls.
- She may respond appropriately to "no," "bye-bye," or her own name and may perform an action, such as clapping her hands, when told to.
- She will repeat simple sounds and words, such as "mama."

12 to 18 months
- By 18 months, most children have learned to say several words with appropriate meaning.
- Pronunciation is far from perfect; baby may say "tup" when you point to a cup or "goggie" when she sees a dog.
- She communicates by pointing and perhaps saying a word or two.
- She responds to simple commands such as "Give me the cup" and "Open your mouth."

18 to 24 months
- Most children go through a stage of echolalia, in which they repeat, or echo, the speech they hear. Echolalia is a normal phase of language development, and most children outgrow it by about the age of 2½.
- There is a great spurt in acquisition and use of speech; baby begins to combine words into short sentences, such as "Daddy bye-bye" and "Want cookie."
- Receptive vocabulary grows even more rapidly; at 2 years of age she may understand more than 1,000 words.
- Understands such concepts as "soon" and "later" and makes more subtle distinctions between objects such as cats and dogs and knives, forks, and spoons.

2 to 3 years
- The 2-year-old child talks, saying sentences such as "I won't tell you" and asking questions such as "Where my daddy go?"
- She participates in conversations.
- She identifies colors, uses plurals, and tells simple stories about her experiences.
- She can follow compound commands such as "Pick up the doll and bring it to me."
- She uses most vowel sounds and some consonant sounds correctly.

3 to 4 years
- The normal 3-year-old has lots to say, speaks rapidly, and asks many questions.
- She may have an expressive vocabulary of 900–1,000 different words, using sentences of three to four words.

(continues)

FIGURE 2 **OVERVIEW OF TYPICAL LANGUAGE DEVELOPMENT**
(continued)

- Sentences are longer and more varied: "Cindy's playing in water"; "Mommy went to work"; "The cat is hungry."
- She uses speech to request, protest, agree, and make jokes.
- She understands children's stories; grasps such concepts as funny, bigger, and secret; and can complete simple analogies such as "In the daytime it is light; at night it is . . . "
- She substitutes certain sounds, perhaps saying "baf" for "bath" or "yike" for "like."
- Many 3-year-olds repeat sounds or words ("b-b-ball," "l-l-little"). These repetitions and hesitations are normal and do not indicate that the child will develop a habit of stuttering.

4 to 5 years
- The child has a vocabulary of more than 1,500–2,000 words and uses sentences averaging five words in length.
- She begins to modify her speech for the listener; for example, she uses longer and more complex sentences when talking to her mother than when addressing a baby or a doll.
- She can define words such as "hat," "stove," and "policeman" and can ask questions such as "How did you do that?" or "Who made this?"
- She uses conjunctions such as "if," "when," and "because."
- She recites poems and sings songs from memory.
- She may still have difficulty with consonant sounds such as /r/, /s/, /z/ and /j/ and with blends such as "tr," "gl," "sk," and "str."

After 5 years
- Language continues to develop steadily, although less dramatically, after age 5.
- A typical 6-year-old uses most of the complex forms of adult English and has an expressive vocabulary of 2,600 words and a receptive understanding of more than 20,000 words.
- Most children achieve adult speech sound production by age 7.
- Grammar and speech patterns of a child in first grade usually match those of her family, neighborhood, and region.

Sources: Adapted from ASHA (2011); Hart and Risley (1999); Hodson (1994); Hulit, Howard, and Fahey (2011); Owens (2012); Reed (2012).

he is going?"; pronunciations such as "cwackers" and "twuck"; or word forms such as "comed," "goed," or "sheeps" gradually learn to replace them with acceptable adult forms. These early developmental forms drop out as the child matures, usually without intervention or instruction (Hulit et al., 2011; Owens, 2012). Children often produce speech sounds inconsistently. The clarity of a sound may vary according to factors such as where the sound occurs in a word and how familiar the word is to the child.

A major longitudinal study has provided a great deal of information about the social and linguistic environment in which typical children learn to talk. Hart and Risley (1995, 1999) conducted monthly hour-long observations of children from 42 diverse families over a period of 2½ years. The researchers recorded everything said by, to, and around each of the children during unstructured activities in their daily lives at home. Of the many interesting results of this landmark study, two findings are especially notable. First, children between the ages of 11 and 36 months of age are exposed to a tremendous amount of spoken language. "Perhaps most striking of all our findings . . . was the sheer amount of children's exposure to talk and interaction among the people around them. Over the years of observation, we regularly recorded an average of 700–800 utterances per hour within the children's hearing" (Hart & Risley, 1999, p. 34).

Second, children who are learning to talk practice their new skill relentlessly, actively participating in thousands of learning trials every day. They say words again and

Children with spoken vocabularies of fewer than 50 words and/ or who produce limited word combinations at 24 months of age are considered *late talkers.* Kelly (1998) reviews the late-talker literature and makes recommendations for serving this population of children.

again, they repeat what they hear, they describe things, they talk to themselves while playing, they say what they want, they ask questions, and they respond to questions. After the children in the Hart and Risley study said their first word at an average age of 11 months, their number of utterances per hour increased steadily. On average, at 19 months of age the children became talkers: their frequency of utterances containing recognizable words had grown to exceed the frequency of nonword utterances. At 28 months, the children became speakers: their frequency of talking matched their parents'. At age 3, the children said an average of 1,400 words per hour, using an average of 232 different words per hour and almost 20,000 total words in a 14-hour waking day.

Most children learn patterns of speech and language appropriate to their families and neighborhoods before they enter school.

© Olena Teslya/Shutterstock

Communication Disorders Defined

The American Speech-Language-Hearing Association (ASHA) (1993) defines a **communication disorder** as "an impairment in the ability to receive, send, process, and comprehend concepts or verbal, nonverbal and graphic symbols systems. A communication disorder may be evident in the processes of hearing, language, and/or speech" (p. 40).

To be eligible for special education services, a child's communication disorder must have an adverse effect on learning. The Individuals with Disabilities Education Act (IDEA) defines *speech or language impairment* as "a communication disorder, such as stuttering, impaired articulation, a language impairment, or a voice impairment that adversely affects a child's educational performance" (34 *CFR*, Part 300 §300.8[c][11]).

Like all disabilities, communication disorders vary widely by degree of severity. Some children's speech and language deviate from those of most children to such an extent that they have serious difficulties in learning and interpersonal relations. Children who cannot make themselves understood or who cannot comprehend ideas spoken to them by others experience a significant handicap in virtually all aspects of education and personal adjustment. A severe communication disorder may lead others—teachers, classmates, people in the community—to erroneously believe the child does not care about the world around him or simply has nothing to say (Downing, 2005).

Specialists in the field of communication disorders make a distinction between speech impairments and language impairments. A child may have a speech impairment, a language impairment, or both.

SPEECH IMPAIRMENTS A widely used definition considers speech to be impaired "when it deviates so far from the speech of other people that it (a) calls attention to itself, (b) interferes with communication, or (c) provokes distress in the speaker or the listener" (Van Riper & Erickson, 1996, p. 110). Three basic types of **speech impairments** are articulation disorders (errors in the production of speech sounds), fluency disorders (difficulties with the flow or rhythm of speech), and voice disorders (problems with the quality or use of one's voice). Each is discussed later in the chapter.

It is important to keep the speaker's age, education, and cultural background in mind when determining whether speech is impaired. A 4-year-old girl who says, "Pwease weave the woom" would not be considered to have a speech impairment, but a 40-year-old woman would surely draw attention to herself with that pronunciation because it differs markedly from the speech of most adults. A traveler unable to

Definition of speech and language impairments

Council for Exceptional Children

Content Standards for Beginning Teachers—Common Core: Issues in definition and identification of individuals with exceptional learning needs including those from culturally and linguistically diverse backgrounds. (ICC1K5).

articulate the /l/ sound would not be clearly understood when he tries to buy a bus ticket to Lake Charles, Louisiana. A male high school student with an extremely high-pitched voice might be reluctant to speak in class for fear of being mimicked and ridiculed by his classmates.

Many children have mild to moderate speech impairments. Their speech can usually be understood, but they may mispronounce certain sounds or use immature speech, like that of younger children. These problems often disappear as a child matures. If a mild or moderate articulation problem does not improve over an extended period or if it has an adverse effect on the child's interaction with others, referral to a speech-language pathologist is indicated (Owens, 2012).

LANGUAGE IMPAIRMENTS   A **language disorder** is "impaired comprehension and/or use of spoken, written, and/or other symbol systems. The disorder may involve (a) the form of language (phonology, morphology, and syntax), (b) the content of language (semantics), and/or (c) the function of language in communication (pragmatics) in any combination" (ASHA, 1993, p. 40).

Some children have serious difficulties in understanding language or expressing themselves through language. A child with a **receptive language disorder** may struggle learning the days of the week in proper order or following a sequence of commands such as "Pick up the paint brushes, wash them in the sink, and then put them on a paper towel to dry." A child with an **expressive language disorder** may have a limited vocabulary for her age, say sounds or words in the wrong order (e.g., "hostipal," "aminal," "wipe shield winders"), and use tenses and plurals incorrectly (e.g., "Them throwed a balls"). Children with an expressive language disorder may or may not also have difficulty in receptive language. For instance, a child may be able to count out six pennies when asked and shown the symbol 6, but she may not be able to say "six" when shown the symbol. In that case, the child has an expressive difficulty, but her receptive language is adequate.

Communication Differences Are Not Disorders

Dialects and communication differences

 Council for Exceptional Children

Content Standards for Beginning Teachers—Common Core: Issues in definition and identification of individuals with exceptional learning needs including those from culturally and linguistically diverse backgrounds. (ICC1K5).

Before entering school, most children have learned patterns of speech and language appropriate to their families and communities. The way each of us speaks is the result of a complex mix of influences, including race and ethnicity, socioeconomic class, education, occupation, geographical region, and peer group identification. Every language contains a variety of forms, called **dialects**, that result from historical, linguistic, geographic, and sociocultural factors. Each dialect shares a common set of rules with the standard language. Standard American English (as used by most teachers, in textbooks, and on newscasts) is an idealized form seldom used in everyday conversation. As it is spoken in North America, English includes at least 10 regional dialects (e.g., Appalachian English, Southern English, New York dialect, Central Midland) and several sociocultural dialects (e.g., Black English, Latino English) (Payne, 2011).

The dialect of any group of people is neither inferior nor superior to the dialect spoken by another group. "There are dialects of English spoken by many people and dialects spoken by fewer people, but number of speakers does not indicate superiority or correctness. Every dialect of English is linguistically correct within the rules that govern it, and every dialect of English is as valid as any other" (Hulit et al., 2011, p. 334).

A child who uses a dialect different from the dominant culture of the school should not be treated as having a communication disorder. If the teacher does not accept natural communication differences among children and mistakenly assumes that a speech or language impairment is present, problems may arise in the classroom and in parent–teacher communication (Reed, 2012). On the other hand, some children with communication differences have communication disorders within their dialects, and such impairments must not be overlooked (Cheng, 2012; Payne, 2011).

CHARACTERISTICS

Speech-Sound Errors

Four basic kinds of speech-sound errors occur:

- *Distortions.* A speech sound is distorted when it sounds more like the intended phoneme than another speech sound but is conspicuously wrong. The /s/ sound, for example, is relatively difficult to produce; children may produce the word "sleep" as "schleep," "zleep," or "thleep." Some speakers have a lisp; others a whistling /s/. Distortions can cause misunderstanding, although parents and teachers often become accustomed to them.
- *Substitutions.* Children sometimes substitute one sound for another, as in saying "train" for "crane" or "doze" for "those." Children with this problem are often certain they have said the correct word and may resist correction. Substitution of sounds can cause considerable confusion for the listener.
- *Omissions.* Children may omit certain sounds, as in saying "cool" for "school." They may drop consonants from the ends of words, as in "pos" for "post." Most of us leave out sounds at times, but an extensive omission problem can make speech unintelligible.
- *Additions.* The addition of extra sounds makes comprehension difficult. For example, a child might say "buhrown" for "brown" or "hamber" for "hammer."

Traditionally, all speech-sound errors by children were identified as articulation problems and thought to be relatively simple to treat. *Articulation* refers to the movement of muscles and speech organs necessary to produce various speech sounds. Research during the past two decades, however, has revealed that many speech-sound errors are not simply a function of faulty mechanical operation of the speech apparatus but are directly related to problems in recognizing or processing the sound components of language (phonology) (Schwartz & Marton, 2011).

ARTICULATION DISORDERS An **articulation disorder** means that a child is at present not able to produce a given sound physically; the sound is not in his repertoire of sounds. A severe articulation disorder is present when a child pronounces many sounds so poorly that his speech is unintelligible most of the time; even the child's parents, teachers, and peers cannot easily understand him. The child with a severe articulation disorder may say, "Yeh me yuh a da wido," instead of "Let me look out the window," or perhaps "Do foop is dood" for "That soup is good." The fact that articulation disorders are prevalent does not mean that teachers, parents, and specialists should regard them as simple or unimportant. On the contrary, as Haynes and Pindzola (2012) observe, an articulation disorder severe enough to interfere significantly with intelligibility is a debilitating communication problem; and articulation disorders are not necessarily easy to diagnose and treat effectively.

PHONOLOGICAL DISORDERS A child is said to have a **phonological disorder** if she has the ability to produce a given sound and does so correctly in some instances but

Intervention for this student with a speech disorder includes intensive practice sessions with an SLP and supports from his classroom teacher.

Patrick White/Merrill

Articulation and phonological disorders

Council for Exceptional Children

Content Standards for Beginning Teachers—Common Core: Educational implications of characteristics of various exceptionalities (ICC2K2).

does not produce the sound correctly at other times. Children with phonological disorders are apt to experience problems in academic areas, and they are especially at risk for difficulties in reading (Bishop & Snowling, 2004) and writing (Dockrell, Lindsay, Connelly, & Mackie, 2007).

Determining whether a speech-sound error is primarily an articulation or a phonological disorder is important because the treatment goals and procedures differ. General indicators used by clinicians for differentiating between articulation disorders and phonological disorders are shown in Figure 3.

Fluency Disorders

Fluency disorders

Content Standards for Beginning Teachers—Common Core: Educational implications of characteristics of various exceptionalities (ICC2K2).

Typical speech makes use of rhythm and timing. Words and phrases flow easily, with certain variations in speed, stress, and appropriate pauses. A **fluency disorder** is an "interruption in the flow of speaking characterized by atypical rate, rhythm, and repetitions in sounds, syllables, words, and phrases. This may be accompanied by excessive tension, struggle behavior, and secondary mannerisms" (ASHA, 1993, p. 40).

STUTTERING The best-known (and in some ways least understood) fluency disorder is **stuttering**, a condition marked by rapid-fire repetitions of consonant or vowel sounds, especially at the beginnings of words, prolongations, hesitations, interjections, and complete verbal blocks (Ramig & Pollard, 2011). Developmental stuttering is considered a disorder of childhood. Its onset is usually between the ages of 2 and 4, and rarely after age 12 (Bloodstein & Bernstein Ratner, 2007). It is believed that 4% of children stutter for 6 months or more and that 70% to 80% of children 2 to 5 years old who stutter recover spontaneously, some taking until age 8 to do so (Yairi & Ambrose, 1999). Stuttering is far more common among males than females, and it occurs more frequently among twins. It is believed that approximately 3 million people in the United States stutter (Stuttering Foundation of America, 2011). The incidence of stuttering is about the same in all Western countries: regardless of what language is spoken, about 1% of the general population has a stuttering problem at

---

FIGURE 3 DISTINGUISHING ARTICULATION AND PHONOLOGICAL DISORDERS

Articulation Disorder	Phonological Disorder
• Difficulty with only a few sounds, with limited effect on intelligibility	• Multiple sound errors with obvious impairment of intelligibility
• Consistent misarticulation of specific sounds	• Inconsistent misarticulation of sounds
• Sound errors are motoric	• Can motorically produce sound but not in appropriate places
• Co-existing communication disorders possible but not as likely as with phonological disorders	• Errors consistent with a phonological process (e.g., final consonant deletion, making an error on a sound in one position but producing that sound correctly in another position, as in omitting "t" in "post" but producing "t" in "time")
	• Other language delays likely (because phonology is a component of language)

Sources: Haynes and Pindzola, (2012); Sunderland (2004); Schwartz and Marton (2011).

any given time. The causes of stuttering remain unknown, although the condition has been studied extensively with some interesting results. A family member of a person who stutters is 3 to 4 times more likely to stutter than the family member of a person who does not stutter. It is not known whether this is the result of a genetic connection or an environment conducive to the development of the disorder, or a combination of hereditary and environmental factors (Yairi & Seery, 2011).

Stuttering is situational; that is, it appears to be related to the setting or circumstances of speech. A child may be more likely to stutter when talking with people whose opinions matter most to him, such as parents and teachers, and in situations such as being called on to speak in front of the class. Most people who stutter are fluent about 90% of the time; a child with a fluency disorder may not stutter at all when singing, talking to a pet, or reciting a poem in unison with others. Reactions and expectations of parents, teachers, and peers clearly have an important effect on any child's personal and communicative development.

CLUTTERING A type of fluency disorder known as **cluttering** is characterized by excessive speech rate, repetitions, extra sounds, mispronounced sounds, and poor or absent use of pauses. The clutterer's speech is garbled to the point of unintelligibility. "Let's go!" may be uttered as "Sko!" and "Did you eat?" collapsed to "Jeet?" (Yairi & Seery, 2011). Whereas the stutterer is usually acutely aware of his fluency problems, the clutterer may be oblivious to his disorder.

Voice Disorders

Voice is the sound produced by the larynx. A **voice disorder** is characterized by "the abnormal production and/or absences of vocal quality, pitch, loudness, resonance, and/or duration, which is inappropriate for an individual's age and/or sex" (ASHA, 1993, p. 40). A voice is considered normal when its pitch, loudness, and quality are adequate for communication and it suits a particular person. A voice—whether good, poor, or in between—is closely identified with the person who uses it.

Voice disorders are more common in adults than in children. Considering how often some children shout and yell without any apparent harm to their voices, it is evident that the vocal cords can withstand heavy use. In some cases, however, a child's voice may be difficult to understand or may be considered unpleasant (Sapienza, Hicks, & Ruddy, 2011). *Dysphonia* describes any condition of poor or unpleasant voice quality.

The two basic types of voice disorders involve phonation and resonance. A *phonation disorder* causes the voice to sound breathy, hoarse, husky, or strained most of the time. In severe cases, there is no voice at all. Phonation disorders can have organic causes, such as growths or irritations on the vocal cords; but hoarseness most frequently comes from chronic vocal abuse, such as yelling, imitating noises, or habitually talking while under tension. Misuse of the voice causes swelling of the vocal folds, which in turn can lead to growths known as vocal nodules, nodes, or polyps. A breathy voice is unpleasant because it is low in volume and fails to make adequate use of the vocal cords.

A voice with a *resonance disorder* is characterized by either too many sounds coming out through the air passages of the nose (*hypernasality*) or, conversely, not enough resonance of the nasal passages (*hyponasality*). The hypernasal speaker may be perceived as talking through her nose or having an unpleasant twang (Hall et al., 2001). A child with hyponasality (sometimes called *denasality*) may sound as though he constantly has a cold or a stuffed nose, even when he does not.

Language Disorders

Language disorders involve problems in one or more of the five dimensions of language: phonology, morphology, syntax, semantics, and/or pragmatics. Language disorders are usually classified as either receptive or expressive. As described previously, a *receptive*

Voice disorders

 Council for Exceptional Children

Content Standards for Beginning Teachers—Common Core: Educational implications of characteristics of various exceptionalities (ICC2K2).

301

Receptive and expressive
language impairments

 Content
Standards for
Beginning
Teachers—Common Core:
Educational implications of
characteristics of various
exceptionalities (ICC2K2).

Language delays

 Content
Standards for
Beginning
Teachers—Common Core:
Typical and atypical human
growth and development
(ICC2K1).

language disorder interferes with the understanding of language. A child may, for example, be unable to comprehend spoken sentences or follow a sequence of directions. An *expressive* language disorder interferes with the production of language. The child may have a very limited vocabulary, may use incorrect words and phrases, or may not speak at all, communicating only through gestures. A child may have good receptive language when an expressive disorder is present or may have both expressive and receptive disorders in combination. Educators sometimes use the term *language-learning disability (LLD)* to refer to children with significant receptive and/or expressive language disorders.

To say that a child has a language delay does not necessarily mean that the child has a language disorder. As Reed (2012) explains, a *language delay* implies that a child is slow to develop linguistic skills but acquires them in the same sequence as typically developing children do. Generally, all language features are delayed at about the same rate. A *language disorder,* however, suggests a disruption in the usual rate and/or sequence in which specific language skills emerge. For example, a child who consistently has difficulty in responding to who, what, and where questions but who otherwise displays language skills appropriate for her age would likely be considered to have a language disorder.

Children with serious language disorders are almost certain to have problems in school and with social development. They frequently play a passive role in communication. Children with impaired language are less likely to initiate conversations than are their peers. When children with language disorders are asked questions, their replies rarely provide new information related to the topic. It is often difficult to detect children with language disorders; their performance may lead people to mistakenly classify them with disability labels such as intellectual disabilities, hearing impairment, or emotional disturbance, when in fact these descriptions are neither accurate nor appropriate.

Young children with oral language problems are also likely to have reading and writing disabilities (Catts et al., 2002; DeThorne, Petrill, Schatschneider, & Cutting, 2010). For example, Catts (1993) reported that 83% of kindergarteners with speech-language delays eventually qualified for remedial reading services. The problem is compounded because children with speech-language delays are more likely than their typically developing peers to be "treatment-resistors" to generally effective early literacy interventions (Al Otaiba, 2001).

PREVALENCE

Estimates of the prevalence of communication disorders in children vary widely. Reliable figures are hard to come by because investigators often employ different definitions of speech and language disorders and sample different populations. In the 2009–10 school year, 1,107,029 children ages 6 to 21 received special education services under the IDEA category of "speech or language impairments" (U.S. Department of Education, 2011). This number represents about 2.5% of the school-age population and 19% of all students receiving special education services, making speech or language impairments the second-largest category after learning disabilities.

The actual number of children with speech and language impairments is much higher. Approximately 50% of children who receive special education services because of another primary disability (e.g., intellectual disabilities, learning disabilities, hearing impairments) also have communication disorders (Hall et al., 2001).

School-based speech-language pathologists (SLPs) work with a median caseload of 50 students each month (ASHA, 2010). Approximately half of all elementary students who are served by SLPs have speech and language production problems. About 1 in 20 children served by SLPs has fluency disorders.

Speech and language impairments are more prevalent among males than females and are about the same in each of the major geographic regions of the United States. Approximately two-thirds of school-age children served by SLPs are boys (Hall et al., 2001). The percentage of children with speech and language disorders decreases significantly from the earlier to the later school grades.

CAUSES

Many types of communication disorders and numerous possible causes are recognized. A speech or language impairment may be *organic*—that is, attributable to damage, dysfunction, or malformation of a specific organ or part of the body. Most communication disorders, however, are not considered organic but are classified as functional. A *functional communication disorder* cannot be ascribed to a specific physical condition, and its origin is not clearly known.

Causes of Speech Impairments

Examples of physical factors that frequently result in speech impairments are **cleft palate,** paralysis of the speech muscles, absence of teeth, craniofacial abnormalities, enlarged adenoids, and traumatic brain injury. **Dysarthria** refers to a group of speech disorders caused by neuromuscular impairments in respiration, phonation, resonation, and articulation. Lack of precise motor control needed to produce and sequence sounds causes distorted and repeated sounds. An organic speech impairment may be a child's primary disability, or it may be secondary to other disabilities, such as cerebral palsy or intellectual disabilities.

Causes of Language Disorders

Factors that can contribute to language disorders in children include developmental and intellectual disabilities, autism, traumatic brain injury, child abuse and neglect, hearing loss, and structural abnormalities of the speech mechanism (Bacon & Wilcox, 2011). Language is so important to academic performance that it can be impossible to differentiate a learning disability from a language disorder (Silliman & Diehl, 2002).

Some severe disorders in expressive and receptive language result from injury to the brain. **Aphasia** describes a loss of the ability to process and use language. Aphasia is one of the most prevalent causes of language disorders in adults, most often occurring suddenly after a cardiovascular event (stroke). Head injury is a significant cause of aphasia in children. Aphasia may be either expressive or, less commonly, receptive. Children with mild aphasia have language patterns very similar to those of typically developing children but may have difficulty retrieving certain words and tend to need more time than usual to communicate. Children with severe aphasia, however, are likely to have a markedly reduced storehouse of words and language forms.

Research indicates that genetics may contribute to communication disorders (McNeilly, 2011). Scientists in Britain have discovered a gene area that affects speech (Porterfield, 1998), and other researchers have reported genetic links to phonological disorders (Uffen, 1997) and stuttering (Yairi, 1998).

Environmental influences also play an important part in delayed, disordered, or absent language. The communication efforts of some children are reinforced; other children, unfortunately, are punished for talking, gesturing, or otherwise attempting to communicate. A child who has little stimulation at home and few chances to speak, listen, explore, and interact with others will probably have little motivation for communicating and may well experience delays in language development (Kang et al., 2010).

IDENTIFICATION AND ASSESSMENT

"Don't worry; she'll grow out of it."
"Speech therapists can't help a child who doesn't talk."
"He'll be all right once he starts school."

These are common examples of misguided, inaccurate, yet widely held attitudes toward communication disorders. Although some children who experience mild speech impairments or language delays do get better, many do not improve and deteriorate without intervention. To avoid the consequences of unrecognized or untreated speech and language impairments, it is especially important for children to receive professional assessment and evaluation services.

Screening and Teacher Observation

Screening for communication disorders

 Council for Exceptional Children

Content Standards for Beginning Teachers—Common Core: Screening, prereferral, referral, and classification procedures (ICC8K3).

In some school districts, SLPs screen the spoken language abilities of all kindergarten children. These screenings might involve norm-referenced tests, informal assessments developed by the SLP, and questionnaires or checklists for parents and teachers (Justice, 2010; Owens, Metz, & Farinella, 2011). Classroom teachers also play an important role in identifying children who may have speech and language impairments. Teachers can use a checklist such as the one in Figure 4 to identify children with whom the SLP can conduct individualized screening for possible communication disorders. Children who fail a speech and language screening test are candidates for a systematic, in-depth evaluation.

Evaluation Components

Assessment and diagnosis of communication disorders

 Council for Exceptional Children

Content Standards for Beginning Teachers—Common Core: Screening, prereferral, referral, and classification procedures (ICC8K3).

Testing procedures vary according to the suspected type of disorder. Often the specialist conducts broad screenings to detect areas of concern and then moves to more detailed evaluation in those areas. Most examiners will use a variety of assessment devices and approaches in an effort to obtain as much relevant information as possible to inform diagnostic decisions and treatment plans. A comprehensive evaluation to detect the presence and extent of a communication disorder would likely include the following components:

- *Case history and physical examination.* Most professional speech and language assessments begin with the creation of the child's case history. This typically involves completing a biographical form that includes information such as the child's birth and developmental history, health record, scores on achievement and intelligence tests, and adjustment to school. The parents may be asked when the child first crawled, walked, and uttered words. Social skills, such as playing readily with other children, may also be considered. The specialist carefully examines the child's mouth, noting any irregularities in the tongue, lips, teeth, palate, or other structures that may affect speech production. If the child has an organic speech problem, the child is referred for possible medical intervention.
- *Articulation.* Speech errors by the child are assessed. A record is kept of the sounds that are defective, how they are being mispronounced, and the number of errors. Examples of articulation tests include the Photo Articulation Test (Lippke, Dickey, Selmar, & Soder, 1997) and the Goldman-Fristoe Test of Articulation—2 (Goldman & Fristoe, 2000).
- *Hearing.* Hearing is usually tested to determine whether a hearing problem is causing the suspected communication disorder.
- *Phonological awareness and processing.* Competent speakers and users of language can distinguish the presence and absence of speech sounds, differences between and among sounds, and when individual sounds begin and end. They can remember language sounds and reproduce them at a later time. Children without such phonological awareness and processing skills not only have problems with

FIGURE 4	A CHECKLIST FOR IDENTIFYING POSSIBLE LANGUAGE IMPAIRMENT IN THE CLASSROOM

Directions: The following behaviors may indicate that a child in your classroom has a language impairment that is in need of language intervention. Please check the appropriate items.

_____ Child mispronounces sounds and words.

_____ Child omits word endings, such as plural -s and past tense -ed.

_____ Child omits small, unemphasized words, such as auxiliary verbs or prepositions.

_____ Child uses an immature vocabulary, overuses empty words, such as "one" and "thing," or seems to have difficulty recalling or finding the right word.

_____ Child has difficulty comprehending new words and concepts.

_____ Child's sentence structure seems immature or overreliant on forms, such as subject-verb-object. It's unoriginal, dull.

_____ Child has difficulty with one of the following:

    _____ Verb tensing   _____ Articles   _____ Auxiliary verbs

    _____ Pronouns   _____ Irreg. verbs   _____ Prepositions

    _____ Word order   _____ Irreg. plurals   _____ Conjunctions

_____ Child has difficulty relating sequential events.

_____ Child has difficulty following directions.

_____ Child's questions are often poorly formed.

_____ Child has difficulty answering questions.

_____ Child's comments are often off topic or inappropriate for the conversation.

_____ There are long pauses between a remark and the child's reply or between successive remarks by the child. It's as if the child is searching for a response or is confused.

_____ Child appears to be attending to communication but remembers little of what is said.

Source: Robert E. Owens, Jr. _Language Disorders: A Functional Approach to Assessment and Intervention_, 5e. Published by Pearson. Copyright © 2010 by Pearson Education. Reprinted by permission of the publisher.

receptive and expressive spoken language but also have great difficulties in learning to read. Phonological processing measures include the Test of Phonological Awareness (Torgeson & Bryant, 2004) and the Comprehensive Test of Phonological Processing (Wagner, Torgeson, & Rahsotte, 1999).

- _Overall language development and vocabulary._ The amount of vocabulary a child has acquired is generally a good indicator of language competence. Frequently used tests of vocabulary include the Peabody Picture Vocabulary Test—4 (Dunn & Dunn, 2006) and the Comprehensive Receptive and Expressive Vocabulary Test (Wallace & Hammill, 2002). An overall language test, such as the Test of Language Development (Hammill & Newcomer, 2008) or the Clinical Evaluation of Language Fundamentals (Semel, Wiig, & Secord, 2003), assesses the child's understanding and production of language structures (e.g., important syntactical elements such as the concept that conjunctions show relations between the sentence elements they connect).

- _Assessment of language function._ In his account of language and communication, B. F. Skinner (1957; Sundberg, 2007) emphasized the circumstances surrounding the various functions of communication (e.g., requesting, naming) rather than the structure and form of language (e.g., words and sentences). Skinner's analysis of verbal behavior has led to advances in the assessment and treatment of language and communication disorders. (See *Teaching & Learning*, "A Functional Analysis of Language and Applications for Language Intervention.") The *Verbal Behavior Milestones Assessment and Placement Program* (VB-MAPP) is an assessment tool based on Skinner's analysis (Sundberg, 2008). This test identifies a student's strengths and weaknesses across the different language functions, and compares them with the language and communication skills of typically developing children. The VB-MAPP also includes a Barriers Assessment that identifies 24 possible barriers that might be preventing a child from making progress (e.g., prompt dependency, weak motivation) and a Transition Assessment that can help to identify a child's overall educational needs.

- *Language samples.* An important part of any evaluation for communication disorders is obtaining accurate samples of the child's expressive speech and language. The examiner considers factors such as intelligibility and fluency of speech, voice quality, and use of vocabulary and grammar. Some SLPs use structured tasks to evoke language samples, such as asking a child to describe a picture, tell a story, or answer a list of questions. Most specialists, however, use informal conversation to obtain language samples, believing that the child's language sample will be more representative if the examiner uses natural conversation rather than highly structured tasks (Hadley, 1998). Open-ended questions such as "Tell me about your family" are suggested rather than yes–no questions or questions that can be answered with one word, such as "What color is your car?" To ensure a complete and accurate record of the talk and reduce distractions for the child caused by note taking, examiners usually make an audio recording of the child's talking.

- *Observation in natural settings.* Observation and measurement of children's language use in social contexts and everyday activities are important elements of assessment for communication disorders. It is imperative that the observer sample the child's communication behavior across various settings rather than limit it to a clinic or an examining room. A parent–child observation is frequently arranged for young children. The specialist provides appropriate toys and activities and requests the parent to interact with the child in typical fashion.

Because of the large volume of assessment information obtained, some SLPs use computer programs to organize the data and analyze the results. The SLP then develops a treatment plan in cooperation with the child's parents and teachers to set up realistic communication objectives and determine the methods that will be used.

Assessment of Communication Disorders in Children Whose First Language Is Not English or Who Use Nonstandard English

It is often difficult to distinguish between a student whose learning and communication problems result from a disability and a student whose primary need is systematic, culturally responsive instruction that values and builds on the skills he already possesses in his first language (L1) to enable him to

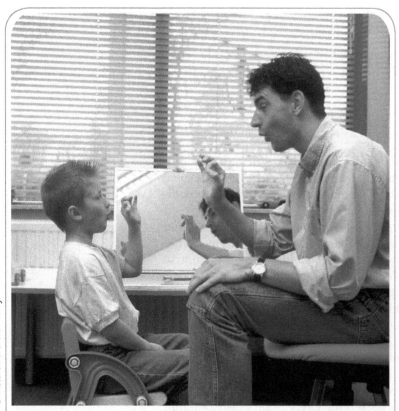

© Picture Partners/Alamy

A comprehensive assessment of communication disorders includes language samples during conversation and naturally occurring activities.

improve his English communicative and literacy skills (Roseberry-McKibbin, 2007). While professionals must be careful not to confuse communication differences with delayed or disordered speech and language, proper assessment of the speech-language skills of children from diverse cultural, linguistic, and socioeconomic backgrounds poses a difficult challenge for language-majority educators (Salend & Salinas, 2003).

IDEA requires that assessment for the purpose of identifying children with disabilities be conducted in the child's native language. Although a few standardized language proficiency tests are available in languages other than English (see McLaughlin & Lewis, 2008, for a review), translation or adaptation of tests into other languages poses certain problems (Díaz-Rico & Weed, 2005; Rhodes, Ochoa, & Ortiz, 2005). For example, DeAvila (1976) pointed out the great variety in language within Hispanic populations and noted that when Mexican American children were given a test in Spanish that was developed with a population of Puerto Rican children, they performed even more poorly than on an admittedly unfair English test. To illustrate the confusion that may result from inappropriate translations, DeAvila observed that, depending on the family's country of origin, a Spanish-speaking child may use any one of five distinct words to describe a kite: *cometa, huila, volantin, papalote,* or *chiringa.* Thus, although translation of tests and other materials into a child's native language may be helpful in many instances, educators must take care to avoid an improper translation that may actually do a disservice to the culturally and linguistically different child.

It should not be surprising that students who are English language learners and students whose first language is English but who speak a nonstandard dialect often perform poorly on formal tests of English speech and language skills. The results of formal language tests should never be the sole basis for diagnosing a speech or language disorder. Determining a culturally and linguistically different child's true communicative competence requires careful assessment of the child's language proficiency in both the first and second languages (L1 and L2) combined with an analysis of authentic conversational behavior (Cheng, 2012). Culturally and linguistically diverse students, and those who speak a nonstandard dialect, should not be diagnosed with a speech-language disorder if "problems" are observed only in English and not in their first language (or dialect). If a student has a genuine language impairment, difficulties will be observed in both L1 and in standard English (Roseberry-McKibbin, 2007).

Best practices in assessing speech and language competence of children who do not speak standard English as their first language include assessments of basic interpersonal communication skills (BICS) and cognitive academic language proficiency (CALP) (Roseberry-McKibbin, 2007, 2008). BICS are a set of language skills required in everyday face-to-face communication situations (e.g., conversing about the weather). CALP refers to proficient use of language specific to academic learning situations (e.g., "Compare formal and functional properties of sand and granite"). A typical English language learner needs about 2 years under ideal conditions to develop BICS to a level similar to native speakers, and achieving a similar level of performance with CALP may require 5 to 7 years (Cummins, 2002).

EDUCATIONAL APPROACHES

Speech-language pathologist (SLP) is the preferred term for the school-based professional with primary responsibility for identifying, evaluating, and providing therapeutic services to children with communication disorders. But terms such as *speech therapist, speech clinician,* and *speech teacher* are still used in some schools. As a key member of a child's IEP team, the SLP's goal is to correct the child's speech and/or language problems or to help the child achieve the maximum communicative potential, which may involve compensatory techniques and/or augmentative and alternative means of communication. Speech-language pathology addresses both organic and functional causes and encompasses practitioners with numerous points of view who use a wide range of accepted intervention techniques.

A Functional Analysis of Language and Applications for Language Intervention

BY MARK L. SUNDBERG

Four-year-old Brittney has learned to say 10 words but doesn't use them to communicate. For example, when shown a ball and asked, "What is this?" Brittney says nothing until her mom or teacher says, "Ball," then she will echo, "Ball." But when Brittney wants something, she whines or grabs at it rather than using her words.

Brittney's communication problems are common among children who fail to acquire language in a typical pattern. Fortunately, intervention procedures can teach Brittney how to use her words instead of whining to get what she wants. B. F. Skinner's (1957) analysis of *verbal behavior* provides the theoretical foundation for these procedures. Departing from traditional expressive/receptive perspectives on communication based on structure and form (e.g., speech sounds, words and sentences spoken), Skinner explored the reasons behind the words and other forms of language (e.g., signs or pictures) that people use to communicate. He emphasized the various functions of language, over its form. For example, when Brittney says, "Ball" (form), why did she say it (i.e., what was the word's function or meaning)? Is she repeating the word because someone else said it, naming an object she sees, or requesting a ball?

WHAT DOES IT MEAN WHEN A CHILD SAYS, "BALL"?

Clearly, the same word can have several different functions, or meanings, in different situations. Skinner described seven classes or types of verbal behavior based on the circumstances controlling the response (see the chart on the next page). The simplest function is the ability to repeat or **echo** words emitted by others (for sign language, to **imitate** a sign). The ability to echo a word is quite different from understanding what that words means. However, the ability to echo words (or imitate signs) is an important early step in teaching nonverbal students to communicate.

Infants learn quickly to communicate their needs and wants to others, a language function Skinner called **manding.** Crying is typically one of the first response forms to function as a mand. Eventually, crying and other nonvocal responses a child may have learned (e.g., pointing, grabbing) are replaced by words (or signs,

or PECS), such as saying "ball" when he wants his ball but cannot find it. Manding is also important for social development because much of social play and interaction involves one child manding to another child.

The ability to name a ball with the word or sign *ball* is called **tacting.** A focus for many students with communication disorders involves teaching them to tact common items (nouns), actions (verbs), properties (adjectives and adverbs), spatial relations (prepositions), possession (pronouns), and so on. Students also need to understand the words spoken by others, or **listener** skills. When someone else says, for example, "Where is the ball?" a student's ability to select the ball from an array of other items demonstrates his listener skills. As with tacting, listener skills must also be developed for verbs, adjectives, prepositions, pronouns, and so forth. Thus far, a single language form, *ball*, has been described as having four separate functions: (a) echoic, (b) mand, (c) tact, and (d) listener understanding.

A typically developing 3- or 4-year-old can describe events, talk about future activities, and maintain a conversation. All of this language can occur in the absence of the items and activities being discussed. Skinner used the term **intraverbal** for language emitted under the control of other verbal stimuli. Intraverbals are the most extensive and complex language function. A typical adult can emit hundreds of thousands of different intraverbal responses (consider the number of different topics found on the Internet or in a library).

Skinner's analysis of verbal behavior also entailed reading (**textual** behavior) and writing (**transcription**). Collectively, these seven functions of language, along with consideration for response forms, can provide the basis for language assessment and intervention for individuals who experience communication disorders (e.g., Sundberg, 2008; Sundberg & Partington, 1998).

INTERVENTION ACROSS COMMUNICATION FUNCTIONS

By pinpointing communication problems related to function as well as form, a wider range of language disorders can be identified, and more effective intervention strategies developed. As described earlier, Brittney

TEACHING & LEARNING

can voice several perfectly articulated words when she hears those words (echoic function), but she does not use those same words to name specific items (tact) or ask for those items when she wants them (the mand function). On the other hand, some students with communication disorders can name many things (tact), but they have limited ability to use those same words to converse with others (intraverbal). This demonstrates that the problem is related not to form but to function. Thus, intervention strategies need to be developed and implemented to teach students the full range of communication functions.

Language Function	Example with Specific Language Form *Ball*
Echoic (or **imitation** for sign language)—repeating words spoken (or signs made) by others	Mom says, *"Ball,"* Brittney says, *"Ball."*
Mand—asking for desired items, actions, properties, information, etc.	Brittney wants to play with a ball; says, *"Ball."*
Tact—naming items, actions, properties, etc.	Teacher points to a ball; Brittney says, *"Ball."*
Listener—responding to the language of others	Brother says, "Get the ball"; Brittney takes a ball from the toy box.
Intraverbal—answering questions or verbally responding to the words spoken by others	Dad says, "What are you going to hit with that bat?" Brittney says, *"Ball."*
Textual—reading	Teacher holds up a card with the word *ball* on it; Brittney says, *"Ball."*
Transcription—spelling	Asked to spell *ball*, Brittney writes *b-a-l-l*.

HOW TO GET STARTED

1. **Include a test of language function when assessing existing language skills (e.g., the VB-MAPP).** Brittney's results on the VB-MAPP would clearly show her strong echoic and listener skills, as well as her weak tacting and manding skills. It would also show that she is not ready for intraverbal, textual, or transcriptive training.

2. **Establish intervention priorities.** The focus for Brittney would be on developing her mand and tact skills. While there are many different language skills that she will eventually need, these are the most important immediately. For other students, there may be other priorities, and the VB-MAPP can help to identify these. For example, if a student can name 500 different items but cannot talk about any of those items when they are absent, intraverbal training will be a priority.

3. **Implement an intervention program.** For children with significant needs like Brittney, it is recommended that a classroom be designed as a language-based environment where every activity across the day incorporates language-training procedures using behavioral teaching methodology, and staff receive regular training and support. The daily schedule should involve specific language-training sessions (e.g., tact, intraverbal), as well as language training during natural and social environment activities (e.g., Hart & Risley, 1975; Sundberg & Partington, 1998).

4. **Track skill acquisition.** The only way to tell if a student is acquiring the targeted language skills is to collect data on those skills. These data can then provide the needed guidance for each student's intervention program.

5. **Practice and generalization.** Once specific language skills are acquired, it is important to maintain them with regular practice. It is easy to forget words if there are not enough opportunities to use them or if new words make it difficult to remember old words. Also, once a student has learned a specific word and function, such as the ability to tact (name) a car, it is important to make sure the student can tact different cars, in different locations, and for different people. The student's peers and family play a valuable role in providing opportunities to practice communication.

About the Author

Mark L. Sundberg, Ph.D., BCBA-D is the founder and a past editor of the journal *The Analysis of Verbal Behavior* and the author of the *VB-MAPP*.

TEACHING & LEARNING

Some SLPs employ structured exercises and drills to correct speech sounds; others emphasize speech production in natural language contexts. Some prefer to work with children in individual therapy sessions; others believe that group sessions are advantageous for language modeling and peer support. Some encourage children to imitate the therapist's speech; others have the child listen to recordings of his own speech. Some specialists follow a structured, teacher-directed approach in which targeted speech and language behaviors are precisely prompted, reinforced, and recorded; others use less structured methods. Some SLPs focus on a child's expressive and receptive communication; others devote attention to other aspects of the child's behavior and environment, such as developing self-confidence and improving interactions with parents and classmates.

Treating Speech-Sound Errors

A general goal of specialists in communication disorders is to help the child speak as clearly and pleasantly as possible so that a listener's attention will focus on the child's message rather than how he says it.

ARTICULATION ERRORS The goals of therapy for articulation problems are acquisition of correct speech sound(s), generalization of the sound(s) to all speaking settings and contexts (especially the classroom), and maintenance of the correct sound(s) after therapy has ended. Traditional articulation therapy involves discrimination and production activities.

Discrimination activities are designed to improve the child's ability to listen carefully and detect the differences between similar sounds (e.g., the /t/ in *tape,* the /k/ in *cape*) and to differentiate between correct and distorted speech sounds. The child learns to match his speech to that of a standard model by using auditory, visual, and tactile feedback. A generally consistent relationship exists between children's ability to recognize sounds and their ability to articulate them correctly.

Production is the ability to produce a given speech sound alone and in various contexts. Therapy emphasizes the repetitive production of sounds in various contexts, with special attention to the motor skills involved in articulation. Exercises are employed to produce sounds with differing stress patterns. The SLP may have the child carefully watch how sounds are produced and then use a mirror to monitor his own speech production. Children are expected to accurately produce problematic sounds in syllables, words, sentences, and stories. They may record their own speech and listen carefully for errors. Therapy progresses from having the child articulate simple sounds in isolation; then in syllables, words, phrases, sentences, and structured conversation; and finally in unstructured conversation. As in all communication training, it is important for the teacher, parent, and specialist to provide good language models, reinforce improving performance, and encourage the child to talk.

SLPs use audition, visual, and tactile feedback to help children match their speech to that of a standard model.

PHONOLOGICAL ERRORS   When a child's spoken language problem includes one or more phonological errors, the goal of therapy is to help the child identify the error pattern(s) and gradually produce more linguistically appropriate sound patterns (Barlow, 2001). For example, a child who frequently omits final consonants might be taught to recognize the difference between minimally contrastive words—perhaps using a set of cards with the words *sea, seed, seal, seam,* and *seat* (Hall et al., 2001). Therapeutic tasks are constructed so that the child is rewarded for following directions (e.g., "Pick up the *seal* card") and speaking clearly enough for the therapist to follow his or her directions (e.g., the child directs the SLP to give him the *seat* card). To respond correctly, the child must attend to and use the information in the final consonant sound.

Sounds are not taught in isolation. Children with phonological problems can often articulate specific sounds but do not use those sounds in proper linguistic context.

Although the distinction between articulation errors and phonological errors is important, many children with communication disorders have problems with both. The therapeutic approaches for articulation and phonological disorders are not incompatible and can be used together for some children.

Treating Fluency Disorders

Throughout history, people who stutter have been subjected to countless treatments—some of them unusual, to say the least. Past treatments included holding pebbles in the mouth, sticking fingers into a light socket, talking out of one side of the mouth, eating raw oysters, speaking with the teeth clenched, taking alternating hot and cold baths, and speaking on inhaled rather than exhaled air (Ham, 1986). For many years, it was widely thought that a tongue that was unable to function properly in the mouth caused stuttering. As a result, it was common for early physicians to prescribe ointments to blister or numb the tongue or even to remove portions of the tongue through surgery!

Application of behavioral principles has strongly influenced contemporary practice in the treatment of fluency disorders. Therapists using this methodology regard stuttering as learned behavior and seek to replace it by establishing and encouraging fluent speech. One example of a behaviorally based stuttering treatment approach is the Lidcombe Program, which trains parents to ignore their child's stuttering initially and reinforce fluent utterances with frequent praise (e.g., "That was smooth talking!") (Jones et al., 2005; Koushick, Shenker, & Onslaw, 2009). Onslow, Packman, and Harrison (2003) report that studies evaluating the effectiveness of the Lidcombe Program with over 750 children worldwide have reported a 95% success rate.

Children may learn to manage their stuttering by deliberately prolonging certain sounds or by speaking slowly to get through a "block." They may increase their confidence and fluency by speaking in groups, where pressure is minimized and successful speech is positively reinforced. They may learn to monitor their own speech and to reward themselves for periods of fluency (Ryan, 2004). They may learn to speak to a rhythmic beat or with the aid of devices that mask or delay their ability to hear their own speech. Audio recorders are often used for drills, simulating conversations, and documenting progress.

Children often learn to control their stuttering and produce increasingly fluent speech as they mature (Ramig & Pollard, 2011). No single method of treatment has been recognized as most effective. Stuttering frequently decreases when children enter adolescence, regardless of which treatment method was used. Often, the problem disappears with no treatment at all. Results from studies of the phenomenon of spontaneous recovery from stuttering have reported that 65% to 80% of children diagnosed as stutterers apparently outgrow or get over their dysfluencies without formal intervention (Yairi & Ambrose, 1999). Nevertheless, an SLP should be contacted when a child exhibits signs of stuttering or when the parents are concerned about speech fluency. Although some children who stutter improve without help, many do

Detailed description of the Lidcombe Program and the research evaluating it is available at the Australian Stuttering Research Centre website: http://sydney.edu.au/health_sciences/asrc/.

not. Early intervention may prevent the child from developing a severe stutter. In its initial stages, stuttering can almost always be treated successfully by teachers, parents, and an SLP working together.

There is no single treatment for stuttering because the causation, type, and severity of nonfluencies vary from child to child. Despite this variability, teachers can significantly help a child who stutters by providing a good speech model, paying attention to what the child is saying rather than to his difficulties in saying it, and reinforcing fluent speech (LaBlance, Steckol, & Smith, 1994; National Institute on Deafness and Other Communication Disorders [NIDCD], 2011). When the child experiences a verbal block, the teacher should be patient and calm, refrain from telling the child to "slow down" or "take a deep breath," and maintain eye contact with the child until he finishes speaking.

Treating Voice Disorders

A thorough medical examination should always be sought for a child with a voice disorder. Surgery or other medical interventions can often treat organic causes. In addition, SLPs often recommend environmental modifications; a person who is consistently required to speak in a noisy setting, for example, may benefit from the use of a small microphone to reduce vocal straining and shouting. Most remedial techniques, however, offer direct vocal rehabilitation, which helps the child with a voice disorder gradually learn to produce more acceptable and efficient speech. Voice therapy often begins with teaching the child to listen to his own voice and learn to identify those aspects that need to be changed. Depending on the type of voice disorder and the child's overall circumstances, vocal rehabilitation may include activities such as exercises to increase breathing capacity, relaxation techniques to reduce tension, vocal hygiene (e.g., drink fluids, avoid excessive throat clearing, vocal rest), and procedures to increase or decrease the loudness of speech (Sapienza et al., 2011).

Because many voice problems are directly attributable to vocal abuse, techniques from applied behavior analysis can be used to help children and adults break habitual patterns of vocal misuse. For example, a child might self-monitor the number of abuses he commits in the classroom or at home, receiving rewards for gradually lowering the number of abuses over time.

Treating Language Disorders

Treatments for language disorders are also extremely varied. Some programs focus on precommunication activities that encourage the child to explore and that make the environment conducive to the development of receptive and expressive language. Clearly, children must have something they want to communicate. And because children learn through imitation, it is important for the teacher or specialist to speak clearly, use correct inflections, and provide a rich variety of words and sentences.

Children with very limited oral language might be taught how to orally "read" pictures as a language enhancement activity (Alberto & Fredrick, 2000). Teachers can use story boards and song boards with pictures illustrating language: The teacher places and removes pictures from the board as she tells the story or points to the appropriate picture while singing a line (Skau & Cascella, 2006). Children with language impairments might develop written language skills by exchanging e-mail letters with pen pals (Harmston, Strong, & Evans, 2001).

VOCABULARY BUILDING Vocabulary has been called the building block of language (Dockrell & Messer, 2004). Children with language disorders have a limited store of words to call upon. Speech-language pathologists and classroom teachers use a wide variety of techniques to build students' vocabulary, including graphic organizers, mnemonics, and learning strategies. Foil and Alber (2003)

Interacting with a child who stutters

 Council for Exceptional Children

Content Standards for Beginning Teachers—Common Core: Teacher attitudes and behaviors that influence behavior of individuals with exceptional learning needs (ICC5K4).

recommend that teachers use the following sequence to help students learn new vocabulary:

1. Display each new word, pronounce it, give the meaning of the word, and have students repeat it.
2. Provide and have students repeat multiple examples of the word used in context.
3. Connect the word and its meaning to students' current knowledge, and prompt students to describe their experiences related to the word.
4. Provide multiple opportunities for students to use the word in context during guided practice, and provide feedback on their responses.
5. Help students discriminate between words with similar meanings but subtle differences (e.g., *separate* and *segregate*).
6. Assign independent practice activities; challenge students to select new vocabulary words to learn independently.
7. Promote generalization and maintenance by prompting students to use their new vocabulary, providing praise and other forms of reinforcement when students' speech and writing contain new vocabulary, and having students self-record how often they use new vocabulary.

NATURALISTIC STRATEGIES Speech-language pathologists are increasingly employing naturalistic interventions to help children develop and use communication skills. Naturalistic approaches were developed as an alternative to didactic language interventions because children often experienced difficulties in generalizing new skills from structured teaching settings to everyday contexts. In contrast to didactic teaching approaches, which use contrived materials and activities (e.g., pictures, puppets) and massed trials to teach specific skills, naturalistic interventions, often called *milieu* or *incidental teaching,* take advantage of naturally occurring activities throughout the day to provide motivation and opportunities for a child to use language skills (Downing, 2011). Naturalistic approaches occur in the context of typical conversational interchanges that follow the child's "attentional lead" (Goldstein, Kaczmarek, & Hepting, 1994).

Kaiser and Grim (2006) make the following recommendations about naturalistic interventions:

- Teach when the child is interested.
- Teach what is functional for the student at the moment.
- Stop while both the student and the teacher are still enjoying the interaction. (pp. 455–456)

Naturalistic interventions involve structuring the environment to create numerous opportunities for desired child responses (e.g., holding up a toy and asking, "What do you want?") and structuring adult responses to a child's communication (e.g., the child points outside and says, "Go wifth me," and the teacher says, "Okay, I'll go with you"). Effective milieu teaching more closely resembles a conversation than a structured instructional episode (Kaiser & Grim, 2006). However, good naturalistic teaching does not mean the teacher should wait patiently to see whether and when opportunities for meaningful and interesting language use by children occur. Environments in which language teaching takes place should be designed to catch students' interest and increase the likelihood of communicative interactions that can be used for teaching purposes. Six strategies for arranging environments that create naturally occurring language teaching opportunities are described in Figure 5.

No matter what the approach to treatment, children with language disorders need to be around children and adults with something interesting to talk about. Educators assumed for many years that a one-to-one setting was the most effective format for language intervention. Emphasis was on eliminating distracting stimuli and focusing

Naturalistic interventions/
milieu teaching strategies

Council for
Exceptional
Children

Content
Standards for
Beginning
Teachers—Common Core:
Design learning environments
that encourage active
participation in individual and
group activities (ICC5S4)

FIGURE 5   SIX STRATEGIES FOR INCREASING NATURALISTIC OPPORTUNITIES FOR LANGUAGE TEACHING

1. **Interesting materials.**   Students are likely to communicate when things or activities in the environment interest them. *Example:* James lay quietly on the rug, with his head resting on his arms. Ms. Davis sat at one end of the rug and rolled a big yellow ball right past James. James lifted his head and looked around for the ball.

2. **Out of reach.**   Students are likely to communicate when they want something that they cannot reach. *Example:* Mr. Norris lifted a drum off the shelf and placed it on the floor between Judy and Annette, who were both in wheelchairs. Mr. Norris hit the drum three times and then waited, looking at his two students. Judy watched and clapped her hands together. Then, she reached for the drum with both arms outstretched.

3. **Inadequate portions.**   Students are likely to communicate when they do not have the necessary materials to carry out an instruction. *Example:* Mr. Robinson gave every student except Mary a ticket to get into the auditorium for the high school play. He told his students to give their tickets to the attendant. Mr. Robinson walked beside Mary toward the entrance. When Mary reached the attendant, Mr. Robinson paused and looked at Mary. She pointed to the tickets in his hand and signed "give me." Mr. Robinson gave her a ticket and she handed it to the attendant who said "Thank you. Enjoy the play."

4. **Choice-making.**   Students are likely to communicate when they are given a choice. *Example:* Peggy's favorite pastime is listening to tapes on her tape recorder. On Saturday morning, Peggy's father said to her, "We could listen to your tapes" (pointing to the picture of the tape recorder on Peggy's communication board) "or we could go for a ride in the car" (pointing to the picture of the car). "What would you like to do?" Peggy pointed to the picture of the tape recorder. "OK, let's listen to this new tape you like," her father said as he put the tape in and turned on the machine.

5. **Assistance.**   Students are likely to communicate when they need assistance in operating or manipulating materials. *Example:* Tammy's mother always places three clear plastic containers with snacks (cookies, crackers, popcorn) on the kitchen table before Tammy returns from school. When Tammy arrives home and is ready for a snack, she goes to the table and chooses what she wants. The containers are hard to open, so Tammy usually brings the container with her chosen snack to her mother. Her mother responds to this nonverbal request by modeling a request form that specifies Tammy's choice (e.g., "Open popcorn.").

6. **Unexpected situations.**   Students are likely to communicate when something happens that they do not expect. *Example:* Ms. Esser was helping Kathy put on her socks and shoes after rest time. After assisting with the socks, Ms. Esser put one of the shoes on her own foot. Kathy stared at the shoe for a moment and then looked up at her teacher, who was smiling. "No," laughed Kathy, "my shoe."

Source: From Kaiser, A. P., & Grim, J. C. (2006). Teaching functional communication skills. In M. E. Snell & F. Brown (Eds.), *Instruction of students with severe disabilities* (6th ed., p. 464). Upper Saddle River, NJ: Pearson Education, Inc. Reprinted by permission.

a child's attention on the desired communication task. Today, however, it is generally recognized that language is an interactive, interpersonal process and that educators should use naturally occurring intervention formats to expose children with language disorders to a wide range of stimuli, experiences, contexts, and people that cannot be replicated in one-to-one therapy.

Augmentative and Alternative Communication

Augmentative and alternative communication (AAC) refers to a diverse set of strategies and methods to assist individuals who cannot meet their communication needs through speech or writing. AAC entails three components (Kangas & Lloyd, 2011):

- A representational symbol set or vocabulary
- A means for selecting the symbols
- A means for transmitting the symbols

Each of the three components of AAC may be unaided or aided. *Unaided AAC techniques* do not require a physical aid or device. They include oral speech, gestures, facial expressions, general body posture, and manual signs. Of course, individuals without disabilities use a wide range of unaided augmentative communication techniques. *Aided AAC techniques* of communication involve an external device or piece of equipment. AAC devices range from no-tech (e.g., paper and pencil) to low-tech (e.g., the child pushes a switch to transmit a single word or phrase) to high-tech electronic equipment (e.g., computerized voice-output device) (Owens et al., 2011). (See *Teaching & Learning,* "Talking with Pictures? Using PECS to Teach Functional Communication Skills".)

Individuals who do not speak so that others can understand must have access to vocabulary that matches as nearly as possible the language they would use in various situations if they could speak. Beukelman and Miranda (1998) suggest that decisions about what to include in a student's augmentative vocabulary should take into account the following:

- Vocabulary that peers in similar situations and settings use
- What communication partners (e.g., teachers, parents) think will be needed
- Vocabulary the student is already using in all modalities
- Contextual demands of specific situations

SYMBOL SETS AND SYMBOL SYSTEMS   After selecting the vocabulary for an AAC system, the educator must choose or develop a collection of symbols to represent the vocabulary. Symbol sets are graphic, which means that the symbols look like the object or concept they represent as much as possible. Numerous *symbol sets* are available both commercially and free. These sets are a collection of pictures or drawings in which each symbol has one or more specified meanings, from which a person's AAC vocabulary might be constructed. Using software programs such as Mayer-Johnson's Boardmaker, teachers can create individualized sets of communication symbols. Symbol sets may also be homemade, consisting of photos, pictures, and perhaps words and the alphabet.

In contrast to symbol sets, *symbol systems* are structured around an internal set of rules that govern how new symbols are added to the system. One of the best-known symbol systems is Blissymbolics, an international graphical language of over 4,000 symbols, first developed for use by people with physical disabilities. (Blissymbolics Communication International, 2011). Bliss characters combine multiple symbols to create new meanings (e.g., "school" is communicated by selecting the symbols "house-gives-knowledge"). Simple shapes are used to keep the symbols easy and fast to draw. Because many of the Blissymbolics are abstract, however, and do not look like the concept they represent, some individuals have difficulty learning the system.

SELECTING THE SYMBOLS   Students select symbols in augmentative communication by direct selection, scanning, or encoding responses (Kangas & Lloyd, 2011). *Direct selection* involves pointing to the symbol one wishes to express with a finger or fist or sometimes with a wand attached to the head or chin. With a limited number of selections widely spaced from one another, the user can select symbols by "eye pointing." *Scanning* techniques present choices to the user one at a time, and the user makes a response at the proper time to indicate which item or group of selections she wants to communicate. Scanning can be machine or listener assisted (e.g., the listener may point

Augmentative and alternative communication

Content Standards for Beginning Teachers—Common Core: Augmentative and assistive communication strategies (ICC6K4).

To see examples and learn more about Blissymbolics, go to http://www.blissymbolics.org/pfw/. To explore a wide range of symbol systems available for AAC users, search the Internet for "AAC picture communication symbols."

Talking with Pictures? Using PECS to Teach Functional Communication Skills

BY ANDY BONDY AND LORI FROST

Patrick, a not quite 3-year-old with autism who has never spoken, sleepily walks down the stairs dragging his PECS communication book behind. He goes to the kitchen, and Mom helps him into his highchair. Patrick uses his pictures to form the sentence "I want toast butter." Mom reads the pictures out loud and then helps him butter some toast. Patrick takes his pictures again, this time creating "I want toast butter jelly." Mom happily helps her son add some jelly to his toast. Although Patrick has not said a single word, he surely has communicated effectively with his mom. What is PECS, and how does it help children like Patrick?

A form of augmentative and alternative communication (AAC), the Picture Exchange Communication System (PECS) teaches nonverbal users to successfully request highly motivating items and outcomes before moving on to other aspects of language. PECS is unique among language-training programs in that it teaches users to approach a communicative partner before introducing lessons on vocabulary—in this case, what the picture "means." Users learn to request highly motivating items and outcomes before moving on to other aspects of language. PECS has been demonstrated to be effective with children with autism and other disabilities (Charlop-Christy, Carpenter, Le, LeBlanc, & Kellet, 2002), as well as with adults with severe disabilities (Chambers & Rehfeldt, 2003).

EXPANDING COMMUNICATION FROM SINGLE PICTURES TO COMPLEX REQUESTS

The PECS program is divided into several phases, each with its own teaching strategies and error correction procedures. Phase I involves getting a user to pick up, reach for, and release a single picture into the hands of someone who is holding a desired item. Patrick learned to be a spontaneous, independent communicator via a unique training strategy, the Two-Person Prompting Procedure, that prevents prompt dependency—a common dilemma inherent in many training protocols. Phase II involves increasing the distance between the user and her communicative partner and between the user and her pictures. In Phase III, the user learns to discriminate between pictures, beginning with simple choices (e.g., *cookie* vs. *sock*), and moving to more difficult choices (e.g., *cracker* vs. *pretzel*). Phase IV introduces a simple sentence structure—"I want X"—on which additional language skills are later built. At this point, the teacher or SLP focuses on adding attributes, such as "*I want blue car.*" Phase V introduces simple questions, such as "*What do you want?*"; and in the final Phase VI, users

learn to make comments such as "*I see the train*" or "*I hear the bird.*"

Teachers and SLPs most often apply PECS, but several recent studies show that parents, such as Patrick's family, can learn to apply the PECS (BenChaabane, Alber Morgan, & DeBar, 2009; Park, Alber Morgan, & Cannella-Malone, 2011). For detailed description of the PECS training protocol, see Frost and Bondy (2002). A video of Patrick requesting his breakfast toast can be seen at http://www.pecsusa.com/.

BUT WILL MY CHILD TALK?

Because PECS teaches nonverbal users to communicate with pictures, some people are concerned that PECS may interfere or delay the development of speech. In fact, there is no research showing that any AAC system, including PECS, deters speech acquisition or development. To the contrary, several peer-reviewed studies show that PECS, especially for young children, actually increases the likelihood in speech production compared to pretraining vocal skills.

HOW TO GET STARTED

1. **Conduct preference assessment.** Before beginning a PECS lesson, teachers must determine what the user likes. They will need to complete a reinforcer assessment either by systematic observation or a formal analysis. It may be helpful to begin with items that are highly reinforcing and that tend to be "consumable"— that is, things that naturally disappear (e.g., drinks, food items, spinning toys, bubbles that pop, etc.).

2. **Create a set of pictures.** Choose pictures that are easily manipulated by the student. What the picture looks like is not critical because at the beginning of training, we are teaching the student how to interact with it rather than what each picture means (Angermeier et al., 2008). Typically, the pictures are from 2.5- to 5.0-cm squares of card-stock quality paper, often laminated to provide some degree of protection.

3. **Teach basic picture exchange.** This phase works best with two trainers: the communicative partner (CP) controls access to the rewarding item (e.g., child's favorite toy), and the physical prompter (PP) helps the user manipulate the picture. The CP shows the items but says nothing. No picture discrimination is being taught yet, so begin with a single picture between the student and the

Andy Bondy

This girl constructs picture sentences to make requests, answer questions, and comment on her world.

CP. When the user reaches for the item, the PP immediately helps him pick up the picture card and hand it to the CP. As soon as the picture touches the CP's hand, the CP says the name of the item in an excited voice and gives it to the user. The PP fades out physical prompts as rapidly as possible over subsequent training trials.

4. **"Stretch" the lesson.** When the user is reliably handing over a single picture, start increasing the distance between the user and CP, introduce new CPs and different pictures/rewards, and conduct lessons in varied locations.

5. **Teach discrimination.** Although some children carefully select distinct pictures in distinct situations without direct training, most users need to be taught to discriminate between pictures. One strategy is to have the user begin choosing between items that are highly reinforcing and items that are not reinforcing (e.g., a cookie and a sock). If the user selects the cookie picture, give some of the cookie. However, if the user gives the sock picture, then you know a mistake or error has occurred and an error correction strategy would be used. After the user has mastered such easy discriminations, make the choices involve equally reinforcing items.

6. **Teach simple sentence structure.** Give the user a new icon for "*I want*" and a "sentence strip" on which a sequence of pictures can adhere (see photo). Teach the user to place "I want" and a picture of the requested item on the sentence strip, and then hand the entire strip to the CP. Once this new skill is acquired, the CP helps the user touch each picture as the CP says the corresponding word. This is an exciting time because some users begin to speak as this strategy

is introduced. If speech occurs, the CP should provide enthusiastic praise. If the user doesn't speak, give encouragement but don't try to force the user to speak. It's much more effective to create frequent opportunities for speech and reinforce any approximations of speech as they occur.

7. **Teach attributes.** Identify the attributes of the most powerful reinforcers that are likely to be most appealing to the child. If a big cookie is likely to be preferred over a small cookie, teach the user to request, "*I want big cookie.*" A child who consistently picks out all the red blocks from a pile of blocks of different colors can be taught to request, "*I want red block.*" Taking advantage of a child's current interests will be more motivating and effective than asking the child to "Point to the big cup" or "Give me the red spoon."

8. **Teach responding to questions.** Teach the user to use pictures to respond to the simple question "What do you want?"

9. **Teach commenting.** Create interesting sights, sounds, and tactile events that will capture the user's attention. When the user creates and hands over a comment (e.g., "*I see car*"), the CP should not give the car to the child. Comments lead to social reactions, not the receipt of the item. Once the user begins to comment and attributes have been acquired, arrange for the user to incorporate any attributes learned within a comment ("I see the big brown bear").

About the Authors

Lori Frost, a speech-language pathologist, and Andy Bondy, a behavior analyst, are the developers of PECS.

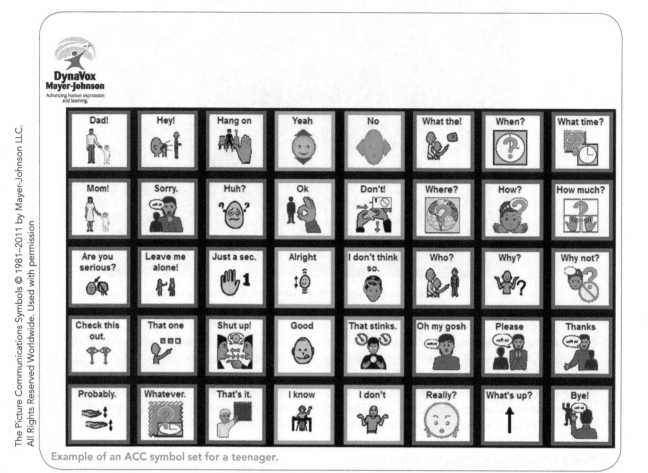

Example of an ACC symbol set for a teenager.

to symbols one at a time while watching for the user's eye blink, which signals selection). *Encoding* involves giving multiple signals to indicate the location of the symbol or the item to be selected. Usually, the user makes a pair of responses that directs the listener to a specific printed message on a reference list. In a display in which symbols are organized by color and number, for example, a student can first touch one card (to select the red group of messages) and then make a second pointing response to indicate which number message in the red group is intended.

TRANSMITTING THE SYMBOLS After meaningful vocabulary and an appropriate symbol set have been determined, a method of transmitting the symbols must be considered.

An ever-more sophisticated variety of AAC devices offer a wide range of alternatives for transmitting communication symbols. Software developers have created numerous AAC apps for smart phones, such as the iPhone and Android, and for portable tablets, such as the iPad. Dedicated communication aids—such as the Dynavok Maestro and Prentke Romich Intro Talker—offer computerized speech selection and transmission and large vocabulary that can be individualized for the user.

In spite of the high-tech "arms race" among developers and providers of computer-based AAC systems, one of the most common and effective AAC tools is the *communication board,* a flat area (often a tray or a table attached to a wheelchair) on which the symbols are arranged for the user to select. A student may have a basic communication board of common words, phrases, numbers, and so forth, for use across many situations. A student may also have various situational boards, or miniboards, with specific vocabulary for certain situations (e.g., at a restaurant, in science class). Students can also transport and display symbols in a wallet or a photo album.

EDUCATIONAL PLACEMENT ALTERNATIVES

During the 2008–09 school year, approximately 87% of children with speech or language impairments were served in the general education classroom—6% in resource rooms and 4.6% in separate classes (U.S. Department of Education, 2010b). A wide variety of service delivery models for students with communication disorders are used within and across these three educational placement options. ASHA recognizes the following seven service delivery models (ASHA, 2000).

Monitoring

The SLP monitors or checks on the student's speech and language performance in the general education classroom. This option is often used just before a student is dismissed from therapy.

Pull-Out

The traditional and still most prevalent model of service delivery is the pull-out approach, sometimes called *intermittent direct service*. SLPs spend two-thirds of their time working with a child individually or with small groups of up to three children (ASHA, 2010). Depending on the needs of the individual child, pull-out may involve sessions of up to 1 hour 5 days per week.

According to ASHA (2010), most of the students receiving services from school-based SLPs during the school year met with the SLP at least two times a week, most often for 21- to 30-minute sessions. The classroom teacher and the SLP collaborate so that curriculum materials used in the classroom can be incorporated into the child's speech and language therapy sessions.

Many SLPs believe it is impossible to adequately serve a child with speech or language impairments with an isolated, pull-out approach (two or three 30-minute sessions each week with a specialist) (Harn, Bradshaw, & Ogletree, 1999). Because communication is seen as occurring most meaningfully in the natural environment, remedial procedures are increasingly carried out in the general education classroom during ongoing routines rather than in a special speech room.

Collaborative Consultation

Increasingly, communication disorders specialists serve as consultants for regular and special education teachers (and parents) rather than spending most of their time providing direct services to individual children (Dohan & Schulz, 1998). SLPs who work in school settings more often function as team members concerned with children's overall education and development. The SLP often provides training and consultation for the general education classroom teacher, who may do much of the direct work with a child with communication disorders. The specialist concentrates on assessing communication disorders, evaluating progress, and providing materials and techniques. Teachers and parents are encouraged to follow the specialist's guidelines.

Classroom or Curriculum Based

Increasingly, SLPs are working as educational partners in the classroom, mediating between students' communication needs and the communication demands of the academic curriculum. SLPs report devoting about one-fourth of time in helping teachers integrate language and speech goals into daily curriculum activities. The advantage is that services are brought to the child and the teacher, and communication connections with the curriculum are made more directly.

Training classroom teachers and parents to promote children's speech and language development has become an increasingly important aspect of the SLP's responsibilities. A growing controversy among some members of the SLP profession is the extent to which services for students with speech and language impairments provided in general education classrooms should take "a therapeutic focus" versus an

Placement alternatives

Content Standards for Beginning Teachers—Common Core: Issues, assurances, and due process rights related to assessment, eligibility, and placement with a continuum of services (ICC1K6).

Collaboration with SLPs

Content Standards for Beginning Teachers—Common Core: Models and strategies of consultation and collaboration (ICC10K1).

Hall and colleagues (2001) and Lue (2001) offer numerous suggestions for how teachers can help children with communication disorders in the classroom.

"educational focus" (Prelock, 2000a, 2000b). Although SLPs in the schools are being encouraged to provide services within inclusive models, they often express concern that they are becoming more like classroom teachers and that the therapy they should be providing to students on their caseloads is becoming watered down as a result. Ehren (2000) discusses these concerns and offers solutions to the role confusion and dissatisfaction of many SLPs who provide in-classroom speech-language services. Ehren suggests that SLPs can preserve their role identity and the integrity of services provided by maintaining a therapeutic focus and sharing the responsibility for student success with classroom teachers.

Separate Classroom

Students with the most severe communication disorders are served in special classrooms for children with speech or language impairments. During the 2009–10 school year, approximately 1 in 20 children with speech or language impairments were served in separate classes (U.S. Department of Education, 2011).

Community Based

In community-based models, speech and language therapy is provided outside the school, usually in the home. This model is most often used with preschoolers and sometimes for students with severe disabilities, with an emphasis on teaching functional communication skills in the community.

Combination

Variations of all these models exist, and many schools and SLPs serve children using combinations of two or more models.

▼ TIPS FOR BEGINNING TEACHERS

Supporting Students with Language Disorders

BY STEVE EVERLING

LANGUAGE IMPAIRMENTS

Although each student with a language impairment presents a unique profile, teachers can implement some general strategies when working with these students.

- **Thoroughly explain new vocabulary.** Students with language impairments often have problems learning and retaining new words, so explicitly explaining new vocabulary is essential. To create an environment for success for these students, present the new vocabulary orally and in writing with a definition, and then provide visual cues (pictures), gestural cues, and examples. After presenting and explaining these words, post the visual cues in the classroom so that students can refer to them as needed.
- **Embed new vocabulary across the curriculum.** Students will need a lot of practice and repetition with new vocabulary. The best way to provide this practice is to create opportunities for the students to use new vocabulary across content areas and in different contexts. For example, if you are teaching farm animal vocabulary, have students read books about farm animals during reading, design a farm animal habitat during science,

and graph animal characteristics (e.g., animals that eat hay) as part of their math lesson.

- **Provide longer wait time.** Students with language impairments sometimes need a little longer to formulate and express responses to questions. Wait 3 or 4 seconds longer than you normally would to give the student a chance to answer, and don't interrupt or hurry the student with her answer.
- **Break multistep directions into smaller components.** Complying with a teacher's complex, multistep direction, "Put your paper in your desk and push in your chair before you go to the bathroom," may be overwhelming for a student with a language impairment. To lessen frustration and create more opportunities for compliance, break up your directions into smaller tasks:

Step 1: "Put your paper in your desk."
Step 2: "Stand up and push in your chair."
Step 3: "Now you may go to the bathroom."

Do not move on to a new direction until the student completes each task successfully. Once the student consistently follows shorter directions, you can start to give longer directions.

ARTICULATION ERRORS

Although students in the primary grades exhibit variability in speech-sound development, most typically developing children consistently make most speech sounds by the time they begin kindergarten.

- **Do not confuse typical speech-sound development with serious articulation errors.** Even typically developing children sometimes have difficulty with the /r/ and /l/ sounds and complex consonant blends, like the /str/ in *street*, which may not fully develop until first or second grade. However, a kindergarten child who is difficult to understand may be at risk for communication and literacy learning problems, so be sure to monitor her progress.
- **Consult with your school's SLP if you have a hard time understanding a child's speech.** Whenever you are uncertain whether a student's speech-sound development is where it should be, consult with your school's SLP. The SLP will be able to answer your questions and, if need be, begin a formal evaluation and intervention process with the student.

STUTTERING

Many teachers are unsure of what to do with a student who stutters. Here are a few general guidelines:

- **Don't anticipate what the student wants to say and finish the utterance for her.** Instead, try to listen attentively, letting the student work through the stuttering moment on her own.
- **Consistently model a relaxed and unhurried speaking style.** Your calm and steady speech will have a more positive effect on the student than telling her to "slow down" or "relax."
- **Ask the student what strategies she uses to speak more fluently.** It is okay to speak openly and individually with the student about her stuttering. Implementing these strategies in the classroom can make the educational process more effective and enjoyable for the student and give her a sense of empowerment.

▼ KEY TERMS AND CONCEPTS

aphasia
articulation disorder
augmentative and alternative communication
    (AAC)
cleft palate
cluttering
communication
communication disorder
dialects
dysarthria
echoic
expressive language disorder
fluency disorder
graphemes
imitate
intraverbal
language
language disorder

listener
mand
morphemes
morphology
phoneme
phonological disorder
phonology
pragmatics
receptive language disorder
semantics
speech
speech impairments
stuttering
syntax
tact
textual
transcription
voice disorder

▼ SUMMARY

Definitions

- *Communication* is any interaction that transmits information. Narrating, explaining, informing, requesting, and expressing are major communicative functions.
- A *language* is an arbitrary symbol system that enables a group of people to communicate. Each language has rules of phonology, morphology, syntax, semantics, and

pragmatics that describe how users put sounds and ideas together to convey meaning.
- *Speech* is the oral production of language; it is the fastest and most efficient method of communication by language.
- Typical language development follows a relatively predictable sequence. Most children learn to talk and

use language without any formal instruction; by the time they enter first grade, their grammar and speech patterns match those of the adults around them.

- A *communication disorder* is "an impairment in the ability to receive, send, process, and comprehend concepts or verbal, nonverbal and graphic symbol systems" (ASHA, 1993, p. 40).
- A child has a speech impairment if his speech draws unfavorable attention to itself, interferes with the ability to communicate, or causes social or interpersonal problems.
- The three basic types of speech impairments are articulation disorders (errors in the production of speech sounds), fluency disorders (difficulties with the flow or rhythm of speech), and voice disorders (problems with the quality or use of one's voice).
- Some children have trouble understanding language (receptive language disorders); others have trouble using language to communicate (expressive language disorders); still others have language delays.
- Speech or language differences based on cultural or regional dialects are not communication disorders. However, children who use a different dialect may also have speech or language disorders.

Characteristics

- Four basic kinds of speech-sound errors exist: distortions, substitutions, omissions, and additions.
- A child with an articulation disorder cannot produce a given sound physically.
- A child with a phonological disorder can produce a given sound and does so correctly in some instances but not at other times.
- Stuttering, the most common fluency disorder, is marked by rapid-fire repetitions of consonant or vowel sounds, especially at the beginnings of words, prolongations, hesitations, interjections, and complete verbal blocks.
- A voice disorder is characterized by abnormal vocal quality, pitch, loudness, resonance, and/or duration for the speaker's age and sex.
- Language impairments involve problems in phonology, morphology, syntax, semantics, and/or pragmatics; they are usually classified as either receptive or expressive.

Prevalence

- About 2.5% of school-age children receive special education for speech and language impairments, the second-largest disability category under IDEA.
- Nearly twice as many boys as girls have speech impairments.
- Children with articulation and spoken language problems represent the largest category of speech-language impairments.

Causes

- Although some speech and language impairments have physical (organic) causes, most are functional disorders that cannot be directly attributed to physical conditions.

Identification and Assessment

- Assessment of a suspected communication disorder may include some or all of the following components: (a) case history and physical examination, (b) articulation test, (c) hearing test, (d) auditory discrimination test, (e) phonological awareness and processing, (f) vocabulary and overall language development test, (g) assessment of language function, (h) language samples, and (i) observation in natural settings.

Educational Approaches

- Speech-language pathologists (SLPs) employ a wide range of techniques for identifying, evaluating, and providing therapeutic services to children. These include structured exercises and drills as well as individual and group therapy sessions.
- A general goal of treating speech-sound errors is to help the child speak as clearly as possible. Addressing articulation and phonological errors involves discrimination and production activities. Fluency disorders can be treated with the application of behavioral principles and self-monitoring, although many children recover spontaneously.
- Voice disorders can be treated surgically or medically if the cause is organic. Most remedial techniques offer direct vocal rehabilitation. Behavioral principles help break habitual patterns of misuse.
- Language disorder treatments vary widely. Precommunication activities encourage exploration of expressive language. SLPs connect oral language to literacy components of the curriculum. Naturalistic interventions disperse learning trials throughout the natural environment and normal conversation.
- Augmentative and alternative communication may be aided or unaided and consists of three components: a representational symbol set or vocabulary, a means for selecting the symbols, and a means for transmitting the symbols.

Educational Placement Alternatives

- Most children with speech and language problems (87%) attend general education classes.
- ASHA recognizes seven service delivery models: monitoring, pull-out, collaborative consultation, classroom based, separate classroom, community based, and combination.

MyEducationLab™

Go to Topic 13, Communication Disorders, in the MyEducationLab (www.myeducationlab.com) for *Exceptional Children,* where you can

- Find learning outcomes for communication disorders along with the national standards that connect to these outcomes.
- Complete Assignments and Activities that can help you more deeply understand the chapter content.
- Apply and practice your understanding of the core teaching skills identified in the chapter with the Building Teaching Skills and Dispositions learning units.
- Examine challenging situations and cases presented in the IRIS Center Resources.
- Access video clips of CCSSO National Teachers of the Year award winners responding to the question "Why do I teach?" in the Teacher Talk section.
- Check your comprehension of the content covered in the chapter with the Study Plan. Here you will be able to take a chapter quiz, receive feedback on your answers, and then access Review, Practice, and Enrichment activities to enhance your understanding of chapter content.
- Use the Online Lesson Plan Builder to practice lesson planning and integrating national and state standards into your planning.

▼ GLOSSARY

aphasia: The loss of speech functions; often, but not always, refers to inability to speak because of brain lesions.

articulation disorder: Abnormal production of speech sounds.

augmentative and alternative communication (AAC): A diverse set of nonspeech communication strategies and methods to assist individuals who cannot meet their communication needs through speech; includes sign language, symbol systems, communication boards, and synthetic speech devices.

cleft palate: A congenital split in the palate that results in an excessive nasal quality of the voice. Can often be repaired by surgery or a dental appliance.

cluttering: A type of fluency disorder in which speech is very rapid, with extra sounds or mispronounced sounds; speech may be garbled to the point of unintelligibility; compare to *stuttering.*

communication: An interactive process requiring at least two parties in which messages are encoded, transmitted, and decoded by any means, including sounds, symbols, and gestures.

communication disorder: "An impairment in the ability to receive, send, process, and comprehend concepts or verbal, nonverbal, and graphic symbols systems. . . . [D]isorder may be evident in the processes of hearing, language, and/or speech" (ASHA, 1993, p. 40).

dialect: A variety within a specific language; can involve variation in pronunciation, word choice, word order, and inflected forms.

dysarthria: A group of speech disorders caused by neuromuscular impairments in respiration, phonation, resonation, and articulation.

echoic: An elementary verbal operant evoked by a verbal discriminative stimulus that has point-to-point correspondence and formal similarity with the response (e.g., parent says, "Cookie," and child says, "Cookie"). Learning to repeat the words of others is essential to acquiring the other elementary verbal operants.

expressive language disorder: A language impairment that interferes with the production of language; contrast with *receptive disorder.*

fluency disorder: A speech disorder characterized by atypical rate, rhythm, and repetitions in sounds, syllables, words, and phrases; see *stuttering, cluttering.*

grapheme: The smallest level of written language that corresponds to one phoneme; for example,, the grapheme *t* represents the phoneme /t/.

intraverbal: An elementary verbal operant evoked by a verbal discriminative stimulus that does *not* have point-to-point correspondence with that verbal stimulus (e.g., parent says, "What tastes good with milk?"; child says, "Cookie."). Intraverbal behavior constitutes the basis for social interaction, conversations, and much of academic and intellectual behavior. Questions are mands, and answers are intraverbal.

language: A system used by a group of people for giving meaning to sounds, words, gestures, and other symbols to enable communication with one another. Languages can use vocal (speech sounds) or nonvocal symbols, such as American Sign Language, or use movements and physical symbols instead of sounds.

language disorder: Impaired comprehension and/or use of spoken, written, and/or other symbol systems.

listener: Responding to the language of others. Someone who provides reinforcement for verbal behavior. (e.g., a classmate says, "Hand me a cookie," and child picks out and gives cookie."). A listener may also serve as an audience evoking verbal behavior. The distinction between listener and speaker is often blurred by the fact that much of a listener's behavior may involve being a speaker at the covert level (e.g., thinking about what was said). A speaker may be his own listener (contrast with *speaker*).

mand: An elementary verbal operant motivated by and followed by specific reinforcement (e.g., child wants a cookie and says, "Cookie"). Manding allows speakers to get their wants and needs reinforced by listeners. Manding plays an important role in language acquisition.

morpheme: The smallest element of a language that carries meaning.

morphology: Refers to the basic units of meaning in a language and how those units are combined into words.

phoneme: The smallest unit of sound that can be identified in a spoken language. The English language has 45 phonemes, or sound families.

phonological disorder: A language disorder in which the child produces a given sound correctly in some instances but not at other times.

phonology: Refers to the linguistic rules governing a language's sound system.

pragmatics: Refers to the rules that govern how language is used in a communication context.

receptive language disorder: A language impairment characterized by difficulty in understanding language; contrast with *expressive language disorder*.

semantics: Refers to the meaning in language.

speech: Using breath and muscles to create the specific sounds of spoken language.

speech impairment: Speech that "deviates so far from the speech of other people that it (1) calls attention to itself, (2) interferes with communication, or (3) provokes distress in the speaker or the listener" (Van Riper & Erickson, 1996, p. 110). The three basic types of speech impairments are articulation, fluency, and voice.

stuttering: Fluency disorder of speaking marked by rapid-fire repetitions of consonant or vowel sounds, especially at the beginning of words; prolongations; hesitations; interjections; and complete verbal blocks; compare to *cluttering*.

syntax: The system of rules governing the meaningful arrangement of words in a language.

tact: An elementary verbal operant evoked by a nonverbal discriminative stimulus and followed by generalized conditioned reinforcement (e.g., teacher points to a cookie and child says, "Cookie"). Tacting enables a speaker to name the features of the physical environment such as items, actions, and properties.

textual: An elementary verbal operant involving a response that is evoked by a verbal discriminative stimulus that has point-to-point correspondence, but no formal similarity, between the stimulus and the response product. Reading is textual behavior—decoding printed words into spoken language—comprehending what one has decoded, however, requires other verbal skills such as intraverbal behavior (vocabulary) and listener skills (receptive language).

transcription: An elementary verbal operant involving a spoken verbal stimulus that evokes a written, typed, or finger-spelled response.

voice disorder: The "abnormal production and/or absences of vocal quality, pitch, loudness, resonance, and/or duration, which is inappropriate for an individual's age and/or sex" (ASHA, 1993, p. 40).

Blindness and Low Vision

Blindness and Low Vision

► **FOCUS QUESTIONS**

- What are the instructional implications of the three general classifications of visual impairments that educators use?

- How do blindness and low vision affect learning, motor development, and social interaction?

- Why is it important that teachers know about the types of visual impairments affecting children in their classrooms?

- How do the educational goals and instructional methods for children with low vision differ from those for children who are blind?

- How might the educational placement of a student with visual impairments affect her opportunities to learn the expanded core curriculum of nonacademic skills necessary for overall success in life?

▼ FEATURED TEACHER

CECELIA PEIRANO

Ohio State School for the Blind • Columbus, Ohio

EDUCATION—TEACHING CREDENTIALS—EXPERIENCE

- B.A., elementary education, The Ohio State University, 1977

- M.A., visual impairment, K–12, The Ohio State University, 1978

- Ohio Professional Elementary, 1–8; Professional Special Education, Visually Impaired, K–8; National Board Certification, Exceptional Needs Specialist, Vision, 2004

- 34 years of experience as a teacher of students with visual impairments

CURRENT TEACHING POSITION AND STUDENTS

The Ohio State School for the Blind serves both day students from the surrounding area and also residential students from throughout the state. I currently teach eight fifth and sixth graders ages 10 to 13. My students' academic abilities vary greatly; several of my students have learning disabilities, and two are gifted. They attend special classes for technology, orientation and mobility, physical education, and music and art. I also serve as the coordinator of the elementary department to facilitate the activities, curriculum, and programs of the elementary classes.

CURRICULUM MODIFICATIONS

Success for students with visual impairments is contingent on their ability to access the core curriculum and receiving specialized instruction in the unique areas of the expanded core curriculum for students with visual impairments (braille, listening skills, orientation and mobility, social skills, visual efficiency, and technology, to name a few). Teachers need to work in teams to assure that students are receiving the appropriate visual, tactile, and auditory modifications. A comprehensive functional vision assessment and learning media assessment will inform a teacher of the specific modification each student needs to be successful.

In math, for example, students will need more manipulatives and hands-on time to explore concepts. The materials need to be enlarged or made tactually accessible. In addition to Nemeth, the braille code for math, modifications for math instruction include three-dimensional objects, tactile graphics, talking calculators, computer with assistive software, and extended time.

Since keyboarding is necessary for students to access technology, we start teaching keyboarding in first grade. Our students use the Talking Typer program available from the American Printing House for the Blind. It uses touch typing method with both auditory and large-print capabilities. You don't want to use large print, braille or adaptive keyboards unless the student has a physical disability. The students just need to feel the raised marks on the *f* and *j* keys that are on all standard keyboards. Because they don't try to visually scan the keyboard, my totally blind students are almost always my best typists.

TECHNOLOGY OPENS MANY DOORS Technology today is wonderful for both teachers of students with visual impairments and especially their students. It gives students many opportunities to be included in regular activities with their sighted peers and the skills they will need to join the job market as a teenager or adult. Accessing print material has always been difficult for students with visual impairments, but technology has definitely leveled the playing field.

Students with low vision can learn to use closed-circuit televisions, ZoomText, pocket viewers, and many additional pieces of equipment to enlarge, store, and manipulate print, access computers, or have material read to them. Students who use braille can access material with BrailleNote, JAWS or other screen readers, special keyboards for smart phones, and the list goes on! Students just soak up all of the information available through new technology, and our students with visual impairments need to be a part of it!

Teachers also can make curriculum more easily accessible to students through programs that translate print to braille such as Duxbury, transmit whiteboard material directly to students' computers where they can enlarge or listen to what the teacher is writing on the board, or download books or presentations to notetakers such as the BrailleNote. Teachers need to stay current on what devices would benefit each student, get the training needed to teach students to use it, and then teach them to use it. I can't tell you how many students have transferred into our school with equipment they've had for several years that has been stored in a closet. Don't be scared off by the price of technological devices. Many Lions' Clubs, grant programs, or other service groups will step up to help.

And last but not least, don't ever listen to people who say braille is being replaced by technology. Braille is necessary for the independent reading and writing of students who cannot access print. The technology only allows them greater ease in accessing, producing, and storing their work.

ADVICE TO SOMEONE CONSIDERING A CAREER IN SPECIAL EDUCATION Just jump right in! Throughout high school and college, I volunteered in a local public school classroom for the visually impaired. You need to volunteer with other teachers and professionals to see if you have what it takes to succeed in this challenging and rewarding profession. And by all means, if you find that you are not passionate about special needs kids, find another profession because life is too short to not love your career for the next 40 years. There is a great joy in teaching a child to read braille, to explore a tactile map in which he realizes he has traveled from Ohio to Florida, and adapt a science lesson and see a student's smile when she finally understands that gas molecules expand when heated. I have one student this year, Casey, who always turns his head toward me, grins, and says, "Oh, now I get it!" That says it all!

To meet Ms. Peirano and some of her students, go to the book resources for this text on MyEducationLab.

MyEducationLab™

Visit the **MyEducationLab** for *Exceptional Children* to enhance your understanding of chapter concepts with a personalized Study Plan. You'll also have the opportunity to hone your teaching skills through video- and case-based Assignments and Activities, IRIS Center Resources, and Building Teaching Skills and Dispositions lessons.

SIXTEEN-YEAR-OLD MARIA IS A BRIGHT, COLLEGE-BOUND STUDENT who has been totally blind since birth. She took a series of intellectual and psychological tests and performed well, scoring at about her expected age and grade level. Something unusual happened, however, on one of the test items. The examiner handed Maria an unpeeled banana and asked, "What is this?" Maria held the banana and took several guesses but could not answer correctly. The examiner was astonished, as were Maria's teachers and parents. After all, this section of the test was intended for young children. Even though Maria had eaten bananas many times, she had missed out on one important aspect of the banana experience: she had never held and peeled a banana by herself.

This true story illustrates the tremendous importance of vision in obtaining information about our world. Although students with visual impairments may learn to make good use of their other senses (hearing, touch, smell, and taste) as channels for contacting the environment, they do not totally compensate for loss of vision. Touch and taste cannot tell a child much about things that are far away or even just beyond her arms' reach. And while hearing can provide a good deal of information about the near and distant environment, it seldom provides information that is as complete, continuous, or exact as the information people obtain from seeing their surroundings.

Vision plays a critical role in learning in the classroom. Normally sighted students are routinely expected to exercise several important visual skills. They must be able to focus on different objects and shift their vision from near to far as needed. They must have good hand-to-eye coordination, maintain visual concentration, discriminate among colors and letters, see and interpret many things simultaneously, and remember what they have seen. Children with visual impairments have deficits in one or more of these abilities. As a result, they need special equipment and/or adaptations in instructional materials or procedures.

Importance of visual experience

Content Standards for Beginning Teachers—B&VI: Impact of B&VI on learning and experience (B&VISK4).

DEFINITIONS

Unlike other disabilities covered by the Individuals with Disabilities Education Act (IDEA), visual impairment has both legal and educational definitions.

Legal Definition of Blindness

The statutory definition of blindness is based on visual acuity and field of vision. **Visual acuity**—the ability to clearly distinguish forms or discriminate among details—is most often measured by reading letters, numbers, or other symbols from the Snellen Eye Chart. The familiar phrase "20/20 vision" does not, as some people think, mean perfect vision; it simply indicates that at a distance of 20 feet, the eye can see what a normally seeing eye sees at that distance. As the bottom number increases, visual acuity decreases.

Visual acuity, field of vision, tunnel vision

Content Standards for Beginning Teachers—B&VI: Specialized terminology used in assessing individuals with B&VI (B&VI8K1) (also B&VI1K4).

A person whose visual acuity is 20/200 or less in the better eye with the use of a corrective lens is considered **legally blind** by the federal government (Social Security Administration, 2011). If Jane has 20/200 vision while wearing her glasses, she needs to stand at a distance of 20 feet to see what a normally sighted person can see from 200 feet. In other words, Jane must get much closer than normal to see things clearly. She will likely find it difficult to use her vision in many everyday situations. But many children with 20/200, or even 20/400, visual acuity succeed in the classroom with special help. Some students' visual acuity is so poor they cannot perceive fine details at any distance, even while wearing glasses or contact lenses. An individual with visual acuity of no better than 20/70 in the better eye after correction is considered **partially sighted** for legal and governmental purposes.

A person may also be considered legally blind if his **field of vision** is extremely restricted. When gazing straight ahead, a normal eye can see objects within a range of approximately 160 to 170 degrees. A person whose vision is restricted to an area of 20 degrees or less is considered legally blind. Some people with **tunnel vision** describe their perception as viewing the world through a narrow tube; they may have good central vision but poor peripheral vision at the outer ranges of the visual field. Conversely, some eye conditions make it impossible for people to see things clearly in the center of the visual field but allow relatively good peripheral vision. Because a person's visual field often deteriorates gradually over a period of years without notice, a thorough visual examination should always include measurement of the visual field as well as visual acuity. Figure 1 shows what a person might see with normal or poor visual acuity or a limited field of vision.

Federal entitlements for children who are legally blind

Content Standards for Beginning Teachers—B&VI: Access rights to specialized equipment and materials for individuals with B&VI (B&VI1K1).

To learn about services available to people with visual impairments, go to the websites of the American Printing House for the Blind (www.aph .org) and the American Foundation for the Blind (www.afb.org).

Children who are legally blind are eligible to receive a wide variety of educational services, materials, and benefits from governmental agencies. They may, for example, obtain Talking Books and playback devices from the Library of Congress. Their schools

FIGURE 1

A STREET SCENE AS IT MIGHT BE VIEWED BY PEOPLE WITH 20/20 VISION (A), 20/200 VISUAL ACUITY (B), AND RESTRICTED FIELDS OF VISION (C & D)

(A) NORMAL VISION   (B) CATARACTS

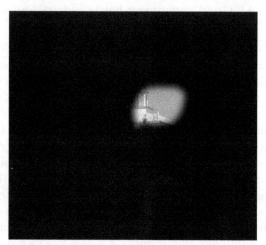

(C) EARLY-STAGE GLAUCOMA   (D) ADVANCED GLAUCOMA

may be able to buy books and educational materials from the American Printing House for the Blind because the federal government allots states and local school districts a certain financial allowance for each legally blind student. A person who is legally blind is also entitled to vocational training, free U.S. mail service, and an income tax exemption.

Even though these services and benefits are important to know about, the legal definition of blindness is not especially useful for teachers. Some children who do not meet the criteria for legal blindness have visual impairments severe enough to require special education. Other students whose visual impairments qualify them as legally blind have little or no need for special education services.

Educational Definitions of Visual Impairments

The definition of *visual impairment* in the Individuals with Disabilities Education Act (IDEA) emphasizes the relationship between vision and learning:

> Visual impairment including blindness means an impairment in vision that, even with correction, adversely affects a child's educational performance.

Definitions of visual impairment

 Council for Exceptional Children

Content Standards for Beginning Teachers—B&VI: Incidence and prevalence figures for individuals with B&VI (B&VI1K3).

The term includes both partial sight and blindness. (20 USC §1401 [2004], 20 *CFR* §300.8[c][13])

Students with visual impairments display a wide range of visual abilities—from total blindness to relatively good vision. The precise measurements of visual acuity and visual field used to determine legal blindness have limited relevance for educators. Instead, educators classify students with visual impairments based on the extent to which they use vision and/or auditory/tactile means for learning.

- A student who is *totally blind* receives no useful information through the sense of vision and must use tactile and auditory senses for all learning.
- A child who is *functionally blind* has so little vision that she learns primarily through the auditory and tactile senses; however, she may be able to use her limited vision to supplement the information received from the other senses and to assist with certain tasks (e.g., moving about the classroom).
- A child with **low vision** uses vision as a primary means of learning but may supplement visual information with tactile and auditory input.

Scott Cunningham/Merrill

Children who have been blind since birth have a background of learning through hearing, touch, and other nonvisual senses.

Age at Onset

Like other disabilities, visual impairment can be congenital (present at birth) or adventitious (acquired). Most visual impairments of school-age children are congenital. It is useful for a teacher to know the age at which a student acquired a visual impairment. A child who has been blind since birth has a different perception of the world than does a child who lost his vision at age 12. The first child has a background of learning through hearing, touch, and the other nonvisual senses, whereas the second child also has a large background of visual experiences on which to draw. Most people who are adventitiously blind retain a visual memory of things they saw. This memory can be helpful in a child's education; an adventitiously blind child may, for instance, remember the appearance of colors, maps, and printed letters. At the same time, however, the need for emotional support and acceptance may be greater than it might be for a congenitally blind child, who does not have to make a sudden adjustment to the loss of vision (Wahl et al., 2006).

Age of onset

 Council for Exceptional Children

Content Standards for Beginning Teachers—B&VI: Development of secondary senses when vision is impaired (B&VI2K2) (also B&VI2K5).

CHARACTERISTICS

Cognition and Language

This chapter began with a story about a bright teenage girl without sight who could not identify the object she was holding as a banana. Maria had eaten bananas many times, she could spell and read the word *banana*, and she could explain the best climate for growing bananas. But because she'd never held and unpeeled a banana, Maria was not able to identify it.

Vision enables children to organize and make connections between different experiences, connections that help the child make the most of those experiences. Children who are blind perform more poorly than sighted children do on cognitive tasks requiring comprehension or relating different items of information. Impaired or absent vision makes it difficult to see (literally, of course, but also cognitively) the connections

Cognition and language development

 Council for Exceptional Children

Content Standards for Beginning Teachers—B&VI: Effects of visual impairment on development (B&VI2K3) (also ICC2K2).

331

between experiences. "It is as though all the educational experiences of the blind child are kept in separate compartments" (Kingsley, 1997, p. 27).

Sighted children without other disabilities are constantly learning from their experiences and interactions with their environment. As they move about, the sense of sight provides a steady stream of detailed information about their environment and about relationships between things in that environment. Without any effort on their part or on the part of others, children with normal sight produce great stores of useful knowledge from everyday experiences. Visual impairments, however, preclude most such incidental learning.

Ferrell (2006) described what two children, one with normal vision and one with limited or absent vision, might learn from their everyday experiences with a family pet. When a child with normal vision hears a cat meow and sees its mouth open, he relates the sound to the cat. When he pets the cat, he feels soft fur and sees the cat's entire body simultaneously. The child with visual impairments hears the meow but cannot see what is producing it; he can feel its soft fur but can feel only part of the cat at a time. And if he gets scratched, the paw comes out of and returns to nowhere. This makes learning even simple language concepts such as "cats have tails" and "bananas are smooth" difficult.

Abstract concepts, analogies, and idiomatic expressions can be particularly difficult for children who cannot see. Jeanna Mora Dowse, a teacher of students with visual impairments, related this experience:

> One morning, the OT was working with a 4-year-old student who was blind. This student was taking his time walking to the therapy room, so the OT told him to "Shake a leg!" The student stopped, shook his right leg, and then continued walking as slowly as before. The OT had to explain to him that "Shake a leg!" was just an expression for "Hurry up" (2009, p. 374).

There is no evidence that these challenges to learning restrict the potential of children with visual impairments. They do, however, magnify the importance of repeated, direct contact with concepts through nonvisual senses (Ferrell & Spungin, 2011).

Direct, repeated contact through nonvisual senses is critical for learning by children with visual impairments. Morgan is learning the concept of cause and effect by hitting the switch that turns the fan on and off.

Elizabeth Young-Dove

Motor Development and Mobility

Motor development

Council for Exceptional Children

Content Standards for Beginning Teachers—B&VI: Effects of visual impairment on development (B&VI2K3) (also ICC2K2).

Blindness or severe visual impairment often leads to delays or deficits in motor development. Vision plays four important functions in the acquisition of motor skills: (a) motivation, (b) spatial awareness, (c) protection, and (d) feedback (Houwen, Visscher, Limmink, & Hartman, 2009). A significant portion of the purposeful movements of fully sighted babies involves reaching for things they see. The child's efforts to grasp objects, especially those that are just out of reach, strengthen muscles and improve coordination, which in turn enable more effective movement. The absence of sight or clear vision, however, reduces the baby's motivation to move. For the child who is blind, the world is no more interesting when sitting up and turning her head from side to side than it is when she is lying on the floor.

Vision provides critical information on the distance of objects and direction of movement. A child without clear vision may move less often because movements in the past have resulted in painful contact with the environment. The continuous feedback vision provides regarding many movements enables the child to correct errors and improve precision of movement. Together, spatial awareness and feedback functions of vision enable the sighted child to observe and imitate the movements of others (Brambring, 2006, 2007).

Even limited vision can have negative effects on motor development. Children with low vision have poorer motor skills than do children who are sighted. Their gross motor skills, especially balance, are weak. They frequently cannot perform motor activities through imitation, and they are usually more careful of space (Bouchard & Tétreault, 2000). Parents' concern for their children's safety may also contribute to reduced opportunities for physical exploration and activity (Stuart, Lieberman, & Hand, 2006).

Social Adjustment and Interaction

Compared with typically sighted children, children with visual impairments play and interact less during free time and are often delayed in the development of social skills (Celeste, 2006; Zebehazy & Smith, 2011). Although many adolescents with visual impairments have best friends, many also struggle with social isolation and must work harder than their sighted peers to make and maintain friendships (Lifshitz, Irit, & Weisse, 2007; Sacks & Wolffe, 2006). Students with visual impairments are often not invited to participate in group activities such as going to a ball game or a movie because sighted peers just assume they are not interested. Over time students with visual impairments and their sighted age mates have fewer and fewer shared experiences and common interests as bases for conversation, social interactions, and friendships.

Rosenblum (2000) identifies several issues influencing the limited social involvement of many adolescents with visual impairments. Because of the low incidence of the disability, many children with visual impairments cannot benefit from peers or adult role models who are experiencing the same challenges because of visual impairments. Social isolation becomes particularly pronounced for many teenagers with visual impairments when sighted peers obtain drivers' licenses.

Another factor contributing to social difficulties is that the inability to see and respond to the social signals of others reduces opportunities for reciprocal interactions (Campbell, 2007). During a conversation, for example, a student who is blind cannot see her conversation partner's gestures, facial expressions, and changes in body posture. This hampers the blind student's understanding of the conversation partner's message. And her failure to respond with socially appropriate eye contact, facial expressions, and gestures suggests lack of interest in her partner's communicative efforts and makes it less likely that the individual will seek out her company in the future.

Some individuals with visual impairments engage in repetitive body movements or other behaviors such as body rocking, eye pressing and poking, hand flapping, and head weaving. These behaviors were traditionally referred to in the visual impairment literature as "blindisms" or "blind mannerisms" (Kingsley, 1997). *Stereotypic behavior* (stereotypy) is a more clearly defined term that subsumes blindisms and mannerisms. It is also a more appropriate term: some sighted children exhibit such behaviors, and they do not occur among all children who are blind (Gense & Gense, 1994).

Although not usually harmful, stereotypic behavior can place a person with visual impairments at a great social disadvantage because these actions are conspicuous and may call negative attention to the person. It is not known why many children with visual impairments engage in stereotypic behaviors, though the vestibular stimulation produced by the behaviors is a suspected source of reinforcement (Bak, 1999). However, behavioral interventions such as self-monitoring and differential reinforcement

Social and emotional development

Content Standards for Beginning Teachers—B&VI: Effects of visual impairment on development (B&VI2K3) (also ICC2K2).

Stereotypic behavior

Content Standards for Beginning Teachers—B&VI: Effects of visual impairment on development (B&VI2K3) (also ICC2K2).

of incompatible behaviors have helped individuals with visual impairments reduce stereotypic behaviors such as repetitive body rocking or head drooping during conversation (McAdam, O'Cleirigh, &Cuvo, 1993).

Many people who have lost their sight report that the biggest difficulty socially is dealing with the attitudes and behavior of sighted people. Wagner-Lampl and Oliver (1994) suggest that many sighted people are influenced by the "folklore of blindness," a collection of superstitions and myths equally divided between negative beliefs that blind people are either helpless and pathetic or evil and contagious, and the beliefs that blind people have special or even magical abilities and special powers of perception, and thus deserve special attention.

PREVALENCE

Although the American Foundation for the Blind (2011b) estimates that more than 25 million people in the United States are living with a vision loss, visual impairment requiring special education is a low-incidence disability. Children with visual impairments constitute a very small percentage of the school-age population—fewer than 2 children in 1,000. Even when viewed as a percentage of the population of students who receive special education services, the prevalence of visual impairments is very small: only about 1 in 200 to 250 of all school-age children with IEPs are served under the disability category of visual impairments. During the 2009–10 school year, 25,813 children ages 6 to 21 received special education services under IDEA within the category of visual impairments (U.S. Department of Education, 2011).

Many students with visual impairments have one or more additional disabilities, and are served and counted under other disability categories such as deaf-blindness and multiple disabilities. Thus, the number of students with visual impairments is larger than the data reported for IDEA. The American Printing House for the Blind (2010) reported that 49,526 children from birth to age 21 were eligible for services for visual impairment.

TYPES AND CAUSES OF VISUAL IMPAIRMENTS

How We See

Effective vision requires proper functioning of three anatomical systems of the eye: the optical system, the muscular system, and the nervous system. A simplified diagram of the eye appears in Figure 2. The eye's optical system collects and focuses light energy reflected from objects in the visual field. As light passes through the eye, several structures bend, or refract, the light to produce a clear image. The light first hits the *cornea*, the curved transparent membrane that protects the eye (much as an outer crystal protects a watch face). It then passes through the *aqueous humor*, a watery liquid that fills the front chamber of the eye. Next the light passes through the *pupil*, a circular hole in the center of the colored *iris*; the pupil contracts or expands to regulate the amount of light entering the eye. The light then passes through the *lens*, a transparent, elastic structure. After the light passes through the *vitreous humor*, a jellylike substance that fills most of the eye's interior, it reaches the innermost layer of the eye, the *retina*. This multilayered sheet of nerve tissue at the back of the eye has been likened to the film in a camera: for a clear image to be seen, the light rays must come to a precise focus on the retina.

The eye's muscular system enables **ocular motility,** the eye's ability to move. Six muscles attached to the outside of each eye enable it to search, track, converge, and fixate on images. These muscles also play a significant part in depth perception (**binocular vision**), the ability to fuse the separate images from each eye into a single, three-dimensional image. Inside the eye, tiny muscles adjust the shape of the lens, making it thicker or thinner, so the eye can bring objects at different distances into sharp focus (**accommodation**).

The eye's nervous system converts light energy into electrical impulses and transmits that information to the brain, where it is processed into visual images. The retina

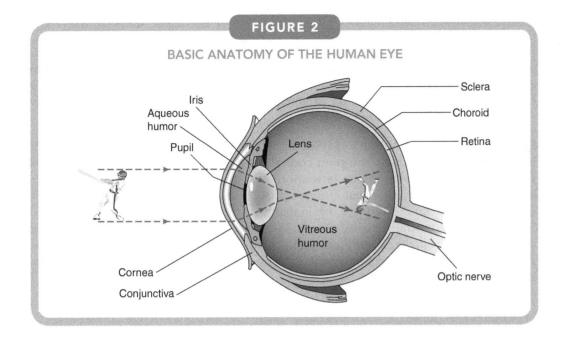

FIGURE 2

BASIC ANATOMY OF THE HUMAN EYE

consists of millions of light receptors called *cones* and *rods*. The cones enable detection of color and detail necessary for tasks such as reading and are located in the center of the retina and function best in good light. The rods, which are responsible for peripheral vision, detection of movement, and vision in dim light, are distributed around the periphery of the retina. The optic nerve carries the electrical messages from the cones and rods directly to the visual cortex at the base of the brain.

Causes of Visual Impairments

Damage or disturbances to any part of the eye's optical, muscular, or nervous systems can result in impaired vision. Causes of visual impairments are grouped into three broad categories: refractive errors, structural impairments, and cortical visual impairments.

REFRACTIVE ERRORS **Refraction** is the process of bending light rays when they pass from one transparent structure into another. As just described, the normal eye refracts, or bends, light rays so that a clear image falls directly on the retina. However, for many people—perhaps half the general population—the size and shape of the eye prevent the light rays from focusing clearly on the retina. In **myopia,** or nearsightedness, the eye is longer than normal from front to back, causing the image to fall in front of the retina instead of exactly on it. A child with myopia can see near objects clearly; but more distant objects, such as a chalkboard or a movie, are blurred or not seen at all (see Figure 1). The opposite of myopia is **hyperopia,** commonly called farsightedness. The *hyperopic eye* is shorter than normal, preventing the light rays from converging on the retina. A child with hyperopia has difficulty seeing near objects clearly but can focus well on more distant objects. Glasses or contact lenses can compensate for many refractive errors by changing the course of light rays to produce as clear a focus as possible.

STRUCTURAL IMPAIRMENTS Visual impairments can be caused by poor development of, damage to, or malfunction of one or more parts of the eye's optical or muscular systems. Cataracts and glaucoma are two of the numerous causes of visual impairment due to damage or disintegration of the eye itself. A **cataract** is a cloudiness in the lens of the eye that blocks the light necessary for seeing clearly. **Glaucoma** is abnormally high pressure within the eye caused by disturbances or blockages of the fluids that normally circulate within the eye. Central and peripheral vision are impaired or lost entirely when the increased pressure damages the optic nerve (see Figure 1).

Types and causes of visual impairment

 Content Standards for Beginning Teachers—B&VI: Basic terminology related to diseases and disorders of the human visual system (B&VI1K4).

Dysfunction of the muscles that control and move the eyes can make it difficult or impossible for a child to see effectively. **Nystagmus**, a rapid, involuntary, back-and-forth movement of the eyes in a lateral, vertical, or rotary direction, can cause problems in focusing and reading. **Strabismus** is an inability to focus on the same object with both eyes because imbalance of the eye muscles creates an inward or outward deviation of one or both eyes. If left untreated, strabismus and other disorders of ocular motility can lead to permanent loss of vision.

CORTICAL VISUAL IMPAIRMENTS   Some children with visual impairments have nothing wrong with their eyes. The term **cortical visual impairment (CVI)** refers to reduced visual functioning due to known or suspected damage to or malfunction of the parts of the brain that interpret visual information. Causes of CVI include insufficient oxygen at birth (anoxia), head injury, brain maldevelopment such as hydrocephalus, and infections of the central nervous system. Visual functioning may fluctuate depending on environment, lighting conditions, and activities. Some children with CVI use their peripheral vision, some are photophobic, some are attracted to bright light, and some will gaze at lights or the sun.

Table 1 summarizes some of the most common types and causes of visual impairments. Although a teacher seldom needs detailed knowledge concerning the etiology of a child's visual impairment, understanding how a student's visual impairment affects classroom performance is important. It is useful to know, for example,

TABLE 1 • Types and causes of visual impairments

CONDITION	DEFINITION/CAUSE	REMARKS/EDUCATIONAL IMPLICATIONS
Albinism	Lack of pigmentation in the eyes, skin, and hair; results in moderate-to-severe visual impairment by reducing visual acuity and causing nystagmus; heredity	Children with albinism almost always have photophobia, a condition in which the eyes are extremely sensitive to light; eye fatigue may occur during close work.
Amblyopia	Reduction in or loss of vision in the weaker eye from lack of use; caused by strabismus, unequal refractive errors, or opacity of the lens or cornea.	Close work may result in eye fatigue, loss of place, poor concentration; seating should favor functional eye.
Astigmatism	Distorted or blurred vision due to irregularities in the cornea or other surfaces of the eye that produce images on retina not in equal focus (refractive error).	Loss of accommodation when object brought close to face; avoid long periods of reading or close tasks that cause discomfort; child may complain of headaches and fluctuating vision.
Cataract	Blurred, distorted, or incomplete vision caused by cloudiness in the lens; caused by injury, malnutrition, or rubella during pregnancy, glaucoma, retinitis pigmentosa, heredity, aging.	Avoid glare of any kind; light source behind child; good contrast between print and paper; variation in near and distant tasks can prevent tiring.
Color deficiency or color blindness	Difficulty distinguishing certain colors; red-green confusion is most common; caused by absent or malformed cones, macular deficiency, heredity	Usually not educationally significant; teach alternative ways to discriminate objects usually identified by color (e.g., tags for clothing colors, position of red and green on traffic lights).
Cortical visual impairment (CVI)	Impaired vision due to damage to or malfunction of the visual cortex and/or optic nerve; causes include anoxia, head injury, and infections of the central nervous system; many children with CVI have additional disabilities, such as cerebral palsy, seizure disorders, intellectual disabilities.	Visual functioning may fluctuate depending on lighting conditions and attention; vision usually does not deteriorate; improvement sometimes occurs over a period of time; some children with CVI use their peripheral vision; some are photophobic; some are attracted to bright light; may fail to blink at threatening motions; visual images should be simple and presented singly.

CONDITION	DEFINITION/CAUSE	REMARKS/EDUCATIONAL IMPLICATIONS
Diabetic retinopathy	Impaired vision as a result of hemorrhages and the growth of new blood vessels in the area of the retina due to diabetes; a leading cause of blindness in adults	Provide good lighting and contrast; magnification; pressure to perform can affect blood glucose.
Glaucoma	Abnormally high pressure within the eye due to disturbances or blockages of the fluids that normally circulate within the eye; vision is impaired or lost entirely when the increased pressure damages the retina and optic nerve.	Fluctuations in visual performance may frustrate child; be alert to symptoms of pain; administer eye drops on schedule; child may be subjected to teasing because of bulging eyes.
Hyperopia (farsightedness)	Difficulty seeing near objects clearly but able to focus on distant objects; caused by a shorter than normal eye that prevents light rays from converging on the retina (refractive error).	Loss of accommodation when object brought close to face; avoid long periods of reading or close tasks that cause discomfort.
Macular degeneration	Central area of the retina gradually deteriorates, causing loss of clear vision in the center of the visual field; common in older adults but fairly rare in children.	Tasks such as reading and writing difficult; prescribed low-vision aid or closed-circuit TV; good illumination; avoid glare.
Myopia (nearsightedness)	Distant objects are blurred or not seen at all but can see near objects clearly; caused by an elongated eye that focuses images in front of the retina (refractive error).	Encourage child to wear prescribed glasses or contact lens; for near tasks, child may be more comfortable working without glasses and bringing work close to face.
Nystagmus	Rapid, involuntary, back-and-forth movement of the eyes, which makes it difficult to focus on objects; when the two eyes cannot focus simultaneously, the brain avoids a double image by suppressing the visual input from one eye; the weaker eye (usually the one that turns inward or outward) can actually lose its ability to see; can occur on its own but is usually associated with other visual impairments.	Close tasks for extended period can lead to fatigue; some children turn or tilt head to obtain the best focus; do not criticize this.
Retinitis pigmentosa (RP)	The most common genetic disease of the eye; causes gradual degeneration of the retina; first symptom is usually difficulty seeing at night, followed by loss of peripheral vision; heredity.	High illumination with no glare; contrasting visual field causes difficulties scanning and tracking; skills necessary for tasks such as reading; teach student to locate visual objects with systematic search grid; as RP is progressive, curriculum should include mobility training, especially at night, and braille training if prognosis is loss of sight.
Retinopathy of prematurity (ROP)	Caused by administering high levels of oxygen to at-risk infants; when the infants are later removed from the oxygen-rich incubators, the change in oxygen levels can produce an abnormally dense growth of blood vessels and scar tissue in the eyes, leading to visual impairment and often total blindness.	High illumination, magnifiers for close work; telescopes for distance viewing; students may have brain damage resulting in intellectual disabiities and/or behavior problems.
Strabismus	Inability to focus on the same object with both eyes due to an inward or outward deviation of one or both eyes; caused by muscle imbalance; secondary to other visual impairments.	Classroom seating should favor student's stronger eye; some students may use one eye for distance tasks, the other eye for near tasks; frequent rest periods may be needed during close work; may need more time to adjust to unfamiliar visual tasks.

Sources: From American Foundation for the Blind (2011a); Braille Institute (2011); Lighthouse International (2011); Lueck (2011), Miller and Menacker (2007); Shaw and Trief (2009).

that Traci's cataracts make it difficult for her to read under strong lights, that Derek has only a small amount of central vision in his right eye, or that Naoko will need to administer eye drops to relieve the pressure caused by her glaucoma before leaving on a class field trip.

EDUCATIONAL APPROACHES

History of education of students with B&VI

 Council for Exceptional Children

Content Standards for Beginning Teachers—B&VI: Historical foundations of education of individuals with B&VI as related to traditional roles of specialized and public schools around the world (B&VI1K2).

For detailed and interesting historical accounts of the education of students with visual impairments, see Geruschat and Corn (2006), Koenig and Holbrook (2000), and Moore (2006).

Educators have developed numerous specialized teaching methods and curriculum materials in an effort to overcome the obstacles to learning presented by blindness and low vision. Recent advances in technology have greatly increased access to the general education curriculum and academic success for students with visual impairments. As one high school student who is blind remarked, "By taking advantage of technology around me, I am able to have an education equal to my sighted peers" (Leigh & Barclay, 2000, p. 129). However, the education of students with visual impairments is a field with a rich history of more than 150 years, and today's developments were made possible by the contributions of many teachers and researchers who came before. Figure 3 highlights some key historical events and their implications for the education of students with visual impairments.

Special Adaptations for Students Who Are Blind

Because they must frequently teach skills and concepts that most children acquire through vision, teachers of students who are blind must plan and carry out activities that will help their students gain as much information as possible through the nonvisual senses and by participation in active, practical experiences (Chen & Downing, 2006a, 2006b; Salisbury, 2008). For example, a child who is blind may hear a bird singing but get no concrete idea of the bird itself from the sound alone. A teacher interested in teaching such a student about birds might plan a series of activities that has the student touch birds of various species and manipulate related objects such as eggs, nests, and feathers. The student might assume the responsibility for feeding a pet bird at home or in the classroom. Through such experiences, the child with visual impairments can gradually obtain a more thorough and accurate knowledge of birds than she could if her education were limited to reading books about birds, memorizing vocabulary, or feeling plastic models.

Braille, brailler, slate, and stylus

 Council for Exceptional Children

Content Standards for Beginning Teachers—B&VI: Select and adapt materials in braille, accessible print, and other formats (B&VI4S1).

BRAILLE Braille is the primary means of literacy for people who are blind. **Braille** is a tactile system of reading and writing in which letters, words, numbers, and other systems are made from arrangements of raised dots (see Figure 4). The Nemeth code consists of braille symbols for mathematical and scientific notation.

In some ways, braille is like the shorthand once used by secretaries. A set of 189 abbreviations, called *contractions*, saves space and permits faster reading and writing. For example, when the letter *r* stands by itself, it means *rather*. The word *myself* in braille is written *myf*. Frequently used words, such as *the, and, with,* and *for,* have their own special contractions. For example, the *and* symbol appears four times in the following sentence:

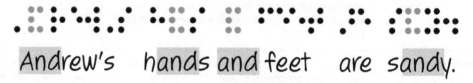

Students who are blind can read braille much more rapidly than they can read the raised letters of the standard alphabet. The speed of braille reading varies a great deal from student to student; however, it is almost always much slower (about 100 words per minute for good braille readers) than reading print (Wetzel & Knowlton, 2006a). Most children who are blind are introduced to braille in the first grade. Rather than

FIGURE 3 KEY HISTORICAL EVENTS IN THE EDUCATION AND TREATMENT OF PEOPLE WITH VISUAL IMPAIRMENTS

Date	Event/Implications
1784	Shocked at seeing people who were blind performing as jesters or begging on the streets of Paris, Victor Hauy resolved to teach them more dignified ways of earning a living. He started the first school for children who were blind. The success of Hauy's students influenced the establishment of other residential schools in Europe in the early 19th century.
1821	Samuel Gridley Howe founded the Perkins School for the Blind, the oldest and best-known residential school for students who are blind. Many methods and materials for teaching students with visual impairments were developed at Perkins. Anne Sullivan and her famous pupil, Helen Keller, spent several years at Perkins.
1829	Louis Braille, a student at a Paris school for children who were blind, published the first draft of a tactile method of reading. Braille's system of embossed six-dot cells proved the most efficient of reading by touch and remains the primary means of literacy for the blind today.
1862	The Snellen chart was developed by a Dutch ophthalmologist. The chart provides a fast, standardized test of visual acuity and is still used today as a visual screening tool.
1900; 1909/1913	The first public school class for children who were blind opened in Chicago; the first classes for children with low vision began in Cleveland and Boston. Children with low vision were educated in special "sight-saving classes" in which all instruction was conducted orally.
1932	The Library of Congress made Talking Books available to any person who is legally blind.
1938	The first itinerant teaching program for children with visual impairments attending general education classrooms began in Oakland, California. This marked the beginning of the long and relatively successful history of including children with visual impairments in general education classrooms.
1940s–1950s	Thousands of children became blind or severely visually impaired by retinopathy of prematurity (ROP). Because residential schools could not accommodate the influx of visually impaired children, public school programs for students with visual impairments became more widely available in the 1950s and 1960s.
1944	Richard Hoover developed a system for teaching orientation and mobility (O&M) skills that featured a long white cane. This system and the "Hoover cane" became standard parts of the curriculum for students with visual impairments.
1951	The Perkins brailler was invented.
Mid-1960s	Natalie Barraga published research showing that children with low vision do not lose their remaining sight by using it and that visual functioning can be improved by use. Barraga's (1964, 1970) work was instrumental in ending the sight-saving classes attended by children with low vision for more than 50 years.
1970s	Development of the Kurzweil Reading Machine, the world's first text-to-speech optical scanning machine, provided access to print materials not available in braille, large-print, or recorded formats. The Kurzweil set the stage for a continuing explosion of technological advancements that have benefited the lives of many people with visual impairments.
1997	The Individuals with Disabilities Education Act (IDEA '97) mandated that orientation and mobility (O&M) services be provided to any student with a disability who needs them.
1996/2004	American Foundation for the Blind (AFB) publishes/revises the "expanded core curriculum" of nonacademic skill needed by blind and visually impaired students for overall success in life (Hatlen, 2011).

have the child learn to write out every word, letter by letter, and later unlearn this approach, teachers introduce contractions early in the program (Wormsley, 2004). Of course, it is important for the child to eventually learn the correct spelling of words, even if not every letter appears in braille.

Children generally learn to write braille by using a **brailler,** a six-keyed mechanical device that somewhat resembles a typewriter. Although it usually takes several years

To learn more about this strategy, go to the Book Resources for this text in MyEducationLab.

339

FIGURE 4

THE BRAILLE SYSTEM FOR REPRESENTING NUMBERS AND LETTERS

The six dots of the Braille cell are arranged and numbered thus:

1 • • 4
2 • • 5
3 • • 6

The capital sign, dot 6, placed before a letter makes it a capital. The number sign, dots 3, 4, 5, 6, placed before a character makes it a figure and not a letter.

1 a	2 b	3 c	4 d	5 e	6 f	7 g	8 h	9 i	0 j

k	l	m	n	o	p	q	r	s	t

u	v	w	x	y	z	Capital Sign	Number Sign	Period	Comma

Source: From the Division for the Blind and Physically Handicapped, Library of Congress, Washington, DC.

for children to become thoroughly familiar with braille, it is no more difficult than learning to read print for sighted children. Koenig (2006) suggests that a child who says that braille is difficult to read has probably heard an adult say so.

Braille technological aids

Council for Exceptional Children

Content Standards for Beginning Teachers—B&VI: Teach the use of Braillewriter, slate and stylus, and computer technology to produce braille materials (B&VI4S2).

Braille Technological Aids. Most braille books are large, expensive, and cumbersome. It can be difficult for students to retrieve information quickly when they must tactilely review many pages of braille books or notes. Technological developments have made braille more efficient, thus enabling students who are blind to function more independently in general education classrooms, universities, and employment settings.

Braille 'n Speak is a battery-powered, portable device for note taking with a standard Perkins-style keyboard for braille entry. It translates braille into synthesized speech or print. The Mountbatten Pro Brailler is an electronic brailler that is easier to use than the manual, mechanical brailler (Cooper & Nichols, 2007). Braille embossers print braille from digital text; some printers produce pages with both braille and print formats, enabling blind and sighted readers to use the same copy.

TACTILE AIDS AND MANIPULATIVES

Tactile-experience books created by gluing, stapling, or otherwise attaching artifacts from actual events experienced by the child to the pages of a simple and sturdy book can help young children who are blind or have severe visual impairments acquire book concepts and early literacy skills (Lewis & Tolla, 2003). Each page of a tactile-experience book includes braille or print related to the artifacts on the page.

Manipulatives are generally recognized as effective tools in teaching beginning mathematics skills to elementary students. When using manipulatives such as Cuisenaire rods, sighted students use length and color to distinguish the various numerical values of the rods. Belcastro (1993) developed a set of rods that enables students who are blind to quickly identify different

This brailler is a six-keyed device that punches the raised braille dots in special paper.

Katelyn Metzger/Merrill

values by feeling the lengths and tactile markings associated with each. Other math manipulatives commonly used include braille math blocks, Digi-Blocks, and APH tools to enhance number system concepts, and Tack-Tiles® Braille Systems.

Another mathematical aid for students who are blind is the Cranmer abacus. Long used in Japan, the abacus has been adapted to assist students who are blind in learning number concepts and making calculations. Manipulation of the abacus beads is particularly useful in counting, adding, and subtracting.

For more advanced mathematical functions, the student is likely to use the Speech-Plus talking calculator, a small electronic instrument that performs most of the operations of any standard calculator. It "talks" by voicing entries and results aloud and also presents them visually in digital form. This is only one of many instances in which the development of synthetic speech technology has helped people who are blind. Talking clocks and spelling aids are also available.

In the sciences and social studies, several adaptations encourage students who are blind to use their tactile and auditory senses for firsthand manipulation and discovery (Chen & Downing, 2006a). Examples are embossed relief maps and diagrams, three-dimensional models, and electronic probes that give an audible signal in response to light. Curriculum modification projects, such as SAVI/SELPH (Science Activities for the Visually Impaired/Science Enrichment for Learners with Physical Handicaps) developed at the University of California, Berkeley, emphasize how students with visual impairments can, with some modifications, participate in learning activities along with normally sighted students.

Technological Aids for Reading Print. Character recognition software for people who are blind or visually impaired converts printed or electronic text into spoken words. For example, the Kurzweil 1000 is a sophisticated computer-based reading system that uses an optical-character recognition system to scan and read text with synthetic speech. The user can regulate the speed, have the machine spell out words letter by letter if desired, and even choose from a variety of natural-sounding voices that can be modified to suit individual preferences.

COMPUTER ACCESS Assistive technology that provides access to personal computers has opened tremendous opportunities for education, employment, communication, and leisure enjoyment by individuals with visual impairments. These technologies include hardware and software that magnify screen images and speech-recognition software that enables the user to tell the computer what to do, and software that converts text files to synthesized speech.

Keyboarding is an important means of communication between children who are blind and their sighted classmates and teachers and is also a useful skill for further education and employment. Instruction in keyboarding should begin as early as feasible in the child's school program. Handwriting is seldom taught to students who are totally blind, with the noteworthy exception of learning to sign one's name for tasks such as maintaining a bank account, registering to vote, and applying for a job.

Special Adaptations for Students with Low Vision

Between 75% and 80% of school-age children enrolled in educational programs for visually impaired students have some potentially useful vision. Learning by students with low vision need not be restricted to the nonvisual senses, and they generally learn to read print (Corn & Erin, 2000).

VISUAL EFFICIENCY *Functional vision* and *visual efficiency* are related terms denoting how well a person uses whatever vision he has (Barraga & Erin, 2001). Visual efficiency cannot be determined or predicted by clinical measures of visual acuity or visual field. Some children with severe visual impairments use the limited vision they have very capably. Other children with relatively minor visual impairments function poorly as visual learners; they may even behave as though they were blind.

Tactile aids and manipulatives

Content Standards for Beginning Teachers—B&VI: Strategies for teaching use of the abacus, talking calculator, tactile graphics, and adapted science equipment (B&VI4S3).

Osterhaus (2011) provides detailed descriptions of materials and practical strategies for teaching math to students who are blind and visually impaired.

To learn more about the SAVI/SELPH project, go to http://www. lawrencehallofscience.org/ cml/saviselph/index.html.

Computer access and keyboarding

Content Standards for Beginning Teachers—B&VI: Strategies for teaching social, daily living, and functional life skills (B&VI4K6) (also B&VI4K5).

Visual efficiency/Visual functioning

Content Standards for Beginning Teachers—B&VI: Strategies for teaching visual efficiency skills and use of print adaptations, optical devices, and nonoptical devices (B&VI4K2).

Visual efficiency encompasses the following skills: awareness (visually sensing the presence of objects or movement), fixing or locating (aligning one or both eyes on a stationary object), scanning (searching for an object or person among multiple visual stimuli), tracking (visually following a moving object), gaze shifting (shifting fixation from one object to another), discriminating (visually determining differences between and among stimuli), and visual sequencing (detecting the sequence in which objects appear, leave, or move in the visual field) (Shaw & Trief, 2009; Utley, Roman, & Nelson, 1998). Students with visual impairments who have acquired these skills enjoy enhanced autonomy and choice in the range of activities they can perform independently in home, school, vocational, and community environments. The fundamental premises underlying the development of visual efficiency is that functional vision is learned (and therefore teachable) behavior and that children must be actively involved in using their own vision (Corn & Erin, 2000).

Merely furnishing a classroom with attractive things for children to see is not sufficient. Without training, a child with low vision may be unable to derive much meaningful information through vision. Forms may be perceived as vague masses and shapeless, indistinct blobs. Children with low vision need systematic training in visual recognition and discrimination to learn to use their visual impressions intelligently and effectively, to make sense out of what they see (Li, 2004; Lueck, 2004). Functional vision instruction should not be isolated to "visual stimulation sessions" but occur within the context of meaningful activities throughout the student's daily schedule (Ferrell & Spungin, 2011) (see Figure 5).

FIGURE 5   EXAMPLE OF EMBEDDING OPPORTUNITIES TO USE AND DEVELOP FUNCTIONAL VISUAL SKILLS THROUGHOUT THE DAILY SCHEDULE FOR PAULA, A 15-YEAR-OLD GIRL WITH CEREBRAL PALSY WHO DEMONSTRATES VISUAL SKILLS ABOUT 50% OF THE TIME

Place and Time	Activity and Visual Skills Needed
At home 7:30–8:30 A.M.: Getting ready for school	Have Paula choose what she wants to wear. Her mother puts 2 sets of clothes in front of her but does not describe them. She asks Paula what she wants to wear either by naming the color or pointing to the clothing. *Visual skills needed to choose:* Localization and shifting attention.
At school, First period class: Daily living skills—Grooming	After brushing and arranging Paula's hair have her look in a magnifying mirror and ask her how she likes her hair. Once in a while change her hairstyle to see if she notices the difference. *Visual skills needed to examine hair:* Visual attending, localization, and scanning.
At school, Second period class: Home economics—Laundry	While sorting clothes into a light and a dark pile, ask Paula to decide into which pile each piece of clothing should go. *Visual skills involved:* Visual attending, localization, shifting attention, and scanning.
At school, lunch	Present Paula with 2 types of food with which she is familiar without telling her what they are. Have her choose what she wants to eat. If she has difficulty identifying the food, allow her to smell it. *Visual skills she will need:* Visual attending, localization, and shifting attention.
Afternoon community outing	While grocery shopping, encourage Paula to identify items that are easily recognizable or that she frequently uses. Encourage her to say what the item is and where it is. For example, place her between the bananas and the apples or near just one item. *Visual skills involved:* Visual attending, localization, and scanning. While outdoors, encourage Paula to tell you what she sees or ask her to point to specific items (e.g., cars, flowers, green grass, fire hydrants). *Visual skills involved:* Visual attending, localization, tracking, and scanning.

Source: From Li. A. (2003). A model for developing programs to improve the use of vision in students who are visually impaired with multiple disabilities. *RE:View, 35(1),* p. 38. Reprinted with permission of the Helen Dwight Reid Educational Foundation. Published by Heldref Publications, 1319 Eighteenth St., NW, Washington, DC 20036-1802. Copyright © 2003.

OPTICAL DEVICES Many ophthalmologists and optometrists specialize in the assessment and treatment of low vision. A professional examination can help determine which types of optical aids, if any, can benefit a particular child with low vision. These special devices might include glasses and contact lenses, small handheld telescopes, and magnifiers placed on top of printed pages. Such aids cannot give normal vision to children with visual impairments but may help them perform better at certain tasks, such as reading small print or seeing distant objects.

Optical aids are usually specialized rather than all-purpose, and children whose vision is extremely limited are more likely to use monocular (one-eye) than binocular (two-eye) aids, especially for seeing things at a distance. Juanita might, for example, use her glasses for reading large print, a magnifier stand for reading smaller print, and a monocular telescope for viewing the chalkboard. A usual disadvantage of corrective lenses and magnifiers is that the more powerful they are, the more they tend to distort or restrict the peripheral field of vision. Some field-widening lenses and devices are now available for students with limited visual fields. These include prisms and fish-eye lenses designed to make objects appear smaller so that a greater area can be perceived on the unimpaired portions of a student's visual field.

Closed-circuit television systems are used in some classrooms to enable students with low vision to read regular-sized printed materials. These systems usually include a sliding table on which a book is placed, a television camera with a zoom lens mounted above the book, and a television monitor nearby. The student can adjust the size, brightness, and contrast of the material and can select either an ordinary black-on-white image or a negative white-on-black image, which many students prefer. The teacher may also have a television monitor that lets him see the student's work without making repeated trips to the student's desk. A disadvantage of closed-circuit television systems is that they are usually not portable, so the student who uses television as a primary reading medium is largely restricted to the specially equipped classroom or library. Many students with low vision use ZoomText, a computer program that enlarges and enhances images and text on their computer screens.

Recent advances in computer and optical technologies have led to the development of a number of low-vision devices called *augmented reality systems*. These lightweight, head-mounted devices track the position of the user's head and project the desired images onto beam-splitting optics that allow the user to see an overlay or superimposed image on the environment (Feiner, 2002). One augmented reality system for people with low vision, called Nomad, uses a high-resolution laser to project an image directly onto the user's retina. Studies have shown that Nomad can function as a substitute computer monitor (Kleweno, Seibel, Viirre, Kelly, & Furness, 2001) and that users can read print with the device (Goodrich, Kirby, Wagstaff, Oros, & McDevitt, 2004).

READING PRINT Students with low vision use three basic approaches for reading print: (a) approach magnification (reducing the distance between the eye and the page of print from 40 cm to 5 cm results in 8× magnification), (b) lenses (optical devices), and (c) large print. Many books and other materials are available in large print for children with low vision. The American Printing House for the Blind produces books in 18-point type. Some states and other organizations produce large-type materials; but the size and style of the print fonts, spacing, paper, and quality of production vary widely.

Optical devices

Council for Exceptional Children

Content Standards for Beginning Teachers—B&VI: Strategies for teaching visual efficiency skills and use of print adaptations, optical devices, and nonoptical devices (B&VI4K2).

To learn more about this strategy, go to the Book Resources for this text in MyEducationLab.

Most optical aids are designed for special purposes. Brennan uses his monocular telescope to focus on distance targets for independent travel.

Katelyn Metzger/Merrill

The sentence you are reading now is set in 10-point type. Here are four examples of different large-print type sizes:

This is 14-point type.
This is 18-point type.
This is 20-point type.
This is 24-point type.

Although print size is an important variable, other equally important factors to consider are the print quality of the material, the font or typeface, the contrast between print and page, the spacing between lines, and the illumination of the setting in which the child reads (Griffin, Williams, Davis, & Engelman, 2002; Russell-Minda et al., 2007). Educators generally agree that a child with visual impairments should use the smallest print size that she can read comfortably. A child may be able to transfer from large print to smaller print as reading efficiency increases, just as most normally sighted children do. Figure 6 compares advantages and disadvantages of large-print materials and optical devices.

Most children with low vision learn to read regular-sized print with or without the use of optical aids. This makes a much wider variety of materials available and eliminates the added cost of obtaining large-print books or enlarging texts with special duplicating machines. Additionally, regular-sized print books are easier to store and carry around than are large-print books. Some children with visual impairments are dual-media learners, who learn to use both print and braille simultaneously (Lusk & Corn, 2006a, 2006b).

Teachers can accommodate the slower reading rates of most children with low vision by (a) providing 1½ to 2 times as much time as sighted children need for reading, (b) ensuring sufficient time to study and use auditory reading aids such as talking books or text-to-speech computer software if time is not available, and (c) allowing extra time on tests (Gompel, van Bon, & Schreuder, 2004).

CLASSROOM ADAPTATIONS Minor classroom adaptations, such as proper lighting, can be very important for students with low vision. Although most classrooms have adequate lighting, adjustable lamps are helpful for some children. Rosenthal and Williams (2000) recommend that additional lighting should come from the side of the eye with the greatest usable vision. Many students benefit from desks with adjustable or tilting tops so that they can read and write at close range without constantly bending over and casting a shadow. Writing paper should have a dull finish to reduce glare; an off-white color such as buff or ivory is generally better than white. Worksheets photocopied on colored paper can be difficult for students with low vision to use; if needed, an aide or a classmate can first go over the worksheet with a dark pen or marker. Some teachers have found it helpful to give students with low vision chairs with wheels so that they can easily move around the chalkboard area or other places in the classroom where instruction is taking place

Katelyn Metzger/Merrill

This student with low vision is using ZoomText, a software program that enables her to produce and read large print.

FIGURE 6 ADVANTAGES AND DISADVANTAGES OF LARGE-PRINT MATERIALS AND OPTICAL DEVICES FOR READERS WITH LOW VISION

LARGE-PRINT MATERIALS	OPTICAL DEVICES
Advantages	**Advantages**
• Little or no instruction is needed to use a large-print book or other materials.	• Users have access to materials of various sizes, such as regular texts, newspapers, menus, and maps.
• A low vision clinical evaluation is not needed.	
• Students carry large-print books like other students carry books in their classes.	• Optical devices have a lower cost per child than large-print materials do.
• Funds for large-print books come from school districts that may require parental or other funding for optical devices.	• Devices are lighter weight and more portable than large-print materials are.
	• There is no waiting time for production or availability.
	• Users have access to distant print and objects, such as chalkboards, signs, and people.
Disadvantages	**Disadvantages**
• Fewer words can be seen at once; large-print materials are more difficult to read smoothly with a natural sweep of eye movements.	• A low vision clinical evaluation must be obtained for the prescription of optical devices.
• Enlarging print by photocopy emphasizes imperfect letters.	• Funding for clinical evaluation and optical devices must be obtained.
• Pictures are in black, white, and shades of gray.	• Instruction in the use of the optical devices is needed.
• Fractions, labels on diagrams, maps, and so forth are enlarged to a print size smaller than 18-point type.	• The cosmetics of optical devices may cause self-consciousness.
• The size and weight of large-print texts make them difficult to handle.	• Optical problems associated with the optics of devices need to be tolerated.
• Large-print materials are not readily available after the school years, and students may be nonfunctional readers with regular-size type.	

Source: A. Corn & G. Ryser. (1989). "Access to Print for Students with Low Vision." *Journal of Visual Impairment & Blindness, 83,* 340–349 . Reprinted with permission from American Foundation for the Blind, 15 West 16th St., New York, NY 10011.

without constantly getting up and down. A teacher can make many other modifications using common sense and considering the needs of the individual student with low vision. For suggestions on helping students with low vision in the classroom, see *Teaching & Learning*, "Helping the Student with Low Vision."

For detailed information on lighting recommended for various environments and tasks for low vision, see Takeshita (2011).

Expanded Core Curriculum

In addition to communication and sensory skills such as reading and writing braille, functional vision skills, and assistive technology, the *expanded core curriculum* for students with visual impairments includes orientation and mobility, listening skills, social interaction skills, independent living skills, recreation and leisure skills, and career education.

To learn more about the expanded core curriculum, see Hatlen (2011).

ORIENTATION AND MOBILITY *Orientation* is knowing where you are, where you are going, and how to get there by interpreting information from the environment. *Mobility* involves moving safely and efficiently from one point to another. Although the two sets of skills are complementary, orientation and mobility are not the same thing. A person can know where he is but not be able to move safely in that environment, and a person may be mobile but become disoriented or lost.

Helping the Student with Low Vision

What does a child with low vision actually see? It is difficult for us to know. Even when two children share the same cause of visual impairment, it is unlikely that they see things in exactly the same way. And each child may see things differently at different times (Guerette, Lewis, & Mattingly, 2011). Corn believes that curriculum development and instructional planning for children with low vision should be guided by the following basic premises about low vision and its effects on a person (Corn & Erin, 2000; Corn et al., 2004):

- **Children with congenital low vision view themselves as whole.** Although it may be proper to speak of residual vision in reference to those who experience adventitious low vision, those with congenital low vision do not have a normal vision reference. They view the world with all of the vision they have ever had.

- **Children with low vision generally view the environment as stationary and clear.** Although there are exceptions, it is a misconception that people with low vision live in an impressionistic world in which they are continuously wanting to clear the image.

- **Low vision offers a different aesthetic experience.** Low vision may alter an aesthetic experience, but it does not necessarily produce a lesser one.

- **Using low vision is not always the most efficient or preferred method of functioning.** For some tasks, the use of vision alone or in combination with other senses may reduce one's ability to perform. For example, using vision may not be the most efficient method for determining how much salt has been poured on one's food.

- **Those who have low vision may develop a sense of visual beauty, enjoy their visual abilities, and use vision to learn.**

HOW TO GET STARTED

The following suggestions for teachers of students with low vision are from The Vision Team, a group of specialists in visual impairment who work with general education classroom teachers in 13 school districts in Hennepin County, Minnesota.

- Using the eyes does not harm them. The more children use their eyes, the greater their efficiency will be.

- Holding printed material close to the eyes may be the best way for the child with low vision to see. It will not harm the eyes.

- Although eyes cannot be strained from use, the eyes of a child with low vision may tire more quickly. A change of focus or activity helps.

- Copying is often a problem for children with low vision. The child may need a shortened assignment or more time to do classwork.

- It is helpful if the teacher verbalizes as much as possible while writing on the chalkboard or using projected images and text.

- One of the most important things a child with low vision learns in school is to accept the responsibility of seeking help when necessary rather than waiting for someone to offer help.

- In evaluating quality of work and applying discipline, the teacher best helps the child with low vision by using the same standards that he uses with other children.

Orientation and mobility (O&M) instruction is considered a related service by IDEA and is included in the IEP of virtually all children with significant visual impairments. O&M specialists have developed many specific techniques (e.g., trailing, squaring off, using arms as bumpers) and mobility devices (e.g., a shopping cart, a suitcase on wheels) to teach students with visual impairments to understand their environment and maneuver through it safely and effectively (Wiener, Welsh, & Blasch, 2010).

For most students, more time and effort are spent on orientation training than on learning specific mobility techniques. It is extremely important that from an early age, children with visual impairments be taught basic concepts that will familiarize them with their own bodies and their surroundings. For example, they must be taught that the place where the leg bends is called a "knee" and that rooms have walls, doors, windows, corners, and ceilings. Perla and O'Donnell (2004) stress the importance of systematically teaching students to respond to orientation and mobility obstacles and puzzles as problem-solving opportunities so that they will not have to depend on others each time they find themselves in a novel environment.

Cane Skills. The long cane is the most widely used device for adults with severe visual impairments who travel independently. The traveler does not tap the cane but sweeps it lightly in an arc while walking to gain information about the path ahead (Sauerburger &

USING LOW-VISION AIDS

Here are some tips for teachers to share with children to help them get the most from their low-vision aids:

- **Low-vision aids take time to get used to.** At first, it seems like just a lot more things to take care of and carry around, but each aid you have will help you with a special job of seeing. In time, reaching for your telescope to read the chalkboard will seem as natural as picking up a pencil or pen to write. It's all a matter of practice.

Low-vision aids should be portable and easy to use.

- **Lighting is very important.** Always work with the most effective light for you. It makes a big difference in how clear things will look. Some magnifiers come with a built-in light, but most times you will have to use another light. A desk lamp is best. (The overhead light casts a shadow on your book or paper as you get close enough to see it.) Be sure the light is along your side, coming over your shoulder.
- **Keep your aids clean.** It's hard to see through dust, dirt, and fingerprints. Clean the lenses with a clean, soft cloth (never paper). Always be sure your hands are clean to begin with.
- **Keep your aids in their cases when you are not using them.** They will be more protected and always ready for you to take with you wherever you go.
- **Carry your low-vision aids with you.** Most aids are small and lightweight. In that way, you will have them when you need them. If you have aids you use only at school, you may want to ask your teacher to keep them in a safe place for you.
- **Experiment in new situations.** Can you see the menu at McDonald's? Watch the football game? See prices on toys? Find your friend's house number? The more often you use your low-vision aid, the better you will get at using it.
- **Try out different combinations of aids with and without your glasses or contact lenses.** In this way, you will find the combinations that work best for you.

Sources: Allman and Lewis (2000); Bennett (1997); Brilliant (1999); Lidoff and Massof (2000); Tips for using low-vision aids from M. Dean, *A Closer Look at Low Vision Aids.* Connecticut State Board of Education and Services for the Blind, Division of Children's Services, 184 Windsor Ave., Windsor, CT 06095. Reprinted by permission.

Bourquin, 2010). Properly used, the cane serves as both a bumper and a probe. It acts as a bumper by protecting the body from obstacles such as parking meters and doors; it is also a probe to detect in advance things such as drop-offs or changes in travel surface (e.g., from grass to concrete or from a rug to a wooden floor).

Even though mastery of cane skills can do much to increase a person's independence and self-esteem, cane use exacts physical effort and poses certain disadvantages (Gitlin, Mount, Lucas, Weirich, & Gramberg, 1997). The cane cannot detect overhanging obstacles such as tree branches and provides only fragmentary information about the environment, particularly if the person who is blind is in new or unfamiliar surroundings.

Preschool children benefit from the services of an O&M specialist; but there is disagreement over which, if any, mobility device is most suitable for initial use by very young children (Dykes, 1992). Professionals recognize the long cane's benefits of increased protection and confidence while traveling but question whether preschoolers can handle the motor and conceptual demands of long cane use. These concerns have led to the development of a variety of alternative mobility devices, including modified and smaller canes such as the Connecticut precane, kiddie canes, and canes with T-bar handles (American Foundation for the Blind, 2011c).

TEACHING & LEARNING

Guide Dogs. Fewer than 2% of people with visual impairments travel with the aid of guide dogs (Hill & Snook-Hill, 1996). Like the cane traveler, the guide dog user must have good O&M skills to select a route and to be aware of the environment. The dog wears a special harness and has been trained to follow several basic verbal commands, to provide protection against obstacles, and to ensure the traveler's safety. Guide dogs are especially helpful when a person must travel over complicated or unpredictable routes, as in large cities. Several weeks of intensive training at special guide dog agencies are required before the person and the dog can work together effectively (Guerette & Zabihaylo, 2010). Guide dogs are not usually available to children under 16 years of age or to people with multiple disabilities. Young children, however, should have exposure to and positive experiences with dogs so they are comfortable with them and can make informed choices later about the possibilities of working with a guide dog.

Although owning a guide dog is a major responsibility and sometimes inconvenient, many owners report increased confidence and independence in traveling and say that their dogs often serve as icebreakers for interactions with sighted people (Minor, 2001). However, guide dogs are not pets but working companions for their owners, and sighted people should not pet a guide dog without first obtaining the owner's permission or take hold of the dog's harness, as this might confuse the dog and the owner.

Katelyn Metzger/Merrill

Under the watchful eyes of an orientation and mobility specialist, Creighton is learning how to gain information about the path ahead by sweeping his cane in an arc.

Additional information on guide dog etiquette and tips for meeting and interacting with a person who is blind can be found at VisionServe Alliance (2011).

Sighted Guides. Most people who are blind find it necessary to rely occasionally on the assistance of others. The **sighted guide technique** is a simple method of helping a person with visual impairments to travel:

- When offering assistance to a person who is blind, speak in a normal tone of voice and ask, "May I help you?" This helps the person locate you.
- Do not grab the person's arm or body. Permit him to take your arm.
- The person with visual impairment should lightly grasp the sighted person's arm just above the elbow and walk half a step behind in a natural manner. Young children might hold on to the index finger or pinky of an adult sighted guide.
- The sighted person should walk at a normal pace, describing curbs or other obstacles and hesitating slightly before going up or down. Never pull or push a person who is blind.
- Do not try to push a person who is blind into a chair. Simply place his hand on the back of the chair, and the person will seat himself.

When students with visual impairments attend general education classes, it may be a good idea for one of the students and the O&M specialist to demonstrate the sighted guide technique to classmates. To promote independent travel, however, overreliance on the sighted guide technique should be discouraged once the student has learned to get around the classroom and the school.

Electronic Travel Aids. A variety of electronic travel aids facilitate the orientation and mobility of individuals with visual impairments. The laser beam cane converts infrared light into sound as the light beam strikes objects in the traveler's path. Different levels of vibration in the cane signal relative proximity to an obstacle. Other electronic travel aids are designed for use in conjunction with a standard cane or guide dog. The Mowat

Sensor is a flashlight-sized device that bounces ultrasound off objects and gives the traveler information about the distance and location of obstacles through changes in vibration. The SonicGuide, which is worn on the head, converts reflections of ultrasound into sounds of varied pitch, amplitude, and tone that enable the traveler to determine distance, direction, and characteristics of objects in the environment.

Recent research has developed accessible and affordable global positioning system (GPS) technologies and other way-finding products for people with visual impairments that can announce present location, interpret traffic signals, read street signs, give distance and direction information, and more (Marston, Loomis, Klatzky, & Golledge, 2007; Ponchillia et al., 2007).

Whatever the preferred method of travel, most students with visual impairments learn to negotiate familiar places, such as school and home, on their own. Many students with visual impairments can benefit from learning to use a systematic method for obtaining travel information and assistance with street crossing. Good orientation and mobility skills have many positive effects. A child with visual impairments who can travel independently is likely to develop more physical and social skills and more self-confidence than will a child who must continually depend on other people to get around. Good travel skills also expand a student's opportunities for employment and independent living (Wolffe & Kelly, 2011).

LISTENING SKILLS Children with visual impairments, especially those who are blind, must obtain an enormous amount of information by listening. Vision is thought to be the coordinating sense, and it has been estimated that 80% of information received by a normally sighted person comes through the visual channel (Arter, 1997). Children who are blind must use other senses, predominately touch and hearing, to contact and comprehend their environment. A widely held misconception is that people who are blind automatically develop a better sense of hearing to compensate for their loss of sight. Children with visual impairments do not have a super sense of hearing, nor do they necessarily listen better than their normally sighted peers do. It is more accurate to say that, through proper instruction and experiences, children with visual impairments learn to use their hearing more efficiently (Koenig, 2006).

The systematic development of listening skills is an important component of the educational program of every child with visual impairments. Listening is not the same thing as hearing; it is possible to hear a sound without understanding it. Listening involves being aware of sounds, discriminating differences in sounds, identifying the source of sounds, and attaching meaning to sounds (Ferrell & Spungin, 2011).

Learning-to-listen activities can take an almost unlimited variety of forms. Young children, for example, might learn to discriminate between sounds that are near and far, loud and soft, high pitched and low pitched. A teacher might introduce a new word into a sentence and ask the child to identify it or ask children to clap each time a key word is repeated. In the "shopping game," a child begins by saying, "I went to the store and I bought _____." Each player repeats the whole list of items purchased by previous students and then adds his or her own item to the list (Arter, 1997). It is important to arrange the rules of such games so that children who fail to remember the list are not eliminated, which would result in fewer opportunities to practice for the children with the weakest listening and auditory memory skills. Older students might practice higher-order listening skills such as identifying important details with distracting background noises, differentiating between fact and opinion, or responding to verbal analogies.

Students with visual impairments, particularly in high school, make frequent use of recorded materials. In addition to using recordings of texts, lectures, and class discussions, students with visual impairments and their teachers can obtain on a free-loan basis thousands of recorded books and magazines and playback equipment through the Library of Congress, the American Printing House for the Blind (APH), the Canadian National Institute for the Blind, Recordings for the Blind, and various other organizations. A listener can process auditory information at more than twice the speed of

Listening skills

Content Standards for Beginning Teachers—B&VI: Strategies for teaching listening and compensatory auditory skills (B&VI6K2).

the average oral reading rate of about 120 words per minute (Aldrich & Parkin, 1989). With practice, students can listen to accelerated and compressed speech at speeds of up to 275 words per minute without affecting comprehension (Arter, 1997). The Book Port Plus, a portable player/recorder available from the American Printing House for the Blind (2011), lets the user adjust the playback rate and sound quality of recorded text and includes a speech-compression feature that electronically shortens the length of selected words.

FUNCTIONAL LIFE SKILLS Some special educators have expressed concern that efforts to help students with visual impairments match the academic achievement of their sighted age mates have too often come at the expense of sufficient opportunities to learn daily living and career skills (Lohmeier, 2005; Sacks, Wolffe, & Tierney, 1998). Specific instruction and ongoing supports should be provided to ensure that students with visual impairments learn skills such as cooking, personal hygiene and grooming, shopping, financial management, transportation, and recreational activities that are requisites for an independent and enjoyable adulthood (Corn & Erin, 2000; Kaufman, 2000; Rosenblum, 2000). To find out how three secondary students who are blind were taught to prepare some of their favorite snack foods, see *Teaching & Learning,* "I Made It Myself, and It's Good!"

EDUCATIONAL PLACEMENT ALTERNATIVES

In the past, most children with severe visual impairments were educated in residential schools. Today, however, 88% of children with visual impairments are educated in public schools, and three of four receive at least some of their education in general education school classrooms: 62% of all school-age students with visual impairments are members of general education classes, and 13% attend resource rooms for part of each day (U.S. Department of Education, 2010). Separate classrooms in public schools serve another 12% of the school-age population of children with visual impairments, and about 6% attend special day schools.

Inclusive Classroom and Itinerant Teacher Model

Students with visual impairments were among the first students with disabilities to be included in general education classrooms. Although Cruickshank (1986) suggested that "the blind child is perhaps the easiest exceptional child to integrate into a regular grade in the public schools" (p. 104), successful inclusion requires a full program of individualized special education and related services (Salisbury, 2008).

Most students with visual impairments in general education classrooms receive support from itinerant teacher-consultants, sometimes called vision specialists. These specially trained teachers may be employed by the school district; a nearby residential school; or a regional, state, or provincial education agency. Although their roles and caseloads vary widely, most itinerant teacher-consultants have some or all of the following responsibilities (Olmstead, 2005):

- Help identify the child's current level of performance, learning goals and objectives, and need for related services as member of IEP team.
- Collaborate with the general education classroom teacher on curricular and instructional modifications according to the child's individual needs.
- Provide direct instruction on compensatory skills (e.g., braille, listening, keyboarding).
- Obtain or prepare specialized learning materials (e.g., math manipulatives).
- Adapt reading assignments and text-based curriculum material into braille, large-print, or audio-recorded form.
- Make referrals for low-vision aids and services, and train students in the use and care of low-vision aids.

Functional life skills

Content Standards for Beginning Teachers—B&VI: Strategies for teaching social, daily living, and functional life skills to individuals with B&VI (B&VI4K6).

Placement alternatives

Content Standards for Beginning Teachers—Common Core: Issues, assurances, and due process right related to assessment, eligibility, and placement with a continuum of services (ICC1K6).

- Provide information about the child's visual impairment and visual functioning to parents and other school personnel.
- Initiate and maintain contact with various agencies that provide services for children with visual impairments.
- Consult with the child's parents and other teachers.

The itinerant teacher-consultant may or may not provide instruction in O&M. Some schools, particularly in rural areas, employ dually certified teachers who are also O&M specialists. Other schools employ one teacher for educational support and another for O&M training. Students on an itinerant teacher's caseload may range from infants to young adults and may include children who are blind, those with low vision, and students with multiple disabilities.

Patrick is getting along fine in the general education classroom—thanks to the instructional adaptations jointly planned by his itinerant vision specialist and his classroom teacher.

© Nathan Benn/Alamy

The amount of time the itinerant teacher-consultant or resource room teacher spends with a visually impaired student who attends general education classes varies considerably. Some students may be seen every day because they require a great deal of specialized assistance. Others may be seen weekly, monthly, or even less frequently because they can function well in the general education class with less support.

For inclusion to succeed, a child with visual impairments needs a skilled and supportive general education classroom teacher. This was underscored by a study that asked adolescents to assess the impact of visual impairments on their lives (Rosenblum, 2000). All 10 students in the study attended public school general education classrooms for at least 50% of the school day. Several students reported that a general education teacher made it difficult for them to use disability-specific skills such as braille or computerized speech output in the classroom. ("It took him about a quarter to get the stuff [tests and worksheets] to the braillist in the first place" [p. 439].) Other participants reported that insensitive teachers caused them to feel humiliation and frustration about having a visual impairment. ("The science teacher wanted me to identify rocks by a visual method and I told her I can't. She goes, 'Well, you're going to have to if you want to get a good grade'" [p. 439].) Several other participants reported that general education teachers treated them like younger children. ("The teachers talk to me differently like I'm more of a 6 year old rather than a 13 year old" [p. 43].) Figure 7 provides tips for supporting a student with visual impairments in the general education classroom.

Residential Schools

About 4% of school-age children with visual impairments attend residential schools (U.S. Department of Education, 2010). Residential schools continue to meet the needs of a sizable number of children with visual impairments. The current population of residential schools consists largely of children with visual impairments with additional disabilities, such as intellectual disabilities, hearing impairment, behavioral disorders, and cerebral palsy. Some parents cannot care for their children adequately at home; others prefer the greater concentration of specialized personnel, facilities, and services that a residential school usually offers.

Residential schools

 Council for Exceptional Children

Content Standards for Beginning Teachers—B&VI: Historical foundations of education of individuals with B&VI as related to traditional roles of specialized and public schools around the world (B&VI1K2).

TEACHING & LEARNING

▼ I Made It Myself, and It's Good!

Being able to prepare one's own food is a critical skill for independent living. Steve, Lisa, and Carl were 17 to 21 years old and enrolled in a class for students with multiple disabilities at a residential school for the blind (Trask-Tyler, Grossi, & Heward, 1994). None had any functional vision or braille skills, and their IQ scores ranged from 64 to 72 on the Perkins Binet Test of Intelligence for the Blind. They were living in an on-campus apartment used to teach daily living skills. Teachers had made several unsuccessful attempts to teach basic cooking skills to the three.

Students like Steve, Lisa, and Carl require intensive instruction over many sessions to learn new skills, especially those involving long chains of responses such as following a recipe. The challenge was to discover a method for teaching cooking skills that would be effective initially but also would enable the students to prepare recipes for which they had not received instruction and that resulted in long-term maintenance of their new skills.

AN AUDIO COOKBOOK

Because Steve, Lisa, and Carl were blind, it was not possible to use picture cookbooks or color-coded recipes, which have been used successfully with learners with intellectual and other disabilities (e.g., Book, Paul, Gwalla-Ogisi, & Test, 1990). Instead, the students used audio-recorded recipes. Each student wore a cooking apron with two pockets. One pocket at the waist held a small tape recorder; the second pocket, located at the chest, held a switch that turned the tape player on and off. Each step from the task-analyzed recipes was prerecorded in sequence on a cassette tape (e.g., "Open the bag of cake mix by tearing it at the tab"). A beep signaled the end of each direction.

PERFORMANCE MEASURES

The number of recipe steps each student independently completed was measured in probes conducted before, during, and after instruction. Additional probes on two classes of recipes on which the students received no training were conducted to assess generalization. Simple generalization recipes could be prepared using the same cooking skills learned in a related trained recipe. Complex generalization recipes required a combination of skills learned in two different trained recipes. Each attempt was also scored as to whether the food prepared was edible.

INSTRUCTION

Students were told that the taped recipes explained exactly what to do and where to find the food items and utensils. They practiced controlling the rate of instructions by starting and stopping the tape each time they heard a beep. Training for each step of the task analysis consisted of a three-component least-to-most prompt hierarchy (verbal, physical, and hand-over-hand guidance) following errors and verbal praise for correct responses. Training on a recipe continued until a student correctly performed all steps on two consecutive trials over two sessions.

RESULTS

Lisa, Carl, and Steve needed a total of 12, 19, and 35 instructional trials, respectively, to learn to make three different recipes. (Steve required a greater number of trials to master the coffee and cheesecake recipes due to repeated spills when pouring liquids. His teacher solved this problem by teaching Steve to use his fingers to feel where and how much liquid he was pouring.) After mastering the trained recipes, each student was able to prepare both the simple and the complex generalization recipes with the tape recorder, even though they had not received any instruction on those recipes.

The ultimate evaluation of cooking skills instruction is whether or not the food can be eaten: does it taste good? A mistake on any one of several crucial steps in the 27-step task analysis for making microwave cake (e.g., not stirring the egg into the batter) would result in a cake no one would want to eat. Before training, none of Steve's 13 attempts to make any of the trained recipes could be eaten, whereas all 6 of his posttraining attempts were edible. Before training, Steve was unsuccessful in all 20 of his attempts to make the simple generalization recipes and on each of 4 attempts to prepare the complex generalization recipes. After learning how to make the related recipes, he was able to follow tape-recorded recipes to successfully prepare the recipes for which he had received no direct training: on 82% of the trials (9 of 11) with the simple generalization recipes and on all 3 trials with the complex generalization recipes. In two follow-up probes conducted 6 weeks and 4 months after the study ended, Steve was still able to prepare all of the recipes successfully. Lisa and Carl showed similar gains in their ability to prepare food for themselves.

Larry Hammill/Merrill

Steve learned to accurately pour and measure the milk for his cake by placing his fingers in the bowl.

INDIVIDUALIZED, NORMALIZED, AND SELF-DETERMINED

Self-operated audio prompting systems (SOAPS), such as the one used by Steve, Lisa, and Carl, offer several advantages (also see Grossi, 1998; Lancioni, O'Reilly, & Oliva, 2001; Mechling, 2007; Post, Storey, & Karabin, 2002). First, the prerecorded instructions or prompts can be individualized. For example:

- Audio-recorded instructions can be as precise or general as necessary, depending on known or probable tasks and environments.
- Vocabulary can be modified, pacing of instructions speeded up or slowed down, and instructions for particularly difficult steps repeated or given in more detail.
- Students might use their own voice to record special prompts or reminders relevant to certain steps of the task (e.g., "Have I checked for spills?").
- Verbal praise and encouragement from teachers, parents, friends, or the student himself could also be included in the instructions.

Second, individuals with disabilities are currently using a variety of assistive devices to increase their independence in domestic, community, and employment settings. The learner in natural settings, however, may not use some assistive devices. A student in a crowded restaurant, for example, may hesitate to remove a laminated ordering card from her pocket or purse because it marks her as different. By contrast, the popularity of personal mp3 devices such as iPods enables the user to listen to self-delivered prompts in a private, unobtrusive, and normalized manner that does not impose on or bother others.

Third, the self-operated feature of the system puts the student in control of the environment, thereby increasing the probability of independent functioning and level of self-determination. As Carl remarked when sharing with his girlfriend the microwave cake he had just made, "I made it myself, and it's good!"

HOW TO GET STARTED

If the SOAPS will be used to help a student complete multistep activities (e.g., making macaroni and cheese):

1. Create a task analysis of the activity.
2. Write a script of instructions for each step of the task analysis using language that the student understands.
3. Record the script, embedding a standard phrase or distinct tone between instructions to cue the student when to stop and start the playback device.

If the SOAPS will be used to help a student stay on task and be productive during an ongoing activity (e.g., washing dishes):

1. Write a variety of simple statements that are likely to function for the student as prompts to keep working, encouragement and praise, and/or cues to self-evaluate her performance.
2. Record the prompts, praise statement, and/or cues to self-evaluate in a random sequence at irregular intervals.
3. If listening to music would be appropriate for the student while doing the activity, consider embedding the instructions or prompts within a recording of the student's favorite singer or band.

For all SOAPS:

1. If necessary, teach the student how to operate the portable audio device before introducing the prerecorded instructions or prompts.
2. Observe and monitor the student's initial use of the SOAPS to determine whether the length and complexity of the steps/instructions are appropriate and efficient.
3. Ask the student whether any changes in the instructions or prompts would make the system more effective or enjoyable to use.

MyEducationLab™

To see how this strategy works, go to the Book Resources for this text in MyEducationLab.

TEACHING & LEARNING

FIGURE 7   SUPPORTING A STUDENT WITH VISUAL IMPAIRMENTS IN THE GENERAL EDUCATION CLASSROOM

Although each student with a visual impairment is unique and requires a specially designed set of accommodations and modifications to meet her own academic and social goals, teachers should follow some fundamental guidelines when working with any student who relies on nonvisual senses for communication and learning. Using the following tips and techniques will increase the effectiveness of your communication with students who have visual impairments and encourage and promote their confidence and independence.

Communicate with Clarity and Respect

- Always state the name of the student you are speaking to in the classroom. The student with a visual impairment will not notice eye contact.

- Indefinite pronouns such as 'this,' 'that,' and 'there' can be confusing to students with visual impairments. It is better to name specific items, events, or people.

- Individuals with visual impairments frequently make idiomatic references to sight, and it is okay for their teachers and peers to do so also: e.g., "Do you see what I mean?" or "Let's take a look at this next sentence."

- Always give a verbal warning when you are about to hand something to a student with visual impairments. This avoids unnecessary surprises and helps the student respond efficiently.

- Include specific spatial references when giving your student directions. For example, telling the student, "The book is on your left," or "The desk is 10 feet in front of you," is better than saying, "It's over there," or "It's near the table."

- When writing or drawing on the board, describe your actions verbally in a manner useful for all students in the class. Be sure not to talk down to the student with a visual impairment.

- Introduce yourself by name when meeting your student outside the classroom. Do not assume that he will recognize your voice, and do not ask, "Guess who this is?"

- When you are about to leave the student's vicinity, tell him that you are going.

- When you need to physically show your student how to do something, use the hand-under-hand technique. Have the student place her hands on top of yours so she can feel the movement of your hands. This is usually more effective than placing your hands over the student's hands.

Expect and Enable Independence

- If students are expected to perform jobs or responsibilities in your classroom, be sure also to assign a meaningful job to your students with visual impairments.

- Allow students with visual impairments time to obtain and put away materials. If a student had to use glue and scissors for an activity, make sure she returns those items to their proper places. Although it is often much easier to get and put away materials for students with visual impairments, it is critical that they learn to become self-sufficient and pick up after themselves.

- Peers are often the most effective and efficient teachers of social skills. Cooperative groups are a great way for students with visual impairments to learn important social skills.

- Always make safety a priority, but do not overprotect students with visual impairments. Hands-on experiences are the best way for a student to learn new concepts.

- Provide real-life experiences whenever possible. When on a school field trip, give the student with a visual impairment sufficient time to explore her environment.

Source: Suggestions courtesy of Jeanna Mora Dowse, who worked for many years as an itinerant teacher of students with visual impairments in two school districts in Apache County, Arizona.

Parents and educators who support residential schools for children with visual impairments frequently point to the leadership that such schools have provided over a long period and their range of services. These supporters argue that a residential school can be the least restrictive environment for some students with visual impairments and multiple disabilities. Among the advantages cited are specialized curriculum and equipment, participation in extracurricular activities, individualized instruction, small classes, and improved self-esteem.

As with any other point in the continuum of educational settings, placement in a residential school should not be regarded as permanent. Many children with visual impairments move from residential schools into public schools (or vice versa) as their needs change. Some students in residential schools attend nearby public schools for part of the school day. Most residential schools encourage parent involvement and have recreational programs that bring students with visual impairments into contact with sighted peers. Independent living skills and vocational training are important parts of the program at virtually all residential schools.

Residential schools have long played an important role in training teachers of children with visual impairments. Most residential schools are well equipped to serve as a resource center for instructional materials and as a place where students with visual impairments can receive specialized evaluation services. Some residential schools offer short-term training to students with visual impairments who attend regular public schools. One example is a summer workshop emphasizing braille, mobility, and vocational training.

Can a Neighborhood School Provide the Needed Specialized Services?

Some vision professionals resist noncategorical special education programs for students with visual impairments. It is unrealistic, they argue, to expect general education teachers or teachers trained in other areas of special education to be competent in specialized techniques such as braille, O&M, and visual efficiency. The Council for Exceptional Children's Division of Visual Impairments (DVI) recognizes that a student's need for instruction in the expanded core curriculum may require different educational placements at various times during his or her school years (Huebner, Garber, & Wormsley, 2006). (See *Current Issues and Future Trends*, "Inclusion of Students with Visual Impairments.")

Although financial restrictions may require some public school and residential school programs for children with visual impairments to close down or consolidate with programs for children with other disabilities, strong support exists for the continuation of highly specialized services. It is likely that both public school and state-run residential programs for children with visual impairments will continue to operate well into the future, occasionally challenging each other for the privilege of serving the relatively small number of available students. The results of this competition may well prove favorable if both types of programs are encouraged to improve the quality of their educational services.

Fighting Against Discrimination and For Self-Determination

Like other groups of individuals with disabilities, people with visual impairments have become increasingly aware of their rights as citizens and consumers. They are fighting discrimination based on their disabilities (Koestler, 2004; Lunsford, 2006) and experiencing the benefits of self-determination (Agran, Hong, & Blankenship, 2007). Many people—even some special educators who work with students with visual impairments—underestimate their students' capacities and deny them a full range of occupational and personal choices. The future should bring a shift away from some of the vocations and settings in which people with visual impairments have traditionally worked (e.g., piano tuning, rehabilitation counseling) in favor of a more varied and rewarding range of employment opportunities.

In an essay describing the importance of the expanded core curriculum, Hatlen (1996) tells of a prominent blind woman who, when asked, "What is it that blind people want from society?" replied, "The opportunity to be equal and the right to be different."

> What did this woman mean by two remarks that seem diametrically opposite? Perhaps she meant that print and braille are equal, but very different; that the need for independent travel is similar for sighted and blind persons, but the skills are learned very differently by blind people; and that concepts and learning that occur for sighted people in a natural, spontaneous manner require different learning experiences for blind persons. Perhaps she was emphasizing that blind persons should have the opportunity to learn the same knowledge and skills as sighted people, but that their manner of learning will be different. (www.afb.org)

The Texas School for the Blind and Visually Impaired is an outstanding resource for schools, teachers, and parents about serving students with visual impairments. See http://www.tsbvi.edu/outreach.

Inclusion

Council for Exceptional Children

Content Standards for Beginning Teachers—B&VI: Historical foundations and research evidence on which educational practice is based (DH&H1K2).

CURRENT ISSUES

AND FUTURE TRENDS

▶ Inclusion of Students with Visual Impairments

AMERICAN FOUNDATION FOR THE BLIND

"INCLUSION," "FULL INCLUSION" AND "inclusive education" are terms which recently have been narrowly defined by some (primarily educators of students with severe disabilities) to espouse the philosophy that ALL students with disabilities, regardless of the nature or the severity of their disability, receive their TOTAL education within the general education environment. This philosophy is based on the relatively recent placement of a limited number of students with severe disabilities in general education classrooms. Research conducted by proponents of this philosophy lacks empirical evidence that this practice results in programs which are better able to prepare ALL students with visual impairments to be more fully included in society than the current practice, required by federal law, of providing a full range of program options. Educators and parents of students with visual impairments have pioneered special education and inclusive program options for over 164 years. It is significant that the field of education of visually impaired students was the first to develop a range of special education program options, beginning with specialized schools in 1829 and extending to inclusive (including "full inclusion") public school program options since 1900.

Experience and research clearly support the following three position statements outlining the essential elements which must be in place in order to provide an appropriate education in the least restrictive environment for students with visual impairments.

I. Students with visual impairments have unique educational needs which are most effectively met using a team approach of professionals, parents and students. In order to meet their unique needs, students must have specialized services, books and materials in appropriate media (including braille), as well as specialized equipment and technology to assure equal access to the core and specialized curricula, and to enable them to most effectively compete with their peers in school and ultimately in society.

The unique educational needs of all students with visual impairments cannot be met in a single environment, even with unlimited funding. It is critical that a team approach be used in identifying and meeting these needs and that the team must include staff who have specific expertise in educating students with visual impairments. The proposal that ALL of the needs of ALL students can be met in one environment, the regular classroom, violates the spirit as well as the letter of the law—IDEA.

II. There must be a full range of program options and support services so that the Individualized Education Program (IEP) team can select the most appropriate placement in the least restrictive environment for each individual student with a visual impairment. The right of every student

---

▼ TIPS FOR BEGINNING TEACHERS

Supporting Your Students with Visual Impairments

BY CECELIA PEIRANO

COMMUNICATION

Be specific when communicating with your students, their parents, and professionals.

- Use the student's name when you are speaking only to him or her, directional words to give specific locations, and descriptive language to avoid confusion. For example, "Seth, please place your science assignment in the basket to the left of the pencil sharpener," will give you better results than "Put your paper over there."

- When meeting with aides, teachers, or other professionals, give specific instructions—written, if possible—about what your student needs. That way if the meeting is interrupted or cut short, you will have left clear directions for what your student needs in your absence. Include specific timelines so they have a goal set.

PREPARATION

Be prepared with materials ahead of time so your students are active participants.

---

with a visual impairment to an appropriate placement in the least restrictive environment, selected by the IEP team from a full range of program options and based upon each student's needs, is nothing more or less than is mandated by federal law.

III. There must be adequate personnel preparation programs to train staff to provide specialized services that address the unique academic and non-academic curriculum needs of students with visual impairments. There must also be ongoing specialized personnel development opportunities for all staff working with these students as well as specialized parent education. Students with visual impairments have the right to an appropriate education that is guided by knowledgeable specialists who work collaboratively with parents, the student and other education team members. Access to training on an ongoing basis is essential for all team members, especially parents who provide the necessary continuity and support in their child's education.

PLACEMENT DOES NOT NECESSARILY PROVIDE ACCESS

Providing equal access to all individuals with disabilities is the key element of the Rehabilitation Act of 1973 and the Americans with Disabilities Act of 1992. Access involves much more than providing ramps. Access is also the key element of inclusion, which involves much more than placement in a particular setting. The relationship of access and inclusion may not be obvious to individuals who are not familiar with the educational and social impact of a vision loss. Placing a student with a visual impairment in a regular classroom does not, necessarily, provide access and the student is not, necessarily, included. A student with a visual impairment, who does not have access to social and physical information because of the visual impairment, is not included, regardless of the

physical setting. Students with visual impairments will not be included unless their unique educational needs for access are addressed by specially trained personnel in appropriate environments and unless these students are provided with equal access to core and specialized curricula through appropriate specialized books, materials and equipment.

Conclusion: Students with visual impairments need an educational system that meets the individual needs of ALL students, fosters independence, and is measured by the success of each individual in the school and community. Vision is fundamental to the learning process and is the primary basis upon which most traditional education strategies are based. Students who are visually impaired are most likely to succeed in educational systems where appropriate instruction and services are provided in a full array of program options by qualified staff to address each student's unique educational needs, as required by Public Law 101-476, The Individuals with Disabilities Education Act (IDEA).

WHAT DO YOU THINK?

1. Should the least restrictive environment (LRE) for students with visual impairments be defined differently from the LRE for students with other disabilities? Why or why not?

2. Can a residential school be the LRE for a student who has been blind from birth? for a child who lost her sight in elementary school? Why or why not?

3. Do you think any single educational setting can serve as an LRE for a student with visual impairment? Why or why not?

Source: "Educating Students with Visual Impairments for Inclusion in Society: A Paper on the Inclusion of Students with Visual Impairments," by the American Foundation for the Blind's Josephine L. Taylor Leadership Institute, Education Work Group. Copyright 2011 by the American Foundation for the Blind. Reprinted with permission. The full text of this paper is available at http://www.afb.org/Section.asp?SectionID=44&TopicID=189&DocumentID=1344.

- Encourage other staff to get all materials to you ahead of time so that they can be put into the appropriate format such as braille, large print, or into an auditory file. You will also have the opportunity to gather any manipulatives, make tactile graphics, or review the material ahead of time if they will need additional explanation. This might be the case if students are being introduced to Southeast Asia or the periodic table.

- Have a scheduled meeting time that works for the staff involved. They will be more likely to have a quick conference to pass on lesson plans or information that helps in preparing material for your student if they know exactly when you're coming.

- Try to agree on specific schedules and responsibilities while collaborating with the entire staff involved with your student. This will avoid confusion if the student will be missing class for orientation and mobility or other

special services and has assignments to make up. A good resource for this is *Classroom Collaboration* (Hudson, 1997), which is written specifically for working with students with visual impairments.

SELF-ADVOCACY AND THE RIGHT TO STRUGGLE A BIT

Provide your students with the skills and confidence to be independent.

- Expect your students to have the same responsibilities as other students, and provide them with the tools to do it successfully. For example, if they need to take the lunch count, help them set up a file on their BrailleNote, or use the closed-caption TV to prepare the information needed.

- Teach your students how to request help if they need it and politely decline it when they don't need assistance.

Use role playing with their peers to act out the most common situations they encounter.

- Let them try difficult tasks so they can learn new skills. Sit on your hands if you need to so you don't reach in and do it for them. As they discover new methods, provide just enough help that they can then continue on in the process. Be careful that one-on-one aides are assisting only

when needed because students with visual impairments will need additional time at first to become independent learners.

- Peer interaction and group projects can be great for all types of social skills and confidence building because sometimes you need to hear it from a good friend!

▼ KEY TERMS AND CONCEPTS

accommodation
binocular vision
braille
brailler
cataract
cortical visual impairment (CVI)
field of vision
glaucoma
hyperopia
legally blind
low vision
myopia

nystagmus
ocular motility
orientation and mobility (O&M)
partially sighted
refraction
sighted-guide technique
strabismus
tunnel vision
visual acuity
visual efficiency

▼ SUMMARY

Definitions

- Legal blindness is defined as visual acuity of 20/200 or less in the better eye after correction with glasses or contact lenses or a restricted field of vision of 20 degrees or less.
- An educational definition classifies students with visual impairments based on the extent to which they use vision and/or auditory/tactile means for learning.
- A student who is totally blind receives no useful information through the sense of vision and must use tactile, auditory, and other nonvisual senses for all learning.
- A child who is functionally blind has so little vision that she learns primarily through the auditory and tactile senses; however, she may be able to use her limited vision to supplement the information received from the other senses.
- A child with low vision uses vision as a primary means of learning.
- The age at onset of a visual impairment affects a child's educational and emotional needs.

Characteristics

- Children with severe visual impairments do not benefit from incidental learning that normally sighted children obtain in everyday experiences and interactions with the environment.
- Visual impairment often leads to delays or deficits in motor development.
- Some students with visual impairments experience social isolation and difficulties in social interactions due

to limited common experiences with sighted peers; inability to see and use eye contact, facial expressions, and gestures during conversations; and/or stereotypic behaviors.

- The behavior and attitudes of sighted people can be unnecessary barriers to the social participation of individuals with visual impairments.

Prevalence

- Visual impairment is a low-incidence disability affecting fewer than 2 of every 1,000 children in the school-age population. About one half of all students with visual impairments have additional disabilities.

Types and Causes of Visual Impairment

- The eye collects light reflected from objects and focuses the objects' image on the retina. The optic nerve transmits the image to the visual cortex of the brain. Difficulty with any part of this process can cause vision problems.
- Refractive errors mean that the size and shape of the eye prevent the light rays from focusing clearly on the retina.
- Structural impairments are visual impairments caused by poor development of, damage to, or malfunction of one or more parts of the eye's optical or muscular systems.
- Cortical visual impairment (CVI) refers to decreased vision or blindness due to damage to or malfunction of the parts of the brain that interpret visual information.

Educational Approaches

- Braille—a tactile system of reading and writing in which letters, words, numbers, and other systems are made from arrangements of embossed six-dot cells—is the primary means of literacy for students who are blind.
- Students who are blind may also use special equipment to access standard print through touch, reading machines, and prerecorded materials.
- Children with low vision should be taught to use their vision as much and as efficiently as possible.
- Students with low vision use three basic methods for reading print: magnification, optical devices, and large print.
- Students who are blind or have severe visual impairments need instruction in orientation (knowing where they are, where they are going, and how to get there) and mobility (moving safely and efficiently from one point to another).
- Systematic development of listening skills is an important component of the educational program of every child with visual impairments.

- The curriculum for students with visual impairments should also include systematic instruction in functional living skills such as cooking, personal hygiene and grooming, shopping, financial management, transportation, and recreational activities.

Educational Placement Alternatives

- Three of four children with visual impairments spend at least part of each school day in general education classes with sighted peers.
- In many districts, a specially trained itinerant vision specialist provides support for students with visual impairments and their general education classroom teachers.
- Some large school districts have resource room programs for students with visual impairments.
- About 4% of children with visual impairments, especially those with other disabilities, attend residential schools.

MyEducationLab™

Go to Topic 16, Sensory Impairment, in the MyEducationLab (www.myeducationlab.com) for *Exceptional Children*, where you can

- Find learning outcomes for sensory impairment along with the national standards that connect to these outcomes.
- Complete Assignments and Activities that can help you more deeply understand the chapter content.
- Apply and practice your understanding of the core teaching skills identified in the chapter with the Building Teaching Skills and Dispositions learning units.
- Examine challenging situations and cases presented in the IRIS Center Resources.
- Access video clips of CCSSO National Teachers of the Year award winners responding to the question "Why Do I Teach?" in the Teacher Talk section.
- Check your comprehension of the content covered in the chapter with the Study Plan. Here you will be able to take a chapter quiz, receive feedback on your answers, and then access Review, Practice, and Enrichment activities to enhance your understanding of chapter content.
- Use the Online Lesson Plan Builder to practice lesson planning and integrating national and state standards into your planning.

▼ GLOSSARY

accommodation: The adjustment of the eye for seeing at different distances; accomplished by muscles that change the shape of the lens to bring an image into clear focus on the retina.

binocular vision: Vision using both eyes working together to perceive a single image.

braille: A system of writing letters, numbers, and other language symbols with a combination of six raised dots. A person who is blind reads the dots with his fingertips.

brailler: A six-keyed device for writing braille.

cataract: Clouding of the crystalline lens of the eye that results in a reduction or loss of vision.

cortical visual impairments (CVI): Decreased vision or blindness due to known or suspected damage or malfunction of the parts of the brain that interpret visual information.

field of vision: The expanse of space visible with both eyes looking straight ahead, measured in degrees; 160 to 170 degrees is considered normal.

glaucoma: An eye disease characterized by abnormally high pressure inside the eyeball. If left untreated, it can cause total blindness; but if detected early, most cases can be arrested.

hyperopia: Farsightedness; condition in which the image comes to a focus behind the retina instead of on it, causing difficulty in seeing near objects.

legally blind: Visual acuity of 20/200 or less in the better eye after the best possible correction with glasses or contact lenses, or vision restricted to a field of 20 degrees or less. Acuity of 20/200 means the eye can see clearly at 20 feet what the normal eye can see at 200 feet.

low vision: Visual impairment severe enough so that special educational services are required. A child with low vision can learn through the visual channel and generally learns to read print.

myopia: Nearsightedness; results when light is focused on a point in front of the retina, resulting in a blurred image for distant objects.

nystagmus: A rapid, involuntary, rhythmic movement of the eyes that may cause difficulty in reading or fixating on an object.

ocular motility: The eye's ability to move.

orientation and mobility (O&M): Two complementary sets of skills that are critical for people with visual impairments. *Orientation* is knowing where you are, where you are going, and how to get there by interpreting information from the environment; *mobility* involves moving safely and efficiently from one point to another.

partially sighted: The term used for legal and governmental purposes that means visual acuity of no better than 20/70 in the better eye after correction.

refraction: The bending or deflection of light rays from a straight path as they pass from one medium (e.g., air) into another (e.g., the eye). Used by eye specialists in assessing and correcting vision.

sighted-guide technique: A method by which a sighted person can help a person with visual impairments travel. The person with visual impairment grasps the sighted person's arm just above the elbow and walks half a step behind in a natural manner.

strabismus: A condition in which one eye cannot attain binocular vision with the other eye because of imbalanced muscles.

tunnel vision: Visual impairment in which a person has good central vision but poor peripheral vision.

visual acuity: The ability to clearly distinguish forms or discriminate details at a specified distance.

visual efficiency: A term used to describe how effectively a person uses his or her vision. Includes such factors as control of eye movements, near and distant visual acuity, and speed and quality of visual processing. See also *functional vision*.

Deafness and Hearing Loss

Deafness and Hearing Loss

Will & Deni McIntyre/Photo Researchers, Inc.

▶ FOCUS QUESTIONS

- What distinguishes a child who is deaf from a child who is hard of hearing in terms of the primary sensory mode used for learning and communication?
- How might deafness affect a child's acquisition and use of speech and language, academic achievement, and social functioning?
- What implications for a child's education result from the type of hearing loss and age of onset?
- How do students who are deaf and hard of hearing use technologies and supports to amplify, supplement, or replace sound?

- How do oral/aural, total communication, and bilingual-bicultural approaches to educating children who are deaf and hard of hearing differ in their philosophies and methods?
- How might membership in the Deaf culture influence a student's and his family's perspectives and wishes regarding educational placement?

▼ FEATURED TEACHER

DOUGLAS JACKSON

El Paso Regional Day School Program for the Deaf • El Paso, Texas

EDUCATION—TEACHING CREDENTIALS—EXPERIENCE

- B.A., social studies education, University of Northern Colorado, 1978
- M.S., education of the deaf, University of Rochester/National Technical Institute for the Deaf, New York, 1982
- Texas and Florida certifications in hearing impaired, K–12; social studies (secondary); and gifted, K–12
- 26 years of experience teaching students with special needs

CURRENT TEACHING POSITION I teach science, social studies, math, and art to elementary-age deaf students at Hillside Elementary. Texas is divided into regional day school programs for deaf education. At Hillside Elementary, a neighborhood school of about 700 students, five deaf-education teachers, two speech therapists, and interpreters serve 45 deaf students. We serve the students of 13 school districts in our region. Some students travel an hour each way to come to school. This is not unusual. Deafness is a low-incidence disability and a very cost-intensive one. We are a total communication program, which means the simultaneous use of speech and sign.

STUDENTS Four students in my fifth-grade homeroom receive special education and related services under the IDEA category of hearing impairment. Most of our students are Hispanic; some come from homes in which Spanish is the primary or only language. Some of our students come from middle-class families, and some come from poor families—sometimes desperately so. We get to know our students very well, and our students get to know each other better than their own siblings sometimes.

CURRICULUM MATERIALS AND TEACHING STRATEGIES We parallel the units covered in the general education curriculum, adapting a lot of the language in the texts. I often turn textbook content into plays that incorporate the students' personalities and interests and take advantage of the resources provided by the local community and culture. Sometimes students draw backgrounds and create props, and we videotape these plays. I use participatory theater as a teaching tool for several reasons: (a) plays help the students understand the material better; (b) active responding is always better than passive attending; (c) plays personalize the material, helping the students understand that the events and concepts they're learning about are central to the history and current life of their world; (d) plays bring out the students' natural creativity; and (e) plays help the students feel less daunted by the textbook. Our greatest role-playing academic exercise is our annual mock trial held in the 243rd District Courtroom of Judge David Guaderrama. With the assistance of Assistant District Attorney Lori Hughes and Federal Public Defender Bruce Weathers, our students are defendants, witnesses, attorneys, bailiffs, and jurors. Over the years we have brought Goldilocks, Snow White's stepmother, the third Little Pig, Hansel and Gretel, and others to justice, and along the way we have taught our students about our system of justice and the services (especially interpreters) they require to ensure their constitutional rights. With all of the costumes and preparation, a mock trial is the coolest school play imaginable.

Technology has had a tremendous impact on my teaching and my students. I feel blessed to be working at a time when there are so many tools that allow my students to use their strengths as visual learners. My Smart Board™, for example, enables students to manipulate digital images, streaming video, websites, and PowerPoints, to understand the relationships in everything from the water cycle to fractions and decimals to the causes and effects of the Civil War. The Smart Board is a blank canvas on which I can create lessons on literally any topic imaginable. There are so many possibilities, but you must choose the ones that you are actually going to invest your time, energy, and passion in. Other ways we use technology include video letters to deaf students in other schools, distance-learning sessions with the Texas School for the Deaf, and structured Internet research assignments.

My students frequently conceive, create, and give PowerPoint presentations to classmates, teachers, and civic groups. This practice began in 2003 with a presentation on effective inclusion for teachers at our district's elementary, middle, and high school campuses. It has continued with presentations on the rights and responsibilities of deaf people in the criminal justice system (for the El Paso Bar Association), in medical situations (for Texas Tech med students), and in the workplace (for business people in a civic group). Recent presentations were on deaf artists and optical illusions—two topics for which my students are very passionate—to all of the second to fifth graders

in our school. Watching my students master the tools that can help them overcome their communication challenges and seeing their individual personalities emerge as smart, funny, charming, and dynamic young people is extremely rewarding.

PERSONAL QUALITIES IMPORTANT FOR SPECIAL EDUCATORS Being an effective teacher is like being an effective lawyer, doctor, chef, or artist. At some point it stops being a role you "play" and becomes who you "are." Look at Van Gogh or Picasso or Renoir. Every brushstroke by these artists was a fingerprint. You can't tell where the self ends and the profession begins. Great teachers are like that. They're always seeing the world through the eyes of a teacher; and when something new and interesting happens to them, they think about how they can share that experience with their students. I didn't possess this skill on day 1 as a teacher. Many of my early efforts were two steps forward and one step back—sometimes 1 step forward and two steps back. It is something that I am still working on now—I am very much a work in progress.

A MEMORABLE MOMENT Our students love school. Many come from hearing families that struggle to communicate with them, and all are frequently in social situations with people who can't communicate with them. Consequently, school is an oasis of communication for them. Once, while gathering for a field trip, we passed the marquee in front of school. One of my students looked at the sign and read, "Saturday School," which referred, of course, to a mandatory program for students who had misbehaved during the week. Several other students gasped, "Saturday school! Can we come?" It's always great to learn that your customers want more, not less, of your service. And the only thing more meaningful than realizing you have provided an oasis of communication for a deaf child is understanding that it is your mission to expand the boundaries of that oasis into his world outside the classroom.

MyEducationLab™

Visit the **MyEducationLab** for *Exceptional Children* to enhance your understanding of chapter concepts with a personalized Study Plan. You'll also have the opportunity to hone your teaching skills through video- and case-based Assignments and Activities, IRIS Center Resources, and Building Teaching Skills and Dispositions lessons.

A SIGHTED PERSON CAN SIMULATE BLINDNESS by closing her eyes or donning a blindfold, but it is virtually impossible for a hearing person to turn off his ears. Throughout life, all hearing animals obtain information about their world, from all directions, 24 hours a day. When a twig snaps behind us, we don't have to be looking to know that we are not alone.

In addition to its tremendous survival advantage, hearing plays the lead role in the natural, almost effortless manner by which most children acquire speech and language. Hearing infants as young as 1 month can discriminate speech sounds (Hulit, Howard, & Fahey, 2011). By the time they are 1 year old, hearing children can produce many of the sounds of their language and are speaking their first words. In contrast, for children who cannot hear speech sounds, learning a spoken language is anything but natural or effortless.

DEFINITIONS

Children who are deaf and hard of hearing receive special education and related services under the federal disability category of hearing impairments. IDEA defines **deafness** and **hearing loss** as follows:

> Deafness means a hearing loss that is so severe that the child is impaired in processing linguistic information through hearing, with or without amplification, [and] that adversely affects a child's educational performance. (PL 108-446, 20 U.S.C. §1401 [2004], 20 *CFR* §300.8[c][3])
>
> Hearing loss means a loss in hearing, whether permanent or fluctuating, that adversely affects a child's education performance but that is not included under the definition of deafness in this section. (PL 108-446, 20 U.S.C. §1401 [2004], 20 *CFR* §300.8[c][5])

Most special educators distinguish between children who are deaf and those who are hard of hearing. A child who is deaf cannot use hearing to understand speech. *Normal hearing* generally means that a person has sufficient hearing to understand speech. Under adequate listening conditions, a person with normal hearing can interpret speech without using any special device or technique. Even with a hearing aid, the hearing loss is too great to allow a deaf child to understand speech through the ears alone. Although most deaf people perceive some sounds through **residual hearing**, they use vision as the primary sensory mode for learning and communication.

Children who are **hard of hearing** can use their hearing to understand speech, generally with the help of a hearing aid. The speech and language skills of a child who is hard of hearing, though they may be delayed or deficient, are developed mainly through the auditory channel.

Many deaf people do not view themselves as disabled and consider *hearing loss* an inappropriate and demeaning term because it suggests a deficiency or pathology. Like other cultural groups, members of the Deaf community share a common language and social practices (Woll & Ladd, 2011). When the cultural definition of hearing loss is used, *Deaf* is spelled with a capital *D*, just as an uppercase letter is used to refer to a French, Japanese, or Jewish person. While person-first language is the appropriate way to refer to individuals with disabilities, people who identify with the **Deaf culture** prefer terms such as *teacher of the Deaf, school for the Deaf,* and *Deaf person.*

Definitions: *hearing loss, deaf, residual hearing, hard of hearing*

 Council for Exceptional Children — Content Standards for Beginning Teachers—D/HH: Educational definitions and identification criteria for individuals who are D/HH (DH&H1K1).

Deaf culture and community

 Council for Exceptional Children — Content Standards for Beginning Teachers—D/HH: Sociocultural, historical, and political forces unique to deaf education (DH&H1K2).

Hearing plays the lead role in the natural, almost effortless manner by which most children acquire speech and language.

Silver Burdett Ginn

How We Hear

Audition, the sense of hearing, is a complex and not completely understood process. The ear gathers sounds (acoustical energy) from the environment and transforms that energy into a form (neural energy) that can be interpreted by the brain. Figure 1 shows the major parts of the human ear. The *outer ear* consists of the external ear and the auditory canal. The part of the ear we see, the **auricle** (or *pinna*), funnels sound waves into the **auditory canal (external acoustic meatus)** and helps distinguish the direction of sound.

When sound waves enter the external ear, they are slightly amplified as they move toward the **tympanic membrane** (eardrum). Pressure variations in sound waves move the eardrum in and out. These movements of the eardrum change the acoustical energy into mechanical energy, which is transferred to the three tiny bones of the *middle ear* (the *hammer, anvil,* and *stirrup*). The base (called the *footplate*) of the third bone in the sequence, the stirrup, rests in an opening called the *oval window*, the place where sound energy enters the inner ear. The vibrations of the three bones (together called the **ossicles**) transmit energy from the middle ear to the inner ear with little loss.

The *inner ear*, the most critical and complex part of the entire hearing apparatus, is covered by the *temporal bone*, the hardest bone in the entire body. The inner ear contains the **cochlea**, the main receptor organ for hearing, and the *semicircular canals*, which control the sense of balance. The cochlea, named for its resemblance to a coiled snail shell, consists of two fluid-filled cavities that contain 30,000 tiny hair cells arranged in four rows. Energy transmitted by the ossicles moves the fluid in the cochlea, which in turn stimulates the hair cells. Each hair cell has approximately a hundred tiny spines, called *cilia,* at the top. When the hair cells are stimulated, they displace the fluid around them, which produces minute electrochemical signals that are transmitted along the auditory nerve to the brain. High tones are picked up by the hair cells at the basal, or lowest turn of the cochlea; low tones stimulate hair cells at the apex, or top, of the cochlea.

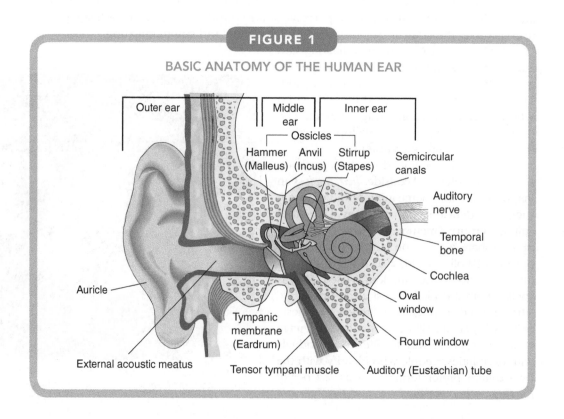

FIGURE 1

BASIC ANATOMY OF THE HUMAN EAR

The Nature of Sound

Sound is measured in units that describe its intensity and frequency. Both dimensions of sound are important in considering the needs of a child who is deaf or hard of hearing. The intensity or loudness of sound is measured in **decibels (dB)**. Zero dB represents the smallest sound a person with normal hearing can perceive, which is called the *zero hearing-threshold level (HTL),* or **audiometric zero.** Larger-decibel numbers represent increasingly louder sounds on a ratio scale in which each increment of 10 dB is a 10-fold increase in intensity. A low whisper 5 feet away registers about 10 dB; conversational speech 10 to 20 feet away ranges from 20 to 50 dB. Traffic on a city street produces sound at about 70 dB, and a lawnmower about 90 to 100 dB. Sounds of 125 dB or louder cause pain to most people.

The frequency, or pitch, of sound is measured in cycles per second, or **hertz (Hz)**; 1 Hz equals 1 cycle per second. Pure tones consist of one frequency only. Speech and most environmental sounds are complex tones containing different frequencies. The lowest note on a piano has a frequency of about 30 Hz, middle C about 250 Hz, and the highest note about 4,000 Hz. The human hearing can detect sounds ranging from approximately 20 to 20,000 Hz. Although a person who cannot hear very low sounds (e.g., a foghorn) or very high sounds (e.g., a piccolo) may experience some inconvenience, she will encounter no significant problems in the classroom or everyday life. A person with a severe hearing loss in the speech range, however, is at a great disadvantage in acquiring and communicating in a spoken language.

The frequency range most important for hearing spoken language is 500 to 2,000 Hz, but some speech sounds have frequencies below or above that range. For example, the /s/ phoneme (as in the word *sat*) is a high-frequency sound, typically occurring between 4,000 and 8,000 Hz (Northern & Downs, 2002). A student whose hearing loss is more severe at the higher frequencies will thus have particular difficulty in discriminating the /s/ sound. Conversely, phonemes such as /dj/ (the sound of the *j* in *jump*) and /m/ occur at low frequencies and will be more problematic for a student with a low-frequency hearing loss. As you might expect, a student with a high-frequency hearing loss tends to hear men's voices more easily than women's voices.

Degree and frequency range of hearing loss

 Content
Council for
Exceptional Standards for
Children Beginning
Teachers—D/HH: Effects of sensory input on the development of language and cognition (DH & H6K3).

CHARACTERISTICS

Any discussion of characteristics of students who are deaf or hard of hearing should include three qualifications. First, students who receive special education because of hearing loss comprise an extremely heterogeneous group (Karchmer & Mitchell, 2011). It is a mistake to assume that a commonly observed behavioral characteristic or average level of academic achievement is representative of all children with hearing loss.

Second, the effects of hearing loss on a child's communication and language skills, academic achievement, and social and emotional functioning are influenced by many factors, including the type and degree of hearing loss, the age at onset, the attitudes of the child's parents and siblings, opportunities to acquire a first language (whether through speech or sign), and the presence or absence of other disabilities.

Third, generalizations about how deaf people are supposed to act and feel must be viewed with extreme caution. Lane (1988), who makes a strong case against the existence of the so-called psychology of the deaf, notes the similarity of the traits attributed to deaf people in the professional literature to traits attributed to African people in the literature of colonialism and suggests that those traits do not "reflect the characteristics of deaf people but the paternalistic posture of the hearing experts making these attributions" (p. 8).

English Literacy

A child with a hearing loss—especially a prelingual loss of 90 dB or greater—is at a great disadvantage in acquiring English language skills. From early infancy, hearing children typically acquire a large vocabulary and a knowledge of grammar, word order, idiomatic expressions, fine shades of meaning, and many other aspects of verbal expression by listening to others and to themselves. A child who, from birth or soon after, cannot hear the speech of other people will not learn speech and language spontaneously, as do typically developing children with normal hearing. Because reading and writing involve graphic representations of a phonologically based language, the deaf child who has not benefited from exposure to a rich grammatical model of spoken English must strive to decode, comprehend, and produce text based on a language for which she may have little or no understanding. How does one teach letter–sound correspondence, a critical component of reading, to children who cannot hear? *Visual phonics,* a multisensory system of hand cues and written symbols that represent sounds, is a promising approach (Narr & Cawthon, 2011). See *Teaching & Learning,* "Phonemic Awareness and Phonics Instruction with Deaf and Hard-of-Hearing Students."

Students with hearing loss have smaller vocabularies when compared to peers with normal hearing, and the gap widens with age (American Speech-Language-Hearing Association [ASHA], 2011a). Children with hearing loss learn concrete words such as *tree, run,* and *book* more easily than abstract words such as *before, after, equal to,* and *jealous.* They also have difficulty with function words such as *the, an, are,* and *a.*

They may omit endings of words, such as the plural *-s, -ed,* or *-ing.* Because the grammar and structure of English often do not follow logical rules, a person with prelingual hearing loss must exert a great deal of effort to read and write with acceptable form and meaning. For example, if the past tense of *talk* is *talked,* then why doesn't *go* become *goed*? If the plural of *man* is *men,* then shouldn't the plural of *pan* be *pen*? Learning words with multiple meanings is difficult. It is not easy to explain the difference between the expressions "He's beat" (tired) and "He was beaten" to a person who has never had normal hearing.

Many deaf students have difficulty differentiating questions from statements and understanding and writing sentences with passive voice ("The assignment was given yesterday") and relative clauses ("The gloves I left at home are made of leather"). They typically compose sentences that are short, incomplete, or improperly arranged. The following sentences written by elementary deaf students illustrate some of the English literacy problems attributable to not hearing the spoken language on which the written form is based:

Bobby is walked.
The boy sees a brown football on the hold hand.
The trees is falling a leaves.
The happy children is friending.

Speaking

Atypical speech is common in many children who are deaf or hard of hearing. On top of all of the challenges hearing loss poses to learning the vocabulary, grammar, and syntax of English, not being able to hear one's own speech makes it difficult to assess and monitor it. The speech of some children who are deaf and hard of hearing is difficult to understand because they omit quiet speech sounds such as /s/, /sh/, /f/, /t/, and /k/, which they cannot hear. Some speak too loudly or not loudly enough. Their speech may be abnormally high pitched or sound mumbled because of improper stress or inflection.

Academic Achievement

Students who are deaf and hard of hearing continue to lag behind their general education peers in academic achievement (Antia, Jones, Reed, & Kreimeyer 2009; Shaver, Newman, Huang, Yu, & Knokey, 2011). Most children with hearing loss have difficulty with all areas of academic achievement, especially reading and math. Studies of the academic achievement of students with hearing loss have routinely found them to lag far behind their hearing peers, and the gap in achievement between children with normal hearing and those with hearing loss usually widens as they get older (ASHA, 2011a). The average deaf student who leaves high school at age 18 or 19 is reading at about the fourth-grade level (Kuntze, 1998), and her mathematics performance is in the range of fifth to sixth grade (Traxler, 2000). Approximately 30% of deaf students leave school functionally illiterate (Paul & Jackson, 1993).

Academic performance must not be equated with intelligence. Deafness itself imposes no limitations on the cognitive capabilities of individuals, and some deaf students read very well and excel academically (Karchmer & Mitchell, 2011; Williams & Finnegan, 2003). The problems that deaf students often experience in education and adjustment are largely attributable to inadequate development of a first language as well as the mismatch between the demands of spoken and written English and the students' ability to understand and communicate in English.

Social Functioning

Children with severe to profound hearing loss often report feeling isolated, without friends, and unhappy in school, particularly when their socialization with other children with hearing loss is limited. These social problems appear to be more frequent in children with mild or moderate hearing loss than in those with severe to profound losses (ASHA, 2011a). Children with hearing loss are more likely to have behavioral difficulties in school and social situations than are children with normal hearing. A study of more than 1,000 deaf adolescents who were considered disruptive in the classroom (Kluwin, 1985) found that the most frequently related factor was reading ability; that is, students who were poorer readers were more likely to exhibit problem behaviors in school. Even a slight hearing loss can cause a child to miss important auditory information, such as the tone of a teacher's voice while telling the class to get out their spelling workbooks, which can lead to the child's being considered inattentive, distractible, or immature (Easterbrooks, 1999).

Children and adults who are deaf frequently express feelings of depression, withdrawal, and isolation, particularly those with adventitious hearing loss (Connolly, Rose, & Austen, 2006; Scheetz, 2004). Research has not provided clear insights into the effects of hearing loss on behavior; however, it appears that the extent to which a child with hearing loss successfully interacts with family members, friends, and people in the community depends largely on others' attitudes and the child's ability to communicate in some mutually acceptable way (Ita & Friedman, 1999). Certainly, communication plays a major role in anyone's adjustment. Figure 2 lists some tips for making your speech more accessible to an individual who is speechreading.

PREVALENCE

Approximately 36 million Americans report some degree of hearing loss (NIDCD, 2011c). Males are more likely than females to experience hearing loss. The majority of all people with hearing loss are 65 years or older. About 2 to 3 out of every 1,000 children are born deaf or hard of hearing (NIDCD, 2011a).

During the 2009–10 school year, 70,548 students ages 6 to 21 received special education services under the disability category of hearing impairment (U.S. Department of Education, 2011). This represents 1.2% of all school-age students who received special education services and about 0.1% of the resident student population. The actual number of school-age children with hearing loss in special education programs is somewhat higher because some children with hearing losss are counted under another primary disability category (e.g., intellectual disabilities, multiple disabilities deaf-blind). It is not known precisely the percentage of these students who are deaf or hard of hearing. A national survey of deaf or hard-of-hearing students found that 41% had severe or profound hearing loss and that 40% had another disabling condition (Gallaudet Research Institute, 2008).

Academic achievement

Content Standards for Beginning Teachers—D/HH: Effects of sensory input on the development of language and learning (DH&H6K3) (also ICC2K2, DH&H2K2).

Social functioning

Content Standards for Beginning Teachers—D/HH: Impact of educational placement options with regard to cultural identity and linguistic, academic, and social-emotional development (DH&H3K1) (also DH&H3K2).

Phonemic Awareness and Phonics Instruction with Deaf and Hard-of-Hearing Students

BY BARBARA R. SCHIRMER AND RACHEL A. FRIEDMAN NARR

TEACHING & LEARNING

Teaching phonemic awareness and phonics to deaf and hard-of-hearing students has seemed illogical and a poor use of valuable instruction time to many teachers. Yet phonemic awareness and phonics not only *can* be taught to children who do not fully hear the sounds of English but *should* be taught so that these children have more tools to use as they navigate learning to read.

Phonological awareness and phonics instruction have been found to be so important in reading development that children without these skills are at a great disadvantage in learning to read English (e.g., Ehri, 2005; Eldredge, 2005; National Reading Panel, 2000a). As in all alphabetic languages, the basic unit of writing in English reflects a correspondence (though not a perfect match) between phonemes and graphemes, or sounds and letters. If the reader is aware of the phonemes that make up spoken words, then she can map these sounds to English letters, letter combinations, syllables, and words.

These findings suggest that phonemic awareness may well be related to the reading performance of deaf children, given that research has shown considerably greater similarities than differences between the reading processes of deaf and hearing readers (Schirmer & McGough, 2005). And, indeed, results have shown that deaf readers, particularly more skilled readers, can access phonological information (e.g., Harris & Moreno, 2004; Mayberry, del Giudice, & Lieberman, 2011).

Furthermore, recent findings are very promising in demonstrating that deaf children can be taught to access phonological information and apply it effectively in reading (Colin, Magnan, & Ecalle, 2007; Trezek, Wang, Wood, Gampp, & Paul, 2007; Wang, Trezek, Luckner, & Paul, 2008). The key has been finding a medium through

which deaf children can become aware of the sounds of spoken language and teaching them explicitly and systematically how to link these sounds to decoding written words within the child's vocabulary. (This is important because if the child's vocabulary does not include the written word, then the ability to link sounds and letters will not help the child identify the word's meaning.)

HOW TO GET STARTED WITH STUDENTS WHO SIGN

When young children develop phonemic awareness, they internalize rules and patterns associated with the sound-based properties of words. For children who are deaf and hard of hearing, the concept of the *phoneme* can be a mental representation. While deaf and hard-of-hearing students may choose to vocalize or talk during these activities, voicing is not *necessary* to demonstrate comprehension of phonemes.

Students who are deaf and hard of hearing and students who are deaf in oral/aural programs may benefit from the strategies for beginning reading instruction described in Figure 4. Students who rely on sign-based communication, either through simultaneous communication or American Sign Language, need the phonological properties of words to be represented through visual, tactile, and kinesthetic stimuli, as the following suggestions demonstrate:

- **Use a variety of sensory stimuli to teach phonemic awareness and phonics to promote well-developed mental representations.** Teach phonemes through a systematic multimodal method that capitalizes on the student's intact senses (vision, tactile, kinesthetic). Visual phonics and cued speech are systems that use hand cues to represent the

Rachel Friedman Narr

Visual phonics hand cues for /b/, /ae/, and /g/ sounds.

44 to 46 phonemes in spoken English visually. These are two distinct systems that are not used interchangeably. (For a comparison of Visual Phonics and Cued Speech, see Friedman Narr, 2006.)

- **Teach speechreading cues directly to show how sounds and words look when other people say them.** For example, when students know that only three sounds are made with both lips together (/m/, /b/, /p/), they can make reasonable choices about decoding and spelling options. Instruction in speechreading can be paired with phonemic awareness and phonics lessons. In the *sandwich technique*, you sign and say (or mouth) the whole word, then fingerspell or write the word but leave out the target phoneme, then say (or mouth) that phoneme (not the letter name), and finally sign and say (or mouth) the whole word again.

- **Teach students how to analyze words and decode in chunks.** One technique is to directly teach spelling patterns and regularities (e.g., b*oat*; l*ight*), onsets and rimes (e.g., *b*-ook, th-*ink*), and prefixes and suffixes (e.g., *re*-play, walk-*ing*). Another technique is to fingerspell words in chunks, such as syllable by syllable (e.g., el-e-phant) instead of letter by letter.

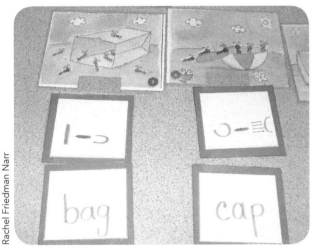

Rachel Friedman Narr

Examples of grapheme cues used in visual phonics.

- **Teach phonics in context to support skills taught in isolation.** Students will be more engaged and motivated, and they will realize that the point of phonics is to identify words during reading, not simply to learn lists of letter–sound correspondences. For example, when reading, point out the similarities between new words in the material and previously learned words with the same number of syllables; words that have a particular spelling pattern; or words that begin with a certain sound, letter, or lip shape.

LEARNING VISUAL PHONICS

The International Communication Learning Institute (ICLI) is the parent organization that regulates training in See the Sound—Visual Phonics. Groups or individuals who want to use it can receive training from licensed ICLI trainers. Trainings range from 8 to 14+ hours, depending on the amount of time desired for guided practice. Learning visual phonics is generally quick and easy. Like most newly acquired skills, the more you use it, the more fluent you will become.

Teachers can use visual phonics in conjunction with any reading curriculum. When teaching phonemic awareness and phonics instruction, the teacher uses the visual phonics hand cues and grapheme symbols (see photos) to *show* sounds in words, which makes the *concept of the phoneme* completely accessible, even if the acoustic properties are not. Visual phonics is not used for communication; instead, it is used at the phoneme and word level only. Trezek and her colleagues have demonstrated efficacy with visual phonics when teachers use it in conjunction with established reading instructional curricula (Trezek & Malmgren, 2005; Trezek & Wang, 2006; Trezek et al., 2007). (You can find contact information for finding a trainer at www.icli.org.)

About the Authors

Barbara R. Schirmer is provost, vice president of academic affairs, and professor of education at Defiance College. She is the author of *Teaching the Struggling Reader* (Allyn & Bacon, 2010). Rachel A. Friedman Narr is an associate professor of special education at California State University–Northridge.

TEACHING & LEARNING

TIPS FOR COMMUNICATING WITH SOMEONE WHO IS DEAF

When presented with an opportunity to communicate with a person who is deaf, many people with normal hearing are unsure of themselves. As a result, they may avoid deaf people altogether or use ineffective and frustrating strategies when they do attempt to communicate. The following tips for facilitating communication were suggested by the Community Services for the Deaf program in Akron, Ohio. These tips provide basic information about three common ways that deaf people communicate: through speechreading, with sign language or the assistance of an interpreter, and by written communication. Usually, the person will indicate the approach with which he is most comfortable.

If the person relies mainly on speechreading, here are things you can do to help:

- Face the person and stand or sit no more than four feet away.
- The room should have adequate illumination, but don't seat yourself in front of a strong or glaring light.
- Try to keep your whole face visible.
- Speak clearly and naturally and not too fast.
- Don't exaggerate your mouth movements.
- Don't raise the level of your voice.
- Some words are more easily read on the lips than others are. If you are having a problem being understood, try substituting different words.
- It may take a while to become used to the deaf person's speech. If at first you can't understand what she is saying, don't give up.
- Don't hesitate to write down any important words that are missed.

If the deaf person communicates best through sign language (and you do not), it will probably be necessary to use an interpreter. Here are some considerations to keep in mind:

- The role of the interpreter is to facilitate communication between you and the person who is deaf. The interpreter should not be asked to give opinions, advice, or personal feelings.
- Maintain eye contact with the deaf person and speak directly to him. The deaf person should not be made to take a back seat in the conversation. For example, say, "How are you today?" instead of "Ask him how he is today."
- Remain face-to-face with the deaf person. The best place for the interpreter is behind you and a little to your side. Again, avoid strong or glaring light.
- Remember, it is the interpreter's job to communicate everything that you and the deaf person say. Don't say anything that you don't want to be interpreted.

Written messages can be helpful in exchanging information. Consider the following:

- Avoid the temptation to abbreviate your communication.
- Write in simple, direct language.
- The deaf person's written English may not be grammatically correct, but you will probably be able to understand it. One deaf person, for example, wrote, "Pay off yesterday, finish me," to convey the message, "I paid that loan off yesterday."
- Use visual aids, such as pictures, diagrams, and business cards.
- Don't be afraid to supplement your written messages with gestures and facial expressions.
- Written communication has limitations, but it is often more effective than no communication at all.

TYPES AND CAUSES OF HEARING LOSS

Types and Age of Onset

Types of hearing loss

 Council for Exceptional Children

Content Standards for Beginning Teachers—D/HH: Effects of sensory input on the development of language and learning (DH&H6K3).

Type of hearing loss is determined by the affected region of the auditory system. **Conductive hearing impairment,** as its name implies, involves a problem with the conduction, or transmission, of sound vibrations to the inner ear. A conductive hearing loss results from abnormalities or complications of the outer or middle ear. A buildup of excessive wax in the auditory canal can cause a conductive hearing loss, as can a disease that leaves fluid or debris. Some children are born with incomplete or malformed auditory canals. Conductive hearing loss can occur if the eardrum or ossicles do not move properly. Surgery or other medical treatment can often correct a conductive hearing loss, and hearing aids are usually beneficial.

A **sensory hearing impairment** entails damage to the cochlea, while **neural hearing impairment** is attributed to abnormality or failure of the auditory nerve pathway. Both types are often subsumed by the term *sensorineural hearing impairment.* Hearing aids may not help people with sensorineural hearing impairments because the electromechanical energy corresponding to sound is delivered to the brain in distorted fashion or not delivered at all. Surgery or medication cannot correct most sensorineural hearing loss. Any combination of conductive, sensory, and neural hearing loss is called a *mixed hearing impairment.*

Hearing loss is also described in terms of being *unilateral* (present in one ear only) or *bilateral* (present in both ears). Most deaf and hard-of-hearing students have bilateral losses, although the degree of loss may not be the same in both ears. Children with unilateral hearing loss generally learn speech and language without major difficulties, although they tend to have problems localizing sounds and listening in noisy or distracting settings.

It is important to consider the age of onset—whether a hearing loss is **congenital** (present at birth) or **acquired** (appears after birth). The terms **prelingual hearing loss** and **postlingual hearing loss** identify whether a hearing loss occurred before or after the development of spoken language. A child who cannot hear the speech of other people from birth or soon after will not learn speech and language spontaneously, as do typically developing children with normal hearing. To approximate the experience of a child who is deaf from birth, watch a television program in a foreign language with the sound turned off. You would face the double problem of being unable to read lips and understand an unfamiliar language.

A child who acquires a hearing loss after speech and language are well established, usually after age 2, has educational needs very different from the prelingually deaf child. The educational program for a child who is prelingually deaf usually focuses on acquisition of language and communication, whereas the program for a child who is postlingually deaf usually emphasizes the maintenance of intelligible speech and appropriate language patterns.

Scott Cunningham/Merrill

Prelingual deafness imposes tremendous challenges to learning to comprehend and produce spoken language.

Age of onset

Content Standards for Beginning Teachers—D/HH: Effects of the interrelationship among onset of hearing loss, age of identification, and provision of services on the development of the individual who is D/HH (DH&H2K2).

Causes of Congenital Hearing Loss

Although more than 400 causes of hearing loss have been identified, a national survey of more than 36,000 deaf and hard-of-hearing students found that the cause was undetermined in 57% of cases (Gallaudet Research Institute, 2008).

GENETIC FACTORS About one half of all congenital deafness is attributed to genetic abnormalities (Debonis & Donohue, 2008). More than 200 types of genetically caused deafness have been identified. Genetic hearing loss may be autosomal dominant, autosomal recessive, or X-linked (related to the sex chromosome). *Autosomal dominant hearing loss* exists when one parent, who carries the dominant gene for hearing loss and typically has a hearing loss, passes the gene on to the child. In this case, each offspring has a 50% probability of receiving the gene and having a hearing loss. The probability is higher if both parents have the dominant gene or if both grandparents on one side of the family have hearing loss due to genetic causes. About 20% of inherited deafness is the result of dominant inheritance.

Approximately 80% to 90% of inherited hearing loss is caused by *autosomal recessive hearing loss,* in which both parents typically have normal hearing and carry a recessive gene. In this case, there is a 25% probability that each child will have a hearing loss. Because both parents usually have normal hearing, and because no other family members have hearing loss, there is no prior expectation that the child may have a hearing loss. Because most hereditary deafness is the result of recessive genetic traits, a child of two deaf people has only a slightly increased risk of deafness because there is a small chance that both parents' deafness was affected by the same exact genetic syndrome (Northern & Downs, 2002).

Causes of hearing loss

Content Standards for Beginning Teachers—D/HH: Etiologies of hearing loss that can result in additional learning challenges (DH&H1K3).

In *X-linked hearing loss*, the mother carries the recessive trait for hearing loss on the sex chromosome and passes it on to male offspring but not to females. X-linked transmission accounts for about 2% to 3% of hereditary hearing loss.

Hearing loss is a characteristic of more than 400 genetic syndromes, such as Down syndrome, Usher syndrome, Treacher Collins syndrome, and fetal alcohol syndrome (Todd, 2011).

MATERNAL RUBELLA Although rubella (also known as German measles) has relatively mild symptoms, it can cause deafness, visual loss, heart disorders, and a variety of other serious disabilities in the developing child when contracted by a pregnant woman, particularly during the first trimester. A major rubella epidemic in the United States and Canada in 1963–1965 accounted for more than 50% of the students with hearing loss in special education programs in the 1970s and 1980s. Since an effective vaccine was introduced in 1969, the incidence of hearing loss caused by rubella has decreased significantly.

CONGENITAL CYTOMEGALOVIRUS Both rubella and **cytomegalovirus (CMV)** are members of a group of infectious agents known as TORCHES (toxoplasmosis, rubella, cytomegalovirus, herpes simplex, and syphilis). CMV is a common viral infection, and most people infected with it experience minor symptoms such as respiratory infections that soon disappear. Approximately 1 in 150 children are born with congenital CMV, and 10% to 20% of those may later develop conditions such as developmental disabilities, visual impairment, and, most often, hearing loss (CDC, 2010). At present, no prevention or treatment for CMV exists. However, a blood test can determine if a woman of childbearing age is at risk for developing an initial CMV infection during pregnancy.

PREMATURITY It is difficult to precisely evaluate the effects of prematurity on hearing loss, but early delivery and low birth weight are more common among children who are deaf than among the general population.

Causes of Acquired Hearing Loss

OTITIS MEDIA A temporary, recurrent infection of the middle ear, **otitis media** is the most common medical diagnosis for children. Nearly 90% of all children will experience otitis media at least once, and about one-third of children under age 5 have recurrent episodes (Bluestone & Klein, 2007). Left untreated, otitis media can result in a buildup of fluid and a ruptured eardrum, which causes permanent conductive hearing loss.

MENINGITIS The leading cause of postlingual hearing loss is meningitis, a bacterial or viral infection of the central nervous system that can, among its other effects, destroy the sensitive acoustic apparatus of the inner ear. Children whose deafness is caused by meningitis generally have profound hearing losses. Difficulties in balance and other disabilities may also be present.

MÉNIÈRE'S DISEASE A disorder of the inner ear, Ménière's disease is characterized by sudden and unpredictable attacks of vertigo (dizziness), fluctuations in hearing, and *tinnitus* (the perception of sound when no outside sound is present). In its severest form, Ménière's disease can be incapacitating. Little is understood about the mechanisms underlying the condition, and at present no reliable treatment or cure exists. Ménière's disease most often occurs between the ages of 40 and 60, but it can affect children under the age of 10 (Minor, Schessel, & Carey, 2004).

NOISE EXPOSURE Repeated exposure to loud sounds is a common cause of hearing loss. It is estimated that 10 million Americans have noise-related permanent hearing loss and that 22 million U.S. workers are exposed to hazardous noise levels at work. Occupational hearing loss is the most common work-related injury in the U.S. (Centers for Disease Control and Prevention, 2011).

Noise-induced hearing loss (NIHL) caused by chronic exposure to recreational and occupational noise often occurs gradually, and the person may not realize his hearing is being damaged until it is too late. Sources of noise that can cause NIHL include motorcycles, jet aircraft, target shooting, leaf blowers, and amplified music, all emitting sounds from 120 to 150 decibels. Prolonged or repeated exposure to noise above 85 dB can cause gradual hearing loss. Regular exposure of more than 1 minute to noise at 110 dB risks permanent hearing loss (NIDCD, 2011a). Herer, Knightly, and Steinberg (2007) identified the following warning signs for excessive noise: being within 3 feet of someone and having to shout to be understood, experiencing ringing in the ears (tinnitus) after leaving the area, and hearing only muffled or soft sounds 1 to 2 hours later.

To learn more about noise-induced hearing loss and how to prevent it, visit the Wise Ears! website, www .nidcd.nih.gov/health/wise.

IDENTIFICATION AND ASSESSMENT

Assessment of Infants

Newborns respond to sounds by startling or blinking. At a few weeks of age, infants with normal hearing can listen to quiet sounds, recognize their parents' voices, and pay attention to their own gurgling and cooing sounds. All infants, hearing and deaf alike, babble. In children with normal hearing, vocalizations containing a minimum of a consonant and vowel sound, called canonical babbling, emerge between 7 and 12 months (Bass-Ringdahl, 2010). Children who are deaf tend to stop babbling and vocalizing because they cannot hear themselves or their parents, but the baby's increasing silence may go unnoticed for a while and then be mistakenly attributed to other causes.

The Joint Committee on Infant Hearing (2007) recommends that all infants be screened by 1 month of age. Today a "1-3-6" model of Early Hearing Detection and Intervention programs in most states is working toward the goal of having all babies being screened by 1 month, diagnosed by 3 months, and enrolled in early intervention programs no later than 6 months of age. The two most widely used methods of screening for hearing loss in infants measure physiological reactions to sound. With *auditory brain stem response*, sensors placed on the scalp measure electrical activity as the infant responds to auditory stimuli. In *otoacoustic emission* screening, a tiny microphone placed in the baby's ear detects the "echoes" of hair cells in the cochlea as they vibrate to sound (Ross & Levitt, 2000).

Even though an infant passes screening in the hospital, hearing loss can develop later. Figure 3 lists some common auditory behaviors emitted by infants with normal hearing. An infant who fails to demonstrate these responses may indicate a hearing loss, and an audiological exam is recommended.

Early identification of hearing loss

 Council for Exceptional Children — Content Standards for Beginning Teachers—D/HH: Specialized terminology used in assessing individuals who are D/HH (DH&H8K1) (also DH&H2K2).

Typical development of behaviors related to sound

 Council for Exceptional Children — Content Standards for Beginning Teachers—D/HH: Effects of sensory input on the development of language and learning (DH&H6K3) (also ICC2K5).

See the National Center for Hearing Assessment and Management site at http:// www.infanthearing.org/.

Pure-Tone Audiometry

A procedure called *pure-tone audiometry* is used to assess the hearing of older children and adults. The test determines how loud sounds at various frequencies must be for the child to hear them. The examiner uses an **audiometer,** an electronic device that generates pure tones at different levels of intensity and frequency. Most audiometers deliver tones in 5-dB increments from 0 to 120 dB, with each decibel level presented in various frequencies, usually starting at 125 Hz and increasing in octave intervals (doubling in frequency) to 8,000 Hz. The child, who receives the sound either through earphones (air conduction) or through a bone vibrator (bone conduction), is instructed to depress a button when he hears a sound and to release the button when he hears no sound. To obtain a hearing level on an audiogram, the child must detect a sound at that level at least 50% of the time. For example, a child who

An audiometer generates tones of precise intensity and frequency.

© Michael Newman/PhotoEdit

FIGURE 3 — SOME EXPECTED AUDITORY BEHAVIORS DURING BABY'S FIRST YEAR

Birth to 3 Months

- Startles to loud noises
- Coos and makes pleasurable gurgling sounds
- Turns to voices
- Quiet downs or smiles when spoken to
- Stirs or awakens from sleep to a loud sound relatively close

4 to 6 Months

- Engages in vocal play when alone; gurgles
- Babbles with speechlike sounds
- Turns eyes toward direction of sounds
- Notices toys that make sounds
- Laughs and chuckles

7 Months to 1 Year

- Responds differently to a cheerful versus angry voice
- Responds to music or singing
- Vocalizes emotions
- Babbling acquires inflection and contains short and long groups of speech sounds ("tata, upup, bibibi")
- Tries to imitate the speech sounds of others
- Turns head in the direction of the source of a sound
- Ceases activity when parent's voice is heard
- Responds to own name and requests such as "Want more?" or "Come here."
- Uses a few words (e.g., *Mama* or *Dada, Doggie*) by first birthday

Sources: Adapted from American Speech-Language-Hearing Association (2011c); Hulit, L. M., Howard, M. R., & Fahey, K. R. (2011); and National Institute on Deafness and Other Communication Disorders (2011c).

Audiometry and audiograms

Content Standards for Beginning Teachers—D/HH: Specialized terminology used in assessing individuals who are D/HH (DH&H8K1) (also DH&H8K2).

has a 60-dB hearing loss cannot detect a sound until it is at least 60 dB loud. The results of the test are plotted on a chart called an **audiogram** (see Figure 4).

Speech Reception Test

A complete hearing exam includes testing a person's detection and understanding of speech sounds. A list of phonetically balanced one- and two-syllable words is presented at different decibel levels. The **speech reception threshold (SRT),** the lowest decibel level at which the individual can repeat half of the words, is measured and recorded for each ear.

Alternative Audiometric Techniques

Several alternative techniques have been developed for testing the hearing of very young children and individuals with severe disabilities who may not understand and follow conventional audiometry procedures. In **play audiometry,** the child is taught to perform simple but distinct activities, such as picking up a toy or putting a ball into a cup whenever she hears the signal, either pure tones or speech. A similar procedure is **operant conditioning audiometry,** in which the child receives a token or a small candy when she pushes a button in the presence of a light paired with a sound. No reinforcer is given for pushing the button when the light and sound are off. Next, the sound is presented without the light. If the child pushes the button in response to the sound alone, the examiner knows the child can hear that sound. **Behavior observation audiometry** is

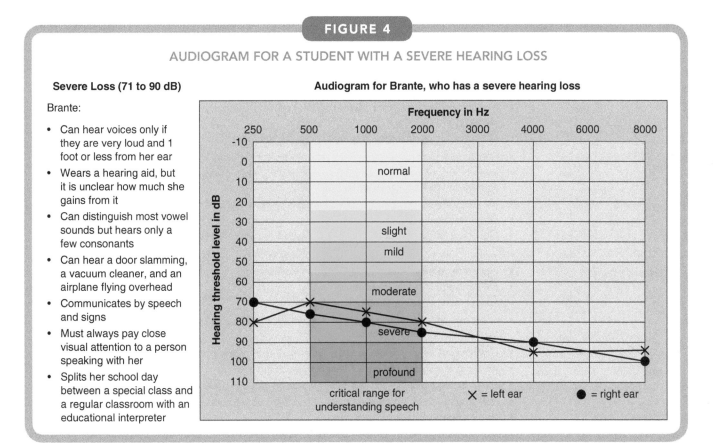

FIGURE 4

AUDIOGRAM FOR A STUDENT WITH A SEVERE HEARING LOSS

Severe Loss (71 to 90 dB)

Brante:

- Can hear voices only if they are very loud and 1 foot or less from her ear
- Wears a hearing aid, but it is unclear how much she gains from it
- Can distinguish most vowel sounds but hears only a few consonants
- Can hear a door slamming, a vacuum cleaner, and an airplane flying overhead
- Communicates by speech and signs
- Must always pay close visual attention to a person speaking with her
- Splits her school day between a special class and a regular classroom with an educational interpreter

Audiogram for Brante, who has a severe hearing loss

a passive assessment procedure in which the child's reactions to sounds are observed. A sound is presented at an increasing level of intensity until a response, such as head turning, eye blinking, or cessation of play, is reliably observed.

Classification of Hearing Loss

Hearing loss is usually described by the terms *slight, mild, moderate, severe,* and *profound,* depending on the average hearing level, in decibels, across the frequencies most important for understanding speech (500 to 2,000 HZ). Figure 5 lists some of the impacts of levels of hearing loss on speech and language and classroom supports that may be needed. It is important to recognize, however, that no two children have exactly the same pattern of hearing, even if their responses on a hearing test are similar. Just as a single intelligence test cannot provide sufficient information to plan a child's educational program, the special education needs of a child who is deaf or hard of hearing cannot be determined from an audiometric test alone. Children hear sounds with differing degrees of clarity, and the same child's hearing ability may vary from day to day. Some children with very low levels of measurable hearing can benefit from hearing aids and can learn to speak. On the other hand, some children with less measurable hearing loss do not function well through the auditory channel and rely on vision as their primary means of communication.

Degree and frequency range of hearing loss

 Council for Exceptional Children

Content Standards for Beginning Teachers—D/HH: Effects of sensory input on the development of language and learning (DH&H6K3).

TECHNOLOGIES AND SUPPORTS

Technologies That Amplify or Provide Sound

It was once assumed that people who were deaf simply did not hear at all, but nearly all deaf children have some degree of residual hearing. Modern technology for amplifying and clarifying sound enable many children with severe and profound hearing loss to use their residual hearing productively.

FIGURE 5 CLASSIFICATION OF HEARING LOSS AND EFFECTS ON SPEECH AND LANGUAGE AND PROBABLE EDUCATIONAL NEEDS

Degree of Hearing Loss	Classification	Impact on Speech and Language
27 to 40 dB	Slight	• No difficulty understanding speech in quiet settings, but noisy environments pose problems to learning • May benefit from favorable seating and sound field amplification
41 to 55 dB	Mild	• Can understand face-to-face conversation with little difficulty • Misses much of classroom discussion—particularly when the speaker cannot be seen clearly or several students are speaking at once • May have some classmates who are unaware she has a hearing loss • Benefits from a hearing aid • Most benefit from speech and language assistance from a speech-language pathologist
56 to 70 dB	Moderate	• Without hearing aid can hear conversational speech only if it is near, loud and clear • Finds it extremely difficult to follow group discussions • Full-time amplification is necessary • Speech noticeably impaired but intelligible • Many benefit from time in a special class where intensive instruction in language and communication can be provided
71 to 90 dB	Severe	• Can hear voices only if they are very loud and 1 foot or less from her ear • Wears a hearing aid, but it is unclear how much it helps • Can hear loud sounds such as a slamming door, vacuum cleaner, and airplane flying overhead • May distinguish most vowel sounds but few if any consonants • Communicates by speech and sign • May split school day between a special class and a general education classroom with an educational interpreter
91 dB or more	Profound	• Cannot hear conversational speech • Hearing aid enables awareness of certain very loud sounds, such as a fire alarm or a bass drum • Vision is primary modality for learning • American Sign Language likely to be first language and principal means of communication • Has not developed intelligible speech • Most require full-time program special education program for students who are deaf

Sources: Paul and Whitlow (2011); Scheetz (2012); Schirmer (2001); Schow and Nerbonne (2007).

Hearing aids

 Council for Exceptional Children Content Standards for Beginning Teachers—D/HH: Strategies for stimulating and using residual hearing (DH&H6K8).

HEARING AIDS A hearing aid makes sounds louder. A hearing aid is like a miniature public address system, with a microphone, an amplifier, a receiver, and controls to adjust volume and tone. Hearing aids come in a variety of designs and can be worn behind the ear, in the ear, completely in the ear canal, on the body, or incorporated into eyeglass frames. Children can wear hearing aids in one or both ears (monaural or binaural aids). Whatever its shape, power, or size, a hearing aid picks up sound, magnifies its energy, and delivers this louder sound to the user's middle ear.

Early versions indiscriminately amplified all sounds and were ineffective for most children with sensorineural hearing loss. Today's digital programmable hearing aids employ computer microchips that distinguish and separate speech sounds from background noise, and deliver a clear, distortion-free signal that differentially amplifies selected frequencies tailored to the user's individual pattern of hearing loss. The user can select preprogrammed settings for optimal listening in different environments, such as a classroom or outdoors.

The earlier in life a child can be fitted with an appropriate hearing aid, the more likely she will learn to use hearing for communication and awareness (Moeller, Hoover, Peterson, & Stemachowicz, 2009). Today, it is not unusual to see infants and preschoolers wearing hearing aids; the improved listening conditions become an important part of the young child's speech and language development. To derive maximum benefit from a hearing aid, a child should wear it throughout the day.

GROUP ASSISTIVE LISTENING DEVICES Group assistive listening devices can solve the problems caused by distance, noise, and reverberation in the classroom. In most systems, a radio link is established between the teacher and the children with hearing loss, with the teacher wearing a small microphone transmitter (often on the lapel, near the lips) and each child wearing a receiver that doubles as a personal hearing aid. An FM radio frequency is usually employed, and wires are not required, so teacher and students can move freely around the classroom.

COCHLEAR IMPLANTS Unlike hearing aids, which deliver amplified sound to the ear, a **cochlear implant** bypasses damaged hair cells and stimulates the auditory nerve directly. The implant is surgically placed under the skin behind the ear. An implant has four basic parts: an external *microphone,* which picks up sound from the environment; an external *speech processor,* which selects and arranges sounds picked up by the microphone; a *transmitter;* and a *receiver/ stimulator,* which receives signals from the speech processor and converts them into electric impulses. *Electrodes* collect the impulses from the stimulator and send them directly to the brain via the auditory nerve (see Figure 6).

Cochlear implant surgery usually takes 2 to 3 hours, and the child stays overnight in the hospital. About 4 weeks later, the child returns to the implant center for initial stimulation of the device and tune-up sessions over 2 to 3 days. Approximately 188,000 people worldwide have received cochlear implants, including 25,500 children and 41,500 adults in the United States (NIDCD, 2011a). A national survey found that 14% of deaf and hard-of-hearing students had cochlear implants (Gallaudet Research Institute, 2008).

A cochlear implant does not restore or create normal hearing. It can, however, give a deaf person a useful auditory understanding of the environment and help him or her understand speech. When coupled with intensive postimplantation therapy, cochlear implants can help young children acquire speech, language, developmental, and social skills. Although many questions about cochlear implants remain to be answered, initial research reports have described significant improvements in speech perceptions, speech production, and language skills compared to peers without cochlear implants (e.g., Schorr, Roth, & Fox, 2008, 2009; Vermeulen, van Bon, Schreuder, Knoors, & Snik, 2007).

Tremendous controversy surrounds cochlear implants (National Association for the Deaf, 2000). Some members of the Deaf community are vehemently opposed to cochlear implants and consider the procedure to be a form of genocide of the Deaf culture (e.g., Hyde & Power, 2006; Komesaroff, 2007). Luterman (1999) offered the following explanation of a position that is difficult for most hearing people to understand:

> People who have never heard do not experience hearing loss as a loss. This is why they can believe, much to the consternation of the normally hearing population, that deafness is a cultural difference rather than a deficit. It would be analogous, for example, to those who had ESP thinking that the rest of us were terribly handicapped in our communication abilities, while we who do not possess ESP and have never had it do not feel the least handicapped. The only way we would is if those with ESP constantly reminded us of our deficiency and tried to "fix" us. (p. 75)

To derive maximum benefit from a hearing aid, a child should wear it throughout the day.

Scott Cunningham/Merrill

Group listening devices

Content Standards for Beginning Teachers—D/HH: Strategies for stimulating and using residual hearing (DH&H6K8).

Cochlear implants

Content Standards for Beginning Teachers—D/HH: Sociocultural, historical, and political forces unique to deaf education (DH&H1K4) (also DH&H3K2).

379

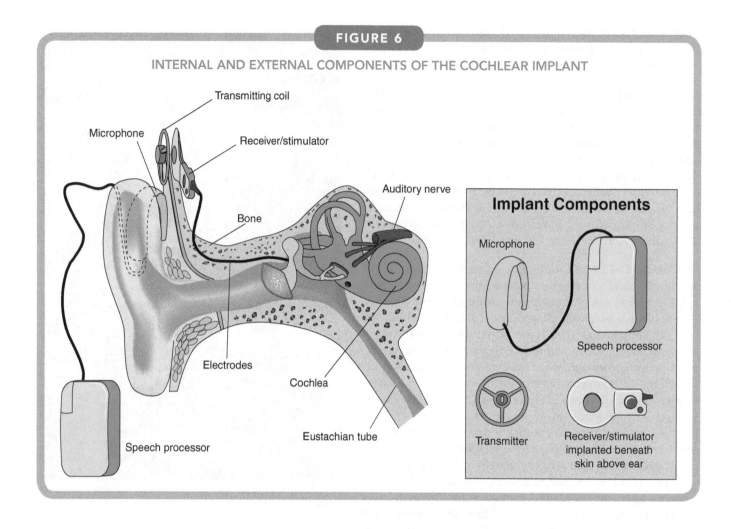

FIGURE 6

INTERNAL AND EXTERNAL COMPONENTS OF THE COCHLEAR IMPLANT

To hear eight deaf people talk about their experiences living in a hearing world and their diverse opinions on cochlear implant surgery, go to "Voices of Deafness" at http://www.pbs.org/wnet/soundandfury/culture/voices.html. Detailed information about cochlear implants appears in Nussbaum (2011).

Interpreters

 Council for Exceptional Children Content Standards for Beginning Teachers—D/HH: Spoken and visual communication modes (DH&H6K4) (also DH&H4K3, DH&H6K1).

To read more about the contrasting views of deafness as a cultural difference or as a sensory loss to be remedied, see *Current Issues* and *Future Trends*, "Deafness: The Dilemma."

Supports and Technologies That Supplement or Replace Sound

SIGN LANGUAGE INTERPRETERS *Interpreting*—signing the speech of a teacher or other speaker for a person who is deaf—began as a profession in 1964 with the establishment of the Registry of Interpreters for the Deaf (RID). Many states have programs for training interpreters, who must meet certain standards of competence to be certified by the RID. The organization was initially composed primarily of freelance interpreters, who interpret primarily for deaf adults in situations such as legal or medical interactions.

Sign language interpretation (sometimes called *transliteration*) has enabled many deaf and hard-of-hearing students to successfully complete college and other postsecondary education programs. The use of educational interpreters for deaf and hard-of-hearing students in elementary and secondary classrooms has increased (Monikowski & Winston, 2011). An interpreter must provide the deaf or hard-of-hearing student with all speech and other auditory information in the classroom, a formidable task for even the most highly skilled interpreter.

A skilled interpreter in the classroom is no guarantee that students with hearing loss will receive and participate in accurate communication. Garay (2003) recommends that deaf students be taught how to effectively use interpreters—for example, how to let interpreters know when they do not understand something, and how to appropriately and effectively indicate that they have something to ask the teacher or contribute to the class discussion.

SPEECH-TO-TEXT TRANSLATION Computer-aided speech-to-text translation increases access by deaf students to live presentations, such as public or classroom lectures. An example of this technology is the C-Print speech-to-text service developed at the National Technical Institute for the Deaf at the University of Rochester (Stinson, Elliot, Kelly, & Liu, 2008). A trained captionist types the teacher's lecture and students' comments into a laptop computer using a shorthand code. Special software translates the code (e.g., typing "kfe" produces "coffee"), and the text appears on a screen or a student's personal laptop computer monitor about 3 seconds after the words are spoken. The text display remains on the screen for approximately 1 minute, which provides students with much more time to consider the words than using an interpreter or speechreading would. The system provides a meaning-for-meaning (not verbatim) translation of the lecture, which would be impossible at speech rates of 150 words per minute. Captionists eliminate redundancies, identify key points, and condense information on the fly, keeping as close as possible to the original. Text files can be saved, edited, and printed after class.

TELEVISION, VIDEO, AND MOVIE CAPTIONING Most programming today on commercial and public network television is captioned (printed text appears at the bottom of the screen, similar to watching a film with subtitles). Since 1993, a federal law has required that all new television sets sold in the United States be equipped with an internal device that allows the user to position captions anywhere on the screen. Many videos are movies are captioned, and an ever-increasing number of movie theaters are offering a captioning system called Rear Window. Captions from an LED panel at the back of the theater are projected on an adjustable, clear Lucite panel attached to the viewer's seat.

TEXT TELEPHONES The telephone presented a major barrier to people with hearing impairments in employment and social interaction until acoustic couplers made it possible to send immediate messages over conventional telephone lines in typed or digital form. Text telephones (TT)—also called TTYs (teletypes) or TDDs (telecommunication devices for the deaf)—enable the user to send a typed message over telephone lines to anyone else who has a TT. As a result of the Americans with Disabilities Act, TTs are now available in most public places such as airports and libraries, and every state has a relay service that enables TT users to communicate with a person on a conventional telephone via a sign language interpreter who relays the messages. Relay numbers are published in every phone directory.

COMPUTER TECHNOLOGY Ever-improving personal computer and mobile digital technologies have opened and expanded avenues of communication and connectivity for people with hearing impairments. Smart phones and other mobile devices with video capability such as the iPad enable people who are deaf to instant message, tweet, email, and surf the Web.

ALERTING DEVICES Some individuals who are deaf or hard of hearing use special devices to alert them to certain sounds or events. For example, to signal the doorbell, a

Technically, sign language *interpretation* means translating spoken English into American Sign Language, which has its own vocabulary and syntax. *Transliteration* is the use of sign in the same word order as spoken English.

Speech-to-text translation and TV captioning

Council for Exceptional Children

Content Standards for Beginning Teachers—D/HH: Spoken and visual communication modes (DH&H6K4) (also DH&H4K3, DH&H6K1).

Hearing dogs are trained to alert a deaf person to important sounds such as a ringing telephone.

photo courtesy: Dogs for the Deaf, Inc., www.dogsforthedeaf.org

AND

FUTURE TRENDS

▶ Deafness: The Dilemma

BY BONNIE TUCKER

CURRENT ISSUES

DURING THE LAST 20 YEARS, technological advances to assist people with hearing loss surpassed the expectations of many. Hearing aids improved tremendously, both with respect to quality and aesthetics. The newer aids block out background noise and emphasize sound in the speech range, which has enabled some severely hearing-impaired people to benefit from aids for the first time. . . . Cochlear implants have enabled some profoundly deaf people, both children and adults, to understand speech without having to rely on speechreading or interpreters; some cochlear implantees are able to converse on the voice telephone with strangers.

Twenty years ago I, for one, did not foresee these transformations. Today, however, my vision for the future is unlimited. Given the rapidly advancing state of technology in this area, it is not unrealistic to assume that 20 years hence the technological advances of the past two decades will seem outmoded, even ancient. It is not unrealistic to assume that in 20 years cochlear implants will enable profoundly deaf people to understand speech in most circumstances, including on the telephone. We are not there yet, but we are on our way.

Many members of the Deaf community, including leaders of the National Association of the Deaf (NAD),

do not want cochlear implants. They do not want to hear. They want their children to be Deaf, and to be a part of the Deaf world. "We like being Deaf," they state. "We are proud of our Deafness. . . ." They claim the right to their own "ethnicity, with our own language and culture, the same way that Native Americans or Italians bond together"; they claim the right to "personal diversity," which is "something to be cherished rather than fixed and erased." And they strongly protest the practice of placing cochlear implants in children. These same individuals, however, are among the strongest advocates for laws and special programs to protect and assist people with hearing loss. They argue fiercely for the need for interpreters, TTYs, telephone relay services, specially funded educational programs, and closed captioning, at no cost to themselves. On the one hand, therefore, they claim that deafness is not a disability, but a state of being, a "right" that should not be altered. On the other hand, they claim that deafness is a disability that society should compensate for by providing and paying for services to allow deaf people to function in society.

Do Deaf people have the right to refuse to accept new technology, to refuse to "fix" their Deafness if such repair becomes possible? Yes, absolutely. They do have

Figure 7 highlights some key historical events in deaf education. For interesting historical accounts of deaf education, see Scheetz (2012), Van Cleve (2007), Winzer (2009), and the "Timeline of Deaf History" at http://www.pbs.org/wnet/soundandfury/culture/deafhistory.html.

fire alarm, or an alarm clock, a sound- or vibration-sensitive switch can be connected to a flashing light or to a vibrator. Hearing dogs are trained to alert a deaf person to important sounds in the environment (Guest, Collis, & McNicholas, 2006).

EDUCATIONAL APPROACHES

Over the years, many philosophies, theories, and specialized methods and materials have been developed for teaching children who are deaf. Most of these approaches have been enthusiastically promoted by their advocates and critically denounced by others. Indeed, for more than 100 years, people have waged an impassioned debate over how best to teach children who do not hear.

Most programs for students who are deaf and hard of hearing emphasize one of three approaches: the oral/aural approach, total communication, or the bilingual-bicultural approach (Estabrooks, 2006).

Oral/Aural Approaches

Educational programs with an oral/aural emphasis view speech as essential if students who are deaf are to function in the hearing world. Training in producing and

the right, if they wish to exercise that right, to cherish their Deaf culture, their Deaf ethnicity, their "visually oriented" personal diversity. Do Deaf people have the right to demand that society pay for the resulting cost of that choice, however? No, I do not believe they do.

By way of analogy, suppose that blindness and quadriplegia were "curable" due to advanced technology. Blind people could be made to "see" via artificial means such as surgical implantation or three-dimensional eyeglasses; quadriplegic individuals could be made to "walk" and use their arms via artificial means such as surgical nerve implantation or specially built devices. Oh, the blind people might not see as perfectly as sighted people—they might still miss some of the fine print. And the quadriplegic individuals might walk with a limp or move their arms in a jerky fashion. But, for the most part, they would require little special assistance.

Suppose that 10 blind people chose not to make use of available technology for the reason that blindness is not a "disability," not something to be fixed, but that blind people are simply "auditory oriented," and 20 quadriplegic people chose not to make use of available technology for the reason that quadriplegics are simply "out-of-body oriented." How long will society agree to pay for readers, attendants, and other services and devices to assist those blind and quadriplegic individuals who have exercised their right to be diverse? More important, how long should society be asked to pay for such services and devices?

When technology advances to the extent that profoundly deaf people could choose to "hear"—which, eventually, it surely will—Deaf people will have to resolve the dilemma,

both for reasons of practicality and morality. Deaf people will have to decide whether to accept hearing or to remain Deaf. They have every right to choose the latter course. If they do so, however, they must assume responsibility for that choice and bear the resultant cost, rather than thrust that responsibility upon society. As our grandparents used to say, "You can't have your cake and eat it too."

WHAT DO YOU THINK?

1. If your newborn were diagnosed with profound deafness, would you consider cochlear implants? Why or why not?
2. Do you think there are interventions or treatments for people with other disabilities that should be discussed and debated as cochlear implants have for Deaf children? Why or why not?
3. Does society have the right or responsibility to deny supports and services to a person who has chosen not to use an available technology that would make those supports and services unnecessary?

About the Author

Bonnie Tucker is Emerita Professor of Law at Arizona State University. Deaf since infancy and unable to wear hearing aids, Dr. Tucker had cochlear implant surgery at the age of 52. She is the editor and part author of *Cochlear Implants: A Handbook* (McFarland, 1998).

Source: From Tucker, B. (1993). Deafness: 1993–2013—The dilemma. *The Volta Review, 95,* 105–108. Reprinted with permission from the Alexander Graham Bell Association for the Deaf and Hard of Hearing. www.agbell.org.

---

understanding speech and language is incorporated into virtually all aspects of the child's education. A purely oral approach without any manual communication was used widely in the United States before the 1970s. Today, about one-fourth of special schools and educational programs for students who are deaf or hard of hearing identify themselves as solely oral/aural programs. However, with rising numbers of deaf and hard-of-hearing children educated in general education classrooms, the actual proportion educated orally is increasing.

A child who attends a program with an oral emphasis typically uses several means to develop residual hearing and the ability to speak as intelligibly as possible. Auditory, visual, and tactile methods of input are frequently used. Much attention is given to amplification, auditory training, speechreading, the use of technological aids, and, above all, talking. A few schools maintain a purely oral environment and may even prohibit children from pointing, using gestures, or spelling out words to communicate. Children in these programs are required to express themselves and learn to understand others through speech alone. Other programs emphasize speech and listening skills but also use and encourage a variety of approaches to help students produce and understand spoken language.

Educators who use an oral approach acknowledge that teaching speech to deaf children is difficult, demanding, and time-consuming for the teacher, the parents,

History of education of students who are D/HH

Content Standards for Beginning Teachers—D/HH: Historical foundations and research evidence upon which educational practice is based (DH&H1K4) (also DH&H7K1).

Speech is the primary communication mode in classrooms attended by 52% of deaf and hard-of-hearing students (Gallaudet Research Institute, 2008).

FIGURE 7	KEY HISTORICAL EVENTS IN THE EDUCATION OF STUDENTS WHO ARE DEAF OR HARD OF HEARING

Date	Historical Event
Late 16th century	Pedro Ponce de Leon (1520–1584), an Augustinian monk and scholar, established a school for the deaf children of noble families in Spain.
18th century	Schools for children who were deaf were begun in England, France, Germany, Holland, and Scotland. Both oral and manual methods of instruction were used.
1817	Thomas Gallaudet and Laurent Clerc, a deaf French educator, open the American Asylum for the Education of the Deaf and Dumb (renamed the American School for the Deaf) in Hartford, CT. Some consider Clerc the father of deaf education in the United States.
Early 19th century	The prevailing philosophy that people who were deaf could not benefit from oral instruction led to segregation in asylums or special sanctuaries and removed from normal society.
1864	Gallaudet University (then called the National College for the Deaf and Dumb) is founded.
Mid- to late 19th century	Oral approaches dominated to such a great degree that the use of sign language in schools was officially prohibited at an international conference in 1880. This era marked the beginning of what some have called "the Hundred Years War" over what methods of communication are best for deaf children.
Mid- to late 20th century	Enrollments in residential schools for children with hearing losss declined sharply as most students whose deafness was caused by the rubella epidemics of the 1960s left high school and public school programs became more widely available.
1960s	Research by linguist William Stokoe at Gallaudet showed that sign language used by the deaf community was a legitimate language in its own right. What had been called "the Sign Language" was given a new name, American Sign Language (ASL).
1968	Congress funded the National Technical Institute for the Deaf (NTID) at the Rochester Institute of Technology.
1970s	The majority of deaf education programs adopted total communication (TC) as the method of communication and instruction. While TC is still used frequently today, it has not raised the academic achievement of deaf students.
1986	Concerned over academic and employment outcomes of deaf students, Congress established the Commission on Education of the Deaf (CED) with the Education of the Deaf Act of 1986.
1988	Students at Gallaudet University protested the hiring of a hearing president at their college. The Deaf President Now movement galvanized the Deaf community, increased awareness in hearing society of concerns and issues facing the Deaf culture, and led to the hiring of Gallaudet's first deaf president, I. King Jordan.
1989	FDA approved cochlear implant surgery as a means of bypassing the inner ear and providing a sense of sound directly through the auditory nerve for those with sensorineural hearing loss. Many in the Deaf community view cochlear implants as a threat to the existence of their language and culture.
1990s	The Deaf community increased its activism and self-advocacy, especially with regard to ASL as a Deaf child's first language.
2010	Attendees at the International Congress on Education of the Deaf (ICED) unanimously passed a statement formally rejecting the 1880 edict that had banned sign language in school programs for the deaf.

Oral/aural approach

 Council for Exceptional Children

Content Standards for Beginning Teachers—D/HH: Historical foundations and research evidence upon which educational practice is based (DH&H1K4) (also DH&H4K4, DH&H6K5).

and—most of all—the student. Speech comes hard to the deaf child. The rewards of successful oral communication, however, are thought to be worth the effort. And indeed, most students with hearing loss no worse than severe can learn speech well enough to communicate effectively with hearing people. The best results are obtained with students who are enrolled in indisputably comprehensive oral programs or who are integrated most of the school day into general education programs (Paul & Whitlow, 2011).

AUDITORY LEARNING Listening comprises 45% of daily communication for adults, and children spend up to 60% of the school day in situations where they are expected to be listening effectively (Crandell & Smaldino, 2001). Many children with hearing loss have much more auditory potential than they use, and their residual hearing can be improved in the context of actual communication and daily experiences. All children with hearing loss, regardless of whether their preferred method of communication is oral (speech) or manual (signs), should receive training and practice with improving their listening skills.

Auditory training for young children with hearing loss begins by teaching awareness of sound. Parents might direct their child's attention to sounds such as a doorbell ringing or water running. They might then focus on localization of sound—for example, by hiding a radio somewhere in the room and encouraging the child to look for it. Discrimination of sounds is another important part of auditory training; a child might learn to notice the differences between a man's voice and a woman's voice, between a fast song and a slow song, or between the words *rack* and *rug*. Identification of sounds comes when a child can recognize a sound, word, or sentence through listening.

The focus today is on auditory learning—that is, teaching the child to learn to listen and to learn by listening instead of simply learning to hear (Ling, 2002). Advocates of auditory learning contend that the first three levels of auditory training—detecting, discriminating, and identifying sounds—are important but insufficient for developing the student's residual hearing. Auditory learning emphasizes a fourth and highest level of listening skills: the comprehension of meaningful sounds.

Practitioners of an approach called *auditory-verbal therapy* conduct some sessions in which a child is required to use only hearing to recognize sounds and words without looking at the speaker's lips (Estabrooks, 2006). Parental involvement is critical to success as auditory training opportunities are integrated into family and social activities as well as in school (Dornan et al., 2010). In actual practice, however, the child gains useful information from vision and the other senses to supplement the information received from hearing. Consequently, all senses should be effectively developed and constantly used.

SPEECHREADING Speechreading is the process of understanding a spoken message by observing the speaker's lip movements, facial expressions, eye movements and body gestures. Some sounds are readily distinguished by watching the speaker's lips. For example, the word *pail* begins with the lips in a shut position, whereas the lips are somewhat drawn together and puckered at the corners for the word *rail*. Paying careful attention to a speaker's lips may help an individual with hearing loss derive important clues—particularly if she also can gain additional information through residual hearing, signs or gestures, facial expressions, and the context or situation.

A combination of amplification and auditory training can help a child make the most of his residual hearing.

Speechreading, however, is extremely difficult and has many limitations. About half of all English words have some other word(s) that appear the same in pronunciation; that is, although they sound quite different, they look alike on the lips. Words such as *bat, mat,* and *pat,* for example, look exactly alike and simply cannot be discriminated by watching the speaker's lips. To complicate matters, visual clues may be blocked by a hand or a pencil, chewing gum, or a mustache. Many speakers are virtually unintelligible through speechreading; they may seem not to move their lips at all. In addition, it is extremely tiring to watch lips for a long time, and it may be impossible to do so at a distance, such as during a lecture. Walker (1986) estimates that even the best speechreaders detect only about 25% of what is said through visual clues alone; "the rest is contextual piecing together of ideas and expected constructions" (p. 19).

Despite the problems inherent in speechreading, it can be a valuable tool in a deaf or hard-of-hearing person's communication repertoire (Paul & Whitlow, 2011). When deaf people practice speechreading their own speech and others via computer-assisted video instruction, their speechreading skills can improve (Sims & Gottermeier, 1995). Initial evaluations of a computer-based, interactive videodisc program developed at

Auditory training/learning

Content Standards for Beginning Teachers—D/HH: Apply strategies to facilitate cognitive and communicative development (DH&H6S1).

Speechreading

Content Standards for Beginning Teachers—D/HH: Apply strategies to facilitate cognitive and communicative development in individuals who are D/HH (DH&H6S1).

Scott Cunningham/Merrill

Bloomsburg (Pennsylvania) University helps people with hearing loss make better use of their vision to decode speech (Slike, Thornton, Hobbis, Kokoska, & Job, 1995).

CUED SPEECH **Cued speech** supplements oral communication with a visual system of hand signals that represent the 44 phonemes of spoken English. The hand signals must be used in conjunction with speech; they are neither signs nor manual alphabet letters and cannot be read alone. Eight hand shapes identify consonant sounds, and four locations around the chin identify vowel sounds. A hand shape coupled with a location gives a visual indication of a syllable. Cued speech helps students identify syllabic and phonetic features of speech that cannot be distinguished through speechreading. According to Orin Cornett, who developed the system in 1964, cued speech does not disrupt the natural rhythm of speech (Cornett & Daisey, 2001). Some research shows that students taught with cued speech develop reading and spelling at levels comparable to hearing children (Hage & Leybaert, 2006).

Total Communication

As Scheetz (2012) points out, **total communication** refers to an educational philosophy as well as to a mode of communication. Advocates use a variety of forms of communication to teach English to students with hearing loss. Practitioners of total communication maintain that the simultaneous presentation of English language by speech and manual communication (signing and fingerspelling) makes it possible for children to use either one or both types of communication (Hawkins & Brawner, 1997). Since its introduction as a teaching philosophy in the 1960s, total communication has become the most widely used method of instruction in schools for the deaf. A survey of 137 early intervention programs for deaf and hard-of-hearing students in 39 states found that 66% of the programs used total communication (Meadow-Orlans et al., 1997).

MANUALLY CODED ENGLISH Teachers who practice total communication generally speak as they sign and make a special effort to follow the form and structure of spoken English as closely as possible. Several English-based sign systems have been designed for educational purposes, with the intention of facilitating the development of reading, writing, and other language skills in students with hearing loss. *Manually coded English* refers to several educationally oriented sign systems, such as Signing Essential English (commonly known as SEE I) (Anthony, 1971), Signing Exact English (SEE II) (Gustafson, Pfetzing, & Zawolkow, 1980), and Signed English (Bornstein, 1974). While manually coded English borrows many signs and incorporates some of the features of American Sign Language (to be discussed), it follows standard English usage and word order. Unfortunately, deaf students must often learn and use two or more sign language systems, depending on the person with whom they are communicating.

FINGERSPELLING Fingerspelling, the manual alphabet, is used to spell out proper names for which no signs exist and to clarify meanings. Fingerspelling is an integral part of American Sign Language (ASL) and an important aspect of becoming bilingual in English and ASL (Haptonstall-Nykaza & Schick, 2007). It consists of 26 distinct hand positions, one for each English letter. A one-hand manual alphabet is used in the United States and Canada (see Figure 8). Some manual letters—such as *C, L,* and *W*—resemble the shape of printed English letters, whereas others—such as *A, E,* and *S*—have no apparent similarity. As in typewriting, each word is spelled out letter by letter.

Deaf babies' first attempts at fingerspelling emerge shortly after their first birthday, and their fingerspelled word at 2 years of age (Erting, Thumann-Prezioso, & Benedict, 2000). Fingerspelling can help deaf and hard-of-hearing students with reading by providing a link to English vocabulary and syntax (Baker, 2010).

Cued speech

Content Standards for Beginning Teachers—D/HH: Apply strategies to facilitate cognitive and communicative development in individuals who are D/HH (DH&H6S1).

Total communication

Content Standards for Beginning Teachers—D/HH: Historical foundations and research evidence upon which educational practice is based (DH&H1K4) (also DH&H4K3, DH&H6K5).

Manually coded English and fingerspelling

Content Standards for Beginning Teachers—D/HH: Apply strategies to facilitate cognitive and communicative development in individuals who are D/HH (DH&H6S1).

About 36% of students who are deaf and hard of hearing attend classrooms where speech and manual sign are the primary language and mode of communication (Gallaudet Research Institute, 2008).

FIGURE 8

THE MANUAL ALPHABET USED TO FINGERSPELL ENGLISH IN NORTH AMERICA

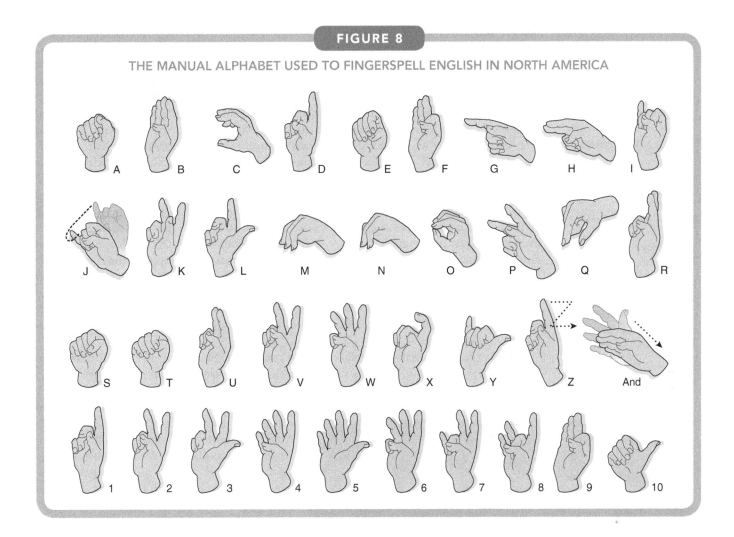

American Sign Language and the Bilingual-Bicultural Approach

American Sign Language (ASL) is the language of the Deaf culture in the United States and Canada. Although the sign languages used by native deaf speakers were once thought to be nonlanguages (alinguistic), work by the linguist William Stokoe (Stokoe, 1960; Stokoe, Armstrong, & Wilcox, 1995) showed that ASL is a legitimate language in its own right rather than an imperfect variation of spoken English. ASL is a visual-spatial language in which the shape, location, and movement pattern of the hands; the intensity of motions; and the signer's facial expressions all communicate meaning and content. Because ASL has its own rules of phonology, morphology, syntax, semantics, and pragmatics, it does not correspond to spoken or written English (Valli, Lucas, & Mulrooney, 2005). Articles, prepositions, tenses, plurals, and word order are expressed differently from English. It is as difficult to make precise word-for-word translations between ASL and English as it is to translate many foreign languages into English word for word.

Some ASL signs are *iconic*; that is, they convey meaning through hand shapes or motions that look like or appear to imitate or act out their message. In making the sign for "cat," for example, the signer seems to be stroking feline whiskers on her face; in the sign for "eat," the hand moves back and forth into an open mouth. Most signs, however, have little or no iconicity; they do not resemble the objects or actions they represent. If ASL were simply a form of pantomime, then most nonsigners would be able to understand it with relative ease. But the vast majority of signs cannot be guessed by people who are unfamiliar with sign language.

During the 1990s, the Deaf community and a sizeable number of both hearing and deaf special educators began calling for ASL to be the language of instruction

ASL

 Council for Exceptional Children

Content Standards for Beginning Teachers—D/HH: Spoken and visual communication modes used by and with individuals who are hearing and those who are D/HH (DH&H6K4) (also DH&H4K3, DH&H6K1).

An ASL video dictionary is available at Handspeak http://www.handspeak .com/.

Bilingual–bicultural approach

Content Standards for Beginning Teachers—D/HH: Historical foundations and research evidence upon which educational practice is based (DH&H1K4) (also DH&H6K5, DH&H7K1).

(Baker & Baker, 1997; Drasgow, 1998). They believe that ASL provides a natural pathway to linguistic competence and that English is better learned in the context of a **bilingual-bicultural (bi-bi) approach** after the child has mastered his native or first language (ASL) (Baker, 2011). Proponents of this model view deafness as a cultural and linguistic difference, not a disability, and recognize ASL as the deaf child's natural language. The goal of the bilingual-bicultural education approach is to help deaf students become bilingual adults who are competent in their first language, ASL, and who can read and write with competence in their second language, English.

The theoretical argument for bilingual education is that students who have a solid foundation in their native language (L1) will be able to use their literacy-related L1 skills as a springboard for learning the majority second language (L2) (Musselman, 2000). Deaf infants and toddlers form families where ASL is the primary language achieve language development milestones at about the same rate as hearing children do with spoken language (Emmorey, 2002; Goldin-Meadow, 2003). Children from deaf families enter school ready to learn because as infants and toddlers, they learn their first language through communicating with family members (Marschark, Schick, & Spencer, 2006). Research demonstrating a correlation between early exposure to and development of fluency in ASL and increased competence and English literacy (Prinz & Stong, 1998; Yoshinaga-Itano, 2006) provides some empirical support for the bilingual-bicultural approach.

Mayer and Akamatsu (1999), however, question the extent of L1–L2 interdependence when the two languages under consideration are a native sign language and the written form of an oral language. They also point out the logical inconsistency and danger of not providing deaf students with direct instruction and practice in the bottom-up literacy skills such as English language principles and phonics just because those are the skills with which they have the most difficulty. To date, although there is solid philosophical and theoretical reasoning for bilingual-bicultural approach and many programs have been implemented, much more objective data on effectiveness and long-term program outcomes are needed (DeLana, Gentry, & Andrews, 2007).

American Sign Language (ASL) is a complete language with its own vocabulary, syntax, and grammatical rules.

© Michael Newman/PhotoEdit

Which Approach for Whom?

Educators, scientists, philosophers, and parents—both hearing and deaf—have for many years debated the most appropriate instructional methods for children who are deaf. The controversy continues today. In the past, however, fundamental disagreement focused on the extent to which deaf children should express language through speech and perceive the communication of others through speechreading and residual hearing. Today, the debate has switched to which language—English or ASL—should be a deaf child's first language.

Different children communicate in different ways. Some deaf children, unfortunately, have experienced deep frustration and failure because of rigid adherence to an oral-only program. They have left oral programs without having developed a usable avenue of communication. Equally unfortunate is the fact that other children have not been given an adequate opportunity to develop their auditory and oral skills because they were placed in educational programs that did not provide good oral instruction. In both cases, children have been unfairly penalized. Every child who is deaf should have access to an educational program that uses a communication method best suited to her unique abilities and needs (Marschark, 2007). Mahshie (1995) recommends letting the child choose her first language:

> In environments where the Deaf child encounters both spoken and signed language separately—as whole languages—during the course of natural interactions, it has become apparent to both parents and professionals that the child will be the guide regarding his or her predisposition toward a more oral or more visual language. In this win-win situation, the choice of a first language is clearly the child's. (p. 73)

Early and continued access to language and the communication modality best suited to their individual needs and preferences, effective instruction with meaningful curriculum, and self-determination are the keys to increasing the number of deaf or hard-of-hearing people who can access and enjoy the full spectrum of educational, social, vocational, and recreational opportunities society has to offer.

EDUCATIONAL PLACEMENT ALTERNATIVES

In most areas of the United States today, parents of deaf and hard-of-hearing students can choose between local public school programs and residential schools. The majority of students who are deaf or hard of hearing attend local public schools: 54% receive most of their education in general education classrooms with hearing students, 17% attend resource rooms for part of the school day, and 16% are served in separate classrooms. About 8% of students who are deaf attend special day schools and 4% attend residential schools for the deaf (U.S. Department of Education, 2010d). Most students with hearing loss who are included in general education classrooms have hearing losses of less than 90 dB.

The question of where students who are deaf should be educated has produced some research evidence—and much strong opinion—in support of both inclusive and segregated settings (Cerney, 2007). As Bat-Chava (2000) notes, where a child who is deaf is educated also influences the likelihood of his or her cultural identity. In schools in which oral English is the language of instruction, supplemented by fingerspelling and English-based sign systems, students are more likely to view hearing loss as a disability. Schools in which ASL is the language of instruction foster the perspective of Deaf culture.

In a study of the effects of inclusion on the academic achievement of high school students who are deaf, Kluwin (1993) reported that although those students who were included in general education classrooms for academic content fared better on achievement measures than did students who spent all or most of the day in a separate class, the difference may have been the result of curriculum programming and class selection, not the actual place where instruction took place. After assessing the self-concepts of 90 deaf secondary students across different educational placements, Van Gurp (2001) concluded there were academic advantages to more integrated, resource room–type placements and social advantages in attending segregated schools.

Instruction and support services provided to deaf and hard-of-hearing students in general education classrooms leave much to be desired. Cawthon (2001) found that elementary teachers in inclusive classrooms directed about half as many utterances to deaf students as they did to hearing students and that educational interpreters were critical factors in how well the deaf students understood and participated in classroom discourse and learning activities. Recent national surveys found that only about 20% of all school-age deaf and hard-of-hearing students reported receiving interpreting service as an instructional support (Gallaudet Research Institute, 2008), and 45% of secondary students with severe or profound hearing loss included in general education academic classes were provided interpreting service (Shaver et al., 2011).

The skill level of an educational interpreter plays a critical role in the success and appropriateness of a general education classroom placement for students who are deaf. After finding that about 60% of 2,100 educational interpreters across the United States had inadequate skills, researchers concluded that "many deaf and hard-of-hearing students receive interpreting services that will seriously hinder reasonable access to the classroom curriculum and social interaction" (Schick, Williams, & Kupermintz, 2006, p. 3).

While many deaf students have benefited from full inclusion, all of the professional and parent organizations involved with educating students who are deaf have issued position statements strongly in favor of maintaining a continuum of placement options (e.g., Commission on Education of the Deaf, 1988; National Association of the Deaf, 2002). As one respected leader in the field of deaf education noted, including a deaf child in a classroom with hearing children may actually have an exclusionary effect that isolates the child academically and socially due to unequal access to curriculum (Moores, 1993).

As with all learners, we should never overlook the most fundamental factor in determining how successful a student will be in a general education classroom (or any other placement): quality of instruction. After studying the math achievement of 215 secondary students with hearing loss who were either in self-contained classrooms or mainstreamed into general education classes with or without an interpreter, Kluwin and Moores (1989) concluded, "Quality of instruction is the prime determinant of achievement, regardless of placement" (p. 327).

Postsecondary Education

Gallaudet University and NTID

 Council for Exceptional Children Content Standards for Beginning Teachers—D/HH: Model programs for individuals who are D/HH (DH&H7K1).

To learn more about postsecondary educational programs and supports, visit the Postsecondary Education Programs Network website at www.pepnet.org.

The percentage of students with hearing loss who attend postsecondary educational programs has risen dramatically since the 1980s. About 40% of all students with hearing loss go on to college education (Gallaudet Research Institute, 2005). A growing number of educational opportunities are available to students with hearing loss after completion of high school. The oldest and best known is Gallaudet University in Washington, DC, which offers a wide range of undergraduate and graduate programs in the liberal arts, sciences, education, business, and other fields. The National Technical Institute for the Deaf (NTID), located at the Rochester Institute of Technology, provides wide-ranging programs in technical, vocational, and business-related fields such as computer science, hotel management, photography, and medical technology. Both Gallaudet and NTID are supported by the federal government, and each enrolls approximately 1,500 students who are deaf or hard of hearing.

More than 100 other institutions of higher education have developed accredited programs specifically for students with hearing loss (King, DeCaro, Karchmer, & Cole, 2001). Among these are regional postsecondary programs that enroll substantial numbers of students with hearing loss: St. Paul (Minnesota) College, Seattle (Washington) Central Community College, the University of Tennessee, and California State University at Northridge.

▼ TIPS FOR BEGINNING TEACHERS

Taking Advantage of Resources in School and Community

BY DOUGLAS JACKSON

VISUALIZE, INTERNALIZE, REFLECT

As teachers, we are responsible for covering a variety of academic courses using spoken and signed language; for addressing the auditory, speech, and other needs of our students; and for documenting our efforts on IEPs thicker than some metropolitan phone books. With all of this in mind, our task becomes how to do all of this effectively and successfully.

- Visualize what you want to accomplish and how you want to accomplish it. Imagine the obstacles in your way (time and resource limitations, red tape, etc.) and how you can overcome them (collaboration, grants, activities).
- When you learn new skills or information, whether they are new signs or Visual Phonics or high-tech resources, internalize the new skills and information so that they are entwined with your personality, sensibilities, and particular gifts as an educator.
- Take time to reflect. Think about what worked, what didn't, what you could do differently in the future, and what's next.

KNOCK DOWN THE CLASSROOM WALLS

We are never more powerful than when we realize not only our strengths but also our weaknesses. That is particularly true now when we try to counter great challenges with the new resources available to us.

- Use your resources. There are dozens of people in your school who can do things that you can't do and who know things that you don't know. Their skills and knowledge can benefit both you and your students.
- Communicate and collaborate with your peers. You can begin to foster this communication and collaboration by sharing your ideas and materials. Everyone has a different perspective that can be helpful in difficult situations in the classroom with students or outside the classroom with parents.

KNOCK DOWN THE SCHOOL WALLS

Beyond your school walls are doctors, lawyers, artists, business owners, police officers, and civic and government leaders. These professionals can teach your students things they cannot always learn in a classroom. Some may be the parents of your students.

- Create partnerships. Identify professionals who are willing to become potential partners with your class by sharing their time, skills, and knowledge—or those who are interested in mentoring specific students. In this way you can become an educational bridge between your students and these professionals.
- Design activities (simulations, presentations, art, drama, etc.) to maximize the impact of these work-world opportunities. Ask your professional partners for any feedback and input.

PICK YOUR BATTLES

As educators we are surrounded by situations crying out for change, challenges we feel compelled to take on but battles we can't always fight simultaneously. Pick the battles that are most important, and devote your energy, creativity, and passion to them.

- Choose initiatives that make your school a better place for your students. Hold off (for now) on those that don't seem to have a clear outcome or impact.
- Create opportunities in your class to infuse the curriculum with hands-on, meaningful lessons that connect with your students.
- Develop a list of the goals, behaviors, and values that are important to you as an educator. This will ultimately help you decide which battles to pick when they all seem worth fighting.

ENJOY THE RIDE

Sometimes I find myself walking down the hall of my school, obsessing about this meeting or that bit of paperwork or whatever the slings and arrows of outrageous bureaucracy happen to be that day. I will look up and see a small child walking down the hall, wide-eyed with the many possibilities of educational discovery in front of her, a voyage that she might feel is as important as those of Columbus, Isaac Newton, and Neil Armstrong. And, of course, she is absolutely right. When I see this look of wonder, I realize that we teachers have the coolest job in the world. We are eyewitnesses for many amazing voyages of discovery.

▼ KEY TERMS AND CONCEPTS

acquired
American Sign Language (ASL)
audiogram
audiometer
audiometric zero
audition
auditory canal (external acoustic meatus)
auditory training
auricle
behavior observation audiometry
bilingual-bicultural (bi-bi) approach
cochlea
cochlear implant
conductive hearing impairment
congenital
cued speech
cytomegalovirus (CMV)
Deaf culture
deafness

decibels (dB)
fingerspelling
hard of hearing
hearing loss
hertz (Hz)
neural hearing impairment
operant conditioning audiometry
ossicles
otitis media
play audiometry
postlingual hearing loss
prelingual hearing loss
residual hearing
sensory hearing impairment
speech reception threshold (SRT)
speechreading
total communication
tympanic membrane

▼ SUMMARY

Definitions

- Hearing loss exists on a continuum from mild to profound, and most special educators distinguish between children who are deaf and those who are hard of hearing. A deaf child cannot understand speech through the ears alone. A hard-of-hearing child can use hearing to understand speech, generally with the help of a hearing aid.
- Many Deaf people do not view hearing loss as a disability. Like other cultural groups, members of the Deaf community share a common language (ASL) and social practices.
- Sound is measured by its intensity (decibels [dB]) and frequency (Hertz [Hz]); both dimensions are important in considering the special education needs of a child with a hearing loss. The frequencies most important for understanding speech are 500 to 2,000 Hz.

Characteristics

- Deaf children—especially those with a prelingual hearing loss of 90 dB or greater—are at a great disadvantage in acquiring English literacy skills, especially reading and writing.
- The speech of many children with hearing loss may be difficult to understand because they omit speech sounds they cannot hear, speak too loudly or softly, speak in an abnormally high pitch, speak with poor inflection, and/or speak at an improper rate.
- As a group, students who are deaf and hard of hearing lag far behind their hearing peers in academic achievement, and the achievement gap usually widens as they get older.
- Children with severe to profound hearing losses often report feeling isolated and unhappy in school, particularly when their socialization with other children with hearing loss is limited.
- Many deaf individuals choose membership in the Deaf community and culture.

Prevalence

- Students with hearing loss represent about 1.2% of all school-age students receiving special education.

Types and Causes of Hearing loss

- Hearing loss is described as conductive (outer or middle ear) or sensorineural (inner ear) and unilateral (in one ear) or bilateral (in both ears).
- A prelingual hearing loss occurs before the child has developed speech and language; a postlingual hearing loss occurs after that time.
- Causes of congenital hearing loss include genetic factors, maternal rubella, heredity, congenital cytomegalovirus (CMV), and prematurity.

- Causes of acquired hearing loss include otitis media, meningitis, Ménière's disease, and noise exposure.

Identification and Assessment

- Auditory brain-stem response and otoacoustic emission are two methods of screening for hearing loss in infants.
- A formal hearing test generates an audiogram, which graphically shows the intensity of the faintest sound an individual can hear 50% of the time at various frequencies.
- Hearing loss is classified as slight, mild, moderate, severe, or profound, depending on the degree of hearing loss.

Technologies and Supports

- Technologies that amplify or provide sound include hearing aids, assistive listening devices, and cochlear implants.
- Technologies and supports that supplement or replace sound include educational interpreters, speech-to-text translation, television captioning, text telephones, and alerting devices.

Educational Approaches

- The oral/aural approach views speech as essential if students are to function in the hearing world; much emphasis is given to amplification, auditory training, speechreading, the use of technological aids, and, above all, talking.
- Total communication uses speech and simultaneous manual communication via signs and fingerspelling in English word order.
- In the bilingual-bicultural approach, deafness is viewed as a cultural and linguistic difference, not a disability, and American Sign Language (ASL) is used as the language of instruction.

Educational Placement Alternatives

- About half of all students who are deaf or hard of hearing are educated in regular classrooms; of the others, approximately 17% attend resource rooms, 16% are served in separate classrooms, 8% go to special schools, and 4% attend residential programs.
- All of the professional and parent organizations involved in deaf education have issued position statements strongly in favor of maintaining a continuum of placement options.
- Access to the language and communication modality best suited to their individual needs and preferences, effective instruction with meaningful curriculum, and self-advocacy are the keys to improving the future for people who are deaf or hard of hearing.

MyEducationLab™

Go to Topic 16, Sensory Impairment, in the MyEducationLab (www.myeducationlab.com) for *Exceptional Children*, where you can

- Find learning outcomes for sensory impairment along with the national standards that connect to these outcomes.
- Complete Assignments and Activities that can help you more deeply understand the chapter content.
- Apply and practice your understanding of the core teaching skills identified in the chapter with the Building Teaching Skills and Dispositions learning units.
- Examine challenging situations and cases presented in the IRIS Center Resources.
- Access video clips of CCSSO National Teachers of the Year award winners responding to the question "Why do I teach?" in the Teacher Talk section.
- Check your comprehension of the content covered in the chapter with the Study Plan. Here you will be able to take a chapter quiz, receive feedback on your answers, and then access Review, Practice, and Enrichment activities to enhance your understanding of chapter content.
- Use the Online Lesson Plan Builder to practice lesson planning and integrating national and state standards into your planning.

▼ GLOSSARY

acquired (condition or disability): A disability or condition that develops at any time after birth, from disease, trauma, or any other cause; contrast with *congenital*.

American Sign Language (ASL): A visual-gestural language with its own rules of syntax, semantics, and pragmatics; does not correspond to written or spoken English. ASL is the language of the Deaf culture in the United States and Canada.

audiogram: A graph of the faintest level of sound a person can hear in each ear at least 50% of the time at each of several frequencies, including the entire frequency range of normal speech.

audiometer: A device that generates sounds at specific frequencies and intensities; used to examine hearing.

audiometric zero: The smallest sound a person with normal hearing can perceive; also called the *zero hearing-threshold level (HTL)*.

audition: The act or sense of hearing.

auditory canal (external acoustic meatus): The part of the ear that slightly amplifies and transports sound waves from the external ear to the middle ear.

auditory training: A program that works on listening skills by teaching individuals with hearing impairments to make as much use as possible of their residual hearing.

auricle: The external part of the ear; collects sound waves into the auditory canal.

behavior observation audiometry: A method of hearing assessment in which an infant's reactions to sounds are observed; a sound is presented at an increasing level of intensity until a response, such as head turning, eye blinking, or cessation of play, is reliably observed.

bilingual-bicultural (bi-bi) approach: An approach to teaching students who are deaf in which American Sign Language (ASL) is used as the child's native language and

English is taught as a second language; also stresses teaching of Deaf culture.

cochlea: Main receptor organ for hearing located in the inner ear; tiny hairs within the cochlea transform mechanical energy into neural impulses that then travel through the auditory nerve to the brain.

cochlear implant: A surgically implanted device that converts sound from the environment into electric impulses that are sent directly to the brain via the auditory nerve. Enables some people who are deaf to achieve a useful auditory understanding of the environment and to understand speech.

conductive hearing loss: Hearing loss caused by obstructions in the outer or middle ear or malformations that interfere with the conduction of sound waves to the inner ear. Can often be corrected surgically or medically.

congenital: Any condition that is present at birth (contrasts with *adventitious*).

cued speech: A method of supplementing oral communication by adding cues in the form of eight different hand signals in four different locations near the chin.

cytomegalovirus (CMV): A common virus that infects most people worldwide; can remain alive but dormant in the body for life; usually harmless, but in a very small percentage of children infected at birth, CMV may later develop and lead to various conditions, including mental retardation, visual impairment, and, most often, hearing impairment.

Deaf culture: Shared language (in the United States, American Sign Language [ASL]), social practices, literature, and beliefs of the Deaf community; members do not view deafness as a disability.

deafness: See *deaf*.

decibel (dB): The unit of measure for the relative intensity of sound on a logarithmic

scale beginning at zero. Zero decibels refers to the faintest sound a person with normal hearing can detect.

fingerspelling: The manual alphabet used to spell out proper names for which no signs exist and to clarify meanings; an integral part of American Sign Language (ASL).

hard of hearing: A level of hearing loss that makes it difficult, although not impossible, to comprehend speech through the sense of hearing alone.

hearing loss: As defined in IDEA is "a loss in hearing, whether permanent or fluctuating, that adversely affects a child's education performance but that is not included under the definition of deafness in this section." Because it suggests a deficiency or pathology, many members of the Deaf community consider *hearing loss* an inappropriate and demeaning term.

hertz (Hz): A unit of sound frequency equal to one cycle per second; used to measure pitch.

neural hearing impairment: Hearing impairment attributed to abnormality or failure of the auditory nerve pathway.

operant conditioning audiometry: A method of measuring hearing by teaching the individual to make an observable response to sound. For example, a child may be taught to drop a block into a box each time a light and a loud tone are presented. Once this response is learned, the light is no longer presented and the volume and pitch of the tone are gradually decreased. When the child no longer drops the block into the box, the audiologist knows the child cannot hear the tone. Sometimes used to test the hearing of nonverbal children and adults.

ossicles: Three small bones (hammer, anvil, and stirrup) that transmit sound energy from the middle ear to the inner ear.

otitis media: An infection or inflammation of the middle ear that can cause a conductive hearing loss.

play audiometry: A method for assessing a child's hearing ability by teaching the child to perform simple but distinct activities, such as picking up a toy or putting a ball into a cup whenever he hears the signal, either pure tones or speech.

postlingual hearing loss: Occurring after the development of language; usually used to classify hearing losses that begin after a person has learned to speak.

prelingual hearing loss: Describes a hearing impairment acquired before the development of speech and language.

residual hearing: The remaining hearing, however slight, of a person who is deaf.

sensory hearing impairment: Hearing impairment that entails damage to the cochlea.

speech reception threshold (SRT): The decibel (sound-volume) level at which an individual can understand half of the words during a speech audiometry test; the SRT is measured and recorded for each ear.

speechreading: A process of understanding a spoken message by observing the speaker's lips in combination with information gained from facial expressions, gestures, and the context or situation.

total communication: An approach to educating deaf students that combines oral speech, sign language, and fingerspelling.

tympanic membrane (eardrum): Located in the middle ear, the eardrum moves in and out to variations in sound pressure, changing acoustical energy to sound energy.

Physical Disabilities, Health Impairments, and ADHD

From Chapter 11 of *Exceptional Children* and *An Introduction to Special Education*, Tenth Edition. William L. Heward.

Physical Disabilities, Health Impairments, and ADHD

Katelyn Metzger/Merrill

▶ FOCUS QUESTIONS

- How might the effects of an acute health condition on a student's classroom participation and educational progress differ from those due to a chronic condition?

- Why is the prevalence of chronic medical conditions in children much higher than the number of students receiving special education under the disability categories of orthopedic impairments and other health impairments?

- What does a classroom teacher need to know about physical disabilities and health impairments in children?

- Why do you think attention-deficit/hyperactivity disorder (ADHD) is not included as a separate disability category in IDEA?

- How might the visibility of a physical disability or health impairment affect a child's self-perception, social development, and level of independence across different environments?

- What are some of the problems that members of transdisciplinary teams for students with physical disabilities and multiple health needs must guard against?

- Of the many ways that the physical environment, social environment, and instruction can be modified to support the inclusion of students with physical disabilities, health impairments, and ADHD, which are most important?

▼ FEATURED TEACHER

CAROL MOSS

Colerain Elementary School • Columbus, Ohio

EDUCATION—TEACHING CREDENTIALS—EXPERIENCE

- B.S., Home Economics, Family and Child Development, The Ohio State University, 1975
- M.Ed., Education of students with exceptional needs, The Ohio State University, 1989
- Ohio, Orthopedic Handicaps, K–12 and Pre-K certification
- National Board Certification, Early Childhood Generalist, 1997
- 7 years community day care and Head Start teacher
- 28 years as a special education teacher

MY SCHOOL AND STUDENTS Colerain Elementary is a K–5 public school that serves children without disabilities from the surrounding neighborhood and children with significant physical disabilities and health care needs from the Columbus public and nearby school districts. Our school includes many architectural design elements and a staff to enable us to educate children in an inclusive neighborhood school setting. The playground, for example, was designed with ramps for wheelchair and walker accessibility and extra handholds and pads for additional stability and safety.

I teach second graders, ages 8 and 9 years old, who receive special education and related services under the disability categories of orthopedic impairments, other health impairments, and multiple disabilities. Let me introduce four of my students.

Carson's athetoid cerebral palsy makes all of his movements, especially efforts at fine motor control, very shaky. Before coming to Colerain, Carson attended a county program for preschoolers with intellectual and developmental disabilities. He depends a lot on primitive reflexes and has developed compensatory strategies that allow him to function in the school environment. When speaking, he places his chin against his right shoulder to help stabilize his head and enable improved voice output. When sitting, Carson stabilizes his head by placing his elbow on the desk and resting his chin in his hand. Minimizing his head-bobbing also positively influences his social acceptance by others.

Pamela has sickle-cell anemia, which requires pain medicine, affects her vision, and sometimes makes her fatigued and feverish. Pamela also has cerebral palsy that affects her balance. She must be careful that she doesn't fall and strike her head. Pamela often gets deeply involved in an activity and often is reluctant to transition to the next thing on her schedule. The other day when the speech therapist came in the room Pamela shouted, "You barged in! I'm reading now," refused to join the speech-therapy group, and started tantruming. A behavior intervention plan, which entails ignoring Pamela's resistance and provides her with positive attention when she does or says the first appropriate thing, is helping her transition better.

When he was born at 27 weeks gestation, Norrece weighed just 2 pounds. He contracted pneumonia at 3 months of age and suffered permanent brain injury when the ventilator that was helping him breathe was accidentally turned off. Norrece also has cerebral palsy. He uses a wheelchair and takes medication to control seizures. Large-print materials with distinctive figure-ground contrast help compensate for his visual impairment. When Norrece arrives at school in the morning, school staff help him switch from his manual wheelchair to an electric powered chair he's learning to drive. He loves the power chair and smiles broadly when motoring it around the classroom and school. He doesn't like it when adults provide hand-over-hand prompts on his joystick to help him steer through crowded situations such as assemblies and the lunchroom, but his driving skills are improving.

Bethany has Joubert syndrome, a rare brain malformation characterized by the absence or underdevelopment of the part of the brain that controls coordination and balance. Common features of Joubert syndrome include abnormally rapid breathing (hyperpnea), decreased muscle tone (hypotonia), jerky eye movements, cognitive disability, and the inability to coordinate her voluntary muscle movements (ataxia). Bethany must lie flat to drink fluids to prevent the liquid from entering her lungs.

The physical and health challenges of these students can lead people to think they are extremely fragile and that working with them might be depressing. Nothing could be further from the truth. The children are vibrant, active, and very interested in their world. Carson's favorite book is *Winter's Tail,* the true story of a dolphin with a prosthetic tail. Pamela and Bethany are huge fans of Pinkalicious, a fun character in books by Victoria and Elizabeth Kann. Anything at all having to do with trucks makes Norrece excited and ready to engage and learn.

ALTERNATIVE MEANS OF RESPONDING My students spend part of each school day in their general education homeroom and part in my classroom. A real key to an effective lesson, in any classroom setting they are in, is providing an alternative means for each student to participate and demonstrate his or her knowledge. Computer access is a good example: Carson responds to questions generated by a math software program by depressing a big red button; he can't manipulate a mouse, but a joystick wrapped in a heavy sock works just fine. Norrece uses a touch screen with enlarged icons. Standing up makes it easier for Carson to point to his choices or answers, a fine motor movement that's nearly impossible for him while sitting.

All of my students love engaging with and learning on the iPad. Some of the apps my students are benefiting from are Flash to Pass, ABC Phonics, and Jumpstart Preschool. Norrece loves Starfall, and Carson likes Pocket Frogs. Carson curls up on the floor with the iPad resting on his legs and uses his thumbs to work with it. A good source of iPad apps is the Ohio Center for Autism and Low Incidence (http://www.ocali.org/up_archive_doc/Apps_Designed_with_Disability_in_Mind.pdf).

Accommodations and adaptations for my students when they take district- and statewide assessments include but are not limited to slant boards, extra time, small-group setting, frequent breaks, readers, scribes, and adapted keyboards.

INSTRUCTIONAL PRACTICES I am a big believer in hands-on, project-based learning activities that integrate objectives across the curriculum. For example, during social studies recently, my students created city and farm environments using materials such as milk cartons, pipe cleaners, Play-Doh, clay, and foam, along with two large boxes with one side cut out. Students worked on reading, writing, language arts, and math objectives by naming, labeling, counting, and classifying the buildings, places, people, and animals.

When observing students with significant physical disabilities and health impairments doing such activities, it's often apparent how much their orthopedic and health conditions have limited their opportunities to experience the everyday world in ways that we take for granted. For example, I recently asked students to name things you might expect to see in a garden. They came up with words such as *plants*, *flowers*, *bugs* and *dirt*, but little else. I showed them a basket of small potatoes from my garden and asked what was in it. Two students said rocks, one of whom continued to call a potato a rock even after holding it.

Potatoes played a central role in a series of related lessons over the next 2 days. The students cleaned and then cooked potatoes from my garden in an occupational therapy group lesson. They tried several types of potato peelers; all were too difficult for children with physical challenges. So as a group we decided to leave the skins on and discussed how eating the skins is a healthier option anyway.

We C-clamped an old-fashioned French fry cutter onto the table, and the students pushed down the handle and sent the small potatoes through the cutter. We also cut up some potatoes and boiled them. When summarizing the activity, students discussed which way of cooking and eating potatoes they liked the best. Science and math objectives were integrated by observing changing matter as the potatoes cooked and observing and counting the potatoes' "eyes" using math concepts and terms such as *part/whole*, *half/fourths*, and so on. The next day the students' regular classroom teacher selected a nonfiction book about potatoes, and the students made potato prints (potatoes were cut into the stamp of a house), and they stamped house prints on a map of their community.

Our school is focused on academic excellence; however, our students also need life skills. Lately we have been fortunate to participate in LifeTown field trips in the community, teaching our students to effectively navigate in real-life situations. LifeTown includes mock but realistic stores and environments such as a deli, library, movie theater, and bank where children learn to order and pay for items and learn the social skills expected in those settings. (To learn about LifeTown's programs, go to http://www .lifetowncolumbus.org/.)

TOGETHER WE CAN Parents and families are the ones who help me the most. By the time these children are in second grade, their parents are very realistic. They understand their children have lifelong disabiities and aren't expecting a teacher to perform miracles. They are pragmatic and want me to help their children acquire practical skills that will positively affect their quality of life. I strive to teach the skills they see as most important. I work closely with all faculty members, including the school psychologist, school nurses, PTs, OTs, and speech-language pathologists. The principal, assistant principal, and social worker are key players as well. Each of us holds a "thread," and I play a vital role in helping weave all the threads together as we strive to provide the best education for each individual student.

To meet Carol Moss and some of her students and colleagues and go on a video tour of Colerain Elementary School led by the principal, go to the book resources for this text on MyEducationLab.

MyEducationLab™

Visit the **MyEducationLab** for *Exceptional Children* to enhance your understanding of chapter concepts with a personalized Study Plan. You'll also have the opportunity to hone your teaching skills through video- and case-based Assignments and Activities, IRIS Center Resources, and Building Teaching Skills and Dispositions lessons

CHILDREN WITH PHYSICAL DISABILITIES AND HEALTH IMPAIRMENTS are an extremely varied population. Their physical disabilities may be mild, moderate, or severe. Some children with special health care needs are extremely restricted in their activities and intellectual functioning; others have no major limitations on what they can do and learn. Some appear no different than the typical child; others have highly visible impairments or health conditions. Children may have a single impairment or a combination of disabilities. They may have lived with the physical disability or health impairment since birth or have acquired it recently. Some children must use special assistive devices that call attention to their disability; others display behaviors they cannot control. Some disabilities are always present; others occur only from time to time. Over an extended period, the degree of disability may increase, decrease, or remain about the same.

Natalie has undergone long periods of hospitalization and finds it difficult to keep up with her academic work. Gary takes medication that controls his seizures most of the time, but it also tends to make him drowsy in class. Janella tires easily and attends school for only 3 hours per day. Ken does his schoolwork in a specially designed chair that helps him sit more comfortably in the classroom.

As you can see, the students whose special education needs we consider in this chapter have a great many individual differences. Although general statements about some physical disabilities and health conditions are appropriate, a host of variables determine the effects on the child and his educational needs. These variables include the degree and severity of the impairment, age of onset, and environmental context. Thus, general information and suggested guidelines form the basic content of this chapter.

DEFINITIONS OF PHYSICAL DISABILITIES AND HEALTH IMPAIRMENTS

Definitions of orthopedic impairments and other health impairments

 Council for Exceptional Children Content Standards for Beginning Teachers—P&HD: Issues and educational definitions of individuals with P&HD (PH1K1).

Children with physical disabilities and health conditions who require special education are served under two of the disability categories of the Individuals with Disabilities Education Act (IDEA) disability categories: orthopedic impairments and other health impairments. According to IDEA, a

> severe orthopedic impairment adversely affects a child's educational performance. The term includes impairments caused by a congenital anomaly (e.g., clubfoot, absence of some member, etc.), impairments caused by disease (e.g., poliomyelitis, bone tuberculosis), and impairments from other causes (e.g., cerebral palsy, amputations, and fractures or burns that cause contractures). (20 USC §1401 [2004], 20 *CFR* §300.8[c][8])

Although IDEA uses the term *orthopedic impairment,* children with physical disabilities may have orthopedic impairments or neuromotor impairments. An **orthopedic impairment** involves the skeletal system—bones, joints, limbs, and associated muscles. A **neuromotor impairment** involves the central nervous system, affecting the ability to move, use, feel, or control certain parts of the body. Although orthopedic and neuromotor impairments are two distinct and separate types of disabilities, they may cause similar limitations in movement. Many of the same educational, therapeutic, and recreational activities are appropriate for students with orthopedic and neuromotor impairments (Best, Heller, & Bigge, 2010). And a close relationship exists between the two types: for example, a child who cannot move his legs because of damage to the central nervous system (neuromotor impairment) may develop disorders in the bones and muscles of the legs (orthopedic impairment), especially if he does not receive proper therapy and equipment.

Health impairments include diseases and special health conditions that affect a child's educational activities and performance such as cancer, diabetes, and cystic fibrosis. According to IDEA

> **Other health impairment** means having limited strength, vitality, or alertness, including a heightened alertness to environmental stimuli, that results in limited alertness with respect to the educational environment, that—
>
> (i) Is due to chronic or acute health problems such as asthma, attention deficit disorder or attention deficit hyperactivity disorder, diabetes, epilepsy, a heart condition, hemophilia, lead poisoning, leukemia, nephritis, rheumatic fever, sickle cell anemia, and Tourette syndrome; and
> (ii) Adversely affects academic performance. (20 USC §1401 [2004], 20 *CFR* §300.8[c][9])

Children with attention-deficit/hyperactivity disorder (ADHD) may be served under the other health impairments category of IDEA, with the reasoning that their condition results in a heightened alertness that adversely affects their educational performance. However, many children with ADHD who meet eligibility requirements for special education are served under other disability categories, most often emotional disturbance or learning disabilities. ADHD is discussed later in this chapter.

Note in each IDEA definition the common clause: *that adversely affects a child's educational performance.* A child is entitled to special education services if her educational performance is adversely affected by a physical disability or a health-related condition. Physical disabilities and health conditions may be congenital (e.g., a child is born with a missing limb) or acquired (a child without disabilities sustains a spinal cord injury at age 15). Not all students with physical disabilities and health conditions need special education. Most physical disabilities and health impairments that result in special education are **chronic conditions**—that is, they are long-lasting and most often permanent (e.g., cerebral palsy is a permanent disability that will affect a child throughout his life). By contrast, an **acute condition,** while it may produce severe and debilitating symptoms, is of limited duration (e.g., a child with pneumonia will experience symptoms, but the disease itself is not permanent). Some children with chronic physical disabilities and health conditions experience flare-ups or episodes of acute symptoms (e.g., a child with cystic fibrosis may experience periods of acute respiratory difficulties).

PREVALENCE

Studies of the number of children with physical disabilities and health impairments have produced hugely diverse findings. One review of prevalence studies found estimates of chronic health conditions in childhood ranging from as low as 0.22% to as high as 44%, depending on the researchers' concepts and definitions (van der Lee, Mokkink, Grootenhuis, Heymans, & Offringa, 2007). In the middle of that range is Sexson and Dingle's (2001) estimate that chronic medical conditions affect up to 20% (approximately 12 million) of school-age children in the United States. Whatever the actual number, researchers widely accept that the incidence of chronic health conditions has increased considerably in recent decades. In 1960, data showed that just 1.8% of American children and adolescents had a chronic health condition that limited their activities, compared to 7% in 2004 (Perrin, Bloom, & Gortmaker, 2007).

Clearly, a great many children's lives are affected by physical disabilities and health impairments. During the 2009–10 school year, however, only 57,930 children between the ages of 6 and 21 received special education services under the disability category of orthopedic impairment compared with 678,970 children served under the category of other health impairments (U.S. Department of Education, 2011). These two disability categories represent 1% and 11.6% of all school-age children receiving special education services, respectively.

Two factors make the actual number of children with physical disabilities and health conditions much higher than the number of children receiving special education services under these two IDEA categories. First, numerous children have chronic health conditions or physical impairments that do not adversely affect their educational performance sufficiently to warrant special education (Hill, 1999). Second, because physical and health impairments often occur in combination with other disabilities, children may be counted under other categories, such as multiple disabilities, speech impairment, or intellectual disabilities. For example, for the purpose of special education eligibility, a diagnosis of intellectual disabilities often takes precedence over a diagnosis of physical impairment.

TYPES AND CAUSES

Literally hundreds of physical impairments and health conditions can adversely affect children's educational performance. Here we address only those that are encountered most frequently in school-age children.

Chronic and acute conditions

Content Standards for Beginning Teachers—P&HD: Medical terminology related to P&HD (PH2K4).

Types and causes of physical disabilities and health impairments

Content Standards for Beginning Teachers—P&HD: Etiology and characteristics of P&HD across the life span (PH2K1) (also PH2K2).

For a more extensive discussion of the many physical impairments and chronic health conditions that may result in the need for special education, see Batshaw, Pellegrino, and Roizen (2007) or Best et al. (2010).

Cerebral Palsy

Cerebral palsy—a disorder of voluntary movement and posture—is the most prevalent physical disability in school-age children. Cerebral palsy is a permanent condition resulting from a lesion to the brain or an abnormality of brain growth. Many diseases can affect the developing brain and lead to cerebral palsy (Batshaw et al., 2007). Children with cerebral palsy experience disturbances of voluntary motor functions that may include paralysis, extreme weakness, lack of coordination, involuntary convulsions, and other motor disorders. They may have little or no control over their arms, legs, or speech, depending on the type and degree of impairment. More severe forms of cerebral palsy are often diagnosed in the first few months of life. In many cases, however, cerebral palsy is not detected until the child is 2 to 3 years old, when parents notice that their child is having difficulty balancing or standing. The motor dysfunction usually does not get progressively worse as a child ages. Cerebral palsy can be treated but not cured; it is not a disease, not fatal, not contagious, and, in the great majority of cases, not inherited.

Between 23% and 44% of children with cerebral palsy have cognitive impairments, ranging from mild to severe intellectual disabilities (Odding, Roebroeck, & Stam, 2006). Sensory impairments are also common in children with cerebral palsy; 5% to 15% have hearing loss (Nehring, 2010), and 60% to 70% have impaired vision, particularly strabismus (Odding et al.). No clear relationship exists between the degree of motor impairment and the degree of intellectual impairment (if any) in children with cerebral palsy (or other physical disabilities). A student with mild motor impairment may experience severe developmental delays, whereas a student with severe motor impairments may be intellectually gifted (Willard-Holt, 1998).

The causes of cerebral palsy are varied and not clearly known (Pellegrino, 2007). It has most often been attributed to the occurrence of injuries, accidents, or illnesses that are *prenatal* (before birth), *perinatal* (at or near the time of birth), or *postnatal* (soon after birth) and that result in decreased oxygen to low-birth-weight newborns. Recent improvements in obstetrical delivery and neonatal care, however, have not changed the incidence of cerebral palsy, which has remained at about 2 per 1,000 live births for more than 40 years (NICHCY, 2010a). Factors most often associated with cerebral palsy are intellectual disabilities of the mother, premature birth (gestational age of 32 weeks or less), low birth weight, and a delay of 5 minutes or more before the baby's first cry.

Because the location and extent of brain damage are so variable in individuals with cerebral palsy, a diagnosis of the condition is not descriptive of its effects. Cerebral palsy is classified in terms of the affected parts of the body and by the nature of its effects on muscle tone and movement (Best & Bigge, 2010). The term *plegia* (from the Greek "to strike") is used in combination with a prefix indicating the location of limb involvement:

- *Monoplegia*—only one limb (upper or lower) is affected.
- *Hemiplegia*—two limbs on same side of the body are involved.
- *Triplegia*—three limbs are affected.
- *Quadriplegia*—all four limbs (both arms and legs) are involved; movement of the trunk and face may also be impaired.
- *Paraplegia*—only legs are impaired.
- *Diplegia*—impairment primarily involves the legs, with less severe involvement of the arms.
- *Double hemiplegia*—impairment primarily involves the arms, with less severe involvement of the legs.

Cerebral palsy is defined according to its effects on muscle tone (hypertonia or hypotonia) and quality of movement (athetosis or ataxia) (Pellegrino, 2007). Approximately 50% to 60% of all individuals with cerebral palsy have *spastic cerebral palsy,* which is characterized by tense, contracted muscles (**hypertonia**). Their movements

Limbs affected by cerebral palsy

Content Standards for Beginning Teachers—P&HD: Medical terminology related to P&HD (PH2K4).

Hypertonia, athetosis, ataxia, and hypotonia

Content Standards for Beginning Teachers—P&HD: Medical terminology related to P&HD (PH2K4) (also PH2K2, PH3K1, ICC2K1).

may be jerky, exaggerated, and poorly coordinated. They may be unable to grasp objects with their fingers. When they try to control their movements, they may become even jerkier. If they can walk, they may use a scissors gait, standing on the toes with knees bent and pointed inward. Deformities of the spine, hip dislocation, and contractures of the hand, elbow, foot, and knee are common.

Athetosis occurs in about 20% of all cases of cerebral palsy. Children with *athetoid cerebral palsy* make large, irregular, twisting movements they cannot control. When they are at rest or asleep, little or no abnormal motion occurs. An effort to pick up a pencil, however, may result in wildly waving arms, facial grimaces, and extension of the tongue. These children may not be able to control the muscles of their lips, tongue, and throat and may drool. They may also seem to stumble and lurch awkwardly as they walk. At times their muscles may be tense and rigid; at other times, they may be loose and flaccid. Extreme difficulty in expressive oral language, mobility, and activities of daily living often accompanies this form of cerebral palsy.

Ataxia is the primary type of involvement in 1% to 10% of cases of cerebral palsy (Hill, 1999). Children with *ataxic cerebral palsy* have a poor sense of balance and hand use. They may appear to be dizzy while walking and may fall if not supported. Their movements tend to be jumpy and unsteady, with exaggerated motion patterns that often overshoot the intended objects. They seem to be constantly attempting to overcome the effect of gravity and stabilize their bodies.

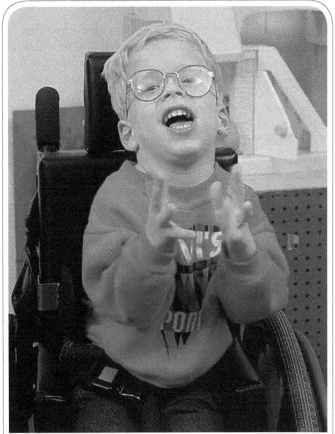

Although cerebral palsy affects Joey's control over his movements, it has not dampened his enthusiasm and determination for learning.

Scott Cunningham/Merrill

Rigidity and *tremor* are additional but much less common types of cerebral palsy. Children with the rare rigidity type of cerebral palsy display extreme stiffness in the affected limbs; they may be fixed and immobile for long periods. Rhythmic, uncontrollable movements mark tremor cerebral palsy; the tremors may actually increase when the children attempt to control their actions. Because most children with cerebral palsy have diffuse brain damage, pure types of cerebral palsy are rare. Children may be described as having *mixed cerebral palsy,* consisting of more than one of these types, particularly if their impairments are severe.

Most infants born with cerebral palsy have **hypotonia,** or weak, floppy muscles, particularly in the neck and trunk. When hypotonia persists throughout the child's first year without being replaced with spasticity or athetoid involvement, the condition is called *generalized hypotonia.* Hypotonic children typically have low levels of motor activity, are slow to make balancing responses, and may not walk until 30 months of age. Severely hypotonic children must use external support to achieve and maintain an upright position.

Cerebral palsy is a complex condition that is most effectively managed through the cooperative involvement of physicians, teachers, physical therapists, occupational therapists, communication specialists, counselors, and others who work directly with children and families. Regular exercise and careful positioning in school settings help the child with cerebral palsy move as fully and comfortably as possible and prevent or minimize progressive damage to muscles and limbs. Most children with cerebral palsy can learn to walk, although many need to use wheelchairs, braces, and other assistive devices, particularly for moving around outside the home. Orthopedic surgery may increase a child's range of motion or obviate complications such as hip dislocations and permanent muscle contractions.

Dormans and Pellegrino (1998) have compiled a handbook to guide the education of children with cerebral palsy by interdisciplinary teams. Bower (2009) details procedures for supporting the young child with cerebral palsy at home.

Spina Bifida

Spina bifida and related terms

Council for Exceptional Children

Content Standards for Beginning Teachers—P&HD: Medical terminology related to P&HD (PH2K4) (also PH2K2, PH3K1).

Congenital malformations of the brain, spinal cord, or vertebrae are known as *neural tube defects.* The most common neural tube defect is **spina bifida,** a condition in which the vertebrae do not enclose the spinal cord. As a result, a portion of the spinal cord and the nerves that control muscles and feeling in the lower part of the body fail to develop normally. Of the three types of spina bifida, the mildest form is **spina bifida occulta,** in which only a few vertebrae are malformed, usually in the lower spine. The defect is usually not visible externally. Approximately 40% of Americans may have spina bifida occulta, but because they experience few or no symptoms, very few ever know that they have it (NICHCY, 2004). If the flexible casing (meninges) that surrounds the spinal cord bulges through an opening in the infant's back at birth, the condition is called **meningocele.** These two forms do not usually cause any loss of function for the child.

In **myelomeningocele**—the most common and most serious form of spina bifida— the spinal lining, spinal cord, and nerve roots all protrude. The protruding spinal cord and nerves are usually tucked back into the spinal column shortly after birth. This condition carries a high risk of paralysis and infection. In general, the higher the location of the lesion on the spine, the greater the effect on the body and its functioning. About 7 in 10,000 live births in the United States result in myelomeningocele; and it affects girls at a higher rate than boys (Spina Bifida Association, 2011).

About 70% to 90% of children born with myelomeningocele develop **hydrocephalus,** the accumulation of cerebrospinal fluid in tissues surrounding the brain (NICHCY, 2004). Left untreated, this condition can lead to head enlargement and severe brain damage. Hydrocephalus is treated by the surgical insertion of a **shunt,** a one-way valve that diverts the cerebrospinal fluid away from the brain and into the bloodstream. Replacements of the shunt are usually necessary as a child grows older. Teachers who work with children who have shunts should be aware that blockage, disconnection, or infection of the shunt may result in increased intracranial pressure. Warning signs such as drowsiness, vomiting, headache, irritability, seizures, and change in personality should be heeded because a blocked shunt can be life-threatening (Dias, 2003). Shunts can be removed in many school-age children when the production and absorption of cerebrospinal fluid are brought into balance.

Clean intermittent catheterization (CIC)

Council for Exceptional Children

Content Standards for Beginning Teachers—P&HD: Specialized health care interventions for individuals with P&HD (PH1K3). (also IIC5K1).

Spina bifida usually results in some degree of paralysis of the lower limbs. Most children with spina bifida have good use of their arms and upper body (although some children experience fine-motor problems). They usually walk with braces, crutches, or walkers; they may use wheelchairs for longer distances. Some children need help dressing and toileting; others manage these tasks on their own.

Because the spinal defect usually occurs above where nerves that control the bladder emerge from the spinal cord, most children with spina bifida have urinary incontinence and need to use a *catheter* (tube) or bag to collect their urine. Medical personnel teach **clean intermittent catheterization (CIC)** to children with urinary complications so that they can empty their bladders at convenient times (Rues, Graff, & Ault, 2011). CIC is effective with both boys and girls, works best if used every 2 to 4 hours, and does not require an absolutely sterile environment (McLone & Ito, 1998).

Scott Cunningham/Merrill

"I think the best part of the story was when . . ." Learning self-catheterization has given Kristine more control over her classroom schedule and increased her participation.

Muscular Dystrophy

Muscular dystrophy refers to a group of about 40 inherited diseases marked by progressive *atrophy* (wasting away) of the body's muscles. **Duchenne muscular dystrophy (DMD)** is the most common and most severe type. DMD affects only boys (1 in 3,500 male births), but about one-third of cases are the result of genetic mutation in families with no history of the disease (Best, 2010b). Muscle weakness is usually evident between the ages of 2 and 6, when the child begins to experience difficulty in running or climbing stairs. The child may walk with an unusual gait, showing a protruding stomach and hollow back. The calf muscles of a child with muscular dystrophy may appear unusually large because the degenerated muscle has been replaced by fatty tissue.

Children with muscular dystrophy often have difficulty getting to their feet after lying down or playing on the floor. They may fall easily. By age 10 to 14, the child loses the ability to walk; the small muscles of the hands and fingers are usually the last to be affected. Treatment focuses on maintaining function of unaffected muscles for as long as possible, facilitating ambulation, helping the child and the family cope with limitations imposed by the disease, and providing emotional support and counseling to the child and the family (Hill, 1999). Regular physical therapy, exercise, and the use of appropriate aids and appliances can maintain a good deal of independence. The child should be encouraged to be as active as possible. However, a teacher should be careful not to lift a child with muscular dystrophy by the arms: even a gentle pull may dislocate the child's limbs.

At this time, no known treatment exists to stop or reverse any form of muscular dystrophy. Although some cases may be mild and progress very slowly, enabling the person to live into adulthood with only moderate disability, muscular dystrophy is often fatal in adolescence or young adulthood (National Institutes of Neurological Disorders and Stroke, 2010). Death is often caused by heart failure or respiratory failure due to atrophied chest muscles.

> For discussions of how classroom teachers can help themselves, classmates, and parents deal with the death of a student, see Munson and Hunt (2005), Kreicbergs, et al. (2004), Rues et al. (2011), and Spinelli (2004).

Spinal Cord Injuries

Spinal cord injuries are usually the result of a lesion to the spinal cord caused by a penetrating injury (e.g., a gunshot wound), stretching of the vertebral column (e.g., whiplash during an auto accident), fracture of the vertebrae, or compression of the spinal cord (e.g., a diving accident). Motor vehicle accidents (41.3%), falls (27.3%), acts of violence (15%), and sports (7.9%) are the most common causes of spinal cord injuries (National Spinal Cord Injury Statistical Center, 2010). Injury to the spinal column is generally described by letters and numbers indicating the site of the damage; for example, a C5–6 injury means the damage has occurred at the level of the fifth and sixth cervical vertebrae, a flexible area of the neck susceptible to injury from whiplash and diving or trampoline accidents. A T12 injury refers to the 12th thoracic (chest) vertebra, and an L3 to the 3rd lumbar (lower back) area. In general, paralysis and loss of sensation occur below the level of the injury. The higher the injury on the spine and the more the injury (lesion) cuts through the entire cord, the greater the paralysis.

> Location and effects of spinal cord injuries

> Content Standards for Beginning Teachers—P&HD: Medical terminology related to P&HD (PH2K4).

Males represent 80% of the approximately 12,000 people in the United States who are victims of traumatic spinal cord injuries each year, and most are between 16 and 30 years old (National Spinal Cord Injury Statistical Center, 2010). Students who have sustained spinal cord injuries usually use wheelchairs for mobility. Motorized wheelchairs, though expensive, are recommended for those with **quadriplegia** (also called *tetraplegia*), whereas children with **paraplegia** can use self-propelled wheelchairs. Children with quadriplegia may have severe breathing problems because the muscles of the chest, which normally govern respiration, are affected. Most children with spinal cord injuries lack bladder and bowel control and need to follow a careful management program to maintain personal hygiene and avoid infection and skin irritation.

Rehabilitation programs for children and adolescents who have sustained spinal cord injuries usually involve physical therapy, the use of adaptive devices for mobility and independent living, and psychological support to help them adjust to a sudden disability. Personal care attendants (PCAs) assist many individuals with spinal cord injury with activities of daily living. Adolescents and adults are often particularly concerned about sexual function. Even though most spinal cord injuries do affect sexuality, with understanding partners and positive attitudes toward themselves, many people with spinal cord injuries enjoy satisfying sexual relationships (Byzek, 2001).

Epilepsy

Epilepsy and types of seizures

Council for Exceptional Children

Content Standards for Beginning Teachers—P&HD: Medical terminology related to P&HD (PH2K4) (also PH2K2, PH3K1).

Whether we are awake or asleep, electrical activity continually occurs in the brain. A *seizure* is a disturbance of movement, sensation, behavior, and/or consciousness caused by abnormal electrical discharges in the brain. "Some have likened the event, known as a seizure, to an engine misfiring or to a power surge in a computer" (Hill, 1999, p. 231). Anyone can have a seizure. It is common for a seizure to occur when someone has a high fever, drinks excessive alcohol, or experiences a blow to the head.

When seizures occur chronically and repeatedly, the condition is known as a *seizure disorder* or, more commonly, **epilepsy.** Epilepsy is not a disease, and it constitutes a disorder only while a seizure is actually in progress. It is estimated that 3% of the population is prone to seizures and about 3 million Americans have epilepsy (Goldman, 2006; NICHCY, 2010b).

The cause of epilepsy for approximately 30% of cases is identified from among at least 50 different conditions known to result in seizure activity, such as cerebral palsy; infections of the brain or central nervous system; metabolic disorders such as hypoglycemia, genetics, and alcohol or lead poisoning; an underlying lesion caused by scar tissue from a head injury; high fever; an interruption in blood supply to the brain; or rough handling of a baby (shaken-baby syndrome) (Lowenthal, 2001; Weinstein & Gaillard, 2007). Epilepsy can occur at any stage of life but most frequently begins in childhood. A wide variety of psychological, physical, and sensory factors can trigger seizures in susceptible people—for example, fatigue, excitement, anger, surprise, hyperventilation, hormonal changes (as in menstruation or pregnancy), withdrawal from drugs or alcohol, and exposure to certain patterns of light, sound, or touch.

Many misconceptions about epilepsy have circulated in the past, and some remain prevalent even today (Bishop & Boag, 2006; Kanner & Schafer, 2006). Negative public attitudes, in fact, have probably been more harmful to people with epilepsy than has the condition itself. During a seizure, a dysfunction in the electrochemical activity of the brain causes a person to lose control of the muscles temporarily. Between seizures (i.e., most of the time), the brain functions normally. Several types of seizures occur.

The **generalized tonic-clonic seizure** (formerly called *grand mal*) is the most conspicuous and serious type of seizure. The affected child usually has little or no warning that a seizure is about to occur; the muscles become stiff, and the child loses consciousness and falls to the floor. Then the entire body shakes violently as the muscles alternately contract and relax. Saliva may be forced from the mouth, legs and arms may jerk, and the bladder and bowels may be emptied. In mos t cases, the contractions diminish in 2 to 3 minutes, and the child either goes to sleep or regains consciousness in a confused or drowsy state. Generalized tonic-clonic seizures may occur as often as several times a day or as seldom as once a year. They are more likely to occur during the day than at night. A tonic-clonic seizure, although very frightening to someone who has never witnessed one, is not a medical emergency unless it lasts a very long time or unless the seizures occur frequently without a return to consciousness between seizures (Dean, 2006). Figure 1 describes first aid for tonic-clonic seizures in the classroom.

The **absence seizure** (previously called *petit mal*) is far less severe than the generalized tonic-clonic seizure but may occur much more frequently—as often as 100 times per day in some children. Usually a brief loss of consciousness occurs, lasting from a few seconds to half a minute or so. The child may stare blankly, flutter or blink her eyes, grow pale, or drop whatever she is holding. She may be mistakenly viewed as daydreaming or not listening. The child may or may not be aware that she has had a seizure, and no special first aid is necessary.

FIRST AID FOR GENERALIZED TONIC-CLONIC SEIZURES

First aid for a convulsive seizure protects the child from injury while the seizure runs its course. The seizure itself triggers mechanisms in the brain to bring it safely to an end. There are no other first aid steps that can hasten that process. When this type of seizure happens, the teacher should:

- Keep calm. Reassure the other children that the child will be fine in a minute.
- Ease the child gently to the floor and clear the area around him of anything that could hurt him.
- Put something flat and soft (like a folded jacket) under his head so it will not bang against the floor as his body jerks.
- Turn him gently onto his side. This keeps his airway clear and allows any fluid in his mouth to drain harmlessly away. DON'T try to force his mouth open. DON'T try to hold on to his tongue. DON'T put anything in his mouth. DON'T restrain his movements.
- When the jerking movements stop, let the child rest until full consciousness returns.
- Breathing may have been shallow during the seizure, and may even have stopped briefly. This can give the child's lips or skin a bluish tinge, which corrects naturally as the seizure ends. In

the unlikely event that breathing does not begin again, check the child's airway for any obstruction. It is rarely necessary to give artificial respiration.

Some children recover quickly after this type of seizure; others need more time. A short period of rest, depending on the child's alertness following the seizure, is usually advised.

If the child is able to remain in the classroom afterwards, he should be encouraged to do so. Staying in the classroom (or returning to it as soon as possible) allows for continued participation in classroom activity and is psychologically less difficult for the child. Of course, if he has lost bladder or bowel control, he should be allowed to go to the rest room first. A change of clothes kept in the health room or the principal's office will reduce embarrassment when this happens.

If a child has frequent seizures, handling them can become routine once teacher and classmates learn what to expect. One or two of the children can be assigned to help while the others get on with their work.

Source: Epilepsy Foundation. (2011). *Managing seizures at school.* Landover, MD. Available: http://www.epilepsyfoundation.org/living/children/education/managing.cfm

A **complex partial seizure** (also called *psychomotor*) may appear as a brief period of inappropriate or purposeless activity. The child may smack her lips, walk around aimlessly, or shout. She may appear to be conscious but is not actually aware of her unusual behavior. Complex partial seizures usually last from 2 to 5 minutes, after which the child has amnesia about the entire episode. Some children may respond to spoken directions during a complex partial seizure.

Sudden jerking motions with no loss of consciousness characterize a **simple partial seizure.** Partial seizures may occur weekly, monthly, or only once or twice a year. The teacher should keep dangerous objects out of the child's way and, except in emergencies, should not try to physically restrain him.

Many children experience a warning sensation, known as an *aura,* a short time before a seizure. The aura takes various forms: distinctive feelings, sights, sounds, tastes, and even smells. The aura can be a useful safety valve enabling the child to leave the class or the group before the seizure actually occurs. Some children report that the warning provided by the aura helps them feel more secure and comfortable.

In some children, absence and partial seizures can go undetected for long periods. An observant teacher can be instrumental in detecting the presence of a seizure disorder and in referring the child for appropriate medical help. The teacher can also assist parents and physicians by noting both the effectiveness and the side effects of any medication. With proper medical treatment and the support of parents, teachers, and peers, most students with seizure disorders lead full and normal lives. Antiepileptic drugs provide complete control in more than 50% of children and reduce the frequency of seizures in another 20% to 30% (Epilepsy Foundation, 2011). Some children require such heavy doses of medication, however, that their learning and behavior are adversely affected; and some medications have undesirable side effects, such as excessive fatigue, nausea, slurred speech, lack of appetite, and thickening of the gums. All children with seizure disorders benefit from a realistic understanding of their condition and accepting attitudes on the part of teachers and classmates (Shafer & DiLorio, 2006). Although the student with seizure disorders may be uncomfortable about letting friends know about the condition, classmates should be aware, so that they will know how to respond—and how *not* to respond—in the event of a seizure (Mittan, 2008, 2009).

Procedures for handling seizures

 Content Standards for Beginning Teachers—P&HD: Specialized health care interventions for individuals with P&HD (PH5K2).

Diabetes

Diabetes is a chronic disorder of metabolism that affects an estimated 25.8 million children and adults in the U.S., or 8.3% of the population (American Diabetes Association, 2011). Without proper medical management, the diabetic child's system cannot obtain and retain adequate energy from food. Not only does the child lack energy but also many important parts of the body (particularly the eyes and the kidneys) can be affected by untreated diabetes. Early symptoms of diabetes include thirst, headaches, weight loss (despite a good appetite), frequent urination, and cuts that are slow to heal.

Children with **type 1 diabetes** (formerly called *juvenile diabetes* or *early-onset diabetes*) have insufficient insulin, a hormone normally produced by the pancreas and necessary for the metabolism of glucose, a form of sugar produced when food is digested. To regulate the condition, the patient must receive daily injections of insulin under the skin. Most children with diabetes learn to inject their own insulin—in some cases as frequently as four times per day. Children with diabetes must follow a specific a diet prescribed by a physician or a nutrition specialist.

Type 2 diabetes, the most common form of diabetes, results from insulin resistance (the body failing to properly use insulin), combined with relative insulin deficiency. Type 2 diabetes occurs most often in adults who are overweight, but the recent increase in childhood obesity has led to a dramatic rise in the incidence of type 2 diabetes in children (Hannon, Rao, & Arslanian, 2005).

Teachers who have a child with diabetes in their classrooms should learn how to recognize the symptoms of both too little sugar and too much sugar in the child's bloodstream and the kind of treatment indicated by each condition (Getch, Bhukhanwala, & Neuharth-Pritchett, 2007). *Hypoglycemia* (low blood sugar), also called *insulin reaction* or *diabetic shock,* can result from taking too much insulin, unusually strenuous exercise, or a missed or delayed meal (the blood sugar level is lowered by insulin and exercise and raised by food). Symptoms of hypoglycemia include faintness, dizziness, blurred vision, drowsiness, and nausea. The child may appear irritable or have a marked personality change. In most cases, giving the child some form of concentrated sugar (e.g., a sugar cube, a glass of fruit juice, a candy bar) ends the insulin reaction within a few minutes. The child's doctor or parents should inform the teacher and school health personnel of the appropriate foods to give in case of insulin reaction.

Hyperglycemia (high blood sugar) is more serious; it indicates that too little insulin is present and the diabetes is not under control. Its onset is gradual rather than sudden. The symptoms of hyperglycemia, sometimes called *diabetic coma,* include fatigue; thirst; dry, hot skin; deep, labored breathing; excessive urination; and fruity-smelling breath. A doctor or nurse should be contacted immediately if a child displays such symptoms.

Asthma

Asthma is a chronic lung disease characterized by episodic bouts of wheezing, coughing, and difficulty breathing. An asthmatic attack is usually triggered by allergens (e.g., pollen, certain foods, pets); irritants (e.g., cigarette smoke, smog); exercise; or emotional stress. The result is a narrowing of the airways in the lungs, which increases resistance to the airflow in and out of the lungs and makes it harder for the individual to breathe. The severity of asthma varies greatly, from mild coughing to extreme difficulty in breathing that requires emergency treatment. Many asthmatic children experience normal lung functioning between episodes.

Asthma is the most common lung disease of children; estimates of its prevalence range from 7% to as high as 10% of school-age children (Asthma and Allergy Foundation of America, 2011). The causes of asthma are not completely known, though most consider it the result of an interaction of heredity and environment.

Primary treatment for asthma begins with a systematic effort to identify the stimuli and environmental situations that trigger attacks. Asthma can be controlled effectively in most children with a combination of medications and limiting exposure to known allergens. Most children whose breathing attacks are induced by physical exercise can still enjoy physical exercise and sports through careful selection of activities (e.g., swimming generally provokes less exercise-induced asthma than running) and/or taking certain medications before rigorous exercise. Although asthma is biochemical in origin, an interrelationship exists between emotional stress and asthma. Periods of psychological stress or higher emotional responses increase the likelihood of asthmatic attacks, and asthmatic episodes produce more stress. Treatment often involves an asthma teaching program, in which children and their families are taught ways to reduce and cope with emotional stress.

Asthma accounts for more hospitalizations than any other childhood disease and is the leading cause of absenteeism in school. It is estimated that 14 million school days are lost each year because of asthma (approximately 8 days for each student with asthma) (Asthma and Allergy Foundation of America, 2011). Chronic absenteeism makes it difficult for the child with asthma to maintain performance at grade level, and homebound instructional services may be necessary. The majority of children with asthma who receive medical and psychological support, however, successfully complete school and lead normal lives. By working cooperatively with parents and medical personnel to minimize the child's contact with provoking factors and constructing a plan to assist the child during attacks, the classroom teacher can play an important role in reducing the impact of asthma.

Cystic Fibrosis

Cystic fibrosis is a genetic disease of children and adolescents in which the body's exocrine glands excrete thick mucus that block the lungs and parts of the digestive system. Cystic fibrosis occurs predominantly in Caucasians, but it can affect all races. Children with cystic fibrosis often have difficulty breathing and are susceptible to pulmonary disease (lung infections). Malnutrition and poor growth are common characteristics of children with cystic fibrosis because of pancreatic insufficiency that causes inadequate digestion and malabsorption of nutrients, especially fats. Affected children often have large and frequent bowel movements because food is only partially digested. Getting children with cystic fibrosis to consume enough calories is critical to their health and development.

Medical research has not determined exactly how cystic fibrosis functions, and no reliable cure has yet been found. Medications prescribed for children with cystic fibrosis include enzymes to facilitate digestion and solutions to thin and loosen the mucus in the lungs. Children with cystic fibrosis undergo daily physiotherapy in which the chest is vigorously thumped and vibrated to dislodge mucus, followed by positioning the body to drain loosened secretions.

Many children and young adults with cystic fibrosis lead active lives. During vigorous physical exercises, some children may need help from teachers, aides, or classmates to clear their lungs and air passages. Although the life expectancy of people with cystic fibrosis used to be very short—in the 1950s, few children with cystic fibrosis lived to attend elementary school—the prognosis for affected children continues to improve. More than 45% of the cystic fibrosis population today is age 18 and older, and in 2008 the predicted median age of survival was 37.4 years (Cystic Fibrosis Foundation, 2011).

HIV and AIDS

HIV is the **human immunodeficiency virus (HIV)** that can lead to **acquired immune deficiency syndrome (AIDS)**. A person with AIDS cannot resist and fight off infections because of a breakdown in the immune system. Opportunistic infections such as tuberculosis, pneumonia, and cancerous skin lesions attack the person's body, grow in severity, and ultimately result in death. Although no known cure or vaccine exists for AIDS, advances in antiretroviral drug treatment have dramatically reduced mortality rates.

Cystic fibrosis

 Content Standards for Beginning Teachers—P&HD: Characteristics, treatment, and course of physical and health disabilities (PH2K1) (also PH2K2, PH3K1, ICC2K2).

HIV/AIDS

 Content Standards for Beginning Teachers—P&HD: Types and transmission routes of infectious and communicable diseases (PH2K4) (also PH2K1, PH3K1).

HIV, which is found in the bodily fluids of an infected person (blood, semen, vaginal secretions, and breast milk), is transmitted from one person to another through sexual contact and blood-to-blood contact (e.g., intravenous drug use with shared needles, transfusions of unscreened contaminated blood). Pregnant women can transmit HIV to their unborn children. Most people who become infected with HIV show no symptoms of AIDS for 8 to 12 years, and not all people who are infected with HIV develop AIDS (Centers for Disease Control and Prevention [CDC], 2011c).

Because of fear generated by misconceptions about the spread of the disease, some school districts have barred children with HIV/AIDS from attending school in defiance of the IDEA principle of zero reject (Turnbull, Stowe, & Huerta, 2007). However, saliva, nasal secretions, sweat, tears, urine, and vomit do not transmit HIV unless those fluids contain blood (CDC, 2011d). A child with HIV/AIDS in the classroom presents no undue health risks to other children. Children with HIV/AIDS cannot legally be excluded from attending school unless they are deemed a direct health risk to other children (e.g., exhibit biting behavior, have open lesions).

Parents are not required to inform the school that their child has HIV (or any other medical or health condition). All teachers and school personnel should be trained in **universal precautions,** a set of standard safety techniques that interrupt the chain of infection spread by potential biohazards such as blood and bodily fluids. Universal precautions include safe administration of first aid for a cut, nosebleed, or vomiting.

Students receiving special education services may be more prone to contracting HIV because of a lack of knowledge about the disease. For recommendations on developing and implementing an HIV/AIDS prevention and education curriculum for students with disabilities, see Kelker, Hecimovic, and LeRoy (1994) and Sileo (2005).

ATTENTION-DEFICIT/ HYPERACTIVITY DISORDER

Everyone has difficulty attending at times (attention deficit), and we all sometimes engage in high rates of purposeless or inappropriate movement (hyperactivity). A child who consistently exhibits this combination of behavioral traits may be diagnosed with **attention-deficit/hyperactivity disorder (ADHD).** Children with ADHD present a difficult challenge to their families, teachers, and classmates. Their inability to stay on task, impulsive behavior, and fidgeting impair their ability to learn and increase the likelihood of unsatisfactory interactions with others.

Although the last decade of the 20th century witnessed an explosion of interest in ADHD, historical references to the symptoms that are diagnosed as ADHD today suggest that such children have been with us for centuries (Barkley, 2005; Conners, 2000). The first published account of the disorder in the medical or scientific literature appeared in 1902, when British physician George Still described Still's disease. Still believed that children who were restless and exhibited problems maintaining attention suffered from a "defect of moral control" that he presumed to be the result of brain injury or dysfunction. Over the years, researchers have used a variety of terms to refer to this combination of behavioral symptoms: *postencephalitic disorder* in the 1920s, *brain damage syndrome* in the 1940s, *minimal brain dysfunction* in the 1960s, and *hyperkinetic impulse disorder of children* in the 1970s (Mather & Goldstein, 2001). Because medical science has found no clear-cut evidence of brain damage, emphasis in defining and diagnosing the condition has focused and relied on the description and identification of a combination of behavioral symptoms.

Definition and Diagnosis

"The essential feature of attention-deficit/hyperactivity disorder is a persistent pattern of inattention and/or hyperactivity-impulsivity that is more frequent and severe than is typically observed in individuals at a comparable level of development" (American Psychiatric Association, 2000a, p. 85). The proposed diagnostic criteria for ADHD for the fifth edition of the *Diagnostic and Statistical Manual of Mental Disorders (DSM-5)*, scheduled for publication in May 2013, state that six or more symptoms of inattention and/or hyperactivity-impulsivity must have persisted for at least 6 months, with the onset of several noticeable symptoms present by age 12.

> *Inattention*—not attending to details, difficulty sustaining attention to tasks or activities, does not seem to listen, not following through on instructions (e.g., starts a task but soon gets sidetracked), difficulty organizing tasks and activities (e.g., work is messy and disorganized), dislikes tasks that require sustained mental effort, frequently loses things, easily distracted, often forgetful.
>
> *Hyperactivity and impulsivity*—fidgeting, restlessness, runs about or climbs on furniture, often excessively loud or noisy, often "on the go" as if "driven by a motor," talks excessively, blurts out answers, difficulty waiting to take his or her turn, interrupts others, acts without thinking (e.g., starts a task without reading or listening to the instructions), impatient, rushes through activities or tasks, has difficulty resisting temptations. (adapted from American Psychiatric Association, 2011c)

These symptoms must occur in two or more environments; interfere with or reduce the quality of the individual's functioning in social, academic, or occupational tasks; and not be the result of another mental disorder (e.g., mood disorder, anxiety disorder). Depending on the constellation of symptoms presented by the child, one of four ADHD subtypes are assigned: combined presentation (inattention and hyperactivity/impulsivity); predominantly inattentive presentation; predominantly hyperactivity-impulsive presentation; and inattentive presentation (restrictive). Within the population of children with ADHD, approximately 55% have been diagnosed with the combined type, 27% with the predominantly inattentive subtype, and 18% with the hyperactive-impulsive subtype (Wilens, Biederman, & Spencer, 2002).

The diagnostic criteria for ADHD are highly subjective. For example, what is the basis for deciding whether a child is "often 'on the go'"? And how does one determine that a child who avoids or dislikes schoolwork or homework does so because of an attention deficit as opposed to one of many other possible reasons? A child who is regarded by one physician as not having ADHD may very well be diagnosed by another as having it.

Because no valid, independent test for ADHD exists, diagnosis rests on information obtained from parents and teachers. One study found that teachers were the most likely to be the first to suggest the diagnosis of ADHD, followed by parents (Sax & Kautz, 2003). Parents have been known to engage in "physician shopping," taking their child from one doctor to another until a diagnosis of ADHD is made (Reid, Maag, & Vasa, 1994).

Prevalence

The most frequently cited estimate of the prevalence of ADHD is 3% to 7% of school-age children (American Psychiatric Association, 2004). As of 2007, approximately 5.4 million children ages 4 to 17, or 9.5%, had at some point been diagnosed with ADHD, and boys are about three times more likely to be diagnosed with ADHD than are girls, with the ratio being higher at younger ages (CDC, 2011d). The typical classroom will have one or two children either diagnosed with ADHD or presenting the problems typically associated with ADHD.

Child count data reported by the states reveal a large increase in the numbers of students served under IDEA's other health impairments category, because the federal government stipulated that students with ADHD were eligible for special education under that disability category. Some states reported increases of 20% in the number of children served under the other health impairments category between the 1997–98 and 1998–99 school years (U.S. Department of Education, 2000). Nationwide, the number of children served in the other health impairments category increased from 63,982

While changes, if any, to the diagnostic criteria for ADHD by the DSM-5 work group were likely to be minor, readers should consult the DSM-5 for the final version officially adopted by the American Psychiatric Association.

in 1992–93 to 678,970 in 2009–10, the biggest proportional increase of any disability category other than autism (U.S. Department of Education, 2011).

Academic Achievement and Comorbidity with Other Disabilities

Most children with ADHD struggle in the classroom. They score lower than their age mates on IQ and achievement tests, more than half require remedial tutoring for basic skills, and about 30% repeat one or more grades (Barkley, 2005). A national study of more than 1,400 students found that 58% of those students receiving special education services under the disability category of emotional disturbance had ADHD and that 20% of those students receiving special education in the intellectual disability and learning disability categories had ADHD (Schnoes, Reid, Wagner, & Marder, 2006). Many children with Asperger syndrome and Tourette syndrome are identified as having ADHD (Kube, Peterson, & Palmer, 2002; Prestia, 2003).

Eligibility for Special Education

Researchers estimate that between 40% and 50% of students with ADHD qualify for special education services, the majority being served under the disability categories of emotional disturbance and learning disabilities (Reid & Maag, 1998; Zentall, 2006). Students with ADHD can be served under the other health impairment category if the outcome of the disorder is a "heightened alertness to environmental stimuli that results in limited alertness with respect to the educational environment that adversely affects academic performance" (20 USC §1401 [2004], 20 *CFR* §300.8[c][9]).

Many children with ADHD who are not served under IDEA are receiving services under Section 504 of the Rehabilitation Act. Section 504 is a civil rights law that provides certain protections for people with disabilities. Under Section 504, schools may be required to develop and implement accommodation plans to help students with ADHD succeed in the general education classroom. Accommodation plans often include such adaptations and adjustments as extended time on tests, preferred seating, additional teacher monitoring, reduced or modified class or homework assignments and worksheets, and monitoring the effects of medication on the child's behavior in school.

Causes

The causes of ADHD are not well understood. Similar patterns of behavior leading to the diagnoses of ADHD in two different children likely, if not certainly, will be caused by completely different factors or sets of factors (Gresham, 2002; Maag & Reid, 1994). Although many consider ADHD to be a neurologically based disorder, no clear and consistent causal evidence links brain damage or dysfunction to the behavioral symptoms of ADHD (National Institute of Health Consensus Statement, 1998). However, significant evidence indicates that genetic factors may place individuals at a greater than normal risk of an ADHD diagnosis (Willcutt, Pennington, & DeFries, 2000). Genetics may provide certain risk or resilience factors, and environmental influences (i.e., life experiences) then determine whether an individual receives a diagnosis of ADHD (Goldstein & Goldstein, 1998).

ADHD is associated with a wide range of genetic disorders and diseases (Levy, Hay, & Bennett, 2006). For example, individuals with fragile X syndrome, Turner syndrome, and Williams syndrome frequently have attention and impulsivity problems. Symptoms of ADHD are also associated with conditions such as fetal alcohol syndrome, prenatal exposure to cocaine, and lead poisoning.

Research using neuroimaging technologies has shown that some individuals with ADHD have structural or biochemical differences in their brains (e.g., Cherkasova & Hechtman, 2009; Sowell et al., 2003). Not all individuals diagnosed with ADHD, however, have brains that appear different from those of individuals without ADHD. And some people without ADHD have brain structures similar to those with ADHD.

Achievement of students with ADHD and comorbidity with other disabling conditions

 Council for Exceptional Children Content Standards for Beginning Teachers—Common Core: Educational implications of characteristics of various exceptionalities (ICC2K2) (also LD3K1).

ADHD and eligibility for special education

 Council for Exceptional Children Content Standards for Beginning Teachers—Common Core: Issues, assurances, and due process rights related to assessment, eligibility, and placement within a continuum of services (ICC1K6).

Causes of ADHD

 Council for Exceptional Children Content Standards for Beginning Teachers of Students with LD: Etiologies of LD (LD2K1).

Treatment

Drug therapy and behaviorally based interventions are the two most widely used treatment approaches for children with ADHD.

MEDICATION Prescription stimulant medication is the most common intervention for children with ADHD. Methylphenidate, sold under the trade name Ritalin, is the most frequently prescribed medication for ADHD. Other stimulants such as dextro-amphetamine (Dexedrine), dextroamphetamine sulfate (Adderall), methamphetamine hydrochloride (Desoxyn), and pemoline (Cylert) are also widely prescribed.

The number of children on stimulant medication has increased tremendously since the the late 1980s, when it was estimated that 700,000 children received medication for ADHD. By 1995 the number had more than doubled to 1.6 million children (Safer, Zito, & Fine, 1996). The Centers for Disease Control and Prevention (2011a) estimated that as of 2007 2.7 million children ages 4 to 17 were receiving medication treatment for ADHD. Diller (1998) reports that sales of Ritalin for children in the United States account for 90% of the worldwide consumption of the drug. Klein (2007) reported that children in the United States are 10 times more likely to take a stimulant medication for ADHD than are kids in Europe, and that the United States consumes about 85% of the stimulants manufactured for ADHD.

When prescribed and monitored by a competent physician, Ritalin has proven to be a safe and often effective intervention (Multimodal Treatment Study Group, 1999). Reviews of controlled studies show that 70% to 80% of school-age children diagnosed with ADHD respond positively to Ritalin, at least in the short term (Barkley, 2005; Swanson, McBurnett, Christian, & Wigal, 1995); 20% to 30% show either no response or a negative response (i.e., their symptoms get worse) (Gresham, 2002). A positive response typically includes a reduction in hyperactivity, increased attention and time on task, increased academic productivity, and improvements in general conduct. Although teachers and parents generally report favorable outcomes for children who are taking stimulant medication, common side effects include insomnia, decreased appetite, headaches, weight loss, decrease of positive affect, and irritability. These side effects are usually of short duration and can often be controlled with a reduction in dosage (Goldstein & Goldstein, 1998).

Mather and Goldstein (2001) believe that "the immediate short-term benefits of stimulant medications far outweigh the liabilities and thus appear to justify the continued use of these medications in the treatment of ADHD" (p. 63). Based on their assessment of two meta-analyses of medication studies, Forness, Kavale, Crenshaw, and Sweeney (2000) suggest that it is unwise and could be considered malpractice not to include drug therapy as part of a comprehensive treatment program for children with ADHD.

No clear evidence indicates that stimulant medications lead to improved academic achievement (e.g., better grades and scores on achievement tests) (Flora, 2007; Pelham, 1999). A longitudinal study that followed children with ADHD who had taken Ritalin for 4 years found the children did not make gains in either specific or general areas of academic achievement from the first through the fifth grade (Frankenberger & Cannon, 1999). Some professionals have voiced concerns that educators and parents rely too much on medical interventions (Flora, 2007; Northup, Galley, Edwards, & Fountain, 2001). They view drug treatment as an inappropriate, easy way out that might produce short-term improvements in behavior but result in long-term harm.

Because the diagnosis of ADHD often leads to the prescription of stimulant medication, it is important that teachers have valid knowledge of the condition and its treatment. Unfortunately, educators hold many misconceptions about ADHD and its treatment by stimulant medication. Snider, Busch, and Arrowood (2003) asked 145 teachers to rate how much they agreed or disagreed with 13 statements about ADHD and its treatment by stimulant medication. All of the questions were either true or false on the basis of scientific research, and more than half of the teachers answered only 5 of the 13 questions correctly (see Table 1).

Drug treatment of ADHD

 Council for Exceptional Children

Content Standards for Beginning Teachers—Common Core: Effects of various medications on individuals with exceptional learning needs (ICC2K7).

Sources of information for educators and parents on safe and effective use of stimulant medication in treating children are Gadow and Nolan (1993), DuPaul and Stoner (2003), Goldstein and Goldstein (1998), and the *ADHD Parents Medication Guide* (2010).

TABLE 1 • Percentage of classroom teachers who correctly rated statements about ADHD and its treatment by stimulant medication

ITEM	PERCENTAGE CORRECT
ADHD is the most commonly diagnosed psychiatric disorder of childhood. (True)	58
There are data to indicate that ADHD is caused by a brain malfunction. (False)	10
ADHD symptoms (e.g., fidgets, does not follow through on instruction, easily distracted) may be caused by academic deficits. (True)	63
Stress and conflict in the student's home life can cause ADHD symptoms. (True)	71
Diagnosis of ADHD can be confirmed if stimulant medication improves the child's attention. (False)	33
Stimulant medication use may decrease the physical growth rate (i.e., height) of students. (True)	38
Stimulant medication use may produce tics in students. (True)	45
Adderall, Ritalin, and Dexedrine have abuse potential similar to Demerol, cocaine, and morphine. (True)	46
The long-term side effects of stimulant medications are well understood. (False)	67
Over time, stimulant medication loses its effectiveness. (True)	46
While on stimulant medication, students exhibit similar amounts of problem behaviors as their normally developing peers. (False)	27
Short-term studies show that stimulant medication improves the behaviors associated with ADHD. (True)	86
Studies show that stimulant medication has a positive effect on academic achievement in the long run. (False)	6

Note: Statements were rated using a 5-point Likert-type scale (1 = *strongly disagree* to 5 = *strongly agree*). Percentage correct indicates percentage of respondents who answered 4 or 5 to an item that was true and 1 or 2 to an item that was false.

Source: Figure from "Teacher Knowledge of Stimulant Medication and ADHD" by Linda Arrowood, Tracey Busch and Vickie E. Snider, from REMEDIAL AND SPECIAL EDUCATION, January 2003, Volume 24(1). Copyright © 2003 by Arrowood et al. Reprinted with permission by SAGE publications.

Behavioral interventions for ADHD

 Council for Exceptional Children

Content Standards for Beginning Teachers—Common Core: Teach individuals to use self-assessment, problem solving, and other cognitive strategies to meet their needs (ICC4S2) (also ICC5K2).

BEHAVIORAL INTERVENTION The principles and methods of applied behavior analysis provide teachers and parents with practical strategies for teaching and living with children with ADHD (Pelham & Fabiano, 2008). These methods include positive reinforcement for on-task behavior, modifying assignments and instructional activities to promote success, and systematically gradually teaching self-control. Teacher-administered interventions for children with ADHD include restructuring the environment (e.g., seating the child close to the teacher and breaking assignments into small, manageable chunks); providing frequent opportunities to actively respond within ongoing instruction; and providing differential consequences for child behavior (e.g., positive reinforcement such as praise and tokens for appropriate behavior, ignoring inappropriate behavior, and time out or response cost for inappropriate behavior) (Garrick Duhaney, 2003; Harlacher, Roberts, & Merrell, 2006; Salend, Elhoweris, & van Garderen, 2003). Interventions based on functional assessment of off-task, disruptive, and distracting behavior by students with ADHD have also proven effective (e.g., Lo & Cartledge, 2006; Stahr, Cushing, Lane, & Fox, 2006).

414

An important line of research with major implications for treating children with ADHD is exploring how to teach self-control to children whose impulsivity adversely affects learning. A deficit of *executive function,* or the ability to verbally think through and control one's actions, has been hypothesized as a primary characteristic of children with ADHD (Barkley, 2005; Brocki, Eninger, Thorell, & Bohlin, 2010). According to this hypothesis, children with ADHD would be unlikely candidates for, and perhaps incapable of, learning self-control (Abikoff, 1991). Recent research has demonstrated, however, that children with ADHD can learn to self-regulate their behavior and reduce impulsiveness (Reid, Trout, & Schartz, 2005).

Neef, Bicard, and Endo (2002) demonstrated that children with ADHD can learn

Since learning to self-monitor his behavior, Brandon's impulsiveness has decreased.

self-control when treatment regimens are directly tied to assessment. Results of a subsequent study demonstrated that children with ADHD can learn to follow rules and describe their own behavior, provided they receive clear instructions and consistent reinforcement (Bicard & Neef, 2002). Results of these studies and research on self-regulation (Reid et al., 2005) and correspondence training show promise for treating children who have ADHD. Correspondence training is a procedure in which children are reinforced for "do–say" verbal statements about what they had done previously and "say–do" statements describing what they plan to do (e.g., Shapiro, DuPaul, & Bradley-King, 1998). See *Teaching & Learning*, "Self-Monitoring Helps Students Do More Than Just Be on Task."

CHARACTERISTICS OF CHILDREN WITH PHYSICAL AND HEALTH IMPAIRMENTS

The characteristics of children with physical disabilities and health impairments are so varied that attempting to describe them is nearly impossible. Knowing the underlying cause of a student's physical impairment or health condition provides limited guidance in planning needed special education and related services. One student with cerebral palsy may need few special modifications in curriculum, instruction, or environment, while the severe limitations in movement and intellectual functioning experienced by another student with cerebral palsy require a wide array of curricular and instructional modifications, adaptive equipment, and related services. Some children with health conditions have chronic but relatively mild health conditions; others have extremely limited endurance and vitality, requiring sophisticated medical technology and around-the-clock support to maintain their very existence. And a given physical or health condition may take markedly different *trajectories* (Best, 2010a). For example, treatment of cancer may prolong and enhance the life of a child, lead to complete remission of the disease, or have little or no positive effects on a child's life.

These variables render lists of learning and behavioral characteristics of children with physical disabilities and health impairments highly suspect at best. Nevertheless, two cautiously qualified statements can be made concerning the academic and socioemotional characteristics of children with physical disabilities and health impairments. First, although many students with physical disabilities or health impairments achieve well above grade level, as a group, these students function below grade level academically. In addition to the neuromotor and orthopedic impairments that hamper their academic performance, the daily health care routines and medications that some children must endure have negative side effects on academic achievement. For example, Frueh (2007) described how the mother of a 15-year-old with epilepsy helps teachers understand the effects of seizures and medication on a student's school performance.

> I tell them, "Imagine you have the flu. Plus, you've taken a nighttime cold medicine. You head off to school and must perform on par all day, feeling awful, and do all of your work. In addition to that, the teacher pats you on the back and speaks to you the whole time to encourage you along. Now, write the alphabet backwards with your non-dominant hand, while swinging your opposite foot backwards in a circle." Kids with epilepsy take medication every day that makes them feel that way.

The educational progress of some children is also hampered by frequent and sometimes prolonged absences from school for medical treatment when flare-ups or relapses require hospitalization.

Second, as a group, students with physical disabilities and health impairments perform below average on measures of social-behavioral skills. Coster and Haltiwanger (2004) reported that classroom teachers and other school professionals, such as physical and occupational therapists, rated more than 40% of the 62 elementary students with physical disabilities below mean on six of seven social-behavioral tasks considered necessary for optimal functioning and learning in school (e.g., following social conventions, compliance with adult directives, positive interaction with peers and adults, constructive responses to feedback, and personal care awareness).

Coping emotionally with a physical disability or a chronic health impairment presents a major problem for some children (Antle, 2004; Kanner & Schafer, 2006). Maintaining peer relationships and a sense of belonging to the group can be difficult for a child who must frequently leave the instructional activity or the classroom to participate in therapeutic or health care routines. Anxiety about fitting in at school may be created by prolonged absences from school (Olsen & Sutton, 1998). Students with physical disabilities and health impairments frequently identify concerns about physical appearance as reasons for emotional difficulties and feelings of depression (Sexson & Dingle, 2001).

Variables Affecting the Impact of Physical Disabilities and Health Impairments on Educational Performance

Effects of P&HD on academic achievement and social/emotional development

 Council for Exceptional Children

Content Standards for Beginning Teachers—Common Core: Educational implications of various exceptionalities (ICC2K2) (also PH3K1).

Many factors must be taken into consideration in assessing the effects of a physical disability or health impairment on a child's development and behavior. A physical impairment or medical condition can limit a child's ability to engage in age-appropriate activities, mobility, cognitive functioning, social and emotional development, sensory functioning, and communication across a continuum ranging from normal functioning (no impact) to extremely impaired. A minor or transient physical or health impairment, such as those most children experience while growing up, is not likely to have lasting effects; but a severe, chronic impairment can greatly limit a child's range of experiences. In addition to the severity with which the condition affects different areas of functioning, two particularly important factors are age of onset and visibility.

AGE OF ONSET Some conditions are congenital (present at birth); other conditions are acquired during the child's development as a result of illness, accident, or unknown cause. As with all disabilities, it is important for the teacher to be aware of the child's age at the time he acquired the physical or health impairment. A child who has not had the use of his legs since birth may have missed out on some important developmental experiences, particularly if he did not receive early inter-vention services. In contrast, a teenager who suddenly loses the use of her legs in an accident has likely had a normal range of experiences throughout childhood but may need considerable support from parents, teachers, specialists, and peers in adapting to life with this newly acquired disability.

VISIBILITY Physical impairments and health conditions range from highly visible and conspicuous to not visible. How children think about themselves and the degree to which others accept them often are affected by the vis-ibility of a condition. Some children use a variety of spe-cial orthopedic appliances, such as wheelchairs, braces, crutches, and adaptive tables. They may ride to school on a specially equipped bus or van. In school they may need assistance using the toilet or may wear helmets. Although such special devices and adaptations help children meet important needs, they have the unfortunate side effect of making the physical impairment more visible, thus making the child look even more different from her class-mates without disabilities.

The visibility of some physical disabilities may cause other children and adults to underestimate the child's abilities and limit opportunities for participation. By con-trast, many health conditions such as asthma or epilepsy are not visible, and others may not perceive that the child needs or deserves accommodations. This misperception is supported by the fact that the child functions normally most of the time (Best, 2010a).

The severity, visibility, and age of acquisition of a physical disability or health impairment affect a child's development and behavior.

Katelyn Metzger/Merrill

EDUCATIONAL APPROACHES

Special education of children with physical disabilities and health impairments in the United States has a history of more than 100 years (see Figure 2). While some students with physical and health impairments can fully access and benefit from education with minimal accommodations or environmental modifications, the in-tensive health and learning needs of other students require a complex and coordi-nated array of specialized instruction, therapy, and related services. In addition to progressing in the general education curriculum to the maximum extent possible, many students with physical disabilities or health impairments also need intensive instruction in a "parallel curriculum" on ways of "coping with their disabilities" (Bowe, 2000, p. 75). Similar in function to the "expanded core curriculum" for stu-dents with visual impairments, the parallel curriculum for students with physical and health impairments includes using adaptive methods and assistive technologies for mobility, communication, and daily-living tasks; increasing independence by self-administering special health care routines; and learning self-determination and self-advocacy skills.

History of education of students with P&HD

 Council for Exceptional Children

Content Standards for Beginning Teachers—P&HD: Historical foundations related to knowledge and practices in P&HD (PH1K2).

Teaming and Related Services

The transdisciplinary team approach has special relevance for students with physical disabilities and health impairments. No other group of exceptional children comes into contact, both in and out of school, with as many different teachers, physicians,

▼ Self-Monitoring Helps Students Do More Than Just Be on Task

Self-monitoring is a relatively simple procedure in which a person observes his behavior systematically and records the occurrence or nonoccurrence of a specific behavior. Self-monitoring not only often changes the behavior observed and recorded but also typically changes the behavior in the desired direction.

Self-monitoring has helped students with and without disabilities be on task more often in the classroom (Wood, Murdock, Cronin, Dawson, & Kirby, 1998), decrease talk-outs and aggression (Martella, Leonard, Marchand-Martella, & Agran, 1993), improve their performance in a variety of academic subject areas (Maag, Reid, & DiGangi, 1993; Wolfe, Heron, & Goddard, 2000), and complete homework assignments (Trammel, Schloss, & Alper, 1994). In addition to improving the target behavior, self-monitoring enables students to achieve a form of self-determination by taking responsibility for their learning (Wehmeyer et al., 2000; Wehmeyer & Schalock, 2001).

CAN STUDENTS WITH ADHD SELF-MONITOR THEIR OWN BEHAVIOR?

How can a a student who seldom sits still, pays little attention to instruction, and frequently disrupts the class be expected to carefully observe his own behavior and accurately self-record it? Asking a child with ADHD to self-monitor whether he is on task and productive may seem a bit like asking the fox to guard the hen house. How can a student with ADHD pay attention to his own paying attention? Isn't he likely to forget? And if he does remember, what will keep him from recording that he was on task even if he wasn't? Although these are understandable and legitimate questions and concerns, research has shown self-monitoring to be an effective intervention for students diagnosed with ADHD (e.g., Barry & Messer, 2003; Harris, Friedlancer, Saddler, Frizzelle, & Graham, 2005; Lo & Cartledge, 2006).

HOW TO GET STARTED

Following are suggestions based on more than 30 years of research on self-monitoring. For a review of principles and strategies for self-monitoring, see Cooper, Heron, and Heward (2007). Detailed procedures and materials for teaching students self-monitoring and other self-management skills are described in Joseph and Konrad (2009) and Rafferty (2010).

1. **Specify the target behavior and performance goals.** In general, students should self-monitor their performance of academic or social tasks (e.g., number of math problems answered, participating in class discussions, transitioning between activities, having materials ready for class) instead of an on-task behavior such as "paying attention." On-task behavior does not necessarily result in

a collateral increase in productivity. By contrast, when productivity is increased, improvements in on-task behavior almost always occur as well. However, a student whose persistent off-task and disruptive behaviors create problems for him or others in the classroom may benefit more from self-monitoring on-task behavior, at least initially.

Encourage students' participation in selecting and defining the behaviors to be self-monitored and in setting performance goals. Some students will work harder to achieve self-selected goals than teacher-determined goals (Olympia, Sheridan, Jenson, & Andrews, 1994).

2. **Select or create materials that make self-monitoring easy.** Simple paper-and-pencil recording forms, wrist counters, hand-tally counters, and countdown timers can make self-monitoring easy and efficient. Self-recording forms consisting of nothing more than a series of boxes or squares are often effective. At various intervals, the student might write a + or –, circle *yes* or *no*, or mark an × through a smiling face or sad face; or record tally marks for the number of target responses made during a just-completed interval.

For example, elementary students with ADHD used the form shown on the opposite page to self-monitor whether they worked quietly, evaluated their work, and followed a prescribed sequence for obtaining teacher assistance during independent seat-work activities (Lo & Cartledge, 2006). The form served the dual purpose of reminding the students of the expected behaviors and as a device on which to self-record those behaviors. Countoons are self-monitoring forms that illustrate the target behaviors to be self-monitored and the consequences for meeting the performance contingency (Daly & Ranalli, 2003).

KidTools are free software programs children can use to create charts and tools for self-monitoring and other self-management tasks. KidTools can be downloaded at http://kidtools.missouri.edu. Also available at this site are training modules for teachers with video demonstrations and practice materials.

3. **Provide supplementary cues to self-monitor.** Although the self-monitoring device or form itself provides a visual reminder to self-monitor, additional prompts or cues are often helpful. Teachers should provide frequent prompts at the beginning of a self-monitoring intervention and gradually reduce their number as the student becomes accustomed to self-monitoring. Auditory

TEACHING & LEARNING

Date:

Work quietly

1. "Am I working quietly?"

2. Check my work

3. "Do I need teacher?"

4. Raise my hand

5. "How am I Doing?"

6. Say "thank you"

THANK YOU

Source: Self-monitoring form from *Functional Assessment and Individualized Intervention Plans: Increasing the Behavioral Adjustment of Urban Learners in General and Special Education Settings* by Y. Lo, 2003. Unpublished doctoral dissertation. Columbus, OH: The Ohio State University: Reprinted by permission.

of the target behavior and how and when it should be recorded, provide repeated opportunities to practice, and give praise and corrective feedback.

5. **Reinforce accurate self-monitoring.** Although self-monitoring often positively affects behavior even when inaccurate (e.g., Maag et al., 1993; Marshall, Lloyd, & Hallahan, 1993), accurate self-monitoring is desirable, especially when students use self-recorded data as the basis for self-evaluation or self-administered consequences. One proven method for increasing the accuracy of self-monitoring is rewarding students when their self-recorded data match teacher-collected data for the same period (Rhode, Morgan, & Young, 1983). Check student's data frequently at the beginning of a self-monitoring program, then gradually reduce the number of checks to a random check every now and then.

6. **Reward improvements in the target behavior.** Self-monitoring is often part of an intervention package that includes reinforcement for meeting self- or teacher-selected performance goals (e.g., Olympia et al., 1994). The reinforcer may be self-administered or teacher-delivered (Martella et al., 1993).

7. **Encourage self-evaluation.** Self-evaluation entails comparing one's performace with a predetermined goal or standard (e.g., Grossi & Heward, 1998). Show the student how to self-evaluate and make self-evaluative statements about his behavior (e.g., "That was my best score ever. Excellent!" "I missed my goal by two problems. I'll work harder tomorrow.").

8. **Evaluate the program.** Take some data on the student's behavior for several days before the student begins self-monitoring. Use these data as a baseline against which to compare the data you obtain during the first several sessions of self-monitoring.

prompts in the form of prerecorded beeps or tones can cue self-monitoring. For example, Todd, Horner, and Sugai (1999) had a student place a check mark next to *yes* or *no* under the heading "Was I paying attention?" each time he heard a prerecorded tone that sounded at random intervals.

Tactile prompts can also signal self-recording moments. The MotivAider® (www.habitchange.com) is a small, battery-operated device the user can program to vibrate at fixed or variable time intervals. Flaute, Peterson, Van Norman, Riffle, and Eakins (2005) describe 20 ways for using a MotivAider to improve behavior and productivity in the classroom.

4. **Provide explicit instruction.** Self-monitoring is easy, but don't assume that simply telling the student how to do it will suffice. Model examples and nonexamples

Courtesy of Behavioral Dynamics, Inc. Developer of MotivAider®

The MotivAider can be programmed to vibrate at fixed or variable time intervals. (Courtesy of Behavioral Dynamics, Inc., Developer of MotivAider®.)

Figure from FUNCTIONAL ASSESSMENT AND INDIVIDUALIZED INTERVENTION PLANS: INCREASING THE BEHAVIORAL ADJUSTMENT OF URBAN LEARNERS IN GENERAL AND SPECIAL EDUCATION SETTINGS by Ya-yu Lo. Copyright © 2003 by Ya-yu Lo. Reprinted with permission.

TEACHING & LEARNING

therapists, and other specialists. Because the medical, educational, therapeutic, vocational, and social needs of these students are often complex, educational and health care personnel must openly communicate and cooperate with one another. Two particularly important members of the team for many children with physical disabilities and health impairments are the physical therapist and the occupational therapist. Each is a licensed health professional who must complete a specialized training program and meet rigorous standards.

Physical therapists (PTs) are involved in the development and maintenance of motor skills, movement, and posture. They may prescribe specific exercises to help a child increase control of muscles and use specialized equipment, such as braces, effectively. Massage and prescriptive exercises are perhaps the most frequently applied procedures; but physical therapy can also include swimming, heat treatment, special positioning for feeding and toileting, and other techniques. PTs encourage children to be as motorically independent as possible; help develop muscular

PTs, OTs, and other related-services specialists

 Council for Exceptional Children Content Standards for Beginning Teachers—P&HD: Roles and responsibilities of school and community-based medical and related-services personnel (PH10K1).

FIGURE 2 KEY HISTORICAL EVENTS IN THE EDUCATION OF CHILDREN WITH PHYSICAL DISABILITIES AND HEALTH IMPAIRMENTS

Date	Historical Event	Educational Implications
1893	Industrial School for Crippled and Deformed Children is established in Boston.	This was the first special institution for children with physical disabilities in the United States (Eberle, 1922).
Circa 1900	The first special classes for children with physical impairments begin in Chicago.	This was the first time children with physical disabilities were educated in public schools (La Vor, 1976).
Early 1900s	Serious outbreaks of tuberculosis and polio occur in the United States.	This led to increasing numbers of children with physical impairments being educated by local schools in special classes for the "crippled" or "delicate" (Walker & Jacobs, 1985).
Early 20th century	Winthrop Phelps demonstrated that children could be helped through physical therapy and the effective use of braces. Earl Carlson (who himself had cerebral palsy) was a strong advocate of developing the intellectual potential of children with physical disabilities through appropriate education.	The efforts of these two American physicians contributed to increased understanding and acceptance of children with physical disabilities and to recognition that physical impairment did not preclude potential for educational achievement and self-sufficiency.
Early 20th century to 1970s	Decisions to "ignore, isolate, and institutionalize these children were often based on mental incompetence presumed because of physical disabilities, especially those involving communication and use of upper extremities" (Conner, Scandary, & Tullock, 1988, p. 6).	Increasing numbers of children with mild physical disabilities and health conditions were educated in public schools. Most children with severe physical disabilities were educated in special schools or community agencies (e.g., the United Cerebral Palsy Association).
1975	PL 94-142 mandated a free appropriate public education for all children with disabilities and required schools to provide related services (e.g., transportation services, physical therapy, school health services) necessary for students to be educated in the least restrictive environment.	No longer could a child be denied the right to attend the local public school because there was a flight of stairs at the entrance, bathrooms were not accessible, or school buses were not equipped to transport wheelchairs. The related services provision of IDEA transformed schools from "solely scholastic institutions into therapeutic agencies" (Palfrey, 1995, p. 265).

(continues)

function; and reduce pain, discomfort, or long-term physical damage. They may also suggest do's and don'ts for sitting positions and activities in the classroom and may devise exercise or play programs that children with and without disabilities can enjoy together.

Occupational therapists (OTs) are concerned with a child's participation in activities, especially those that will be useful in self-help, employment, recreation, communication, and aspects of daily living (e.g., dressing, eating, personal hygiene). They may help a child learn (or relearn) diverse motor behaviors such as drinking from a modified cup, buttoning clothes, tying shoes, pouring liquids, cooking, and typing on a computer keyboard. These activities can enhance a child's physical development, independence, vocational potential, and self-concept. OTs conduct specialized assessments and make recommendations to parents and teachers regarding the effective use of appliances, materials, and activities at home and

To find out how a PT and an OT worked with a third-grade student with spastic cerebral palsy and other members of the student's IEP team to support five learning outcomes, see Szabo (2000).

	FIGURE 2	*Continued*	
1984		The Supreme Court rules in *Independent School District v. Tatro* that schools must provide intermittent catheterization as a supportive or related service if necessary to enable a student with disabilities to receive a public education.	The *Tatro* ruling expanded the range of related services that schools are required to provide and clarified the differences between school health services, which can be performed by a nonphysician, and medical services, which are provided by physicians for diagnostic or eligibility purposes.
1984		The World Institute on Disability is cofounded by Ed Roberts, an inspirational leader for self-advocacy by people with disabilities.	This was a major milestone in the civil rights and self-advocacy movement by people with disabilities.
1990		Americans with Disabilities Act (PL 101-336) is passed.	ADA provided civil rights protections to all people with disabilities in private sector employment and mandated access to all public services, accommodations, transportation, and telecommunications.
1990		Traumatic brain injury is added as a new disability category in the reauthorization of IDEA (PL 101-476).	This addition raised teachers' awareness of the educational needs of children with TBI and led to increased services and research dedicated to meeting those needs.
1999		The U.S. Supreme Court rules in *Cedar Rapids v. Garret F.* that a local school district must pay for the one-on-one nursing care for a medically fragile student who required continuous monitoring of his ventilator and other health-maintenance routines.	The decision reaffirmed and extended the Court's ruling in the 1984 *Tatro* case that schools must provide any and all health services needed for students with disabilities to attend school, as long as performance of those services does not require a licensed physician.
2004		Improving Access to Assistive Technology Act of 2004 (PL 108-364); third time Congress amended and extended provisions of the Technology-Related Assistance for Individuals with Disabilities Act of 1988.	Congress funds an Assistive Technology Act Project (ATAP) in each state to assist people with disabilities in obtaining AT services throughout their entire life span. ATAP activities include product demonstrations, AT device loan programs, financing assistance, and public awareness regarding the availability, benefits, and costs of AT. For more info, go to www.resna.org/taproject.

A physical therapist leads Kavana through exercises to increase her muscular strength and postural control.

Katelyn Metzger/Merrill

school. Many OTs also work with vocational rehabilitation specialists in helping students find opportunities for work and independent living after completing an educational program.

Other specialists who frequently provide related services to children with physical disabilities and health impairments include the following:

- *Speech-language pathologists (SLPs),* who provide speech therapy, language interventions, oral motor coordination (e.g., chewing and swallowing), and augmentative and alternative communication (AAC) services
- *Adapted physical educators,* who provide physical education activities designed to meet the individual needs of students with disabilities
- *Recreation therapists,* who provide instruction in leisure activities and therapeutic recreation
- *School nurses,* who provide certain health care services to students, monitor students' health, and inform IEP teams about the effects of medical conditions on students' educational programs
- *Prosthetists,* who make and fit artificial limbs
- *Orthotists,* who design and fit braces and other assistive devices
- *Orientation and mobility specialists,* who teach students to navigate their environment as effectively and independently as possible
- *Biomedical engineers,* who develop or adapt technology to meet a student's specialized needs
- *Health aides,* who carry out medical procedures and health-care services in the classroom
- *Counselors and medical social workers,* who help students and families adjust to disabilities

Environmental Modifications

Environmental modifications

![Council for Exceptional Children] Content Standards for Beginning Teachers—P&HD: Adaptations of educational environments necessary to accommodate individuals with P&HD (PH5K1) (also ICC5K1).

Environmental modifications are frequently necessary to enable a student with physical and health impairments to participate more fully and independently in school. Environmental modifications include adaptations to provide increased access to a task or an activity, changing the way in which instruction is delivered, and changing the manner in which the task is done (Best, Heller, & Bigge, 2010; Heller, Dangel, & Sweatman, 1995). Although barrier-free architecture is the most publicly visible type of environmental modification for making community buildings and services more accessible, some of the most functional adaptations require little or no cost:

- Install paper-cup dispensers near water fountains so students in wheelchairs can use them.
- Move a class or an activity to an accessible part of a school building so that a student with a physical impairment can participate.
- Provide soft-tip pens that require less pressure for writing.
- Provide a head-mounted pointer stick and keyboard guard that enable a student with limited fine-motor control to strike one computer key at a time.
- Change desks and tabletops to appropriate heights for students who are very short or use wheelchairs.

- Provide a wooden pointer to enable a student to reach the upper buttons on an elevator control panel.
- Modify response requirements by allowing written responses instead of spoken ones, or vice versa.

Assistive Technology

Although the term *technology* often conjures up images of sophisticated computers and other hardware, technology includes any systematic method based on scientific principles for accomplishing a practical task or purpose. IDEA defines **assistive technology** as both assistive technology devices and the services needed to help a child obtain and effectively use the devices.

> *Assistive technology device* means any item, piece of equipment, or product system, whether acquired commercially off the shelf, modified, or customized, that is used to increase, maintain, or improve the functional capabilities of a child with a disability. The term does not include a medical device that is surgically implanted or the replacement of such device. (20 USC §1401 [2004], 20 *CFR* §300.5)
>
> *Assistive technology service* means any service that directly assists a child with a disability in the selection, acquisition, or use of an assistive technology device. (20 USC §1401 [2004], 20 *CFR* §300.6)

Individuals with physical disabilities use both low-tech assistive devices (e.g., adapted eating utensils, a "grabber" or "reacher" that enables a person in a wheelchair to reach items on a shelf) and high-tech assistive devices (e.g., computerized synthetic speech devices, electronic switches activated by eye movements) for a wide variety of purposes, including mobility, performance of daily life skills, improved environmental manipulation and control, better communication, access to computers, recreation and leisure, and enhanced learning (Best, Reed, & Bigge, 2010; Dell, Newton, & Petroff, 2008). IEP team members should not view a student's acquisition and use of assistive technology as an educational outcome in itself but as a means of increasing the student's independence and access to various activities and opportunities.

Some students cannot move freely from place to place without the assistance of a mobility device. Many children as young as 3 to 5 years old can learn to explore their environment with freedom and independence in "energy efficient, creative, wheeled scooter boards and wheeled go-carts that provide mobility without restricting upper or lower extremity functions" (Evans & Smith, 1993, p. 1418). Adapted bicycles enable children with disabilities to enjoy the thrill of bicycle riding and reap the health benefits (Klein, McHugh, Harrington, Davis, & Lieberman, 2005).

Advances in wheelchair design have made manual chairs lighter and stronger, powered chairs have been adapted for use in rural areas, and new environmental controls have put the wheelchair user into contact with both immediate and distant parts of her world. A student should not be described as being "confined to a wheelchair." This expression suggests that the person is restrained or even imprisoned. Most students who use wheelchairs leave them from time to time to exercise, travel in an automobile, or lie down. The preferred language is "has a wheelchair" or "uses a wheelchair to get around."

New technological aids for communication are used increasingly by children whose physical impairments

Assistive technology

Council for Exceptional Children — Content Standards for Beginning Teachers—P&HD: Continuum of nonsymbolic to symbolic forms of communication (PH6K1).

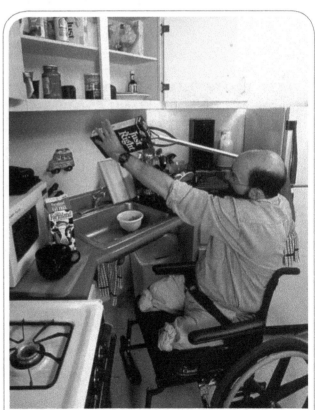

Assistive technology includes low-tech devices such as this simple "reacher."

© Will Hart/PhotoEdit

prevent them from speaking clearly. For students who can speak but have limited motor function, voice input/output products enable them to access computers (Dell et al., 2008). Such developments allow students with physical impairments to communicate expressively and receptively with others and take part in a wide range of instructional programs. Many individuals with physical disabilities use telecommunications technologies to expand their world, gain access to information and services, and meet new people. Many children and adults with disabilities use e-mail, Facebook, and other social media to communicate with others, make new friends, and build and maintain relationships.

Technology can seldom be pulled off the shelf and serve a student with disabilities with maximum effectiveness. Before purchasing and training a child to use any assistive technology device, the IEP team should carefully consider certain characteristics of the child and the potential technologies that might be selected as well as the impact of using those technologies on the child's family (Alper & Raharinirina, 2006; Parette & Brotherson, 2004). An assessment of the child's academic skills, social skills, and physical capabilities should help identify the goals and objectives for the technology and narrow down the kinds of devices that may be effective. The team should also determine the child's preferences for certain types of technology. The IEP team should then consider the characteristics of potentially appropriate technologies, including availability, simplicity of operation, initial and ongoing cost, adaptability to meet the child's changing needs, and the device's reliability and repair record.

Bausch and Ault (2008) detail how IEP teams can design an assistive technology implementation plan to ensure devices are used and have their intended outcomes.

Animal Assistance

Animals can help children and adults with physical disabilities in many ways. Nearly everyone is familiar with guide dogs, which can help people who are blind travel independently. Some agencies now train hearing dogs to assist people who are deaf by alerting them to sounds. Another recent and promising approach to the use of animals by people with disabilities is the helper or service dog. Depending on a person's needs, dogs can be trained to carry books and other objects (in saddlebags), pick up telephone receivers, turn light switches on or off, and open doors. Dogs can also be used for balance and support—for example, to help a person propel a wheelchair up a steep ramp or stand up from a seated position. And dogs can be trained to contact family members or neighbors in an emergency.

Monkeys also have been trained to serve as personal care attendants for people with disabilities. See *Current Issues and Future Trends*, "Monkey Helpers: Personal Care Attendants and Companions for People with Disabilities."

In addition to providing practical assistance and enhancing the independence of people with disabilities, animals also have social value as companions. People frequently report that their helper animals serve as icebreakers in opening up conversations and contacts with people without disabilities in the school and community.

photo provided by Canine Companions for Independence®

Helper or service dogs can be trained to assist with many daily living and work-related tasks.

Special Health Care Routines

Many students with physical disabilities have health care needs that require specialized procedures such as taking prescribed medication or self-administering insulin shots, CIC (described earlier in this chapter), tracheotomy care, ventilator/respirator care, and managing special nutrition and dietary needs. These special health-related needs are prescribed in an

individualized health care plan (IHCP), which is included as part of the student's IEP. In addition to general information describing the history, diagnosis, and assessment data relevant to the condition, the IHCP "includes precise information about how to handle routine healthcare procedures, physical management techniques, and medical emergencies that may arise while the child is at school" (Getch et al., 2007, p. 48). Teachers and school personnel must be trained to safely administer the health care procedures they are expected to perform (Heller, Fredrick, Best, Dykes, & Cohen, 2000).

Often, well-meaning teachers, classmates, and parents tend to do too much for a child with a physical or health impairment. It may be difficult, frustrating, and/or time-consuming for the child to learn to care for his own needs, but the confidence and skills gained from independent functioning are well worth the effort in the long run (Rues et al., 2011). Students who learn to perform all or part of their daily health care needs increase their ability to function independently in nonschool environments and lessen their dependence on caregivers (Betz & Nehring, 2007; Collins, 2007). Self health-care skills must be thoroughly analyzed for *time-limited steps*, which must be completed within a certain time frame or injury may occur (e.g., in tube feeding, adding more to the syringe barrel before it empties to avoid air going into the stomach), and *caution steps*, in which the student could injure himself by making jerking or incorrect movement (e.g., in tube feeding, attaching the syringe barrel to the G-tube without pulling out the G-tube) (Heller, Bigge, & Allgood, 2010).

IMPORTANCE OF POSITIONING, SEATING, AND MOVEMENT Proper positioning, seating, and regular movement are critically important for children with physical disabilities. Proper positioning and movement encourage the development of muscles and bones and help maintain healthy skin (Heller, Forney, Alberto, Schwartzman, & Goeckel, 2000). In addition to these health benefits, positioning can influence how a child with physical disabilities is perceived and accepted by others. Simple adjustments can contribute to improved appearance and greater comfort and increased health for the child with physical disabilities (Best, Reed, & Bigge, 2010; Cantu, 2004):

- Good positioning results in alignment and proximal support of the body.
- Stability positively affects use of the upper body.
- Stability promotes feelings of physical security and safety.
- Good positioning distributes pressure evenly and provides comfort for seating tolerance and long-term use.
- Good positioning can reduce deformity.
- Positions must be changed frequently.

Proper seating helps combat poor circulation, muscle tightness, and pressure sores and contributes to proper digestion, respiration, and physical development. Be attentive to the following (Heller, Forney et al., 2000):

- Face should be forward, in midline position.
- Shoulders should be in midline position, not hunched over.
- Trunk should be in midline position; maintain normal curvature of spine.
- Seatbelt, pommel or leg separator, and/or shoulder and chest straps may be necessary for shoulder/upper trunk support and upright positions.
- Pelvic position: hips as far back in the chair as possible and weight distributed evenly on both sides of the buttocks.
- Foot support: both feet level and supported on the floor or wheelchair pedals.

Skin care is a major concern for many children with physical disabilities. Caregivers should check the skin underneath braces or splints daily to identify persistent red spots that indicate an improper fit. Someone should perform skin checks at least twice daily. Students who can conduct self-checks of their skin should be taught to do so. Use of a long-handled mirror can reduce the student's dependence on others for this self-care task (Ricci-Balich & Behm, 1996). A health care professional should be contacted if any spot does not fade within 20 minutes after the pressure is relieved (Campbell,

IHCPs

 Content Standards for Beginning Teachers—P&HD: Integrate an individual's health care plan into daily programming (PH7S2).

In-depth information on health care procedures, including sample IHCP objectives, task analysis, and teaching techniques, can be found in Heller, Forney et al. (2000).

Positioning, seating, and movement

 Content Standards for Beginning Teachers—P&HD: Use proper positioning techniques and equipment to promote participation in academic and social environments (PH5S1) (also PH2K3).

CURRENT ISSUES AND

FUTURE TRENDS

▶ Monkey Helpers: Personal Care Attendants
and Companions for People with Disabilities

THE FIRST EDITION OF *EXCEPTIONAL CHILDREN*, in 1980, included a description of an exciting research project by M. J. Willard at Tufts New England Medical Center exploring the possibility of capuchin monkeys as service animals for people with spinal cord injuries. Dr. Willard described her early work with Crystal, one of the first monkeys to participate in her noble experiment.

> One of the first things I taught Crystal was to feed me. I used a shaping procedure. If Crystal would just touch the spoon she was rewarded with a pellet of food and "Good girl!" Then she had to learn to grasp the spoon on the right end. Once Crystal got to holding the spoon, then any movement where she raised it was reinforced.... Once she could raise the spoon and put it into my mouth, I taught her to touch the bowl first and do scooping motions. Then we went to fake food, Styrofoam bits, because she had to learn not to touch the food. Finally we went to real food, applesauce, and about 95% of it would get into me—and that took about 3 months of 20-minute training sessions every day. But we learned a lot and we're getting much better now. Teaching new skills in a matter of days. (quoted in Heward & Orlansky, 1980, p. 265)

Crystal proved such a capable learner that she was eventually placed with Bill Powell, a computer engineer living in Boston. Dr. Willard's pioneering work laid the foundation for Helping Hands, a nonprofit organization that trains and places helper monkeys with individuals with spinal cord injuries, muscular dystrophy, multiple sclerosis, Lou Gehrig's disease, and other mobility-limiting diseases.

Courtesy of Helping Hands: Monkey Helpers for the Disabled, Inc.

Dr. Willard uses a shaping procedure to teach Crystal to feed her with a spoon. Crystal's success is immediately reinforced with a bit of *her* favorite food.

2011). Students who can use their arms should be taught to perform "chair pushups" in which they lift their buttocks off the seat for 5 to 10 seconds. Doing chair pushups every 30 to 60 minutes may prevent pressure sores. Children who cannot perform pushups can shift their weight by bending forward and sideways.

LIFTING AND TRANSFERRING STUDENTS To prevent the development of pressure sores and help students maintain proper seating and positioning, teachers must know how to move and transfer students with physical disabilities. Teachers should follow routines for lifting and transferring a child with disabilities that entail standard procedures for each child for (a) making contact with the child, (b) communicating what is going to happen in a manner the child can understand, (c) preparing the child physically for the transfer, and (d) requiring the child to participate in the routine as much as possible (Stremel et al., 1990). Figure 3 shows an example of an individualized routine for lifting and carrying a preschool child with cerebral palsy and spastic

Lifting and transferring students

 Council for Exceptional Children

Content Standards for Beginning Teachers—P&HD: Demonstrate appropriate body mechanics to ensure student and teacher safety in transfer, lifting, positioning, and seating (PH5S2).

Crystal unlocks the door to Bill's apartment, pushes it open, and turns on the light.

Courtesy of Helping Hands: Monkey Helpers for the Disabled, Inc.

WHY MONKEYS

Capuchin monkeys are especially well suited to be monkey helpers. Capuchins are natural tool users in the wild, and their small size (6 to 10 pounds) is well suited to a home environment. Only positive reinforcement is needed to teach capuchins new tasks. Training is accomplished by rewarding the monkeys for doing activities that already come naturally to them.

Monkeys can do a wider range of tasks for a much longer time than other animals. It costs about $38,000 to support each monkey from breeding through placement.

A helper monkey can provide care and companionship for 20 to 30 years. This compares favorably to $50,000 needed to train and support a service dog with a 10-year life span.

HELPING HANDS

Helping Hands has learned that although task assistance is fundamentally valuable to its recipients, the true magic of the program is the emotional benefit of companionship and the animal–human bond. Chris Watts, who has no feeling from the chest down and limited use of his arms and hands as the result of breaking his neck in a diving accident, describes what his capuchin monkey helper, Sadie, means to him:

> "It's somewhere between having a daughter and a friend, and a pet and a personal care attendant all wrapped in one."
>
> "We give something to each other," says Watts. "She needs my affection just as much as I need hers. It just feels really good just to know there's something that loves you unconditionally like she does." (from television news report by Scott Wahle, CBS 4 Boston, January 17, 2006)

To learn more about Helping Hands and see videos of people and their helper monkeys, go to http://www.monkeyhelpers.org/

WHAT DO YOU THINK?

1. How might having a monkey helper and companion contribute to the quality of life experienced by a person with disabilities?
2. What skills would a person need to be a responsible partner for a helper monkey?
3. How might animal species other than dogs and monkeys help people with disabilities?

quadriplegia. Posting charts and photos of recommended positions for individual students can remind teachers and other staff to use proper transferring and positioning techniques.

Independence and Self-Esteem

All children, whether or not they face the challenges presented by a physical disability or a chronic health condition, need to develop respect for themselves and feel that they have a rightful place in their families, schools, and communities. Effective teachers accept and treat children with physical impairments and special health care needs as worthwhile and whole individuals rather than as disability cases. They encourage the children to develop a positive, realistic view of themselves and their physical conditions. They enable the children to experience success, accomplishment, and, at times, failure. They expect the children to meet reasonable standards of performance and

Developing independence and self-esteem

 Council for Exceptional Children

Content Standards for Beginning Teachers—

P&HD: Barriers to accessibility by individuals with P&HD (PH5K2) (also ICC5K4).

FIGURE 3   EXAMPLE OF A ROUTINE FOR LIFTING AND CARRYING A CHILD WITH PHYSICAL DISABILITIES

Name: Susan   **Date:** 5/12/2010
Lifting and Carrying Routine
Follow these steps each time you pick Susan up from the floor or move her from one piece of equipment to another or move her in the classroom from one location to another.

Step	Activity	Desired response
Contacting	Touch Susan on her arm or shoulder and tell her you are going to move her from _____ to _____.	Wait for Susan to relax.
Communicating	Tell Susan where you are going and show her a picture or object that represents where she is going. For example, show her coat and say, "We are going outside now to play."	Wait for Susan to respond with facial expressions and vocalizations. (Try not to get her so hyped that she becomes more spastic.)
Preparing	Make sure Susan's muscle tone is not stiff before you move her. Use deep pressure touch with a flat hand on her chest area to help relax her.	Wait to make sure that Susan's body is relaxed and in alignment (as much as possible).
Lifting	Place Susan in a sitting position and lift her from sitting unless she is in the stander, where she will need to be lifted from standing. Tell her that you are going to lift her. Put your arms around Susan's back and under her knees and bend her knees to her chest so that you maintain her in a flexed position.	Wait for Susan to reach her arms forward toward you and facilitate at her shoulders if she does not initiate reach within 10 seconds.
Carrying	Turn Susan away from you so that she is facing away and can see where you are moving. Lean her back against your body to provide support and hold her with one arm under her hips with her legs in front. If her legs become stiff, use your other arm to hold her legs apart by coming under one leg and between the two legs to hold them gently apart.	Susan will be able to see where she is going and can use her arms to indicate location (grossly).
Repositioning	Put Susan in the next position she is to use for the activity. Tell her what is happening; "Music is next, and you are going to sit on the floor so you can play the instruments with Jilly and Tommy."	Susan is ready to participate in the next activity.

Source: From Campbell, P. H. (2010). Addressing motor disabilities. In M. E. Snell & F. Brown (Eds.), *Instruction of students with severe disabilities* (7th ed., p. 362). © 2010 by Merrill/Prentice Hall. Reprinted by permission of Pearson Education, Inc., Upper Saddle River, NJ.

behavior. They help the children cope with disabilities wherever possible and realize that, beyond their physical impairments, these children have many qualities that make them unique individuals.

Students with physical limitations should be encouraged to develop as much independence as possible (Angell, Stoner, & Fulk, 2010; Enright, 2000). Nevertheless, most people with physical disabilities find it necessary to rely on others for assistance at certain times and in certain situations. Effective teachers can help students cope with their disabilities, set realistic expectations, and accept help gracefully when it is needed.

Many people with disabilities report that their hardware (wheelchairs, prosthetic limbs, communication devices, etc.) creates a great deal of curiosity and leads to frequent, repetitive questions from strangers. Learning how to explain their physical disabilities or health condition and to respond to questions can be an appropriate component of the educational programs for some children. They may also benefit from discussing concerns such as when to ask for help from others and when to decline offers of assistance (see Figure 4).

Many self-help groups are available for people with disabilities. These groups can help provide information and support to children affected by similar disabilities. It is usually encouraging for a child and parent to meet and observe capable, independent adults who have disabilities; and worthwhile helping relationships can be established. Teachers can help promote self-knowledge and self-confidence in their students with physical disabilities by introducing them to such adults and groups. Some self-advocacy groups operate centers for independent living, which emphasize adaptive devices, financial benefits, access to jobs, and provision of personal care attendants.

EDUCATIONAL PLACEMENT ALTERNATIVES

For no group of exceptional children is the continuum of educational services and placement options more relevant than for students with physical impairments and special health needs. Most children with physical and health impairments today spend at least part of the school day in general education classrooms. During the 2008–09 school year, about 52% of all students who received special education services under the disability category of orthopedic impairments and 60% of those with other health impairments were educated in

Jose has learned how to get in and out of his wheelchair, which helps him take part in his health care and increases his independence.

Katelyn Metzger/Merrill

general education classrooms (U.S. Department of Education, 2010b). The percentage of students in each disability category served in resource rooms was 17% and 24%, respectively.

Many children with physical disabilities are also served in special classes in the public schools. During the 2008–09 school year, about 24% of all students who received special education services under the disability category of orthopedic impairments and 11% of those with other health impairments were educated in separate classrooms (U.S. Department of Education, 2010b). Special classes usually provide smaller class size, more adapted equipment, and easier access to the services of professionals such as physicians, physical and occupational therapists, adapted physical educators, and specialists in communication disorders and therapeutic recreation. Some districts build or adapt school buildings especially for students with physical disabilities.

Some children with the most severe physical and health impairments are served in homebound or hospital education programs. If a child's medical condition necessitates hospitalization or treatment at home for a lengthy period (generally 30 days or more), the local school district is obligated to develop an IEP and provide appropriate educational services to the child through a qualified teacher. Some children need home- or hospital-based instruction because their life support equipment cannot be made portable.

A **technology-dependent student** is "one who needs both a medical device to compensate for the loss of a vital body function and substantial and ongoing nursing care to avoid death or further disability" (Office of Technology Assessment, 1987, p. 3). Educators also use the term *medically fragile* to refer to students "who are in constant need of medical supervision to prevent life-threatening situations" (Katsiyannis & Yell, 2000, p. 317). As Lehr and McDaid (1993) pointed out, however, many of these children are "survivors of many adverse conditions, who in fact are not fragile at all, but remarkably strong to be able to rebound from periods of acute illness" (p. 7).

Placement alternatives

Council for Exceptional Children

Content Standards for Beginning Teachers—Common Core: Demands of learning environments (ICC5K1).

FIGURE 4 PROMOTING THE INDEPENDENCE OF STUDENTS WITH PHYSICAL DISABILITIES AND SPECIAL HEALTH CARE NEEDS

by Mary Kate Ryan-Griffith

Encourage Independent Movement

Sometimes efforts to assist and be nice to a student with physical and health challenges can contribute to learned helplessness, which becomes increasingly difficult to overcome as the child grows older. Teachers should help children with physical and health challenges learn to be as motorically independent and self-sufficient as possible. Doing things for themselves develops and maintains children's muscular function and enhances their self-esteem.

- A student's independence can be sabotaged by inefficient room arrangement. Plan the layout of your classroom so that students can access the water fountain, the blackboard, the reading area, the small-group-activities area, and the computer and can enter and exit the classroom for bathroom and emergency situations.
- If one of your students uses a wheelchair, obtain one (ask the school nurse or the PT), get in it, and navigate the classroom layout yourself. Looking at wheelchair access from this level is very sobering.
- Troubleshoot each activity in the classroom and around the school building and grounds that students should do themselves if they can: opening doors, turning pages in a book, feeding the class pet, holding up a test tube in science lab, going through the lunch line in the cafeteria, and so forth. Look for ways to adapt the task and/or provide an assistive device that will enable the student to participate as independently as possible. A student who moves purposively throughout the day develops and maintains muscular function and interacts more naturally with classmates.

Teach Students to Ask For and Decline Help

As important as it is to build their independence, students with physical and special health needs must also learn to recognize and accept their limits.

- Teach students that it is okay to politely request assistance with tasks or situations that they cannot do independently. Manners should always be stressed! The pendulum can swing very quickly from a student who does not self-advocate to an imperious leader barking orders at one and all.
- A student who has politely requested and received assistance from others will likely experience an increase in unsolicited offers of help. Teach the student that it is also okay to say, "No, thanks, I don't need help now."

Don't be Afraid of the Equipment

The special equipment used by some students with physical disabilities and their special health needs—braces, wheelchairs, ventilators, and voice boxes—can be intimidating to other students and to adults.

- If one of your students uses special equipment, get to know it. Ask the PT, the OT, the school nurse, or other health professionals on the student's IEP team to demonstrate and explain the equipment before the first week of school begins. The student should participate in this demonstration and discussion as much as possible. Ask what to look for to ensure that the equipment is in good working order and who to contact if you notice any problems.
- Ask the student with physical disabilities or special health care needs to do a show-and-tell of his equipment for the class. This not only helps classmates become comfortable with the equipment but also helps build friendships and quickly puts the equipment in the background where it should be so that children can see their classmate as just another kid.

Source: Mary Kate Ryan-Griffith, a special education teacher in Silver Spring, Maryland, was the Featured Teacher for this chapter in the previous three editions of *Exceptional Children.* Ms. Ryan-Griffith is paralyzed from the chest down as the result of an auto accident and has used a wheelchair for 28 years.

Home or hospital settings are usually regarded as the most restrictive placements because little or no interaction with students without disabilities is likely. Most large hospitals and medical centers employ educational specialists who cooperate with the hospitalized student's home school district in planning and delivering instruction. Homebound children are visited regularly by itinerant teachers or tutors hired by the school district. Some school programs use a closed-circuit TV system to enable children to see, hear, and participate in class discussions and demonstrations from their beds.

One should not assume that a technology-dependent child cannot be educated in the public schools. After examining the experiences of 77 families of children who are ventilator assisted, the authors of a study on the educational placements of such children concluded that "barriers to the integration of these children into school-based programs are attitudinal more than technological" (Jones, Clatterbuck, Marquis, Turnbull, & Moberly, 1996, p. 47).

Related Services in the Classroom

We will likely see a continuation of the trend to serve children with physical and health impairments in general education classrooms as much as possible. Therapists and other related service and support personnel will come into the classroom to assist the teacher, the child, and classmates (Szabo, 2000).

Including students with physical impairments and special health care needs in general education classrooms, however, has raised several controversial issues. Many questions center on the extent of responsibility properly assumed by teachers and schools for a child's physical health care needs. Some educators and school administrators believe that services such as catheterization, tracheotomy care, and tube feeding are more medical than educational and should not be the school's responsibility. The expense of such services, the training and supervision of personnel, and the availability of insurance pose potential problems for school districts. Similar questions have been raised with regard to the assistive devices and special therapeutic services that children with physical or health impairments may need to access and benefit from a public education. For example, who should bear the cost of an expensive computerized communication system for a child with cerebral palsy—the parents, the school, both, or some other agency?

Two landmark U.S. Supreme Court cases have made clear the government's position. In *Irving Independent School District v. Tatro* (1984), the Court decided that a school district was obligated to provide CIC to a young child with spina bifida. The Court considered catheterization to be a related service, necessary for the child to remain in the least restrictive educational setting and able to be performed by a trained layperson.

Cedar Rapids Community School District v. Garret F. (1999) involved nursing care for a middle school student who was paralyzed in a motorcycle accident at the age of 4 and could breathe only with an electric ventilator or by someone pumping an air bag attached to his tracheotomy tube. In addition to having someone monitor and check the settings on his ventilator, Garret required continuous assistance with his tracheotomy, positioning in his wheelchair, observations to determine if he was in respiratory distress, catheterization, assessments of his blood pressure, and assistance with food and drink. Garret's mother had used money from insurance and a settlement with the motorcycle company to hire a nurse to care for his medical needs. When Garret reached middle school, his mother asked the school district to assume the cost of his physical care during the school day. The school district refused, believing it was not responsible under IDEA for providing continuous nursing care. The Supreme Court agreed with lower courts that the nursing services were related services because Garret could not attend school without them and ruled that the school district had to pay for continuous one-on-one nursing care. These two rulings used what is known as a "bright-line test" for making decisions about related services (Katsiyannis & Yell, 2000). A bright-line test is clearly stated and easy to follow. The bright-line test established in the *Tatro* case and upheld by the *Garret* case is that if a licensed physician is required to perform a service, the school district is not responsible for paying for it. If a nurse or a health aide can perform the service, even if it is medical in nature, it is considered a related service that the school district must provide under IDEA to give the child access to a free appropriate public education.

You can find reviews and discussions of special education law and legal precedents concerning the schools' responsibility for providing assistive technology and special health care services in Heller, Fredrick, and colleagues (2000); Katsiyannis and Yell (2000); Murdick, Gartin, and Crabtree (2007); Wright and Wright (2006b); and Yell (2012).

Inclusive Attitudes

After health care objectives, acceptance is the most basic need of children with physical disabilities and health impairments. How parents, teachers, classmates, and others react to a child with physical disabilities is at least as important as the disability itself. Many children with physical disabilities suffer from excessive pity, sympathy, and overprotection; others are cruelly rejected, stared at, teased, and excluded from participating in activities with nondisabled children (Pivik, McComas, & LaFlamme, 2002). Turner-Henson, Holaday, Corser, Ogletree, and Swan (1994) conducted interviews

Tatro and Garret cases

 Content Standards for Beginning Teachers—P&HD: Laws and policies related to specialized health care in the educational setting (PH1K3).

Attitudes and practices that hinder or support inclusion of students with P&HD

 Content Standards for Beginning Teachers—P&HD: Barriers to accessibility by individuals with P&HD (PH5K2) (also ICC5K4).

431

with the parents of 365 children with chronic illnesses and reported that one third (34.5%) of the parents had experienced specific incidences of discrimination concerning their children. Although the study did not focus on the schools, more than half (55%) of the problems cited by the parents occurred at school (e.g., child not allowed to participate in play activities because of a brace or excluded from parties because of food limitations; teacher thinks child is faking low blood sugar). Peers were the second-most common source of discrimination (36%).

The classroom can be a useful place to discuss disabilities and encourage understanding and acceptance of a child with a physical disability or health impairment. Some teachers find that simulation or role-playing activities are helpful. Classmates might, for example, have the opportunity to use wheelchairs, braces, or crutches to expand their awareness of some barriers a classmate with physical disabilities faces. Factual information can also help build a general understanding of impairment. Classmates should learn to use accurate terminology and offer the correct kind of assistance when needed.

▼ TIPS FOR BEGINNING TEACHERS

Promoting the Success of Students with Physical Disabilities and Special Health Care Needs in the Regular Classroom

BY CAROL MOSS

All teachers, whether general or special educators, will at various times during their careers have students with physical disabilities or special health care needs in their classrooms. When teachers ask me what they should do to help these students have academic and social success, I always recommend the following.

KEEP A BOX OF TOOLS AT THE READY

Access to a "toolbox" containing a variety of effective instructional strategies and tactics is a common denominator among highly successful teachers. Alongside their toolbox of instructional techniques, most teachers of children with physical disabilities and special health care needs have an actual box containing real tools and accessories as recommended by the PTs and OTs on their students' IEP teams. Here are some of the items in my toolbox:

- Screwdrivers, pliers, and an adjustable wrench to tighten screws and nuts on students' adapted desks, standers, braces, and mobility equipment
- C-clamps and Velcro for securing instructional materials to desks and tables
- Dycem, a blue, rubberlike, self-adhesive material that, when attached to walkers, canes, writing utensils, and so forth, enables students with spasticity or impaired mobility to grasp and manipulate those items; provides a secure surface that anchors items such as games or note pads to tables; and prevents cups from slipping off trays or tables
- Tennis balls to put on desk and chair legs so they can move easily without excessive noise
- Painter's tape of varied colors to provide visual cues

HOLD HIGH EXPECTATIONS FOR ALL STUDENTS

Some teachers feel sorry for students with significant physical disabilities or health conditions and, as result, tend to hover and baby them. As Mary Kate Ryan-Griffith so wisely points out earlier in this chapter (see Figure 4), an oversupply of assistance can foster learned helplessness and limit a student's opportunity to build skills and self-confidence.

- **Expect and support maximum independence.** Most students want to do things for themselves. Let them know that this is what you expect but that you or a classmate will assist when help is necessary. Putting desired materials just out of reach may motivate students to stretch their abilities. Most children with physical disabilities and health care needs are not fragile, but their safety while at school is paramount. To be sure you are expecting realistic levels of independence and not creating potentially dangerous situations, consult with the PT, school nurse, any medical personnel on the IEP team, and the child's parents.
- **Allow the freedom to fail.** Encouraging students to push themselves—literally and figuratively—will necessarily result in their struggling and failing now and then. How you react to those failures will help determine whether they get back up and try again.
- **Provide supports and other forms of scaffolding to help, and then gradually withdraw those supports as much as possible.**
- **Expect and require appropriate social behavior.** Consistently enforce classroom rules for all students, and teach social skills directly. My students best learn social

skills such as taking turns or greeting a new student or adult who enters the classroom when instruction includes role playing and discriminating the correct and incorrect ways to behave.

- **Correct errors as you would those of any other student.** Reluctance to correct mistakes by a student with physical disabilities can be an unfortunate by-product of feeling sorry for a student, perhaps with the idea that correction may harm his self-esteem. But letting a student repeat the same mistake again and again does him no favors.

TRUST YOURSELF, BUT SEEK HELP, TOO

As a beginning teacher, you will sometimes feel overwhelmed, unsettled by your lack of effectiveness, and unsure of what to do next. These feelings are normal; veteran teachers also experience them. After 28 years in the classroom, I still have days when I question my effectiveness and what I'm doing. I'd be

worried if I didn't. When you find yourself struggling, consider these tips:

- **Don't ever get too comfortable with your teaching.** Just as you hold high expectations for your students, expect the best from yourself. Practice and become good at reflection. Look at your teaching practices objectively with the aim of becoming a more effective teacher.
- **Go back to fundamentals of sound instructional lesson design and delivery.** Ask questions such as these: Do my lessons have clearly defined and observable learning outcomes? Are materials individualized for maximum accessibility by each student? Do all students have multiple opportunities for guided and independent practice?
- **Seek assistance from colleagues and other professionals.** Feel free to ask for help, especially with students who are challenging. Ask a colleague to observe in your classroom and suggest ways you might improve.

▼ KEY TERMS AND CONCEPTS

absence seizure
acquired immune deficiency syndrome (AIDS)
acute condition
assistive technology
asthma
ataxia
athetosis
attention-deficit/hyperactivity disorder (ADHD)
cerebral palsy
chronic conditions
clean intermittent catheterization (CIC)
complex partial seizure
cystic fibrosis
diabetes
Duchenne muscular dystrophy
epilepsy
generalized tonic-clonic seizure
human immunodeficiency virus (HIV)
hydrocephalus
hypertonia

hypotonia
individualized health care plan (IHCP)
meningocele
muscular dystrophy
myelomeningocele
neuromotor impairment
occupational therapist (OT)
orthopedic impairment
other health impairment
paraplegia
physical therapist (PT)
quadriplegia
shunt
simple partial seizure
spina bifida
spina bifida occulta
technology-dependent student
type 1 diabetes
type 2 diabetes
universal precautions

▼ SUMMARY

Definitions of Physical Disabilities and Health Impairments

- Children with physical disabilities and health impairments are eligible for special education under two disability categories of IDEA: orthopedic impairments and other health impairments.
- Orthopedic impairments involve the skeletal system; a neuromotor impairment involves the nervous system.

Both are frequently described in terms of the affected parts of the body.

- Physical disabilities and health impairments may be congenital or acquired, chronic or acute.

Prevalence

- In 2009–10, 12.6% of all school-age children who received special education services were served under the disability categories of orthopedic impairments and other health impairments. This figure does not include all children with physical or health impairments because some are reported under other disability categories and some do not require special education services.

Types and Causes

- Cerebral palsy is a long-term condition arising from impairment to the brain and causing disturbances in voluntary motor functions.
- Spina bifida is a congenital condition that may cause loss of sensation and severe muscle weakness in the lower part of the body. Children with spina bifida can usually participate in most classroom activities but need assistance in toileting.
- Muscular dystrophy is a long-term condition; most children gradually lose the ability to walk independently.
- Spinal cord injuries are caused by a penetrating injury, stretching of the vertebral column, fracture of the vertebrae, or compression of the spinal cord and usually result in some form of paralysis below the site of the injury.
- Epilepsy produces disturbances of movement, sensation, behavior, and/or consciousness.
- Diabetes is a disorder of metabolism that can often be controlled with injections of insulin.
- Children with cystic fibrosis, asthma, HIV/AIDS, and other chronic health conditions may require special education and other related services, such as health care services and counseling.

Attention-Deficit/Hyperactivity Disorder

- To be diagnosed with attention-deficit/hyperactivity disorder (ADHD), a child must consistently display six or more symptoms listed in the DSM of inattention or hyperactivity-impulsivity for a period of at least 6 months.
- Students with ADHD are eligible for special education under the other health impairment category if they have a heightened alertness to environmental stimuli that results in limited alertness with respect to the educational environment that adversely affects academic performance. Many children with ADHD who meet eligibility requirements for special education are served under other disability categories, most often emotional disturbance or learning disabilities. Some children with ADHD are eligible for services under Section 504 of the Rehabilitation Act.
- The prevalence of ADHD is estimated to be 3% to 7% of all school-age children.
- Boys are much more likely to be diagnosed with ADHD than are girls.
- Genetic factors may place individuals at a greater-than-normal risk of an ADHD diagnosis. ADHD is associated with a wide range of genetic disorders and diseases such as fragile X syndrome, Turner syndrome, Williams syndrome, fetal alcohol syndrome, prenatal exposure to cocaine, and lead poisoning.

- Some individuals with ADHD have structural or biochemical differences in their brains that may play a causal role in their behavioral deficits and excesses.
- Ritalin is the most frequently prescribed medication for children with ADHD. About 70% to 80% of children with ADHD respond positively to Ritalin, at least in the short term. Common but usually manageable side effects of Ritalin and other stimulant medications include insomnia, decreased appetite, headaches, weight loss, and irritability.
- The use of stimulant medications with children is controversial. Some professionals believe the benefits outweigh the liabilities and that drug therapy should be part of a comprehensive treatment program for children with ADHD. Other professionals are concerned that stimulant medications have few long-term benefits and that educators and parents rely too heavily on medical interventions.
- Behavioral interventions for students with ADHD include reinforcing on-task behavior, modifying assignments and instructional activities to promote success, and teaching self-control strategies.

Characteristics

- Many factors must be taken into consideration when assessing the effects of a physical impairment or health condition on a child's development and behavior. Two particularly important variables are the age of onset and the visibility of the impairment.

Educational Approaches

- Most children with physical disabilities and health impairments require services from an interdisciplinary team of professionals.
- Physical therapists (PTs) use specialized knowledge to plan and oversee a child's program for making correct and useful movements. Occupational therapists (OTs) are concerned with a child's participation in activities, especially those that will be useful in self-help, employment, recreation, communication, and other aspects of daily living.
- Modifications to the physical environment and to classroom activities can enable students with physical and health impairments to participate more fully in the school program.
- An assistive technology device is any piece of equipment used to increase, maintain, or improve the functional capabilities of a child with disabilities.
- Animals, particularly dogs and monkeys, can assist people with physical disabilities in various ways.
- Students can increase their independence by learning to take care of their personal health care routines such as clean intermittent catheterization and self-administration of medication.
- Proper positioning and seating are important for children with physical disabilities. All teachers and other staff should follow a standard routine for lifting and moving a child with physical disabilities.

- How parents, teachers, classmates, and others react to a child with physical disabilities is at least as important as the disability itself.
- Students with physical limitations should be encouraged to develop as much independence as possible. Effective teachers help students cope with their disabilities, set realistic expectations, and accept help gracefully when needed.
- Children with physical disabilities and health impairments can gain self-knowledge and self-confidence by meeting capable adults with disabilities and joining self-advocacy groups.

Educational Placement Alternatives

- About 50% of students with physical impairments and chronic health conditions are served in general education classrooms.
- The amount of support and accommodations required to enable a student with physical disabilities to function effectively in a general education class varies greatly according to each child's condition, needs, and level of functioning.
- Special classes usually provide smaller class size, more adapted equipment, and easier access to the services of professionals such as physicians, physical and occupational therapists, and specialists in communication disorders and therapeutic recreation.
- Some technology-dependent children require home- or hospital-based instruction because their life-support equipment cannot be made portable.
- The education of students with physical and health impairments in general education classrooms has raised several controversial issues, particularly with regard to the provision of medically related procedures in the classroom.
- Successful reentry of children who have missed extended periods of school because of illness or the contraction of a disease requires preparation of the child, parents, classmates, and school personnel.

MyEducationLab™

Go to Topic 15, Physical Disabilities and Health Impairments, and Topic 12, ADHD, in the MyEducationLab (www.myeducationlab.com) for *Exceptional Children*, where you can

- Find learning outcomes for sensory impairment along with the national standards that connect to these outcomes.
- Complete Assignments and Activities that can help you more deeply understand the chapter content.
- Apply and practice your understanding of the core teaching skills identified in the chapter with the Building Teaching Skills and Dispositions learning units.
- Examine challenging situations and cases presented in the IRIS Center Resources.
- Access video clips of CCSSO National Teachers of the Year award winners responding to the question "Why Do I Teach?" in the Teacher Talk section.
- Check your comprehension of the content covered in the chapter with the Study Plan. Here you will be able to take a chapter quiz, receive feedback on your answers, and then access Review, Practice, and Enrichment activities to enhance your understanding of chapter content.
- Use the Online Lesson Plan Builder to practice lesson planning and integrating national and state standards into your planning.

▼ GLOSSARY

absence seizure: A type of epileptic seizure in which the individual loses consciousness, usually for less than half a minute; can occur very frequently in some children.

acquired immune deficiency syndrome (AIDS): A fatal illness in which the body's immune system breaks down. At present there is no known cure for AIDS or a vaccine for the virus that causes it (see *human immunodeficiency virus*).

acute condition: A serious state of illness or injury, but not permanent; contrast with *chronic*.

assistive technology: "Any item, piece of equipment, or product system, whether acquired commercially off the shelf, modified, or customized, that is used to increase, maintain, or improve the functional capabilities of children with disabilities" (the

Individuals with Disabilities Education Act [IDEA] regulations, 34 *CFR* § 300.5).

asthma: A respiratory condition characterized by recurrent episodes of wheezing, coughing, and difficulty breathing.

ataxia: A poor sense of balance and body position and lack of coordination of the voluntary muscles; characteristic of one type of cerebral palsy.

athetosis: A type of cerebral palsy characterized by large, irregular, uncontrollable twisting motions. The muscles may be tense and rigid or loose and flaccid. Often accompanied by difficulty with oral language.

attention-deficit/hyperactivity disorder (ADHD): A diagnostic category of the American Psychiatric Association for a condition in which a child exhibits

developmentally inappropriate inattention, impulsivity, and hyperactivity.

cerebral palsy: Motor impairment caused by brain damage, which is usually acquired during the prenatal period or during the birth process. Can involve a wide variety of symptoms (see *ataxia, athetosis, rigidity, spasticity,* and *tremor*) and range from mild to severe. Neither curable nor progressive.

chronic condition: A long-lasting, often permanent condition; contrast with *acute*.

clean intermittent catheterization (CIC): A clean (not sterile) catheter (tube) is inserted into the urethra and advanced into the bladder; catheter remains in place until urine is released into a bag.

complex partial seizure: A type of seizure in which an individual goes through a brief period of inappropriate or purposeless activity (also called *psychomotor seizure*). Usually lasts from 2 to 5 minutes, after which the person has amnesia about the entire episode.

cystic fibrosis: An inherited disorder that causes a dysfunction of the pancreas and mucus, salivary, and sweat glands. Cystic fibrosis causes severe, long-term respiratory difficulties. No cure is currently available.

diabetes: A chronic disease in which the body does not produce or properly use insulin, a hormone needed to convert sugar, starches, and other food into energy (see *type 1 diabetes*).

Duchenne muscular dystrophy: The most common form of muscular dystrophy, a group of long-term diseases that progressively weaken and waste away the body's muscles.

epilepsy: A condition marked by chronic and repeated seizures, disturbances of movement, sensation, behavior, and/or consciousness caused by abnormal electrical activity in the brain (see *generalized tonic-clonic seizure, complex partial seizure, simple partial seizure,* and *absence seizure*). Can usually be controlled with medication, although the drugs may have undesirable side effects. May be temporary or lifelong.

generalized tonic-clonic seizure: The most severe type of seizure, in which the individual has violent convulsions, loses consciousness, and becomes rigid. Formerly called *grand mal seizure.*

human immunodeficiency virus (HIV): The virus that causes *acquired immune deficiency syndrome (AIDS).*

hydrocephalus: An enlarged head caused by accumulation of cerebrospinal fluid in the cranial cavity; often causes brain damage and severe retardation. A condition present at birth or developing soon afterward. Can sometimes be treated successfully with a *shunt.*

hypertonia: Muscle tone that is too high; tense, contracted muscles.

hypotonia: Muscle tone that is too low; weak, floppy muscles.

individualized health care plan (IHCP): The individualized education program (IEP) component for students with special health care needs; specifies health care procedures and services administered by school personnel and a plan for emergencies.

meningocele: A type of spina bifida in which the covering of the spinal cord protrudes through an opening in the vertebrae but the cord itself and the nerve roots are enclosed.

muscular dystrophy: A group of diseases that gradually weakens muscle tissue; usually becomes evident by the age of 4 or 5.

myelomeningocele: A protrusion on the back of a child with spina bifida, consisting of a sac of nerve tissue bulging through a cleft in the spine.

neuromotor impairment: Involves the central nervous system, affecting the ability to move, use, feel, or control certain parts of the body.

occupational therapist (OT): A professional who programs and/or delivers instructional activities and materials to help children and adults with disabilities learn to participate in useful activities.

orthopedic impairment: Impairment of the skeletal system—bones, joints, limbs, and associated muscles.

other health impairment: A disability category in the Individuals with Disabilities Education Act under which a child is eligible for special education; includes diseases and special health conditions such as cancer, diabetes, and cystic fibrosis that affect a child's educational activities and performance.

paraplegia: Paralysis of the lower part of the body, including both legs; usually results from injury to or disease of the spinal cord.

physical therapist (PT): A professional trained to help people with disabilities develop and maintain muscular and orthopedic capability and make correct and useful movements.

quadriplegia: Paralysis of all four limbs.

shunt: A tube that diverts fluid from one part of the body to another; often implanted in people with hydrocephalus to remove extra cerebrospinal fluid from the head and send it directly into the heart or intestines.

simple partial seizure: A type of seizure characterized by sudden jerking motions with no loss of consciousness. Partial seizures may occur weekly, monthly, or only once or twice a year.

spina bifida: A congenital malformation of the spine in which the vertebrae that normally protect the spine do not develop fully; may involve loss of sensation and severe muscle weakness in the lower part of the body.

spina bifida occulta: A type of spina bifida that usually does not cause serious disability. Although the vertebrae do not close, no protrusion of the spinal cord and membranes is present.

technology-dependent student: A "student who needs both a medical device to compensate for the loss of a vital body function and substantial and ongoing nursing care to avoid death or further disability" (Office of Technology Assessment, 1987, p. 3).

type 1 diabetes: (formerly called *juvenile diabetes* or *early-onset diabetes*) A disease characterized by inadequate secretion or use of insulin and the resulting excessive sugar in the blood and urine. Managed with diet and/or medication but can be difficult to control. Can cause coma and eventually death if left untreated or treated improperly. Can also lead to visual impairments and limb amputation. Not curable at the present time.

type 2 diabetes: The most common form of diabetes; results from insulin resistance (the body's failure to properly use insulin), combined with relative insulin deficiency. Occurs most often in adults who are overweight, but the recent increase in childhood obesity has led to a rise in the incidence of type 2 diabetes in children.

universal precautions: A set of safety guidelines (e.g., wearing protective gloves, hand washing) that interrupt the chain of infection spread by potential biohazards such as blood and bodily fluids.

Low-Incidence Disabilities: Severe/Multiple Disabilities, Deaf-Blindness, and Traumatic Brain Injury

From Chapter 12 of *Exceptional Children* and *An Introduction to Special Education*, Tenth Edition. William L. Heward.

Low-Incidence Disabilities: Severe/Multiple Disabilities, Deaf-Blindness, and Traumatic Brain Injury

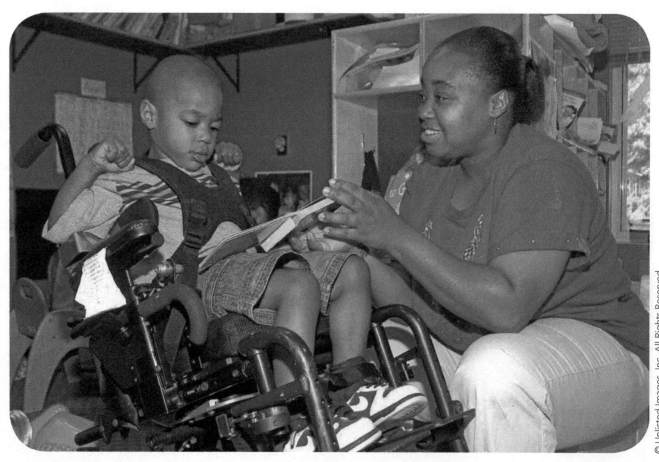

► FOCUS QUESTIONS

- Why is a curriculum based on typical developmental stages and milestones inappropriate for students with severe and multiple disabilities?

- How can a teacher assist a child who has been hospitalized with a traumatic brain injury return to school?

- Why are functional and age-appropriate curricula so critical for students with severe and multiple disabilities?

- How does access to the general academic curriculum benefit students with severe disabilities?

- What are the most important skills for a teacher of students with severe and multiple disabilities? Why?

- How much time should a student with severe and multiple disabilities spend in the general education classroom?

▼ FEATURED TEACHER

CAREY CREECH-GALLOWAY

George Rogers Clark High School • Winchester, Kentucky

EDUCATION—CERTIFICATION—EXPERIENCE

- B.S., special education, University of Kentucky in 2004

- M.Ed., special education: moderate and severe disabilities, University of Kentucky, 2011

- Kentucky Moderate and Severe Disabilities, P–12

- 7 years as a special education teacher; 3 years as an instructional assistant for secondary students with moderate and severe disabilities

I enjoy the student-centered approach and individual programming that occurs in special education. With each student, I must continually try to achieve the most beneficial balance of functional skills and academic curriculum and instructional methods. That and the incredibly varied student ability levels keep me fresh and on my toes. To be an effective teacher of students with severe disabilities requires organization, flexibility, and knowledge of systematic instruction strategies.

COLLABORATION AND PREPARATION FOR MEANINGFUL INCLUSION Each of my students is included in a general education classroom for at least two class periods per day. While I am not an advocate of full inclusion for every student with severe disabilities, when appropriate supports are in place, meaningful and beneficial inclusion occurs.

Inclusion has gone well for my students because we provide appropriate adaptations and modifications in the general education setting. It is important to look at the core content that the general education teacher is focusing on and obtain the essential information. Teachers can embed functional self-care, communication, and vocational goals into the general education setting in numerous ways. Sarah, for example, is included in health and PE classes and uses her switch to answer yes/no questions and make choices during group work with her peers. During the lecture portion of the class, Sarah accesses her switch to give information to the class that corresponds with the teacher's lecture. Another student, Charles is taking an agricultural class that entails some greenhouse activities and some lecture and seat work. A peer tutor reads items to Charles and supports him on daily assignments.

We have established a very strong peer tutoring program at my high school, and every semester we have to turn away students who want to participate. These peers without disabilities facilitate relationships throughout the building, modify work, provide support in the general education setting, and act as a liaison between me and the general education teachers in the building. The relationships between our peer tutors and my students are some of the most important connections that are made during the school year.

EVIDENCE-BASED INSTRUCTION AND POSITIVE BEHAVIOR SUPPORT

I am a dedicated user of evidence-based teaching methods. Three techniques with significant research supporting their effectiveness with students with significant disabilities are constant time delay, the system of least prompts, and simultaneous prompting. I have found that these methods are easy to implement and apply to many different skills, and they are effective in helping my students achieve a wide variety of functional and academic learning objectives. For example, consistent use of the system of least prompts has enabled Mandy to progress from needing physical assistance to feed herself to needing only gesture and verbal prompts. The goal is to continue until the naturally occurring stimulus of setting the food in front of her occasions Mandy's eating. These procedures are easy to reteach to general education teachers, paraprofessionals, and even peer tutors who work with my students.

The all-important question that many special educators always ask one another is "How do you handle challenging behaviors?" Every teacher will have students whose inappropriate or defiant behaviors test their ability to be effective. When faced with such behaviors, I begin by keeping a daily log of the frequency of the behavior and the circumstances surrounding each occurrence (called ABC, or antecedent-behavior-consequence observations). These data help me understand the function of the behavior for the student, which in turn points to likely solutions such as teaching a replacement behavior or altering the motivation for the behavior with a curriculum modification. In every case, I make sure to provide positive reinforcement to promote the desired behaviors.

This year I have a student, Brian, who often has a difficult time keeping his hands to himself and, when asked to perform a task that he doesn't like, exhibits some very aggressive behaviors. I began pairing working on his IEP goals with an activity he really enjoys in order to reinforce good behavior during instruction. I observed Brian's behavior while he worked on different activities with each of the two paraprofessionals in my classroom. After those observations, I had one of the paraprofessionals

observe me working with Brian. We used ABC observation forms during these observations and compiled them to try to find a function and pattern for the behavior. We developed a plan for a DRO (differential reinforcement of zero rates or other behaviors) that we implemented on a 5-minute fixed-interval schedule. At the end of each interval, if Brian displayed no aggressive behavior and kept his hands and feet to himself, he received a choice of pretzels, popcorn, time with an iPod, or a favorite magazine. Soon after implementing the DRO, however, it was clear that Brian could anticipate when each interval ended and that he behaved appropriately at just those moments required to receive reinforcement. We applied the DRO procedure at random intervals, ranging from 3 to 8 minutes. Brian's aggressive behavior worsened over the first 3 days of this intervention but then improved dramatically over the next 2 weeks. I gradually increased the duration of the intervals until Brian was working for reinforcement once per hour.

Dealing with students' aggressive behaviors is very stressful on a new teacher. I think it is important to remember to stick with your behavior management plan for the student, but I also think it is important that your staff have some training on how to deescalate behaviors and safely manage the students physically if they become aggressive. It is important to ask your school about their protocol or management plan for students with aggressive behaviors.

KEEPING ON TOP OF THE DATA

I collect and graph data on every instructional objective I teach, and I graph all of the data. Each of my students receives instruction on a minimum of six to eight instructional objectives each school day, so I may be collecting data on up to 50 IEP objectives. Keeping up with progress data is very challenging Whenever possible, I group students with similar objectives in small groups and collect data using that model, but some students have individual objectives that require 1:1 instruction to collect data. I cannot stress enough how important direct and frequent measurement is when teaching students with severe disabilities. It allows the teacher to make data-based decisions about instruction and gives information about the student's independence level. For example, I may have a student learning to use a communication board to request items. At the beginning of the school year, that student may require physical or model prompts, but by school year's end, she may need only verbal prompts to perform the skill. This is a huge amount of progress that may not be evident without data collection. I have excellent paraprofessionals who can assist me in keeping up with records and data collection, which in my opinion is one of the most important aspects of my job.

I recently moved from teaching in a middle school to teaching high school students. Both have been challenging, but I have really come to understand the importance focusing on students' life after high school. When developing IEP goals, you begin to think more about the big picture and what the student's life will look like after high school. Those ideas or goals drive your instruction, which gives teachers of high school students with severe disabilities I have developed a feeling of urgency as I watch my students' school years drawing to a close. I think it is so important for teachers of elementary children with severe disabilities

to ask themselves, "How will learning this skill or bit of knowledge increase this student's independence in the future?"

If I could share only one piece of advice with those who plan to become teachers of students with severe disabilities, it is this: get as much hands-on experience with this population as possible. My experiences working as an instructional assistant, an employment trainer, and being involved in local Special Olympics were as valuable to me as my schoolwork and helped me get the most from the excellent education I received at the University of Kentucky.

MyEducationLab™

Visit the **MyEducationLab** for *Exceptional Children* to enhance your understanding of chapter concepts with a personalized Study Plan. You'll also have the opportunity to hone your teaching skills through video- and case-based Assignments and Activities, IRIS Center Resources, and Building Teaching Skills and Dispositions lessons.

PRESCHOOLER ZACK SHOWS A CARD with a symbol and picture that says, "I want toy," to a classmate, who responds, "Here's the toy, Zack." First grader Emily is learning to feed herself with a spoon. A teacher shows 13-year-old Terrence that when first meeting someone, a handshake is more appropriate than a hug. Manuela, who is 20, is learning to ride a city bus to her afternoon job busing tables at a diner.

Zack, Emily, Terrence, and Manuela have severe disabilities or multiple disabilities. Without direct and systematic instruction, many students with severe and multiple disabilities will not learn even the most basic, everyday activities that most of us take for granted, such as eating, toileting, and communicating our needs and feelings to others. Despite the severity and multiplicity of their disabilities, these students can and do learn.

DEFINING SEVERE, PROFOUND, AND MULTIPLE DISABILITIES

Severe Disabilities

As used by most special educators, the term **severe disabilities** includes students with significant impairments in intellectual, motor, and/or social functioning. Students with multiple disabilities and deaf-blindness—two of the three IDEA disability categories described in this chapter—as well as those with severe intellectual disabilities, severe emotional disturbance, and severe physical disabilities or health impairments are encompassed by the term.

No single widely accepted definition of severe disabilities exists. Most definitions are based on scores on tests of cognitive functioning, developmental progress based on age, or the extent of educational and other supports needed. According to the system once used to classify levels of intellectual disabilities, a person obtaining IQ scores of 35 to 40 would be considered to have severe intellectual disabilities. In

Definitions of severe disabilities, profound disabilities, and multiple disabilities

 Council for Exceptional Children

Content Standards for Beginning Teachers—INDEP CURR: Definitions and issues related to the identification of individuals with disabilities (IIC1K1) (also ICC1K5).

Students with severe disabilities require systematic instruction to learn basic skills.

© Robin Nelson/PhotoEdit

practice, however, the term *severe disabilities* often includes many individuals who score in the moderate level of intellectual disabilities (IQ scores of 40 to 55).

A developmental approach to defining severe disabilities was once common. For example, Justen (1976) defined students with severe disabilities as those individuals "age 21 and younger who are functioning at a general developmental level of half or less than the level which would be expected on the basis of chronological age" (p. 5). Today, special educators realize that developmental levels have little relevance to this population and instead emphasize that a student with severe disabilities, regardless of age, is one who needs instruction in basic skills that most children without disabilities acquire in the first 5 years of life.

The organization TASH (formerly The Association for Persons with Severe Handicaps) describes the people for whom it advocates as "people with significant disabilities and support needs who are most at risk for being excluded from society; perceived by traditional service systems as most challenging; most likely to have their rights abridged; most likely to be at risk for living, working, playing and learning in segregated environments; least likely to have the tools and opportunities necessary to advocate on their behalf; and are most likely to need ongoing, individualized supports to participate in inclusive communities and enjoy a quality of life similar to that available to all people" (TASH, 2011).

Special educators who serve children with severe disabilities have generated very little concern and debate over definitional issues compared to their colleagues in intellectual disabilities, learning disabilities, and emotional and behavioral disorders. This is not indication that professionals in the field of severe disabilities are uninterested in defining the population of students they serve; instead, it is a reflection of two inherent features of severe disabilities. First, a definition that delineates precisely who is and is not to be identified by the term *severe disabilities* is unnecessary. While the specific criteria used to define learning disabilities have a major impact on which students are eligible for special education services, whether or not any child who *might* be considered to have severe disabilities needs special education is never an issue. Second, the tremendous diversity of learning and physical challenges that these students experience renders any single set of descriptors inadequate.

Profound Disabilities

Some professionals make a distinction between children with severe disabilities and those with profound disabilities. According to Sternberg (1994), an individual with **profound disabilities** functions at a level no higher than that of a typically developing 2-year-old in all five areas of cognition, communication, social skills, motor mobility, and activities of daily living; and requires continuous monitoring and observation. IQ scores of 20 to 25 and below typically result in a classification of profound intellectual disabilities. Although some people with profound disabilities are able to achieve semi-independent functioning in some tasks of daily living, many do not speak, are nonambulatory, and are unresponsive to sensory stimuli (Petry & Maes, 2007).

IDEA mandates that all children are entitled to a free public education in the least restrictive environment no matter how complicated or challenging their learning, behavioral, or medical problems may be. However, some individuals have questioned whether children with profound disabilities can benefit from education. To read one viewpoint on whether children with the most severe disabilities are "educable," see Figure 1.

Traditional intelligence tests are virtually useless with children who have profound disabilities. Imagine the difficulty, as well as the inappropriateness, of giving an IQ test to a student who cannot hold up his head or point, let alone talk. If tested, such students tend to be assigned IQ scores at the extreme lower end of the continuum. Knowing that a particular student has an IQ of 25, however, is of no value in designing an appropriate educational program.

FIGURE 1   ARE ALL CHILDREN EDUCABLE?

Some people question the wisdom of spending large amounts of money, time, and human resources attempting to educate children who have such profound disabilities that they may never be able to function independently. Some would prefer to see resources spent on children with higher apparent potential—especially when economic conditions limit the quality of educational services for all children in the public schools. "Why bother with children who fail to make meaningful progress?" they ask.

Our knowledge of the learning and developmental processes of individuals with severe and profound disabilities is still primitive and incomplete. We do know, however, that children with severe disabilities can benefit from intensive and "customized" special education (Smith, Gast, Logan, & Jacobs, 2001). Even when a student shows little or no progress, it would be wrong to conclude that the student is incapable of learning. Instead, our teaching methods may be imperfect, and the future may bring improved methods and materials to enable that student to learn useful skills. No matter how severe their disabilities, all children have the right to the best possible public education society can offer them.

No one knows for certain the true learning potential of children whose disabilities are complex and pervasive. We do know that students with the most severe disabilities will go no farther than we let them; it is up to us to open doors and to raise our sights, not to create additional barriers.

The late Don Baer, a pioneer in the development of effective teaching methods for people with disabilities, offered this perspective on the debate over who may or may not be educable:

> Some of us have ignored both the thesis that all persons are educable and the thesis that some persons are ineducable, and instead have experimented with ways to teach some previously unteachable people. Over a few centuries, those experiments have steadily reduced the size of the apparently ineducable group relative to the obviously educable group. Clearly, we have not finished that adventure. Why predict its outcome, when we could simply pursue it, and just as well without a prediction? Why not pursue it to see if there comes a day when there is such a small class of apparently ineducable persons left that it consists of one elderly person who is put forward as ineducable. If that day comes, it will be a very nice day. And the next day will be even better.

(D. M. Baer, February 15, 2002, personal communication)

Multiple Disabilities

IDEA defines **multiple disabilities** as

> concomitant impairments (such as intellectual disability–blindness, intellectual disability–orthopedic impairment), the combination of which causes such severe educational needs that they cannot be accommodated in special education programs solely for one of the impairments. Multiple disabilities does not include deaf-blindness. (20 §1401 [2004], 20 *CFR* §300.8[c][7])

Deaf-Blindness

IDEA defines **deaf-blindness** as

> concomitant hearing and visual impairments, the combination of which causes such severe communication and other developmental and educational needs that they cannot be accommodated in special education programs solely for children with deafness or children with blindness. (20 U.S.C. §1401 [2004], 20 *CFR* §300.8[c][2])

Although the term *deaf-blind* implies the absence of hearing and vision, the vast majority of children with deaf-blindness have some functional hearing and/or vision. The combined effects of the dual impairments severely impede learning, communication, and social skills. An educational program for children who are deaf is often inappropriate for a child who also has limited vision because many methods of instruction and communication rely heavily on the use of sight. On the other hand, programs for students with visual impairments usually require good hearing because much instruction is auditory. The majority of children who have both visual and hearing impairments at birth experience major difficulties in acquiring communication skills, motor and mobility skills, and appropriate social behavior.

The absence of clear and consistent input from either sensory modality is thought to be a reason that many children who are deaf-blind engage in various forms of self-stimulatory behavior (e.g., finger flicking, hand mouthing, head/body rocking) (Downing & Eichinger, 1990). Because students with dual sensory impairments may not

Definition of deaf-blindness

Content Standards for Beginning Teachers—INDEP CURR: Definitions and issues related to the identification of individuals with disabilities (IIC1K1) (also ICC1K5).

Impact of deaf-blindness

Content Standards for Beginning Teachers—INDEP CURR: Impact of sensory impairments, physical and health disabilities on individuals, families, and society (IIC2K2) (also ICC2K2, ICC2K6).

Teaching techniques involving the sense of touch are used to provide and supplement instructional stimuli for students with dual sensory impairments.

Scott Cunningham/Merrill

initiate interactions or respond to the efforts of others to gain their attention, they appear passive or even noncompliant. The unresponsiveness of a child with deaf-blindness can lead parents and caregivers to do things for the child that unwittingly contribute to his passivity and communication difficulties. With increasingly fewer opportunities and no requirements to exert control over his environment, "learned helplessness" often develops, and the child becomes a passive recipient of care (Pease, 2000).

More than 90% of children who are deaf-blind have one or more additional disabilities: 57% also have physical disabilities, 66% have cognitive impairments, and 38% have complex health care needs (Malloy & Killoran, 2007). Educational programs for students with dual sensory impairments who require instruction in basic skills are generally similar to those for other students with severe disabilities. Although most students with dual sensory impairments can make use of information presented in visual and auditory modalities, when used in instruction, these stimuli must be enhanced and the students' attention directed toward them. Tactile teaching techniques involving the sense of touch are used to supplement the information obtained through visual and auditory modes (Chen & Downing 2001, 2006b; Downing & Chen, 2003).

A wealth of information about educating children who are deaf-blind can be found at the National Consortium on Deaf-Blindness, at http://www .nationaldb.org.

Characteristics of severe disabilities

Content Standards for Beginning Teachers—INDEP CURR: Psychological and social-emotional characteristics of individuals with disabilities (IIC2K4) (also ICC2K2).

CHARACTERISTICS OF STUDENTS WITH SEVERE AND MULTIPLE DISABILITIES

Throughout this text, we have seen how definitions and lists of characteristics used to describe the children within a disability category have limited meaning at the level of the individual student. And, of course, it is at the level of the individual student where decisions about what and how to teach should be made. As the various physical, behavioral, and learning characteristics associated with severe disabilities are described, keep in mind that students with severe disabilities constitute the most heterogeneous group of all exceptional children. As Westling and Fox (2009) point out, the differences among students with severe disabilities are greater than their similarities.

Most students with severe disabilities exhibit significant deficits in intellectual functioning. The majority of students with severe disabilities have more than one disability. Many need special services and supports because of motor impediments; communication, visual, and auditory impairments; and seizure disorders. Treatment of medical conditions and health problems results in frequent and often extended absences from school (Zijlstra & Vlaskamp, 2005). Even with the best available methods of diagnosis and assessment, it is often difficult to identify the nature and intensity of a child's multiple disabilities. Some children, for example, do not respond in any apparent way to visual stimuli, such as bright lights or moving objects. Is this because the child is blind as a result of eye damage, or is the child's unresponsiveness a feature of profound intellectual disability caused by brain damage? Such questions arise frequently in planning educational programs for students with severe disabilities.

The one defining characteristic of students with severe disabilities is that they exhibit significant and obvious deficits in multiple life-skill or developmental areas. No specific set of behaviors is common to all individuals with severe disabilities. Although each student presents a unique combination of physical, intellectual, and social characteristics, the following learning and behavioral characteristics are frequently observed in students with severe disabilities (Collins, 2007; Kim & Arnold, 2006; Westling & Fox, 2009):

- *Slow acquisition rate of new skills.* Compared to other students with disabilities, students with severe disabilities learn at a slower rate, require more instructional trials to learn a new skill, learn a fewer number of skills, and have extreme difficulty learning abstract concepts.
- *Poor generalization and maintenance of newly learned skills. Generalization* refers to the performance of a skill in settings or under conditions different from those in which the skill was learned initially. *Maintenance* refers to the continued use of a skill after instruction has been terminated. Without instruction that has been meticulously planned and implemented to facilitate generalization and maintenance, students with severe disabilities seldom show such outcomes.
- *Limited communication skills.* Almost all students with severe disabilities have difficulty expressing themselves and understanding others. Some cannot talk or gesture meaningfully and might not respond when communication is attempted.
- *Impaired physical and motor development.* Many children with severe disabilities have limited physical mobility. Many cannot walk; some cannot stand or sit up without support. They are slow to perform such basic tasks as rolling over, grasping objects, and holding up their heads. Physical impairments and health conditions are common.
- *Deficits in self-help skills.* Some children with severe disabilities cannot independently care for their most basic needs, such as dressing, eating, exercising bowel and bladder control, and maintaining personal hygiene. They often require special training involving prosthetic devices and/or adapted skill sequences to learn these basic skills.
- *Infrequent constructive behavior and interaction.* Children without disabilities and those whose disabilities are less severe typically play with other children, interact with adults, and seek out information about their surroundings. Some children with severe disabilities do not. They may appear to be completely out of touch with reality and may not show normal human emotions. It may be difficult to capture the attention of or evoke any observable response from a child with profound disabilities.
- *Stereotypic and challenging behavior.* Some children with severe disabilities engage in behaviors that are ritualistic (e.g., rocking back and forth, waving fingers in front of the face,); self-stimulatory (e.g., grinding the teeth, patting the body); self-injurious (e.g., head banging, hair pulling, eye poking); and/or aggressive (e.g., hitting or biting others). In addition to safety issues, the high frequency with which some children emit these challenging behaviors interferes with learning more adaptive behaviors and with acceptance and functioning in integrated settings.

Descriptions of characteristics such as those just mentioned can easily give an overly negative impression. Despite the intense challenges their disabilities impose on them, many students with severe disabilities exhibit warmth, persistence, determination, cheerfulness, a sense of humor, sociability, and various other desirable traits

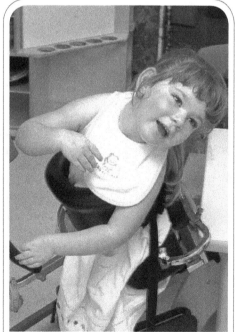

Every child with severe and multiple disabilities presents a unique combination of physical, intellectual, and social characteristics.

445

(Collins, 2007; Petry & Maes, 2007). Many teachers find great satisfaction in working with students who have severe disabilities and in observing their progress in school, home, and community settings.

PREVALENCE OF SEVERE AND MULTIPLE DISABILITIES

Because no definition of severe disabilities is universally accepted, no accurate and uniform figures on prevalence exist. Estimates of the prevalence of severe disabilities range from 0.1% to 1% of the population (Kim & Arnold, 2006). Brown (1990) considers students with severe disabilities to be those who function intellectually in the lowest-functioning 1% of the school-age population.

Because the category of severe disabilities is not one of the disability categories under which the states make their annual report to the federal government, the number of students with severe disabilities who receive special education services under IDEA cannot be determined from data supplied by the U.S. Department of Education. Students who have severe disabilities are served and reported under several disability categories, including intellectual disability, multiple disabilities, other health impairments, autism, traumatic brain injury, and deaf-blindness.

In the 2009–10 school year, 124,380 school-age children received special education and related services under the IDEA disability category of multiple disabilities. Deaf-blindness is a very low-incidence disability. Before the passage of IDEA in 1975, fewer than 100 children with dual-sensory impairments were receiving specialized education services, virtually all of which were located at residential schools for children who are blind. Although just 1,359 school-age children were served under the deaf-blindness disability category in the 2009–10 school year (U.S. Department of Education, 2011), a national census counted 9,131 children with deaf-blindness from birth through age 18 (National Consortium on Deaf-Blindness, 2011).

The term *low-incidence disabilities* refer to disabilities that do not occur very often. Multiple disabilities, traumatic brain injury, and deaf-blindness (the three IDEA disability categories described in this chapter) combined represent fewer than 3 of every 100 school-age children who receive special education.

CAUSES OF SEVERE AND MULTIPLE DISABILITIES

Causes of severe disabilities

 Council for Exceptional Children

Content Standards for Beginning Teachers—INDEP CURR: Etiologies and medical aspects of conditions affecting individuals with disabilities (IIC2K3).

Severe intellectual disabilities can be caused by a wide variety of conditions, largely biological, that may occur before (prenatal), during (perinatal), or after birth (postnatal). In almost every case, a brain disorder is involved. Brain disorders are the result of either *brain dysgenesis* (abnormal brain development) or *brain damage* (caused by influences that alter the structure or function of a brain that had been developing normally up to that point). From a review of 10 epidemiological studies, Coulter (1994) estimated that prenatal brain dysgenesis accounts for most cases of severe cognitive limitations and that perinatal and postnatal brain damage for a minority of cases. A brain disorder is "the only condition that will account for the existence of profound disabilities" (p. 41).

A significant percentage of children with severe disabilities are born with chromosomal abnormalities, such as Down syndrome, or with genetic or metabolic disorders that can cause serious problems in physical or intellectual development. Complications of pregnancy—including prematurity, Rh incompatibility, and infectious diseases contracted by the mother—can cause severe disabilities. A pregnant woman who uses drugs, drinks alcohol excessively, or is poorly nourished has a greater risk of giving birth to a child with severe disabilities.

Severe disabilities also may develop later in life from head trauma caused by automobile and bicycle accidents, falls, assaults, or abuse. Malnutrition, neglect, ingestion of poisonous substances, and certain diseases that affect the brain (e.g., meningitis, encephalitis) also can cause severe disabilities. Although hundreds of medically related causes of severe disabilities have been identified, in many cases the cause cannot be clearly determined.

TRAUMATIC BRAIN INJURY

Definition

When it was originally passed, IDEA did not mention the needs of children who have experienced head trauma and/or coma. However, when Congress amended the law in 1990 (PL 101-476), it added traumatic brain injury to the list of disability categories under which children could be eligible for special education services. IDEA defines **traumatic brain injury** as

> an acquired injury to the brain caused by an external physical force, resulting in total or partial functional disability or psychosocial impairment, or both, that adversely affects a child's educational performance. Traumatic brain injury applies to open or closed head injuries resulting in impairments in one or more areas, such as cognition; language; memory; attention; reasoning; abstract thinking; judgment; problem-solving; sensory, perceptual, and motor abilities; psychosocial behavior; physical functions; information processing; and speech. Traumatic brain injury does not apply to brain injuries that are congenital or degenerative, or to brain injuries induced by birth trauma. (20 §1401 [2004], 20 *CFR* §300.8[c][12])

Definition of TBI

Content Standards for Beginning Teachers—PH: Issues and educational definitions of individuals with PH (PH1K1).

Prevalence of Traumatic Brain Injury

About 1.7 million people sustain a traumatic brain injury each year in the United States (Centers for Disease Control and Prevention, 2011f). Of those, 52,000 will die of their injury and 275,000 will be hospitalized. Traumatic brain injury is the leading cause of death in children and the most common acquired disability in childhood. It is estimated that 5.3 million Americans have long-term need for help in performing activities of daily living as a result of traumatic brain injury (Brain Injury Association of America, 2011).

In spite of the sobering statistics on head injuries, the number of children receiving special education under the category of traumatic brain injury is quite small. In 1991–92, the first school year after traumatic brain injury was added to IDEA as a separate disability category, only 330 school-age children were served nationally. By the 2009–10 school year, the number had increased to 24,395 (U.S. Department of Education, 2011).

What accounts for the huge difference between incidence of traumatic brain injury and the number of children served? First, the vast majority of head injuries sustained by children are mild and do not adversely affect educational performance to the degree where special education is needed. Second, the human brain has a remarkable capacity to naturally compensate for injury, and recovery is good following most mild to moderate brain injuries (Vu, Babikian, & Asarnow, 2011). Third, many students with mild brain injuries are identified and served under another disability category, most likely learning disabilities or emotional or behavioral disorders. Nevertheless, special educators and neurologists are concerned that schools fail to identify many children with mild traumatic brain injury who would benefit from special education and related services (Deidrick & Farmer, 2005; Hotz, 2011).

Types and Causes of Traumatic Brain Injury

Head injuries are classified by the type of injury (open or closed), by the kind of damage sustained by the brain, and by the location of the injury. An **open head injury** is the result of penetration of the skull, such as that caused by a bullet or a forceful blow to the head with a hard or sharp object. Open head injuries that are not fatal often result in the loss of behavioral or sensory functions controlled by the part of the brain where the injury occurred (see Figure 2).

The most common type of head injury does not involve penetration of the skull. A **closed head injury** occurs when the head hits or is hit by an object with such force

Types and causes of TBI

Content Standards for Beginning Teachers—PH: Characteristics, treatment, and course of physical and health disabilities (PH2K1) (also PH2K2).

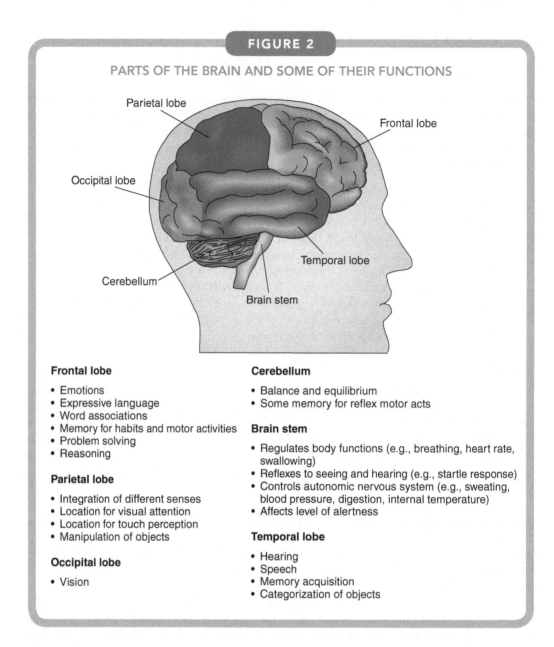

FIGURE 2

PARTS OF THE BRAIN AND SOME OF THEIR FUNCTIONS

Frontal lobe

- Emotions
- Expressive language
- Word associations
- Memory for habits and motor activities
- Problem solving
- Reasoning

Parietal lobe

- Integration of different senses
- Location for visual attention
- Location for touch perception
- Manipulation of objects

Occipital lobe

- Vision

Cerebellum

- Balance and equilibrium
- Some memory for reflex motor acts

Brain stem

- Regulates body functions (e.g., breathing, heart rate, swallowing)
- Reflexes to seeing and hearing (e.g., startle response)
- Controls autonomic nervous system (e.g., sweating, blood pressure, digestion, internal temperature)
- Affects level of alertness

Temporal lobe

- Hearing
- Speech
- Memory acquisition
- Categorization of objects

that the brain slams against the inside of the cranium. The rapid movement and impact tears nerve fibers, or axons, breaking connections between different parts of the brain. Primary causes of closed head injuries are car and bicycle accidents, falls, and accidents while playing sports. *Shaken baby syndrome* is another unfortunate but common cause of traumatic brain injury in children. Violent shaking of a baby causes rapid acceleration and deceleration of the head, which in turn causes the baby's brain whip back and forth, bouncing off the inside of the skull.

The effects of traumatic brain injury on learning and behavior are determined by the severity of the injury and the part of the brain that sustained damage. A mild brain injury results in a *concussion,* a brief or momentary loss of consciousness (from seconds or minutes, up to 30 minutes) without any subsequent complications or damage. Even a mild concussion, however, is often followed by postconcussion syndrome, which can include temporary headaches, dizziness, and fatigue. Repeated mild traumatic brain injuries over a period of months or years can result in cumulative neurological and cognitive deficits. Repeated mild traumatic brain injuries occurring within short period of time (i.e., hours, days, or weeks) can be catastrophic or fatal (Centers for Disease Control and Prevention, 2011f).

Contusions (bruising, swelling, and bleeding) usually accompany a moderate brain injury. Blood vessels in the brain may also rupture, causing a *hematoma* (aggregation or clotting of blood) that may grow and put pressure on vital brain structures. A moderate brain injury usually results in a loss of consciousness lasting more than 30 minutes up to 24 hours followed by several days or weeks of confusion. Individuals who sustain a moderate brain injury will experience significant cognitive and behavioral impairments for many months. Most, however, will make a complete or nearly complete recovery (Vu et al., 2011).

Severe head trauma almost always results in a *coma,* a state of prolonged unconsciousness lasting days, weeks, or even longer. A person in a coma cannot be awakened and makes no meaningful response to external stimulation. In addition to brain contusions and hematomas or damage to the nerve fibers, or axons, a person with severe brain injury may have suffered from **anoxia** (loss of oxygen to the brain for a period of time). Although many people with severe brain injuries make significant improvements during the 2 years postinjury and continue to improve at a more gradual pace for many years, most will have permanent physical, behavioral, and/or cognitive impairments (Vu et al., 2011).

Effects and Educational Implications of Traumatic Brain Injury

Though not always visible and sometimes seemingly minor or inconsequential, traumatic brain injury is complex. The symptoms vary widely depending on the severity of the injury, its extent and site, the age of the child at the time of the injury, and time passed since the injury (von Hahn, 2004).

Impairments caused by brain injuries fall into three main categories: (a) physical and sensory changes (e.g., lack of coordination, spasticity of muscles); (b) cognitive impairments (e.g., short- and long-term memory deficits, difficulty maintaining attention and concentration, language problems); and (c) social, behavioral, and emotional problems (e.g., mood swings, self-centeredness, lack of motivation). Figure 3 provides additional examples of characteristics that may be signs of traumatic brain injury.

Recovery from a brain injury is a long and unpredictable process. A student might make excellent progress, then regress to an earlier stage, and then make a rapid series of gains. Individuals with brain injuries sometimes reach plateaus in their recovery during which no improvements occur for some time. A plateau does not signal the end to functional improvement. Ylvisaker (2005) recommends that the child return to school when she is physically capable, can respond to instructions, and can sustain attention for 10 to 15 minutes.

Students who have been hospitalized with head injuries reenter school with deficits from their injuries compounded by their extended absence from school. Students with head injuries are likely to require comprehensive programs of academic, psychological, and family support (Tyler & Mira, 1999). IEP goals and services may need to be reviewed and modified as often as every 30 days because of the dramatic changes in behavior and performance by some children during the early stages of recovery. Educators can assist students with traumatic brain injury by doing the following (Babikian & Asarnow, 2009; Deidrick & Farmer, 2005; von Hahn, 2004; Vu et al., 2011):

- Schedule academic instruction during peak performance periods, and provide frequent breaks. Chronic fatigue may necessitate a reduced class load and shortened school day.
- Rehearse social situations in advance, and provide explicit instructions and prompts about social interactions such as maintaining socially accepted body space and tone of voice.
- Provide clear, uncomplicated instructions; break multistep instructions into simplified steps.
- Pair auditory instructions with visual cues.

Signs and effects of TBI

 Content Standards for Beginning Teachers—Common Core: Educational implications of various exceptionalities (ICC2K2) (also PH3K1).

Accommodations for students with TBI

 Content Standards for Beginning Teachers—PH: Adaptations of educational environments to enhance the potential of individuals with PH (PH5K1) (also ICC5K1).

FIGURE 3 POSSIBLE SIGNS AND EFFECTS OF TRAUMATIC BRAIN INJURY

Physical and sensory changes

- Chronic headaches, dizziness, light-headedness, nausea
- Vision impairments (e.g., double vision, visual field defects, blurring, sensitivity to light)
- Hearing impairment (e.g., increased sensitivity to sound)
- Alterations in sense of taste, touch, and smell
- Sleep problems (e.g., insomnia, day/night confusion)
- Stress-related disorders (e.g., depression)
- Poor body temperature regulation
- Recurrent seizure activity
- Poor coordination and balance
- Reduced speed of motor performance and precision of movement

Cognitive changes and academic problems

- Difficulty keeping up with discussions, instructional presentations, note taking
- Difficulty concentrating or attending to task at hand (e.g., distractible, confused)
- Difficulty making transitions (e.g., home to school, class to class, switching from fractions to decimal problems on same math worksheet)
- Inability to organize work and environment (e.g., difficulty keeping track of books, assignments, lunch box)
- Problems in planning, organizing, pacing tasks and activities
- Extremely sensitive to distraction (e.g., unable to take a test in a room with other students)

- Tendency to perseverate; inflexibility in thinking
- Impairments in receptive oral language (e.g., difficulty following directions; misunderstanding what is said by others)
- Inability to perceive voice inflections or nonverbal cues
- Impairments in reading comprehension
- Impairments in expressive oral or written language (e.g., aphasia, difficulty retrieving words, poor articulation, slow speech, difficulty in spelling or punctuation)

Social, emotional, and behavioral problems

- Chronic agitation, irritability, restlessness, or anxiety
- Increased aggressiveness
- Impaired ability to self-manage; lowered impulse control; poor anger control
- Difficulty dealing with change (i.e., rigid); poor coping strategies
- May overestimate own ability (often evidenced as "bragging")
- Decreased insight into self and others; reduced judgment
- Decreased frustration tolerance; frequent temper outbursts and overreactions to events
- May talk compulsively and excessively
- Inability to take cues from the environment (often leading to socially inappropriate behavior)

Source: Adapted from Hill, J. L. (1999). *Meeting the needs of children with special physical and health care needs* (pp. 259–260). Upper Saddle River, NJ: Merrill/ Prentice Hall. © 1999 by Merrill/Prentice Hall. Used by permission.

- Have a teacher, counselor, or aide meet with the student at the beginning and end of each school day to review the day's schedule, keep track of assignments, and monitor progress.
- Have a peer to help the student move efficiently from class to class, and permit early dismissal from class to allow time to get to the next room.
- Adapted physical education is often indicated difficulties with mobility, balance, or coordination.
- Provide behavior management and/or counseling interventions to help with poor judgment, impulsiveness, overactivity, aggression, destructiveness, and socially uninhibited behavior often experienced by students with head injury.
- Tape-record lectures, assign a note taker, and allow extra time to take tests.

EDUCATIONAL APPROACHES

How does one go about teaching students with severe and multiple disabilities? To begin to answer this question, three fundamental and interrelated questions must be considered:

1. What skills should be taught?
2. What instructional methods should be used?
3. Where should instruction take place?

Of course, answers to each of these questions must be determined for all students with special educational needs, but the answers take on enormous importance for students with severe disabilities.

Curriculum: What Should Be Taught?

Because students with the most significant disabilities learn new skills more slowly and acquire a much smaller set of skills than any group of students, deciding what to teach them is of paramount importance. For many years, a student's "mental age" as determined by norm-referenced tests was the primary factor in the selection of curriculum content and teaching activities. This practice led to an emphasis on activities thought to be essential prerequisites for higher-level skills because typically developing children of a given age demonstrated these skills. As a result, students with severe disabilities spent years sorting blocks by color and placing wooden pegs in pegboards. These contrived activities contributed little, if anything of value to the student's daily functioning (see Figure 4).

If developmental age is a poor basis for determining curriculum content and instructional activities for students with severe disabilities, what factors should drive those decisions? Of the many factors that should be considered when selecting individualized curriculum content for students with severe disabilities, two considerations that should always be at the top the list are functionality and age-appropriateness.

FUNCTIONALITY Functional skills are immediately useful to a student. They are frequently required in the student's daily activities, and they are valued by people in those settings. Dressing oneself, preparing a snack, riding a public bus, purchasing items from vending machines, and responding appropriately to common sight words in community settings are functional skills for many students with severe disabilities. Functional skills mean less dependence on others and enable more meaningful participation in current and future educational, domestic, work, and community environments. Brown and colleagues (1982) suggested the following tests for determining the functionality of a particular skill: if the student could not perform the task, (a) would someone else would have to do it for the student, and (b) could the student function as an adult without the skill?

Functional and age-appropriate skills

 Council for Exceptional Children

Content Standards for Beginning Teachers—Common Core: Theories and research that form the basis of curriculum developments and instructional practice (ICC7K1) (also ICC4S4, ICC7K2, IIC5S2, IIC5S12).

FIGURE 4 MY BROTHER DARRYL: A CASE FOR TEACHING FUNCTIONAL SKILLS

Eighteen years old, moderately/severely handicapped, Darryl has been in school for 12 years. He's never been served in any setting other than an elementary school. He has had a number of years of "individualized instruction." Darryl can now do lots of things he couldn't do before:

- He can put 100 pegs in a board in less than 10 minutes with 95% accuracy, but he can't put quarters into a vending machine.

- Upon command he can touch his nose, shoulder, leg, hair, ear. He is still working on wrist, ankle, hips, but he can't blow his nose when needed.

- He can do a 12-piece Big Bird puzzle with 100% accuracy and color an Easter bunny and stay in the lines. He prefers music but has never been taught to use a radio or record player.

- He can now fold primary paper in half and even quarters, but he can't sort clothes, white from colors, for washing.

- He can roll Play-Doh and make wonderful clay snakes, but he can't roll bread dough and cut out biscuits.

- He can string beads in alternating colors and match it to a pattern on a DLM card, but he can't lace his shoes.

- He can sing his ABCs and tell me the names of all the letters in the alphabet with 80% accuracy when they are presented on a card in upper case, but he can't tell "Men's" room from "Ladies'" when we go to McDonald's.

- He can be told it's cloudy/rainy and take a black felt cloud and put it on the day of the week on an enlarged calendar (with assistance), but he still goes out in the rain without a raincoat or hat.

- He can identify with 100% accuracy 100 different Peabody Picture Cards by pointing, but he can't order a hamburger by pointing to a picture or gesturing.

- He can walk on a balance beam forward, sideways, and backward, but he can't walk up the steps of the bleachers unassisted in the gym or go to basketball games.

- He can count to 100 by rote memory, but he doesn't know how many dollars to pay the waitress for a $2.59 McDonald coupon special.

- He can put a cube in the box, under the box, beside the box, and behind the box, but he can't find the trash bin in McDonald's and empty his trash into it.

- He can sit in a circle with appropriate behavior and sing songs and play "Duck Duck Goose," but nobody else in his neighborhood his age seems to want to do that.

I guess he's just not ready yet.

Written by Preston Lewis, a curriculum specialist in the Kentucky Department of Education.

Laura Bolesta/Merrill

Functional curriculum activities use authentic, age-appropriate materials with meaningful outcomes. Every school day, Kevin sorts, labels, and delivers the newspaper to "customers" in his school.

AGE-APPROPRIATENESS Students with severe disabilities should participate in activities that are appropriate for their same-age peers without disabilities. Having teenagers sit on the floor and play clap-your-hands games highlights their differences and discourages integration. Such activities also contribute to the perception by some that students with severe disabilities are eternal children. Teaching secondary students with severe disabilities how to play video games and operate an iPod would give them more age-appropriate recreation and leisure skills.

Age-appropriate behaviors are expected in most settings, and they are modeled and valued by peers without disabilities. As a result, age-appropriate skills are more likely to be practiced and reinforced, and thus maintained in the student's repertoire, than are behaviors typical of a much younger child.

Specific curriculum areas that IEP teams for students with severe disabilities should consider are communication, literacy, recreation and leisure, choice making, and the general education academic curriculum.

COMMUNICATION Communication is an essential quality of human life. Communication enables us to express our needs and desires, obtain and provide information, and, most important, form and maintain relationships with others. Communication does not develop naturally or easily for children with severe and multiple disabilities. As Chen (1999) noted, the communicative efforts by an infant severe and multiple disabilities may be subtle or unusual, and thus difficult for parents and caregivers to identify and interpret. At the same time, the infant may not even perceive that his parents and caregivers are gesturing, talking or signing to him.

Early research and training in communication for people with severe disabilities focused on remediation of specific forms of communication, such as the production of speech sounds, words, and descriptive phrases. However, the focus of and methods used to teach communication skills to these students have undergone significant changes during the past 20 years. Three perspectives regarding the nature of communication have helped shape contemporary research and instructional practices (Downing, 2011; Ferguson, 1994; Kaiser & Goetz, 1993); these changes encompass shared meanings, modes of communication, and function:

1. *Communication occurs when communication partners establish shared meanings.* The responsibility for successful communication rests with both partners. However, shared meaning is more likely when the partner who is relatively more skilled uses the principles of responsive interaction, such as following the lead of the less skilled communicator balancing turns between conversation partners, and responding with interest and affect.

2. *Communication is independent of the specific form or mode that is used.* Speech is always a desirable goal for those who can attain it, and many students with severe disabilities learn to understand and produce spoken language. But the sensory, motor, and/or cognitive limitations that some students with severe disabilities have keep them from learning to speak intelligibly even after intensive and extensive instruction. Many students who do not acquire speech are successful users of augmentative and alternative communication (AAC)—including gestures, various sign language systems,

AAC

 Council for Exceptional Children Content Standards for Beginning Teachers—Common Core: Augmentative and assistive communication strategies (ICC6K4).

communication boards, picture exchange communication systems (PECSs), and electronic communication aids.

Communication is achieved only with great difficulty by people who are deaf-blind and requires greater effort on the part of communication partners. The use of dual-communication boards can help students who are deaf-blind discriminate the receptive or expressive functions of responses from a partner (Heller & Bigge, 2010). When a communication partner points to pictures or symbols on her board, a receptive message is provided to the student, requiring a response from the student on his board. The partner can point to the student's board and provide imitative prompts or corrective feedback to help the student make expressive messages.

Because the contrived and idiosyncratic nature of their systems requires specialized knowledge from the communication partner, specialized forms of communication used by some individuals with severe disabilities limit the number of people with whom they can communicate (Heller & Bigge, 2010). However, they do enable many students with severe disabilities to receive and express basic information, feelings, needs, and wants. A student's teachers, peers, parents, and employers can learn sign language and other communication systems, thus encouraging use outside the classroom.

3. *Communication must "work" for the child by influencing the behavior of others.* Communication is functional when it enables a child to do things such as the following: tell people what to do, get help, convey social pleasantries ("Hi," "Bye"), show interest in an activity, protest, express an emotional or physical state, make a choice, and request and/or report information (Cascella & McNamara, 2005).

Some deaf-blind people use finger braille to communicate. See http://deafandblind.com/blind.html.

LITERACY Literacy is important in that it provides increased access to information and further learning. For many years it was assumed that students with significant disabilities were not able to benefit from instruction in reading and math (Fenlon, McNabb, & Pidlypchak, 2010). Recent research, however, has shown that even children who communicate on a presymbolic level can benefit from instruction in early literacy skills (e.g., Browder, Ahlgrim-Delzell, Courtade, Gibbs, Flowers, 2008; Mims, Browder, Baker, Lee, & Spooner, 2009; Spooner, Knight, Browder, Jimenez, & DiBiase, in press). Diane Browder, a pioneer in development of early literacy instruction for children with significant disabilities, described a visit to a classroom in which an elementary-aged child was learning the book version of the movie *Toy Story*. At one point, the teacher, Bree Jimenez, asked her visitor to hold up a board of pictures for the child to see, then asked, "When did Buzz Lightyear first come into the story?" The girl leaned over to a picture of a cake symbolizing a birthday party and blew on it. "That girl reads now," said Browder. See *Teaching & Learning*, "'Eighth Grade Work!' Teaching General Curriculum Content to Students with Severe Disabilities."

RECREATION AND LEISURE Most children develop the ability to play and later to occupy themselves constructively and pleasurably during their free time. But children with severe disabilities may not learn to enjoy recreation and leisure skills without explicit instruction and supports. Teaching appropriate leisure and recreational skills helps students with severe disabilities interact socially, maintain their physical health and motor skills, and become more involved in community activities. Many people with severe disabilities do not use their unstructured time appropriately; rather than participate in enjoyable pursuits, they may spend excessive time sitting, wandering, or looking at television. Recreation and leisure now acknowledged as an extremely important part of the curriculum for students with severe disabilities, and a variety of instructional programs and adapted equipment have been developed.

In one study, picture prompts and modified game materials enabled elementary children with moderate and severe disabilities learn to independently play a board game (Raschke, Dedrick, Heston, & Farris, 1996). Changing the way in which team games are played can enable an individual with severe disabilities to participate in

"Eighth Grade Work!" Teaching General Curriculum Content to Students with Severe Disabilities

BY DIANE M. BROWDER

TEACHING & LEARNING

When Lance, a student with a severe intellectual disability, was in elementary school, his typical day involved learning to communicate basic needs (e.g., "Eat" and "Toilet"), eat with a spoon, zip his jacket, and perform other basic life skills. His teachers also introduced a few sight words and how to identify coins. When Lance was included in general education classes, he worked on his own goals (e.g., matching coins) while other students were learning to read and solve math problems. Lance's life changed when the 1997 reauthorization of IDEA required that all students with disabilities have access to the general curriculum and be included in general assessments.

By the eighth grade, Lance's teacher began to have much higher expectations for him. Now Lance's day includes applying his emerging literacy and numeracy skills to activities adapted from grade-level content. For example, to access eighth grade novels Lance interacts with a teacher or a peer who reads the text aloud. To answer comprehension questions, he selects a picture from an array of four pictures. He has learned how to make and interpret bar graphs using small pictures to represent and compare quantities (e.g., who got more votes). In science, Lance participates in experiments and selects pictures that complete concept statements (e.g., "A solvent and solute form a _____"; selects picture of "solution"). In social studies he uses pictures and a graphic organizer to summarize the key facts of a historical event. When one of his recently praised Lance for working so hard, he smiled and said with pride, "Eighth grade work!"

OPPORTUNITIES AND CHALLENGES FOR TEACHERS AND STUDENTS

Many students like Lance were denied the opportunity to learn academic skills because of past assumptions about their ability based on their IQ or other characteristics of their disability. However, comprehensive reviews of research demonstrate that students with moderate and severe intellectual disability have learned reading (Browder, Wakeman, Spooner, Ahlgrim-Delzell, & Algozzine, 2006), mathematics (Browder, Spooner,

Ahlgrim-Delzell, Harris, & Wakeman, 2008), and science skills (Spooner et al., in press).

What is not yet known is how much students with severe disabilities can learn because educators are just now trying new interventions to teach state standards. Although not all students may learn to read, it is important for all students to have the opportunity. Students who do not learn to read may learn to understand text through read-alouds. Similarly, the opportunity to learn "real" academic content such as math and science may help the students acquire important skills needed for future jobs or leisure pursuits.

Some educators worry that teaching state standards may rob students with severe disabilities of time needed to learn daily living skills. Teachers do need to find time in the day to continue to promote learning of skills needed to be independent in daily routines (e.g., eating, toileting, street crossing). The challenge of balancing access to general curriculum with instruction of functional skills needs to be identified through the IEP process.

HOW TO GET STARTED

1. **Define a specific objective for mastery.** Identify what the target is for student learning. In science, it may be defining a science term or finding the term that labels the outcome of an experiment. In a read-aloud of a novel, the objective may be for the student to answer comprehension questions (e.g., "Who knew the woods best?"). In math, the target for mastery may be performing the specific operation (e.g., using a calculator to add the sides of a figure to find the perimeter).

2. **Develop text summaries and other resources.** Whether teaching students academic content in general or special education, a good place to begin is by creating more accessible versions of the text that other students will read. For example, the chapter of a novel may be summarized in a simple paragraph as shown on the opposite page. Some pictures may be used to help students track the text as a teacher or peer reads the passage aloud.

She asked three of her brothers to go with her.

The brothers followed her because Harriet knew the

woods best. They made a lot of noise, crashing through

the underbrush and scaring themselves. She told them

to be quiet. They complained it was too dark. She told

them with all the stars shining bright, there was plenty

of light.

3. Why did the brothers follow Harriet?

Source: Example of text from a middle school biography on Harriet Tubman adapted for a student with severe disabilities. Created by Melissa Hudson and reprinted with permission.

3. **Determine how the student will respond.** Students may need to use assistive technology or other materials to make the target response. Sometimes responses can be made more accessible by giving the student an array of options (e.g., four pictures). For example, a second grader with severe disabilities might select from a list of word/picture options to complete an opinion statement or simply to complete a sentence with an opinion (e.g,. "I like _____").

Students with the most severe disabilities might approximate this skill in an alternative way. For example, the student might complete the sentence "I like _____" by choosing between objects and then pasting a picture of the object into the sentence. What is most important is that the student has achieved a parallel outcome of producing a written sentence that expresses an opinion. Some students may need to select the correct answer by gazing at their choice with their eyes or by hitting a switch.

4. **Teach the student to respond.** Students with severe disabilities may need to have the material presented multiple times to learn the content and be able to show the correct response. The teacher may read the same adapted chapter every day for a week. Even with this repetition, the student may need systematic prompting to make the correct response. For example, in teaching the student to enter the numbers to compute the perimeter, the teacher may use a system of least intrusive prompting. First, the teacher tells the student what to do ("Enter 5"). If the student does not respond, the teacher models the response ("Enter 5 like this; now you do it"). If the student still needs help, the teacher physically guides the correct response ("Enter 5 like this. Let's do it together"). When the student gets the correct response, the teacher offers praise ("Good, you entered 5").

5. **Promote and test for generalization.** Use a wide range of materials including some that students will encounter in their daily routines. To teach perimeter, the teacher might use a variety of shapes, materials, sizes, and some activities that have a real-life application (e.g., "Compute how much packing tape we need to go around this box"). Test students with untrained materials (e.g., a new story; packing tape and a different-size box) to see whether they have learned the target concept versus memorizing the correct answers for the instructional examples.

About the Author

Diane Browder is Snyder Distinguished Professor of Special Education & Ph.D. Program Coordinator at the University of North Carolina–Charlotte. Among her more than 100 publications is *Teaching Academics to Students with Significant Cognitive Disabilities* (Brookes, 2006) (co-authored with her UNCC colleague Fred Spooner). Her research focuses on access to general curriculum, early literacy, and alternative assessment for students with severe disabilities.

TEACHING & LEARNING

FIGURE 5 EXAMPLE OF EQUIPMENT AND RULE MODIFICATIONS ENABLING
A STUDENT WITH SEVERE AND MULTIPLE DISABILITIES TO
PARTICIPATE MEANINGFULLY IN A TEAM SPORT

David and Basketball
David is a tenth-grade student with cerebral palsy and severe
mental retardation. He moves around in his wheelchair with full
support from others. One of David's IEP objectives addresses
participation in recreational activities that include a movement of
picking up and throwing a ball.

In basketball games, two types of baskets are placed side
by side: one has a higher rim, the other has a lower rim. To
ensure David's essential involvement in the game, which basket
his team can use depends totally on the degree of effort David
makes. During a basketball game, David engages in picking up
and throwing a basketball to make an adapted shot outside of the

basketball court. Each time he successfully makes an adapted
shot, his team is allowed to use the lower basket.

Thus, David's efforts to throw a ball are converted
momentarily and proportionally into the height of a basket. In this
way, he can assist team players without disabilities, who are not
good at shooting, in making more successful shots. Therefore,
David is considered an active participant in an essential part of
the basketball game.

Source: Ohtake, Y. (2004). Meaningful inclusion of all students in team sports.
Teaching Exceptional Children, 37(2), 25. Reprinted with permission.

For information and
guidelines for selecting
and teaching recreation,
leisure, and sport activities,
see Bambara, Koger, and
Bartholomew (2011); Block
(2007); Juarez, Best, and
Bigge (2010); and Kleinert,
Miracle, and Sheppard-
Jones (2007).

Teaching choice making

 Council for
Exceptional
Children
Content
Standards for
Beginning
Teachers—INDEP CURR:
Teach individuals to give
and receive meaningful
feedback from peers and
adults (IIC5S5) (also IIC4K3,
ICC4S5).

Information and lesson
plans for teaching choice
making to students with
severe disabilities can be
found in Bambara and
Koger (1996), Mithaug
(2002), and Stafford (2005).

team sports. Figure 5 shows how equipment and rule modifications enabled a 10th-grade student with cerebral palsy and severe intellectual disabilities to play basketball in a way that maintained the integrity of the game for players without disabilities.

MAKING CHOICES Imagine going through an entire day without being able to make a choice, any choice at all. Someone else—a teacher, a staff person, a parent—will decide what you will wear, what you will do next, what you will eat for lunch, whom you will sit next to, and so on throughout the day, every day. In the past, students with severe disabilities had few opportunities to express preferences and make choices. People with severe disabilities were simply cared for and taught to be compliant. It is easier and faster to complete a task for a person with severe disabilities than it is to teach her the task. Such treatment deprives the individual of potentially valuable learning experiences and fostered learned helplessness.

Special educators today recognize that opportunities to choose and the ability to make choices are important indicators of a student's quality of life (Agran & Hughes, 2006; Wehmeyer, 2006). Educators are increasing efforts to help students with severe disabilities express their preferences and make decisions about matters that will affect them. For example, a child might be presented with pictures of two activities and asked to point to the one she would rather engage in. Another might be asked, "Whom would you like for your partner?" Or the teacher might say, "Should we do this again?" Of course, in presenting such choices, the teacher must be prepared to accept whichever alternative the student selects and to follow through accordingly.

Several researchers have found that nonverbal students with severe disabilities can learn to use picture activity schedules to indicate their preferences for learning and leisure-time activities (e.g., Bryan & Gast, 2000; Morrison, Sainato, BenChaaban, & Endo, 2002). Other researchers have discovered ways to help people with severe disabilities indicate whether they want to participate in daily routines and activities (Lancioni et al., 2006), express preferences for what foods they will purchase and eat (Cooper & Browder, 1998), make choices regarding leisure activities (Kreiner & Flexer, 2009), and choose where they will live (Faw, Davis, & Peck, 1996).

ACCESS TO GENERAL EDUCATION CURRICULUM IDEA requires that all students with disabilities have access to the general curriculum taught to students without disabilities. State standards specify expected learning outcomes by grade level for each content area. For example, according to Common Core State Standards for English Language Arts and Mathematics, a first grader is expected "to represent and solve problems involving addition and subtraction," and a fifth grader should be able "perform operations with multi-digit whole numbers and with decimals to hundreds." IDEA and No Child Left Behind require students with disabilities participate in statewide assessments of student learning. Most students with severe disabilities participate in alternative assessments as measures of their progress on state standards.

Participation in the general curriculum by students with severe disabilities has enabled some teachers to discover that their students with the most significant disabilities can do much more than they had thought, particularly in reading and math (Kohl, McLaughlin, & Nagle, 2006). Many experienced teachers in this study reported confidence in integrating academic standards into lessons on functional skills. Two basic strategies for combining functional and academic content are (a) embedding core academic content into functional activities and (b) adding functional applications to instructional objectives based on core content standards (Collins, Hager, & Galloway, 2011).

Some special educators view teaching academic versus functional life skills as competing priorities (Kohl et al., 2006). The expectation that all students show progress in the general education curriculum has caused some special educators to fear that teaching practical skills to students with severe disabilities is taking a backseat to the academic demands of No Child Left Behind (Ayres, Lowrey, Douglas, & Sievers, 2011). See *Current Issues and Future Trends*, "What Happened to Functional Curriculum?"

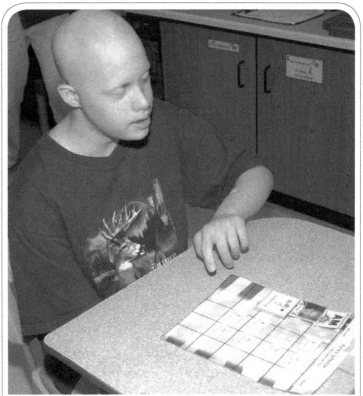

Learning to choose what he wants to do next is an important IEP goal for Daniel.

Laura Bolesta/Merrill

SELECTING AND PRIORITIZING INSTRUCTIONAL TARGETS Students with severe disabilities present numerous skill deficits, which are often compounded by the presence of challenging behavior. Each of those skill deficits and behavioral challenges could (but not necessarily should) be targeted as an IEP goal. It is seldom, if ever, possible, however, to design and implement a teaching program to deal simultaneously with all of the learning needs of a student with severe disabilities. Selecting and prioritizing instructional objectives is one of the greatest responsibilities a special educator undertakes as an IEP team member.

Accurate predictions of how much any particular skill—functional or academic—ultimately will contribute to a student's overall quality of life are difficult to make. In many cases, we simply do not know how useful a new skill or bit of knowledge will prove to be. But when deciding which academic standards to incorporate into student's program, common sense and, most of all, the student's best interests must rule the day. As Ayers, and colleagues (2011) note, "there is no reasonable way to integrate Chaucer and volcanoes into a community based lesson related to paying for a meal in a restaurant" (p. 15). This author agrees with Ayers and others who contend that a functional approach must remain a priority when developing curriculum for students with severe disabilities.

Whichever skills are targeted for instruction, they ultimately need to be meaningful for the learner and her family. A variety of person-centered planning methods are available to help IEP teams work with the individual and family members to identify and prioritize the relative significance of skills or learning activities (e.g., Browder, 2001; Giangreco, Cloninger, & Iverson, 2011; Keyes & Owens-Johnson, 2003). Figure 6 shows a form on which an IEP team summarized the outcomes of various assessments and IEP goal recommendations for a student with severe disabilities in an inclusive classroom setting.

Most states have adopted the Common Core State Standards for English Language Arts and Mathematics (see http://www.corestandards.org/). States also have standards in other content areas such as science and social studies.

Carey Creech-Galloway, the featured teacher for this chapter, is an active contributor to the emerging research literature exploring ways that teachers can design lessons that blend effective instruction of both functional skills and academic goals (Collins, Evans, Creech-Galloway, Karl, & Miller, 2010; Collins, Karl, Riggs, Galloway, & Hager, 2010). A summary and practical examples of this work can be found in Collins, Hager, and Galloway (2011).

FUTURE TRENDS
▶ What Happened to Functional Curriculum?

BY BELVA C. COLLINS

FOR THE LAST 40 YEARS, I have been a participant-observer of special education's ongoing efforts to improve educational opportunities and outcomes for students with severe disabilities. Those efforts have produced tremendous changes in schooling for students with severe disabilities. They have moved from institutions to special schools, then to segregated classrooms in neighborhood schools, and, most recently, to inclusive classrooms serving all students. The movement from segregated to inclusive settings was fueled by the belief that every child has the right to receive a free and appropriate public education and supported by research showing that membership in inclusive classrooms benefits students with severe disabilities, especially in learning social and communication skills. What began as philosophically logical practice became law when IDEA mandated that students be educated in the least restrictive environment.

ORIGINS OF FUNCTIONAL CURRICULUM

What students with severe disabilities are taught also has changed dramatically. When I began my career as a special education teacher in the 1970s, curriculum was based on a developmental approach in which a student's mental age rather than chronological age determined what he was taught. It was thought that the most these students might learn in a lifetime would be to identify letters of the alphabet, indicate their names, count from 1 to 10, name farm animals, and recognize community helpers. Like "My Brother Darryl" (see Figure 4), our students were not considered ready to learn meaningful skills.

In 1979, Lou Brown and his colleagues changed the entire focus of the curriculum by asserting that students with severe disabilities needed to be taught the life skills that would enable them to transition successfully to adulthood in less restrictive community, domestic, leisure, and vocational environments. This change in curricular focus was supported by numerous research studies demonstrating that systematic instruction enabled many students with severe disabilities to acquire functional skills and generalize and maintain them across settings, people, and materials.

A DOOR OPENS TO THE GENERAL CURRICULUM

The field took another major turn with the reauthorization of IDEA and the passage of NCLB requiring that all students, regardless of ability, should have access to the same curriculum and that their progress should be assessed on the same academic standards expected for all students. The prevailing thought this time was that we had been underestimating the ability of students with severe disabilities to acquire knowledge from the general education curriculum and that we should challenge all students to acquire this knowledge. This produced a seismic shift in curriculum for students with severe disabilities: from a sole focus on functional skills to teaching both functional and academic core content. Too often, this has resulted in curriculum that lacked meaning for students with severe disabilities. Now, when I go into classrooms, I am more likely to observe students with severe disabilities engaging in lessons such as the following:

A young girl with severe disabilities (poor motor skills, no verbal expressive language, significant intellectual disability) is positioned in an adapted chair at a table in a segregated elementary classroom surrounded by other students with severe disabilities. Two button switches are in front of her: a blue one labeled "beneficial" and a red one labeled "harmful." The teacher stands in front of her and holds up a photograph of a car being driven on a public street. "Is this beneficial or harmful to the environment?" she asks. The student is looking at everything in the room except the photograph, so the teacher calls her name, moves her head to focus her eye gaze on the photograph, and then repeats the question. The student's arms flail out to the sides as she jerks her head to look at something more interesting. The teacher physically moves the student's hand to press the red switch, and a prerecorded voice says "Harmful." "Good job! A car is harmful to the environment," the teacher says, recording the student's response before moving to the next photograph that shows a recycling bin.

What is happening? The teacher is using sound systematic instruction to teach required elementary science core content (i.e., "Students will describe human interactions in the environment where they live and will classify the interactions as beneficial or harmful to the environment using data/evidence to support conclusions"). After several weeks of daily instruction, the student most likely will learn to hit the red or the blue switch in response to the pictures and perform well on the state's alternative assessment. The important questions, however, are not being asked: Does she understand the concepts behind the responses she has been taught? (The teacher had conducted no assessment to determine if the student could distinguish a car from a recycling bin or match the photograph to the object or demonstrate understanding of the words *beneficial* or *environment*. Pollution and recycling are abstract concepts to be inferred from the photographs.) Will the skill be meaningful in her life or allow her to function with less support as an adult? Will she generalize the skill of hitting a switch to more meaningful tasks with other recorded messages? Is she missing instruction on meaningful skills or exposure to peers without disabilities to spend time working on this task?

I recently served on a team of special educators charged with identifying new academic standards for our state's alternative assessment. I began with high hopes this would be an opportunity to identify skills from core content that would have meaning in the lives of students with severe disabilities. To my dismay, our task was to take isolated general education academic core content standards across age levels that had been preselected in a survey and try, by deleting words, to reduce each to a minimum standard that a student with severe disabilities might achieve. As we worked, we discovered two problems: (a) the isolated standards selected across age levels had no logical progression, and (b) no apparent thought had been given to whether the selected standards had relevance to the everyday real life of a person with severe disabilities. I point out these problems not to be critical but to highlight how much special education is still struggling to identify what to teach students with severe disabilities.

MY COUSIN JEFFREY

In the 1960s, my cousin Jeffrey was born with multiple disabilities that included a significant intellectual disability and numerous physical challenges and medical conditions. He was legally blind and had a hearing impairment. Jeffrey never learned to walk or to talk. His primary mode of ambulation and communication was to roll across the floor toward the object or person he desired. He could not sit up independently or perform basic self-care skills. Jeffrey never went to school, but he was an integral part of every gathering of family and friends.

Jeffrey died this past year, at the age of 45. As I struggled to find the right words for the eulogy, I found myself wondering what Jeffrey's life would have been like if he had been born after the doors to local schools were open to children like him or what he might have learned if today's assistive technology had been available to him from an early age. While Jeffrey taught everyone in our family a lot about unconditional love and acceptance, how much more could he have learned from us?

Perhaps Jeffrey would have benefited from well-designed functional skills lessons and thoughtful engagement with core academic content. I would have hated, however, to see Jeffrey spend his precious time in school pressing colored switches in an isolated activity with no relevance to his daily life, when he could have benefited from a more functional core content

approach that strengthened his muscle tone by assisting him in crushing cans for recycling or that taught him to distinguish between beneficial or harmful choices when he was thirsty or hungry. Somewhere along the way, in our vigor to defend the rights of all students with severe disabilities to access the general curriculum and be assessed on high standards, it seems that we lost our ability to rationally think through a way to make all content meaningful and relevant to all students.

WE CAN AND MUST DO BETTER

Perhaps it is time to abandon "functional curriculum" for a "functional approach." Perhaps we should take a step back and think about how to find a compromise so that students with severe disabilities can access core content and still learn functional skills. In a recent research investigation, my colleagues and I systematically taught core academic content to middle school students with moderate to severe disabilities in ways we hoped would be relevant to their lives (Collins et al., 2011). For example, we taught the students to read vocabulary from current events in the news, identify states of matter as they related to cooking and the weather, and worked math problems using order of operations to compute sales tax with calculators. We found that core content can be embedded in functional skill instruction and that functional skills can be embedded in core content instruction. Special educators must establish high standards for our students yet also retain an emphasis on functional applications. Only then can we be satisfied that students can successfully transition to adulthood with the highest degree of independence possible.

WHAT DO YOU THINK?

1. How should teachers determine the value and effectiveness of a lesson for students with severe disabilities?
2. How should core academic content be selected for students with severe disabilities?
3. Your state curriculum standards require secondary students to describe the relationship between sexual reproduction (cell meiosis) and the transmission of genetic information. How would you design a meaningful lesson on this standard for a student with significant intellectual disabilities and no verbal expressive language?

About the Author

Belva C. Collins is professor of special education and the chair of the Department of Special Education and Rehabilitation Counseling at the University of Kentucky, where she trains teachers to work with students with severe disabilities and conducts research on how to improve the effectiveness and efficiency of instruction. She is author of *Moderate and Severe Disabilities: A Foundational Approach* (Pearson, 2007) and a soon-to-be published text on systematic instruction to teach functional core content.

FIGURE 6   SUMMARY OF ASSESSMENT, PERSONALIZED CURRICULUM NEEDS, AND IEP FOR A STUDENT WITH SEVERE DISABILITIES

Summary of Ecological Assessment
for an Individualized Education Plan (IEP)

Student's Name: Roddie Sprankle   Date: May 26, 2011

Planning Team: Roddie, Ms. Sprankle (Roddie's mother), Ms. Durham (current special education teacher), Mr. Lindquist (current physical therapist) Mr. Adzima (special education teacher at Colby), Ms. Gomez (principal of Colby), Ms. Townsend (third-grade teacher at Colby), Ms. Karpowicz (math and computer teacher at Colby), Mr. Preston (language arts teacher at Colby)

1. Background on Student

Roddie Sprankle is an 8-year-old boy who has traumatic brain injury as the result of an accident at age 5. Roddie made a remarkable recovery from the accident and has continued to show important progress over the last 3 years. He can now walk with a walker and speak in short phrases. Last year Roddie mastered writing a cursive signature and putting on his jacket. He made good progress on learning sight words and some math facts, which he often practiced using computer software. Roddie did not learn to initiate conversation. Although he talks more this year, his comments are often difficult to comprehend as he searches for the words he wants to use. He also made little progress on reading phrases. A prior evaluation by a neurologist, Dr. Hauster, notes that Roddie needs continued training in memory strategies and cognitive stimulation.

2. Person-Centered Planning with Student and Family

Roddie's mother's priorities are that he (1) be treated well by other students (social inclusion); (2) continue to learn life skills, given his excellent progress this year in learning to put on his jacket; and (3) be taught reading. Roddie has expressed an interest in trying out the cafeteria. Currently he eats in his special education classroom with only five other students present.

3. Encouraging Student Self-Determination

Roddie has been learning goal setting and decision making this year. He has presented the planning team with a photo album of his preferences, which he placed in rank order. His top five include food (tacos, hamburgers, French fries), working on the computer, playing computer games, swimming at the YMCA, and music. He has also presented the team with his goals, which include being able to walk without his walker and getting his own computer.

4. Development of Personalized Curriculum

Because Roddie has emerging functional academic skills, these can be used to create curricular parallels in general education. Expanding his sight word vocabulary, teaching him to read and write short phrases, and helping him build on his knowledge of math facts by learning to add are important priorities. These skills should be embedded in as many academic subjects as possible (e.g., learning sight word vocabulary in math). Roddie also has priority needs related to communication, self-direction, social interaction skills, and motor development that can be taught within the typical classroom.

5. Recommendations for the IEP

The team has determined that the priorities for Roddie's IEP include (1) functional academics (Roddie wants this work to be computer-assisted); (2) continued improvement of his balance and fine-motor skills (Roddie's priority is to walk without his walker); (3) initiation of conversations; (4) self-direction (goal setting, self-managed seatwork); and (5) mastery of personal care skills. Roddie will spend most of his day in Ms. Townsend's third grade classroom and will receive specially designed instruction from Mr. Adzima and a teaching assistant. He will also receive individual assistance for toileting and individual physical therapy sessions, based on his preference for privacy in these activities.

Source: Courtesy Diane M. Browder, University of North Carolina Charlotte. Used by permission.

Prioritizing instructional targets

Council for Exceptional Children

Content Standards for Beginning Teachers—Common Core: Identify and prioritize areas of the general curriculum and accommodations for individuals with exceptional learning needs (ICC7S1) (also ICC7S2, ICC7S3).

Instructional Methods: How Should Students with Severe and Multiple Disabilities Be Taught?

Concern for the well-being of students with severe disabilities and assuring their access to meaningful curricular content and extracurricular activities are important. By themselves, however, concern and access are not enough. To learn effectively, students with severe disabilities need more than love, care, and a supportive school environment. They seldom acquire complex skills through imitation and observation alone; they are not likely to blossom on their own.

Because their skill deficits and learning problems are so significant, students with severe disabilities need instruction that is carefully planned, systematically executed, and continuously monitored for effectiveness. Collectively, the authors of leading texts on teaching students with severe disabilities recommend that teachers attend to the following components of an instructional program (e.g., Browder & Spooner, 2011; Collins, 2007; Snell & Brown, 2011; Westling & Fox, 2009):

- *Assess the student's current level of performance.* Precise assessment of current performance is necessary to determine which skills to teach and at what level instruction should begin. Unlike traditional assessments, which rely heavily on standardized scores and developmental levels, assessment of students with severe disabilities emphasizes each learner's ability to perform specific, observable behaviors under specific conditions. Can Keeshia hold her head up without support? For how many seconds? Under what conditions? In response to what verbal or physical signals? Assessment should not be a one-shot procedure but take place at different times, in different settings, and with different people. The fact that a student with severe disabilities does not demonstrate a skill at a particular time or place does not mean she is incapable of demonstrating that skill.

- *Clearly define the skill to be taught.* "Carlos will feed himself" is too broad a goal for many students with severe disabilities. A more appropriate statement might be "When applesauce is applied to Carlos's right index finger, he will put the finger in his mouth within 5 seconds." A clear statement like this enables the teacher and other observers to determine whether Carlos attains this objective. If, after repeated trials, he has not, a different method of instruction should be tried.

- *Break the skill down into component steps.* Effective teachers of students with severe disabilities know how to use **task analysis** to break down a skill into a series of specific, observable steps. Assessment of student performance on each step of the task analysis helps the teacher determine where to begin instruction. She can systematically teach each required step until the student can accomplish the entire task independently. Without this sort of structure and precision in teaching, a great deal of valuable time is likely to be wasted.

- *Determine how the learner can actively participate in the lesson.* Active engagement and repeated practice, important elements of effective instruction for all students, are crucial for learners with severe disabilities. Some students with severe disabilities can participate in the same way that typical students might, such as using response cards in a lesson on number identification (Skibo, Mims, & Spooner, 2011). Active participation by some students, however, requires alternative response modes or topographies—for example, an adapted mouse for selecting choices of vocabulary words on a computer screen or eye gaze to indicate yes/no picture symbols in a shared reading lesson (Fenlon et al., 2010).

- *Provide a clear response prompt.* It is important for the child to know what action or response is expected. A prompt can be verbal; the teacher might say, "Bev, say, 'Apple,'" to indicate what Bev must do before she will receive an apple. A prompt can be physical; the teacher might point to a light switch to indicate that Bev should turn on the light. The teacher also may need to demonstrate an activity many times and to physically guide the child through some or all of the tasks required in the activity.

- *Provide immediate feedback.* Students with severe disabilities must receive immediate and clear information about

Components of systematic instruction

 Council for Exceptional Children

Content Standards for Beginning Teachers—Common Core: Theories and research that form the basis of curriculum developments and instructional practice (ICC7K1) (also ICC4S4, ICC7S5, ICC7S13, IIC1K7, IIC4S6).

Collins (2007) and Snell and Brown (2011) provide in-depth information on how to deliver and fade instructional prompts.

Katelyn Metzger/Merrill

Megan's teacher provides response prompts and physical guidance to help her learn new tasks.

461

To learn how to use time delay and other methods for delivering and fading instructional prompts to students with severe disabilities, see Collins (2007) and Snell and Brown (2011).

Cooper, Heron, and Heward (2007) and Westling and Fox (2009) describe in detail strategies and tactics for helping students generalize and maintain what they have learned.

Some teachers record video of their students' performance on specific tasks, adding an important dimension to documenting learning over extended periods. Denham and Lahm (2001) describe how students with severe disabilities can use computer and assistive technologies to create alternative portfolios as a means to document their accomplishments.

Naturalistic teaching strategies

Content Standards for Beginning Teachers—INDEP CURR: Strategies for integrating student-initiated learning experiences into ongoing instruction (IIC4K3) (also ICC4S4).

Partial participation

Content Standards for Beginning Teachers—Common Core: Use procedures to increase the individual's self-awareness, self-management, self-control, self-reliance, and self-esteem (ICC4S5) (also IIC5S6).

their performance: reinforcement for correct responses (e.g., praise statement and giving child access to preferred toy for 5 seconds) and corrective feedback for errors and nonresponses (e.g., "No, that's not it" in a calm voice and repeating the response prompt) (e.g., Leaf et al., 2011). It is critical that effective reinforcers be identified for students with severe disabilities. Unfortunately, it is not always easy to determine what items or events a noncommunicative child finds motivating. Many teachers devote extensive efforts attempting to find out which items and activities will function as reinforcers to a particular child, and they keep careful records of what is and is not effective. For descriptions of methods for assessing stimuli that may serve as reinforcers for people with severe and profound disabilities, see Cannella-Malone, O'Reilly, and Lancioni (2005) and Logan and Gast (2001).

- *Gradually withdraw response prompts.* Contrived prompts must be withdrawn so that a student's correct responses come under control of naturally occurring stimuli. One evidence-based teaching tactic for transferring control from contrived to natural stimuli is **time delay** (Browder, Ahlgrim-Delzell, Spooner, Mims, & Baker, 2009).
- *Promote maintenance and generalization.* Effective teachers ensure that their students can perform targeted skills in different settings and with different instructors, cues, and materials before concluding with confidence that the student has acquired and generalized a skill. Authentic materials help promote generalization to real-life situations and should be used in lessons whenever possible. For example, students learning to make purchases should practice with real money instead of simulated bills and coins. Using naturalistic teaching strategies is one of the best ways to facilitate a student's generalization and maintenance of important skills (Kaiser & Grim, 2006; Koegel & Koegel, 2006).
- *Directly and frequently assess student learning.* Learning by students with severe disabilities most often occurs in very small steps that may be missed without direct measurement. Learning is shown most clearly when some measure of student performance is collected during every lesson. Recording a student's performance of each step of a task-analyzed skill or routine or level of prompts is needed (e.g., see Collins, Karl, et al., 2010).

PARTIAL PARTICIPATION   The principle of **partial participation**, first described by Baumgart and colleagues (1982), acknowledges that even though some individuals with severe disabilities cannot independently perform all steps of a given task or activity, they often can be taught to perform selected components or an adapted version of the task. Partial participation can be used to help a learner be more active in a task, make more choices in how the task will be carried out, and provide more control over the activity (Udvari-Solner, Causton-Theoharis, & York-Barr, 2004). Ongoing evaluation determines when various components of assistance can be faded or eliminated and that partial participation enables "meaningful involvement in all school and classroom activities" (Janney & Snell, 2011, p. 225).

Like any instructional strategy or technique, partial participation can be misused. Ferguson and Baumgart (1991) describe and offer suggestions for avoiding four types of misapplications of partial participation: (a) *passive participation*—the learner is present but not actively participating; (b) *myopic participation*—the student's participation is limited to only some parts of the activity, which are chosen for the convenience of others; (c) *piecemeal participation*—partial participation and the accompanying concepts of functional, activity-based, age-appropriate curriculum activities are used only part of the time; and (d) *missed participation*—in trying to help students become independent, the point of partial participation is missed altogether.

POSITIVE BEHAVIORAL SUPPORT   In the not-too-distant past, a student who engaged in hand mouthing and stereotypic head weaving may have had his arms put in splints while a teacher manipulated his head up and down for several minutes. A student who tantrumed or screamed may have been "treated" by being sprayed with water mist or given an extended time-out from instruction. A student who repeatedly struck out at others was restrained and held motionless on the floor for several minutes. Although some programs still use such techniques as part of treatment plans, little evidence exists for their therapeutic value, especially the use of restraint. It is widely accepted that "restraint is not treatment; it is the failure of treatment" (Alliance to Prevent Restraint, Aversive Interventions and Seclusion [APRAIS], 2011a).

Today, special educators are helping students with severe disabilities learn to replace disruptive, aggressive, self-injurious or socially unacceptable behaviors with a treatment approach called *positive behavioral support* (APRAIS, 2011b). Elements of positive behavior support include (a) understanding the meaning that a behavior has for a student, (b) teaching the student a positive alternative behavior, (c) restructuring the environment to make the undesired behaviors less likely, and (d) using strategies that are socially acceptable and intended for use in integrated school and community settings (Carr et al., 2002).

Positive behavioral support begins with a functional assessment of the problem behavior. Results of functional assessments guide the development of positive behavior support plans. For example, functional assessments conducted by Roscoe et al. (2010) revealed that aggressive outbursts during instructional activities by a 13-year-old student with multiple disabilities were maintained by teacher attention in the form of preferred conversational topics (e.g., zoo, dogs). This information led to the design of a function-based intervention that decreased the child's aggression by teaching her a socially accepted alternative behavior (pointing to an "I want to talk" card) to access highly preferred conversation topics.

Compared to interventions that do not consider the function of problem behavior, treatments informed by functional assessment are more likely to produce durable improvements in behavior, are less restrictive in nature, and are more likely to be viewed by consumers as acceptable (Hastings & None, 2005; Neef & Peterson, 2007).

Problem behaviors such as noncompliance, aggression, acting out, and self-injury can sometimes be reduced in frequency or prevented altogether through relatively simple environmental modifications of curriculum or the way in which learning activities are conducted (Cannella-Malone et al., 2006; Ferro, Carbone, Morgenstern, & Zecchin-Tirri, 2010; O'Reilly et al., 2006). For example:

- Providing students with a choice of tasks or a task sequence (Peterson, Neef, Van Norman, & Ferreri, 2005).
- Interspersing easy or high-probability tasks or requests with more difficult items or low-probability requests (Killu, Sainato, Davis, Ospelt, & Paul, 1998).
- Maintaining a rapid pace of instruction (Tincani, Ernsbarger, Harrison, & Heward, 2005).
- Using a response-prompting procedure that results in fewer errors (Ebanks & Fisher, 2003; Heckaman, Alber, Hooper, & Heward, 1998).
- Increasing response effort required to perform the challenging behavior (Carter, 2009).
- Delivering reinforcement noncontingently on a fixed time schedule (Kodak, Miltenberger, & Romaniuk, 2003).
- Providing free access to leisure items and activities (Cannella-Malone, O'Reilly, Sigafoos, & Chan, 2008; Lindberg, Iwata, Roscoe, Worsdell, & Hanley, 2003).

SMALL-GROUP INSTRUCTION For many years, it was thought that one-to-one instruction was the only effective teaching arrangement for students with severe disabilities. The rationale was that one-to-one teaching minimized distractions and increased the likelihood that the student would respond only to the teacher. Although one-to-one teaching formats enable the intensive, systematic instruction that is effective with students with severe disabilities, research has shown that well-designed and -executed small-group instruction has advantages and can also be effective (Kamps, Dugan, Leonard, &

APRAIS was established in 2004 to protect children with significant disabilities who exhibit challenging behaviors from abuse in schools, treatment programs and residential facilities. The Council for Exceptional Children's policy on restraint and seclusion is available at http://www.cec.sped.org.

Positive behavioral support

 Content Standards for Beginning Teachers—Common Core: Laws, policies, and ethical principles regarding behavior management planning and implementation (ICC1K2) (also ICC5S5).

Functional assessment, functional analysis

 Content Standards for Beginning Teachers—Common Core: Use functional assessments to develop intervention plans (ICC7S4) (also ICC8K1, IIC7S1, IIC8S1).

For detailed procedures and guidelines for developing positive behavioral support plans, see Cipani and Schock (2007); Horner, Albin, Todd, Newton, and Sprague (2011); O'Neill et al. (1997); and Umbreit, Ferro, Liaupsin, and Lane (2007).

Small-group instruction

 Content Standards for Beginning Teachers—INDEP CURR: Methods for ensuring individual academic success in one-to-one, small-group, and large-group settings (IIC5K4) (also ICC5K3).

Daoust, 1994; Leaf et al., 2011; Munk, Laarhoven, Goodman, & Repp, 1998; Snell & Brown, 2011, Traubman et al., 2001):

- Skills learned in small-group instruction may be more likely to generalize to group situations and settings.
- Small-group instruction provides opportunities for social interaction and reinforcement from peers that are missed when a student is taught alone and isolated from other students.
- Small-group instruction provides opportunities for incidental or observation learning from other students.
- In some instances, small-group instruction may be a more cost-effective use of the teacher's time.

Teachers can enhance the effectiveness of small-group instruction for all students by

- Ensuring that students possess basic prerequisite skills such as (a) sitting quietly for a period of time, (b) maintaining eye contact, and (c) following simple instructions or imitating simple responses.
- Encouraging students to listen and watch other group members and then praise them for doing so.
- Making instruction interesting by keeping individual turns short, giving all members turns, giving turns contingent on attending, and using demonstrations and a variety of materials that can be handled.
- Using methods that produce high rates of active student response, such as choral responding and response cards, which enable every student in the group to respond to each instructional trial.
- Teaching at a lively pace with very brief intertrial intervals.
- Involving all members by using multilevel instruction individualized to each student's targeted skills and mode of response.
- Using partial participation and material adaptation to enable all students to respond.
- Eliminating unnecessary teacher talk and limiting the amount/length of student response in a single turn.

Where Should Students with Severe Disabilities Be Taught?

What is the most appropriate educational setting for a student with severe disabilities? This important question continues to be the subject of much debate and discussion (Gallagher et al., 2000; Giangreco, 2011).

Benefits of neighborhood schools

 Council for Exceptional Children
Content Standards for Beginning Teachers—INDEP CURR: Advantages and disadvantages of placement options and programs on the continuum of services for individuals with disabilities (IIC5K5) (also IIC1K6, ICC5K1).

BENEFITS OF NEIGHBORHOOD SCHOOLS Lou Brown (who has long championed the inclusion of people with severe disabilities in integrated school, vocational, and community settings) and his colleagues at the University of Wisconsin made a strong case for why students with severe disabilities should attend the same school they would attend if they were not disabled:

The environments in which students with severe intellectual disabilities receive instructional services have critical effects on where and how they spend their postschool lives. Segregation begets segregation. We believe that when children with intellectual disabilities attend separate schools, they are denied opportunities to demonstrate to the rest of the community that they can function in integrated environments and activities; their nondisabled peers do not know or understand them and too often think negatively of them; their parents become afraid to risk allowing them opportunities to learn to function in integrated environments later in life; and taxpayers assume they need to be sequestered in segregated group homes, enclaves, work crews, activity centers, sheltered workshops, institutions, and nursing homes. (Brown et al., 1989a, p. 1)

Brown and his colleagues offered four reasons why students with severe disabilities should be educated in neighborhood schools. First, when students without disabilities go to an integrated school with peers who have disabilities, they are more likely to develop a greater acceptance of diversity and are likely to function responsibly as adults in a pluralistic society (Downing, Spencer, & Cavallaro, 2004). Second, integrated schools are more meaningful instructional environments (Fisher & Meyer, 2002). Third, parents and families have greater access to school activities when children are attending their home schools. Fourth, attending one's home school provides greater opportunities to develop a wide range of social relationships with nondisabled peers (Zambo, 2010). While each rationale has received various types and levels of research support in the literature (Ryndak & Fisher, 2007), the benefits of inclusion on social skills and relationships have the most extensive empirical support.

Friendships and after-school relationships between students with disabilities and their peers are more likely to develop when all students attend their home school.

© Bill Aron/PhotoEdit

SOCIAL RELATIONSHIPS Establishing and maintaining a network of social relationships are among the desired outcomes of inclusive educational practices for students with severe disabilities (Schwartz, 2000; Carter, 2011). Table 1 presents examples of 11 kinds of social relationships that might develop between students with severe disabilities and their nondisabled peers when they attend the same school. Although research has shown that simply placing students with disabilities into neighborhood schools and classrooms does not necessarily lead to increased positive social interactions, participation in a general education class can provide additional opportunities for positive social contacts and the development of friendships (e.g., Carter, Clark, Cushing, & Kennedy, 2005; Staub, Spaulding, Peck, Gallucci, & Schwartz, 1996). See *Teaching & Learning*, "Including Students in General Education: The Peer Buddy Program."

Educators have developed a wide variety of strategies for promoting social interactions and friendship. One strategy is teaching the student with disabilities a specific skill for initiating and maintaining interaction (Hughes et al., 2000). For example, Jolly, Test,

and Spooner (1993) taught two nonverbal boys with severe and profound intellectual disabilities and multiple physical disabilities to initiate play activities with nondisabled peers by showing badges with photographs of activities. Other strategies focus on teaching classmates without disabilities to initiate social contacts during free time, cooperative learning, or peer tutoring and peer buddy activities (Copeland et al., 2004; Hughes et al., 2001). Still other approaches involve changes in the roles and responsibilities of instructional faculty, such as collaborative teaching teams (Dettmer, Thurston, & Dyck, 2005; Snell & Janney, 2005).

Many of these strategies for facilitating the inclusion of students with severe disabilities are compatible with one another; and programs typically incorporate multiple, concurrent methods for identifying and providing supports for students, their teachers, and their peers.

Inclusion and social relationships

Council for Exceptional Children

Content Standards for Beginning Teachers—INDEP CURR: Advantages and disadvantages of placement options and programs on the continuum of services for individuals with disabilities (IIC5K5) (also IIC5K2, ICC5K1).

In the end, the best inclusion facilitators are the students themselves.

© Robin Nelson/PhotoEdit

465

TABLE 1 • **Social relationships that can develop between students with severe disabilities and their peers without disabilities when they attend the same school**

SOCIAL RELATIONSHIP	EXAMPLE
Peer tutor	Leigh role-plays social introductions with Margo, providing feedback and praise for Margo's performance.
Eating companion	Jennifer and Rick eat lunch with Linda in the cafeteria and talk about their favorite music groups.
Art, home economics, industrial arts, music, physical education companion	In art class, students were instructed to paint a sunset. Tom sat next to Dan and offered suggestions and guidance about the best colors to use and how to complete the task.
Regular class companion	A fifth-grade class is doing a "Know Your Town" lesson in social studies. Ben helps Karen plan a trip through their neighborhood.
During-school companion	"Hangs out" and interacts on social level: after lunch and before the bell for class rang, Molly and Phyllis went to the student lounge for a soda.
Friend	David, a member of the varsity basketball team, invites Ralph, a student with severe disabilities, to his house to watch a game on TV.
Extracurricular companion	Sarah and Winona prepare their articles for the school newspaper together and then work on the layout in the journalism lab.
After-school-project companion	The sophomore class decided to build a float for the homecoming parade. Joan worked on it with Maria, a nondisabled companion, after school and on weekends in Joan's garage.
After-school companion	On Saturday afternoon, Mike, who is not disabled, and Bill go to the shopping mall.
Travel companion	David walks with Ralph when he wheels from last-period class to the gym, where Ralph helps the basketball team as a student manager.
Neighbor	Interacts with student in everyday environments and activities. Parents of nondisabled students in the neighborhood regularly exchange greetings with Mary when they are at school, around the neighborhood, at local stores, at the mall, at the grocery.

Source: Table adapted from "The Home School: Why Students with Severe Disabilities Must Attend the Schools of Their Brothers, Sisters, Friends, and Neighbors" by L. Brown, from JOURNAL FOR THE ASSOCIATION FOR PERSONS WITH SEVERE HANDICAPS, 1987, Volume 14. Copyright © 1987 by TASH. Reprinted with permission.

HOW MUCH TIME IN THE GENERAL EDUCATION CLASSROOM? Although research has clearly shown the social benefits of general education class membership for students with disabilities, as well as for their peers without disabilities, the effects of full inclusion on the attainment of IEP goals are not yet known. Although the functional IEP goals and objectives for students with severe disabilities can be embedded within the academic instruction in the general education classroom, doing so meaningfully if often very difficult, especially at the secondary level. Making the most effective use of available instructional time is critical to students who by definition require direct, intensive, and "customized" instruction to acquire basic skills that students without disabilities learn without instruction (Smith, Gast, Logan, & Jacobs, 2001). A major challenge for both special and general educators is to develop models and strategies for including students with severe disabilities in general education classroom activities without sacrificing their opportunities to acquire, practice, and generalize the functional skills they need most.

The question of how much time students with severe disabilities should spend in the general education classroom is an important one. Although a few full-inclusion advocates might argue that every student with disabilities should have a full-time general education class placement regardless of the nature of her educational needs, most special educators probably would agree with Brown and colleagues (1991), whose position is that students with severe disabilities should be based in the same schools and classrooms they would attend if they were not disabled but that they should also spend some time elsewhere.

> There are substantial differences between being based in and confined to regular education classrooms. "Based in" refers to being a member of a real class, where and with whom you start the school day, you may not spend all your time with your class, but it is still your group and everyone knows it.... It is our position that it is unacceptable for students with severe disabilities to spend either 0% or 100% of their time in regular education classrooms.... How much time should be spent in regular classes? Enough to ensure that the student is a member, not a visitor. A lot, if the student is engaged in meaningful activities. Quite a bit if she is young, but less as she approaches 21. There is still a lot we do not know. (pp. 40, 46)

The Challenge and Rewards of Teaching Students with Severe and Multiple Disabilities

Teachers—special as well as general educators—who are providing instruction to students with severe and multiple disabilities can rightfully be called pioneers on an exciting new frontier of education. In 1984, Orelove stated that professionals who were involved in educating students with severe disabilities could "look back with pride, and even awe, at the advances they have made. In a relatively brief period, educators, psychologists, and other professionals have advocated vigorously for additional legislation and funds, extended the service delivery model into the public schools and community, and developed a training technology" (p. 271).

Although significant progress has been made in the nearly 30 years since Orelove's positive assessment, a great deal more can and must be accomplished. Future research must increase our understanding of how students with severe disabilities acquire, maintain, and generalize functional skills. As we develop more effective techniques for changing behavior, they must be balanced with concern for the personal rights and dignity of individuals with severe disabilities. Current and future teachers of students with severe disabilities have the opportunity to be at the forefront of those developments.

Teaching students with severe disabilities is difficult and demanding. The teacher must be well organized, firm, and consistent. He must be able to manage a complex educational operation, which usually involves supervising paraprofessional aides, student teachers, peer tutors, and volunteers. The teacher must be knowledgeable about one-to-one and small-group instruction formats and be able to work cooperatively with other teachers and related-services professionals. He must maintain accurate records and constant planning for the future needs of his students. Effective communication with parents and families, school administrators, vocational rehabilitation personnel, and community agencies is also vital.

Detailed descriptions of administrative, curricular, and instructional strategies that support the education of students with severe disabilities in inclusive schools and inclusive classrooms are available in Bauer and Brown (2001), Downing and Eichinger (2003), Ryndak and Fisher (2007), Giangreco and Doyle (2007), and Snell and Janney (2005).

467

Including Students in General Education: The Peer Buddy Program

BY CAROLYN HUGHES, ERIK CARTER, MARILEE DYE, AND CORIE BYERS

TEACHING & LEARNING

As inclusion of students with disabilities into general education classes and activities is sought in more and more schools, educators are seeking direction in how to actually accomplish this goal. Peer buddy programs—in which general education students interact with and support special education students—are an effective strategy for increasing inclusion and access to the general education environment and curriculum (Hughes & Carter, 2006).

At the secondary level, classroom teachers often find it especially difficult to get special and general education students together. Most high school schedules are broken into 50- to 90-minute class periods—often with no free periods—which makes it difficult to include students with disabilities in the mainstream of school life. In addition, many special education students are involved in community-based training, which requires longer blocks of time. Scheduling constraints may be one reason why most inclusion projects and research studies take place at the preschool and elementary levels.

The Peer Buddy Program attempts to remove scheduling barriers to inclusion by providing daily class times in which general education and special education students may interact. The program was developed and is being implemented in all comprehensive high schools in the Metropolitan Nashville Public Schools—an urban school district of 78,000 students. This program has become a prototype for peer interaction and inclusion programs adopted by many schools and school districts nationwide. An elective, one-credit course allows peer buddies to spend at least one period each day with their special education partners. Peer buddies serve as positive role models for social interaction and provide the support their partners need to be included within general education and career/technical classes and the extracurricular activities that make up a typical high school day. They also are effective in teaching conversational skills to their classmates with intellectual disabilities and autism (Hughes et al., 2011). Benefits reported by peer buddies include an increase in disability awareness, friendships, understanding of themselves and others, and appreciation of individual differences (Copeland et al., 2004).

A TEACHER'S PERSPECTIVE: MARILEE DYE, SPECIAL EDUCATION TEACHER AT MCGAVOCK HIGH SCHOOL

My classroom includes the entire spectrum of students with severe disabilities: students with intellectual disabilities, multiple disabilities, communication deficits, sensory impairments, and autism. Peer tutors from the peer buddy program have been effective with all of these students. In my classroom, peer buddies perform a wide variety of activities. But the main thing they do is develop a friendship with the student to whom they are assigned.

Social interaction skills are a deficit for all of my students, and they are the single most difficult set of skills for an adult to teach a teenager. Peer buddies are much more successful at teaching social skills. Often, they are not trying to work on social skills, but through the course of a regular conversation or interaction, it just seems to occur. My first peer buddy, Amy, worked with Melissa on reading skills every day. Also during the school year, the two often discussed personal hygiene issues. I had absolutely nothing to do with these conversations. In a period of 2 months, we saw positive changes in Melissa's cleanliness and appearance. I had been working with Melissa for 1 year on these same issues, as had other teachers for the past several years. We had had no impact on her behavior either singly or collectively. It was amazing to me what a peer accomplished in such a short time and with very little effort. After 2 years, Melissa continues to use the skills she learned from Amy; with no prompting, she keeps her hair washed and combed, brushes her teeth, and wears clothes that match.

This year I have a student with autism in my class. When Kim first came into my room, she appeared to have no interest in others and initiated interactions only when she wanted to eat or go to the rest room. Then Kim developed a friendship with her peer buddy, Corie. Now she watches the door for Corie every day. When they are together, Kim makes eye contact with her buddy frequently, laughs often, and even initiates conversations. We never saw Kim do these behaviors before. Kim also has increased her verbal repertoire from 4 to 11 words. I have been truly amazed at the difference peer buddies have made in the lives of my students.

A STUDENT'S PERSPECTIVE: CORIE BYERS, SENIOR AT MCGAVOCK HIGH SCHOOL

I heard about the peer buddy program from my guidance counselor and because I didn't have another class for one of my class periods, I decided to take it. I was kind of interested in it anyway, because I had been a peer tutor in seventh and eighth grade, and I wondered if I could get into it again.

I learned a lot about different people and different aspects of handicaps. My second semester as a peer buddy I spent mostly with Kim in Ms. Dye's room. And that girl—whew! She was a handful. When I first got into the classroom, Kim would just sit there and either sleep all day or cry about something. Or kind of just wander around with her eyes and look and not do anything. After my first semester, I noticed how she wouldn't deal with anybody. She was just always by herself. So I would go over there and tickle her and, all of a sudden, she just livened up! It was like someone had to just talk to her one time, and she burst out with life. When I first started talking to her, she really didn't have many words that she could say. Mostly she just said, "Milk," if she wanted milk, or if she had to go to the bathroom, she would tell us. That was about it. Then I got to talking to her, and toward the end of the year, she developed more language and everything.

We played games like hand-slap games and tickled each other. The bean bag chair was the best because she just loved that thing. Kim would just lay on it and wallow all over the floor and just laugh. It was so cool!

Well, that's Kim! She's cool now.

HOW TO GET STARTED

Steps for implementing a peer buddy program are well established and can easily be adapted to your individual situation (Hughes & Carter, 2008):

1. **Develop a one-credit course.**
   - Incorporate a peer-tutoring course into your school's curriculum that allows peer buddies to spend at least one period each day with their special education partners.
   - Follow the school district's established procedures when you apply for the new course offering.
   - Include the course description in your school's official class schedule.

2. **Recruit peer buddies.**
   - Present information about the new program at a faculty meeting.
   - Actively recruit peer buddies during the first year. After that, peer buddies will recruit for you.
   - Include announcements, posters, and articles in the school newspaper and parent–teacher organization newsletter and videos on the school's closed-circuit television. Have peer buddies speak in school clubs and classes.
   - Have guidance counselors refer students who have interest, good attendance, and adequate grades.

3. **Screen and match students.**
   - Allow students to observe in the special education classroom to learn about the role of a peer buddy and decide if they would be an appropriate match for the class.
   - Have students interview with the special education teachers and meet potential partners.
   - Have students provide information on past experiences with students with disabilities and clubs or activities they are involved in that their special education partners could join.

4. **Teach instructional strategies to peer buddies.**
   - Conduct a peer buddy orientation that includes people-first language, disability awareness, communication strategies, and suggested activities.
   - Communicate teachers' expectations for the peer buddy course, including attendance and grading policies.
   - Model prompting and reinforcement techniques.
   - Provide suggestions for dealing with inappropriate behavior, setting limits, and modifying general education curricula.

5. **Provide feedback and evaluate the program.**
   - Schedule observations and feedback sessions with peer buddies to address their questions or concerns.
   - Give peer buddies feedback on their interaction skills, time management, use of positive reinforcement, and activities engaged in with their partners.
   - Have peer buddies keep a daily journal of their activities and reflections, which the classroom teacher should review weekly.
   - Establish a peer buddy club that allows students to share experiences and ideas.

6. **Hold a lunch bunch.**
   - Invite peer buddies to join special education students in the cafeteria for lunch.
   - Encourage buddies to invite their general education friends to join the group, increasing social contacts for special education partners.

7. **Establish an advisory board.**
   - Develop an advisory board that includes students (buddies and partners), their parents, participating general and special education teachers, administrators, and guidance counselors.
   - Include community representatives to expand the peer buddy program to community-based activities, such as work experiences.

About the Authors

Carolyn Hughes is a professor of Special Education and Human and Organizational Development at Vanderbilt University. Erik Carter is associate professor of Special Education at Vanderbilt University. Marilee Dye is a special education teacher, and Corie Byers was a senior at McGavock High School in Nashville.

Students with the most severe disabilities sometimes give little or no apparent response, so their teachers must be very sensitive to small changes in behavior. The effective teacher is consistent and persistent in designing and implementing strategies to improve learning and behavior. The effective teacher should not be too quick to remove difficult tasks or requests that result in noncompliance or misbehavior. It is better to teach students to request assistance and to intersperse tasks that are easy for the student to perform.

There is a difference between either expecting miracles or being passively patient and simply working each day at the job of designing, implementing, and evaluating systematic instruction and supports. It can be a mistake to expect a miracle:

> In the beginning, we were expecting a sudden step forward, that we might somehow turn a cognitive, emotional, or social key inside the child's mind that would produce a giant leap ahead.... Such a leap would have been so gratifying, and it would have made our work so much easier. But it never happened. Instead, progress followed a slow, step-by-step progression, with only a few and minor spurts ahead from time to time. We learned to settle in for hard work. (Lovaas, 1994, n.p.)

Some might consider it undesirable to work with students with severe and multiple disabilities because of the extent of their behavioral challenges and learning problems. Yet teaching students who require instruction at its very best can offer many highly rewarding teaching experiences. Much satisfaction can be felt in teaching a child to feed and dress herself independently; helping a student make friends with nondisabled peers; and supporting a young adult's efforts to live, travel, and work as independently as possible in the community. Both the challenge and the potential rewards of teaching students with severe disabilities are great.

▼ TIPS FOR BEGINNING TEACHERS

Tips for Teaching Students with Severe Disabilities

BY CAREY CREECH-GALLOWAY

DEVELOP A SCHEDULE AND STICK TO IT

- List all of the students' IEP objectives and related services first and other activities that have set times during the school day. Schedule the students, instructional assistants, and the teacher all on the same schedule so that everyone knows their responsibilities for that block of time.
- List the student(s) and instructor and the goal or activity for that time period. You may even want to list the materials needed until your paraprofessionals become familiar with your expectations. Don't forget to have several generalization activities on hand so that students have an opportunity to apply the concepts taught during direct instruction.
- You'll probably revise this schedule five or six times before it runs smoothly, but stick with it!

PAIR PICTURE CUES WITH PRINT AS MUCH AS POSSIBLE

- Pairing pictures with print is especially important when you are teaching at the elementary level. Students with severe disabilities acquire and generalize language quicker when the words are paired with pictures. Secondary students can also benefit from this strategy—just make sure that your pictures are age-appropriate.
- Use this approach with schedules, labeling items, learning centers, communication boards, choice boards, and class rules.

GET ORGANIZED WITH YOUR INSTRUCTIONAL DATA

- Develop a system for keeping each student's instructional data organized. You could begin with a binder with each IEP objective on a tab with the data sheet and graph behind the tab. You can organize this per student or per IEP objective if that applies (e.g., all students working on brushing teeth in one binder).
- Secondary teachers may find it more beneficial to break into instructional groups per the IEP goals first, and then set up group instruction binders that contain the probe data collection, data collection sheets for the skills being taught, graphs for each student's performance, and a list of instructional materials required.

- Take data on the IEP objective every time you provide instruction, because you need the data to make decisions on instruction. As one University of Kentucky professor told me, "If you aren't taking data on the skill, why teach it?"

EMBED FUNCTIONAL SKILLS INSTRUCTION THROUGHOUT THE SCHOOL DAY

- To maintain functional skills or independent living skills, the student needs opportunities during the day to practice those skills when they may occur naturally.
- With an increasing emphasis on core content instruction, it is important for teachers of students with moderate and severe disabilities to keep in mind long-term and transition goals for their students so they can increase their independence.
- Start with a list of daily living skills and which students need to work or those skills. List any vocational skills, cooking skills, community living skills, or recreation leisure skills that your students may need in the future. Target two or three skills for each student and schedule time during the day for those skills to be taught. For example, you could embed some of those skills in the following way brushing teeth after lunch wiping tables at the end of the day; preparing breakfast for another student, sorting items in the school bank.

COLLABORATE WITH GENERAL EDUCATION TEACHERS

- Meet with the teachers individually, if possible, and determine how you will communicate—whether through a paraprofessional, a peer tutor, e-mail, or weekly meetings.
- Set clear goals for your students in the general education setting. Talk with the general education teacher about what opportunities there are in their classroom for your student to participate, and discuss how work will be modified.
- Have a plan if the time may present itself that the setting is not appropriate for your students; for example, the entire class is taking a standardized test or the schedule is changed for some reason.
- Look at each student's IEP goals and determine when those goals could be worked on in the general education setting as well.
- **Be flexible.** Plan lessons that are focused on a measurable, observable outcomes, and look at how to teach core content skills in a functional way. Remember you can—and should—use systematic instructional strategies to teach core content objectives as well as functional skills.

▼ KEY TERMS AND CONCEPTS

anoxia
closed head injury
deaf-blindness
multiple disabilities
open head injury
partial participation

profound disabilities
severe disabilities
task analysis
time delay
traumatic brain injury

▼ SUMMARY

Defining Severe, Profound, and Multiple Disabilities

- Students with severe disabilities need instruction in basic skills that most children without disabilities acquire without instruction in the first 5 years of life.
- TASH defines people with severe disabilities as individuals "who require ongoing support in more than one major life activity in order to participate in an integrated community and enjoy a quality of life similar to that available to all citizens."
- Students with profound disabilities have pervasive delays in all domains of functioning at a developmental level no higher than 2 years.
- Students with severe disabilities frequently have multiple disabilities, including physical impairments and health conditions.
- Students with deaf-blindness cannot be accommodated in special education programs designed solely for students with hearing or visual impairments. Although the vast majority of children who are deaf-blind have some functional hearing and/or vision, the dual impairments severely impede learning.

Characteristics of Students with Severe and Multiple Disabilities

- Students with severe disabilities need instruction in many basic skills that most children without disabilities learn without help. Children with severe disabilities may show some or all of the following behaviors or skill deficits: slow acquisition rates for learning new skills, difficulty in generalizing and maintaining newly learned skills, severe deficits in communication skills, impaired physical and motor development, deficits in self-help skills, infrequent constructive behavior and interaction, and frequent inappropriate behavior.

- Despite their intense challenges, students with severe disabilities often exhibit many positive characteristics, such as warmth, humor, sociability, and persistence.
- Despite their limitations, children with severe disabilities can and do learn.

Prevalence of Severe and Multiple Disabilities

- Estimates of the prevalence of severe disabilities range from 0.1% to 1% of the population.
- Together, children served under the IDEA disability categories of multiple disabilities, traumatic brain injury, and deaf-blindness represent less than 3% of all children who receive special education.

Causes of Severe and Multiple Disabilities

- Brain disorders, which are involved in most cases of severe intellectual disabilities, are the result of either brain dysgenesis (abnormal brain development) or brain damage (caused by influences that alter the structure or function of a brain that had been developing normally up to that point).
- Severe and profound disabilities most often have biological causes, including chromosomal abnormalities, genetic and metabolic disorders, complications of pregnancy and prenatal care, birth trauma, and later brain damage.
- In about one-sixth of all cases of severe disabilities, the cause cannot be clearly determined.

Traumatic Brain Injury

- IDEA defines traumatic brain injury (TBI) as an acquired injury to the brain caused by an external physical force, resulting in total or partial functional disability or psychosocial impairments, or both, that adversely affects a child's educational performance.
- Traumatic brain injury is the leading cause of death in children and the most common cause of acquired disability in childhood.
- Causes of TBI are open head injuries, which are the result of penetration of the skull, and closed head injuries, which are more common and result from the head hitting or being hit by an object with such force that the brain slams against the inside of the cranium.
- Major causes of traumatic brain injury in children are car and bicycle accidents, falls, accidents during contact sports, and shaken baby syndrome.
- A mild brain injury results in a concussion (a brief or momentary loss of consciousness), usually without any subsequent complications.
- A moderate brain injury usually results in contusions (bruising, swelling, and bleeding), hematomas (aggregation or clotting of blood), loss of consciousness, and significant cognitive and behavioral impairments for many months.
- In addition to brain contusions, hematomas, and damage to the nerve fibers or axons, a severe brain injury results in a coma and often permanent impairments in functioning.

- Impairments caused by brain injuries fall into three main categories: (a) physical and sensory changes (e.g., lack of coordination, spasticity of muscles); (b) cognitive impairments (e.g., short- and long-term memory deficits, difficulty maintaining attention and concentration); and (c) social, behavioral, and emotional problems (e.g., mood swings, self-centeredness, lack of motivation).

Educational Approaches

- A curriculum based on typical developmental milestones is inappropriate for most students with severe disabilities.
- Students with severe disabilities must be taught skills that are functional, age-appropriate, and directed toward current and future environments.
- Students with severe disabilities should be taught choice-making skills.
- The emphasis of research and training in communication for people with severe disabilities has shifted from instruction of specific forms of communication to a focus on functional communication in any mode that enables communication partners to establish shared meanings.
- Some students with severe disabilities use augmentative and alternative systems of communication (AAC), such as gestures, various sign language systems, pictorial communication boards, picture exchange communication systems (PECS), and electronic communication aids.
- Students with severe disabilities should be taught age-appropriate recreation and leisure skills.
- Because each student with severe disabilities has many learning needs, teachers must carefully prioritize and choose IEP objectives and learning activities that will be of most benefit to the student and his family.
- Effective instruction of students with severe disabilities is characterized by these elements:
  - The student's current level of performance is precisely assessed.
  - The skill to be taught is defined clearly.
  - The skills are ordered in an appropriate sequence.
  - The teacher provides clear prompts or cues to the student.
  - The student receives immediate feedback and reinforcement from the teacher.
  - Strategies that promote generalization of learning are used.
  - The student's performance is directly and frequently assessed.
- Partial participation is both a philosophy for selecting activities and a method for adapting activities and supports to enable students with severe disabilities to actively participate in meaningful tasks they cannot perform independently.
- The teacher of students with severe disabilities must be skilled in positive, instructionally relevant strategies for assessing and dealing with challenging and problem behaviors.

- Research has shown that integrated small-group instructional arrangements with students with severe disabilities can be effective.
- Students with severe disabilities are more likely to develop social relationships with students without disabilities if they attend their home school and are included in the general education classroom.
- Although the initial reactions of many general education teachers who have a student with severe disabilities placed in their classrooms are negative, those apprehensions and concerns often transform into positive experiences as the student becomes a regular member of their classroom.
- Teachers must be sensitive to small changes in behavior. The effective teacher is consistent and persistent in evaluating and changing instruction to improve learning and behavior.
- Working with students who require instruction at its very best can be highly rewarding to teachers.

MyEducationLab™

Go to Topic 17, Multiple Disabilities and Traumatic Brain Injury, in the MyEducationLab (www.myeducationlab.com) for *Exceptional Children*, where you can

- Find learning outcomes for multiple disabilities and traumatic brain injury along with the national standards that connect to these outcomes.
- Complete Assignments and Activities that can help you more deeply understand the chapter content.
- Apply and practice your understanding of the core teaching skills identified in the chapter with the Building Teaching Skills and Dispositions learning units (optional).
- Examine challenging situations and cases presented in the IRIS Center Resources.
- Access video clips of CCSSO National Teachers of the Year award winners responding to the question "Why do I teach?" in the Teacher Talk section.
- Check your comprehension the content covered in the chapter with the Study Plan. Here you will be able to take a chapter quiz, receive feedback on your answers, and then access Review, Practice, and Enrichment activities to enhance your understanding of chapter content.
- Use the Online Lesson Plan Builder to practice lesson planning and integrating national and state standards into your planning.

▼ GLOSSARY

anoxia: A lack of oxygen severe enough to cause tissue damage; can cause permanent brain damage and mental retardation.

closed head injury: Caused by the head hitting a stationary object with such force that the brain slams against the inside of the cranium; stress of this rapid movement and impact pulls apart and tears nerve fibers, or axons, of the brain.

deaf-blindness: Any combination of hearing and visual impairments that causes such severe communication, developmental, and educational needs that the individual cannot be accommodated in a special education program designed solely for children with hearing impairments or visual impairments.

multiple disabilities: Two or more disabilities in the same person; defined as a disability category in the Individuals with Disabilities Education Act as "concomitant impairments, the combination of which causes such severe educational needs that they cannot be accommodated in special education programs solely for one of the impairments."

open head injury: Result of penetration of the skull, such as caused by a bullet or a forceful blow to the head with a hard or sharp object.

partial participation: A teaching approach that acknowledges that even though an individual with severe disabilities may not be able to independently perform all the steps of a given task or activity, she can often be taught to do selected components or an adapted version of the task.

profound disabilities: Functioning at a level no higher than a typically developing 2-year-old in all behavioral and cognitive domains and requiring intensive supports and continuous monitoring.

severe disabilities: A term used to refer to challenges faced by individuals with severe and profound mental retardation, autism, and/or physical/sensory impairments combined with marked developmental delay. People with severe disabilities exhibit extreme deficits in intellectual functioning and need systematic instruction for basic skills such as self-care and communicating with others.

task analysis: Breaking a complex skill or chain of behaviors into smaller, teachable units.

time delay: A teaching technique for transferring control of a student's response from a teacher-provided prompt (e.g., teacher saying the word on a printed card) to the target stimulus (e.g., printed word); in a progressive time delay procedure in which using the target stimulus and prompt are presented concurrently in initial trials and a gradually increasing amount of time (e.g., 1 second, 2 seconds) is then inserted between the presentation of the target stimulus and the prompt, which may result in few or no errors by the learner.

traumatic brain injury: An acquired injury to the brain caused by an external physical force, resulting in total or partial functional disability, psychosocial impairments, or both that adversely affect a child's educational performance.

Gifted and Talented

From Chapter 13 of *Exceptional Children* and *An Introduction to Special Education*, Tenth Edition. William L. Heward.

Gifted and Talented

by William L. Heward and Donna Y. Ford

© Laurence Gough/Shutterstock

▶ FOCUS QUESTIONS

- How has the dynamic and evolving definition of giftedness changed the ways in which students are identified and served?

- Why do students who are very capable need special education?

- What provisions should and can be made to accurately identify students who are from racially, culturally, and economically different groups or who have disabilities?

- How can general education classroom teachers provide curriculum and instruction at the pace, breadth, and depth needed by gifted and talented

- students, while meeting the needs of other students in the classroom?

- What are some strategies for differentiating curriculum for gifted and talented learners through acceleration and enrichment?

- Should gifted students be educated with their same-age peers (in general education classes) or in heterogeneous groups of students who share similar intellectual and academic talents and interests?

- Should special education for gifted and talented students be required by federal law, as it is for students with disabilities?

▼ FEATURED TEACHER

LINDA MICHAEL

Edison Elementary School • Ashland City Schools, Ashland, Ohio

EDUCATION—TEACHING CREDENTIALS— EXPERIENCE

- B.A. in anthropology and history, Miami University

- M.S. in textiles and clothing, Ohio University

- M.Ed. in curriculum and instruction: talent development, Ashland University

- Ohio teacher licenses: Middle Grades (4–9) Science and Language Arts and Reading, Gifted Intervention Specialist

I have been a teacher of the gifted for 7 years, having come to the field of teaching after many work and life experiences. Some refer to this as a second career. I disagree. I view all the choices I have made as preparation to my first career—teaching.

MY CLASSROOM My first 2 years I taught fourth to sixth graders in a pull-out program. I then began teaching a self-contained gifted class of students identified as gifted in specific academic areas and/or as superior cognitive, and continue to do so. We require the students to be identified in at least math and language arts to be considered for the self-contained classes. We attempt to serve students identified in only one area through a gifted intervention specialist that pulls the student out for that discipline and is the

teacher of record. In my self-contained class, I have taught a combination of grade levels (fourth and fifth graders and fifth and sixth graders) as well as only sixth graders. The configuration is based on the number of students identified in the grade and the number of openings in my class. The class size is limited by state guidelines. In my state a self-contained class may have 25 sixth-grade students or 20 students in the lower grades or a multiage class.

I feel that the self-contained classroom is the best way to meet the needs of the students identified as superior cognitive or in multiple areas. Pull-out programs offer enrichment, but usually only for a few hours, once or twice a week. In my state, inclusion of a gifted intervention specialist in the regular classroom is replacing pull-out programs, or districts are offering inclusion along with pull-out programs. Most districts do not have enough teachers to meet the needs of all the identified gifted and talented students. Students aren't just gifted for part of the day or in increments throughout the week; they must have their needs met throughout the school day. I have found the self-contained classroom gives me the opportunity to do that. Because the curriculum can be compacted, we have the opportunity to focus on in-depth topics. Inquiry-based and project-based lessons are the norm in my classroom. Also, as I have the students all the time, we aren't stuck in a scheduling "box." If we need 2 hours for a science lab, we have it. Our school day is driven by our academic pursuits, not a bell schedule. Questions and interests of the students often mean we don't complete all the lesson plans I have for the day, and that's okay. I still cover all the material required in the state standards and so much more.

The self-contained class option is often controversial. More than one teacher has told me she was against the idea because I would be taking away the best and brightest students, the "sparkplugs." I have several responses to this viewpoint. The first is if the "sparkplugs" are the only students that regularly participate in class, the rest of the students are not being adequately reached. My second response is those "sparkplugs" may be draining the other students who are too intimidated to respond or who have grown complacent to be in a nonresponsive role.

The third response I have is a question: what is more important, a student's education or a teacher's routine? Gifted students who must wait for others to catch up or who are used as tutors in the classroom are not having their needs met. My final response is "Don't stereotype the gifted kid!" Gifted students are individuals and are not all "sparkplugs," constantly raising their hands in class. A gifted and talented student can just as often be the troublemaker, the quiet kid staring out the window, or the class clown who frequently forgets his assignments.

The birth of my self-contained class was not without its problems, but it has been worth the struggle, and my district now has two self-contained classes for fourth to sixth graders. Students and parents are excited, and my day is never dull. Teachers are beginning to understand that gifted education is not a threat to the general classroom but another positive way to serve students. Teachers are also recognizing that teachers of the gifted are an excellent resource to go to for help and suggestions for teaching gifted students in the regular classroom.

TEACHING STRATEGIES I've discovered how important it is to understand the learning strengths and challenges of your students. Sometimes it can be difficult getting students to step out of their comfort zones and to try new approaches in problem solving. For example, one of my students this year would rather read than do anything else. Once, during a math lesson, the students were creating isometric figures with cubes and then drawing their figures on grid paper. This activity was very difficult for my reader because she couldn't visualize the 3-D figure on a 2-D surface. But I didn't let her give up. And I didn't give up on her. When she finally saw the patterns, she got very excited about her accomplishment. Will she ever be an architect or engineer? Probably not, but that's not the point. She realized that she has even more talents and abilities than she thought, and she learned the value of persistence when faced with a challenging activity.

Becoming involved in a cause one feels strongly about is an excellent way for students to feel their education has personal meaning. In my first year of teaching, two of my students approached me with a petition to save the Mountain Gorillas. They had read about them and wanted to help in some way. The entire class began researching Mountain Gorillas, the causes of their dwindling population, and organizations that were helping alleviate the problems. The students discovered the Dian Fossey Foundation for Gorilla Research and decided to have a fund-raiser to adopt as many Mountain Gorillas as possible. They sold brownies, called Gorilla Bars, at the elementary schools. A parent who is a chef helped us bake the bars in one of the school kitchens. The experience brought the kids together for a cause they believed in and became a great lesson in math as the students estimated the quantity of the ingredients they needed and what the cost of the bars should be to make a profit. I must stress, I didn't initiate the idea. I guided and suggested, but the kids made it their own.

One of the best pieces of teaching advice I have encountered comes from an article by Steven Reinhart in the journal *Mathematics Teaching in the Middle School* (April 2000). Reinhart simply stated, "Never say anything a kid can say" (p. 1). Instead of answering a question, ask good questions that require students to think. This approach isn't easy. It demands that the teacher have a mastery of the academic content areas she is teaching. It also means the teacher must recognize her role is one of facilitator, not of lecturer. This isn't to say lecturing does not have its place, but it should be a brief introduction to a lesson, not the beginning, middle, and end.

Teaching gifted and talented students is a daily challenge that I wouldn't trade for anything. My classroom always seems to have a buzz about it because the students are excited to be there. This can be exhausting, especially when I feel like I can't do it all. Most of the time, however, it is exhilarating because I believe so much in the students and their potential.

MyEducationLab™

Visit the **MyEducationLab** for *Exceptional Children* to enhance your understanding of chapter concepts with a personalized Study Plan. You'll also have the opportunity to hone your teaching skills through video- and case-based Assignments and Activities, IRIS Center Resources, and Building Teaching Skills and Dispositions lessons.

OUR STUDY OF EXCEPTIONAL CHILDREN THUS FAR HAS FOCUSED on students with intellectual, behavioral, or physical disabilities—children who require individual programs of specially designed instruction and related services to benefit from education. On the other end of the continuum of cognitive, academic, artistic, and social abilities are gifted and talented students who find that traditional curriculum and methods of instruction do not provide the advanced and unique challenges they require to learn most effectively. They, too, need special education to reach their potential.

Janie has just completed her report on the solar system for class tomorrow. She looks out her bedroom window and wonders what might be happening on the countless planets that circle all of those stars. And she thinks about the circumstances that made life possible on the third planet from the star called Sol. What Janie is doing may not seem special; after all, most students write school reports and wonder about extraterrestrial life—until we learn that she is just 6 years old. Janie is functioning years ahead of her peers. She writes in complete sentences, expresses herself exceptionally well, and has a powerful urge to know the answers to many and varied problems.

Twelve-year-old Toney saunters down a dusty back road near his home in the southwest. He is excited because today his mentor and great-aunt has promised to teach him the process of applying the rich charcoal slip to the pottery he is making. His ancestors and family have been making pottery for hundreds of years, but somehow it seems to take on multiple meanings in his hands. He uses small variations in color and texture to embed symbolism into his pieces. Perhaps this one will have the winged serpent that he favors so much, reminding everyone that an immense trade network existed in prehistoric America that reached from present-day Canada to South America. Toney sees much in his pottery, in his ancestors who have inspired him, in the beauty that is the earth made functional, and in a desire for continuity in his life. Toney does not say much in school or express himself very well in writing, but he understands everything that is being said and talked about. This is clear when he is able to show his learning on projects and performance-based assignments. He is very patient and humble, and seems tentative and reserved in his behavior, not wanting to create a disturbance that would draw attention to himself.

Ninth grader Malcolm runs from school for the bus that will take him to the local university, where he is taking his second course on creative writing. He is excited about showing his latest short story to the professor. Malcolm's prose brings into focus all of the pain he sees around him, critically analyzing the leadership of his community and nation. He believes he has a message that must be heard; he is powerfully moved to reach out to the disaffected, the disenfranchised, as well as the ambivalent of all races. He has many ideas for changing what he believes is wrong with his government. He believes deeply in his vision and knows he can make a difference once he learns how to communicate his message as effectively as possible. Bursting with energy and desire, Malcolm struggles to sit still while the bus moves him ever closer to his training ground for the future.

Janie, Toney, and Malcolm need special education—in the form of curriculum modifications and specialized instructional activities—to enhance and develop their individual talents. These precocious youngsters, and others like them, will become the outstanding scientists, artists, writers, inventors, and leaders of the future. Understanding and working to develop the talents of these exceptional children is the mission of special educators who work with gifted and talented students.

DEFINITIONS

Intelligence, creativity, and talent have been central to the various definitions of giftedness that have been proposed over the deacades. Lewis Terman (1925), one of the pioneers of the field, defined the gifted as those who score in the top 2% on standardized tests of intelligence. Guilford (1967) called for the identification of people with creative potential. Witty (1951) described gifted and talented children as those "whose performance is consistently remarkable in any potentially valuable area" (p. 62). These three concepts continue to be reflected in the current and still-evolving definitions of gifted and talented children.

Federal Definitions

The first federal definition of gifted and talented students was included in a 1972 report to Congress titled *Education of the Gifted,* by then U.S. commissioner of education Sydney Marland:

> [T]he term "gifted and talented children" means children, and whenever applicable, youth, who are identified at the preschool, elementary, or secondary level as possessing demonstrated or potential high performance capabilities in areas such as intellectual, creative, specific academic, or leadership ability or in the performing and visual arts and who by reason thereof require services or activities not ordinarily provided by the school.... [G]ifted and talented will encompass a minimum of 3 to 5 percent of the school population. (p. 5)

The Marland definition encompassed multiple forms of giftedness in addition to superior intellectual ability and had significant influence on states' definitions.

A 1993 federal report, *National Excellence: A Case for Developing America's Talent,* featured a revised definition of gifted and talented children that was motivated by new cognitive research and concerns about inequity in participation in programs for the intellectually gifted. The word *gifted* was eliminated, and the terms *outstanding talent* and *exceptional talent* were embraced. Potential was retained in the definition, which stated that giftedness—or talent—occurs in all groups, across all cultures, and is not necessarily apparent in test scores but in a person's "high-performance capability" in intellectual, creative, and artistic realms. Giftedness is said to connote "a mature power rather than a developing ability." Talent is to be found by "observing students at work in rich and varied educational settings" (Part III, p. 2).

The current federal definition, first promulgated in the Jacob K. Javits Gifted and Talented Students Education Act of 1988 (PL 100-297) as part of the Elementary and Secondary Education Act and now included in the No Child Left Behind Act of 2001, reads as follows:

> Students, children, or youth who give evidence of high achievement capability in areas such as intellectual, creative, artistic, or leadership capacity, or in specific academic fields, and who need services and activities not ordinarily provided by the school in order to fully develop those capabilities. (Title IX, Part A, Section 9101 [22])

National Association for Gifted Children

The National Association for Gifted Children (NAGC, 2010a) defines gifted individuals as

> those who demonstrate outstanding levels of aptitude (defined as an exceptional ability to reason and learn) or competence (documented performance

Early definitions of G&T and Marland Report

Content Standards for Beginning Teachers—G&T: Historical foundations of gifted and talented education including points of view and contributions of individuals form diverse backgrounds (GT1K1).

In addition to CEC Content Standards, prospective teachers of gifted and talented students should also be familiar with the National Association for Gifted Children's PreK–12 Gifted Education Programming Standards (available at http://www.nagc.org).

Federal definition of G&T

Content Standards for Beginning Teachers—G&T: Issues in conceptions, definitions, and identification of individuals with gifts and talents, including those from culturally and linguistically diverse backgrounds (GT1K4).

or achievement in top 10% or rarer) in one or more domains. Domains include any structured area of activity with its own symbol system (e.g., mathematics, music, language) and/or set of sensorimotor skills (e.g., painting, dance, sports). (p. 1)

NAGC views the development of ability or talent as a lifelong process. Exceptional performance in young children may be evident on tests and other measures of ability or as an exceptionally rapid rate of learning, compared to other students of the same age, experience, and environment, or in actual achievement in a domain. As children reach adolescence, achievement and high motivation in the domain are often the primary characteristics of their giftedness.

Other Contemporary and Complementary Definitions

Contemporary conceptions of giftedness represent a growing recognition of the importance of balancing theoretical with practical definitions of giftedness that emphasize situated problem solving (Sternberg & Grigorenko, 2000); talents that are culture, context, and domain related (Gagné, 2003; Gardner, 1983/1994, 2006; Piirto, 2004a, 2004b; Sternberg, 2007); and the influence of sustained, deliberate practice on the realization of exceptional talent (Ericsson, Nadogapal, & Roring, 2005). The following definitions of gifted and talented students, offered by Joseph Renzulli, Jane Piirto, and June Maker, are examples of these contemporary views.

Renzulli's, Piirto's, and Maker's conceptions of G&T

Content Standards for Beginning Teachers—G&T: Issues in conceptions, definitions, and identification of individuals with gifts and talents, including those from culturally and linguistically diverse backgrounds (GT1K4).

RENZULLI'S THREE-TRAIT DEFINITION Renzulli's (2003) definition of giftedness is based on an interaction among three basic clusters of human traits: (a) above-average general intellectual abilities, (b) a high level of task commitment, and (c) creativity. Gifted and talented children are those

> possessing or capable of developing this composite set of traits and applying them to any potentially valuable area of human performance. Children who manifest or are capable of developing an interaction among the three clusters require a wide variety of educational opportunities and services that are not ordinarily provided through regular instructional programs. (p. 184)

Figure 1 illustrates how the three components of ability (demonstrated or potential), task commitment, and creative expression are jointly applied to a valuable area of human endeavor. Like the most recent federal definitions, Renzulli's definition casts a wide net; it provides a great deal of freedom in determining who is considered capable of high potential for gifted and talented performance.

PIIRTO'S CONCEPT OF TALENT DEVELOPMENT
Piirto (2007) defines the gifted as

> those individuals who, by way of having certain learning characteristics such as superior memory, observational powers, curiosity, creativity, and the ability to learn school-related subject matters rapidly and accurately with a minimum of drill and repetition, have a right to an education that is differentiated according to those characteristics. (p. 37)

Many gifted and talented students display characteristics such as superior memory, observational powers, curiosity, creativity, and the ability to learn school-related subject matter with a minimum of drill and repetition.

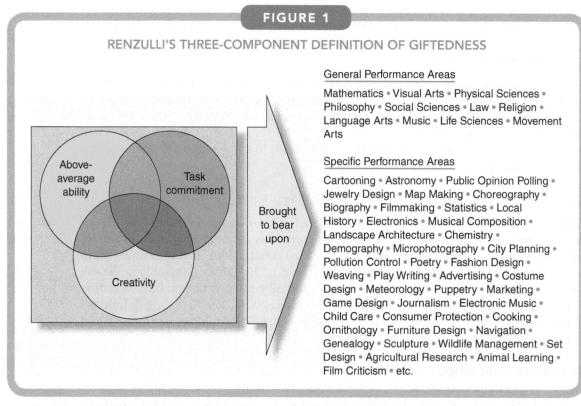

Piirto believes such children become apparent early and should be served throughout their educational lives, from preschool through college. While they may or may not become producers of knowledge or makers of novelty, their education should give them the background to become adults who do produce knowledge or make new artistic and social products.

MAKER'S PROBLEM-SOLVING PERSPECTIVE Maker's dynamic perspective incorporates the three elements that appear most often within contemporary definitions of the gifted and talented: high intelligence, high creativity, and excellent problem-solving skills. She characterizes a gifted person as

> a problem solver—one who enjoys the challenge of complexity and persists until the problem is solved in a satisfying way. Such an individual is capable of: a) creating a new or more clear definition of an existing problem, b) devising new and more efficient or effective methods, and c) reaching solutions that may be different from the usual, but are recognized as being effective, perhaps more effective, than previous solutions. (Maker, 1993, p. 71; also see Maker, 2005)

These and other contemporary conceptions of giftedness and talent, such as Sternberg's (2003, 2007) triarchic theory of intelligence, Gagné's (2003) differentiated model of giftedness and talent, and Gardner's (2006) theory of multiple intelligences, radically depart from earlier definitions that focused primarily on high IQ, by recognizing special talents and emphasizing an understanding of the role of opportunity as well as environmental and personality factors.

State-by-State Definitions

Many states have now incorporated aspects of the 2001 federal definition into their definitions of giftedness and talent. Although the general intelligence element prevails across states' definitions of giftedness and talent (30 states consider superior ability as

To learn how your state defines giftedness and types of educational programs and supports it provides for gifted students and their teachers, go to the NAGC website (http://www.nagc.org/) and click on Gifted By State.

giftedness), different states feature other aspects of special abilities and performance: specific academic ability (27 states), visual and performing arts (18 states), creative thinking (20 states), and unusual leadership capacity (16 states) (NAGC, 2010b). Three states have no official definition of gifted and talented students.

CHARACTERISTICS

Giftedness is a complex human characteristic that encompasses a wide range of abilities, skills, and traits. Whereas definitions of giftedness are social constructs (i.e., they are not absolute but vary according to situation), without doubt, gifted students have special educational needs. Some students have special talents, but rarely do these match the stereotypes and myths that people may have of giftedness. These students may not be outstanding in academics, but they may have exceptional abilities in areas such as music, dance, art, or leadership. Gifted and highly talented individuals are found in all gender, cultural, economic, linguistic, and disability groups. Learning and intellectual characteristics evidenced by many gifted and talented children include superior ability to (Clark, 2008; Davis, Rimm, & Siegle, 2011; Maker, 2005; Piirto, 2007):

- rapidly acquire, retain, and use large amounts of information;
- relate one idea to another;
- make sound judgments;
- appreciate multiple and opposing points of view;
- perceive the operation of larger systems of knowledge that may not be recognized by the typical person;
- acquire and manipulate abstract symbol systems; and
- solve problems by reframing the question and creating novel solutions.

Some children may have exceptional intellectual abilities found only in 1 child in 1,000 or 1 child in 10,000. Silverman (1995) identified the following characteristics for the highly gifted—children with IQ scores 3 standard deviations or greater above the mean (IQ >145):

- intense intellectual curiosity
- fascination with basic words and simple ideas
- perfectionism and need for precision
- learning with great/large/murky intuitive leaps
- intense need for mental stimulation and challenge
- difficulty conforming to the thinking/logic/reasoning of others
- early moral and existential concerns
- tendency toward introversion–independence and isolation

Many gifted children have a highly developed sense of moral judgment, fair play, compassion, and empathy for others for their age (Gross, 2004). As a result, teachers and parents may find themselves in heated discussons with gifted children over issues such as why adults litter or politicians want to cut aid programs for the elderly and poor (Davis et al., 2011). For examples of thoughtful observations on making the world a better place by young gifted students, see Figure 2.

Many discussions and lists of gifted characteristics portray gifted children as having only strengths and virtues but no flaws. The very attributes by which we identify gifted children, however, can cause or contribute to a multitude of problems (Cross, 2006; Nugent, 2005). Giftedness is not without costs. For example, strong verbal ability may be evident in gifted students who talk themselves out of troublesome situations or who dominate class discussions. High curiosity may give them the appearance of being aggressive or snoopy as they pursue interests and challenges. Educators need substantive preparation in gifted education: (a) to avoid unrealistic positive stereotypes of gifted students and (b) to avoid letting students' shortcomings be used to deny gifted education assessment and services (Ford, 2010a).

For common myths about gifted education, go to http://www.nagc.org/commonmyths.aspx.

Cognitive and learning characteristics of G&T

 Council for Exceptional Children Content Standards for Beginning Teachers—G&T: Cognitive and affective characteristics of individuals with gifts and talents in intellectual, academic, creative, leadership, and artistic domains (GT2K1).

FIGURE 2   MAKING THE EARTH A BETTER PLACE: WHO SAID IT?

Who do you think made each of these observations? Check your selections with the correct answers at the end.

1. After the strife of war begins the strife of peace.
   a. Napoleon Bonaparte
   b. Carl Sandburg
   c. Dwight Eisenhower
   d. Matthew O'Brien
   e. Abraham Lincoln

2. Global peace is a powerful weapon. If we have it, we can use it to make the earth a better place.
   a. Tom Brokaw
   b. Winston Churchill
   c. Henry David Thoreau
   d. Robert Campbell
   e. Mahatma Gandhi

3. The truth is more important than the facts.
   a. Frank Lloyd Wright
   b. Oscar Wilde
   c. Alyce Jaspers
   d. Albert Einstein
   e. Golda Meir

4. Cooperation is a crucial part of survival. Cooperation is key in human life because humans' needs are so diverse, requiring for their fulfillment more skills, more talents, and more learning than any one individual can possess.
   a. Lester Brown
   b. Buckminster Fuller
   c. Polao Salori
   d. Andrea Goldberg
   e. John Nesbit

5. The only way for earth to even come near perfection is for the people in our society who are in the best position to create a perfect earth to become somewhat competent.
   a. John F. Kennedy
   b. Margaret Mead
   c. John Lennon
   d. Nelson Mandela
   e. Peter Bret Lamphere

6. After much deep thinking and evaluation of those thoughts, I have come to the realization that, without a shadow of a doubt, the most crucial global issue today, and for years to come, is arms reduction.
   a. Edward Kennedy
   b. Mikhail Gorbachev
   c. Roy Stoner
   d. Jimmy Carter
   e. George Bush

7. Change lately has given us humans quite a stir. Berlin wall down, democracy up; Noriega down, taxes up. What a fast-changing world we live in.
   a. Barbara Walters
   b. Peter Jennings
   c. Walter Cronkite
   d. Connie Chung
   e. Robert Campbell

8. People should feel obligated to leave the world a little better than they found it.
   a. Pippa Bowde
   b. Carl Sagan
   c. Robert Redford
   d. Teddy Roosevelt
   e. Mother Teresa

9. Death in the rain forest used to be a natural part of life. The message was simple: death was the beginning of a new generation. Now that man has entered the picture, death has come to have a new meaning: an end to birth.
   a. Barry Lopez
   b. Andrea Goldberg
   c. Carl Sagan
   d. Manuel Lujan
   e. Abbie Hoffman

10. If there is no personal concern, nothing happens.
    a. Martin Luther King Jr.
    b. Carl Rogers
    c. Benjamin Spock
    d. Thomas Jefferson
    e. Danielle Eckert

Answers: (1) Carl Sandburg; (2) Robert Campbell, age 10; (3) Frank Lloyd Wright; (4) Andrea Goldberg, age 9; (5) Peter Bret Lamphere, age 9; (6) Roy Stoner, age 9; (7) Robert Campbell, age 10; (8) Pippa Bowde, age 11; (9) Andrea Goldberg, age 9; (10) Danielle Eckert, age 9. Except for numbers 1 and 3, all the statements were written by gifted students. We are grateful to Sandy Lethem and Dennis Higgins, facilitators for the gifted at the Zuni Elementary Magnet School, Albuquerque, New Mexico, for sharing their students' thoughts on the environment.

Inter- and intraindividual differences

Council for Exceptional Children

Content Standards for Beginning Teachers—G&T: Similarities and differences within the group of individuals with gifts and talents as compared to the general population (GT2K5).

Individual Differences Among Gifted and Talented Students

Awareness of individual differences is essential in understanding gifted students. Like other children, gifted children show both inter- and intraindividual differences. For example, if two students are given the same reading achievement test but obtain a different score, we can speak of *interindividual* differences in reading achievement. If a student who obtains a high reading achievement score obtains a much lower score on an arithmetic achievement test, we say the student has an *intraindividual* difference between the two areas of performance. Intraindividual differences are also evident when a child is high in intelligence or achievement, yet less mature

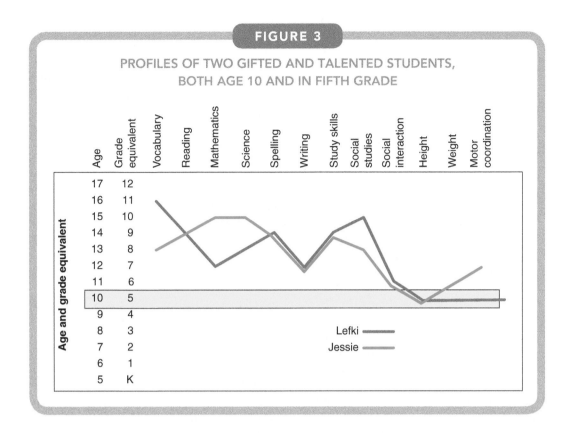

FIGURE 3

PROFILES OF TWO GIFTED AND TALENTED STUDENTS,
BOTH AGE 10 AND IN FIFTH GRADE

emotionally and/or socially. A graph or profile of any student's abilities would reveal some high points and some lower points; scores would not be the same across all dimensions. **Asynchrony** is a term used to describe disparate rates of intellectual, emotional, social, and physical growth or development displayed by some gifted children.

The gifted student's overall pattern of performance, however, may be well above the average for that grade, age, and/or experience, as shown in Figure 3. Lefki performs higher in vocabulary and social studies than Jessie does; however, Jessie shows higher performance in science and mathematics than Lefki. These are interindividual and possibly cultural differences (Ford, 2010b; Sternberg, 2007). Each student also has intraindividual differences in scores. For example, Lefki has the vocabulary of an 11th grader, but scores at a 7th-grade equivalent in mathematics; Jessie earned grade equivalents of 10th grade in science and mathematics and 7th grade in writing. All students, including gifted students, have strengths and weaknesses. No inidividual is perfect or flawless, and to believe and expect otherwise is unrealistic and places an unnecessary burden on gifted and talented students.

Creativity

Some scholars and teachers believe that creative ability is central to the definition of giftedness. Although we all profess to know creativity when we see it, no universally accepted definition of creativity exists. Guilford (1967, 1987), who studied the emergence of creativity, described these dimensions of cognitive creative behavior, which he called *divergent production,* in his structure of intellect model:

- *Fluency.* The creative student or individual can and does produce many ideas.
- *Flexibility.* The individual or student offers a wide variety of ideas, unusual ideas, and alternative solutions.
- *Novelty/originality.* The student uses words in unique ways and uses low-probability words and responses; the creative person has novel ideas.

Guilford's elements of creativity

Content Standards for Beginning Teachers—G&T: Cognitive and affective characteristics of individuals with gifts and talents in intellectual, academic, creative, leadership, and artistic domains (GT2K1) (also GT2K2, GT7K3).

- *Elaboration*. The individual provides details.
- *Synthesizing ability*. The person can link unlikely ideas together.
- *Analyzing ability*. The individual can organize ideas into larger, inclusive patterns. Symbolic structures must often be broken down before they can be reformed into new ones.
- *Ability to reorganize or redefine existing ideas*. The creative individual shows the ability to transform an existing object into one of different design, function, or use.
- *Complexity*. The person shows the ability to manipulate many interrelated ideas.

Creativity is quite subjective and heavily dependent on the times, context, and culture. In many of his writings, Torrance proposed that the most creative individuals come from economically disadvantaged backgrounds; they tend to be resourceful students who find a way to use their imagination and lack of resources to think outside the box (see Grantham et al., 2011).

Clark (2008) suggests that the purpose of creativity is "to recognize and bring forth that which is new, diverse, advanced, complex, and/or previously unknown so that humankind can experience life as fuller, richer, and/or more meaningful" (p. 158). Many gifted and talented individuals become scientists, physicians, inventors, and great artists and performers. However, they have no obligation to do so—this may not be their interest, passion, or goal.

After studying the characteristics of highly creative individuals in a variety of fields, Piirto (2004a, 2004b) concluded that (a) each field has specific behaviors in childhood that are predictive of creativity, (b) a developmental process in the emergence of talent occurs in various domains, and (c) IQ scores should be minimized in importance and subsumed into a more contextual view of children who are performing tasks within specific domains. The relationship between intelligence (IQ) and creativity is debatable. Regardless, testing for creative potential is often invalid and unreliable (Gagné, 2003; Piirto, 2004b), with the exception of the Torrance Tests of Creative Thinking (Torrance, 2006).

It is also difficult to differentiate between talent and creativity, perhaps because they may exist on a continuum rather than as separate entities. If we examine the life of a highly talented individual, such as the famous dancer Martha Graham, we can see the relationship between creativity and talent; in this case, the talent is in the visual and performing arts. Graham's creativity was evident in her pioneering modern dance techniques and innovative methods of expression in the choreography of the dance. However, her great talent as a dancer, seen in elegant movements, was equally impressive and deserves notice. Gifted and talented children often show creativeness, talents, or intellectual abilities that are highly advanced for their age. See *Current Issues and Future Trends*, "Precocity as a Hallmark of Giftedness."

Gifted and talented children are often identified by their precociousness. The unique abstract style of Alexandra Nechita, shown here at age 16, was evident when she was 4 years old.

PREVALENCE

If giftedness were defined solely on the basis of superior cognitive ability as evidenced by scores on a standardized intelligence test, then, theoretically, 2.3% of the general population would be gifted by virtue of an IQ score 2 standard deviations or more above the mean (roughly 130). The same theoretical statistical approach predicts that about 1 in 1,000 people would be highly gifted by attaining an IQ score of 145 (3 standard deviations above the mean), and roughly 1 in 10,000 would be considered exceptionally or profoundly gifted (IQ 160, at 4 standard deviations above the mean).

Not only is intelligence testing a theoretically thorny, inexact, and sometimes biased process (particularly when applied to children from culturally and linguistically different backgrounds on whom the tests were not normed), the concept of giftedness has long been expanded to encompass special talents and the potential for intellectual, creative, and superior performance. Some estimates of the prevalence of giftedness range as high as 10% to 15% of the total school-age population (e.g., Gagné, 2003; Renzulli & Reis, 2003).

Most federal reports and related legislation have estimated the prevalence of gifted and talented children at 3% to 5% of the student population. The percentage of school-age students identified as gifted and talented varies widely from state to state; for instance, six states identified more than 10% of the student population as gifted and talented, and six states identified 3% or less. A biannual survey conducted by the National Association for Gifted Children and the Council of State Directors of Gifted Education (2010) showed that the United States has approximately 3 million gifted students in grade pre-K to grade 12.

HISTORICAL BACKGROUND

Two major themes in the history of gifted and talented education are (a) theories of intelligence and its measurement and (b) the schools' provision of differentiated curriculum and services for gifted students.

Defining and Measuring Intelligence

Early 19th-century works, including a classic study by Sir Francis Galton (1869), focused on the concept of genius. He was the first to offer a definition of genius that used observable characteristics or outcomes. Galton thought that the largest proportion of human intelligence was fixed and immutable. This view eventually came to be enshrined as the theory of fixed intelligence, wherein people believed they were born and died with the same amount of intelligence regardless of their life experiences.

Two events in the early 1900s cemented the marriage of the theory of fixed intelligence to a method of measuring it. First, in 1905 the French government commissioned two psychologists, Alfred Binet and Theophile Simon, to develop a means of separating groups of slow learners from other children in order to provide them appropriate educational services. Second, these scales were translated into English and refined by Lewis Terman at Stanford University in 1916 for the U.S. government to use in sorting soldiers for a variety of duties in World War I. Known as the Stanford-Binet Intelligence Scale, it was published in 1916 and most recently revised in 2003 (Roid, 2003b). It has become the scale against which all other measures of intelligence are compared. (As we described, Binet and Simon's test has also played a critical role in the history of special education for children with intellectual disabilities.)

The result of these events was the emergence of a single number, the "intelligence quotient" or "IQ," which came to represent the overall intellectual abilities of a person. IQ tests and related tools became the dominant process for determining the intellectual differences among human beings and continues to be used widely today. Although the use of any measure of intelligence as the sole criterion for giftedness has been out of favor for many years and is considered inappropriate and unethical practice today, it is important to remember that Binet and Simon made a significant contribution to the education of gifted children. A standardized objective measure, however crude, makes it possible to identify some children with superior academic potential. Intelligence tests offered the first means of locating bright children, and plans for meeting their special needs could then be developed.

To read about the personalities and family backgrounds of child prodigies and children with extraordinarily high IQs, including six children well above IQ 200, see Morelock and Feldman (2003).

AND

FUTURE TRENDS

► Precocity as a Hallmark of Giftedness

BY JANE PIIRTO

Four-year-old Maria has been waiting and waiting to go to school. She plays school all the time. She is the teacher, and her dolls are the students. At her day-care center, she is the one who always leads the other kids in games because she is the only one who can read. The other kids look up to her, except when she tries to make them do things they really don't want to do, such as count by twos. The day-care center teacher told Maria's mother that Maria was very bright. When Maria went for her preschool screening, the district recommended that the school psychologist test her. The school psychologist told Maria's mother that Maria had an IQ of 145 on the Stanford-Binet Intelligence Scale, a score that put her in the 99th percentile. This score would qualify her for the district's program for the academically talented, which started at the third grade, although they did have enrichment lessons in first and second grade.

Finally, it is the first day of school; Maria turned 5 in August. She has her new dress and new shoes on. Her mother braids her hair and fastens it with new barrettes. When she gets to school, she is anxious for her mother to leave, yet still she feels shy, with all of these children here. Half of them are crying as their parents leave them.

Maria looks around the room and sees a shelf of books. She always reads when she doesn't know what else to do, so she goes over to the shelf and waits for things to calm down. After all of the parents have gone, the teacher tells the children to sit on a line painted on the floor. As the children have come into the room, they have been given large name tags. The teacher sits on a small chair with the children in a semicircle around her and says, "My name is Mrs. Miller, boys and girls. Welcome to kindergarten. In kindergarten, we will learn our letters and our numbers so that we can learn to read in first grade."

"I can read already," Maria says, jumping up.

"That's nice," says Mrs. Miller. "Maria, when we want to talk, first we must stand, and then we must wait until Mrs. Miller calls on us."

"But I can read already!" Maria's voice gets petulant, and tears form in the corners of her eyes.

"Maria, that's nice," said Mrs. Miller. "But in kindergarten, we will learn how to read right. Please sit down now."

Maria is chagrined. Feeling shame and embarrassment, she sits down. She has taken the first step to underachievement.

School Programs and National Agendas

The provision of educational services to students identified as gifted and talented has a long but sporadic history. The first special education services aimed at accommodating gifted and talented students were initiated in St. Louis in 1868 and involved a plan for flexible promotion. Around 1900, rapid advancement classes were established, in which children could complete 2 years worth of academic work in 1 year, or 3 years worth of work in 2. This and other "acceleration" strategies, such as multiple tracking options and advanced course work, were practiced as the primary intervention strategies until the early 1900s.

The Progressive education movement in the 1920s advocated "enrichment," which involved more in-depth instruction and ability grouping as the appropriate interventions for students who were gifted and talented. One of the earliest enrichment programs for gifted children began in the early 1920s in Cleveland, Ohio. In 1922, a group of "publicly spirited" women organized to promote special classes for gifted students. The Cleveland program remains one of the longest-running, continuous programs for gifted children in the United States. However, relatively few school districts developed formal, systematic programs for enriching curriculum content for academically talented students.

In 1957, the Soviet Union launched a small satellite called *Sputnik* into space. This event precipitated a questioning of the academic and scientific capabilities of Americans and resulted in the National Defense Education Act of 1958, which funded a nationwide revival of mathematics, science, and foreign language studies. After a relatively brief period of interest, the needs of gifted and talented students were

UNDERACHIEVEMENT IS THE PREVAILING SITUATION in the education of academically talented young children in most schools today. By the time she has been socialized into the kindergarten milieu, Maria will have learned to keep quiet about her abilities and even to suppress that she can read and do well in other school subjects. In the first grade, she will learn to comply with reading tasks in order to fit in. By second grade, even though she will get all of her work correct, she will have learned that she doesn't have to put forth any effort in school to be the top-performing student. By third grade, she will have learned that boredom (as long as she's quietly bored) and waiting (as long as she's not disruptive) are what the school seems to expect of her. By fourth grade, when she participates in a pull-out program for academically gifted/talented students, she will likely resent it when the teacher tries to challenge her. Maria's story, unfortunately, is all too typical of many young academically gifted or talented students.

Like other gifted and talented children, Maria can easily do things typically seen only in older children. Even without testing, their talents can be spotted by teachers who are sensitive to the concept of precocity. I believe the main way to recognize gifted and talented students is by their precocity: achievements resembling those of older children

or even adults. These children are often difficult to find and identify because they might wish to fit in and not create disturbances; but parents/caregivers, teachers and other educators who have formal training and who look closely can find their talents.

WHAT DO YOU THINK?

1. How do you think Mrs. Miller should have responded to Maria's insisting that "I can read already!"?

2. As the parent of a highly precocious kindergartner, what would your hopes and expectations be for your child's academic and social opportunities in the classroom? How would you communicate those to her or his teacher and the school?

3. How should a teacher's efforts to accommodate and build on a child's precocity differ depending upon the child's areas of advanced knowledge and skill, age, grade level, and experience and environment?

4. Where do culture and cultural differences fit into the topics and issues just addressed? Do issues and responses to questions 1–3 change or differ when culture is considered?

generally ignored, until the publication of the Marland Report in 1972. In 1975, gifted and talented students were passed over for inclusion in IDEA (PL 94-142), but they received recognition and a small amount of funding from the Title IV-C Grants program in 1977. In 1982, the Office of the Gifted and Talented in the U.S. Department of Education was closed after being in existence for just 6 years. The next federal recognition of the needs of gifted and talented students was the enactment of the Jacob K. Javits Gifted and Talented Student Education Act (PL 100-297), enacted in 1988. The Javits Act provides federal support for demonstration programs, a national research center on the gifted talented, competitive grants to institutions of higher education and state and local school districts to develop and expand models serving students who are underrepresented in gifted and talented programs, and competitive grants for state agencies and school districts to enhance gifted education curricula and programs. While the purposes of the Javits Act are laudable, it has been "chronically underfunded" (Council for Exceptional Children, 2011). The $7.5 million Congress appropriated for the Act in fiscal year 2010 represents less than 2 cents of every $100 of the federal K–12 education budget.

A timeline of milestones in gifted education can be found on the NAGC website: http://www.nagc.org/.

IDENTIFICATION AND ASSESSMENT

Most states and school districts rely on intelligence and achievement tests, respectively, to identify gifted and talented students. Some schools use both. Just as cognitive disabilities exist on a continuum (mild, moderate, severe), so too does intellectual giftedness. The same applies to achievement tests, where students can be proficient, at grade level, and advanced. Many schools identify students as academically gifted when they score at or above the 93rd percentile.

While not illegal, it is uninformative and disadvantageous to rely on one test or instrument to formally identify or label gifted students; there is too much room for error in doing so, such as missing students who do not test well and ignoring or discounting test bias. A multidimensional and multimodal assessment approach that collects information from a variety of sources (e.g., parents, teachers, psychologists) and in a variety of ways (e.g, tests, interviews, performance) is more accurate and equitable in the identification of gifted and talented students (Ford, 2010b; Ford, Grantham, & Whiting, 2008). Comprehensive and equitable assessment for identification of gifted and talents students includes the following:

- Group and individual intelligence tests
- Achievement tests
- Proficiency/state tests
- Portfolios of student work
- Authentic performances and/or products
- Teacher nomination based on reports of student behavior in the classroom
- Parent/family/caregiver nomination
- Self-nomination
- Peer nomination
- Extracurricular or leisure activities

Equity-minded professionals in gifted education recommend a comprehensive and proactive approach for identifying students who require specialized services (e.g., Ford, 2010b; Renzulli & Reis, 2004). Clark (2008) described an approach to identification based on a model first developed by the California Association for Gifted Children. The approach features a progressive filtering process that refines a large pool of potentially gifted students down to a smaller, formally identified group. The process is time-consuming and thorough, beginning with the development of a large pool of potentially gifted students in the initial stage (screening); testing, consulting, and analyzing data (development of profile and case study); identification decisions and placement (committee meeting for consideration; placement in gifted program); and finally the development of an appropriate educational program for the child. Clearly, such important decisions ought not be made quickly and with minimal information.

Quantitative and qualitative approaches to assessment should be part of the identification process (Ryser, 2004). Qualitative assessment includes portfolios, interviews, and observations. Educators can use observations to find students who are demonstrating characteristics that indicate giftedness, talent, and potential. Observations can include checklists or rating scales, as well as simple "jot-down" procedures (Renzulli & Reis, 2004). Interviews of peers and parents/caregivers can also indicate potential talent. A word of caution is that the majority of checklists and all nomination forms are subjective, which necessarily includes personal biases; some students may be missed for this reason.

Let's examine how this process would work with a student thought to have great potential, using Janie, described at the beginning of this chapter. First, Janie's highly refined intellectual behaviors would have to be noticed by a teacher, a parent, her peers, or another person, who would then forward a nomination for additional screening. Figure 4 shows questions that Janie's teacher might ask. The teacher's report would contribute to the multidimensional, or multifactored, screening approach that is gaining in popularity among educators of the gifted and talented.

Multidimensional screening is equitable and involves a rigorous examination of teacher reports, family history, student inventories, and work samples and perhaps the administration of group achievement and/or group or individual intelligence tests. In many states, the coordinator of gifted services at the school, district, or regional level reviews this information and determines whether the results indicate a potential for

FIGURE 4 QUESTIONS ABOUT CLASSROOM BEHAVIOR THAT CAN HELP TEACHERS IDENTIFY STUDENTS WHO MAY BE GIFTED AND TALENTED

Does the child
- Ask a lot of questions?
- Show a lot of interest in progress?
- Have in-depth information on many things?
- Often want to know why, why not, or how something is so?
- Become unusually upset at injustices?
- Seem interested in and concerned about social or political problems?
- Often have a better reason for not doing what you want done than you have asking them to do it?
- Refuse to drill on spelling, mathematics, facts, flash cards, or handwriting?
- Criticize others for dumb ideas?
- Become impatient if work is not "perfect"?
- Seem to be a loner?
- Seem bored and often have nothing to do?
- Complete only part of an assignment or project and then take off in a new direction?
- Stick to a subject long after the class has gone on to other things?
- Seem restless and leave his or her seat often?
- Daydream?
- Seem to understand easily?
- Like solving puzzles and problems?
- Have his or her own idea about how something should be done? And stay with it?
- Talk a lot?
- Love metaphors and abstract ideas?
- Love debating issues?

This child may be showing giftedness through cognitive ability.

Does the child
- Show unusual ability in some area—maybe reading or mathematics?
- Show fascination with one field of interest? And manage to include this interest in all discussion topics?

Does the child
- Enjoy meeting or talking with experts in this field?
- Get answers correct, but find it difficult to tell you how?
- Enjoy graphing everything? Seem obsessed with probabilities?
- Invent new obscure systems and codes?

This child may be showing giftedness through academic ability.

Does the child
- Try to do things in different, unusual, imaginative ways?
- Have a really zany or odd sense of humor?
- Enjoy new routines or spontaneous activities?
- Love variety and novelty?
- Create problems with no apparent solutions? And enjoy asking you to solve them?
- Love controversial and unusual questions?
- Have a vivid imagination?
- Seem never to proceed sequentially?

This child may be showing giftedness through creative ability.

Does the child
- Organize and lead group activities? Sometimes take over?
- Enjoy taking risks?
- Seem cocky, self-assured?
- Enjoy decision making? Stay with that decision?
- Synthesize ideas and information from a lot of different sources?

This child may be showing giftedness through leadership ability.

Does the child
- Seem to pick up skills in the arts—music, dance, drama, or painting, for example—without instruction?
- Invent new techniques? Experiment?
- See minute detail in products or performances?
- Have high sensory sensitivity?

This child may be showing giftedness through visual or performing arts ability.

Source: From Barbara Clark, *Growing Up Gifted*, 7th ed. (p. 201), © 2008. Reproduced by permission of Pearson Education, Inc., Upper Saddle River, NJ

giftedness and justify referral to a placement committee. If the coordinator or counselor believes the information is sufficient to continue assessment, the parents/caregivers are asked if they would like to refer Janie for more extensive testing. The coordinator then manages the development of a case study that includes screening data, parent/caregvier interviews, test protocols, an individual intelligence test, tests in specific content areas, and creativity tests. The coordinator compiles, organizes, and presents the data to the placement committee for consideration. The committee determines whether Janie qualifies for or would benefit from services and what type of program or service would best suit her particular pattern of giftedness. The parents or caregivers are an integral part of this meeting and have to agree with the results and placement decisions that the committee develops. Janie is then placed in a gifted program, and the special education teacher or person in charge of the program initiates the approproriate services.

Multicultural Assessment and Identification

"One of the most persistent and pervasive problems in education is the underrepresentation of African American, Hispanic American, and Native American students in gifted education programs and advanced placement (AP) classes" (Ford, 2010b, p. 371). For decades, reports and census studies have shown that these three groups of culturally different students have consistently been underrepresented in gifted education (Artiles, Trent, & Palmer, 2004; Donovan & Cross, 2002; Ford, 1998, 2010b). This underrepresentation and great loss of gifts and talent stand at about 55% for African Americans, almost 40% for Latinos/Hispanics, and about 30% for Native Americans. Biases inherent throughout the identification process, from low rates of referrals due to educators' low expectations through the use of culturally biased tests and instruments, are primarily to blame for the underrepresentation of students from different economic, racial/ethnic, cultural, and language groups (Castellano & Frazier, 2010; Ford, 2004b; Grantham, 2003; Klug, 2004).

Frasier, Garcia, and Passow (1995) described 10 core attributes of giftedness across socioeconomic, ethnic, and racial groups. Gifted and talented people across ethnic groups demonstrate (a) communication skills, (b) imagination/creativity, (c) humor, (d) inquiry, (e) insight, (f) interests, (g) memory, (h) motivation, (i) problem solving, and (j) reasoning. Many youth from special populations have not had the extensive opportunities to develop such a broad pattern of gifts and talents, but they have often developed special abilities within a particular domain. The identification process should be designed to find the special talent. Subsequent educational service should focus on facilitating growth in this talent area. Current best practices for identifying gifted and talented students from different racial and cultural groups involve a multifactored, or multidimensional and multimodal, assessment process that meets these criteria (Castellano, 2003; Castellano & Frazier, 2010; Ford, 2010a, 2010b; Frasier, Hunsaker, et al., 1995; Montgomery, 2001):

- Identification should have the goal of inclusion rather than exclusion.
- Data should be gathered from multiple sources providing both objective and subjective information (e.g., parent interviews, individual intelligence testing, performance on group problem-solving tasks, motivational and behavioral factors, individual conferences with candidates).
- A combination of formal and informal testing techniques, including teacher input, family input, and the results of intelligence tests, and achievement tests, should be used.
- Identification procedures should begin as early as possible—before children are exposed to prejudice and stereotyping—and be continuous.
- Unconventional or nontraditional measures involving arts and aesthetic expression, such as dance, music, and creative writing, as well as nonverbal measures should be used.
- Information gathered during the screening and identification process should be used to help determine the curriculum, programs, and services.

Maker (1996, 2005) developed a procedure called DISCOVER (Discovering Strengths and Capabilities while Observing Varied Ethnic Responses) that educators have used to identify gifted children from different racial and cultural groups. The DISCOVER assessment process involves a series of five progressively more complex problems that provide children with various ways to demonstrate their problem-solving competence by interacting with the content and with one another.

Maker (2005) states that an assessment emphasis on problem solving instead of formal tests of acquired knowledge has the potential to "level the playing field," enabling students who solve problems on a daily basis to demonstrate their abilities.

"Little Claudia," a 5-year-old Mexican American girl, who was responsible for dressing her 2-year-old brother and making sure he was taken to daycare before she went to kindergarten class, had extensive practice in problem solving. However, she was not exposed to advanced knowledge through visits to museums or a home environment with many sources of information, nor was she given opportunities to produce sophisticated products through special courses, lessons, or other opportunities afforded to children from middle and upper socioeconomic status (SES) families. Many children from diverse economic, geographic, and cultural groups face challenges similar to Little Claudia's. (p. 12)

Maker (2001, 2005) and other researchers (e.g., Powers, 2003; Sarouphim, 2001) report positive results from using the DISCOVER model to assess the problem-

Assessment of young children's abilities to solve mathematical-spatial problems might include the time used to complete puzzles, the number of puzzles completed, and the particular problem-solving strategies used by the child.

solving abilities of students from African American, Navajo, Tohono O'odham, and Mexican American cultural groups: (a) the children identified by the process closely resemble the cultural characteristics of the communities from which they come; (b) equitable percentages of children from various ethnic, cultural, linguistic, and economic groups are identified; (c) the process is equally effective with boys and girls; and (d) students identified through the process make gains equal to or greater than those of students who were identified by traditional standardized tests when placed in special enrichment programs.

Other means of identifying culturally different gifted learners have been tried and found to have moderate success. Tests that do not require the use of verbal symbol systems have also been recommended and adopted, such as the Raven's Standard Progressive Matrices Test (Raven, Court, & Raven, 1983) and the Naglieri Nonverbal Ability Test (Naglieri & Ford, 2003, 2005). Naglieri and Ford argue that traditional tests of intelligence and achievement penalize students from low-socioeconomic-status backgrounds and culturally different groups who have not had the opportunity to learn the language or extensive vocabulary required for success on such tests.

As noted all across the literature about culturally different students, the identification procedure must not contain merely an IQ score or only one score; rather, educators must use a multitude of methods (Joseph & Ford, 2006). More researchers realize and theories show that test scores and checklists themselves can be and have been harmful to students because they are scored in the aggregate (the total, the accumulation): a gifted and talented child may have only one of the characteristics and thus not be selected for gifted education services.

All gifted and talented children come from a family with goals, a history, and a background. For example, it is far more likely for a child to be identified as talented if she or he has books in the home and is read to regularly. This is as true for bilingual children as it is for monolingual children. Other promising alternative assessment methods that would resolve underrepresentation are (a) the Frasier method (1991), which focuses on the 10 characteristics mentioned earlier; (b) the Renzulli Revolving Door method (2003), which identifies the top 25% of students; (c) the "quota" method (Mitchell, 1988), which identifies a certain, representative quota of students; however, quotas by race are not legal; (d) the case study method (Borland & Wright, 1994), which conducts in-depth case studies of students; (e) the use of portfolios, which assess achievement without testing; (f) performance assessment (VanTassel-Baska, Johnson & Avery, 2002), which assesses how students perform on certain universal tasks;

(g) dynamic assessment (Chaffey, 2004), which gives the assessment, teaches the assessment, and then gives it again; and (h) multiple intelligence (MI) assessment, based on Gardner's (2006) theory of multiple intelligences. All alternative assessments must be nondiscriminatory, taking into account the culture, race, income, gender, language, and home life of the child being assessed.

Identifying gifted and talented children from culturally different and underrepresented groups is, of course, just the beginning. In the absence of high-quality curriculum and instruction that are sensitive and responsive to their cultural heritage, culturally and racially different gifted and talented students may "distance" themselves from the gifted label and be hesitant to enter and unwilling to stay in gifted education programs (Foley & Seknandore, 2003; Ford, 2004a, 2010; Ford et al., 2008; Henfield, Moore, & Wood, 2008). To reverse this problem, educators need formal training in both gifted education and multicultural education. This will help to improve their expectations for these students, appreciate their gifts and talents, increase referrals, and select the most culturally fair tests and instruments, as well as policies and procedures. See *Current Issues and Future Trends*, "Gifts Unopened and Denied: The Persistent Underrepresentation of Black Students in Gifted Education."

Gifted and Talented Females

Cultural barriers, test and social biases, organizational reward systems, sex-role stereotyping, and conflicts among career, marriage, friends, and family all act as external impediments to the advancement of gifted and talented females—girls and women (Kerr, 1997). In reviewing the topic of gifted females, Silverman (1986) noted that the history of genius and women's roles has been contradictory (eminent contributions cannot be made from a subservient status) and that identification procedures reflect masculine (product-oriented) versus feminine (development-oriented) concepts of giftedness.

Thus, some of the key issues that appear in the literature concerning the identification and education of females who are gifted and talented involve conflicts concerning role definitions (Cross, 2006; Rimm, 2000, 2002), stress related to a lack of self-esteem (Genshaft, Greenbaum, & Borovosky, 1995), poor course selection based on academic choices made in middle school and high school (Boothe, 2004; Clark, 2008), and a lack of parental/caregiver and general community support for female achievements (Hollinger, 1995).

Since few studies have been reported on the characteristics, issues, and needs of gifted females who are African American, Latino/Hispanic, Asian American, and Native American, readers should avoid generalizing the above findings to them (Ford, in press).

Gifted and Talented Males

The problems and situations of gifted and talented males have been highlighted as well (Kerr & Cohen, 2001; Neu & Weinfeld, 2006), but the database and discussion are much less extensive. More scholarship has focused on gifted females than males. Among the key issues are negative stereotyping for males who have talent in and want to enter the arts, a "boy code" (Pollack, 1998) that operates against the expression of feelings and emotions, and a reluctance on the part of parents and teachers to permit males' creative behavior. However, despite the stereotyping and name-calling ("nerds," "geeks," etc.) that is present in U.S. schools, white males continue to outscore girls at the highest levels on tests such as the Scholastic Aptitude Test, the American College Test, the Differential Aptitude Test, and most achievement tests (Boothe, 2004). The reverse is true for African American and Latino/Hispanic males who consistently underperform compared to white males and to all female groups (Ford, 2010b).

Low-Income Gifted Students

Too few students who are low-income are identified and represented in gifted education. Many of these low-income students live in rural and urban communities.

Identification of G&T girls and boys

Content Standards for Beginning Teachers—G&T: Processes and procedures for the identification of individuals with exceptional learning needs (GT8K1) (also GT8K2, GT8S1).

Whiting's (2009) Scholar Identity Institute was codeveloped with Ford to increase black males' academic identity and self-efficacy. Watch a video at www.youtube.com/watch?v=YrNP1zqMr3A.

In 1993, the U.S. Department of Education reported that gifted programs have only 10% of students who are poor. As with cultrally different students, tests must be selected and interpreted carefully, identification and assessment must be proactive and comprehensive, and teacher expectations for this group must increase. More recent information along with recommendations on identifying and serving low-come gifted learners can be found in the appropriately titled book *Overlooked Gems*, by VanTassel-Baska and Stambaugh (2007).

Gifted and Talented Students with Disabilities

It surprises many people to learn that many students with disabilities are also gifted and talented. Some disabilities, such as learning disabilities, mask giftedness on both the tests and in classroom academic performance. The combination of a disability and giftedness brings with it a complicated set of behaviors and attitudes that confuse and challenge educators and parents (Nielsen & Higgins, 2005). Students with dual exceptionalities whose giftedness goes unidentified are especially likely to underachieve or even drop out of school.

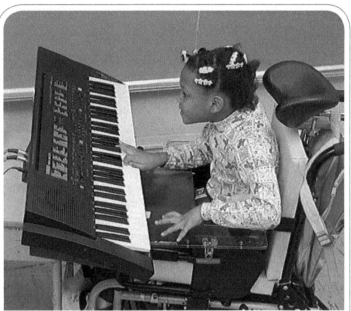

The intellectual abilities and talents of children with disabilities are fostered by daily opportunities to practice superior abilities and enjoy the feelings of success.

Affective concerns for twice-exceptional and second-language learners include issues of acculturation, such as culture shock, loss of first language and second-language acquisition, and delayed identity formation (Rance-Roney, 2004). King (2005) recommended that teachers support the social and emotional needs of twice-exceptional students by doing the following:

- Foster clear understanding of students' disabilities as well as their strengths to promote self-understanding and self-acceptance.
- Encourage students to succeed, and enlist support of parents and other teachers in this endeavor.
- Teach strategies for coping with frustration.
- If needed, encourage counseling to monitor each student's emotions that accompany frustration and perceived failures.
- Think of these children not only as having a disability or as being gifted but as having needs in both areas.
- Provide support in establishing and maintaining social relationships.
- Ensure caregivers'/parents' understanding of their child's giftedness and disabilities, emphasizing the child's potential.
- Support students with future goals and career planning; make sure students are aware of their potential and encourage them not to sell themselves short.
- Provide an adult mentor who is also gifted/learning disabled or gifted with another exceptionality (e.g., autism, visual or hearing or physicial impairment).

An appropriate education for gifted students with disabilities requires the creation of what Neu (2003) terms a *dually differentiated* curriculum that recognizes and "meets the needs of students who exhibit two contradictory sets of learning characteristics by creating a balance between nurturing the students' strengths and compensating for their learning deficits" (p. 158). Special education and related services implemented to meet the student's needs that result from the disability must not trump the student's need to be challenged in his/her domain(s) of giftedness and talent.

Valuable information on identifying and serving twice-exceptional children can be found in Baum (2004), Neihart (in press), and many documents published by the National Research Center on the Gifted and Talented (http://www.gifted.uconn.edu/nrcgt.html).

Scott Cunningham/Merrill

CURRENT ISSUES AND FUTURE TRENDS

▶ Gifts Unopened and Denied: The Persistent Underrepresentation of Black Students in Gifted Education

BY DONNA Y. FORD

I entered the field of gifted education in 1991, earning a Ph.D. in urban education with a dissertation focusing on the perplexing question of how and why any child identified as gifted would and could underachieve. My interest was first personal and, then, professional. Here's my story.

PART 1

I was identified as gifted very early in school. Every teacher I can recall praised my reading skills, writing skills, and vocabulary skills in particular, but I excelled in all subject areas. In 10th grade, I received an academic scholarship for low-income black students to attend a local private high school for females. I entered this school armed with pride, confidence, motivation, and goals. I could be anything I wanted to be!

While attending the high school for 1 year—that's all I could handle socially and emotionally—I started underachieving. That 10th-grade year unraveled 16 years of academic and intellectual pride. I quickly lost confidence in my academic and intellectual abilities. I questioned whether I was as smart as my mother, as so many educators and others had professed for as long as I could remember.

I was an outsider among wealthy, white females who refused to associate with me and made it clear I wasn't welcome—not sitting with me in the cafeteria, leaving the tables in class when I approached them for a seat, accusing me of stealing, and so much more.

I was an enigma to the white teachers who seemed unaccustomed to and uninterested in teaching a poor black girl on scholarship. Some of the teachers treated me worse than classmates. One teacher constantly asked "who helped" me with my work. She was often surprised that I wrote "so well" and the like. To me, this treatment was worse because she was an adult and a *professional*—a teacher! Mind you, I had been admitted based on test scores and school performance, so this was an academic scholarship for low-income, high-performing black students. I was indeed capable of excelling there. Why was my high performance questioned, even on in-class

assignments? The curriculum and academic expectations challenged me, but that was just what I wanted and needed. Academically, this was the school for me; socially, it was not. I withdrew after 1 year, mentally, emotionally, socially, and academically drained. I transferred to an all-black public school with a curriculum that left a lot to be desired. While I sometimes felt physically unsafe at the all-black school due to fights and an anti-achievement ethic among students, at least I was not hated by classmates or mistreated by teachers.

PART 2

When my son was born (I was 18 and in college), I was determined to make him "smart and gifted." From birth, I focused on challenging him and put a premium on academics (school readiness). He on caught so quickly, it was amazing! He exceeded milestones for typical development: sitting up at 4 months, walking at 9 months, talking in complete sentences at 12 months.

Armed with the notion, confidence, and pride that my son was gifted, I had him tested for early entrance into kindergarten. Living in a low-income black community, and aware of some of the research about the achievement gap and failing schools, I thought he was a shoo-in, as they say. After all, since age 3, he had been reading and spelling, and doing simple math problems. At 5, how could teachers and decision makers not realize he was ready for formal schooling? The school psychologist, a white female in an all-black school, tested my son. After scoring the results, she professed to having a dilemma. She said he scored well on the test (I never asked which one) but was "socially incompetent." I have never forgotten those two words.

On whose culture were these skills being judged? I recall asking her if he had poor manners and social skills. Did he sneeze without covering his mouth? Did he pick his nose? Was he rude? Was he defiant? Exasperated, I was desperate for answers. I had raised him well, so how could he be socially incompetent? Her response was matter-of-fact, delivered by someone just doing her job. She responded: he does not know such things as *butler*, *veranda*, and *pasture*. Darn! I didn't know what the word *veranda* meant, either. So, was I socially incompetent? Doubt and anger surfaced. Had I failed my son?

The school psychologist recommended that I not enter him into school early; she thought he would not do well socially. Against my better judgment, I took her advice. This was one of the worst academic decisions I ever made for him. He was bored and underchallenged. Thankfully, both his kindergarten and first-grade teachers recommended him for the gifted education class in second grade. Like I had as a high schooler, my son experienced a teacher from hell in the second grade. He did not do well. He hated her (it was mutual) and school.

PART 3

In 1995, I was now a professor, conducting research on and writing about underrepresentation and underachievement among gifted black students. Based on the collective experiences of myself and my son (and too many other stories to tell), I began to write my first book on gifted black underachievers. I was seeing our story told too many times as I worked in schools and taught teachers interested in gifted education. Underachievement and underrepresentation were (and are) the norm. My son and I were just two people in the bigger scheme of inequities. My passion was and is both personal and professional.

PART 4

The future is now. But as I reflect on over 20 years in gifted education professionally, it is disheartening to see too little progress regarding black students' underrepresentation in gifted education. As of 2006, using data from the Civil Rights Elementary and Secondary Education Survey, some 253,000 black students are not identified as gifted and not participating in gifted education (Ford, in press). Nationally, every study and report has found that black students have been and are the most underrepresented group in gifted education. As I and others have found (e.g., Mary Frasier, Alexinia Baldwin, Tarek Grantham), a number of factors contribute to black students' underrepresentation. First and foremost is the lack of teacher referrals of black students for gifted education screening, identification, and placement. Underreferral is pervasive and significant (Ford, Grantham, & Whiting, 2008). Deficit thinking, the worst form of low expectations and stereotypes, blinds teachers and counselors from seeing gifts and talents in black students. In some schools, the identification process—based on educator referrals—ends here.

If black students are referred for gifted education services or if all students in the school are screened without referrals to develop talent pools, they often take an intelligence and/or achievement test. For a myriad of reasons associated with the test and policies and procedures, black students tend not to score at the designated level (e.g., cutoff score, matrix criteria, etc.). At this point, the identification process often stops, despite underrepresentation.

Interpretations of low test scores vary. But most educators seem wedded to the notion that they are fair and representative of students' potential and capacity to achieve or excel in gifted education. The debates regarding test bias are too extensive to capture here. Having reviewed both sides, which are often entrenched and polemic, I believe that most traditional, standardized tests continue to be biased against black students on cultural and linguistic grounds. Having said this, one type of test, nonverbal intelligence tests, have shown to be more effective at reducing test bias. Curiously, schools seldom adopt them, preferring traditional tests that favor white and middle-class students. Should such practices as teacher referral continue when *every* study has shown that black students are significantly underreferred, and should nonverbal tests continue to be discounted, then business will continue as unusual—gifts will continue to be unopened. The unnecessary waste of human potential should be evident. Not only do black students lose academically, socially, and professionally; we all lose nationally and globally.

WHAT DO YOU THINK?

1. Examine the representation of black students in your district's gifted education program as well as instruments, policies, and procedures. If underrepresentation exists, to what do you and school personnel attribute it? If the district does not share these data, visit http://ocrdata.ed.gov/.

2. Many standardized intelligence tests have been renormed and evaluated for bias. As such, it is easy and/or logical to conclude that they are no longer biased against black students. What is your opinion? Do you support the use of nonverbal tests?

3. If underrepresentation exists in your school district, design policies and procedures, along with recommended instruments, to eliminate barriers and increase access to gifted education.

About the Author

Donna Y. Ford is professor of special education at Vanderbilt University, where she prepares teachers to work with students who are culturally different and low-income. Her work focuses on underrepresentation among black students in gifted education and underachievement. She is the author of several books, including *Multicultural Gifted Education* (2011) and *Reversing Underachievement Among Gifted Black Students* (2010), and many articles.

EDUCATIONAL APPROACHES

The overall goal of educational programs for gifted and talented students should be the fullest possible development of every child's demonstrated and potential abilities. In addition to maximum academic achievement, exemplary programs help students develop feelings of self-worth, self-sufficiency, and pride in one's race and ethnicity, civic responsibility, and vocational and avocational competence. In the broadest sense, then, the educational goals for gifted youngsters do not differ from those for any child. Some additional specific educational outcomes, however, are especially important for gifted and talented students.

Gifted students need both content knowledge and the opportunity to develop and use that knowledge effectively. These students have a distinct need for increased relevance and depth of current curriculum, with changes in the pace to address what they already know and how quickly they learn.

Educators of gifted students, often guided by research and scholarship, recommend the following for curriculum and instruction for gifted and talented students; appropriate, challenging, and respectful curriculum (Ford, 2011; Piito, 2007; Tomlinson et al., 2009; VanTassel-Baska & Stambaugh, 2006).

Functions and characteristics of differential curriculum

 Content Standards for Beginning Teachers—G&T: Features that distinguish differentiated curriculum from general curricula for individuals with exceptional learning needs (GT7K6) (also GT7K2, GT7K5).

- *Possess academic rigor.* The widespread abuse of grading practices, the dumbing down of the curriculum, and the lowered expectations of teachers all have sapped the general education curriculum of its strength and rigor. The curriculum should include systematic teaching of research skills, keyboarding and computer use, speed reading, at least one foreign language, and interpersonal and affective development. Gifted students have a distinct need for increased relevance and depth of current curriculum, especially within the general education classroom, where most gifted students are most frequently educated.
- *Be thematic and interdisciplinary.* Gifted and talented students should be exposed to the structures, terminologies, and methodologies of various disciplines. Gifted students thrive on big ideas and concepts, and they enjoy learning that borrows from and is informed by more than one discipline. Connecting the lesson or content, when applicable, to sociology, anthropology, medicine, science, language arts, history, the arts, music, and so on, helps gifted students to make connections in various subject areas and to appreciate the complexity of the topic they are studying.
- *Be responsive to and respectful of gifted students' learning characteristics.* These characteristics include "their ability to learn at a faster rate; their ability to think abstractly about content that is challenging; their ability to think productively, critically, creatively, and analytically; and their ability to constantly and rapidly increase their store of knowledge, both knowledge of facts and knowledge of processes and procedures" (Piirto, 2007, p. 429).

Educators of gifted and talented students agree that the most important concern in developing appropriate curriculum is to match students' specific abilities, potentials, and interests with a qualitatively different curricular intervention.

Curriculum Differentiation

Differentiation is a broad term referring to the need to tailor teaching environments, curricula, and instructional practices to create appropriately different learning experiences for students with different needs, interests, readiness, and learning profiles, as noted particulary in the work of Carol Tomlinson (2005, 2011). The reality that gifted learners differ in meaningful ways is the guiding premise of differentiation. The main objective is to engage learners in instruction through different learning modalities, appealing to differing interests, using varied rates of instruction, and providing varied degrees of complexity within and across a challenging and conceptually rich curriculum.

Meaningful curriculum differentiation for gifted and talented students requires that educators recognize the individual strengths of these learners and acknowledge the inadequacy of the regular curriculum to meet those needs (Kaplan, 2005). Differentiating instruction to accommodate also "involves a healthy dose of common sense" (Tomlinson, 2011).

To help teachers discover and apply their common sense within theoretically and pragmatically sound approaches to differentiating lessons, Tomlinson developed a planning tool she calls "the equalizer." The equalizer reminds teachers they can tailor any lesson to provide a motivating challenge best suited to gifted learner's interests, abilities, and emerging skills by adjusting the "volume" of eight dimensions (e.g., concrete ↔ abstract, simple ↔ complex, structured ↔ open, slow ↔ fast).

A schematic of Tomlinson's equalizer can be found at http://www.scgifted.org/TomlinsonEqualizer.pdf

Acceleration and Enrichment

Acceleration and enrichment are two fundamental strategies that respect and take advantage of gifted students' learning characteristics and strengths by differentiating curriculum in its pace, breadth, and depth.

ACCELERATION Acceleration is the general term for a variety of methods for increasing the speed with which a student moves through curriculum content. Early admission (to kindergarten, junior high, high school, or college), grade skipping, self-paced instruction, curriculum compacting, telescoping curriculum, concurrent/dual enrollment in high school and college, advanced placement, and credit by examination are some of the most commonly used grade acceleration practices (Southern & Jones, 2004). Subject acceleration would take the form of a fourth grader taking math (or another class) with fifth or even seventh graders. The NAGC (2004) believes that a variety of acceleration options should be available at each stage of a student's development, from early entrance to kindergarten through early college enrollment.

Silverman (1995) called acceleration a "necessary response to a highly gifted student's faster pace of learning" (p. 229). The NAGC (2004) states that "educational acceleration is one of the cornerstones of exemplary gifted education practices, with more research supporting this intervention than any other in the literature on gifted education" (p. 1).

One common concern is that early admission and grade skipping will lead to social or emotional problems because the child will be in a classroom with older students who are more advanced physically and emotionally. Some educators and parents are also concerned that gifted and talented students will suffer from the pressure to achieve at higher levels and will burn out or lose their excitement for learning. Although these concerns are understandable and real, when acceleration is done properly, few, if any, socioemotional or achievement problems result (Davis et al., 2011). In 2004, the Templeton Foundation published a major report on the benefits of acceleration. With the somewhat hyperbolic title *A Nation Deceived* (Colangelo, Assouline, & Gross, 2004), it detailed cases where acceleration was the solution to the curriculum problems of bright children, showing that acceleration is not the social and emotional bugaboo it has been called by many educators. As a result of this report, which was featured on the front page of many newspapers across the country, many states and school districts have formulated acceleration policies, whereby individual students can receive an education at their intellectual and academic levels, rather than age level.

ENRICHMENT Enrichment enables students to probe or study specific subject matter, a topic of interest, or a discipline at a greater detail and depth than would occur in the standard curriculum. Independent study, mentorships, and shadowing are widely used methods for enrichment. Enrichment is the most commonly applied strategy by general education teachers who are attempting to differentiate curriculum for gifted and talented students in their classrooms.

Acceleration

 Content Standards for Beginning Teachers—G&T: Acceleration, enrichment, and counseling within a continuum of service options for individuals with gifts and talents (GT5K4) (also GT7K2).

VanTassel-Baska (2005) gives excellent practical guidance for implementing numerous acceleration techniques.

Enrichment

 Content Standards for Beginning Teachers—G&T: Provide opportunities for indivduals with gifts and talents to explore, develop, or research their areas of interest or talent (GT4S3) (also GT7S5).

The most successful enrichment activities accomplish both process- and content-related goals (Davis et al., 2011). Process goals entail the development of skills such as creative thinking, problem solving, and research skills; content goals entail the additional enhanced and nuanced knowledge about the topic the student acquires.

Topics of investigation may be derived from the ongoing activities of the classroom or from beyond the limits of the day-to-day instructional offerings. By allowing the students to help define the area of interest and independently access a variety of information and materials, the teacher can learn to facilitate the development of gifted and talented students' competencies and skills. Enrichment is not a "do your own thing" approach without structure or guidance—students should not be released to do a random, haphazard project. A basic framework that defines limits and sets outcomes is necessary. Projects should have purpose, direction, and specified outcomes. Teachers must provide guidance where necessary to keep students working efficiently. To learn about enrichment activities in language arts for gifted students, see *Teaching & Learning,* "Using the Literary Masters to Inspire Written Expression in Gifted Students."

ACCELERATE OR ENRICH? Whether acceleration or enrichment is the most appropriate strategy for differentiation depends on the subject matter and the student. Some curriculum material, such as reading or social studies, readily lends itself to enrichment. Mathematics and foreign languages, because of their sequential nature, are ideally suited to acceleration. In mathematics, a child must learn to add before subtracting, must learn to multiply before dividing. By the time a gifted and talented child is in the fourth grade, he or she probably will have mastered the skills of reading; enrichment with more complex reading matter is a way of differentiation. In mathematics, however, the subject matter proceeds from arithmetic to algebra to calculus, and so on. Often, one of the most difficult tasks for teachers is to persuade the administration and fellow teachers that acceleration in mathematics is necessary for gifted and talented students. A first grader who is fluent with the basic arithmetic operations will benefit little from several more years of adding, subtracting, multiplying, and dividing.

A young gifted and talented student interested in fractal geometry and attending the Johns Hopkins University summer program told how he had sat, bored, during a plane geometry class that was required at his school for intellectually and academically talented students but where testing out of a course was not permitted. To this student, plane geometry consisted of nothing but "two points on a line, two points on a line." Even though the plane geometry class was being offered to eighth graders, whereas in most schools it is offered to sophomores, this student had already mastered the material and was interested in fractal geometry. The high point in his day was being able to ask the teacher one or two questions about fractal geometry at the end of the period when the students began their homework. Although the teacher kept him pointed in the right direction, and he experimented with fractal geometry on his home computer, an accelerated curriculum would have saved this student from having to sit day after day through content he had already mastered.

Although acceleration and enrichment are often viewed as separate options for talented students, as Southern and Jones (1991) pointed out, the two strategies are intertwined: "advanced study in any discipline may entail the kind of activities normally associated with enrichment" (p. 22). Enrichment broadens the curriculum and includes material that is not in the general education course of study. However, acceleration often involves advanced material also not contained in the general education course of study. Still, Davis and colleagues (2011) offer a functional distinction between the two approaches: any curriculum differentiaton technique that involves advanced placement or potential course credit (e.g., in an AP course) is acceleration; any strategy that supplements or goes beyond the standard grade-level curriculum that does not entail advanced placement or potential credit is enrichment.

Lesson Differentiation in the General Education Classroom

Methods for differentiation within the general education classroom include curriculum compacting, tiered lessons, and using Bloom's taxonomy as frameworks for modifying questions and creating instructional activities.

CURRICULUM COMPACTING Many gifted and talented students have already mastered much of the content of the general education curriculum when the school year begins. **Curriculum compacting** involves compressing the instructional content and materials so that academically able students have more time to work on more challenging materials (Reis & Renzulli, 2005). Reis and coworkers studied the effects of curriculum compacting on 336 students in grades 2 through 6 with demonstrated advanced content knowledge and superior academic ability. When teachers used curriculum compacting to eliminate 36% to 54% of content in mathematics or language arts curricula, no significant differences resulted in achievement test scores between gifted students whose curriculum had been compacted and those who had received the general education curriculum (Reis, Westberg, Kulikowich, & Purcell, 1998). Another study showed that when teachers compacted the curriculum, gifted and talented students scored significantly higher on tests of mathematics and science concepts after the content was altered (Reis, 1995).

Curriculum compacting entails three steps: (a) assess students' knowledge and skills in the target content areas, (b) determine the content to be eliminated, and (c) substitute the more appropriate content. Most teachers find the third step to be the most difficult as they "lack expertise in knowing what to substitute for high-ability students" (Renzulli & Reis, 2004, p. 98). When pretesting academically talented students to find out what they already know, the most difficult problems or content should be presented first. Students who can solve the most difficult problems do not need to do the other, easier problems (Winebrenner, 2001).

For curriculum compacting to be effective, teachers must have a substantial understanding of the curricular content and not only condense the material but also modify its presentation, create more meaningful instruction, and evaluate that instruction for individual students. For example, Juan's teacher, Mr. Dominguez, suspects that Juan has already mastered substantial amounts of the mathematics that students are doing in the fourth grade, perhaps by as much as two grade levels. To discover if Juan is a good candidate for curriculum compacting, Mr. Dominguez first determines the scope and sequence of the mathematics problems that Juan should be able to do in the fifth and sixth grades. Then he constructs an evaluation process that will accurately determine at what level Juan can perform the mathematics problems. If Juan has mastered the content and strategies of the higher-level math, then Mr. Dominguez must design and provide replacement activities that are a more challenging and productive use of Juan's time.

TIERED LESSONS A **tiered lesson** provides different extensions of the same basic lesson for groups of students of differing abilities. For example, after the whole class is exposed to a basic lesson on a poem, three groups of students might work on follow-up activities or assignments of basic, middle, and high difficulty. Figure 5 shows an example of a tiered lesson on riddles.

USING BLOOM'S TAXONOMY FOR PHRASING QUESTIONS AND ASSIGNING STUDENT PRODUCTS Bloom and his colleagues (Bloom, Englehart, Furst, Hill, & Krathwohl, 1956) formulated a taxonomy of educational objectives that has proven very useful for differentiating curriculum. The original **Bloom's taxonomy** contains six levels or types of cognitive understanding: knowledge, comprehension, application, analysis, synthesis, and evaluation. In 2001, the taxonomy was revised (Anderson et al., 2001). Nouns have become active verbs in the revised taxonomy. Knowledge is called *remember,* comprehension is called *understand,* application is *apply,* analysis is *analyze,* evaluation is *evaluate,* and synthesis is called *create.* A contributor to

Curriculum compacting

Content Standards for Beginning Teachers—G&T: Pace delivery of curriculum and instruction consistent with needs of indivduals with gifts and talents (GT4S5) (also GT7S3, GT7S5).

Detailed explanations, examples, and resources for implementing tiered lessons and many other strategies for differentiating curriculum and instruction are available at http://www.differentiation central.com/ and http://www.caroltomlinson.com/.

Bloom's taxonomy

Content Standards for Beginning Teachers—G&T: Theories and research that form the basis of curriculum development and instructional practice (GT7K1).

Using the Literary Masters to Inspire Written Expression in Gifted Students

BY SHEILA R. ALBER-MORGAN, CHRISTA M. MARTIN, AND DEIDRA M. GAMMILL

Gifted children's inclination to explore ideas and manipulate linguistic expressions endows them with the potential to become great writers (Fraser, 2003; Kaufman & Gentile, 2002). Exposing gifted students to important literature, including multicultural literature, can inspire them to find their own voices and attain personal growth while making contributions to their culture (Ford, in press).

HOW TO GET STARTED

The instructional activities described here are for students in grades 8 through 12, but you can easily adapt them for younger children.

1. **Provide an overview and structural framework.** Provide an overview of the history and substance of great literature by showing how authors and their works can be categorized by period and culture, literary movements, and genres. Students can use a matrix classifying literature by genre (e.g. allegory, adventure, fantasy, realism, romance, satire, tragedy), to create a structural framework for the following activities.

2. **Encourage independent exploration.**
   - **Biographical author study.** Each student selects one author from the matrix and researches the author's time period, culture, and major life events, and then explores how those experiences may have influenced his or her work writing.
   - **Compare and contrast.** The student compares and contrasts several authors from a given time period and culture. For example, how were the lives and works of Homer, Aesop, Sophocles, and Euripides similar and different? What aspects of 1st-century AD Greek culture influenced each author?
   - **Literary evolution within a culture.** Each student researches how the development of the literature of a selected culture evolved from its origins to the present. For example, what events in 17th-century North America set the stage for authors such as Cotton Mather and Anne Bradstreet?
   - **Literary evolution within a time period.** The student researches literary masters from around the world who lived during a specific historical period and describes the relationship between those authors and the historical events that may have shaped their writing. For example, this can be done using the 19th century, which produced writers such as Karl Marx in the German culture and Victor Hugo in the French culture. What world events might have inspired or influenced these authors?

3. **Encourage cooperative learning.**
   - **Learn and teach.** Each student writes a critical analysis of a selected book in the context of its place in history. What events influenced this literature? What was the author trying to tell us? For example, Ernest Hemingway became involved with Spain's loyalist army during the Spanish Civil War, and his novel *For Whom the Bell Tolls* tells the story of an American fighting the fascist forces in Spain. Students should elaborate on their analyses and provide references from the literature to support their viewpoints. After each student completes this writing assignment, they take turns teaching the other members of their cooperative learning group what they learned about their selected work.
   - **Common threads.** After the students have shared their literature with their cooperative learning groups, each group attempts to identify common threads across the selected works. Students can discuss how their selected readings

both the original and the revised taxonomies, Krathwohl (2002) noted that the original hierarchy implied that activities become more complex as one moves from level to level, while the new hierarchy "gives much greater weight to teacher usage, the requirement of a strict hierarchy has been relaxed to allow the categories to overlap one another" (p. 215).

Teachers most often ask knowledge (remember, recall) and comprehension (understand) questions. Figure 6 illustrates how Bloom's taxonomy could guide the types of questions asked and possible student products in a unit based on the

are similar to one another in terms of theme, mood, characters, plot, setting, style, or any other aspect they wish to explore, and then create a cohesive class presentation.

- **Panel discussion or debate.** Group members examine a single piece of literature and present their collective interpretations to the class in the form of a panel discussion or debate.

4. **Help students discover their own voices.** In-depth study of a piece of literature provides students with many launching points for examining their own perspectives, making personal connections, and producing their own inspired work. The following example of Mary Shelley's work illustrates how to use a piece of literature to inspire written expression.

Since its publication in 1818, Mary Shelley's *Frankenstein* has been regarded as a novel of horror and science fiction. Many students are familiar with the novel's protagonist: the nameless monster. Immortalized by 1930s Hollywood, the monster has become an icon for the dangers and hubris of unchecked scientific research. But those who read the actual novel find that while Frankenstein's monster does commit terrible acts, so does his creator. Both give birth to evil through their irresponsibility and their isolation. Frankenstein's monster levels a terrible accusation at his maker: "How dare you thus sport with life? Do your duty towards me, and I will do mine towards you and the rest of mankind" (Shelley, 1818, p. 145). "Sporting with life" serves as a focal point for the tension that exists between maker and monster. Frankenstein sports with life by creating and then abandoning his creature; the creature sports with life as he attempts, unsuccessfully, to participate in his creator's world. This tension opens up a wealth of writing opportunities within the gifted classroom. Students can explore *Frankenstein* from several vantage points often overlooked in the traditional English classroom.

The following activities are designed to enhance gifted students' understanding of the novel and to encourage creative, critical writing.

- **Role-play and debate.** Each student adopts the role of Victor Frankenstein or the monster and seeks to justify his character's desire to "sport with life." Each student writes a defense of her character's actions, either in creating life or in participating in it. Once students are satisfied with their positions, ask them to break into pairs and debate each other.

- **Contemporary first-person short story.** Students imagine a modern counterpart for their character. Encourage students to move beyond obvious connections such as cloning and harvesting embryos for stem cells and to think of other parallels that affect them on a personal and emotional level (e.g., teen pregnancy/parenthood, plastic surgery). Once the students have decided on a parallel issue, have them write a short story in first-person narrative in which their character personifies the scientist/creator or the victim/monster. How does their character "sport with life," and what are the outcomes? Does their story contain a moral or a warning? Or does it simply paint a vignette and allow the reader to decide?

- **Contemporary short story with narrator.** Mary Shelley tells Frankenstein's story through her narrator, Robert Walton, in his series of letters to his sister. This stylistic device allows Walton to serve as a go-between for Frankenstein and the reader. Had Frankenstein related his story directly, the reader would have questioned his objectivity and honesty. Have students consider adopting this same device by employing an outside narrator to convey their tale. What type of character is best suited to be objective yet involved enough to offer accurate insight? This activity should take approximately three to five class periods, if students work on their stories at home and bring them to class for peer editing and revision.

Source: Adapted from "Using the Literary Masters to Inspire Written Expression in Gifted Students," by S. R. Alber, C. M. Martin, and D. M. Cammill, 2005. *Gifted Child Today, 28*(2), 50–59. Copyright © 2005 by Prufrock Press. Adapted with permission

Cinderella story. Although both average and high-ability students should have learning opportunities at all levels of Bloom's taxonomy, opportunities and expectations to work at the advanced levels of the taxonomy are especially important for academically talented students. It is a mistake to think that gifted and talented learners do not need instructional activities at the lower levels of the taxonomy (Clark, 2008; Ford, in press). To analyze, evaluate, and create meaningful concepts and relationships, students must remember and understand basic information about the topic.

Ford (in press) presents a matrix for designing curriculum and lesson plans based on Bloom's taxonomy and James Banks's (2007) multicultural curriculum model. The 24-cell matrix addresses critical thinking and multicultural education.

TEACHING & LEARNING

A TIERED LESSON USING RIDDLES TO PROMOTE THINKING AND PROBLEM-SOLVING SKILLS

Author: Ms. Erin Morris Miller (National Research Center/Gifted and Talented)	**Author's e-mail:** HOTLINX@virginia.edu
Curriculum area(s): math, science, social studies	Grade Level: 3
Time required: 30 minutes	Instructional grouping: heterogeneous

Overview

This is a thinking skills lesson to help students practice thinking openly and flexibly. Use this lesson as a mental warm-up session before beginning a challenging lesson that requires the students to think flexibly or counterintuitively. Use this lesson to prepare the students for times when making assumptions would be bad. Examples: solving word problems in math, finding patterns in math, drawing conclusions from reading selections, and making decisions during a unit on economy. (Idea inspired by a high school advanced placement calculus teacher, Fred Pence, who began class with a puzzle to get students in the mood to problem-solve. The concept was adapted for younger students.) In this lesson students first solve a riddle as a whole class and then divide into small groups to solve additional riddles. Groups are formed according to the students' readiness to read and understand difficult vocabulary. Each group works independently as the teacher moves from group to group, facilitating discussions.

Standards

This lesson helps students develop the skills necessary to achieve any standard that involves problem solving. Examples include math and science problems as well as dilemmas in social studies and analysis of literature.

Materials

There are three levels of riddles. Level 1 consists of three simple riddles, level 2 consists of one medium-hard riddle, and level 3 consists of one difficult riddle.

As a result of this lesson, students should

know . . .
  Riddles are written puzzles.
understand . . .
  Riddles require people to think creatively.
  Riddles require people to not make assumptions.
be able to do . . .
  Students should be able to solve riddles.

Preassessment

One main difference between the riddles is the difference in the vocabulary involved. Groups should be formed based on the students' verbal proficiency.

Basic riddles

What can go up a chimney down but can't go down a chimney up? (an umbrella)

If a rooster laid a brown egg and a white egg, what kind of chicks would hatch? (None. Roosters don't lay eggs!)

What needs an answer, but doesn't ask a question? (the phone)

Medium-hard riddle

I can sizzle like bacon,
I am made with an egg,
I have plenty of backbone but lack a good leg,
I peel layers like onions but still remain whole,
I can be long like a flagpole yet fit in a hole.
What am I?
(a snake)

Challenging riddle

This thing devours all,
Birds, beasts, trees, flowers,
Gnaws iron, bites steel,
Grinds hard stones to meal,
Slays kings, ruins towns,
And beats high mountains down.
(time) (by J. R. R. Tolkien)

FIGURE 6 USING BLOOM'S TAXONOMY AS A GUIDE FOR DIFFERENTIATING INSTRUCTION BASED ON THE CINDERELLA STORY

Level	Common Verbs to Use to Phrase Questions	Example from Cinderella Story	Possible Student Products
Remember	know, collect, cite, repeat, recall, define, enumerate, list, name, label, tell, recount, relate, specify, memorize, identify	1. How many stepsisters did Cinderella have? 2. Do you recall what the slipper was made of?	Test, list, definition, fact, reproduction.
Understand	restate, recognize, locate, summarize, explain, report, convert, discuss, express, retell, describe, identify, translate, estimate	1. Discuss the events on the night of the ball. 2. Describe what happened to the pumpkin.	Same as for knowing level.
Apply	exhibit, apply, dramatize, solve, employ, practice, compute	1. Make an exhibit of the ball gowns Cinderella's two sisters and stepmother wore. 2. Dramatize what happened when the Prince came to Cinderella's house with the glass slipper.	Illustration, diagram, map, diary, model, collection, diorama, puzzle.
Analyze	interpret, categorize, dissect, analyze, classify, diagram, outline, compare, group, arrange, contrast, examine, inventory, subdivide	1. Compare and contrast Cinderella's treatment by her stepmother and by the Prince. 2. Examine why the stepmother was so cruel to Cinderella.	Questionnaire, survey, report, graph, chart, outline.
Evaluate	judge, criticize, prove, decide, assess, revise, appraise, estimate, rate, evaluate, determine, conclude	1. Prove that Cinderella deserves to go to the ball. 2. Determine what would have happened if Cinderella had run away but had not lost her slipper.	Panel discussion, evaluation scale, report, survey, editorial, verdict, recommendation.
Create	compose, propose, produce, invent, imagine, formulate, create, design, predict, construct, improve, develop, rearrange	1. Compose a song that Cinderella would sing while she did her work in the cinders. 2. Design Cinderella's ball gown; chariot; slipper.	Formula, invention, film, new game, story, poem, art product, machine, advertisement.

Source: Jane Piirto, © 2007. Used with permission

Curriculum Differentiation Outside the Classroom

For some students with outstanding talents, what takes place outside the classroom may be more important and rewarding than many of the activities within it. The teacher should always attempt to connect classwork with human and physical resources available in the community.

INTERNSHIPS AND MENTOR PROGRAMS The value and power of a viable mentor to the realization of talent or creativity have been recognized since the Middle Ages. The importance of mentors cannot be overestimated in certain artistic and scientific fields, where the development of both conceptual and performance skills is critical to success. Mentors are also critically important for low-income and culturally different students (Whiting, 2009). Internship and mentor programs expose gifted students to one of the most powerful and proven educational strategies—modeling, practice, and direct feedback and reinforcement of important behaviors—within a real-world setting (Siegle & McCoach, 2005).

Differentiating curriculum outside the classroom

 Content Council for Exceptional Children Standards for Beginning Teachers—G&T: School and community resources, including content specialists, which support differentiation (GT4K1).

A mentor provides opportunities for students with exceptional talents to develop their conceptual and performance skills in a real-world setting.

© Roger Hutchings/Alamy

SPECIAL COURSES Specialized courses and workshops are offered in many communities, arts and cultural venues, museums, and recreation centers. These courses, which may or may not award high school or college continuing education credits, form a rich variety of opportunities for students to encounter mentors, make new friends, and explore concepts that may not be available in the confines of the school curriculum.

JUNIOR GREAT BOOKS This is a highly structured educational program in which students read selections from a number of areas, including classics, philosophy, fiction, and poetry, and then discuss their meaning with teachers. The teachers must undergo special training and use specific questioning techniques designed to evoke high-quality responses from the students.

SUMMER PROGRAMS Many summer programs are available to gifted and talented students that offer educational experiences as diverse as environmental studies and space and aeronautical studies. A number of new program offerings have been aimed at gifted minority students at the state and local levels; they are often located on college and university campuses. Summer programs are usually relatively brief but intensive learning experiences that concentrate on specific areas of intellectual, artistic, or cultural affairs.

INTERNATIONAL EXPERIENCES New Zealanders have a cultural rite of passage they refer to as "the trek," wherein they pack their bags and travel in modest fashion to the far reaches of the planet. It is an eye-opening experience for people from a remote Pacific island nation and one that gives them an exceptional opportunity to see and touch the world in an intimate fashion. An international curricular experience can merge this act of exploration with the demands of a structured learning experience—for example, the International Baccalaureate Program. Numerous international programs offer academic credits for study at participating educational agencies around the world. They are excellent opportunities for students to develop global interactional skills with academically rigorous studies.

Program Models

Each of the three instructional models described in this section engages students in similar ways, by focusing on independent exploration and inquiry, making substantial modifications to the learning environment, and expecting tangible products as outcomes of the learning activities. These models were selected because they offer solid examples of how special education for gifted and talented students can truly be differentiated from the general education curriculum. Although the Schoolwide Enrichment Model (SEM) is the only model that provides activities for both typically developing and gifted students, each of the other models includes components that can be modified and applied to a broad range of student abilities and talents within general education classrooms.

THE SCHOOLWIDE ENRICHMENT MODEL The SEM not only attempts to meet the needs of gifted and talented students within the general education classroom setting but also is meant to be used with other students in the class (Renzulli & Reis, 2003).

The Schoolwide Enrichment Model (SEM) focuses on applying the know-how of gifted education to a systematic plan for total school improvement. This plan is not intended to replace existing services to students who are identified

Schoolwide Enrichment Model

Council for Exceptional Children

Content Standards for Beginning Teachers—G&T: Key philosophies, theories, models, and research supporting gifted and talented education (GT1K2) (also GT7K3, GT7S4).

as gifted according to various state or local criteria. Rather, the model should be viewed as an umbrella under which many different types of enrichment and acceleration services are made available to targeted groups of students, as well as all students within a given school or grade level. (Renzulli, 1998, p. 1)

The first step of the SEM is identifying a talent pool of high-ability students (usually 15% to 25% of the school's enrollment) by using a multifactored assessment approach, including achievement tests, teacher and peer nominations, and creativity assessments. Once the students are identified, they can take part in specialized services, many of which are also available and appropriate for other learners in the same classroom. Reis (1995) discussed some of the relevant features of this instructional approach:

- Teachers use interest and learning styles assessments with talent pool students. Teachers also use informal and formal methods to create and/or identify individual students' interests and to encourage students to further develop and pursue their interests in various ways.
- Teachers offer curriculum compacting to all eligible students. The general education curriculum of the classroom is modified by eliminating redundant or repetitious information and materials.
- Teachers offer three types of enrichment activities to students: Type I, general exploratory experiences; Type II, purposefully designed instructional methods and materials; and Type III, advanced-level studies with greater depth and complexity.

All children in the talent pool participate in Type I and Type II enrichment activities. Only students who show serious interest in a specific topic evolve into Type III investigators. Students are never compelled to begin Type III projects; the level remains an open option for them.

MAKER'S ACTIVE PROBLEM SOLVER MODEL   Maker proposes a process by which the key elements of content, process, products, and the environment of a child's learning situation can be modified (Maker, 2005; Maker & Schiever, 2010). Maker and coworkers have conducted extensive research on reliability and validity of the DISCOVER assessment and curriculum model, showing that teachers whose beliefs parallel the theory behind the model can help students raise their test scores. Arts infusion with this model also has been successful. The teachers use four kinds of modifications:

- *Content modifications.* The content of a curriculum is the type of subject matter being taught. In general, the goal is to develop content that is more advanced, complex, innovative, and original than what is usually encountered in the classroom.
- *Process modifications.* The strategies and methods used in delivering the content to learners are key features of instruction. The goal is to provide students with many opportunities to actively respond to the content, including independent research, cooperative learning, peer coaching, simulations, and apprenticeships.
- *Product modifications.* The products of learning are the outcomes associated with instruction. The goal is to encourage a variety of ways that students can present their thoughts, ideas, and results.

A wide range materials and web-based resources for implmenting SEM can be found at the Neag Center for Gifted Education and Talent Development (http://www.gifted.uconn.edu/sem/) and Renzulli Learning (http://www.gifted.uconn.edu/sem/).

Maker's Problem-Solving Model

 Content Standards for Beginning Teachers—G&T: Key philosophies, theories, models, and research supporting gifted and talented education (GT1K2) (also GT7K3, GT7S4).

Letting students choose the kinds of problems they wish to study and how they will go about their investigations is one method for differentiating curriculum for students with outstanding academic abilities.

Anthony Magnacca/Merrill

- *Environment modifications.* The learning environment includes both the physical characteristics of the setting(s) and the ambiance created by the teachers or facilitators. The goal is first to establish a positive working environment and then to rearrange the layout.

Problem-Based
Learning Units

Content
Standards for
Beginning
Teachers—G&T: Key
philosophies, theories,
models, and research
supporting gifted and
talented education (GT1K2)
(also GT7K3, GT7S4).

PROBLEM-BASED LEARNING Problem-based learning (PBL) challenges students to "learn to learn" while working cooperatively in groups to seek solutions to real-world problems. The problems are used to engage students' curiosity and initiate learning of subject matter. Since the mid-1990s, Joyce VanTassel-Baska has served as overall project director for a series of federally funded grants to develop a thematic, interdisciplinary, problem-based curriculum for gifted students. Gifted educators throughout the country created and field-tested units in science, language arts, and the social sciences. (Figure 7 describes several examples.)

An ill-formed, real-world problem serves as the basis for each of the science units, and understanding and applying the concept of systems compose the overarching theme. These units give students experience in collecting, organizing, analyzing, and evaluating scientific data and learning to communicate their understanding to others. The PBL language arts units feature change as the overarching theme; the social studies units focus on the concept of interdependence.

FIGURE 7   EXAMPLES OF COLLEGE OF WILLIAM & MARY PROBLEM-BASED LEARNING UNITS IN SCIENCE, LANGUAGE ARTS, AND SOCIAL STUDIES

SCIENCE

What a Find! (Grades 2-4)	Students are put in the role of a newly hired archaeologist who is contacted by a construction company crew that has just unearthed some artifacts. The construction company needs your input to determine what the next steps should be. Through the concept of systems, a simulation and scientific investigations of the archaeological processes, students will uncover a solution to the problem.
Acid, Acid Everywhere (Grades 4-6)	This unit presents the structure of systems through chemistry, ecological habitats, and transportation. The unit poses an ill-structured problem that leads students into an interdisciplinary inquiry about the structure and interaction of several systems, centering around the study of an acid spill on a local highway.

LANGUAGE ARTS

The 1940s: A Decade of Change (Grades 6-10)	This unit looks at the historical events and social issues of the 1940s through the literature of the decade, including novels, short stories, poetry, essays, letters, and newspapers. The unit is rich in materials that highlight the concept of change, including works such as Hersey's *Hiroshima*, *The Diary of Anne Frank*, and Spiegelman's *Maus II*.
Change Through Choices (Grades 10-12)	Choices and the consequences of choices that people make have an important impact on life and the success of individuals. This unit, designed for high-ability students, focuses on catalytic choices that determine change in a variety of situations. Rich in content, the world literature chosen can be analyzed and synthesized for depth in understanding cultural similarities and differences. This unit attempts to give the student a chance to question real-world choices and problems and decide what valuable lessons can be learned through careful individual examination of options. (Author: Felicia Dixon) (1997)

SOCIAL STUDIES

Ancient Egypt: Gift of the Nile (Grades 2-3)	This unit is designed around the idea that human civilizations develop and sustain themselves as a collection of interdependent systems. The unit also provides opportunities for students to broaden their understanding by comparing ancient Egyptian civilization with aspects of their own lives and communities.
The 1930s in America: Facing Depression (Grades 6-7)	This unit explores Depression-era America from the perspective of many different groups of people, utilizing a variety of primary sources to illustrate events and the social-political context. The concept of cause and effect is employed to support student understanding of the complexity of history.

Source: For more information on these and other problem-based curriculum units, go to http://cfge.wm.edu/curriculum.htm.

The PBL units have won many major curriculum awards from discipline-based subject matter groups, as well as the National Association for Gifted Children's "red apple" award for excellence. PBL units are used by teachers in almost 20 countries and have been adopted by the American Embassy Schools and the Department of Defense Schools. Although the PBL units were developed initially for gifted and talented students, they can be used with students of all ability levels by modifying the activities depending on students' skills and interests.

EDUCATIONAL PLACEMENT ALTERNATIVES: ABILITY GROUPING

> Providing special services for the gifted and talented students almost inevitably requires some special grouping. (Feldhusen, 1989, p. 9)

Ability grouping has been used in schools, both formally and informally, for more than 100 years. As soon as the number of students in any classroom or school became so large that the differences in their abilities to learn stood out, teachers automatically placed students in groups for subject matter instruction. These groups were often informal, consisting of two or more students who could keep pace with each other.

An issue that has generated considerable debate and strong opinions over the years is the extent to which gifted and talented students should be taught in homogeneous groups composed of their intellectual and academic peers or in heterogeneous groups of students encompassing a wide range of abilities. Social injustices and upheavals have resulted in increased calls for equity in all of society's institutions. For some, equity in education includes the idea that all students should be taught in heterogeneous groups so that no single group can progress faster than any other. But virtually all educators and researchers in the field of gifted education believe that *flexible* heterogeneous grouping that does not result in tracking helps students reach their full potential.

The NAGC (2009) states that "[g]rouping gifted children is one of the foundations of exemplary gifted education practice" (p. 1) and contends that the many myths surrounding ability grouping for gifted students—that it damages the self-esteem of struggling students, creates an elitist group who think too highly of themselves, and is undemocratic and even racist at times—have no research support. The NAGC believes that grouping gifted learners is usually the "least restrictive environment" in which their learning can occur, and it affords schools the most effective and efficient means to provide the differentiated curriculum and instruction the students need.

A variety of grouping practices are used for both full-time and part-time gifted education programming.

Full-Time Grouping Options

SPECIAL SCHOOLS Special high schools for gifted students of both genders began in the early 20th century with the establishment of Stuyvesant High School in New York City. The establishment of the Hunter College High School for Gifted Girls came even earlier. The Hunter College Elementary School for gifted students opened in 1941. Children are selected for admission to these schools on the basis of competitive examinations and scores on individual IQ tests. These arrangements for academically talented children became popular in the 1980s as mandates for desegregation caused urban school systems to change the concept of the neighborhood school to the concept of the magnet school. Even on the elementary school level in many urban areas, special magnet schools emphasize various themes: for example, Columbus, Ohio, has a French-language school; some large cities have a special high school for the visual and performing arts and special schools for mathematics and science. Recently, special charter schools for gifted and talented students have been established in some states.

Placement alternatives and ability grouping

Council for Exceptional Children

Content Standards for Beginning Teachers—G&T: Key issues and trends including diversity and inclusion, connecting general, special, and gifted and talented education (GT1K7) (also GT5S2).

Ability grouping issues and concerns

Council for Exceptional Children

Content Standards for Beginning Teachers—G&T: Key issues and trends including diversity and inclusion, connecting general, special, and gifted and talented education (GT1K7) (also GT5S2).

SPECIAL CLASSROOMS The primary advantage of the self-contained classroom is that all curriculum and instruction can be focused on the needs of gifted and talented students. Other advantages of self-contained classrooms are that students are more likely to work at a pace commensurate with their abilities, and membership in a class of intellectual equals may challenge some gifted students to excel even further. The self-contained classroom model may also be more efficient because gifted education teachers do not have to move from classroom to classroom or school to school to serve students.

In addition to sharing many of the disadvantages of self-contained classrooms for students with disabilities (e.g., limited opportunity to interact with peers in general education), self-contained classroom programs for gifted and talented students must often deal with the stigma of being viewed as elitist. Some districts may be too small to support the self-contained classroom option, even multiage or across-grade-level classes.

CLUSTER ABILITY GROUPING In *cluster ability grouping,* the top five to eight gifted and talented students at a given grade level are placed as a group in a regular classroom of mixed-ability students. The cluster receives specialized instruction from a teacher with training in gifted education. A cluster group of 8 students in a class of 24 would receive one-third of the teacher's time and instruction. Cluster grouping can be especially effective when there are not enough students to form an advanced placement section for a particular subject. An advantage of this type of cluster grouping is that it fits philosophically with the special educational practice of inclusion yet still provides intensive differentiated instruction to gifted students within a peer group.

Research shows that gifted students educated with full-time ability grouping options gain from 1.3 to 2 years' academic growth per year and show small but positive gains in social maturity, self-efficiency, self-esteem, and motivation for learning (Rogers, 2006).

Part-Time Grouping Options

RESOURCE ROOM OR PULL-OUT PROGRAMS Some educators believe that the resource room, or pull-out model, is the best option for serving gifted and talented students. Although pull-out programs offer many of the advantages of a self-contained classroom without the disadvantages of complete segregation from the general education classroom, they pose a number of challenges and disadvantages as well. Administrators and teachers in schools that provide resource room/pull-out services for gifted and talented students should recognize that these children do not stop being gifted when they leave the resource room and return to the general education classroom. Although the learning opportunities and instruction provided to talented students in the resource room may be of the highest quality, they do not eliminate the need to differentiate curriculum for these students when they are in the general education classroom during the rest of the school day.

In cluster performance grouping, students within a heterogeneous class are grouped for instruction in each subject area according to their achievement.

CLUSTER PERFORMANCE GROUPING In *cluster performance grouping,* the teacher groups students within the same heterogeneous class for instruction in each subject area according to their achievement. The most common form of within-class grouping is regrouping by subject; students are generally grouped into three or more levels, and they study material from different textbooks at different levels.

LIKE-ABILITY COOPERATIVE LEARNING GROUPS When the teacher uses cooperative learning activities, the three to four highest-ability students are grouped together and assigned a differentiated cooperative learning task with differentiated expected outcomes and assessment criteria.

Research shows small, positive gains in academic, social, and self-esteem measures for gifted students in part-time ability grouping options. More than a year's academic growth will be achieved when the learning activities in these options focus on extensions of the general curriculum or on critical thinking or creative production (Rogers, 2006).

Ability grouping options facilitate the provision of differentiated curriculum and instruction to gifted and talented learners, but that is all grouping does. Educators must realize that just putting children into like-ability or performance groups is insufficient. What matters most is what happens in the groups rather than grouping itself. Challenging curriculum, well-designed lessons, and effective instructional practices are needed to get the most of any group arrangement. Although this may seem obvious, some teachers think that just putting children into different ability groups is enough, and they do not provide differentiated curriculum.

Consulting Teacher Model

Most gifted and talented students are served in general education classrooms. If the school district has a program for gifted and talented students, a teacher with special training in gifted education provides direct and indirect support for the general education classroom teacher. Working in consultation with the general education classroom teacher, this special educator—sometimes called a facilitator, a consulting teacher, or an intervention specialist for the gifted—might provide specialized instruction in science, math, the humanities, or other subjects to flexibly grouped students. She may work with a high-ability reading or math group while the rest of the class works in these domains. She may mentor independent projects, design special learning centers, plan special field trips, and help students prepare for academic competitions.

An advantage of this model is that the gifted education teacher is no longer isolated and alone, working in her resource room or pull-out classroom without knowledge of what the students are doing in their home classrooms. She is in partnership with general education classroom teachers, collaborating on curriculum planning teams as they plan multilevel lessons. Another important advantage of the consultant teacher model is that students of all ability levels in the general education classroom can benefit from smaller student–teacher ratios, participating in multitiered lessons and learning activities on creativity, critical thinking, or study strategies that the gifted specialist may teach to the whole class.

Many schools, however, do not have a gifted education specialist, and the general education classroom teachers are responsible for differentiating curriculum for students with advanced educational needs. We cannot stress this enough: to most effectively understand, teach, and challenge gifted and talented students, teachers, counselors, and other educators must be formally trained. Unfortunately, most colleges and universities do not offer course work or degrees in gifted education.

CONTINUING CHALLENGES

Whereas access to individually planned special education to meet their unique educational needs is no longer an issue for students with disabilities, only a small percentage of gifted and talented children enjoy the benefits of differentiated curriculum and instruction. For gifted and talented children from culturally and linguistically different backgrounds and those who live in poverty, access to high-quality differentiated curriculum is especially rare.

Consider this: the No Child Left Behind Act, which emphasizes the measurement of educational progress for all students, especially those who may risk lack of academic success, may not serve gifted and talented students adequately (e.g., Gallagher, 2004;

Consulting teacher model

Content Standards for Beginning Teachers—G&T: Key issues and trends including diversity and inclusion, connecting general, special, and gifted and talented education (GT1K7) (also GT5S2).

Advocate for gifted and talented students

Content Standards for Beginning Teachers—G&T: Advocate for the benefit of individuals with gifts and talents and their families (GT10S3).

Kaplan, 2004). Since 2001, all NAGC presidents have taken this position. DeLacy (2004) asked, "What group of students makes the lowest achievement gains in school?" and "What group of students has been harmed most by the No Child Left Behind Act?" The answer was "The brightest students" (p. 40). She explained that studies by various states had shown that the emphasis on bringing up the lowest-achieving students has too often resulted in teachers neglecting the highest-achieving students while they concentrate on the lowest-achieving students. This finding is not new, as shown by Donna Ford and Tarek Grantham, who discuss the notion of "academic triage": Who is deemed unsalvageable? Who is worthy of being saved? DeLacy (2004) asserted that

> gifted students are truly our forgotten children. Neglected in our schools and ignored by our policymakers, they spend their days dozing through classes in which they aren't learning. Many suffer from depression. It is time to take them out of their holding pens and give them a chance to stretch and to grow. (p. 40)

The biggest challenge facing the field of gifted education is instilling recognition by society in general and by policy makers in particular that gifted and talented children deserve and need specially designed instruction.

One of the greatest challenges, not yet achieved, is a federal mandate (akin to IDEA) to identify, fund, and serve gifted and talented children and youth. Debates abound regarding whether gifted and talented students need educational services to meet their needs and to promote achievement. Given that there is no mandate, it appears that policy makers do not believe that such students have special needs like those with other exceptionalities. However, any teacher and parent or caregiver knows that gifted and talented students have special educational needs that must be addressed to reach their potential. Countless stories exist of gifted and talented individuals who failed to achieve, do well in school, and contribute to society. Large numbers of students who qualify for gifted and talented services drop out of school, and many more students who are culturally different, in need of special education, and/or economically disadvantaged are never even identified. Estimates of this group of underachieving gifted students range from 10% to 25% of all high school dropouts (Davis et al., 2011) and are even higher for gifted students who are low-income and/or Hispanic and African American, especially males (Ford, 2010).

Gifted and talented students from all walks of life need an appropriate education; they need differentiated curriculum, instructional strategies, materials, and experiences that will enable them to realize their potential. There are new approaches and perspectives concerning the manner in which these students are identified and how services are delivered that reflect insights into the way humans develop, learn, and create. These innovations promise a brighter future for students with gifts and talents—a future that will benefit the world in which they live.

▼ TIPS FOR BEGINNING TEACHERS

Teaching Gifted and Talented Children

BY LINDA MICHAEL

If you become a general education teacher, you may never have a student who is blind, a student who is deaf, or a student with severe and multiple disabilities in your classroom. You will, however, have students who are gifted and talented. The general education classroom is where most gifted and talented students spend most of their time in school. Here are some tips that may help.

DIFFERENTIATE

Curriculum content can be compacted and accelerated to provide learning experiences appropriate to gifted students' advanced abilities; you should be prepared to do the following:

- **Pretest.** You may find that a gifted and talented student already knows most or all of the material planned for a unit of study. After pretesting, have your students work in fluid small groups based on their ability in that specific area.

- **Compact.** Even after you have placed gifted and talented students ahead in the curriculum based on their pretest performances, you will probably find that those students can move through the advanced material faster than most students. You might give them an independent project, a more advanced lesson, or an assignment in the same area but based on their interests.

- **Accelerate.** Accelerating a gifted student one, two, or even three grade levels in certain subject areas is often easier and less costly than developing your own materials within the classroom.

DON'T BE AFRAID TO CREATE YOUR OWN CURRICULUM

Many schools do not have established curricular plans or preexisting menus of enriched learning opportunities for gifted and talented students. This gives classroom teachers the responsibility, and the opportunity, to develop differentiated curriculum.

- **Administer an interest survey.** Find out what the students are studying and learning on their own, and tailor class activities and assignments to these interests. For example, young science students may have elaborate collections, and young math students might be interested in elaborate, complicated number games.
- **Build a library of curriculum materials spanning several years above grade level, and keep those materials in your classroom.** These materials will provide ideas and content for developing tiered lessons.
- **Take advantage of curriculum guides and materials for gifted students.** Have advanced materials available in your classroom. In my classroom, I have fourth- to eighth-grade curriculum materials and reference sources spanning from elementary to college level. I don't rely solely on textbooks. Some of the best problem-based units for gifted and talented students that I have used are Interact Simulations (www.interact-simulations.com), the GEMS Program (Great Explorations in Math and Science) from the Lawrence Hall of Science at the University of California at Berkeley (www.lhs.org), and the William and Mary Units developed by the Center for Gifted Education at the College of William and Mary.
- **Provide learning opportunities outside the classroom.** Take advantage of the opportunities in your region. Too often, field trips are taken as a reward or a day off from the classroom. Field trips are much more meaningful if they have relevance and are connected to what is happening in the classroom. I live in a college town and am lucky to have professors willing to share their expertise with my students. This may be a chemistry or physics professor doing hands-on science demonstrations or a

visit to the campus television and radio station to see a production in action. Our regional theater also has several offerings for schools throughout the year.

- **Involve your students in academic contests.** Gifted and talented students are often competitive. They like to participate in regional and national competitions to see how their abilities compare. For the past 4 years, I have taken a team to a First Lego League (FLL) competition in our state. These competitions require teams to not only program a Lego Mindstorms robot but to create a research project. FLL stresses teamwork and cooperation as well as healthy, friendly competition.

I require my students to participate in our district science fair. Science fair competitions require students to research, inquire, analyze, and draw conclusions. Science fairs also help students understand the importance of written and spoken communication skills. Science fairs also offer students the opportunity to earn scholarships and awards.

Local and districtwide academic challenges are also a great way for kids from other schools to meet and compete. *Power of the Pen, Odyssey of the Mind, Math Olympiad,* spelling bees, and geography bees are just a few examples of competitions your students may choose to enter.

TAILOR YOUR INSTRUCTIONAL ARRANGEMENTS AND TEACHING METHODS

Gifted and talented children do not need specialized methods of instruction as much as they need opportunities to explore challenging curriculum in a supportive environment. Tier, or layer, lessons so that the top students are always challenged.

- **Provide regular opportunities for gifted and talented students to share their ideas and talk about what they have learned.**
- **Challenge them to think, not just pass tests.** Many gifted students already can pass grade-level tests. Encourage and require them to explore the deeper meaning, extensions, and implications of concepts.
- **Use cooperative or collaborative groups that encourage pair sharing.** It is a mistake to make gifted and talented students responsible for the learning of the whole group.
- **Don't assume that because a gifted and talented student is advanced in some skills she has mastered the entire subject area.** A student who has no trouble with the abstract aspects of algebra may struggle with geometry. When you notice gaps in a student's learning, you will often find that she can quickly catch up with direct instruction in the skills that are missing.

▼ KEY TERMS AND CONCEPTS

ability grouping
acceleration
asynchrony
Bloom's taxonomy

curriculum compacting
enrichment
tiered lesson

▼ SUMMARY

Definitions

- The federal government defines gifted and talented children as those who give evidence of high-achievement capability in areas such as intellectual, creative, artistic, or leadership capacity or in specific academic fields, and who need services and activities not ordinarily provided by the school in order to fully develop those capabilities.
- The National Association for Gifted Children defines gifted individuals as those who demonstrate outstanding levels of aptitude (defined as an exceptional ability to reason and learn) or competence (documented performance or achievement in top 10% or rarer) in one or more domains.
- Renzulli's definition of giftedness is based on the traits of above-average general abilities, high level of task commitment, and creativity.
- Piirto defines the gifted as having superior memory, observational powers, curiosity, creativity, and ability to learn.
- Maker defines the gifted and talented student as a problem solver who can (a) create a new or clearer definition of an existing problem, (b) devise new and more efficient or effective methods, and (c) reach solutions that may differ from the usual.

Characteristics

- Learning and intellectual characteristics of gifted and talented students include the ability to do the following:
  - Rapidly acquire, retain, and use large amounts of information
  - Relate one idea to another
  - Make sound judgments
  - Appreciate multiple and opposing points of view
  - Perceive the operation of larger systems of knowledge that others may not recognize
  - Acquire and manipulate abstract symbol systems
  - Solve problems by reframing the question and creating novel solutions
- Characteristics that have been noted in highly gifted students with IQs of 145 and above include the following:
  - Intense intellectual curiosity
  - Fascination with basic words and simple ideas
  - Perfectionism and need for precision
  - Learning with great/large/murky intuitive leaps
  - Intense need for mental stimulation and challenge
  - Difficulty conforming to the thinking/logic/reasoning of others
  - Early moral and existential concerns
  - Tendency toward introversion
- *Asynchrony* is a term used to describe disparate rates of intellectual, emotional, and physical growth or development often displayed by gifted children.
- Many gifted children are highly creative. Although there is no standard definition of creativity, most researchers and educators agree that fluency, flexibility, originality, and elaboration are important dimensions.

Prevalence

- Most federal reports estimate that gifted and talented children are 3% to 5% of the student population.
- The NAGC reports there are 3 million school-age gifted students in the United States.

Historical Background

- Much of the history of the field of gifted and talented education has revolved around theories and measurement of intelligence and schools' provision of differentiated curriculum for gifted students.
- Congressional appropriations for the Javits Gifted and Talented Students Education Act, enacted in 1988 to provide federal support to develop and enhance programs for gifted and talented students, represent less than 2 cents of every $100 of the federal K–12 education budget.

Identification and Assessment

- Comprehensive and equitable identification of gifted and talented students includes a combination of intelligence tests; achievement measures; checklists; teacher, parent, community, and peer nominations; self-nomination; and leisure interests.
- Some states/school districts use a progressive filtering process to identify students for gifted education services that refines a large pool of potentially gifted students down to a smaller, formally identified group.
- African American, Hispanic American, and Native American students are underrepresented in gifted education programs and advanced placement classes.
- Identification instruments, policies, and procedures must not be discriminatory or biased; they must be valid and reliable for all groups, and take into account cultural, linguistic, and economic differences.
- Maker's DISCOVER procedure can be used to equitably identify gifted and talented students from different cultural groups and low-socioeconomic-status backgrounds.
- Teachers of gifted students with disabilities must strive for a balance between nurturing the students' strengths and teaching and providing accommodations and supports to meet the needs resulting from their disabilities.

Educational Approaches

- Curriculum for gifted and talented students should possess academic rigor, be thematic and interdisciplinary, and be responsive to the learning characteristics of gifted students.
- *Differentiation* is a broad term referring to a variety of strategies for providing gifted and talented students with a challenging and conceptually rich curriculum.

- *Acceleration* is the general term for modifying the pace at which a student moves through the curriculum.
- *Enrichment* means probing or studying a subject in greater depth than would occur in the general education curriculum.
- Curriculum compacting involves compressing instructional content so students have time to work on more challenging materials.
- Tiered lessons provide extensions of the same basic lesson for groups of students of differing abilities.
- Bloom's taxonomy of educational objectives provides a framework for differentiating curriculum by asking questions and assigning activities that require students to demonstrate different types of knowledge.
- Options for learning outside school include internships and mentorships, special courses and workshops in the community, Junior Great Books, summer programs, competitions and fairs, and international experiences.
- Three models for differentiating curriculum for gifted students are Renzulli's Schoolwide Enrichment Model, Maker's Active Problem Solver Model, and the William & Mary Problem-Based Learning units.
- Ford's multicultural gifted education matrix, designed for all gifted students, targets critical thinking and multicultural education.

Educational Placement Alternatives and Ability Grouping

- Grouping gifted students is usually the "least restrictive enviornment" for their learning and affords schools an effective and efficient means to provide differentiated curriculum and instruction.
- Full-time options for ability grouping—teaching gifted and talented students in homogeneous groups composed of their intellectual and academic peers—include special magnet schools, special classrooms, and cluster ability groups within regular classrooms.
- Part-time options for ability grouping include resource rooms/pull-out programs, cluster performance grouping, and like-ability cooperative learning groups.
- Most gifted and talented students are served in general education classrooms. A consultant teacher trained in gifted education often helps the general education classroom teacher plan and deliver specialized instruction.

Continuing Challenges

- The biggest challenge facing the field of gifted education is instilling recognition by society in general and by educational policy makers in particular that gifted and talented children deserve and need specially designed instruction.

MyEducationLab™

Go to Topic 18, Gifted and Talented, in the MyEducationLab (www.myeducationlab.com) for *Exceptional Children*, where you can

- Find learning outcomes for gifted and talented learners, along with the national standards that connect to these outcomes.
- Complete Assignments and Activities that can help you more deeply understand the chapter content.
- Apply and practice your understanding of the core teaching skills identified in the chapter with the Building Teaching Skills and Dispositions learning units.
- Examine challenging situations and cases presented in the IRIS Center Resources.
- Access video clips of CCSSO National Teachers of the Year award winners responding to the question "Why do I teach?" in the Teacher Talk section.
- Check your comprehension of the content covered in the chapter with the Study Plan. Here you will be able to take a chapter quiz, receive feedback on your answers, and then access Review, Practice, and Enrichment activities to enhance your understanding of chapter content.
- Use the Online Lesson Plan Builder to practice lesson planning and integrating national and state standards into your planning.

▼ GLOSSARY

ability grouping: Placing students with similar levels of achievement and skill into the same classes or instructional groups.

acceleration: An educational approach that provides a child with learning experiences usually given to older children; most often used with gifted and talented children.

asynchrony: A term used to describe the disparate rates of intellectual, emotional, and physical growth or development characteristic of many gifted and talented children.

Bloom's taxonomy: A hierarchy of educational objectives consisting of six types of cognitive understanding: (a) knowledge, (b) comprehension, (c) application, (d) analysis, (e) synthesis (creation), and (f) evaluation. Can be used as a framework for differentiating curriculum by asking questions and assigning activities that require students to demonstrate different types of learning.

curriculum compacting: Strategy for differentiating curriculum for gifted and talented students by replacing content that students have already mastered with more challenging material.

enrichment: An educational approach that provides a child with extra learning experiences that the standard curriculum would not normally include. Most often used with gifted and talented children.

tiered lesson: A lesson that entails different extensions of the same basic lesson for groups of students of differing abilities. For example, after the whole class is exposed to a basic lesson on a poem, three groups of students might work on follow-up activities or assignments of basic, medium, and high difficulty.

Early Childhood Special Education

From Chapter 14 of *Exceptional Children* and *An Introduction to Special Education*, Tenth Edition. William L. Heward.

Early Childhood
Special Education

Laura Bolesta/Merrill

► **FOCUS QUESTIONS**

- Why is it so difficult to measure the impact of early intervention?
- How can we provide early intervention for a child whose disability is not yet present?
- How are the four different purposes of assessment and evaluation in early childhood special education related to one another?

- Which do you think are the most important goals of early childhood special education?
- How can a play activity or an everyday routine become a specially designed learning opportunity for a preschooler with disabilities?

▼ FEATURED TEACHER

MARK FRALEY

Madrona Elementary School • Seattle Public School District • Seattle, Washington

EDUCATION—TEACHING CREDENTIALS—EXPERIENCE

- B.S., physical education, Mid America Nazarene University, 1999
- M.Ed., early childhood special education, University of Kansas, 2003
- Washington State, Professional Teaching Certificate, Special Education, PreK–3
- 9 years as an early childhood special education teacher and 2 years of paraprofessional work in a self-contained special education preschool classroom

MY STUDENTS Twenty preschool children attend my classroom, each for 2.5 hours per day, 4 days per week. Two instructional assistants and I teach 9 students in the morning session and 11 in the afternoon. Most of my students qualify for special education services under the IDEA category developmental delay, several have a diagnosis of autism, and nearly all receive speech and language services for a communication delay.

My students are an extremely diverse mix of cultural and ethnic backgrounds, languages, and socioeconomic levels. Two of my students are West African refugees, one from Sierra Leone and one from Gambia. Many of my students have multiple cultural heritages, such as Ethiopian/American, African American/Thai, Latino/African American, and Russian/American. There are Spanish, Soninke, Amharic, Russian, Cambodian, Thai, and English speakers. Some

days I feel like I am hosting a United Nations summit! I'll introduce you to two of my students.

Five-year-old Omaru receives services for delays in expressive and receptive communication and social/emotional development. Omaru was painfully shy when he first joined my class 2 years ago. He seldom left my side and would duck behind me whenever someone entered the room. Today, any new volunteer or visitor who enters the room is greeted by Omaru's ear-to-ear smile and big "Hello!" or high five. Omaru's growing confidence and skill in communication are the result of the wide variety of language- and vocabulary-rich activities in my classroom. For example, the last day of the week when the students conduct a play based on our book of the week, Omaru repeats his favorite story lines with our classroom microphone.

Frederick, another 5-year-old who joined my classroom 2 years ago, was adopted from Vietnam shortly after his second birthday. Challenged by global developmental delays, Frederick receives services in social/emotional, adaptive, motor, communication, and preacademic domains. For the first few months in my classroom, Frederick rarely spent more than 30 seconds on any activity. He often stumbled over toys and other children. His play skills consisted of running about the classroom bumping into his peers to get a reaction. Although still a mischievous attention-getter at times, Frederick has improved his attention and motor-sequencing skills by following visual supports that cue each step in an activity. Today, as he is about ready to transition to kindergarten, Frederick can play in the centers for at least 5 minutes without disrupting ongoing activity and participate purposefully in group activities such as circle time for 10 minutes, with no more than two teacher prompts or redirections.

A TYPICAL DAY Most of my students arrive by bus, often from a day care or other preschool program such as Head Start. We begin our day with a tabletop activity, such as puzzles, bins with small building materials or blocks, or thematic coloring pages. During this time I engage in informal discussions to learn about their day. I use an emotions chart to help them indicate what feeling they relate to most. This helps me gauge who needs a little extra attention. Circle time is next. A standard circle time routine each day gives my students a sense of predictability and security and me a structure in which to embed a variety of IEP goals such as group participation, turn taking, and color/number/letter/shape recognition.

Next, my assistants and I split the students into three groups and accompany them through a sequence of three 10-minute activity centers for small-group instruction. While one group works on a thematic project involving a sequence of steps (e.g., color, cut, and paste), another is doing hands-on activities such as counting and sorting, and the third group is learning to follow a play script. If the dramatic play area is featuring a beach theme for the week, our students can play with blankets, sun glasses, and an umbrella. Special attention is paid to each student's ability to complete each activity as independently as possible. Omaru uses a notebook to record his observations and results of a science experiment. Frederick benefits from a series of pictures followed by a selected reward for completing an activity.

Time outdoors on the playground or covered play area comes next. Specially adapted tricycles and other equipment enable the students to develop gross motor skills and social skills while playing as independently as possible. After being outside, the children are ready for a snack. Snack time is a wonderful opportunity to teach skills in multiple domains: social-communicative skills such as requesting, asking and responding to

questions, and appropriately getting someone's attention; fine-motor skills such as eating with a spoon and drinking from a cup; and adaptive skills such as cleaning up and washing hands.

Free-choice center time comes next. A choice board contains photos of each center and Velcro-backed pictures of the students below. Each student sticks his picture next to the center of his choice. Observing the student during free-choice time helps me judge the effectiveness of our teaching. If, during small-group instruction time, we have taught them well, how to play appropriately with materials in a new center, the children will need little to no teacher support during free-choice play.

I make music a part of many of our class activities. Music captures children's attention and encourages them to participate, and I have found that a musical rhyme or song can redirect inappropriate behavior such as fidgeting in line or refusing to wash hands. Our day ends with a slow-tempo song that helps children transition from the activity centers to gathering their belongings and lining up for the buses in an orderly manner.

COMMUNICATING WITH PARENTS AND FAMILIES I cannot stress enough the importance of ongoing, open communication with parents and families. I make my classroom a welcoming place from day one by inviting the families to participate in volunteer opportunities and visits. I strive for complete transparency with everything I do in the classroom, and parents of my students have come to expect no less from me. Knowing that I have to explain the reasoning behind every teaching method and curriculum materials I use has made me a better teacher and more reflective about my practice.

I also help my students' parents find out something that all parents of young children want to know. Significant communication delays prevent many of my students from providing a satisfactory answer when their parents ask, "What did you do in school today?" To help in that regard, my students take home several pictures of their activities in school that day. I keep a digital camera handy and take countless pictures during the school year. These photos are a powerful, effective form of communication that lets parents and families see what they participated in and who they interacted with. Creating these take-home sheets is easy and fast. I import the day's photos from my digital camera to the computer in my classroom, paste two or three of the most telling shots in PowerPoint, add a sentence or two of description, and make copies on a printer in the school work office.

REWARDS AND LESSONS AS A SPECIAL EDUCATOR A student of mine passed away a few years ago. He had a juvenile form of pancreatic cancer. You never would have picked him out of a crowd of kids as being "the one" with cancer. He was rough-and-tumble, a 100% boy. He had both a colostomy bag and a urostomy bag. This meant a lot of extra work and not the type anybody signs up for. His time in my classroom was challenging in the sense that he was given only a short time to live and would be on strong chemotherapy. However, his determination and always ready-to-go attitude provided a spark in my teaching and led this particular group of students to a terrific school year. When he passed away in the fall of his kindergarten year, his mother shared with me how meaningful his time was in my classroom. In his short life, being a member of my classroom played an important role in giving him a rich quality of life. I look back on this with sadness but at the same time realize that my role as a special

educator is always meaningful and purposeful. The stigma that can follow a child with special needs really gets to me. Because children with disabilities may act and learn in a different way, some students, teachers, or parents may look at them in a way that is often demeaning. I have trouble with that. I am constantly educating people about what special education is and is not. We meet students where their needs are and treat them as individuals with dignity and respect, fully capable to be part of the educational process! My role as a special education teacher extends beyond my classroom and influences how I interact not only with other teachers, administrators, and families but even grocery store clerks! I take great responsibility in, and great pleasure from, being a spokesman and advocate for exceptional children.

MyEducationLab™

Visit the **MyEducationLab** for *Exceptional Children* to enhance your understanding of chapter concepts with a personalized Study Plan. You'll also have the opportunity to hone your teaching skills through video- and case-based Assignments and Activities, IRIS Center Resources, and Building Teaching Skills and Dispositions lessons.

CHILDREN LEARN A PHENOMENAL AMOUNT from the moment they are born until they enter school. They grow and develop in orderly, predictable ways, learning to move about their world, communicate, and play. Typical rates and patterns of child development contrast sharply with the progress of many young children with disabilities. If they are to master the basic skills that most children acquire naturally, young children with disabilities need carefully planned and implemented early childhood special education services.

THE IMPORTANCE OF EARLY INTERVENTION

The earlier intervention begins, the better. Burton White, who conducted years of research with typically developing infants and preschoolers at Harvard University's Preschool Project, believes that the period between 8 months and 3 years is critical to cognitive and social development: "to begin to look at a child's educational development when he is 2 years of age is already much too late" (White, 1995, p. 4). If the first years of life are the most important for children without disabilities, they are even more critical for the child with disabilities, who, with each passing month, risks falling even further behind her typically developing age mates.

What Is Early Intervention?

In the early childhood and special education literature, the term *early intervention* often refers only to services provided to infants and toddlers from birth through age 2. *Early childhood special education* refers to educational and related services provided to preschoolers ages 3 to 5. Early intervention consists of a comprehensive system of therapies, educational, nutritional, child care, and family supports, all designed to reduce the effects of disabilities or prevent the occurrence of learning and developmental problems later in life for children presumed to be at risk for such problems (Smith & Guralnick, 2007).

Does Early Intervention Work?

Hundreds of studies have been conducted in an effort to answer that question. We'll look at a few of those studies here. First, we'll consider two of the earliest examples of what Guralnick (1997) calls first-generation research: studies that try to answer the question "Does early intervention make a difference for children and their families?" Then we'll look at two examples of second-generation research studies designed to discover what factors make early intervention more or less effective for particular groups of children.

SKEELS AND DYE The earliest and one of the most dramatic demonstrations of the potential impact of early intervention was conducted by Skeels and Dye (1939). They found that intensive stimulation, one-to-one attention, and a half-morning kindergarten program with 1- to 2-year-old children who were classified as intellectually disabled resulted in IQ gains and eventual independence and success as adults when compared to similar children who received adequate medical and health services but no individual attention. Although the Skeels and Dye study can be justly criticized for its lack of tight experimental methodology, it challenged the widespread belief at the time that intelligence was fixed and that little could be expected from intervention efforts. This study served as the catalyst for many subsequent investigations into the effects of early intervention.

THE MILWAUKEE PROJECT The goal of the Milwaukee Project was to reduce the incidence of intellectual disabilities through a program of parent education and infant stimulation for children considered at risk for developmental delay because of their mothers' levels of intelligence (IQs below 70) and conditions of poverty (Garber & Heber, 1973). The mothers received training in child care and were taught how to interact with and stimulate their children through play. Beginning before the age of 6 months, the children also participated in an infant stimulation program conducted by trained teachers. By the age of 3½, the experimental children tested an average of 33 IQ points higher than did a control group of children who did not participate in the program. (Play is critically important to children's learning and development. See *Teaching & Learning*, "Selecting Toys for Young Children With Disabilities.")

Although the Milwaukee Project was criticized for its research methods (e.g., Page, 1972), this study is sometimes offered as evidence that a program of maternal education and early infant stimulation can reduce the incidence of intellectual disabilities caused by psychosocial disadvantage. Psychosocial disadvantage is a combination of social and environmental deprivation early in a child's life, and it is believed to be a major cause of mild intellectual disabilities.

THE ABECEDARIAN PROJECT The Abecedarian Project is one of the longest-running and most carefully controlled and respected studies on early education ever conducted in the United States. It was an experiment to test whether intellectual disabilities caused by psychosocial disadvantage could be prevented by intensive, early education preschool programs (in conjunction with medical and nutritional

The first years of life are critical for children with disabilities, who, with each passing month, risk falling even further behind their typically developing age mates.

Skeels and Dye study and Milwaukee Project

Council for Exceptional Children

Initial Standards for Special Education Professionals in ECSE: Historical, philosophical foundations, and legal basis of services for infants and young children both with and without exceptional needs (ECSE1K1).

supports) beginning shortly after birth and continuing until children enter kindergarten (Campbell & Ramey, 1994). The 57 children randomly assigned to the experimental group received early intervention that was both intensive and long: full-day preschool, 5 days per week, 50 weeks per year. The 54 children in the control group received supplemental medical, nutritional, and social services, and some attended a child care center, but they received no daily early educational intervention. Outcome measures were taken for both groups at multiple points in time.

By age 3, children in the early intervention group scored higher on IQ tests than did the children in the control group; at age 12, in addition to higher IQ scores, the early intervention participants had achieved better reading and mathematics scores and were 50% less likely to have failed a grade. At the age of 21, 104 of the original 111 infants in the project were measured for cognitive functioning, academic skills, educational attainment, employment, parenthood, and social adjustment. Early intervention participants fared better on every measure (e.g., 35% were attending a 4-year college compared about 14% in the control group). Additionally, mothers of the children who received intensive early intervention were more likely to be employed, had higher levels of education, and held higher-paying jobs than mothers of children in the control group.

THE INFANT HEALTH AND DEVELOPMENT PROGRAM The Infant Health and Development Program (IHDP) provided early intervention services to infants who were born prematurely and at low birth weight (less than 2,500 grams, or about 5½ pounds), two conditions that place children at risk for developmental delays (Ramey et al., 1992). This large-scale study involved nearly 1,000 children and their families in eight locations throughout the United States. Early intervention specialists conducted home visits for newborns through age 3. Because of health problems associated with prematurity and low birth weight, the children did not begin attending the center-based early education program until 12 months of age and continued until age 3. Improvements in intellectual functioning were noted, with babies of comparatively higher birth weight showing increases similar in magnitude to those found in the Abecedarian Project.

The IHDP study found a positive correlation between how much children and their families participated in early intervention and the intellectual development of the children. The percentages of children whose IQ scores fell into the intellectual disabilities range based on tests administered at age 3 for each of the groups were 17% for the control group, 13% for those with low participation, 4% for medium participation, and less than 2% for high participation. The most active participants had an almost ninefold reduction in the incidence of intellectual disabilities compared to the control group and a sixfold reduction compared to low-participation children.

Studies such as the Abecedarian Project and IHDP provide strong evidence that children at risk for developmental delays and poor school outcomes respond favorably to systematic early intervention. They also point to two factors that appear highly related to the outcome effectiveness of early intervention: the *intensity of the intervention* and the *level of participation* by the children and their families (Guralnick & Conlon, 2007).

SUMMARIZING THE RESEARCH BASE Numerous methodological problems make it difficult to conduct early intervention research in a scientifically sound manner. Among the problems are the wide disparity among children in the developmental effects of their disabilities; the tremendous variation across early intervention programs in curriculum focus, teaching strategies, length, and intensity; and the ethical concerns of withholding early intervention from some children so that they may form a control group for comparison purposes (Guralnick, 2005; Hill, Brooks-Gunn, & Waldfogel, 2003).

Despite these problems, most educators agree with Guralnick's (2005) conclusion that on balance, the research evidence shows that comprehensive, experientially based

To see a video of the Abecedarian Project, go to http://www.fpg.unc.edu/~abc/fpg_abc-video.cfm.

The National Early Intervention Longitudinal Study (NEILS) followed a nationally representative sample of 3,338 children between birth and 31 months of age and their families who began early intervention services for the first time from 1997 through 2001. The study provides information about the characteristics of the children and families, the services they received, and the outcomes they experienced in early intervention and into early elementary school. Information about NEILS is available at http://www.sri.com/neils/reports.html.

Selecting Toys for Young Children with Disabilities

John Dewey said, "Children learn by doing." He might just as well have said, "Children learn by playing." Play provides children with natural, repeated opportunities for critical learning. An infant bats at a mobile with her hand, observes the motion, bats at it again, and discovers something about how the world works and her own capabilities in it. As a toddler, her play with objects teaches her to discriminate and compare shapes and sizes and to learn concepts such as cause and effect and fast and slow (Malone & Langone, 1999). A preschooler's increasingly complex play develops gross- and fine-motor skills, requires her to communicate and negotiate plans with others, and exposes her to preacademic math and literacy skills (Barton & Wolery, 2008; DiCarlo & Reid, 2004; Mastrangela, 2009).

If play is the work of childhood, then toys are the child's tools. Play materials, whether store-bought toys or everyday household items such as pots and pans, should provide meaningful, motivating activities that serve as a precursor to more complex learning (Carter, 2006; Hamm, Mistrett, & Goetz Ruffino, 2006). Not all toys, however, are accessible to children with disabilities.

HOW TO GET STARTED

The National Lekotek Center is a nationwide, nonprofit network of play centers, toy lending libraries, and computer loan programs dedicated to making play accessible for children with disabilities and to those living in poverty. Lekotek recommends keeping the following 10 tips in mind when selecting toys for young children with disabilities:

- **Multisensory appeal.** Does the toy respond with lights, sounds, or movements? Are there contrasting colors? Does it have scent? Texture?
- **Method of activation.** Will the toy provide a challenge without frustration? What force is required to activate it? What are the number and complexity of steps required?
- **Adjustability.** Does the toy have adjustable height, sound, volume, speed, and level of difficulty?
- **Opportunities for success.** Can play be open-ended with no definite right or wrong way?
- **Child's individual characteristics.** Does the toy provide activities that reflect both developmental and chronological ages? Does it reflect the child's interests?
- **Self-expression.** Does the toy allow for creativity and choice making? Will it give the child experience with a variety of media?
- **Potential for interaction.** Will the child be an active participant during use? Will the toy encourage social and language engagement with others?

Anthony Magnacca/Merrill

In addition to enhancing the development of infants and toddlers with disabilities, early intervention can help reduce the need for special education and related services after those children reach school age.

early intervention enhances the development of young children who already exhibit delays and helps children who are at risk of developmental delays by preventing those delays entirely or by minimizing their magnitude.

Our national policy makers also believe that early intervention produces positive results for young children with disabilities, those who are at risk for developmental delays, and their families. Citing research and testimony from families, Congress identified the following outcomes for early intervention in the Individuals with Disabilities Education Improvement Act of 2004:

1. to enhance the development of infants and toddlers with disabilities, to minimize their potential for developmental delay, and to recognize the significant brain development that occurs during a child's first 3 years of life;
2. to reduce the educational costs to our society, including our Nation's schools, by minimizing the need for special education and related services after infants and toddlers with disabilities reach school age;

Play provides children with natural, repeated opportunities for critical learning.

- **Safety and durability.** Are the toy and its parts sized appropriately given the child's size and strength? Can it be washed and cleaned? Is it moisture-resistant?
- **Where the toy will be used.** Will the toy be easy to store? Is there space in the home? Can the toy be used in a variety of positions (e.g., by a child lying on his side) or on a wheelchair tray?
- **Current popularity.** Is it a toy almost any child would like? Does it tie in with popular books, TV programs, or movies?

Information on specific toys can be found in Lekotek's Toy Guide for Differently-Abled Kids!, a free resource published in conjunction with Toys 'R' Us® and endorsed by the National Parent Network on Disabilities. The catalog includes pictures and descriptions of more than 100 toys that have been tested with preschoolers with disabilities. Each toy is identified according to its likelihood of promoting growth in 10 developmental or skill areas: auditory, language, visual, tactile, gross motor, fine motor, social skills, self-esteem, creativity, and thinking.

Information about Lekotek and its services to families can be obtained at its website (http://www.lekotek.org). Lekotek also operates a toy resource helpline at (800)366-PLAY, a toll-free service that anyone can use to talk directly to trained play experts who will recommend appropriate toys and play activities for a particular child as well as make referrals to other disability-related resources for families.

3. to maximize the potential for individuals with disabilities to live independently in society;
4. to enhance the capacity of families to meet the special needs of their infants and toddlers with disabilities; and
5. to enhance the capacity of State and local agencies and service providers to identify, evaluate, and meet the needs of all children, particularly minority, low-income, inner city, and rural children, and infants and toddlers in foster care. (PL 108-446, USC 1431, Sec. 631[a])

IDEA AND EARLY INTERVENTION/ EARLY CHILDHOOD SPECIAL EDUCATION

Since 1975, Congress has enacted five bills reauthorizing and amending the original IDEA. The second of those bills, PL 99-457, has been called the most important legislation ever enacted for young children with developmental delays (Shonkoff & Meisels, 2000). Before passage of this law, Congress estimated that states served at most about 70% of preschool children with disabilities, and systematic early intervention services for infants and toddlers with disabilities from birth through age 2 were scarce or nonexistent in many states. PL 99-457 mandated preschool services for children with disabilities ages 3 to 5 and included a voluntary incentive grant program for early intervention services to infants and toddlers and their families.

High-quality early intervention is expensive, but the improved educational, health, and employment outcomes of the recipients can save society the high costs of extended services and care. A benefit-cost analysis of the Abecedarian Project found that every $1 invested in the program yielded a $4 return to society (Masse & Barnett, 2011).

Early Intervention for Infants and Toddlers

If a state chooses to provide comprehensive early intervention services to infants and toddlers and their families, it can receive federal funds under IDEA's early intervention provisions. Currently, all states are participating. Each state receives federal funds under this program based on the number of children birth through age 2 in the state's general population. In 2009–10, approximately 352,000 infants and toddlers were served nationally.

IDEA mandates early intervention services for any child under 3 years of age who

(i) needs early intervention services because of developmental delays, as measured by appropriate diagnostic instruments or procedures, in 1 or more of the areas of cognitive development, physical development, communication development, social or emotional development, or adaptive development; or

(ii) has a diagnosed physical or medical condition that has a high probability of resulting in developmental delay. (PL 108-446, 20 USC 1432, Sec. 632[5])

Thus, states that receive IDEA funds for early intervention services must serve all infants and toddlers with developmental delays or established risk conditions. Each state may also, at its discretion, serve at-risk infants and toddlers "who would be at risk of experiencing a substantial developmental delay if early intervention services were not provided" (PL 108-446, 20 USC 1432, Sec. 632[1]). Although not required to do so, states may also use IDEA funds to provide early intervention services to infants and toddlers who fall under two types of *documented risk,* biological and environmental.

- *Developmental delays* are significant delays or atypical patterns of development that make children eligible for early intervention. Each state's definition of developmental delay must be broad enough to include all disability categories covered by IDEA, but children do not need to be classified or labeled according to those categories to receive early intervention services.
- *Established risk conditions* include diagnosed physical or medical conditions that almost always result in developmental delay or disability. Examples are Down syndrome, fragile X syndrome, fetal alcohol spectrum disorder (FASD), brain or spinal cord damage, sensory impairments, and maternal acquired immune deficiency syndrome (AIDS).
- *Biological risk conditions* include pediatric histories or current biological conditions (e.g., significantly premature birth, low birth weight) that result in a greater than usual probability of developmental delay or disability.
- *Environmental risk conditions* include factors such as extreme poverty, parental substance abuse, homelessness, abuse or neglect, and parental intellectual impairment, which are associated with a higher than normal probability of developmental delay.

INDIVIDUALIZED FAMILY SERVICES PLAN IDEA requires that early intervention services for infants and toddlers be delivered according to an **individualized family services plan (IFSP)** developed by a multidisciplinary team that includes the child's parents and other family members and must include each of the following eight elements:

1. a statement of the infant's or toddler's present levels of physical development, cognitive development, communication development, social or emotional development, and adaptive development, based on objective criteria;

2. a statement of the family's resources, priorities, and concerns relating to enhancing the development of the family's infant or toddler with a disability;

3. a statement of the measurable results or outcomes expected to be achieved for the infant or toddler and the family, including preliteracy and language skills, as developmentally appropriate for the child, and the criteria,

procedures, and timelines used to determine the degree to which progress toward achieving the results or outcomes is being made and whether modifications or revisions of the outcomes or services are necessary;

4. a statement of the specific early intervention services based on peer-reviewed research, to the extent practicable, necessary to meet the unique needs of the infant or toddler and the family, including the frequency, intensity, and method of delivering services;

5. a statement of the natural environments in which early intervention services will appropriately be provided, including a justification of the extent, if any, to which the services will not be provided in a natural environment;

6. the projected dates for initiation of services and the anticipated length, duration, and frequency of services;

7. the identification of the service coordinator from the profession most immediately relevant to the infant's or toddler's or family's needs (or who is otherwise qualified to carry out all applicable responsibilities under this part) who will be responsible for the implementation of the plan and coordination with other agencies and persons, including transition services; and

8. the steps to be taken to support the transition of the toddler with a disability to preschool or other appropriate services. (PL 108-446, 20 USC 1436, Sec. 636[d])

IFSPs differ from IEPs in several important ways. Unlike an IEP, an IFSP

- revolves around the family as the constant and most important factor in the child's life;
- defines the family as the recipient of early intervention services rather than the child alone;
- focuses on the natural environments in which the child and family live, extending the settings in which services can be provided beyond formal settings such as preschools to everyday routines in home and community; and
- includes interventions and services provided by a variety of health and human service agencies in addition to education.

The IFSP must be evaluated once a year and reviewed with the family at 6-month intervals (sooner if requested by the family). Recognizing the critical importance of time for the infant with disabilities, IDEA allows early intervention services to begin before the IFSP is completed if the parents give their consent. Figure 1 shows portions of an IFSP developed with and for the family of a 26-month-old child with disabilities.

Special Education for Preschoolers

IDEA requires states to provide special education services to all children with disabilities ages 3 to 5. The regulations governing these programs are similar to those for school-age children, with the following exceptions:

- Preschool children do not have to be diagnosed with and reported under one of the traditional disability categories (e.g., intellectual disabilities,

IDEA requires states to provide special education to all children with disabilities ages 3 to 5.

Laura Bolesta/Merrill

FIGURE 1 PORTION OF AN IFSP WRITTEN WITH THE FAMILY OF A 26-MONTH-OLD CHILD WITH DISABILITIES

INDIVIDUALIZED FAMILY SERVICE PLAN (IFSP) for Children Birth to Three Years   SANTA CLARA COUNTY

Child's name: _Cathy Rae Wright_   Birth Date: _11-15-09_   Age: _26_ months   Sex: _F_

Parent(s)/Guardian(s): _Martha and Gary Wright_   Address: _1414 Coolidge Drive Cupertino_   Zip: _95014_

Home phone: 408 _398-2461_   Work phone: 408 _554-2490_   Primary language of the home: _English_   Other languages _____

Date of this IFSP _1/15/12_   **Projected periodic review** _7/15/12_   **Projected annual review** _1/15/13_   **Tentative IFSP exit** _11/15/12_
(at 6 months or before)

Service Coordinator Name	Agency	Phone	Date Appointed	Date Ended
Sandy Drohman	Regional Center	408-461-2192	12/10/08	/ /

Family's strengths and preferred resources (With the family, identify the family strengths and the resources they might find helpful in addressing family concerns and priorities.) Mr. and Mrs. Wright are well-educated and constantly seek additional information about Cathy's condition. They are anxious to help Cathy in any way possible. Mrs. Wright's family is very supportive. They provide child care for Cathy's older brother.

Because of Cathy's tendency to be medically fragile, Mr. and Mrs. Wright prefer a home-based early intervention program. They appreciate receiving written materials to help them understand how to work with Cathy. Mrs. Wright wants to be home when the home visitor comes so she can learn from her.

Family's concerns and priorities (With the family, identify major areas of concerns for the child with special needs and the family as a whole.) Mr. and Mrs. Wright are very concerned about Cathy's delays in walking, using her fingers to pick up things, and in talking with other children. They also worry about her small size. Cathy is their second child and was born at 24 weeks gestation. Mr. and Mrs. Wright would like to have more information on the issues of prematurity and they would like to find an appropriate support group for themselves.

CHILD'S STRENGTHS AND PRESENT LEVELS OF DEVELOPMENT

With the family, identify what the child can do and what the child is learning to do. Include family and professional observations in each of the following areas:

PHYSICAL *Based on parent report and HELP Strands

Health _Cathy is said by her parents to be healthy but is very petite. Her parents are working with a nutritionist to help Cathy gain weight._

Vision _Cathy has had corrective surgery for strabismus._

Hearing _She has had numerous ear infections and currently has tubes in her ears._

Gross Motor (large movement) _Cathy stands on tiptoes, runs on toes, makes sharp turns around corners when running, walks upstairs with one hand held_

Fine Motor (small movement) _Cathy grasps crayon adaptively and points with index finger; imitates horizontal strokes, builds 6 block tower, turns pages one at a time; has trouble picking up small objects._

COGNITIVE (responsiveness to environments, problem-solving) _Cathy finds hidden object; attempts and succeeds in activating mechanical toy; demonstrates use of objects appropriate for age_

COMMUNICATION (language and speech)

RECEPTIVE (understanding) _Cathy points to body parts when asked; obeys two-part commands._

EXPRESSIVE (making sounds, talking) _Cathy names 8 pictures, interacts with peers using only gestures; attempts to sing songs with words_

SOCIAL/EMOTIONAL (how relates to others) _Cathy expresses affection, is beginning to obey and respect simple rules, tends to be physically aggressive_

ADAPTIVE/SELF-HELP (sleeping, eating, dressing, toileting, etc.) _Cathy can put on socks and shoes, verbalizes need to use the toilet, but is not potty trained, feeds self_

DIAGNOSIS (if known) _____

(continued)

FIGURE 1 *continued*

INDIVIDUALIZED FAMILY SERVICE PLAN (IFSP) for Children Birth to Three Years   SANTA CLARA COUNTY

Child's name: *Cathy Rae Wright*

IFSP OUTCOMES
With the family, identify the goals they would like to work on in the next six months.
These should be directly related to the family's priorities and concerns as stated on page one.

OUTCOME: *Cathy will increase her attempts to vocally communicate in order to make her needs known and to positively interact with others.*

Strategy or activity to achieve the outcome	Service Type (Individual = **I** Group = **G**) Location	Frequency of sessions / Length of each session	Start Date	End Date (anticipated)	Responsible Agency/ Group Including payment arrangements (if any)
(Who will do what and when will they do it?) AIM Infant Educator will model for Mr. and Mrs. Wright techniques to solicit Cathy's vocalization efforts. **Criteria** (How will we know if we are making progress?) Increased vocalization will be observed by parents and infant educator.	**I** — Home-based infant program	1 hour each week	1-23-12	11-10-12	AIM (funded by SARC) Family
(Who will do what and when will they do it?) Mrs. Wright will take Cathy to play with neighborhood children and will invite children to her home. She will encourage play and vocalization. **Criteria** (How will we know if we are making progress?) Mrs. Wright will observe and note extent of interaction.	**G** — Home and in the neighborhood	once each week for at least 30 minutes	2-1-12	ongoing	Mrs. Wright
(Who will do what and when will they do it?) Cathy will be assessed by a speech pathologist by 2-15-12 and followed on an as needed basis. **Criteria** (How will we know if we are making progress?) A follow-up report will be submitted.	**I** — Regional Center Speech and Language Clinic	1 hour play-based assessment	2-15-12	as needed	Sandy Drohman will make arrange-ments (funded by SARC)

OUTCOME: *Mr. and Mrs. Wright will join Parents Helping Parents in order to receive peer parent support and learn more about Cathy's condition.*

Strategy or activity to achieve the outcome	Service Type / Location	Frequency / Length	Start Date	End Date	Responsible Agency/ Group
(Who will do what and when will they do it?) Sandy Drohman will provide all referral information to Mr. and Mrs. Wright and will accompany them to their first meeting if they desire. **Criteria** (How will we know if we are making progress?) Mr. and Mrs. Wright will find satisfaction in increased support and knowledge.	**G** — Parents Helping Parents	(up to parents' discretion)			Sandy Drohman Mr. and Mrs. Wright Parents Helping Parents
(Who will do what and when will they do it?) AIM Infant Educator will assist Mr. and Mrs. Wright in obtaining additional information about Cathy's condition. **Criteria** (How will we know if we are making progress?) Mr. and Mrs. Wright will express satisfaction over the assistance received in becoming more informed.	**I** — Home	ongoing	2-1-12	11-10-12	AIM Infant Educator

Source: Adapted figure from ADAPTING EARLY CHILDHOOD CURRICULA FOR CHILDREN WITH SPECIAL NEEDS by Ruth E. Cook, Diane M. Klein and Annette Tessier, 7th Ed. Copyright © 2008 by Cook, Klein and Tessier. Reprinted by permission of Pearson Education, Inc., Upper Saddle River, NJ.

emotional disturbance, orthopedic impairments) to receive services. They may instead receive services under the eligibility category developmental delay.

- Each state, at its discretion, may also serve children from ages 3 through 9 under the developmental disability category who are

  a. experiencing developmental delays as defined by the State and as measured by appropriate diagnostic instruments and procedures in 1 or more of the following areas: physical development, cognitive development, communication development, social or emotional development, or adaptive development; and
  b. who, by reason thereof, need special education and related services. (PL 108-446, 20 USC 1401, Sec. 602[3][B][I])

- IEPs for preschoolers must include a section with suggestions and information for parents.
- Local education agencies may elect to use a variety of service delivery options (home-based, center-based, or combination programs), and the length of the school day and year may vary.
- The state education agency must administer preschool special education programs, but it may contract services from other agencies to meet the requirement of a full range of services. For example, many preschoolers with disabilities are served in community-based Head Start programs.

SCREENING, IDENTIFICATION, AND ASSESSMENT

Assessment and evaluation in early childhood education are conducted for at least four different purposes, with specific evaluation tools for each (Bagnato, Neisworth, & Pretti-Frontczak, 2010; Elliott, Huai, & Roach, 2007; Pool & Hourcade, 2011):

- *Screening.* Quick, easy-to-administer tests to identify children who may have a disability and who should receive further testing
- *Diagnosis.* In-depth, comprehensive assessment of all major areas of development to determine a child's eligibility for early intervention or special education services
- *Program planning.* Curriculum-based, criterion-referenced assessments to determine a child's current skill level, identify IFSP/IEP objectives, and plan intervention activities
- *Evaluation.* Curriculum-based, criterion-referenced measures to determine progress on IFSP/IEP objectives and evaluate program effectiveness

Screening Tools

Before young children and their families can be served, the children must be identified. Some children's disabilities are so significant that no test is needed. As a general rule, the more severe a disability, the earlier it is detected. In the delivery room, medical staff can identify certain physical disabilities and health impairments, such as microcephaly and cleft palate, as well as most instances of Down syndrome. Within the first few weeks, other physical conditions such as paralysis, seizures, or rapidly increasing head size can signal possible disabilities. But most children who experience developmental delays are not identifiable by obvious physical characteristics or behavioral patterns, especially at very young ages. That is where screening comes into play.

THE APGAR SCALE The Apgar scale, which measures the degree of *asphyxia* (oxygen deprivation) an infant experiences during birth, is administered to virtually all babies born in U.S. hospitals. The test administrator—nurse, nurse anesthetist, or pediatrician—evaluates the newborn twice on five physiological measures: heart rate, respiratory effort, response to stimulation, muscle tone, and skin color. The child is

FIGURE 2   THE APGAR EVALUATION SCALE

			60 sec.	5 min.
Heart rate	Absent Less than 100 100 to 140	(0) (1) (2)	1	2
Respiratory effort	Apneic Shallow, irregular Lusty cry and breathing	(0) (1) (2)	1	1
Response to catheter stimulation	No response Grimace Cough or sneeze	(0) (1) (2)	1	2
Muscle tone	Flaccid Some flexion of extremities Flexion resisting extension	(0) (1) (2)	1	2
Color	Pale, blue Body pink, extremities blue Pink all over	(0) (1) (2)	0	1
	Total		4	8

given a score of 0, 1, or 2 on each measure according to the criteria described on the scoring form (see Figure 2).

The first administration of the test, which is conducted 60 seconds after birth, measures how the baby fared during the birth process. If the newborn receives a low score, the delivery room staff takes immediate resuscitation action. The scale is given again 5 minutes after birth. At that point a total score of 0 to 3 (out of a possible 10) indicates severe asphyxia, 4 to 6 moderate asphyxia, and 7 to 10 mild asphyxia. Some stress is assumed on all births, and the 5-minute score measures the success of any resuscitation efforts. A 5-minute score of 6 or less indicates follow-up assessment to determine what is causing the problem and what interventions may be needed. The Apgar has been shown to identify high-risk infants—those with a greater than normal chance of developing later problems. Research has shown that oxygen deprivation at birth contributes to neurological impairment, and the 5-minute Apgar score correlates well with eventual neurological outcomes.

NEWBORN BLOOD TEST SCREENING   Some form of newborn screening is mandated in all states, but the components of the newborn screen vary from state to state. Phenylketonuria (PKU) is screened in all states. It causes severe intellectual disabilities, which can be easily prevented if the condition is detected before symptoms develop and the child is treated with a special diet. Testing is also done for *hypothyroidism*, which can likewise lead to intellectual disabilities if not detected early. Affected individuals are treated with supplemental thyroid hormone.

The American College of Medical Genetics (2004) submitted a report to the federal Health Resources and Services Administration identifying national standards for state newborn screening programs. The report identified a core of 29 conditions that screening should target, plus an additional 25 "secondary" conditions for which test results should be reported. States may also screen for conditions beyond the 54. Today, all states and the District of Columbia have newborn screening programs, but the conditions screened for vary across states (U.S. Department of Health and Human Services, 2011).

Screening tests require a few small drops of blood collected from each newborn, usually taken in the hospital 24 to 48 hours after birth. This is done by a heel stick and

More information is available from the National Newborn Screening and Genetics Resource Center at http://genes-r-us .uthscsa.edu/.

spotting a few small drops of blood on a paper card, which is then sent for laboratory analysis that can test for as many as 30 congenital conditions or diseases that can lead to physical and health problems, sensory impairments, and/or developmental delays. Other common testing includes (but is not limited to) biotinidase deficiency, congenital adrenal hyperplasia, congenital hypothyroidism, cystic fibrosis, sickle cell diseases, maple syrup urine disease, and galactosemia and hemoglobinopathy (diseases of the red blood cells).

DEVELOPMENTAL SCREENING TESTS A widely used screening test for developmental delays is the Denver II (Frankenburg & Dodds, 1990). It can be used with children from 2 weeks to 6 years of age, using both testing–observation and a parent report format. The Denver II assesses 125 skills arranged in four developmental areas: gross motor, fine motor–adaptive, language, and personal-social. Each test item is represented on the scoring form by a bar showing at what ages 25%, 50%, 75%, and 90% of typically developing children can perform that skill. The child is allowed up to three trials per item. A child's performance on each item is scored as "pass" or "fail" and then interpreted as representing "advanced," "OK," "caution," or "delayed" performance by comparing the child's performance with those of the same age in the standardized population. Physicians most often administer the Denver II, and the test form was designed to fit the schedule of well-baby visits recommended by the American Academy of Pediatrics.

Help Me Grow is list of developmental milestones for children ages 3 months to 5 years and some things that their families can do to help developed by the Minnesota Department of Health. It can be obtained at http://www.health.state .mn.us/divs/fh/mcshn/pdfd ocs/wheel.pdf.

No one observes a child more often, more closely, and with more interest than his parents. Mothers' estimates of their preschool children's levels of development often correlate highly with those that professionals produce by using standardized scales, and parental involvement in screening has been found to reduce the number of misclassifications (Henderson & Meisels, 1994). Recognizing this fact, early childhood specialists have developed numerous screening tools for parent use. One such tool is the Ages and Stages Questionnaires (ASQ-3) (Squires & Bricker, 2009). The ASQ includes 11 questionnaires that the parents complete when the child is 4, 6, 8, 12, 16, 18, 20, 24, 30, 36, and 48 months old. Each questionnaire consists of 30 items covering 5 areas of development: gross motor, fine motor, communication, personal-social, and adaptive. Many of the items include illustrations to help the parents evaluate their child's behavior.

Diagnostic Tools

Assessment of developmental domains

Council for Exceptional Children

Content Standards for Beginning Teachers—Initial Common Core: Use and limitations of assessment instruments (ICC8K4).

When the results of a screening test raise suspicion of disability or developmental delay, the child is referred for diagnostic testing. The specific diagnostic tests to be used depend on the suspected delay or disability. Tests designed to determine presence and extent of a developmental delay usually measure performance in five major developmental areas or domains:

- *Motor development*. The ability to move one's body and manipulate objects within the environment provides a critical foundation for all types of learning. Motor development involves improvements in strength, flexibility, endurance, and eye–hand coordination and includes gross-motor movement and mobility (e.g., walking, running, throwing) and fine-motor control (e.g., pick up a toy, tie a shoe).
- *Cognitive development*. Children use cognitive skills when they sort or count objects, remember things they have done in the past, plan and make decisions about what they will do in the future, integrate newly learned information with previously learned knowledge and skills, solve problems, and generate novel ideas.
- *Communication and language development*. Children use communication and language skills when they receive information from others, share information with others, and use language to effectively control the environment. This domain encompasses all forms of communicative development, including the ability to respond nonverbally with gestures, smiles, or actions and the acquisition of spoken language—sounds, words, phrases, sentences, and so on.

- *Social and emotional development.* Children who have developed competence in social skills share toys and take turns, cooperate with others, and resolve conflicts. Children should feel good about themselves and know how to express their emotions and feelings.
- *Adaptive development.* Learning self-care and adaptive skills such as dressing/undressing, eating, toileting, tooth brushing, and hand washing, enable young children to function independently across multiple environments, which provides and enhances opportunities for additional kinds of learning.

Generally, these five areas are broken down into specific, observable tasks and sequenced developmentally—that is, in the order in which most children learn them. Sometimes each task is tied to a specific age at which the majority of typically developing children can perform it. This arrangement allows the examiner to note significant delays or gaps as well as other unusual patterns in a child's development. These developmental domains are not mutually exclusive; considerable overlap exists between domains as well as across skills within a specific domain. Most activities of children in everyday settings involve skills from multiple domains. For example, playing marbles typically requires a child to use skills from the motor, cognitive, communication, and social domains.

Two widely used tests for diagnosing developmental delays are the Battelle Developmental Inventory (BDI-2) (Newborg, 2006) and the Bayley Scales of Infant and Toddler Development—III (Bayley, 2005). The Battelle can be administered to children with and without disabilities, from birth through age 7 years, 11 months; and it has adapted testing procedures for use with children with different disabilities. The Bayley III evaluates development in cognition, language, social-emotional motor, and adaptive behavior in infants and toddlers from 1 to 42 months.

The Bayley Scales can be used to diagnose developmental delays in children from 2 months to 30 months.

© Laura Dwight/PhotoEdit

Program Planning and Evaluation Tools

A growing number of early intervention programs have moved away from assessments based entirely on developmental milestones to curriculum-based assessment (CBA) (Grisham-Brown & Pretti-Frontczak, 2011). CBA tools enable early childhood teams to (a) identify a child's current levels of functioning, (b) select IFSP/IEP goals and objectives, (c) determine the most appropriate interventions, and (d) evaluate the child's progress. Each item in a CBA relates directly to a skill in the program's curriculum, thereby providing a direct link among testing, teaching, and progress evaluation (Bagnato et al., 2010).

One empirically tested CBA tool is the Assessment, Evaluation, and Programming System: For Infants and Young Children (AEPS) (Bricker, 2002). The AEPS is divided into two levels: one for infants and toddlers from birth to 3 years, one for children from 3 to 6 years. The AEPS is divided into six areas of development: fine motor, gross motor, adaptive, cognitive, social-communication, and social. Each domain is divided into strands that group related behaviors and skills considered essential for infants and young children to function independently. The AEPS can be used in conjunction with the associated AEPS curricula (Bricker & Waddell, 2002a, 2002b) or with other similar early childhood curricula such as the Carolina Curriculum for Preschoolers with Special Needs (Johnson-Martin, Attermeier, & Hacker, 2004a, 2004b).

Curriculum-based assessment in ECSE

 Council for Exceptional Children Initial Standards for Special Education Professionals in ECSE: Conduct ongoing formative child, family, and setting assessments to monitor instructional effectiveness (ECSE8S11).

CURRICULUM AND INSTRUCTION IN EARLY CHILDHOOD SPECIAL EDUCATION

Curriculum and Program Goals

Goals for ECSE

 Initial Standards for Special Education Professionals in ECSE: Involve the individual and family in setting instructional goals and monitoring progress (ICC7S3).

Most professionals in early childhood special education agree that programs should be designed and evaluated with respect to the following outcomes or goals (Cook, Klein, & Chen, Tessier, 2012; Odom & Wolery, 2003; Pretti-Frontczak & Bricker, 2004; Sandall, Hemmeter, Smith, & McLean, 2005; Wolery & Sainato, 1996):

- *Support families in achieving their own goals.* Although the child with special needs is undoubtedly the focal point, a major function of early intervention is helping families achieve the goals most important to them. Families function as a system, and separating the child from the system results in limited and fragmented outcomes (Trivette, Dunst, & Hamby, 2010).

- *Promote maximum child independence and mastery.* Early childhood special education seeks to minimize the extent to which children depend on others and differ from their age-mates. To achieve that goal, intervention strategies should promote active engagement, initiative and autonomy (choice making, self-directed behavior), and self-sufficiency with age-appropriate tasks in many typical routines and situations (Wolery & Sainato, 1993). In situations in which independence is not safe, possible, or practical, support and assistance should be provided to enable the child to participate as much as she can.

- *Promote development in all important domains.* Successful early intervention programs help children make progress in each of the developmental areas already described. Because young children with disabilities are already behind their typically developing age mates, early childhood special educators should use only instructional strategies that lead to rapid learning. Strategies that produce rapid learning move the child closer to typical developmental levels and free up time to work on other goals.

- *Build and support social competence.* Social skills, such as learning to get along with others and making friends, are among the most important skills anyone can learn. Most children learn such skills naturally, but many children with disabilities do not learn to interact effectively and properly simply by playing with others.

- *Facilitate the generalization of learned skills.* Most typically developing children effortlessly generalize what they learn in one situation to another place and time. But many children with disabilities have extreme difficulty remembering and using previously learned skills in other situations.

- *Prepare and assist children for typical life experiences with their families, in school, and in their communities.* Early intervention should be characterized by the principle of normalization; that is, services should be provided in settings that are as much like the typical settings in which young children without disabilities play and learn as is possible. A large and growing body of published research demonstrates the benefits of inclusive practices for children with disabilities and their families and suggests strategies for effective inclusion programs (Grisham-Brown, Hemmeter, & Pretti-Frontczak, 2005; Odom, 2000; Purcell, Horn, & Palmer, 2007; Sandall & Schwartz, 2008).

- *Help children and their families make smooth transitions.* A transition occurs when a child and his family

Early childhood preschool programs should promote children's development in all important domains.

© Bill Aron/PhotoEdit

move from one early intervention program or service delivery mode to another. For example, program transitions typically occur at age 3 when a child with disabilities moves from a home-based program to an early childhood special education classroom and again at age 5 when the child moves from a preschool classroom to a general education kindergarten classroom. Preparing and assisting children and their families for smooth transitions ensures continuity of services, minimizes disruptions to the family system, and is another important way for promoting the success of young children with disabilities as they move into more normalized environments (Brandes, Ormsbee, & Haring, 2007; Hanson et al., 2000). Cooperative planning and supports for transitions must come from professionals in both the sending and the receiving programs (Epley et al., 2010; Rous & Hallam, 2006).

- *Prevent or minimize the development of future problems or disabilities.* Early intervention programs that serve at-risk infants and toddlers are designed with prevention as their primary goal.

Developmentally Appropriate Practice

Virtually all early childhood educators—whether they work with typically developing children and/or those with special needs—believe that learning environments, teaching practices, and other components of programs serving young children should be based on what is typically expected of and experienced by children of different ages and developmental stages (Cook et al., 2012; Howard, Williams, & Lepper, 2012; Morrison, 2012; Jalongo & Isenberg, 2012). **Developmentally appropriate practice (DAP)** is a philosophy and set of practice guidelines based on that belief. According to the National Association for the Education of Young Children (NAEYC, 2011a), "DAP is a framework of principles and guidelines that outline practice that promotes young children's *optimal* learning and development."

DAP rests on core principles that early childhood educators should consider in their decision making (NAEYC, 2011b):

- *Knowledge must inform decision making.* Practitioners must know (a) about child development and learning, (b) about each child as an individual, and (c) about the social and cultural contexts each child lives in.
- *Goals must be challenging and achievable.* Meeting children where they are is essential, but no good teacher simply leaves them there. Learning and development are most likely to occur when new experiences build on what a child already knows and is able to do and when those experiences also entail the child stretching a reasonable amount in acquiring new skills, abilities, or knowledge.
- *Teaching must be intentional to be effective.* Good teachers are intentional in everything they do—setting up the classroom, planning curriculum, making use of various teaching strategies, assessing children, interacting with them, and working with their families.

While most early childhood special educators view the DAP guidelines as the foundation on which to provide early intervention, they also recognize that specially designed, individualized instruction (i.e., special education) is necessary to properly serve young children with disabilities and their families (Cook et al., 2012; Noonan & McCormick, 2006; Odom & Wolery, 2003). Researchers and practitioners in early childhood special education have developed effective methods for incorporating instruction aimed at children's IFSP/IEP goals into the context of the typical play and preschool activities of young children. For example, preschoolers often enjoy sociodramatic play with make-believe objects and stuffed animals (McDevitt & Ormrod, 2010). Early childhood special educators have shown how stuffed animals and puppets can help children acquire IEP goals and objectives (e.g., Michael, Meese, Keith, & Mathews, 2009; Salmon & Sainato, 2005). To learn how puppets can help preschoolers with disabilities learn language skills, see *Teaching & Learning*, "Using Puppets in the Early Childhood Classroom."

A joint position statement by CEC's Division for Early Childhood and the National Association for the Education of Young Children on the value of inclusion and how it can be used to improve early childhood services can be found at http://community. fpg.unc.edu/resources/ articles/Early_Childhood_ Inclusion.

Developmentally appropriate practice

Initial Standards for Special Education Professionals in ECSE: Plan, implement, and evaluate developmentally appropriate curricula, instruction, and adaptations based on knowledge of individual children, the family, and the community (ECSE4S1).

TEACHING & LEARNING

Using Puppets in the Early Childhood Classroom

BY MARY D. SALMON, STACIE MCCONNELL, DIANE M. SAINATO, AND REBECCA MORRISON

Early childhood educators promote active engagement, independence, and mastery across developmental domains for all children by providing a rich variety of experiences, materials, and ideas. Puppets can be effective tools for presenting activities that are engaging, interesting, and developmentally appropriate for the wide range of abilities of young children in early childhood settings (Salmon & Sainato, 2005).

Most young children are delighted by puppets. Their vivid colors, interesting textures, and larger-than-life expressions encourage curiosity and heighten attention levels among typically developing children as well as children with a range of developmental disabilities. A puppet's physical characteristics, overstated smiles or frowns, and motivational value make it a valuable prop for use with many young children. With this knowledge, we can put puppets to instructional use in inclusive early childhood classrooms.

USING PUPPETS DURING CIRCLE TIME

Circle time is important in the preschool day because it introduces activities and provides a time for review. Introducing new concepts and skills, while reinforcing previously learned material, requires upbeat, appropriately paced, and highly interactive instructional strategies. One way to incorporate these strategies and add dimension and excitement to circle time is by embedding the actions of a variety of puppets into songs, stories, or games.

USING PUPPETS DURING TRANSITION TIMES

Like circle time, transition times in the preschool classroom can be chaotic, noisy, disruptive, or difficult for some young children. A puppet may help the teacher signal transitions between classroom activities, making them smoother and less stressful for students and teacher alike.

USING PUPPETS TO ENHANCE SOCIAL AND EMOTIONAL SKILLS

Young children frequently have difficulty expressing their emotions and interpreting the feelings of others. When paired with social stories and role-play activities, the exaggerated facial features of many character puppets make them especially well suited to modeling appropriate emotions. The actions of the puppets' large hands and feet may encourage an unwilling youngster to imitate their movement. Puppets can also help children match their own experiences with language, teach them to be an attentive audience, as well as help them develop more elaborate sociodramatic and symbolic play.

Carl Harris/Merrill

Puppets can help children express their feelings and learn to empathize with others.

Selecting IFSP/IEP Goals and Objectives

IFSP/IEP goals and objectives

Council for Exceptional Children

Initial Standards for Special Education Professionals in ECSE: Plan and implement developmentally and individually appropriate curriculum (ECSE7S2).

The breadth of developmental domains and the activities that young children typically engage in provide an almost unlimited number of possibilities for instructional objectives. Early childhood special educators can judge the value of potential IFSP/IEP goals and objectives according to five quality indicators (e.g., Notari-Syverson & Shuster, 1995; Pretti-Frontczak & Bricker, 2000):

1. *Functionality.* A functional skill (a) increases the child's ability to interact with people and objects in her daily environment and (b) may have to be performed by someone else if the child cannot do it.
2. *Generality.* In this context, a skill has generality if it (a) represents a general concept as opposed to a particular task; (b) can be adapted and modified to meet

FINDING RESOURCES

A wide variety of puppets are available from many sources to stimulate the interest and active engagement of young students. Entertaining, engaging puppets such as glove or stick puppets, finger puppets, and sock puppets are quickly adapted for uncomplicated use by younger students or students with special needs.

HOW TO GET STARTED

Circle Time

- **Calendar helper.** The teacher or a child can be the puppeteer, leading the class during calendar time.
- **Weather helper.** Dress a large, full-bodied puppet in child-sized clothing to reinforce weather concepts. Spice up his wardrobe with a variety of hats, sunglasses, and mittens as well as attire appropriate for all types of weather.
- **Rule bunny.** Teaching classroom rules is an important and ongoing process. To increase impact, designate a puppet to teach these common procedures: "Rule Bunny says, 'Play nicely with your friends,' or 'Put materials away neatly.'"
- **Other activities.** Puppets can read stories, sing songs, play "Simon Says," and model a variety of motor skills.

Transitions

- **Transition prompter.** To signal transition times, a puppet can shake a bell or ring a chime to indicate when it is time to clean up or move to the next activity.
- **Attention getter.** Using a puppet to lead the way to the next activity can capture the attention of a busy (and noisy) group of youngsters.
- **Transition helper.** Classroom helpers can take turns using a puppet to ready the class for special activities. Line leaders can guide the class to the library, gym, music, or art class, using a puppet to improve group attention.
- **Clean-up time.** Puppets can model appropriate clean-up behaviors such as placing blocks in a bin or putting away art materials.

Sociodramatic Play and Social Skills

- Assume different roles, such as police officer or firefighter, with simple hand puppets and a few accessories (e.g., hats, badges).
- Puppets representing familiar adults can be made by printing photos of faces onto transfer paper using a computer and an inkjet printer. Iron the pictures onto simple hand puppets made from durable fabric, and embellish the body with fabric markers or paint.
- Many characters from favorite books are available as puppets. Children can act out their favorite story and become any character they wish.
- Combine favorite stories with representative puppets to teach appropriate social behaviors. For example, use *Rainbow Fish* by Marcus Pfister to teach sharing.

Dealing with Emotions

- Puppets can make emotions "larger than life." Use them to demonstrate appropriate emotional responses while watching or acting out short skits.
- A child may be more inclined to express her feelings through a puppet. Teachers can also talk through a puppet to discuss appropriate classroom expectations and behavior.
- Help children solve simple problems by using puppets in role-play activities.

About the Authors

Mary Salmon coordinates the REACH program for children with autism spectrum disorders in the Columbus, Ohio, City Schools. An avid puppet collector, she was an early childhood special education teacher for more than 15 years. Stacie McConnell teaches in an early childhood special needs preschool classroom in Reynoldsburg, Ohio. Diane Sainato is a member of the special education faculty at The Ohio State University, where she directs the program in early childhood special education and conducts research on young children's independent engagement, social, and communicative behavior. Rebecca Morrison is the founder and director of Oakstone Academy and The Children's Center for Development Enrichment in Columbus.

the child's disability; and (c) can be used across different settings, with various materials, and with different people.

3. *Instructional context.* The skill should be easily integrated into the child's daily routines and taught in a meaningful way that represents naturalistic use of the skill.

4. *Measurability.* A skill is measurable if its performance or a product produced by its performance can be seen, felt, and/or heard. Measurable skills can be counted or timed and enable objective determination of learning progress.

5. *Hierarchical relation between long-range goals and short-term objectives.* Short-term objectives should be hierarchically related; the achievement of short-term objectives should contribute directly to the attainment of long-term goals.

Figure 3 shows 11 questions that teachers can use to assess potential IFSP/IEP objectives according to those five criteria.

FIGURE 3 FIVE CRITERIA FOR EVALUATING IEP/IFSP OBJECTIVES FOR INFANTS, TODDLERS, AND PRESCHOOLERS WITH DISABILITIES

FUNCTIONALITY	GENERALITY	INSTRUCTIONAL CONTEXT	MEASURABILITY	HIERARCHICAL RELATION BETWEEN LONG-RANGE GOAL AND SHORT-TERM OBJECTIVE
1. Will the skill increase the child's ability to interact with people and objects within the daily environment? The child needs to perform the skill in all or most of the environments in which he or she interacts. *Skill:* Places object into container. *Opportunities:* Home—Places sweater in drawer, cookie in paper bag. School—Places lunch box in cubbyhole, trash in trash bin. Community—Places milk carton in grocery cart, rocks and soil in flower pot. **2. Will the skill have to be performed by someone else if the child cannot do it?** The skill is a behavior or event that is critical for completion of daily routines. *Skill:* Looks for object in usual location. *Opportunities:* Finds coat on coat rack, gets food from cupboard.	**3. Does the skill represent a general concept or class of responses?** The skill emphasizes a generic process, rather than a particular instance. *Skill:* Fits objects into defined spaces. *Opportunities:* Home—Puts mail in mailbox, places crayon in box, puts cutlery into sorter. **4. Can the skill be adapted or modified for a variety of disabling conditions?** The child's sensory impairment should interfere as little as possible with the performance. *Skill:* Correctly activates simple toy. *Opportunities:* Motor impairments—Activates light, easy-to-move toys (e.g., balls, rocking horse, toys on wheels, roly-poly toys). Visual impairments: Activates large, bright, noise-making toys (e.g., bells, drums, large rattles). **5. Can the skill be generalized across a variety of settings, materials, and/or people?** The child can perform the skill with interesting materials and in meaningful situations. *Skill:* Manipulates two small objects simultaneously. *Opportunities:* Home—Builds with small interlocking blocks, threads laces on shoes. School—Sharpens pencil with pencil sharpener. Community—Takes coin out of small wallet.	**6. Can the skill be taught in a way that reflects the manner in which the skill will be used in daily environments?** The skill can occur in a naturalistic manner. *Skill:* Uses object to obtain another object. *Opportunities:* Uses fork to obtain food, broom to rake toy; steps on stool to reach toy on shelf. **7. Can the skill be elicited easily by the teacher/parent within classroom/home activities?** The skill can be initiated easily by the child as part of daily routines. *Skill:* Stacks objects. *Opportunities:* Stacks books, cups/plates, wooden logs.	**8. Can the skill be seen and/or heard?** Different observers must be able to identify the same behavior. *Measurable skill:* Gains attention and refers to object, person, and/or event. *Nonmeasurable skill:* Experiences a sense of self-importance. **9. Can the skill be directly counted (e.g., by frequency, duration, distance measures)?** The skill represents a well-defined behavior or activity. *Measurable skill:* Grasps pea-sized object. *Nonmeasurable skill:* Has mobility in all fingers. **10. Does the skill contain or lend itself to determination of performance criteria?** The extent and/or degree of accuracy of the skill can be evaluated. *Measurable skill:* Follows one-step directions with contextual cues. *Nonmeasurable skill:* Will increase receptive language skills.	**11. Is the short-term objective a developmental subskill or step thought to be critical to the achievement of the long-range goal?** *Appropriate:* Short-Term Objective—Releases object with each hand. Long-Range Goal—Places and releases object balanced on top of another object. *Inappropriate:* 1. The Short-Term Objective is a restatement of the same skill as the Long-Range Goal, with the addition of an instructional prompt (e.g., Short-Term Objective—Activates mechanical toy with physical prompt. Long-Range Goal—Independently activates mechanical toy) or a quantitative limitation to the extent of the skill (e.g., Short-Term Objective—Stacks 5 1-inch blocks; Long-Range-Goal—Stacks 10 1-inch blocks). 2. The Short-Term Objective is not conceptually or functionally related to the Long-Range Goal (e.g., Short-Term Objective—Releases object voluntarily; Long-Range Goal—Pokes with index finger).

Source: Adapted from Notari-Syverson, A. R., & Shuster, S. L. (1995). Putting real-life skills into IEP/IFSPs for infants and young children. *Teaching Exceptional Children, 27*(2), 31. Used by permission.

Instructional Adaptations and Modifications

Providing specialized instruction to "remediate delays caused by the child's disabilities and prevent any secondary disabilities from developing" is the cornerstone of what early childhood special educators do (Sandall, Schwartz, & Joseph, 2000, p. 3). Like their colleagues who work with school-age students with disabilities, teachers who work with young children with disabilities must be skilled in using a wide range of instructional strategies and tactics.

Modifications and adaptations of the physical environment, materials, and activities are often sufficient to support successful participation and learning. Such modifications range from subtle, virtually invisible supports (e.g., changing the duration or sequence of activities, using a child's preferences as a conversation topic while playing) to more obvious interventions and support (e.g., providing the child with an adaptive device, teaching peers to prompt and reward participation) (Sandall et al., 2000). The challenge is determining how much support a child needs for a given skill in a specific context. Too much support may lead to overreliance on adult help; too little support may result in frustration, reduced participation, and increased frequency of challenging behavior (Sandall et al., 2000).

EMBEDDED LEARNING OPPORTUNITIES One effective method for incorporating intentional instruction into typical preschool activities is called **embedded learning opportunities.** The concept is based on the premise that although quality early childhood programs offer opportunities for learning across the day, many children with disabilities need guidance and support to learn from those opportunities (Barton & Wolery, 2010; Horn, Lieber, Li, Sandall, & Schwartz, 2000; Tate, Thompson, & McKerchar, 2005). Therefore, teachers should look and plan for ways to embed brief, systematic instructional interactions that focus on a child's IEP objectives in the context of naturally occurring classroom activities. Figure 4 shows a teacher's plan for embedding learning opportunities into four different activity centers to support an IEP objective in the fine-motor domain for a 4-year-old boy with cerebral palsy.

Embedding learning opportunities to support the development of communication and language skills is an especially important teaching responsibility for an early childhood special educator. Many children with disabilities do not acquire language in the spontaneous manner of their peers without disabilities. And as children with disabilities slip further and further behind their peers, their language deficits make social and academic development even more difficult. Preschoolers with disabilities need repeated opportunities for language use and development (Goldstein, 2002; Justice, 2004). In addition to providing systematic, explicit instruction of language skills to children in individual and small-group learning activities, teachers should embed meaningful opportunities for children to communicate throughout the day. Even transitions between activities can provide opportunities for learning (Wolery, Anthony, & Heckathorn, 1998).

A creative and effective example of embedding language learning opportunities into mealtimes was reported by Robinson Spohn, Timko, and Sainato (1999). Each child was seated at the table in front of a placemat showing a picture of a food item, a cartoon character, an animal, and something silly (e.g., a cat wearing glasses and reading a book) (see Figure 5). Twelve different placemats were used in the study, and each child sat before a different one each day. At first, the teacher played "The Talking Game" with the children while they ate breakfast in the school lunchroom. The children took turns picking an index card from a shuffled set of cards. Each card had a photo of one of the children in

Modifying and adapting the physical environment

 Initial Standards for Special Education Professionals in ECSE: Select, develop, and evaluate developmentally and functionally appropriate materials, equipments, and environments (ECSE5S1) (also (EC5S2 and CC5K1).

For an annotated bibliography of research and teacher resources on naturalistic teaching methods featuring embedded learning opportunities and activities-based interventions for young children with and without disabilities, see Pretti-Frontczak, Barr, Macy, and Carter (2003).

Embedded learning opportunities

 Initial Standards for Special Education Professionals in ECSE: Embed learning opportunities in everyday routines, relationships, activities, and places (ECSE5S23).

Effective early childhood special educators are experts at embedding learning opportunities in the context of naturally occurring classroom activities.

Lori Whitley/Merrill

FIGURE 4 EXAMPLE OF A PLAN FOR EMBEDDING LEARNING
OPPORTUNITIES INTO FOUR DIFFERENT ACTIVITY
CENTERS TO SUPPORT A CHILD'S IEP OBJECTIVE
IN THE FINE-MOTOR DOMAIN

Embedded Learning Opportunities at a Glance for: _Alex_

Objective: _Will pour liquid or other fluid material (e.g., sand, beans) from one_
container to another with no spillage.

Date: _8/14_   Activity: _Center Time_
Material: _All centers available_

Modifications Needed:	What are you going to do?
—Water table: add a variety of containers with spouts (e.g., plastic measuring cups, teapot, play pitcher)	Move through center modeling use of these new activities/materials. Provide physical guidance for Alex
—Snack Center: Add to Alex's workjob pouring juice for other children	What are you going to say? Use natural cues— Let's see you do it. Can you do it and get all the beans in the pot?
—Art Center: Place tempera paint in small pitcher, have children pour into individual bowls	How will you respond? Praise, acknowledgment, feedback on accuracy Engagement in activity created
—Housekeeping: Add beans to kitchen cabinet in a small pitcher for pouring into pots, cups or plates	What materials do you need? Need to be prepared with clean-up supplies for spills—(see under modifications)

Source: "Supporting Young Children's IEP Goals in Inclusive Settings Through Embedded Learning Opportunities" by E. Horn, J. Lieber, S. Li, S. Sandall, & I. Schwartz, 2000. *Topics in Early Childhood Education, 20,* 208–223. Copyright 2000 by the Hammill Institute on Disability. Reprinted with permission.

the group. After a child selected a card, the teacher prompted him to say something to the child pictured on the card. If the child could not think of anything to say, the teacher prompted him to talk about one of the pictures on his placemat. After several weeks, the teacher no longer used the index cards and stopped prompting the children's interactions. The children continued talking with one another during mealtimes at rates higher than they had before, often using the pictures on their placemats as conversation starters.

Preschool Activity Schedules

Teachers in preschool programs for children with disabilities face the challenge of organizing the program day into a schedule that meets each child's individual learning needs and provides children with many opportunities to explore the environment and

---

Preschool activity schedules

 Council for Exceptional Children

Content Standards for Beginning Teachers— Initial Common Core: Demands of learning environments (ICC5K1) (also ECSE5S3).

FIGURE 5

A PLACEMAT USED TO ENCOURAGE PRESCHOOLERS WITH DEVELOPMENTAL DISABILITIES TO COMMUNICATE WITH ONE ANOTHER DURING MEALTIME

Source: Courtesy of Diane M. Sainato, The Ohio State University.

communicate with others throughout the day. The schedule should include a balance of child-initiated and planned activities, large- and small-group activities, active and quiet times, and indoor and outdoor activities; it should allow easy transition from activity to activity (Cook et al., 2012). In short, the schedule should provide a framework for maximizing children's opportunities to develop new skills and practice what they have learned while remaining manageable and flexible (Pretti-Frontczak & Bricker, 2004). In addition, how activities are scheduled and organized has considerable effect on the frequency and type of interaction that occurs between children with and without disabilities (Harris & Handleman, 2008) and on the extent to which children with disabilities benefit from instructional activities.

A Supportive Physical Environment

The physical arrangement of the classroom must support the planned activities. Designing an effective preschool classroom requires thoughtful planning to ensure that play areas and needed materials are accessible to and safe for all students, boundaries between areas minimize distractions, and, most important, the environment makes children want to explore and play. Suggestions for setting up a preschool classroom include the following (Cook et al., 2012; Johnson-Martin et al., 2004b; Morrison, 2012; Pretti-Frontczak & Bricker 2004):

- Organize the classroom into a number of different well-defined areas to accommodate different kinds of activities (e.g., quiet play, messy play, dramatic play, constructive play, active play).
- Locate quiet activities together, away from avenues of traffic, and loud activities together.

Physical arrangement of preschool classroom

 Council for Exceptional Children — Initial Standards for Special Education Professionals in ECSE: Organize space, time, materials, peers, and adults to maximize progress in natural and structured environments (EC5S2) (also ICC5S4).

- Equip each area with abundant, appropriate materials that are desirable to children.
- Locate materials where children can easily retrieve them and do not depend on adults.
- Have an open area, perhaps a large rug, to conduct large-group activities such as circle time and story reading.
- Label or color code all storage areas so that aides and volunteers can easily find needed materials.
- Arrange equipment and group areas so that students can move easily from one activity to another. Apply pictures or color codes to various work areas.
- Provide lockers or cubbies for students so they know where to find their belongings. Again, add picture cues to help students identify their lockers.

SERVICE DELIVERY ALTERNATIVES FOR EARLY INTERVENTION

Early intervention services are delivered in a variety of settings, depending on the age of the child and the type and intensity of supports she and her family need. Hospitals are frequently the setting for early intervention services for infants and newborns with significant disabilities. Most early childhood special education services, however, are provided in the child's home, in a center- or school-based facility, or in a combination of both settings. Young children with mild developmental delays are often served by itinerant special education teachers in general education preschool settings (Sadler, 2003).

Hospital-Based Programs

Low-birth-weight and other high-risk newborns who require specialized health care are placed in neonatal intensive care units (NICUs). NICUs include a variety of professionals, such as neonatologists who provide medical care for infants with special needs, nurses who provide ongoing medical assistance, psychologists and social workers who help parents and families with emotional and financial concerns, and infant education specialists who promote interactions between parents and infants.

Home-Based Programs

Home-based programs are built around family involvement and support. The parents typically assume primary responsibility as caregivers and teachers for their child with disabilities. They are usually supported by an early intervention specialist who visits the home regularly. Home visitors (or home teachers or home advisors, as they are often called in some programs) are specially trained paraprofessionals. They may visit as frequently as several times a week but probably no less than a few times a month. They sometimes carry the results of their in-home evaluations back to supervisors, who may recommend changes in the program.

One of the best-known and most widely replicated home-based programs, the Portage Project, was begun in 1969 by a consortium of 23 school districts in south-central Wisconsin (Portage Project, 2011). A project teacher typically visits the home one day each week to review the child's progress during the previous week, describe activities for the upcoming week, demonstrate to the parents how to carry out activities with the child, observe parents and children interacting, offer suggestions and advice as needed, summarize where the program stands, and indicate what records parents should keep during the next week. The Portage Project has produced its own assessment materials, curriculum guides, and teaching activities. The New Portage Guide: Birth to Six, contains descriptions, resources, and supporting materials for 364 activities/routines sequenced developmentally and classified into self-help, cognition, socialization, language, and motor skills.

To learn more about the Portage Project, go to www.portageproject.org.

Home-based early intervention programs have several advantages:

- The home is the child's natural environment, and parents can often give more time and attention to the child than even the most adequately staffed center or school.
- Other family members, such as siblings and grandparents, have more opportunity to interact with the child during instruction and socially. These significant others can play an important role in the child's growth and development.
- Home learning activities and materials are more likely to be natural and appropriate.
- Parents who are actively involved in helping their child learn and develop have an advantage over parents who feel guilt, frustration, or defeat at their seeming inability to help their child.
- Home-based programs can be less costly to operate.

Home-based programs, however, can have disadvantages:

- Because home-based programs place so much responsibility on parents, they are not effective with all families. Not all parents are able or willing to spend the time required to teach their children, and some who try are not effective teachers.
- A large and growing number of young children do not reside in the traditional two-parent family—especially children with teenage mothers who are single, un-educated, and poor. It is unlikely that a young mother struggling with the realities of day-to-day survival will be able to meet the added demands of involvement in a home-based early intervention program (Turnbull et al., 2011).
- Children in home-based programs may not receive as wide a range of services as they would in a center-based program, where they can be seen by a variety of professionals. (Note, however, that the services of professionals such as physical therapists, occupational therapists, and speech-language therapists are sometimes provided in the home.)
- The child may not receive sufficient opportunities for social interaction with peers.

Center-Based Programs

Center-based programs provide early intervention services in a special educational setting outside the home. The setting may be part of a hospital complex, a special day care center, or a preschool. Some centers provide a wide range of services for children with varying types and degrees of disabilities, combining services of professionals from several different fields.

Center-based programs encourage social interaction among children, and many integrate children with disabilities and typically developing children in day care or preschool classes. Some children attend a center each weekday for all or most of the day; others may come less frequently, although most centers expect to see each child at least once a week. Parents may participate as classroom aides or be encouraged to act as their child's primary teacher. Most centers offer parent education programs (some programs require parents to attend training sessions). Virtually all effective programs for young children with disabilities recognize the critical need to involve parents, and they welcome parents in every aspect of the program.

Center-based programs generally offer four advantages that are difficult to build into home-based efforts:

- A team of specialists from different fields has an increased opportunity to directly observe each child and collaborate in planning, implementing, and evaluating the effectiveness of interventions.
- The intensive instruction and related services that can be provided in a center-based program are especially important for children with severe disabilities.
- The opportunity for interaction with typically developing peers makes center programs especially effective for some children.
- Most parents involved in center programs feel some relief at the support they get from the professionals who work with their child and from other parents with children at the same center.

Differences between home-based, center-based, and combined programs

Content Standards for Beginning Teachers—Initial Common Core: Family systems and the role of families in supporting development (ICC2K4) (also ICC5K1).

LifeSpan Circle Schools in Charlotte, North Carolina, teach parents to identify and increase the frequency of positive behaviors by their infants, such as smiling or imitating.

Disadvantages of center-based programs include the expense of transportation, the cost and maintenance of the center itself, and the possibility of less direct parent involvement than in home-based programs.

Combined Home–Center Programs

Many early intervention programs combine center-based activities and home visitation. Few center programs take children for more than a few hours a day or more than 5 days per week. But because young children with disabilities require more intervention than a few hours a day, many programs combine the intensive help of a variety of professionals in a center with the continuous attention and care of parents at home. Coordinated intervention carried out in both home and center environments offers many of the advantages of the two types of programs and negates some of their disadvantages.

LifeSpan Circle Schools in North Carolina offer a combination home- and center-based early intervention program for infants and toddlers with severe/profound disabilities. The program is based on the social reciprocity model, which views the child's behavior as affecting the parent, whose behavior in turn affects the behavior of the child—hence the "circle" in the program's name. Nonresponsiveness, nonvocal behavior, irritability, lack of imitation responses, and the need for special health care routines (e.g., tube feeding, suctioning) all present special challenges to infant–parent interactions; behaviors associated with these problems are often viewed negatively. The program attempts to identify and increase the frequency of alternative positive behaviors that will cause parents to want to continue their interactions with their child (Calhoun & Kuczera, 1996; Calhoun, Rose, Hanft, & Sturkey, 1991). The center-based component consists of classroom instruction from 9:00 a.m. to 1:00 p.m. throughout the year. The home-based/family-services component entails monthly home visits that include family-focused assessment and planning, demonstrations of instructional techniques, and provision of information and other support. Between regularly scheduled home visits, ongoing individualized consultation and collaboration with parents and families are available as needed.

Families: Most Important of All

The success of efforts to prevent disabilities in children and to identify, assess, and intervene with children who have special needs as early as possible requires the training, experience, and cooperation of a wide range of professionals. Current best-practice guidelines for early childhood services call for a transdisciplinary approach to the delivery of related services in which parents and professionals work together to assess needs, develop the IFSP or IEP, provide services, and evaluate outcomes (Horn, Ostrosky, & Jones, 2004; Howard et al., 2010).

Of all the people needed to make early intervention work, parents and families are the most important. Given enough information and support, parents can help prevent many risks and causes of disabilities—before pregnancy, before birth, and certainly before a child has gone months or years without help. Given the chance and support, parents can take an active role in determining their children's educational needs and goals. And given some guidance, training, and support, many parents can teach their children at home and even at school.

It is no wonder, then, that all successful intervention programs for young children with disabilities take great care to involve parents. Parents are the most frequent and constant observers of their children's behavior. They usually know better than anyone else what their children need, and they can help educators set realistic goals. They can report on events in the home that outsiders might never see—for instance, how a child responds to other family members. They can monitor and report on their children's progress at home, beyond the more controlled environment of the early intervention center or preschool. In short, parents can contribute to their children's programs at every stage—assessment, planning, classroom activities, and evaluation. Many parents even work in preschool classrooms as teacher aides, volunteers, or other staff members.

But in our efforts to involve parents, we must recognize that while professionals come and go, parents and families are in it for the long haul. In their focus to help young children attain critical developmental gains, it is easy for early childhood professionals to overlook that parents are just beginning a lifetime of commitment and responsibility.

As Hutinger, Marshall, and McCarten (1983) aptly reminded us 30 years ago, we must not forget that early childhood is supposed to be a fun, happy time for children and for the adults who are fortunate enough to work with them.

> Part of our mission as professionals in the field of early childhood special education is to possess an art of enjoyment ourselves and to help instill it in the young children and families with whom we work.
>
> Early childhood comes but once in a lifetime.... Let's make it count!

▼ TIPS FOR BEGINNING TEACHERS

Early Childhood Special Education

BY MARK FRALEY

CREATE AN ENVIRONMENT THAT'S RESPONSIVE AND PREDICTABLE FOR EVERYONE

- Make a poster of your daily routine with pictures, icons, and words your students can understand. Refer to your schedule to help. Transitions can be challenging times for young children, and a visual reference of what is going to happen next can guide them to more independent functioning. Some students benefit from a individualized visual schedule they can carry with them.
- Create a master schedule showing what activities everyone in your classroom, professionals and children, should be doing during each time period of the day. One matrix hanging on my classroom wall indicates the roles that I and every member of the teaching team—my instructional assistants, the speech-language pathologist, PTs, and OTs—are to assume throughout the day (e.g., who will be lead teacher, who is responsible for collecting child performance data).
- Another matrix makes it easy for parents and classroom volunteers to quickly see what's going on and how they might help.
- Posting your plans and intentions in this way reduces the chance of conflicts with staff or parents over misunderstandings of who was supposed to be doing what with whom when. When a conflict occurs or if there is breakdown in the way services are delivered, the master schedule can be a reference tool to review and troubleshoot.

USE THESE THREE TEACHING TACTICS

- **Put yourself on the child's level.** If a child is on the floor playing with building blocks, I sit on the floor and simply join her. This shows I value her as a person and respect what she has to say or contribute. Once I am at the student's level, I will follow her lead. By allowing students to self-direct their learning to a certain degree, it is easy to find what they are interested in and plan activities that incorporate these things.
- **Don't ask too many questions during play.** Asking questions is not only intrusive to play, it changes my role from cooperative play partner to test giver. How much fun is it to play with a test giver? Not much! Instead, I'll make comments like a sports broadcaster: "I see you are building a green tower with long rectangle blocks. It is very tall!" Many of my students have communication delays, and providing a vocabulary-rich environment with opportunities to hear and say words and sentences builds social-communicative skills.
- **Let students make and learn from their mistakes.** I used to get upset when my students responded incorrectly or took too long to complete a task. I have to remember that young children, and especially those with developmental disabilities, need many, many opportunities to master a skill. Allowing room for mistakes gives them a chance to try another strategy or method. It is fun as teacher to make a mistake in front of students, such as

trying to put the wrong lid on a bin during clean-up. Your students will see this and step in to help or guide you as you have taught them through problem solving. Making mistakes can also encourage more communication opportunities as they will need to request items or identify the problem.

COLLECT DATA FROM MULTIPLE SOURCES

All teachers should collect data to assess student learning and evaluate their teaching. For special education teachers, direct and frequent measurement of student progress on IEP goals and objectives is not just good practice; it is required by law. The data I gather in my classroom shed light onto what skills are beginning to emerge and how I can help support these developing skills through thoughtfully planned activities and lessons. Over the years I have learned the value of obtaining data from a wide variety of sources

and how to do so efficiently. Here are a few of those approaches:

- Keeping counts of important student behaviors with tally marks on a piece of masking tape placed on my leg or shirt
- Marking the number, type, and prompt level of responses by students in various activities on specifically designed data sheets kept in a clipboard next to each classroom center or activity area
- Writing anecdotal observations of student accomplishments on note cards kept in a folder beside my desk
- Taking digital photos throughout the day of where students spend their time and how they are interacting with peers
- Photocopying coloring pages or other student products before sending them home with the student
- Taking videos of my circle time and other instructional activities group times to review my teaching and their performance

▼ KEY TERMS AND CONCEPTS

developmentally appropriate practice (DAP)
embedded learning opportunities

individualized family services
plan (IFSP)

▼ SUMMARY

The Importance of Early Intervention

- Early intervention consists of educational, nutritional, child care, and family supports designed to reduce the effects of disabilities or prevent the occurrence of developmental problems later in life for children at risk for such problems.
- Research has documented that early intervention can provide both intermediate and long-term benefits for young children with disabilities and those at risk for developmental delay. Benefits of early intervention include the following:
  - Gains in physical development, cognitive development, language and speech development, social competence, and self-help skills
  - Prevention of secondary disabilities
  - Reduction of family stress
  - Reduced need for special education services or placement during the school year
  - Savings to society of the costs of additional educational and social services that would be needed later without early intervention
  - Reduced likelihood of social dependence in adulthood
  - Increased effectiveness of early intervention when it begins as early in life as possible and is intensive and long-lasting

IDEA and Early Childhood Special Education

- States that receive IDEA funds for early intervention services must serve all infants and toddlers birth to age 3 with developmental delays or established risk conditions. At their discretion, states may serve infants and toddlers who are at risk for acquiring disabilities because of certain biological or environmental risk conditions.
- Early intervention services for infants and toddlers are family centered, transdisciplinary, and described by IFSPs.
- IDEA requires states to provide special education services (via IEPs) to all preschool children with disabilities, ages 3 through 5.
- Preschool children do not have to be identified and reported under disability categories to receive services.

Screening, Identification, and Assessment

- Four major types of assessment purposes/tools are used in early childhood special education:
  - Screening involves quick, easy-to-administer tests to identify children who may have a disability and who should receive further testing.
  - Diagnosis requires in-depth, comprehensive assessment of all major areas of development to determine a child's eligibility for early intervention or special education services.

- Program planning uses curriculum-based, criterion-referenced assessments to determine a child's current skill level, identify IFSP/IEP objectives, and plan intervention activities.
- Evaluation uses curriculum-based, criterion-referenced measures to determine progress on IFSP/IEP objectives and evaluate a program's effects.
- Many early intervention programs are moving away from assessments based entirely on developmental milestones and are incorporating curriculum-based assessment, in which each item relates directly to a skill included in the program's curriculum. This provides a direct link among testing, teaching, and program evaluation.

Curriculum and Instruction in Early Childhood Special Education

- Early intervention and education programs for children with special needs should be designed and evaluated according to these outcomes or goals:
  - Support families in achieving their own goals
  - Promote child engagement, independence, and mastery
  - Promote development in all important domains
  - Build and support social competence
  - Facilitate the generalized use of skills
  - Prepare for and assist children with normalized life experiences in their families, schools, and communities
  - Help children and their families make smooth transitions
  - Prevent or minimize the development of future problems or disabilities
- Developmentally appropriate practices provide a foundation or context from which to build individualized programs of support and instruction for children with special needs.
- IEP/IFSP objectives for infants and young children should be evaluated according to their functionality, generality, instructional context, measurability, and relation between short- and long-range goals.
- Embedded learning opportunities are brief, systematic instructional interactions that focus on a child's IEP objectives in the context of naturally occurring classroom activities. They are an effective method for incorporating specialized instruction into typical preschool activities.

- A preschool activity schedule should maximize children's opportunities to develop new skills and practice what they have learned previously while remaining manageable and flexible.
- How activities are scheduled and organized affects the interaction between children with and without disabilities.
- Suggestions for setting up a preschool classroom include the following:
  - Organize the classroom into different, well-defined areas to accommodate different kinds of activities.
  - Locate quiet activities together, away from avenues of traffic, and locate loud activities together.
  - Equip each area with appropriate and desirable materials.
  - Locate materials where children can retrieve them without help from adults.
  - Have an open area to conduct large-group activities.
  - Label or color code all storage areas.
  - Arrange equipment and group areas so that students can move easily from one activity to another.
  - Provide lockers or cubbies for students.

Service Delivery Alternatives for Early Intervention

- In hospital-based programs, early intervention services are provided to low-birth-weight and other high-risk newborns in neonatal intensive care units (NICUs).
- In home-based programs, a child's parents act as the primary teachers, with regular training and guidance from a teacher or specially trained paraprofessional who visits the home.
- In center-based programs, a child comes to the center for instruction, although the parents are usually involved. Center programs allow a team of specialists to work with the child and enable the child to meet and interact with other children.
- Many programs offer the advantages of both models by combining home visits with center-based programming.
- Parents and families are the most important people in an early intervention program. They can act as advocates, participate in educational planning, observe their children's behavior, help set realistic goals, work in the classroom, and teach their children at home.

MyEducationLab™

Go to Topic 19, Early Intervention, in the MyEducationLab (www.myeducationlab.com) for *Exceptional Children*, where you can

- Find learning outcomes for early intervention along with the national standards that connect to these outcomes.
- Complete Assignments and Activities that can help you more deeply understand the chapter content.
- Apply and practice your understanding of the core teaching skills identified in the chapter with the Building Teaching Skills and Dispositions learning units.
- Examine challenging situations and cases presented in the IRIS Center Resources.
- Access video clips of CCSSO National Teachers of the Year award winners responding to the question "Why do I teach?" in the Teacher Talk section.
- Check your comprehension of the content covered in the chapter with the Study Plan. Here you will be able to take a chapter quiz, receive feedback on your answers, and then access Review, Practice, and Enrichment activities to enhance your understanding of chapter content.
- Use the Online Lesson Plan Builder to practice lesson planning and integrating national and state standards into your planning.

▼ GLOSSARY

developmentally appropriate practice (DAP): A philosophy and guidelines for practice based on the belief that the learning environments, teaching practices, and other components of programs that serve young children should be based on educators' typical expectations and children's experiences for children of different ages and developmental stages.

embedded learning opportunities: Incorporating intentional instruction into typical preschool activities by embedding brief, systematic instructional interactions that focus on a child's IEP objectives in the context of naturally occurring classroom activities.

individualized family services plan (IFSP): A requirement of the Individuals with Disabilities Education Act for the coordination of early intervention services for infants and toddlers with disabilities from birth to age 3. Similar to the individualized education program (IEP), which is required for all school-age children with disabilities.

Transitioning to Adulthood

Transitioning to Adulthood

► FOCUS QUESTIONS

- Why should postschool outcomes drive educational programming for secondary students with disabilities?
- What key factors influence the success of an individualized transition plan?
- How can teachers of elementary students with disabilities help them prepare for successful life as adults?
- Why is self-determination so important to the success of students with disabilities in postsecondary education?

- How do the philosophy and principles of supported living differ from traditional residential placement services?
- How can teachers help school-age children with disabilities achieve satisfying recreation and leisure as adults?
- Is quality of life for adults with disabilities the ultimate outcome measure for special education? Why or why not?

▼ FEATURED TEACHER

BRADLEY BAUMGARTNER

East Anchorage High School • Anchorage, Alaska

EDUCATION—TEACHING CREDENTIALS—EXPERIENCE

- B.A. English, University of Iowa, 2001; B.S. Special Education/Cross-Categorical, University of Wisconsin–Stout, 2006
- 5 years as a job coach and personal support provider for individuals with disabilities
- 2 years as grade 9–12 resource and collaborative teacher; 2 years as a life skills special educator

CURRENT TEACHING ROLE AND STUDENTS

I came to be a special educator through the experiences I gained working with individuals at their agency-supported job sites and group homes. When I began teaching, I was immediately interested in postschool goals and transition plans. As a job coach and personal care provider, I came equipped with the knowledge of the options that are available to many individuals with cognitive disabilities. My two teaching assistants and I currently work with 17 students who receive special education and transition services for a wide variety of disabilities: mild to moderate intellectual disabilities, autism, emotional-behavior disorder, attention-deficit/hyperactivity, fetal alcohol syndrome, and physical impairments. The goal of our life skills program has always been to strike a balance between the academic goals of high school and the very real problem-solving and necessary vocational skill sets that

will enrich a student's life beyond school.

GOING BEYOND THE CLASSROOM TO LEARN LIFE LESSONS The

activities most valued by the students are community-based work and recreation experience. Most of the students participate in our school's Partners Club, which connects students with disabilities to those without disabilities through athletics and social outings. Student volunteers and students from our program run an espresso shop that is open daily before school. The machine and much of the equipment were obtained through fund-raising and a school business partnership with a local coffee purveyor. The local business teaches our students how to make and serve espresso, maintain the machines, and use customer service skills. Each morning, our classroom is open to the students and staff of our school to buy coffee, muffins, and granola bars. Students deliver coffee to staff throughout the building. Not only does the Partners Espresso shop help the club fund-raise for community outings; it makes our classroom and students a positive hub for socialization, cooperation, and camaraderie.

After the morning rush, students settle in for 2 to 3 hours of instruction focusing on basic communication skills, money skills, and reading. After lunch, while

11th and 12th graders are at community-based job sites, the 9th and 10th graders clean the kitchen, wrap muffins, count out and deposit the day's receipts, and prepare the espresso shop for business the next morning. Because the work experiences, student connections, and funds raised are real, students see the positive results of working hard and are quick to buy in to the process.

The program works well because it empowers the students to be the stakeholders in the social, athletic, and community events in which we take part. Throughout the life of the program, students have traveled to the Special Olympics National Games, state and regional athletic competitions, in addition to skiing at an adaptive ski school three times a year.

The combination of real work, social, and recreational opportunities that are available to our students is quite amazing. I was lucky to come to a life skills education program that had been established by an unbelievably creative, bright, and dedicated veteran teacher and leader. I feel that I'm a good fit for this program because I have seen both the positive and the negative aspects of vocational, social, and living arrangements beyond school. I'm lucky to have the opportunity to work with these students on a daily basis at skills such as self-care, personal responsibility, and self-advocacy so that they will have the skills to participate to the greatest extent in every opportunity life has to offer them.

CHALLENGES TO TRANSITION TO ADULTHOOD

One of the most important things I do as a teacher of transition-age students is highlighting those moments that provide opportunities to build critical thinking and problem-solving skills. Many of our students' lives are so routine driven that when a problem arises, they don't feel capable of solving it independently. That's when I tell them to step back and brainstorm ways they might solve the problem. When given the chance and responsibility to solve problems for themselves, students soon realize how important it is to possess certain knowledge and skills—for example, knowing their phone number, reading a bus schedule, leaving a message for an employer or friend, and so on.

I believe it's important to allow students to experience the natural consequences of some of their choices or preparation, especially when they are capable of showing those independence skills. Lessons such as "If you don't have your bus pass, you can't go to the lunch

outing with us" sound so simple, but I've noticed that students are more likely to take personal responsibility seriously when the consequences are real. When natural consequences are rarely enforced, students are often quite happy to let everyone else take care of their problems. Sometimes, it can be hard to stay out of the situation, but students often learn more as a result. Of course, all of us need a little help at times, which is why we teach lessons about how to communicate effectively to supervisors, parents, and community helpers.

All my 9th and 10th graders have jobs within school. When they turn 16, they are placed in a community job site for 1-hour shifts twice a week. The vocational experience is ripe with opportunity to practice those aforementioned critical thinking skills. It's a big moment when a student begins to understand that work does come first. One of my students was shocked recently when I told her that attending a pep assembly wasn't a valid excuse for missing her shift at the job site. A big lesson the teacher assistants and I try to instill is that having a job requires planning your social activities around it. This idea is a whole new concept to most high school students, let alone those with significant cognitive disabilities. The work experience give students opportunities to interact with their employers, practice communication skills, and solve their own problems. Of course we'll be there to help when we're truly needed, but I am a big believer in letting students attempt to problem-solve on their own first. In many cases, community work experience is the first opportunity they've had to encounter natural consequences, learn from their mistakes, and achieve success and a paycheck.

Mr. Baumgartner shared his experiences during the 2009–10 school year on the, Council for Exceptional Children's blog for new teachers, Reality 101. To learn more about Brad and his perspectives on special education, go to http://www.cecreality101.org/meet-brad.html.

MyEducationLab™

Visit the **MyEducationLab** for *Exceptional Children* to enhance your understanding of chapter concepts with a personalized Study Plan. You'll also have the opportunity to hone your teaching skills through video- and case-based Assignments and Activities, IRIS Center Resources, and Building Teaching Skills and Dispositions lessons.

WHAT DOES IT MEAN TO BECOME AN ADULT? Ferguson and Ferguson (2011) suggest that adulthood is expressed through autonomy, membership, and change. Adults express autonomy by self-sufficiency (e.g., having the financial and emotional resources to take care of themselves), self-determination, and completeness (a sense of having "arrived"). Adults experience and enjoy membership in the form of connectedness with the community, citizenship activities, and affiliations. Adulthood is characterized by change: moving to a new community, going back to school, taking a new job, watching old friends move away, and making new friends.

Transitioning from high school to the increased privileges and responsibilities of adulthood, while difficult for most young people, is especially challenging for youth with disabilities. Skill deficits, limited opportunities created by low expectations or discrimination, and the absence of needed supports are just some of the obstacles to successful transition faced by many youth with disabilities.

HOW DO FORMER SPECIAL EDUCATION STUDENTS FARE AS ADULTS?

What happens to students with disabilities when they leave high school and enter the adult world? Do they find work? Where do they live? How do the lives of adults with disabilities compare with the expectations and experiences of most citizens?

Obtaining answers to such questions has become one of the highest priorities in special education today. More than 75 studies of graduates and leavers of secondary special education programs provide enlightening information on their experiences as young adults. The largest and most comprehensive studies of the adult adjustment of youth with disabilities after they leave secondary special education programs are the two National Longitudinal Transition Studies (NLTS1 and NLTS2) funded by the U.S. Office of Special Education Programs. NLTS1 assessed and monitored changes in the lives of 8,000 youths with disabilities who left U.S. secondary special education programs between 1985 and 1987. The recently completed NLTS2 was a 10-year study of the experiences of a nationally representative sample of more than 11,000 youth with disabilities who were in at least seventh grade and receiving special education services in the 2000–01 school year, as they moved from secondary school into adult roles.

A detailed description and results of the NLTS2 can be found at http://www.nlts2.org.

High School Completion

Students who do not complete high school are likely to face more difficulties in adult adjustment than are those who do. Special education students who do not complete high school face lower levels of employment and wages, reduced access to postsecondary education and training opportunities, higher rates of problems with the criminal justice system, and less overall satisfaction with life in general (Holub & Rusch, 2008; Wagner, Newman, Cameto, Garza, & Levine, 2005). Parents interviewed from NLTS2 (2005) indicated that 72% of youth with disabilities completed high school by receiving either a regular diploma or a certificate of completion or similar document. Major differences were found in high school completion rates by disability, ranging from a high of 95% of high school students with visual impairment to 56% of students with behavioral disorders and emotional disturbance.

Studies have reported school dropout rates for secondary students with disabilities ranging from 28% (NLTS2) to "a staggering" 37.6%, more than twice that of peers without disabilities (Pacer Center, 2006). Dropout rates vary considerably by disability type, ranging from about 17% for students with autism and visual impairments to 61% for students with emotional or behavioral disorders (U.S. Department of Education, 2006).

Results of the NLTS

 Knowledge and Skill Base for Beginning Special Education Transition Specialists: Research on relationships between individual outcomes and transition practices (TS3K2).

Employment

The NLTS2 found that 57% of youth with disabilities were working for pay outside the home during the first 4 years after leaving high school, compared to a 66% employment

© James Shaffer/PhotoEdit

Judah's after-school job gives him a sense of autonomy and connectedness with the community.

rate among same-age youth in the general population (Newman, Wagner, Cameto, & Knokey, 2009). Employment outside the home by students with disabilities who had completed high school (received a diploma or certification of completion) was 61% versus 41% for noncompleters. The three most common types of jobs held by youth with disabilities were food service (17%), skilled laborer (11%), and cashier (10%).

Slightly more than half (58%) of young adults with disabilities who are employed have full-time jobs. Youth with disabilities out of high school 1 to 4 years earned an average hourly wage of $8.20, compared to $9.20 per hour earned by youth in the general population. Only 44% of working youth with disabilities receive any employment benefits such as health insurance, sick leave, paid vacation, or health benefits.

The Bureau of Labor Statistics (2010) reported that just 18% of individuals with disabilities of working age were employed versus 64% of individuals without disabilities. Adults with intellectual, developmental, or severe disabilities are even less likely to be employed. Exceedingly high unemployment rates for individuals with disabilities are a major factor for the persistently high poverty rates for adults with disabilities, especially those with severe disabilities (Hughes & Avoke, 2010; Lindstrom, Doren, & Miesch, 2011). A nationwide survey of Americans with disabilities aged 18 to 64 found three times as many people with disabilities living in poverty compared with those who do not have disabilities (26% vs. 9%) (Kessler Foundation/National Organization on Disability, 2010).

Postsecondary Education

Attending college and postsecondary vocational programs greatly increases the likelihood of employment and generally experiencing success as an adult and raises earning potential, even for those who have not earned a degree (Marcotte, Bailey, Borkoski, & Kienzel, 2005). NLTS2 found that 45% of youth with disabilities had at some time been enrolled in a postsecondary education program since leaving high school 1 to 4 years earlier, compared to 41% of youth without disabilities.

At the time of the interview, 24% of the NLTS2 participants were enrolled in a postsecondary school program, compared to a current enrollment rate of 41% by their peers in the general population. Enrollment in postsecondary programs by NLTS2 participants at some point since leaving high school varied widely by disability category, ranging from 78% of students with visual impairment to 27% of students with intellectual disabilities.

Community Involvement: Positive and Negative

Successful adulthood involves much more than holding a job; it includes becoming an independent and active member of society. Independence for an adult includes the ability to participate in society, work, have a home, raise a family, and share the joys and responsibilities of community life (Ferguson & Ferguson, 2011). Adults with disabilities face numerous obstacles in day-to-day living that affect where and how they live, how well they can use community resources, and what opportunities they have for social interaction.

Just one-half (49%) of young adults in the NLTS2 had participated in some type of community social activity outside work or school in the preceding year, from lessons or classes outside school (22%) and a volunteer community service activity (25%), to a community group of some kind (31%). As with other postschool outcome measures, community participation varied greatly by disability, ranging from 82% of youth with visual impairments having taken part in at least one social activity to 28% of students with intellectual disabilities.

Young adults with disabilities are involved with the criminal justice system at a higher rate than same-age peers without disabilities. Overall 28% of out-of-high-school youth in NLTS2 had been arrested at some time, a rate more than twice that of youth in the general population (12%). The percentage of out-of-high-school youth who had been arrested ranged across disability categories, from a high of 62% of youth with emotional and behavioral disorders to 3% with orthopedic impairments.

The postschool outcomes summarized here represent improvements over measures obtained by earlier studies (e.g., NLTS1). That's the good news. The bad is that far too many youth with disabilities leave high school to discover to their dismay and discouragement that "the fiscal and logistical demands of daily life [are] far more complex than what they learned in functional math, home-economics, or life skills classes . . . [and that the] protective nature of their experiences in special education had left them ill-prepared for the real world" (Knoll & Wheeler, 2005, pp. 502–503). And it is not just students with major cognitive limitations or severe physical, sensory, or behavioral disabilities who have trouble adjusting to life after high school. Former special education students with high-incidence disabilities face significant challenges in every aspect of adult life (Carter, Trainer, Sun, & Owens, 2009; Johnson, Mallard, & Lancaster, 2007).

It is clear that many secondary students and recent school leavers do not view themselves as ready for adulthood. Only about 60% of youth with disabilities ages 15–19 who participated in the NLTS2 reported that they thought of themselves as being able to handle challenges or feeling "useful and important" (Wagner et al., 2007).

IDEA AND TRANSITION SERVICES

Congress first authorized funding for secondary education and transitional services for youth with disabilities when it amended IDEA in 1983 (PL 98–199). In 1984, Madeleine Will, director of the U.S. Office of Special Education and Rehabilitation Services, proposed a model of transition services that encompassed three levels of service, each conceptualized as a bridge between the secondary special education curriculum and adult employment (Will, 1986). Each level—generic, time limited, and ongoing support—differed in the nature and extent of the services an individual with disabilities needs to make a successful transition from school to work.

While Will's "bridges model" of school-to-work transition showed that the federal government recognized the need to improve employment outcomes for special education students, many special educators thought that its perspective on transition was too limited. Halpern (1985) wrote that it is a mistake to focus on adult employment as the sole purpose and outcome of transition services: "Living successfully in one's community should be the primary target of transitional services" (p. 480). Halpern proposed a transition model that directed Will's generic, time-limited, and ongoing support services toward helping students with disabilities adjust to adult life in the community in three domains: (a) quality of residential environment, (b) adequacy of social and interpersonal network, and (c) meaningful employment. Halpern's view that secondary education for students with disabilities must focus on all domains of adult functioning greatly influenced subsequent amendments to IDEA that have made transition services a central component of special education designed to achieve the national goal of "equality of opportunity, full participation, independent living, and economic self-sufficiency for individuals with disabilities" (IDEA 2004, Sec. 614[d][2][D][5]).

Will's bridges model

 Council for Exceptional Children

Knowledge and Skill Base for Beginning Special Education Transition Specialists: Theoretical and applied models of transition (TS3K1) (also TS1K2).

Halpern's transition model

 Council for Exceptional Children

Knowledge and Skill Base for Beginning Special Education Transition Specialists: Theoretical and applied models of transition (TS3K1) (also TS1K2).

Transition Services

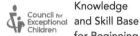

IDEA definition of transition services

Council for Exceptional Children

Knowledge and Skill Base for Beginning Special Education Transition Specialists: Transition-related laws and policies (TS1K2).

IDEA defines **transition services** as

> A coordinated set of activities for a child with a disability that is designed to be within a results-oriented process, that is focused on improving the academic and functional achievement of the child with a disability to facilitate the child's movement from school to post-school activities, including postsecondary education, vocational education, integrated employment (including supported employment), continuing and adult education, adult services, independent living, or community participation. (20 USC § 1401 [602][34])

TRANSITION PLANNING

Beginning no later than the first IEP to be in effect when the child is 16 (or 14 in some states) and updated annually thereafter, each child's IEP must contain the following:

1. appropriate measurable postsecondary goals based upon age appropriate transition assessments related to training, education, employment, and, where appropriate, independent living skills;
2. the transition services (including courses of study) needed to assist the child in reaching those goals. (20 USC § 1401 (614) [d][1][A][8])

Individualized transition planning

Council for Exceptional Children

Knowledge and Skill Base for Beginning Special Education Transition Specialists: Transition-related laws and policies (TS1K2) (also ICC1K4).

This portion of the student's IEP, called an **individualized transition plan (ITP)**, details the curricular programming and other supports that will prepare the student for a smooth and successful transition to adult life (Mazzotti et al., 2009). The purpose of the ITP is "to ensure that all of our students step into the adult life they desire. This doesn't mean locking a student into a life plan. It means that each student will leave high school recognizing her personal strengths, knowing where to turn for support, and looking toward adult life with confidence" (Horvath, 2006, p. 603).

IDEA 2004 and the regulations that govern its implementation require IEP teams to follow a specific transition planning process (see Figure 1).

Age-Appropriate Transition Assessment

Detailed information and materials to help educators, students, and their families develop effective transition plans are available from the National Secondary Transition Technical Assistance Center (NSTTAC) (http://www.nsttac.org/) and Seattle University's Center for Change in Transition Services http://www.seattleu.edu/ccts/.

Age-appropriate assessment is the all-important initial and ongoing component of transition planning. The intention helps the student answer the following questions:

- Who am I?
- What are my unique talents and interests?
- What do I want in life, now and in the future?
- What are some of life's demands that I can meet now?
- What are the main barriers to getting what I want from school and my community?
- What are my options in the school and community for preparing me for what I want to do, now and in the future? (NSTTAC, 2011)

A combination of formal and informal assessment methods are used to determine the student's needs, strengths, preferences, and interests in terms of current and future work, education, domestic, and social environments. Informal assessments often include interviews, direct observations, anecdotal records, curriculum-based assessments, interest inventories, preference assessments, and job-site evaluations. Formal measures include adaptive behavior and independent living assessments, aptitude tests, interest assessments, personality or preference tests, career development measures, and measures of self-determination.

Age-appropriate transition assessment

Council for Exceptional Children

Knowledge and Skill Base for Beginning Special Education Transition Specialists: Transition-related laws and policies (TS4S22) (also TS4S3, TS4S4, ICC8S44).

The *Transition Planning Inventory* (Clark & Patton, 2006) is widely used to determine the student's transition-related knowledge and skills. The 46-item assessment tool asks teachers, parents, and the student to rate the student's current competence across nine transition domains (e.g., employment, further education and training, daily living, leisure). Examples of items in the self-determination domain are recognizes and accepts own strengths and limitations, expresses feelings and ideas to others appropriately, and sets personal goals.

FIGURE 1 STEPS IN THE TRANSITION-PLANNING PROCESS

Conduct Age-Appropriate Transition Assessments

Needs | Strengths | Preferences | Interests

⬇

Write Measurable Postsecondary Goals

Education/Training | Employment | Independent Living (as appropriate)

⬇

Identify Transition Services

Instruction | Related Services | Community Experiences | Employment & Daily Living Skills | Courses of Study

⬇

Develop Annual IEP Goals in Support of Postsecondary Goals

Education/Training | Employment | Independent Living (as appropriate)

⬇

Coordinate Transition Services with Adult Services Agencies

Postsecondary Ed/Training Programs | State Vocational Rehabilitation Dept. | Supported Living Agencies

⬇

Provide Student with Summary of Performance

Supports That Have Helped | Supports Needed for Continued Success

---

Source: Adapted from the Center for Change in Transition Services, Seattle University and the National Secondary Transition Technical Assistance Center (NSTTAC) at University of North Carolina at Charlotte; and Mazzotti et al. (2009).

Measurable Postsecondary Goals

A postsecondary goal is "generally understood to refer to those goals that a child hopes to achieve after leaving secondary school (i.e., high school)" (IDEA 2004 Part B Regulations, §300.320[b]). IDEA requires that each student's IEP contain at least one postsecondary goal in education or training, one in employment, and, where appropriate for the student, independent living (i.e., life skills in the following domains: leisure/recreation, home and personal care, community participation).

A postsecondary goal is not the process of pursuing or moving toward a desired outcome. A measurable goal must contain a time frame, a clear behavior (i.e., "The student will _____"), and a situation. For example, "The summer after leaving high school, Lynn will obtain a part-time position working in a pet store." Figure 2 contains examples of postsecondary goals for three transition-age students.

Parent and family involvement, important at all stages of the transition from school to adult life, is particularly helpful during assessment and determining of postsecondary goals (Ankeny, Wilkins, & Spain, 2009). Person-centered planning, which entails a variety of strategies and activities for determining the desires, concerns, hopes, and dreams of individuals with disabilities and their families, can be an excellent way to engage the student and his or her family in the transition process (e.g., Meadan, Sheldon, Appel, & DeGrazia, 2010; Michaels & Ferrara, 2005).

Parents of students with disabilities can call the PACER Center at (952) 838-9000 to speak with a trained advocate who will help them understand their rights and find resources to help with all aspects of transition. Transition resources for parents are also available online at www.pacer.org/.

557

| FIGURE 2 | POSTSECONDARY GOALS FOR THREE HIGH SCHOOL STUDENTS |

	Education/Training	Employment	Independent Living
Allison—18 year-old with learning disabilities	Allison will obtain a 4 year degree from a liberal arts college with a major in child development.	After college, Allison will be employed in the field of early childhood education.	N/A
Jodi—17 year-old with mild intellectual disabilities	The fall after high school, Jodi will attend the Customer Service Representative course offered through the Pathways to Employment program at Central Piedmont Community College.	Within 3 months after graduation, Jodi will be competitively employed, working 20 or more hours, in the retail industry with time-limited supports of a job coach.	After high school, Jodi will assume responsibility for a share of living expenses by saving money earned at work and following a budget set by Jodi and her parents.
Kevin—18 year-old with significant intellectual disabilities—plans to stay in school until age 21 to obtain 3 more years of services.	Immediately after graduation, Kevin will participate in habilitative and functional skill training through CAP services and will attend courses designed to provide specialized academic, functional, and occupational preparation for individuals with disabilities (two times per week) at the community college.	Within 3 months of graduation, Kevin will obtain a supported employment position that allows him to work to his maximum stamina and incorporates the use of assistive technology.	Immediately following graduation, Kevin will participate in one to two age-appropriate community and individual community-based activities per week related to horticulture, socialization with young adults, animals, and music.

Source: Adapted from *NSTTAC Indicator 13 Checklist: Form B (Enhanced for Professional Development)*. Charlotte: University of North Carolina, National Secondary Transition Technical Assistance Center (NSTTAC). Available: http://www.nsttac.org/content/nsttac-indicator-13-checklist-form-b-enhanced-professional-development

Identify Transition Services

This section of the ITP addresses a coordinated set of transition-related strategies and activities in the areas of instruction, employment, community experiences, independent living, related services, and, if necessary, daily living and functional vocational assessment. For each of the student's postsecondary goals, the team identifies at least one instructional strategy, experience, or activity to assist the student in reaching it, the person or agency responsible for implementing the strategy or service, and the timeline for these responsibilities. Mazzotti and colleagues (2009) described the following transition services to support a student's postsecondary goals in education/training and employment of completing a welding course and gaining a job as an entry-level welder: job safety instruction, community-based experiences related to automotive construction, and work-based experience with a local welder.

Decisions about needed transition services should be guided by answers to questions such as the following (Blalock, Patton, Kohler, & Bassett, 2009; Flexer, Simmons, Luft, & Baer, 2008; Sitlington, Neubert, & Clark, 2010; Test, Aspel, & Everson, 2006; Wehman, 2011a):

• What are the student's strengths? How can she build on them to facilitate a successful transition?

- What skills does the student need to develop or improve to make progress toward her postschool goals?
- Will the student seek a regular high school diploma? If so, what course of study and proficiency tests will be required?
- Will she work toward a vocational certificate of completion instead of a regular diploma?
- Is the student likely to remain in high school through the maximum age of eligibility for special education services? If so, what curriculum and work experiences will be needed after age 18?
- In what school and community activities will the student participate?
- Does she have an expressed career interest now? If not, what can the team do to help her explore career possibilities and discover her preferences?

© Jim West/Alamy

Brett's individualized transition plan includes instruction and community-based experiences to help him reach his goal of obtaining a job in food services.

- What supports are necessary in the student's current and future environments that will enable the desired postschool goals and outcomes to become reality?

Annual IEP Goals

For each postsecondary goal, at least one annual IEP goal must be written that helps the student make progress toward that goal. Figure 3 shows IEP goals aligned with one or more postsecondary goals of the three students shown in Figure 2. IEP goals can be linked to more than one postsecondary goal. For example, Allison's IEP goal to improve algebra skills is consistent with her postsecondary goals of attending college and obtaining a job in early childhood education.

Secondary special educators are becoming increasingly skilled in creating instructional materials and activities that simultaneously teach academic and transition-related skills (Baer, Simmons, Bauder, & Flexer, 2008; Hughes, Wood, Konrad, & Test, 2006). For example, the EnvisionIT Program developed at The Ohio State University's Nisonger Center integrates Internet research skills and transition planning with national and state academic content standards (Izzo, Yurick, Nagaraja, & Novak, 2010). Students complete online lessons that present information technology (IT) content and career activities using the Internet. In the process of creating an electronic and print-based transition portfolio, students take assessment items that correlate to the high-stakes test that students must pass to earn a high school diploma. To learn about another example of combining transition and academic skill instruction, see *Teaching & Learning*, "Two for One: Teaching Self-Determination and Writing Together."

Relating transition services to IEP goals and objectives

 Council for Exceptional Children

Knowledge and Skill Base for Beginning Special Education Transition Specialists: Methods for linking academic content to transition goals (TS2K3) (also ICC4S6).

To learn about the EnvisionIT Program, go to http://nisonger.osu.edu/transition/envisionit.htm.

Coordinate Transition Services with Adult Agencies

Nowhere in special education are interdisciplinary teaming and interagency collaboration more important than when planning and delivering transition services for secondary students (Kochhar-Bryant, 2008; Sitlington et al., 2010; Wehman, 2011a). Successful, seamless transition requires the coordination, delivery, and transfer of services from the secondary school program to receiving agencies (e.g., employers, postsecondary education and vocational training programs, and residential service providers). While work-study and vocational training programs for special education students and vocational rehabilitation services for adults with disabilities have long

Two for One: Teaching Self-Determination and Writing Together

BY MOIRA KONRAD AND DAVID W. TEST

Although educators believe it is important to teach self-determination skills to students with disabilities, they are overwhelmed with a broad range of roles and responsibilities. Teachers must balance standards-based instruction with students' individualized transition needs, including the development of self-determination. In response, we developed the IEP Template and the GO 4 IT . . . NOW! strategies that teachers can use to involve students in the IEP process and teach an academic skill (written expression) simultaneously.

THE IEP TEMPLATE

The IEP Template is essentially a fill-in-the-blank IEP that students can use to write a draft of a first-person IEP.

The template serves as an organizer to help students understand the content and format of an IEP. It also helps students draft components of their IEPs in complete sentences.

GO 4 IT . . . NOW!

Once students have successfully used the IEP Template, they can move seamlessly to the GO 4 IT . . . NOW! learning strategy and apply their knowledge and skills. GO 4 IT . . . NOW! is a strategy that teaches students how to write paragraphs while simultaneously teaching them to write IEP goals and objectives (Konrad & Test, 2007; Konrad, Trela, & Test, 2006). Specifically, students learn that each paragraph is about one particular goal. The

---

Example of a vision statement <u>before</u> template instruction:

After high school I plan to . . .
Live _____ in New York _____
Learn _____
Work _____ as a lawyer _____
Play _____

Example of an academic strength <u>before</u> template instruction:

I can _____ math _____

Example of a goal <u>before</u> template instruction:

I will _____ writing _____

Example of a vision statement <u>after</u> template instruction:

After high school I plan to . . .
Live _____ in an apartment _____
Learn _____ how to be a lawyer _____
Work _____ in a restaurant _____
Play _ basketball at the YMCA with my friends _

Example of an academic strength <u>after</u> template instruction:

I can _ say my multiplication facts quickly _

Example of a goal <u>after</u> template instruction:

I will _____ write and edit paragraphs _____

---

existed in every state, systematic communication and coordination of service among schools and community-based adult service agencies is a relatively new phenomenon with variable degrees of success from state to state and community to community.

Although interagency cooperation is critical to the success of transition, IDEA gives the ultimate responsibility of implementing transition goals and activities to special education. Secondary special education teachers often play key roles in the lives of transition-age students with disabilities. Teachers such as Brad Baumgartner (this chapter's Featured Teacher) serve as role models and mentors, help youth with disabilities successfully complete high school, connect them to the world of work, and encourage self-directed decision making (Lindstrom et al., 2011).

Summary of Performance

The 2006 federal regulations for IDEA added a new transition-related requirement. Every student who exits special education services through graduation or by exceeding

goal itself serves as the topic sentence of the paragraph. The objectives are the supporting details in the paragraph, and a restatement of the goal with an indication of how long it will take to complete (a timeline) serves as a concluding sentence. The mnemonic GO 4 IT . . . NOW! helps students remember the structure of the paragraph, and, more specifically, what to include:

G—Goals
O—Objectives
4—4 objectives
IT—Identify timeline
N—Did I NAME my topic?
O—Did I ORGANIZE my details?
W—Did I WRAP it up and restate my topic?

TIPS FOR TEACHING THE IEP TEMPLATE AND THE GO 4 IT . . . NOW! STRATEGY

1. Help students identify their visions for the future.
   - Use online interest, career inventories, and school guidance counselors to help students develop vision statements about what they want to do when they finish high school.
   - Discuss with students how these vision statements will drive their transition planning.
2. Teach students how to turn visions into goals and objectives.
   - Help students identify their academic, functional, social, and behavioral needs, and teach them how to turn a need into a goal using an "I will" statement.
   - Provide explicit instruction in how to write a goal paragraph, using modeling, guided and independent practice, and explicit feedback.
   - Emphasize the use of transition words to teach students how to put objectives into logical order.
3. Build in writing and communication skills.
   - Use the sentences students develop in their IEP Templates to teach capitalization, punctuation, and parts of speech.

- Teach students how to use transition words and phrases to string sentences into paragraphs. For example, have students write sentences about a specific topic such as "My Strengths" or "My Services and Accommodations" and then use transition words to turn them into paragraphs.
- Weave letter-writing skills into the curriculum by having students write letters to invite the IEP team members to attend annual review meetings.
- Suggest that students prepare to participate in their IEP meetings by (a) bringing their completed templates and/or paragraphs to the meetings or (b) developing presentations about their templates.

4. Take it a step further.
   - Emphasize, teach, and model how GO 4 IT . . . NOW! can be used to write all kinds of paragraphs.
   - Encourage students to create essays (once they can write effective paragraphs) by combining paragraphs.
   - Suggest that students bring their paragraphs/essays to their IEP team meetings and share them with the team, or send out the essays with the IEP invitation letters as preparation for the meeting.

Detailed instructions and examples on using GO 4 IT can be found in Konrad and Trela (2007).

About the Authors

Moira Konrad is an associate professor of special education at The Ohio State University. Her research interests include self-determination and writing strategy instruction. David Test, a professor of special education at the University of North Carolina at Charlotte, is co–principal investigator of the National Secondary Transition Technical Assistance Center (www.nsttac.org), coeditor of the journal *Career Development for Exceptional Individuals*, and senior author of the text *Transition Methods for Youth with Disabilities*.

the age of eligibility, must receive a **summary of performance (SOP).** The SOP summarizes the student's performance in academic achievement and functional performance and provides specific recommendations for what the student should do to continue progressing toward his or her goals and the kinds of community-based education/training, vocational, and independent living agencies and services that may have a role in helping the student achieve those goals.

As with every step of the transition-planning process, the student should take an active role in developing the SOP. Considering along with his IEP team members which supports and services have been most helpful in high school and the types of services or supports likely to be needed in the future, the student may develop a better understanding of his needs for support and make him more able to self-advocate for services from adult agencies.

FIGURE 3 ANNUAL IEP GOALS ALIGNED WITH POSTSECONDARY GOALS SHOWN IN FIGURE 2

	Annual IEP Goal
Allison—18-year-old with learning disabilities	Allison will develop algebra skills, as measured by her homework completion and quiz scores, by using a planner to record assignments, prepare questions for class, and record formulas for study in the Algebra II course during her senior year.

This is an appropriate transition-related IEP goal because

- developing algebra skills in her Algebra II course is consistent with Allison's postsecondary goal of attending a 4-year liberal arts university; and
- Allison's employment goal is contingent upon her completion of college; therefore, annual goals that support her college completion also support her employment goal.

Jodi—17-year-old with mild intellectual disabilities	Given explicit instruction on balancing a checkbook, Jodi will demonstrate how to write a check, make checking account deposits and withdrawals, and balance a checkbook, four out of six opportunities during the duration of her IEP.

This is an appropriate transition-related IEP goal because

- it focuses directly on Jodi's postsecondary goal of sharing living expenses and following a budget.

Kevin—18-year-old with significant intellectual disabilities—plans to stay in school until age 21 to obtain 3 more years of services.	Given the GoTalk20+ augmentative communication device and weekly community practice, Kevin will independently use the device to communicate a desire for an item in community settings, including restaurants and ticket counters, using single words with 80% accuracy.

This is an appropriate transition-related IEP goal because

- Kevin is not able to use a GoTalk20+ effectively, and learning to do so will prepare him to participate in a habilitative and vocational training program, recreational opportunities, and educational opportunities after high school;
- learning to use a GoTalk20+ effectively will prepare Kevin to incorporate assistive technology use in future employment; and
- communicating choices will prepare Kevin for the goal of participating in leisure activities that interest him.

Source: Adapted from *NSTTAC Indicator 13 Checklist: Form B (Enhanced for Professional Development)*. Charlotte: University of North Carolina, National Secondary Transition Technical Assistance Center (NSTTAC). Available: http://www.nsttac.org/content/nsttac-indicator-13-checklist-form-b-enhanced-professional-development

EMPLOYMENT

Work can be defined as using one's physical and/or mental energies to accomplish something productive. Our society is based on a work ethic: we place a high value on work and on people who contribute. Besides providing economic support, work offers opportunities for social interaction and a chance to use and enhance skills in a chosen area. Work generates the respect of others and provides a sense of pride and self-satisfaction. Individuals with disabilities who are employed report a higher-quality life (Kraemer, McIntyre, & Blacher, 2003).

All young adults face important questions about what to do with their lives—attend college or technical school, work as a bricklayer or an accountant—but for the person without disabilities, answering those questions involves choosing from a number of options. By contrast, the young adult with disabilities typically has fewer options from which to choose. Occupational choices decrease if the person with disabilities has limited skills; they may decrease even more due to the nature of the disability and still further because of employers' prejudices and misconceptions about people with disabilities. For most adults with disabilities, obtaining and holding a job are major life challenges and goals.

Beginning Career Education Early

Numerous models for conceptualizing and guiding the delivery of employment-related transition services have been developed (e.g., Kochhar-Bryant & Greene, 2009; Martin, Woods, & Sylvester, 2008; Sitlington et al., 2010; Wehman, 2011a). Every transition model with research to support its effectiveness stresses the importance of providing career education at an early age, the students choosing goals, a functional secondary school curriculum that offers work experiences in integrated community job sites, systematic coordination between the school and adult service providers, and parental involvement and support.

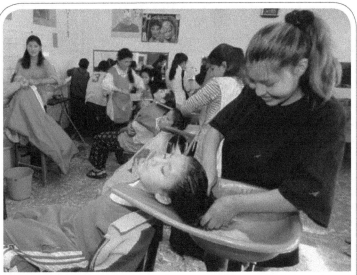

Giving secondary students regular opportunities to participate in integrated work settings in the community builds career awareness and teaches valuable vocational skills.

The Council for Exceptional Children's Division on Career Development and Transition (DCDT) recommends that career development and transition services begin in the elementary grades for all children with disabilities (Blalock et al., 2003). Developing career awareness and vocational skills during the elementary years does not mean placing 8-year-old children on job sites for training. Appropriate work-related curriculum and instructional objectives should be selected at each age level (Brolin, 2004; Cronin, Patton, & Wood, 2005; Wehman, 2011b). For example, elementary students might sample different types of jobs through classroom responsibilities such as watering plants, cleaning chalkboards, or taking messages to the office. Middle school students should begin to spend time at actual community job sites, with an increasing amount of in-school instruction devoted to the development of associated work skills, such as being on time, hygiene, dressing properly, staying on task, asking for help, and accepting direction (Beakley & Yoder, 1998).

Developing and operating a school-based business enterprise can help high school students learn functional academic, work, problem-solving, and social skills. Lindstrom, Benz, and Johnson (1997) describe four school-based businesses that students with disabilities in several high schools in Oregon helped develop and operate: an espresso and baked-goods bar (like the one described by Bradley Baumgartner), a take-out meals operation, a mail-order seed business, and a winter produce garden. Secondary students with moderate and severe disabilities should also spend an increasing amount of time experiencing and receiving instruction at actual community job sites (Test & Mazzotti, 2011). The remaining hours of in-school instruction should focus on acquisition of functional skills needed in the adult work, domestic, community, and recreational/leisure environments toward which the student is headed. Table 1 shows examples of transition-related curriculum activities in the domestic, community, leisure, and vocational domains that might be incorporated into a student's IEP.

Competitive Employment

Federal law defines **competitive employment** as work in a competitive labor market on a full- or part-time basis in an integrated setting that earns at or above the federal minimum wage, but not less than the customary wage and level of benefits paid by the employer for the same or similar work performed by individuals who are not disabled (Rehabilitation Act, 1998, Sections 7(11) & 7 [35][a], 29 USC 705[11] and 709[c]). Virtually all special educators who have studied the transition of students with disabilities from school to

CEC-DCDT

 Knowledge and Skill Base for Beginning Special Education Transition Specialists: Organizations and publications relevant to the field of transition (TS5K3).

Career awareness and transition-related curriculum activities

 Knowledge and Skill of the three students for Beginning Special Education Transition Specialists: Methods for linking academic content to transition goals (TS2K2) (also TS2K5, ICC4S6).

Jorgen Schytte/Peter Arnold, Inc./Photolibrary

563

TABLE 1 • **Examples of transition-related curriculum activities in four domains that might be included in a student's IEP**

	DOMESTIC	COMMUNITY	LEISURE	VOCATIONAL
ELEMENTARY	• Grooming • Put away clean clothes • Keep room uncluttered • Feed pet • Clear table • Dust • Vacuum • Answer telephone • Make bed • Make sandwich	• Buy nutritious snack • Use proper table etiquette • Learn to make emergency calls • Open bank account	• Play video games • Take turns • Practice conversational skills (i.e. listening, subject matter etc.) • Share • Make friends • Ride bike • Play little league sport	• Make choices • Tell time • Complete assignment on time • Wait calmly • Show concern for others • Introduce self to others • Answer telephone • Ask for permission to leave table
MIDDLE SCHOOL	• Take care of personal clothes • Straighten bathroom after use • Use microwave oven to prepare simple meal • Wash and clean inside of car • Sweep floors • Water plants • Take phone messages • Learn emergency and first aid procedures	• Make small personal purchases • Deposit money in bank account • Cross street with stop light	• Attend dance class • Take swimming lessons • Join club • Search the internet • Attend event out with a friend	• Set a schedule • Follow a schedule • Set alarm clock • Introduce others • Remain calm if plans are altered • Keep a to do list • Organize paperwork • Stay focused on tasks
HIGH SCHOOL	• Handle family laundry • Prepare more complicated meals • Initiate/do things that have to be done • Fix and maintain things (e.g. replace lightbulbs, clean coffeemaker) • Auto care (gas, oil etc...) • Lawn maintenance	• Shop for week's groceries • Learn how to solve problems (lodge complaints etc.) • Comparison shop • Balance bank statement • Control impulse buying	• Volunteer • Go to school sports events • Shop with friends • Go out to eat with friends • Hang out at friend's house • Go on a date • Make new friends	• Pay bills • Perform patient transport duties at hospital • Perform stocking at large retailer • Perform food preparation at hotel restaurant

Source: Table courtesy of Paul Wehman (2011a).

adult life believe that only through significant revision of the public school curriculum and improved coordination of school and adult vocational habilitation services can the prospects of competitive employment be enhanced for young adults with disabilities (e.g., Flexer et al., 2008; Wehman, 2011a; Patton et al., 1997; Sitlington et al., 2010).

We have already identified some key characteristics of school programs that increase the likelihood of successful employment outcomes for students. First, the curriculum must stress functional skills; that is, students must learn vocational skills that they will actually need and use in local employment situations (Swedeen, Carter, & Molfenter, 2010). The instruction of academic skills is seen as "minimally important" by many providers of employment opportunities for young adults with disabilities (Moon, Simonsen, & Neubert, 2011). Second, students with disabilities must receive ample opportunities to learn the social and interpersonal skills necessary to work effectively with colleagues in integrated work sites (Gear, Bobzien, Judge, & Raver, 2011; Hughes, Washington, & Brown, 2008). Third, community-based work experience and employment skill instruction should begin as early as ages 10 to 13 for students with severe disabilities and be used for progressively extended periods as students near graduation. While on community work sites, students should receive direct instruction

Characteristics of secondary school programs and competitive employment outcomes

 Council for Exceptional Children — Knowledge and Skill Base for Beginning Special Education Transition Specialists: Research on relationships between individual outcomes and transition practices (TS2K5).

in areas such as specific job skills, ways to increase production rates, and transportation to and from employment sites. Although students should train and work in the community whenever possible so they learn "the communication, behavior, dress and other codes critical for success in integrated environments...[and] to get to and from important places on time or to produce consistently" (Brown, Farrington, Suomi, & Zeigler, 1999, p. 6), the effectiveness of job site training can be increased when supplemented with simulation training in the classroom (Lattimore, Parsons, & Reid, 2006).

Research shows a positive correlation between paid work experiences during the last 2 years of high school and postschool employment and total earnings (e.g., Baer et al., 2003; Benz, Lindstrom, Unruh, & Waintrup, 2004; Benz, Lindstrom, & Yavanoff, 2000). Unpaid and volunteer work experience is also valuable for students with disabilities (Brown et al., 1999).

Students should experience community jobs that match their vocational interests. Martin et al. (2008) describe how Christopher, a 17-year-old student with moderate intellectual disabilities, used the Choose and Take Action vocational assessment software program (Martin et al., 2004) to select an entry-level job he would like to observe or try. The Choose and Take Action process includes four steps:

Step 1: *Choice making.* During choice making, Christopher viewed pairs of randomly presented videos showing different employment settings, activities, and job characteristics (see Figure 4). From each pair, he selected the one he liked the best. After viewing all the videos once, the chosen videos were paired and Christopher chose again. This continued until he picked one final video.

Step 2: *Plan.* During the planning part of the program, Christopher determined if he wanted to watch someone do the activity at the selected setting or if he wanted to do the activity. A printed plan showed what Christopher chose. Evaluation questions regarding these choices are also printed on the plan.

> Carter et al. (2009) describe several practical strategies educators can use to discover and expand community-based employment opportunities for students with disabilities.

FIGURE 4

EXAMPLE OF SCREEN SHOT FROM VOCATIONAL ASSESSMENT SOFTWARE PROGRAM

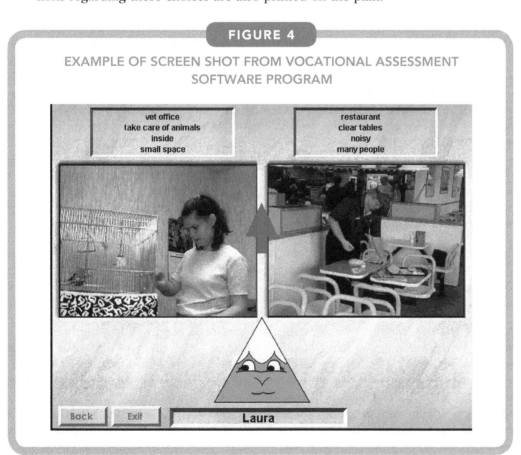

Source: From Martin, J. E., Marshall, L. H., Wray, D., Wells, L., O'Brien, J., Olvey, G., et al. (2004). *Choose and take action: Finding the right job for you.* Longmont, CO: Sopris West. Used by permission.

Step 3: *Try it.* Based on the plan, Christopher went into the community to "try it" at the chosen setting.

Step 4: *Evaluate.* Christopher, with his teacher's guidance, evaluated the experience, and then entered that information into the computer. (adapted from Martin et al., 2008, pp. 95–96)

Supported Employment

Definition of supported employment

Knowledge and Skill Base for Beginning Special Education Transition Specialists: Transition-related laws and policies (TS1K1).

Supported employment helps adults with severe disabilities, who have historically been unemployed or restricted to sheltered settings, earn real wages for real work. **Supported employment** means

(i) Competitive employment in an integrated setting with ongoing support services for individuals with the most severe disabilities—(A) For whom competitive employment has not traditionally occurred or for whom competitive employment has been interrupted or intermittent as a result of a severe disability; and (B) Who, because of the nature and severity of their disability, need intensive supported employment services from the designated State unit and extended services after transition in order to perform this work; or (ii) Transitional employment for individuals with the most severe disabilities due to mental illness. (34 *CFR* 363.6 [c][2][iv])

Supported employment has grown rapidly since its inception. In 1986, fewer than 10,000 individuals were working in federally assisted supported employment demonstration projects in 20 states. Just 2 years later, the supported employment movement had grown to a total of 32,342 participants nationally; the cumulative wages these workers earned grew from $1.4 million to $12.4 million in the 15 states that reported earnings data (Wehman, Kregel, Shafer, & West, 1989). In 2009, 117,638 people with disabilities were working through supported employment (Braddock et al., 2011). Supported employees earned more than $750 million in annual wages in 1995, many becoming taxpayers for the first time in their lives. Vermont's supported employees earned an average hourly wage of $8.59 in 2009 (Braddock et al., 2011). A statewide study in Maryland found that average weekly earnings of individuals placed in supported employment was 3.5 times greater than the earnings of individuals in sheltered work environments ($134.33 compared to weekly wages of $40.69) (Conley, 2003; see also Association for Persons in Supported Employment [APSE] at www.apse.org).

The success of supported employment depends in large part on job development—the identification and creation of community-based employment opportunities for individuals with disabilities (Griffin, Hammis, & Geary, 2007). Four distinct models of supported employment have evolved: small business enterprise, mobile work crew, work enclave, and individual placement.

Supported employment models

Knowledge and Skill Base for Beginning Special Education Transition Specialists: Theoretical and applied models of transition (TS1K1) (also TS2K6).

SMALL BUSINESS ENTERPRISE This model provides supported employment for people with disabilities by establishing a business that takes advantage of existing commercial opportunities within a community. The business hires a small number of individuals with disabilities as well as several employees without disabilities.

MOBILE WORK CREW A mobile work crew involves a small group of supported employees organized around a small, single-purpose business, such as building or grounds maintenance, working in an integrated community employment setting. A general manager may be responsible for finding and coordinating the work of several small crews of three to eight individuals, with each crew supervised by a supported employment specialist. Mobile work crews are organized as not-for-profit corporations; the extra costs the organizations incur because their employees do not work at full productivity levels are covered by public funds. Such costs are usually less than would be needed to support the work crew employees in activity centers, which provide little or no real work or reimbursement.

ENCLAVE (OR CLUSTERED PLACEMENT) In this model of supported employment, a small group of people with disabilities performs work with special training or job supports within a typical business or industry. Work enclave employees typically receive wages commensurate with their productivity rates. The work enclave provides a useful alternative to traditional segregated sheltered employment, offering many of the benefits of community-based integrated employment as well as the ongoing supports necessary for long-term job success.

INDIVIDUAL PLACEMENT The individual placement model of supported employment consists of developing jobs with employers in the community, systematically assessing clients' job preferences, carefully placing employees in jobs they want, implementing intensive job site training and advocacy, building systems of natural supports on the job site, monitoring client performance, and taking a systematic approach to long-term job retention (Wehman, Inge, Revell, & Brooke, 2006).

An approach to individual placement, used increasingly in recent years, known as **customized employment** entails carving out or creating a job within an integrated competitive work environment based on the current skills of the employee (Griffin et al., 2007; Office of Disability Employment Policy, 2011). Customized employment is a "value exchange between

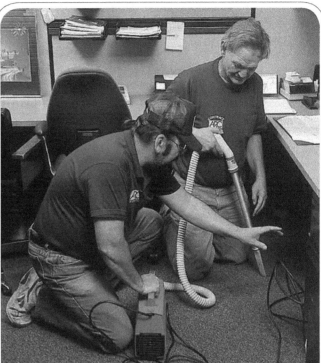

Supported employment has enabled tens of thousands of people like Barry to experience, for the first time in their lives, the benefits of real work for real pay.

the employer and employee based on the unique needs and contributions of the individual and the discrete and emerging needs of the employer" (Parent et al., 2008, p. 114). Supported self-employment offers another possibility for meaningful employment by some people with significant disabilities (Griffin & Hammis, 2003).

EMPLOYMENT SPECIALIST The supported employment specialist is the key to making a supported work program effective. The supported employment specialist, sometimes called a job coach or employment consultant, is a community-based professional who works in a nonprofit job placement program, a public vocational or adult services program, or a secondary special education program.

In a typical supported employment program, the employment specialist provides direct, on-site job training to the employee with disabilities and serves as the primary source of support and assistance. Although the job coach gradually reduces the time spent in direct, on-site training and support, this model of outside assistance has several inherent drawbacks (Mank, Cioffi, & Yovanoff, 2000; Simmons & Flexer, 2008; Trach, 2008):

- The arrival and presence of the job coach can disrupt the natural work setting.
- The supported employee may perform differently in the presence of the job coach.
- The job coach's presence can reduce the frequency of interaction between the supported employee and coworkers without disabilities.
- It is difficult for the employment specialist to be sensitive to the changing demands of the job over time and provide continued support and training consistent with those changes.
- The cost for an employment specialist who must travel to the job site is higher and the efficiency of the approach is lower than one that takes advantage of the natural interactions of coworkers.
- The always-on-call job coach may prevent the employer and coworkers from figuring out and implementing natural solutions to problems.

Roles of employment specialist

 Council for Exceptional Children

Knowledge and Skill Base for Beginning Special Education Transition Specialists: Scope and role of agency personnel related to transition services (TS2K6).

The Job Accommodation Network (JAN) provides free, expert, and confidential guidance on workplace accommodations and disability employment issues. JAN helps people with disabilities enhance their employability, and shows employers how to capitalize on the value and talent that people with disabilities add to the workplace. Go to http://askjan.org/.

- This approach may foster too much dependence on the job coach, working against the supported employee's success in learning how to solve problems and assuming responsibility for her own management.

NATURAL SUPPORTS The role of the employment specialist/job coach has evolved from one of primary supporter for the employee with disabilities to one of working with the employer and coworkers to help identify, develop, and facilitate the typical or indigenous supports of the workplace. Rogan, Hagner, and Murphy (1993) define natural supports as "any assistance, relationships or interactions that allow a person to secure or maintain a community job...in a way that corresponds to the typical work routines and social interactions of other employees" (p. 275). Figure 5 describes and gives examples of seven categories of natural supports identified by Rogan's SPANS model (1996).

NATURAL CUES AND SELF-MANAGEMENT The belief that employees with disabilities should be taught independence in the workplace has gained widespread acceptance among supported employment professionals and has spawned exciting and promising

---

FIGURE 5   SEVEN TYPES OF NATURAL SUPPORTS FOR ASSISTING A PERSON WITH DISABILITIES TO OBTAIN AND MAINTAIN A JOB

Organizational supports involve the preparation and organization of activities in the job setting, including, but not limited to, scheduling, order of tasks, and locations of materials. Supported employment professionals may be uneasy requesting such supports from employers, but the reality is that employers provide similar accommodations regularly to employees without disabilities. Examples include:

- All necessary supplies are moved to a storage area accessible to the supported employee.
- The supervisor adjusts the supported employee's schedule to accommodate the public bus schedule. For example, Brad needs wheelchair-accessible transportation to get to and from work. The paratransit system is unreliable on the weekends, so his supervisor excuses him from weekend shifts.
- The supervisor works with the employment consultant to carve out job responsibilities that will be most appropriate for the supported employee.

Physical supports involve the design and function of physical objects and equipment in a job setting, whether technical or nontechnical. These supports can range from the simplest jig to specialized computer equipment. Examples include:

- Greg's boss purchased mail pouches, which he attached to Greg's wheelchair every morning. Greg collects recyclables in the pouches.
- The supported employee purchases an augmentative communication device through vocational rehabilitation.

Social supports involve interactions with other individuals. Although social supports often include individuals in the work environment, they can involve individuals from any environment that affects the supported employee's outcomes at work. Examples include:

- With help from the supervisor, John's employment consultant identified a co-worker who has similar interests with John and requested that the co-worker take breaks with John occasionally.
- A neighbor gives the supported employee a ride to and from work.

Training supports involve the extension of personal competence and skill through direct training and instruction. The most common

training support used in supported employment is direct training by a job coach. Examples of other training supports include:

- A co-worker receives consultation from an employment specialist on suggested training activities and then provides training to the supported employee.
- A supported employee shadows a co-worker performing the job that she is to perform.

Social service supports involve accessing professional and nonprofessional disability-related services. Examples include:

- The supported employee uses Social Security Plan for Achieving Self-Support (PASS) to pay for transportation to and from work.
- A residential service provider assists the supported employee in finding an apartment near a bus line.

Community supports involve accessing community agencies and services that are available to all individuals. Examples include:

- The supported employee uses public transportation to get to and from work.
- The supported employee takes adult education courses to upgrade his skills.

Personal and family supports involve accessing family and personal resources. These supports often fall into another category, but the category itself is important as a reminder that a supported employee and his or her family or personal network often hold the answers to addressing many of the support needs that are identified. Examples include:

- The supported employee joins a self-advocacy group to learn to better advocate for herself at work.
- Family members provide employment referrals to the job seeker and the job developer.

Source: Adapted from Trach, J. S. (2008). Natural supports in the workplace and beyond. In F. R. Rusch (Ed.), *Beyond high school: Preparing adolescents for tomorrow's challenges* (2nd ed., pp. 259–261). Reproduced by permission of Pearson Education, Inc., Upper Saddle River, NJ.

research in the use of natural cues and self-management. Natural cues are features already existing in the work environment that the employee can see, hear, touch, or smell and use as a signal for what to do next (Inge & Moon, 2006). For example, clocks or whistles may signal that it is time to go to a job station, the sight of coworkers' stopping work and leaving the job station might be the prompt for break time, and a growing pile of dirty dishes should be the cue to increase the rate of dishwashing. The employment specialist's role expands from training the employee how to perform various vocational and social skills to teaching him how to respond independently to the cues that occur naturally in the workplace. When those cues are insufficient to prompt the desired behavior, the supported employee can be taught to respond to contrived cues, such as picture prompts depicting individual steps in a multistep task (Cihak, Kessler, & Alberto, 2008) or prerecorded verbal prompts interspersed within favorite music that the employee might listen to on a personal audio player (Grossi, 1998; Mechling, 2007).

Self-monitoring can also be effectively used in employment training. Research has shown that employees with disabilities can use self-monitoring (observing and recording one's performance) and self-evaluation (comparing self-monitored performance with a goal or production criterion) to increase their job productivity and independence (Ganz & Sigafoos, 2005; Grossi & Heward, 1998; Storey, 2007).

Employees with disabilities can also learn to self-manage their work performance by providing their own verbal prompts and self-instructions. For example, Browder and Minarovic (2000) taught four adults with intellectual disabilities to self-initiate job tasks in their community job settings (e.g., cafeteria, grocery store, garment factory). The employees were taught to complete and initiate the next job activity on their list of work tasks by verbalizing a "did-next-now" strategy (e.g., "I did fill the bags; next I'm going to sweep the floor, now I'm sweeping the floor").

Natural and contrived cues, self-monitoring, and self-instruction in the workplace

 Content Standards for Beginning Teachers—Common Core: Use procedures to increase the individual's self-awareness, self-management, self-control, self-reliance, and self-esteem (TS4S5) (also ICC4S5, ICC4S6, TS5S1, TS8S5).

Sheltered Employment

Sheltered employment refers to work by people with disabilities at an accredited occupationally oriented facility, including a work activities center, operated by a private nonprofit agency, which, except for its administrative and support staff, employs disabled people certified under special provisions of federal minimum wage laws by the Wage and Hour Division, U.S. Department of Labor. Sheltered employment is the most common type of vocational activity for adults with severe disabilities. A national survey of employment programs funded by state agencies serving this population found that 435,443 individuals worked in sheltered employment and work activity centers settings in 2009, roughly 4 times the number of people with intellectual and developmental disabilities working in supported employment (Braddock et al., 2011).

Sheltered employment

 Knowledge and Skill Base for Beginning Special Education Transition Specialists: Range of postschool options within specific outcome areas (TS2K7).

Sheltered workshops provide one or more of three types of programs: (a) evaluation and training for community-based employment (commonly referred to as *transitional workshops*), (b) extended or long-term employment, and (c) work activities. A **work activity center** offers programs of activities for individuals whose disabilities are viewed by local decision makers as too severe for productive work. Rehabilitation and training revolve around concentration and persistence at a task. Intervals of work may be short, perhaps only an hour long, interspersed with other activities—such as training in social skills, self-help skills, household skills, community skills, and recreation.

Many sheltered work programs offer both transitional and extended employment within the same building. Transitional workshops try to place their employees in community-based jobs. Extended employment workshops are operated to provide whatever training and support services are necessary to enable individuals with severe disabilities to work productively within the sheltered environment. The Wage and Hour Division of the U.S. Department of Labor allows sheltered workshops to pay employees hourly wages based on the employee's ability to produce in relation to a nondisabled standard. Workshops are required to determine prevailing wage rates for like-type work done by experienced workers in the surrounding community. Employees are evaluated in relation to a competitive standard at least once every 6 months. For example, if an employee is producing 50 units per hour and the competitive standard is 100 units, then his rate of pay is 50% of the prevailing wage rate for that job. If the prevailing wage rate is $9.00, the employee will receive $4.50 per hour. The workshop still pays the employee $9.00 for each 100 units produced, the same amount a nondisabled worker would make.

Most special educators and related employment services professionals no longer consider sheltered employment an appropriate transition outcome for young people with disabilities (Targett & Wehman, 2011). The theoretical purpose of sheltered workshops is to train individuals in specific job-related skills that will enable them to obtain competitive employment; however, few employees of sheltered workshops are ever placed in jobs in the community, and many who are placed do not keep their jobs for long (Rogan et al., 2002).

Many professionals believe that the poor competitive employment record of sheltered workshop graduates may indicate the limitations inherent in these sites rather than in the employment potential of people with disabilities (Migliore, Grossi, Mank, & Rogan, 2008; Wehman et al., 2006). Because sheltered employment is conducted in segregated settings, affords limited opportunities for job placement in the community, and provides extremely low pay, it has been called a dead-end street for individuals with intellectual disabilities (Frank & Sitlington, 1993). See the TASH Resolution on Integrated Employment for people with significant disabilities (Figure 6).

Poor prospects for sheltered employees

Council for Exceptional Children

Knowledge and Skill Base for Beginning Special Education Transition Specialists: Research on relationships between individual outcomes and transition practices (TS1K4).

FIGURE 6 TASH RESOLUTION ON INTEGRATED EMPLOYMENT

TASH, an international advocacy association of people with disabilities, their family members, other advocates and people who work in the disability field, endorses the following features of employment for all people with significant disabilities:

- **Integration:** Employment of people with significant disabilities must be in regular employment settings where they work along side people without disabilities. Frequent and ongoing interactions and the development of relationships must be assured.

- **Income and benefits:** Employment must result in paid compensation of at least the minimum wage, up to prevailing wage, for work performed and should include benefits comparable to coworkers performing similar work.

- **Customization and Choice:** Job seekers should be offered access to a customized process that allows for a negotiated relationship with the employer. This process serves to avoid strict competitive employment by focusing on the discrete contributions of the individual in relation to specific needs of the employer. Job selection and the duration of any job must be based on the choice of the individual.

- **Control of resources:** People with disabilities and those they choose to support them should be given the option of controlling and directing the funding and resources allocated on their behalf for employment.

- **Ongoing career advancement:** Employment for persons with significant disabilities must be viewed as careers that evolve over time driven by the individual's interests where positive job changes and advancement occur with access to higher pay, greater responsibility and variety, better working conditions that meet personal needs.

- **Individualized and natural supports:** The assistance and support provided persons with significant disabilities should be individualized according to their conditions for success, and their abilities. The supports provided should maximize natural features of support provided by personnel in the workplace.

- **Funding:** Funding for "day" services at the federal, state and local levels should be directed towards employment as the first and most important outcome for adults with significant disabilities. Funding for community participation, recreation and other non-work outcomes should be designed around the work routines of the individual.

- **Education:** Employment should be an expected outcome of the educational process for students with significant disabilities of both high school and college settings. Educational settings should provide information, supports and experiences to all students, including students with significant disabilities, on employment and the importance of a working life.

- **Business ownership:** For those individuals with significant disabilities who wish to own their own business, access to funding, services and supports should be provided in a manner similar to that of wage employment.

- **Equal access:** People with the greatest support needs must be given high priority for employment.

Source: TASH, 1001 Connecticut Avenue, NW, Suite 235, Washington, D.C. 20036. Full text available at http://tash.org/advocacy-issues/employment/

POSTSECONDARY EDUCATION

Going to college is no longer a fantasy for individuals with disabilities; it is a reality occurring with greater frequency. In the 2008–09 academic year, 707,700 students with disabilities were enrolled in 2- and 4-year postsecondary institutions (Raue & Lewis, 2011). In 2007–08, 10.8% of all undergraduate students and 7.6% of graduate students reported having a disability. The most prevalent types of disability reported by postsecondary students are specific learning disabilities (31%), ADD/ADHD (18%), mental illness or psychiatric condition (15%), and health impairment (11%). Data from NLTS2 showed that enrollment in postsecondary education programs by former high school special education students more than doubled from 19% in 1990 to 46% in 2005 (Newman, Wagner, Cameto, Knokey, & Shaver, 2010).

Individuals with disabilities are increasingly attending postsecondary education programs of all types.

Many high school students look ahead to college. However, access to postsecondary education may be even more important for people with disabilities than it is for individuals without them. Postsecondary education significantly improves chances of meaningful employment. Among adults with disabilities, only 15.6% of those who leave high school without a diploma are employed; participation in the labor force doubles to 30.2% for those who have completed high school and triples to 45.1% for those with some postsecondary education (Yelin & Katz, 1994). For individuals with disabilities who obtain a 4-year degree, the employment rate rises to 50.3%.

Individuals with disabilities who obtain a postsecondary education—whether it be completing a technical training program, a community college's 2-year associate's degree, or a 4-year bachelor's degree—enjoy increased vocational options and greater lifetime earnings (Madaus, 2006). Overall, college graduates can expect to have better health, greater self-confidence, increased career options, higher-level problem-solving skills, improved interpersonal relationships, and a higher level of open-mindedness as well as more involvement in politics, community affairs, recreation, and leadership activities (Madaus, 2006). They will also be less dependent on parents and governmental benefits than will individuals who do not pursue postsecondary education (Turnbull, Turnbull, Wehmeyer, & Park, 2003).

Postsecondary education is increasingly becoming an option for students with significant disabilities such as intellectual disabilities, autism, or multiple disabilities. Some school districts allow students who require special education services past the age of 18 to graduate with their nondisabled peers and continue educational programming on the campuses of community colleges, universities, or vocational-technical schools (Pappay & Bambara, 2011). These programs enable youth with moderate and severe disabilities to continue their education in a more age-appropriate learning environment and to participate in some aspects of traditional college life, including auditing academic classes and enjoying recreation and physical education activities in an integrated setting with same-age peers (Casale-Giannola & Wilson Kamens, 2006; Goldrich Eskow & Fisher, 2004). Most programs offer a combination of college classes, basic or functional skills classes, and job experiences.

Although the range and availability of services offered by colleges and universities for students with disabilities have increased greatly in recent years, the success of students with disabilities as measured by graduation is well below that of students without disabilities. One study found that 80% of students with learning disabilities

Relationship between postsecondary education and employment

Knowledge and Skill Base for Beginning Special Education Transition Specialists: Research on relationships between individual outcomes and transition practices (TS3K2).

who had attended postsecondary education programs had not graduated 5 years after high school compared to 56% of students without disabilities (Murray, Goldstein, Nourse, & Edgar, 2000). Ten years after they had left high school, 56% of the students with learning disabilities had not graduated from postsecondary education compared to 32% of those without disabilities.

Becoming aware of the demands of postsecondary education environments is a necessary first step for high school teachers who want to help students acquire the skills, supports, and accommodations needed to succeed in those environments. Other key components and strategies for preparing and supporting secondary students with disabilities for successful transition to postsecondary education include the following (Cunningham, 2007; Hong, Ivey, Gonzalez, & Ehrensberger, 2007; Walker & Test, 2011):

- Students need exposure to increasingly rigorous curriculum content at the secondary level.
- Students need training in learning strategies for solving new content.
- Students need to be trained how to use assistive technology devices that will increase their access to and ability to manipulate curriculum content.
- Students need to learn self-determination skills that enable effective goal setting, planning, self-management, and advocacy skills to succeed in college.
- Students need to make early application to college.
- To be eligible for accommodations and support services at the postsecondary level, students must identify themselves as a student with a disability and provide documentation of the disability.
- Students must learn to identify the accommodations that supported their academic success at the secondary level and how to request these supports as needed at the postsecondary level.

Good social skills are also key to success, not only in college, but at work and in every area of adult life (Gear et al., 2011; Jantz, 2011). Wenzel and Rowley (2010) describe a semester-long course that helps college students with Asperger's syndrome learn critical social skills for survival and success on campus. Dating and romantic involvement are particularly challenging for many youth with disabilities. To read about one young woman's perspectives, see *Current Issues and Future Trends*, "Try a Little Tenderness: A Firsthand Perspective on Asperger's Syndrome and Dating."

RESIDENTIAL ALTERNATIVES

Where one lives determines a great deal about how one lives. It influences where a person can work, what community services and resources will be available, who her friends will be, what opportunities for recreation and leisure exist, and, to a great extent, what feelings of self and place in the community will develop. At one time, the only place someone with severe disabilities could live, if she did not live with family, was a large, state-operated institution. Although she had done no wrong to society, an institution was considered the best place for the person. There were no other options— no such thing as residential alternatives.

Today, however, most communities provide a continuum of residential options for adults with disabilities. Increased community-based residential services have meant a greater opportunity for adults with severe disabilities to live in more normalized settings.

Residential options

Knowledge and Skill Base for Beginning Special Education Transition Specialists: Range of postschool options within specific outcome areas (TS2K7).

Apartment Living

A rented apartment is one of the most common living arrangements for adults without disabilities. Today, an increasing number of adults with disabilities are enjoying the freedom and independence that apartment living offers. Three types of apartment living for adults with disabilities are common: the apartment cluster, the co-residence apartment, and the maximum-independence apartment. An *apartment cluster* consists of a small number of apartments housing people with disabilities and another nearby apartment for a support person or staff member. An apartment cluster allows for a great deal of flexibility in the amount and degree of support needed by residents in the various apartments. Whereas some people might require direct help with such things as shopping, cooking, or even getting dressed, others need only limited assistance or suggestions and prompts. To facilitate social integration, people without disabilities may also occupy some apartments in an apartment cluster.

A *co-residence apartment* is shared by an individual with disabilities and a roommate without disabilities. Although this arrangement is sometimes permanent, most co-residence apartments are used as a step toward independent living. The live-in roommates are often unpaid volunteers.

Two to four adults with disabilities usually cohabit *maximum-independence apartments*. These adults have all of the self-care and daily living skills required to take care of themselves and their apartment on a day-to-day basis. A supervisory visit is made once or twice a week to help them deal with any special problems they may be having.

Foster Homes

When a family opens its home to an unrelated person for an extended period, the term *foster home* applies. Although foster homes have provided temporary residential services and family care for children (usually wards of the court) for many years, more and more families have begun to share their homes with adults with disabilities. In return for providing room and board for their new family member, foster families receive a modest financial reimbursement.

Julian's transition plan includes learning housecleaning skills for independent apartment living.

Katelyn Metzger/Merrill

Life in a foster family home can have numerous advantages for an adult with disabilities. Instead of interacting with paid group-home staff who may or may not actually live at the same address, the person with disabilities lives in a residence that is owned or rented by individuals or families as their primary domicile. The person can participate and share in day-to-day family activities, receive individual attention from people vitally interested in his continued growth and development, and develop close interpersonal relationships. As part of a family unit, the adult with disabilities also has more opportunities to interact with and be accepted by the community at large.

Group Homes

Group homes provide family-style living for a small group of individuals, usually three to six people. Most group homes serve adults with intellectual disabilities, although some have residents with other disabilities. A 2009 national census found 196,211 people with intellectual and developmental disabilities living in group homes of six or fewer residents, a huge increase over the 20,400 people living in similar-sized group homes in 1977 (Braddock et al., 2011; Lakin, Larson, Salmi, & Webster, 2010).

Some group homes are principally a permanent place to live for their residents. Staff in this type of home help the people who live there develop self-care and daily living skills, form interpersonal relationships, and participate in recreation and leisure skills. During the day, most residents work in the community or in a sheltered workshop. Other group homes operate more as halfway houses. Their primary function is to prepare individuals with disabilities for a more independent living situation, such as a supervised apartment. These transitional group homes typically serve residents who have recently left institutions, bridging the gap between institutional and community living.

Compared to institutions, two aspects of group homes make them a much more normalized place to live: their size and their location. Most people grow up in a typical family-sized group with opportunity for personal attention, care, and privacy. The

CURRENT ISSUES AND FUTURE TRENDS

▶ Try a Little Tenderness: A Firsthand Perspective on Asperger Syndrome and Dating

BY AMY GRAVINO

HE WAS HER FIRST. First love, first everything. She can remember her skin tingling just from knowing she was about to see him. He knew that boys had traditionally been more likely to run *away* from her than run after her. Even though she was older than he was by a few years, he was the one with experience on his side. Experience taught him what to say to her, how to make her feel special, and she fell for him more every day. There was a picnic in the park one sunny afternoon, the blanket spread out, homemade sandwiches sitting on plates. Just before he left, he ran back to where she sat, kissing her good-bye once more.

Experience also taught him how to lie. Long after she found out the truth; long after his deception came to light and her world crashed down around her, she still remembered how he made her feel. Only now, she couldn't tell if it was real. He knew she had Asperger syndrome and had taken advantage of her vulnerability, her willingness to trust. But she was not blameless; she had acted foolishly by letting love blind her. In the end, it was not her trust in him that was destroyed, but more her trust in herself. Today, she still carries it with her. I carry it. Because I am this girl, and she is me.

One of the most pressing, and least often talked-about, issues faced by adolescents and adults with Asperger syndrome is entering into and maintaining a romantic relationship. Other issues such as job training, self-care, and independent living skills have been rigorously addressed by the existing research literature, and while many social skills between individuals on the spectrum and their caregivers, teachers, and peers have been taught, the dating skills arena remains largely untouched.

HOW MUCH EYE CONTACT IS TOO MUCH?

As a graduate student in applied behavior analysis, I designed a research study that sought to teach adult men with Asperger syndrome how to ask someone out on a date. The desire to do this came from the dearth of reliable research on the subject, from knowing that the many children who are diagnosed with autism and Asperger syndrome will soon be teenagers and adults who will benefit from these skills, and from my own experiences with Asperger syndrome.

Behaving effectively and appropriately in a dating situation is different from and more challenging than many other facets of the adult world. Attempting to operationally define specific parameters for dating behavior is an even more daunting task. When I was designing this study, I had to make a number of considerations, such as, How much eye contact is too much when asking someone out? What are the "right" and "wrong" things to say? How long should one wait after beginning a conversation before asking the person out on a date?

To answer the first question, I sat in a coffee shop observing various couples. I quickly realized that just as every person is unique, the dynamics between these twosomes are also unique. Eye contact between two friends has a certain "look" to it, and so does the eye contact between two people who are in love—the way they gaze at each other. This type of eye contact was not appropriate for the people for whom my study was geared, and I had to recognize this, not only as a researcher but as a person who has Asperger syndrome for whom reading social cues is frequently a source of great difficulty.

When it comes to surmounting a challenge, the idiomatic expression "Getting there is half the battle" is frequently heard. For individuals with Asperger syndrome, getting there is *all* of the battle—and then some. It's been said that the best foundation for a romantic relationship is a solid friendship. Although studies have been conducted to teach social skills and foster the development of casual friendships between individuals on the spectrum and their neurotypical peers, the number of meaningful,

congregate-living arrangement of an institution cannot provide a normalized lifestyle, no matter how much effort a hardworking, caring staff makes. Because the number of people in a group home is small, there is a greater chance for a family-like atmosphere to develop. Size is also directly related to the neighborhood's ability to assimilate the members of the group home into typical activities within the community. Large groups tend to become self-sufficient, orienting inward and thereby resisting

close friendships that these individuals have is usually very low. A step that I did not undertake in my research but that could have significant implications for adolescents and adults with Asperger is developing strategies to bridge that gap, and help this population more effectively learn the ins and outs of dating.

As teachers of students with special needs, the key to developing such strategies lies in creating a balance. Most teenagers, whether on the autism spectrum or not, are more likely to listen to their peers and friends than their parents or teachers. The responsibility of teachers lies in working with both the ASD student and the neurotypical peers, in different capacities. A step-by-step, concrete task analysis seems to be effective for many individuals with Asperger (e.g., "When this happens, I do #1. If I need more help, I do #2. If I still need help, I do #3"). Task analyses for building friendships could be potentially powerful tools for individuals on the spectrum and can be altered and shaped based on the specific social situation.

Teachers need to impart to neurotypical peers the importance of meaning what you say and saying what you mean. Individuals on the autism spectrum are very likely to interpret statements literally, to take them to heart. A neurotypical peer who says something in jest may find that AS student does not understand the joke but instead takes what is said seriously. Teenagers are also not known for giving the best advice, so while a neurotypical teen would probably understand when an offered "helpful suggestion" is actually a bad idea, the ASD teenager probably would not. Educating neurotypical peers not just about what Asperger syndrome is or how to handle a classmate who has it, but how to act with compassion toward these students, can make an entire world of difference.

As a woman with Asperger syndrome, my own experiences with dating have been marked by few friendship-to-relationships situations and more "barely being friends with someone before falling head over heels for them" situations. Emotions have no "halfway" for many of us on the spectrum. When we care for someone, we give ourselves and our hearts completely. This blinded me to the fact that the person I cared for not only did not reciprocate those feelings but was untruthful with me about very serious issues, and when the truth finally came out (as it always does), it left me devastated. The inability to "dial down" the intensity of these emotions also means that rejection for individuals with Asperger's becomes even more difficult to cope with.

Rejection is an unpleasant subject, but if we are to develop strategies for teaching individuals with Asperger syndrome about dating, it is necessary to include methods for coping with rejection. The scope of my thesis research did not allow for me to address rejection, but it was mentioned to me by one of the participants at the conclusion of the study as something they thought would have improved it. Perhaps the most difficult aspect of rejection for individuals with Asperger's is that, for some, it will diminish their motivation to ask another person out on a date for fear of facing the same rejection again and again, resigning themselves to a life of isolation and loneliness.

Having Asperger syndrome or autism does not preclude one from having the same desires as a neurotypical person—to date, and to find love, and to make mistakes in the process. Although we live in a world that is often difficult for us to navigate, through the lens of science, strategies to learn the skills involved in dating can be custom designed and can act as one brick of many in the path to finding fulfilling romantic relationships. The wisdom of individuals with Asperger syndrome may be unconventional, but we have far more to offer than people might expect from us, if only we could get the chance to show it.

WHAT DO YOU THINK?

1. What are some challenges individuals with Asperger syndrome might face when trying to establish a romantic relationship?
2. When developing a strategy or intervention to teach adults or adolescents with Asperger syndrome how to date, what considerations must be made?
3. How can individuals with Asperger syndrome learn to cope with rejection in a dating situation?

About the Author

Amy Gravino, the founder of A.S.C.O.T. Coaching, LLC, currently serves on the board of directors for the Global and Regional Asperger Syndrome Partnership (www.grasp.org). Diagnosed with Asperger syndrome at age 10, Amy is a writer, consultant, and public speaker who recently obtained her M.A. in applied behavior analysis at Caldwell College and sat on a panel of autism experts at the United Nations. To learn more about Amy and her work coaching transition-age students and young adults with Asperger syndrome, go to www.amygravino.com.

movement outward into the community. In groups of more than six or eight people, care providers can no longer relate properly to individuals. Large group homes tend to acquire the characteristics of a place of work for direct-care staff rather than a home where people live (Ferguson & Ferguson, 2011). Indeed, some evidence suggests that quality of life is better for people residing in smaller rather than larger group homes (Burchard, Hasazi, Gordon, & Yoe, 1991; Conroy, 1996).

The location and physical characteristics of the group home itself are also vital determinants of its ability to provide a normalized lifestyle. A group home must be located within the community in a residential area, not a commercially zoned district. It must be in an area where the people who live there can conveniently access shopping, schools, churches, public transportation, and recreational facilities. In other words, a group home must be located in a typical residential area where any one of us might live. And it must look like a home not conspicuously different from other family dwellings on the same street.

Supported Living

Several innovative models for residential services for adults with disabilities have been developed based on the belief that residential placements must be adapted to the needs of the person with disabilities, not vice versa (Baer & Daviso, 2008). **Supported living** helps people with disabilities live in the community as independently and normally as possible. Similar to the way in which supported employment provides ongoing, individualized supports to help a person with disabilities perform meaningful work in a community-based employment setting, supported living entails a personalized network of various types and levels of natural supports.

Klein (1994, 2011) explains what supported living is by describing what it is not. There are no criteria for participation (e.g., people in this program must be able to cook for themselves, have a physical disability, need more or less than 3 hours per day of attendant care, have visual impairments). Supported living is not based on readiness and movement through a continuum. Participation in traditional residential services is based on a professional's assessment of the person's readiness or ability to live in a particular program, and a person must perform well (learn new skills on her individual habilitation plan) in order to move ("earn" the right) to the next, less restrictive rung on the continuum. Guiding principles of supported living are described in Figure 7. A 2009 survey of state departments of developmental disabilities found 246,822 people with intellectual and developmental disabilities were participating in supported living in the U.S. (Braddock, 2011).

Institutions

Most of the large, state-operated institutions in the United States were founded in the 19th or early 20th century, when it was generally believed that people with intellectual disabilities could not be educated or trained. Large custodial institutions (some housed 1,000 or more people with intellectual and other disabilities) kept people with disabilities segregated from the rest of society; they were never designed to help people learn to live in the community. In the 1960s and 1970s, these institutions came under intense criticism for their inability to provide individualized residential services in a comfortable, humane, and normalized environment (Blatt, 1976; Kugel & Wolfensberger, 1969). The complaints were not leveled against the concept of residential programs; there will probably always be people whose disabilities are so severe that they require the kind of 24-hour support that residential facilities can offer. The problem lies with the inherent inability of an institutional environment to allow a person to experience a normal lifestyle.

© Janine Wiedel Photolibrary/Alamy

Supported living provides flexible supports when and as they are needed. Once or twice each week, Kay's neighbor stops by to see if she needs any help with her apartment.

FIGURE 7   WHAT IS SUPPORTED LIVING?

What is Supported Living?

Supported living is not a specialized method, program or technique for providing assistance, nor is it a model or approach with a complex set of procedures that will guarantee that all people will live happily in their own homes. Adopting the concept of supported living means abandoning the idea of a perfect model, a uniform answer, or the absence of barriers, disappointment, imperfections or failure in providing assistance to people to live in their own homes. Instead, we focus on assisting each individual to create the life he or she desires.

Precepts of Supported Living

If we are to embrace supported living, the following assertions must be at the core of assisting people with the label of disability to control their own homes:

1. *Housing is separate from assistance.* No one is forced to live in any situation based on the type or amount of assistance he or she may need. People choose and control their homes as well as the assistance they receive; these are separate.

2. *Personalized assistance.* Supported living is, by definition, provided to one individual at a time. There are no exceptions. This does not necessarily mean that everyone lives alone; it means that the person chooses whether and with whom he or she shares his or her home. Individuals receive the appropriate, individualized assistance they need in a home of their choosing. If the person chooses to live with other(s), that/those individual(s) will receive his or her own separate personalized assistance as necessary.

3. *Everyone is ready.* There are no prerequisites to living in a home of one's choosing, regardless of disability. Likewise, support is individually designed, flexible, mobile, and based on the person's needs at any given time. No person lives in a simulated environment in order to "prepare" for living in his or her home.

4. *Person-centered planning.* Support providers, friends, family members and the person with whom life planning is occurring must get to know each other. To assist the person to live in an ideal environment, we must have answers to these questions: What are the person's dreams, desires, and preferences? How would this person describe his or her ideal living situation? After determining the answers to these questions, the person's planning group convenes regularly to develop and implement a plan for creating the person's ideal future and to modify that plan as the person's life changes.

5. *Connections and generic community resources.* Traditional residential services rely on system solutions to problems, referring to the procedures and policy manual to seek answers and using existing agency resources. Supported living relies on the assistance of all who are invested in the person's future. "Who do we know who we can engage?" is asked over and over as the process of planning and arranging for assistance evolves. People use generic community services that are available to all community members.

6. *Flexible supports.* Supports are based upon the person's specific needs and schedule versus on a program or agency's schedule. Support is provided where, when, how, and by whom it is needed. Supports are flexible enough to adjust to the person's changing life needs, preferences, and desires.

7. *Combining natural assistance, learning, and technology.* Assistance is provided in a manner that is natural to the time, place, and person. Each person is assisted to recruit, hire, design, and manage his or her own support and use technology to gain the maximum possible amount of control over his or her environment.

8. *A focus on what people can do.* Traditional residential programs often focus on what people cannot do and how to remediate those skill deficiencies, Supported living focuses on the person's capacities, skills, and gifts, provides support for things the person cannot do, and provides opportunities for the person to learn what he or she determines is important.

9. *Language that is natural to the setting.* The places where people live are described as "Joe's home" or "Mary's house." People clean their homes and do their laundry rather than learn programs; people live with roommates, not with staff or care providers; friends, not volunteers, visit; and people are referred to as neighbors, friends, and citizens rather than clients, consumers, and residents.

10. *Ownership.* Last and most important, the person living in the home "owns" the home. Home ownership does not mean that every person will hold the mortgage to a home. It does mean, however, that the person will sign his or her lease; that items in the home are chosen by and belong to the person, reflecting his or her taste; roommates, if any, sublet from the person, support people are hired by the person and the place is his or her home.

Source: Jay Klein, August 14, 2011, personal communication (adapted and revised by Jay Klein from Klein, 1994).

Tremendous improvements have been made in the abysmal living conditions in institutions that Blatt and Kaplan (1966) exposed over 45 years ago in their book *Christmas in Purgatory*. During the 1970s, the U.S. Department of Health, Education, and Welfare and the Joint Commission on the Accreditation of Hospitals developed extensive standards for residential facilities for individuals with intellectual disabilities. A facility must meet these standards—which cover topics as diverse as building construction, staffing, and habilitative and educational programming—to qualify for federal and state Medicaid funding. Residential units that meet the standards are referred to as ICF-MR Medicaid facilities. Today, an ICF-MR facility serving 16 or more residents is considered an institution. Although the ICF-MR Medicaid system of rules and regulations has eliminated the inhumane conditions that had defined institutional life, the system has become the target of criticism because of residents' quality of life, the high operating costs, and the prevalence of lifetime placements for people in these transitional programs (e.g., Baer & Daviso, 2008; Knoll & Wheeler, 2005).

Deinstitutionalization—the movement of people with disabilities out of large institutions and into smaller, community-based living environments such as group homes or apartments—has been an active reality over the past four decades. The number of people with intellectual and developmental disabilities living in large state institutions has decreased steadily from a high of 194,650 in 1967 to 32,909 people in 2009 (Lakin, Larson, & Kim, 2011). As of January 2010, more than half of 354 state institutions and residential units for people with intellectual and developmental disabilities that have been operating within the previous 50 years had been closed, and 11 states had closed all of their institutions.

Lakin and colleagues (2011) reviewed 36 studies of the outcomes of deinstitutionalization for nearly 5,000 people with intellectual disabilities. They found 31 of the studies indicated generally positive outcomes for residents, and studies that specifically assessed changes in social skills, language and communication skills, self-care and domestic skills, and community-living skills after leaving large institutions to live in the community "overwhelmingly showed positive outcomes." They concluded that "to overlook such substantial and consistent findings cannot be easily justified in either public policy or treatment practices" (p. 4). The organization TASH (2000) has a resolution on deinstitutionalization calling for the termination of residential facilities and programs.

Deinstitutionalization

Knowledge and Skill Base for Beginning Special Education Transition Specialists: Range of postschool options within specific outcome areas (TS3K2).

RECREATION AND LEISURE

Recreation and the enjoyable use of leisure time are important components of a self-satisfying adult life. Most of us take for granted our ability to pursue leisure and recreational activities. We benefit from a lifetime of learning how to play and how to enjoy personal hobbies or crafts.

Recreation and leisure activities do not come easily for many adults with disabilities, however. To use community recreational resources, one must have transportation, the physical ability or skills to play the game, and, usually, other willing and able friends with whom to play. These three factors, alone or in combination, severely limit the recreation and leisure activities available to many adults with disabilities (Matheson, Olsen, & Weisner, 2007). Transportation is not available; the person's disability does not allow him to swim, bowl, or play tennis; and he has no friends with similar skills and interests. Because of these problems, the majority of recreation and leisure experiences for many adults with disabilities have consisted of segregated, disabled-only outings. Too often, the so-called leisure activities for adults with disabilities consist of watching great amounts of television, listening to music in the solitude of their rooms, and spending discretionary time socially isolated (Strand & Kreiner, 2005).

Special educators must realize the importance of including training for recreation and leisure in curricula for school-age children with disabilities. Juarez, Best, and Bigge (2010) describe how numerous games, hobbies, crafts, and projects can be adapted to become enjoyable, worthwhile leisure-time pursuits for people with disabilities. Areas they suggest include music appreciation and study, photography, card games, collecting, and nature study. Suggestions are also available for adapting leisure activities for young adults who are deaf-blind, such as using permanent tactile prompts (e.g., attaching fabric to the flipper buttons of a pinball machine), adequately stabilizing materials, enhancing the visual or auditory input provided by the materials (e.g., using large-print, low-vision playing cards), and simplifying the requirements of the task (e.g., raising the front legs on a pinball machine, thereby reducing the speed with which the ball approaches the flippers).

Active recreation that includes physical exercise not only can increase life satisfaction for an adult with disabilities but also can help the person maintain a job by

Teaching recreation and leisure activities

Knowledge and Skill Base for Beginning Special Education Transition Specialists: Arrange and evaluate instructional activities in relation to postschool goals (TS2S2) (also TS4S1).

improving overall vitality and health condition (Ispen, 2006). Learning appropriate recreation and leisure skills is particularly important for adults with severe disabilities (Bambara, Koger, & Bartholomew, 2011). Most people with severe disabilities have ample free time, but many do not use it constructively and may instead engage in inappropriate behaviors such as body rocking, hand flapping, or bizarre vocalizations. A number of studies have demonstrated how to teach recreation and leisure skills to secondary students and adults with moderate and severe intellectual disabilities (e.g., Collins, Hall, & Branson, 1997; Cooper & Browder, 1997; Jerome, Frantino, & Sturmey, 2007; Zhang, Gast, Horvat, & Datillo, 1995). In one interesting demonstration of age-appropriate instruction, four adults with moderate intellectual disabilities learned to order drinks in an Irish pub (O'Reilly, Lancioni, & Kiernans, 2000).

Sebine likes to dance. Choice is crucial to the enjoyment of leisure activities.

Scott Cunningham/Merrill

Programs that encourage and support recreational and leisure activities among secondary students with disabilities and their classmates without disabilities are especially valuable for all parties involved (Hughes et al., 2002). Participating in community recreation and leisure activities with an adult with disabilities is an excellent way for prospective teachers to appreciate the value of a functional curriculum for school-age students and in the process perhaps make a good friend (Dardig, 2006). To read about one such program, see *Teaching & Learning*, "Next Chapter Book Club: Lifelong Learning and Community Inclusion."

Best Buddies is a nonprofit organization dedicated to helping school-age students, college students, and adults with intellectual and developmental disabilities establish one-to-one friendships with same-age peers without disabilities. To learn more, go to www.bestbuddies .org.

The Ultimate Transition Goal: A Better Quality of Life

Significant strides have been made in the lives of many people with disabilities. Tens of thousands of people who previously were relegated to institutions and other segregated settings now live in real homes in regular neighborhoods. Many who never had an opportunity to learn meaningful job skills go to work each day and bring home a paycheck each week. But living in a community-based residence and having a job in an integrated setting do not translate automatically into a better life. Two in five (42%) employed people with disabilities feel that their work requires them to use their full abilities, and only 34% of adults with disabilities say they are very satisfied with life in general compared to 61% of those without disabilities (Kessler Foundation/National Organization on Disability, 2010).

Most advocates and professionals now realize what people with disabilities have long understood: that inclusion in typical employment, housing, and recreation settings is a necessary first step but that the only truly meaningful outcome of human service programs is an improved quality of life. How highly would you judge the quality of life for a woman who always sits alone during lunch and breaks at work because she has not developed a social relationship with any of her coworkers?

And what about the quality of life for a young man who lives in a group home in a residential neighborhood but seldom gets to choose what he will eat for dinner or when he will go to bed and whose only "friends" are the paid staff responsible for supervising him on his weekly trip to the shopping mall? One measure of the quality of a person's life is the extent to which he can make choices. The choices we make play a significant role in defining our individual identities—from everyday matters, such as what to eat or wear, to the choices we make on larger matters, such as where to live or what kind of work to do (Ferguson & Ferguson, 2011).

Next Chapter Book Club: Lifelong Learning and Community Inclusion

BY TOM FISH, VICKI GRAFF, AND ANKE GROSS-KUNKEL

TEACHING & LEARNING

Although many adults with intellectual disabilities are living independently in the community, they often experience loneliness, isolation, and lack of friendships. Too often people with intellectual disabilities live in the community but are not part of the community. There are those in our society who believe that people with special needs are not capable of lifelong learning and not interested in books. Beyond school, meaningful opportunities for literacy and ongoing learning are rare. Lower literacy skills usually result in a lower quality of life, with fewer employment and leisure opportunities.

The Next Chapter Book Club (NCBC) promotes literacy learning, community inclusion, and social connectedness for adolescents and adults with intellectual disabilities (Fish, Rabidoux, Ober, & Graff, 2009). Developed in 2002 at The Ohio State University's Nisonger Center, NCBC has expanded from two clubs in Columbus, Ohio, to more than 190 clubs: 89 U.S. cities in 22 states, more than 5 cities in Germany, 5 cities in Canada, 2 cities in the U.K., and 1 city in Spain.

THE NEXT CHAPTER BOOK CLUB MODEL

The premise is simple. A group of five to eight people with intellectual disabilities and two or three trained volunteer facilitators gather in a local bookstore or café to read and discuss a book for 1 hour a week. The members take turns reading aloud. Everyone has a copy of the same book, so they can follow along when it is not their turn to read. Much like members of other book clubs, NCBC members choose the book they want to read and how they want to structure their club. Books in the NCBC library include adapted classic novels such as *The Secret Garden* and *Treasure Island* as well as current and sports-related literature. Let's take a closer look at the three model components.

Literacy Learning. Although it isn't planned, each club is racially and ethnically diverse, and includes both readers and nonreaders. That's right—readers and nonreaders are in all clubs. In fact, 60% to 70% of members are not conventionally literate but demonstrate emerging literacy. At first we purchased tape players, thinking that members who couldn't read would want to listen to books on tape before coming to the club. The tape players remain unopened to date; it soon became clear that members wanted to read the books aloud together. That leads to a question often asked: What do we do about the emergent readers?

Our training program for volunteer facilitators includes a variety of strategies to help everyone join in. For example, facilitators often use "echo reading": After a brief pause, they say a word or phrase and let the member "echo" the words back. Over time, many members recognize more words. When any member is stuck on a word, facilitators encourage other members to help. Emergent readers can also participate by describing what's happening in the pictures.

The primary goal of the weekly meetings is to include everyone in the process of reading and talking about the story. It's not so much about reading as many pages as possible. The NCBC challenges as well as assists the members to read in a group setting with other adults who share their interests. It takes 12 to 16 weeks to complete one book in this way.

The NCBC provides people with intellectual disabilities a place where they can enjoy reading and don't feel obliged to do so. Scot, age 51, says, "I didn't like reading at school because I was teased by the other kids." Many members tell us that their motivation to read is to relax. Even though they often had bad experiences with learning to read and felt left out in school, they are still eager to participate in a book club.

The results of being a member are often amazing. Rob, age 49, says he wants to learn to drive, and the book club is helping him read the words on traffic signs. Angela, age 29, can see but is legally blind and can't read. Yet her mother, Kathy, says Angela's favorite place to go is the bookstore or library; she loves to be read to. Jessica, age 23, is an emergent reader who always loved books. Her mother, Minda, says since coming to the NCBC, Jessie pretends to read by imitating other beginning readers.

Community Inclusion. Unlike book clubs that meet in private homes or libraries, NCBCs meet in busy, inviting community settings such as bookstores, coffee shops,

There have been many different conceptions and definitions of quality of life, debates over how or even whether it can be measured, and recommendations about what should or must be done to improve it (e.g., Hughes, Copeland, Fowler, & Church-Pupke, 2002; Lachapelle et al., 2005; Schalock, Gardner, & Bradley, 2007; Sheppard-Jones, Thompson Prout, & Kleinert, 2005).

Volunteer facilitators use a variety of strategies to help Next Chapter Book Club members enjoy reading and discussing books.

and cafés. This follows the paradigm of normalization. Our host sites include Barnes & Noble, Borders, Panera Bread, Starbucks, and Target cafés, among others. These venues have become popular social gathering places for the larger society. Not only does meeting in such places provide the opportunity for people with intellectual disabilities to experience café culture; it also helps raise public awareness of exceptional people.

Tony, the night manager at a local Caribou Coffee, says he and his staff have a good time serving book club members each week. "It's an opportunity to see everybody socialize and participate like other people," he said. Because the store has no large table, the staff assembles several tables before the club arrives. Such things happen in our clubs spontaneously.

Community inclusion for exceptional people means more than simply living in the community. It should translate to going wherever and whenever one wants. Dependence on others for transportation and accessibility issues remain challenges. Phoebe says it's hard to get to her club, because the store has no ramp for her wheelchair. But somehow she gets there.

Ideally, people with disabilities hanging out with friends in cafés on their own will become commonplace. We recognize that the NCBC is merely a structured platform for people with intellectual disabilities to participate in mainstream society. But it's a start.

Social Connectedness. Interpersonal connections, friendships, and belonging play important roles in a person's emotional and physical well-being. Over and over we hear from members, parents, and support staff how much members enjoy making friends and hanging out in the book club. Angela's mother, Kathy, says Angela was shy at first but has improved her social skills and now greets other members and initiates conversations. "Angela's more outgoing and definitely happier. She has a more joyful attitude and . . . a brighter life!"

Reading in a group is an essential part of the book club that empowers the members. They have the chance to relate what is happening in the story to their own lives and learn from one another. Richard, age 32, says, "When I'm helping the others in the book club, I feel high-level."

CONCLUSION

People with intellectual disabilities have the right to participate as full and equal members of society. We encourage students, professionals in the field, and family members of people with intellectual disabilities to embrace activities such as the NCBC and seek similar opportunities for the people they support and advocate with.

HOW TO GET STARTED

Special education teachers can help promote adult literacy:

- Recognize that literacy experiences for adults with intellectual disabilities are severely lacking.
- Recognize that adults with intellectual disabilities enjoy reading, especially when literacy experience is combined with hanging out with friends in a bookstore or café.
- Find local groups or organizations (e.g., service providers, disability organizations, and advocacy or parent groups) interested in cosponsoring an NCBC in your community.
- Contact the NCBC staff to schedule a training workshop and help you take the next steps. Details are on the website: www.nextchapterbookclub.org.
- Introduce community literacy experiences as part of the classroom curriculum, e.g., visits to the library or reading books in a local bookstore or café.

About the Authors

Thomas R. Fish, director of Social Work & Family Support Services, and Vicki L. W. Graff, program manager, both work at The Ohio State University's Nisonger Center. Anke Gross-Kunkel is program coordinator, University of Cologne, Germany.

One widely used measure of the quality of life of a person with intellectual disabilities is the Quality of Life Questionnaire (Schalock & Keith, 1993). The instrument consists of 40 items in four domains: (a) overall satisfaction (e.g., "Does your job make you feel good?"), (b) competence/productivity, (c) empowerment/independence (e.g., "How much control do you have in when you go to bed and when you get up?"), and

(d) social belonging/community integration (e.g., "How frequently do you spend time in recreational activities in town?"). For individuals with sufficient language skills, the instrument is administered in an interview format. For people who lack the necessary language skills, the instrument is completed by two raters who know the individual well and who are familiar with the individual's current activities and living environment.

Misguided and Limiting Presumptions

A continuing problem for many adults with disabilities is lack of acceptance as full members of our society, with all the rights, privileges, and services granted to any citizen. Progress has been made in this regard, but we still have a long way to go. Courts can decree and laws can require, but neither can alter the way in which individuals treat people with disabilities.

Most adults with disabilities believe the biggest barriers to full integration into society are not inaccessible buildings or the actual restrictions imposed by their disabilities but the differential treatment afforded them by people without disabilities. Just as the terms *racism* and *sexism* indicate prejudiced, discriminatory treatment of racial groups and women, **handicapism** describes biased reactions toward people with disabilities. Those reactions are not based on an individual's qualities or performance but on a presumption of what a person with a disability must feel or be like because of the disability (Ohio Developmental Disabilities Council, 2009). When asked how people generally react toward them, 28% of adults with disabilities in a national survey reported that people act as if they are sorry for them, 27% said they are treated differently, and 14% said people tend to avoid further contact with them (Kessler Foundation/National Organization on Disability, 2010). People with severe disabilities in this study were much more likely to describe negative experiences than were those with mild or moderate disabilities.

Only when a man or a woman with a disability is allowed to be simply an ordinary person—given the opportunity to strive and perhaps succeed but also allowed the freedom and dignity to strive and sometimes fail—can full membership and participation in society become a reality. Only then can people with disabilities enjoy a quality of life that citizens without disabilities take for granted.

Self-Advocacy and Self-Determination

Advocacy on behalf of children and adults with disabilities has had a tremendous impact, especially during the past 30 years. Indeed, most of the pervasive changes in education, employment opportunities, and residential services have occurred because of the efforts of advocates. Family members, friends, professionals, and attorneys have traditionally undertaken advocacy for people with disabilities.

Increasingly, people with disabilities are asserting their legal and human rights, challenging the view that they are incapable of speaking for themselves. An interesting finding of the NLTS2 was that among age-eligible young adults with disabilities, 67% had registered to vote, compared to just 58% of 18- to 24-year olds in the general population. Perhaps most conspicuous has been the self-advocacy of individuals with physical disabilities, who have been highly effective in their lobbying as part of the independent living movement. Individuals with sensory impairments have also engaged in self-advocacy. A striking and successful example was Gallaudet University students' refusal in 1988 to accept the appointment of a hearing president who did not know American Sign Language. People with intellectual disabilities have engaged in little self-advocacy, perhaps because many have not learned to recognize when their rights are being violated and because they lack the verbal skills to advocate on their own behalf. Evidence indicates, however, that people with intellectual and developmental disabilities are beginning to use Internet resources and tools to further their civil rights (Zubal-Ruggieri, 2007).

Still a Long Way to Go

In general, the quality of life for most adults with disabilities is better today than it has ever been. Not only do more adults with disabilities live, work, and recreate in

Handicapism

Content Standards for Beginning Teachers—Initial Common Core: Teacher attitudes and behaviors that influence behavior of individuals with exceptional learning needs (IC5K4).

To view a slide show about handicapism, go to http://www.mncdd.org/parallels2/one/sidebar/Handicapism.html.

Self-advocacy and self-determination

Knowledge and Skill Base for Beginning Special Education Transition Specialists: Use support systems to facilitate self-advocacy in transition planning (TS2S4) (also ICC5S8).

community-based, integrated environments, but more adults with disabilities have acquired or are acquiring the personal, social, vocational, and leisure skills that enable them to enjoy the benefits of those settings. But more people with disabilities is not the same as all people with disabilities. And individuals don't live life "in general"; they experience specific instances of joy and sadness, success and failure. There is still a long way to go.

True, the quality of life for someone who now has his own bedroom in a group home and works for wages in a sheltered workshop is appreciably better than it was before he left the institution where he ate and slept communally, and his "work" consisted of an endless series of arts-and-crafts projects. But do the unacceptable standards of the past mean that a relatively better quality of life today is therefore good? Would it be good enough for you?

▼ TIPS FOR BEGINNING TEACHERS

Teaching the Transition Process to Students with Disabilities and Their Families

BY BRADLEY BAUMGARTNER

PRESENT REAL OPPORTUNITIES

Rather than justify to students why a certain behavior or skill is important, present opportunities that require those behaviors or skills from the outset. Real experiences require that students demonstrate social or vocational skills starting today—not tomorrow.

- **Connect students with job shadow opportunities within the community.** Emphasize the importance of social skills and independence to students at every job shadow.
- **Give students the opportunity to work at three or four different job sites.** Even if a student loves and excels at the very first job, it's important to transition to a new set of skills and coworkers. Let a work-experience program provide those experiences to students before they enter the "real world."
- **Run a school-based business that provides work experience and doubles as fund-raising for the life skills program.** Nothing creates interest and commitment by students and administration as a student-run business providing a real and valued service in exchange for program funding. Buy an espresso machine or printing press and let your students compete with Starbucks and Kinko's!
- **Provide leadership opportunities for students.** As younger students enter the program, allow more experienced students to set the tone by taking the lead at worksites, on outings in the community, and at school events.

INFORM FAMILIES ABOUT AVAILABLE RESOURCES

Supports available through community, state, and federal agencies are major factors in the quality of life for adults with disabilities.

- **Schedule a transition night for parents and family members.** Gather those involved and hammer out dates that everyone will stick to. As the school year progresses, events that aren't prioritized early on fall off the radar. The next thing you know, what seemed like a solid plan in August becomes a good idea for next year. Early commitment to dates builds momentum and allows time for discussing and distributing the work among colleagues.
- **Invite local experts.** Every school works with agencies that coordinate information, applications, and services for individuals with disabilities. Many communities also have other support groups or legal agencies whose sole goal is to advocate for those with disabilities. Invite a representative from each to speak briefly about your state's waiver process.
- **Maximize face time with families.** The school schedule is busy as it is. Economize time by offering your Transition Night as a part of parent conferences, the school open house, or a similar existing event. If families are already in the building, they're more likely to drop in for another half-hour or so, especially if you provide refreshments. (Ask your administration for a $100 stipend, or ask a local restaurant to cater for a discounted rate.)
- **Enhance your ability to be understood.** If your school has the resources, provide bilingual interpreters to decrease the communication gap. Use visuals in addition to pertinent literature on the subject. Giving a glimpse of the real locations/offices in your community can be a great first step in getting families to connect to them.
- **Facilitate discussion between families.** Encourage those parents who have experience with the system to share with others. If there is a particularly knowledgeable or outgoing parent or family, encourage them to invite other families to the next Transition Night.
- **Follow up and check in.** Do this step within a month of your first meeting with students and families. Ask if they've completed the waiver process or if they need help with the application. Be prepared to refer them to your local agencies and coordinators again. Whatever you do, don't miss the opportunity to impress how important it is that their child receives the services for which he or she is eligible.

FOCUS EFFORT TO HELP STUDENTS ACHIEVE

As a new special educator, it was very tempting for me to take on more work than the day permitted. The result was week after week of putting in long hours and still feeling as though I hadn't finished. Since then, I've become better at focusing on what's most important.

- **When speaking to colleagues or parents, don't say, "I'll try to . . . [do something] ."** Nothing disappoints so much as a professional who doesn't follow through. Make the decision on whether it's important enough to do it or not do it on the spot—and then stick to your word.
- **Hold high expectations for student learning, behavior, and vocational discipline.** Most students with disabilities will reach their postsecondary goals as long as they are expected to achieve them as much as the next. Students are highly sensitive to uneven levels of expectation or fairness. Push all students to achieve their greatest potential.

▼ KEY TERMS AND CONCEPTS

competitive employment
customized employment
deinstitutionalization
handicapism
individualized transition plan (ITP)
sheltered employment

sheltered workshops
summary of performance (SOP)
supported employment
supported living
transition services
work activity center

▼ SUMMARY

How Do Former Special Education Students Fare as Adults?

- About 7 in 10 students with disabilities complete high school by receiving either a regular diploma or a certificate of completion.
- Data from the National Longitudinal Transition Study-2 (NLTS2) found that 57% of youth with disabilities were working for pay outside the home during the first 4 years after leaving high school, 58% were employed full-time, and 44% received benefits.
- A nationwide survey found three times as many adults with disabilities living in poverty as those without disabilities.
- NLTS2 found that 45% of youth with disabilities had taken postsecondary education classes within 4 years of leaving high school, and their rate of current enrollment (24%) was less than that of same-age peers in the general population (41%).
- One-half (49%) of young adults in NLTS2 had participated in some type of community social activities outside work or school in the preceding year.
- More than twice as many out-of-high-school youth with disabilities in NLTS2 had been arrested (28%) than had youth in the general population (12%).

IDEA and Transition Services

- Will's "bridges model" for transition from high school to adult employment entailed three levels of support—generic, time-limited, and ongoing—depending on the student's needs.
- Halpern's view that secondary special education must help students with disabilities achieve maximum success in all domains of adult functioning greatly influenced amendments to IDEA.

- Transition services are a coordinated set of activities designed to assist a child with disabilities achieve postsecondary goals in education/training, employment, and, where appropriate, independent living.

Transition Planning

- Beginning no later than age 16, each child's IEP must contain measurable postsecondary goals based on age-appropriate transition assessments and a description of the transition services needed to assist the child in reaching those goals.
- IDEA regulations stipulate the following transition-planning process:
  - Conduct age-appropriate transition assessment
  - Write measurable postsecondary goals
  - Identify transition services
  - Develop annual IEP goals that align with postsecondary goals
  - Coordinate transition services with adult services agencies
  - Provide student with summary of performance

Employment

- For most adults with disabilities, obtaining and holding a job are major life challenges and goals.
- Development of career awareness and vocational skills should begin in the elementary grades for children with severe disabilities.
- Middle school students should begin to spend time on actual community job sites.
- Secondary students should spend more time on actual community job sites, with in-school instruction focusing on the functional skills needed in adult

work, domestic, community, and recreational/leisure environments.

- Secondary school programs can enhance the competitive employment prospects for young adults with disabilities by (a) stressing functional, vocational skills; (b) conducting school-based instruction in integrated settings as much as possible; and (c) beginning community-based instruction as early as age 12 for students with severe disabilities and for progressively extended periods as the student nears graduation.

- Supported employment recognizes that many adults with severe disabilities require ongoing support to obtain and hold a job. Supported employment is characterized by performance of real, paid work in regular, integrated work sites; it requires ongoing support from a supported work specialist.

- The role of the employment specialist has evolved from one of primary supporter for the employee with disabilities to one who works with the employer and coworkers to create innovative and natural support networks.

- Self-monitoring, self-evaluation, learning how to respond to naturally occurring cues, and self-instruction are four ways that employees with disabilities can increase their independence and productivity in the workplace.

- Many adults with severe disabilities work in sheltered workshops that provide one or a combination of three kinds of programs: training for competitive employment in the community, extended or long-term employment, and work activities.

Postsecondary Education

- Participation in postsecondary education significantly improves chances of meaningful employment for people with disabilities.

- Although the percentage of postsecondary students who indicate they have a disability has increased significantly in recent years, graduation rates of college students with disabilities remain far below those of students without disabilities.

- The difficulties reported by many college students with disabilities reveal the need for greater emphasis on postsecondary education goals and outcomes during high school transition planning.

Residential Alternatives

- Apartment living offers the greatest opportunities for integration into the community and interaction with people without disabilities. Three common forms of apartment living for adults with disabilities are the apartment cluster, the co-residence apartment, and the maximum-independence apartment.

- Foster home placement allows an adult with disabilities to participate in day-to-day activities of family life, receive attention from people interested in his development, and experience close personal relationships.

- Group homes provide family-style living for three to six people. Most group homes serve adults with intellectual disabilities, although some have residents with other disabilities. Staff people in this type of home help the people who live there develop self-care and daily living skills, form interpersonal relationships, and participate in recreation and leisure skills.

- Supported living is an approach toward helping people with disabilities live in the community as independently and normally as they can by providing a network of various kinds and levels of natural supports.

- Despite deinstitutionalization—the movement of people with intellectual disabilities out of large public institutions and into smaller, community-based residences such as group homes—in 2009, nearly 33,000 people in the United States, mostly adults with severe or profound intellectual disabilities, still lived in large institutions.

Recreation and Leisure

- Learning to participate in age-appropriate recreation and leisure activities is necessary for a satisfying lifestyle.

The Ultimate Transition Goal: A Better Quality of Life

- Many adults with disabilities continue to face lack of acceptance as full members of society.

- Handicapism—discriminatory treatment and biased reactions toward someone with a disability—occurs on personal, professional, and societal levels. It must be eliminated before normalization can become a reality for every man and woman with a disability.

- People with disabilities have begun to assert their legal rights, challenging the view that they are incapable of speaking for themselves.

MyEducationLab™

Go to Topic 20, Transition, in the MyEducationLab (www.myeducationlab.com) for *Exceptional Children*, where you can

- Find learning outcomes for transition along with the national standards that connect to these outcomes.
- Complete Assignments and Activities that can help you more deeply understand the chapter content.
- Apply and practice your understanding of the core teaching skills identified in the chapter with the Building Teaching Skills and Dispositions learning units.
- Examine challenging situations and cases presented in the IRIS Center Resources.
- Access video clips of CCSSO National Teachers of the Year award winners responding to the question "Why Do I Teach?" in the Teacher Talk section.
- Check your comprehension of the content covered in the chapter with the Study Plan. Here you will be able to take a chapter quiz, receive feedback on your answers, and then access Review, Practice, and Enrichment activities to enhance your understanding of chapter content.
- Use the Online Lesson Plan Builder to practice lesson planning and integrating national and state standards into your planning.

▼ GLOSSARY

competitive employment: Full- or part-time work in a competitive labor market in an integrated setting, at or above the federal minimum wage, but not less than the customary wage and level of benefits paid by the employer for the same or similar work performed by individuals who are not disabled.

customized employment: A form of supported employment in which a job is created within an integrated competitive work environment based on the current skills of the potential employee and needs of the employer.

deinstitutionalization: The movement of individuals with disabilities, especially people with mental retardation, from large institutions to smaller, community-based residences and work settings.

handicapism: Prejudice or discrimination based solely on a person's disability, without regard for individual characteristics.

individualized transition plan (ITP): Specifies desired postschool outcomes in four areas (employment, postsecondary education, residential, and recreation/leisure) and instructional programming and supports to help the student attain those outcomes;

required part of each student's individualized education program (IEP) by age 16.

sheltered employment: Work by people with disabilities in a segregated setting, including a work activities center, operated by a private nonprofit agency that employs people with disabiities certified under special provisions of federal minimum wage laws.

sheltered workshop: A structured work environment where people with disabilities receive employment training and perform work for pay. May provide transitional services for some individuals (e.g., short-term training for competitive employment in the community) and permanent work settings for others.

summary of performance (SOP): 2006 Federal regulations for IDEA require that every student who exits special education services through graduation or by exceeding the age of eligibility receives an SOP that summarizes the student's performance in academic achievement and functional performance, provides recommendations for what the student should do to continue progressing toward his or her transition goals, and suggests

community-based education/training, vocational, and independent living agencies and services that may help the student achieve those goals.

supported employment: Providing ongoing, individualized supports to people with disabilities to help them find, learn, and maintain paid employment at regular work sites in the community.

supported living: Personalized networks of natural supports to help people with disabilities live successfully in homes of their own in the community.

transition services: A coordinated set of activities for a child with a disability designed to facilitate the child's movement from school to postschool activities, including postsecondary education, employment, independent living, and community participation; see *individualized transition plan.*

work activity center: A sheltered work and activity program for adults with severe disabilities; teaches concentration and persistence, along with basic life skills, for little or no pay.

Developing Your Own View of Special Education

ALL INTRODUCTORY TEXTBOOKS contain a great deal of information, and this text is no different from any other in that respect. I hope, however, that you have gained more than a collection of basic facts and information about learners with exceptional educational needs and special education, the profession dedicated to meeting those needs. I hope you have examined your own attitudes toward and relationships with children and adults with disabilities. The 10 beliefs that underlie my personal, but by no means unique, view of special education are as follows:

- *People with disabilities have a fundamental right to live and participate in the same settings and programs—in school, at home, in the workplace, and in the community—as do people without disabilities.* People with and without disabilities have a great deal to contribute to and learn from one another. We cannot do that without regular, meaningful interactions in shared environments.

- *People with disabilities have the right to as much self-determination as they can achieve.* Special educators have no more important teaching task than helping students with disabilities learn how to increase the level of autonomy over their own lives.

- *Special education must expand and improve the effectiveness of its early identification and prevention efforts.*

- *Special education must do a better job of helping students with disabilities transition from school to adult life.*

- *Special education must continue to improve its cultural competence.*

- *School and family partnerships enhance both the meaningfulness and the effectiveness of special education.*

- *The work of special educators is most effective when supplemented by the expertise and services of all of the disciplines in the helping professions.*

- *Students with disabilities have the right to an effective education.* The special educator's primary responsibility is designing, implementing, and evaluating instruction that helps students with disabilities acquire, generalize, and maintain knowledge and skills that improve the quality of their lives in school, at home, in the community, and in the workplace—now and in the future. To put it another way, the proof of the special education process is in the product. Therefore . . .

- *Teachers must demand effectiveness from curriculum materials and instructional tools.* Although students with disabilities often need more instructional trials to master a skill than do their peers without disabilities (a reality that sometimes requires a heightened level of perseverance and energy by their teachers), the notion that teaching students with disabilities requires unending patience is a disservice to students with special needs and to their educators—both special and general education teachers. Teachers should not wait patiently for exceptional children to learn but should modify the instructional program to improve its effectiveness.

- *The future for people with disabilities holds great promise.* We have only begun to discover ways to improve teaching, increase learning, prevent or minimize the conditions that cause and exacerbate the effects of disabilities, and use technology to compensate for disabilities. We have not come as far as we can in learning how to help exceptional children and adults build and enjoy fuller, more independent lives.

AS A MEMBER OF THE PROFESSION If you consider yourself a prospective special educator, view special education as a profession and yourself as a professional in the making. A professional commands a specific skill set and knowledge. Becoming a special educator will make you different from people without your professional training. This has nothing to do with arrogance but everything to do with recognizing that students with disabilities depend on their teachers' developing and responsibly using as much professional competence as they can muster.

Obtaining an objective understanding of the nature and scope of a special educator's responsibilities is the first step toward professional competence. Special education is serious business. The learning problems faced by students with disabilities are real, and they require intensive and systematic intervention. Be wary of the notion that disability is merely a socially constructed phenomenon: that all children diagnosed with a disability would be successful and happy learners if others simply viewed them more positively. This romantic ideology is seldom promoted by people with disabilities or by their parents and families. Children with disabilities have skill deficits and difficulties in acquiring and generalizing new knowledge and skills—real learning challenges that cannot be deconstructed away. Don't let the needs of exceptional children and their families get lost in such postmodern ideologies. They need and deserve systematic, effective special education.

It is commendable that you have the commitment and the desire to teach children with exceptional educational needs. You will probably hear often that you are "wonderful" or "patient" because of this. Good intentions are fine, but desire and commitment are only a first step. What learners with disabilities need most are teachers who are in some ways impatient— impatient with curriculum, instructional methods, and policies that do not help their students learn and subsequently use new knowledge and skills required for successful functioning in the home, school, workplace, and community. So, my recommendation to you as a future teacher is this: Don't be patient; be effective.

You will increase your effectiveness as a teacher by using only those curriculum and instructional methods that are backed by sound, empirical research evidence. Special education research has produced a significant and reliable knowledge base about effective teaching practices. While no knowledgeable person believes that research has discovered everything we need to know about teaching exceptional students—many important questions remain to be answered—today's special educator can turn to a research base that includes many instructional strategies and tactics that did not exist when the Education of All Handicapped Children Act was signed into law in 1975.

When considering a new curriculum, program, or instructional method, teachers should ask questions such as the following:

- Has this program been tested in the classroom?
- What evidence shows that this program works?
- What measures of student performance were used to evaluate this program?
- Has any research on this program been published in peer-reviewed journals?
- Does any evidence suggest the program will succeed if modified to meet the skill levels and ages of my students?

Educating students with disabilities has always presented teachers with complex and difficult challenges. And today's special education teachers are expected to do more than ever before. For example, special educators must help ensure students' access to the general education curriculum while teaching them the functional skills needed for daily living and successful transition from school to adult life in the community and workplace. Prepare yourself for meeting this challenge as best you can. Demand relevant, up-to-date information and hands-on practical experiences from your teacher education program. Continue your education and professional development throughout your career. Stay abreast of advances in special education by reading professional journals, actively participate in your school's in-service training opportunities, and attend professional conferences. Even better, experiment with instructional methods, and share the results of your research with colleagues through presentations and publications.

Special education is not a grim, thankless business. Quite the opposite: special education is an exciting, dynamic field that offers personal satisfaction and feelings of accomplishment unequaled in many professions. Welcome aboard!

AS A MEMBER OF THE COMMUNITY The degree of success and happiness that a person with disabilities enjoys in the normal routines of everyday life is not determined solely by his skills and abilities. In large measure, the integration of people with disabilities into contemporary society depends on the attitudes and actions of citizens with little knowledge of or experience with exceptional learners. How can people come to accept and support a group they do not know?

Society controls who enters and who is kept out, much as a gatekeeper lets some visitors pass but refuses others. For a particular individual, society's gatekeeper may have been a physician who urged parents to institutionalize their child or a teacher who resisted having difficult-to-teach students in her classroom. It may have been an employer who refused to hire workers with disabilities. It may have been a social worker, a school board member, or a voter. Saddest of all, it may even have been a parent whose low expectations kept the gate closed.

How society views people with disabilities influences how individual members of the community respond. For several decades, society's views have been changing gradually for the better; changed by people who believe that past practices of exclusion and denial of opportunities were primitive, unfair, and ultimately detrimental to everyone. But to have maximum impact, the movement toward integration and opportunities must ultimately translate into personal terms for those of you who will not choose careers in special education. People with disabilities and people without disabilities do experience certain aspects of life differently, but we are more like one another than we are different. And the conclusion I hope you have reached is this: Every child and adult with disabilities must be treated as an individual, not as a member of a category or a labeled group.

IN SUM Viewing every individual with disabilities first as a person and second as a person with a disability may be the most important step in integrating the individual into the mainstream of school and community life. But changing our attitudes will not diminish the disability. What it will do is give us a new outlook—a more objective and positive one—and allow us to see a disability as a set of special needs. Viewing exceptional people as individuals with special needs tells us much about how to respond to them—and how we respond is the essence of special education.

REFERENCES

AAIDD Ad Hoc Committee on Terminology and Classification. (2010). *Intellectual disability: Definition, classificati on, and systems of supports* (11th ed.). Washington, DC: American Association on Intellectual and Developmental Disabilities.

Abikoff, H. (1991). Cognitive training in ADHD children: Less to it than meets the eye. *Journal of Learning Disabilities, 24,* 205–209.

Abrams, B. J. (2005). Becoming a therapeutic teacher for students with emotional and behavioral disorders. *Teaching Exceptional Children, 38*(2), 40–45.

Accardo, P. (Ed.). (2008). *Capute and Accardo's neurodevelopmental disabilities in infancy and childhood* (3rd ed.). Baltimore: Brookes.

Achenbach, T. M., & McConaughy, S. H. (2003). *The Achenbach System of Empirically Based Assessment.* In C. R. Reynolds & R. W. Kamphaus (Eds.), *Handbook of psychological and educational assessment of children: Personality, behavior, and context* (2nd ed., pp. 406–432). New York: Guilford.

ADHD Parents Medication Guide. (2010). Joint publication of the American Academy of Child and Adolescent Psychiatry and the American Psychiatric Association. Retrieved February 14, 2011, from http://www.parentsmedguide.org/pmg_adhd.html

Agran, M., Blanchard, C., Wehmeyer, M., & Hughes, C. (2002). Increasing problem-solving skills of students with developmental disabilities participating in general education. *Remedial and Special Education, 23,* 279–288.

Agran, M., Hong, S., & Blankenship, K. (2007). Promoting the self-determination of students with visual impairments: Reducing the gap between knowledge and practice. *Journal of Visual Impairment and Blindness, 101,* 453–464.

Agran, M., & Hughes, C. (2006). Introduction to special issue: Self-determination reexamined: How far have we come? *Research and Practice for Persons with Severe Disabilities, 30,* 105–107.

Agran, M., King-Sears, M., Wehmeyer, M. L., & Copeland, S. R. (2003). *Teachers' guides to inclusive practices: Student-directed learning strategies.* Baltimore: Brookes.

Agran, M., Sinclair, T., Alper, S., Cavin, M., Wehmeyer, M., & Hughes, C. (2005). Using self-monitoring to increase following-direction skills of students with moderate to severe disabilities in general education. *Education and Training in Developmental Disabilities, 40,* 3–13.

Ahearn, W. H. (2010). What every behavior analyst should know about the "MMR causes autism" hypothesis. *Behavior Analysis in Practice, 3*(1), 46–52.

Aiello, B. (1976, April 25). Up from the basement: A teacher's story. *New York Times,* p. 14.

Akshoomoff, N. (2000). *Neurological underpinnings of autism* (Vol. 9). Baltimore: Brookes.

Al Otaiba, S. (2001). IRA outstanding dissertation award for 2001: Children who do not respond to early literacy instruction: A longitudinal study across kindergarten and first grade [Abstract]. *Reading Research Quarterly, 36,* 344–345.

Alber, S. R., & Heward, W. L. (1996). "GOTCHA!" Twenty-five behavior traps guaranteed to extend your students' academic and social skills. *Intervention in School and Clinic, 31,* 285–289.

Alber, S. R., & Heward, W. L. (1997). Recruit it or lose it! Training students to recruit positive teacher attention. *Intervention in School and Clinic, 32,* 275–282.

Alber, S. R., & Heward, W. L. (2000). Teaching students to recruit positive attention: A review and recommendations. *Journal of Behavioral Education, 10,* 177–204.

Alber, S. R., Anderson, L. L., Martin, C. M., & Moore, K. J. (2004). Teaching elementary students with behavior disorders to recruit positive teacher attention: Effects on math proficiency. *Journal of Early and Intensive Behavioral Intervention, 1,* 218–231.

Alber, S. R., Heward, W. L., & Hippler, B. J. (1999). Training middle school students with learning disabilities to recruit positive teacher attention. *Exceptional Children, 65,* 253–270.

Alber, S. R., Nelson, J. S., & Brennan, K. B. (2002). A comparative analysis of two homework study methods on elementary and secondary school students' acquisition and maintenance of social studies content. *Education and Treatment of Children, 26,* 172–196.

Alber Morgan, S. R. (2007). Ten ways to enhance the effectiveness of repeated readings. *Journal of Early and Intensive Behavioral Intervention, 3,* 257–263.

Alber Morgan, S. R. (2010). *Using RTI to teach literacy to diverse learners, K–8.* Thousand Oaks, CA: Corwin.

Alber Morgan, S. R., Hessler, T. L., & Konrad, M. (2007). Teaching writing for keeps. *Education and Treatment of Children, 30*(3), 107–128.

Alber Morgan, S. R., Ramp, E. M., Anderson, L. L., & Martin, C. M. (2007). The effects of repeated readings, error correction, and performance feedback on the fluency and comprehension of middle school students with behavior problems. *Journal of Special Education, 41,* 17–30.

Alberto, P. A., & Fredrick, L. D. (2000). Teaching picture reading as an enabling skill. *Teaching Exceptional Children, 33*(6), 60–64.

Alberto, P. A., & Troutman, A. C. (2009). *Applied behavior analysis for teachers* (8th ed.). Upper Saddle River, NJ: Pearson.

Aldrich, F. K., & Parkin, A. J. (1989). Listening at speed. *British Journal of Visual Impairment, 7*(1), 16–18.

Al-Hassan, S., & Gardner, R., III. (2002). Involving immigrant parents of students with disabilities in the educational process. *Teaching Exceptional Children, 35*(2), 52–58.

Ali, Z. (2001). Pica in people with intellectual disability: A literature review of etiology, epidemiology and complications. *Journal of Intellectual and Developmental Disability, 26,* 205–215.

Allen, K. E., Hart, B. M., Buell, J. S., Harris, F. R., & Wolf, M. M. (1964). Effects of social reinforcement on isolate behavior of a nursery school child. *Child Development, 35,* 511–518.

Alliance to Prevent Restraint, Aversive Interventions and Seclusion. (2011a). *Overview of ARS.* Washington, DC: Author. Retrieved June 23, 2011, from http://tash.org/advocacy-issues/restraint-and-seclusion-aprais/overview-of-ars/

Alliance to Prevent Restraint, Aversive Interventions and Seclusion. (2011b). *Positive alternatives.* Washington, DC: Author. Retrieved June 23, 2011 from http://tash.org/advocacy-issues/restraint-and-seclusion-aprais/positive-alternatives/

Allman, C. B., & Lewis, S. (2000). *Seeing eye to eye: An administrator's guide.* New York: AFB Press.

Allor, J. H., Mathes, P. G., Jones, F. G., Champlin, T. M., & Cheatham, J. P. (2010). Individualized research-based reading instruction for student with intellectual disabilities: Success stories. *Teaching Exceptional Children, 42*(3), 6–12.

Alper, S., & Raharinirina, S. (2006). Assistive technology for individuals with disabilities: A review and synthesis of the literature. *Journal of Special Education Technology, 21,* 47.

American Association on Intellectual and Developmental Disabilities. (2012). *Diagnostic adaptive behavior scale.* Washington, DC: Author.

American Association on Mental Retardation. (1994). Policy on facilitated communication. *AAMR News & Notes, 7*(5), 1.

American College of Medical Genetics. (2004). *Newborn screening: Toward a uniform screening panel and system.* Report commissioned by the Health Resources and Services Administration. Available: http://mchb.hrsa.gov/screening/

American Diabetes Association. (2011). *Total prevalence of diabetes & pre-diabetes.* Alexandria, VA: Author. Retrieved February 10, 2011, from http://www.diabetes.org/diabetes-basics/diabetes-statistics/

American Foundation for the Blind. (2011a). *Glossary of eye conditions.* Retrieved May 18, 2011, from http://www.afb.org/seniorsite.asp?SectionID=63&DocumentID=2139

American Foundation for the Blind. (2011b). *Living with vision loss.* Retrieved May 18, 2011, from http://afb.org/section.asp?SectionID=40

American Foundation for the Blind. (2011c). *Mobility devices for young children.* Retrieved June 21, 2011, from http://www.afb.org/section.asp?SectionID=40&TopicID=168&DocumentID=804

American Printing House for the Blind. (2010). *Distribution of eligible students based on the federal quota census of January 7, 2008 (Fiscal Year 2009).* Louisville, KY: Author. Retrieved May 18, 2011, from http://www.aph.org/fedquotpgm/dist09.html

American Printing House for the Blind. (2011). *Book Port Plus user guide.* Louisville, KY: Author. Retrieved June 21, 2011, from http://tech.aph.org/bt_info.htm

American Psychiatric Association. (2000). *Diagnostic and statistical manual of mental disorders, text revision: DSM-IV-TR* (4th ed.). Washington, DC: Author.

American Psychiatric Association. (2004). *Diagnostic and statistical manual of mental disorders, text revision: DSM-IV-TR* (4th ed.). Washington, DC: Author.

American Psychiatric Association. (2006). *Quick reference to the American Psychiatric*

Association practice guidelines for the treatment of psychiatric disorders: Compendium 2006. Washington, DC: Author.

American Psychiatric Association. (2011a). DSM V Development. A 09 Autism Spectrum Disorder: Proposed revision. Washington, DC: Author. Retrieved August 16, 2011, from http://www.dsm5.org/ProposedRevision/Pages/proposedrevision.aspx?rid=94

American Psychiatric Association. (2011b). DSM-V Development. A 10 Attention deficit/hyperactivity disorder: Proposed revision. Washington, DC: Author. Retrieved October 20, 2011, from http://www.dsm5.org/ProposedRevisions/Pages/proposedrevision.aspx?rid=383

American Psychological Association. (1994, August). Resolution on facilitated communication by the American Psychological Association. Washington, DC: Author.

American Speech-Language-Hearing Association. (1993). Definitions of communication disorders and variations [Relevant Paper]. Available from www.asha.org/policy

American Speech-Language-Hearing Association. (2000). Guidelines for the roles and responsibilities of speech-language pathologists [Guidelines]. Rockville, MD: Author. Available from www.asha.org/policy

American Speech-Language-Hearing Association. (2007). The prevalence and incidence of hearing loss in adults. Retrieved June 6, 2011, from http://asha.org/public/hearing/disorders/prevalence_adults.htm

American Speech-Language-Hearing Association. (2010a). Roles and responsibilities of speech-language pathologists in schools [Professional issues statement]. Rockville, MD: Author.

American Speech-Language-Hearing Association. (2010b). Schools survey summary report: Number and type of responses, SLPs. Rockville, MD: Author.

American Speech-Language-Hearing Association. (2011a). Effects of hearing loss on development. Rockville, MD: Author. Retrieved June 6, 2011, from http://www.asha.org/public/hearing/disorders/effects.htm

American Speech-Language-Hearing Association. (2011b). How does your child hear and talk? Birth to one year. Rockville, MD: Author. Retrieved June 6, 2011, from http://asha.org/public/speech/development/01.htm

American Speech-Language-Hearing Association. (2011c). Social language use: Pragmatics. Rockville, MD: Author. Retrieved June 14, 2011, from http://www.asha.org/public/speech/development/Pragmatics.htm

Anastasiou, D., & Kauffman, J. M. (2011). A social constructionist approach to disability: Implications for special education. Exceptional Children, 77, 367–384.

Anderegg, M. L., Vergason, G. A., & Smith, M. C. (1992). A visual representation of the grief cycle for use by teachers with families of children with disabilities. Remedial and Special Education, 13(2), 17–23.

Anderson, A., Moore, D. W., & Bourne, T. (2007). Functional communication and other concomitant behavior change following PECS training: A case study. Behaviour Change, 24, 173–181.

Anderson, D. H., Fisher, A., Marchant, M., Young, K. R., & Smith, J. A. (2006). The cool card intervention: A positive support strategy for managing anger. Beyond Behavior, 16, 3–13.

Anderson, L. W. (Ed.), Krathwohl, D. R. (Ed.), Airasian, P. W., Cruikshank, K. A., Mayer, R. E., Pintrich, P. R., Raths, J., & Wittrock, M. C. (2001). A taxonomy for learning, teaching, and assessing: A revision of Bloom's Taxonomy of Educational Objectives (Complete ed.). New York: Longman.

Anderson, N. B., & Shames, G. H. (2006). Human communication disorders: An introduction (8th ed.). Upper Saddle River, NJ: Pearson.

Anekny, E. M., Wilkins, J., & Spain, J. (2009). Mothers' experiences of transition planning for their children with disabilities. Teaching Exceptional Children, 41(6), 28–36.

Angell, M. E., Stoner, J. B., & Fulk, B. M. (2010). Advice from adults with physical disabilities on fostering self-determination during the school years. Teaching Exceptional Children, 42(3), 64–75.

Angermeier, K., Schlosser, R. W., Luiselli, J. K., Harrington, C., & Carter, B. (2008). Effects of iconicity on requesting with the Picture Exchange Communication System in children with Autism spectrum disorders. Research in Autism Spectrum Disorders, 2, 430–446.

Ankeny, E. M., Wilkins, J., & Spain, J. (2009). Mothers' experiences of transition planning for their children with disabilities. Teaching Exceptional Children, 41(6), 28–36.

Annie E. Casey Foundation. (2011). Children in poverty (percent)—2010. Baltimore: Author. Retrieved October 4, 2011, from http://datacenter.kidscount.org/data/acrossstates/Rankings.aspx?ind=43

Anthony, D. (1971). Signing essential English. Anaheim, CA: Anaheim School District.

Antia, S., Jones, P., Reed, S., & Kreimeyer, K. (2009). Academic status and progress of deaf and hard of hearing students in general education courses. Journal of Deaf Studies and Deaf Education, 14, 293–311.

Antle, B. J. (2004). Factors associated with self-worth in young people with physical disabilities. Health and Social Work, 29, 167–175.

Antunez, B. (2000). When everyone is involved: Parents and communities in school reform. National Council for Bilingual Education. Available: http://www.ncbe.gwu.edu/ncbepubs/tasynthesis/framing/6parents.htm

Anxiety Disorders Association of America. (2011). Brief overview of anxiety disorders. Silver Spring, MD: Author. Retrieved July 26, 2011, from http://www.adaa.org/understanding-anxiety

Araujo, B. E. (2009). Best practices in working with linguistically diverse families. Intervention in School and Clinic, 45, 116–123.

Armbruster, B. B., Lehr, F., & Osborn, J. (2006). Put reading first: The research building blocks for teaching children to read (3rd ed.). Jessup, MD: Center for the Improvement of Early Reading Achievement.

Armendariz, F., & Umbreit, J. (1999). Using active responding to reduce disruptive behavior in a general education classroom. Journal of Positive Behavior Interventions, 1, 152–158.

Arndt, S. A., Konrad, M., & Test, D. W. (2006). Effects of the self-directed IEP on student participation in planning meetings. Remedial and Special Education, 27, 194–207.

Arnold, J. B., & Dodge, H. W. (1994). Room for all. American School Board Journal, 181(10), 22–26.

Arnold, L. E., Christopher, J., Huestis, R. D., & Smeltzer, D. J. (1978). Megavitamins for minimal brain dysfunction: A placebo controlled study. Journal of the American Medical Association, 240, 2642–2643.

Arter, C. (1997). Listening skills. In H. Mason & S. McCall (Eds.), Visual impairment: Access to education for children and young people (pp. 143–148). London: Fulton.

Artiles, A. J., & Bal, A. (2008). The next generation of disproportionality research: Toward a comparative model in the student of equity in ability differences? Journal of Special Education, 42, 4–14.

Artiles, A. J., Harris-Murri, N., & Rostenberg, D. (2006). Inclusion as social justice: Critical notes on discourses, assumptions, and the road ahead. Theory into Practice, 45, 260–268.

Artiles, A. J., Trent, S. C., & Palmer, J. D. (2004). Culturally diverse students in special education Legacies and prospects. In J. A. Banks & C. A. M. Banks (Eds.), Handbook of research of multicultural education (2nd ed., pp. 716–735). San Francisco: Jossey-Bass.

Asthma and Allergy Foundation of America. (2011). Asthma facts and figures. Washington, DC: Author. Retrieved February 10, 2011, from http://www.aafa.org/display.cfm?id=8&sub=42

Astley, S. J., & Clarren, S. K. (2000). Diagnosing the full spectrum of fetal alcohol–exposed individuals: Introducing the 4-digit diagnostic code. Alcohol & Alcoholism, 35, 400–410.

Attwood, T. (2003). Understanding and managing circumscribed interests. In M. Prior (Ed.), Learning and behavior problems in Asperger syndrome (pp. 126–147). New York: Guilford.

Attwood, T. (2007). The complete guide to Asperger's syndrome. London: Jessica Kingsley.

Autism and Developmental Disabilities Monitoring Network. (2007). Prevalence of autism spectrum disorders: Six sites, United States, 2000. Available: http://www.cdc.gov/mmwr/preview/mmwrhtml/ss5601a1.htm

Autism Research Institute. (1998). Another genetic defect linked to autistic behavior, retardation. Autism Research Review International, 12(1), 4.

Ayres, K. M., & Langone, J. (2008). Video supports for teaching students with developmental disabilities and autism: Twenty-five years of research and development. Journal of Special Education Technology, 23(3), 1–8.

Ayres, K. M., Lowrey, K. A., Douglas, K. H., & Sievers, C. (2011). I can identify Saturn but I can't brush my teeth: What happens when the curricular focus for students with severe disabilities shifts. Education and Training in Autism and Developmental Disabilities, 46, 11–21.

Babikian, T., & Asarnow, R. F. (2009). Neuro-cognitive outcomes and recovery after pediatric TBI: Meta-analytic review of the literature. Neuropsychology, 23, 283–296.

Bacon, C. K., & Wilcox, M. J. (2011). Developmental language delay in infancy and early childhood. In N. B. Anderson & G. H. Shames (Eds.), Human communication disorders: An introduction (8th ed., pp. 305–330). Upper Saddle River, NJ: Pearson.

Baer, D. M. (1999). How to plan for generalization (2nd ed.). Austin, TX: PRO-ED.

Baer, D. M. (2005). Letters to a lawyer. In W. L. Heward, T. E. Heron, N. A. Neef, S. M. Peterson, D. M. Sainato, G. Cartledge, R. Gardner III, L. D. Peterson, S. B. Hersh, & J. C. Dardig (Eds.), Focus on behavior analysis in education: Achievements, challenges, and opportunities (pp. 3–30). Upper Saddle River, NJ: Merrill/Pearson.

Baer, D. M., & Daviso, A. W. III. (2008). Independent living and community participation. In R. W. Flexer, T. J. Simmons, P. Luft, & R. M. Baer (Eds.), Transition planning for secondary students with disabilities (3rd ed., pp. 290–316). Upper Saddle River, NJ: Merrill/Pearson.

Baer, D. M., & Wolf, M. M. (1970). The entry into natural communities of reinforcement. In R. Ulrich, T. Stachnick, & J. Mabry (Eds.), Control of human behavior (pp. 319–324). Glenview, IL: Scott, Foresman.

Baer, R. M., Simmons, T. J., Bauder, D., & Flexer, R. W. (2008). Standards based curriculum and transition. In R. W. Flexer, T. J. Simmons, P. Luft, & R. M. Baer (Eds.), Transition planning for secondary students with disabilities (3rd ed., pp. 134–160). Upper Saddle River, NJ: Merrill/ Pearson.

Bagnato, S. J., Neisworth, J. T., & Pretti-Frontczak, K. (2010). LINKing assessment and early intervention: An authentic curriculum-based approach (2nd ed.). Baltimore: Brookes.

Bahr, M. W., & Kovalesk, J. F. (2006). The need for problem-solving teams: Introduction to the special issue. Remedial and Special Education, 27, 2–5.

Bailey, D., Skinner, D., Correa, V., Arcia, E., Reyes-Blanes, M., Rodriguez, P., Vazquez, E., & Skinner, M. (1999). Needs and supports reported by Latino families of young children with developmental disabilities. American Journal on Mental Retardation, 104, 437–451.

Bailey, D., Skinner, D., Correa, V., Blanes, M., Vasquez, E., & Rodriguez, P. (1999). Awareness, use, and satisfaction with services for Latino parents of young children with disabilities. Exceptional Children, 65, 367–381.

Bak, S. (1999). Relationships between inappropriate behaviors and other factors in young children with visual impairments. RE:view, 31, 84–91.

Baker, E., Wang, M., & Walberg, H. (1995). The effects of inclusion in learning. Educational Leadership, 52(4), 33–34.

Baker, S. (2010). Research brief 1: The importance of fingerspelling for reading. Washington, DC: Gallaudet University Science of Learning Center on Visual Language and Visual Learning.

Baker, S. (2011). Research brief 2: Advantages of early visual language. Washington, DC: Gallaudet University Science of Learning Center on Visual Language and Visual Learning.

Baker, S., & Baker, K. (1997). Educating children who are deaf or hard of hearing: Bilingual-bicultural education. ERIC Digest #553. (ERIC Document Reproduction Service No. ED 416 671).

Baker, S., Gersten, R., & Scanlon, D. (2002). Procedural facilitators and cognitive strategies: Tools for unraveling the mysteries of comprehension and the writing process, and for providing meaningful access to the general curriculum. Learning Disabilities Research & Practice, 17, 65–77.

Baker, S., Smolkowski, K., Katz, R., Fien, H., Seeley, J., Kame'enui, E. J., et al. (2008). Reading fluency as a predictor of reading proficiency in low-performing, high-poverty schools. School Psychology Review, 37(1), 18–37.

Bambara, L. M., & Koger, F. (1996). Innovations: Providing opportunities for choice throughout the day. Washington, DC: American Association on Mental Retardation.

Bambara, L. M., Koger, F., & Bartholomew, A. (2011). Building skills for home and community. In M. E. Snell & F. Brown (Eds.), Instruction of students with severe disabilities (7th ed., pp. 529–568). Upper Saddle River, NJ: Pearson.

Banda, D. R., & Grimmett, E. (2008). Enhancing social and transition behaviors of persons with autism through activity schedules: A review. Education and Training in Developmental Disabilities, 43(3), 324–333.

Bandura, A. (1962). Social learning through imitation. Lincoln: University of Nebraska Press.

Banks, J. A. (2007). Educating citizens in a multicultural society (2nd ed.). New York: Teachers College Press.

Banks, J. A., & Banks, C. A. M. (Eds.). (2013). Multicultural education: Issues and perspectives (8th ed.). Boston: Allyn & Bacon.

Barbera, M. L., with Rasmussen, T. (2007). The verbal behavior approach: How to teach children with autism and related disorders. Philadelphia: Jessica Kingsley.

Barkley, R. A. (2005). Attention-deficit hyperactivity disorder: A handbook for diagnosis and treatment (3rd ed.). New York: Guilford.

Barlow, J. A. (2001). Prologue: Recent advances in phonological theory and treatment. Language, Speech, and Hearing Services in Schools, 32, 225–228.

Barnard-Brak, L., & Lechtenberger, D. (2010). Student IEP participation and academic achievement across time. Remedial and Special Education, 31, 343–349.

Baron-Cohen, S., Allen, J., & Gillberg, C. (1992). Can autism be detected at 18 months? The needle, the haystack, and the CHAT. British Journal of Psychiatry, 161, 839–843.

Barr, R., Dowden, A., & Hayne, H. (1996). Developmental changes in deferred imitation by 6- to 24-month-old infants. Infant Behavior and Development, 19, 159–171.

Barraga, N. C. (1964). Increased visual behavior in low vision children. New York: American Foundation for the Blind.

Barraga, N. C. (1970). Teacher's guide for development of visual learning abilities and utilization of low vision. Louisville, KY: American Printing House for the Blind.

Barraga, N. C., & Erin, J. N. (2001). Visual impairments and learning (4th ed.). Austin, TX: Exceptional Resources.

Barrera, I. (1995). To refer or not to refer: Untangling the web of diversity, "deficit," and disability. New York State Association for Bilingual Education Journal, 10, 54–66.

Barry, L. M., & Messer, J. J. (2003). A practical application of self-management for students diagnosed with attention-deficit/hyperactivity disorder. Journal of Positive Behavior Interventions, 5, 238–248.

Bartlett, L. D., Etscheidt, S., & Weisentstein, G. R. (2007). Special education law and practice in public schools (2nd ed.). Upper Saddle River, NJ: Merrill/Pearson.

Barton, E. E., Wolery, M. (2008). Teaching pretend play to children with disabilities: A review of the literature. Topics in Early Childhood Special Education, 28, 109–125.

Barton, E. E., Wolery, M. (2010). Training teachers to promote pretend play in young children with disabilities. Exceptional Children, 77, 85–106.

Bass-Ringdahl, S. M. (2010). The relationship of audibility and the development of canonical babbling in young children with hearing impairment. Journal of Deaf Studies and Deaf Education, 14, 287–310.

Bat-Chava, Y. (2000). Diversity of deaf identities. American Annals of the Deaf, 145, 420–428.

Bateman, B. (2005). The play's the thing. Learning Disability Quarterly, 28, 115–118.

Bateman, B. D., & Herr, C. M. (2006). Writing measurable IEP goals and objectives. Verona, WI: Attainment Company.

Bateman, B. D., & Linden, M. L. (2006). Better IEPs: How to develop legally correct and educationally useful programs (4th ed.). Verona, WI: Attainment Company.

Bateman, D. F. (2008). Due process hearing case study. Teaching Exceptional Children, 41(2), 73–75.

Bateman, D. F. (2010). Due process hearing case study. Teaching Exceptional Children, 42(4), 80–82.

Batshaw, M. L., Pellegrino, L, & Roizen, N. J. (Eds.). (2007). Children with disabilities (6th ed.). Baltimore: Brookes.

Bauer, A. M., & Brown, G. M. (2001). Adolescents and inclusions: Transforming secondary schools. Baltimore: Brookes.

Bauer, P. E. (2008). Perspective: Prenatal screening for Down syndrome. Intellectual and Developmental Disabilities, 46, 247–251.

Baum, S. (2004). Twice-exceptional and special populations of gifted students. Thousand Oaks, CA: Corwin.

Baumgart, D., Brown, L., Pumpian, I., Nisbet, J., Ford, A., Sweet, M., Messina, R., & Schroeder, J. (1982). Principle of partial participation and individualized adaptations in educational programs for severely handicapped students. Journal of the Association for Persons with Severe Handicaps, 7, 17–27.

Bausch, M. E., & Ault, M. J. (2008). Assistive technology implementation plan: A tool for improving outcomes. Teaching Exceptional Children, 41(1), 6–14.

Bayley, N. (2005). Bayley Scales of Infant and Toddler Development (3rd ed.). San Antonio, TX: PsychCorp.

Beadle-Brown, J., Murphy, G., & Wing, L. (2005). Long-term outcome for people with severe intellectual disabilities: Impact of social impairment. American Journal on Mental Retardation, 110, 1–12.

Beakley, B. A., & Yoder, S. L. (1998). Middle schoolers learn community skills. Teaching Exceptional Children, 30(3), 16–21.

Beard, L., Bowden Carpenter, L., & Johnston, L. (2011). Assistive technology: Access for all students (2nd ed.). Upper Saddle River, NJ: Merrill/Pearson.

Beatty, L. S., Madden, R., Gardner, E. F., & Karlsen, B. (2003). Stanford Diagnostic Mathematics Test—Fourth edition. San Antonio, TX: Harcourt Brace Educational Measurement.

Beck, J., Broers, J., Hogue, E., Shipstead, J., & Knowlton, E. (1994). Strategies for functional community-based instruction and inclusion for children with mental retardation. Teaching Exceptional Children, 26(2), 44–48.

Beck, R., Conrad, A. D., & Anderson, P. (2010). One-minute fluency builders series. Longmont, CO: Sopris West.

Becker-Cottrill, B., McFarland, J., & Anderson, V. (2003). A model of positive behavioral support for individuals with autism and their families: The family focus project. Focus on Autism and Other Developmental Disabilities, 18, 113–123.

Behr, S. K., Murphy, D. L., & Summers, J. A. (1992). *User's manual: Kansas inventory of parental perceptions (KIPP)*. Lawrence: University of Kansas, Beach Center on Families and Disability.

Beilke, J. R., & Yssel, N. (1999). The chilly climate for students with disabilities in higher education. *College Student Journal, 33*(3), 364–371.

Beirne-Smith, M., Patton, J. R., & Kim, S. H. (2006). *Mental retardation* (7th ed.). Upper Saddle River, NJ: Merrill/Pearson.

Belcastro, F. (1993). Teaching addition and subtraction of whole numbers to blind students: A comparison of two methods. *Focus on Learning Problems in Mathematics, 15* (1), 14–22.

Bellini, S., & Akullian, J. (2007). A meta-analysis of video modeling and video self-modeling interventions for children and adolescents with autism spectrum disorders. *Exceptional Children, 73*, 264–287.

Belmont, J. M. (1966). Long-term memory in mental retardation. *International Review of Research in Mental Retardation, 1*, 219–255.

BenChaabane, D., Alber Morgan, S. R., & DeBar, R. M. (2009). The effects of parent-implemented PECS training on improvisation of mands by children with autism. *Journal of Applied Behavior Analysis, 42*, 671–677.

Benner, G. J., Nelson, J. R., Ralston, N. C., & Mooney, P. (2010). A meta-analysis of the effects of reading instruction on the reading skills of students with or at-risk of behavioral disorders. *Behavioral Disorders, 35*, 86–102.

Bennett, D. (1997). Low vision devices for children and young people with a visual impairment. In H. Mason & S. McCall (Eds.), *Visual impairment: Access to education for children and young people* (pp. 64–75). London: Fulton.

Benz, M. R., Lindstrom, L., Unruh, D., & Waintrup, M. (2004). Sustaining secondary transition programs in local schools. *Remedial and Special Education, 25*, 39–50.

Bergeron, R., & Floyd, R. G. (2006). Broad cognitive abilities of children with mental retardation: An analysis of group and individual profiles. *American Journal on Mental Retardation, 111*, 417–432.

Benz, M. R., Lindstrom, L., & Yavanoff, P. (2000). Improving graduation and employment outcomes of students with disabilities: Predictive factors and student perspectives. *Exceptional Children, 66*, 509–529.

Berkson, G. (2004). Intellectual and physical disabilities in prehistory and early civilization. *Mental Retardation, 42*, 195–208.

Berney, T. P. (2000). Autism: An evolving concept. *British Journal of Psychiatry, 176*, 20–25.

Bernheimer, L. P., Keogh, B. K., & Guthrie, D. (2006). Young children with developmental delays as young adults: Predicting developmental and personal-social outcomes. *American Journal on Mental Retardation, 111*, 263–272.

Best, S. J. (2010a). Health impairments and infectious diseases. In S. J. Best, K. W. Heller, & J. L. Bigge (Eds.), *Teaching individuals with physical or multiple disabilities* (6th ed., pp. 82–109). Upper Saddle River, NJ: Merrill/Pearson.

Best, S. J. (2010b). Physical disabilities. In S. J. Best, K. W. Heller, & J. L. Bigge (Eds.), *Teaching individuals with physical or multiple disabilities* (6th ed., pp. 32–58). Upper Saddle River, NJ: Merrill/Pearson.

Best, S. J., & Bigge, J. L. (2010). Cerebral palsy. In S. J. Best, K. W. Heller, & J. L. Bigge (Eds.), *Teaching individuals with physical or multiple*

disabilities (6th ed., pp. 60–81). Upper Saddle River, NJ: Merrill/Pearson.

Best, S. J., Heller, K. W., & Bigge, J. L. (2010). *Teaching individuals with physical or multiple disabilities* (6th ed.). Upper Saddle River, NJ: Merrill/Pearson.

Best, S. J., Reed, P., & Bigge, J. L. (2010). Assistive technology. In S. J. Best, K. W. Heller, & J. L. Bigge (Eds.), *Teaching individuals with physical or multiple disabilities* (6th ed., pp. 175–220). Upper Saddle River, NJ: Merrill/Pearson.

Bettelheim, B. (1967). *The empty fortress: Infantile autism and the birth of the self*. London: Collier-Macmillan.

Betz, C. L., & Nehring, W. M. (2007). *Promoting health care transitions for adolescents with special health care needs and disabilities*. Baltimore: Brookes.

Beukelman, D. R., & Miranda, P. (1998). *Augmentative and alternative communication: Management of severe communication disorder in children and adults* (2nd ed.). Baltimore: Brookes.

Bevill, A. R., Gast, D. L., MaGuire, A. M., & Vail, C. O. (2001). Increasing engagement of preschoolers with disabilities through correspondence training and picture cues. *Journal of Early Intervention, 24*, 129–145.

Bianco, M. (2005). The effects of disability labels on special education and general education teachers' referrals for gifted programs. *Learning Disability Quarterly, 28*, 285–293.

Bicard, D. F., & Neef, N. A. (2002). Effects of strategic versus tactical instructions on adaptation to changing contingencies in children with ADHD. *Journal of Applied Behavior Analysis, 35*, 375–389.

Bierman, K. L. (2005). *Peer rejection: Developmental processes and intervention strategies*. New York: Guilford.

Bigby, L. (2007). Legal, historical, and cultural perspectives. In J. Anderson Downing (Ed.), *Students with emotional and behavioral problems: Assessment, management, and intervention strategies* (pp. 2–19). Upper Saddle River, NJ: Merrill/Pearson.

Bigge, J. L., Stump, C. S., Spagna, M. E., & Silberman, R. K. (1999). *Curriculum, assessment, and instruction for students with disabilities*. Belmont, CA: Wadsworth.

Biklen, D. (1990). Communication unbound: Autism and praxis. *Harvard Educational Review, 60*, 291–314.

Biklen, D. (2005). *Autism and the myth of the person alone*. New York: New York University Press.

Biklen, D., & Cardinal, D. N. (1997). *Contested words, contested science: Unraveling the facilitated communication controversy*. New York: Teachers College Press.

Billingsley, G., Scheuermann, B., & Webber, J. (2009). A comparison of three instructional methods for teaching math skills to secondary students with emotional/behavioral disorders. *Behavioral Disorders, 35*, 4–18.

Binder, C. (1996). Behavioral fluency: Evolution of a new paradigm. *The Behavior Analyst, 19*, 163–197.

Bishop, D. V. M., & Snowling, M. (2004). Developmental dyslexia and specific language impairment: Same or different? *Psychological Bulletin, 130*, 858–886.

Bishop, M., & Boag, E. M. (2006). Teachers' knowledge about epilepsy and attitudes toward

students with epilepsy: Results of a national survey. *Epilepsy & Behavior, 8*, 397–405.

Blacher, J. (1984). A dynamic perspective on the impact of a severely handicapped child on the family. In J. Blacher (Ed.), *Severely handicapped children and their families* (pp. 3–50). Orlando, FL: Academic Press.

Blacher, J., & Baker, B. L. (2007). Positive impact of intellectual disability on families. *American Journal on Mental Retardation, 112*, 330–348.

Blake, C., Wang, W., Cartledge, G., & Gardner, R. (2000). Middle school students with serious emotional disturbances serve as social skills trainers and reinforcers for peers with SED. *Behavioral Disorders, 25*, 280–298.

Blalock, G., Kochhar-Bryant, C., Test, D. W., Kohler, P., White, W., Lehmann, J., Bassett, D., & Patton, J. (2003). The need for comprehensive personnel preparation in transition and career development: DCDT position statement. *Career Development for Exceptional Individuals, 26*, 207–226.

Blalock, G., Patton, J. R., Kohler, P., & Bassett, D. (2009). *Transition and students with learning disabilities: Facilitating the movement from school to adult life* (2nd ed.). Austin: Pro-Ed.

Blatt, B. (1976). *Revolt of the idiots: A story*. Glen Ridge, NJ: Exceptional Press.

Blatt, B., & Kaplan, F. (1966). *Christmas in purgatory: A photographic essay on mental retardation*. Boston: Allyn & Bacon.

Blaxhill, M. F. (2004). What's going on? The question of time trends in autism. *Public Health Reports, 119*, 536–551.

Blisssymbolics Communication International. (2011). *About Blisssymbolics*. Toronto: Author. Retrieved June 15, 2011, from http://www.blisssymbolics.org/pfw/index.php?option=com_content&view=article&id=4&Itemid=1

Block, M. E. (2007). *A teacher's guide to including students with disabilities in general physical education* (3rd ed.). Baltimore: Brookes.

Bloodstein, O., & Bernstein Ratner, N. (2007). *A handbook on stuttering* (6th ed.). Florence, KY: Cengage Learning.

Bloom, B. S. (1980). The new direction in educational research: Alterable variables. *Phi Delta Kappan, 61*, 382–385.

Bloom, B. S., Englehart, M., Furst, E., Hill, W., & Krathwohl, D. (1956). *Taxonomy of educational objectives: The classification of educational goals. Handbook I: Cognitive domain*. New York: Longman's Green.

Blue-Banning, M., Summers, J. A., Frankland, H. C., Nelson, L. L., & Beegle, G. (2004). Dimensions of family and professional partnerships: Constructive guidelines for collaboration. *Exceptional Children, 70*, 167–184.

Bluestone, C. D., & Klein, J. O. (2001). *Otitis media in infants and children* (3rd ed.). Philadelphia: Saunders.

Board of Education of the Hendrick Hudson Central School District v. Rowley, 102 S. Ct. 3034 (1982).

Boothe, D. (2004). Gender differences in achievement and aptitude test results: Perspectives from the recent literature. In D. Boothe & J. Stanley (Eds.), *In the eyes of the beholder: Critical issues for diversity in gifted education* (pp. 179–189). Waco, TX: Prufrock.

Borland, J. H., & Wright, L. (1994). Identifying young, potentially gifted, economically disadvantaged students. *Gifted Child Quarterly, 44*, 33–42.

Bornstein, H. (1974). Signed English: A manual approach to English language development. *Journal of Speech and Hearing Disorders, 3*, 330–343.

Botts, B. H., Hershfeldt, P. A., & Christensen-Sandfort, R. J. (2089). Snoezelen®: Empirical review of product representation. *Focus on Autism and Other Developmental Disabilities, 24*, 17

Bouchard, D., & Tétreault, S. (2000). The motor development of sighted children and children with moderate low vision aged 8–13. *Journal of Visual Impairments and Blindness, 94*, 564–573.

Bouck, E. C. (2009). A snapshot of secondary education for students with mild intellectual disabilities. *Education and Training in Developmental Disabilities, 4*, 435–443.

Bouck, E. C. (2011). Functional curriculum models for secondary students with mild mental impairment. *Education and Training in Autism and Developmental Disabilities, 46*, 399–409.

Bouffard, S. (July, 2008). *Tapping into technology: The role of the internet in family–school communication.* Cambridge, MA: Harvard Family Research Project. Retrieved September 6, 2011, from http://www.hfrp.org/publications-resources/browse-our-publications/tapping-into-technology-the-role-of-the-internet-in-family-school-communication

Boushey, A. (2001). The grief cycle—One parent's trip around. *Focus on Autism and Other Developmental Disabilities, 16*, 27–30.

Boutot, E. A., & Bryant, D. P. (2005). Social integration of students with autism. *Education and Training in Developmental Disabilities, 40*, 14–23.

Boutot, E. A., & Tincani, M. (Eds.). (2009). *Autism encyclopedia: The complete guide to autism spectrum disorders.* Waco, TX: Prufrock.

Bowe, F. (2000). *Teaching individuals with physical and multiple disabilities* (4th ed.). Upper Saddle River, NJ: Merrill/Pearson.

Bower, E. (2009). *Finnie's handling the young child with cerebral palsy at home.* Philadelphia: Elsevier.

Bower, E. M. (1960). *Early identification of emotionally handicapped children in the schools.* Springfield, IL: Thomas.

Bower, E. M. (1982). Defining emotional disturbance: Public policy and research. *Psychology in the Schools, 19*, 55–60.

Boyd-Ball, A. (2007, June). *Native Americans with disabilities.* Eugene: University of Oregon.

Boykin, A. W. (1983). The academic performance of Afro-American children. In J. Spence (Ed.), *Achievement and achievement motives* (pp. 324–371). San Francisco: Freeman.

Boyle, C., Van Naarden Braun, K., & Yeargin-Allsopp, M. (2005). The prevalence and the genetic epidemiology of developmental disabilities. In M. Butler & J. Meany (Eds.), *Genetics of developmental disabilities* (pp. 716–717). Oxford: Blackwell.

Boyle, J. R. (2001). Enhancing the note-taking skills of students with mild disabilities. *Intervention in School and Clinic, 36*(4), 221–224.

Boyle, J. R. (2010). Note-taking skills of middle school students with and without learning disabilities. *Journal of learning disabilities, 43*(6), 530–540.

Boyle, J. R. (2011). Strategic note-taking for inclusive middle school science classrooms. *Remedial and Special Education.* Published online before print June 27, 2011, doi: 10.1177/0741932511410862

Braddock, D., Hemp, R., Rizzolo, M. C., Hafner, L., Tanis, E. S., & Wu, J. (2011). *The state of the states in developmental disabilities: 2011.* Boulder: University of Colorado, Coleman Institute for Cognitive Disabilities.

Bradley, R., Danielson, L., & Doolitte, J. (2007). Responsiveness to intervention: 1997–2007. *Teaching Exceptional Children, 39*(5), 8–12.

Bradley, V. J., Knoll, J., & Agosta, J. M. (Eds.). (1992). *Emerging issues in family support.* Washington, DC: American Association on Mental Retardation.

Braille Institute. (2011). *Leading eye diseases.* Los Angeles: Author. Retrieved June 16, 2011, from http://brailleinstitute.org/About_Sight_Loss/Leading_Eye_Diseases.aspx

Brain Injury Association of America. (2011). *Brain injury and you.* Vienna, VA: Author.

Brambring, M. (2006). Divergent development of gross motor skills in children who are blind or sighted. *Journal of Visual Impairment and Blindness, 100*, 620–634.

Brambring, M. (2007). Divergent development of manual skills in children who are blind or sighted. *Journal of Visual Impairment and Blindness, 101*, 212–225.

Brame, P. (2000). Using picture storybooks to enhance the social skills training of special needs students. *Middle School Journal, 32*(1), 41.

Bramlett, V., Ayres, K. M., Douglas, K. H., & Cihak, D. F. (2011). Effects of computer and classroom simulations to teacher student with various exceptionalities to locate apparel sizes. *Education and Training in Autism and Developmental Disabilities, 46*, 454–469.

Brandes, J. A., Ormsbee, C. K., & Haring, K. A. (2007). From early intervention to early childhood programs: Timeline for early successful transitions (TEST). *Intervention in School and Clinic, 42*, 204–211.

Brandon, R. R., & Brown, M. R. (2009). African American families in the special education process. *Intervention in School and Clinic, 45*, 251.

Brantlinger, E., Jimenez, R., Klingner, J., Pugach, M., & Richardson, V. (2005). Qualitative studies in special education. *Exceptional Children, 71*, 195–207.

Bricker, D. (Ed.). (2002). *Assessment, evaluation, and programming system (AEP) for infants and children* (2nd ed.). Baltimore: Brookes.

Bricker, D., & Waddell, M. (Eds.). (2002a). *AEPS curriculum for birth to three years* (2nd ed.). Baltimore: Brookes.

Bricker, D., & Waddell, M. (Eds.). (2002b). *AEPS curriculum for three to six years* (2nd ed.). Baltimore: Brookes.

Brigance, A. H. (2010). *Brigance Comprehensive Inventory of Basic Skills—II.* N. Billerica, MA: Curriculum Associates.

Brigham, N., Morocco, C. C., Clay, K., & Zigmond, N. (2006). What makes a high school good for students with disabilities. *Learning Disabilities Research & Practice, 21*, 184–190.

Brilliant, R. L. (1999). *Essentials of low vision practice.* Boston: Butterworth-Heinemann.

Bristol, M., Cohen, D., Costello, J., Denckla, M., Eckberg, T., Kallen, R., Kraemer, H., Lord, C. Maurer, R., McIlvane, W., Minshew, N. Sigman, M., & Spence, M. (1996). State of the science in autism: Report to the National Institute of Health. *Journal of Autism and Developmental Disorders, 26*, 121–154.

Brobst, J. B., Clopton, J. R., & Hendrick, S. S. (2009). Parenting children with autism spectrum disorders. *Focus on Autism and Other Developmental Disabilities, 24*, 38–49.

Broicki, K. C., Eninger, L., Thorell, L. B., & Bohlin, G. (2010). Interrelations between executive function and symptoms of hyperactivity/impulsivity and inattention in preschoolers: A two year longitudinal study. *Journal of Abnormal Child Psychology, 38*, 163–171.

Brolin, D. E. (2004). *Life-centered career education: A competency-based approach* (5th ed.). Arlington, VA: Council for Exceptional Children.

Bronicki, G. J., & Turnbull, A. P. (1987). Family–professional interactions. In M. E. Snell (Ed.), *Systematic instruction of persons with severe handicaps* (3rd ed., pp. 9–35). Upper Saddle River, NJ: Merrill/Pearson.

Browder, D. M. (2000). *Comments made as guest faculty for OSU teleconference seminar: Contemporary issues in special education.* Columbus, OH: The Ohio State University.

Browder, D. M. (2001). *Curriculum and assessment for students with moderate and severe disabilities.* New York: Guilford.

Browder, D. M., Ahlgrim-Delzell, L., Courtade Little, G., & Snell, M. E. (2006). General curriculum access. In M. E. Snell & F. Brown (Eds.), *Instruction of students with severe disabilities* (6th ed., pp. 489–525). Upper Saddle River, NJ: Merrill/Pearson.

Browder, D. M., Ahlgrim-Delzell, L., Courtade, G., Gibbs, S., & Flowers, C. (2008). Evaluation of the effectiveness of an early literacy program for students with significant disabilities. *Exceptional Children, 75*, 33–52.

Browder, D. M., Ahlgrim-Delzell, L., Spooner, F., Mims, P. J., & Baker, J. N. (2009). Using time delay to teach literacy to students with severe developmental disabilities. *Exceptional Children, 75*, 343–364.

Browder, D. M., Flowers, C., Ahlgrim-Delzell, L., Karvonen, M., Spooner, F., & Algozzine, B. (2004). The alignment of alternate assessment content with academic and functional curricula. *Journal of Special Education, 37*, 211–223.

Browder, D. M., & Minarovic, T. J. (2000). Utilizing sight words in self-instruction training for employees with moderate mental retardation in competitive jobs. *Education and Training in Mental Retardation and Developmental Disabilities, 35*, 78–89.

Browder, D. M., Schoen, S. F., & Lentz, F. E. (2001). Learning to learn through observation. *Journal of Special Education, 20*, 447–461.

Browder, D. M., & Spooner, F. (2006). *Teaching language arts, math, and science to students with significant cognitive disabilities.* Baltimore: Brookes.

Browder, D. M., & Spooner, F. (2011). *Teaching students with moderate and severe disabilities.* New York: Guilford.

Browder, D. M., Spooner, F., Ahlgrim-Delzell, L., Harris, A., & Wakeman, S. (2008). A meta-analysis on teaching mathematics to students with significant cognitive disabilities. *Exceptional Children, 74*, 407–432.

Browder, D. M., Wakeman, S. Y., Spooner, F., Ahlgrim-Delzell, L., & Algozzine, B. (2006). Research on reading instruction for individuals with significant cognitive disabilities. *Exceptional Children, 72*, 392–408.

Brown v. Board of Education of Topeka, 347 U.S. 483 (1954).

Brown, J. E., & Doolittle, J. (2008). A cultural, linguistic, and ecological framework for response to intervention with English language learners. *Teaching Exceptional Children, 40*(5), 66–72.

Brown, L. (1990). Who are they and what do they want? An essay on TASH. *TASH Newsletter, 16*(9), 1.

Brown, L., Farrington, K., Suomi, J., & Zeigler, M. (1999). Work-wage relationships and individuals with disabilities. *Journal of Vocational Rehabilitation, 13*(1), 5–13.

Brown, L., Ford, A., Nisbet, J., Sweet, M., Shiraga, B., & Gruenewald, L. (Eds.). (1982). *Educational programs for severely handicapped students: Vol. XII.* Madison, WI: MMSD.

Brown, L., Long, E., Udvari-Solner, A., Davis, L., VanDeventer, P., Ahlgren, C., Johnson, F., Gruenewald, L., & Jorgensen, J. (1989a). The home school: Why students with severe disabilities must attend the schools of their brothers, sisters, friends, and neighbors. *Journal of the Association for Persons with Severe Handicaps, 14*, 1–7.

Brown, L., Long, E., Udvari-Solner, A., Davis, L., VanDeventer, P., Ahlgren, C., Johnson, F., Gruenewald, L., & Jorgensen, J. (1989b). Should students with severe intellectual disabilities be based in regular or in special education classrooms in home schools? *Journal of the Association for Persons with Severe Handicaps, 14*, 8–12.

Brown, L., Schwartz, P., Udvari-Solner, A., Kampschroer, E. F., Johnson, F., Jorgensen, J., & Gruenewald, L. (1991). How much time should students with severe intellectual disabilities spend in regular education classrooms and elsewhere? *Journal of the Association for Persons with Severe Handicaps, 16*, 39–47.

Brown, V. L., Cronin, M. E., & McEntire, E. (1994). *Test of Mathematical Abilities* (2nd ed.). Bloomington, MN: Pearson.

Brown, V. L., Wiederholt, J. L., & Hammill, D. D. (2008). *Test of reading comprehension* (4th ed.). Bloomington, MN: Pearson.

Brownell, M. T., Sindelar, P. T., Kiely, M. T., & Danielson, L. C. (2010). Special education teacher quality and preparation: Exposing foundations, constructing a new model. *Exceptional Children, 76*, 357–377.

Bryan, L. C., & Gast, D. L. (2000). Teaching on-task and on-schedule behaviors to high-functioning children with autism via picture activity schedules. *Journal of Autism and Developmental Disorders, 30*, 553–567.

Bryan, T. (2005). Science-based advances in the social domain of learning disabilities *Learning Disability Quarterly, 28*, 119–121.

Bryan, T., & Ryan, A. (2001). Jacob's story: Amazing discoveries. In A. K. Ryan, *Strengthening the safety net: How school can help youth with emotional and behavioral needs complete their high school education and prepare for life after school* (p. 10). Burlington: School Research Office, University of Vermont.

Bryant, D. P., & Bryant, B. R. (2012). *Assistive technology for people with disabilities* (2nd ed.). Upper Saddle River, NJ: Pearson.

Buggey, T. (2007). A picture is worth . . . : Video self-modeling applications at school and home. *Journal of Positive Behavior Interventions, 9*(3), 151–158.

Bui, Y. N., Schumaker, J. B., & Deshler, D. D. (2006). Effects of a strategies writing program for students with and without learning disabilities in inclusive fifth-grade classes. *Learning Disabilities Research & Practice, 22*, 129–136.

Bulgren, J. A. (2006). Integrated content enhancement routines: Responding to the needs of adolescents with disabilities in rigorous inclusive secondary content classes. *Teaching Exceptional Children, 38*(6), 54–58.

Bullock, C., & Foegen, A. (2002). Constructive conflict resolution for students with behavioral disorders. *Behavioral Disorders, 27*, 289–295.

Burchard, S. N., Hasazi, J. S., Gordon, L. R., & Yoe, J. (1991). An examination of lifestyle and adjustment in three community residential alternatives. *Research in Developmental Disabilities, 12*, 127–142.

Bureau of Labor Statistics. (2010). *Economic news release: Table A-6. Employment status of the civilian population by sex, age, and disability, not seasonally adjusted.* Washington, DC: Bureau of Labor Statistics, US. Department of Labor. Retrieved from http://www.bls.gov/news .release/empsit.tO6.htm

Burke, M. D., Hagan-Burke, S., Kwok, O., & Parker, R. (2009). Predictive validity of early literacy indicators from the middle of kindergarten to second grade. *Journal of Special Education, 42*(4), 209–226.

Burns, M., & Ysseldyke, J. (2009). Reported prevalence of evidence-based instructional practices in special education. *Journal of Special Education, 43*, 3–11.

Bursuck, W. D., & Damer, M. (2011). *Teaching reading to students who are at risk or have disabilities: A multi-tier approach* (2nd ed.). Upper Saddle River, NJ: Pearson.

Bybee, J., & Zigler, E. (1998). Outerdirectedness in individuals with and without mental retardation: A review. In J. A. Burack, R. M. Hodapp, & E. Zigler (Eds.), *Handbook of mental retardation* (pp. 434–460). Cambridge: Cambridge University Press.

Byrd, E. S. (2011). Educating and involving parents in the response to intervention process: The school's important role. *Teaching Exceptional Children, 43*(3), 32–39.

Byzek, J. (2001, February). Committed couples. *New Mobility: The Magazine for Active Wheelchair Users.* Retrieved September 2, 2007, from http://www.newmobility.com/ articleView.cfm?id=333&action=browse

Calhoun, M. L., & Kuczera, M. (1996). Increasing social smiles of young children with disabilities. *Perceptual and Motor Skills, 82*, 1265–1266.

Calhoun, M. L., Rose, T. L., Hanft, B., & Sturkey, C. (1991). Social reciprocity interventions: Implications for developmental therapists. *Physical and Occupational Therapy in Pediatrics, 11*, 45–46.

Callahan, K., Rademacher, J. A., & Hildreth, B. L. (1998). The effect of parent participation in strategies to improve the homework performance of students who are at risk. *Remedial and Special Education, 19*(3), 131–141.

Cameron, J. (2005). The detrimental effects of reward hypothesis: Persistence of a view in the face of disconfirming evidence. In W. L. Heward, T. E. Heron, N. A. Neef, S. M. Peterson, D. M. Sainato, G. Cartledge, R. Gardner III, L. D. Peterson, S. B. Hersh, & J. C. Dardig (Eds.), *Focus on behavior analysis in education: Achievements, challenges, and opportunities* (pp. 304–315). Upper Saddle River, NJ: Merrill/Pearson.

Cameron, J., Banko, K. M., & Pierce, W. D. (2001). Pervasive negative effects of rewards on intrinsic motivation: The myth continues. *Behavior Analyst, 24*, 1–44.

Campbell, F. A., & Ramey, C. T. (1994). Effects of early intervention on intellectual and academic achievement: a follow-up study of children from low-income families. *Child Development, 65*, 684–689.

Campbell, J. (2007). Understanding the emotional needs of children who are blind. *Journal of Visual Impairment and Blindness, 101*, 351–355.

Campbell, P. H. (2011). Addressing motor disabilities. In M. E. Snell & F. Brown (Eds.), *Instruction of students with severe disabilities* (7th ed., pp. 340–376). Upper Saddle River, NJ: Merrill/Pearson.

Campbell Miller, M., Cooke, N. L., Test, D. W., & White, R. (2003). Effects of friendship circles on the social interactions of elementary age student with mild disabilities. *Journal of Behavioral Education, 12*, 167–184.

Cannella-Malone, H. I., O'Reilly, M. F., & Lancioni, G. (2005). Choice and preference assessment research with people with severe to profound developmental disabilities: A review of the literature. *Research in Developmental Disabilities, 26*, 1–15.

Cannella-Malone, H. I., O'Reilly, M. F., Sigafoos, J., & Chan, J. M. (2008). Combined curricular interventions with brief hands down to decrease hand mouthing and the use of arm splints for a young boy with profound disabilities. *Education and Training in Developmental Disabilities, 43*, 360–366.

Cantu, C. O. (2004). Wheelchair positioning: Foundation in wheelchair selection. *Exceptional Parent, 34*(5), 33–35.

Capizzi, A. M. (2008). From assessment to annual goal: Engaging a decision-making process in writing measurable IEPs. *Teaching Exceptional Children, 41*(1), 18–25.

Carbone, V. J., Morgenstern, B., & Zecchin-Tirri, G. (2010). The role of the reflexive-conditioned motivating operation (CMO-R) during discrete trial instruction of children with autism. *Focus on Autism and Other Developmental Disabilities, 25*, 110–124.

Carlin, M. T., Chrysler, C., & Sullivan, K. (2007). Conjunctive search in individuals with and without mental retardation. *American Journal on Mental Retardation, 112*, 54–65.

Carlin, M. T., Soraci, S. A., & Strawbrige, C. P. (2005). Generative learning during visual search for scene changes: Enhancing free recall of individuals with and without mental retardation. *American Journal on Mental Retardation, 110*, 13–22.

Carlin, M. T., Soraci, S. A., Strawbrige, C. P., Dennis, N., Loiselle, R., & Chechile, N. A. (2003). Detection of changes in naturalistic scenes: Comparisons of individuals with and without mental retardation. *American Journal on Mental Retardation, 108*, 181–193.

Carnahan, C. R., Williamson, P., Clarke, L., & Sorensen, R. (2009). A systematic approach for supporting paraeducators: A guide for teachers. *Teaching Exceptional Children, 41*(5), 34–43.

Carnine, D. (1997). Bridging the research to practice gap. *Exceptional Children, 63*, 513–521.

Carnine, D. W., Silbert, J., Kame'enui, E. J., & Tarver, S. G. (2010). *Direct instruction reading* (5th ed.). Upper Saddle River, NJ: Pearson.

Carnine, D. W., Silbert, J., Kame'enui, E. J., Tarver, S. G., & Jongjohann, K. (2006). *Teaching struggling and at risk readers: A direct instruction approach.* Upper Saddle River, NJ: Merrill/Pearson.

Carr, E. G., Dunlap, G., Horner, R. H., Koegel, R. L., Turnbull, A. P., Sailor, W., Anderson, J., Albin, R. W., Koegel, L. K., & Fox, L. (2002). Positive behavioral support: Evolution of an applied science. *Journal of Positive Behavior Interventions, 4,* 4–16.

Carter, E. W. (2011). Supporting peer relationships. In M. E. Snell & F. Brown (Eds.), *Instruction of students with severe disabilities* (7th ed., pp. 431–460). Upper Saddle River, NJ: Pearson.

Carter, E. W., Clark, N. M., Cushing, L. S., & Kennedy, C. H. (2005). Number of peers in peer support programs for students with severe disabilities: Effects on social interactions and access to the general education curriculum. *Research and Practice for People with Severe Disabilities, 30,* 15–25.

Carter, E. W., Trainor, A. A., Ditchman, N., Swedeen, B., Sun, Y., & Owens, L. (2010). Summer employment and community experiences of transition-age youth with severe disabilities. *Exceptional Children, 76,* 194–212.

Carter, E. W., Trainor, A. A., Sun, Y., & Owens, L. (2009). Assessing the transition-related strengths and needs of adolescents with high-incidence disabilities. *Exceptional Children, 76,* 74–94.

Carter, N. J., Prater, M. A., & Dyches, T. T. (2009). *What every teacher should know about: Adaptations and accommodations for students with mild to moderate disabilities.* Upper Saddle River, NJ: Pearson.

Carter, S. L. (2006). Everything you ever wanted to know in a bubble. *Teaching Exceptional Children, 39*(2), 40–43.

Carter, S. L. (2009). Treatment of pica using a pica exchange procedure with increasing response effort. *Education and Training in Developmental Disabilities, 43,* 360–366.

Cartledge, G., & Kleefeld, J. (2009). *Taking part: Introducing social skills to children* (2nd ed.). Champaign, IL: Research Press.

Cartledge, G., & Kourea, L. (2008). Culturally responsive classrooms for culturally diverse students with and at risk for disabilities. *Exceptional Children, 74,* 351–371.

Cartledge, G., Gardner III, R., & Ford, D. Y. (2009). *Teaching diverse learners in general education classrooms.* Upper Saddle River, NJ: Pearson.

Cartledge, G., Kea, C. D., & Ida, D. J. (2000). Anticipating differences—celebrating strengths: Providing culturally competent services for students with serious emotional disturbance. *Teaching Exceptional Children, 32*(3), 6–12.

Casale-Giannola, D., & Wilson Kamens, M. (2006). Inclusion at a university: Experiences of a young woman with Down syndrome. *Mental Retardation, 44,* 344–352.

Cascella, P. W., & McNamara, K. M. (2005). Empowering students with severe disabilities to actualize communication skills. *Teaching Exceptional Children, 37*(3), 38–43.

Caspi, A., Henry, B., McGee, R. O., Moffitt, T. W., & Silva, P. A. (1995). Temperamental origins of child and adolescent behavior problems: From age three to age fifteen. *Child Development, 66,* 55–68.

Castellano, J. A. (2003). *Special populations in gifted education: Working with diverse gifted learners.* Boston: Allyn & Bacon.

Castellano, J., & Frazier, A. D. (2010). *Special populations in gifted education.* Waco, TX: Prufrock.

Catania, A. C. (2007). *Learning* (interim 4th ed.). Beverly, MA: Cambridge Center for Behavioral Studies.

Catts, H. W. (1993). The relationship between speech-language impairments and reading disabilities. *Journal of Speech and Hearing Research, 36,* 948–958.

Catts, H. W., Fey, M. E., Tomblin, J. B., & Zhang, Z. (2002). A longitudinal investigation of reading outcomes in children with language impairments. *Journal of Speech, language, and Hearing Research, 45,* 1142–1157.

Causton-Theoharis, J. N. (2009). The golden rule of providing support in inclusive classrooms: Support others as you would wish to be supported. *Teaching Exceptional Children, 42*(2), 36–43.

Cavanaugh, R. A., Heward, W. L., & Donelson, F. (1996). Effects of response cards during lesson closure on the academic performance of secondary students in an earth science course. *Journal of Applied Behavior Analysis, 29,* 403–406.

Cavkaytar, A. (2007). Turkish parents as teachers: Teaching parents how to teach self-care and domestic skills to their children with mental retardation. *Education and Training in Mental Retardation and Developmental Disabilities, 42,* 85–93.

Cawley, J. F., Parmar, R. S., Foley, T. E., Salmon S., & Roy, S. (2001). Arithmetic performance of students: Implications for standards and programming. *Exceptional Children, 67,* 311–328.

Cawley, J. F., Parmar, R. S., Yan, W., & Miller, J. H. (1998). Arithmetic computation performance of students with learning disabilities: Implications for curriculum. *Learning Disabilities Research and Practice, 13,* 68–74.

Cawthon, S. W. (2001). Teaching strategies in inclusive classrooms with deaf students. *Journal of Deaf Studies and Deaf Education, 6,* 212–225.

Cedar Rapids Community School District v. Garret F., 67 U. S. L. W. 4165 (1999).

Celeste, M. (2006). Play behaviors and social interactions of a child who is blind: In theory and practice. *Journal of Visual Impairment and Blindness, 100,* 75–90.

Centers for Disease Control and Prevention. (2010). Cytomegalovirus (CMV) and congenital CMV infection. Retrieved June 12, 2011, from http://www.cdc.gov/cmv/overview.html

Centers for Disease Control and Prevention. (2011a). *Attention deficit/hyperactivity disorder: Data & statistics in the United States.* Retrieved February 10, 2011, from http://www.cdc.gov/ncbddd/adhd/data.html

Centers for Disease Control and Prevention. (2011b). *Autism spectrum disorders (ASDs): Data and statistics.* Retrieved August 15, 2011, from http://www.cdc.gov/ncbddd/autism/data.html

Centers for Disease Control and Prevention. (2011c). *Concussion in sports.* Atlanta: Author. Retrieved June 25, 2011, from http://www.cdc.gov/concussion/sports/index.html

Centers for Disease Control and Prevention. (2011d). *HIV in the United States.* Retrieved February 10, 2011, from http://www.cdc.gov/hiv/resources/factsheets/us.htm

Centers for Disease Control and Prevention. (2011e). *HIV transmission.* Retrieved February 10, 2011, from http://www.cdc.gov/hiv/resources/qa/transmission.htm

Centers for Disease Control and Prevention. (2011f). *How many people have TBI.* Atlanta: Author. Retrieved June 25, 2011, from http://www.cdc.gov/TraumaticBrainInjury/index.html

Centers for Disease Control and Prevention. (2011g). *Summary of autism/ASD prevalence studies.* Retrieved August 15, 2011, from http://www.cdc.gov/ncbddd/autism/documents/Autism_PrevalenceSummaryTable_2011.pdf

Cerney, J. (2007). *Deaf education in America: Voices of children from inclusion settings.* Washington, DC: Gallaudet University Press.

Chaffey, G. (2004, August). *Coolabah Dynamic Assessment: A paradigm shift in the identification of giftedness?.* Paper presented at the Australian Association for the Gifted meeting, Melbourne, Australia.

Chakrabarti, S., & Fombonne, E. (2001). Pervasive developmental disorders in preschool children. *Journal of the American Medical Association, 285,* 3093–3099.

Chamberlain, S. P. (2010a). Don Hammill: A personal perspective on the field of learning disabilities, 3-tier, and RTI. *Intervention in School and Clinic, 45,* 312–316.

Chamberlain, S. P. (2010b). Tom Lovitt: Reflections on a career and the field of learning disabilities. *Intervention in School and Clinic, 46,* 54–59.

Chambers, C. R., Wehmeyer, M L., Saito, Y., Lida, K. M., Lee, Y., & Singh, V. (2007). Self-determination: What do we know? Where do we go? *Exceptionality, 15,* 3–15.

Chambers, M., & Rehfeldt A. (2003). Assessing the acquisition and generalization of two mand forms with adults with severe developmental disabilities. *Research in Developmental Disabilities, 24*(4), 265–280.

Chance, P. (1992). The rewards of learning. *Phi Delta Kappan, 74*(3), 200–207.

Chance, P. (1993). Sticking up for rewards. *Phi Delta Kappan, 74*(10), 787–790.

Charania, S. M., LeBlanc, L. A., Carr, J. E., & Gunby, K. (2010). Teaching effective hand raising to children with autism during group instruction. *Journal of Applied Behavior Analysis, 43,* 493–497.

Chard, D. J., & Kame'enui, E. J. (2000). Struggling first-grade readers: The frequency and progress of their reading. *Journal of Special Education, 34,* 28–38.

Charlop-Christy, M. H. (2007, February). *Social and interpersonal skills interventions for children with autism.* Presentation at the conference Progress and Challenges in the Behavioral Treatment of Autism Conference, Boston. [Available on DVD from the Association for Behavior Analysis International.]

Charlop-Christy, M. H., Carpenter, M., Le, L., LeBlanc, L. A., & Kellet, K. (2002). Using the picture exchange communication system (PECS) with children with autism: Assessment of PECS acquisition, speech, social-communicative behavior, and problem behavior. *Journal of Applied Behavior Analysis, 35,* 213–231.

Chen, D. (1999). Learning to communicate: Strategies for developing communication with infants whose multiple disabilities include visual impairment and hearing loss. *reSources, 10*(5), 1–6. Published by California Deaf-Blind Services. Available: http://www.sfsu.edu/~cadbs/Summer99.pdf

Chen, D., & Downing, J. E. (2001). Tactile learning strategies for children who are deaf-blind: Concerns and considerations from Project SALUTE. *Deaf-Blind Perspectives, 8*(2), 1–6.

Chen, D., & Downing, J. E. (2006a). *Tactile learning strategies: Interacting with children who have visual impairments and multiple disabilities.* New York: AFB Press.

Chen, D., & Downing, J. E. (2006b). *Tactile strategies for children who have visual impairments and multiple disabilities: Promoting communication and learning skills.* New York: AFB Press.

Cheney, D., Flower, A., & Templeton, T. (2009). Applying response to intervention metrics in the social domain for students at risk of developing emotional or behavioral disorders. *Journal of Special Education, 42,* 108–126.

Cheng, L-R. L. (2012). Language and linguistically-culturally diverse children. In V. A. Reed, *An introduction to children with language disorders* (4th ed., pp. 352–392). Upper Saddle River, NJ: Pearson.

Cherkasova, M. V., & Hechtman, L. (2009). Neuroimaging in attention-deficit hyperactivity disorder: Beyond the frontostriatal circuitry. *Canadian Journal of Psychiatry. 54,* 651–664.

Chesley, G. M., & Calaluce, P. D. (1997). The deception of inclusion. *Mental Retardation, 35,* 488–490.

Chiasson, K., & Reilly, A. (2008). Families and their children with disabilities. In G. Olsen & M. L. Fuller (Eds.), *Home-school relations: Working successfully with parents and families* (pp. 151–174). Boston: Allyn & Bacon.

Christensen, L., Young, K. R., & Marchant, M. (2004). The effects of a peer-mediated positive behavior support program on socially appropriate classroom behavior. *Education and Treatment of Children, 27,* 199–234.

Christle, C. A., & Schuster, J. W. (2003). The effects of using response cards on student participation, academic achievement, and on-task behavior during whole-class, math instruction. *Journal of Behavioral Education, 12,* 147–165.

Cihak, D., Alberto, P. A., Taber-Doughty, T., & Gama, R. I. (2006). A comparison of static picture prompting and video prompting simulation strategies using group instructional procedures. *Focus on Autism and Other Developmental Disabilities, 21,* 89–99.

Cihak, D. F., Kessler, K., & Alberto, P. A. (2008). Use of a handheld prompting system to transition independently through vocational tasks for students with moderate and severe intellectual disabilities. *Education and Training in Developmental Disabilities, 43,* 102–110.

Cipani, E. (2008). *Classroom management for all teachers: Plans for evidence-based practice* (3rd ed.). Upper Saddle River, NJ: Pearson.

Cipani, E., & Schock, K. (2007). *Functional behavioral assessment, diagnosis, and treatment: A complete system for education and mental health settings.* New York: Springer.

Clark, B. A. (2008). *Growing up gifted* (7th ed.). Upper Saddle River, NJ: Pearson.

Clark, G. M., & Patton, J. R. (2006). *Transition Planning Inventory: Administration and resource guide.* Austin: PRO-ED.

Clausen, J. A. (1967). Mental deficiency: Development of a concept. *American Journal of Mental Deficiency, 71,* 727–745.

Clements, S. D. (1966). *Minimal brain dysfunction in children* (NINDS Monograph No. 3, Public Health Service Bulletin No. 1415). Washington, DC: U.S. Department of Health, Education, and Welfare.

Cobb, B., Lehmann, J., Newman-Gonchar, R., & Morgen, A. (2009). Self-determination for students with disabilities: A narrative metasynthesis. *Career Development for Exceptional Individuals, 32*(2), 108–114.

Cobb Morocco, C., Clay, K., Parker, C. E., & Zigmond, N. (2006). Walter Cronkite High School: A culture of freedom and responsibility. *Learning Disabilities Research & Practice, 21,* 146–158.

Codding, R. S., Burns, M. K., & Lukito, G. (2011). Meta-analysis of mathematic basic-fact fluency interventions: A component analysis. *Learning Disabilities Research & Practice, 26,* 36–47.

Cohen, H., Amerine-Dickens, M., & Smith, T. (2006). Early intensive behavioral treatment: Replication of the UCLA Model in a community setting. *Journal of Developmental and Behavioral Pediatrics, 27,* S145–S155.

Colangelo, N., Assouline, S. G., & Gross, M. U. M. (2004). *A nation deceived: How schools hold back America's brightest students.* Iowa City: University of Iowa Press.

Cole, C. M., Waldron, N., & Majd, M. (2004). Academic progress of students across inclusive and traditional settings. *Mental Retardation, 42,* 136–144.

Colin, S., Magnan, A., & Ecalle, J. (2007). Relation between deaf children's phonological skills in kindergarten and word recognition performance in first grade. *Journal of Child Psychology and Psychiatry and Allied Disciplines, 48,* 139–146.

Collins, B. C. (2007). *Moderate and severe disabilities: A foundational approach.* Upper Saddle River, NJ: Merrill/Pearson.

Collins, B. C., Evans, A., Creech-Galloway, C., Karl, J., & Miller, A. (2010). Comparison of the acquisition and maintenance of teaching functional core content sight words in special and general education settings. *Focus on Autism and Other Developmental Disabilities, 22,* 220–233.

Collins, B. C., Hager, K. D., & Galloway, C. C. (2011). Addition of functional content during core content instruction with students with moderate disabilities. *Education and Training in Autism and Developmental Disabilities, 46,* 22–39.

Collins, B. C., Hall, M., & Branson, T. A. (1997). Teaching leisure skills to adolescents with moderate disabilities. *Exceptional Children, 63,* 499–512.

Collins, B. C., Karl, J. Riggs, L, Galloway, C. C., & Hager, K. D. (2010). Teaching core content with real-life applications to secondary students with moderate and severe disabilities. *Teaching Exceptional Children, 43*(1), 52–59.

Collins, D. W., & Rourke, B. (2003). Learning-disabled brains: A review of the literature. *Journal of Clinical and Experimental Neuropsychology, 25,* 1011–1034.

Comacho, M. R. (2007, April). *TENFEE: Spanish workshops for the needs of families in special education.* Poster presented at the 85th Annual Convention of the Council for Exceptional Children, Louisville, KY.

Commission on Education of the Deaf. (1988). *Toward equality: Education of the deaf.* Washington, DC: U.S. Government Printing Office.

Coniglio, S. J., Lewis, J. D., Lang, C., Burns, T. G., Subhani-Siddique, R., Weintraub A., et al. (2001). A randomized, double-blind, placebo-controlled trial of a single-dose intravenous secretin as treatment for children with autism. *Journal of Pediatrics, 138*(5), 649–655.

Conley, R. W. (2003). Supported employment in Maryland: Successes and issues. *Mental Retardation, 41,* 237–249.

Conner, E. P., Scandary, J., & Tullock, D. (1988). Education of physically handicapped and health impaired individuals: A commitment to the future. *DPH Journal, 10*(1), 5–24.

Conners, C. K. (2000). Attention-deficit/hyperactivity disorder: Historical development and overview. *Journal of Attention Disorders, 3,* 173–191.

Connolly, A. J. (2007). *KeyMath—3: A Diagnostic Inventory of Essential Skills.* Bloomington, MN: Pearson.

Connolly, C. M., Rose, J., & Austen, S. (2006). Identifying and assessing depression in prelingually deaf people: A literature review. *American Annals of the Deaf, 151,* 49–60.

Conroy, J. W. (1996). The small ICF/MR program: Dimensions of quality and cost. *Mental Retardation, 34,* 13–26.

Conroy, M. A., & Brown, W. H. (2006). Early identification, prevention, and early intervention with young children at risk for emotional and behavioral disorders: Issues, trends, and a call for action. *Behavioral Disorders, 29,* 224–236.

Consortium for Appropriate Conflict Resolution in Special Education (CADRE). (2008).

Cook, B. G. (2001). A comparison of teachers' attitudes toward their included students with mild and severe disabilities. *Journal of Special Education, 34,* 203–213.

Cook, B. G. (2004). Inclusive teachers' attitudes toward their students with disabilities: A replication and extension. *The Elementary School Journal, 104,* 307–320.

Cook, B. G., Cameron, D. L., & Tankersley, M. (2007). Inclusive teachers' attitudinal ratings of their students with disabilities. *Journal of Special Education, 40,* 230–238.

Cook, B. G., & Cook, S. C. (2010). Evidence-based practices, research-based practices, and best and recommended practices: Some thoughts on terminology. *Savage Controversies, 4*(1), 2–4.

Cook, B. G., Tankersley, M., Cook, L., & Landrum, T. J. (2000). Teachers' attitudes toward their included students with disabilities. *Exceptional Children, 67,* 115–135.

Cook, B. G., Tankersley, M., & Landrum, T. (2009). Determining evidence-based practices in special education. *Exceptional Children, 75,* 365–383.

Cook, R. E., Klein, M. D., Chen, D., & Tessier, A. (2012). *Adapting early childhood curricula for children with special needs* (8th ed.). Upper Saddle River, NJ: Pearson.

Cooke, N. L., Mackiewicz, S. M., Wood, C. L., & Helf, S. (2009). The use of audio prompting to assist mothers with limited English proficiency in teaching their pre-kindergarten children English vocabulary. *Education and Treatment of Children, 32*(2), 213–229.

Coolican, J., Bryson, S. E., & Zwaigenbaum, L. (2008). Brief report: Data on the Stanford-Binet Intelligence Scales (5th ed.) in children with autism spectrum disorder. *Journal of Autism and Developmental Disorders, 38,* 190–197.

Cooper, H. L., & Nichols, S. K. (2007). Technology and early braille literacy: Using the Mountbatten Pro Brailler in primary-grade classrooms.

Journal of Visual Impairment and Blindness, 101, 22–31.

Cooper, J. O., Heron, T. E., & Heward, W. L. (2007). *Applied behavior analysis* (2nd ed.). Upper Saddle River, NJ: Merrill/Pearson.

Cooper, J. O., Heron, T. E., & Heward, W. L. (2007). Applied behavior analysis (2nd ed.). Upper Saddle River, NJ: Pearson.

Cooper, K. J., & Browder, D. M. (1997). The use of a personal trainer to enhance participation of older adults with severe disabilities in community water exercise classes. *Journal of Behavioral Education, 7,* 421–434.

Cooper-Duffy, K., Szedia, P., & Hyer, G. (2010). Teaching literacy to students with significant cognitive disabilities. *Teaching Exceptional Children, 42*(3), 30–39.

Copeland, S. R., Hughes, C., Carter, W. W., Guth, C., Presley, J. A., Williams, C. R., & Fowler, S. E. (2004). Increasing access to general education: Perspectives of participants in a high school peer support program. *Remedial and Special Education, 25,* 342–352.

Coplan, J., Souders, M. C., Mulberg, A. E., et al. (2003). Children with autistic spectrum disorders. II: Parents are unable to distinguish secretin from placebo under double-blind conditions. *Archives of Disease in Childhood, 88,* 739.

Corn, A. L., & Erin, J. N. (Eds.). (2000). *Foundations of low vision: Clinical and functional perspectives* (2nd ed.). New York: AFB Press.

Com, A. L., Erin, J. N., Ferrenkipf, C., Huebner, K. M., McNear, D., Spungin, S. J., & Torres, I. (Eds.). (2004). *When you have a visually impaired student in your classroom: A guide for teachers.* New York: AFB Press.

Cornett, R., & Daisey, M. (2001). *The cued speech resource book for parents of deaf children.* Cleveland, OH: National Cued Speech Association.

Correa, V. I., Gollery, T., & Fradd, S. (1988). The handicapped undocumented alien student dilemma: Do we advocate or abdicate? *Journal of Educational Issues of Language Minority Students, 3,* 41–47.

Correa, V. I., Jones, H. A., Thomas, C. C., & Morsink, C. V. (2005). *Interactive teaming: Enhancing programs for students with special needs* (4th ed.). Upper Saddle River, NJ: Merrill/Pearson.

Cosden, M., Brown, C., & Elliott, K. (2002). Development of self-understanding and self-esteem in children and adults with learning disabilities. In B. Wong & M. Donahue (Eds.), *The social dimensions of learning disabilities* (pp. 33–51). Hillsdale, NJ: Erlbaum.

Coster, W. J., & Haltiwanger, J. T. (2004). Social-behavioral skills of elementary students with physical disabilities included in general education classrooms. *Remedial and Special Education, 25,* 95–103.

Cott, A. (1972). Megavitamins: The orthomolecular approach to behavioral disorders and learning disabilities. *Academic Therapy, 7,* 245–258.

Coulter, D. L. (1994). Biomedical conditions: Types, causes, and results. In L. Sternberg (Ed.), *Individuals with profound disabilities: Instructional and assistive strategies* (3rd ed., pp. 41–58). Austin, TX: PRO-ED.

Council for Children with Behavioral Disorders. (1993, June). Staff position statement: Inclusion. CCBD *Newsletter,* p. 1.

Council for Children with Behavioral Disorders. (2000, October). *Draft position paper on terminology and definition of emotional or behavioral disorders.* Reston, VA: Author, A Division of the Council for Exceptional Children. Available: http://www.ccbd.net/advocacy

Council for Exceptional Children. (2006). *Evidence-based professional practices proposal.* Reston, VA: Professional Standard & Practice Committee, Council for Exceptional Children. Available: http://www.cec.sped.org/Content/NavigationMenu/ProfessionalDevelopment/ProfessionalStandards/EVP_revised_03_2006.pdf

Council for Exceptional Children. (2009). *What every special educator must know: Ethics, standards, and guidelines* (6th ed.). Arlington, VA: Author.

Council for Exceptional Children. (2011). *Federal outlook for exceptional children.* Arlington, VA: Author.

Court, D., & Givon, S. (2003). Group intervention: Improving social skills of adolescents with learning disabilities. *Teaching Exceptional Children, 36*(2), 46–51.

Cox, A. L., Gast, D. L., Luscre, D., & Ayers, K. M. (2009). The effects of weighted vests on appropriate in-seat behaviors of elementary-age students with autism and severe to profound intellectual disabilities. *Focus on Autism and Other Developmental Disabilities, 24,* 17–26.

Coyne, M. D., Kame'enui, E. J., & Carnine, D. W. (Eds.). (2011). *Effective teaching strategies that accommodate diverse learners* (4th ed.). Upper Saddle River, NJ: Pearson.

Craft, M. A., Alber, S. R., & Heward, W. L. (1998). Teaching elementary students with developmental disabilities to recruit teacher attention in a general education classroom: Effects on teacher praise and academic productivity. *Journal of Applied Behavior Analysis, 31,* 399–415.

Crandell, C. C., & Smaldino, J. J. (2001). Rehabilitative technologies for individuals with hearing loss and normal hearing. In J. Katz (Ed.), *Handbook of clinical audiology* (5th ed., pp. 607–630). New York: Lippincott, Williams, & Wilkins.

Crone, D., Horner, R. H., & Hawken, L. (2004). *Responding to problem behavior in schools: The behavior education program.* New York: Guilford.

Cronin, M. E., Patton, J. R., & Wood, S. J. (2005). *Life skills instruction: A practical guide for integrating real-life content into the curriculum at the elementary and secondary levels for students with special needs or who are placed at risk* (2nd ed.). Austin: PRO-ED.

Cross, T. L. (2006). *On the social and emotional lives of gifted kids: Understanding and guiding their development* (3rd ed.). Waco, TX: Prufrock.

Crossley, R. (1988). *Unexpected communication attainments by persons diagnosed as autistic and intellectually impaired.* Caulfield, Australia: Deal Communication Centre.

Crossley, R., & Remington-Guerney, J. (1992). Getting the words out: Facilitated communication training. *Topics in Language Disorders, 12*(4), 29–45.

Crozier, S., & Sileo, N. M. (2005). Encouraging positive behavior with social stories: An intervention for children with autism spectrum disorders. *Teaching Exceptional Children, 37*(6), 26–31.

Crozier, S., & Tincani, M. J. (2005). Using a modified social story to decrease disruptive behavior of a child with autism. *Focus on Autism and Other Developmental Disabilities, 20,* 150–157.

Cruickshank, W. M. (1986). *Disputable decisions in special education.* Ann Arbor: University of Michigan Press.

Cruz, L., & Cullinan, D. (2001). Awarding points, using levels to help children improve behavior. *Teaching Exceptional Children, 33*(3), 16–23.

Culatta, B., & Wiig, E. H. (2006). Language disabilities in school-age children and youth. In N. B. Anderson & G. H. Shames (Eds.), *Human communication disorders: An introduction* (8th ed., pp. 331–360). Upper Saddle River, NJ: Pearson.

Cullinan, D. (2007). *Students with emotional and behavioral disorders: An introduction for teachers and other helping professionals* (2nd ed.). Upper Saddle River, NJ: Pearson.

Cullinan, D., Epstein, M. H., & Sabornie, E. J. (1992). Selected characteristics of a national sample of seriously emotionally disturbed adolescents. *Behavioral Disorders, 17,* 273–280.

Cullinan, D., & Kauffman, J. M. (2005). Do race of student and race of teacher influence ratings of emotional and behavioral problem characteristics of students with emotional disorders? *Behavioral Disorders, 30,* 393–402.

Cullinan, D., & Sabornie, E. J. (2004). Characteristics of emotional disturbance in middle and high school students. *Journal of Emotional and Behavioral Disorders, 12,* 157–168.

Cummins, J. (2002). Foreword. In P. Gibbons, *Scaffolding language, scaffolding learning: Teaching second language learners in the mainstream classroom.* Portsmouth, NH: Heinemann.

Cunningham, B. (2007). *Student transitional guide to college.* National Secondary Transition Technical Assistance Center. Retrieved September 26, 2007, from http://www.nsttac.org/?FileName=student_transitional_guide&type=1

Cystic Fibrosis Foundation. (2011). *About cystic fibrosis.* Bethesda, MD: Author. Retrieved February 10, 2011, from http://www.cff.org/AboutCF/Faqs/

Daane, M. C., Campbell, J. R., Grigg, W. S., Goodman, M. J., & Oranje, A. (2005). *Fourth-grade students reading aloud: NAEP 2002 special study of oral reading* (NCES 2006-469). U.S. Department of Education. Institute of Education Sciences, National Center for Education Statistics. Washington, DC: Government Printing Office.

Daley, T. C., & Carlson, E. (2009). Predictors of change in eligibility status among preschoolers in special education. *Exceptional Children, 75,* 412–426.

Daly, P. M., & Ranalli, P. (2003). Using countoons to teach self-monitoring skills. *Teaching Exceptional Children, 35*(5), 30–35.

Danforth, S., & Navarro, V. (1998). Speech acts: Sampling the social construction of mental retardation in everyday life. *Mental Retardation, 36,* 31–43.

Dardig, J. C. (2005). The *McClurg Monthly Magazine* and 14 more practical ways to involve parents. *Teaching Exceptional Children, 38*(2), 46–51.

Dardig, J. C. (2006). A friendship program for future special education teachers. In W. L. Heward, *Exceptional children: An introduction to special education* (8th ed., pp. 624–626). Upper Saddle River, NJ: Merrill/Pearson.

Dardig, J. C. (2008). *Involving parents of students with special needs: 25 ready-to-use strategies.* Thousand Oaks, CA: Corwin.

Davenport, T. N., & Eidelman, S. M. (2008). Affordability of family care for an individual with intellectual and developmental disabilities. *Intellectual and Developmental Disabilities, 46,* 396–399.

Davern, L. (2004). *School-to-home notebooks: What parents have to say. Teaching Exceptional Children, 36*(5), 22–27.

Davis, G. A., Rimm, S. B., & Siegle, D. (2011). *Education of the gifted and talented* (6th ed.). Upper Saddle River, NJ: Pearson.

Davis, L. L., & O'Neill, R. E. (2004). Use of response cards with a group of students with learning disabilities including those for whom English is a second language. *Journal of Applied Behavior Analysis, 37,* 219–222.

Dawson, G., Toth, K., Abbott, R., Osterling, J., Munson, J., & Estes, A. (2004). Early social attention impairments in autism: Social orienting, joint attention, and attention to distress. *Developmental Psychology, 40*(2), 271–283.

De La Paz, S., & Graham, S. (1997). Strategy instruction in planning: Effects on the writing performance and behavior of students with learning difficulties. *Exceptional Children, 63,* 167–181.

De Martini-Scully, D., Bray, M. A., & Kehle, T. J. (2000). A packaged intervention to reduce disruptive behaviors in general education students. *Psychology in the Schools, 37,* 149–156.

De Valenzuela, J. S., Copeland, S. R., Huaqing Qi, C., & Park, M. (2006). Examining educational equity: Revisiting the disproportionate representation of minority students in special education. *Exceptional Children, 72,* 425–441.

Dean, P. (2006). Seizures and teens: When emergencies happen, what to do? *Exceptional Parent, 36*(8), 30–33.

DeAvila, E. (1976). Mainstreaming ethnically and linguistically different children: An exercise in paradox or a new approach? In R. I. Jones (Ed.), *Mainstreaming and the minority child* (pp. 93–108). Reston, VA: Council for Exceptional Children.

Debonis, D. A., & Donohue, C. L. (2008). *Survey of audiology fundamentals for audiologists and health professionals.* Boston: Allyn & Bacon.

DEC/NAEYC. (2009). *Early childhood inclusion: A joint position statement of the Division for Early Childhood (DEC) and the National Association for the Education of Young Children (NAEYC).* Chapel Hill: The University of North Carolina, FPG Child Development Institute. Retrieved June 29, 2011, from http://community.fpg.unc.edu/resources/articles/Early_Childhood_Inclusion

Deci, E. L., Koestner, R., & Ryan, R. M. (1999). A meta-analytic review of experiments examining the effects of extrinsic rewards on intrinsic motivation. *Psychological Bulletin, 125,* 627–668.

Deer, B. (2010, January 31). "Callous, unethical and dishonest": Dr. Andrew Wakefield. Retrieved August 18, 2011, from http://www.timesonline.co.uk/tol/news/uk/health/article7009882.ece

Deidrick, K. K. M., & Farmer, J. E. (2005). School reentry following traumatic brain injury. *Preventing School Failure, 49,* 23–33.

Dekker, M., Koot, H., van der Ende, J., & Verhulst, F. (2002). Emotional and behavioral problems in children and adolescents with and without intellectual disability. *Journal of Child Psychology and Psychiatry, 43,* 1087–1098.

DeLacy, M. (2004, June 23). The "No Child" Law's biggest victims? An answer that may surprise. *Education Week, 23*(41), 40.

DeLana, M., Gentry, M. A., & Andrews, J. (2007). The efficacy of ASL/English bilingual education: Considering public schools. *American Annals of the Deaf, 152.*

Dell, A. G., Newton, D., & Petroff, J. (2008). *Assistive technology in the classroom: Enhancing the school experiences of students with disabilities.* Upper Saddle River, NJ: Merrill/Pearson.

Denham, A., & Lahm, E. A. (2001). Using technology to construct alternate portfolios of students with moderate and severe disabilities. *Teaching Exceptional Children, 33*(5), 10–17.

Denning, C. B., Chamberlain, J. A., & Polloway, E. A. (2000). An evaluation of state guidelines for mental retardation: Focus on definition and classification practices. *Education and Training in Mental Retardation and Developmental Disabilities, 35,* 226–232.

Deno, S., Lembke, E., & Anderson, R. (no date). *Progress monitoring: Study group content module.* Minneapolis: Institute on Progress Monitoring, University of Minnesota. Available: http://www.progressmonitoring.net/

Deno, S., Maruyama, G., Espin, C., & Cohen, C. (1990). Educating students with mild disabilities in general education classrooms: Minnesota alternatives. *Exceptional Children, 57,* 150–161.

Denton, C., & Mathes, P. (2002). Reading Recovery (Use caution). *Current Practice Alerts, Issue 7.* Reston, VA: Division for Learning Disabilities and Division for Research, Council for Exceptional Children. Available: http://www.teachingld.org/ld%5Fresources/alerts/

Deshler, D. (2005). *Intervention research and bridging the gap between research and practice.* ERIC Clearinghouse on Disabilities and Gifted Education. Retrieved June 25, 2007, from www.ldonline.org/article/5596

Deshler, D. D., & Lenz, B. K. (1989). The strategies instructional approach. *International Journal of Disability, Development, and Education, 6*(3), 203–244.

Deshler, D. D., & Schumaker, J. B. (2006). *Teaching adolescents with disabilities: Accessing the general education curriculum.* Thousand Oaks, CA: Corwin.

Deshler, D. D., Schumaker, J. B., Bulgren, J. A., Lenz, B. K., Jantzen, J., Adams, G., Carnine, D., Grossen, B., Davis, B., & Marquis, J. (2001). Making things easier: Connecting new knowledge to things students already know. *Teaching Exceptional Children, 33*(4), 82–85.

DeSimone, J. R., & Parmar, R. S. (2006). Middle school math teachers' beliefs about inclusion of students with learning disabilities. *Learning Disabilities Research & Practice, 21,* 98–110.

DeThorne, L. S., Petrill, S. A., Schatschneider, C., & Cutting, L. (2010). Conversational language use as a predictor of early reading development: Language history as a moderating variable. *Journal of Speech, Language, Hearing Research, 53,* 209–223.

Dettmer, P., Thurston, L. P., & Dyck, N. J. (2005). *Consultation, collaboration, and teamwork for students with special needs* (5th ed.). Boston: Allyn & Bacon.

Dias, M. S. (2003). *Hydrocephalus and shunts in the person with spina bifida.* Washington, DC: Spina Bifida Association. Available: http://www.sbaa.org/atf/cf/{99DD789C-904D-467E-A2E4-DF1D36E381C0}/fs_hydrocephalus.pdf

Díaz-Rico, L. T., & Weed, K. Z. (2005). *The cross-cultural, language, and academic development handbook: A complete K–12 reference guide* (3rd ed.). Boston: Allyn & Bacon.

DiCarlo, C. F., & Reid, D. H. (2004). Increasing pretend toy play of toddlers with disabilities in an inclusive setting. *Journal of Applied Behavior Analysis, 37,* 197–207.

Dickson, C. A., Deutsch, C. K., Wang, S. S., & Dube, W. V. (2006). Matching-to-sample assessment of stimulus overselectivity in students with intellectual disabilities. *American Journal on Mental Retardation, 111,* 447–453.

Didden, R., Korzilius, H., van Oorsouw, W., & Sturmey, P. (2006). Behavioral treatment of challenging behaviors in individuals with mild mental retardation: Meta-analysis of single-subject research. *American Journal on Mental Retardation, 111,* 290–298.

Dietrich, R., Keyworth, R., & States, J. (2008). A road-map to evidence-based education: Building an evidence-based culture. In R. Dietrich, R. Keyworth, & J. States (Eds.). *Advances in evidence-based education (Vol. 1): A roadmap to evidence-based education* (pp. 3–19). Oakland, CA: Wing Institute.

Diller, L. H. (1998). *Running on Ritalin.* New York: Bantam.

Dimitropoulos, A., Feurer, I. D., Butler, M. G., & Thompson, T. (2001). Emergence of compulsive behavior and tantrums in children with Prader-Willi syndrome. *American Journal of Mental Retardation, 106,* 39–51.

Dion, E., Fuchs, D., & Fuchs, L. S. (2005). Differential effects of Peer-Assisted Learning Strategies on students' social preference and friendship making. *Behavioral Disorders, 30,* 421–429.

Division for Learning Disabilities. (2011). *DLD's views on response to intervention and learning disabilities.* Arlington, VA: Author. Retrieved August 8, 2011, from http://www.cec.sped.org/

Dockrell, J. E., & Messer, D. (2004). Later vocabulary acquisition. In R. Berman (Ed.), *Language development across childhood and adolescence: Psycholinguistic and crosslinguistic perspectives* (pp. 35–52). Trends in Language Acquisition Research 3. Amsterdam: John Benjamins.

Dockrell, J. E., Lindsay, G., Connelly, V., & Mackie, C. (2007). Constraints in the production of written text in children with specific language impairments. *Exceptional Children, 73,* 147–164.

Dodge, K. (1993). The future of research on conduct disorder. *Development and Psychopathology, 5*(1/2), 311–320.

Dogoe, M., & Banda, D. R. (2009). Review of research using constant time delay to teach chained tasks to persons with developmental disabilities. *Education and Training in Autism and Developmental Disabilities, 44,* 177–186.

Doll, E. A. (1941). The essentials of an inclusive concept of mental deficiency. *American Journal of Mental Deficiency, 46,* 214–219.

Donley, C. R., & Williams, G. (1997). Parents exhibit children's progress at a poster session. *Teaching Exceptional Children, 29*(4), 46–51.

Donovan, M. S., & Cross, C. T. (Eds.). (2002). *Minority students in special education and gifted education.* Washington, DC: National Academy of Sciences.

Doren, B., Bullis, M., & Benz, M. R. (1996a). Predicting the arrest status of adolescents with disabilities in transition. *Journal of Special Education, 29*, 363–380.

Dormans, J. P., & Pellegrino, L. (Eds.). (1998). *Caring for children with cerebral palsy: A team approach.* Baltimore: Brookes.

Dornan, D., Hickson, L., Murdoch, B., Houston, T., & Constantinescu, G. (2010). Is auditory-verbal therapy effective for children with hearing loss? *Volta Review, 110*, 361–387.

Dosen, A., & Day, K. (Eds.). (2001). *Treating mental illness and behavior disorders in children and adults with mental retardation.* Washington, DC: American Psychiatric Press.

Douma, J. C. H., Dekker, M. C., de Ruiter, K. P., Tick, N. T., & Koot, H. M. (2007). Antisocial and delinquent behaviors in youths with mild or borderline disabilities. *American Journal on Mental Retardation, 112*, 207–220.

Downing, J. (2000). Augmentative communication services: A critical aspect of assistive technology. *Journal of Special Education Technology, 15*(3), 35–38.

Downing, J. (2005). *Teaching communication skills to students with severe disabilities* (2nd ed.). Baltimore: Brookes.

Downing, J. (2011). Teaching communication skills. In M. E. Snell & F. Brown (Eds.), *Instruction of students with severe disabilities* (7th ed., pp. 461–491). Upper Saddle River, NJ: Pearson.

Downing, J. E., & Chen, D. (2003). Using tactile strategies with students who are blind and have severe disabilities. *Teaching Exceptional Children, 36*(2), 56–60.

Downing, J. E., & Eichinger, J. (1990). Instructional strategies for learners with dual sensory impairments in integrated settings. *Journal of the Association for Persons with Severe Handicaps, 15*, 98–105.

Downing, J. E., Spencer, S., & Cavallaro, C. (2004). The development of an inclusive elementary school: Perceptions from stakeholders. *Research and Practice for People with Severe Disabilities, 29*, 11–24.

Downs, R. C., & Downs, A. (2010). Practice in early intervention for children with autism: A comparison with the National Research Council recommended practices. *Education and Training in Autism and Developmental Disabilities, 45*(2), 150–159.

Dowse, J. M. (2009). Jeanna Mora Dowse: Featured teacher. In W. L. Heward, *Exceptional Children: An introduction to special education* (9th ed., pp. 370–371, 374). Upper Saddle River, NJ: Pearson.

Drasgow, E. (1998). American Sign Language as a pathway to linguistic competence. *Exceptional Children, 64*, 329–342.

Drew, C. J., & Hardman, M. L. (2007). *Intellectual disabilities across the lifespan* (9th ed.). Upper Saddle River, NJ: Merrill/Pearson.

Dunlap, G., Iovannone, R., Kincaid, D., Wilson, K., Christiansen, K., Strain, P. S., & English, C. (2010). *Prevent, teach, reinforce: The school-based model of individualized positive behavior support.* Baltimore: Brooks.

Dunlap, G., Iovannone, R., Kincaid, D., Wilson, K., Christiansen, K., Strain, P. S., & English, C. (2010). *Prevent, teach, reinforce: The school-based model of individualized positive behavior support.* Baltimore: Brookes.

Dunlap, G., Strain, P. S., Fox, L., Carta, J. J., Conroy, M., Smith, B. J., Kern, L., Hemmeter, M. L., Timm, M. A., McCart, A., Sailor, W., Markey, U.,

Markey, D. J., Lardieri, S., & Sowell, C. (2006). Prevention and intervention with young children's challenging behavior: Perspective regarding current knowledge: A review of reviews. *Behavioral Disorders, 32*, 29–45.

Dunn, L. M., & Dunn, D. M. (2006). *Peabody Picture Vocabulary Test—4.* Bloomington, MN: Pearson.

Dunn-Geier, J., Ho, H. H., Auersberg, E., Doyle, D., Eaves, L., Matsuba, C., et al. (2000). Effects of secretin on children with autism: A randomized controlled trial. *Developmental Medicine and Child Neurology, 42*(12), 796–802.

Dunst, C. (2001). Participation of young children with disabilities in community learning activities. In M. Guralnick (Ed.), *Early childhood inclusion: Focus on change* (pp. 307–333). Baltimore: Brookes.

DuPaul, G. J., & Stoner, G. (2003). *ADHD in the schools: Assessment and intervention strategies* (2nd ed.). New York: Guilford.

Durand, V. M., & Crimmins, D. (1992). *The Motivation Assessment Scale.* Topeka, KS: Monaco & Associates.

Dyches, T. T., Carter, N. J., & Prater, M. A. (2012). *A teacher's guide to communicating with parents: Practical strategies for developing successful partnerships.* Upper Saddle River, NJ: Pearson.

Dye, G. A. (2000). Graphic organizers to the rescue! Helping student link—and remember—information. *Teaching Exceptional Children, 32*(3), 72–76.

Dykens, E. M., Hodapp, R. M., & Finucane, B. M. (2000). *Genetics and mental retardation syndromes: A new look at behavior and interventions.* Baltimore: Brookes.

Dykes, J. (1992). Opinions of orientation and mobility instructors about using the long cane with preschool-age children. *RE:view, 24*, 85–92.

Dyson, L. (1996). The experiences of families of children with learning disabilities: Parental stress, family functioning, and sibling self-concept. *Journal of Learning Disabilities, 29*(3), 280–286.

Easterbrooks, S. (1999). Improving practices for students with hearing impairments. *Exceptional Children, 65*, 537–554.

Easterbrooks, S. R., & Baker, S. K. (2001). Considering the communication needs of students who are deaf or hard of hearing. *Teaching Exceptional Children, 33*(3), 70–76.

Ebanks, M. E., & Fisher, W. W. (2003). Altering the timing of academic prompts to treat destructive behavior maintained by escape. *Journal of Applied Behavior Analysis, 36*, 355–359.

Eberle, L. (1922). The maimed, the halt and the race. Reprinted in R. H. Bremner (Ed.), *Children and youth in America: A documentary history. Vol. 2: 1866–1932* (pp. 1026–1028). Cambridge, MA: Harvard University Press.

Edens, R. M., Murdick, N. L., & Gartin, B. C. (2003). Preventing infection in the classroom: The use of universal precautions. *Teaching Exceptional Children, 35*(4), 62–66.

Editors of The Lancet. (2010, February 2). Retraction—Ileal-lymphoid-nodular hyperplasia, non-specific colitis, and pervasive developmental disorder in children. *The Lancet.* doi:10.1016/S0140-6736 (10)60175-4

Ehlers, S., Gillberg, C., & Wing, L. (1999). A screening questionnaire for Asperger syndrome and other high-functioning autism spectrum disorders in school age children. *Journal of*

Autism and Developmental Disorders, 29, 129–141.

Ehren, B. J. (2000). Maintaining a therapeutic focus and sharing responsibility for student success: Keys to in-classroom speech-language services. *Language, Speech, and Hearing Services in Schools, 31*, 219–229.

Ehri, L. C. (2005). Learning to read words: Theory, findings, and issues. *Scientific Studies of Reading, 9*, 167–188.

Eikeseth, S. (2009). Outcome of comprehensive psycho-educational interventions for young children with autism. *Research in Developmental Disabilities, 30*, 158–178.

Eikeseth, S., & Lovaas, O. I. (1992). The autistic label and its potentially detrimental effect on the child's treatment. *Journal of Behavioral Therapy and Experimental Psychiatry, 23*(3), 151–157.

Eikeseth, S., Smith, T., Jahr, E., & Eldevik, S. (2002). Intensive behavioral treatment at school for 4- to 7-year-old children with autism: A 1-year comparison controlled study. *Behavior Modification, 26*, 49–68.

Elbaum, B. (2002). The self-concept of students with learning disabilities: A meta-analysis of comparison across different placements. *Learning Disabilities Research and Practice, 17*, 216–226.

Eldevik, S., Hastings, R. P., Hughes, J. C., Jahr, E., Eikeseth, S., & Cross, S. (2010). Using participant data to extend the evidence base for intensive behavioral intervention for children with autism. *American Journal on Intellectual and Developmental Disabilities, 115*, 364–380.

Eldredge, J. L. (2005). Foundations of fluency: An exploration. *Reading Psychology, 26*, 161–181.

Elksnin, L. K., & Elksnin, N. (2006). *Teaching social-emotional skills at school and home.* Denver: Love.

Ellet, L. (1993). Instructional practices in mainstreamed secondary classrooms. *Journal of Learning Disabilities, 26*, 57–64.

Elliott, S. N., Huai, N., & Roach, R. T. (2007). Universal and early screening for educational difficulties: Current and future approaches. *Journal of School Psychology, 45*, 137–161.

Ellis, E. S., Deshler, D. D., Lenz, B. K., Schumaker, J. B., & Clark, F. L. (1991). An instructional model for teaching learning strategies. *Focus on Exceptional Children, 24*(1), 1–14.

Ellis, E. S., & Howard, P. W. (2007). Graphic organizers: Power tools for teaching students with learning disabilities. *Current Practice Alerts*, Issue 13. Reston, VA: Division for Learning Disabilities and Division for Research, Council for Exceptional Children. Retrieved September 12, 2011, from http://teachingld .org/alerts#the-alert-series

Ellis, E. S., Worthington, L. A., & Larkin, M. J. (2002). *Executive summary of the research synthesis on effective teaching principles and the design of quality tools for educators.* Available: http://idea.uoregon.edu/-ncite/ documents/techrep/tech06.html

Ellis, N. R. (1963). The stimulus trace and behavior inadequacy. In N. R. Ellis (Ed.), *Handbook of mental deficiency* (pp. 134–158). New York: McGraw-Hill.

Emmorey, K. (2002). *Language, cognition, and the brain: Insights from sign language research.* Mahwah, NJ: Erlbaum.

Engelmann, S. (1977). Sequencing cognitive and academic tasks. In R. D. Kneedler & S. G. Tarver (Eds.), *Changing perspectives in special education* (pp. 46–61). Upper Saddle River, NJ: Merrill/Pearson.

Engelmann, S., & Bruner, E. C. (2008). *Reading mastery signature edition, grade K.* Columbus, OH: SRA/McGraw-Hill.

Engelmann, S., & Bruner, E. C. (2008). *Reading mastery signature edition, Grade K.* Columbus, OH: SRA/McGraw-Hill.

Englert, C. S., Wu, X., & Zhao, Y. (2005). Cognitive tools for writing: Scaffolding the performance of students through technology. *Learning Disabilities Research & Practice, 20,* 184–198.

Englund, L. W. (2009). Designing a Web site to share information with parents. *Intervention in School and Clinic, 45,* 45–51.

Enright, R. (2000). If life is a journey, make it a joyride: Some tips for young people. *Exceptional Parent, 31*(7), 50–51.

Epilepsy Foundation. (2011). *Treatment options: Medications.* Landover, MD: Author. Retrieved February 14, 2011, from http://www.epilepsyfoundation.org/about/treatment/medications/

Epley, P., Gotto IV, G. S., Summers, J. S., Brotherson, M. J., Turnbull, A. P., & Friend, A. (2010). Supporting families of young children with disabilities: Examining the role of administrative structure. *Topics in Early Childhood Special Education, 30*(1), 20–31.

Epstein, M. H. (2004). *Behavioral and Emotional Rating Scale (BERS-2): A strength-based approach to assessment.* Austin, TX: PRO-ED.

Epstein, M. H., Hertzog, M. A., & Reid, R. (2001). The Behavioral and Emotional Rating Scale: Long term test-retest reliability. *Behavioral Disorders, 26,* 314–320.

Ericsson, K. A., Nadogapal, K., & Roring, R. W. (2005). Giftedness from the expert-performance perspective. *Journal for the Education of the Gifted, 28,* 287–311.

Erting, C. J., Thumann-Prezioso, C., & Benedict, B. (2000). Bilingualism in a deaf family: Finger-spelling in early childhood. In P. E. Spencer, C. J. Erting, & M. Marschark (Eds.), *The deaf child in the family and at school: Essays in honor of Kathryn P. Meadow-Orlans* (pp. 41–54). Mahwah, NJ: Erlbaum.

Eshleman, J. (2000). *SAFMEDS on the web: Guidelines and considerations for SAFMEDS.* Available: http://standardcelerationcharttopics.pbworks.com/w/page/15573489/SAFMEDS-on-the-Web

Estabrooks, W. (2006). *Auditory-verbal therapy and practice.* Washington, DC: A. G. Bell.

Estell, D. B., Jones, Pearl, M. H., Pearl, R., & Van Acker, R. (2009). Best friendships of students with and without learning disabilities across late elementary school. *Exceptional Children, 76,* 110–124.

Etscheidt, S. (2006). Behavioral intervention plans: Pedagogical and legal analysis of issues. *Behavioral Disorders, 31,* 223–243.

Evans, J. C., & Smith, J. (1993). Nursing planning, intervention, and evaluation for altered neurologic function. In D. B. Jackson & R. B. Saunders (Eds.), *Child health nursing: A comprehensive approach to the care of children and their health* (pp. 1353–1430). Philadelphia: Lippincott.

Fairbanks, S., Sugai, G., Guardino, D., & Lathrop, M. (2007). Response to intervention: Examining classroom behavior support in second grade. *Exceptional Children, 73,* 288–310.

Fan, X., & Chen, M. (2001). Parental involvement and students' academic achievement: A meta-analysis. *Educational Psychology Review, 13,* 1–22.

Faw, G. D., Davis, P. K., & Peck, C. (1996). Increasing self-determination: Teaching people with mental retardation to evaluate residential options. *Journal of Applied Behavior Analysis, 29,* 173–188.

Fazzio, D., Martin, G. L., Arnal, L., & Yu, C. T. (2009). Instructing university students to conduct discrete-trials teaching with children with autism. *Research in Autism Spectrum Disorders, 3*(1), 57–66.

Feil, E. G, Small, J. W., Forness, S. R., Serna, L. A., Kaiser, A. P., Hancock, T. B., Brooks-Gunn, J., Bryant, D., Kuperschmidt, J., Burchinal M. R., Boyce, C. A., & Lopez, M. L. (2005). Using different measure, informants, and clinical cut-off points to estimate prevalence of emotional or behavior disorders in preschoolers: Effects on age, gender, and ethnicity. *Behavioral Disorders, 30,* 375–391.

Feinberg, E., & Vacca, J. (2000). The drama and trauma of creating public policies on autism: Critical issues to consider in the new millennium. *Focus on Autism and Other Developmental Disabilities, 15*(3), 130–137.

Feingold, B. F. (1975). *Why your child is hyperactive.* New York: Random House.

Feingold, B. F. (1976). Hyperkinesis and learning disabilities linked to ingestion of artificial food colors and flavorings. *Journal of Learning Disabilities, 9,* 551–559.

Feldhusen, J. F. (1989). Synthesis of research on gifted youth. *Educational Leadership, 46,* 6–11.

Fenlon, A. G., McNabb, J., & Pidlypchak, H. (2010). "So much potential in reading! Developing meaningful literacy routines for students with multiple disabilities. *Teaching Exceptional Children, 43*(1), 42–48.

Ferguson, D. L. (1994). Is communication really the point? Some thoughts on interventions and membership. *Mental Retardation, 1,* 7–18.

Ferguson, D. L., & Baumgart, D. (1991). Partial participation revisited. *Journal of the Association for Persons with Severe Handicaps, 16,* 218–227.

Ferguson, P. M. (2003). A place in the family: An historical interpretation of research on parental reactions to having a child with a disability. *Journal of Special Education, 36,* 124–130.

Ferguson, P. M., & Ferguson, D. L. (2011). The promise of adulthood. In M. E. Snell & F. Brown (Eds.), *Instruction of students with severe disabilities* (7th ed., pp. 612–641). Upper Saddle River, NJ: Pearson.

Ferrell, K. A. (2006). Your child's development. In M. C. Holbrook (Ed.), *Children with visual impairments: A parents' guide* (2nd. ed., pp. 85–108). Bethesda, MD: Woodbine House.

Ferrell, K. A., & Spungin, S. J. (Eds.). (2011). *Reach out and teach: Helping your child who is visually impaired learn and grow.* New York: American Federation for the Blind.

Ferro, J., Foster-Johnson, L., & Dunlap, G. (1996). Relations between curricular activities and problem behaviors of students with mental retardation. *American Journal on Mental Retardation, 101,* 184–194.

Fidler, D. J., Hepburn, S. L., Mankin, G., & Rogers, S. J. (2005). Praxis skills in young children with Down syndrome, other developmental disabilities, and typically developing children. *American Journal on Occupational Therapy, 59,* 129–138.

Fidler, D. J., Hepburn, S. L., Most, D. E., Philofsky, A., & Rogers, S. J. (2007). Emotional responsivity in young children with Williams syndrome. *American Journal on Mental Retardation, 110,* 312–322.

Fidler, D. J., Philofsky, A., Hepburn, S. L., & Rogers, S. J. (2005). Nonverbal requesting and problem-solving by toddlers with Down syndrome. *American Journal on Mental Retardation, 110,* 312–322.

Fiedler, C. R., Chiang, B., Van Haren, B., Jorgensen, J., Halberg, S., & Boreson, L. (2008). Culturally response practices in schools. A checklist to address disproportionality in special education. *Teaching Exceptional Children, 40*(5), 52–59.

Fiedler, C. R., Simpson, R. L., & Clark, D. M. (2007). *Parents and families of children with disabilities: Effective school-based support services.* Upper Saddle River, NJ: Merrill/Pearson.

Filipek, P. A., Accardo, P., Ashwal, S., Baranek, G., Cook, E., Dawson, G., et al. (2000). Practice parameter: Screening and diagnosis of autism. *Neurology, 55,* 468–477.

Filter, K., Benedict, E., McKenna, M., Horner, R. H., Todd, A., & Wilson J. (2007). Check in/check out: A post-hoc evaluation of an efficient secondary-level targeted interventions for reducing behavior problems. *Education and Treatment of Children, 30,* 69–84.

Finn, C. E., Rotherham, A. J., & Hokanson, C. R., Jr. (Eds.). (2001). *Rethinking special education for a new century.* Washington, DC: Thomas B. Fordham Foundation and the Progressive Policy Institute.

Firth, U. (2003). *Autism: Explaining the enigma* (2nd ed.). Malden, MA: Blackwell.

Fish, T., Rabidoux, P., Ober, J., & Graff, V. L. W. (2009). *Next Chapter Book Club: A model community literacy program for people with intellectual disabilities.* Bethesda, MD: Woodbine.

Fisher, M., & Meyer, L. H. (2002). Development and social competence after two years for students enrolled in inclusive and self-contained educational programs. *Research and Practice for People with Severe Disabilities, 27,* 165–174.

Fisher, S. E., & Francks, C. (2006). Genes, cognition and dyslexia: Learning to read the genome. *Trends in Cognitive Science, 10,* 250–257.

Fitzgerald, J. L., & Watkins, M. W. (2006). Parents' rights in special education: The readability of procedural safeguards. *Exceptional Children, 72,* 497–510.

Flaherty, E., & Glidden, L. M. (2000). Positive adjustment in parents rearing children with Down syndrome. *Early Education and Development, 11,* 407–422.

Flaute, A. J., Peterson, S. M., Van Norman, R. K., Riffle, T., & Eakins, A. (2005). Motivate me! 20 tips for using a MotivAider® for improving your classroom. *Teaching Exceptional Children Plus, 2*(2), Article 3. Retrieved July 3, 2006.

Fleischmann, A. (2004). Narratives published on the Internet by parents of children with autism: What do they reveal and why is it important? *Focus on Autism and Other Developmental Disabilities, 19,* 25–43.

Fletcher, J. M., Lyon, G. R., Barnes, M., Stuebing, K. K., Francis, D. J., Olson, R. K., Shaywitz, S. E., & Shaywitz, B. A. (2002). Classification of learning disabilities: An evidence-based evaluation. In R. Bradley, L. Danielson, & D. P. Hallahan (Eds.), *Identification of learning disabilities: Research* to practice (pp. 185–250). Mahwah, NJ: Erlbaum.

Flexer, R. W., Simmons, T. J., Luft, P., & Baer, R. M. (2008). *Transition planning for secondary students with disabilities* (3rd ed.). Upper Saddle River, NJ: Merrill/Pearson.

Flora, S. R. (2004). *The power of reinforcement.* Albany: State University of New York Press.

Flora, S. R. (2007). *Taking America off drugs: Why behavioral therapy is more effective for treating ADHD, OCD, depressions, and other psychological problems.* Ithaca, NY: SUNY Press.

Flores, M. M., & Ganz, J. B. (2009). Effects of direct instruction on the reading comprehension of students with autism and developmental disabilities. *Education and Training in Developmental Disabilities, 44*(1), 39–53.

Florian, L., Hollenweger, J., Simeonsson, R. J., Wedell, K., Riddell, S., Terzi, L., & Holland, A. (2006). Cross-cultural perspectives on the classification of children with disabilities: Part I. Issues in the classification of children with disabilities. *Journal of Special Education, 40,* 36–45.

Florian, V., & Findler, L. (2001). Mental health and marital adaptation of mothers of children with cerebral palsy. *American Journal of Orthopsychiatry, 71,* 358–367.

Flynn, J. R. (1987). WAIS-III and WISC-III: IQ gains in the United States from 1972 to 1995: How to compensate for obsolete norms. *Perceptual & Motor Skills, 86,* 1231–1239.

Flynn, J. R. (2006). Tethering the elephant: Capital cases, IQ, and the Flynn effect. *Psychology, Public Policy, and Law, 12,* 170–198.

Flynn, J. R. (2007). *What is intelligence: Beyond the Flynn effect.* New York: Cambridge University Press.

Foil, C. R., & Alber, S. R. (2002). Fun and effective ways to build your students' vocabulary. *Intervention in School and Clinic, 37,* 131–139.

Foley, K., & Seknandore, O. (2003). Gifted education for the Native American student. In J. A. Castellano (Ed.), *Special populations in gifted education: Working with diverse gifted learners* (pp. 117–118). Boston: Allyn & Bacon.

Fombonne, E. (2003). The prevalence of autism. *Journal of the American Medical Association, 289*(1), 87–89.

Foorman, B. R. (2007). Primary prevention in classroom reading instruction. *Teaching Exceptional Children, 39*(5), 24–30.

Ford, D. Y. (1998). The underrepresentation of minority students in gifted education. *Journal of Special Education, 32*(1), 4–14.

Ford, D. Y. (2004a). A challenge for culturally diverse families of gifted children: Forced choices between achievement or affiliation. *Gifted Child Today, 27*(3), 26–27, 65.

Ford, D. Y. (2004b). *Intelligence testing and cultural diversity: Concerns, cautions, and considerations.* Storrs, CT: National Research Center on the Gifted and Talented.

Ford, D. Y. (2010a). Recruiting and retaining gifted students from diverse ethnic, cultural, and language groups. In J. A. Banks & C. A. M. Banks (Eds.), *Multicultural education: Issues and perspectives* (7th ed., pp. 371–391). New York: Wiley.

Ford, D. Y. (2010b). *Reversing underachievement among gifted Black students* (2nd ed.). Waco, TX: Prufrock.

Ford, D. Y. (in press). *Multicultural gifted education.* Waco, TX: Prufrock.

Ford, D. Y., Grantham, T. C., & Whiting, G. W. (2008). Culturally and linguistically diverse students in gifted education: Recruitment and retention issues. *Exceptional Children, 74,* 289–306.

Forgatch, M. S., & Paterson, G. R. (1998). Behavioral family therapy. In F. M. Dattilo (Ed.), *Case studies in couple and family therapy: Systematic and cognitive perspectives* (pp. 85–107). New York: Guilford.

Forness, S. R., & Kavale, K. A. (2000). Emotional or behavior disorders: Background and current status of the E/BD terminology and definition. *Behavioral Disorders, 25,* 264–269.

Forness, S. R., Kavale, K. A., Crenshaw, T. M., & Sweeney, D. P. (2000). Best practice in treating children with ADHD: Does not using medication in a comprehensive intervention program verge on malpractice? *Beyond Behavior, 10*(2), 4–7.

Fowler, C. H., Konrad, M., Walker, A., Test, D. W., & Wood, W. M. (2007). Self-determinatoin interventions' effects on the academic perfromance of students with developmental disabilities. *Education and Training in Developmental Disabilities, 42*(3), 270–285.

Fox, L., Vaughn, B. J., Wyatte, M. L., & Dunlap, G. (2002). "We can't expect other people to understand": Family perspectives on problem behavior. *Exceptional Children, 68,* 437–450.

Frank, A. R., & Sitlington, P. L. (1993). Graduates with mental disabilities: The story three years later. *Education and Training in Mental Retardation, 28,* 30–37.

Frankenberger, W., & Cannon, C. (1999). Effects of Ritalin on academic achievement from first to fifth grade. *International Journal of Disability, Development, and Education, 46,* 199–221.

Frankenburg, W. K., & Dodds, J. B. (1990). *The Denver II training manual.* Denver: Denver Developmental Materials.

Fraser, D. (2003). From the playful to the profound: What metaphors tell us about gifted children. *Roeper Review, 25,* 180–185.

Frasier, M. (1991). Disadvantaged and culturally diverse gifted students. *Journal for the Education of the Gifted, 14,* 234–245.

Frasier, M., Garcia, J., & Passow, A. (1995). *A review of assessment issues in gifted education and their implications for identifying gifted minority students.* Storrs: University of Connecticut, National Research Center on the Gifted and Talented. (Research Monopoly RM95204).

Frasier, M., Hunsaker, S., Lee, J., Mitchell, S., Cramond, B., Krisel, S., Garcia, J., Martin, D., Frank, E., & Finley, S. (1995). *Core attributes of giftedness: A foundation for recognizing the gifted potential of minority and economically disadvantaged students.* Storrs: University of Connecticut, National Research Center on the Gifted and Talented.

Freeman, F., & Alkin, M. (2000). Academic and social attainments of children with mental retardation in general education and special education settings. *Remedial and Special Education, 21,* 3–18.

Friedman Narr, R. A. (2006). Teaching phonological awareness with deaf and hard-of-hearing students. *Teaching Exceptional Children, 38*(4), 53–58.

Friend, M., & Bursuck, W. D. (2012). *Including students with special needs: A practical guide for classroom teachers* (6th ed.). Upper Saddle River, NJ: Pearson.

Friend, M., & Cook, L. (2010). *Interactions: Collaboration skills for school professionals* (6th ed.). Upper Saddle River, NJ: Pearson.

Friend, M., & Hurley-Chamberlain, D. (2011). Is co-teaching effective? *CEC Today.* Retrieved September 13, 2011, from http://www.cec.sped.org/AM/Template.cfm?Section=Home&TEMPLATE=/CM/ContentDisplay.cfm&CONTENTID=7504

Frost, L., & Bondy, A. (2002). *The Picture Exchange Communication System training manual* (2nd ed.). Newark, DE: Pyramid Products.

Frostig, M., & Horne, D. (1973). *The Frostig program for the development of visual perception* (rev. ed.). Chicago: Follett.

Frostig, M., Lefever, D. W., & Whittlesey, J. R. B. (1964). *The Marianne Frostig development test of visual perception.* Palo Alto, CA: Consulting Psychologists Press.

Frueh, E. (2007). *Back to school: Creating a safe and supporting school environment for kids with epilepsy.* Landover, MD: Epilepsy Foundation. Retrieved September 2, 2007, from http://www.epilepsyfoundation.org/living/back-to-school-2007.cfm

Fuchs, D., & Deshler, D. D. (2007). What we need to know about responsiveness to intervention (and shouldn't be afraid to ask). *Learning Disabilities Research & Practice, 22,* 129–136.

Fuchs, D., & Fuchs, L. S. (1994). Inclusive schools movement and the radicalization of special education reform. *Exceptional Children, 60,* 294–309.

Fuchs, D., & Fuchs, L. S. (2009). Creating opportunities for intensive intervention for students with learning disabilities. *Teaching Exceptional Children, 42*(2), 60–62.

Fuchs, D., Fuchs, L. S., Mathes, P. G., & Simmons, D. C. (1996). *Peer-assisted learning strategies in reading: A manual.* (Available from Box 328 Peabody, Vanderbilt University, Nashville, TN 37203.)

Fuchs, D., Fuchs, L. S., & Stecker, P. M. (2010). The "blurring" of special education in a new continuum of general education placements. *Exceptional Children, 76,* 301–323.

Fuchs, D., Fuchs, L. S., Thompson, A., Svenson, E., Yen, L., Al Otaiba, S., Yang, N., McMaster, K. N., Prentice, K., Kazdan, S., & Saenz, L. (2001). Peer-assisted learning strategies in reading: Extension for kindergarten, first grade, and high school. *Remedial and Special Education, 22,* 15–21.

Fuchs, D., & Young, C. L. (2006). On the irrelevance of intelligence in predicting responsiveness to reading instruction. *Exceptional Children, 73*(1), 8–30.

Fuchs, L. S. (2011). *A framework for preventing academic failure and identifying LD: Success and challenges, 2011.* Presentation at the 87th Annual Convention of the Council for Exceptional Children. National Harbor, MD.

Fuchs, L. S., & Fuchs, D. (2001). Principles for the prevention and intervention of mathematics disabilities. *Learning Disabilities Research and Practice, 16,* 85–95.

Fuchs, L. S., & Fuchs, D. (2005). Responsiveness-to-intervention: A blueprint for practitioners, policymakers, and parents. *Teaching Exceptional Children, 38*(1), 57–61.

Fuchs, L. S., & Fuchs, D. (2007a). A model for implementing responsiveness to intervention. *Teaching Exceptional Children, 39*(5), 14–20.

Fuchs, L. S., & Fuchs, D. (2007b). *What is scientifically based research on progress monitoring?* Washington, DC: National Center on Student Progress Monitoring. Available online: http://www.studentprogress.org/library/articles.asp#ann

Fuchs, L. S., Fuchs, D., Hamlett, C. L., & Steecker, P. M. (1991). Effects of curriculum-based measurement and consultation on teacher planning and student achievement in mathematics operations. *American Educational Research Journal, 28,* 617–641.

Fuchs, L. S., Fuchs, D., & Hollenbeck, K. N. (2007). Extending responsiveness to intervention to mathematics at first and third grade. *Learning Disabilities Research & Practice, 22,* 13–24.

Fuchs, L. S., Powell, S. R., Seethaler, P. M., Fuchs, D., Hamlett, C. L., Cirino, P. T., & Fletcher, J. M. (2010). A framework for remediating number combination deficits. *Exceptional Children, 76,* 135–156.

Fujiura, G. T. (2003). Continuum of intellectual disabilities: Demographic evidence for the "forgotten generation." *Mental Retardation, 41,* 420–429.

Fujiura, G. T., & Yamaki, K. (2000). Trends in demography of childhood poverty and disability. *Exceptional Children, 66,* 187–199.

Fujiura, J. E., & Yamaki, K. (1997). Analysis of ethnic variations in developmental disability prevalence and household economic status. *Mental Retardation, 35,* 286–294.

Fullerton, E. K., Conroy, M. A., & Correa, V. I. (2009). Early childhood teachers' use of specific praise statements with young children at risk for behavioral disorders. *Behavioral Disorders, 34,* 118–135.

Furlong, M. J., Morrison, G. M., & Jimerson, S. (2004). Externalizing behaviors of aggression and violence in the school context. In R. B. Rutherford, M. M. Quinn, & S. R. Mathur (Eds.), *Handbook of research in emotional and behavioral disorders* (pp. 243–261). New York: Guilford.

Gabel, S. (2004). South Asian Indian cultural orientations toward mental retardation. *Mental Retardation, 42,* 12–25.

Gabrieli, J. D. E. (2009). Dyslexia: A new synergy between education and neuroscience. *Science, 325,* 280–323.

Gabriels, R. L., Agnew, J. A., Miller, L. J., Gralla, J., Pan, Z., Goldson, E., Ledbetter, J. C., Dinkins, J. P., & Hooks, E. (2008). Is there a relationship between restricted, repetitive, stereotyped behaviors and interests and abnormal sensory response in children with autism spectrum disorders? *Research in Autism Spectrum Disorders, 2,* 660–670.

Gadow, K. D., & Nolan, E. E. (1993). Practical considerations in conducting school-based medication evaluations for children with hyperactivity. *Journal of Emotional and Behavioral Disorders, 1,* 118–126.

Gagné, F. (2003). Transforming gifts into talents: The DMGT as a developmental theory. In N. Colangelo & G. A. Davis (Eds.), *Handbook of gifted education* (3rd ed., pp. 60–74). Needham Heights, MA: Allyn & Bacon.

Gagnon, J. C., Barber, B. R., Van Loan, C. O., & Leone, P. E. (2009). Juvenile correctional schools: Characteristics and approaches to curriculum. *Education & Treatment of Children, 32,* 673–696.

Galaburda, A. M. (2005). Neurology of learning disabilities: What will the future bring? The answer comes from the successes of the recent past. *Learning Disability Quarterly, 28,* 107–109.

Gallagher, D. J., Heshusius, L., Iano, R. P., & Skrtic, T. M. (2004). *Challenging orthodoxy in special education: Dissenting voices.* Denver, CO: Love.

Gallagher, J. J. (1984). The evolution of special education concepts. In B. Blatt & R. J. Morris (Eds.), *Perspectives in special education: Personal orientations* (pp. 210–232). Glenview, IL: Scott, Foresman.

Gallagher, J. J. (2004). No Child Left Behind and gifted education. *Roeper Review, 26*(3), 121–123.

Gallagher, P. A., Floyd, J. H., Stafford, A. M., Taber, T. A., Brozovic, S. A., & Alberto, P. A. (2000). Inclusion of students with moderate and severe disabilities in educational and community settings: Perspectives from parents and siblings. *Education and Training in Mental Retardation and Developmental Disabilities, 35,* 135–147.

Gallaudet Research Institute. (2008, November). *Regional and national summary report of data from the 2007–2008 annual survey of deaf and hard of hearing children and youth.* Washington, DC: GRI, Gallaudet University.

Galton, F. (1869). *Hereditary genius.* London: Macmillan.

Ganz, J. B., & Sigafoos, J. (2005). Self-monitoring: Are young adults with MR and autism able to utilize cognitive strategies independently? *Education and Training in Developmental Disabilities, 40,* 24–33.

Garay, S. V. (2003). Listening to the voices of deaf students: Essential transition issues. *Teaching Exceptional Children, 35*(4), 44–48.

Garber, H., & Heber, R. (1973). *The Milwaukee Project: Early intervention as a technique to prevent mental retardation* [Technical paper]. Storrs: University of Connecticut.

Gardner, H. (1983/1994). *Frames of mind: The theory of multiple intelligences.* New York: Basic Books.

Gardner, H. (2006). *Multiple intelligences: New horizons in theory and practice.* New York: Basic Books.

Gardner, R., III, Cartledge, G., Seidl, B., Woolsey, M. L., Schley, G. S., & Utley, C. A. (2001). Mt. Olivet after-school program. *Remedial and Special Education, 22,* 22–33.

Gardner, R., III, Heward, W. L., & Grossi, T. A. (1994). Effects of response cards on student participation and academic achievement: A systematic replication with inner-city students during whole-class science instruction. *Journal of Applied Behavior Analysis, 27,* 63–71.

Gardner, R., III, Nobel, M. M., Hessler, T., Yawn, C. D., & Heron, T. E. (2007). Tutoring system innovations: Past practice to future prototypes. *Intervention in School and Clinic, 43*(2), 71–81.

Garrick Duhaney, L. M. (2003). A practical approach to managing the behaviors of students with ADD. *Intervention in School and Clinic, 38,* 267–279.

Garrick Duhaney, L. M., & Salend, S. (2000). Parental perceptions of inclusive educational placement. *Remedial and Special Education, 21,* 121–128.

Gear, S., Bobzien, J., Judge, S., & Raver, S. A. (2011). Teaching social skills to enhance work performance in a child care setting. *Education and Training in Autism and Developmental Disabilities, 46,* 40–51.

Geary, D. C. (2004). Mathematics and learning disabilities. *Journal of Learning Disabilities, 37,* 4–15.

Gense, M. H., & Gense, D. J. (1994). Identifying autism in children with blindness and visual impairments. *RE:view, 26,* 55–62.

Genshaft, J. L., Greenbaum, S., & Borovosky, S. (1995). Stress and the gifted. In J. L. Genshaft, M. Bireley, & C. L. Hollinger (Eds.), *Serving gifted and talented students: A resource for school personnel* (pp. 257–268). Austin, TX: PRO-ED.

George, C. L. (2010). Effects of response cards on performance and participation in social studies for middle school students with emotional and behavioral disorders. *Behavioral Disorders, 35*(3), 200–213.

Gerber, M. M. (2011). A history of special education. In J. M. Kauffman & D. P. Hallahan (Eds.), *Handbook of special education* (pp. 3–14). New York: Routledge.

Gersten, R. (1998). Recent advances in instructional research for students with learning disabilities: An overview. *Learning Disabilities Research and Practice, 13,* 162–170.

Gersten, R. (2011). *Understanding RTI in mathematics.* Baltimore: Brookes.

Gersten, R., Beckmann, S., Clarke, B., Foegen, A., Marsh, L., Star, J. R., & Witzel, B. (2009). *Assisting students struggling with mathematics: Response to Intervention (RtI) for elementary and middle schools* (NCEE 2009-4060). Washington, DC: National Center for Education Evaluation and Regional Assistance, Institute of Education Sciences, U.S. Department of Education. Retrieved from http://ies.ed.gov/ncee/wwc/publications/practiceguides

Gersten, R., Fuchs, L. S., Compton, D., Coyne, M., Greenwood, C., & Innocenti, M. S. (2005). Quality indicators for group experimental and quasi-experimental research in special education. *Exceptional Children, 71,* 149–164.

Geruschat, D. R., & Corn, A. L. (2006). A look back: 100 years of literature on low vision. *Journal of Visual Impairment and Blindness, 100,* 646–671.

Getch, Y., Bhukhanwala, F., & Neuharth-Pritchett, S. (2007). Strategies for helping children with diabetes in elementary and middle schools. *Teaching Exceptional Children, 39*(3), 46–51.

Getty, L. A., & Summey, S. E. (2004). The course of due process. *Teaching Exceptional Children, 36*(3), 40–44.

Giangreco, M. F. (2007). *Absurdities and realities of special education: The complete digital set.* Minnetonka, MN: Peytral Publications.

Giangreco, M. F. (2011). Educating students with severe disabilities: Foundational concepts and practices. In M. E. Snell & F. Brown (Eds.), *Instruction of students with severe disabilities* (7th ed., pp. 1–30). Upper Saddle River, NJ: Pearson.

Giangreco, M. F., & Broer, S. M. (2007). School based screening to determine overreliance on paraprofessionals. *Focus on Autism and Other Developmental Disabilities, 22,* 149–159.

Giangreco, M. F., Cloninger, C. J., & Iverson, V. S. (2011). *Choosing options and accommodations for children: A guide to educational planning for students with disabilities* (3rd ed.). Baltimore: Brookes.

Giangreco, M. F., & Doyle, M. B. (2007). *Quick-guides to inclusion: Ideas for education students with disabilities* (2nd ed.). Baltimore: Brookes.

Giangreco, M. F., Edelman, S., & Dennis, R. (1991). Common professional practices that interfere with the integrated delivery of related services. *Remedial and Special Education, 12*(2), 16–24.

Gitlin, L. N., Mount, J., Lucas, W., Weirich, L. C., & Gramberg, L. (1997). The physical costs and psychosocial benefits of travel aids for persons who are visually impaired or blind. *Journal of Visual Impairment and Blindness, 91,* 347–359.

Glaeser, B. C., Pierson, M. R., & Fritschman, N. (2003). Comic strip conversation: A positive behavioral support strategy. *Teaching Exceptional Children, 36*(2), 14–19.

Glassberg, L. A., Hooper, S. R., & Mattison, R. E. (1999). Prevalence of learning disabilities at enrollment in special education students with behavioral disorders. *Behavioral Disorders, 26,* 164–172.

Glidden, L. M., & Switzky, H. N. (2006). *International review of research in mental retardation, Vol. 31: Mental retardations, personality, and motivational systems.* Maryland Heights, MO: Elsevier.

Goffreda, C. T., Diperna J. C., & Pedersen, J. A. (2009). Preventive screening for early readers: Predictive validity of the Dynamic Indicators of Basic Early Literacy Skills (DIBELS). *Psychology in the Schools, 46*(6), 539–552.

Goin, R. P., & Myers, B. J. (2004). Characteristics of infantile autism: Moving toward earlier detection. *Focus on Autism and Other Developmental Disabilities, 19,* 5–12.

Goin-Kochel, R. P., Mackintosh, V. H., & Myers, B. J. (2006). How many doctors does it take to make an autism spectrum diagnosis? *Autism and Other Developmental Disabilities, 10,* 439–451.

Goldin-Meadow, S. (2003). *The resilience of language: What gesture creation in deaf children can tell us about how all children learn language.* New York: Psychology Press.

Goldman, A. M. (2006). Genes, seizures, and epilepsy. *Exceptional Parent, 36*(9), 52, 54–59.

Goldman, R., & Fristoe, M. (2000). *Goldman-Fristoe Test of Articulation—2.* Austin, TX: PRO-ED.

Goldman, R., Fristoe, M., & Woodcock, R. W. (1990). *Goldman-Fristoe-Woodcock test of auditory discrimination.* Upper Saddle River, NJ: Pearson.

Goldrich Eskow, K., & Fisher, S. (2004). Getting together in college: An inclusion program for young adults with disabilities. *Teaching Exceptional Children, 36*(3), 26–32.

Goldstein, A. P. (2000). *The prepare curriculum: Teaching prosocial competencies* (rev. ed.). Champaign, IL: Research Press.

Goldstein, H. (2002). Communication intervention for children with autism: A review of treatment efficacy. *Journal of Autism and Developmental Disabilities, 32,* 373–396.

Goldstein, H., Kaczmarek, L., & Hepting, N. (1994). Communication interventions: The challenges of across-the-day implementation. In R. Gardner III, D. M. Sainato, J. O. Cooper, T. E. Heron, W. L. Heward, J. Eshleman, & T. A. Grossi (Eds.), *Behavior analysis in education: Focus on measurably superior instruction* (pp. 101–113). Pacific Grove, CA: Brooks/Cole.

Goldstein, S., & Brooks, R. B. (2007). *Understanding and managing children's classroom behavior: Creating sustainable, resilient classrooms* (2nd ed.). New York: Wiley.

Goldstein, S., & Goldstein, M. (1998). *Managing attention-deficit hyperactivity disorder in children: A guide for practitioners* (2nd ed.). New York: Wiley.

Goldstein, S., Naglieri, J. A., & DeVries, M. (2011). *Learning and attention disorders in adolescence and adulthood: assessment and treatment* (2nd ed.). New York: Wiley.

Gollnick, D. M., & Chinn, P. C. (2009). *Multicultural education in a pluralistic society* (8th ed.). Upper Saddle River, NJ: Pearson.

Gompel, M., van Bon, W. J. J., & Schreuder, R. (2004). Reading by children with low vision. *Journal of Visual Impairments and Blindness, 98,* 77–89.

Gonzalez-Mena, J. (2006). *The young child in the family and the community* (4th ed.). Upper Saddle River, NJ: Merrill/Pearson.

Good, R. H., Kaminski, R. A., et al. (2011). *DIBELS next assessment manual.* Eugene, OR: Dynamic Measurement Group. Available: http://www.dibels.org/

Goodey, C. F. (2005). Blockheads, roundheads, pointed heads: Intellectual disability and the brain before modern medicine. *Journal of the History of the Behavioral Sciences, 41,* 165–183.

Goodman, G., & Williams, C. M. (2007). Interventions for increasing the academic engagement of students with autism spectrum disorders in inclusive classrooms. *Teaching Exceptional Children, 36*(6), 53–61.

Goodman, L. V. (1976). A bill of rights for the handicapped. *American Education, 12*(6), 6–8.

Goodrich, G. L., Kirby, J., Wagstaff, P., Oros, T., & McDevitt, B. (2004). A comparative study of reading performance with a head-mounted laser display and conventional low vision devices. *Journal of Visual Impairments and Blindness, 98,* 148–159.

Graham, S., & Harris, K. R. (2003). Students with learning disabilities and the process of writing. In H. L. Swanson, K. R. Harris, & S. Graham (Eds.), *Handbook of learning disabilities* (pp. 323–344). New York: Guilford.

Graham, S., & Harris, K. R. (2005). *Writing better: Effective strategies for teaching students with learning difficulties.* Baltimore, MD: Brookes.

Graham-Day, K. J., Gardner, R. III, Hsin, Y-W. (2010). Increasing on-task behaviors of high school students with attention deficit hyperactivity disorder: Is it enough? *Education and Treatment of Children, 33,* 205–211.

Grandin, T. (1995). *Thinking in pictures and other reports of my life with autism.* New York: Vintage Books.

Grandin, T. (2006, August 14). Seeing in beautiful, precise pictures. *On Morning Edition* [Radio program]. Washington, DC: National Public Radio. Retrieved July 24, 2007, from http://www.npr.org/templates/story/story.php?storyId=5628476

Grantham, T. (2003). Increasing black student enrollment in gifted programs: An exploration of the Pulaski County Special School District's advocacy efforts. *Gifted Child Quarterly, 47,* 46–65.

Grantham, T. C., Ford, D. Y., Henfield, M. S., Trotman Scott, M., Harmon, D. A., Procher, S., & Price, C. (2011). *Gifted and advanced Black students in school.* Waco, TX: Prufrock.

Gray, C. A., & Attwood, T. (2010). *The new social story book* (10th ed.). Arlington, TX: Future Horizons.

Gray, C., & Garand, J. (1993). Social stories: Improving responses of student with autism with accurate social information. *Focus on Autistic Behavior, 8,* 1–10.

Green, K. B., Mays, N. M., & Jolivette, K. (2011). Making choices: A proactive way to improve behaviors for young children with challenging behavior. *Beyond Behavior, 20*(1), 25–31.

Green, V. A., Pituch, K. A., Itchon, J., Choi, A., O'Reilly, M., & Sigafoos, J. (2006). Internet survey of treatments used by parents of children with autism. *Research in Developmental Disabilities, 27,* 70–84.

Greenspan, S., & Weider, S. W. (1997). Developmental patterns and outcomes in infants and children with disorders in relating and communicating: A chart review of 200 cases of children with autistic spectrum diagnoses. *Journal of Developmental and Learning Disorders, 1,* 87–141.

Greenwood, C. R., Delquadri, J., & Carta, J. J. (1997). *Together we can: Classwide peer tutoring to improve basic academic skills.* Longmont, CO: Sopris West.

Greenwood, C. R., Delquadri, J., & Hall, R. V. (1984). Opportunity to respond and student academic achievement. In W. L. Heward, T. E. Heron, D. S. Hill, & J. Trap-Porter (Eds.), *Focus on behavior analysis in education* (pp. 58–88). Upper Saddle River, NJ: Merrill/Pearson.

Greenwood, C. R., & Maheady, L. (1997). Measurable change in student performance: Forgotten standard in teacher preparation? *Teacher Education and Special Education, 20,* 265–275.

Greenwood, C. R., Maheady, L., & Delquadri, J. C. (2002). Classwide peer tutoring. In G. Stoner, M. R. Shinn, & H. Walker (Eds.), *Interventions for achievement and behavior problems* (2nd ed., pp. 611–649). Washington, DC: National Association of School Psychologists.

Grenot-Scheyer, M., Fisher, M., & Staub, D. (2001). *Lessons learned in inclusive education at the end of the day.* Baltimore: Brookes.

Gresham, F. (2002). Responsiveness to intervention: An alternative approach to the identification of learning disabilities. In R. Bradley, L. Danielson, & D. P. Hallahan (Eds.), *Identification of learning disabilities: Research to practice* (pp. 467–519). Mahwah, NJ: Erlbaum.

Gresham, F. M., Cook, C. R., Crews, S. D., & Kern, L. (2004). Social skills training for children and youth with emotional and behavior disorders: Validity considerations and future directions. *Behavioral Disorders, 30,* 32–46.

Gresham, F. M., Lane, K. L., MacMillan, D.L., & Bocian, K. M. (1999). Social and academic profiles of externalizing and internalizing groups; Risk factors for emotional and behavioral disorders. *Behavioral Disorders, 24,* 231–245.

Gresham, F. M., & MacMillan, D. L. (1997a). Autistic recovery? An analysis and critique of the empirical evidence on the Early Intervention Project. *Behavioral Disorders, 22,* 185–201.

Gresham, F. M., & MacMillan, D. L. (1997b). Denial and defensiveness in the place of fact and reason: Rejoinder to Smith and Lovaas. *Behavioral Disorders, 22,* 219–230.

Grice, D. W., & Buxbaum, J. D. (2006). The genetics of autism spectrum disorders. *NeuroMolecular Medicine, 8,* 451–460.

Griffin, C., & Hammis, D. (2003). *Making self-employment work for people with disabilities.* Baltimore: Brookes.

Griffin, C., Hammis, D., & Geary, T. (2007). *The job developer's handbook: Practical tactics for customized employment*. Baltimore: Brookes.

Griffin, H. C., Williams, S. C., Davis. M. L., & Engelman, M. (2002). Using technology to enhance cues for children with low vision. *Teaching Exceptional Children, 35*(2), 36–42.

Grigal, M., Test, D. W., Beattie, J., & Wood, W. (1997). An evaluation of transition components of individualized education programs. *Exceptional Children, 63*, 357–372.

Grigorenko, E. L. (2003). The first candidate gene for dyslexia: Turning the page of a new chapter of research. *Proceedings of the National Academy of Sciences of the USA, 100*(20), 11190–11192.

Grisham-Brown, J., Hemmeter, M. L., & Pretti-Frontczak, K. (2005). *Blended practices for teaching young children in inclusive settings*. Baltimore: Brookes.

Grisham-Brown, J., & Pretti-Frontczak, K. (2011). *Assessing young children in inclusive settings: The blended practices approach*. Baltimore: Brookes.

Gross, M. (2004). *Exceptionally gifted children* (2nd ed.). London: Routledge Falmer.

Grossi, T. A. (1998). Using a self-operated auditory prompting system to improve the work performance of two employees with severe disabilities. *Journal of the Association for Persons with Severe Handicaps, 23*, 149–154.

Grossi, T. A., & Heward, W. L. (1998). Using self-evaluation to improve the work productivity of trainees in a community-based restaurant training program. *Education and Training in Mental Retardation and Developmental Disabilities, 33*, 248–263.

Guerette, A. R., Lewis, S., & Mattingly, C. (2011). Students with low vision describe their visual impairments and visual functioning. *Journal of Visual Impairment and Blindness, 105*, 287–298.

Guerette, H., & Zabihaylo, C. (2010). Mastering the environment through audition, kinesthia, and cognition: An O&M approach to *training for guide dog travel*. New York: AFB Press.

Guest, C. M., Collis, G. M., & McNicholas, J. (2006). Hearing dogs: A longitudinal study of social and psychological effects on deaf and hard-of-hearing recipients. *Journal of Deaf Studies and Deaf Education, 11*, 252–261.

Guilford, J. P. (1967). *The nature of human intelligence*. New York: McGraw-Hill.

Guilford, J. P. (1987). Creativity research: Past, present and future. In S. Isaksen (Ed.), *Frontiers of creativity research* (pp. 33–66). Buffalo, NY: Bearly.

Gunter, P. L., Denny, R. K., Jack, S. L., Shores, R. E., & Nelson, C. M. (1993). Aversive stimuli in academic interactions between students with serious emotional disturbance and their teachers. *Behavioral Disorders, 18*, 265–274.

Guralnick, M. J. (1997). *The effectiveness of early intervention*. Baltimore: Brookes.

Guralnick, M. J. (2005). Early intervention for children with intellectual disabilities: Current knowledge and future prospects. *Journal of Applied Research in Intellectual Disabilities, 18*, 313–324.

Guralnick, M. J., & Conlon, C. (2007). Early intervention. In M. Batshaw, L. Pelligrino, & N. Roizen (Eds.), *Children with Disabilities* (6th ed., pp. 511–521). Baltimore: Brookes.

Guralnick, M. J., Connor, R. T., Neville, B., & Hammond, M. A. (2006). Promoting the peer-related social development of young children with mild developmental delays: Effectiveness of a comprehensive intervention. *American Journal on Mental Retardation, 111*, 336–356.

Gurney, J. G., Fritz, M. S., Ness, K. K., Sievers, P., Newschaffer, C. J., & Shapiro, E. G. (2003). Analysis of prevalence trends of autism spectrum disorders in Minnesota. *Archives of Pediatric Adolescent Medicine, 157*, 622–627.

Gursel, O., Tekin-Iftar, E., & Boxkurt, F. (2006). Effectiveness of simultaneous prompting in small group: The opportunity of acquiring non-target skills through observational learning and instructive feedback. *Education and Training in Developmental Disabilities, 41*, 225–243.

Gustafson, G., Pfetzing, D., & Zawolkow, E. (1980). *Signing exact English*. Los Alamitos, CA: Modern Signs.

Hadley, P. A. (1998). Language sampling protocols for eliciting text-level discourse. *Language, Speech, and Hearing Services in the Schools, 29*, 132–147.

Hage, C., & Leybaert, J. (2006). The effect of cued speech on the development of spoken language. In P. E. Spencer & M. Marschark (Eds.), *Advances in the spoken-language development of deaf and hard-of-hearing children* (pp. 193–211). New York: Oxford University Press.

Hale, J. E. (2001). *Learning while black: Creating educational excellence for African American children*. Baltimore: Johns Hopkins University Press.

Hall, B. J., Oyer, H. J., & Haas, W. H. (2001). *Speech, language, and hearing disorders: A guide for the teacher* (3rd ed.). Boston: Allyn & Bacon.

Hall, S. S., Lightbody, A. A., & Reiss, A. L. (2008). Compulsive, self-injurious, and autistic behavior in children and adolescents with fragile X syndrome. *American Journal on Mental Retardation, 113*, 44–53.

Hall, T. E., Wolfe, P. S., & Bollig, A. A. (2003). The home-to-school notebook: An effective communication strategy for students with severe disabilities. *Teaching Exceptional Children, 36*(2), 68–73.

Hallahan, D. P. (1998). Teach. Don't flinch. *DLD Times, 16*(1), 1, 4.

Halpern, A. S. (1985). Transition: A look at the foundations. *Exceptional Children, 51*, 479–486.

Ham, R. (1986). *Techniques of stuttering therapy*. Upper Saddle River, NJ: Prentice Hall.

Hamilton, S. L., Seibert, M. A., Gardner, R., III, & Talbert-Johnson, C. (2000). Using guided notes to improve the academic achievement of incarcerated adolescents with learning and behavior problems. *Remedial and Special Education, 21*, 133–140.

Hamm, E. M., Mistrett, S. G., & Goetz Ruffino, A. (2006). Play outcomes and satisfaction with toys and technology of young children with special needs. *Journal of Special Education Technology, 21*(1), 29–35.

Hammill, D., & Larsen, S. (1978). The effectiveness of psycholinguistic training: A reaffirmation of position. *Exceptional Children, 44*, 402–417.

Hammill, D. D., & Newcomer, P. L. (2008). *Test of Language Development Intermediate—3*. Austin, TX: PRO-ED.

Hanhan, S. F. (2008). Parent-teacher communication: Who's talking? In G. Olsen & M. L. Fuller (Eds.), *Home-school relations: Working successfully with parents and families* (pp. 104–126). Boston: Allyn & Bacon.

Hannah, M. E., & Midlarsky, E. (2005). Helping by siblings of children with mental retardation. *American Journal on Mental Retardation, 110*, 87–99.

Hannon, T. S., Rao, G., & Arslanian, S. A. (2005). Childhood obesity and Type 2 diabetes mellitus. *Pediatrics, 116*, 473–480.

Hanson, M. J., Beckman, P. J., Horn, E., Marquart, J., Sandall, S., Greig, D., & Breenan, E. (2000). Entering preschool: Family and professional experiences in this transition process. *Journal of Early Intervention, 23*, 279–293.

Haptonstall-Nykaza, T. S., & Schick, B. (2007). The transition from fingerspelling to English print: Facilitating English decoding. *Journal of Deaf Studies and Deaf Education, 12*, 172–183.

Hardman, M. L., McDonnell, J., & Welch, M. (1997). Perspectives on the future of IDEA. *Journal of the Association for Persons with Severe Handicaps, 22*, 61–77.

Harlacher, J. E., Roberts, N. E., & Merrell, K. W. (2006). Classwide interventions for students with ADHD. *Teaching Exceptional Children, 39*(2), 6–12.

Harmston, K. A., Strong, C. J., & Evans, D. D. (2001). International pen-pal correspondence for students with language-learning disabilities. *Teaching Exceptional Children, 33*(3), 46–51.

Harris, F. R., Johnston, M. K., Kelly, C. S., & Wolf, M. M. (1964). Effects of positive social reinforcement on regressed crawling of a nursery school child. *Journal of Educational Psychology, 55*, 35–41.

Harris, K. R., Friedlander, B. D., Saddler, B., Frizzelle, R., & Graham, S. (2005). Self-monitoring of attention versus self-monitoring of academic performance: Effects among students with ADHD in the general education classroom. *Journal of Special Education, 39*(3), 145–156.

Harris, M., & Moreno, C. (2004). Deaf children's use of phonological coding: Evidence from reading, spelling, and working memory. *Journal of Deaf Studies and Deaf Education, 9*, 253–268.

Harris, S. L., & Handleman, J. S. (Eds.). (2008). *Preschool programs for children with autism* (3rd ed.). Austin, TX: PRO-ED.

Harrison, J., & Hare, D. J. (2004). Brief report: Assessment of sensory abnormalities in people with autistic spectrum disorders, *Journal of Autism and Developmental Disorders, 34*, 727–730.

Harrison, P. L., & Oakland, T. (2003). *Adaptive Behavior Assessment System manual* (2nd ed.). San Antonio, TX: Harcourt Assessment.

Harrop, A., & Swinson, J. (2000). Natural rates of approval and disapproval in British infant, junior, and secondary classrooms. *British Journal of Educational Psychology, 70*, 473–483.

Harry, B. (2003). Trends and issues in serving culturally diverse families of children with disabilities. *Journal of Special Education, 36*, 131–138.

Harry, B. (2008). Collaboration with culturally and linguistically diverse families: Ideal versus reality. *Exceptional Children, 74*, 372–388.

Harry, B., & Klingner, J. K. (2006). *Why are so many minority students in special education? Understanding race and disability in schools*. New York: Teachers College Press.

Harry, B., & Klingner, J. (2007). Discarding the deficit model. *Educational Leadership, 64*(5), 16–21.

Harry, B., Rueda, R., & Kalyanpur, M. (1999). Cultural reciprocity in sociocultural perspective: Adapting the normalization principle for family collaboration. *Exceptional Children, 66*, 123–136.

Hart, B. M., Allen, K. E., Buell, J. S., Harris, F. R., & Wolf, M. M. (1964). Effects of social reinforcement on operant crying. *Journal of Experimental Child Psychology, 1*, 145–153.

Hart, B., & Risley, T. R. (1995). *Meaningful differences in the everyday experience of young American children.* Baltimore: Brookes.

Hart, B., & Risley, T. R. (1999). *The social world of children learning to talk.* Baltimore: Brookes.

Harte, H. A. (2009). What teachers can learn from mothers of children with autism. *Teaching Exceptional Children, 42*(1), 24–30.

Hartman, M. A. (2009). Step by step: Creating a community-based transition program for students with intellectual disabilities. *Teaching Exceptional Children, 41*(6), 6–11.

Hartnedy, S. L., Mozzoni, M. P., & Fahoum, Y. (2005). The effect of fluency training on math and reading skills in neuropsychiatric diagnosis children: A multiple baseline design. *Behavioral Interventions, 20*(1), 27–36.

Hastings, R. P., Beck, A., & Hill, C. (2005). Positive contributions made by children with an intellectual disability in the family: Mothers' and fathers' perceptions. *Journal of Intellectual Disabilities, 9*, 155–165.

Hastings, R. P., & Noone, S. J. (2005). Self-injurious behavior and functional analysis: Ethics and evidence. *Education and Training in Developmental Disabilities, 40*, 335–342.

Hatlen, P. (1996). *The core curriculum for blind and visually impaired students, including those with additional disabilities.* New York: American Foundation for the Blind. Retrieved June 21, 2011, from http://www.afb.org/Section.asp?SectionID=44&TopicID=395&DocumentID=2115

Hatlen, P. (2011). *Core curriculum—The right to be different.* New York: American Foundation for the Blind. Retrieved June 20, 2011, from http://www.afb.org/Section.asp?SectionID=44&TopicID=395&DocumentID=2117

Havey, J. M. (1999). School psychologists' involvement in special education due process hearings. *Psychology in the Schools, 36*(2), 117–121.

Hawken, L., & Horner, R. H. (2003). Evaluation of a targeted intervention within a schoolwide system of behavior support. *Journal of Behavioral Education, 12*, 225–240.

Hawkins, L., & Brawner, J. (1997). *Educating children who are deaf/hard of hearing: Total communication.* Reston, VA: ERIC Clearinghouse on Disabilities and Gifted Education. (ERIC Document Reproduction Service No. ED 414 677)

Haynes, W., & Pindzola, R. (2012). *Diagnosis and evaluation in speech pathology* (8th ed.). Upper Saddle River, NJ: Pearson.

Haywood, H. C. (2006). Broader perspectives on mental retardation. In H. N. Switzky & S. Greenspan (Eds.), *What is mental retardation? Ideas for an evolving disability in the 21st century* (rev. ed., pp. xv–xx). Washington, DC: American Association on Intellectual and Developmental Disabilities.

Heaton, P., & Wallace, G. L. (2004). Annotation: The savant syndrome. *Journal of Child Psychology and Psychiatry, 45*, 899–911.

Heber, R. F. (1961). *A manual on terminology and classification in mental retardation. A monograph supplement to the American Journal of Mental Deficiency, 64* (Monograph Suppl.).

Heckaman, K. A., Alber, S. R., Hooper, S., & Heward, W. L. (1998). A comparison of least-to-most prompts and progressive time delay on the disruptive behavior of students with autism. *Journal of Behavior Education, 8*, 171–201.

Heckaman, K., Conroy, M., Fox, J., & Chait, A. (2000). Functional assessment-based interventions research on students with or at risk for emotional and behavioral disorders in school settings. *Behavioral Disorders, 25*, 196–210.

Heering P. W., & Wilder, D. A. (2006). The use of dependent group contingencies to increase on-task behavior in two general education classrooms. *Education & Treatment of Children, 29*, 459–468.

Heikua, U., Linna, S-L., Olsén, P., Hartikaiinen, A-L., Taanila, A., & Järvelin, M-R. (2005). Etiological survey on intellectual disabilities in the Northern Finland birth cohort 1986. *American Journal on Mental Retardation, 110*, 171–180.

Heller, K. W., & Bigge, J. (2010). Augmentative and alternative communication. In S. J. Best, K. W. Heller, & J. L. Bigge (Eds.), *Teaching individuals with physical or multiple disabilities* (6th ed., pp. 221–254). Upper Saddle River, NJ: Pearson.

Heller, K. W., Bigge, J. L., & Allgood, P. (2010). Adaptations for personal independence. In S. J. Best, K. W. Heller, & J. L. Bigge (Eds.), *Teaching individuals with physical or multiple disabilities* (6th ed., pp. 289–310). Upper Saddle River, NJ: Merrill/Pearson.

Heller, K. W., Dangel, H., & Sweatman, L. (1995). Systematic selection of adaptations for students with muscular dystrophy. *Journal of Developmental and Physical Disabilities, 7*, 253–265.

Heller, K. W., Forney, P. E., Alberto, P. A., Best, S. J., & Schwartzman, M. N. (2009). *Understanding physical, health and multiple disabilities* (2nd ed.). Upper Saddle River, NJ: Merrill/Pearson.

Heller, K. W., Forney, P. E., Alberto, P. A., Schwartzman, M. N., & Goeckel, T. M. (2000). *Meeting physical and health needs of children with disabilities: Teaching student participation and management.* Pacific Grove, CA: Brooks/Cole.

Heller, K. W., Fredrick, L. D., Best, S., Dykes, M. K., & Cohen, E. T. (2000). Specialized health care procedures in the schools: Training and service delivery. *Exceptional Children, 66*, 173–186.

Hempenstall, K. (2004). The importance of effective instruction. In N. Marchand-Martella, T. Slocum, & R. Martella, R. C. (Eds.), *Introduction to direct instruction* (pp. 1–27). Boston: Allyn & Bacon.

Henderson, K., & Bradley, R. (2004). A national perspective on mental health and children with disabilities: Emotional disturbances in children. *Emotional and Behavioral Disorders in Youth, 4*, 67–74.

Henderson, L. W., & Meisels, S. J. (1994). Parental involvement in the developmental screening of their young children: A multiple-source perspective. *Journal of Early Intervention, 18*, 141–154.

Henfield, M. S., Moore, J. L., III, & Wood, C. (2008). Inside and outside gifted education programming: Challenges for African American students. *Exceptional Children, 74*, 433–450.

Henry, L. (2008). Short-term memory coding in children with intellectual disabilities. *American Journal on Mental Retardation, 113*, 187–200.

Herer, G. R., Knightly, C. A., & Steinberg, A. G. (2007). Hearing: Sounds and silences. In M. L. Batshaw (Ed.), *Children with disabilities* (6th ed.). Baltimore: Brookes.

Heron, T. E., & Harris, K. C. (2001). *The educational consultant: Helping professionals, parents, and students in inclusive classrooms* (4th ed.). Austin, TX: PRO-ED.

Heron, T. E., Heward, W. L., Cooke, N. L., & Hill, D. S. (1983). Evaluation of a classwide peer tutoring system: First graders teach each other sight words. *Education & Treatment of Children, 6*, 137–152.

Hertz-Picciotto, I., & Delwiche, L. (2009). The rise of autism and the role of age at diagnosis. *Epidemiology, 20*, 94–90.

Hessler, T., & Konrad, M. (2008). Using curriculum-based measurement to drive IEPs and instruction in written expression. *Teaching Exceptional Children, 41*(2), 28–37.

Hetzner, A. (2007, March 30). Disparity shows in special ed: State deems 25 districts' minority enrollment disproportionate. *Milwaukee Journal Sentinel.*

Heumann, J. (1993). Building our own boats: A personal perspective on disability policy. In L. O. Gostin & H. A. Beyer (Eds.), *Implementing the Americans with Disabilities Act: Rights and responsibilities of all Americans.* Baltimore: Brookes.

Heumann, J. (1995). Terminology. *TASH Newsletter, 20*(4), 1.

Heward, W. L. (1994). Three "low-tech" strategies for increasing the frequency of active student response during group instruction. In R. Gardner III, D. M. Sainato, J. O. Cooper, T. E. Heron, W. L. Heward, J. Eshleman, & T. A. Grossi (Eds.), *Behavior analysis in education: Focus on measurably superior instruction* (pp. 283–320). Pacific Grove, CA: Brooks/Cole.

Heward, W. L. (2001). *Guided notes: Improving the effectiveness of your lectures.* Columbus: Ohio State University Partnership Grant for Improving the Quality of Education for Students with Disabilities. Available: http://ada.osu.edu/resources/fastfacts/Guided-Notes-Fact-Sheet.pdf

Heward, W. L. (2003). Ten faulty notions about teaching and learning that hinder the effectiveness of special education. *Journal of Special Education, 36*(4), 186–205.

Heward, W. L. (2005). Reasons applied behavior analysis is good for education and why those reasons have been insufficient. In W. L. Heward, T. E. Heron, N. A. Neef, S. M. Peterson, D. M. Sainato, G. Cartledge, R. Gardner III, L. D. Peterson, S. B. Hersh, & J. C. Dardig (Eds.), *Focus on behavior analysis in education: Achievements, challenges, and opportunities* (pp. 316–348). Upper Saddle River, NJ: Merrill/Pearson.

Heward, W. L. (2011). *Helping school-age students with autism succeed in the regular classroom.* Invited address at the Association for Behavior Analysis International's 2011 Autism Conference, Washington, DC.

Heward, W. L., Courson, F. H., & Narayan, J. S. (1989). Using choral responding to increase active student response during group instruction. *Teaching Exceptional Children, 21*(3), 72–75.

Heward, W. L., & Dardig, J. C. (2001, Spring). What matters most in special education. *Education Connection*, 41–44.

Heward, W. L., Heron, T. E., & Cooke, N. L. (1982). Tutor huddle: Key element in a classwide peer tutoring system. *Elementary School Journal, 83*, 115–123.

Heward, W. L., Heron, T. E., Gardner, R., III, & Prayzer, R. (1991). Two strategies for improving students' writing skills. In G. Stoner, M. R. Shinn, & H. M. Walker (Eds.), *A school psychologist's interventions for regular education* (pp. 379–398). Washington, DC: National Association of School Psychologists.

Heward, W. L., & Orlansky, M. D. (1980). *Exceptional children: An introductory survey of special education*. Columbus, OH: Merrill.

Heward, W. L., & Silvestri, S. M. (2005). The neutralization of special education. In J. W. Jacobson, J. A. Mulick, & R. M. Foxx (Eds.), *Controversial therapies in developmental disabilities: Fads, fashion, and science in professional practice* (pp. 193–214). Hillsdale, NJ: Erlbaum.

Hill, E. W., & Snook-Hill, M. (1996). Orientation and mobility. In M. C. Holbrook (Ed.), *Children with visual impairments: A parents' guide* (pp. 259–286). Bethesda, MD: Woodbine House.

Hill, J. L. (1999). Meeting the needs of students with special physical and health care needs. Upper Saddle River, NJ: Merrill/Pearson.

Hill, J. L., Brooks-Gunn, J., & Waldfogel, J. (2003). Sustained effects of high participation in an early intervention for low-birth-weight premature infants. *Developmental Psychology, 39*, 730–744.

Hirose, M., & Amemiya, T. (2003). Wearable finger-braille interface for navigation of deaf-blind in ubiquitous barrier-free space. In *Proceedings of 10th International Conference on Human-Computer Interaction (HCI International 2003): Universal access in human-computer interaction*, HCII 2003 (Vol. 4, pp. 1417–1421).

Hobbs, N. (Ed.). (1976a). *Issues in the classification of children (Vol. 1)*. San Francisco: Jossey-Bass.

Hobbs, N. (Ed.). (1976b). *Issues in the classification of children (Vol. 2)*. San Francisco: Jossey-Bass.

Hock, M. F., Schumaker, J. B., & Deshler, D. D. (1999). Closing the gap to success in secondary schools: A model for cognitive apprenticeship. In S. Graham, K. R. Harris, & M. Pressley (Series Eds.) & D. D. Deshler, K. R. Harris, & S. Graham (Vol. Eds.), *Advances in teaching and learning, teaching every child every day: Learning in diverse schools and classrooms* (pp. 1–52). Cambridge, MA: Brookline.

Hodapp, R. M., & Dykens, E. M. (2001). Strengthening behavioral research on genetic mental retardation syndromes. *American Journal of Mental Retardation, 106*, 4–15.

Hodapp, R. M., & Dykens, E. M. (2007). Behavioral effects of genetic retardation disorders. In J. W. Jacobson, J. A. Mulick, & J. Rojahn (Eds.), *Handbook of intellectual and developmental disabilities* (pp. 115–131). New York: Springer.

Hodge, J., Riccomini, P. J., Buford, R., & Herbst, M. H. (2006). A review of instructional interventions in mathematics for students with emotional and behavioral disorders. *Behavioral Disorders, 31*, 297–311.

Hoffman, C. D., Sweeney, D. P., Gilliam, J. E., & Lopez-Wagner, M. C. (2006). Sleep problems in children with autism and in typically developing children. *Focus on Autism and Other Developmental Disabilities, 21*, 146–152.

Holland, K. D. (2006). Understanding the parent of the special needs child. *Exceptional Parent, 36*(8), 60–62.

Hollinger, C. L. (1995). Counseling gifted young women about educational and career choices. In J. L. Genshaft, M. Bireley, & C. L. Hollinger (Eds.), *Serving gifted and talented students: A resource for school personnel* (pp. 269–283). Austin, TX: PRO-ED.

Holub, T., & Rusch, F. R. (2008). Dropout preventions: Using self-determination to achieve desired postschool outcomes. In F. R. Rusch (Ed.). *Beyond high school: Preparing adolescents for tomorrow's challenges* (2nd ed., pp. 288–303). Upper Saddle River, NJ: Pearson.

Hong, B. S. S., Ivey, W. F., Gonzalez, H. R., & Ehrensberger, W. (2007). Preparing students for postsecondary education. *Teaching Exceptional Children, 40*(1), 32–38.

Honig v. Doe, 485 U.S. 305, 108 S.Ct. 592, 98 L.Ed. 2d 686 (1988).

Hoover, H. D., Dunbar, S. B., & Frisbie, D. A. (2007). *Iowa Tests of Basic Skills*. Rolling Meadows, IL: Riverside.

Hoover, J. J., Klinger, J. J., Baca, L. M., & Patton, M. M. (2008). *Methods for teaching culturally and linguistically diverse exceptional learners*. Upper Saddle River, NJ: Merrill/Pearson.

Hoover-Dempsey, K. V., Walker, J. M. T., Sandler, H. M., Whetsel, D., Green, C. L., . . . , & Closen, K. (2005). Why do parents become involved? Research findings and implications. *The Elementary School Journal, 106*, 105–130.

Horn, C. (2010). Response cards: An effective intervention for students with disabilities. *Education and Training in Autism and Developmental Disabilities, 45*, 116–123.

Horn, C., Shuster, J. W., & Collins, B. C. (2006). Use of response cards to teach telling time to students with moderate and severe disabilities. *Education and Training in Developmental Disabilities, 41*, 382–391.

Horn, E., Lieber, J., Li, S., Sandall, S., & Schwartz, I. (2000). Supporting young children's IEP goals in inclusive settings through embedded learning opportunities. *Topics in Early Childhood Special Education, 20*, 208–223.

Horn, E., Ostrosky, M., & Jones, X. (2004). *Interdisciplinary teams* (Monograph series no. 6). Reston, VA: Council for Exceptional Children, Division for Early Childhood.

Homer, R. H., Albin, R. W., Todd, A. W., Newton, J. S., & Sprague, J. R. (2011). Designing and implementing individualized positive behavior support. In M. E. Snell & F. Brown (Eds.), *Instruction of students with severe disabilities* (7th ed., pp. 257–303). Upper Saddle River, NJ: Pearson.

Horner, R. H., Carr, E. G., Halle, J., McGee, G., Odom, S., & Wolery, M. (2005). The use of single-subject research to identify evidence-based practices in special education. *Exceptional Children, 71*, 165–179.

Horvath, B. (2006). Helping students step into adult life with confidence. In W. L. Heward, *Exceptional children: An introduction to special education* (8th ed., pp. 602–603). Upper Saddle River, NJ: Merrill/Pearson.

Horvath, K., Stefanatos, G., Sokolski, K. N., Wachtel, R., Nabors, L., & Tildon, J. T. (1998). Improved social and language skills after secretin administration in patients with autistic spectrum disorders. *Journal of the Association for Academic Minority Physicians, 9*(1), 9–15.

Hotz, G. A. (2011). *The importance of early neurocognitive assessment in children recovering from brain injury*. Alexandria, VA: International Brain Injury Association. Retrieved June 23, 2011, from http://www.internationalbrain.org/?q=node/156

Houwen, S., Visscher, C., Limmink, K. A. P. M., & Hartman, E. (2009). Motor skill performance of children and adolescents with visual impairments: A review. *Exceptional Children, 75*, 464–492.

Howard, J. S., Sparkman, C. R., Cohen, H. G., Green, G., & Stanislaw, H. (2005). A comparison of intensive behavior analytic and eclectic treatments for young children with autism. *Research in Developmental Disabilities, 26*, 359–383.

Howard, L., &. Potts, E. A. (2009). Using co-planning time: Strategies for a successful co-teaching marriage. *TEACHING Exceptional Children Plus, 5*(4), article 2. Retrieved September 12, 2011, from http://escholarship.bc.edu/education/tecplus/vol5/iss4/art2

Howard, V. F., Williams, B. F., & Lepper, C. E. (2010). *Very young children with special needs: A foundation for educators, families, and service providers* (5th ed.). Upper Saddle River, NJ: Pearson.

Howlin, P. (2003). Outcome of high-functioning adults with autism with and without early language delays: Implications for the differentiating between autism and Asperger syndrome. *Journal of Autism and Developmental Disorders, 33*, 3–13.

Hudson, L. J. (1997). *Classroom collaboration*. Watertown, MA: Perkins School for the Blind.

Huebner, K. M., Garber, M., & Wormsley, D. P. (2006). *Student-centered educational placement decisions: The meaning, interpretation, and application of least restrictive environment for students with visual impairments*. Arlington, VA: Division of Visual Impairments (DVI) of the Council for Exceptional Children.

Hughes, C., & Avoke, S. K. (2010). The elephant in the room: Poverty, disability, and employment. *Research and Practice for Persons with Severe Disabilities, 35*, 5–15.

Hughes, C., & Carter, E. W. (2006). *Success for all students: Promoting inclusion in secondary schools through peer buddy programs*. Boston: Allyn & Bacon.

Hughes, C., Copeland, S., Fowler, S., & Church-Pupke, P. (2002). Quality of life. In K. Storey, P. Bates, & D. Hunter (Eds.), *The road ahead: Transition to adult life for persons with disabilities* (pp. 157–171). St. Augustine, FL: Training Resource Network.

Hughes, C., Golas, M., Cosgriff, J., Brigham, N., Edwards, C., & Cashen, K. (2011). Effects of a social skills intervention among high school students with intellectual disabilities and autism and their general education peers. *Research and Practice for Persons with Severe Disabilities, 36*, 46–61.

Hughes, C., Washington, B. H., & Brown, G. L. (2008). Supporting students in the transition from school to adult life. In F. R. Rusch (Ed.), *Beyond high school: Preparing adolescents for tomorrow's challenges* (2nd ed., pp. 266–287). Upper Saddle River, NJ: Merrill/Pearson.

Hughes, W., Wood, W. M., Konrad, M., & Test, D. W. (2006). Get a life: Students practice being self-determined. *Teaching Exceptional Children, 38*(5), 57–63.

Huguenin, N. H. (2000). Reducing overselective attention to compound visual cues with extended training in adolescents with severe mental retardation. *American Journal on Mental Retardation, 111*, 447–453.

Hulit, L. M., Howard, M. R., & Fahey, K.R. (2011). *Born to talk: An introduction to speech and language development* (5th ed.). Upper Saddle River, NJ: Pearson.

Hunt, P., Soto, G., Maier, J., & Doering, K. (2003). Collaborative teaming to support students at risk and students with severe disabilities in general education classrooms. *Exceptional Children, 69*, 315–332.

Hutinger, P. L., Marshall, S., & McCarten, K. (1983). *Core curriculum: Macomb 0–3 regional project* (3rd ed.). Macomb: Western Illinois University.

Hutton, A. M., & Caron, S. L. (2005). Experience of families with children with autism in rural New England. *Focus on Autism and Other Developmental Disabilities, 20*, 180–189.

Hyde, M., & Power, D. (2006). Some ethical dimensions of cochlear implantation for Deaf children and their families. *Journal of Deaf Studies and Deaf Education, 11*, 102–111.

Hyman, S. L., & Towbin, K. E. (2007). Autism spectrum disorders. In M. L. Batshaw, L. Pellegrino, & N. J. Roizen (Eds.), *Children with disabilities* (6th ed.). Baltimore: Brookes.

Inge, K. J., & Moon, M. S. (2006). Vocational preparation and transition. In M. E. Snell & F. Brown (Eds.), *Instruction of students with severe disabilities* (6th ed., pp. 328–374). Upper Saddle River, NJ: Merrill/Pearson.

Institute on Communication and Inclusion at Syracuse University. (2011). *Workshop materials: 2011 ICI Summer Institute.* Syracuse, NY. Retrieved August 17, 2011, from http://soe.syr.edu/centers_institutes/institute_communication_inclusion/

Interactive Autism Network. (2011). *IAN research findings: Treatment series.* Retrieved August 17, 2011, from http://www.iancommunity.org/cs/ian_treatment_reports/overview

Interagency Autism Coordinating Committee. (2011, January). *2011 Strategic plan for autism spectrum disorder research.* Retrieved from the Department of Health and Human Services Interagency Autism Coordinating Committee website, http://iacc.hhs.gov/strategic-plan/2011/index.shtml

International Dyslexia Association. (2008). *Just the facts: Definition of dyslexia.* Baltimore: Author. Available: http://www.interdys.org/

Irving Independent School District v. Tatro, 104 S. Ct. 3371, 82 L.Ed. 2d 664 (1984).

Iscoe, I., & Payne, S. (1972). Development of a revised scale for the functional classification of exceptional children. In E. P. Trapp & P. Himelstein (Eds.), *Readings on the exceptional child* (pp. 7–29). New York: Appleton-Century-Crofts.

Ispen, C. (2006). Health, secondary conditions, and employment outcomes for adults with disabilities. *Journal of Disability Policy Studies, 17*, 77–87.

Ita, C. M., & Friedman, H. A. (1999). The psychological development of children who are deaf or hard of hearing: A critical review. *Volta Review, 101*, 165–181.

Itard, J. M. G. (1806/1962). *The wild boy of Aveyron* (G. Humphrey & M. Humphrey, Eds. and Trans.). Englewood Cliffs, NJ: Prentice Hall. (Original work published in Paris by Guoyon).

Ives, B. (2007). Graphic organizers applied to secondary algebra instruction for students with learning disorders. *Learning Disabilities Research & Practice, 22*, 110–118.

Ivey, M. L., Heflin, L. J., & Alberto, P. (2004). The use of social stories to promote independent behaviors in novel events for children with PDD-NOS. *Focus on Autism and Other Developmental Disabilities, 19*, 164–176.

Iwata, B. A., Dorsey, M., Slifer, K., Bauman, K., & Richman, G. (1994). Toward a functional analysis of self-injury. *Journal of Applied Behavior Analysis, 27*, 197–209.

Izzo, M. V., Yurick, A., Nagaraja, H. N., & Novak, J. A. (2010). Effects of a 21st-century curriculum on students' information technology and transition skills. *Career Development for Exceptional Individuals, 33*, 95–105.

Jacobson, J. W., Foxx, R. M., & Mulick, J. A. (Eds.). (2005a). *Controversial therapies for developmental disabilities: Fads, fashion, and science in professional practice.* Mahwah, NJ: Erlbaum.

Jacobson, J. W., Foxx, R. M., & Mulick, J. A. (2005b). Facilitated communication: The ultimate fad treatment. In J. W. Jacobson, R. M. Foxx & J. A. Mulick (Eds.), *Controversial therapies for developmental disabilities: Fads, fashion, and science in professional practice* (pp. 363–383). Mahwah, NJ: Erlbaum.

Jalongo, M. R., & Isenberg, J. P. (2012). *Exploring your role: An introduction to early childhood education* (4th ed.). Upper Saddle River, NJ: Pearson.

Janney, R. E., & Snell, M. E. (2011). Designing and implementing instruction for inclusive classes. In M. E. Snell & F. Brown (Eds.), *Instruction of students with severe disabilities* (7th ed., pp. 224–256). Upper Saddle River, NJ: Pearson.

Jantz, K. M. (2011). Support groups for adults with Asperger's syndrome. *Focus on Autism and Other Developmental Disabilities, 26*, 119–118.

Jenkins, J. R., & O'Conner, R. E. (2001). *Early identification and intervention for young children with reading/learning disabilities* (Executive Summary). Paper presented at the LD Summit, Washington, DC. http://ldsummit.air.org/download/Jenkins%20final%208-14-01.pdf

Jernigan, K. (1993, August). The pitfalls of political correctness: Euphemisms excoriated. *Braille Monitor,* 865–867.

Jerome, J. Frantino, E. P., & Sturmey, P. (2007). The effects of errorless learning and backward chaining on the acquisition of internet skills in adults with developmental disabilities. *Journal of Applied Behavior Analysis, 40*, 185–189.

Johnson, C. E., & Viramontez Anguiano, R. P. (2004). Latino parents in the rural Southeast: A study of family and school partnerships. *Journal of Family and Consumer Sciences, 96*, 4, 29–33.

Johnson, D. R., Mallard, D. F., & Lancaster, P. (2007). Road to success: Helping young adults with learning disabilities plan and prepare for employment. *Teaching Exceptional Children, 39*(6), 26–32.

Johnson, D. W., & Johnson, R. T. (2009). *Joining together: Group theory and group skills* (10th ed.). Upper Saddle River, NJ: Pearson.

Johnson, E., Mallard, D. F., Fuchs, D., & McKnight, M. A. (2006). *Responsiveness to intervention: How to do it.* Lawrence, KS: National Research Center on Learning Disabilities. Available: www.nrcld.org

Johnson, H. L. (1993). Stressful family experiences and young children: How the classroom teacher can help. *Intervention in School and Clinic, 28*(3), 165–171.

Johnson, K. R., & Layng, T. V. J. (1994). The Morningside Model of generative instruction. In R. Gardner III, D. M. Sainato, J. O. Cooper, T. E. Heron, W. L. Heward, J. Eshleman, & T. A. Grossi (Eds.), *Behavior analysis in education: Focus on measurably superior instruction* (pp. 173–197). Monterey, CA: Brooks/Cole.

Johnson, T. P. (1986). *The principal's guide to the educational rights of handicapped students.* Reston, VA: National Association of Secondary School Principals.

Johnson-Martin, N. M., Attermeier, S. M., & Hacker, B. J. (2004). *The Carolina Curriculum for infants and toddlers with special needs* (3rd ed.). Baltimore: Brookes.

Johnston, M. K., Kelly, C. S., Harris, F. R., & Wolf, M. M. (1966). An application of reinforcement principles to the development of motor skills of a young child. *Child Development, 37*, 370–387.

Joint Committee on Infant Hearing. (2007). Year 2007 position statement: Principles and guidelines for early hearing detection and intervention. *Pediatrics, 120*(4), 898–921.

Joint United Nations Programme on HIV/AIDS. (2010). *UNAIDS report on the global AIDS epidemic: 2010.* Geneva, Switzerland: Author. Retrieved February 10, 2011, from http://www.unaids.org/en/resources/unaidspublications/2010/

Jolivette, K., Lingo, A. S., Houchins, D. E., Barton-Arwood, S. M., & Shippen, M. E. (2006). Building math fluency for students with developmental disabilities using *Great Leaps Math. Education and Training in Developmental Disabilities, 41*, 392–400.

Jolly, A. C., Test, D. W., & Spooner, F. (1993). Using badges to increase initiations of children with severe disabilities in a play setting. *Journal of the Association for Persons with Severe Handicaps, 18*, 46–51.

Jones, D. E., Clatterbuck, C. C., Marquis, J., Turnbull, H. R., & Moberly, R. L. (1996). Educational placements for children who are ventilator assisted. *Exceptional Children, 63*, 47–57.

Jones, E. A., & Carr, E. G. (2004). Joint attention in children with autism: Theory and intervention. *Focus on Autism and Other Developmental Disabilities, 19*, 13–26.

Jones, M., Onslow, M., Packman, A., Williams, S., Ormond, T., Schwarz, I., & Gebski, V. (2005). A randomised controlled trial of the Lidcombe Program for early stuttering intervention. *British Medical Journal, 331*, 659–661.

Joseph, L. M., & Ford, D. Y. (2006). Nondiscriminatory assessment: Considerations for gifted education. *Gifted Child Quarterly, 50*, 42–51.

Joseph, L. M., & Konrad, M. (2009). Twenty ways to help students self-manage their academic performance. *Intervention in School and Clinic, 44*, 246–249.

Juarez, A., Best, S. J., & Bigge, J. L. (2010). Adaptations in physical education, leisure education, and recreation. In S. J. Best, K. W. Heller, & J. L. Bigge (Eds.), *Teaching individuals with physical or multiple disabilities* (6th ed., pp. 311–341). Upper Saddle River, NJ: Pearson.

Jung, L. A. (2007). Writing SMART objectives and strategies that fit the routine. *Teaching Exceptional Children, 39*(4), 54–58.

Jurgens, A., Anderson, A., & Moore, D. W. (2009). The effect of teaching PECS to a child with autism on verbal behaviour, play, and social functioning. *Behaviour Change, 26,* 66–81.

Justen, J. E. (1976). Who are the severely handicapped? A problem in definition. *AAESPH Review, 1*(2), 1–12.

Justice, L. M. (2004). Creating language-rich preschool classroom environments. *Teaching Exceptional Children, 37*(2), 36–44.

Justice, L. M. (2010). *Communication sciences and disorders: A contemporary perspective* (2nd ed.). Upper Saddle River, NJ: Pearson.

Kaderavek, J. N. (2011). *Language disorders in children: Fundamental concepts of assessment and intervention.* Upper Saddle River, NJ: Pearson.

Kadesjo, B., Gillberg, C., & Hagberg, B. (1999). The prevalence of autism and autism spectrum disorders. In F. C. Verhult & H. N. Koot (Eds.), *The epidemiology of child and adolescent psychopathology* (pp. 227–257). Oxford: Oxford University Press.

Kagan, J., & Snidman, N. (2004). *The long shadow of temperament.* Cambridge, MA: Harvard University Press.

Kaiser, A. P., & Goetz, L. (1993). Enhancing communication with persons labeled severely disabled. *Journal of the Association for Persons with Severe Handicaps, 18,* 137–142.

Kaiser, A. P., & Grim, J. C. (2006). Teaching functional communication skills. In M. E. Snell & F. Brown (Eds.), *Instruction of students with severe disabilities* (6th ed.). Upper Saddle River, NJ: Merrill/Pearson.

Kalyanpur, M. (2008). The paradox of majority of underrepresentation in special education in India. *Journal of Special Education, 42,* 55–64.

Kame'enui, E. J. (1993). Diverse learners and the tyranny of time: Don't fix blame; fix the leaky roof. *The Reading Teacher, 46,* 376–383.

Kame'enui, E. J. (2007). A new paradigm: Responsiveness to intervention. *Teaching Exceptional Children, 39*(5), 6–7.

Kame'enui, E. J., Good, R., III, & Harn, B. A. (2005). Beginning reading failure and the quantification of risk: Reading behavior as the supreme index. In W. L. Heward, T. E. Heron, N. A. Neef, S. M. Peterson, D. M. Sainato, G. Cartledge, R. Gardner III, L. D. Peterson, S. B. Hersh, & J. C. Dardig (Eds.), *Focus on behavior analysis in education: Achievements, challenges, and opportunities* (pp. 69–89). Upper Saddle River, NJ: Pearson.

Kamps, D. M., Dugan, E. P., Leonard, B. R., & Daoust, P. M. (1994). Enhanced small group instruction using choral responding and student interactions for children with autism and developmental disabilities. *American Journal on Mental Retardation, 99,* 60–73.

Kanaya, T., Scullin, M. H., & Ceci, S. J. (2003). The Flynn effect and U.S. policies: The impact of rising IQs on American society via mental retardation diagnoses. *American Psychologist, 58,* 778–790.

Kang, C., Riazuddin, S., Mundorff, J., Krasnewich, D., Friedman, P., Mullikin, J. C., & Drayna, D. (2010). Mutations in the lysosomal enzyme-targeting pathway and persistent stuttering. *New England Journal of Medicine, 362*(8), 677–685.

Kangas, K. A., & Lloyd, L. L. (2011). Augmentative and alternative communication. In N. B. Anderson & G. H. Shames (Eds.), *Human communication disorders: An introduction* (8th ed., pp. 406–439). Upper Saddle River, NJ: Pearson.

Kanner, A. M., & Schafer, P. O. (2006). Seizures and teens: When seizures aren't the only problem. *Exceptional Parent, 36*(11), 50, 52–55.

Kanner, L. (1943/1985). Autistic disturbance of affective contact. *Nervous Child, 2,* 217–250.

Kaplan, D. E., Gayan, J., Ahn, J., Won, T. W., Pails, D. L., Olson, R. K., DeFries, C., Wood, F. B., Pennington, B. F., Page, G. P., Smith, S. D., & Gruen, J. R. (2002). Evidence for linkage and association with reading disability. *American Journal of Human Genetics, 70,* 1287–1298.

Kaplan, S. (2004). Where we stand determines the answers to the question: Can the No Child Left Behind legislation be beneficial to gifted students? *Roeper Review, 26*(3), 124–125.

Kaplan, S. (2005). Layering differentiated curricula for the gifted and talented. In F. A. Karnes & S. M. Bean (Eds.), *Methods and materials for teaching the gifted* (2nd ed., pp. 107–132). Waco, TX: Prufrock.

Karchmer, M. A., & Mitchell, R. E. (2011). Demographic and achievement characteristics of deaf and hard-of-hearing students. In M. Marschark & P. E. Spencer (Eds.), *Oxford handbook of deaf studies, language, and education* (2nd ed., pp. 18–31). New York: Oxford University Press.

Karnick, N. S. (2004). The social environment. In H. Steiner (Ed.), *Handbook of mental health interventions in children and adolescents* (pp. 51–72). San Francisco: Jossey-Bass.

Kasari, C., Freeman, S., & Paparella, T. (2006). Joint attention and symbolic play in young children with autism: A randomized controlled intervention study. *Journal of Child Psychology and Psychiatry, 47,* 611–620.

Katsiyannis, A., & Maag, J. W. (2001). Manifestation determination as a golden fleece. *Exceptional Children, 68,* 85–96.

Katsiyannis, A., & Yell, M. L. (2000). The Supreme Court and school health services: Cedar Rapids v. Garret F. *Exceptional Children, 66,* 317–326.

Katsiyannis, A., & Yell, M. L. (2004). Critical issues and trends in the education of students with emotional or behavioral disorders [Introduction to special issue]. *Behavioral Disorders, 29,* 209–210.

Kauffman, J. M. (1999). How we prevent the prevention of emotional and behavioral disorders. *Exceptional Children, 65,* 448–468.

Kauffman, J. M. (2003). Appearance, stigma, and prevention. *Remedial and Special Education, 24,* 195–198.

Kauffman, J. M. (2005). *Characteristics of emotional and behavioral disorders of children and youth* (8th ed.). Upper Saddle River, NJ: Merrill/Pearson.

Kauffman, J. M. (2010). Commentary: Current status of the field and future directions. *Behavioral Disorders, 35,* 180–184.

Kauffman, J. M. (2011). *Toward a science of education: The battle between rogue and real science.* Verona, WS: Full Court Press.

Kauffman, J. M., & Hallahan, D. K. (2005). *The illusion of full inclusion: A comprehensive critique of a current special education bandwagon* (2nd ed.). Austin, TX: PRO-ED.

Kauffman, J. M., & Konold, T. R. (2007). Making sense in education: Pretense (including No Child Left Behind) and realities in rhetoric and policy about schools and schooling. *Exceptionality, 15,* 75–96.

Kauffman, J. M., & Landrum, T. J. (2009). *Characteristics of emotional and behavioral disorders of children and youth* (9th ed.). Upper Saddle River, NJ: Pearson.

Kauffman, J. M., Bantz, J., & McCullough, J. (2002). Separate and better: A special public school class for students with emotional and behavioral disorders. *Exceptionality, 10,* 149–170.

Kaufman, A. (2000). Clothing-selection habits of teenage girls who are sighted and blind. *Journal of Visual Impairments and Blindness, 94,* 527–531.

Kaufman, J. C., & Gentile, C. A. (2002). The will, the wit, the judgment: The importance of an early start in productive and successful creative writing. *High Ability Studies, 13,* 115–124.

Kavale, K. A. (2002). Discrepancy models in the identification of learning disability. In R. Bradley, L. Danielson, & D. P. Hallahan (Eds.), *Identification of learning disabilities: Research to practice* (pp. 369–426). Mahwah, NJ: Erlbaum.

Kavale, K. A., & Forness, S. R. (1996). Social skills deficits and learning disabilities: A meta-analysis. *Journal of Learning Disabilities, 29,* 226–237.

Kavale, K. A., & Forness, S. R. (2000). History, rhetoric and reality: Analysis of the inclusion debate. *Remedial and Special Education, 21,* 279–296.

Kavale, K. A., Holdnack, J. A., & Mostert, M. P. (2006). Responsiveness to intervention and the identification of learning disabilities: A critique and alternative proposal. *Learning Disability Quarterly, 29,* 113–127.

Kavale, K. A., & Mattson, P. D. (1983). One jumped off the balance beam: Meta-analysis of perceptual-motor training. *Journal of Learning Disabilities, 16,* 165–173.

Kavale, K. A., & Reese, J. H. (1992). The character of learning disabilities: An Iowa profile. *Learning Disability Quarterly, 15,* 74–94.

Kavale, K. A., & Spaulding, L. S. (2008). I response to intervention good policy for specific learning disability? *Learning Disabilities Research and Practice, 23*(4), 169–179.

Kehle, T. J., Bray, M. A., Theodore, L. A., Jenson, W. R., & Clark, E. (2000). A multi-component intervention designed to reduce disruptive classroom behavior. *Psychology in the Schools, 37,* 475–481.

Kelker, K., Hecimovic, A., & LeRoy, C. H. (1994). Designing a classroom and school environment for students with AIDS: A checklist for teachers. *Teaching Exceptional Children, 26*(4), 52–55.

Kellems, R. O. (2011). *Using video iPods to teach vocational tasks to young adults with autism spectrum disorders.* Poster presented at the 87th annual convention of the Council for Exceptional Children, National Harbor, MD.

Keller, C. L., & Duffy, M. L. (2005). "I said that?" How to improve our instructional behavior in just 5 minutes per day through data-based self-evaluation. *Teaching Exceptional Children, 37*(4), 36–39.

Kelley, K. R., Bartholomew, A., & Test, D. W. (2011). Effects of the *Self-Directed IEP* delivered using computer-assisted instruction on student participation in educational planning meetings. *Remedial and Special Education, 32*(5).

Published online before print August 8, 2011, doi: 10.1177/0741932511415864

Kelly, D. J. (1998). A clinical synthesis of the "late talker" literature: Implications for service delivery. *Language, Speech and Hearing Services in the School, 29,* 76–84.

Kelly, M. L. (1990). *School-home notes: Promoting children's classroom success.* New York: Guilford.

Kelly, S. J., Macaruso, P., & Sokol, S. M. (1997). Mental calculations in an autistic savant: A case study. *Journal of Clinical and Experimental Neuropsychology, 19*(2), 172–184.

Kennedy, C., & Jolivette, K. (2008). The effects of positive verbal reinforcement on the time spent outside the classroom for students with emotional and behavior disorders in a residential setting. *Behavioral Disorders, 33,* 211–221.

Kennedy, C. H., & Fisher, D. (2001). *Inclusive middle schools.* Baltimore: Brookes.

Keogh, B. K. (2005). Revisiting classification and identification: Labeling. *Learning Disability Quarterly, 28,* 100–102.

Kephart, N. C. (1971). *The slow learner in the classroom* (2nd ed.). Columbus, OH: Merrill.

Kern, J. K., Miller, V. S., Evans, P. A., & Trivedi, M. H. (2002). Efficacy of porcine secretin in children with autism and pervasive development disorder. *Journal of Autism and Developmental Disorders, 32,* 153–160.

Kerr, B., & Cohen, S. (2001). *Smart boys.* Tempe, AZ: Great Potential Press.

Kerr, B. A. (1997). *Smart girls: A new psychology of girls, women and giftedness* (rev. ed.). Great Potential Press.

Kerr, M. M., & Nelson, C. M. (2010). *Strategies for managing behavior problems in the classroom* (6th ed.). Upper Saddle River, NJ: Pearson.

Kessler Foundation/National Organization on Disability. (2010). *The ADA, 20 years later.* New York: Author.

Keyes, M. W., & Owens-Johnson, L. (2003). Developing person-centered IEPs. *Intervention in School and Clinic, 38,* 145–152.

Kiewra, K. A. (2002). How classroom teachers can help students learn and teach them how to learn. *Theory and Practice, 41,* 71–80.

Killoran, J. (2007). *The national deaf-blind child count: 1998–2005 in review.* Monmouth, OR: National Technical Assistance Consortium for Children and Young Adults Who Are Deaf-Blind.

Killu, K., Sainato, D. M., Davis, C. A., Ospelt, H., & Paul, J. N. (1998). Effects of high-probability request sequences on preschoolers' compliance and disruptive behavior. *Journal of Behavioral Education, 8,* 347–368.

Kim, S. H., & Arnold, M. B. (2006). Characteristics of persons with severe mental retardation. In M. Beirne-Smith, J. R. Patton, & S. H. Kim (Eds.), *Mental retardation* (7th ed.). Upper Saddle River, NJ: Merrill/Pearson.

Kimball, J. W., Kinney, E. M., Taylor, B. A., & Stromer, R. (2004). Video-enhanced activity schedules for children with autism: A promising package for teaching social skills. *Education and Treatment of Children, 27,* 280–298.

King, E. W. (2005). Addressing the social and emotional needs of twice-exceptional learners. *Teaching Exceptional Children, 38*(1), 16–20.

King, G., Baxter, D., Rosenbaum, P., Zwaigenbaum, L., & Bates, A. (2009). Belief systems of families of children with autism spectrum disorders or Down syndrome.

Focus on Autism and Other Developmental Disabilities, 24, 50–64.

King, N. J., Heyne, D., & Ollendick, T. H. (2005). Cognitive-behavioral interventions for anxiety and phobic disorders in children: A review. *Behavioral Disorders, 30,* 241–257.

King, S. J., DeCaro, J. J., Karchmer, M. A., & Cole, K. J. (2001). *College and career programs for deaf students* (11th ed.). Washington, DC, and Rochester, NY: Gallaudet University and National Technical Institute for the Deaf.

King-Sears, M. E., & Bowman-Kruhm, M. (2010). Attending to specialized reading instruction for adolescents with mild disabilities. *Teaching Exceptional Children, 42*(4), 30–40.

Kingsley, M. (1997). The effects of a visual loss. In H. Mason & S. McCall (Eds.), *Visual impairment: Access to education for children and young people* (pp. 23–29). London: Fulton.

Kirk, S. A., McCarthy, J. J., & Kirk, W. D. (1968). *Illinois test of psycholinguistic abilities* (rev. ed.). Urbana: University of Illinois Press.

Klein, J. (1994). Supported living: Not just another "rung" on the continuum. *TASH Newsletter, 20*(7), 16–18.

Klein, K. (2007, August 20). Pencils, pens, meds" As kids head to class, pharmaceutical companies ramp up their drug marketing—and it works. *Los Angeles Times.* Retrieved September 3, 2007, from http://www.latimes.com/news/opinion/laoeklein20aug20,0,6706516.story?coll=la-opinion-center

Klein, R. E., McHugh, E., Harrington, S. L., Davis, T., & Lieberman, L. J. (2005). Adapted bicycles for teaching riding skills. *Teaching Exceptional Children, 37*(6), 50–56.

Kleinert, H. L., Miracle, S. A., & Sheppard-Jones, K. (2007). Including students with moderate and severe disabilities in extracurricular and community activities. *Teaching Exceptional Children, 39*(6), 33–38.

Kleinert, J. O., Harrison, E. M., Fisher, T. L., & Kleinert, H. L. (2010). "I can" and "I did"—Self-advocacy for young students with developmental disabilities. *Teaching Exceptional Children, 43*(42), 16–26.

Kleinheksel, K. A., & Summy, S. E. (2003). Enhancing student learning and social behavior through mnemonic strategies. *Teaching Exceptional Children, 36*(2), 30–35.

Kleweno, C. P., Seibel, E. J., Viirre, E. S., Kelly, J. P., & Furness, T. A. (2001). The virtual-retinal display as a low-vision computer interface: Pilot study. *Journal of Rehabilitation Research and Development, 38,* 431–441.

Kliewer, C., Biklen, D., & Kasa-Hendrickson, C. (2006). Who may be literate? *American Education Research Journal, 43,* 163–192.

Klimes-Dougan, B., Lopez, J. A., Nelson, P., & Adelman, H. S. (1992). Two studies of low-income parents involvement in schooling. *The Urban Review, 24,* 185–202.

Klug, B. J. (2004). Children of the starry cope: Gifted and talented Native American students. In D. Boothe & J. Stanley (Eds.), *In the eyes of the beholder: Critical issues for diversity in gifted education* (pp. 49–72). Waco, TX: Prufrock.

Kluth, P. (2004). Autism, autobiography, and adaptations. *Teaching Exceptional Children, 36*(4), 42–47.

Kluwin, T. N. (1985). Profiling the deaf student who is a problem in the classroom. *Adolescence, 20,* 863–875.

Kluwin, T. N. (1993). Cumulative effects of mainstreaming on the achievement of deaf adolescents. *Exceptional Children, 60,* 73–81.

Kluwin, T. N., & Moores, D. F. (1989). Mathematics achievement of hearing impaired adolescents in different placements. *Exceptional Children, 55,* 327–335.

Knoll, J. A., & Wheeler, C. B. (2005). My home and community: Developing supports for adult living. In R. W. Flexer, T. J. Simmons, P. Luft, & R. M. Baer (Eds.), *Transition planning for secondary students with disabilities* (2nd ed., pp. 499–539). Upper Saddle River, NJ: Merrill/Pearson.

Knoors, H., & Vervloed, M. P. J. (2011). Educational programming for deaf children with multiple disabilities: Accommodating special needs. In M. Marschark & P. E. Spencer (Eds.), *Oxford handbook of deaf studies, language, and education* (2nd ed., pp. 82–96). New York: Oxford University Press.

Knowlton, E. (1998). Considerations in the design of personalized curricula supports for students with developmental disabilities. *Education and Training in Mental Retardation and Developmental Disabilities, 33,* 95–107.

Kober, N. (2006). *A public education primer: Basic (and sometimes surprising) facts about the U.S. education system.* Washington, DC: Center for Education Policy.

Kochhar-Bryant, C. A. (2008). *Collaboration and system coordination for students with special needs: From early childhood to the postsecondary years.* Upper Saddle River, NJ: Merrill/Pearson.

Kochhar-Bryant, C. A., & Greene, G. (2009). *Pathways to successful transition for youth with disabilities: A developmental approach* (2nd ed.). Upper Saddle River, NJ: Pearson.

Kochhar-Bryant, C. A., & Price, T. (2008). How does cultural and linguistic diversity affect school collaboration and system coordination? In C. A. Kochhar-Bryant, *Collaboration and system coordination for students with special needs: From early childhood to the postsecondary years* (pp. 228–253). Upper Saddle River, NJ: Merrill/Pearson.

Kodak, T., Miltenberger, R. G., & Romaniuk, C. (2003). The effects of differential negative reinforcement of other behavior and non-contingent escape on compliance. *Journal of Applied Behavior Analysis, 36,* 379–382.

Koegel, R. L., & Koegel, L. K. (2006). *Pivotal response treatments for autism.* Baltimore: Brookes.

Koegel, R. L., Openden, D., & Koegel, L. K. (2004). A systematic desensitization paradigm to treat hypersensitivity to auditory stimuli in children with autism in family contexts. *Research and Practice for Persons with Severe Disabilities, 29,* 122–134.

Koenig, A. J. (2006). Growing into literacy. In M. C. Holbrook (Ed.), *Children with visual impairments: A parents' guide* (2nd ed., pp. 265–295). Bethesda, MD: Woodbine House.

Koenig, A. J., & Holbrook, M. C. (Eds.). (2000b). *Foundations of education: Vol. 1: History and theory of teaching children and youths with visual impairments* (2nd ed.). New York: AFB Press.

Koestler, F. A. (2004). *The unseen minority: A social history of blindness in the United States.* New York: AFB Press.

Kogan, M. D., Blumberg, S. J., Schieve, L. A., Boyle, C. A., Perrin, J. M., Ghandour, R. M., & van Dyck, P. C. (2009). Prevalence of parent-reported diagnosis of autism spectrum disorder among children in the US, 2007. *Pediatrics, 124*(5), 1395–1403.

Kohl, F. L., McLaughlin, M. J., & Nagle, K. (2006). Alternative achievement standards and assessments: A descriptive investigation of 16 states. *Exceptional Children, 73*, 107–123.

Kohn, A. (1993). *Punished by rewards.* Boston: Houghton Mifflin.

Kohn, A. (2001). Five reasons to stop saying "Good job!" *Young Children, 56*(5), 24–28.

Komesaroff, L. (2007). *Disabling pedagogy: Power, politics, and Deaf education.* Washington, DC: Gallaudet Press.

Konold, K. E., Miller, S. P., & Konold, K. B. (2004). Using teaching feedback to enhance student learning. *Teaching Exceptional Children, 36*(6), 64–69.

Konold, T. R., Walthall, J. C., & Pianta, R. C. (2004). The behavior of child behavior ratings: Measurement structure of the Child Behavior Checklist across time, informants, and child gender. *Behavioral Disorders, 29*, 372–383.

Konrad, K., Joseph, L. M., & Itoi, M. (2011). Using guided notes to enhance instruction for all students. *Intervention in School and Clinic, 46,* 131–140.

Konrad, M. 2008. Twenty ways to involve students in the IEP process. *Intervention in School and Clinic, 43*(4), 236–239.

Konrad, M., Joseph, L. M., & Eveleigh, E. (2009). A meta-analytic review of guided notes. *Education and Treatment of Children, 32*, 421–444.

Konrad, M., & Test, D. W. (2004). Teaching middle-school students with disabilities to use an IEP Template. *Career Development for Exceptional Individuals, 27*, 101–124.

Konrad, M., & Test, D. W. (2007). Effects of GO 4 IT?NOW! strategy instruction on the written IEP goal articulation and paragraph-writing skills of middle school students with disabilities. *Remedial and Special Education, 28*, 277–291.

Konrad, M., & Trela, K. (2007). Go 4 it . . . NOW! Extending writing strategies to support all students. *Teaching Exceptional Children, 39*(4), 42–51.

Konrad, M., Trela, K., & Test, D. W. (2006). The effects of Go 4 IT . . . NOW! instruction on paragraph-writing and goal-setting skills of students with orthopedic and cognitive disabilities. *Education and Training in Developmental Disabilities, 41*, 111–124.

Konrad, M., Walker, A. R., Fowler, C. H., Test, D. W., & Wood, W. M. (2008). A model for aligning self-determination and general curriculum standards. *Teaching Exceptional Children, 40*(3), 53–64.

Kostewicz, D. E., & Kubina, R. M. (2010). A comparison of two reading fluency methods: Repeated reading to a fluency criterion and interval sprinting. *Reading Improvement, 47*, 43–63.

Kostewicz, D. E., Kubina, R. M., & Ruhl, K. L. (2008). Creating classroom rules for students with emotional and behavioral disorders: A decision-making guide. *Beyond Behavior, 17*(3), 14–21.

Koushik, S., Shenker, R., & Onslow, M. (2009). Follow-up of 6- to 10-year-old stuttering children after Lidcombe Program treatment: A phase I trial. *Journal of Fluency Disorders, 34*, 279–290.

Kozleski, E. B., Engelbrecht, P., Hess, R., Swart, E., Eloff, I., Oswald, M., Molina, A., & Jain, S. (2008). Where differences matter: A cross-cultural analysis of family voice. *Journal of Special Education, 42*, 26–35.

Kraemer, B. R., McIntryre, L. L., & Blacher, J. (2003). Quality of life for young adults with mental retardation during transition. *Mental Retardation, 41*, 250–262.

Krathwohl, D. R. (2002). A revision of Bloom's Taxonomy: An overview. *Theory into Practice, 41*, 212–218.

Kratochwill, T. R., & Stoiber, K. C. (2000). Empirically supported interventions and school psychology. *School Psychology Quarterly, 15*, 233–253.

Kreicbergs, U., Valdimarsdottir, U., Onelov, E., et al. (2004). Talking about death with children who have severe malignant disease. *New England Journal of Medicine, 351*, 1175–1186.

Kreiner J., & Flexer, R. (2009). Assessment of leisure preferences for students with severe developmental disabilities and communication difficulties. *Education and Training in Developmental Disabilities, 44*, 280–288.

Kretlow, A. G., & Blatz, S. L. (2011). The ABC's of evidence-based practice for teachers. *Teaching Exceptional Children, 43*(5), 8–19.

Kroth, R. L., & Edge, D. (2007). *Communicating with parents and families of exceptional children* (4th ed.). Denver: Love.

Kube, D. A., Peterson, M. C., & Palmer, F. B. (2002). Attention deficit hyperactivity disorder: Comorbidity and medication use. *Clinical Pediatrics, 41*, 461–469.

Kubina, R., & Cooper, J. O. (2001). Changing learning channels: An efficient strategy to facilitate instruction and learning. *Intervention in School and Clinic, 35*, 161–166.

Kubina, R. M., & Hughes, C. (2005). Fluency instruction. *Current Practice Alerts, 15.* Reston, VA: Division for Learning Disabilities and Division for Research, Council for Exceptional Children. Retrieved July 15, 2011, from http://www.teachingld.org/pdf/alert15.pdf

Kubina, R. M., & Hughes, C. (2007). *Fluency instruction. Current Practice Alerts,* Issue 15. Reston, VA: Division for Learning Disabilities and Division for Research, Council for Exceptional Children. Retrieved September 12, 2011, from http://teachingld.org/alerts#the-alert-series

Kubina, R. M., & Morrison, R. S. (2000). Fluency in education. *Behavior and Social Issues, 10*, 83–99.

Kubina, R. M., Jr. (2005). The relations among fluency, rate building, and practice: A response to Doughty, Chase, and O'Shields (2004). *The Behavior Analyst, 28*, 73–76.

Kugel, R. B., & Wolfensberger, W. (Eds.). (1969). *Changing patterns in residential services for the mentally retarded.* Washington, DC: Superintendent of Documents.

Kulik, J. A. (1992b). An analysis of the research on ability grouping: Historical and contemporary perspectives. *Research-Based Decision Making Series.* Storrs: University of Connecticut, National Research Center on the Gifted and Talented.

Kuna, J. (2001). The Human Genome Project and eugenics: Identifying the impact on individuals with mental retardation. *Mental Retardation, 39*, 158–160.

Kuntze, M. (1998). Literacy and deaf children: The language question. *Topics in Language Disorders, 18*(4), 1–15.

LaBlance, G. R., Steckol, K. F., & Smith, V. L. (1994). Stuttering: The role of the classroom teacher. *Teaching Exceptional Children, 26*(2), 10–12.

Lachapelle, Y., Wehmeyer, M. L., Haelewyck, M. C., Courbois, Y., Keith, K. D., Schalock, R., Verdugo, M. A., & Walsh, P. N. (2005). The relationship between quality of life and self-determination: An international study. *Journal of Intellectual Disability Research, 49*, 740–744.

Lackaye, T., Margalit, M., Ziv, O., & Ziman, T. (2006). Comparison of self-efficacy, mood, effort, and hope between students with learning disabilities and their non-LD-matched peers. *Learning Disabilities Research & Practice, 21*, 111–112.

Lago-Delello, E. (1998). Classroom dynamics and the development of serious emotional disturbance. *Exceptional Children, 64*, 479–492.

Lake, J. F., & Billingsley, B. S. (2000). An analysis of factors that contribute to parent-school conflict in special education. *Remedial and Special Education, 21*, 240–251.

Lakin, C., Larson, S., & Kim, S. (March, 2011). *The effects of community vs. institutional living on the daily living skills of persons with developmental disabilities?* Evidence-Based Policy Brief published by the National Association of State Directors of Developmental Disability Services and the Association of University Centers on Disability. Retrieved July 11, 2011, from http://www.aucd.org/docs/councils/core/Evidence-Based%20Policy%20Brief_1.pdf

Lakin, K. C., Larson, S. A., Salmi, P., & Webster, A. (2010). *Residential services for persons with developmental disabilities: Status and trends through 2009.* Minneapolis: University of Minnesota, Research and Training Center on Community Living, Institute on Community Integration.

Lalvani, P. (2008). Mothers of children with Down syndrome: Constructing the sociocultural meaning of disability. *Intellectual and Developmental Disabilities, 46*, 436–455.

Lambert, M. C., Cartledge, G., Lo, Y., & Heward, W. L. (2006). Effects of response cards on disruptive behavior and participation by fourth-grade students during math lessons in an urban school. *Journal of Positive Behavioral Interventions, 8*, 88–99.

Lambert, N., Nihira, K., & Leland, H. (1993). *Adaptive Behavior Scale—School* (2nd ed.). Austin, TX: PRO-ED.

Lancaster, J. (1806). *Improvements in education.* London: Collins & Perkins.

Lancioni, G. E., O'Reilly, M. F., & Oliva, D. (2001). Self-operated verbal instruction for people with intellectual and visual disabilities: Using instructor cluster after task co acquisition. *International Journal of Disability, Development and Educator, 48*, 304–312.

Lancioni, G. E., O'Reilly, M. F., Singh, N. N., Sigafoos, J., Didden, R., Oliva, D., & Severini, L. (2006). A microswitch-based program to enable students with multiple disabilities to choose among environmental stimuli. *Journal of Visual Impairment and Blindness, 100*, 488–493.

Landa, R. J., Holman, K. C., & Garrett-Mayer, E. (2007). Social and communication development in toddlers with early and later diagnosis of autism spectrum disorders. *Archives of General Psychiatry, 64*(7), 853–864.

Landrum, T., Katsiyannis, A., & Archwamety, T. (2004). An analysis of placement and exit patterns of students with emotional and behavioral disorders. *Behavioral Disorders, 29*, 140–153.

Landrum, T., Tankersley, M., & Kauffman, J. M. (2003). What is special about special education for students with emotional or behavioral disorders? *Journal of Special Education, 37*, 148–156.

Lane, H. L. (1988). Is there a "psychology of the deaf"? *Exceptional Children, 55*, 7–19.

Lane, K. L., Carter, E. W., Pierson, M. R., & Glaeser, B. C. (2006). Academic, social, and behavioral characteristics of high school students with emotional disturbances and learning disabilities. *Journal of Emotional and Behavioral Disorders, 14*, 108–117.

Lane, K. L., Falk, K., & Wehby, J. H. (2006). Classroom management in special education classrooms and resource rooms. In C. M. Evertson & C. S. Weinstein (Eds.), *Handbook of classroom management: Research, practice, and contemporary issues* (pp. 439–460). Mahwah, NJ: Erlbaum.

Lane, K. L., Givner, C. C., & Pierson, M. R. (2004). Teacher expectations of student behavior: Social skills are necessary for success in elementary classrooms. *Journal of Special Education, 38*, 104–110.

Lane, K. L., & Menzies, H. M. (2005). Teacher-identified students with and without academic and behavioral concerns: Characteristics and responsiveness. *Behavioral Disorders, 31*, 65–83.

Lane, K. L., & Menzies, H. M. (2010). Reading and writing interventions for students with and at risk for emotional and behavioral disorders: An introduction. *Behavioral Disorders, 35*, 82–85.

Lane, K. L., Menzies, H., Barton-Arwood, S. M., Doukas, G. L., & Munton, S. M. (2005). Designing, implementing, and evaluating social skills interventions for elementary students: Step-by-step procedures based on actual school-based investigations. *Preventing School Failure, 49*, 18–26.

Lane, K. L., Wehby, J. H., & Cooley, C. (2006). Teacher expectations of student's classroom behavior across the grade span: Which social skills are necessary for success? *Exceptional Children, 72*, 153–167.

Lanfranchi, S., Baddeley, A., Gathercole, S., & Vianello, R. (2011). Working memory in Down syndrome: Is there a dual task deficit? *Journal of Intellectual Disability Research*. First published online, July 5, 2011, doi:10.1111/j.1365-2788.2011.01444.x

Langdon, H. W., Novak, J. M., Quintanar, R. S. (2000). Setting the teaching-learning wheel in motion in assessing language minority students. *Multicultural Perspectives, 2*(2), 3–9.

Lannie, A. L., & McCurdy, B. L. (2007). Preventing disruptive behavior in the urban classroom: Effects of the Good Behavior Game on student and teacher behavior. *Education & Treatment of Children, 30*, 85–98.

Larson, S. A., Lakin, K. C., Anderson, L., Kwak, N., Hak Lee, J., & Anderson, D. (2001). Prevalence of mental retardation and developmental disabilities: Estimates from the 1994/1995 National Health Interview Survey Disability Supplements. *American Journal of Mental Retardation, 105*, 231–252.

LaRue, R. H., Jr., Northup, J., Baumeister, A. A., Hawkins, M. F., Seale, L., Williams, T., & Ridgway, A. (2008). An evaluation of stimulant medication on the reinforcing effects of play. *Journal of Applied Behavior Analysis, 41*, 143–147.

Lattimore, L. P., Parsons, M. B., & Reid, D. H. (2006). Enhancing job-site training of supported workers with autism: A reemphasis on simulation. *Journal of Applied Behavior Analysis, 39*, 91–102.

La Vor, M. L. (1976). Federal legislation for exceptional persons: A history. In F. J. Weintraub, A. Abeson, J. Ballard, & M. L. La Vor (Eds.), *Public policy and the education of exceptional children* (pp. 96–111). Reston, VA: Council for Exceptional Children.

Lazarus, B. D. (1996). Flexible skeletons: Guided notes for adolescents with mild disabilities. *Teaching Exceptional Children, 28*(3), 37–40.

Leaf, J. B., Opprenheim-Leaf, M. L., Dotson, W. H., Johnson, V. A., Courtemanhce, A. B., Sheldon, J. B., & Sherman, J. A. (2011). Effects of no-no prompting on teaching expressive labeling of facial expressions to children with and without a pervasive developmental disorder. *Education and Training in Autism and Developmental Disabilities, 46*, 186–203.

Learned, J. E., Dowd, M. V., & Jenkins, J. R. (2009). Instructional conferencing: Helping students succeed on independent assignments in inclusive settings. *Teaching Exceptional Children, 41*(5), 46–51.

Lee, D., L., Belifore, P. J., & Budin, S. G. (2008). Riding the wave: Creating a momentum of school success? *Teaching Exceptional Children, 40*(3), 65–70.

Leekam, S. R., Nieto, C., Libby, S. J., Wing, L., & Gould, J. (2007). Describing the sensory abnormalities of children and adults with autism. *Journal of Autism and Developmental Disorders, 37*, 894–910.

Lehr, D. H., & Macurdy, S. (1994). Meeting special health care needs of students. In M. Agran, N. E. Marchand-Martella, & R. C. Martella (Eds.), *Promoting health and safety: Skills for independent living* (pp. 71–84). Pacific Grove, CA: Brooks/Cole.

Leigh, S. A., & Barclay, L. A. (2000). High school braille readers: Achieving academic success. *RE:view, 32*, 123–131.

Lemay, R. (2006). Social role valorization insights into the social integration conundrum. *Mental Retardation, 44*, 1–12.

Lemov, D. (2010). *Teach like a champion: 49 techniques that put students on the path to college.* San Francisco: Jossey-Bass.

Leno, M. (2011). *Expenditures on children by families, 2010.* U.S. Department of Agriculture, Center for Nutrition Policy and Promotion. Miscellaneous Publication No. 1528-2010.

Leonard, C. M. (2001). Imaging brain structure in children: Differentiating language disability and reading disability. *Learning Disability Quarterly, 24*, 158–176.

Lerner, J. W., & Johns, B. (2008). *Learning disabilities and related disorders: Characteristics and teaching strategies* (11th ed.). Boston: Houghton Mifflin.

Levendoski, L. S., & Cartledge, G. (2000). Self-monitoring for elementary school children with serious emotional disturbances: Classroom applications for increased academic responding. *Behavioral Disorders, 25*, 211–224.

Levine, K., & Wharton, R. (2000). Williams syndrome and happiness. *American Journal of Mental Retardation, 105*, 363–371.

Levy, F., Hay, D., & Bennett, K. (2006). Genetics of attention deficit hyperactivity disorder: A current review and future prospects. *International Journal of Disability, Development and Education, 53*, 5–20.

Lewis, M. P. (Ed.). (2009). *Ethnologue: Languages of the world* (16th ed.). Dallas, TX: SIL International.

Lewis, R. B., & Doorlag, D. H. (2011). *Teaching special education in general education classrooms* (8th ed.). Upper Saddle River, NJ: Pearson.

Lewis, S., & Tolla, J. (2003). Creating and using tactile experience books for young children with visual impairments. *Teaching Exceptional Children, 35*(3), 22–28.

Lewis, T. J., Hudson, S., Richter, M., & Johnson, N. (2004). Scientifically supported practices in emotional and behavioral disorders: A proposed approach and brief review of current practices. *Behavioral Disorders, 29*, 247–259.

Li, A. (2004). Classroom strategies for improving and enhancing visual skills in students with disabilities. *Teaching Exceptional Children, 36*(6), 38–46.

Lian, M. G. J., & Fontánez-Phelan, S. M. (2001). Perceptions of Latino parents regarding cultural and linguistic issues and advocacy for children with disabilities. *Journal of the Association for Persons with Severe Handicaps, 26*, 189–194.

Lidoff, L., & Massof, R. W. (Eds.). (2000). *Issues in low vision rehabilitation: Service delivery, policy, and funding.* New York: AFB Press.

Lienemann, T., Graham, S., Leader-Janssen, B., & Reid, R. (2006). Improving the writing performance of struggling writers in second grade. *Journal of Special Education, 40*, 66–78.

Lien-Thorne, S., & Kamps, D. (2005). Replication study of the First Step to Success intervention program. *Behavioral Disorders, 31*, 18–32.

Lifshitz, H., Irit, H., & Weisse, I. (2007). Self-concept, adjustment to blindness, and quality of friendship among adolescents with visual impairments. *Journal of Visual Impairment and Blindness, 101*, 96–107.

Lighthouse International. (2011). *Eye conditions glossary.* Retrieved May 18, 2011, from http://www.lighthouse.org/about-low-vision-blindness/glossary/

Lim, S-Y. (2008). Parent involvement in education. In G. Olsen & M. L. Fuller (Eds.), *Home-school relations: Working successfully with parents and families* (pp. 127–150). Boston: Allyn & Bacon.

Lin, F. Y., & Kubina, R. M. (2005). The relationship between fluency and application for multiplication. *Journal of Behavioral Education, 14*, 73–87.

Lin, J. (2011, February 4). Autism rate triples among K–12 students. *California Watch.*

Lindberg, J. S., Iwata, B. A., Roscoe, E. M., Worsdell, A. S., & Hanley, G. P. (2003). Treatment efficacy of noncontingent reinforcement during brief and extended application. *Journal of Applied Behavior Analysis, 36*, 1–19.

Lindstrom, L. E., Benz, M. R., & Johnson, M. D. (1997). From school grounds to coffee grounds: An introduction to school-based enterprises. *Teaching Exceptional Children, 29*(4), 20–24.

Lindstrom, L., Doren, B., Metheny, J., Johnson, P., & Zane, C. (2007). Transition to employment: Role of the family in career development. *Exceptional Children, 73*, 348–366.

Lindstrom, L., Doren, B., & Miesch, J. (2011). Waging a living: Career development and long-terms employment outcomes for young adults with disabilities. *Exceptional Children, 77*, 13.

Ling, D. (2002). *Speech and the hearing-impaired child: Theory and practice* (2nd ed.). San Diego: Plural Publishing.

Lingo, A. S., Barton-Arwood, S. M., & Jolivette, K. (2011). Teachers working together: Improving learning outcomes in the inclusive classroom—Practical strategies and examples. *Teaching Exceptional Children, 43*(3), 6–13.

Lingo, A. S., Bott Slaton, D., & Jolivette, K. (2006). Effects of Corrective Reading on the reading abilities and classroom behaviors of middle school students with reading deficits and challenging behavior. *Behavioral Disorders, 31*, 265–283.

Lippke, B. A., Dickey, S. E., Selmar, J. W., & Soder, A. L. (1997). *Photo Articulation Test* (3rd ed.). Austin, TX: PRO-ED.

Lipsey, M. W., & Derzon, J. H. (1998). Predictors of violent or serious delinquency in adolescence and early adulthood: A synthesis of longitudinal research. In R. Loeber & D. P. Farrington (Eds.), *Serious and violent juvenile offenders: Risk factors and successful interventions* (pp. 6–105). Thousand Oaks, CA: Sage.

Llewellyn, G., Gething, L., Kendig, H., & Cant, R. (2004). Older parent caregiver's engagement with the service system. *American Journal of Mental Retardation, 109*, 379–396.

Lo, Y., & Cartledge, G. (2006). FBA and BIP: Increasing the behavior adjustment of African American boys in schools. *Behavioral Disorders, 31*, 147–161.

Lockshin, S. B., Gillis, J. M., & Romanczyk, R. G. (2005). *Defying autism: Keep your sanity and take control.* New York: DRL.

Loftin, R. L., Odom, S. L., & Lantz, J. F. (2007). Social interaction and repetitive motor behaviors. *Journal of Autism and Developmental Disorders, 38*, 1124–1135.

Logan, K. R., & Gast, D. L. (2001). Conducting preference assessments and reinforcer testing for individuals with profound multiple disabilities: Issues and procedures. *Exceptionality, 9*(3), 123–134.

Long, C. E., Gurka, M. J., & Blackman, J. A. (2008). Family stress and children's language and behavior problems: Results from the National Survey of Children's Health. *Topics in Early Childhood Special Education November, 28*, 148–157.

Lord, C. (2007, February). *Autism in the twenty-first century.* Presentation at the conference Progress and Challenges in the Behavioral Treatment of Autism, Boston. [Available on DVD from the Association for Behavior Analysis International.]

Lord, C., Rutter, M., & Le Couteur, A. (1994). Autism diagnostic interview—revised: A revised version of a diagnostic interview for caregivers of individuals with possible pervasive developmental disabilities. *Journal of Autism and Developmental Disorders, 24*, 659–685.

Lovaas, O. I. (1987). Behavioral treatment and normal educational and intellectual functioning in young autistic children. *Journal of Consulting and Clinical Psychology, 55*, 3–9.

Lovaas, O. I. (1994, October). Comments made during Ohio State University teleconference on applied behavior analysis, The Ohio State University, Columbus.

Lovaas, O. I., & Newsom, C. D. (1976). Behavior modification with psychotic children. In H. Leitenberg (Ed.), *Handbook of behavior modification and behavior therapy* (pp. 303–360). Englewood Cliffs, NJ: Prentice Hall.

Lovett, M. W., Steinbach, K. A., & Frijters, J. C. (2000). Remediating the core deficits of developmental reading disability: A double-deficit perspective. *Journal of Learning Disabilities, 33*, 334–358.

Lovitt, T. C. (1977). *In spite of my resistance . . . I've learned from children.* Upper Saddle River, NJ: Merrill/Pearson.

Lowenthal, B. (2001). *Abuse and neglect: The educator's guide to the identification and prevention of child maltreatment.* Baltimore: Brookes.

Luckasson, R., Coulter, D. L., Polloway, E. A., Reiss, S., Schalock, R. L., Snell, M. E., Spitalnik, D. M., & Stark, J. A. (1992). *Mental retardation: Definition, classification, and systems of supports* (9th ed.). Washington, DC: American Association on Mental Retardation.

Luckasson, R., Coulter, D. L., Polloway, E. A., Reiss, S., Schalock, R. L., Snell, M. E., Spitalnik, D. M., & Stark, J. A. (2002). *Mental retardation: Definition, classification, and systems of supports* (10th ed.). Washington, DC: American Association on Mental Retardation.

Lue, M. S. (2001). *A survey of communication disorders for the classroom teacher.* Boston: Allyn & Bacon.

Lueck, A. H. (Ed.). (2004). *Functional vision: A practitioner's guide to evaluation and intervention.* New York: AFB Press.

Lusk, K. E., & Corn, A. L. (2006a). An initial study of dual-media learning: Part 2. *Journal of Visual Impairment and Blindness, 100*, 653–665.

Lusk, K. E., & Corn, A. L. (2006b). Learning and using print and Braille: A study of dual-media learners Part 1. *Journal of Visual Impairment and Blindness, 100*, 606–619.

Luterman, D. (1999). Emotional aspects of hearing loss. *Volta Review, 99*(5), 75–83.

Lynch, E. W., & Hanson, M. J. (2011). *Developing cross-cultural competence: A guide for working with children and their families* (4th ed.). Baltimore: Brookes.

Lyon, G. R. (1999, December 12). Special education in state is failing on many fronts. *Los Angeles Times*, p. A1.

Lyon, G. R., Shaywitz, S. E., & Shaywitz, B. A. (2003). Defining dyslexia. *Annals of Dyslexia, 53*, 1–14.

Lyon, R., & Riccards, P. (2007, June 4). The continued need for Reading First. *EdNews.org.*

Lytle, R. K., & Bordin, J. (2001). Enhancing the IEP team: Strategies for parents and professionals. *Teaching Exceptional Children, 33*(5), 28–33.

Maag, J. W. (2001). Rewarded by punishment: Reflections on the disuse of positive reinforcement in schools. *Exceptional Children, 67*, 173–186.

Maag, J. W. (2006). Social skills training for students with emotional and behavioral disorder: A review of reviews. *Behavioral Disorders, 32*, 5–17.

Maag, J. W., & Reid, R. (1994). Attention-deficit hyperactivity disorder: A functional approach to assessment and treatment. *Behavioral Disorders, 20*, 5–23.

Maag, J. W., & Swearer, S. M. (2005). Cognitive-behavioral interventions for depression: Review and implications for school personnel. *Behavioral Disorders, 30*, 259–276.

Maag, J. W., Reid, R., & DiGangi, S. A. (1993). Differential effects of self-monitoring attention, accuracy, and productivity. *Journal of Applied Behavior Analysis, 26*, 329–344.

MacGinitie, W. H., MacGinitie, R. K., Maria, K., Dreyer, L. G., & Hughes, K. E. (2006). *Gates-MacGinitie Reading Tests—Fourth Edition.* Rolling Meadows, IL: Riverside.

Machek, G. R., & Nelson, J. M. (2007). How should reading disabilities be operationalized? A survey of practicing school psychologists. *Learning Disabilities Research & Practice, 22*, 147–157.

Mackiewicz, S. M., Wood, C. L., Cooke, N. L., & Mazzotti, V. L. (2011). Effects of peer tutoring with audio prompting on vocabulary acquisition for struggling readers. *Remedial and Special Education, 32*, 345–354.

Macy, M., & Hoyt-Gonzales, K. (2007). A linked system approach to early childhood special education eligibility assessment. *Teaching Exceptional Children, 39*(3), 40–44.

Madaus, J. W. (2005). Navigating the college transition maze: A guide for students with learning disabilities. *Teaching Exceptional Children, 37*(23), 32–37.

Madaus, J. W. (2006). Employment outcomes of university graduates with learning disabilities. *Learning Disability Quarterly, 29*, 19–31.

Madaus, J. W., Pivarnick, L., Patnoad, M., Scarpati, S., Richard, N., Wright Hirsch, D., Carbone, E., & Gable, R. K. (2010). Teaching food safety skills to students with disabilities. *Teaching Exceptional Children, 42*(4), 44–51.

Madaus, M. M., Kehle, T. J., Madaus, J., & Bray, M. A. (2003). Mystery motivator as in intervention to promote homework completion and accuracy. *School Psychology International, 24*, 369–377.

Maggin, D. M., Wehby, J. J., Moore Partin, T. C., Robertson, R., & Oliver, R. M. (2011). A comparison of the instructional context for students with behavioral issues enrolled in self-contained and general education classrooms. *Behavioral Disorders, 36*, 84–99.

Maheady, L., & Gard, J. (2010). Classwide peer tutoring: Practice, theory, research, and personal narrative. *Intervention in School and Clinic, 46*(2), 71–78.

Maheady, L., & Jabot, M. (2011). Using research-to-practice studies to increase general educators' use of empirically-supported practices. *Savage Controversies, 4*(2), 2–5.

Maheady, L., Mallette, B., & Harper, G. F. (2006). Four classwide peer tutoring models: Similarities, differences, and implications for research and practice. *Reading and Writing Quarterly, 22*, 65–89.

Maheady, L., Michielli-Pendl, J., Mallette, B., & Harper, G. F. (2002). A collaborative research project to improve the academic performance of a diverse sixth grade science class. *Teacher Education and Special Education, 25*, 55–70.

Maheady, L., Sacca, M. K., & Harper, G. F. (1987). Classwide peer tutoring teams: Effects on the academic performance of secondary students. *Journal of Special Education, 21*(3), 107–121.

Mahshie, S. N. (1995). *Educating deaf children bilingually.* Washington, DC: Gallaudet University Press.

Maker, C. J. (1993). Creativity, intelligence, and problem solving: A definition and design for cross-cultural research and measurement related to giftedness. *Gifted Education International, 9*(2), 68–77.

Maker, C. J. (1996). Identification of gifted minority students: A national problem, needed changes, and a promising solution. *Gifted Child Quarterly, 40*, 41–50.

Maker, C. J. (2001). DISCOVER: Assessing and developing problem solving. *Gifted Education International, 15*, 232–251.

Maker, C. J. (2005). *The DISCOVER project: Improving assessment and curriculum for diverse gifted learners (RM05206)*. Storrs, CT: National Research Center of the Gifted and Talented.

Maker, C. J., & Schiever, S. W. (2010). *Curriculum development and teaching strategies for gifted learners* (3rd ed.). Austin: TX: PRO-ED.

Maker, C. J., Nielson, A. B., & Rogers, J. A. (1994). Giftedness, diversity, and problem-solving. *Teaching Exceptional Children, 27*(1), 4–19.

Malloy, P., & Killoran, J. (2007). *Children who are deaf-blind*. Monmouth, OR: National Consortium on Deaf-Blindness. Retrieved June 25, 2011, from http://nationaldb.org/documents/products/population.pdf

Malone, D. M., & Langone, J. (1999). Teaching object-related play skills to preschool children with developmental concerns. *International Journal of Disability, Development and Education, 46*(3), 325–336.

Mancil, G. R. (2006). Functional communication training: A review of the literature related to children with autism. *Education and Training in Developmental Disabilities, 41*, 213–224.

Mank, D., Cioffi, A., & Yovanoff, P. (1998). Employment outcomes for people with severe disabilities: Opportunities for improvement. *Mental Retardation, 36*, 205–216.

Mank, D. M., & Horner, R. H. (1987). Self-recruited feedback: A cost-effective procedure for maintaining behavior. *Research in Developmental Disabilities, 8*, 91–112.

Marchant, M., & Womack, S. (2010). Book in a bag: Blending social skills and academics. *Teaching Exceptional Children, 42*(4), 6–12.

Marcotte, D. E., Bailey, T., Borkoski, C., & Kienzel, G. S. (2005). The returns of a community college education: Evidence from the national education longitudinal survey. *Educational Evaluation and Policy Analysis, 27*(2),157–175.

Marder, C. (2009). *Facts from the Special Education Elementary Longitudinal Study: Perspective on students' disabilities classifications*. Washington, DC: U.S. Department of Education.

Markwardt, F. C., Jr. (1998). *Peabody Individual Achievement Test—4*. Circle Pines, MN: Bloomington, MN: Pearson.

Marland, S. (1972). *Education of the gifted and talented (Vol. 1)*. Report to the U.S. Congress by the U.S. Commissioner of Education. Washington, DC: Office of Education (DHEW). (ERIC Document Reproduction Service No. ED 056 243)

Marschark, M. (2007). *Raising and educating a deaf child: A comprehensive guide to the choices, controversies, and decisions faced by parents and educators* (paperback ed.). New York: Oxford University Press.

Marschark, M., Schick, B., & Spencer, P. (2006). Understanding sign language development of deaf children. In B. Schick, M. Marschark, & P. Spencer (Eds.), *Advances in the sign language development of deaf children* (pp. 3–18). New York: Oxford University Press.

Marshall, K. J., Lloyd, J. W., & Hallahan, D. P. (1993). Effects of training to increase self-monitoring accuracy. *Journal of Behavioral Education, 3*, 445–459.

Marston, J. R., Loomis, J. M., Klatzky, R. L., & Golledge, R. G. (2007). Nonvisual route following with guidance from a simple haptic or auditory display. *Journal of Visual Impairment and Blindness, 101*, 203–211.

Martella, R. C., Leonard, I. J., Marchand-Martella, N. E., & Agran, M. (1993). Self-monitoring negative statements. *Journal of Behavioral Education, 3*, 77–86.

Martella, R. C., Nelson, J. R., Marchand-Martella, N. E., & O'Reilly, M. (2012). *Comprehensive behavior management: Individualized, classroom, and schoolwide approaches* (2nd ed.). Thousand Oaks, CA: Sage.

Martin, D., Bat-Chava, Y., Lalwani, A., & Waltzman, S. B. (2011). Peer relationships of deaf children with cochlear implants: Predictors of peer entry and peer interaction success. *Journal of Deaf Studies and Deaf Education, 16*, 108–120.

Martin, J. E., Huber Marshall, L., & Sale, P. (2004). A 3-year study of middle, junior high, and high school IEP meetings. *Exceptional Children, 70*, 285–297.

Martin, J. E., Marshall, L. H., Wray, D., Wells, L., O'Brien, J., Olvey, G., et al. (2004). *Choose and take action: Finding the right job for you*. Longmont, CO: Sopris West.

Martin, J. E., Van Dycke, J. L., Christensen, W. R., Greene, B. A., Gardner, J. E., & Lovett, D. L. (2006). Increasing student participation in IEP meetings: Establishing the Self-Directed IEP as evidence-based practice. *Exceptional Children, 72*, 187–200.

Martin, J. E., Woods, L. L., & Sylvester, L. (2008). Building an employment vision: Culturally attuning vocational interests, skills, and limits. In F. R. Rusch (Ed.), *Beyond high school: Preparing adolescents for tomorrow's challenges* (2nd ed., pp. 78–109). Upper Saddle River, NJ: Merrill/Pearson.

Masse, L. N., & Barnett, W. S. (2011). *A benefit-cost analysis of the Abecedarian early childhood intervention*. National Institute for Early Education Research, Rutgers, The State University of New Jersey. Retrieved June 27, 2011, from http://nieer.org/resources/research/AbecedarianStudy.pdf

Mastrangela, S. (2009). Harnessing the power of play: Opportunities for children with autism spectrum disorders. *Teaching Exceptional Children, 42*(1), 34–44.

Mastropieri, M. A., & Scruggs, T. E. (2010). *The inclusive classroom: Strategies for effective instruction* (4th ed.). Upper Saddle River, NJ: Pearson.

Mather, N., & Goldstein, S. (2001). *Learning disabilities and challenging behaviors*. Baltimore: Brookes.

Matheson, C., Olsen, R. J., & Weisner, T. (2007). A good friend is hard to find: Friendship among adolescents with disabilities. *American Journal on Mental Retardation, 112*, 319–329.

Matuszny, R. M., Banda, D. R., & Coleman, T. J. (2007). A progressive plan for building collaborative relations with parents from diverse backgrounds. *Teaching Exceptional Children, 39*(4), 24–31.

Maurice, C. (2004, August). *Effective advocacy for children with autism*. Invited address at the Penn State National Autism Conference, State College, PA.

Maurice, C., & Taylor, B. A. (2005). Early intensive behavioral intervention for autism. In W. L. Heward, T. E. Heron, N. A. Neef, S. M. Peterson, D. M. Sainato, G. Cartledge, R. Gardner III, L. D. Peterson, S. B. Hersh, & J. C. Dardig (Eds.), *Focus on behavior analysis in education: Achievements, challenges, and opportunities* (pp. 31–52). Upper Saddle River, NJ: Merrill/Pearson.

Mayberry, R. I., del Giudice, A. A., & Lieberman, A. M. (2011). Reading achievement in relation to phonological coding and awareness in deaf readers: A meta-analysis. *Journal of Deaf Studies and Deaf Education, 16*, 164–188.

Mayer, C., & Akamatsu, C. T. (1999). Bilingual-bicultural models of literacy education for deaf students: Considering the claims. *Journal of Deaf Studies and Deaf Education, 4*, 1–8.

Mayo, L. W. (1962). A proposed program for national action to combat mental retardation. *Report of the President's Committee on Mental Retardation*. Washington, DC: U.S. Government Printing Office.

Mazzotti, V. L., Rowe, D. A., Kelley, K., Test, D. W., Fowler, C. H., Kohler, P., & Kortering, L. J. (2009). Linking transition assessment and postsecondary goals: Key elements in the secondary transition planning process. *Teaching Exceptional Children, 42*(2), 44–51.

McAdam, D. B., O'Cleirigh, C. M., & Cuvo, A. J. (1993). Self-monitoring and verbal feedback to reduce stereotypic body rocking in a congenitally blind adult. *RE:view, 24*, 163–172.

McCabe, H. (2007). Parent advocacy in the face of adversity: Autism and families in the People's Republic of China. *Focus on Autism and Other Developmental Disabilities, 22*, 39–50.

McClannahan, L. E., & Krantz, P. J. (2010). *Activity schedules for children with autism: Teaching independent behavior* (2nd ed.). Woodbine House.

McConnell, S. (2002). Interventions to facilitate social interactions for young children with autism: Review of available research and recommendations for education intervention and future research. *Journal of Autism and Developmental Disabilities, 32*, 351–372.

McDevitt, T. M., & Ormrod, J. E. (2010). *Child development and education* (4th ed.). Upper Saddle River, NJ: Pearson.

McDonough, C. S., Covington, T., Endo, S., Meinberg, D., Spencer, T. D., & Bicard, D. F. (2005). The Hawthorne Country Day School: A behavioral approach to schooling. In W. L. Heward, T. E. Heron, N. A. Neef, S. M. Peterson, D. M. Sainato, G. Cartledge, R. Gardner III, L. D. Peterson, S. B. Hersh, & J. C. Dardig (Eds.), *Focus on behavior analysis in education: Achievements, challenges, and opportunities* (pp. 188–210). Upper Saddle River, NJ: Merrill/Pearson.

McEachin, J. J., Smith, T., & Lovaas, I. O. (1993). Long-term outcome for children with autism who received early intensive behavioral treatment. *American Journal on Mental Retardation, 97*, 359–372.

McEvoy, A., & Welker, R. (2000). Antisocial behavior, academic failure, and school climate: A critical review. *Journal of Emotional and Behavioral Disorders, 8*, 130–140.

McGill, T., & Vogle, L. K. (2001). Driver's education for students with physical disabilities. *Exceptional Children, 67*, 455–466.

McGonigel, M. J., Woodruff, G., & Roszmann-Millican, M. (1994). The transdisciplinary team: A model for family-centered early intervention. In L. J. Johnson, R. J. Gallagher, M. J. LaMontagne, J. B. Jordan, J. J. Gallagher, P. L. Hutinger, & M. B. Karnes (Eds.). *Meeting early intervention challenges: Issues from birth to three* (pp. 95–131). Baltimore: Brookes.

McHale, S. M., & Gamble, W. W. (1989). Sibling relationships of children with disabled and nondisabled brothers and sisters. *Developmental Psychology, 25*(3), 421–429.

McHugh, M. (2003). *Special siblings: Growing up with someone with a disability.* Baltimore: Brookes.

McIntosh, K., & MacKay, L. D. (2008). Enhancing generalization of social skills: Making social skills curricula effective after the lesson. *Beyond Behavior, 18*(1), 18–25.

McIntosh, R., Vaughn, S., & Zaragoza, N. (1991). A review of social interventions for students with learning disabilities. *Journal of Learning Disabilities, 24,* 451–458.

McIntyre, L. L. (2008). Parent training for young children with developmental disabilities: Randomized controlled trial. *American Journal of Mental Retardation, 113,* 356–368.

McLamed, J. C., & Reiman, J. W. (2011). *Collaboration and conflict resolution in education.* The National Center on Dispute Resolution in Special Education Retrieved August 31, 2011, from http://www.directionservice.org/cadre/edu.cfm

McLaughlin, J. A., & Lewis, R. B. (2008). *Assessing students with special needs* (7th ed.). Upper Saddle River, NJ: Merrill/Pearson.

McLaughlin, M. J. (1995). *Consolidated special education funding and services: A local perspective.* Policy Paper No. 5. Palo Alto, CA: Center for Special Education Finance, American Institutes for Research.

McLaughlin, M. J. (2010). Evolving interpretations of educational equity and student with disabilities. *Exceptional Children, 76,* 265–278.

McLaughlin, M. J., Dyson, A., Nagle, K., Thurlow, M., Rouse, M., Hardman, M., Norwich, B., Burke, P. J., & Perlin, M. (2006). Cross-cultural perspectives on the classification of children with disabilities: Part II. Implementing classification systems in schools. *Journal of Special Education, 40,* 46–58.

McLeskey, J., Landers, E., Hoppey, D., & Williamson, P. (2011). Learning disabilities and the LRE mandate: An examination of national and state trends. *Learning Disabilities Research & Practice, 26,* 60–66.

McLeskey, J., Rosenberg, M., & Westling, D. (2010). *Inclusion: Effective practices for all students.* Upper Saddle River, NJ: Pearson.

McLeskey, J., & Waldron, N. L. (2011). Educational programs for elementary students with learning disabilities: Can they be both effective and inclusive? *Learning Disabilities Research & Practice, 26*(1), 46–57.

McLone, D. G., & Ito, J. (1998). *An introduction to spina bifida.* Chicago: Children's Memorial Hospital, Spina Bifida Team.

McMaster, K. L., Fuchs, D., & Fuchs, L. S. (2006). Peer-assisted learning strategies: The promise and limitations of peer-mediated instruction. *Reading and Writing Quarterly, 22,* 5–25.

McMaster, K. L., Kung, S.-H., Han, I., Cao, M. (2008). Peer-assisted learning strategies: A "Tier 1" approach to promoting English learners' response to intervention. *Exceptional Children, 74,* 194–214.

McNamara, J. K., & Willoughby, T. (2010). A longitudinal study of risk-taking behavior in adolescents with learning disabilities. *Learning Disabilities Research and Practice, 25,* 11–24.

McNaughton, D., & Vostal, B. R. (2010). Using active listening to improve collaboration with parents: The LAFF don't CRY strategy. *Intervention in School and Clinic, 45,* 251–256.

McNeilly, L. G. (2011). Genetics: Basis for development and disorders. In N. B. Anderson & G. H. Shames (Eds.), *Human communication disorders: An introduction* (8th ed., pp. 110–131). Upper Saddle River, NJ: Pearson.

Meadan, H., & Halle, J. W. (2004). Social perceptions of students with learning disabilities who differ in social status. *Learning Disabilities Research and Practice, 19,* 71–82.

Meadan, H., Halle, J. W., & Ebata, A. T. (2010). Families with children who have autism spectrum disorders: Stress and support. *Exceptional Children, 77,* 7–36.

Meadan, H., Ostrosky, M. M., Triplett, B., Michna, A. M., & Fettig, A. (2011). Using visual supports with young children with autism spectrum disorder. *Teaching Exceptional Children, 43*(6), 28–35.

Meadan, H., Sheldon, D. L., Appel, K., & DeGrazia, R. L. (2010). Developing a long-term vision: A road map for students' success. *Teaching Exceptional Children, 43*(2), 8–14.

Meadow-Orlans, K. P., Mertens, D. M., Sass-Lehrer, M. A., & Scott-Olson, K. (1997). Support services for parents and their children who are deaf or hard of hearing. *American Annals of the Deaf, 142,* 278–288.

Meadows, N. B., Neel, R. S., Scott, C. M., & Parker, G. (1994). Academic performance, social competence, and mainstream accommodations: A look at mainstreamed and nonmainstreamed students with serious behavioral disorders. *Behavioral Disorders, 19,* 170–180.

Mechling, L. C. (2007). Assistive technology as a self-management tool for prompting students with intellectual disabilities to initiate and complete daily tasks: A literature review. *Education and Training in Developmental Disabilities, 42,* 253–269.

Mechling, L. C. (2008). High-tech cooking: A review of evolving technologies for teaching a functional skill. *Education and Training in Developmental Disabilities, 43,* 474–485.

Mechling, L. C. (in press). Review of twenty-first-century portable electronic devices for persons with moderate intellectual disabilities and autism spectrum disorders. *Education and Training in Autism and Developmental Disabilities.*

Mechling, L. C., Gast, D. M., & Gustafson, M. R. (2009). Use of video modeling to teach extinguishing of cooking related fires to individuals with moderate intellectual disabilities. *Education and Training in Developmental Disabilities, 44*(1), 67–79.

Mechling, L. C., & O'Brien, E. (2010).Computer-based video instruction to teach students with intellectual disabilities to use public bus transportation. *Education and Training in Autism and Developmental Disabilities, 45,* 230–241.

Mechling, L. C., Pridgen, L. S., & Cronin, B. A. (2005). Computer-based video instruction to teach students with intellectual disabilities to verbally respond to questions and make purchases in fast food restaurants. *Education and Training in Developmental Disabilities, 40,* 47–59.

Mechling, L. C., & Stephens, E. (2009). Comparison of self-prompting of cooking skills via picture-based cookbooks and video prompts. *Education and Training in Developmental Disabilities, 44,* 218–236.

Meier, C. R., DiPerna, J. C., & Oster, M. M. (2006). Importance of social skills in the elementary grades. *Education & Treatment of Children, 29,* 409–419.

Mellard, D., McKnight, M., & Jordan, J. (2011). RTI tier structures and instructional intensity. *Learning Disabilities Research & Practice, 25,* 217–225.

Menard, C. (1999, September 2). Pica and the brain. Message posted to St. John's University Autism and Developmental Disabilities List, archived at http://maelstrom.stjohns.edu/archives/autism.html.

Mercer, C. D., Mercer, A. R., & Pullen, P. C. (2011). *Teaching students with learning problems* (8th ed.). Upper Saddle River, NJ: Pearson.

Mercer, C. D., & Pullen, P. C. (2009). *Students with learning disabilities* (7th ed.). Upper Saddle River, NJ: Pearson.

Merrill, E. C. (2005). Preattentive orienting in adolescents with mental retardation. *American Journal on Mental Retardation, 110,* 28–35.

Mervis, C. B., Klein-Tasman, B. P., & Mastin, M. E. (2001). Adaptive behavior of 4- through 8-year-old children with Williams syndrome. *American Journal of Mental Retardation, 106,* 82–93.

Metz, B., Mulick, J. A., & Butter, E. M. (2005). Autism: A late 20th century fad magnet. In J. W. Jacobson, R. M. Foxx, & J. A. Mulick (Eds.), *Controversial therapies for developmental disabilities: Fads, fashion, and science in professional practice* (pp. 237–263). Mahwah, NJ: Erlbaum.

Michael, M., Meese, R. L., Keith, S., & Mathews, R. (2009). Bob Bear: A strategy for improving behaviors of preschoolers identified as at risk or developmentally delayed. *Teaching Exceptional Children, 41*(5), 54–59.

Michaels, C. A., & Ferrara, D. L. (2005). Promoting post-school success for all: The role of collaboration in person-centered transition planning. *Journal of Educational and Psychological Consultation, 16,* 287–313.

Migliore, A., Grossi, T. A., Mank, D., & Rogan, P. (2008). Why do adults with intellectual disabilities work in sheltered workshops? *Journal of Vocational Rehabilitation, 28*(1), 29–40.

Miller, A. D., Barbetta, P. M., & Heron, T. E. (1994). START tutoring: Designing, training, implementing, adapting, and evaluating tutoring programs for school and home settings. In R. Gardner III, D. M. Sainato, J. O. Cooper, T. E. Heron, W. L. Heward, J. Eshleman, & T. A. Grossi (Eds.), *Behavior analysis in education: Focus on measurably superior instruction* (pp. 75–85). Pacific Grove, CA: Brooks/Cole.

Miller, A. D., Hall, S. W., & Heward, W. L. (1995). Effects of sequential 1-minute time trials with and without intertrial feedback and self-correction on general and special education students' fluency with math facts. *Journal of Behavioral Education, 5,* 319–345.

Miller, C. J., Sanchez, J., & Hynd, G. W. (2003). Neurological correlates of reading disabilities. In H. L. Swanson, K. R. Harris, & S. Graham (Eds.), *Handbook of learning disabilities* (pp. 242–255). New York: Guilford.

Miller, M. M., & Menacker, S. J. (2007). Vision: Our window to the world. In M. L. Batshaw, L. Pellegrino, & N. J. Roizen (Eds.), *Children with disabilities* (6th ed.). Baltimore: Brookes.

Mims, P. J., Browder, D. M., Baker, J. N., Lee, A., & Spooner, F. (2009). Increasing comprehension of students with significant intellectual disabilities and visual impairments during shared stories. *Education and Training in Developmental Disabilities, 44,* 409–420.

Ming, K., & Dukes, C. (2010). Gimme five: Creating a comprehensive reading lesson with all the essential elements. *Teaching Exceptional Children, 42*(3), 22–28.

Minor, L. B., Schessel, D. A., & Carey, J. P. (2004). Meniere's disease. *Current Opinion in Neurology, 17*(1), 9–16.

Minor, R. J. (2001). The experience of living with and using a dog guide. *RE:view, 32,* 183–190.

Misquitta, R. (2011). A review of the literature: Fraction instruction for struggling learning in mathematics. *Learning Disabilities Research & Practice, 26,* 109–119.

Mitchell, B. M. (1988). A strategy for the identification of the culturally different gifted/talented child. *Roeper Review, 10,* 163–164.

Mitchell, D. (Ed.). (2004a). *Contextualizing inclusive education: Evaluating old and new international paradigms.* London: Routledge Falmer.

Mitchell, D. (Ed.). (2004b). *Special educational needs and inclusive education: Major themes in education.* London: Routledge Falmer.

Mitchell, R. E., & Karchmer, M. A. (2004). Chasing the mythical ten percent: Parental hearing status of deaf and hard of hearing students in the United States. *Sign Language Studies, 4*(2), 138–163.

Mithaug, D. K. (2002). "Yes" means success: Teaching students with multiple disabilities to self-regulate during independent work. *Teaching Exceptional Children, 35*(1), 22–27.

Mittan, R. J. (2008). Managing stigma in school. *Exceptional Parent, 38*(9), 42–43.

Mittan, R. J. (2009). How to tell friends and dates about epilepsy. *Exceptional Parent, 39*(6/7), 94–96.

Mock, D. R., & Kauffman, J. M. (2005). *The delusion of full inclusion* In J. W. Jacobson, R. M. Foxx, & J. A. Mulick (Eds.), *Controversial therapies in developmental disabilities: Fads, fashion, and science in professional practice* (pp. 113–128). Hillsdale, NJ: Erlbaum.

Moeller, M.P., Hoover, B., Peterson, B., & Stelmachowicz, P. (2009). Consistency of hearing aid use in infants with early-identified hearing loss. *American Journal of Audiology, 18,*14–23.

Molloy, C. A., Manning-Courtney, P., Swayne, S., Bean, J., Brown, J. M., Murray, D. S., Kinsman, A. M., Brasington, M., & Ulrich II, C. D. (2002). Lack of benefit of intravenous synthetic human secretin in the treatment of autism. *Journal of Autism and Developmental Disorders, 32,* 545–551.

Monikowski, C., & Winston, E. A. (2011). Interpreters and interpreter education. In M. Marschark & P. E. Spencer (Eds.), *Oxford handbook of deaf studies, language, and education* (paperback ed., pp. 367–378). New York: Oxford University Press.

Montague, M., Enders, C., Cavendish, W., & Castro, M. (2011). Academic and behavioral trajectories for at-risk adolescents in urban schools. *Behavioral Disorders, 36,* 141–156.

Montgomery, D. (2001). Increasing Native American Indian enrollment in gifted programs in rural schools. *Psychology in the Schools, 38,* 467–475.

Montgomery, D. J. (2005). Communicating without harm: Strategies to enhance parent-teacher communication. *Teaching Exceptional Children, 37*(5), 50–55.

Moody, S. W., Vaughn, S., Hughes, M. T., & Fischer, M. (2000). Reading instruction in the resource room: Set up for failure. *Exceptional Children, 66,* 305–316.

Moon, S., Simonsen, M. L., & Neubert, D. A. (2011). Perceptions of supported employment providers: What students with developmental disabilities, families, and educators need to know for transition planning. *Education and Training in Autism and Developmental Disabilities, 46,* 94–105.

Mooney, P., Epstein, M. H., Reid, R., & Nelson, J. R. (2003). Status of and trends in academic intervention research for students with emotional disturbance. *Remedial and Special Education, 24,* 273–287.

Mooney, P., Ryan, J. B., Uhing, B. M., Reid, R., & Epstein, M. H. (2005). A review of self-management interventions targeting academic outcomes for students with emotional and behavioral disorders. *Journal of Behavioral Education, 14,* 203–221.

Moore, J. E. (2006). 100 years of trends and issues in employment, rehabilitation, and legislation. *Journal of Visual Impairment and Blindness, 100,* 453–458.

Moores, D. F. (1993). Total inclusion/zero rejection models in general education: Implication for deaf children. *American Annals of the Deaf, 138,* 251.

Morelock, M. J., & Feldman, D. H. (2003). Extreme precocity: Prodigies, savants, and children of extraordinarily high IQ. In N. Colangelo & G. A. Davis (Eds.), *Handbook of gifted education* (3rd ed., pp. 455–469). Needham Heights, MA: Allyn & Bacon.

Morgan, P. L., Young, C., & Fuchs, D. (2006). Peer-Assisted Learning Strategies: An effective intervention for young readers. *Insights on Learning Disabilities, 3*(1), 23–41.

Morocco, C. C., Brigham, N., & Aguilar, C. M. (2006). *Visionary middle schools: Signature practices and the power of local innovation.* New York: Teachers College Press.

Morris, R. J., Shah, K., & Morris, Y. P. (2002). Internalizing behavior disorders. In K. L. Lane, F. M. Gresham, & T. E. O'Shaughnessy (Eds.), *Children with or at risk for emotional and behavior disorders* (pp. 223–241). Boston: Allyn & Bacon.

Morris, T. L., & March, J. (Eds.). (2004). *Anxiety disorders in children and adolescents* (2nd ed.). New York: Guilford.

Morrison, G. S. (2012). *Early childhood education today* (12th ed.). Upper Saddle River, NJ: Pearson.

Morrison, G., & D'Incau, B. (2000). Developmental and service trajectories of students with disabilities recommended for expulsion from school. *Exceptional Children, 66,* 55–66.

Morrison, R. S., Sainato, D. M., BenChaaban, D., & Endo, S. (2002). Increasing play skills of children with autism using activity schedules and correspondence training. *Journal of Early Intervention, 25,* 58–72.

Morse, T. E., & Schuster, J. W. (2000). Teaching elementary students with moderate intellectual disabilities how to shop for groceries. *Exceptional Children, 66,* 273–288.

Morse, W. C. (1985). *The education and treatment of socioemotionally impaired children and youth.* Syracuse, NY: Syracuse University Press.

Most, T., & Greenbank, A. (2000). Auditory, visual, and auditory-visual perception of emotions by adolescents with and without learning disabilities, and their relationship to social skills. *Learning Disabilities Research and Practice, 15,* 171–178.

Mostert, M. P. (2001). Facilitated communication since 1995: A review of published studies. *Journal of Autism and Developmental Disorders, 31,* 287–313.

Mostert, M. P. (2010). Facilitated communication and its legitimacy: 21st century developments. *Exceptionality, 18,* 31–41

Mottram, L., & Berger-Gross, P. (2004). An intervention to reduce disruptive behaviours in children with brain injury. *Pediatric Rehabilitation, 7,* 133–143.

Moyson, T., & Roeyers, H. (2011). The quality of life of siblings of children with autism spectrum disorder. *Exceptional Children, 78,* 41–55.

Mueller, R. A., & Courchesne, E. (2000). Autism's home in the brain: Reply. *Neurology, 54*(1), 270.

Mueller, T. G. (2009). IEP facilitation: A promising approach to resolving conflicts between families and schools. *Teaching Exceptional Children, 41*(3), 60–67.

Multimodal Treatment Study Group. (1999). A 14-month randomized clinical trial of treatment strategies for attention-deficit/hyperactivity disorder. *Archives of General Psychiatry, 56,* 1088–1096.

Mulvey, E. P. (2011, March). Highlights from Pathways to Desistance: A longitudinal study of serious adolescent offenders. *OJJDP Juvenile Justice Fact Sheet.* Washington, DC: Office of Juvenile Justice and Delinquency Prevention. Retrieved July 28, 2011, from https://ncjrs.gov/pdffiles1/ojjdp/230971.pdf

Munk, D. D., Van Laarhoven, T., Goodman, S., & Repp, A. C. (1998). Small-group direct instruction for students with moderate to severe disabilities. In A. Hilton & R. Ringlaben (Eds.), *Best and promising practices in developmental disabilities* (pp. 127–138). Austin, TX: PRO-ED.

Munson, L. J., & Hunt, N. (2005). Teachers grieve! What can we do for our colleagues and ourselves when a student dies? *Teaching Exceptional Children, 37*(4), 48–51.

Murawaski, W. W., & Dieker, L. (2008). 50 ways to keep your co-teacher. Strategies for before, during, and after co-teaching. *Teaching Exceptional Children, 40*(4), 40–48.

Murdick, N. L., Gartin, B. C., & Crabtree, T. (2007). *Special education law* (2nd ed.). Upper Saddle River, NJ: Merrill/Pearson.

Murphy, C. M. (2003). *Using functional assessment to determine the maintaining contingencies of non-contextual speech by children with autism.* Unpublished master's thesis, The Ohio State University, Columbus.

Murphy, K. A., Theodore, L. A., Danielle Aloiso, D., Alric-Edwards, J. M., & Hughes, T. L. (2006). Interdependent group contingency and mystery motivators to reduce preschool disruptive behavior. *Psychology in the Schools, 44,* 53–63.

Murray, C., Goldstein, D. E., Nourse, S., & Edgar, E. (2000). The postsecondary school attendance and completion rates of high school graduates with learning disabilities. *Learning Disabilities Research and Practice, 15,* 119–127.

Musselman, C. (2000). How do children who can't hear learn to read an alphabetic script? A review of the literature on reading and deafness. *Journal of Deaf Studies and Deaf Education, 5,* 9–31.

Musti-Rao, S., & Haydon, R. (2011). Strategies to increase behavior-specific teacher praise in an inclusive environment. *Intervention in School and Clinic.* Published online July 29, 2011, doi:10.1177/1053451211414187

Musti-Rao, S., Kroeger, S. D., & Schumacher-Dyke, K. (2008). Using guided notes and response cards at the postsecondary level. *Teacher Education and Special Education, 31,* 149–163.

Myers, P. I., & Hammill, D. D. (1976). *Methods for learning disorders* (2nd ed.). New York: Wiley.

Myers, S. M., Plauché Johnson, C., & the Council on Children with Disabilities. (2007). Management of children with autism spectrum disorders. *American Academy of Pediatrics, 120,* 1162–1182.

Naglieri, J. A., & Ford, D. Y. (2003). Addressing under representation of minority children using the Naglieri Nonverbal Ability Test. *Gifted Child Quarterly, 47,* 155–160.

Naglieri, J. A., & Ford, D. Y. (2005). Increasing minority children's participation in gifted classes using the NNAT: A response to Lohman. *Gifted Child Quarterly, 49,* 29–31.

Narr, R. F., & Cawthon, S. W. (2011). The "wh" questions of visual phonics: What, who, where, when, and why. *Journal of Deaf Studies and Deaf Education, 16,* 66–78.

National Association for the Education of Young Children. (2011a). *The core of DAP.* Washington, DC: Author. Retrieved June 28, 2011, from http://www.naeyc.org/dap/core

National Association for the Education of Young Children. (2011b). *Developmentally appropriate practice (DAP).* Washington, DC: Author. Retrieved June 28, 2011, from http://www.naeyc.org/DAP

National Association for the Gifted. (2010). *State of the nation in gifted education (2008–2009).* Washington, DC: Author.

National Association for Gifted Children. (2004, September). *Acceleration* (NAGC Position Paper). Washington, DC: Author. Available: http://www.nagc.org/index.aspx?id=383

National Association for Gifted Children. (2009). *Grouping* (NAGC Position Paper). Washington, DC: Author. Available: http://www.nagc.org/index.aspx?id=4450

National Association for Gifted Children. (2010a). *Redefining giftedness for a new century: Shifting the paradigm* (NAGC Position Paper). Washington, DC: Author. Available: http://www.nagc.org/index2.aspx?id=375#definition

National Association for Gifted Children. (2010b). *State definitions of giftedness (as of 8-22-10).* Washington, DC: Author. Retrieved July 22, 2011, from http://www.nagc.org/uploadedFiles/Advocacy/State%20definitions%20(8-24-10).pdf

National Association for Gifted Children and Council of State Directors of Gifted Education. (2010). *2008–2009 State of the states.* (2010). Washington, DC: Author.

National Association of State Boards of Education. (1992). *Winners all: A call for inclusive schools.* Alexandria, VA: Author.

National Association of the Deaf. (2000). *Cochlear implants: NAD position statement* [Approved by NAD Board of Directors, October 6, 2000]. Washington, DC: Author. Available: http://www.nad.org/issues/technology/assistive-listening/cochlear-implants

National Association of the Deaf. (2002). *Position statement on inclusion.* [Approved by the NAD Board of Directors on January 26, 2002.] Silver Spring, MD: Author. Available: http://www.nad.org/issues/education/k-12/inclusion

National Autism Center. (2009a). *Evidence-based practice and autism in the schools.* Randolf, MA: Author.

National Autism Center. (2009b). *The National Autism Center's national standards project: Findings and conclusions.* Randolf, MA: Author.

National Center on Response to Intervention. (2010, March). *Essential components of RTI: A closer look at response to intervention.* Washington, DC: U.S. Department of Education, Office of Special Education Programs, National Center on Response to Intervention. Available: http://www.rti4success.org

National Center on Universal Design for Learning. (2011). *UDL principles and practice.* Wakefield, MA: Author. Retrieved July 18, 2011, from http://www.udlcenter.org/resource_library/videos/udlcenter/guidelines

National Clearinghouse for English Language Acquisition. (2011, February). *The growing numbers of English learner students, 1998/99–2008/09.* Washington, DC: U.S. Department of Education.

National Coalition for Parent Involvement in Education. (2011). *Putting partnerships into practice.* Washington, DC: Author. Retrieved September 1, 2011, from http://ncpie.org/Resources/

National Consortium on Deaf-Blindness. (2011). *2009 national deaf-blind child count maps.* Monmouth, OR: Author. Retrieved June 25, 2011, from http://www.nationaldb.org/censusMaps.php

National Dissemination Center for Children with Disabilities (NICHCY). (2004, January). *Spina bifida: Disability fact sheet #12.* Washington, DC: Author. Retrieved February 17, 2011, form http://www.nichcy.org/disabilities/specific/pages/spinabifida.aspx

National Dissemination Center for Children with Disabilities (NICHCY). (2009, September). *Attention-deficit/hyperactivity disorder (AD/HD), Disability fact sheet #19.* Washington, DC: Author. Retrieved February 8, 2011, from http://www.nichcy.org/InformationResources/Documents/NICHCY%20PUBS/fs19.pdf

National Dissemination Center for Children with Disabilities (NICHCY). (2010a, June). *Cerebral palsy, Disability fact sheet #2.* Washington, DC: Author. Retrieved February 8, 2011, from http://www.nichcy.org/Disabilities/Specific/Pages/CerebralPalsy.aspx

National Dissemination Center for Children with Disabilities (NICHCY). (2010b, June). *Epilepsy, Disability fact sheet #6.* Washington, DC: Author. Retrieved February 8, 2011, from http://www.nichcy.org/InformationResources/Documents/NICHCY%20PUBS/fs6.pdf

National Down Syndrome Society. (2011). *Down syndrome fact sheet.* New York: Author. Retrieved August 25, 2011, from http://www.ndss.org/index.php?option=com_content&view=article&id=54&Itemid

National Education Association. (1992). *The integration of students with special needs into regular classrooms: Policies and practices that work.* Washington, DC: Author.

National Education Association. (2010). *Status of the American public school teacher, 2005–2006.* Washington, DC: Author.

National Institute for Literacy (NIFL). (2007). *What content-area teachers should know about adolescent literacy.* Retrieved from http://www.nifl.gov/nifl/publications/adolescent_literacy07.pdf

National Institute of Child Health and Human Development. (2000). *Report of the National Reading Panel. Teaching children to read: An evidence-based assessment of the scientific research literature on reading and its implications for reading instruction: Reports of the subgroups* (NIH Publication No. 00-4754). Washington, DC: U.S. Government Printing Office.

National Institute of Health Consensus Statement. (1998). Diagnosis and treatment of attention deficit/hyperactivity disorder. *NIH Consensus Statement, 16*(2), 1–37.

National Institute of Mental Health (NIH). (2004). *Congressional appropriations report on the state of autism research.* Bethesda, MD: Author.

National Institute of Mental Health (NIH). (2007). Tiny, spontaneous gene mutations may boost autism risk. Bethesda, MD: Author. Retrieved March 17, 2007, from http://www.sciencedaily.com/releases/2007/03/070315161043.htm

National Institute on Deafness and Other Communication Disorders. (2011a). *Noise-induced hearing loss.* Retrieved June 12, 2011, from http://www.nidcd.nih.gov/health/hearing/noise.asp

National Institute on Deafness and Other Communication Disorders. (2011b). *Quick statistics.* Retrieved June 12, 2011, from http://www.nidcd.nih.gov/health/statistics/quick.htm

National Institute on Deafness and Other Communication Disorders. (2011c). *Stuttering.* Retrieved June 14, 2011, from http://www.nidcd.nih.gov/health/hearing/noise.asp

National Institute on Deafness and Other Communication Disorders. (2011d). *Your baby's hearing and communicative development checklist.* Retrieved June 12, 2011, from http://www.nidcd.nih.gov/health/hearing/silence.html

National Institutes of Neurological Disorders and Stroke. (2010, December). *Muscular dystrophy information page.* Bethesda, MD: Author. Retrieved February 8, 2011, from http://www.ninds.nih.gov/disorders/md/md.htm

National Joint Committee on Learning Disabilities. (1991). Learning disabilities: Issues on definition. *ASHA, 33* (Suppl. 5), 18–20. Available at http://www.ldonline.org/about/partners/njcld/archives

National Joint Committee on Learning Disabilities. (2011, March). *Learning disabilities: Implications for policy regarding research and practice.* Available: http://www.ldonline.org

National Longitudinal Transition Study 2. (2005). *Facts from NLTS2: High school completion by youth with disabilities.* Menlo Park, CA: SRI International.

National Parent Information and Resource Coordination Center. (2011). *About the PIRCS.* Washington, DC: Author. Retrieved September 1, 2011, from http://www.nationalpirc.org

National Parent Teacher Association. (2011). *Family–school partnerships.* Alexandria, VA: Author. Retrieved September 1, 2011, from http://www.pta.org/family_school_partnerships.asp

National Reading Panel. (2000a). *Report of the National Reading Panel. Teaching children to read: An evidence-based assessment of the scientific research literature on reading and its implications for reading instruction.* Washington, DC: U.S. Department of Health and Human Services.

National Reading Panel. (2000b). *Teaching children to read: An evidence-based assessment of the scientific research literature on reading and its implications for reading instruction—Reports of the subgroups.* Available: http://www.nichd.nih.gov/publications/nrp/smallbook.htm

National Research Council. (2001). *Educating children with autism.* Washington, DC: National Academy Press.

National Secondary Transition Technical Assistance Center (NSTTAC). (2011). *Transition assessment toolkit.* Washington, DC: U.S. Office of Special Education Programs. Retrieved July 7, 2011, from http://www.nsttac.org/products_and_resources/tag.aspx

National Spinal Cord Injury Statistical Center. (2010. February). *Spinal cord injury facts and figures at a glance.* Birmingham, AL: Author. Retrieved February 8, 2011, from https://www.nscisc.uab.edu/public_content/pdf/Facts%20and%20Figures%20at%20a%20Glance%202010.pdf

NCHAM. (2011). *The NCHAM eBook: A resource guide for early hearing detection and intervention (EHDI).* Utah State University: National Center for Hearing Assessment and Management.

Neef, N. A., Bicard, D. F., & Endo, S. (2001). Assessment of impulsivity and the development of self-control in students with attention-deficit hyperactivity disorder. *Journal of Applied Behavior Analysis, 34,* 397–407.

Neef, N. A., & Peterson, S. M. (2007). Functional behavior assessment. In J. O. Cooper, T. E. Heron, & W. L. Heward, *Applied behavior analysis* (2nd ed., pp. 500–524). Upper Saddle River, NJ: Merrill/Pearson.

Neely-Barnes, S., Graff, J. C., Marcenko, M., & Weber, L. (2008). Family decision making: Benefits to persons with developmental disabilities and their families. *Intellectual and Developmental Disabilities, 46,* 93–105.

Neely-Barnes, S., Marcenko, M., & Weber, L. (2008). Does choice influence quality of life for people with mild intellectual disabilities? *Intellectual and Developmental Disabilities, 46,* 12–26.

Nehring, W. M. (2010). Cerebral palsy. In P. Jackson Allen & J. A. Vessey (Eds.), *Primary care of the child with a chronic condition* (5th ed., pp. 326–346). Philadelphia: Elsevier.

Neihart, M. (in press). The identification and provision of services to twice exceptional children. In S. Pfeifer (Ed.). *Handbook of the gifted and talented: A psychological approach.* New York: Kluwer Academic/Plenum.

Neilsen, M. E., & Higgins, L. D. (2005). The eye of the storm: Services and programs for twice-exceptional learners. *Teaching Exceptional Children, 38*(1), 8–15.

Neisworth, J. T., & Bagnato, S. J. (2005). Recommended practices: Assessment. In S. Sandall, M. L. Hemmeter, B. J. Smith, & M. E. McLean (Eds.), *DEC recommended practices: A comprehensive guide for practical application in early intervention/early childhood special education* (pp. 45–69). Arlington, VA: Council for Exceptional Children, Division for Early Childhood.

Nelson, C. M. (2000). Educating students with emotional and behavioral disabilities in the 21st century: Looking through windows, opening doors. *Education and Treatment of Children, 23,* 204–222.

Nelson, L. G. L., Summers, J. A., & Turnbull, A. P. (2004). Boundaries in family-professional relationships: Implications for special education. *Remedial and Special Education, 25,* 153–165.

Nelson, J. A. P., Caldarella, P., Young, K. R., & Webb, N. (2008). Using peer praise notes to increase the social involvement of withdrawn adolescents. *Teaching Exceptional Children, 41*(2), 6–13.

Nelson, J. R., Benner, G. J., & Cheney, D. (2005). An investigation of the language skills of students with emotional disturbance served in public school settings. *Journal of Special Education, 39,* 97–105.

Nelson, J. R., Benner, G. J., Lane, K., & Smith, B. W. (2004). Academic achievement of K–12 students with emotional and behavioral disorders. *Exceptional Children, 71,* 59–73.

Nelson, J. R., Martella, R. M., & Marchand-Martella, N. (2002). Maximizing student learning: The effects of a comprehensive school-based program for preventing problems behaviors. *Journal of Emotional and Behavioral Disorders, 10,* 136–148.

Nelson, J. R., Stage, S., Duppong-Hurley, K. Synhorst, L., & Epstein, M. H. (2007). Risk factors predictive of the problem behavior of children at risk for emotional and behavioral disorders. *Exceptional Children, 73,* 367–379.

Neu, T. (2003). When the gifts are camouflaged by disability: Identifying and developing the talent in gifted students with disabilities. In J. A. Castellano (Ed.), *Special populations in gifted education: Working with diverse gifted learners* (pp. 151–162). Boston: Allyn & Bacon.

Neu, T., & Weinfeld, R. (2006). *Helping boys succeed in school.* Waco, TX: Prufrock.

Newborg, J. (2006). *Battelle developmental inventory (BDI-2)* (2nd ed.). Rolling Meadows, IL: Riverside.

Newman, L. (2004). *Family involvement in the educational development of youth with disabilities. A Special Topic Report from the National Longitudinal Transition Study-2 (NLTS-2).* Menlo Park, CA: SRI International.

Newman, L., Wagner, M., Cameto, R., & Knokey, A. M. (2009). *The post-high school outcomes of youth with disabilities up to 4 years after high school. A report of findings from the National Longitudinal Transition Study-2 (NLTS2)* (NCSER 2009-3017). Menlo Park, CA: SRI International. Available: www.nlts2.org/reports/2009_04/nlts2_report_2009_04_complete.pdf.

Newman, L., Wagner, M., Cameto, R., Knokey, A.M., & Shaver, D. (2010). *Comparisons across time of the outcomes of youth with disabilities up to 4 years after high school: A report of Findings from the National Longitudinal Transition Study-2 (NLTS2).* Menlo Park, CA: SRI International. Available: www.nlts2.org/reports/2010_09/nlts2_report_2010_09_complete.pdf.

Nihira, K., Leland, H., & Lambert, N. K. (1993). *Adaptive Behavior Scale—Residential and Community* (2nd ed.). Austin, TX: PRO-ED.

Nikopoulos, C. K., & Keenan, M. (2004). Effects of video modeling on social initiations by children with autism. *Journal of Applied Behavior Analysis, 37,* 93–96.

Nirje, B. (1969). The normalization principle and its human management implications. In R. Kugel & W. Wolfensberger (Eds.), *Changing patterns in residential services for the mentally retarded* (pp. 181–195). Washington, DC: President's Committee on Mental Retardation.

Noens, I. L. J., & van Berckelaer-Onnes, I. A. (2005). Captured by details: Sense-making, language and communication in autism. *Journal of Communication Disorders, 38,* 123–141.

Noonan, M. J., & McCormick, L. (2006). *Young children with disabilities in natural environments: Methods and procedures.* Baltimore: Brookes.

Northern, J. L., & Downs, M. P. (2002). *Hearing in children* (5th ed.). Baltimore: Lippincott, Williams & Wilkins.

Northup, J., Galley, V., Edwards, S., & Fountain, L. (2001). The effects of methylphenidate in the classroom: What dosage, for which children, for what problems? *School Psychology Quarterly, 16,* 303–323.

Notari-Syverson, A. R., & Shuster, S. L. (1995). Putting real-life skills into IEP/IFSPs for infants and young children. *Teaching Exceptional Children, 27*(2), 29–32.

Nugent, S. A. (2005). Affective education: Addressing the social and emotional needs of gifted students in the classroom. In F. A. Karnes & S. M. Bean (Eds.), *Methods and materials for teaching the gifted* (2nd ed., pp. 409–438). Waco, TX: Prufrock.

Nussbaum, D. (2011). *Cochlear implants: Navigating a forest of information . . . one tree at a time.* Washington DC: Laurent Clerc National Deaf Education Center. Retrieved June 13, 2011, from http://www.gallaudet.edu/Clerc_Center/Information_and_Resources/Cochlear_Implant_Education_Center.html

Obiakor, F. E. (2007). *Multicultural special education: Culturally response teaching.* Upper Saddle River, NJ: Merrill/Pearson.

O'Conner, R. E. (2000). Increasing the intensity of intervention in kindergarten and first grade. *Learning Disabilities Research and Practice, 15,* 44–54.

Odding, E., Roebroeck, M. E., & Stam, H. J. (2006). The epidemiology of cerebral palsy: Incidence, impairments and risk factors. *Disability Rehabilitation, 28,* 183–191.

Odom, S. L. (2000). Preschool inclusion: What we know and where we go from here. *Topics in Early Childhood Special Education, 20,* 20–27.

Odom, S. L., Brantlinger, E., Gersten, R., Horner, R. H., Thompson, B., & Harris, K. R. (2005). Research in special education: Scientific methods and evidence-based practices. *Exceptional Children, 71,* 137–148.

Odom, S. L., Collet-Klingenberg, L., Rogers, S. J., & Hatton, D. D. (2010). Evidence-based practices in interventions for children and youth with autism spectrum disorders. *Preventing School Failure, 54,* 275–282.

Odom, S. L., & Wolery, M. (2003). A unified theory of practice in early intervention/early childhood special education: Evidence-based practices. *Journal of Special Education, 37,* 164–173.

Office of Disability Employment Policy. (2011). *Customized employment: Principles and indicators.* Washington, DC: U.S. Department of Labor. Retrieved July 11, 2011, from http://www.dol.gov/odep/pubs/custom/indicators.htm

Office of Juvenile Justice and Delinquency Prevention. (December 2009). *Juvenile Justice Bulletin.* Washington, DC: U.S. Department of Justice. Available: https://www.ncjrs.gov/pdffiles1/ojjdp/228479.pdf

Office of Technology Assessment. (1987). *Technology-dependent children: Hospital v. home care—A technical memorandum*. OTA-TM-H-38. Washington, DC: Author.

Ohio Developmental Disabilities Council. (2009). *Handicapism: A report from the Center on Human Policy*. Columbus, OH: Author.

Ohtake, Y. (2004). Meaningful inclusion of *all* students in team sports. *Teaching Exceptional Children, 37*(2), 22–27.

Olivos, E. M. (2009). Collaboration with Latino families: A critical perspective of home-school interactions. *Intervention in School and Clinic, 45*, 109–115.

Olmstead, J. E. (Ed.). (2005). *Itinerant teaching: Tricks of the trade for teachers of students with visual impairments* (2nd ed.). New York: AFB Press.

Olsen, R., & Sutton, J. (1998). More hassle, more alone: Adolescents with diabetes and the role of formal and informal support. *Child: Care, Health, and Development, 24*(1), 31–39.

Olympia, D. W., Andrews, D., Valum, L., & Jenson, W. (1993). *Homework teams: Homework management strategies for the classroom*. Longmont, CO: Sopris West.

Olympia, D. W., Sheridan, S. M., Jenson, W. R., & Andrews, D. (1994). Using student-managed interventions to increase homework completion and accuracy. *Journal of Applied Behavior Analysis, 27*, 85–99.

O'Neill, R. E., Horner, R. H., Albin, R. W., Sprague, J. R., Storey, K., & Newton, J. S. (1997). *Functional assessment and program development for problem behavior: A practical handbook* (2nd ed.). Pacific Grove, CA: Brooks/Cole.

Onslow, M., Packman, A., & Harrison, E. (2003). *The Lidcombe Program of early stuttering intervention: A clinician's guide*. Austin, TX: PRO-ED.

O'Reilly, M. F., Lancioni, G. E., & Kierans, I. (2000). Teaching leisure social skills to adults with moderate mental retardation: An analysis of acquisition, generalization, and maintenance. *Education and Training in Mental Retardation and Developmental Disabilities, 35*, 250–258.

Orelove, F. P. (1984). The educability debate: A review and a look ahead. In W. L. Heward, T. E. Heron, D. S. Hill, & J. Trap-Porter (Eds.), *Focus on behavior analysis in education* (pp. 271–281). Upper Saddle River, NJ: Merrill/Pearson.

Orsillo, S. M., McCaffrey, R. J., & Fisher, J. M. (1993). Siblings of head-injured individuals: A population at risk. *Journal of Head Trauma Rehabilitation, 8*(1), 102–115.

Orsmond, G. I., & Seltzer, M. M. (2000). Brothers and sisters of adults with mental retardation: Gendered nature of the sibling relationship. *American Journal of Mental Retardation, 105*, 486–508.

Ortiz, A. (1997). Learning disabilities occurring concomitantly with linguistic differences. *Journal of Learning Disabilities, 30*, 321–333.

Osborne, L. A., & Reed, P. (2009). The relationship between parenting stress and behavior problems of children with autism spectrum disorders. *Exceptional Children, 76*, 54–73.

Osher, D., Cartledge, G., Oswald, D., Sutherland, K. S., Artiles, A. J., & Coutinho, M. (2004). Issues of cultural and linguistic competency in disproportionate representation. In R. B. Rutherford, M. M. Quinn, & S. R. Mathur (Eds.), *Handbook of research in emotional and behavioral disorders* (pp. 54–77). New York: Guilford.

Osterhaus, S. A. (2011). *Teaching math to visually impaired students*. Austin: Texas School for the Blind and Visually Impaired. Retrieved June 20, 2011, from http://www.tsbvi.edu/math/

Oswald, D. P. (1994). Facilitator influence in facilitated communication. *Journal of Behavioral Education, 4*, 191–200.

Overton, T. (2012). *Assessing learners with special needs: An applied approach* (7th ed.). Upper Saddle River, NJ: Pearson.

Owens, R. E., Jr. (2012). *Language development: An introduction* (8th ed.). Upper Saddle River, NJ: Pearson.

Owens, R. E., Jr., Metz, D. E., & Farinella, K. A. (Eds.). (2011). *Introduction to communication disorders: A lifespan evidence-based perspective* (4th ed.). Upper Saddle River, NJ: Pearson.

Ozcan, N., & Cavkaytar, A. (2009). Parents as teachers: Teaching parents how to teach toilet skills to their children with autism and mental retardation. *Education and Training in Autism and Developmental Disabilities, 44*, 237–243.

Ozonoff, S., Young, G. S., Carter, A., Messinger, D., Yirmiya, N., Zwaigenbaum, L., et al. (2011). Recurrence risk for autism spectrum disorders: A baby siblings research consortium study. *Pediatrics*. Originally published online August 15, 2011: doi: 10.1542/peds.2010-2825

Pacer Center. (2006). *Drop-out prevention: Parents play a key role*. Minneapolis, MN: Author. Available: http://www.pacer.org/parent/php/PHP-c114.pdf

Paclawsky, T. R., Matson, J. L., Rush, K. S., Smalls, Y., & Vollmer, T. R. (2000). Questions about behavioral function (QABF): A behavioral checklist for functional assessment of aberrant behavior. *Research in Developmental Disabilities, 21*, 223–229.

Page, E. B. (1972). Miracle in Milwaukee: Raising the IQ. *Educational Researcher, 15*, 8–16.

Palfrey, J. S. (1995). Amber, Katie, and Ryan: Lessons from children with complex medical conditions. *Journal of School Health, 65*, 265–267.

Palmer, D. S., Fuller, K., Arora, T., & Nelson, M. (2001). Taking sides: Parents' views on inclusion for their children with severe disabilities. *Exceptional Children, 67*, 467–484.

Pappay, C. K., & Bambara, L. M. (2011). Postsecondary education for transition-age students with intellectual and other developmental disabilities. *Education and Training in Autism and Developmental Disabilities, 46*, 78–93.

Parent, W., Gossage, D., Jones, M., Turner, P., Walker, C., & Feldman, R. (2008). Working with parents: Using strategies to promote planning and preparation, placement, and support. In F. R. Rusch (Ed.), *Beyond high school: Preparing adolescents for tomorrow's challenges* (2nd ed., pp. 110–133). Upper Saddle River, NJ: Merrill/Pearson.

Parette, H. P., & Brotherson, M. J. (1996). Family participation in assistive technology assessment for young children with mental retardation and developmental disabilities. *Education and Training in Mental Retardation and Developmental Disabilities, 31*, 29–43.

Parette, H. P., Brotherson, M. J., & Huer, M. B. (2000). Giving Families a Voice in Augmentative and Alternative Communication Decision-Making. *Education and Training in Mental Retardation and Developmental Disabilities, 35*(2), 77–90.

Parette, H. P., & Petch-Hogan, B. (2000). Approaching families: Facilitating culturally/linguistically diverse family involvement. *Teaching Exceptional Children, 33*(2), 4–10.

Parish, S. L., Rose, R. A., Grinstein-Weiss, M., Richman, E. L., & Andrews, M. E. (2008). Material hardship in U.S. families raising children with disabilities. *Exceptional Children, 75*, 71–92.

Park, J. H., Alber Morgan, S. R., & Cannella-Malone, H. I. (2011). Effects of mother-implemented Picture Exchange Communication System training on spontaneous communicative behaviors of young children with autism spectrum disorders. *Topics in Early Childhood Special Education, 31*(1), 37–47.

Park, J. H., Alber Morgan, S. R., & Fleming, C. (2011). Collaborating with parents to implement behavioral interventions for children with challenging behaviors. *Teaching Exceptional Children, 43*(3), 22–30.

Parson, L. R., & Heward, W. L. (1979). Training peers to tutor: Evaluation of a tutor training package for primary learning disabled students. *Journal of Applied Behavior Analysis, 12*, 309–312.

Partington, J. W. (2008). *The assessment of basics language and learning skills—Revised*. Pleasant Hill, CA: Behavior Analysts.

Patterson, G. R. (1982). *Coercive family process*. Eugene, OR: Castilia.

Patterson, G. R., Reid, J. B., & Dishion, T. J. (1992). *Antisocial boys. Vol. 4: A social interactional approach*. Eugene, OR: Castalia.

Patterson, K. B. (2005). Increasing positive outcomes for African American males in special education with the use of guided notes. *Journal of Negro Education, 74*, 311–320.

Patton, B., Jolivette, K., & Ramsey, M. (2006). Students with emotional and behavioral disorders *can* manage their own behavior. *Teaching Exceptional Children, 39*(2), 14–21.

Patton, J. R., Jayanthi, M., & Polloway, E. A. (2001). Home-school collaboration about homework: What do we know and what should we do? *Reading and Writing Quarterly: Overcoming Learning Difficulties, 17*, 227–242.

Paul, P. V., & Jackson, D. (1993). *Towards a psychology of deafness* (2nd ed.). San Diego: Singular.

Paul, P. V., & Whitlow, G. M. (2011). *Hearing and deafness: An introduction for health and education professionals*. Sudbury, MA: Jones Bartlett.

Payne, K. T. (2011). Multicultural differences in human communication disorders. In N. B. Anderson & G. H. Shames (Eds.), *Human communication disorders: An introduction* (8th ed., pp. 84–109). Upper Saddle River, NJ: Pearson.

Payne, L., Marks, L. J., & Bogan, B. L. (2007). Using curriculum-based assessment to address the academic and behavioral deficits of students with emotional and behavioral disorders. *Beyond Behavior, 16*, 3–6.

Pease, L. (2000). Creating a communication environment. In S. Aitken, M. Buultjenns, C. Clark, J. T. Eyre, & L. Pease (Eds.), *Teaching children who are deafblind: Contact communication and learning* (pp. 35–82). London: Fulton.

Pelham, W. (1999). The NIMH multimodal treatment study for attention-deficit hyperactivity disorder: Just say yes to drugs? *Canadian Journal of Psychiatry, 44,* 981–990.

Pelham, W., & Fabiano, G. A. (2008). Evidence-based psychosocial treatments for attention deficit/hyperactivity disorder. *Journal of Clinical Child Psychology, 37,* 184–214.

Pellegrino, L. (2007). Cerebral palsy. In M. L. Batshaw, L. Pellegrino, L, & Roizen, N. J. (Eds.), *Children with disabilities* (6th ed.). Baltimore: Brookes.

Pennington, B. F. (2002). *The development of psychopathology: Nature and nurture.* New York: Guilford.

Pennsylvania Association for Retarded Children (PARC) v. Commonwealth of Pennsylvania, 343 F. Supp. 279 (1972).

Pennsylvania Department of Education. (2011). *Resolution meetings: A guide for parents and educators.* Harrisburg, PA: Bureau of Special Education. Available: http://www.pattan.net/ category/Resources/PaTTAN%20Publications/ Browse/Single/?id=4dc09560cd69f9ac7f920000

Perla, F., & O'Donnell, B. (2004). Encouraging problem solving in orientation and mobility. *Journal of Visual Impairments and Blindness, 98,* 47–52.

Perrin, J. M., Bloom, S. R., & Gortmaker, S. L. (2007). The increase of childhood chronic conditions in the United States. *Journal of the American Medical Association, 297,* 2755–2759.

Perske, R. (2004). Nirje's eight planks. *Mental Retardation, 42,* 147–150.

Peterson, S. M., Neef, N. A., Van Norman, R., & Ferreri, S. J. (2005). Choice making in educational settings. In W. L. Heward, T. E. Heron, N. A. Neef, S. M. Peterson, D. M. Sainato, G. Cartledge, R. Gardner III, L. D. Peterson, S. B. Hersh, & J. C. Dardig (Eds.), *Focus on behavior analysis in education: Achievements, challenges, and opportunities* (pp. 125–136). Upper Saddle River, NJ: Merrill/Pearson.

Petry, K., & Maes, B. (2007). Description of the support needs of people with profound multiple disabilities using the 2002 AAMR System: An overview of the literature. *Education and Training in Developmental Disabilities, 42,* 130–143.

Petursdottir, A., McComas, J., McMaster, K., & Horner, K. (2007). The effects of scripted peer tutoring and programming common stimuli on social interactions of a student with autism spectrum disorder. *Journal of Applied Behavior Analysis, 40,* 353–357.

Pierce, C. D., Reid, R., & Epstein, M. H. (2004). Teacher mediated interventions for children with EBD and their academic outcomes. *Remedial and Special Education, 25,* 175–188.

Piirto, J. (2004a). The creative process in poets. In J. Kaufman & J. Baer (Eds.), *Creativity in domains: Faces of the muse* (pp. 1–15). Mahwah, NJ: Erlbaum.

Piirto, J. (2004b). *Understanding creativity.* Scottsdale, AZ: Great Potential.

Piirto, J. (2007). *Talented children and adults: Their development and education.* Waco, TX: Prufrock.

Pivik, J., McComas, J., & LaFlamme, M. (2002). Barriers and facilitators to inclusive education. *Exceptional Children, 67,* 97–102.

Plauché Johnson, C. P., Myers, S. M., & the Council on Children with Disabilities. (2007). Identification and evaluation of children with autism spectrum disorders. *American Academy of Pediatrics, 120,* 1183–1215.

Ploessl, D. M., Rock, M. L., Schoenfeld, N., & Blanks, B. (2010). On the same page: Practical techniques to enhance co-teaching interactions. *Intervention in School and Clinic, 45,* 158–168.

Plomin, R. (1995). Genetics and children's experiences in the family. *Journal of Child Psychology and Psychiatry, 36,* 33–68.

Plumer, P. J., & Stoner, G. (2005). The relative effects of classwide peer tutoring and peer coaching on the positive social behaviors of children with attention deficit hyperactivity disorder. *Journal of Attention Disorders, 9*(1), 1–11.

Pollack, W. (1998). *Real boys: Rescuing our sons from the myths of boyhood.* New York: Holt.

Polloway, E. A., Smith, J. D., Patton, J. R., & Smith, T. E. C. (1996). Historic changes in mental retardation and developmental disabilities. *Education and Training in Mental Retardation and Developmental Disabilities, 31,* 3–12.

Pomerantz, E. M., Moorman, E. A., & Litwack, S. D. (2007). The how, when, and why of parents' involvement in children's academic lives. More is not always better. *Review of Educational Research, 77,* 373–410.

Ponchillia, P. E., MacKenzie, N., Long, R. G., Denton-Smith, P., Hicks, T. L., & Miley, P. (2007). Finding a target with an accessible global positioning system. *Journal of Visual Impairment and Blindness, 101,* 479–488.

Pool, J. L., & Hourcade, J. J. (2011). Developmental screening: A review of contemporary practice. *Education and Training in autism and Developmental Disabilities, 46,* 267–275.

Popkin, J., & Skinner, C. H. (2003). Enhancing academic performance in a classroom serving students with serious emotional disturbance: Interdependent group contingencies with randomly selected components. *School Psychology Review, 32,* 271–284.

Portage Project. (2011). *About us.* Portage, WS: Author. Retrieved June 30, 2011, from http:// www.portageproject.org/ABOUTUS.HTM

Porterfield, K. (1998). British researchers identify genetic area affecting speech. *ASHA Leader, 3*(4), 1, 4.

Post, M., Storey, K., & Karabin, M. (2002). Cool headphones for effective prompts: Supporting students and adults in work and community environments. *Teaching Exceptional Children, 34,* 60–65.

Potts, E. A., & Howard, L. (2011). *How to co-teach: A guide for general and special educators.* Baltimore: Brookes.

Poulson, C. L., & Kymissis, E. (1988). Generalized imitation in infants. *Journal of Experimental Child Psychology, 46,* 324–336.

Powell, L., Houghton, S., & Douglas, J. (1997). Comparison of etiology-specific cognitive functioning profiles for individuals with fragile X and individuals with Down syndrome. *Journal of Special Education, 34,* 362–376.

Powers, S. (2003). Evaluation report for Project LISTO: Paradise Valley Unified School District, Arizona. Tucson, AZ: Creative Research Associates.

Poyadue, F. S. (1993). Cognitive coping at Parents Helping Parents. In A. P. Turnbull, J. M. Paterson, S. K. Behr, D. L. Murphy, J. G. Marquis, & M. J. Blue-Banning (Eds.), *Cognitive coping, families, and disability* (pp. 95–110). Baltimore: Brookes.

Prabhala, A. (2007, February 10). Mental retardation is no more—new name is intellectual and developmental disabilities. *AAIDD News.*

Prelock, P. A. (2000a). Epilogue: An intervention focus for inclusionary practice. *Language, Speech, and Hearing Services in Schools, 31,* 296–298.

Prelock, P. A. (2000b). Prologue: Multiple perspectives for determining the roles of speech-language pathologists in inclusionary classrooms. *Language, Speech, and Hearing Services in Schools, 31,* 213–218.

Prestia, K. (2003). Tourette's syndrome: Characteristics and interventions. *Intervention in School & Clinic, 39,* 67.

Pretti-Frontczak, K., Barr, D. M., Macy, M., & Carter, C. (2003). Research and resources related to activity-based intervention, embedded learning opportunities, and routines-based instruction. *Topics in Early Childhood Special Education, 23*(1), 29–39.

Pretti-Frontczak, K. L., & Bricker, D. (2000). Enhancing the quality of Individualized Education Plan (IEP) goals and objectives. *Journal of Early Intervention, 23,* 92–105.

Pretti-Frontczak, K., & Bricker, D. (2004). *An activity-based approach to early intervention* (3rd ed.). Baltimore: Brookes.

Price, L., Field, S., & Patton, J. R. (Guest Eds.). (2003). Adults with learning disabilities (Special Issue). *Remedial and Special Education, 24,* 322–382.

Prinz, P., & Strong, M. (1998). ASL proficiency and English literacy within a bilingual deaf education model of instruction. *Topics in Language Disorders, 18*(4), 47–60.

Professional Development in Autism Center. (2004). *Professional development in autism.* Seattle: University of Washington.

Pullen, P. C., & Lloyd, J. W. (2007). *Phonics instruction. Current Practice Alerts,* Issue 14. Reston, VA: Division for Learning Disabilities and Division for Research, Council for Exceptional Children. Retrieved September 12, 2011, from http://teachingld.org/alerts#the-alert-series

Purcell, M. L., Horn, E., & Palmer, S. (2007). A qualitative study of the initiation and continuation of preschool inclusion programs. *Exceptional Children, 74,* 85–99.

Qi, C. H., & Kaiser, A. P. (2003). Behavior problems of preschool children from low-income families: Review of the literature. *Teaching Early Childhood Special Education, 23,* 188–216.

Quinn, M. M., Rutherford, R. B., Leone, P. E., Osher, D. M., & Poirier, J. M. (2005). Youth with disabilities in juvenile corrections: A national survey. *Exceptional Children, 71,* 339–345.

Quintero, N., & McIntyre, L. L. (2010). Sibling adjustment and maternal well-being: An examination of families with and without a child with autism spectrum disorders. *Focus on Autism and Other Developmental Disabilities, 25,* 37–46.

Rafferty, L. A. (2010). Step-by-step: Teaching students to self-monitor. *Teaching Exceptional Children, 43*(2), 50–58.

Ramey, C. T., Bryant, D. M., Wasik, B. H., Sparling, J. J., Fendt, K. H., & LaVange, L. M. (1992). The Infant Health and Development Program for low birthweight, premature infants: Program elements, family participation, and child intelligence. *Pediatrics, 89,* 454–465.

Ramig, P. R., & Pollard, R. (2011). Stuttering and other disorders of fluency. In N. B. Anderson & G. H. Shames (Eds.), *Human communication disorders: An introduction* (8th ed., pp. 132–163). Upper Saddle River, NJ: Pearson.

Ramirez, A. Y. (2003). Dismay and disappointment: Parental involvement of Latino immigrant parents. *Urban Review, 35,* 93–110.

Rance-Roney, J. A. (2004). The affective dimension of second culture/second language acquisition in gifted adolescents. In D. Boothe & J. Stanley (Eds.), *In the eyes of the beholder: Critical issues for diversity in gifted education* (pp. 73–85). Waco, TX: Prufrock.

Randolph, J. J. (2007). Meta-analysis of the research on response cards: Effects on test achievement, quiz achievement, participation, and off-task behavior. *Journal of Positive Behavioral Interventions, 9,* 113–128.

Rao, S. S. (2000). Perspectives of an African American mother on parent-professional relationships in special education. *Mental Retardation, 38,* 475–488.

Raschke, D. B., Dedrick, C. V. L., Heston, M. L., & Farris, M. (1996). Everyone can play! Adapting the Candy Land board game. *Teaching Exceptional Children, 28*(4), 28–33.

Raskind, M. H., Margalit, M., & Higgins, E. L. (2006). "My LD": Children's voices on the Internet. *Learning Disability Quarterly, 29,* 253–268.

Raue, K., & Lewis, L. (2011). *Students with disabilities at degree-granting postsecondary institutions: First look.* Washington, DC: U.S. Department of Education Institute of Education Sciences. National Center for Education Statistics. Retrieved July 11, 2011, from http://nces.ed.gov/pubs2011/2011018.pdf

Raven, J. C., Court, J. H., & Raven, J. (1983). *Manual for Raven's Progressive Matrices and vocabulary scales: Advanced progressive matrices.* London: Lewis.

Rea, P. J., McLaughlin, V. L., & Walther-Thomas, C. (2002). Outcomes for students with learning disabilities in inclusive and pullout programs. *Exceptional Children, 68,* 203–222.

Reed, V. A. (2012). *An introduction to children with language disorders* (4th ed.). Upper Saddle River, NJ: Pearson.

Reeve, S. A., Reeve, K. F., Townsend, D. B., & Poulson, C. L. (2007). Establishing a generalized repertoire of helping behavior in children with autism. *Journal of Applied Behavior Analysis, 40,* 123–136.

Rehfeldt, R. A., Kinney, E. M., Root, S., & Stromer, R. (2004). Creating activity schedules using Microsoft® PowerPoint®. *Journal of Applied Behavior Analysis, 37,* 115–128.

Reid, R., Gonzalez, J. E., Nordness, P. D., Trout, A., & Epstein, M. H. (2004). A meta-analysis of the academic status of students with emotional/behavioral disturbance. *Journal of Special Education, 38,* 130–143.

Reid, R., & Maag, J. W. (1998). Functional assessment: A method for developing classroom-based accommodations and interventions. *Reading & Writing Quarterly, 14,* 7–15.

Reid, R., Maag, J. W., & Vasa, S. F. (1994). Attention deficit hyperactivity disorder as a disability category: A critique. *Exceptional Children, 60,* 198–214.

Reid, R., Trout, A. L., & Schartz, M. (2005). Self-regulation interventions for children with attention deficit/hyperactivity disorder. *Exceptional Children, 71,* 361–377.

Reinhart, S. (2000, April). Never say anything a kid can say! *Mathematics Teaching in the Middle School, 5,* 478–483.

Reis, S. (1995). What gifted education can offer the reform movement: Talent development. In J. L. Genshaft, M. Bireley, & C. L. Hollinger (Eds.), *Serving gifted and talented students: A resource for school personnel* (pp. 371–387). Austin, TX: PRO-ED.

Reis, S. M. (2004). *Twice-exceptional and special populations of gifted students.* Thousand Oaks, CA: Corwin.

Reiss, S. M., & Reiss, M. M. (2004). Curiosity and mental retardation: Beyond IQ. *Mental Retardation, 42,* 77–81.

Reis, S. M., & Renzulli, J. S. (2005). *Curriculum compacting: An easy start to differentiating for high-potential students.* Waco, TX: Prufrock.

Reis, S. M., Westberg, K. L., Kulikowich, J. M., & Purcell, J. H. (1998). Curriculum compacting and achievement test scores: What does the research say? *Gifted Child Quarterly, 42,* 123–129.

Renzulli, J. S. (1998). *Relationship between gifted programs and total school improvement using the schoolwide enrichment model.* Storrs: University of Connecticut, National Resource Center on the Gifted and Talented.

Renzulli, J. S. (2003). Conception of giftedness and its relationship to the development of social capital. In N. Colangelo & G. A. Davis (Eds.), *Handbook of gifted education* (3rd ed., pp. 75–87). Needham Heights, MA: Allyn & Bacon.

Renzulli, J. S. (2011). Kappan Classic: What makes giftedness? Reexamining a definition. *Phi Delta Kappan, 92*(8), 81–88.

Renzulli, J. S., & Reis, S. M. (2003). The schoolwide enrichment model: Developing creative and productive giftedness. In N. Colangelo & G. A. Davis (Eds.), *Handbook of gifted education* (3rd ed., pp. 184–203). Needham Heights, MA: Allyn & Bacon.

Renzulli, J. S., & Reis, S. M. (2004). *Identification of students for gifted and talented programs.* Thousand Oaks, CA: Corwin.

Reschly, D. J. (2005). Learning disabilities identification: Primary intervention, secondary intervention, and then what? *Journal of Learning Disabilities, 38,* 510–515.

Resetar, J. L., Noell, G. H., & Pellegrin, A. L. (2006). Teaching parents to use research supported systematic strategies to tutor their children in reading. *School Psychology Quarterly, 21,* 241–261.

Reynhout, G., & Carter, M. (2006). Social stories for children with disabilities. *Journal of Autism and Developmental Disorders, 36,* 445–469.

Reynolds, M. C., Zetlin, A. G., & Heistad, D. (1996). *A manual for 20/20 analysis.* Philadelphia: Temple University, Center for Research in Human Development and Education. (ERIC Document Reproduction Service No. ED 358 183)

Rhee, S. H., & Waldman, I. D. (2002). Genetic and environmental influences on antisocial behavior: A meta-analysis of twin and adoption studies. *Psychological Bulletin, 128,* 490–529.

Rhode, G., Jenson, W. R., & Morgan, D. P. (2003). *Tough kid new teacher kit.* Longmont, CO: Sopris West.

Rhode, G., Jenson, W. R., & Reavis, H. K. (1998). *The tough kid book: Practical classroom management strategies.* Longmont, CO: Sopris West.

Rhode, G., Morgan, D. P., & Young, K. R. (1983). Generalization and maintenance of treatment gains of behaviorally handicapped students from resource rooms to regular classrooms using self-evaluation procedures. *Journal of Applied Behavior Analysis, 16,* 171–188.

Rhodes, R. L., Ochoa, S. H., & Ortiz, S. O. (2005). *Assessing culturally and linguistically diverse students: A practical guide.* Arlington, VA: Council for Exceptional Children.

Ricci-Balich, J., & Behm, J. A. (1996). Pediatric rehabilitation nursing. In S. P. Hoeman (Ed.), *Rehabilitation nursing: Process and application* (pp. 660–682). St. Louis: Mosby.

Richards, T. L. (2001). Functional magnetic resonance imaging and spectroscopic imaging of the brain: Application of fMRI and fMRS to reading disabilities and education. *Learning Disability Quarterly, 24,* 189–203.

Richardson, B. G., & Shupe, M. J. (2003). The importance of teacher self-awareness in working with students with emotional and behavior disorders. *Teaching Exceptional Children, 36*(2), 8–13.

Rigby. (2004). *Rigby literacy teacher's guide, grade 1.* Barrington, IL: Author.

Rimland, B. (1993). Beware the advozealots: Mindless good intentions injure the handicapped. *Autism Research Review International, 7*(4), 1.

Rimland, B. (1994). The modern history of autism: A personal perspective. In J. L. Matson (Ed.), *Autism in children and adults: Etiology, assessment, and intervention.* Pacific Grove, CA: Brooks/Cole.

Rimland, B., & Fein, D. A. (1988). Special talents of autistic savants. In L. K. Obler & D. A. Fein (Eds.), *The exceptional brain: Neuropsychology of talent and special abilities.* New York: Guilford.

Rimm, S. (2000). *See Jane win.* New York: Crown.

Rimm, S. (2002). *How Jane won.* New York: Crown.

Rimm-Kaufman, S. E., & Kagan, J. (2005). Infant predictors of kindergarten behavior: The contribution of inhibited and uninhibited temperament types. *Behavioral Disorders, 30,* 331–347.

Risley, T. (2005). Montrose M. Wolf (1935–2004). *Journal of Applied Behavior Analysis, 38,* 279–287.

Ritvo, E. R. (2006). *Understanding the nature of autism and Asperger's disorder.* London: Jessica Kingsley.

Roberts, C. D., Stough, L. M., & Parrish, L. H. (2002). The role of genetic counseling in the elective termination of pregnancies involving fetuses with disabilities. *Journal of Special Education, 36,* 48–55.

Roberts, J. E., Schaaf, J. M., Skinner, M., Wheeler, A., Hooper, S., Hatton, D. D., & Bailey, D. B. (2005). Academic skills of boys with fragile X syndrome: Profiles and predictors. *American Journal on Mental Retardation, 110,* 107–120.

Roberts, R. E., Attkisson, C. C., & Rosenblatt, A. (1998). Prevalence of psychopathology among children and adolescents. *American Journal of Psychiatry, 155,* 715–725.

Robins, D., Fein, D., Barton, M., & Green, J. (2001). The modified checklist for autism in toddlers: An initial study investigating the early detection of autism and pervasive developmental disorders. *Journal of Autism and Developmental Disorders, 31,* 131–144.

Robinson, K. E., & Sheridan, S. M. (2000). Using the mystery motivator to improve child bedtime compliance. *Child & Family Behavior Therapy, 22,* 29–49.

Robinson Spohn, J. R., Timko, T. C., & Sainato, D. M. (1999). Increasing the social interactions of preschool children with disabilities during mealtimes: The effects of an interactive placemat game. *Education and Treatment of Children, 22*, 1–18.

Rockwell, S., & Guetzloe, E. (1996). Group development for students with emotional/behavioral disorders. *Teaching Exceptional Children, 29*(1), 38–43.

Rogan, P. (1996). Natural supports in the workplace: No need for a trial. *Journal of the Association for Persons with Severe Handicaps, 21*(4), 178–180.

Rogan, P., Grossi, T. A., Mank, D., Haynes, D. Thomas, E., & Majd, C. (2002). What happens when people leave the workshop? Outcomes of workshop participants now in SE. *Supported Employment Infolines, 13*(4), 1, 3.

Rogan, P., Hagner, D., & Murphy, S. (1993). Natural supports: Reconceptualizing job coach roles. *Journal of the Association for Persons with Severe Handicaps, 18*, 275–281.

Rogers, E. (2010). *Kasey to the rescue: The remarkable story of a monkey and a miracle.* New York: Hyperion.

Rogers, K. (2006). *A menu of options for grouping gifted students.* Waco, TX: Prufrock.

Rogers, M. F., & Myles, B. S. (2001). Using social stories and comic strip conversations to interpret social situations for an adolescent with Asperger's Syndrome. *Intervention in School and Clinic, 36*, 310–313.

Roid, G. H. (2003a). *Stanford-Binet Intelligence Scales* (5th ed.). Itasca, IL: Riverside.

Roid, G. (2003b). *The Stanford-Binet Intelligence Scales: Examiner's handbook* (5th ed.). Itasca, IL: Riverside.

Roscoe, E. M., Kindle, A. E., & Pence, S. E. (2010). Functional analysis and treatment of aggression maintained by preferred conversational topics. *Journal of Applied Behavior Analysis, 43*, 723–727.

Roseberry-McKibbin, C. (2007). *Language disorders in children: A multicultural and case perspective.* Boston: Allyn & Bacon.

Roseberry-McKibbin, C. (2008). *Multicultural students with special language needs: Practical strategies for assessment and intervention* (3rd ed.). Oceanside, CA: Academic Communication Associates.

Rosenblum, L. P. (2000). Perceptions of the impact of visual impairments on the lives of adolescents. *Journal of Visual Impairments and Blindness, 94*, 434–445.

Rosenshine, B. V. (1986). Synthesis of research on explicit teaching. *Educational Leadership, 43*(7), 60–69.

Rosenshine, B. V. (1987). Explicit teaching and teacher training. *Journal of Teacher Education, 38*(3), 34–36.

Rosenthal, B., & Williams, D. (2000). Devices primarily for people with low vision. In B. Silverstone, M. Lang, B. Rosenthal, & E. Faye (Eds.), *The lighthouse handbook on vision impairment and vision rehabilitation* (pp. 951–982). New York: Oxford University Press.

Ross, M., & Levitt, H. (2000). Developments in research and technology: Otoacoustic emissions. *Volta Voices, 7*, 30–31.

Rourke, B. (2005). Neuropsychology of learning disabilities: Past and future: *Learning Disability Quarterly, 28*, 111–114.

Rous, B. S., & Hallam, R. A. (2006). *Tools for transition in early childhood: A step-by-step guide for agencies, teachers, and families.* Baltimore: Brookes.

Rowland, C., & Schweigert, P. (2000). *Tangible symbol systems: Making the right to communicate a reality for individuals with severe disabilities.* Portland, OR: Design to Learn Products.

Rueda, R., Monzo, L., Shapiro, J., Gomez, J., & Blacher, J. (2005). Cultural models of transition: Latina mothers of young adults with developmental disabilities. *Exceptional Children, 71*, 401–414.

Rues, J. P., Graff, J. C., & Ault, M. M. (2011). Understanding special health care procedures. In M. E. Snell & F. Brown (Eds.), *Instruction of students with severe disabilities* (7th ed., pp. 304–339). Upper Saddle River, NJ: Pearson.

Rush, A. J., & Francis, A. (2000). Expert consensus guideline series: Treatment of psychiatric and behavioral problems in mental retardation. *American Journal of Mental Retardation, 105*, 159–228.

Russell-Minda, E., Jutai, J. W., Graham Strong, J., Campbell, K. A., Gold, D., Pretty, L., & Wilmot, L. (2007). The legibility of typefaces for readers with low vision: A research review. *Journal of Visual Impairment and Blindness, 101*, 402–415.

Rutherford, R. B., Quinn, M. M., & Sathur, R. (Eds.). (2004). *Handbook of research in emotional and behavioral disorders.* New York: Guilford.

Rutter, M. (1976). *Helping troubled children.* New York: Plenum.

Rutter, M. (2002). Address to the Second International Annual Meeting for Autism Research.

Rutter, M. (2006). *Genes and behavior: Nature-nurture interplay explained.* Malden, MA: Blackwell.

Rutter, M., Bailey, A., & Lord, C. (2003). *Social communication questionnaire.* Torrance, CA: Western Psychological Services.

Ryan, B. P. (2004). Contingency management and stuttering in children. *Behavior Analyst Today, 5*, 144–150.

Ryan, J. B., Saunders, S., Katsiyannis, A., & Yell, M. L. (2007). Using time-out effectively in the classroom. *Teaching Exceptional Children, 39*(4), 60–67.

Ryan, S., & Ferguson, D. L. (2006). On, yet under, the radar: Students with fetal alcohol syndrome disorder. *Exceptional Children, 72*, 363–379.

Ryan, S. M., Boxmeyer, C. L., & Lochman, J. E. (2009). Influence of risk factors for child disruptive behavior on parent attendance at a prevention intervention. *Behavioral Disorders, 35*, 41–55.

Ryndak, D. L., & Fisher, D. (Eds.). (2007). *The foundations of inclusive education: A compendium of articles on effective strategies to achieve inclusive education* (2nd ed.). Baltimore: Association for Persons with Severe Handicaps.

Ryser, G. (2004). Qualitative and quantitative approaches to assessment. In S. Johnsen (Ed.), *Identifying gifted students: A practical guide* (pp. 23–40). Waco, TX: Prufrock.

Sabornie, E. J., & Kauffman, J. M. (1986). Social acceptance of learning disabled adolescents. *Learning Disabilities Quarterly, 9*, 55–60.

Sack-Min, J. (2007). The issues of IDEA. *American School Board Journal, 194*(3), 20–25.

Sacks, S. Z., & Wolffe, K. E. (2006). *Teaching social skills to students with visual impairments: From theory to practice.* New York: AFB Press.

Sacks, S. Z., Wolffe, K. E., & Tierney, D. (1998). Lifestyles of students with visual impairments—adolescents. Preliminary studies of social networks. *Exceptional Children, 64*, 463–478.

Sadler, F. H. (2003). The itinerant special education teacher in the early childhood classroom. *Teaching Exceptional Children, 35*(3), 8–15.

Safer, D. J., Zito, J. M., & Fine, E. M. (1996). Increased methylphenidate usage for attention-deficit disorder in the 1990s. *Pediatrics, 98*, 1084–1088.

Salend, S. J. (2006). Explaining your inclusion program to families. *Teaching Exceptional Children, 38*(4), 6–11.

Salend, S. J. (2011). *Creating inclusive classrooms: Effective and reflective practices* (7th ed.). Upper Saddle River, NJ: Pearson.

Salend, S. J., Elhoweris, H., & van Garderen, D. (2003). Educational interventions for students with ADD. *Intervention in School and Clinic, 38*, 280–288.

Salend, S. J., & Garrick Duhaney, L. M. (2005). Understanding and addressing the disproportionate representation of students of color in special education. *Intervention in School and Clinic, 40*, 213–221.

Salisbury, R. (Ed.). (2008). *Teaching pupils with visual impairment: A guide to making the school curriculum accessible.* New York: Routledge.

Salmon, M. D., & Sainato, D. M. (2005). Beyond Pinocchio: Puppets as teaching tools in inclusive early childhood programs. *Young Exceptional Children, 8*(3), 12–19.

Salvia, J., Ysseldyke, J. E., & Bolt, S. (2007). *Assessment in special and inclusive education* (11th ed.). Belmont, CA: Wadsworth.

Salvia, J., Ysseldyke, J. E., & Bolt, S. (2013). *Assessment in special and inclusive education* (12th ed.). Belmont, CA: Wadsworth.

Sandall, S., Hemmeter, M. L., Smith, B. J., & McLean, M. E. (Eds.). (2005). *DEC recommended practices: A comprehensive guide for practical application in early intervention/early childhood special education.* Arlington, VA: Council for Exceptional Children, Division for Early Childhood.

Sandall, S., & Schwartz, I. (2008). *Building blocks for teaching preschoolers with special needs* (2nd ed.). Baltimore: Brookes.

Sandall, S., Schwartz, I., & Joseph, G. (2000). A building blocks model for effective instruction in inclusive early childhood settings. *Young Exceptional Children, 4*(3), 3–9.

Sandler, A. (2005). Placebo effects in developmental disabilities: Implications for research and practice. *Mental Retardation and Developmental Disabilities Research Reviews, 11*, 164–170.

Sandmel, K. N., Brindle, M., Harris, K. R., Lane, K. L., Graham, S., Nackel, J., Mathias, R., & Little, A. (2009). Making it work: Differentiating tier two self-regulated strategies development in writing in tandem with school wide positive behavioral support. *Teaching Exceptional Children, 42*(2), 22.33.

Santelli, B., Poyadue, F. S., & Young, J. L. (2001). *The parent to parent handbook: Connecting families of children with special needs.* Baltimore: Brookes.

Santelli, B., Turnbull, A., Marquis, J., & Lernet, E. (1997). Parent to parent programs: A resource for parents and professionals. *Journal of Early Intervention, 21*(1), 73–83.

Santsosti, F. J., & Powell-Smith, K. A. (2008). Using computer-presented social stories and video models to increase the social communication skills of with high-functioning autism spectrum

623

disorder. *Journal of Positive Behavior Interventions, 10,* 162–178.

Santsosti, F. J., Powell-Smith, K. A., & Kincaid, D. (2004). A research synthesis of social story interventions for children with autism spectrum disorders. *Focus on Autism and Other Developmental Disabilities, 19,* 194–204.

Sapienza, C., Hicks, D. M., & Ruddy, B. H. (2011). Voice disorders. In N. B. Anderson & G. H. Shames (Eds.), *Human communication disorders: An introduction* (8th ed., pp. 202–237). Upper Saddle River, NJ: Pearson.

Sapon-Shevin, M. (2007). *Widening the circle: The power of inclusive classrooms.* Boston: Beacon.

Sarouphim, K. M. (2001). DISCOVER: Concurrent validity, gender differences, and identification of minority students. *Gifted Child Quarterly, 45*(2), 130–139.

Sass-Lehrer, M. (2011). Early intervention for children birth to 3: Families, communities, and communication. In NCHAM, *The NCHAM eBook: A resource guide for early hearing detection and intervention* (pp. 9.1–9.16). Utah State University: National Center for Hearing Assessment and Management

Sauerburger, D., & Bourquin, E. (2010). Teaching the use of a long cane step by step: suggestions for progressive, methodical instruction. *Journal of Visual Impairment and Blindness, 104,* 203–214.

Sax, L., & Kautz, K. J. (2003). Who suggests the diagnosis of attention-deficit/hyperactivity disorder? *Annals of Family Medicine, 1,* 171–174.

Sayeski, K. L. (2009). Defining special educators' tools: The building blocks of effective collaboration. *Intervention in School and Clinic, 45,* 38–44.

Scattone, D., Wilczynski, S. M., Edwards, R. P., & Rabian, B. (2002). Decreasing disruptive behaviors of children with autism using social stories. *Journal of Autism and Developmental Disorders, 32,* 535–543.

Schafer, P. O., & DiLorio, C. (2006). Self-management in epilepsy care: Putting teen and families in the center. *Exceptional Parent, 36*(6), 46–48.

Schalock, R. L. (Ed.). (1999). *Adaptive behavior and its measurement.* Washington, DC: American Association on Intellectual and Developmental Disabilities.

Schalock, R. L., Gardner, J. F., & Bradley, V. J. (2007). *Quality of life: Applications for people with intellectual and developmental disabilities.* Washington, DC: American Association on Intellectual and Developmental Disabilities.

Schalock, R. L., & Keith, K. D. (1993). *Quality of Life Questionnaire.* Worthington, OH: IDS.

Schalock, R. L., Luckasson, R., & Shogren, K. A. (2007). The renaming of *mental retardation:* Understanding the change to the term *intellectual disability. Intellectual and Developmental Disabilities, 45,* 116–124.

Scheetz, N. A. (2004). *Psychosocial aspects of deafness.* Boston: Allyn & Bacon.

Scheetz, N. A. (2012). *Deaf education in the 21st century: Topics and trends.* Boston: Allyn & Bacon.

Scheuermann, B., & Webber, J. (2002). *Autism: Teaching does make a difference.* Belmont, CA: Wadsworth.

Schick, B., Williams, K., & Kupermintz, H. (2006). Look who's being left behind: Educational interpreters and access to education for deaf and hard-of-hearing students. *Journal of Deaf Studies and Deaf Education, 11,* 3–20.

Schirmer, B. R. (2001). *Psychological, social, and educational dimensions of deafness.* Boston: Allyn & Bacon.

Schirmer, B. R., & McGough, S. M. (2005). Teaching reading to children who are deaf: Do the conclusions of the National Reading Panel apply? *Review of Educational Research, 75,* 83–117.

Schnoes, C., Reid, R., Wagner, M., & Marder, C. (2006). ADHD among students receiving special education services: A national survey. *Exceptional Children, 72,* 483–496.

Schnorr, R. F., & Fenlon, A. (2008). *A literacy framework: Stages of literacy development.* Albany, NY: New York Higher Education Support Center for Systems Change. Retrieved June 23, 2011, from http://www.inclusion-ny.org/node/2078

Schonert-Reichl, K. A. (1993). Empathy and social relationships in adolescents with behavioral disorders. *Behavioral Disorders, 18,* 189–204.

Schopler, E., Van Bourgondien, M. E., Wellman, G. J., & Love, S. R. (2009). *The childhood autism rating scale CARS2)* (2nd ed.). Torrance, CA: Western Psychological Services.

Schorr, E. A., Roth, F. P., & Fox, N. A. (2008). A comparison of the speech and language skills of children with cochlear implants and children with typical hearing. *Communicative Disorders Quarterly, 29*(4), 195–210.

Schorr, E. A., Roth, F. P., & Fox, N. A. (2009). Quality of life for children with cochlear implants perceived benefits and problems and the perception of single words and emotional sounds. *Journal of Speech, Language and Hearing Research, 52,* 141–152.

Schow, R., & Nerbonne, M. (2007). *Introduction to audio logic rehabilitation* (5th ed.). New York: Pearson.

Schreibman, L. (2005). *The science and fiction of autism.* Cambridge, MA: Harvard University Press.

Schultz, T. R., Schmidt, C. T., & Stichter, J. P. (2011). A review of parent education programs for parents of children with autism spectrum disorders. *Focus on Autism and Other Developmental Disabilities, 26,* 96–104.

Schulz, J. B. (1985). The parent–professional conflict. In H. R. Turnbull & A. P. Turnbull (Eds.), *Parents speak out: Then and now* (pp. 3–11). Upper Saddle River, NJ: Merrill/Pearson.

Schum, R. L. (2002, September 24). Selective mutism: An integrated treatment approach. *The ASHA Leader Online.* Available: http://www.asha.org/about/publications/leader-online/archives/2002/q3/020924ftr.htm

Schumaker, J. B., & Deshler, D. D. (1992). Validation of learning strategy interventions for students with learning disabilities: Results of a programmatic research effort. In B. Y. L. Wong (Ed.), *Contemporary intervention research in learning disabilities* (pp. 22–46). New York: Springer.

Schumaker, J. B., & Deshler, D. D. (2006). Teaching adolescents to be strategic learners. In D. D. Deshler & J. B. Schumaker (Eds.), *Teaching adolescents with disabilities: Accessing the general education curriculum* (pp. 121–156). New York: Corwin.

Schumaker, J. B., & Deshler, D. D. (2009). Teaching adolescents with disabilities to write: Are we selling them short? *Learning Disabilities Research & Practice, 24,* 81–92.

Schumm, J. S., Moody, S. W., & Vaughn, S. (2000). Grouping for reading instruction: Does one size fit all? *Journal of Learning Disabilities, 33,* 477–488.

Schumm, J. S., Vaughn, D., Haager, D., McDowell, J., Rothlein, L., & Saumell, L. (1995). General education teacher planning: What can students with learning disabilities expect? *Exceptional Children, 61,* 335–352.

Schwartz, C. E., Snidman, N., & Kagan, J. (1999). Adolescent social anxiety and outcome of inhibited temperament in childhood. *Journal of the American Academy of Child and Adolescent Psychiatry, 38,* 1008–1015.

Schwartz, I. (2000). Standing on the shoulders of giants: Looking ahead to facilitating membership and relationships for children with disabilities. *Topics in Early Childhood Special Education, 20,* 123–128.

Schwartz, I. S., Staub, D., Peck, C. A., & Gallucci, C. (2006). Peer relationships. In M. E. Snell & F. Brown (Eds.), *Instruction of students with severe disabilities* (6th ed.). Upper Saddle River, NJ: Merrill/Pearson.

Schwartz, R. G., & Marton, K. (2011). Articulatory and phonological disorders. In N. B. Anderson & G. H. Shames (Eds.), *Human communication disorders: An introduction* (8th ed., pp. 132–163). Upper Saddle River, NJ: Pearson.

Schwartz, S. (Ed.). (2007). *Choices in deafness* (3rd ed.). Bethesda, MD: Woodbine.

Scorgie, K., & Sobsey, D. (2000). Transformational outcomes associated with parenting children who have disabilities. *Mental Retardation, 38,* 195–206.

Scullin, M. H. (2006). Large state-level fluctuations in mental retardation classifications related to introduction of renormed intelligence test. *American Journal on Mental Retardation, 111,* 322–335.

Semel, E., Wiig, E. H., & Secord, W. (2003). *Clinical evaluation of language fundamentals* (4th ed.). San Antonio, TX: Psychological Corporation.

Serna, L. A., Forness, S. R., & Nielson, M. E. (1998). Intervention versus affirmation: Proposed solutions to the problem of disproportionate minority representation in special education. *Journal of Special Education, 32,* 48–51.

Sexson, S. B., & Dingle, A. D. (2001). Medical disorders. In F. M. Kline, L. B. Silver, & S. C. Russell (Eds.), *The educator's guide to medical issues in the classroom* (pp. 29–48). Baltimore: Brookes.

Shapiro, E. S., DuPaul, G. J., & Bradley-King, K. L. (1998). Self-management as a strategy to improve the classroom behavior of adolescents with ADHD. *Journal of Learning Disabilities, 31,* 545–555.

Shapiro, E. S., Miller, D. N., Swaka, K., Gardill, M. C., & Handler, M. W. (1999). Facilitating the inclusion of students with EBD into general education classrooms. *Journal of Emotional and Behavioral Disorders, 7,* 83–93.

Shapiro, S., Zigmond, N., Wallace, T., & Marsten, D. (Eds.). (2011). *Models of response to intervention.* New York: Guilford.

Shaver, D., Newman, L., Huang, T., Yu, J., & Knokey, A. (2011). *Facts from NLTS2: The secondary school experiences and academic performance of students with hearing impairments.* Washington, DC: U.S. Department of Education.

Shaw, R., & Trief, E. (2009). *Everyday activities to promote visual efficiency: A handbook for working with young children with visual impairments.* New York: AFB Press.

Shaywitz, B. A., Shaywitz, S. E., Blachman, B. A., Pugh, K. R., Fulbright, R. K., Skudlarski, P., Menci, W. E., Constable, R. T., Holahan, J. M., Marchione, K. E., Fletcher, J. M., Lyon, G. R., & Gore, J. C. (2004). Development of left occipitotemporal systems for skilled reading in children after a phonologically-based intervention. *Biological Psychiatry, 55,* 926–933.

Sheffield, K., & Waller, R. J. (2010). A review of single-case studies utilizing self-monitoring interventions to reduce problem classroom behaviors. *Beyond Behavior, 19*(2), 7–13.

Sheppard-Jones, K., Thompson Prout, H., & Kleinert, H. (2005). Quality of life dimensions for adults with developmental disabilities: A comparative study. *Mental Retardation, 43,* 281–291.

Shogren, K., Palmer, S., Wehmeyer, M.L., Williams-Diehm, K., & Little, T. (2011 Effect of intervention with the *Self-Determined Learning Model of Instruction* on access and goal attainment. *Remedial and Special Education.* Published online before print June 16, 2011, doi:10.1177/0741932511410072

Shonkoff, J. P., & Meisels, S. J. (Eds.). (2000). *Handbook of early childhood intervention* (2nd ed.). New York: Cambridge University Press.

Sickmund, M. (2010, February). Juveniles in residential placement: 1997–2008. *OJJDP Fact Sheet.* Washington, DC: Office of Juvenile Justice and Delinquency Prevention, U.S. Department of Justice. Retrieved July 28, 2011, from https://www.ncjrs.gov/pdffiles1/ojjdp/229379.pdf

Sidman, M. (1989). *Coercion and its fallout.* Boston: Authors Group.

Siegle, D., & McCoach, D. B. (2005). Expanding learning through mentorships. In F. A. Karnes & S. M. Bean (Eds.), *Methods and materials for teaching the gifted* (2nd ed., pp. 473–518). Waco, TX: Prufrock.

Sigafoos, J., O'Reilly, M., Cannella, H., Edrisinha, C., de la Cruz, B., Upadhyaya, M., Lancioni, G. E., Hundley, A., Andrews, A., Garver, C., & Young, D. (2007). Evaluation of a video prompting and fading procedure for teaching dish washing skills to adults with developmental disabilities. *Journal of Behavioral Education, 16*(2), 93–109.

Sigafoos, J., O'Reilly, M., & de la Cruz, B. (2007). *How to use video modeling and video prompting.* Austin, TX: Pro-Ed.

Sileo, J. M. (2010). Co-teaching: Getting to know your partner. *Teaching Exceptional Children, 42*(5), 32–38.

Sileo, J. M., & van Garderen, D. (2010). Creating optimal opportunities to learn mathematics: Blending co-teaching structures with research-based practices. *Teaching Exceptional Children, 42*(3), 14–21.

Sileo, N. M. (2005). Design HIV/AIDS prevention education: What are the roles and responsibilities of classroom teachers? *Intervention in School and Clinic, 40,* 177–181.

Sileo, N. M., & Prater, M. A. (2012). *Working with families of children with special needs: Family and professional partnerships and roles.* Upper Saddle River, NJ: Pearson.

Silliman, E. R., & Diehl, S. F. (2002). Assessing children with language learning disabilities. In D. K. Berstein & E. Tiegerman-Farber (Eds.), *Language and communication disorders in children* (5th ed.). Needham Heights, MA: Allyn & Bacon.

Silverman, L. K. (1986). Parenting young gifted children. *Journal of Children in Contemporary Society, 18,* 73–87.

Silverman, L. K. (1995). Highly gifted children. In J. L. Genshaft, M. Bireley, & C. L. Hollinger (Eds.), *Serving gifted and talented students: A resource for school personnel* (pp. 124–160). Austin, TX: PRO-ED.

Simmons, D. C., Kame'enui, E. J., Coyne, M. D., Chard, D. J., & Hairrell, A. (2011). Effective strategies for teaching beginning reading. In M. D. Coyne, E. J. Kame'enui, & D. W. Carnine (Eds.), *Effective teaching strategies that accommodate diverse learners* (4th ed., pp. 51–84). Upper Saddle River, NJ: Pearson.

Simmons, T. J., & Flexer, R. W. (2008). Transition to employment. In R. W. Flexer, T. J. Simmons, P. Luft, & R. M. Baer (Eds.), *Transition planning for secondary students with disabilities* (3rd ed., pp. 230–257). Upper Saddle River, NJ: Merrill/Pearson.

Simos, P. G., Breier, J. I., Fletcher, J. M., Bergman, E., & Papanicolaou, A. C. (2000). Cerebral mechanisms involved in word reading in dyslexic children: A magnetic source imaging approach. *Cerebral Cortex, 10,* 809–816.

Simpson, C. G., Swicegood, P. R., & Gaus, M. D. (2006). Nutrition and fitness curriculum: Designing instructional interventions for children with developmental disabilities. *Teaching Exceptional Children, 38*(6), 50–53.

Simpson, R. L. (2004a). Finding effective intervention and personnel preparation practices for students with autism spectrum disorders. *Exceptional Children, 70,* 135–144.

Simpson, R. L. (2004b). Inclusion of students with behavior disorders in general education settings. *Behavioral Disorders, 30,* 19–31.

Simpson, R. L. (2005). Evidence-based practices and students with autism spectrum disorders. *Focus on Autism and Other Developmental Disabilities, 20,* 140–149.

Simpson, R. L., & Myles, B. S. (1995). Effectiveness of facilitated communication with children and youth with autism. *Journal of Special Education, 28,* 424–439.

Sims, D. G., & Gottermeier, L. (1995). Computer-assisted, interactive video methods for speech-reading instruction: A review. In K. Erik-Spens & G. Plant (Eds.), *Speech, communication and profound deafness* (pp. 220–241). London: Whurr.

Siperstein, G. N., Parker, R. C., Norins Bardon, J., & Widaman, K. F. (2007). A national study of youth attitudes toward the inclusion of students with intellectual disabilities. *Exceptional Children, 73,* 435–455.

Sitlington, P. L., Neubert, D. A., & Clark, G. M. (2010). *Comprehensive transition education and services for students with disabilities* (5th ed.). Upper Saddle River, NJ: Pearson.

Skau, L., & Cascella, P. W. (2006). Using assistive technology to foster speech and language skills at home and in preschool. *Teaching Exceptional Children, 38*(6), 12–17.

Skeels, H. M., & Dye, H. B. (1939). A study of the effects of differential stimulation on mentally retarded children. *Convention Proceedings, American Association on Mental Deficiency, 44,* 114–136.

Skiba, R. (2002). Special education and school discipline: A precarious balance. *Behavioral Disorders, 27,* 81–97.

Skiba, R. J., Poloni-Staudinger, L., Galine, S., Simmons, A. B., & Feggins-Azziz, R. (2006). Disparate access: The disproportionality of African American students with disabilities across environments. *Exceptional Children, 72,* 411–424.

Skiba, R. J., Simons, A. B., Ritter, S., Gibb, A. C., Rausch, M. K., Cuadrado, J., & Chung, C-G. (2008). Achieving equity in special education: History, status, and current challenges. *Exceptional Children, 74,* 264–288.

Skibo, H., Mims, P., & Spooner, F. (2011). Teaching number identification to students with severe disabilities using response cards. *Education and Training in Developmental Disabilities, 46,* 124–133.

Skinner, B. F. (1957). *Verbal behavior.* New York: Appleton-Century-Crofts.

Skinner, B. F. (1989). *Recent issues in the analysis of behavior.* Columbus, OH: Merrill.

Skinner, C. H., Williams, R. L., & Neddenriep, C. E. (2004). Using interdependent group-oriented reinforcement to enhance academic performance in general education classrooms. *School Psychology Review, 33,* 384–397.

Skinner, D., Bailey, D. D., Jr., Correa, V. I., & Rodriguez, P. (1999). Narrating self and disabilities: Latino mothers' construction of identities vis-à-vis their children with special needs. *Exceptional Children, 65,* 481–495.

Skinner, D., Correa, V., Skinner, M., & Bailey, D. (2001). Role of religion in the lives of Latino families of young children with developmental delays. *American Journal on Mental Retardation, 106,* 297–313.

Slavin, R. E. (1986). *Using student team learning* (3rd ed.). Baltimore: Johns Hopkins University, Center for Research on Elementary and Middle Schools.

Slavin, R. E. (1995). *Cooperative learning: Theory, research and practice* (2nd ed.). Boston: Allyn & Bacon.

Slike, S. B., Thornton, N. E., Hobbis, D. H., Kokoska, S. M., & Job, K. A. (1995). The development and analysis of interactive videodisc technology to teach speechreading. *American Annals of the Deaf, 140*(4), 346–351.

Small, L. H. (2012). *Fundamental of phonetics: A practical guide for students* (3rd ed.). Upper Saddle River, NJ: Pearson.

Smith, B. J., & Guralnick, M. J. (2007). Definition of early intervention. In R. S. New & M. Cochran (Eds.), *Early childhood education: An international encyclopedia* (pp. 329–332). Westport, CT: Greenwood Publishing Group.

Smith, B. W., & Sugai, G. (2000). A self-management functional assessment-based behavior support plan for a middle school student with EBD. *Journal of Positive Behavior Interventions, 2,* 208–217.

Smith, C. R., Marchand-Martella, N. E., & Martella, R. C. (2011). Assessing the effects of the *Rocket Math* program with a primary elementary school student at risk for school failure: A case study. *Education & Treatment of Children, 34,* 1–12.

Smith, J. D. (2000). The power of mental retardation: Reflections on the value of people with disabilities. *Mental Retardation, 38,* 70–72.

Smith, J. D. (2004). The historical contexts of special education: Framing our understanding of contemporary issues. In A. McCray Sorrells, H. J. Rieth, & P. T. Sindelar (Eds.), *Critical* issues in special education: *Access, diversity, and accountability* (pp. 1–15). Boston: Allyn & Bacon.

Smith, J. D., & Hilton, A. (1997). The preparation and training of the educational community for the inclusion of students with developmental disabilities: The MRDD position. *Education and Training of Mental Retardation and Developmental Disabilities, 32,* 3–10.

Smith, J. D., & Mitchell, A. L. (2001a). Disney's Tarzan, Edgar Rice Burroughs' eugenics, and visions of utopian perfection. *Mental Retardation, 39,* 221–225.

Smith, J. D., & Mitchell, A. L. (2001b). "Me? I'm not a drooler. I'm the assistant": Is it time to abandon mental retardation as a classification? *Mental Retardation, 39,* 144–146.

Smith, J. D., & Prior, M. (1995). Temperament and stress resilience in school-age children: A within-families study. *Journal of the American Academy of Children and Adolescent Psychiatry, 34,* 168–179.

Smith, P. D., Gast, D. L., Logan, K. R., & Jacobs, H. A. (2001). Customizing instruction to maximize functional outcomes for students with profound disabilities. *Exceptionality, 9,* 135–145.

Smith, S. W., & Brownell, M. T. (1995). Individualized education programs: From intent to acquiescence. *Focus on Exceptional Children, 28*(1), 1–12.

Smith, T., & Lovaas, O. I. (1998). Intensive and early behavioral intervention with autism: The UCLA young autism project. *Infants and Young Children, 10*(3), 67–78.

Smith, T., Eikeseth, S., Klevstrand, M., & Lovaas, O. I. (1997). Intensive behavioral treatment for preschoolers with severe mental retardation and pervasive developmental disorders. *American Journal on Mental Retardation, 102,* 238–249.

Smith, T., Groen, A. D., & Wynn, J. W. (2000). Randomized trial of intensive early intervention for children with pervasive developmental disorder. *American Journal on Mental Retardation, 105,* 269–285.

Smith, T. E. C. (2002). Section 504: What teachers need to know. *Intervention in School and Clinic, 37,* 259–266.

Smith, T. J., & Adams, G. (2006). The effect of comorbid AD/HD and learning disabilities on parent-reported behavioral and academic outcomes of children. *Learning Disability Quarterly, 29,* 101–112.

Smith Myles, B. S., Jones-Bock, S., & Simpson, R. L. (2000). *Asperger syndrome diagnostic scale.* Austin: PRO-ED.

Smith Myles, B. S., & Simpson, R. L. (2001). Effective practices for students with Asperger syndrome. *Focus on Exceptional Children, 34*(3), 1–14.

Smyth, P., & Keenan, M. (2002). Compound performance: The role of free and controlled operant components. *Journal of Precision Teaching and Celeration, 18*(2), 3–15.

Snell, M. E., & Brown, F. (Eds.). (2011). *Instruction of students with severe disabilities* (7th ed.). Upper Saddle River, NJ: Pearson.

Snell, M. E., & Janney, R. E. (2005). *Practices for inclusive schools: Collaborative teaming* (2nd ed.). Baltimore: Brookes.

Snider, V. E., Busch, T., & Arrowood, L. (2003). Teacher knowledge of stimulant medication and ADHD. *Remedial and Special Education, 24,* 46–56.

Snow, K. (2001). *Disability is natural.* Woodland Park, CO: Braveheart.

Social Security Administration. (2011). *Titles II and XVI: Basic disability evaluation guides.* Available: http://www.ssa.gov/OP_Home/rulings/di/01/SSR82-53-di-01.html

Solomon, B. (2007). When all you need is rest. *Exceptional Parent, 37*(4), 38–39.

Sonnenschein, S. (1981). Parents and professionals: An uneasy relationship. *Teaching Exceptional Children, 14,* 62–65.

Sontag, E., Sailor, W., & Smith, J. (1977). The severely/profoundly handicapped: Who are they? Where are we? *Journal of Special Education, 11*(1), 5–11.

Soukup, J. H., Wehmeyer, M. L., Bashinski, S. M., & Bovaird, J. A. (2007). Classroom variables and access to the general curriculum for students with disabilities. *Exceptional Children, 74,* 101–120.

Southall, C. M., & Gast, D. L. (2011). Self-management procedures: A comparison across the autism spectrum. *Education and Training in Autism and Developmental Disabilities, 46*(2), 155–177.

Southern, W. T., & Jones, E. (1991). *The academic acceleration of gifted children.* New York: Teachers College Press.

Sowell, E. R., Thompson, P. M., Welcome, S. E., Henkenius, A. L., Toga, A.W., & Peterson, B. S. (2003). Cortical abnormalities in children and adolescents with attention-deficit hyperactivity disorder. *The Lancet, 362,* 1699–1707.

Sparrow, S. S., Balla, D. A., & Cicchetti, D. V. (2005). *Vineland Adaptive Behavior Scales: Second edition (Vineland—II).* Upper Saddle River, NJ: Pearson Assessments.

Spencer, V. G. (2006). Peer tutoring and students with emotional or behavioral disorders: A review of the literature. *Behavioral Disorders, 31,* 204–222.

Speth, T., Saifer, S., & Forehand, G. (2008). *Parent involvement activities in school improvement plans in the Northwest Region.* Issues & Answers Report, REL 2008—No. 064. Washington, DC: U.S. Department of Education, Institute of Education Sciences, National Center for Education Evaluation and Regional Assistance, Regional Educational Laboratory Northwest. Retrieved from http://ies.ed.gov/ncee/edlabs

Spina Bifida Association. (2011). *Frequently asked questions about spina bifida.* Retrieved February 17, 2011, from http://www.spinabifidaassociation.org/site/c.liKWL7PLLrF/b.2642327/k.5899/FAQ_About_Spina_Bifida.htm

Spinelli, C. G. (2004). Dealing with cancer in the classroom: The teacher's role and responsibilities. *Teaching Exceptional Children, 36*(4), 14–21.

Spinelli, C. G. (2012). *Classroom assessment for students in special and general education* (3rd ed.). Upper Saddle River, NJ: Pearson.

Spirito, A., & Overholser, J. C. (Eds.). (2003). *Evaluating and treating adolescent suicide attempters: From research to practice.* New York: Academic Press.

Spooner, F., Knight, V., Browder, D. M., Jimenez, B., & DiBiase, W. (in press). Evaluating evidence-based practice in teaching science content to students with severe developmental disabilities. *Research and Practice in Severe Disabilities.*

Sprague, J., & Walker, H. (2000). Early identification and intervention for youth with antisocial and violent behavior. *Exceptional Children, 66,* 367–379.

Spriggs, A. D., Gast, D. L., & Ayres, K. M. (2007). Using picture activity schedules to increase on-schedule and on-task behaviors. *Education and Training in Developmental Disabilities, 42,* 209–223.

Spring, C., & Sandoval, J. (1976). Food additives and hyperkinesis: A critical evaluation of the evidence. *Journal of Learning Disabilities, 9,* 560–569.

Squires, J., & Bricker, D. (2009). *Ages and Stages Questionnaires (ASQ-3)* (3rd ed.). Baltimore: Brookes.

SRI International. (2005). *Declassification—students who leave special education: A special topic report from the special education elementary longitudinal study.* Menlo Park, CA: Author.

Stafford, A. M. (2005). Choice making: A strategy for students with severe disabilities. *Teaching Exceptional Children, 37*(6), 12–17.

Stahr, B., Cushing, D., Lane, K., & Fox, J. (2006). Efficacy of a function-based intervention in decreasing off-task behavior exhibited by a student with ADHD. *Journal of Positive Behavioral Interventions, 8,* 201–211.

Stainback, S., & Stainback, W. (Eds.). (1996). *Inclusion: A guide for educators* (2nd ed.). Baltimore: Brookes.

Stainback, S., Stainback, W., & Ayres, B. (1996). Schools as inclusive communities. In S. Stainback & W. Stainback (Eds.), *Controversial issues confronting special education: Divergent perspectives* (2nd ed., pp. 31–43). Boston: Allyn & Bacon.

Staub, D., Spaulding, M., Peck, C. A., Gallucci, C., & Schwartz, I. S. (1996). Using nondisabled peers to support the inclusion of students with disabilities at the junior high school level. *Journal of the Association for Persons with Severe Handicaps, 21,* 194–205.

Stecker, P. M. (2007). Tertiary intervention: Using progress monitoring with intensive services. *Teaching Exceptional Children, 39*(5), 50–57.

Stecker, P. M., & Fuchs, L. S. (2000). Effecting superior achievement using curriculum-based measurement: The importance of individual progress monitoring. *Learning Disabilities Research and Practice, 15,* 128–134.

Stephens, T. M., & Wolf, J. S. (1989). *Effective skills in parent/teacher conferencing* (2nd ed.). Columbus: Ohio State University, College of Education, School Study Council of Ohio.

Stephenson, J., & Carter, M. (2011). Use of multisensory environments in school for students with severe disabilities: Perceptions from schools. *Education and Training in Autism and Other Developmental Disabilities, 46,* 276–290.

Sterling, R., Barbetta, P. M., Heward, W. L., & Heron, T. E. (1997). A comparison of active student response and on-task instruction on the acquisition and maintenance of health facts by fourth grade special education students. *Journal of Behavioral Education, 7,* 151–165.

Sternberg, L. (Ed.). (1994). *Individuals with profound disabilities: Instructional and assistive strategies.* Austin, TX: PRO-ED.

Sternberg, R. J. (2003). Giftedness according to the theory of successful intelligence. In N. Colangelo & G. A. Davis (Eds.), *Handbook of gifted education* (3rd ed., pp. 88–99). Needham Heights, MA: Allyn & Bacon.

Sternberg, R. J. (2007). Who are the bright children? *Educational Researcher, 36*(3), 148–155.

Sternberg, R. J., & Grigorenko, E. (2000). *Teaching for successful intelligence.* Upper Saddle River, NJ: Pearson.

Stetter, M. E., & Hughes, M. T. (2010). Using story grammar to assist students with learning disabilities and reading difficulties improve their comprehension. *Education and Treatment of Children, 33*(1), 115–1351.

Stevens, R., & Rosenshine, B. (1981). Advances in research on teaching. *Exceptional Education Quarterly, 2,* 1–9.

Stiegler, L. N. (2005). Understanding pica behavior: A review for clinical and education professionals. *Focus on Autism and Other Developmental Disabilities, 20,* 27–38.

Stiegler, L. N., & Davis, R. (2010). Understanding sound sensitivity in individuals with autism spectrum disorder. *Focus on Autism and Other Developmental Disabilities, 25,* 65–75.

Stinson, M., Elliot, L., Kelly, R., & Liu, Y. (2009). Deaf and hard-of-hearing students' memory of lectures with speech-to-text and interpreting/note taking services. *Journal of Special Education, 43,* 52–64.

Stokoe, W. (1960). *The calculus of structure.* Washington, DC: Gallaudet University Press.

Stokoe, W., Armstrong, D. F., & Wilcox, S. (1995). *Gesture and the nature of language.* New York: Cambridge University Press.

Stoneman, Z., & Gavidia-Payne, S. (2006). Marital adjustment in families of young children with disabilities: Associations with daily hassles and problem-focused coping. *American Journal on Mental Retardation, 111,* 1–14.

Stoner, J. B., Jones Bock, S., Thompson, J. R., Angell, M. E., Heyl, B. S., & Crowley, E. P. (2005). Welcome to our world: Parent perceptions of interactions between parents of young children with ASD and education professionals. *Focus on Autism and Other Developmental Disabilities, 20,* 39–51.

Storey, K. (2007). Review of research on self-management interventions in supported employment settings for employees with disabilities. *Career Development for Exceptional Individuals, 30,* 24–34.

Stormont, M., & Reinke, W. (2009). The importance of precorrective statements and behavior-specific praise and strategies to increase their use. *Beyond Behavior, 18*(3), 26–32.

Strain, P. S., & Joseph, G. E. (2004). A not so good job with "Good job." *Journal of Positive Behavior Interventions, 6*(1), 55–59.

Strain, P. S., & Timm, M. A. (2001). Remediation and prevention of aggression: An evaluation of the Regional Intervention Program over a quarter century. *Behavioral Disorders, 26,* 297–313.

Strand, J., & Kreiner, J. (2005). Recreation and leisure in the community. In R. W. Flexer, T. J. Simmons, P. Luft, & R. M. Baer (Eds.), *Transition planning for secondary students with disabilities* (2nd ed., pp. 460–482). Upper Saddle River, NJ: Merrill/Pearson.

Strauss, A. C., Lehtinen, L. E., & Kephart, N. C. (1947). *Psychopathology and education of the brain-injured child.* New York: Grune & Stratton.

Stremel, K., Molden, V., Leister, C., Matthews, J., Wilson, R., Goodall, D. V., & Hoston, J. (1990). *Communication systems and routines: A decision making process.* Washington, DC: U.S. Office of Special Education.

Strickland, B. B., & Turnbull, A. P. (1993). *Developing and implementing Individualized*

Education Programs (3rd ed.). Upper Saddle River, NJ: Merrill/Pearson.

Stromer, R., Kimball, J., Kinney, E., & Taylor, B. (2006). Activity schedules, computer technology, and teaching children with autism spectrum disorders. *Focus on Autism and Other Developmental Disabilities, 21,* 14–24.

Strunk, J. A. (2010). Respite care for families of special needs children: A systematic review. *Journal of Developmental and Physical Disabilities, 22,* 615–630.

Stuart v. Nappi, 443 F. Supp. 1235 (D. Conn. 1978).

Stuart, M. E., Lieberman, L., & Hand, K. E. (2006). Beliefs about physical activity among children who are visually impaired and their parents. *Journal of Visual Impairment and Blindness, 100,* 223–234.

Stuart, S. K., Flis, L. D., & Rinaldi, C. (2006). Connecting with families: Parents speak up about preschool services for their children with autism spectrum disorders. *Teaching Exceptional Children, 39*(1), 46–51.

Stuttering Foundation of America. (2011). *Facts on stuttering.* Memphis, TN: Author. Retrieved April 20, 2011, from http://www.stutteringhelp.org/Default.aspx?tabid=17

Sugai, G., & Horner, R. H. (2005). Schoolwide positive behavior supports: Achieving and sustaining effective learning environments for all students. In W. L. Heward, T. E. Heron, N. A. Neef, S. M. Peterson, D. M. Sainato, G. Cartledge, R. Gardner III, L. D. Peterson, S. B. Hersh, & J. C. Dardig (Eds.), *Focus on behavior analysis in education: Achievements, challenges, and opportunities* (pp. 90–102). Upper Saddle River, NJ: Merrill/Pearson.

Sugai, G., Horner, R. H., Algozzine, R., Barrett, S., Lewis, T., Anderson, C., Bradley, R., Choi, J. H., Dunlap, G., Eber, L., George, H., Kincaid, D., McCart, A., Nelson, M., Newcomer, L., Putnam, R., Riffel, L., Rovins, M., Sailor, W., & Simonsen, B. (2010). *School-wide positive behavior support: Implementers' blueprint and self-assessment.* Eugene: University of Oregon.

Sullivan, A. L. (2011). Disproportionality in special education identification and placement of English language learners. *Exceptional Children, 77,* 317–334.

Sulzer-Azaroff, B., & Associates. (2008). *Applying behavior analysis across the autism spectrum: A field guide for practitioners.* Cornwall-on-Hudson, NY: Sloan.

Sundberg, M. L. (2007). Verbal behavior. In J. O. Cooper, T. E. Heron, & W. L. Heward, *Applied behavior analysis* (2nd ed., pp. 526–547). Upper Saddle River, NJ: Pearson.

Sundberg, M. L. (2008). *Verbal Behavior Milestones Assessment and Placement Program: The VB-MAPP.* Concord, CA: AVB Press.

Sundberg, M. L., & Partington, J. W. (1998). *Teaching language to children with autism or other developmental disabilities.* Concord, CA: AVB Press.

Sutherland, K. S., Alder, N., & Gunter, P. L. (2003). The effect of varying rates of opportunities to respond to academic requests on the classroom behavior of students with EBD. *Journal of Emotional and Behavioral Disorders, 11,* 239–248.

Sutherland, K. S., Wehby, J. H., & Copeland, S. R. (2000). Effects of varying rates of behavior specific praise on the on-task behavior of students with emotional and behavioral disorders. *Journal of Emotional and Behavioral Disorders, 8,* 2–8.

Swanson, E. A. (2008). Observing reading instruction for students with learning disabilities: A synthesis. *Learning Disability Quarterly, 31,* 115–133.

Swanson, H. L. (2000). Issues facing the field of learning disabilities. *Learning Disability Quarterly, 23,* 37–50.

Swanson, H. L., & Hoskyn, M. (2001). Instructing adolescents with learning disabilities: A component and composite analysis. *Learning Disabilities Research and Practice, 16,* 109–119.

Swanson, J., McBurnett, K., Christian, D., & Wigal, T. (1995). Stimulant medication and treatment of children with ADHD. In T. H. Ollendick & R. J. Prinz (Eds.), *Advances in clinical child psychology* (Vol. 17, pp. 265–322). New York: Plenum.

Swedeen, B. L., Carter, E. W., & Molfenter, N. (2010). Getting everyone involved: Identifying transition opportunities for youth with severe disabilities. *Teaching Exceptional Children, 43*(2), 38–49.

Sweeney, W. J., Ehrhardt, A. M., Gardner, R., Jones, L., Greenfield, R., & Fribley, S. (1999). Using guided notes with academically at-risk high school students during a remedial summer social studies class. *Psychology in the Schools, 36,* 305–318.

Symons, F. J., Butler, M. G., Sanders, M. D., Feurer, I. D., & Thompson, T. (1999). Self-injurious behavior in Prader-Willi syndrome: Behavioral forms and body location. *American Journal of Mental Retardation, 104,* 260–269.

Szabo, J. L. (2000). Maddie's story: Inclusion through physical and occupational therapy. *Teaching Exceptional Children, 33*(2), 26–32.

Szymanski, L., & King, B. H. (1999). Practice parameters for the assessment and treatment of children, adolescents, and adults with mental retardation and co-morbid mental disorders. *Journal of the American Academy of Children and Adolescent Psychiatry, 38*(12 Suppl.), 5S–31S.

Takeshita, B. (2011). *Lighting tips for people with low vision.* Los Angeles: Braille Institute. Retrieved June 20, 2011, from http://brailleinstitute.org/About_Sight_Loss/Medical_News/Lighting_Tips.aspx

Talbott, E., & Thiede, K. (1999). Pathways to antisocial behavior among adolescent girls. *Journal of Emotional and Behavioral Disorders, 7,* 31–39.

Tam, K. Y. B., & Heng, M. A. (2005). A case involving culturally and linguistically diverse parents in prereferral intervention. *Intervention in School and Clinic, 40,* 222–230.

Tam, K. Y. B., Heward, W. L., & Heng, M. A. (2006). Effects of vocabulary instruction, error correction, and fluency-building on oral reading rate and comprehension of English-language learners who are struggling readers. *Journal of Special Education, 40,* 79–93.

Tardáguila-Harth, J. M., & Correa, V. I. (2007). *Supporting the language development of migrant children with language delays using story books.* Poster presented at the 85th Annual Convention of the Council for Exceptional Children, Louisville, KY.

Targett, P. S., & Wehman, P. (2011a). Employment: Community-based choices. In P. Wehman, *Essentials of transition planning* (pp. 127–143). Baltimore: Brookes.

TASH. (2000, March). *TASH resolution on deinstitutionalization.* Washington, DC: Author.

Retrieved October 8, 2007, from www.tash.org/IRR/resolutions/res02deinstitut.htm

TASH. (2009). *TASH resolution on integrated employment*. Washington, DC: Author. Retrieved April 20, 2011, from http://tash.org/advocacy-issues/employment/

TASH. (2011). *Mission and vision*. Washington, DC: Author. Retrieved June 25, 2011, from http://tash.org/about/mission/

Tate, T. L., Thompson, R. H., & McKerchar, P. M. (2005). Training teachers in an infant classroom to use embedded teaching strategies. *Education and Treatment of Children, 28,* 206–221.

Taylor, B. A., & Hoch, H. (2008). Teaching children with autism to respond to and initiate bids for joint attention. *Journal of Applied Behavior Analysis, 41,* 377–391.

Taylor, S. J. (2005). Caught in the continuum: A critical analysis of the principle of the least restrictive environment. *Research and Practice for Persons with Severe Disabilities, 30,* 218–230.

Teglasi, H. (2006). Temperament. In G. G. Bear & K. M. Minke (Eds.), *Children's needs III: Development, prevention, and intervention* (pp. 391–403). Bethesda, MD: National Association of School Psychologists.

Terman, L. (Ed.). (1925). *Genetic studies of genius* (Vol. 1). Stanford, CA: Stanford University Press.

Terzi, L. (2005). Beyond the dilemma of difference: The capability approach to disability and special education needs. *Journal of Philosophy of Education, 39,* 443–459.

Test, D. W., Aspel, N., & Everson, J. M. (2006). *Transition methods for youth with disabilities.* Upper Saddle River, NJ: Merrill/Pearson.

Test, D. W., & Ellis, M. R. (2005). The effects of LAP fractions on addition and subtraction of fractions with students with mild disabilities. *Education and Treatment of Children, 28*(1), 11–24.

Test, D. W., Fowler, C. H., Brewer, W. M., & Wood, W. (2005). A content and methodological review of self-advocacy intervention studies. *Exceptional Children, 72,* 101–125.

Test, D. W., Mason, C., Hughes, C., Konrad, M., Neale, M., & Wood, W. M. (2004). Student involvement in Individualized Education Program meetings. *Exceptional Children, 70,* 391–412.

Test, D. W., & Mazzotti, V. L. (2011). Transitioning from school to employment. In M. E. Snell & F. Brown (Eds.), *Instruction of students with severe disabilities* (7th ed., pp. 569–611). Upper Saddle River, NJ: Pearson.

Test, D. W., Richter, S., Knight, V., & Spooner, F. (2011). A comprehensive review and meta-analysis of the social stories literature. *Focus on Autism and Other Developmental Disabilities, 26,* 49–62.

Test, D. W., Spooner, F. H., Keul, P. K., & Grossi, T. A. (1990). Teaching adolescents with severe disabilities to use the public telephone. *Behavior Modification, 14,* 157–171.

Thoma, C. A., & Wehman, P. (2010). *Getting the most out of IEPs: An educator's guide to the student-directed approach.* Baltimore: Brookes.

Thompson, B., Diamond, K. E., McWilliam, R., Snyder, P., & Snyder, S. W. (2005). Evaluating the quality of evidence from correlational research for evidence-based practice. *Exceptional Children, 71,* 181–194.

Thompson, J. R., Bryant, B., Campbell, E. M., Craig, E. M., Hughes, C., Rothholz, D. A., Schalock, R. L., Silverman, W., Tassé, M., & Wehmeyer, M. L. (2004). *Supports Intensity Scale: User's manual.* Washington, DC: American Association on Intellectual and Developmental Disabilities.

Thompson, S. J., Quenemoen, R. F., Thurlow, M. L., & Ysseldyke, J. E. (2001). *Alternate assessments for students with disabilities.* Thousand Oaks, CA: Corwin.

Thompson, T. (2009). *Freedom from meltdowns: Dr. Thompson's solutions for children with autism.* Baltimore: Brookes.

Thompson, T. (2011). *Individualized autism intervention for young children: Blending discrete trial and naturalistic strategies.* Baltimore: Brookes.

Thorndike, R. L., Hagen, E. P., & Sattler, J. M. (1986). *Technical manual, the Stanford-Binet Intelligence Scale: Fourth edition.* Chicago: Riverside.

Timothy W. v. Rochester, N. H., School District, 875 F.2d 954 (1st Cir. 1989), *cert. denied* 493 U.S. 983, 110 S.Ct. 519 (1989).

Tincani, M., Ernsbarger, S., Harrison, T. J., & Heward, W. L. (2005). Effects of two instructional paces on pre-K students' participation rate, accuracy, and off-task behavior in the Language for Learning program. *Journal of Direct Instruction, 5,* 97–109.

Todd, A. W., Horner, R. H., & Sugai, G. (1999). Self-monitoring and self-recruited praise: Effects on problem behavior, academic engagement, and work completion in a typical classroom. *Journal of Positive Behavior Interventions, 1,* 66–76.

Todd, N. W. (2011). *The etiologies of childhood hearing impairment* (5.4–5.11). In *The NCHAM eBook: A resource guide for early hearing detection and intervention (EHDI).* Logan: Utah State University, National Center for Hearing Assessment and Management.

Tomlinson, C. A. (2005). *How to differentiate instruction in mixed ability classrooms* (2nd ed.). Upper Saddle River, NJ: Pearson.

Tomlinson, C. A. (2011). *Fulfilling the promise of differentiation.* Available: http://www.caroltomlinson.com/

Tomlinson, C. A., Kaplan, S. N., Renzulli, J. S., Purcell, J. H., Leppien, J. H., Burns, D. E., Strickland, C. A., & Imbeau, M. B. (2009). *The parallel curriculum: A design to develop learner potential and challenge advanced learners* (2nd ed.). Thousand Oaks, CA: Corwin.

Tomporowski, P. D., & Hagler, L. D. (1992). Sustained attention in mentally retarded individuals. In N. W. Bray (Ed.), *International review of research on mental retardation* (Vol. 18, pp. 111–136). New York: Academic Press.

Torgesen, J. K. (2001). Individual differences in response to early intervention in reading: The lingering problem of treatment resisters. *Learning Disabilities Research & Practice, 15,* 55–644.

Torgesen, J. K., & Bryant, B. (2004). *Test of phonological awareness—Second edition: PLUS.* Austin, TX: PRO-ED.

Torgesen, J. K., & Wagner, R. K. (1998). Alternative diagnostic approaches for specific developmental reading disabilities. *Learning Disabilities Research and Practice, 13,* 220–232.

Torrance, E. P. (2006). *Torrance tests of creative thinking.* Bensonville, IL: Scholastic Testing Service.

Tourette Syndrome Association. (2011). *What is Tourette syndrome?* Bayside, NY: Author. Retrieved July 26, 2011, from http://www.tsa-usa.org/Medical/whatists_cov.html.

Townsend, B. L. (2000). The disproportionate discipline of African American learners: Reducing school suspensions and expulsions. *Exceptional Children, 66,* 381–391.

Trach, J. S. (2008). Natural supports in the workplace and beyond. In F. R. Rusch (Ed.). *Beyond high school: Preparing adolescents for tomorrow's challenges* (2nd ed., pp. 250–265). Upper Saddle River, NJ: Merrill/Pearson.

Trammel, D. L., Schloss, P. J., & Alper, S. (1994). Using self-recording, evaluation, and graphing to increase completion of homework assignments. *Journal of Learning Disabilities, 27,* 75–81.

Trask-Tyler, S. A., Grossi, T. A., & Heward, W. L. (1994). Teaching young adults with developmental disabilities and visual impairments to use tape-recorded recipes: Acquisition, generalization, and maintenance of cooking skills. *Journal of Behavioral Education, 4,* 283–311.

Traubman, M., Brierley, S., Wishner, J. Baker, D., McEachin, J., & Leaf, R. B. (2001). The effectiveness of a group discrete trial instructional approach for preschoolers with developmental disabilities. *Research in Developmental Disabilities, 22,* 205–219.

Traxler, C. (2000). Measuring up to performance standards in reading and mathematics: achievement of selected deaf and hard-of-hearing students in the national norming of the 9th Edition Stanford Achievement Test. *Journal of Deaf Studies and Deaf Education, 5,* 337–348.

Treffert, D. A. (2011a). *Kim Peek: The real Rain Man.* Wisconsin Medical Society. Retrieved August 16, 2011, from http://www.wisconsinmedicalsociety.org/savant_syndrome/savant_profiles/kim_peek

Treffert, D. A. (2011b). *Savant syndrome: An extraordinary condition—A synopsis: Past, present, future.* Wisconsin Medical Society. Retrieved August 16, 2011, from http://www.wisconsinmedicalsociety.org/savant_syndrome/overview_of_savant_syndrome/synopsis

Trent, J. W. (1994). *Inventing the feeble-minded: A history of mental retardation in the United States.* Berkeley: University of California Press.

Trezek, B. J., & Malmgren, K. (2005). The efficacy of utilizing a phonics treatment package with middle school deaf and hard of hearing students. *Journal of Deaf Studies and Deaf Education, 10,* 256–271.

Trezek, B. J., & Wang, Y. (2006). Implications of using a phonics-based reading curriculum with children who are deaf or hard of hearing. *Journal of Deaf Studies and Deaf Education, 11,* 202–213.

Trezek, B. J., Wang, Y., Luckner, J. L., & Paul, P. V. (2008). The role of phonology and phonologically related skills in reading instruction for students who are deaf or hard of hearing. *American Annals of the Deaf, 153*(4), 396–407.

Trezek, B. J., Wang, Y., Wood, D. G., Gampp, T. L., & Paul, P. V. (1997). Using Visual Phonics to supplement beginning reading instruction for students who are deaf or hard of hearing. *Journal of Deaf Studies and Deaf Education, 12,* 373–384.

Trivette, C. M., Dunst, C. J., & Hamby, D. W. (2010). Influences of family-systems interventions practices on parent–child interactions and child development. *Topics in Early Childhood Special Education, 30*(1), 3–19.

Troia, G. A. (2007). Writing instruction for students with learning disabilities. In C. A. MacArthur, S. Graham, & J. Fitzgerald (Eds.), *Handbook of writing research* (pp. 324–336). New York: Guilford.

Trout, A., Nordness, P. D., Pierce, C. D., & Epstein, M. H. (2003). Research on the academic status of children and youth with emotional and behavioral disorders: A review of the literature from 1961–2000. *Journal of Emotional and Behavioral Disorders, 11,* 198–210.

Tryon, P. A., Mayes, S. D., Rhodes, R. L., & Waldo, M. (2006). Can Asperger's disorder be differentiated from autism using DSM-IV criteria? *Focus on Autism and Other Developmental Disabilities, 21,* 2–6.

Turnbull, A., Turnbull, H., Erwin, E., Soodak, L., & Shogren, K. A. (2011). *Families, professionals, and exceptionality: Positive outcomes through partnerships and trust* (6th ed.). Upper Saddle River, NJ: Pearson.

Turnbull, A., Zuna, N., Hong, J. Y., Hu, X., Kyzar, K., Obremski, S., Summers, J. A., Turnbull, R., & Stowe, M. (2010). Knowledge-to-action guides: Preparing families to be partners in making educational decisions. *Teaching Exceptional Children, 42*(3), 42–53.

Turnbull, A. P., & Ruef, M. (1996). Family perspectives on problem behavior. *Mental Retardation, 34,* 280–293.

Turnbull, H. R., Huerta, N. E., & Stowe, M. J. (2009). *What every teacher should know about the Individuals with Disabilities Act as amended in 2004* (2nd ed.). Upper Saddle River, NJ: Pearson.

Turnbull, H. R., Stowe, M. J., & Huerta, N. E. (2007). *Free appropriate public education: The law and children with disabilities* (7th ed.). Denver: Love.

Turnbull, H. R., Turnbull, A., Warren, S., Eidelman, S., & Marchand, P. (2002). Shakespeare redux, or *Romeo and Juliet* revisited: Embedding a terminology and name change in a new agenda for the field of mental retardation. *Mental Retardation, 40,* 65–70.

Turnbull, H., Turnbull, P., Wehmeyer, M., & Park, J. (2003). A quality of life framework for special education outcomes. *Remedial and Special Education, 24,* 67–74.

Turner-Henson, A., Holaday, B., Corser, N., Ogletree, G., & Swan, J. H. (1994). The experiences of discrimination: Challenges for chronically ill children. *Pediatric Nursing, 20,* 571–577.

Turton, A. M. Umbreit, J., & Mathur, S. R. (2011). Systematic function-based intervention for adolescents with emotional and behavioral disorders in an alternative settings: Broadening the context. *Behavioral Disorders, 36,* 117–128.

Tyler, J. S., & Mira, M. P. (1999). *Traumatic brain injury in children and adolescents: A sourcebook for teachers and other school personnel* (2nd ed.). Austin, TX: PRO-ED.

U.S. Department of Education. (2000). *Twenty-second annual report to Congress on the implementation of the Individuals with Disabilities Education Act.* Washington, DC: Author.

U.S. Department of Education. (2006). *26th annual report to Congress on the implementation of the Individuals with Disabilities Education Act, 2004.* Washington, DC: Author.

U.S. Department of Education. (2009). *Individuals with Disabilities Education Act (IDEA) Data* (Table 2-2). Washington, DC: Author. Available: http://www.ideadata.org/arc_toc10 .asp#partbLRE

U.S. Department of Education. (2010a, March). *A blueprint for reform: The reauthorization of the Elementary and Secondary Education Act.* Washington, DC: Author.

U.S. Department of Education. (2010b). *Individuals with Disabilities Education Act (IDEA) data* (Table 2-2i). Washington, DC: Author. Available: http://www.ideadata.org/arc_toc10.asp# partbLRE

U.S. Department of Education. (2010c). *Twenty-ninth annual report to Congress on the implementation of the Individuals with Disabilities Education Act* (Table 1-13). Washington, DC: Author.

U.S. Department of Education. (2011). *Individuals with Disabilities Education Act (IDEA) data* (Table 1-3). Washington, DC: Author. Retrieved May 18, 2011, from https://www.ideadata.org/ arc_toc11.asp#partbCC

U.S. Department of Health and Human Services. (2011). *Newborn screening: Toward a uniform screening panel and system.* Washington, DC: Health Resources and Services Administration. Retrieved June 30, 2011, from http://mchb .hrsa.gov/programs/newbornscreening/ screeningreport.html

U.S. Drug Enforcement Agency. (2002). *Yearly aggregate production quotas (1990–1999).* Washington, DC: Office of Public Affairs, U.S. Drug Enforcement Agency.

U.S. Office of Education. (1977). Procedures for evaluating specific learning disabilities. *Federal Register, 42,* 65082–65085.

Udvari-Solner, A., Causton-Theoharis, J., & York–Barr, J. (2004). Developing adaptations to promote participation in inclusive environments. In F. P. Orelove, D. Sobsey, & R. K. Silberman (Eds.), *Education children with multiple disabilities: A collaborative approach* (4th ed., pp. 151–192). Baltimore: Brookes.

Uffen, E. (1997). Speech and language disorders: Nature or nurture? *ASHA Leader, 2*(14), 8.

Umbreit, J., Ferro, J., Liaupsin, C., & Lane, K. (2007). *Functional behavioral assessment and function-based intervention: An effective, practical approach.* Upper Saddle River, NJ: Merrill/Pearson.

Utley, B. L., Roman, C., & Nelson, G. L. (1998). Functional vision. In S. Z. Sacks & R. K. Silberman (Eds.), *Educating students who have visual impairments with other disabilities* (pp. 371–412). Baltimore: Brookes.

Utley, C. A., & Obiakor, F. E. (2001). Learning problems or learning disabilities of multicultural learners: Contemporary perspectives. In C. Utley & F. Obiakor (Eds.), *Special education, multicultural education, and school reform: Components of quality education for learners with mild disabilities* (pp. 90–117). Springfield, IL: Thomas.

Valli, C., Lucas, C., & Mulrooney, K. (2005). *The linguistics of American Sign Language: An introduction* (4th ed.). Washington, DC: Gallaudet University Press.

Van Acker, R., Grant, S. H., & Henry, D. (1996). Teacher and student behavior as a function of risk for aggression. *Education and Treatment of Children, 19,* 316–334.

Van Cleve, J. V. (Ed.). (2007). *The Deaf history reader.* Washington, DC: Gallaudet Press.

van der Lee, J. H., Mokkink, L. B., Grootenhuis, M. A., Heymans, H. S., & Offringa, M. (2007). Definitions and measurement of chronic health conditions in childhood: A systematic review. *Journal of the American Medical Association, 297,* 2741–2751.

Van Dycke, J. L., Martin, J. E., & Lovett, D. L. (2006). Why is this cake on fire? Inviting student into the IEP process. *Teaching Exceptional Children, 38*(3), 42–47.

Van Gurp, S. (2001). Self-concept of deaf secondary school students in different educational settings. *Journal of Deaf Studies and Deaf Education, 6,* 54–69.

van Karnebeek, C. D. M., Scheper, F. Y., Abeling, N. G., Alders, M. K., Barth, P. G., Hoovers, J. M. N., Koevoets, C., Wanders, R. J. A., & Hennekam, R. C. M. (2005). Etiology of mental retardation in children referred to a tertiary care center: A prospective study. *American Journal on Mental Retardation, 110,* 253–267.

Van Laarhoven, T., Johnson, J. W., Van Laarhoven-Myers, T., Grider, G. L., & Grider, K. M. (2009). The effectiveness of using a video iPod as a prompting device in employment settings. *Journal of Behavioral Education, 18,* 119–141.

Van Riper, C., & Erickson, R. L. (1996). *Speech correction: An introduction to speech pathology and audiology* (9th ed.). Boston: Allyn & Bacon.

Van Riper, M. (2007). Families of children with Down syndrome: Responding to "a change in plans" with resilience. *Journal of Pediatric Nursing, 22,* 116–128.

VanTassel-Baska, J. (2005). *Acceleration strategies for teaching gifted learners.* Waco, TX: Prufrock.

VanTassel-Baska, J., Johnson, D., & Avery, L. D. (2002). Using performance tasks in the identification of economically disadvantaged and minority gifted learners: Findings from Project STAR. *Gifted Child Quarterly, 46,* 110–123.

VanTassel-Baska, J., & Stambaugh, T. (2006). *Comprehensive curriculum for gifted learners* (3rd ed.). Upper Saddle River, NJ: Pearson.

VanTassel-Baska, J., & Stambaugh, T. (2007). *Undiscovered gems: A national perspective on low-income promising learners.* Washington, DC: National Association for Gifted Children.

Vannest, K., Burke, M., & Adiguzel, T. (2006). *Electronic Daily Behavior Report Card (e-DBRC): A web based system for progress monitoring* (Beta Version) [Web-based application]. College Station: Texas A&M University. Retrieved August 31, 2011, from http://e-dbrc.tamu.edu/

Vannest, K. J., Burke, M. D., Payne, T. E., Davis, C. R., & Soares, D. A. (2011). Electronic progress monitoring of IEP goals and objectives. *Teaching Exceptional Children, 43*(5), 40–51.

Vannest, K. J., Davis, J. L., Davis, C. R., Mason, B. A., & Burke, M. D. (2010). Effective intervention and measurement with a daily behavior report card: A meta-analysis. *School Psychology Review, 39*(4), 654–672.

Vaughn, S., & Fuchs, L. S. (2003). Redefining learning disabilities as inadequate response to instruction: The promise and potential problems. *Learning Disabilities Research & Practice, 18,* 137–146.

Vaughn, S., Linan-Thompson, S., & Hickman, P. (2003). Response to instruction as a means of identifying students with reading/learning disabilities. *Exceptional Children, 69,* 391–409.

Vaughn, S., McIntosh, R., Schumm, J. S., Haager, D., & Callwood, D. (1993). Social status, peer acceptance, and reciprocal friendships revisited.

Learning Disabilities Research and Practice, 8, 82–88.

Vaughn, S., & Roberts, G. (2007). Secondary interventions in reading: Providing additional instruction for students at risk. *Teaching Exceptional Children, 39*(5), 40–46.

Venn, J. J. (2007). *Assessing students with special needs* (4th ed.). Upper Saddle River, NJ: Pearson.

Vermeulen, A. M., van Bon, W., Schreuder, R., Knoors, H., & Snik, A. (2007). Reading comprehension of deaf children with cochlear implants. *Journal of Deaf Studies and Deaf Education, 12,* 283–302.

VisionServe Alliance. (2011). *Dog guide etiquette.* St. Louis: Author. Retrieved June 21, 2011, from http://www.agenciesfortheblind.org/DogGuide.asp

Voltz, D. L. (1994). Developing collaborative parent-teacher relationships with culturally diverse parents. *Intervention in School and Clinic, 29*(5), 288–291.

von Hahn, L. (2004). Traumatic brain injury: Medical considerations and educational implications. *Exceptional Parent, 33*(11), 40–42.

Voyager Expanded Learning. (2008). *Voyager passport.* Dallas: Author.

Vu, J. A., Babikian, T., & Asarnow, R. F. (2011). Academic and language outcomes in children after traumatic brain injury: A meta-analysis. *Exceptional Children, 77,* 263–281.

Wagner, B. W. (2000). Presidential address 2000—Changing visions into reality. *Mental Retardation, 38,* 436–443.

Wagner, L. (2009, June). *Juvenile re-offense report.* Eugene, OR: Lane County Department of Youth Services.

Wagner, M., & Blackorby, J. (2002). *Disability profiles of elementary and middle school students with disabilities.* Menlo Park, CA: SRI International.

Wagner, M., & Cameto, R. (2004). *NLTS2 data brief: The characteristics, experiences, and outcomes of youth with emotional disturbances.* Minneapolis: National Center on Secondary Education and Transition. Available: http://www.ncset.org/publications/

Wagner, M., Kutash, K., Duchnowski, A. J., Epstein, M. H., & Sumi, C. (2005). The children and youth we serve: A national picture of the characteristics of students with emotional disturbances receiving special education. *Journal of Emotional and Behavioral Disorders, 11,* 194–197.

Wagner, M., Newman, L., Cameto, R., Garza, N., & Levine, P. (2005). *After high school: A first look at the post-school experiences of youth with disabilities. A report from the National Longitudinal Transition Study-2 (NLTS-2).* Menlo Park, CA: SRI International. Available: www.nlts2.org/reports/2005_04/nlts2_report_2005_04_complete.pdf

Wagner, M., Newman, L., Cameto, R., Levine, P., & Marder, C. (2003). *Going to school: Instructional contexts, programs, and participation of secondary school students with disabilities. A report from the National Longitudinal Transition Study-2 (NLTS-2).* Menlo Park, CA: SRI International. Available: http://www.nlts2.org/reports/2003_12/nlts2_report_2003_12_execsum.pdf

Wagner, M., Newman, L., Cameto, R., Levine, P., & Marder, C. (2007). *Perceptions and expectations of youth with disabilities. A special topic report of findings from the National Longitudinal Transition Study-2 (NLTS2) (NCSER 2007-3006).* Menlo Park, CA: SRI International.

Wagner, R. K., Torgeson, J. K., & Rahsotte, C. A. (1999). *Comprehensive Test of Phonological Processing.* Austin, TX: PRO-ED.

Wagner-Lampl, A., & Oliver, G. W. (1994). Folklore of blindness. *Journal of Visual Impairment and Blindness, 88,* 267–276.

Wahl, H., Kämmerer, A., Holz, F., Miller, D., Becker, S., Kaspar, R., & Himmelsbach, I. (2006). Psychosocial intervention for age-related macular degeneration: A pilot project. *Journal of Visual Impairment and Blindness, 101,* 533–544.

Waitoller, F. R., Artiles, A. J., & Cheney, D. A. (2010). The miner's canary: A review of overrepresentation research. *Journal of Special Education, 44,* 29–49.

Wakefield, A. J., Murch, S. H., Anthony, A., Linnell, J., Casson, D. M., Malik, M., . . . , & Walker-Smith, J. A. (1998). Ileal-lymphoid-nodular hyperplasia, non-specific colitis, and pervasive developmental disorder in children. *The Lancet, 351,* 637–641.

Walker, A. R., Richter, S., Uphold, N. M., & Test, D. W. (2010). Review of the literature on community-based instruction across grade levels. *Education and Training in Autism and Developmental Disabilities, 456*(3), 242–267.

Walker, A. R., & Test, D. W. (2011). Using a self-advocacy intervention on African American college students' ability to request academic accommodations. *Learning Disabilities Research & Practice, 26,* 134–144.

Walker, H. M. (1997). *The acting out child: Coping with classroom disruption* (2nd ed.). Longmont, CO: Sopris West.

Walker, H. M., McConnell, S., Holmes, D., Todis, B., Walker, J., & Golden, N. (1988). *The ACCEPTS program: A curriculum for children's effective peer and teacher skills.* Austin, TX: PRO-ED.

Walker, H. M., Ramsey, E., & Gresham, R. M. (2005). *Antisocial behavior in school: Evidence-based practices* (2nd ed.). Belmont, CA: Wadsworth/Thomson Learning.

Walker, H. M., Seeley, J. R., Small, J., Severson, H. H., Graham, B. A., Feil, E. G., et al. (2009). A randomized control trial of the first steps to success early intervention: Demonstration of program efficacy outcomes in a diverse, urban school district. *Journal of Emotional and Behavioral Disorders, 17,* 197–212.

Walker, H. M., & Severson, H. H. (1992). *Systematic screening for behavior disorders: User's guide and administration manual* (2nd ed.). Longmont, CO: Sopris West.

Walker, H. M., Todis, B., Holmes, D., & Horton, G. (1988). *ACCESS: Adolescent curriculum for communication and effective social skills.* Austin, TX: PRO-ED.

Walker, L. A. (1986). *A loss for words: The story of deafness in a family.* New York: Harper & Row.

Wallace, G., & Hammill, D. (2002). *Comprehensive Receptive and Expressive Vocabulary Test* (2nd ed.). Austin, TX: PRO-ED.

Wang, Y., Trezek, B. J., Luckner, J. L., & Paul, P. V. (2008). The role of phonology and phonologically related skills in reading instruction for students who are deaf or hard of hearing. *American Annals of the Deaf, 153,* 396–407.

Warfield, M. E., & Hauser-Cram, P. (1996). Child care needs, arrangements, and satisfaction of mothers of children with developmental disabilities. *Mental Retardation, 34,* 294–302.

Watson, G. S., & Gross, A. M. (2000). Familial determinants. In M. Hersen & R. T. Ammerman (Eds.), *Advanced abnormal psychology* (2nd ed., pp. 81–99). Hillsdale, NJ: Erlbaum.

Webber, J., & Plotts, C. A. (2008). *Emotional and behavioral disorders: Theory and practice* (5th ed.). Boston: Allyn & Bacon.

Webb-Johnson, G. C. (2003). Behaving while black: A hazardous reality for African American learners. *Beyond Behavior, 12*(2), 3–7.

Wechsler, D. (2003). *Wechsler intelligence scale for children* (4th ed.). San Antonio, TX: Psychological Corporation.

Wehby, J. H., Lane, K. L., & Falk, K. B. (2003). Academic instruction for students with emotional and behavioral disorders. *Journal of Emotional and Behavioral Disorders, 11,* 194–197.

Wehby, J. H., Symons, F. J., Canale, J. A., & Go, F. J. (1998). Teaching practices in classrooms for students with emotional and behavioral disorders: Discrepancies between recommendations and observations. *Behavioral Disorders, 24,* 51–56.

Wehby, J. H., Symons, F. J., & Shores, R. E. (1995). A descriptive analysis of aggressive behaviors in classrooms for children with emotional and behavioral disorders. *Behavioral Disorders, 20,* 87–105.

Wehman, P. (2011a). *Essentials of transition planning.* Baltimore: Brookes.

Wehman, P. (2011b). *Functional curriculum for elementary and secondary students with special needs* (3rd ed.). Austin, TX: PRO-ED.

Wehman, P., Inge, K. J., Revell, W. G., Jr., & Brooke, V. A. (Eds.). (2006). *Real work for real pay: Inclusive employment for people with disabilities.* Baltimore: Brookes.

Wehman, P., Kregel, J., Shafer, M., & West, M. (1989). *Emerging trends in supported employment: A preliminary analysis of 27 states.* Richmond: Virginia Commonwealth University, Rehabilitation Research and Training Center.

Wehmeyer, M. L. (2006). Self-determination and individuals with severe disabilities: Reexamining meanings and misinterpretations. *Research and Practice in Severe Disabilities, 30,* 113–120.

Wehmeyer, M. L., Agran, M., Hughes, C., Martin, J., Mithaug, D. E., & Palmer, S. (2007). *Promoting self-determination in students with intellectual and developmental disabilities.* New York: Guilford.

Wehmeyer, M. L., Palmer, S. B., Agran, M., Mithaug, D. E., & Martin, J. E. (2000). Promoting causal agency: The self-determined learning model of instruction. *Exceptional Children, 66,* 273.

Wehmeyer, M. L., & Schalock, R. L. (2001). Self-determination and quality of life: Implications for special education services and supports. *Focus on Exceptional Children, 33*(8), 1–14.

Wehmeyer, M. L., Shogren, K., Palmer, S., Williams-Diehm, K., Little, T., & Boulton, A. (in press). Impact of the *Self-Determined Learning Model of Instruction* on student self-determination: A randomized-trial placebo control group study. *Exceptional Children.*

Weinstein, S. L., & Gaillard, W. D. (2007). Epilepsy. In M. L. Batshaw, L. Pellegrino, L, & Roizen, N. J. (Eds.), *Children with disabilities* (6th ed.). Baltimore: Brookes.

Weintraub, F. J., & Abeson, A. (1974). New education policies for the handicapped: The quiet revolution. *Phi Delta Kappan, 55,* 526–529, 569.

Wenzel, C., & Rowley, L. (2010). Teaching social skills and academic strategies to college students with Asperger's syndrome. *Teaching Exceptional Children, 42*(5), 44–50.

Werts, M. G., Hoffman, E. M., & Darcy, C. (2011). Acquisition of instructive feedback: Relation to target stimulus. *Education and Training in Autism and Developmental Disabilities, 46,* 134–149.

Werts, M. G., Wolery, M., Gast, D. L., & Holcomb, A. (1996). Sneak in some extra learning by using instructive feedback. *Teaching Exceptional Children, 28*(3), 70–71.

Wesson, C. (1991). Curriculum-based measurement and two models of follow-up consultation. *Exceptional Children, 77,* 246–256.

Wesson, C., Wilson, R., & Higbee Mandlebaum, L. (1988). Learning games for active student responding. *Teaching Exceptional Children, 20*(2), 12–14.

West, E., Leon-Guerrero, R., & Stevens, D. (2007). Establishing codes of acceptable schoolwide behavior in a multicultural society. *Beyond Behavior, 16*(2), 32–38.

Westat and Policy Studies Associates. (2001). *The longitudinal evaluation of school change and performance in Title I schools.* Washington, DC: U.S. Department of Education, Office of the Deputy Secretary, Planning and Evaluation Service.

Westling, D. L., & Fox, L. (2009). *Teaching students with severe disabilities* (4th ed.). Upper Saddle River, NJ: Merrill/Pearson.

Wetherby, A., Woods, J., Allen, L., Cleary, J., Dickinson, H., & Lord, C. (2004). Early indicators of autism spectrum disorders in the second year of life. *Journal of Autism and Developmental Disorders, 34,* 473–493.

Wetzel, R., & Knowlton, M. (2006a). Studies of braille reading rates and implications for the unified English braille code. *Journal of Visual Impairment and Blindness, 100,* 275–284.

Wheeler, D. L., Jacobson, J. W., Paglieri, R. A., & Schwartz, A. A. (1993). An experimental assessment of facilitated communication. *Mental Retardation, 31,* 49–60.

Whitaker, S. (2008). That stability of IQ in people with low intellectual ability: An analysis of the literature. *Intellectual and Developmental Disabilities, 45,* 120–128.

White, B. L. (1995). *The first three years of life* (rev. ed.). New York: Fireside.

White, M. A. (1975). Natural rates of teacher approval and disapproval in the classroom. *Journal of Applied Behavior Analysis, 8,* 367–372.

Whiting, G. W. (2009). The scholar identity institute: Guiding Darnel and other Black males. *Gifted Child Today, 32*(4), 53–56.

Wiederholt, J. L., & Bryant, B. R. (2001). *Gray oral reading tests* (4th ed.). Austin, TX: PRO-ED.

Wiener, J. (2004). Do peer relationships foster behavioral adjustment in children with learning disabilities? *Learning Disability Quarterly, 27,* 21–30.

Wiener, J., & Tardif, C. Y. (2004). Social and emotional functioning of children with learning disabilities: Does special education placement make a difference? *Learning Disabilities Research and Practice, 19,* 20–32.

Wiener, W. R., Welsh, R. L., & Blasch, B. B. (2010). *Foundations of orientation and mobility* (3rd ed.). New York: AFB Press.

Wiggins, L. D., Baio, J., & Rice, C. (2006). Examination of the time between first evaluation and autism diagnosis in a population based sample. *Journal of Developmental and Behavioral Pediatrics, 27,* S79–S87.

Wiggins, L. D., Bakeman, R., Adamson, L. B., & Robins, D. L. (2007). The utility of the Social Communication Questionnaire in screening for autism in children referred for early intervention. *Focus on Autism and Other Developmental Disabilities, 22,* 33–38.

Wilens, T. E., Biederman, J., & Spencer, T. J. (2002). Attention deficit/hyperactivity disorder across the lifespan. *Annual Review of Medicine, 53,* 113–131.

Wilkinson, G. S., & Robertson, G. J. (2006). *Wide Range Achievement Test—4.* Luz, FL: Psychological Assessment Resource, Inc.

Will, M. C. (1986). Educating children with learning problems: A shared responsibility. *Exceptional Children, 52,* 411–415.

Willard-Holt, C. (1998). Academic and personality characteristics of gifted students with cerebral palsy: A multiple case study. *Exceptional Children, 65,* 37–50.

Willcutt, E. G., Pennington, B. F., & DeFries, J. C. (2000). Etiology of inattention and hyper-activity/impulsivity in a community ample of twins. *Journal of Abnormal Child Psychiatry, 28,* 149–159.

Willey, L. H. (Ed.). (2003). *Asperger syndrome in adolescence: Living with the ups, the downs, and things in between.* Philadelphia: Jessica Kingsley.

Williams, B. F., & Williams, R. L. (2011). *Effective programs for treating autism spectrum disorders: Applied behavior analysis models.* New York: Routledge.

Williams, C. B., & Finnegan, M. (2003). From myth to reality: Sound information for teachers about students who are deaf. *Teaching Exceptional Children, 35*(3), 40–45.

Williams, J., Whiten, A., Singh, T. (2004). A systematic review of action imitation in autistic spectrum disorder. *Journal of Autism and Developmental Disorders, 34,* 285–296.

Williams, K. E., & Foxx, R. M. (2007). *Treating eating problems of children with autism spectrum disorders and developmental disabilities.* Austin, TX: PRO-ED.

Williams, K. J., Wray, J. J., & Wheeler, D. M. (2005). Intravenous secretin for autism spectrum disorder. *Cochrane Database of Systematic Reviews* 2005, Issue 3. Art. No.: CD003495. doi: 10.1002/14651858.CD003495.pub2

Williams, K. R., Wishart, J. G., Pitcairn, T. K., & Willis, D. S. (2005). Emotion recognition by children with Down syndrome: Investigation of specific impairments and error patterns. *American Journal on Mental Retardation, 110,* 378–392.

Williams, V. L., & Cartledge, G. (1997). Passing notes to parents. *Teaching Exceptional Children, 30*(1), 30–34.

Williamson, G. G. (1978). The individualized education program: An interdisciplinary endeavor. In B. Sirvis, J. W. Baken, & G. G. Williamson (Eds.), *Unique aspects of the IEP for the physically handicapped, homebound, and hospitalized.* Reston, VA: Council for Exceptional Children.

Wilson, C. L. (1995). Parents and teachers: "Can we talk?" *LD Forum, 20*(2), 31–33.

Winebrenner, S. (2001). *Teaching gifted kids in the regular classroom* (2nd ed.). Minneapolis: Free Spirit.

Wing, L. (1998). The history of Asperger syndrome. In E. Schopler, G. B. Mesibov, & L. J. Kunce (Eds.), *Asperger syndrome or high-functioning autism?* (pp. 11–28). New York: Plenum.

Winter-Messiers, M. A. (2007). From tarantulas to toilet brushes: Understanding the special interest areas of children and youth with Asperger syndrome. *Journal of Remedial and Special Education, 28,* 140–152.

Winter-Messiers, M. A., Herr, C. M., Wood, C. E., Brooks, A. P., Gates, M. A. M., Houston, T. L., & Tingstad, K. I. (2007). How far can Brian ride the Daylight 4449 Express? A strength-based model of Asperger syndrome based on special interest areas. *Focus on Autism and Other Developmental Disabilities, 22,* 67–79.

Winzer, M. (2009). *From integration to inclusion: A history of special education in the 20th century.* Washington, DC: Gallaudet University Press.

Witty, P. A. (Ed.). (1951). *The gifted child.* Boston: Heath.

Witzer, B. S., & Mercer, C. D. (2003). Using rewards to teach students with disabilities: Implications for motivation. *Remedial and Special Education, 24,* 88–96.

Wolery, M. (2000). Recommended practices in child-focused interventions. In S. Sandall, M. E. McLean, & B. J. Smith (Eds.), *DEC recommended practices* (pp. 34–38). Longmont, CO: Sopris West.

Wolery, M., Anthony, L., & Heckathorn, J. (1998). Transition-based teaching: Effects on transitions, teachers' behavior, and children's learning. *Journal of Early Intervention, 21,* 117–131.

Wolery, M., & Sainato, D. M. (1993). General curriculum and intervention strategies. In *DEC Recommended Practices* (pp. 50–57). Reston, VA: Council for Exceptional Children, Division for Early Childhood.

Wolery, M., & Sainato, D. M. (1996). General curriculum and intervention strategies. In S. L. Odom & M. McClean (Eds.), *Recommended practices in early intervention* (pp. 125–158). Austin, TX: PRO-ED.

Wolf, M., & Bowers, P. G. (2000). Naming-speed processes and developmental reading disabilities: An introduction to the special issue on the double-deficit hypothesis. *Journal of Learning Disabilities, 33,* 322–324.

Wolfe, L. H., Heron, T. E., & Goddard, Y. I. (2000). Effects of self-monitoring on the on-task behavior and written language performance of elementary students with learning disabilities. *Journal of Behavioral Education, 10,* 49–73.

Wolfensberger, W. (1972). *Normalization: The principle of normalization in human services.* Toronto: National Institute on Mental Retardation.

Wolfensberger, W. (1983). Social role valorization: A proposed new term for the principle of normalization. *Mental Retardation, 21,* 234–239.

Wolfensberger, W. (2000). A brief overview of social role valorization. *Mental Retardation, 38,* 105–123.

Wolffe, K., & Kelly, S. M. (2011). Instruction in areas of the expanded core curriculum linked to transition outcomes for students with visual impairments. *Journal of Visual Impairment and Blindness, 105,* 340–349.

Wolford, T., Alber, S. R., & Heward, W. L. (2001). Teaching middle school students with learning disabilities to recruit peer assistance during cooperative learning group activities. *Learning Disabilities and Research and Practice, 16,* 161–173.

Wolgemuth, J. R., Cobb, R. B., & Alwell, M. (2008). The effects of mnemonic interventions on academic outcomes for youth with disabilities: A systematic review. *Learning Disabilities Research & Practice, 23*, 1–10.

Woll, B., & Ladd, P. (2011). Deaf communities. In M. Marschark & P. E. Spencer (Eds.), *Oxford handbook of deaf studies, language, and education* (2nd ed., pp. 159–171). New York: Oxford University Press.

Wood, C. L., Mackiewicz, S. M., Van Norman, R. K., & Cooke, N. L. (2007). Tutoring with technology. *Intervention in School and Clinic, 43*(2), 108–115.

Wood, S. J., Murdock, J. Y., Cronin, M. E., Dawson, N. M., & Kirby, P. C. (1998). Effects of self-monitoring on on-task behaviors of at-risk middle school students. *Journal of Behavioral Education, 8*, 263–279.

Woodcock, R. W. (1998). *Woodcock Reading Mastery Tests—Revised.* Circle Pines, MN: American Guidance Services.

Woodcock, R. W., Shrank, F. A., McGrew, K. S., & Mather, N. (2007). *Woodcock-Johnson III.* Rolling Meadows, IL: Riverside.

Woods, L. L., Sylvester, L., & Martin, J. E. (2010). Student-directed transition planning: Increasing student knowledge and self-efficacy in the transition planning process. *Career Development for Exceptional Individuals, 33*, 106–114.

Worcester, N. A., Nesman, T. M., Mendez, L. M., R., & Keller, H. R. (2008). Giving voice to parents of young children with challenging behavior. *Exceptional Children, 74*, 509–525.

World Health Organization. (2011). *International classification of functioning, disability and health (ICF).* Geneva: Author. Retrieved July 18, 2011, from http://www.who.int/classifications/icf/en/

Wormsley, D. P. (2004). *Braille literacy: A functional approach.* New York: AFB Press.

Wright, J. E., Cavanaugh, R. A., Sainato, D. M., & Heward, W. L. (1995). *Somos todos ayudantes y estudiantes:* Evaluation of a classwide peer tutoring program in a modified Spanish class for secondary students identified as learning disabled or academically at-risk. *Education and Treatment of Children, 18*, 33–52.

Wright, P. W. D., & Wright, P. D. (2006a). *From emotions to advocacy: The special education survival guide* (2nd ed.). Hartfield, VA: Harbor House Law Press.

Wright, P. W. D., & Wright, P. D. (2006b). *Wrightslaw: Special education law* (2nd ed.). Hartfield, VA: Harbor House Law Press.

Wright, P. W. D., Wright, P. D., & O'Connor, S. W. (2010). *Wrightslaw: All about IEPs.* Hartfield, VA: Harbor House Law Press.

Wright-Gallo, G. L., Higbee, T. S., Reagon, K. A., & Davey, B. J. (2006). Classroom-based functional analysis and intervention for students with emotional/behavioral disorders. *Education & Treatment of Children, 29*, 421–436.

Xin, J. F., & Sutman, F. X. (2011). Using the Smart Board in teaching social stories to students with autism. *Teaching Exceptional Children, 43*(4), 18–24.

Yairi, E. (1998). Is the basis for stuttering genetic? *American Speech-Language-Hearing Association, 70*(1), 29–32.

Yairi, E., & Ambrose, E. N. (1999). Early childhood stuttering. I: Persistence and recovery rates. *Journal of Speech and Hearing Research, 42*, 1097–1112.

Yairi, E., & Seery, C. H. (2011). *Stuttering: Foundations and clinical applications.* Upper Saddle River, NJ: Pearson.

Yavorcik, C. (2008). *ASA statement on Michael Savage radio comments.* Bethesda, MD: Autism Society of America. Available: http://support.autism-society.org/site/News2?page=NewsArticle&id=11701

Yeargin-Allsopp, M., Rice, C., Karapurkar, T., Doemberg, N., Boyle, C., & Murphy, C. (2003). Prevalence of autism in a U.S. metropolitan community. *Journal of the American Medical Association, 289*, 49–55.

Yelin, E., & Katz, P. (1994). Labor force trends of persons with and without disabilities. *Monthly Labor Review, 72*, 593–620.

Yell, M. L. (2012). *The law and special education* (3rd ed.). Upper Saddle River, NJ: Pearson.

Yell, M. L., Katsiyannis, A., & Bradley, M. R. (2011). The Individuals with Disabilities Education Act: The evolution of special education law. In J. M. Kauffman & D. P. Hallahan (Eds.), *Handbook of special education* (pp. 61–76). New York: Routledge.

Yell, M. L., Ryan, J. B., Rozalski, M. E., & Katsiyannis, A. (2009). The U.S. Supreme Court and special education 2005 to 2007. *Teaching Exceptional Children, 41*(3), 68–75.

Ylvisaker, M. (2005). Children with cognitive, behavioral, communication, and academic difficulties. In W. M. High, A. M. Sander, M. A. Struchen, K. A. Hart (Eds.), *Rehabilitation for traumatic brain injury* (pp. 205–234). New York: Oxford University Press.

Yoder, P., & Stone, W. L. (2006). A randomized comparison of the effect of two prelinguistic communication interventions on the acquisition of spoken communication in preschoolers with ASD. *Journal of Speech, Language, and Hearing Research, 49*, 698–671.

Yoshinaga-Itano, C. (2006). Early identification, communication modality, and the development of speech and spoken language skills: Patterns and considerations. In P.E. Spencer & M. Marschark (Eds.), *Advances in the spoken language development of deaf and hard-of-hearing children* (pp. 298–327). New York: Oxford University Press.

Yurick, A. L., Robinson, P. D., Cartledge, G., Lo, Y., & Evans, T. L. (2006). Using peer-mediated repeated readings as a fluency-building activity for urban learners. *Education & Treatment of Children, 29*, 469–506.

Zambo, D. M. (2010). Strategies to enhance the social identities and social networks of adolescent students with disabilities. *Teaching Exceptional Children, 43*(2), 28–35.

Zane, T. (2011, Summer). Apophenia: One explanation for the adoption of fad treatments in autism. Clinical corner: Educating for inclusion. *Science in Autism Treatment, 8*(2), 12–14.

Zane, T., Davis, C., & Rosswurm, M. (2008). The cost of fad treatments in autism. *Journal of Early and Intensive Behavior Intervention, 5*(2), 44–51.

Zebehazy, K. T., & Smith, T. J. (2011). An examination of characteristics related to the social skills of youths with visual impairments. *Journal of Visual Impairment and Blindness, 105*, 84–95.

Zentall, S. S. (2006). *ADHD and education: Foundations, characteristics, methods, and collaboration.* Upper Saddle River, NJ: Merrill/Pearson.

Zeuschner, R. (2003). *Communicating today* (3rd ed.). Boston: Allyn & Bacon.

Zhang, J., Gast, D., Horvat, M., & Datillo, J. (1995). The effectiveness of a constant time delay procedure on teaching lifetime sports skills to adolescents with severe to profound intellectual disabilities. *Education and Training in Mental Retardation and Developmental Disabilities, 30*, 51–64.

Zhang, J., & Wheeler, J. J. (2011). A meta-analysis of peer-mediated interventions for young children with autism spectrum disorders. *Education and Training in Autism and Developmental Disabilities, 46*, 62–77.

Zigler, E. (1999). The retarded child as a whole person. In E. Zigler & D. Bennett-Gates (Eds.), *Personality development in individuals with mental retardation* (pp. 1–16). Cambridge: Cambridge University Press.

Zigmond, N. (2003). Where should students with disabilities receive special education services? Is one place better than another? *Journal of Special Education, 37*, 193–199.

Zigmond, N. (2007). Delivering special education is a two-person job: A call for unconventional thinking. In J. B. Crockett, M. M. Gerber, & T. J. Landrum (Eds.), *Radical reform of special education: Essays in honor of James M. Kauffman.* Mahwah, NJ: Erlbaum.

Zigmond, N., & Baker, J. M. (1995). Concluding comments: Current and future practices in inclusive schooling. *Journal of Special Education, 29*, 245–250.

Zigmond, N., Kloo, A., & Lemons, C. J. (2011). IEP Team decision-making for more inclusive assessments: Policies, percentages, and personal decisions. In S. Elliott, R. Kettler, P. Beddow, & A. Kirz (Eds.), *Handbook of accessible achievement tests for all students* (pp. 69–82). New York: Springer.

Zigmond, N., Kloo, A., & Volonino, V. (2009). What, where, and how? Special education in the climate of full inclusion. *Exceptionality, 17*, 189–204.

Zigmond, N., & Magiera, K. (2001). *Co-teaching. Current Practice Alerts,* Issue 6. Reston, VA: Division for Learning Disabilities and Division for Research, Council for Exceptional Children.

Zigmond, N., & Matta, D. (2005). Value added of the special education teacher in secondary school co-taught classes. In T. M. Scruggs & M. A. Mastropieri (Eds.), *Advances in learning and behavioral disabilities: Research in secondary schools* (pp. 55–76). Oxford: Elsevier.

Zijlstra, H. P., & Vlaskamp, C. (2005). The impact of medical conditions on the support of children with profound intellectual and multiple disabilities. *Journal of Applied Research in Intellectual Disabilities, 18*, 151–161.

Zirkel, P. A., & D'Angelo, A. (2002). Special trends education case law: An empirical trends analysis. *Education Law Reporter, 161*, 731–753.

Zirkel, P. A., & Thomas, L. B. (2010). State laws for RTI: An updated snapshot. *Teaching Exceptional Children, 42*(3), 56–63.

Zubal-Ruggieri, R. (2007). Making links, making connections: Internet resources for self-advocates and people with developmental disabilities. *Intellectual and Developmental Disabilities, 45*, 209–215.

Zucker, A. (2004). Law and ethics. *Death Studies, 28*, 803–806.